Lawyers' Ethics
and
Professional Regulation

Fourth Edition

Alice Woolley
Richard Devlin
Brent Cotter

 LexisNexis

Lawyers' Ethics and Professional Regulation, Fourth Edition

Library and Archives Canada Cataloguing in Publication

Lawyers' ethics and professional regulation, fourth edition / Alice Woolley . . . [et al.].

Includes index.

ISBN 978-0-433-50607-2

1. Legal ethics—Canada. I. Woolley, Alice

KE339.L39 2008 174'.30971   C2008-903831-2
KF306 L39 2008

Printed and bound in Canada.

LAWYERS' ETHICS AND PROFESSIONAL REGULATION

Editors

Alice Woolley
Court of Queen's Bench of Alberta

Richard Devlin
Schulich School of Law, Dalhousie University

Brent Cotter
College of Law, University of Saskatchewan

Authors by Chapter

Chapter 1: Introduction to Legal Ethics
Alice Woolley
Court of Queen's Bench of Alberta

Chapter 2: The Lawyer-Client Relationship
Richard Devlin
Schulich School of Law, Dalhousie University
Pooja Parmar
Faculty of Law, University of Victoria

Chapter 3: The Lawyer's Duty to Preserve Client Confidences
Amy Salyzyn
Faculty of Law, University of Ottawa

Chapter 4: The Duty of Loyalty and Conflicts of Interest
Brent Cotter
College of Law, University of Saskatchewan

Chapter 5: Ethics in Advocacy
Trevor C.W. Farrow
Osgoode Hall Law School, York University

Chapter 6: Counselling and Negotiation
Stephen G.A. Pitel
Faculty of Law, Western University

Chapter 7: Ethics and Criminal Law Practice .
David Tanovich
Faculty of Law, University of Windsor

Chapter 8: Government Lawyers
Adam Dodek
Faculty of Law, University of Ottawa

Chapter 9: In-House Counsel and Their Unique Considerations
Basil Alexander
Faculty of Law, University of New Brunswick

ABOUT THE EDITORS

ALICE WOOLLEY is a Justice at the Court of Queen's Bench of Alberta. Previously she was a Professor of Law at the Faculty of Law, University of Calgary specializing in the areas of legal ethics and professional responsibility.. She is also the author of the casebook *Understanding Lawyers' Ethics in Canada, 2d ed.*, published by LexisNexis Canada. Justice Woolley received her B.A. and LL.B. from the University of Toronto, and her LL.M. from Yale Law School.

RICHARD F. DEVLIN, FRSC, is a Professor at the Schulich School of Law, Dalhousie University. He has published widely in various areas including legal theory, legal ethics, judicial education and contract law.

BRENT COTTER is a Professor and former Dean at the College of Law at the University of Saskatchewan, having formerly been a professor at Dalhousie law School and a visiting professor at Duke Law School, and at the Faculty of Law at the University of Alberta. He has taught and written in the areas of legal and judicial ethics for most of his academic career. He also served as a deputy minister with the Government of Saskatchewan in various capacities, including as Deputy Attorney General. He was appointed to the Senate of Canada in 2020.

ABOUT THE CONTRIBUTORS

BASIL S. ALEXANDER is an Assistant Professor at the University of New Brunswick's Faculty of Law, who also taught at Osgoode Hall Law School and the Université de Sherbrooke. After receiving a B. Arts Sc. (Hon.) from McMaster University and LL.B./M.P.A. degrees from the University of Victoria, he practised several years in a Toronto public interest & social justice law firm. He then returned to academia, received an LL.M. from the University of Toronto, and is pursuing a Ph.D. at Queen's University. His practical experience informs his teaching and research, which involve law & social change (including cause lawyering), legal ethics & professionalism, civil procedure/litigation, and demonstrations & the law.

JAMIE BAXTER is an Associate Professor at the Schulich School of Law, Dalhousie University where he writes and teaches about access to justice, regulation and the legal profession, among other topics. Jamie has been a visiting Fulbright Scholar at the Appalachian Center, University of Kentucky and a lecturer in the Department of Food, Agriculture and Resource Economics at the University of Guelph. He holds degrees in economics and law from McMaster University, the University of Toronto, and Yale.

ADAM DODEK is Dean of Law at the University of Ottawa's Faculty of Law and one of the founders of the University's Public Law Group. He teaches legal ethics, public law and constitutional law. He is one of the founders of the Canadian Association for Legal Ethics (CALE). His book *Solicitor-Client Privilege* was published by LexisNexis Canada in 2014.

TREVOR C.W. FARROW, A.B. (Princeton), B.A./M.A. (Oxford), LL.B. (Dalhousie), LL.M. (Harvard), Ph.D. (Alberta), is a Professor and former Associate Dean at Osgoode Hall Law School. He is the Chair of the Canadian Forum on Civil Justice and was the founding Academic Director of the Winkler Institute for Dispute Resolution. Professor Farrow's teaching and research focus on the administration of civil justice, including legal process, legal and judicial ethics, advocacy, globalization and development. He was formerly a litigation lawyer at the Torys law firm in Toronto. Professor Farrow has received teaching awards from Harvard University and Osgoode Hall Law School.

Stephen **G.A. PITEL** is a Professor at the Faculty of Law at Western University. His teaching and research is focused on the conflict of laws, civil procedure, torts and legal ethics. He has co-authored, edited or co-edited 19 books including *Conflict of Laws*, 2d ed. (2016). He is a member of the Western University Board of Governors, the Vice-President of the Canadian Association for Legal Ethics and a former President of the University of Western Ontario Faculty Association. He has received several teaching awards.

POOJA PARMAR is an Associate Professor at the University of Victoria Faculty of Law. She teaches and writes about legal ethics and professional responsibility, legal history, property, and human rights. Her published work examines legal pluralism, Indigeneity, and questions of legal epistemology in multi-juridical spaces. One of her current projects is a SSHRC-funded study of Indigenous laws as sources of ethical legal practice. She received PhD in Law and LLM degrees from UBC and her LLB degree from Panjab University. Prior to commencing graduate research, she practiced law in New Delhi for several years.

AMY SALYZYN is an Associate Professor at the University of Ottawa Faculty of Law. Amy received her J.S.D. and LL.M. from Yale Law School and her J.D. from the University of Toronto Law School. Amy has also served as a judicial law clerk at the Court of Appeal for Ontario and has practiced at a Toronto litigation boutique. Her litigation practice included a wide variety of civil and commercial litigation matters including breach of contract, tort, professional negligence, securities litigation and employment law as well as administrative law matters. In addition to legal ethics, Amy's research focuses on gender and the law, law and technology and civil justice reform.

DAVID M. TANOVICH FRSC, is a Professor of Law at the Faculty of Law, University of Windsor. Professor Tanovich teaches and writes in the areas of criminal law, evidence, racial profiling and legal ethics. Prior to joining the University of Windsor in 2003, Professor Tanovich spent six years as criminal appellate counsel with Pinkofsky Lockyer in Toronto where he regularly appeared in the Ontario Court of Appeal and Supreme Court of Canada. He won his last three appeals in the Supreme Court including *R. v. Golden* and *R. v. Lyttle*. Professor Tanovich also clerked at the Supreme Court of Canada for former Chief Justice Antonio Lamer during the 1995-1996 term.

ACKNOWLEDGEMENTS

The editors and contributors thank the following people for their contribution to the preparation of this casebook: Ryan Bencic, Jonathan Clark, John Dickieson, Alex Hartwig, Christine Hicks, Kathryn James, Deanna Kerry, David Layton, Molly Ross, Graham Sharp, Linda Szeto, and Ian Wilenius.

A casebook on such a wide subject necessarily contains a great deal of reference to the work of others in the field, in the cases, the notes, the text and especially in the selected readings. The authors and publishers of the following articles and textbooks have been most generous in giving permission for the reproduction in this text of work already in print. References, of course, appear where necessary and possible in the text. It is convenient for us to list below, for the assistance of the reader, the publisher and authors for whose courtesy we are most grateful. The following list is organized in alphabetical order:

Action Committee on Access to Justice in Civil and Family Matters. Access to Civil & Family Justice: A Roadmap for Change (Ottawa, 2013) [footnotes omitted]. Reproduced with permission.

Canadian Bar Association Ethics and Professional Responsibility Committee/Canadian Corporate Counsel Association, FAQs about Privilege and Confidentiality for In-House Counsel (November 2012), A Checklist for In-house Counsel Strategies to Protect Solicitor-Client Privilege. Reproduced with permission.

Federation of Law Societies, "National Requirement: Approved Law Degree" (November 2015) [footnotes omitted]. Reproduced with permission.

Georgetown University Law Center — Regan, Milton C., Jr., "Professional Responsibility and the Corporate Lawyer", Georgetown Journal of Legal Ethics, 13:2 Geo. J. Legal Ethics, 197-215, 2000. Reprinted with permission of the publisher, Georgetown Journal of Legal Ethics © 2000.

The Honourable Georgina R. Jackson, "The Mystery of Judicial Ethics: Deciphering the 'Code'" (2005) 68 Sask. L. Rev. 1 [footnotes omitted]. Reproduced with permission.

Hadfield, Gillian K., "The Price of Law: How the Market for Lawyers Distorts the Justice System" (2000) 98 Mich. L. Rev. 953 [footnotes omitted]. Author retains copyright. Reproduced with permission.

Hughes, Patricia, "Advancing Access to Justice through Generic Solutions: The Risk of Perpetuating Exclusion" (2013) 31 *Windsor Yearbook of Access Justice* 1 [footnotes omitted]. Reproduced with permission.

Kruse, Katherine R., "The Jurisprudential Turn in Legal Ethics" in Arizona Law Review 493, at 494-495 and 504-505 [footnotes omitted]. Reproduced with permission.

Law Society of British Columbia, "Report of the Independence and Self-

Governance Committee" (March 20, 2008) [modified, footnotes omitted]. Reproduced with permission.

Law Society of British Columbia, "Report of the Legal Services Regulatory Framework Task Force" (2014) [footnotes omitted]. Reproduced with permission.

Law Society of Upper Canada, "Working Together for Change: Strategies to Address Systemic Racism in the Legal Professions" (December, 2016) [footnotes omitted]. © 2016, The Law Society of Upper Canada. Reproduced with permission of The Law Society of Upper Canada.

Layton, David, "The Criminal Lawyer's Role" (2004) 27 Dal. L.J. 379, at 380-383 [footnotes omitted]. Reproduced with permission.

Layton, David & Michel Proulx, *Ethics and Criminal Law, 2d Edition* (Toronto: Irwin Law, 2015), at 33-34 [footnotes omitted]. Reproduced with permission.

Luban, David, "The Adversary System Excuse" in *Legal Ethics and Human Dignity* (Cambridge: Cambridge University Press, 2007). Reproduced with permission.

Luban, David, "Tales of Terror: Lessons for Lawyers from the 'War on Terrorism' " in Kieran Trantler *et al.*, eds., *Reaffirming Legal Ethics: Taking Stock and New Ideas* (New York: Routledge, 2010). Reproduced with permission.

The Prairie Law Societies, Cori Ghitter, Director, Professionalism and Access and Shabnam Datta, Policy Counsel of the Law Society of Alberta, Barbra Bailey, Policy Counsel of the Law Society of Saskatchewan and Darcia Senft, General Counsel, Director of Policy and Ethics of the Law Society of Manitoba, "Innovating Regulation: Discussion Paper" (November 2015) [citations omitted]. Reproduced with permission.

Proulx, Michel & David Layton, *Ethics and Canadian Criminal Law* (Toronto: Irwin Law, 2015). Reprinted with permission © 2001.

Shaffer, Thomas, "Legal Ethics and the Good Client" (1987) 36 Cath. U. L. Rev. 319 [footnotes omitted]. Reproduced with permission.

Wilson, Malliha, Taia Wong & Kevin Hille, "Professionalism and the Public Interest" (2011) 38 The Advocates' Quarterly 1, at 14-17. Reproduced with permission.

Woolley, Alice, "Michelle's Story: Creativity and Meaning in Legal Practice" From: *In Search of the Ethical Lawyer: Stories from the Canadian Legal Profession* (Adam Dodek and Alice Woolley eds.) (Vancouver: UBC Press, 2016) [footnotes omitted]. Reproduced with permission.

TABLE OF CONTENTS

CHAPTER 4: THE DUTY OF LOYALTY AND CONFLICTS OF INTEREST

CHAPTER 8: GOVERNMENT LAWYERS 473

CHAPTER 9: IN-HOUSE COUNSEL AND THEIR UNIQUE CONSIDERATIONS 511

TABLE OF CONTENTS

CHAPTER 1

INTRODUCTION TO LEGAL ETHICS

[1] INTRODUCTION

What is legal ethics? Is it a distinct set of moral obligations that arises from the lawyer's role? Is it the rules of ordinary morality applied to the practice of law? Is it the inquiry into whether the life of a lawyer can be consistent with a life well-lived? Is it the "law of lawyering" — the rules and principles that govern a lawyer's conduct of practice in the same way as the rules of court determine the process of an action? Is it market regulation — how we compensate for and regulate the imperfections associated with the market for legal services?

In this book, you will be introduced to what being an ethical lawyer requires and to how Canadian provinces (and other jurisdictions) have chosen to regulate (or not to regulate) lawyer conduct. You will be introduced to specific controversies and important questions related both to the ethical obligations of the individual lawyer and to the challenges of regulating lawyer conduct. You will be invited to consider how the life of a lawyer can be a life well-lived. Overall, we hope this book will help you to solve the ethical problems that inevitably arise in legal practice, to understand the basic structure of professional regulation and governance, to reflect on the morality of being a lawyer, and to engage critically with the most important policy questions related to the ethics of legal practice and its regulation. To help you think about and address, in other words, the various concepts of "legal ethics" set out above.

This chapter provides introductory materials and discussion on lawyers' ethics and professional regulation. First, it offers a brief overview of the two main topics covered in this book: the ethical obligations of lawyers in legal practice and current approaches to regulation of lawyers' ethics. Second, it discusses the main sources of guidance and obligation for lawyers when making ethical decisions. Third, it outlines some of the ways philosophers have attempted to answer the question, "what does being ethical require?". Fourth, it examines some general and competing conceptions of the duties or qualities of the ethical lawyer: loyal advocacy; lawyers as moral agents in pursuit of justice; and integrity. Finally, it considers the challenges and opportunities for establishing an ethical – meaningful – life working as a lawyer.

In reading these materials, you should consider the following questions and problems:

- Is legal ethics law?
- Who should decide what being an ethical lawyer means? Oneself? Courts?

Law societies? Other lawyers? The legislature? The general public? The reasonable person?

- What is the central quality of an ethical lawyer? What does being an ethical lawyer require as a matter of principle?

- If a lawyer's duties in an individual case conflict, how does a lawyer decide what to do?

- Is being an ethical lawyer applying the values learned in kindergarten,[1] or do different principles apply? What does a lawyer do if the values of ethical lawyering conflict with a lawyer's personal sense of what is right or wrong?

- Whose interests (clients', judges', the general public and/or lawyers') should be taken into account in deciding what is ethical?

- Can I be a good lawyer and a good person?

Consider each of these questions through the excerpt from the Supreme Court's 2018 decision in *Groia v. Law Society of Upper Canada*. The main legal issue in that case, related to the regulation of civility, is discussed in Chapter 5, Ethics in Advocacy. This excerpt sets out the facts and the central conclusion of the majority judgment written by Justice Moldaver.

GROIA v. LAW SOCIETY OF UPPER CANADA

[2018] 1 S.C.R. 772; [2018] 1 R.C.S. 772; [2018] S.C.J. No. 27; 2018 SCC 27

Moldaver J.

I. Overview

The trial process in Canada is one of the cornerstones of our constitutional democracy. It is essential to the maintenance of a civilized society. Trials are the primary mechanism whereby disputes are resolved in a just, peaceful, and orderly way.

To achieve their purpose, it is essential that trials be conducted in a civilized manner. Trials marked by strife, belligerent behaviour, unwarranted personal attacks, and other forms of disruptive and discourteous conduct are antithetical to the peaceful and orderly resolution of disputes we strive to achieve.

By the same token, trials are not - nor are they meant to be - tea parties. A lawyer's duty to act with civility does not exist in a vacuum. Rather, it exists in concert with a series of professional obligations that both constrain and compel a lawyer's behaviour. Care must be taken to ensure that free expression, resolute advocacy and the right of an accused to make full answer and defence are not sacrificed at the altar of civility.

The proceedings against the appellant, Joseph Groia, highlight the delicate interplay that these considerations give rise to. At issue is whether Mr. Groia's courtroom conduct in the case of *R. v. Felderhof*, 2007 ONCJ 345, warranted a finding of professional misconduct by the Law Society of Upper Canada. To be precise, was

---

[1] Susan N. Turner, "Raising the Bar: Maximizing Civility in Alberta Courtrooms" (2003) 41 Alta. L. Rev. 547 at 557.

the Law Society Appeal Panel's finding of professional misconduct against Mr. Groia reasonable in the circumstances? For the reasons that follow, I am respectfully of the view that it was not. . . . .

II. Factual Background

Mr. Groia's alleged misconduct stems from his in-court behaviour while representing John Felderhof. Mr. Felderhof was an officer and director of Bre-X Minerals Ltd., a Canadian mining company. Bre-X collapsed when claims that it had discovered a gold mine proved false. The fraud - one of the largest in Canadian capital markets - cost investors over $6 billion. The Ontario Securities Commission ("OSC") charged Mr. Felderhof with insider trading and authorizing misleading news releases under the *Securities Act*, R.S.O. 1990, c. S.5.

Mr. Felderhof hired Mr. Groia, a former OSC prosecutor, to defend him. The trial proceeded in the Ontario Court of Justice before Justice Peter Hryn. It took place in two phases. Phase One began on October 16, 2000 and lasted 70 days. Phase Two did not begin until March 2004. On July 31, 2007, Mr. Felderhof was acquitted of all charges.

Phase One of the Felderhof trial was characterized by a pattern of escalating acrimony between Mr. Groia and the OSC prosecutors. A series of disputes plagued the proceedings with a toxicity that manifested itself in the form of personal attacks, sarcastic outbursts and allegations of professional impropriety, grinding the trial to a near standstill.

A. Disclosure Disputes

Disputes between Mr. Groia and the OSC prosecutors arose during the disclosure process. The Bre-X investigation yielded an extensive documentary record. The OSC initially disclosed interview transcripts and so-called "C-Binders" - binders of documents the OSC intended to use as part of its case against Mr. Felderhof. It did not, however, disclose a substantial body of additional documents it had in its possession. The OSC prosecutors and Mr. Groia disagreed over the scope and format of further disclosure sought by the defence. According to Mr. Groia, it was the OSC's responsibility to sort through all of the documents it had in its possession and to disclose hard copies of any relevant document to the defence. When the OSC prosecutors refused to do so, Mr. Groia wrote a letter to the OSC alleging that the prosecution was "operating under a serious misapprehension of its disclosure obligation[s]", an error that Mr. Groia described as "an abuse of process". . .He would build on these themes as the trial progressed. In response, the OSC offered to disclose electronic copies of the documents in its possession and provide Mr. Groia "with a reasonable supply of blank paper".

Dissatisfied with the OSC's response, Mr. Groia moved for additional disclosure. Mr. Naster, the lead OSC prosecutor, argued that the OSC was not aware of any relevant document that had not been disclosed to Mr. Felderhof. The trial judge, however, agreed with Mr. Groia and ordered the OSC to disclose a further 235 boxes of documents and hard copies of documents stored on 15 discs in its possession.

B. The Second Disclosure Motion

As the trial neared, the parties were still at odds over disclosure. Adamant that the

OSC had not fulfilled its disclosure obligations, Mr. Groia sent Mr. Naster a letter accusing the OSC of adopting "a 'win at any costs' mentality" which demonstrated "a shocking disregard for [Mr. Felderhof's] rights".

Mr. Groia then brought a motion arguing that the OSC's disclosure was so deficient that it amounted to an abuse of process warranting a stay of proceedings. In the alternative, Mr. Groia sought full disclosure, and in the further alternative, an order prohibiting the OSC from calling witnesses until it made full disclosure. Interspersed throughout Mr. Groia's submissions on the motion were allegations that the prosecutors were "unable or unwilling ... to recognize their responsibilities", motivated by an "animus towards the defence", and determined to make Mr. Felderhof's ability to defend himself "as difficult as possible".

By the end of the motion, Mr. Groia conceded that the stringent test for a stay of proceedings had not been met. Accordingly, the trial judge declined to stay the prosecution. Once again, however, he was satisfied that the OSC had not fulfilled its disclosure obligations and he ordered additional disclosure. The trial judge also admonished the OSC for a comment made by one of its media personnel that the OSC's goal "was simply to seek a conviction on the charges" it had laid.

C. The Admissibility of Documents

Characteristic of most *Securities Act* prosecutions, the case against Mr. Felderhof relied heavily on documentary evidence. Between them, the prosecution and defence had nearly 100 binders containing thousands of documents. Disputes over the admissibility of those documents was a major source of friction throughout the trial. . . .

The disputes resulted in frequent objections and lengthy arguments on the admissibility and use of individual documents. The first OSC witness had to be excused for large periods of time as the parties argued. The disputes became increasingly hostile and ground the trial to a near standstill. After 42 days of evidence, the first OSC witness's testimony had yet to be completed.

Much of the disagreement stemmed from Mr. Groia's honest but mistaken understanding of the law of evidence and the role of the prosecutor. His position on the admissibility of documents was founded on two legal errors. First, Mr. Groia maintained that the prosecution was duty-bound to introduce all authentic, relevant documents and that its failure to introduce relevant exculpatory documents through its own witnesses was a deliberate tactic designed to ensure that Mr. Felderhof did not receive a fair trial.

Second, Mr. Groia believed that he could put documents, acknowledged by the OSC as being authentic, to the first OSC witness even though that witness had not authored them and could not identify them. Mr. Naster's objections to this approach spawned further allegations of prosecutorial impropriety. Mr. Groia argued that the OSC was using "a conviction filter" and thwarting Mr. Groia's attempts to secure a fair trial for his client.

Mr. Groia's mistaken position on the admissibility of documents was reinforced by Mr. Naster's comment in the first disclosure motion that he had "an obligation as a prosecutor to ensure that all relevant materials are placed before [the trial judge]".

4

In addition, Mr. Groia mistook Mr. Naster's concession that he was duty-bound to disclose all relevant documents as a promise that he would consent to the admissibility of those documents at trial. In Mr. Groia's view, Mr. Naster unfairly reneged on this promise.

The OSC was not entirely blameless for these skirmishes. Mr. Naster continued to challenge the trial judge's ruling declining to hear an omnibus document motion, lamenting that he was getting "shafted big time". Both sides stubbornly dug their heels in, refusing to budge and taking every opportunity to quarrel.

Despite the frequency and fervor of the disputes, the trial judge initially adopted a hands-off approach, opting to stay above the fray. . . .

It was not until the 57th day of trial that the judge directed Mr. Groia to stop repeating his misconduct allegations. Instead, whenever Mr. Groia felt the prosecution was acting inappropriately, he was to simply state that he was making "the same objection". The trial judge reiterated his instruction a few days later. Mr. Groia largely followed the trial judge's directions for the remainder of Phase One. . . .

Conclusion and Disposition

The Appeal Panel's finding of professional misconduct against Mr. Groia was unreasonable. The Appeal Panel used Mr. Groia's sincerely held but mistaken legal beliefs to conclude that his allegations of prosecutorial misconduct lacked a reasonable basis. But, as I have explained, Mr. Groia's legal errors - in conjunction with the OSC prosecutor's conduct - formed the reasonable basis upon which his allegations rested. In these circumstances, it was not open to the Appeal Panel to conclude that Mr. Groia's allegations lacked a reasonable basis. And because the Appeal Panel accepted that the allegations were made in good faith, it was not reasonably open for it to find Mr. Groia guilty of professional misconduct based on what he said. The Appeal Panel also failed to account for the evolving abuse of process law, the trial judge's reaction to Mr. Groia's behaviour, and Mr. Groia's response - all factors which suggest Mr. Groia's behaviour was not worthy of professional discipline on account of incivility. The finding of professional misconduct against him was therefore unreasonable.

Looking at the circumstances of this case as a whole, the following becomes apparent. Mr. Groia's mistaken allegations were made in good faith and were reasonably based. The manner in which he raised them was improper. However, the very nature of Mr. Groia's allegations - deliberate prosecutorial misconduct depriving his client of a fair trial - led him to use strong language that may well have been inappropriate in other contexts. The frequency of his allegations was influenced by an underdeveloped abuse of process jurisprudence. The trial judge chose not to curb Mr. Groia's allegations throughout the majority of Phase One. When the trial judge and reviewing courts did give instructions, Mr. Groia appropriately modified his behaviour. Taking these considerations into account, the only reasonable disposition is a finding that he did not engage in professional misconduct.

I would allow the appeal and set aside the decision of the Appeal Panel with respect to the finding of professional misconduct against Mr. Groia and the penalty imposed. I would award costs to Mr. Groia in this Court and in the courts below, as well as in the proceedings before the Law Society. Because Mr. Groia, in the circumstances of this case, could not reasonably be found guilty of professional misconduct, the complaints against him are dismissed and there is no need to remit the matter back to the Law Society. . . . .

NOTES AND QUESTIONS

1. Prior to the Supreme Court's decision, Groia had consistently failed in his challenges to Law Society sanctions arising from his representation of Felderhof. Two panels at the Law Society of Ontario (then Upper Canada), the Ontario Divisional Court and the Ontario Court of Appeal had all agreed that his conduct was uncivil and properly subject to Law Society discipline, although one judge at the Ontario Court of Appeal had dissented. The Law Society Appeal Panel described Groia as having engaged in a "relentless personal attack" on the prosecutor without "reasonable basis" for doing so. It found that his conduct had a "serious adverse impact" on the conduct of the trial.

2. The proceedings against Groia were commenced by the Law Society itself. No complaint was made against Groia by any participant in the *Felderhof* litigation, or by any member of the public.

3. The *Groia* case is an example of the regulation of lawyers by the provincial aw ocieties to which every Canadian lawyer belongs. At the same time, however, it shows one of the ways in which Canadian courts play a central role in defining what constitutes ethical conduct for lawyers. Do you think provincial law societies have greater expertise than courts in determining what constitutes incivility, or do the courts? In assessing whether it was unethical, does it matter whether the alleged incivility occurred in court?

4. In considering whether Groia's conduct was ethical, do you find it more helpful to think about the question from the perspective of his role as a lawyer, or from more general moral values (i.e., that would apply to any person)? In what way does the *Groia* case suggest that role morality aligns with universal moral principles? In what way does it suggest that a lawyer's role morality might conflict with universal moral principles?

   To put it slightly differently, is the behaviour of Groia as described by the majority consistent with being a good person? If not, what, if anything, does that suggest to you about the ethics of the lawyer's role, and whether a good lawyer can be a good person?

5. Do you think Felderhof would have viewed Groia's conduct as ethical? What about the general public? Naster? The presiding justice?

6. To whom or what did Groia owe duties when representing Felderhof? What do you think those duties were? Did they conflict? And if so, in what way?

7. How do you view the conduct of Naster, the OSC prosecutor, when compared to Groia? Why do you think Groia might have been subject to law society discipline, while Naster was not?

8. In later chapters, you will learn about the special ethical responsibilities of

prosecutors in criminal cases - that they are often described as "ministers of justice". What effect, if any, does that have on your assessment of the relative conduct of Naster and Groia as described in the majority decision? What does it mean for defining the "role" morality of prosecutors relative to other lawyers?

Scenario One

Traditionally, Canadian lawyers were prohibited from advertising and, in particular, were subject to much stricter restrictions on fee advertising than exist today. In the 1970s a Vancouver lawyer, Don Jabour, began advertising his services. He listed the type of services he provided accompanied by a list of "sample fees (excluding out-of-pocket expenses)". A "Simple will" had a sample fee of $35, an uncontested divorce was ". . .from $195". The Law Society of British Columbia objected to Jabour's advertising practices and disciplined him for unprofessional conduct. Jabour challenged their jurisdiction to do so but was unsuccessful.

In your view, is Jabour's conduct properly described as unethical? Would you view his conduct as consistent with being a good lawyer? A good person? How do you think a potential client of Jabour would have viewed his conduct? Would that person's perspective be the same as that of the Law Society of British Columbia?

For more about Jabour's case see: *Law Society of British Columbia v Jabour* [1980] B.C.J. No. 833, [1982] 2 S.C.R. 307 (S.C.C.).

Scenario Two

The Federation of Law Societies' Model Code of Conduct does not prohibit a lawyer from having a sexual relationship with a client. It identifies such relationships as potentially creating a conflict of interest, noting that they may conflict with the lawyer's ability to provide "objective, disinterested, professional advice" and might "permit exploitation of the client". The Model Code prohibits lawyers from sexually harassing any person. The Model Code and case law also restrict the ability of a criminal defence lawyer to withdraw from representation, although withdrawal is permitted if an ethical issue has arisen in the representation (See Chapter 2, Section [4]).

Roger Smith is a criminal defence lawyer. He was retained by Jane Jones to represent her in relation to an allegation that she had committed fraud against her former employer. After she retained him, Smith and Jones began a sexual relationship. Six weeks prior to Jones' trial, she ended the sexual relationship with Smith. Smith then withdrew from the representation, telling the Court that "ethical differences" had arisen with his client which prevented his continued representation of her.

Did Smith act ethically? If not, what in your view was the source of his unethical conduct? How important to your analysis is the question of whether Smith's conduct conformed with his obligations under the law – for example, the case law governing lawyer withdrawal in criminal cases, or the provisions of the applicable code of conduct? What other factors influence your assessment of the ethics of Smith's conduct? What additional information, if any, would you want to know in making your assessment? What body do you think is best positioned to respond to any ethical deficiencies in Smith's conduct – the Law Society or the courts conducting Jones' criminal trial? What steps could each of those bodies take in relation to Smith?

[2] WHAT ARE LAWYERS' ETHICS AND PROFESSIONAL REGULATION?

The definition of "legal ethics" has engaged and troubled academic commentators for many years. For our purposes, however, it is sufficient to note some relatively uncontroversial features of lawyers' ethics and professional regulation. Or, to put it slightly differently, to map the landscape of what is covered in the rest of this casebook.

Lawyers' ethics deals with the ethical obligations of the practising lawyer, both as individuals and as members of organizations. Lawyers' ethics addresses the constraints on lawyer conduct: the rules, principles and legal obligations with which lawyers are required to comply in conducting their legal practice. It also addresses the moral or ethical aspirations of the practising lawyer — the type of decision-making processes and decisions which an ethical lawyer will employ and make in deciding how to act, particularly where the lawyer is given discretion by the rules or law. At the level of moral aspiration, of course, there is more controversy, and less agreement, as to what lawyers' ethics requires than there is at the level of legal constraint. There is, for example, far more agreement that a lawyer must not fraudulently bill a client than that a lawyer should represent only clients with a just claim. It is the task of the student and teacher of lawyers' ethics to engage, however, with both sorts of questions. This book is designed to allow you to do so. It considers specific ethical issues related to the selection and representation of clients in a variety of practice contexts, and facilitates analysis of what lawyers are required to do, and should aspire to do, in resolving those issues in those contexts. It considers these questions both as a matter of legal doctrine and as a matter of principle.

Lawyers' ethics also considers the implications for the life of a lawyer of fulfilling the lawyer's role. Specifically, whether helping a client to achieve their legal goals, without necessarily approving of those goals, corrodes the lawyer's ethical life. As Charles Fried asked in the opening sentence of his foundational article about lawyer's ethics, "Can a good lawyer be a good person?"[2] This book, and in particular the final section of this chapter, invites you to reflect on this question.

Like lawyer's ethics, professional regulation is concerned with the ethics of legal practice. Its concern exists, however, at the level of regulation and governance: how do we determine and enforce ethical constraints on lawyer conduct? As presently structured, all Canadian lawyers are regulated in significant part through a form of "self-regulation" in which the rules of ethical conduct, the standards for admission to the profession, and the enforcement of those rules and standards, are set by lawyers themselves. This book also provides information about the current structure of professional regulation, some of its current issues and challenges, and possibilities for change and reform.

---

[2] Charles Fried, "The Lawyer as Friend: The Moral Foundations of the Lawyer-Client Relation" (1976), 85 Yale L.J. 1060 at 1060.

[3] SOURCES

In determining what constitutes ethical conduct, a lawyer can look to a number of sources for guidance. These include:

- Case law and legislation;
- Rules of professional conduct;
- Law society disciplinary decisions; and
- The principles or "norms" of lawyering.

These sources also play a role in how we regulate Canadian lawyers. They flow from and inform the traditional method for regulating lawyers – the law societies who admit lawyers, set professional standards and discipline lawyers who violate them. They also flow from and inform regulation of lawyers in the broader sense of regulation as any consistent and sustained effort to create particular behaviour and to achieve particular outcomes.[3]

---

[3] Julia Black, "Critical Reflections on Regulation" (2002) 27 Austl. J. Leg. Phil. 1 at 26.

[a]   Case Law and Legislation

Case law and legislation (including regulations) place constraints on what lawyers can and cannot do in legal practice. The law of negligence obliges lawyers to meet certain basic standards of competence. The law of fiduciary duties requires lawyers to act with loyalty in furthering the interests of their clients, and to put the interests of their clients before those of themselves or others. The law of contracts governs the specific obligations a lawyer has to a client under a retainer agreement (whether written or oral). The Supreme Court of Canada has held that "the scope of the [lawyer's] retainer is governed by contract".[4] The law on taxation of legal fees, in which clients or lawyers obtain court assessment of a lawyer's bill and an order requiring the bill to be paid as assessed, provides guidance on a lawyer's ethical obligations when charging a client. Cases dealing with the law of evidence and, in particular, the doctrine of solicitor-client privilege, are essential for understanding the lawyer's obligation of confidentiality to clients. The rules of court and the cases interpreting those rules have dealt with lawyer ethics in the conduct of an action. In the criminal law context, ensuring the fair trial of an accused creates legal duties on defence lawyers to provide effective assistance of counsel, and identifies constraints on the proper conduct of a prosecution. Finally, the inherent authority of the court to control its own processes has led to numerous cases dealing with the obligations of lawyers to avoid acting in circumstances where there is a potential conflict of interest between the lawyer and their client, or between the lawyers' various clients, current and former. It has also led to case law dealing with the duty of lawyers not to withdraw from a representation except with ethical justification.

Case law and legislation thus significantly guide and constrain lawyer conduct. Indeed, case law and legislation may be the most significant doctrinal source of guidance for lawyers on what is required to act ethically. Nonetheless, many issues are not addressed by case law or legislation, and direction on what lawyers may not do, or are required to do, with respect to those issues must be found elsewhere.

[b]   Rules of Professional Conduct

Every provincial law society has rules of professional conduct. These rules are generally enacted by the law society pursuant to its legislative authority to regulate the legal profession. The rules cover a variety of matters related to legal practice including client selection, advocacy, competence, fees, conflicts of interest, confidentiality, advising clients, interacting with judges and the business operation of a law practice. Through the Federation of Law Societies of Canada, an umbrella organization to which all the provincial law societies belong, the law societies have created a high degree of uniformity in the rules of conduct across the provinces. In 2009, the Federation published a *Model Code of Professional Conduct*. All Canadian law societies outside of Québec have adopted a version of the Federation's *Model Code*. This casebook references the Federation's *Model Code* when setting out what codes of conduct say about lawyers' obligations.

Provincial law societies rely on codes of conduct in disciplinary prosecutions and

---

[4] *Strother v. 3464920 Canada Inc.*, [2007] S.C.J. No. 24, [2007] 2 S.C.R. 177 at para. 34 (S.C.C.).

proceedings but do not uniformly or comprehensively enforce them. In addition, the codes of conduct in a number of areas rely on general and discretionary guidelines ("should" or "may") rather than specific mandatory obligations. Codes of conduct are therefore an essential but non-exhaustive source of guidance for a lawyer in deciding what to do in circumstances of ethical uncertainty.

[c] Law Society Disciplinary Decisions

Law society disciplinary decisions are publicly available through law society websites, Quicklaw and CanLII. Disciplinary decisions provide insight into what provisions of the codes of conduct mean. They also indicate how law societies generally define professional misconduct (misconduct by the lawyer when practising law) and conduct unbecoming (misconduct by the lawyer outside of their legal practice). Disciplinary decisions set out the standard of proof for establishing that a lawyer has committed professional misconduct and the sorts of sanctions that may be imposed.

Disciplinary decisions provide, however, limited guidance to lawyers in deciding how to act, because they tend to address a relatively narrow range of lawyer conduct, concentrating mostly on clear legal violations such as stealing funds from clients, or on a lawyer's refusal to comply with law society regulatory requirements. Most of the vexing questions of ethics, the questions that do not lend themselves to obvious answers, are not addressed by disciplinary decisions in any meaningful way.

[d] Principles or "Norms"

Because of the wide variety of circumstances that can implicate lawyer ethics, and because of the constrained quantity and quality of the guidance provided by case law, legislation, the rules of conduct and disciplinary decisions, lawyers seeking to be ethical must look beyond those sources. A lawyer who is deciding, for example, whether to disclose information provided by a client where the rules of professional conduct say that they "may" do so needs to know what to consider in deciding what action to take. A lawyer who is deciding which clients to act for, when the rules of conduct and case law leave that matter almost entirely within their discretion, needs to know on what basis to make that choice. A lawyer who perceives a gap between the obligations imposed by the law governing lawyers and the obligations of ordinary morality needs to know how to respond to that gap in deciding what to do, or how to reconcile their decision with a life well-lived. Where, for example, the law governing lawyers requires that information be kept confidential, but ordinary moral principles would require disclosure in order to prevent harm to third parties, a lawyer needs principles and norms to guide their response, and to allow them to determine how that response can be incorporated into a life well-lived. With respect to all these sorts of questions important sources of guidance are principles or "norms" that apply to the work that lawyers do.

Principles or norms play an additional role of importance. To act ethically, lawyers need to be sensitive to when an ethical issue has arisen; they need to have the judgment to respond to that ethical situation appropriately; and they need to have

11

the motivation and courage to put their response into action.[5] Having these qualities requires more than that a lawyer be able to apply the law, or reason through how principles might apply to a particular situation. It requires as well that the lawyer have strong intuitions that will allow them to perceive quickly that an ethical problem has arisen, and what should be done. Developing those intuitions requires the lawyer to have a strong commitment to a principled conception of the lawyer's role, to know to the point of sensing, what being a lawyer means, and does not mean.[6]

What principles or norms best define the lawyer's role is a matter of dispute, with differing emphasis being placed on the important societal role that lawyers fulfill, on the requirements of ordinary morality, on the foundational morality of the legal system or on the lawyer's own ethical integrity. In this book, we will not take a position on which principles or norms can best inform a lawyer's ethical decisions. Instead, we will present different conceptions of the lawyer's role. Students or practitioners can defensibly adopt any conception set out here, provided they do so with respect for its full complexity and the demands it actually places upon a lawyer. Moreover, students and practitioners who do this — who have a fully realized normative conception of what being a lawyer requires — will be better equipped to make morally defensible decisions in circumstances of ethical uncertainty, to reconcile their work as a lawyer with the broader goal of achieving an ethical life (a meaningful life), and to fulfil the function of the lawyer within a free and democratic society.

[4] SOME WAYS OF THINKING ABOUT "ORDINARY" ETHICS

The role of norms and principles means that lawyers' ethics is linked with general ways of thinking about what being ethical[7] requires. Being an ethical lawyer is not just about applying "ordinary" ethics to legal practice; indeed, many theorists argue that lawyer's ethics are better understood as a problem of political theory, not of ordinary morality. At the same time, "ordinary" ways of thinking about ethical problems affect, and may sometimes helpfully inform, how we think about what being an ethical lawyer requires. If nothing else, we need to grapple with the extent to which the answer given by the law governing lawyers about what a lawyer should do differs from what ordinary morality would suggest a lawyer ought to do.

This section provides a brief overview of the main philosophical schools of

---

[5] These are the "four components" of ethical decision-making. See, in general, James Rest, *Development in Judging Moral Issues* (Minneapolis: University of Minnesota Press, 1979).

[6] Alice Woolley, "The Problem of Disagreement in Legal Ethics Theory" (2012) 26 C.J.L.J. 181; David Luban, "Reason and Passion in Legal Ethics" (1999) 51 Stan. L. Rev. 873.

[7] In this section I am using ethics and morality interchangeably, but am referring to the idea of impartial rules about the right way to live (which is how Bernard Williams would define morality) and not to the broader ethical concept of a well-lived life (see in general: Bernard Williams, "Moral Luck" in *Moral Luck: Philosophical Papers 1973-1980* (Cambridge: Cambridge University Press, 1981).

thought on ethics. In the readings listed at the end of this chapter, some of the primary sources for each of these schools of thought are also identified. In reading this overview, recall the two dimensions of ethics previously identified: ethics as a series of rules that constrain human behaviour, and ethics as a set of aspirations that, ideally, we attempt to achieve. General philosophies of ethics, like lawyers' ethics, attempt to explain and justify ethics in both senses.

[a] Virtue Ethics

Aristotelian virtue ethics explains ethical action through the combination of human character, practical judgment and orientation towards human flourishing. It posits that individuals possess virtues (or vices) which orientate them towards (or away from) ethical conduct. Thus, for example, a person possessing the virtue of compassion will be disposed towards compassionate action.

The significance of virtues in virtue ethics is not that they have this effect; rather, it is that the possession and cultivation of the virtues contribute to human flourishing (*eudaimonia*). In addition, the possession of virtues is not sufficient in and of itself to ensure virtuous action. Rather, virtuous action will arise where an individual both possesses the virtues essential for such action *and* has the practical judgment (*phronesis*) essential for applying those virtues in a particular situation.

Thus, a lawyer possessed of the virtues necessary for legal practice, and faced with an ethical dilemma, will resolve that dilemma through exercising judgment about how those virtues are appropriately balanced in the circumstances. The lawyer will recognize the importance of the virtues of loyalty, honesty, care, compassion, justice and integrity to the situation, and will exercise judgment as to what those virtues require given the particular circumstances. Virtue ethics eschews the notion of specific rules as the source of ethical guidance — the Kantian position that, for example, because honesty is required by a categorical imperative, there are no circumstances in which a lie is justified — and argues instead that it is our virtues of character which, when exercised through our practical judgment, lead us to ethical action. Pursuit of the virtues is, ultimately, the precondition for human flourishing.

To understand the application of virtue ethics consider the following problem: Jack and Jane both work for a government agency responsible for combating terrorism. The agency has apprehended X, and has excellent grounds for believing that X and others have been conspiring to set off explosive devices at the Canadian National Exhibition on the following day. X's co-conspirators have not been found. If the devices are set off, many people will be injured and killed. X refuses to talk. Should Jack and Jane torture X to obtain information to prevent the execution of the conspiracy?

A virtue ethics based response to this problem would consider it through the applicable virtues which might include respect, dignity, compassion, justice and fairness. It would then assess the facts and how different responses to the facts (torture or not) would accord with the virtues. The ethical answer to the question would be that most consistent with the pursuit of the virtues as properly assessed through judgment of what the facts require.

[b] Utilitarianism (Consequentialism)

Virtue ethics clearly relies on a conception of human beings as constituted by a series of virtues and vices that motivate human action. Utilitarianism rests on starkly different premises about human nature: human beings want to maximize their self-interest and will seek to do so. Humans possess "instrumental rationality" — they can identify their own interests and will act to pursue them. Utilitarianism also asserts the additional premise that a society in which overall human interests are maximized is the best society. The general aim of a society should be to achieve "the greatest good for the greatest number".

For the utilitarian, therefore, ethics is not a matter of abstractly identified concepts of "right" or "wrong" — and certainly not to character-based assertions such as "virtue" or "vice". Rather, the most ethical action – the right action – is that which is likely to do the greatest good for the greatest number or, where that is not possible, to do the least amount of harm to the fewest number of people. Utilitarianism is fundamentally and unabashedly consequentialist.

It must be noted, though, that utilitarianism does not necessarily require case-by-case analysis of consequences. "Indirect (rule) utilitarianism" posits that while it may be that the application of a particular rule does not maximize utility in a single instance, provided that the rule *in general* has that effect, then the rule is justified on utilitarian grounds. So, for example, although the requirement that lawyers keep their client's secrets in confidence may do harm in a particular case, if the overall rule maximizes social utility, the rule is justified. In addition, utilitarian theory includes numerous assumptions which constrain the assessment of a particular act. For example, utilitarian theory requires "agent neutrality" — that the preferences of one person must not be privileged over the preferences of another. In addition, utilitarians such as John Stuart Mill argued that not all preferences are equal. Mill believed it reasonable to assert that some preferences were inherently more valuable than others, and thus entitled to greater weight in an assessment of an action's consequences. So, for example, Mill might suggest that a preference for maintaining client confidences is more valuable — worthy of greater weight in a utilitarian calculus — than a preference for publicity.

Further, in its most sophisticated forms, utilitarianism is not so much a means of reaching ethical decisions as it is a way of judging whether a decision is ethical. It may be that it is impossible to assess in advance the consequences of one's actions, or of a rule or policy governing human conduct. However, if after the fact it is apparent that an action has had terrible consequences, those consequences justify assessing the action as bad or unethical. For example, in the case of *R. v. Murray*,[8] excerpted later in this chapter and discussed in detail in Chapter 3, the lawyer Murray suppressed for a period of time videotapes showing his client, Paul Bernardo, and Bernardo's then spouse Karla Homolka committing horrific sexual violence against young women. In assessing the ethics of his act, it would be relevant in utilitarianism that one consequence of Murray's decision was that Karla Homolka escaped the criminal sanction she deserved because the Crown felt they had to offer her a favourable plea arrangement in return for her testimony against Bernardo. This consequence of Murray's choice indicates, in part, the ethical (or,

---

[8] [2000] O.J. No. 2182, 48 O.R. (3d) 544 (Ont. S.C.J.).

14

more accurately, unethical) nature of that choice.

Finally, some modern consequentialists are willing to accept that consequentialism is not the only way of assessing conduct, or determining what is ethical. But they argue that any reasonable conception of what constitutes ethical action *must* take into account the consequences of that action. Even if we accept an action with awful consequences as ultimately correct — for example, refusing to torture one person even though we know with certainty that doing so would save five others — we cannot ignore those awful consequences in our assessment of the correctness of that action.

To understand the application of utilitarianism, consider again the Jack and Jane torture hypothetical. The utilitarian analysis of the problem would require consideration of the consequences of the torture choice. What will happen to X, to Jack and Jane, and to others if they torture X? What will happen to X, to Jack and Jane, and to others if they do not torture X? What would be the consequences of a rule permitting torture in this situation? What are the consequences of a rule prohibiting torture in this situation? The ethical response should aim to maximize the positive consequences, and minimize the negative consequences, that are possible given the facts at issue, and given the rules that could be developed to decide what to do in the face of those facts.

[c] Kantian/Deontological Theories of Right Action

Kantian theories of right action — of deciding what is morally required — contrast starkly with both virtue ethics and utilitarianism (consequentialism). Unlike virtue ethics, Kantian theories are strongly rule-based; they assert the possibility and necessity of having universal rules that articulate what morality requires, and that can be applied to particular circumstances. Unlike consequentialism, Kantian theories reject the significance of consequences to the assessment of the morality of a course of conduct. If a rule applies to a circumstance, such as "do not torture", then that rule must be applied regardless of the consequences of doing so in a particular case.

However, like virtue ethics and consequentialism, Kantian theories rest on a particular understanding of human nature. For the Kantian, the essential relevant fact about human nature is that humans have the capacity for reasoning: freedom of choice and action. While what a particular person decides to do may be affected by personal desires or impulses, the existence of free will and the capacity to reason means that personal choice will not be *determined* by personal desires and impulses. Through the exercise of reasoning, a person can decide what to do or not do.

Any moral rule or duty must respect this fact. It must comply with what Kant calls the categorical imperative: the only principles which should guide your actions are those which could also hold as universal law, that is, those that could apply to every other free (reasoning) person. The fundamental moral requirement which follows from the application of the categorical imperative is that you must treat every person as having a free will, and you must not make any other person merely a means for the exercise of your own free will. You must treat every person as an end, and not merely as a means.

Kantian ethics also applies to Jack and Jill's ethical dilemma over whether to

15

torture X, and unlike virtue ethics and utilitarianism, the answer it gives to the torture hypothetical would focus on articulation and application of the appropriate moral law as derived from the categorical imperative. Because the impetus for torture is entirely consequentialist, it is unlikely that a moral rule could justify it; torturing a person to achieve one's own (or society's) goal would seem a *prima facie* denial of that person's moral agency, and a treatment of him as merely a means.

[d] Postmodernism

Postmodernism is, fundamentally, a method of intellectual criticism; it does not posit a new way of ethical reasoning or a new definition of the content of ethical conduct. It simply identifies significant problems with most traditional approaches to questions such as "what does it mean to be ethical?"

The central assumption of postmodernism is that the world is unknowable. It is possible to use language to describe things, but any description of the world is necessarily derived from the position of the person doing the describing (and will be understood from the position of the person hearing the description). Contrary to Kant, postmodernism asserts that a person cannot be removed from their desires and impulses; a person may choose not to pursue them, but their existence will necessarily shape and inform that person's analysis. Further, it is impossible to assess consequences with any degree of objectivity or certainty. Knowing what is good, even for one's self, is a situated assessment. It cannot be known in the abstract or with certainty.

Postmodernism does not reject the idea of ethics, nor does it assert that ethics is a waste of time, or that it is impossible to act ethically. What postmodernism identifies as impossible is a calculus through which moral ideas or judgments can be tested and perfected. It posits that ethical decisions must be made through individual judgment and moral intuitions, through the subjective viewpoint of the individual making them. An ethical individual will take responsibility for a decision that they make, and be accountable for it, but they will not be aided in making that decision by abstract or objectively orientated attempts to follow a rule, or to assess the decision's consequences.

Thus, if Jack and Jill are postmodernists they must apply their individual judgment and moral intuitions to determine the ethical/rightful response to X. Further, and importantly, they must accept that they are the ones who made the decision and take responsibility for it. A postmodernist Jack and Jill must be prepared to explain why they decided to torture X (if they did so) and why they decided not to torture X (if they did not do so). No equation or analytical calculus will identify the correct solution to the problem for them — they must simply apply their intuitions and judgment, make a decision, provide justifications and take responsibility for the decision they have made.

[e] Pluralism

Like postmodernism, pluralism rejects the monistic claims of consequentialism and of Kantian deontology. It does not accept that a single premise — either as to the importance of consequences or to the importance of the human capacity to reason — can ground ethical decision-making. Rather, pluralism asserts both that there are various values, and, that there are various ways of identifying which values are important. Pluralism is *not* relativism; it does not accept that all values are equally valid or equally important. It simply asserts that the attempt to find a single unifying value or way of identifying values is misguided and impossible.

For the pluralist, the heart of ethical decision-making is not, therefore, the pursuit of a single value or source of action-guidance against which we can assess our decisions. Rather, the heart of ethical decision-making is the weighing and measuring of different — and occasionally conflicting — values in different circumstances, and the application of those values in order to decide what ethics requires given those circumstances. This may require, as did virtue ethics, the use of practical judgment. It does not necessarily do so, however. Some pluralists argue simply that in any given situation, we will scale the values and apply them: "We can work out trade-offs between different dimensions of pleasure or happiness. And when we do, we rank in a strong sense: not just choose one rather than the other, but regard it as worth more."[9]

The Jack and Jill pluralist is, like the postmodernist, also somewhat unconstrained in how to assess the torture problem. The pluralist may consider virtues, consequences and the possibility of applying a universal rule. A pluralist will not be neutral in assessing whether to torture X, but also will not be bound by one particular way of reasoning through the problem. In the end, like the postmodernist, the pluralist will be required to exercise judgment, to explain the decision and to take responsibility for what that person has done.

[5] WHAT DOES BEING AN ETHICAL LAWYER REQUIRE?

For the remainder of this chapter, the focus is on the general question of what it means to be an ethical lawyer. The following sections discuss some competing conceptions of the lawyer's central ethical duties.

[a] Loyal Advocacy

Loyalty is the core moral requirement or value traditionally associated with legal practice. It has three defining features: that the lawyer be neutral towards the client's goals, that the lawyer not be morally accountable for the client's goals, and that the lawyer act as a partisan to accomplish the client's goals. Commentators who emphasize the importance of loyalty have analogized the lawyer-client relationship to "friendship" in order to explain what loyalty requires:

> A lawyer is a friend in regard to the legal system. He is someone who enters into a personal relation with you — not an abstract relation as under the concept of justice. That means that like a friend he acts in your interests, not his own; or rather he adopts your interests as his own. I would call that the classic definition of friendship. To be sure, the lawyer's range of concern is sharply limited. But within that limited domain the intensity of the identification with the client's interests is the same.[10]

---

[9] J. Griffin, *Well-Being: Its Meaning, Measurement and Moral Importance* (Oxford: Clarendon Press, 1986) at 90.

[10] C. Fried, "The Lawyer as Friend: The Moral Foundations of the Lawyer-Client Relationship" (1975) 85 Yale L.J. 1060 at 1071-1072.

Loyal partisanship requires the lawyer to place the interests of the client above those of other people. A lawyer will help the client to achieve goals despite the consequences for others. It also requires the lawyer to place the interests of the client above their own. As recently described by the Supreme Court: "A fundamental duty of a lawyer is to act in the best interest of his or her client to the exclusion of all other adverse interests, except those duly disclosed by the lawyer and willingly accepted by the client."[11]

Why does a lawyer have a duty of loyalty to a client? Why would we want lawyers to be neutral partisans who pursue their client's goals without moral accountability for those goals? Those who place loyalty at the heart of the lawyer's ethical obligations often justify its importance for the protection of individual rights and freedoms. The thrust of this argument is that each individual in society is autonomous and, as such, is entitled to be free from unwarranted state interference. Maintaining one's autonomy from improper state interference requires every person to have the right to access the justice system. It is through lawyers that individuals access the justice system. Therefore, individuals have a right to a lawyer, and the lawyer who helps a client to access justice does an ethical act.

In addition, a lawyer cannot provide meaningful help to the client without being loyal to the client's interests. A lawyer must do for the client what the client cannot do alone, namely, access the legal system to its full extent. Indeed, to do otherwise — to sacrifice a client to the goals of justice — is to fail to respect the autonomy of the client, and to act inconsistently with the loyalty to which the client is entitled.

More recently, the loyal advocacy position has shifted away from a focus on client autonomy. Instead, proponents of loyal advocacy emphasize the function of law as a means of achieving a civil society despite the fact that the people in any society will have deeply divergent conceptions of the right way to live. For law to function as a form of social compromise, to allow peaceful resolution of disputes and to enable, regulate or restrict individual action, it must be accessible to the citizenry. That accessibility requires lawyers, and it requires in particular lawyers who act in loyal furtherance of their client's interests without judgment of the client. This model does not ignore the lawyer's role in protecting client autonomy or dignity in the legal system, but it does focus on the broader political and social function of law in understanding the lawyer's role in the legal system.

The model of loyal advocacy does not contemplate unconstrained representation of client interests. Rather, it imposes limits on advocacy derived from the principles that justify it, namely that the purpose of advocacy is to allow clients to access the legal system. Thus, any act which does not further client access, which instead subverts or undermines the legal system, cannot be justified. Bradley Wendel, for example, argues that a lawyer's overarching ethical obligation is one of "fidelity to law". The role of the lawyer is not to substitute their moral judgment for that of a client, nor is it to simply do the client's bidding regardless of what the legal system itself requires. Instead, the lawyer's obligation is to assist their client to pursue that

---

[11] *Strother v. 3464920 Canada Inc.*, [2007] S.C.J. No. 24, [2007] 2 S.C.R. 177 at para. 1 (S.C.C.).

client's legal ends, and to do so in a manner consistent with what the legal system itself requires.

The following excerpt defends the loyal advocacy conception of the lawyer's role. Like most more recent defences of the loyal advocacy conception, it relies on the idea of law as a form of social settlement, arguing that the function of the lawyer is to help law achieve that purpose. It also identifies limits on loyal advocacy, suggesting that a lawyer ought to provide zealous representation of a client, but that zeal should be "mere-zeal" not "hyper-zeal".

TIM DARE
"Mere-Zeal, Hyper-Zeal and the Ethical Obligations of Lawyers"
(2004) 7 Legal Ethics 24
[Footnotes omitted]

According to the "standard conception of the lawyer's role", lawyers owe special duties to their clients that allow and perhaps even require conduct that would otherwise be morally impermissible. But 'the standard conception' has become an ironic epithet. If numbers count, the standard view now is that it cannot be right. The conception has passed from orthodoxy to fair game, replaced by a near consensus that it "must be abandoned, to be replaced by a conception that better allows the lawyer to bring his full moral sensibilities to play in his professional role" and that "[t]he lawyer's role carries no moral privileges and immunities". Much of the criticism of the standard conception is directed at the idea that it requires excessive and immoral advocacy on behalf of clients. "Every lawyer", David Luban claims, "knows tricks of the trade that can be used to do opponents out of their legal deserts". Critics of the standard conception claim that it not only allows, but also requires, them to use such tricks if it is in their client's interests to do so.

But I do not think we should abandon the standard conception. This paper offers an alternative reading of the conception, proceeding from a functional analysis of law and drawing a distinction between "mere-zeal" and "hyper-zeal", in an attempt to show both that the conception is essentially the right way to conceive of the ethical obligations of lawyers and how it is able to avoid the complaint that it requires excessive advocacy. In defense of a moderate version of the conception, I attempt to show that the conception requires and allows only mere and not hyper-zeal. . . .

II. The Standard Conception and the Role of Law

1. Law and Reasonable Pluralism

We begin then, with an account of the function of law. The institutions of law in Western democracies no doubt serve many functions: they are dispute resolution devices; they supply answers to coordination problems (they tell us, for instance, which side of the road to drive on); they secure the provision of certain public goods, such as health care and roading; they allow conduct which would simply not be possible other than in institutional contexts (just as one cannot "hit a six" or "hit a home-run" without the institutions of cricket or baseball, nor can one "incorporate a company" without the institution of company law); they facilitate planning by treating certain kinds of undertakings or arrangements as enforceable; they identify certain forms of conduct as required or prohibited, and lend the power of the state to better ensure compliance.

This is no doubt an incomplete list of the functions of the institutions of western law. Yet, even in this abbreviated form, it may seem so diverse as to render impossible a compelling appeal to law's function: how can one appeal meaningfully to "the function of law" when it has so many functions? The answer is that a common and general function lies behind these more specific ones. John Rawls' later work is suggestive. It is based upon the premise that the citizens of modern democracies are and will remain sharply divided over fundamental questions such as what constitutes human flourishing, what basic goals are intrinsically most worthy of pursuit, and what is the best way for individuals to live their lives. This "plurality of conceptions of the good", Rawls concludes, is inevitable; it is "the natural outcome of the activities of human reason under enduring free institutions".

Not all views about these fundamental matters count as reasonable. But even [excluding extremists], a plurality of reasonable views remains. In modern times, the claim goes, we have come to recognize a multiplicity of ways in which a fulfilled life can be lived, without seeing a hierarchy among them that we feel justified in enforcing. We have been forced to acknowledge that even where we believe that we have discerned the superiority of some ways of life over others, reasonable people may not share our view. Pluralism and reasonable disagreement are ineliminable features of the political landscape in modern constitutional democracies.

The challenge for such communities is to find a way that "there may exist over time a secure stable and just society among free and equal citizens profoundly divided by reasonable though incompatible religious, philosophical and moral doctrine". A central part of the liberal answer to this question has been the adoption of a certain kind of neutrality as a political ideal. The members of a pluralist community, the idea goes, will often be able to agree on the structure of neutral institutions and practices even where they cannot agree on the right outcome of a policy question as a substantive matter. Though it is unlikely they ever reach agreement on the substantive political questions which motivate their disagreement, each may accept as fair a system which allows every view to be expressed, which allows representatives of every view to stand for office, which gives every person a vote, which allocates seats to representatives of the various positions in proportion to the percentage of votes cast in favour of that position, and so on. Procedures such as these are intended to ensure that all reasonable views are taken equally seriously, and that none are preferred by the very structure of the procedures. Of course, such practices cannot guarantee outcomes that will suit all the reasonable views. Often there will be no such universally-acceptable outcome. There simply is no resolution of the abortion debate that will seem substantively correct to every reasonable disputant. The hope of liberalism, however, is that even those whose substantive preferences do not win the day on this or that occasion will have cause to accept as fair the decisions of these institutions because they accept the procedures by which they were reached.

The institutions and practices to which a procedural understanding of neutrality give rise allow the creation of stable and just communities, despite the presence of a widespread diversity of conflicting and perhaps even incommensurable conceptions of the good. They do so by mediating between this diversity of substantive views and concrete decisions that communities must take. . . .

Our continued membership in a common community will sometimes require us to find a way of going on, of deciding what to do, despite our disagreement as to what ought to be done. Perhaps we toss a coin and you win. The toss changes the situation in an important way. If our discussion really was exhaustive, you could not give me any more reasons in favour of your view. After the toss, however, you can give me a new reason, namely the fact that the decision procedure we accepted has selected your preference. The normative force of this reason, however, does not depend upon me thinking that you were right about the substantive matter. I can accept it as a reason for action, while continuing to hold on to my own view of what, from a substantive perspective, ought to have been done.

Of course, we do not settle our political disputes by the toss of a coin. The decision-making procedures that are the focus of the actual accommodations between competing conceptions of the good in our community are enormously complex. Instead of the straightforward coin-tossing procedure, we have a set of procedures which include the procedures for selecting governments, for making and interpreting law, for determining ownership of goods, and so on. . . .

Adherents of the various and diverse conceptions of the good that are represented in our communities cannot be expected to agree on any single conception of the good. They can agree, however, on the form of procedures that will give them, if not what they want, at least what they need. Although we do not and will not agree on fundamental matters such as what constitutes human flourishing, what basic goals are intrinsically most worthy of pursuit, and what is the best way for individuals to live their lives, we can agree on procedures which respect the diversity of views represented in the community, and which issue decisions with which we can live.

This section has addressed the role of law in pluralist communities. It began with the observation that the nature of roles and role obligations depended upon the nature and function of the institutions of which they were a part. I have suggested that the institutions of law are designed and intended to mediate between the diverse range of views of what ought to be done, and particular decisions about what is to be done. That is the general function which lies behind the more specific tasks performed by the institutions of law behind decisions about what public goods are to be secured, about which option is to be rendered salient to solve coordination problems, about which sorts of undertakings will receive the protection of law. These and the other specific tasks listed earlier are addressed by the institutions of law in order to allow people who have different views about such matters to live together, despite their ongoing substantive disagreements.

2. The Role of Law and the Lawyer's Role

We began with the claim that one important strand in the justification of role and role-obligations relied upon the function of the institutions of which they were a part. I have argued that the fundamental function of law in Western democracies is to mediate between reasonable but inconsistent views of what we should do as a community. Our aim now is to draw the appropriate conclusions about the roles and role-obligations of lawyers from this account of the function of law. To show this derivation properly, we would need to give close attention to the specific features of the lawyer's professional ethical obligations, such as the duty to maintain confidences and the duty to avoid conflicts of interest. In this paper, however, we will work at a much broader and cruder level, seeking merely to outline the derivation of the more general principles that make up the standard conception, the principles of neutrality, non-accountability and partisanship.

a. The Principle of Neutrality

Some of these derivations are obvious. According to the principle of neutrality, the lawyer must not allow his or her own view of the moral merits of the client's objectives or character to affect the diligence or zealousness with which they pursue the client's lawful objectives. The principle is explained by appeal to the fact of reasonable pluralism. Given the fact of reasonable pluralism, we do not order our communities by direct appeal to any particular view of the good. Instead, we seek the support and co-operation of the advocates of a diverse range of views by undertaking, in effect, to appeal to the determinations of decision procedures structured to take all reasonable views seriously. Lawyers who calibrate their professional efforts according to their own view of the good, or indeed according to any particular view of the good, not only "privilege" the view they favour and disenfranchise the view of the client, they undercut the strategy by which we secure community between people profoundly divided by reasonable but incompatible views of the good. Where legal rights are established by the procedure, decisions about what is to be done are to be settled by appeal to those rights, not by appeal to particular views of the good, still less any particular individual's views of the good.

In short, the principle of neutrality recognizes that it is not up to lawyers to determine what we will do as a community, what rights we will allocate and to whom. The complexity of the procedures upon which a pluralist community such as ours must rely means that lawyers do have tremendous power in this regard. Their legal expertise means they are better placed than any other group of citizens to work in, and with, our legal and political institutions. The principle of neutrality recognizes this power and its potential for abuse. It guards against the possibility that someone might be denied rights allocated by a legal system because its lawyers find those rights or their allocation to that person morally objectionable. Since legal representation is at least sometimes necessary to secure legal rights, the lawyer or the community of lawyers could render the person's claim to their lawful rights worthless by refusing to represent them at all, or by making a less than zealous effort on behalf of an existing client. Given the function of law in pluralist communities, the principle of neutrality states an important and deeply-moral obligation. It is a central part of adequate legal ethics in such communities.

b. The Principle of Non-accountability

Similarly, the appeal to pluralism explains the principle of non-accountability, the principle according to which lawyers are not to be judged by the moral status of their client's projects, even though the lawyer's assistance was necessary to the pursuit of those projects. If we recognize that there are many plausible views about what interests should receive legal protection, we have reason to leave decisions about which are to be protected to procedures which recognize the fact of reasonable pluralism, and which constrain the influence of individuals who happen to find themselves positioned to act as gatekeepers to the realm of legal rights. If these procedures do serve this mediating role, then we cannot assume that lawyers identify or sympathize with particular rights or with their allocation to particular clients. Lawyers might have strong moral objections to a client's projects, but accept the importance of appealing to the procedurally-allocated rights rather than to their own moral preferences. Furthermore, the appeal to pluralism gives us reason to hope that lawyers will not allocate their expertise in a way which will function as a *de facto* barrier to unpopular but protected views of the good. The principle of non-accountability removes one reason lawyers may have for refusing to act for clients whose moral views and legal goals do not accord with their own. In this guise, the rule is a defence for those who do take on unpopular cases. They may plead the rule in response to the mistaken assumption that they would not have taken on the case or would have not have zealously promoted the interests of an existing client had they not endorsed the goals of the client. Thus, the rule removes a barrier to such clients obtaining representation necessary to avail themselves of legal rights.

c. The Principle of Partisanship

The derivation of the principle of partisanship, the remaining and most problematic strand of the standard conception, may seem less obvious. This principle calls upon lawyers to aggressively and single-mindedly pursue the client's interests all the way up to the limits of the law. How does the appeal to pluralism generate this duty? We can use David Luban as a focus for our discussion. He argues that the principle of partisanship cannot be justified by "[t]he argument ...that the best way to guarantee that an individual's legal rights are protected ... is to provide her with a zealous advocate who will further her interests". For current purposes, we can treat the rights-argument referred to in this passage as equivalent to the appeal to pluralism. So read, Luban's claim is that we cannot derive the principle of partisanship from the sort of arguments advanced in this paper. But I think that his conclusion is based upon a common mischaracterization of the principle of partisanship, which treats it as requiring lawyers to be more zealous than in fact it does require them to be. I think Luban is right when he says that the more zealous version of the principle cannot be derived from the sorts of arguments advanced in this paper. But once the principle of partisanship is characterized in a more moderate form, its derivation from the appeal to pluralism is reasonably straightforward.

i. Mere-zeal and Hyper-zeal

What are these more and less moderate understandings of the principle of partisanship? According to one interpretation, the principle calls upon lawyers to exercise what we may call "mere-zeal". The merely-zealous lawyer is concerned solely with the legal interests of his client. He pursues those interests, "without fear ... and without regard to any unpleasant consequences to himself or to any other person". On this account, the interests various codes require lawyers to "fearlessly uphold ... without regard for personal interests or concerns" are those interests protected by law, not simply anything which happens to be in the client's interests, let alone anything in which the client happens to be interested. It is often in our interest to have more than we are entitled to under law, and no doubt we are often interested in having more than our bare legal entitlement. But this is of no moment to the merely-zealous lawyer. His professional obligation is to zealously pursue the client's legal rights. He is to be partisan in the sense that he must bring all of his professional skills to bear upon the task of securing his client's rights. But he is under no obligation to pursue interests that go beyond the law.

According to the alternative understanding, the principle of partisanship commits lawyers to what we may call hyper-zeal, where the hyper-zealous lawyer is concerned not merely to secure her client's legal rights, but to pursue any advantage obtainable for her client through the law. "My legal rights", says Luban, "are everything I am in fact legally entitled to, not everything the law can be made to give". However:

> Every lawyer knows tricks of the trade that can be used to do opponents out of their
> legal deserts using delaying tactics for example, to make it too costly for an
> opponent without much money to prosecute a lengthy suit even though the law is
> on her side, or filing a nuisance claim carefully calculated to be cheaper to settle
> than defend.

According to Luban and the tradition he draws from, the principle of partisanship *requires* lawyers to use these tricks to get their clients all that the law can be made to give. The standard conception, he implies, calls upon lawyers to secure the goals of mere-zeal, the defense of client's rights, by adopting the tactics of hyper-zeal: "The no-holds-barred zealous advocate", he writes, "tries to get everything the law can give ... and thereby does a better job of defending the client's legal rights than a less committed lawyer would do". But I think this is a mistake. I hope in the next few pages to show that the principle of partisanship requires lawyers to be merely zealous, and not to be hyper-zealous.

ii. The Derivation of Mere-zeal

I begin with the derivation of mere-zeal. The duty of mere-zeal seems to flow from the appeal to pluralism in fairly straight-forward fashion. Those arguments postulate a set of procedures that mediate between the diversity of views of the good and decisions about what is to be done. Individuals often require lawyers if they are to obtain the benefit of the procedures around which their communities are formed. They require lawyers to take advantage of the mechanisms which will allow them to have their property distributed a certain way after their death, to secure money over their property, to advance a defence when they are charged with an offence, and so on. The lawyers in these cases act on behalf of their clients. In effect, they do for clients things that clients would do for themselves were the legal system not so complicated. If clients wish to avail themselves of the rights allocated to them under the legal system, their lawyers, insofar as they act on the client's behalf, must assist them to do so. That is what it is to act on the client's behalf with respect to the legal system.

Sometimes, of course, we feel uneasy about people who stand on their rights. Even if a client does have a legal right to avail himself of a statute of limitations, his decision to do so may show him to be callous and nasty. But the appeal to pluralism shows that decisions about what is for the public good, about what sort of tax system we should have, about how long somebody can wait to seek a remedy in contract, about whether *this* defendant has *this* right, and so on, are things to be decided, not in private in the offices of particular lawyers, but in the public arena of politics where everyone can have a say, or in the public domain of the courts where reasons must be given and opportunities exist for challenge and representation. The arguments show that it is not up to individual lawyers to decide what interests will receive legal protection, what legal rights will be allocated to whom. That is the function of the procedures that make communities such as ours possible. Lawyers who fail to exercise mere-zeal, who take it upon themselves not to pursue legal entitlements available to their clients when their clients wish them to do so, privilege whatever moral view they are following in preference to that of their client and undercut the procedures which allow the advocates of a plurality of views to live in common community.

Furthermore, though we often admire people who sacrifice their own interests for the benefit of others, the moral quality of these sacrifices depends crucially upon it being the rights-holder who makes the sacrifice. It is hard to imagine the circumstances in which I act well by sacrificing some entitlement of yours, though there are many circumstances in which we think well of you for doing so. . .

Lawyers who attempt to be generous by sacrificing their clients' rights whether by not merely-zealously pursuing those rights or perhaps by simply not advising the client that the rights are available display not the virtue of generosity, but instead a vice, "something like arrogance".

iii. The Problem of Hyper-zeal

We turn then to the problem of hyper-zeal. Luban suggests that the principle of partisanship commits lawyers to hyper-zealous advocacy, to pursuing not merely the client's legal rights, but all that the law can be made to give. And, of course, his is not an idiosyncratic view. Lord Brougham's classic characterisation of the advocate as bound to pursue the client's interests "at all hazards and costs to other persons", without "regard [to] the alarm, the torments, the destruction which he may bring others", even to the extent that "it should be his unhappy fate to involve his country in confusion", surely takes us beyond mere-zeal and into the realm of hyper-zeal. In questioning Luban's linking of the standard conception and the principle of partisanship with the duty of hyper-zeal, then, we question a reading of the principle of partisanship that dates back at least to Brougham. Notwithstanding its pedigree, however, I do not think the attempt to pin a duty of hyper-zeal on the standard conception is warranted. Indeed, the appeal to pluralism allows us to see why lawyers do not have a duty of hyper-zealous advocacy.

Much of this discussion has been based upon the idea that the role of the lawyer is to allow clients to avail themselves of rights allocated to them by social institutions. If this is an accurate account of the role of the lawyer, it seems to follow directly that it is not their function to allow clients to satisfy interests beyond those allocated by law. Sometimes, of course, clients may wish to do so, and nothing thus far entails that it is the function of the lawyer to prevent them. But if we understand the lawyer as occupying a role in an institution, then we seem able to say at least that the demands that can be made on them must be demands to the "resources" of the institutions of which they are a part. Lawyers occupy roles in an institution designed to allow pluralist communities by specifying what rights members of the community shall have. The role-obligations are framed by reference to the point of that institution. Hence, lawyers have no special responsibilities to allow their clients to avail themselves of resources or benefits that lie outside the law. The lawyer's responsibility is to further the interests of the client, insofar as the institutional rights and duties of the client allow. The institutional framing of the lawyer's responsibilities means that the lawyer is not required to do just anything that would further the client's interests.

Some cases are simple. It may be that my interests would be served if the witness who saw me rob the bank were bumped-off. But it does not follow that my lawyer is thereby placed under a duty to bump-off the witness. And notice that this is true not just because it is illegal to bump-off witnesses. The lawyer has all the moral and legal reasons everyone has for refusing to advance my interest by bumping-off the witness, and a reason that only lawyers have: The lawyer can point to his role in an institution intended to ensure that I am able to avail myself of all the rights allocated to me by law. I cannot require my lawyer to satisfy my interest in having the witness bumped-off, since that is not one of those rights. This is simply to say that the institutional rights of law structure the lawyer's responsibility. In his capacity as lawyer, he can and should respond to my request for help with these "extra-legal" interests, by pointing out that that is not his job. His job is to act on the client's behalf, relative to the institutions of law.

Other cases seem more difficult. We saw some of Luban's examples earlier: ". . .using delaying tactics for example, to make it too costly for an opponent without much money to prosecute a lengthy suit even though the law is on her side, or filing a nuisance claim carefully calculated to be cheaper to settle than defend". And he adds some others:

> The rules of discovery, initiated to enable one side to find out crucial facts from the other, are used nowadays to delay trial or to impose added expenses on the other side; conversely, one might respond to an interrogatory by delivering to the discoverer tons of miscellaneous documents to run up their legal bills or to conceal a needle in a haystack .... Similarly, rules barring lawyers from representations involving conflicts of interest are now regularly used by adversaries to drive up the other side's costs by having the counsel disqualified.

Luban complains that the principle of partisanship requires lawyers to use such tricks if they can advance their client's interests by doing so. These cases may seem more difficult than that involving the inconvenient witness, since the lawyers involved in them could be acting perfectly legally. And of course, it may be true that responding to the other side's interrogatory with tons of miscellaneous documents is the best way of serving the client's interests: Perhaps the client has a hopeless case. Still, though these cases are more difficult, the rights-argument gives us a response. As Luban describes some of these cases, the lawyer "indulges in overkill to obtain as legal rights benefits that in fact may not be legal rights". Under this description, the rights-argument provides the lawyer with a response similar to that he gave when I wanted him to bump-off the inconvenient witness. His responsibility is structured by the institutional rights of law; his job is to act on the client's behalf, relative to the institutions of law. It is not his job to pursue interests that are not protected by law.

We may also be able to develop this response a little by noting that an aspect of the role of helping clients to avail themselves of their legal rights is helping them ascertain what those rights are. And now we can respond that simply preventing a case coming before the decision procedures of our community, by abusing of the rules of discovery or conflict of interest, is not helping ascertain what rights a client may demand, even if it does further their interests. It is not doing the lawyer's job. It is preventing the job from being done. I have suggested that it is the role of lawyers to assist individuals to avail themselves of the rights allocated to them by their communities. This role does not generate obligations or permissions to avoid determinations of rights claims. Lawyers who abuse processes of discovery, for instance, to prevent a case coming to court quite simply do not perform that role. An understanding of the duty of zealous advocacy that portrays lawyers as being allowed or obliged to use every lawful tactic to prevent the legal system addressing a case is simply mistaken. Note why it is mistaken: it goes wrong because it fails to see how the duties of lawyers are derived from a proper understanding of their roles. I am quite happy to concede that this may be a revision of the standard and well-pedigreed understanding of the standard conception. If it is, then so be it: it is one which gives a proper place to the moral considerations which inform the lawyer's role, while holding on to the idea that such roles are subject to role-differentiated obligations.

The upshot is that Luban is right when he says that the rights-argument does not support excesses of professional zeal. But since these are excesses, their failure to find support in the rights-argument is a mark in that argument's favour. By the same token, the fact that the more moderate version of the principle of partisanship can be derived from the rights-argument is a reason to suppose both that the principle, in this form, expresses a genuine obligation on lawyers in pluralist communities, and that the standard conception has long been misunderstood as requiring more than acceptable zeal from lawyers.

* * * * *

NOTES AND QUESTIONS

1. Dare identifies the key features of the lawyer's role as neutrality, non-accountability and partisanship, with partisanship requiring mere-zeal on behalf of a client, not hyper-zeal. Are all of these features a necessary component of "loyalty"? Why or why not? Are there any other components that ought to be added to the lawyer's role to ensure lawyer loyalty? Where does the duty to put your client's interests before your own fit within Dare's standard conception?

2. Which do you think is the most important quality for achieving loyalty – neutrality, non-accountability or partisanship?

3. Dare goes on to suggest that a useful test for distinguishing between mere-zeal and hyper-zeal can be found in abuse of process jurisprudence, which requires lawyers to identify and pursue the "proper object" of legal proceedings and then "restrict their advocacy to the pursuit of those objects" (at p. 35). Do you think that is a helpful distinction? What other ways could you use to distinguish between proper mere-zeal and improper hyper-zeal?

4. Think back to cases you have read in your other law school classes, such as contracts. Think in particular about the unsuccessful party. Are there any claims made in cases the pursuit of which appears more consistent with hyper-zeal than mere-zeal based on this test (*i.e.*, that could legitimately be

viewed as having been an abuse of process)? If so, why? Is *D.C.B. v. Zellers Inc.*, [1996] M.J. No. 362 (Man. Q.B.), leave to appeal refused [1996] M.J. No. 499 (Man. C.A.), excerpted in Chapter 5 and taught in some contract law classes, an example of hyper-zeal?

5.   Assume you act for a client in litigation, and you have some ability to control which judge will hear your client's case. Assume also that you know that there is one judge who would be particularly unsympathetic to your client's position. Is acting to avoid having that judge hear your client's case consistent with mere-zeal, or is it an example of hyper-zeal?

Compare and contrast the concept of the lawyer as zealous advocate set out by Dare with the approach of the Supreme Court of Canada in the following case.

R. v. NEIL

[2002] S.C.J. No. 72, [2002] 3 S.C.R. 631
(S.C.C., Major, Bastarache, Binnie, Arbour and LeBel JJ.)

[The appellant brought an application for a stay of proceedings in his criminal trial on the basis that there had been an abuse of process. The abuse arose from a conflict of interest of the law firm that initially represented him and that ultimately represented a co-accused. The specific facts and legal principles arising from this case are discussed again with respect to conflicts of interest in Chapter 4.]

BINNIE J.: —

*   *   *   *   *

Appellant's counsel reminds us of the declaration of an advocate's duty of loyalty made by Henry Brougham, later Lord Chancellor, in his defence of Queen Caroline against the charge of adultery brought against her by her husband, King George IV. He thus addressed the House of Lords:

> [A]n advocate, in the discharge of his duty, knows but one person in all the world, and that person is his client. To save that client by all means and expedients, and at all hazards and costs to other persons, and, among them, to himself, is his first and only duty; and in performing this duty he must not regard the alarm, the torments, the destruction which he may bring upon others. Separating the duty of a patriot from that of an advocate, he must go on reckless of consequences, though it should be his unhappy fate to involve his country in confusion . . .

These words are far removed in time and place from the legal world in which the Venkatraman law firm carried on its practice, but the defining principle — the duty of loyalty — is with us still. It endures because it is essential to the integrity of the administration of justice and it is of high public importance that public confidence in that integrity be maintained: . . . Unless a litigant is assured of the undivided loyalty of the lawyer, neither the public nor the litigant will have confidence that the legal system, which may appear to them to be a hostile and hideously complicated environment, is a reliable and trustworthy means of resolving their disputes and controversies: . . . As O'Connor J.A. (now A.C.J.O.) observed in *R. v. McCallen*[12],:

---

[12]   [1999] O.J. No. 202, (1999) 43 O.R. (3d) 56 at 67 (C.A.).

. . . the relationship of counsel and client requires clients, typically untrained in the law and lacking the skills of advocates, to entrust the management and conduct of their cases to the counsel who act on their behalf. There should be no room for doubt about counsel's loyalty and dedication to the client's case.

*   *   *   *   *

The duty of loyalty is intertwined with the fiduciary nature of the lawyer-client relationship. One of the roots of the word fiduciary is *fides*, or loyalty, and loyalty is often cited as one of the defining characteristics of a fiduciary: . . . The lawyer fulfills squarely Professor Donovan Waters' definition of a fiduciary:

> In putting together words to describe a "fiduciary" there is of course no immediate obstacle. Almost everybody would say that it is a person in whom trust and confidence is placed by another on whose behalf the fiduciary is to act. The other (the beneficiary) is entitled to expect that the fiduciary will be concerned solely for the beneficiary's interests, never the fiduciary's own. The "relationship" must be the dependence or reliance of the beneficiary upon the fiduciary ... .

Fiduciary duties are often called into existence to protect relationships of importance to the public including, as here, solicitor and client. Disloyalty is destructive of that relationship.

*   *   *   *   *

The aspects of the duty of loyalty relevant to this appeal do include issues of confidentiality in the Canada Trust matters, but engage more particularly three other dimensions:

(i) the duty to avoid conflicting interests . . . including the lawyer's personal interest

(ii) a duty of commitment to the client's cause (sometimes referred to as "zealous representation") from the time counsel is retained, not just at trial, i.e. ensuring that a divided loyalty does not cause the lawyer to "soft peddle" his or her defence of a client out of concern for another client . . . and,

(iii) a duty of candour with the client on matters relevant to the retainer . . . If a conflict emerges, the client should be among the first to hear about it . . .

NOTES AND QUESTIONS

1. The context of *Neil* was a conflict of interest arising from a law firm's representation of two individuals implicated in a crime (see the more fulsome discussion of the case in Chapter 4). Does the statement of the Court that a lawyer must not "soft peddle" their representation of a client apply more generally? Would a lawyer act ethically were they to refuse to cross-examine a witness having a history of psychiatric illness on the effect of illness on the witness's cognitive function because the lawyer believes that the witness is speaking truthfully?

2. The Court in *Neil* refers to "zealous representation". In Canada, however, the obligation placed on lawyers by the Federation of Law Societies is one

of "resolute" advocacy. Do you think there is any meaningful distinction between being "zealous" and being "resolute"? Is there some other terminology that would be better? Should the lawyer's duty be framed in terms of the lawyer's attitude (*e.g.*, zeal or resolution) or should it be framed in terms of the lawyer's conduct (*e.g.*, acting competently in pursuit of the client's legal goals)?

3. Do you think the three ideas of the duty to avoid conflicting interests, the duty of commitment to the client's cause and the duty of candour set out the proper content for the duty of loyalty? How do they relate to the three core concepts identified by Dare of neutrality, non-accountability and partisanship? See Colin Jackson, Richard Devlin and Brent Cotter, "Of Lodestars and Lawyers: Incorporating the duty of Loyalty into the Model Code of Conduct" (2016) 39 Dal L.J. 37.

The Supreme Court considered the concept of loyal advocacy again in a 2015 decision, in which a majority of the Court held that money-laundering legislation violated both s. 7 and s. 8 of the *Charter of Rights and Freedoms* because of its potential to infringe solicitor-client privilege (s. 8) and because it impaired the lawyer's liberty while violating "the principle of fundamental justice in relation to the lawyer's duty of commitment to the client's cause". The following excerpt sets out the majority's description of the lawyer's duty of commitment to the client's cause (the aspects of the case dealing with solicitor-client privilege are excerpted in Chapter 3). When reading the excerpt, consider whether the Court's judgment endorses or contradicts Dare's view on the difference between mere-zeal and hyper-zeal.

CANADA (ATTORNEY GENERAL) v. FEDERATION OF LAW SOCIETIES OF CANADA

[2015] S.C.J. No. 7, 2015 SCC 7, [2015] 1 S.C.R. 401
(S.C.C., Cromwell, LeBel, Abella, Karakatsanis and Wagner JJ.)

CROMWELL J.: —

*   *   *   *   *

The duty of lawyers to avoid conflicting interests is at the heart of both the general legal framework defining the fiduciary duties of lawyers to their clients and of the ethical principles governing lawyers' professional conduct. This duty aims to avoid two types of risks of harm to clients: the risk of misuse of confidential information and the risk of impairment of the lawyer's representation of the client (see, *e.g.*, *Canadian National Railway Co. v. McKercher LLP*, 2013 SCC 39, [2013] 2 S.C.R. 649 at para. 23 [discussed in Chapter 4]).

The Court has recognized that aspects of these fiduciary and ethical duties have a constitutional dimension. I have already discussed at length one important example. The centrality to the administration of justice of preventing misuse of the client's confidential information, reflected in solicitor-client privilege, led the Court to conclude that the privilege required constitutional protection in the context of law office searches and seizures. . . As Major J. put it in *R. v. McClure*, 2001 SCC 14, [2001] 1 S.C.R. 445 at para. 31: "The important relationship between a client and his or her lawyer stretches beyond the parties and is <u>integral to the workings of the legal system itself</u>". (emphasis added)

The question now is whether another central dimension of the solicitor-client relationship — the lawyer's duty of commitment to the client's cause — also requires some measure of constitutional protection against government intrusion. In my view it does, for many of the same reasons that support constitutional protection for solicitor-client privilege. "The law is a complex web of interests, relationships and rules. The integrity of the administration of justice depends upon the unique role of the solicitor who provides legal advice to clients within this complex system": *McClure*, at para. 2. These words, written in the context of solicitor-client privilege, are equally apt to describe the centrality to the administration of justice of the lawyer's duty of commitment to the client's cause. A client must be able to place "unrestricted and unbounded confidence" in his or her lawyer; that confidence which is at the core of the solicitor-client relationship is a part of the legal system itself, not merely ancillary to it: *Smith v. Jones*, [1999] 1 S.C.R. 455 at para. 45, citing with approval, *Anderson v. Bank of British Columbia* (1876), 2 Ch. D. 644 (C.A.); *McClure*. The lawyer's duty of commitment to the client's cause, along with the protection of the client's confidences, is central to the lawyer's role in the administration of justice.

We should, in my view, recognize as a principle of fundamental justice that the state cannot impose duties on lawyers that undermine their duty of commitment to their clients' causes. Subject to justification being established, it follows that the state cannot deprive someone of life, liberty or security of the person otherwise than in accordance with this principle. . . .

Principles of fundamental justice have three characteristics. They must be legal principles, there must be "significant societal consensus" that they are "fundamental to the way in which the legal system ought fairly to operate" and they must be sufficiently precise so as "to yield a manageable standard against which to measure deprivations of life, liberty or security of the person". . . .

Is the Duty of Commitment to the Client's Cause Such a Principle?

Legal Principle and Sufficient Precision

These two elements of the test are conveniently treated together.

Turning first to the definition of a legal principle, the distinction is between, on one hand, a description of "an important state interest" and "the realm of general public policy" and, on the other, a "normative 'legal' principle" and "the basic tenets of our legal system". . . .

An important indicator that a proposed rule or principle is a legal principle is that it is used as a rule or test in common law, statutory law or international law. The duty of commitment to the client's cause has been recognized by the Court as a distinct element of the broader common law duty of loyalty and thus unquestionably is a legal principle: *McKercher*, at paras. 19 and 43-44; *R. v. Neil*, 2002 SCC 70 at para. 19.

While this standard is far from self-applying, it has proven to be sufficiently precise to enable the courts to apply it in widely divergent fact situations: see, *e.g.*,

McKercher, at paras. 43-44 and 55-56; *Neil*, at para. 19. This body of jurisprudence demonstrates that this principle of commitment to the client's cause is sufficiently precise to provide a workable standard in that it can be applied in a manner that provides guidance as to the appropriate result. . .

Of course the duty of commitment to the client's cause must not be confused with being the client's dupe or accomplice. It does not countenance a lawyer's involvement in, or facilitation of, a client's illegal activities. Committed representation does not, for example, permit, let alone require a lawyer to assert claims that he or she knows are unfounded, or to present evidence that he or she knows to be false or to help the client to commit a crime. The duty is perfectly consistent with the lawyer taking appropriate steps with a view to ensuring that his or her services are not being used for improper ends.

I conclude that the lawyer's duty of commitment to the client's cause is well-entrenched as a sufficiently precise legal principle, and therefore satisfies the first and the third requirements of a principle of fundamental justice. . . .

NOTES AND QUESTIONS

1. Is the idea of "commitment to a client's cause" the same as partisanship? Which description of the lawyer's obligation do you find most helpful? Why?

2. This case is discussed in greater detail in Chapter 3.

3. The Court directs the lawyer not to be involved in or facilitate a client's illegal activities. Is that a broad enough restriction on the lawyer's zeal? How does it compare to Dare's suggestion that a lawyer ought to restrict her advocacy to the pursuit of the true objectives of the client's case (see Note 3 after the Dare excerpt)? Which is more helpful? Which is more appropriate?

In her dissenting judgment in *Strother*,[13] McLachlin C.J.C. argued that it is improper to "superimpose" a fiduciary duty of loyalty beyond that contracted for between the parties. Justice Binnie, writing for the majority, disagreed, holding that fiduciary duties "may include obligations that go beyond what the parties expressly bargained for".[14] The duty of loyalty to a client can arise under contract, but more obviously arises under the fiduciary obligation. Consider whether McLachlin C.J.C.'s or Binnie J.'s approach to a lawyer's obligations is preferable in light of the following case.

SZARFER v. CHODOS

[1986] O.J. No. 256, 54 O.R. (2d) 663
(Ont. H.C.J., Callaghan A.C.J.H.C.)

[The defendant Chodos was the plaintiff Szarfer's lawyer in a personal injury claim.

---

[13] *Strother v. 3464920 Canada Inc.*, [2007] S.C.J. No. 24, [2007] 2 S.C.R. 177 (S.C.C.).

[14] *Strother v. 3464920 Canada Inc.*, [2007] S.C.J. No. 24 at para. 34, [2007] 2 S.C.R. 177 (S.C.C.).

In the course of his representation of the plaintiff, the defendant learned about difficulties in the plaintiff's marriage. The defendant knew the plaintiff's wife because she had worked for him occasionally as a legal secretary. In May 1981, the defendant and the plaintiff's wife had an affair, which lasted approximately six weeks. The plaintiff discovered the affair and was devastated. He had existing psychological problems of which the defendant was also aware as a result of his representation. The plaintiff and his wife ultimately reconciled.]

CALLAGHAN A.C.J.H.C.: —

Nature of claim

The plaintiff claims general, special and punitive damages from the defendant as a result of an alleged breach of fiduciary duty arising from their relationship as solicitor and client. The plaintiff claims the defendant utilized confidential information for his own advantage and placed his personal interest in conflict with his duties as a fiduciary. In addition, the plaintiff pleads that the defendant's conduct was a breach of the contract between the parties resulting in damages. In the alternative, the plaintiff claims the defendant having full knowledge of the vulnerable mental and physical condition of the plaintiff, acted in wanton disregard of such knowledge and inflicted mental suffering on the plaintiff thereby committing an intentional tort or, alternatively, the defendant acted negligently in inflicting the aforesaid injury thereby causing the damage claimed.

* * * * *

Law

The fiduciary relationship between a lawyer and his client forbids a lawyer from using any confidential information obtained by him for the benefit of himself or a third person or to the disadvantage of his client. The crucial question for decision is whether or not the defendant used confidential information for his own purposes or to the disadvantage of the plaintiff. It is conceded that the defendant was in a fiduciary relationship with the plaintiff and owed him all the duties of a fiduciary. The highest and clearest duty of a fiduciary is to act to advance the beneficiary's interest and avoid acting to his detriment. A fiduciary cannot permit his own interest to come into conflict with the interest of the beneficiary of the relationship. The equitable principle is stated in Waters, *Law of Trusts in Canada*, 2d ed. (1984), at 710:

> It is a fundamental principle of every developed legal system that one who undertakes a task on behalf of another must act exclusively for the benefit of the other, putting his own interests completely aside. In the common law system this duty may be enforceable by way of an action by the principal upon the contract of agency, but the modes in which the rule can be breached are myriad, many of them in situations other than contract and therefore beyond the control of the law of contract. It was in part to meet such situations that Equity fashioned the rule that no man may allow his duty to conflict with his interest. Stated in this way, Equity has been able since the sixteenth century to provide a remedy for a whole range of cases where the person with a task to perform has used the opportunity to benefit himself.

While Equity first conceived of the rule in relation to trustees the principle applies to anyone who undertakes a task on behalf of another and is applicable to a wide and varied range of persons including lawyers . . . The breadth of the application of the principle is referred to in Waters, *supra*, at p. 731:

> Private advantage gained through direct dealing with the trust property, while the most familiar abuse of the trustee's office, is not the only conduct resulting in personal benefit which Equity regards as a breach of the duty of loyalty. There are many and various ways in which trustees and other fiduciaries can derive personal benefit, as the authorities demonstrate, and they range from the acceptance of secret commissions and bribes to the use of confidential information for personal gain. In a sense these various activities cannot be distinguished. The acceptance of a bribe or a secret commission, which are examples of obvious profiteering, is a manifestation of the same wrongful act *as the exploitation of office in more sophisticated ways.*

(Emphasis added) Once the fiduciary relationship is established, as it is in this case, the onus is on the trustee to prove that he acted reasonably and made no personal use whatsoever of the confidential information.

* * * * * *

In engaging in sexual intercourse with the plaintiff's wife, the defendant was acting in his own interest and to his personal benefit. I cannot help but conclude that his actions were also to the detriment of his client's interest. Upon discovery of the affair, the client's trust in the solicitor was destroyed. Such conduct which vitiates trust, the essential element of a solicitor-client relationship, and results in physical injury to the client, is a breach of the conflict-of-interest rule referred to above. The defendant has not discharged the onus of proving that he acted reasonably in the circumstances. That in itself is sufficient to hold him liable for damages.

Furthermore, however, I am satisfied that he used confidential information for his own purposes in order to obtain the delights and benefits of the affair. The defendant had known Mrs. Szarfer since 1977 but had no sexual relationship with her until May of 1981. He did not acquire details of the Szarfers' marital and sexual problems until March or April of 1981. At that time he obtained the intimate knowledge of the emotional and mental problems of both the plaintiff and his wife. He obtained such information as part of the process of the wrongful dismissal action. The plaintiff's mental state and the plaintiff's sexual problem were issues in that action. As a solicitor he undertook to prosecute the claim for wrongful dismissal including a claim for damages for mental distress and the state of the marriage and all the information related above was an indivisible part of the task undertaken by him as a solicitor. Again, he was aware of Mrs. Szarfer's vulnerability as a result of the information he obtained about the marriage. I have not accepted the defendant's denial that he did not have any information respecting the marriage except financial nor can I overlook his denial of not knowing of the possibility of the marriage break-up even though his trial notes disclosed that he intended to examine on that very issue at trial of the wrongful dismissal action. These matters together with the time factors involved have led me to conclude that the defendant in fact did use the confidential information that he obtained from the plaintiff and his wife for his own purposes and I so find. In so doing, the defendant was in breach of his professional duty to his client, the plaintiff, and that breach was the cause of the plaintiff's

post-traumatic neurosis. The breach constituted professional negligence and demonstrated an unreasonable lack of skill and fidelity in his professional and fiduciary
duties as a lawyer.

* * * * *

NOTES AND QUESTIONS

1. If Chodos had no particular knowledge of the vulnerability of the Szarfers'
   marriage, but had simply had an affair with the wife of his client, should
   the result in the case have been the same? Assuming that it would not – that
   the breach of confidentiality was central to the finding of a breach of
   fiduciary duty – would Chodos' actions be considered unethical? Would
   the commencement of the affair in those circumstances be a violation of
   his duty of loyalty to his client?

2. Chodos was sued by his former client for breach of a fiduciary obligation.
   Should he also have been subject to discipline by the Law Society?

3. Individuals who are called to the Bar in Alberta swear the following oath:

   > I will as a Barrister and Solicitor conduct all causes and matters faithfully
   > and to the best of my ability. I will not seek to destroy anyone's property.
   > I will not promote suits upon frivolous pretences. I will not pervert the
   > law to favour or prejudice anyone, but in all things will conduct myself
   > truly and with integrity. I will uphold and maintain the Sovereign's
   > interest and that of my fellow citizens according to the law in force in
   > Alberta.

   Is this oath consistent with the identification of loyalty as a primary ethical
   obligation for lawyers?

Scenario Three

Alex Smith is a client of Leslie Jones. Alex retains Leslie to provide legal advice
regarding Alex's plan to open a restaurant and bar and, in particular, with respect to
compliance with municipal by-laws. The restaurant and bar prove to be a great
success. Three years later, Leslie decides to leave legal practice and become a
restaurant proprietor. Using their knowledge of municipal by-laws gained in their
representation of Alex, they build a restaurant/bar two doors down from Alex. The
venture is a success and significantly undermines Alex's profitability. Are Leslie's
actions ethical?

Scenario Four

Frank Johnson is a client of Hilary Smith. Frank is selling the public company in
which he is a major shareholder and CEO. On Hilary's advice, he structures part of
his payment from the purchaser as a "non-compete" agreement as this will result in
a preferable tax treatment. The transaction is legitimate from a tax perspective;
however, Frank ends up being charged with various offences under securities
legislation for his failure to properly disclose the payments to shareholders. Hilary
is asked to testify about the advice she gave him. During her testimony she responds
honestly but makes every effort to distance herself from the transaction, and from
Frank. Is Hilary's conduct ethical? See "Media execs chose to disclose payments",
Associated Press (April 13, 2007).

[b]   The Lawyer as Moral Agent in Pursuit of Justice

The emphasis on loyalty as the central norm of ethical practice arguably suffers from two weaknesses. First, while there is much authority in support of the significance of loyalty to the lawyer-client relationship, there is also significant authority emphasizing the importance of other values. Notably, the word "loyalty" appears 18 times in the Federation of Law Societies' *Model Code of Professional Conduct*, while the word "justice" appears nearly twice as often (32 times). The *Model Code* imposes obligations such as: "A lawyer must encourage public respect for and try to improve the administration of justice" and "Admission to and continuance in the practice of law implies, on the part of a lawyer, a basic commitment to the concept of equal justice for all within an open, ordered and impartial system" (see Rule 5.6-1, and Rule 5.6-1, Commentary 2).

Second, the emphasis on loyal advocacy — especially its central features of advocacy for a client's interests and the absence of moral accountability for a client's aims — has been criticized for creating moral malaise and unethical conduct within the legal profession. Leading American legal ethicists, including David Luban, Robert Gordon and William Simon, have argued for a re-orientation of the model of the ethical lawyer away from loyal advocacy and towards a model under which the lawyer retains moral agency and responsibility for what they do when acting for a client. Gordon argues that lawyers must retain and use their independent judgment of whether a client's proposed course of action is just. Luban argues that an ethical lawyer cannot have an unqualified commitment either to zealous partisanship or to moral non-accountability. While the role morality of the lawyer can make a claim upon them, they can never escape the claims that ordinary moral principles make against all of us.

Simon defines the central moral principle governing lawyering as justice: "The lawyer should take those actions that, considering the relevant circumstances of the particular case, seem most likely to promote justice. This 'seek justice' maxim suggests a kind of noncategorical judgment that might be called pragmatist, ad hoc, or dialectical, but that I will call discretionary."[15] Simon defines justice as equivalent to legal merit, and argues that lawyers should only represent those clients whose cases are meritorious relative to other individuals whom the lawyer could represent. Further, a lawyer should "make her best effort to achieve the most appropriate resolution in each case".[16]

The difference between Simon and Luban is that Simon emphasizes the moral claims of the law, suggesting that the law, correctly interpreted, is co-extensive with morality. Luban, as set out in the following excerpt, sees law and morality as at points in irreducible conflict, with the result that a lawyer must choose between them. While the law has a claim that the lawyer can normally accede to, in some circumstances the lawyer can only ethically follow the dictates of morality, not of law.

---

[15] William Simon, "Ethical Discretion in Lawyering" (1988) 101 Harv. L. Rev. 1083 at 1090.

[16] William Simon, "Ethical Discretion in Lawyering" (1988) 101 Harv. L. Rev. 1083 at 1090.

The following case arguably demonstrates the strength of both Luban and Simon's point of view, insofar as it suggests that a lawyer who focuses exclusively on the interests of their client may improperly lose sight of other moral values, including the obligations imposed by the lawyer's legal duty to protect the fair administration of justice. Following the case will be an excerpt from Luban's famous critique of zealous advocacy, and his assertion of the irreducible importance of ordinary morality. When reading Luban's critique consider whether his view, or Simon's, would have better helped Murray to avoid the ethical morass in which he found himself.

R. v. MURRAY

[2000] O.J. No. 2182, 48 O.R. (3d) 544
(Ont. S.C.J., Gravely J.)

GRAVELY J.: —

The accused, Kenneth Murray, is a member of the Ontario Bar and certified as a specialist in criminal litigation by the Law Society of Upper Canada. He was retained by Paul Bernardo initially in February 1993 in regard to the "Scarborough Rapes" and on May 18, 1993, in connection with the murders of Leslie Mahaffy and Kristen French and additional related offences.

On May 6, 1993, on written instructions of Bernardo, Murray attended at the Bernardo home and removed from it videotapes which depicted gross sexual abuse of Kristen French, Leslie Mahaffy, Jane Doe and Tammy Homolka. Without disclosing their existence to the Crown, he retained the tapes for 17 months. Trial motions were to begin on September 12, 1994. On September 2, 1994, Murray, through his counsel, applied to the Law Society of Upper Canada for advice. Accepting that advice Murray appeared before the trial judge, Associate Chief Justice LeSage (now Chief Justice S.C.O.), who directed that the tapes, their integrity protected by suitable undertakings, go to John Rosen, new counsel for Bernardo, at which time Murray was given leave to withdraw as counsel. Rosen, on September 22, 1994, turned the tapes over to the police and they were used by Crown counsel at the trial. A jury found Bernardo guilty on all charges.

Murray now faces this charge of attempt to obstruct justice by concealment of the videotapes.

PART TWO - THE FACTS

* * * * *

57 BAYVIEW DRIVE

Before his arrest Bernardo lived with his wife, Karla Homolka, in a rented house at 57 Bayview Drive, St. Catharines, Ontario. Between February and April 1993 the police, for 71 days, conducted an intensive search of the premises, virtually destroying the interior of the house in the process. On April 30, 1993 the final search warrant expired and on May 4, Doyle, MacDonald and John Lefurgey (a local lawyer assisting the defence team) attended at 57 Bayview with consent of the landlords to assess the condition of the house, videotape the interior and decide what possessions of the Bernardos should be removed. The landlords agreed that the defence team could return on May 6, to remove the Bernardo belongings. They were also, at that time, to be allowed 20 minutes alone in the house in order to confer as to which of the Bernardo possessions might have some relevance to the defence and thus should be taken away.

THE REMOVAL OF THE VIDEOTAPES

On May 6, MacDonald and Doyle [who were working with Murray on the case] went to 57 Bayview at 8:30 a.m. and, with the assistance of the landlords, began to pack up the Bernardo personal effects. Murray said that on his way to 57 Bayview he got lost and, in attempting to telephone MacDonald for directions, discovered in his slipcase an unsealed envelope given to him on May 3, by MacDonald. It contained a letter from Bernardo, which was wrapped around a sealed envelope. The letter read:

> The following is to be opened only and only if you have underlined 57 Bayview. It is instructions on what is probably in the house that we need for our defence. Alone they may first appear to be irrelevant and thus overlooked but together they can be very important. Note: if we can't have access then return the letter intact.
>
> What I was worried about is I would be moved and hidden for a few days until our possession of the house was up. [underlining in original]

*   *   *   *   *

Murray arrived at 57 Bayview at 11:00 a.m. and, as agreed with the landlords, the defence team was given time alone in the house. Murray then opened the sealed envelope, which contained a map and directions to assist in locating six eight-millimetre videotapes.

Referring to his note and map, Murray led the way to the bathroom and started to take apart a pot light while Doyle and MacDonald watched from the doorway. Unsuccessful in finding anything behind the light, he handed the Bernardo instructions to Doyle, who directed him to another pot light. Murray climbed onto the vanity, dismantled the light and was successful in retrieving six eight-millimetre videotapes. He then reassembled the light and placed the videotapes in his slip case. Doyle and MacDonald hugged each other and Doyle whispered to MacDonald, "what have we got?"

The defence team had lunch together on the balcony of 57 Bayview. Murray told Doyle and MacDonald that they would have to make sure that no one found out about the tapes, and the three of them would have to make a pact that they would be the only ones that ever knew what had been obtained. They shook hands, hugged, and agreed not to say anything to anyone about the tapes. Murray said in his evidence that he knew "they wouldn't tell anybody about the tapes". He felt the discovery of the tapes was a "bonanza" or "gold mine" for the defence.

Murray said MacDonald and Bernardo made up the code words on the instruction letter. "How about those Leafs?" was to be the signal that the search was unsuccessful while "How about those Jays?" meant that the tapes were found. In the afternoon of May 6, Bernardo telephoned Murray at 57 Bayview who said to him, "How about those Jays?"

With the map and directions there was a note from Bernardo that said: ". . .

38

although we will have to go through them in the future. At this time I instruct you not to view them".

Murray, MacDonald and Doyle packed and removed a large number of items from the house. Murray locked the tapes in a safe or a credenza at his office.

THE HOMOLKA RESOLUTION AGREEMENT - BERNARDO CHARGED WITH MURDERS

On May 14, 1993 Homolka's defence counsel and Crown counsel entered into a six-page written agreement. Homolka would plead guilty to two counts of manslaughter in relation to the deaths of Kristen French and Leslie Mahaffy, there would be a joint submission that she be sentenced to 12 years imprisonment and she would provide evidence to assist the Crown.

Sometime between May 14 and 17, 1993 the defence team learned about the charges against Homolka and her release on bail and made the assumption that Homolka had entered into an arrangement with the Crown.

On May 18, 1993 Bernardo was charged with two counts of first-degree murder and additional related offences. Homolka was charged with two counts of manslaughter. Murray's retainer was extended to include the additional charges against Bernardo. Bernardo signed an authorization directing Murray to review the videotapes, make copies and use the tapes as Murray deemed appropriate in Bernardo's outstanding criminal matters.

THE CRITICAL TAPES

Of the six videotapes, two ("the critical tapes") form the basis of the charge against Murray.

The critical tapes are indescribably horrible. Leslie Mahaffy was 14 years of age and Kristen French 15 when they were abducted and murdered by Bernardo, assisted by Homolka. The tapes show each of them being forced to participate with Bernardo and Homolka in the grossest sexual perversions. In the course of sexual assaults they are forced to pretend they are enjoying the experience through scripted dialogue, and, in the case of Kristen French, through being instructed to constantly smile at the camera. Obedience is obtained through physical assault and Bernardo threatens each of them with death if they do not perform as directed.

Everyone exposed to the videotapes has been deeply affected by the experience.

Doyle had to review the tapes by way of trial preparation for Rosen. In giving her evidence she broke down at the recollection and said that she saw the tapes nine times, but "a million times in my head".

Rosen, a veteran criminal defence counsel, was obliged to hesitate part way through his evidence as he recollected the images on the tapes. He described viewing the tapes on September 13, 1994 with MacDonald and Clayton Ruby. MacDonald wept beside him as the tapes were shown and Rosen said he himself was extremely upset. Murray described the tapes as "caustic", "corrosive" and "shocking". Even defence counsel, Mr. Cooper, who must in his career have been exposed to almost everything terrible the Court system has to offer, was obliged to request a brief adjournment in the course of reading in some of this evidence.

In addition to the dreadful acts perpetrated on Kristen French and Leslie Mahaffy, the critical tapes also show the drugging and sexual assaults of Jane Doe and Tammy Homolka, both 15 years of age.

The critical tapes demonstrate conclusively that Bernardo was guilty of forcible confinement, assault and sexual assault of Kristen French and Leslie Mahaffy and the sexual assault of Jane Doe and Tammy Homolka. They provide strong circumstantial evidence to prove Bernardo guilty of the murders.

* * * * *

JOHN ROSEN'S "ADVICE"

John Rosen is a senior and respected Toronto counsel. Tim Breen was the spousal companion of MacDonald and he was also a legal associate of Rosen. Breen had assisted Murray from time to time on the Bernardo case. On May 18, 1993, while visiting Bernardo and receiving his instructions to review and make copies of the tapes, Murray obtained from him some indication of their contents. That same evening he and MacDonald met with Breen to discuss tactics. The following day, May 19, Breen approached Rosen with a hypothetical question to the effect that if the defence had hard evidence that compromised Homolka's credibility, should it be revealed to the prosecution to ensure that Homolka got charged with murder, or should it be saved for trial? Rosen told Breen there was no obligation to assist in the prosecution, but that defence counsel's first duty is to the client and if the evidence would assist the defence, then it should be held in the file and used to cross-examine the witness at trial: "Hammer her with any hard evidence that compromises her plea, her deal, her credibility". Rosen warned against going to the Crown with the evidence because it would allow the Crown to prepare Homolka for cross-examination at trial.

Neither Breen nor Rosen was told anything about videotapes or the nature of the "hard evidence". Rosen assumed it was something like a diary or a letter or a card written to a friend. Both Murray and Rosen looked upon the issue as tactical rather than ethical. (At this time, Murray had not yet viewed the tapes).

THE DEFENCE PLAN

Murray testified he had to retain the critical tapes for Bernardo's defence. Bernardo admitted the crimes shown on the tapes but denied killing Leslie Mahaffy and Kristen French. The tapes, Murray said, supported this position. The Crown was going to portray Homolka as an abused, manipulated victim, while the tapes showed the reverse, that she was not afraid and was an enthusiastic participant in the sexual crimes. He was obliged to keep the existence of the tapes secret so that the Crown could not prepare Homolka for Murray's cross-examination.

It is not entirely clear how Murray planned to utilize the critical tapes. It appears there were two alternatives, to some degree conflicting:

1. Hold back the tapes, tie down Homolka's evidence at the Preliminary Inquiries and then spring the tapes on her in cross-examination at trial;

2. Tie down Homolka at the Preliminary Inquiries and then go to the Crown and attempt to negotiate a resolution of the charges against Bernardo on the

basis that Murray was holding evidence that would demonstrate that Homolka was incredible. Bernardo would acknowledge guilt on most of the charges and the prosecution could extricate itself from the Homolka deal. If resolution could not be achieved, the tapes would be turned over to the prosecution. While it would be no "surprise" for Homolka at trial, at least she would have been tied down by her evidence at the Preliminary Inquiries.

Murray stated it was never his intention to "bury" the tapes and, at the very least, they would come out at the trial.

*   *   *   *   *

[Murray was ultimately acquitted of the charges on the basis that he did not have the necessary *mens rea* to be convicted of obstruction. For a discussion of the specific rules related to the disclosure of "real evidence" in criminal cases, see Chapter 7.]

DAVID LUBAN

"The Adversary System Excuse"
Legal Ethics and Human Dignity
(Cambridge: Cambridge University Press, 2007) at 32-64*
[Footnotes omitted]

[Luban sets out the "standard conception of the lawyer's role", namely, that a lawyer must be a partisan advocate for his client's ends and that the lawyer has no moral accountability for those ends. Luban argues that most justifications for the standard conception arise from the adversary system or, expressed more broadly, from the role lawyers play within the justice system as a whole. In this excerpt, Luban challenges the traditional justifications given for the lawyer's role and argues that while that role may legitimately influence a lawyer's moral decisions, it cannot do so absolutely. The lawyer retains responsibility for her moral choices, whether made on behalf of a client or not.]

V. Consequentialist Justifications of the Adversary System

A. Truth

The question whether the adversary system is, all in all, the best way of uncovering the facts of a case at bar sounds like an empirical question. I happen to think that it is an empirical question, moreover, that has scarcely been investigated, and that is most likely impossible to answer. This last is because one does not, after a trial is over, find the parties coming forth to make a clean breast of it and enlighten the world about what *really* happened. A trial is not a quiz show with the right answer waiting in a sealed envelope. We can't learn directly whether the facts are really as the trier determined them because we don't ever find out the facts.

The kind of empirical research that can be done, then, is laboratory simulations: social psychology experiments intended to model the adversary proceeding. Obviously, there are inherent limitations on how closely such experiments can correspond to actual trials, no matter how skillfully they are done. . . . Even so, the

---

* Reproduced with permission.

results are instructive: they show that in some situations the adversary system works better while in others the inquisitorial system does, and furthermore, that the participants cannot tell which situation they are in. This would hardly surprise us: it would be much more astounding to discover a greater difference in veracity between the Anglo-American and Continental systems, for surely such a difference would after so many centuries have become a commonplace in our folklore.

Given all this, it is unsurprising to discover that the arguments purporting to show the advantages of the adversary system as a fact-finder have mostly been nonempirical, a mix of *a priori* theories of inquiry and armchair psychology.

Here is one, based on the idea, very similar to Sir Karl Popper's theory of scientific rationality, that the way to get at the truth is a wholehearted dialectic of assertion and refutation. If each side attempts to prove its case, with the other trying as energetically as possible to assault the steps of the proof, it is more likely that all of the aspects of the situation will be presented to the fact-finder than if it attempts to investigate for itself with the help of the lawyers.

This theory is open to a number of objections. First of all, the analogy to Popperian scientific methodology is not a good one. Perhaps science proceeds by advancing conjectures and then trying to refute them, but it does not proceed by advancing conjectures that the scientist believes to be false and then using procedural rules to exclude probative evidence.

The two adversary attorneys are each under an obligation to present the facts in the manner most consistent with their client's position to prevent the introduction of unfavorable evidence, to undermine the credibility of opposing witnesses, to set unfavorable facts in a context in which their importance is minimized, to attempt to provoke inferences in their client's favor. The assumption is that two such accounts will cancel out, leaving the truth of the matter. But there is no earthly reason to think this is so; they may simply pile up the confusion.

This is particularly likely in cases turning on someone's sanity or state of mind. Out comes the parade of psychiatrists, what Hannah Arendt once called "the comedy of the soul-experts." Needless to say, they have been prepared by the lawyers, sometimes without knowing it. A clinical law teacher explained to a class that when you first contact a psychiatrist and sketch the facts of the case, you mention only the favorable ones. That way, he or she has an initial bias in your favor and tends to discount the unfavorable facts when you finally get around to mentioning them.

The other side, of course, can cross-examine such a witness to get the truth out. Irving Younger, in his time the most popular lecturer on trial tactics in the country, tells how. Among his famous "Ten Commandments of Cross- Examination" are these:

- Never ask anything but a leading question.
- Never ask a question to which you don't already know the answer.
- Never permit the witness to explain his or her answers.
- Don't bring out your conclusions in the cross-examination. Save them for closing arguments when the witness is in no position to refute them.

Of course, the opposition may be prepared for this; they may have seen Younger's three-hour, $425 videotape on how to examine expert witnesses. They may know, therefore, that the cross-examiner is saving his or her conclusions for the closing argument. Not to worry! Younger knows how to stop an attorney from distorting the truth in closing arguments. "If the opposing lawyer is holding the jury spellbound ... the spell must be broken at all cost. [Younger] suggests the attorney leap to his or her feet and make furious and spurious objections. They will be overruled, but they might at least break the opposing counsel's concentration."

My guess is that this is not quite what Sir Karl Popper had in mind when he wrote, "The Western rationalist tradition ... is the tradition of critical discussion – of examining and testing propositions or theories by attempting to refute them."

A skeptic, in fact, might try this scientific analogy: a beam of invisible electrically charged particles – charge and origin unknown – travels through a distorting magnetic field of unknown strength, then through an opposite field of unknown, but probably different, strength. The beam strikes a detector of undeterminable reliability, from which we are supposed to infer the nature and location of the beam's source. That is the adversary system at its worst.

There is, however, one legal context in which the Popperian defense of the adversary system approximates reality and in which the adversary system is indeed strongly justified. When lawyers debate purely legal questions – particularly in appellate argument, where both sides work from a fixed record and no new evidence can be introduced – we find the kind of give and take that critical rationalists favor. It makes sense to assign each advocate the task of arguing one side's interpretation of the law as forcefully as possible, and doing everything possible to undermine the adversary's arguments. With no facts to hide and everything out in the open, only the arguments and counter-arguments remain. Judges invariably attest that the better the advocates arguing before them, the better decisions they make. Adversary advocacy helps ensure that no arguments or objections get overlooked.

Now, the same thing will often be true when lawyers argue over the interpretation of evidence in a trial of facts, so it may appear that my defense of the adversary system of arguing questions of law proves too much, and provides a defense for adversary arguments about facts as well. To the extent that the lawyers are arguing the interpretation of evidence in the record, that is true. But the problems with the adversary system I have highlighted lie in the fact that trial lawyers view one of their main jobs as keeping damaging information out of the record, or – as in Younger's recommendation that lawyers disrupt their adversaries' closing arguments – clouding the decision-making process. Consider, for example, complaints by the president of a lawyers' organization about a recent American innovation in which jurors are permitted to question witnesses directly. "You work very hard to keep certain information out of the trial. Then all of your finesse and art and technique are thrown out the window when a juror comes in and asks, 'Where were you on the night in question?'" It is hard to defend adversary fact-finding on the ground that it is the best way of ensuring that judges and juries get the most information, when the lawyer's "finesse and art and technique" consists of keeping awkward facts out of court.

Even worse, adversarial tactics sometimes include efforts to ensure that cases never even make it to the stage of fact-finding. Defense counsel for corporate defendants use procedural delays to exhaust their opponents' funds. When they can, lawyers resort to intimidation tactics. A particularly egregious example occurred repeatedly during litigation over the Dalkon Shield, an intrauterine contraceptive device that pharmaceutical manufacturer A. H. Robins marketed during the 1970s to over three million women. Because of a design flaw, the Dalkon Shield caused an estimated 66,000 miscarriages and sterilized thousands of women by infecting them with pelvic inflammatory disease (PID). Faced with staggering liability exposure, Robins and its counsel decided on a scorched-earth defense. One tactic of Robins's counsel soon acquired the nickname "the dirty questions list." Defense lawyers taking depositions asked plaintiffs very specific, very graphic questions about intimate details of their personal hygiene and sexual practices – questions that one plaintiff described as "more like an obscene phone call" than a legal interrogation. Firm lawyers argued that the "dirty questions" were relevant to the law suits because they might reveal alternative sources of PID infection. The questions mainly served, however, to intimidate plaintiffs into dropping their law suits or settling them for inadequate amounts. The message was clear that they might have to answer the same questions in open court. Among other things, defense lawyers asked plaintiffs for the names of all their past and present sexual partners ("besides your husband"), with the clear implication that the partners' names might be revealed and their testimony elicited for purposes of impeaching plaintiffs' answers to the "dirty questions" about what they like to do in bed. Potential plaintiffs filed affidavits indicating that they had dropped their own law suits because of the questions other plaintiffs had been asked.

A similar example is the rise of the so-called "SLAPP suit" – "Strategic Lawsuit Against Public Participation." In a typical SLAPP suit, citizens protesting corporate policies or actions are sued for defamation or tortious interference with business. Some of the alleged defamation has been based on speech as innocuous as testifying against a real estate developer at a zoning hearing, complaining to a school board about incompetent teachers, or collecting signatures on a petition. Although 80 per cent of SLAPP suits are dismissed before trial, the aim of the suits is not legal victory but intimidation. Defendants faced with the prospect of ruinous legal bills and the risk of substantial personal liability agree to cease protest activities in return for withdrawal of the SLAPP suits.

The point of these examples is plain: you cannot defend the adversary system on the basis of its truth-finding function when it licenses (or even requires) behavior designed to ensure that the truth never comes out, because litigants are intimidated into abandoning legitimate cases.

One final difference between "pure" argument, paradigmatically appellate argument of legal issues, and the adversary system of fact-finding, appears in the ethics rules themselves. Ordinarily, lawyers are required to keep facts confidential, and in the adversary system they must never reveal damaging facts to a court unless they are compelled to do so. Matters are very different when we turn from facts to law. Here, the fundamental rule requires lawyers "to disclose to the tribunal legal authority in the controlling jurisdiction known to the lawyer to be directly adverse to the position of the client and not disclosed by opposing counsel." This rule, which law students and lawyers often find counter-intuitive ("why should I do my adversary's legal

44

research for them?"), highlights what makes argument about legal questions different. The idea is to ensure that judges reach the best resolutions they can of questions of law. Their resolutions, after all, become precedents. Getting to the best resolutions requires total transparency, and if my adversary has overlooked a favorable case on point, the rule requires me to throw myself on the sword by telling the judge about the case, to ensure that the judge does not overlook it. By contrast, we have seen that adversarial advocacy on factual matters places lawyers at war with transparency.

[Luban then considers Lon Fuller and John Randall's justification of the adversary system in the 1958 *Joint Conference Report*. Fuller and Randall justify adversarial justice as favourable to the inquisitorial system as a basis for discovering the truth.]

* * * * *

Ultimately, the *Joint Conference Report* seems to take as a premise the idea that truth is served by self-interested rather than disinterested investigation. "The lawyer appearing as an advocate before a tribunal presents, as persuasively as he can, the facts and the law of the case *as seen from the standpoint of his client's interest*" [emphasis added]. The emphasized phrase is accurate, but it gives the game away. For there is all the difference in the world between "the facts seen from X's standpoint" and "the facts seen from the standpoint of X's interest." Of course it is important to hear the former – the more perspectives we have, the better informed our judgment. But to hear the latter is not helpful at all. It is in the murderer's *interest* not to have been at the scene of the crime; consequently, the "facts of the case as seen from the standpoint of [the] client's interest" are that the client was elsewhere that weekend. From the standpoint of my *interest*, the world is my cupcake with a cherry on top; from the standpoint of yours, its streets are paved with gold and you own the streets. Combining the two does not change folly to truth.

All this does not mean that the adversary system may not in fact get at the truth in many hard cases. I suppose that it is as good as its rivals. But, to repeat the point I began with, nobody knows how good that is.

[Luban next considers and refutes the claim that zealous advocacy is necessary to defend a client's legal rights.]

* * * * *

C. Ethical Division of Labor

This argument is no longer that the excesses of zealous advocacy are excused by the promotion of truth or the defense of legal rights. Rather, it is that they are excused by what Thomas Nagel calls "ethical division of labor". He says, in a discussion of the peculiarly ruthless and result-oriented role morality of public officials,

> that the constraints of public morality are not imposed as a whole in the same way on all public actions or on all public offices. Because public agency is itself complex and divided, there is a corresponding ethical division of labor, or ethical specialization. Different aspects of public morality are in the hands of different officials. This can create the illusion that public morality is more consequentialist or less restrictive than it is, because the general conditions may be wrongly identified with the boundaries of a particular role. But in fact those boundaries

usually presuppose a larger institutional structure without which they would be illegitimate. (The most conspicuous example is the legitimacy conferred on legislative decisions by the limitation of constitutional protections enforced by the courts.)

The idea is that behavior that looks wrong from the point of view of ordinary morality can be justified by the fact that other social roles exist whose purpose is to counteract the excesses resulting from role-behavior. Zealous adversary advocacy is justified by the fact that the other side is also furnished with a zealous advocate; the impartial arbiter provides a further check.

This is in fact one of the most commonly heard defenses for pugnacious advocacy: "he had a lawyer, too"; "I'm not supposed to do his lawyer's job for him"; or quoting Sharswood once again, "The lawyer, who refuses his professional assistance because in his judgment the case is unjust and indefensible, usurps the functions of both judge and jury."

The idea is really a checks-and-balances theory, in which social engineering or "wise legislation" is supposed to relieve some of the strain on individual conscience. A functionary in a well-designed checks-and-balances system can simply go ahead and perform his duties secure in the knowledge that injuries inflicted or wrongs committed in the course of those duties will be rectified by other parts of the system.

Will this do the trick? The answer, I am afraid, is no. Suppose that a lawyer is about to embark on a course of action that is unjustified from the point of view of ordinary morality, such as attempting to win an unfair, lopsided judgment for a client from a hapless and innocent party. Or think of our second graymailing example, in which lawyers for a corporation involved in a merger advise their client to fire employees a few at a time to blackmail federal authorities into permitting the merger to go forward. A zealous adversary advocate will do whatever she can to avoid the opposing counsel's attempt to foil her designs. For that reason, she surely cannot claim that the existence of the opposing counsel morally justifies these actions. Certainly the fact that a man has a bodyguard in no way excuses you for trying to kill him, particularly if you bend all your ingenuity to avoiding the bodyguard.

The problem is this. The checks-and-balances notion is desirable because if other parts of the system exist to rectify one's excesses, one will be able to devote undivided energy to the job at hand and do it better. It is analogous to wearing protective clothing in a sport such as fencing: knowing that your opponent is protected, you can go all out in the match. But in the adversary system the situation is different, since the attorney is actively trying to get around the checks and balances. Here the analogy is to a fencer who uses a special foil that can cut through the opponent's protective clothing. To put the point another way, the adversary advocate attempts to evade the system of checks and balances, not rely on it to save her opponents.

There is another problem with the notion of ethical division of labor. It attempts to justify a system of roles by the fact that the system is self-correcting, in other words that injuries perpetrated by one part of the system will be rectified by another. Rectification, however, carries with it high transaction costs in terms of money, time, worry, energy, and (generally) an arduous passage through the bureaucratic straits. These transaction costs create a general background "noise" in the system, a penalty imposed on one simply for becoming embroiled in it. This can be justified only if the system itself is justified, but then the checks-and-balances argument seems merely to gild the lily. Had we found a justification for the adversary system on other grounds, we would not have needed to turn to the ethical division-of-labor argument to begin with.

Division of labor arguments raise a very troubling and difficult topic. The structure of bureaucratic institutions such as the legal system lends itself to divided responsibility. Those who write the rules, those who give the orders, and those who carry them out each have some basis for claiming that they are not at fault for any wrong that results. But this is unacceptable. If moral agency divides along lines of institutional authority, it seems to me that every agent in the institution will wind up abdicating moral responsibility . . . It is for this reason that division-of-labor arguments must walk a thin line between the legitimate notion that different roles have different duties and the unacceptable notion that moral responsibility is itself diminished or "divided down" by institutional structure.

*　*　*　*　*

VI. Nonconsequentialist Justifications of the Adversary System

It may be thought, however, that assessing the adversary system in consequentialist terms of how it will get some job done misses the point. Some social institutions, such as participatory democracy, are justifiable despite the fact that – maybe even because – they are inefficient. The moral standing of such institutions has a noninstrumental basis.

I wish to consider two nonconsequentialist justifications of the adversary system. The first and perhaps boldest is an attempt to justify the adversary system in the wide sense: it is the argument that the traditional lawyer-client relation is an intrinsic moral good. The second is a cluster of related arguments: that adversary adjudication is a valued and valuable tradition, that it enjoys the consent of the governed, and that it is thus an integral part of our social fabric.

A. Adversary Advocacy as Intrinsically Good

When we seek out the services of a professional, it seems to me that we generally see more to the relationship than a mere quid pro quo. Perhaps this is because the quo may be of vital importance to us; perhaps it is because a lot of quid may be required to hire those services. In any event, we have the sense of entrusting a large chunk of our life to this person, and the fact that he or she takes on so intimate a burden and handles it in a trustworthy and skillful manner when the stakes are high seems commendable in itself. Nor does the fact that the professional makes a living by providing this service seem to mitigate the praiseworthiness of it. The business aspect moves along a different moral dimension: it explains how the relationship came about, not what it involves. Finally, our being able to bare our weaknesses and mistakes to the professional and receive assistance without condemnation enhances our sense that beneficence or moral graciousness is at work here. Our lawyer, *mirabile dictu*, forgives us our transgressions.

Feelings such as these are quite real; the question is whether they have merely subjective significance. If they do not, if they mean something more, that may show that Schwartz's two principles, and thus the adversary system and the behavior it countenances, are themselves positive moral goods. Such arguments are, in fact, frequently made: they are based on the idea that providing service is intrinsically good. No finer statement of this exists, in my opinion, than Mellinkoff's. He sees the paradigm client as the "man-in-trouble."

> Cruelty, oppression, deception, unhappiness, worry, strain, incomprehension, frustration, bewilderment – a sorcerer's bag of misery. These become the expected. Then the saddest of all human cries: "Who will help me?" Try God, and politics, and medicine, and a soft shoulder, sooner or later a lawyer. Too many do.

> The lawyer, as lawyer, is no sweet kind loving moralizer. He assumes he is needed, and that no one comes to see him to pass the time of day. He is a prober, an analyzer, a scrapper, a man with a strange devotion to his client. Beautifully strange, or so it seems to the man-in-trouble; ugly strange to the untroubled onlooker.

Charles Fried thinks of the lawyer as a "special-purpose friend" whose activity – enhancing the client's autonomy and individuality – is an intrinsic moral good. This is true even when the lawyer's "friendship" consists in assisting the profiteering slumlord to evict an indigent tenant or enabling the wealthy debtor to run the statute of limitations to avoid an honest debt to an old (and less well-off) friend.

I mention Mellinkoff's and Fried's arguments together because, it seems to me, they express similar ideas, while the unsavory consequences Fried draws from his argument exposes the limitations of Mellinkoff's. Both arguments attempt to show that a lawyer serving a client is engaged in an intrinsic moral good. Mellinkoff's, however, really shows something much weaker, that a lawyer serving a man-in-trouble is (even more cautiously: can be) engaged in an intrinsic moral good. If the client is Fried's profiteering slumlord or unscrupulous debtor, we are confronted with no man-in-trouble, and the intuitions to which Mellinkoff's argument appeals disappear. Indeed, if these were the typical clients, the real men-in-trouble – the victims of these predators – might be better off taking their chances in the war of all against all than seeking to have their "autonomy" vindicated legally. The trouble with Mellinkoff's argument is that he makes clients look more pitiable than many really are.

Fried, on the other hand, bites the bullet and argues that it is morally good to represent the man-in-no-trouble-in-particular, the man-who-troubles-others. The slumlord and the graymailing, anticompetitive multiglomerate are nobly served by a special-purpose friend who helps extract that pound of flesh. Fried constructs a "concentric-circles morality" in which, beginning with an absolute right to self-love based on our own moral standing, we work outward toward those closest to us, then to those whose connections are more remote. Fried argues that the abstract connection between a remote person (even a person-in-trouble) and the agent exercises too slight a claim on the agent to override this inclination toward concrete others. This justifies lavishing special care on our friends, even at the expense of "abstract others"; and because lavishing care is morally praiseworthy, once we grant that a lawyer is a special-purpose friend of his client, we are home free with the intrinsic moral worth of the lawyer-client relation.

Several of Fried's critics focus on the fact that the friendship analogy is question-begging: Fried builds enough lawyerly qualities into his concept of friendship that

48

the argument becomes circular; in the words of Edward Dauer and Arthur Leff, "a lawyer is like a friend . . . because, for Professor Fried, a friend is like a lawyer." It does seem to me, however, that the analogy captures some of the legitimate notion of professionals as devoted by the nature of their calling to the service of their clients. Fried's analogy contains a large grain of truth.

This does not, however, vindicate the adversary system. For the friendship analogy undercuts rather than establishes the Principle of Nonaccountability. Most of us are not willing to do grossly immoral things to help our friends, nor should we be. Lord Brougham's apology may be many things, but it is not a credo of human friendship in any of its forms. Fried realizes the danger, for he confesses that

> not only would I not lie or steal for . . . my friends, I probably also would not pursue socially noxious schemes, foreclose the mortgages of widows or orphans, or assist in the avoidance of just punishment. So we must be careful lest the whole argument unravel on us at this point.

The method for saving the argument, however, proves disappointing. Fried distinguishes between *personal* wrongs committed by a lawyer, such as abusing a witness, and *institutional* wrongs occasioned by the lawyer, such as foreclosing on widows. The latter are precisely those done by the lawyer in his or her proper role of advancing the client's legal autonomy and – preestablished harmony? – they are precisely the ones that are morally acceptable. That is because the lawyer isn't really doing them, the system is.

This last distinction has not been very popular since World War II, and Fried takes pains to restrict it to "generally just and decent" systems, not Nazi Germany. With this qualification, he can more comfortably assert: "We should absolve the lawyer of personal moral responsibility for the result he accomplishes because the wrong is wholly institutional."

This last sentence, however, is nothing but the assertion that institutional excuses work for lawyers, and this should tip us off that Fried's argument will be useless for our purposes. For consider: our whole line of argument has been an attempt to justify the adversary system by showing that the traditional lawyer-client relation is an intrinsic moral good. Now it seems that this can be established by Fried's argument only if we are permitted to cancel the moral debit column by means of an institutional excuse; but that can work only if the institution is justified, and we are back where we started.

Part of the problem is that Fried considers the wrong institution: the context of the lawyer's behavior is not simply the system of laws in general, which he assumes to be just and decent, but the adversary system in particular with its peculiar requirement of one-sided zeal at the margin. It is the adversary system and not the system of laws that shapes the lawyer-client relationship.

The more fundamental problem, however, is that Fried takes the lawyer to be the mere occasion rather than the agent of morally-bad-but-legally-legitimate outcomes. The system did it; it "was just one of those things difficult to pre-visualize – like a cow, say, getting hit by lightning."

This is false in three respects: first, because it discounts the extent to which the lawyer has had a creative hand in advocating the outcome, at times even reversing the law – a skilled lawyer, after all, argues, advocates, bargains, and persuades. Second, because the system is not an abstract structure of impersonal role-descriptions but a social structure of interacting human beings, so that the actions of its agents *are* the system. Third, because the lawyer is indeed acting *in propria persona* by "pulling the levers of the legal machinery." Fried's imagery seems to trade on a Rube Goldberg insight: if the apparatus is complex enough, then the lever-puller doesn't really look like the agent. But that cannot be right. I chop the broccoli, whether I do it with a knife or merely push the button on the blender. The legal levers are pulled by the lawyer: no one else can do it.

* * * * *

VII. The Adversary System Excuse

A. Pragmatic Justification

So far the course of argument has been purely negative, a persecution and assassination of the adversary system. By this time you are entitled to ask what I propose putting in its place. The answer is: nothing, for I think the adversary system is justified.

I do not, let me quickly say, have an argumentative novelty to produce. It would be strange indeed for a social institution to be justified on the basis of virtues other than the tried and true ones, virtues that no one had noticed in it before. My justification is rather a version of the tradition argument, but purged of its ideological overtones. I shall call it the "pragmatic justification" or "pragmatic argument" to suggest its affinity with the relaxed, problem-oriented, and historicist notion of justification associated with American pragmatism. The justification is this:

First, the adversary system, despite its imperfections, irrationalities, loopholes, and perversities, seems to do as good a job as any at finding truth and protecting legal rights. None of its existing rivals is demonstrably better, and some, such as trial by ordeal, are demonstrably worse. Indeed, even if one of the other systems were slightly better, the human costs – in terms of effort, confusion, anxiety, disorientation, inadvertent miscarriages of justice due to improper understanding, retraining, resentment, loss of tradition, you name it – would outweigh reasons for replacing the existing system.

Second, *some* adjudicatory system is necessary.

Third, it's the way we have done things for at least a century.

These propositions constitute a pragmatic argument: if a social institution does a reasonable enough job of its sort that the costs of replacing it outweigh the benefits; and if we need that sort of job done, we should stick with what we have. . . .

That this is a very relaxed sort of justification may be seen from the fact that it works equally well for the inquisitorial system in France and Germany. A pragmatic justification is weak as well because it crumbles in the face of a demonstration that, contrary to what we believe, the institution is awful enough to replace. The argument, in other words, does not really endorse an institution – it only endures it.

Accepting a pragmatic justification of the adversary system, it should be added, does not commit one to a blanket conservatism. One can believe that our society should be drastically changed or that our legal system is scandalously unjust and still accept that a changed society or overhauled legal system should utilize adversary adjudication. Thus, while the argument leads to a conservative conclusion, it does so in a piecemeal, nonideological way, and the conclusion extends no further than the institution for which the argument is offered.

In my opinion, many of our social institutions are like the adversary system in that they admit only of pragmatic justification. Some are not intended to serve any positive moral good; some serve it badly. That these institutions are not worth replacing may be a measure of nothing more than social lethargy and our inability to come up with a better idea; my point is that this is a real reason. A pragmatic argument is logically weak – it justifies institutions without showing that they are better than their rivals, or even that they are particularly good – but in practice it is overwhelmingly powerful. Institutions, like bodies, obey Newton's First Law.

B. Pragmatic Justification and Institutional Excuses

Because this is so typical of institutions it is worth asking about the effect of pragmatic argument on the moral obligations of institutional functionaries (such as lawyers). The position I want to press is roughly that a social institution that can receive only a pragmatic justification is not capable of providing institutional excuses for immoral acts. To do that, an institution must be justified in a much stronger way, by showing that it is a positive moral good. A pragmatic argument, by contrast, need show only that it is not much more mediocre than its rivals.

Let me spell this out by criticizing what I shall call the Transitivity Argument, which goes as follows:

1. The institution is justified.
2. The institution requires its functionary to do A.
3. Therefore, the functionary is justified in doing A.

This plausible-looking defense of institutional excuses can be criticized by denying the first premise; however, I am accepting the pragmatic justification of the adversary system and thus accepting the premise. Or it could be criticized by attacking the second premise: thus, William Simon and Richard Abel have argued that the role morality of lawyers is so riddled with contradictions that it is impossible to derive any coherent set of professional requirements from it. My strategy, however, is to deny that the conclusion follows from the premises. The institutional obligation is only a *prima facie* obligation, and the weaker the justification of the institution, the weaker the force of this obligation in overriding other morally relevant factors.

To get the argument underway, let us look at the way an institutional excuse might work when the institution is strongly justified, when it is a positive moral good.

Consider, as an example, a charitable organization whose sole function is to distribute food to famine-stricken people in impoverished areas of the world. We will call this the *institution*. Division of labor within it creates different jobs or *institutional tasks*, each of which has specified duties or *role-obligations*. These may be quite general: the logistics officer, for example, might have as his role-obligation procuring means of transporting food. To carry out the role-obligation, he must

51

perform various actions, call them the *role-acts*.

Let us suppose that to get food to a remote village the logistics officer must obtain trucks from a local, very powerful gangster, P. As it happens, P is involved in a number of unsavory activities, including a plan to murder a local man, because P wants to sleep with the man's wife. Imagine further that the logistics officer overhears P dispatching a murderer to kill the man that very night, that P discovers that the logistics officer has overheard him, and that P tells the officer that if the man is warned and escapes, P will not provide the trucks.

The officer faces a terrible moral dilemma. Other things being equal, he is under a moral obligation to warn the man. Let us, at any rate, suppose that this is so. But here, if anywhere, we may wish to permit an institutional excuse. Suppose the officer complies with P's demand. Asked to justify this, he says, "My job is more important." This is an institutional excuse, the structure of which may be spelled out as follows: he points out that the role-act of complying with P is required by his role-obligation, which in turn is necessary to perform the institutional task, which (finally) is justified by the positive moral good of the institution – the saving of many innocent lives.

The general problem, which creates the dilemma, is that the propositions

> The institution is a morally good one
>
> and
>
> The institution imposes role-obligations on its officers some of which may mandate morally bad role-acts

can both be true.

In such a case, the institutional excuse, fully spelled out, will take the form I have indicated: the agent justifies the role act by showing it is required by the role obligation, justifies the obligation by showing it derives from the institutional task, justifies the institutional task by appealing to the structure of the institution, and justifies the institution by demonstrating its moral goodness.

* * * * *

If, on the other hand, an institution can be justified only pragmatically, the sides of the dilemma do not have equal weight and the institutional excuse collapses. For in that case it reads as follows:

It is true that I am morally wronging you. But that is required by my role-obligations, which are essential to my institutional task, which is necessary to the structure of the institution, which is justified

- because it is there.
- because it's the way we do things around here.
- because it's not worth the trouble to replace it.

This, I think, will not do. The excuse rests on an elephant that stands on a tortoise that floats in the sky. But the sky is falling.

* * * * *

The basic problem with the Transitivity Argument [from the Adversary system] is that it exempts officers of an institution from ordinary moral requirements that conflict with role-obligations, even though the institution itself is in place only because we have done it that way for a long time. The result is to place conformity to existing institutions beyond the very possibility of criticism. This, however, is no longer justified conservatism: rather, it is fetishism of tradition.

Pragmatic arguments do not really praise institutions; they merely give reason for not burying them. Since their force is more inertial than moral, they create insufficient counterweight to resolve dilemmas in favor of the role-obligation. An excuse based on institutions justified in this way is simply a "good soldier" argument with little more to be said.

VIII. Conclusion and Peroration

It is time to summarize.

Perhaps the best way to see the import of the arguments I have been offering is not as an attack on the adversary system (for, after all, I have not suggested that it should be replaced) so much as an attack on an ideology consisting of these ideas:

1. The adversary system is the most powerful engine of justice ever devised.

2. It is a delicately poised instrument in which the generation of just outcomes depends on the regular functioning of each of its parts.

3. Hence the pursuit of justice morally obligates an attorney to assume a one-sided Broughamesque role.

4. The adversary system, in consequence, institutionally excuses lawyers from ordinary moral obligations conflicting with their professional obligations.

5. Broughamesque advocacy is, moreover, a cornerstone of our system of political liberties, for it is the last defense of the hapless criminal-accused against the awesome power of the state. To restrict the advocate is to invite totalitarianism.

I have argued against the first four of these propositions. About the fifth a more cautious conclusion is in order. The argument it offers that the criminal defense lawyer "must not regard the alarm, the torments, the destruction which he may bring upon others" (Brougham, again) is rather persuasive, but only because of two special features of the criminal context: that we have political reasons for handicapping the government in its role as enforcer, and that the criminal defendant comes closest to the paradigm of the man-in-trouble. The argument, then, countenances adversarial ruthlessness as a blanket policy only in criminal and quasi-criminal defense, and thus only in these situations is the adversary system fully available as an institutional excuse.

What does all this mean in noncriminal contexts, where this institutional excuse based on liberal fear of the state is unavailable? The answer, very simply, is this. The adversary system possesses only slight moral force, and thus appealing to it can excuse only slight moral wrongs. Anything else that is morally wrong for a nonlawyer to do on behalf of another person is morally wrong for a lawyer to do as well. The lawyer's role carries no moral privileges and immunities.

This does not mean that zealous advocacy is immoral, not even when it frustrates the search for truth or violates legal rights. Sometimes frustrating the search for truth may be a morally worthy thing to do, and sometimes moral rights are ill served by legal rights. All I am insisting on is that the standards by which such judgments are made are the same for lawyers and nonlawyers. If a lawyer is permitted to puff, bluff, or threaten on certain occasions, this is not because of the adversary system and the Principle of Nonaccountability, but because, in such circumstances, anyone would be permitted to do these things. Nothing justifies doing them on behalf of a predator.

But, it will be objected, my argument leads to a paradox, for I have claimed to offer a vindication, albeit a weak one, of the adversary system, and therefore of the duties of partisan advocacy that it entails. Am I not saying that a lawyer may be professionally obligated to do A and morally obligated not to do A?

That is indeed the conclusion, but there is no contradiction here. The adversary system and the system of professional obligation it mandates are justified only in that, lacking a clearly superior alternative, they should not be replaced. This implies, I have argued, a presumption in favor of professional obligation, but one that any serious and countervailing moral obligation rebuts. Thus, when professional and serious moral obligation conflict, moral obligation takes precedence. When they don't conflict, professional obligations rule the day. The Principle of Professionalism follows from the fact that we have an adversary system; the Principle of Nonaccountability does not. The point of elaborating the former is to tell the lawyer what, in this system, professionalism requires – to insist that it requires zeal, for example, even when cutting corners might be more profitable or pleasant. Professionalism can tell lawyers not to cut corners; my point is that it cannot mandate them to cut throats. When serious moral obligation conflicts with professional obligation, the lawyer must become a civil disobedient to professional rules.

Not that this is likely to happen. Lawyers get paid for their services, not for their consciences. But so does everyone else. As we do not expect the world to strike a truce in the war of all against all, we should not expect lawyers to.

NOTES AND QUESTIONS

1. Had Murray had a view of the lawyer's role similar to that articulated by Luban, do you think that he might have been quicker to realize that he faced an ethical dilemma? What "ordinary" moral values are implicated by the discovery of the video tapes? In answering this question, you may want to refer back to the "ordinary" theories of ethics discussed earlier in the Chapter.

2. Is it reasonable to expect lawyers to be a "civil disobedient to professional rules"? Does this depend on whether one thinks that civil disobedience to law is generally justified? What are the conditions for the legitimate exercise of civil disobedience? Does, for example, the lawyer need to disobey publicly, accepting the consequences that the society chooses to impose? Or may the lawyer simply ignore the legal requirement, hoping that sanctions can be avoided?

3. If moral decisions are, as suggested earlier, reached normally through intuitive responses to problems, is it more likely that lawyers will have intuitions shaped by ordinary moral reasons, or by the claims of legality? In other words, is one advantage of Luban's theory that it allows lawyers to rely on the intuitions they've developed over the course of their lifetimes, rather than on ones that might have emerged only as a product of their legal training?

4. As Dare notes, Luban describes adversarial practice as featuring hyper-zeal. Do you think it needs to? Do you think it does so in practice in Canadian courtrooms? If not, does that affect your assessment of the merits of Luban's argument?

Scenario Five

John Smith represents a woman, M, who is claiming refugee status in Canada. Part of M's claim is that she was sexually assaulted by government soldiers in her home country. Smith has some reason to believe that M's claim is factually untrue, mostly because his assistant (who speaks the same language as M) overheard M saying that the story was "a stretch" and "more useful than true" while sitting in Smith's waiting room. He also, though, is aware that M's country of origin does not accord equal rights and freedoms to women, and that M's future there is bleak. While speaking with M, Smith learns that she has a brother who lives in Canada and is a Canadian citizen. Given what M said, the brother almost certainly would have information about whether the claim made by M is factually accurate, and is also quite likely to tell the truth (since he and M are estranged). Is it ethical for Smith not to contact the brother to find out more? In answering the question bear in mind that it is unethical to mislead a court or tribunal, or to knowingly assist your client in presenting perjured testimony to the court or tribunal. Also consider what ordinary moral values might be at play and how, if at all, those values conflict with the process or substance of the law as applied to M.

Scenario Six

Samantha Cones is a lawyer in England. While amendments allowing no-fault divorce are pending, under English law at the current time, if a spouse cannot establish cause (adultery, unreasonable behaviour or desertion) and cannot establish the consent of the other spouse, a divorce cannot be obtained for five years. Normally divorce is uncontested; however, Samantha's client Hugo Black wants to contest his wife's divorce application. He tells Samantha that he has not been unfaithful or deserted his wife. He says that everything that his wife has included in her application for divorce is true, but that in Hugo's view it does not amount to "unreasonable behaviour". Samantha's assessment is that Hugo has a legal argument that his behaviour is not unreasonable, but she would not want to be married to a man who acts like Hugo did – he was controlling and difficult. Given Luban's account of the lawyer's role, should Samantha pursue Hugo's position that his behaviour was not "unreasonable"? See Caroline Mortimer, "Wife 'locked in' loveless marriage after judge refuses divorce petition" (*The Independent*, February 15, 2017).

[c] Integrity

As legal ethics has evolved, some scholars have come to criticize the singularity of both the zealous advocacy and moral agency conceptions of the lawyer's role. They view those conceptions as unsatisfactory because they fail to capture the complex and multi-faceted emphasis on different (and sometimes competing) values by courts and professional regulators. In particular, critics note, singular normative approaches may not fully capture the moral complexity of the legal and ethical framework that governs Canadian lawyers. In a 1996 article, Alice Woolley argued that the "standard conception" of the American lawyer differs from the standard conception of the Canadian lawyer.[17] Specifically, Canadian codes of conduct, including the new Federation of Law Societies' *Model Code*, differ from their American counterparts because they have always placed a central emphasis on lawyer "integrity". Rule 2.1-1 of the Federation's *Model Code* provides:

> 2.1-1 A lawyer has a duty to carry on the practice of law and discharge all responsibilities to clients, tribunals, the public and other members of the profession honourably and with integrity.

The *Model Code* does not define integrity, but suggests in the Commentary that practising law requires being trustworthy, honourable and responsible, while always avoiding questionable conduct.

Those definitions do not, on their own, provide all that much guidance to a lawyer seeking to practise with integrity. What does maintaining integrity require? One approach is to see integrity as a response to the problem of conflicts between professional and personal morality. Those conflicts cannot be avoided and no fully satisfactory moral answer can be provided in circumstances where they conflict. Either professional or personal moral claims must be sacrificed. What emphasizing integrity does is assert that lawyers should, where possible, avoid circumstances where personal and professional morality are likely to conflict (by, for example, selecting clients whose moral claims the lawyer can respect). In addition, and more importantly, integrity directs the lawyer to be fully cognizant of, and responsible for, their choices in circumstances of moral conflict. Citing Gerald Postema, Woolley suggested that a lawyer must "recognize and take responsibility for the extent to which her professional life requires her to do things that conflict with what, outside of her profession, she would find morally unacceptable".[18] And, if choosing to privilege personal morality over professional obligation, they must take responsibility for that too.

In the following excerpt, Thomas Shaffer considers the significance of a lawyer's integrity in the lawyer-client relationship, and in particular on the lawyer's role as an advisor to the client in circumstances of moral difficulty or complexity.

---

[17] Alice Woolley, "Integrity in Zealousness: Comparing the Standard Conceptions of the Canadian and American Lawyer" (1996) 9 Can. J.L. & Jur. 61.

[18] Alice Woolley, "Integrity in Zealousness: Comparing the Standard Conceptions of the Canadian and American Lawyer" (1996) 9 Can. J.L. & Jur. 61 at 76.

THOMAS SHAFFER

"Legal Ethics and the Good Client"
(1987) 36 Cath. U. L. Rev. 319*
[footnotes omitted]

The distinctive feature of ethics in a profession is that it speaks to the unequal encounter of two moral persons. Legal ethics, which is a subject of study for lawyers, therefore, often becomes the study of what is good — not for me, but for this other person, over whom I have power. Legal ethics differs from ethics generally: ethics is thinking about morals. Legal ethics is thinking about the morals of someone else. It is *concern* with the *goodness* of someone else. In this view, legal ethics begins and ends with Socrates's question to the law professors of Athens: "Pray will you concern yourself with anything else than how we citizens can be made as good as possible?"

The subject in legal ethics is, in this way, the client's goodness, but legal ethics does not focus on the client's *conscience*. Legal ethics is complicated by the fact that the discussion of this other person's morals is focused not in *his* conscience but in mine. Legal ethics is thinking about my client's morals, but I am the one who is thinking. Most of our discussions — in committees of lawyers, in bull sessions, in law school, and with our spouses at dinner — are on what a lawyer should do about his client's morals.

This is a very difficult situation. Martin Buber, the great, prophetic, modern teacher of the theology of human relationship, the person who formulated the notion of the I-Thou relationship as a foundation for moral life, despaired of *professional* relationships. He thought it was all but impossible for a professional in the modern world to look at his client and see a Thou rather than an It: I can see that you *want* to do it, he said, but you cannot; the sides are too unequal. The situation is not only difficult, Buber said — it is *tragic*.

It is also a morally perilous situation for lawyers. It is an invitation to hubris — to arrogance. Most discussion in legal ethics these days is discussion of how a lawyer can protect herself from her client's bad morals. . . . .

If we can manage to regard our client as a Thou and not an It, and if we manage to avoid hubris, the issue is this: What should I want for my client?

The possible answers are three. (Lectures always have three answers. Ten to fifteen minutes each.) The first answer, to the question, "What should I want for my client?" is: I should want my client to be *right*. The second is: I should want my client to be *free*. And the third is the Socratic one: I should want my client to be *good*.

I. Rectitude

The first answer — I should want my client to be right — is traditional in American legal ethics. . .

Republican legal ethics says that what is important is that the client do the right thing, and that it is the lawyer's job to see to it that his client does the right thing.

---

* Reproduced with permission.

In this, republican legal ethics paralleled the development of professional ethics in journalism, in medicine, in the clergy, and in teaching. It was and is an ethic for professional life that tends to ignore, if not to deny, the possibility that the person served — the client, the patient, the newspaper reader, the parishioner, or the student — can be a source of sound morals for professional people. It was a later generation in ethics that tried to apply in the professions' Karl Barth's principle of conditional advice: He who sets out to counsel his brother, Barth said, must be prepared to be counseled in turn if there is need of it. The legal ethics of rectitude is a one-way street. It speaks to professional responsibility, but it tends to hubris, to regard clients as sources of corruption, as occasions of sin. Hoffman said, in reference to the client who came to him as debtor on a debt barred by the statute of limitations, "If my client is conscious he owes the debt, and has no other defense than the legal bar, he shall never make me a partner in his knavery".

II. Freedom

The second school of thought in modern legal ethics, the legal ethics of freedom, is, if nothing else, a corrective to hubris. It does not talk about responsibility and rectitude. It says that what I should wish for my client is that he be free. He will, if I serve him well, be informed. He will, to use a trendy theological word, be *empowered*. And he will then have, to use a trendy philosophical word, *autonomy*. I will have acted to protect his autonomy. He will be empowered to act autonomously. Autonomy is compounded from the Greek words for self and law. My client will himself, make law; he will, alone, be his own ruler.

One of the most prominent exponents of this view in modern American legal ethics is Professor Monroe Freedman, who argued his position in a frequently quoted lecture, given at this law school, in 1977. He said: "The attorney acts both professionally and morally in assisting clients to maximize their autonomy", and then explained:

> that is, by counseling clients candidly and fully regarding the clients' legal rights and moral responsibilities as the lawyer perceives them, and by assisting clients to carry out their lawful decisions. . . . [T]he attorney acts unprofessionally and immorally [when he deprives] clients of their autonomy, that is, by denying them information regarding their legal rights, by otherwise pre- empting their moral decisions, or by depriving them of the ability to carry out their lawful decisions.

To deny my clients legal services because I disagree with their moral choices is - Freedman argues — to "deprive them of the ability to carry out their law- ful decisions". . . .

Freedman's argument. . . is based not on statism, but on the proposition that the highest good of a human person — at least the highest good that is of social or professional importance — is that he be free. That he be autonomous. That he live according to moral principles that are his own, not his lawyer's.

That position is attractive against hubristic moral authority. It was attractive against an arrogant church in the 18th century, as it is now attractive against any totalitarian moral order, or even against a domineering parent. It works well as an objection to the traditional republican legal ethic that seems so often to call for us to force or trick our clients into doing the right thing. The ethic of autonomy is apparently democratic, not arrogant, and thus is in tune with the American political tradition. The ethic of autonomy is progressive - a word we Americans have always liked too much.

In these instrumental and patriotic applications, the ethic of autonomy is able to hide its anthropology. It is not obvious, although it becomes clear when you think about it, that this second position on what I should want for my client depends on a certain view of the human person — the view that the human person is essentially alone. The vulnerability becomes clear when the human person is described adequately, as in the Bible and in our stories — from great novels to television commercials.

In fact, our stories say, the human person is radically connected to other people. The real challenge to autonomy as a doctrine is the ordinary fact that the person comes to *be* in relationships — in families, congregations, communities, friendships, and associations. It is the contrast between being alone and being connected, rather than the contrast between freedom and rectitude, that seems to me revealing in the legal ethics of autonomy. . . .

The ethics of autonomy leave human context out of account; they posit a here-and-now self that seems unconnected to others or even to his own past. The ethics of autonomy do not reflect ordinary sentiment about what people (Americans) want from one another and celebrate in such places as the 100th birthday party of the Statue of Liberty; they do not reflect what we know from stories about American lawyers.

When you describe our lives carefully, you describe lives of moral influence. That is characteristic of the great novels, from Austen and Eliot to Snow and Faulkner and Anne Tyler; it is also characteristic of almost any thirty-minute situation comedy on television, or of *Hill Street Blues*.

In terms of *social* ethics, autonomy is often seen as a guarantor of diversity in the community — of pluralism, if you like. That is, the argument goes, autonomy guarantees that we are not all alike; if each of us rules himself, we will be different from one another, and our strength lies in our difference. This is a social argument, an argument for the common good; it says the common good is served by diversity. In fact, though, we have never wanted diversity more than we have wanted goodness. We have never preferred diversity or supposed that diversity is adequate. Pursued logically, diversity, as a social justification for the ethics of autonomy, would require us to prefer a community of liars, sluggards, and philanderers — provided they do not resemble one another.

Our stories, and particularly our American lawyer-hero stories, say that we prefer, in our communities, people who are brave, generous, reverent, cheerful, and honest. Our collective moral judgment, such as it still is, is not as spooked by Sunday-School morality as law professors think. When you get down to the point of the social argument, finally, what we want in our lawyers, and from our lawyers, is not the free individual, but the wise individual — what Aristotle called the man of practical wisdom. . . .

Freedman argues for moral influence. He said here in 1977 that lawyers should counsel their clients "regarding ... moral responsibilities as the lawyer perceives them", and he gave examples from his own practice. . . .

59

In one case, the client, a landlord, wanted Freedman to evict a war widow; Freedman said, "If you want to evict her, I will. But why don't you give the matter some thought". The client decided not to evict her. In the other case, the other side had made a damaging error in a contract. Freedman said: "We can clobber them with it", and the client cheered. Then Freedman said: "The other choice is to call them up and point out the error. That way, you are the good guy, and maybe we can put our future relationship with them on a higher plane by setting the example." The client took the latter choice.

But in both cases, Freedman said he would do what the client wanted if the client chose to be ruthless. My argument is that this reservation is inconsistent with moral leadership. It has led my friend Freedman to take untenable positions when he advises other lawyers — even though his own practice is obviously one of persuasive moral advice, and his clients are people of good character, in important part — *no doubt* — because of his influence.

The problem with republican legal ethics was that it put the integrity on the lawyer's side: Hoffman looked at his client and said: "He shall never make me a partner in his knavery". The problem with the legal ethics of autonomy is that it shifts that load the other way. Freedman looks at his client and says, I will tell you what I think you should do, but if you decide to do something else — even something I regard as immoral for you *and* for me — I will help you do it; otherwise I will be depriving you of your ability to carry out your lawful decisions. . . .

III. Goodness

The problem with the legal ethics of rectitude was that it seemed not to understand that moral advice is not good unless it is open to influence from the client; he who counsels his sister must be prepared to be counseled in turn. My client is, as Justice Wilson said it, the noblest work of God; that means *he* may have some wisdom for *me*; it also means that he is capable of being and of becoming a good person, and is therefore worth *my* giving *him* moral advice. This theology of the client argues against the legal ethics of rectitude, which has so often seemed to think of him as no damned good.

But there is integrity on the other side of this relationship as well — on the lawyer's side.

Integrity means that the lawyer has moral limits. There are things you will not ask your friend to do, and if your friend is your lawyer, there are things you will not ask your lawyer to do. In part — usually, I suppose — that is because you love her, and you perceive her character, and you want her to be and to become a good person. But also, I think, it is because you know that it would be futile to ask her. There are some things — some *lawful* things — she would refuse to do. Part of the value of her moral advice is that there are things she will refuse to do. This refusal is part of her character. Her character is what makes her your friend, and you her friend, in the first place.

"Those who wish for their friends' good for their friends' sake are friends in the truest sense," Aristotle said, "since their attitude is determined by what their friends are and not by incidental considerations. Hence their friendship lasts as long as they are good, and (that means it will last for a long time, since) goodness or virtue is a thing that lasts ...[E]ach partner is both good ... . and good for his friend." Because the lawyer is good, her advice is worth having, and worth giving. It's being worth having and worth giving is a function of her character.

Moral counsel, then, depends on character, both inherently — otherwise it would not be moral advice — and in terms of effect. We heed the moral advice of a good person because the person who gives it is good. This is as true of social ethics — of political leadership — as it is of professional ethics. . . . .

What is wrong, then, with Monroe Freedman's interesting notion about moral counsel is that his theory of client autonomy removes the essential character of the lawyer. Freedman argues for moral advice, but he also argues for the lawyer who says, "I will do whatever you want me to do - regardless". I argue that such a hypothetical lawyer would not be a person of integrity. And a person who lacks integrity is not a dependable source of moral advice.

I would not trust my life, my fortune, nor, least of all, my conscience, to such a person.

* * * * *

NOTES AND QUESTIONS

1. Shaffer rejects a concept of lawyer's ethics where the lawyer determines the right thing to do without account for the client, but also a concept where the client determines the right thing to do without account for the lawyer. In his view, a better model has the right thing to do determined between the lawyer and client, with both being moral actors and persons of integrity. What would counselling in that model look like? What would happen if, at the end, of the day, the lawyer and client simply disagreed as to the best course of action: who decides?

2. Implicit in Shaffer's article appears to be the idea that there are "good" people and "bad" people (people who have integrity and those who lack it). Do you think that's a plausible account of human nature? Why or why not? Is integrity an act or a trait?

3. While Shaffer sees Freedman's approach, which like Dare defends the standard conception, as unduly deferential to the client, Katherine Kruse has argued that legal ethics theories take insufficient account of the client's part in determining what the law permits or requires. What account of lawyer's ethics can best account for the lawyer *and* the client as moral actors? Compare Dare, Luban and Shaffer in this respect. See in particular Katherine R. Kruse, "Beyond Cardboard Clients in Legal Ethics" (2010) 23 Geo. J. Leg. Ethics 103.

4. Shaffer begins his article by dividing between wanting your client to be right, wanting your client to be free and wanting your client to be good. Do you think those are the right questions for a lawyer to ask? Do you think they are mutually exclusive?

In reading the following judgment, consider whether the type of lawyer-client relationship and dialogue Shaffer imagines would have changed counsel for the defendant's assessment of their obligations to the plaintiff at the point of settlement.

SPAULDING v. ZIMMERMAN

263 Minn. 346 (1962)
(Supreme Court, Thomas Gallagher, Justice.
Justice Rogosheske took no part in the
consideration or decision of this case.)

[The defendants had reached a settlement with the plaintiff for injuries he had suffered in an automobile accident. The medical report given to the defendants indicated that the plaintiff was suffering from an aneurysm which had not been detected by the plaintiff's own physician. The defendants did not disclose the medical report to the plaintiff. The plaintiff later discovered the existence of the aneurysm and sought to set aside the settlement.]

* * * * *

The principles applicable to the court's authority to vacate settlements made on behalf of minors and approved by it appear well established. With reference thereto, we have held that the court in its discretion may vacate such a settlement, even though it is not induced by fraud or bad faith, where it is shown that in the accident the minor sustained separate and distinct injuries which were not known or considered by the court at the time settlement was approved . . . and even though the releases furnished therein purported to cover both known and unknown injuries resulting from the accident. . . . The court may vacate such a settlement for mistake even though the mistake was not mutual in the sense that both parties were similarly mistaken as to the nature and extent of the minor's injuries, but where it is shown that one of the parties had additional knowledge with respect thereto and was aware that neither the court nor the adversary party possessed such knowledge when the settlement was approved. . . .

From the foregoing it is clear that in the instant case the court did not abuse its discretion in setting aside the settlement which it had approved on plaintiff's behalf while he was still a minor. It is undisputed that neither he nor his counsel nor his medical attendants were aware that at time settlement was made he was suffering from an aorta aneurysm which may have resulted from the accident. The seriousness of this disability is indicated by Dr. Hannah's report indicating the imminent danger of death therefrom. This was known by counsel for both defendants but was not disclosed to the court at the time it was petitioned to approve the settlement. While no canon of ethics or legal obligation may have required them to inform plaintiff or his counsel with respect thereto, or to advise the court therein, it did become obvious to them at the time that the settlement then made did not contemplate or take into consideration the disability described. This fact opened the way for the court to later exercise its discretion in vacating the settlement and under the circumstances described we cannot say that there was any abuse of discretion on the part of the court in so doing under Rule 60.02(6) of Rules of Civil Procedure.

* * * * *

Affirmed.

NOTES AND QUESTIONS

1. Assess how each theory of legal ethics discussed here – loyal advocacy; the lawyer as moral agent in pursuit of justice; and integrity – would have affected the lawyer's decision.

2. In the judgment, the court suggests that the lawyer's ethical obligations did not require disclosure of this information. Assuming that that is correct, does it suggest a deficit in the approach to lawyer ethics, or does it suggest that the judgment here is simply limited in application to the question of when settlements should be overturned?

3. Under the applicable discovery rules, Spaulding's lawyer was entitled to request (and to receive) a copy of the independent medical examination. He did not do so. Does this affect your assessment of the ethics of the decision made by Zimmerman's counsel?

4. At the time of the accident, Zimmerman was 19 years old. Spaulding was 20 years old and riding in Zimmerman's car. The damages that Spaulding would have received would have been covered by the various insurance policies in effect given the substantive tort law then applicable. Zimmerman was not consulted about whether the disclosure should take place, and it appears that the insurance representatives were not consulted either. Does this affect your assessment of the ethics of the decision made by Zimmerman's counsel?[19]

Scenario Seven

Assume that you act for a client who tested positive for HIV after negligently receiving tainted blood products from a blood services agency. You enter into settlement discussions with the agency and they provide you with a generous offer to present to your client. Prior to accepting the offer, however, your client tells you that she has just been advised that the test was in error, and that she does not have HIV. She nonetheless instructs you to accept the settlement offer without disclosing the error. Considering only the ethical principles discussed in this chapter, what should you do?[20]

Scenario Eight

Jane Adams is a wills and estates practitioner. A couple in their 60s comes to her for legal advice. She meets with them together, and also has conversations with them on their own. During the conversation with the wife, the wife tells Jane that prior to getting married she had a child whom she gave up for adoption. She knows where the child is (the adoption was with a family member) but the child does not know she is adopted. In addition, the husband does not know about the child. The wife would like to make some provision for the child in her will, but she does not want to tell her husband. Jane believes that openness and honesty are crucial in a

---

[19] See Roger C. Cramton & Lori P. Knowles, "Professional Secrecy and its Exceptions: *Spaulding v. Zimmerman* Revisited" (1998) 83 Minn. L. Rev. 63.

[20] This hypothetical is adapted from Allan C. Hutchinson, *Legal Ethics and Professional Responsibility* (Toronto: Irwin Law, 1999) at 1-2.

marriage, and that the wife's moral well-being rests on her telling the husband the truth. She also knows that under the applicable code of professional conduct she cannot continue to represent the couple unless the wife tells. Does she urge the wife to tell?

[6] ON BEING AN ETHICAL LAWYER

To this point in the chapter, our primary focus has been on what being an ethical lawyer requires, and on different models of the ideal lawyer as a loyal advocate, as morally accountable or as a person of integrity. A further question to consider, however, is what it means to be the person who discharges the lawyer's role. It may be that we can justify the model of the lawyer as a neutral partisan for their client's objectives, without moral accountability for those objectives. But will the lawyer who acts in that way consider their life to be well-lived? Will they view their life as meaningful, and themself as a good person?

The role of the lawyer as an advocate for the interests of others, however that role is constrained or defined, means that at points the lawyer will do and pursue things other than what they themself would choose to do or pursue in that situation. That means that being a lawyer may conflict with other ethical values of importance to the lawyer. The lawyer's work may be morally justified along the lines argued for by authors like Dare, but that may not make it feel right or ethically satisfactory in light of the lawyer's own values and beliefs.

Daniel Markovits argues that the lawyer's role sometimes requires that lawyers "lie" and "cheat". Specifically, that when acting as an advocate a lawyer must say things that they accurately believe are untrue (lying) and must pursue goals that they accurately believe are unworthy (cheating). Markovits argues that lying and cheating by lawyers is morally justified, for reasons similar to those used to justify the standard conception of the lawyer's role, but that a lawyer's lying and cheating means that the lawyer necessarily has a compromised ethical life. Because modern lawyers do not live in insular communities that permit them to redescribe their unethical acts as ethical, they are necessarily "tragic villain[s]".[21]

An alternative perspective, which considers how a lawyer might achieve an ethical life, is set out in the following excerpt.

ALICE WOOLLEY

"Michelle's Story: Creativity and Meaning in Legal Practice"
From: *In Search of the Ethical Lawyer: Stories from
the Canadian Legal Profession* (Adam Dodek and Alice Woolley eds)[*]
(Vancouver: UBC Press, 2016)
[footnotes omitted]

What would it mean if you couldn't be a lawyer anymore? Take money out of the equation, and assume that you have enough to live comfortably. But a degenerative illness has taken away the physical and mental energy required for legal practice.

---

[21] Daniel Markovits, *A Modern Legal Ethics: Adversary Advocacy in a Democratic Age* (Princeton: Princeton University Press, 2008) at 243.

[*] Reproduced with permission.

What would you lose if that happened to you? Who would you be?

Most lawyers never have to answer such questions. They might never ask them. Michelle, whose story this chapter tells, was not that lucky:

> You asked me something about how I feel, about how my life is different without my practice. The more I've thought about that, the more I've kept feeling like I'm hollowed out. I'm still useful. If I were holding up a plate, and you hollowed out the centre, you will still be holding up the plate, but its core is gone. I do feel hollowed out.
>
> A tree trunk, you hollow it out, and it's a canoe. It's just not a tree anymore.
>
> It took me a long time to accept that I was the canoe and not the tree. My shape is different. And my shape might be different tomorrow. That's a reality for me every day.

For Michelle, as for others who leave legal practice, these questions cannot be avoided, nor can the deeper question that they reflect: what role did being a lawyer play in the construction of the ethics of my life, in making my life meaningful, in making it moral, in making it count as well-lived?

That question can be considered personally through reflection on one's life and what it means to have lived the life that one has. It can also be considered philosophically. The question of whether a lawyer's life counts as well-lived matters not only for the lawyer, but also for the broader human question about the roles that our society wants people to occupy, and about what it means to be one of the people who does so. The general ethical question "how should I live?" is one that I answer for myself (it is, after all, about how *I* should live), but also subject to impartial analysis (since it is also about how I *should* live).

Because of these subjective and objective aspects, the ethical question of how one should live can include a wide variety of things. But in terms of understanding the social role of the lawyer, of what that role ought to require, and the ethical consequences of occupying it, two concepts are especially important: morality and meaning. Morality refers to the duties and obligations that follow from the universal and impartial principles that govern human interaction. Morality identifies what each of us owes to each other by virtue of our common humanity. Its concerns are universal and general, not particular and specific.

In terms of the lawyer's role, the question posed by morality is whether that role, normally understood, necessarily results in violations of moral values. If it does, then the next question is whether some morality-based justification in some way constrains or explains what lawyers ought to do on behalf of clients.

Meaning is more subjective and particular than morality, though it still has an objective component. Meaning as a philosophical concept has roots in the work of Bernard Williams. He suggests that each of us has "ground projects" – "a project or set of projects which are closely related to his existence and which to a significant degree give meaning to his life". Ground projects are distinct from morality in that they are not impartial or universal in their significance, but they are not just those things that happen to interest or attract me. They are foundationally important; they make my life worth living, and they might be worth dying for. Pursuit of my ground projects is as much part of my ethical life as is my compliance with moral norms.

Susan Wolf has further defined meaning as a philosophical concept. For an activity to be meaningful, it must be something that grips, excites, or engages us; it must be something that we love. It must also be something worth focusing on, something of value in an objective sense. The objective criterion for establishing meaning is not necessarily onerous or rigid. It is not some "sort of pure, subject-independent metaphysical property". It only connotes the idea that meaning is not wholly self-generated, but also involves some external assessment. Meaning occupies a halfway point between the pure subjectivity of self-interest and the pure objectivity of morality. It is found in "loving something (or a number of things) worthy of love, and being able to engage with it (or them) in a positive way".

When considering the ethics of the lawyer's role, the question raised by meaning is whether being a lawyer can be a legitimate subject of engagement, a source of meaning for the person who occupies that role. Or does being a lawyer in some way disrupt the ability to achieve a meaningful life, to find and pursue things of value to her?

Surprisingly, perhaps, legal ethics theories, which use philosophical concepts to assess the lawyer's role, have generally focused on the morality of that role. They identify the lawyer's role as creating a moral problem – it involves lawyers in advocating for morally-suspect (but lawful) causes through morally- doubtful (but lawful) procedures. They then consider whether what lawyers do can be justified through the principles of moral or political philosophy, or whether what lawyers should change.

The answers to those questions do not tell us much, though, about the meaningfulness of the life of the person who fills the lawyer's role. The morality (or immorality) of being a lawyer can affect the person's experience of it as meaningful, but it does not necessarily do so, given that morality and meaning are distinct ethical qualities. The translation of moral principles into a source (or disruption) of meaning requires some shift between the impartial moral idea and the subjective personal commitment to that idea. The principle can't just matter. It has to matter to *me*.

So how can meaningfulness and the lawyer's role be assessed? One way is by exploring the lives of ordinary lawyers, and the complex interactions between their passions and interests, the things that mattered to them and that ought to have mattered to them, and the work that they did. Through a careful telling and consideration of the stories of those lives, we can develop a more general understanding of the intersection between being a lawyer and having a meaningful life.

Michelle's professional life is one such story. If Michelle could have practised longer, then professional renown likely would have come her way. But she couldn't. Her life in law was consequentially an ordinary one, in biographical details akin to those of her peers. But ordinariness does not preclude interest. Michelle's story is one of an intelligent, warm, serious-minded, engaged, social, loved, driven, and sometimes self-doubting woman whose "ordinary" legal career included challenges, disappointments, and fulfillment. I know her story because Michelle is my friend, but I tell her story because what law was for her, and the loss that she experienced when it was taken away, show us something that legal ethics scholarship has not accounted for – the possibilities and challenges of accomplishing a meaningful life in law.

[After reviewing Michelle's early years and experiences in law school, Woolley turns to Michelle's time in practice]

After graduation, Michelle moved back to Vancouver with her husband to begin articles at the relatively-small local office of a Toronto-based national firm. It felt like an arrival. The lawyers were young, bright, and totally engaged with their work. The firm paid articling students better than any other firm in the city, and there was no doubt that this was the place to be, with the best work, the best students, the best lawyers, and the tightest team. The firm paid the tab for a weekly breakfast for articling students, gave them supper and a cab ride home if they worked late, and always paid for a drink at the bar if a partner was there. But the work was overwhelming. The transition from law school was almost brutal in its difficulty, especially since the firm was willing to give the students and junior lawyers as much responsibility as they could take and sometimes more. The learning curve was steep and the hours demanded long.

During that time, Michelle was articled to a lawyer specializing in employment law and immediately was exposed to that work, which she enjoyed very much. When the lawyer left the firm halfway through her articles, Michelle and a more-senior lawyer picked up many of his files. As a consequence, by the end of her articles, she had an area of practice on which to concentrate, along with a great deal of practical knowledge and skill. Michelle also began to sense some of the personal and power dynamics in the firm. . . .

Her transition to being an associate at the firm was aided by the senior lawyer working on the employment files with Michelle, and by a partner hired as a lateral, both of whom mentored her through employment and human rights litigation and through managing the employment-law aspects of corporate mergers and acquisitions. Gradually, she started to accumulate expertise and gain the sense of knowing what she was doing; although she was not an expert, she had enough competence in the field to advise someone effectively, and that was rewarding. Michelle also thought that employment law had a structure of fairness built into it. . . . She thought that her advice ensured that people received the notice or other entitlements that the law provides. There was an element of problem solving, and the problems were not always the same....

Those emerging rewards, though, were coupled with some significant challenges. Although being given more responsibility was fulfilling, Michelle felt overwhelmed when the responsibility was beyond her knowledge or ability. . . .

When Michelle looked more closely at the tight firm culture, it also seemed to be more complicated than when she had started. When she praised the courtroom skills of a lawyer whom she admired to a senior partner, that partner responded, "well, there's more to practice", with an evident dismissiveness and a lack of respect. Eventually, Michelle learned that his partners despised the lawyer whom she admired, condemning his disorganized practice and failure to bill clients. Whatever the closeness of the culture, it did not preclude judgment or ensure loyalty. And the things valued by the partners were not necessarily a lawyer's quality or skill as an advocate for clients.

The financial and business aspects of the practice began to seem as if they determined relationships and status in the firm. Only a few could stick it out. Of the lawyers there when Michelle began, over 50 per cent had left by the end of her five years. . . .

The dynamics at the firm could also complicate practice issues. Michelle was asked by a partner to take on a wrongful dismissal case for a family member of a client of the firm, but the employer of the dismissed family member was connected to another client of the firm, represented by a different partner. Michelle was caught between the two clients and the two lawyers, and her representation had the added difficulty of not being obviously meritorious. It left her feeling "boxed in by things completely outside of my control".

The general culture and attitude of the firm became unmanageable for Michelle after she had her first child. No female lawyer at the firm had taken a full maternity leave; the expectation was that the women would return to work as soon as possible. Michelle took six months; she had planned on only four, but a combination of post-partum depression and problems arranging child care kept her away from the firm for an extra two months. The firm was financially supportive during her leave, but on her return, expectations were not adjusted in any way. She was immediately drawn into a significant litigation case, and in her first month back, a February, she billed 220 hours. Yet at the end of that month, during her annual review, the partners who reviewed her said, "you are an exceptional lawyer, but you didn't bill enough hours last year". When she pointed out that she had been on maternity leave, the response was that she should have billed more before she left or come back early to meet her target.

Michelle decided then that she would leave the firm, and after a few months she was able to arrange an in-house position advising on employment-related matters. . . .

After a year in-house, Michelle joined a small firm in which she did work for a more diverse client base, individuals as well as corporations. She found individual client work stimulating and memorable, the importance of the files was "more easily touchable," and the lawyer whom she worked with the most was smart and affable. He was also experiencing some changes in his life, though, that made viability of the firm dubious.

Now pregnant with her second child, Michelle made the difficult decision to return to practice at a large firm, joining the local office of another national firm. This firm immediately felt different from the one at which she had articled. When she told them that she was pregnant and would take a maternity leave soon after joining the firm if she was hired, the lawyer who hired her responded, "what's a maternity leave in a career?" . . .

The firm was also strongly non-hierarchical; . . . . . They also seemed to live more modestly, within their incomes rather than at or beyond them. And they were intellectually engaged, writing articles about legal practice or new developments in law. There was significant expertise in the firm in labour and employment law, and Michelle became part of this expertise. . . .

When acting for individuals, Michelle used her advocacy protectively to ensure that clients avoided legal consequences that they ought not to suffer, and received the legal benefits to which they were entitled. A client referred to her by the Law Society of British Columbia referral service had been employed at a corporation, and Michelle helped him to settle his wrongful dismissal claim. The client, disabled, sought government benefits but, misunderstanding his obligations regarding confidentiality, did not disclose the settlement amounts to the government. Michelle was able to explain to the benefits administrator what had happened, and to ensure that the misunderstanding did not result in the disallowance of his benefits. . .

When representing employers, Michelle was able to ensure that businesses could operate effectively and efficiently, but also fairly. Employers can be reluctant to have "full-sentence conversations" with employees and to tell them honestly what is expected of them and when those expectations are not being met. They also have to accommodate employees' disabilities and develop systems to work through conflicts in the workplace. Michelle put it this way:

> I loved doing HR [human resources] reviews, going to [the client], and finding all the ways in which they were breaching the *Human Rights Code* . . . Someone with a bad back can't be told "you're going to get fired unless you continue to lift those boxes." The law requires them to accommodate the disability to the extent they're able. Surely you can find a job that works for the person with a bad back. I loved doing the teaching on all that, or the workplace mediations, working through conflict, system conflict. I'd always say to my employers, if you have good communication with your employees, they won't have a need to unionize. I loved all of that. I loved the employers who called and said, "I have a big problem. One of my employees stinks. We've bought her soap and bath balms for Christmas, but it doesn't help." [I would respond] that, if she's good at what she does and you want to keep her, you're going to need to have that conversation with her . . . You can't just duck it.

> It really suits my personality . . . because I'm a bit of a practical head. The idea of researching, or working through the courts, that's just not my personality . . . Human beings are interesting to me. And they get themselves into all these kinds of knots because they don't . . . want to hurt each other's feelings. . . .

Michelle actively practised at the firm for three years, becoming involved in firm hiring, as well as continuing with her practice. In March 2003, she travelled to negotiate a collective agreement, and she found herself exhausted and could not feel her feet. She began to develop other symptoms, losing feeling in her hand, so that, when she picked up a glass to drink water, she had no sensation of holding the glass. The exhaustion also continued. Her mother has had multiple sclerosis since Michelle was a child, and Michelle began to be concerned about what these symptoms might indicate. After losing sensation in both her hand and her foot, she went to her family doctor and was quickly referred to the emergency neurology clinic, seeing a neurologist within a few days. She was put on the emergency list for an MRI, and within a few weeks she had an MRI at the Children's Hospital, which had a unit available.

> I remember leaving work that day and [my colleague] handing me a disc for the MRI, and I had this feeling of . . . I guess I had a feeling of resolve but also a feeling of dread. And fear. My recollection is that my in-laws were visiting, and they took me to Children's for the MRI. And what's funny about that is, because it was Children's, there's all these posters and colours and cute little things, and you kind of feel like an imposter, like I was there by accident in more ways than one.

And so when they called me . . . I was at my desk . . . And I remember [the doctor] saying, "so we got the MRI results, this is not going to be a surprise to you, you have eleven (or whatever the number was) holes in your central nervous system. All indications of multiple sclerosis."

Exhaustion kept Michelle at home, but she thought that she would be back at work in a month. Yet a month later, in July, she lost her ability to see properly. She could not read or drive until a heavy dose of steroids corrected the problem.

Throughout this period, the firm was supportive. It had excellent short-term and long-term disability benefits, and it made efforts to incorporate Michelle in practice where she could. "Everyone thought I was coming back. I thought I was coming back. They took me to lunch. They put me in proposals and brochures. I felt like they believed in me."

But the need to reduce stress and manage her exhaustion to keep further attacks at a minimum prevented those efforts from coming to fruition. Michelle also had to deal with regular attacks and an attendant increase in the severity of her symptoms. Over the years, subtle indicators pushed her to the understanding that she was not going back, that she would never go back. After six months, she told her assistant to find another job. After a time, her phone was disconnected. After a few years, the insurer required that Michelle apply for her permanent disability pension from the Canada Pension Plan. And eventually she moved from active to inactive status with the Law Society of British Columbia. The development of that understanding was a process:

> At the beginning, I think I thought "this is just one more thing I have to get through." There's a sense of brutal unfairness. My parents are divorced . . . My cousin committed suicide. I have alcoholism in my family. This was one more thing I had to overcome. At the beginning, I felt resigned to just getting through it. Figuring out a way so I could get back to my life.

> And losing my whole identity. I didn't feel that at the beginning. I didn't feel like I was going to give up. So it's kind of . . . been a slow chipping away, . . . slowly coming to understand that I was going to lose all of that. All of my purpose for being, all of my reason to get up, all of my efforts, my everything. Being a lawyer to me was so much part of who I am and how I think. I still think like a lawyer whether, you know, I'm talking about teacher reviews or how to divide the costs for something or assess a risk for something. I think like a lawyer. It's still part of the way I approach the world. It's just that I can't use any of those [skills] to help anybody who is paying me anymore.

> Part of my identity, that I was compensated for, exercising all those parts of my brain that I had trained to be a certain way, learn a certain topic . . . I lost all my contacts. Nobody called me anymore. It just sort of gradually happened. It's like a slow leak. No one called me for lunch. I didn't get invited to the Christmas parties after a few years. The last time I went to one I felt like the token disabled person in the back. You're not part of it anymore. It took me two years to stop going to firm events.

> I wanted to come back, and then I'd just get sick. I don't know how ten years have passed, and other than that one time, when I worked on that deal, I can't believe I haven't found a way to do [it]. And it's funny, because that's what people say to me: "Oh, Michelle, there's got to be a way for you to work."

But I can't give anymore. Even these meetings [with you] leave me just spent. It's been a slow realization. A slow acceptance of where I'm truly at. Lots of counselling. Lots of tears. Lots of grieving for all of that. For the collegiality in a firm. For the intellectual work and rigour. For being useful in a way that I knew, that I just had become. That's the sad thing. I had really felt like I had properly become an expert at what I did. Not that I wasn't still learning, but overall I felt a level of competence.

Michelle's life after practice has not been bleak or unhappy. Her close network of friends is a source of happiness and support. Michelle lives in a tightly-knit community. And her husband remains her best friend and unwavering in his love and commitment. Her children are still in school, and she feels grateful to have been present for them over the past ten years. She has been as active in their education and in her community as she is able to be, including getting involved in some local issues of policies and politics. She has also found peace through yoga: "That discipline of yoga has been absolutely essential for my healing and my grieving and . . . me taking the shape that I am now."

There is nothing perverse or surprising about Michelle's sense of loss. When you consider what attracted Michelle to being a lawyer, why it engaged her passion and her interest, you would not say that she was wrong or that her sense of loss was misguided. It was meaningful to her, and it makes sense that it was so. Some might argue that employment law could be fairer or more just than it is. But inarguably it creates a fairer and more just world for employees than would exist without it. It also achieves law's function of social settlement, perhaps not satisfying everyone's sense of justice and fairness, but settling on a form of justice and fairness between employers and employees that is recognizable and legitimate. For Michelle, the impartial principle derived from political philosophy, that what lawyers do can be justified because it helps to achieve law's social settlement, was something that she experienced in her work as a lawyer. It was part of her motivation to become a lawyer, and it was what she believed she was doing when she ensured that employers talked to employees, and that employees who had been wrongfully dismissed received the payment and dignity that they deserved. Her passion and commitment, and the impartial objective justification for her work, were matched in her experience.

For that reason, the classic moral problem for lawyers – that they advocate for morally suspect (but lawful) ends through morally dubious (but lawful) means – was not an observed feature of her practice. Michelle did have some legally-weak cases, and at times there was external pressure to pursue cases that created challenging and unsettling situations. But her passion for and engagement in her work were not disrupted by any sense that she was participating in a morally-corrupt system or process.

Michelle's engagement with her work also arose from values and experiences not specific to law – participating in the intellectual community of a law firm, educating and assisting those who could benefit from her knowledge, and developing that knowledge into expertise. When you engage in an activity worth doing, and you develop your skills in that activity to a form of excellence, they can be meaningful, as they clearly were for Michelle.

The challenges of legal practice to the meaningfulness of her life were when profit orientation overwhelmed the practice, when the emphasis was on billable hours, and when the focus was on fitting into an intensely profit-driven culture. These aspects created obvious challenges for Michelle as a parent; immediately after her return to work from her first maternity leave, she did not spend any waking hours with her child, let alone have the opportunity to be actively-engaged in parenting her. But they also disrupted the pursuit of what was meaningful to her about being a lawyer. In those moments, being an excellent lawyer, helping or educating clients or ensuring fairness, was more difficult because they weren't how success was measured or valued. They were still what mattered in one sense – certainly they were what mattered to Michelle – but it is hard to hold on to that when those around you are not interested in looking at it or in valuing your efforts to achieve it.

I have told Michelle's story because it shows us things about being a lawyer that the academy does not always see. It certainly has a claim to our attention as scholars. But that isn't the whole truth. I have also told her story because I want people to know it. I want them to know her gifts and the work that Michelle was capable of doing. I want them to know the challenges that she overcame and her determination to find a place to practise where she could be the lawyer that she wanted to be. And I want them to know that being a lawyer can mean a great deal, that when it is taken away, it can break your heart.

NOTES AND QUESTIONS

1. What made Michelle's experiences as a lawyer meaningful? What parts of legal practice did she find challenging or unrewarding?

2. Michelle did not experience her practice as creating tension between her moral values and the causes she pursued on behalf of her clients. Other lawyers will experience that tension – for example: representing a client whom they personally believe to be factually guilty of an offence; prosecuting an accused for drug offences when they believe drug laws to be unjust; pursuing custody on behalf of a parent that the lawyer believes to be less loving and committed than that parent's former spouse. How might that lawyer create "meaning" in their life as defined by Wolf – having something that they love, that is worthy of love, and that they can engage with in a positive way? Can that lawyer have a meaningful life as a lawyer? What challenges will that lawyer experience? What other sources of meaning might exist for the lawyer?

3. What type of legal practice do you think would be meaningful for you? Why? What type of legal practice do you think would be uncomfortable or difficult for you – that is, that would be inconsistent with your own moral values and beliefs?

[7] FURTHER READING

Applebaum, Arthur Isak, *Ethics for Adversaries: The Morality of Roles in Public and Professional Life* (Princeton: Princeton University Press, 1999).

Arthurs, H.W., "Why Canadian Law Schools Do Not Teach Legal Ethics" in Kim Economides, ed., *Ethical Challenges to Legal Education & Conduct* (Oxford: Hart Publishing, 1999).

Ayers, Andrew, "What if Legal Ethics Can't Be Reduced to a Maxim?" (2013) 26 Geo. J. Leg. Ethics 1.

Bagaric, Mirko & Penny Dimopoulos, "Legal Ethics is (Just) Normal Ethics: Towards a Coherent System of Legal Ethics" (2003) 3(2) Q.U.T.L.J. 367.

Berlin, Isaiah, *The Crooked Timber of Humanity* (New York: Random House, 1991).

Blackburn, Simon, *Being Good: A Short Introduction to Ethics* (Oxford: Oxford University Press, 2002).

Dare, Tim, *The Counsel of Rogues?: A Defence of the Standard Conception of the Lawyer's Role* (Surrey, U.K.: Ashgate, 2009).

Farrow, Trevor, "Sustainable Professionalism" (2008) 46 Osgoode Hall L.J. 51.

Freedman, Monroe, "The Professional Responsibility of the Criminal Defence Lawyer: The Three Hardest Questions" (1966) 64 Mich. L. Rev. 1469.

Freedman, Monroe & Abbe Smith, *Understanding Lawyers' Ethics*, 5th ed. (New York: LexisNexis, 2016).

Fried, Charles, "The Lawyer as Friend" (1975) 85 Yale L.J. 1060.

Gordon, Robert W., "The Independence of Lawyers" (1988) 68 B.U. L. Rev. 1.

Hartwell, Steven, "Promoting Moral Development Through Experiential Teaching" (1994–1995) 1 Clinical L. Rev. 505.

Hursthouse, Rosalind, *On Virtue Ethics* (Oxford: Oxford University Press, 1999).

Hutchinson, Allan C., *Legal Ethics and Professional Responsibility*, 2d ed. (Toronto: Irwin Law, 2006).

Kant, Immanuel, *The Metaphysics of Morals*, transl. Mary Gregor (Cambridge: Cambridge University Press, 1996).

Koniak, Susan P., "The Law Between the Bar and the State" (1992) 70 N.C. L. Rev. 1389.

Kronman, Anthony T., *The Lost Lawyer: Failing Ideals of the Legal Profession* (Cambridge, MA: Harvard University Press, 1993).

Kruse, Katherine, "Beyond Cardboard Clients in Legal Ethics" (2010) 23 Geo. J. Leg. Ethics 103.

Kruse, Katherine, "The Jurisprudential Turn in Legal Ethics" (2011) 53 Ariz. L. Rev. 493.

Luban, David, *Lawyers and Justice* (Princeton: Princeton University Press, 1988).

Luban, David, *Legal Ethics and Human Dignity* (Cambridge: Cambridge University Press, 2007).

Luban, David and Wendel, Brad, "Philosophical Legal Ethics: An Affectionate History" (2017) 30 Geo. J. Leg. Ethics 337-364.

MacIntyre, Alasdair, *After Virtue*, 2d ed. (London: Duckworth, 1985).

Markovits, Daniel, *A Modern Legal Ethics: Adversarial Advocacy in a Democratic Age* (Princeton: Princeton University Press, 2008).

Nicolson, Donald & Julian Webb, *Professional Legal Ethics: Critical Interrogations* (Oxford: Oxford University Press, 1999).

Pepper, Stephen L., "The Lawyer's Amoral Ethics Role: A Defense, a Problem, and Some Possibilities" (1986) A.B.F. Res. J. 613.

Postema, Gerald J., "Moral Responsibility in Professional Ethics" (1980) 55 N.Y.U. L. Rev. 63.

Rhode, Deborah L., *Ethics in Practice: Lawyers' Roles, Responsibilities and Regulation* (New York: Oxford University Press, 2000).

Rhode, Deborah L., *In the Interests of Justice: Reforming the Legal Profession* (New York: Oxford University Press, 2003).

Roiphe, Rebecca, "The Decline of Professionalism" (2016) 29 Geo. J. Leg. Ethics 649.

Roiphe, Rebecca & Bruce A. Green, "Impeaching Legal Ethics" (February 21, 2021). NYLS Legal Studies Research Paper No. 3789957, Online: https://ssrn.com/abstract=3789957.

Salyzyn, Amy, "Positivist Legal Ethics Theory and the Law Governing Lawyers: A Few Puzzles Worth Solving" (2014) 42 Hofstra L. Rev. 1063.

Shaffer, Thomas L. & Mary Shaffer, *American Lawyers and their Communities: Ethics in the Legal Profession* (Notre Dame: Notre Dame University Press, 1999).

Simon, William, "Ethical Discretion in Lawyering" (1988) 101 Harv. L. Rev. 1083.

Simon, William, *The Practice of Justice: A Theory of Lawyer's Ethics* (Cambridge, MA: Harvard University Press, 2000).

Stanford Encyclopedia of Philosophy, online: http://plato.stanford.edu.

Tanovich, David, "Law's Ambition and the Reconstruction of Role Morality in Canada" (2005) 28 Dal. L.J. 267.

Wasserstrom, Richard, "Lawyers as Professionals: Some Moral Issues" (1975) 5 Human Rights 1.

Wendel, W. Bradley, "Lawyer Shaming" (2022) U. Ill. Law Rev. (forthcoming), online: http://ssrn.com/abstract=3778984.

Wendel, W. Bradley, *Lawyers and Fidelity to Law* (Princeton: Princeton University Press, 2010).

Wendel, W. Bradley, "Whose Truth? Objective and Subjective Perspectives on Truthfulness in Advocacy" (2016) 28 Yale J.L. & Human 105.

Williams, Bernard, *Ethics and the Limits of Philosophy* (Cambridge, MA: Harvard University Press, 1985).

Woolley, Alice "Is Positivist Legal Ethics an Oxymoron?" (2019) 32(1) Geo. J. Leg. Ethics 77-107.

Woolley, Alice "Context, Meaning and Morality in the Life of the Lawyer" (2014) 17 Leg. Ethics 1.

Woolley, Alice, "The Lawyer as Advisor and the Practice of the Rule of Law" (2014) 47 U.B.C. L. Rev. 743-783.

Woolley, Alice, "The Lawyer as Fiduciary: Defining Private Law Duties in Public Law Relations" (2015) 65:2 U.T.L.J. 285-334.

Woolley, Alice, *Understanding Lawyers' Ethics in Canada,* 2d ed. (Toronto: LexisNexis Canada, 2016).

Woolley, Alice & W. Bradley Wendel, "Legal Ethics and Moral Character" (2010) 23 Geo. J. Leg. Ethics 1065.

CHAPTER 2

THE LAWYER-CLIENT RELATIONSHIP

[1] INTRODUCTION

In the previous chapter, we reviewed the conceptual frameworks for legal ethics and professional responsibility and identified several governing themes and tensions. In this chapter, we translate these more abstract concerns into the day-to-day realities of legal practice by analyzing three areas of ethical concern: (a) formation of the lawyer-client relationship; (b) the obligations of competence and quality of service; and (c) terminating the lawyer-client relationship. These three broad areas generate several quite specific issues which we review chronologically.

[2] FORMATION OF THE LAWYER-CLIENT RELATIONSHIP

In the context of the formation of the lawyer-client relationship there can sometimes be tension between two different visions of the lawyer.[1] On the one hand, it is argued that because lawyers serve a specific public function in relation to the rule of law, they have an obligation to make legal services available, and in the provision of such services, they must be guided by fiduciary obligations.[2] An alternate vision proposes that lawyers are in essence business persons. It suggests that lawyer-client relations should be governed by the usual market norms, and that the provision of legal services should be guided by the terms of the retainer contract. As we work our way through this section, consider how this tension is manifested in issues of advertising, solicitation, and choice of clients. The starting point for the analysis is Rule 4.1-1 (Making Legal Services Available) of the Federation of Law Societies of Canada's *Model Code of Professional Conduct*,[3] read in conjunction with Rule 4.1-2 (Restrictions).

As you review this rule, consider how it mediates the tension between the professional and business models of legal practice. Is the answer obvious from the general title of Chapter 4 of the *Model Code*, "Marketing of Legal Services"? What regulatory work do the directives of "efficiently" and "conveniently" do? How helpful are these directives for a lawyer in the modern "legal services" marketplace?

---

[1] Colin Jackson, Brent Cotter & Richard Devlin, "Of Lodestars and Lawyers: Incorporating the Duty of Loyalty into the *Model Code of Conduct*" (2016) 39:1 Dal. L.J. 37.

[2] Alice Woolley, "The lawyer as fiduciary: Defining private law duties in public law relations" (2015) 65:4 U.T.L.J. 285.

[3] Federation of Law Societies of Canada, *Model Code of Professional Conduct* (2019), online: https://flsc.ca/wp-content/uploads/2019/11/Model-Code-October-2019.pdf.

[a] Advertising, Fee Sharing and Solicitation

Advertising can be understood in different ways. Some analysts (the traditionalists) worry that advertising and solicitation reduce the professional status of lawyers because they introduce vulgarity and commodification. Others (the modernists) claim that advertising and solicitation are essential to ensure the public has access to justice. Still others (the free marketers) argue that, given the highly competitive legal market, it is important for lawyers to be able to brand and market their work (and themselves) and that, ultimately, it is an issue of consumer choice. Adherents of this third position also sometimes suggest that established lawyers and law firms invoke traditionalist arguments pretextually to limit competition. As you review the following provisions, try to identify which of the foregoing approaches is embedded in the *Model Code*, keeping in mind that there are ongoing reforms in this area.

[i] Advertising

Please review Rules 4.2 through 4.3 of the *Model Code* and supporting Commentaries.

NOTES AND QUESTIONS

1. From a historical perspective it seems that, increasingly, Canada has adopted the free marketer's arguments. Is this trend in the best interests of the general public, the legal profession or both?

2. Some argue that increased advertising increases the cost of doing business and that, inevitably, this will be passed on to clients, thereby increasing fees. Others suggest that increased advertising might reinforce the concentration of legal services in larger firms that can afford advertising, to the detriment of medium and smaller sized firms. The consequence is a decrease in competition. Do you find these concerns persuasive? If so, what might be done about this? Consider: which sectors of the legal profession in fact engage in advertising? Or do different sectors engage in different forms of advertising? Does the emergence of social media affect your analysis?

3. Apart from exceptional cases like *Jabour*,[4] few, if any, law societies have ever disciplined a lawyer for an inappropriate advertisement. Do any of the following advertisements cross the line?

We know Everything

We can do Anything

We stop at Nothing[5]

---

[4] *Jabour v. Law Society of British Columbia et al.*, [1978] B.C.J. No. 1096, 97 D.L.R. (3d) 295, 44 C.P.R. (2d) 68 (B.C.C.A.).

[5] Motto for the law firm Burchell, Smith, Jost, Willis, and Burchell, as mentioned in John Willis, Book Review of *The Lion and the Throne* by Catherine Drinker Bowen (1958) 10 Stan. L. Rev. 782 at 784: see G. Blaine Barker, "Willis on 'Cultured' Public Authorities" (2005) 55:3 U.T.L.J. 335 at 337.

Accidents happen . . . But don't let your choice of lawyers be one of them.[6]

I may be a Son of a Bitch

But I'm your Son of a Bitch

Proven to get You Successful Results!![7]

A Chicago law firm, specializing in divorce, posted a billboard featuring the "six-pack abs of a headless male torso and tanned female cleavage heaving forth from a black lace bra". The accompanying caption announced: "Life's Short. Get a Divorce."[8] Would this run afoul of the rules in your jurisdiction? Would your opinion differ if it was an all-female, all-nonbinary, and/or an all-transgender law firm?

A lawyer's T.V. commercial boasts: "I'm so good, I could get Stevie Wonder a driver's licence."[9]

A law firm claims on its website that it has been voted "No. 1 in Client Satisfaction" and "No. 1 Personal Injury Law Firm" by "Elite Lawyers Canada." However, there is no such organization in Canada.[10]

Another firm's website proclaims: "Voted #1 Personal Injury Law Firm in Canada 3 years in a row!"[11]

Another firm advertises on its website, TV commercials and buses that it is "The Top Multi-Ethnic Law Firm."[12]

A lawyer has a vanity plate on her car which proclaims: "SEEUNCRT."

[13]

---

[6] Richardsons Law Office, "Richardsons Law Office" (2015), online: *Richardsons Law Office* www.novalawyer.com.

[7] Jag Virk Criminal Lawyer, "Jag Virk Criminal Lawyer" (April 13, 2013), online: *weblocal.ca* http://www.weblocal.ca/jag-virk-criminal-lawyer-toronto-on-1.html.

[8] Seth A., "Viagra Triangle" (May 13, 2007), online: *B12 Solipsism* www.b12partners.net/mt/archives/2007/05/viagra-triangle.html.

[9] Max Walters, "Boastful barrister fined and reprimanded" (February 1, 2017), online: *The Law Society Gazette* https://www.lawgazette.co.uk/law/boastful-barrister-fined-and-reprimanded/5059648.article.

[10] Kenyon Wallace, "In 'wild west' world of lawyers' ads, personal injury firms make dubious claims" (February 6, 2017), online: *The Toronto Star* https://www.thestar.com/news/investigations/2017/02/06/in-wild-west-world-of-legal-marketing-personal-injury-firms-make-dubious-claims.html.

[11] Kenyon Wallace, "In 'wild west' world of lawyers' ads, personal injury firms make dubious claims" (February 6, 2017), online: *The Toronto Star* https://www.thestar.com/news/investigations/ 2017/02/06/in-wild-west-world-of-legal-marketing-personal-injury-firms-make-dubious-claims.html.

[12] Kenyon Wallace, "In 'wild west' world of lawyers' ads, personal injury firms make dubious claims" (February 6, 2017), online: *The Toronto Star* https://www.thestar.com/news/investigations/2017/02/06/in-wild-west-world-of-legal-marketing-personal-injury-firms-make-dubious-claims.html.

14

---

[13] The editors thank Mr. Peter John for his permission to reproduce this advertisement.

[14] The editors thank the Honourable Michel Bastarache of the former firm Heenan Blaikie LLP for his permission to reproduce this advertisement.

15

---

[15] The editors thank Miller Titerle + Company for permission to reproduce this advertisement.

4.   The firm Miller Titerle + Co. has since published another advertisement which they describe as 'Desert Pirates'. It is available here: https://perma.cc/J3EP-G5WN.[16] The firm acknowledges that their ads are controversial for some, but suggest that they are "an important way for [them] to communicate who [they] are and showcase [their] evolution over time". Do you think their ads are controversial? Do either of these ads raise any

---

[16] 'Desert Pirates - What Were We Thinking?' (October 14, 2020), Available online and in the October 2020 issue of *Canadian Lawyer*.

ethical issues? Does either violate any provision of the Model Code or the amended LSO Rules of Professional Conduct set out below?

5. Professor Elaine Craig has drawn attention to the websites of criminal defense lawyers as a new form of advertising with its own set of ethical problems. She lists four particularly worrisome trends:

    i.   Promoting the acquittal of 'factually guilty' clients (those who had committed the acts in question) without an explanation as to the reason they were acquitted, leaving the reader to infer that the acquittal was due to the skill of the lawyer rather than the correct application of the law;

    ii. Trivializing sexual violence and the harm caused to its victims;

    iii. Advertising or implying aggressive advocacy; and

    iv. Advertising the use of particular defense strategies at trial.

Consider this example — taken from a criminal defense lawyer's website — that makes light of a home invasion and sexual assault:

> Rico was starting a new business, sourcing contractors for home renovations. He was scouting for work locally, and was exploring a woman's home. Rico explored too much. While in a tight spot, he fell, his wardrobe malfunctioned, and his penis made a brief escape. Rico apologized but it was too little, too late: the police were on their way. They arrested him for sexual assault and [being] unlawfully in a dwelling.[17]

Compare this to the police report describing the same incident, also hosted on the lawyer's website:

> The victim was told by the accused that he was working as the plumber in unit #5 next to the victim and he felt that water had leaked into that unit may have come from the victim's home. . . .

> The accused then was taken to the downstairs bathroom where he convinced the victim to get up on the toilet and then the sink to check on a mold spot. As the victim looked at the spot the accused came behind her and rubbed his body up close to hers as he talked about the spot and pointed...The accused then fell backwards and attempted to pull the victim onto his lap... The accused fell backwards with his legs open and pretended to have hurt his thigh... The accused undid his pants and exposed his penis and scrotum to the victim begging her to feel his injury. The victim again attempted to leave but the accused grabbed her hand and put it on his inner thigh next to his penis and scrotum as he pulled them aside.[18]

The lawyer who made the following website excerpt advertises that his client had his charges withdrawn, despite apparently being factually guilty of the offence. It is listed under the title "Charges Dropped Against Child Sex Offender":

---

[17] Elaine Craig, "Examining the Websites of Canada's 'Top Sex Crime Lawyers': The Ethical Parameters of Online Commercial Expression by the Criminal Defence Bar" (2015) 48:2 U.B.C. L. Rev. 257 at 277.

[18] Elaine Craig, "Examining the Websites of Canada's 'Top Sex Crime Lawyers': The Ethical Parameters of Online Commercial Expression by the Criminal Defence Bar" (2015) 48:2 U.B.C. L. Rev. 257 at 277.

My client attended at a hotel room, where two of his friends had been taking turns engaging in repeated acts of sexual intercourse with each of two 14-year-old girls. Without saying a word, my client removed his clothing and [immediately] proceeded to have sexual intercourse with one of the girls and demand oral sex from her. He then got dressed and left. He had two prior convictions for sexual assault on his record. Then, while on release for this offence, he was accused of committing yet another assault, this time upon a mentally disabled girl. . .At the Preliminary Inquiry, during my cross examination of the complainant, she became so frustrated by my questions that she effectively quit, exclaiming that she no longer desired to proceed any further. The matter was adjourned for several months. On the continuation date, the complainant refused to attend, therefore the Crown stayed all charges as against my client. The other two accused continued with their charges in relation to the other complainant. No criminal convictions.[19]

Should the lawyers who developed these websites be disciplined? If so, what provisions of the *Model Code* are engaged? If the lawyers are found to have violated the standards of professional conduct, what is the appropriate remedy?[20]

Further Reforms of the Marketing Rules

In February 2017, the LSO adopted the following amendments to its Rules of Professional Conduct.[21]

4.2-1

Commentary

[1] This Rule establishes, among other things, requirements for communication in the marketing of legal services. These requirements apply to different forms of marketing, including advertisements about the size, location and nature of the lawyer's practice and about awards, rankings and endorsements from third parties.

. . .

[3] Examples of marketing that do contravene this rule include

    (a)   marketing services that the lawyer is not currently able to perform to the standard of a competent lawyer;

    (b)   bait and switch marketing, that is marketing by which clients are attracted by offers of services, prices or terms different from those commonly provided to clients who respond to the marketing;

    (c)   marketing that fails to clearly and prominently disclose a practice that the lawyer has of referring clients for a fee, or other consideration, to other licensees;

---

[19] Elaine Craig, "Examining the Websites of Canada's 'Top Sex Crime Lawyers': The Ethical Parameters of Online Commercial Expression by the Criminal Defence Bar" (2015) 48:2 U.B.C. L. Rev. 257 at 272.

[20] See *Law Society of Ontario v. Penney*, [2018] L.S.S.D. No. 179, 2018 ONLSTH 121 (Ont. Law Society Tribunal).

[21] Law Society of Ontario, *Rules of Professional Conduct* (October 1, 2014; amendments current to October 24, 2019), online: https://lso.ca/about-lso/legislation-rules/rules-of-professional-conduct.

(d)   failing to expressly state that the marketed services will be provided by licensed lawyers, by licensed paralegals or both, as the case may be;

(e)   referring to awards, rankings and third party endorsements that are not *bona fide* or are likely to be misleading, confusing, or deceptive; and

[4] Paragraphs (a) to (d) of Commentary [3] are intended to ensure that marketing does not mislead by failing to make clear what services are actually available and are intended to be provided. It is important that there be no "bait and switch" aspect to marketing. Paragraph (d) is intended to better ensure that prospective clients are aware whether the marketed services being offered will be performed by lawyers or paralegals.

[5] Paragraph (e) of Commentary [3] addresses marketing by reference to awards, rankings and third party endorsements. The terms "awards" and "rankings" are intended to be interpreted broadly and to include superlative titles such as "best", "super", "#1" and similar indications. Awards, rankings and third party endorsements which contravene this rule include those that:

(a)   do not genuinely reflect the performance of the lawyer and the quality of services provided by the lawyer but appear to do so;

(b)   are not the result of a reasonable evaluative process;

(c)   are conferred in part as a result of the payment of a fee or other consideration rather than as a result of a legitimate evaluation of the performance and quality of the lawyer; or

(d)   the lawyer could not have demonstrated, at the time of reference, they were compliant with this rule.

Particular care should be taken in respect of awards, rankings and third-party endorsements referenced in mass advertising, such as in newspaper and internet advertising, and advertising on television, billboards, taxis, buses and the like. In such contexts, references to awards, rankings and third-party endorsements must be particularly clear and straightforward, as there is little opportunity for reflection or appreciation on the part of the potential client or to provide context.

References to awards and honours that are genuine reflections of professional or civic service do not contravene this rule. For example, a potential client may consider it useful to know that a lawyer has been honoured for their service by the Canadian or the Ontario government, the Law Society or a professional organization. However, the lawyer should take care to ensure that such awards and honours reflect a genuine and responsible assessment of the lawyer in the public interest.[22]

In any event, any reference to awards, rankings and third party endorsements must comply with all of the provisions of Rule 4.2-1.

[6] This Rule also requires marketing to be consistent with a high standard of professionalism. Unprofessional marketing is not in the best interests of the public.

---

[22] For an example of a lawyer being reprimanded for the use of a misleading and inaccurate "award", see *Law Society of Ontario v. Goldfinger*, [2018] L.S.D.D. No. 154, 2018 ONLSTH 103 (Ont. Law Society Tribunal).

It has a negative impact on the reputation of lawyers, the legal profession and the administration of justice. The Law Society has acknowledged in the Rules the special role of the profession to recognize and protect the dignity of individuals and the diversity of the community in Ontario. Marketing practices must conform to the requirements of human rights laws in force in Ontario.

[7] Examples of marketing practices that may be inconsistent with a high degree of professionalism would be images, language or statements that are violent, racist or sexually offensive, that take advantage of a vulnerable person or group or that refer negatively to other licensees, the legal profession or the administration of justice.

4.2-1.1 A lawyer marketing legal services shall specifically identify in all marketing materials that they are licensed as a lawyer.

Commentary

[1] It is important that the public be aware that both lawyers and paralegals are licensed by the Law Society, and of whether it is a lawyer or a paralegal who is offering to provide services.

4.2-1.2 The marketing of second opinion services is prohibited.

Commentary

[1] The provision of second opinions is a valuable service to clients. However, second opinion marketing is commonly undertaken with a view to obtaining the retainer, rather than providing a second opinion. Such "bait and switch" marketing is inappropriate. The marketing of second opinions is prohibited under this rule, whatever the intent of the marketing.

NOTES AND QUESTIONS

1. Do these amendments go far enough? Do they go too far? Do they adequately respond to some of the advertising practices previously identified? Should the *Model Code* be amended to follow the Ontario rules? Do these rules empower law societies to discipline lawyers who engage in problematic advertising practices? Do you anticipate an actual increase in such discipline proceedings?

2. Consider the page on the website for the firm Diamond & Diamond at the following link: https://perma.cc/29HK-T22D. This webpage contains statistics about the high number of deaths of seniors at care homes during the COVID-19 pandemic and refers to the firm's history of class-action lawsuits against care homes. The webpage has a contact form to get in touch with the firm's lawyers. This form includes fields for personal information about a loved one in a care home. Does this webpage comply with the LSO's Rules of Professional Conduct?

3. As lawyers become more comfortable using technology and social media, many have started posting memes to their accounts on Facebook, Twitter, Instagram, etc. As with all memes, these posts can take a variety of forms: some are created by the lawyers and some are reposts/edits of existing content. Does the use of memes count as advertising? What concerns

might you have about the use of memes by lawyers and law firms?[23]

[ii]   Fee Sharing and Referral Fees

One important issue in the marketing of legal services is fee sharing. Consider Rule 3.6-7 of the *Model Code*, which prohibits fee sharing with non-lawyers. What are the ethical justifications for such a rule? Are these justifications persuasive? Now consider the two exceptions to this rule in Rules 3.6-6 and 3.6-8.

NOTES AND QUESTIONS

1.   Is there a principled justification for prohibiting fee sharing with non-lawyers, but permitting it with other lawyers?

2.   Assume you are a lawyer whose main area of practice is commercial real estate transactions. Draft a letter to a client that would give effect to Rule 3.6-6. What are the challenges involved in drafting such a letter?

3.   Does Commentary 1(d) to Rule 3.6-7 seem out of place in a *Model Code*? Is this provision in the public interest? Who ultimately pays for this type of "entertaining"?

4.   Does the exception for multidisciplinary practices and inter-jurisdictional law firms create a two-tier system — one for larger firms, one for smaller firms? If so, is such a distinction justifiable? Would it be both fairer and more efficient to simply abandon the prohibition on fee sharing? Why or why not?

5.   In several jurisdictions, including the U.K. and Australia, legal services can be provided via Alternative Business Structures (ABSs), which can be co-owned by non-lawyers (For further discussion of ABSs see Chapter 12). ABSs are not permitted in Canada, in part because of Rule 3.6-7 of the *Model Code* prohibiting fee sharing. In 2014 the Canadian Bar Association's (CBA) *Legal Futures Report* advanced the following recommendation:

Recommendation #5 — Fee-sharing with and Referral Fees to Non-Lawyers

The FLSC Model Code Rules should be amended to permit fee-sharing with non-lawyers and paying referral fees to non-lawyers, subject to the following:

(a)   the conflict rules apply;

(b)   the confidentiality rules apply and privilege must be protected;

(c)   the candour rule applies, meaning full disclosure of the shared fee and of the nature of the relationship with the entity with which the fee is shared must be made to the client;

---

[23] For example, see the following meme on Instagram user @lawbulldog, a lawyer in New York City: https://www.instagram.com/p/CAIo1fgHOWE/?igshid=9dg46viteuwf. The caption on the image reads, "Where does it hurt[?]". The image depicts the outline of three people with the first depicting the pain from a headache, the second depicting the pain from a stomachache, and the third depicting pain radiating over the whole body. The caption of the third image reads, "Hiring the wrong lawyer and helplessly watching your case turn to shit".

(d)   the referral fee must be fair and reasonable and fully disclosed;

(e)   shared fees may not be contingent on the revenue or profitability of specific matters or as the result of such matters;

(f)   the lawyer shall not accept the referral unless the lawyer and the client discuss any client expectations arising from the referral and mutually agree on the basis of the retainer;

(g)   an accounting record is required of referral fees paid and received indicating the amounts and counterparties to each payment; and

(h)   referral fees shall not be accepted where the lawyer is aware that the referral is exploitive.[24]

Identify the arguments for and against this recommendation.

6.   Rule 3.6-6 of the *Model Code* allows for the paid referral of clients to another lawyer if that lawyer is more competent than the referrer to handle the matter. Does this allow lawyers with very successful marketing campaigns to offload clients to other lawyers for profit? Do lawyers who recruit too many clients have an ethical obligation to make referrals to other lawyers? Consider this question again once you have read section [3] on Competence, Quality of Service, and Candour.

7.   The Law Societies of Ontario and British Columbia both allow fee-sharing in multi-disciplinary practices (MDPs) of lawyer and non-lawyers. See Rule 3.6-8(ii) of the LSO's *Rules of Professional Conduct* and Rule 3.6-8 of the LSBC's *Rules of Professional Conduct*. Why is this practice permitted in some provinces but not others?

8.   In 2017, the LSO's Working Group on Advertising and Fee Arrangements Issues identified a series of concerns with the way in which referral fees between lawyers were operating.[25] In particular, the Group found that

   •   a client is often not aware they are being referred, or that there is a fee involved in the referral;

   •   referral fees that used to be in the 10-15% range had grown to the 25-30% range; and

   •   misleading advertising was fueling the lack of transparency in fee arrangements.[26]

---

[24] The Canadian Bar Association, "Futures: Transforming the Delivery of Legal Services in Canada" (August 2014) at 43, online (pdf): *The Canadian Bar Association* http://www.cba.org/CBAMediaLibrary/cba_na/PDFs/CBA%20Legal%20Futures%20PDFS/Futures-Final-eng.pdf.

[25] Advertising & Fee Arrangements Issues Working Group, "Fifth Report of the Advertising & Fee Arrangements Issues Working Group" (June 29, 2017), online (pdf): https://lawsocietyontario.azureedge.net/media/lso/media/legacy/pdf/c/convocation-june2017-professional-regulation-committee-report.pdf.

[26] Advertising & Fee Arrangements Issues Working Group, "Fifth Report of the Advertising & Fee Arrangements Issues Working Group" (June 29, 2017) at 11, online (pdf):

The Working Group identified two potential solutions: a complete prohibition on referral fees, or modifications of the rules to cap the percentage of referral fees and to provide greater transparency to clients.[27] The Law Society eventually adopted the latter approach. Caps on referral fees were introduced, based on the percentage of the legal fees: 15% for the first $50,000 of legal fees and five percent of all legal fees thereafter, to an absolute cap of $25,000. Clients must now also be made aware of referrals and fees. Identify the strengths and weaknesses of this approach.

[iii] Solicitation

Solicitation can take lawyers quite close to some ethical lines. On the one hand, there are concerns that lawyers may invade people's privacy, take advantage of vulnerable persons, engage in overreaching, succumb to opportunistic ambulance-chasing or stir up unnecessary litigation. On the other hand, it can be argued that people do not always know their rights, and do not always have a sense of the services that lawyers can provide. Solicitation, it is argued, can fill this "market gap". For example, historical research in the United States demonstrates that the NAACP in its early years "stirred up litigation" and engaged in "proselytizing" by

- speaking before large audiences to recruit plaintiffs;

- fundraising for test cases;

- following newspaper stories about violations of rights and then writing to the victims offering to represent them; and

- staging confrontations to create facts for test cases.

All of these activities were criticized as "unethical" at that time. Consider the following Canadian example:

LAW SOCIETY OF SASKATCHEWAN V. MERCHANT
[2000] L.S.D.D. No. 24
(Law Society of Saskatchewan, Hearing Committee: B. Morgan,
Chairperson, D. Plaxton and M.E. Wellsch)

[In the late 1990s, there was growing recognition that Canada's policy of residential schools for Aboriginal peoples had potentially infringed the legal rights of tens of thousands of Aboriginal people. In 1998, one law firm, the Merchant Law Group, wrote letters to survivors of residential schools. This led to a number of consequences. The first was a discipline complaint to the Saskatchewan Law Society.]

*   *   *   *   *

On September 3, 1998, Mr. Merchant forwarded to B . . . a letter with an attached Assignment & Retainer Agreement . . . The letter indicated that his firm acted for

---

https://lawsocietyontario.azureedge.net/media/lso/media/legacy/pdf/c/convocation-june2017-professional-regulation-committee-report.pdf.

[27] Advertising & Fee Arrangements Issues Working Group, "Fifth Report of the Advertising & Fee Arrangements Issues Working Group" (June 29, 2017) at 11-12, online (pdf): https://lawsocietyontario.azureedge.net/media/lso/media/legacy/pdf/c/convocation-june2017-professional-regulation-committee-report.pdf.

a number of Indigenous communities and individual members of various Indian bands across Canada who are "suing the federal government and, in many cases, the church involved for abuse and wrongdoing at the Indian residential schools". The letter went on to state:

> "We believe the compensation that we can achieve for you will be significant and you have nothing to lose. If we do not recover anything, then you will pay nothing. If we recover, then we will receive a percentage of what we recover on your behalf".

* * * * *

The letter ended as follows:

> "If you are prepared to receive the money that we think is due to you, please write out your reflections on what happened in the school and write to me as well as sending back the authorization that is shown with your signature at the bottom . . .".

The letter was signed by E. F. Anthony Merchant, Q.C., under the name "Merchant Law Group".

The enclosed two-page Assignment & Retainer Agreement . . . contained the following:

> ". . . Should the client elect to change lawyers, the client will promptly pay for legal services performed up to that time at the usual hourly rates of the lawyers involved.

> If the client unilaterally decides not to pursue the claim without first getting approval from The Merchant Law Group, or if the The Merchant Law Group decides that the action ought not to be pursued, the client will be responsible for all Court costs and other out-of-pocket expenses incurred by The Merchant Law Group in the investigation and advancement of the client's claim. If the client unilaterally decides not to pursue the case without first getting approval from The Merchant Law Group, settles the case without the approval of The Merchant Law Group, or transfers the carriage of the action to another law firm, then in any of these events the client will also be responsible to The Merchant Law Group for payment . . ."

On October 23, 1998, B forwarded a copy of that letter and attached Assignment & Retainer Agreement, along with her own letter . . ., to Ms. Merilee Rasmussen, a lawyer with whom B was familiar . . .

* * * * *

On November 20, 1998, Mr. Merchant forwarded a letter to H . . ., which was similar to the letter forwarded to B, . . . the final request being for the name and telephone number of "anyone else you think we should be contacting, which incidentally we will do on a confidential basis and they will never even know that you suggested that we call". . . .

On January 6, 1999, H forwarded a formal letter of complaint to The Law Society of Saskatchewan . . . Among other things, he wrote that he was "very distressed that Merchant Law Group received my name", and indicated that Mr. Merchant had no knowledge of H's personal circumstances. He also specifically objected to the suggestion that he provide Merchant Law Group "with the names of my friends who have been in these circumstances", calling that suggestion "reprehensible".

H . . . stated that he met Mr. Merchant a number of years ago in a very brief informal setting, but other than that, had had no contact with Mr. Merchant or any other members of his law firm.

*   *   *   *   *

H's evidence was that when he received the letter from Mr. Merchant, he made the assumption that Mr. Merchant had forwarded it to him based on their prior brief meeting . . . after talking to other members of the First Nation . . . he understood that some other recipients of a similar letter had signed and returned the contract, at which point he decided to make a complaint.

He further specifically stated that he was not misled by anything contained in the letter, but felt others were.

In cross-examination, he acknowledged that he was unable to say whether any of the other letters he referred to had come from Mr. Merchant or from The Merchant Law Group.

*   *   *   *   *

B testified that she was offended upon receiving the letter . . . she felt the differences between the fees referred to in the letter, and the fee structure outlined in the Assignment & Retainer Agreement, were misleading. . . .

She further stated during cross-examination that she was aware of at least one relative of hers who had retained Mr. Merchant for the same type of claim.

B also stated that she had become aware of other members of her First Nation who had received letters, had returned the attachments, and were expecting to get approximately $50,000 within a week or two.

*   *   *   *   *

Count 1

Count 1 of the formal complaint against the member alleges that he is guilty of conduct unbecoming a lawyer in that:

> He did correspond with B . . ., by letter . . ., which letter was likely to create in the mind of the intended recipient, an unjustified expectation about the results which the writer may achieve, contrary to Chapter XIV of The Law Society of Saskatchewan *Code of Professional Conduct*, and did thereby breach Rule 1602(b), 1601(2)(b) and 1601(2)(c) of the Rules of The Law Society of Saskatchewan.

The essential ingredient of Count 1 that must be established in order to find that the charge is well-founded is:

> 1. Was the letter likely to create an unjustified expectation in the mind of the intended recipient about the results that the writer may achieve?

Mr. Merchant's letter to B . . . contained statements that may have been designed to create an expectation about the results which he could achieve. He spoke of claims for "cultural abuse", "a loss of a sense of family", physical abuse and sexual abuse. The paragraph concerning sexual abuse stated that "For sexual assault, the

91

amount of compensation could be $50,000, $75,000, or $150,000 . . .". . . .

* * * * *

The hearing committee has considered that, if indeed Mr. Merchant had no personal knowledge concerning B, the suggested quantum of damages contained in his letter . . . may have been pure speculation. However, given . . . subsequent judgments and the facts that are now known about B, the amounts speculated as damages are not outside the realm of possibility. In addition, B was careful to express that the letter did not create unjustified expectations, because, as she said, no amount of compensation could compensate her for "her life".

The hearing committee finds that the letter was not "likely" to create an unjustified expectation in B about the results the member may achieve, given B's circumstances.

Count 2

The amended Count 2 of the formal complaint against the member alleges he is guilty of conduct unbecoming a lawyer in that:

> He did correspond with H . . ., by letter . . ., and he did correspond with B . . ., by letter . . ., which letters were reasonably capable of misleading the intended recipient, contrary to Chapter XIV of The Law Society of Saskatchewan *Code of Professional Conduct*, and did thereby breach Rule 1601(2)(c) of the Rules of The Law Society of Saskatchewan. [Rule 1602(2)(c) states that marketing activity must not be "reasonably capable of misleading the recipient or intended recipient . . .].

The committee finds that the allegation contained in Count 2 of the complaint is well-founded, and accordingly the member is guilty of conduct unbecoming a lawyer, in that the correspondence directed to H and the correspondence directed to B were reasonably capable of misleading the intended recipient. . . .

* * * * *

Correspondence to B

Firstly . . ., the letter is misleading in that it disregards the possibility that the recipient may not have a sustainable cause of action. Even if the recipient has a good cause of action, the letter fails to explain in even a cursory fashion the potential length and complexity of the litigation process, including preparation, possibly undergoing interviews and examinations by experts, discoveries, pre-trial procedures and the trial itself. It leaves the impression that payment will be forthcoming without any effort other than writing out "reflections" and returning the "authorization".

Further, the reader is told that he or she has "nothing to lose" and "will pay nothing" if the firm does not recover on her behalf. This representation is not only capable of misleading the reader, no matter who he or she is, but is indeed misleading when compared with the agreement attached to same. The letter itself is in larger type and for the most part employs common parlance. The agreement attached to the letter, however, is in smaller type, follows the form of a contract and employs what lay persons often refer to as "legalese". It would not be unexpected that a reader would rely on the representations made in the letter, rather than reading the agreement.

*   *   *   *   *

In summary, the statements referred to in the letter are misleading in that they:

- assume that the recipient likely has a valid cause of action, in the absence of any of the information as to the recipient's circumstances that would need to be known before such a representation could be made;

- fail to disclose to the recipient the rigors, potential length, and uncertainties of litigation, not to mention the personal toll it can take upon the litigant and those near him or her, especially when litigating matters as sensitive as that referred to in the letter.

- fail to disclose that the prospective client has something to lose from an economic perspective and indeed may well pay something, even if the firm recovers nothing; to the contrary, the recipient is told "you have nothing to lose". The inherent inaccuracy in that statement as compared to the terms of the attached agreement is compounded by the letter referring to the agreement simply as an authorization.

[The court found similar issues in correspondence to H.]

*   *   *   *   *

Count 3

Count 3 of the formal complaint against the member alleges that he is guilty of conduct unbecoming a lawyer in that:

> He did undertake a marketing activity which included correspondence with B . . . and . . . H . . ., which marketing activity was undignified, in bad taste or otherwise offensive, so as to be inimical to the best interests of the public or the members, or tending to harm the standing of the legal profession, contrary to Chapter XIV, of the Law Society of Saskatchewan *Code of Professional Conduct*, and did thereby breach Rule 1601(2)(d) of the Rules of the Law Society of Saskatchewan. [Rule 1601(2)(d) states marketing must not be "[i]n the opinion of the discipline committee undignified, in bad taste or otherwise offensive, so as to be inimical to the best interests of the public or the members, or tending to harm the standing of the legal profession"].

*   *   *   *   *

The hearing committee is of the view that the letters are "undignified, in bad taste, and otherwise offensive". The letters possess these qualities to the point of offending the rule. Although each of the letters is slightly different, each has the following characteristics in common:

1. Each makes the assumption that the recipient is a member of a First Nation;

2. Each makes the assumption that the recipient attended a residential school;

3. Each makes the assumption that many or most persons meeting the criteria in (i) and (ii) above were likely to have been victims of cultural, physical and/or sexual abuse;

4. Based on these assumptions, each letter states the belief that "the

93

compensation that we can achieve for you will be significant".

. . . The implicit assumptions in the letters:

1. as to the likely situation of the recipient, in the absence of any knowledge as to the actual circumstances of the recipient;

2. in disregard for the potential impact that receiving such a letter may have on a recipient;

3. coupled as they are with a prediction of "significant compensation", in the absence of information that would be required to be known before being in a position to make that prediction;

render this marketing activity "undignified, in bad taste, or otherwise offensive".

Also meeting that criteria in the letter to H is the suggestion that, if he knows of people who ought to be suing, "have them call us".

* * * * *

[The Hearing Committee went on to find, however, that it did not have the power to subject the member to discipline for Count 3 because of a problem with the wording of the rule in question. The Committee found Merchant guilty of the second count, corresponding in a manner reasonably capable of misleading the recipient, in respect of the letters to B and H, and ordered a reprimand, a $5,000 fine, and $10,000 in costs. The judgment was affirmed by a majority of the Saskatchewan Court of Appeal in *Law Society of Saskatchewan v. Merchant*, [2002] S.J. No. 288, 2002 SKCA 60 (Sask. C.A.).]

NOTES AND QUESTIONS

1. Do you agree with the decision of the Law Society of Saskatchewan to reprimand and fine Merchant? If not, do you feel the fine is too harsh, or too lenient?

2. The CBA passed two resolutions (one in 2000 and another in 2007), stating that: "lawyers should not initiate communications with individual survivors of Aboriginal residential schools to solicit them as clients or inquire as to whether they were sexually assaulted", and "lawyers should not accept retainers until they have met in person with the client, whenever reasonably possible". These resolutions were endorsed by the Yukon, Northwest Territories and the Law Society of Upper Canada. The other provinces and territories did not follow suit.

Do you agree with the CBA resolution? What are its strengths? What are its weaknesses? Are both these resolutions redundant in light of the *Model Code* restrictions identified in Rule 4.1-2 and its Commentaries?

[iv] Solicitation and Public Appearances

A concern sometimes arises that some lawyers are "media hounds" who engage the media not only to promote their client's interests but also to enhance their own profile. In this regard, Rule 7.5-1 (Communication with the Public) of the *Model Code* and its Commentary are pertinent. As you review this rule, consider whether it is always possible to distinguish between promoting the "best interests of the client" and "self-promotion and self-aggrandizement" by the lawyer.

Courts have also been concerned about lawyers who use the media to engage in self-promotion. Consider *Stewart v. Canadian Broadcasting Corp.*,[28] a case we will return to in Chapter 4, "The Duty of Loyalty and Conflicts of Interest".

From 1979 to 1981, Edward Greenspan served as counsel during the sentencing and appeal process for Robert Stewart's charge and conviction of criminal negligence causing death. 10 years later, Greenspan acted as a host and narrator in a televised episode of *Scales of Justice*. The episode was called "Regina v. Stewart". It revisited the crime, the trial and the public's fascination with both. Stewart was very upset that Greenspan had participated in the program, which rekindled interest in the case. He brought a claim against Greenspan for a breach of the implied terms of his contract and a breach of a fiduciary duty of loyalty. In the decision, MacDonald J. took the opportunity to comment on a lawyer's obligations to former clients when the lawyer is in the media.

Justice MacDonald held that, in the context of public media attention directed at a former client or case, lawyers must not engage in behaviour that is motivated by self-promotion or self-aggrandizement:

> In my opinion, Mr. Greenspan's decision to involve himself in this broadcast despite Mr. Stewart's objection was motivated by self interest. I find that the substantial reason for his involvement in the broadcast was not public education about the justice system. That was assured without Mr. Greenspan's involvement. Mr. Greenspan's primary reason for involving himself in the broadcast was self-promotion, promotion on national television of his counsel practice through displaying his success on Mr. Stewart's behalf in difficult circumstances . . . He re-visited and undermined the future benefits and protections which he had provided to Mr. Stewart as his counsel, for personal gain.[29]

The guiding force behind MacDonald J.'s analysis of whether or not Greenspan's actions constituted self-promotion or self-aggrandizement was Rule 6.06 of the *Code of Conduct* of the Law Society of Upper Canada [as it then was], entitled "Public Appearances and Public Statements". The Commentary to this Rule (currently 7.5-1[3] *Model Code*) reads: "Public communications about a client's affairs should not be used for the purpose of publicizing the lawyer and should be free from any suggestion that the lawyer's real purpose is self-promotion or self aggrandizement."

Justice MacDonald made further conclusions about the ways in which Greenspan promoted his personal self-interest through the program:

> There is also Mr. Greenspan's broadcast presence. To the viewer, he explained the case and its legal issues. He was thus seen by close to one million people in the role of knowledgeable professional adviser. His image and his voice were prominent throughout. His name was mentioned and displayed. In my opinion, this broadcast was not just education about the justice system. It was also education about Edward

---

[28] [1997] O.J. No. 2271, 150 D.L.R. (4th) 24 (Ont. Gen. Div.).

[29] *Stewart v. Canadian Broadcasting Corp.*, [1997] O.J. No. 2271, 150 D.L.R. (4th) 24 at para. 273 (Ont. Gen. Div.).

Greenspan, his role in the justice system, and his effectiveness as counsel. I find that Mr. Greenspan's primary purpose in involving himself in this production and broadcast, in which educational content was otherwise assured, was to publicize himself and his services as counsel to a national audience.[30]

Justice MacDonald ordered Greenspan to pay Stewart $2,500 for causing Stewart minor and transitory distress by participating as host and narrator in the "Regina v. Stewart" television program. Justice MacDonald also ordered Greenspan to disgorge the $3,250 profit he received for his role in the program to Mr. Stewart.

NOTES AND QUESTIONS

1. Do you agree with the decision in the case? In particular, do you agree that Greenspan breached his fiduciary obligation by discussing the former client's case for the purpose of personal self-promotion? What are the points in favour of Macdonald J.'s decision? What are the points against his decision?

2. Is the remedy imposed by Macdonald J. appropriate? What penalty would you impose?

3. Should the Law Society have commenced an investigation into Greenspan's conduct? Would you encourage the Law Society to impose a penalty? If so, what penalty would you recommend?

4. What if Greenspan had published an academic article discussing the issues of legal strategy raised by Stewart's case? Should Stewart be able to successfully bring a similar claim? What reasons of law or policy would make such a claim distinguishable (or not)?

[b] Choice of Client

[i] Moral Non-Accountability or "Taking it Personally"?

Having discussed the issue of marketing legal services, the next question is choice of clients. Hutchinson argues that client selection

> is arguably the most important decision that any lawyer makes because, once a client is taken on, the lawyer has become committed to a whole host of ethical and moral obligations. . . . Once the lawyer-client relationship is established a large part of the ethical die is cast; the lawyers' options about what they are and are not prepared to do are severely curtailed and their obligation is closely circumscribed. This is entirely reasonable because, under any realistic vision of professional responsibility, it would be unconscionable to take on clients and represent them in any incompetent or half-hearted way; that would be a travesty of any kind of ethical expectation.[31]

There is ethical consensus that a lawyer should refuse to take a client if: there is a conflict of interest; the lawyer lacks competence in the matter; there is a continuing retainer with a previous lawyer; the lawyer has the potential to be a witness in a

---

[30] *Stewart v. Canadian Broadcasting Corp.*, [1997] O.J. No. 2271, 150 D.L.R. (4th) 24 at para. 234 (Ont. Gen. Div.).

[31] Allan C. Hutchinson, *Legal Ethics and Professional Responsibility* (Toronto: Irwin Law, 2006) at 75.

case; or there is an illegal purpose.[32] However, beyond these scenarios there is disagreement on the ethics of accepting or refusing clients.

Broadly speaking, when it comes to the question of choice of clients the debate oscillates between two extremes of a continuum. At one end are those who advocate the principle of "moral non-accountability"; at the other end are those who advocate in favour of "taking it personally".[33] Moral non-accountability emphasizes the structural dimensions of the lawyer's role: modern legal regimes are extremely complex and citizens need lawyers to guide them; lawyers are part of an adversary system; truth emerges through the thrust and parry of resolute advocacy; it is the task of the judge, not the lawyer, to ultimately decide the legal entitlements of parties; consequently, the lawyer is simply a neutral agent whose obligation is to represent the client's interest without regard to the morality of that client's conduct or attitude, and without necessarily having regard to that morality in deciding whether to represent the client. Moral non-accountability, in short, is a social good that promotes the fair administration of justice. A related defence of moral non-accountability is found in the excerpt from Dare included in Chapter 1.

Those who espouse "taking it personally" acknowledge the importance of these larger systems values but, at the same time, argue that there must be limits. While structures are important, so too are human agency and human accountability. Law is an instrument of power; real people both benefit and suffer as a consequence of legal behaviour. Good and evil pervasively permeate legal practice. Consequently, lawyers must take responsibility for their choice of clients and the strategies they deploy on behalf of those clients. This is the perspective defended by Luban in the excerpt included in Chapter 1.

The classic example of this clash of visions is the situation of the criminal defence lawyer who defends someone they know to be guilty of murder, child abuse, sexual assault, hate crimes or some other morally reprehensible crime.[34] But the dilemma can face every lawyer: tax lawyers whose task is to advise on tax avoidance; contracts lawyers who draft unconscionable contracts; environmental lawyers who seek to avoid environmental impact assessments for their client's projects; family lawyers who represent parents hiding income to avoid support obligations.

Layton and Proulx attempt to steer a middle path between the advocates of moral accountability and taking it personally by outlining the following recommendations for the criminal defence lawyer:

> In our view, and consistent with the Canadian rules of professional conduct, there

---

[32] David Layton & Michel Proulx, *Ethics and Canadian Criminal Law,* 2d ed. (Toronto: Irwin Law, 2015) at 72; Beverley Smith, *Professional Conduct for Lawyers and Judges*, 4th ed. (Fredericton: Maritime Law Book, 2011) at 5-6.

[33] See, *e.g.*, Stephen L. Pepper, "The Lawyer's Amoral Ethical Role: A Defense, A Problem, and Some Possibilities" (1986) 11:4 Am. B. Found. Res. J. 613; Allan C. Hutchinson, *Legal Ethics and Professional Responsibility* (Toronto: Irwin Law, 2006) at 206-218.

[34] A. Smith & M. Freedman, eds., *How Can You Represent Those People?* (New York: Palgrave MacMillan US, 2013).

are different ways in which a lawyer's personal views can legitimately influence the decision whether to accept a client...A lawyer must reject a retainer where personal distaste concerning the potential client or cause is so severe that the lawyer can reasonably conclude that the quality of legal representation would suffer as a result...The same conclusion follows where the potential client's personality is so abrasive to the lawyer as to impede fatally the duties demanded of any competent advocate...Leaving the issue of competence aside, what factors can be taken into account in choosing or refusing a particular client? The aim is to recognize some room for a lawyer's legitimate exercise of personal morality without undermining the potential client's right to access justice or the principles that underlie criminal defence counsel's special role in the legal system. In this regard, primary considerations include the following:

1) In most criminal law matters, the client will be facing possible stigma from a conviction, and perhaps also a serious impingement upon liberty. Access to the protections offered by the legal system through the help of counsel will thus constitute a valuable, perhaps even essential, interest. The strength of this interest must not be ignored or unreasonably discounted. Indeed, defence counsel who accepts this rationale — and virtually all of them do — will be exceedingly slow to reject a client simply because he is the subject of public opprobrium.

2) On a somewhat similar note, most Canadian codes state that a lawyer's private opinion about the guilt of an accused person should not constitute the basis to decline employment. Utilizing this rationale for refusing a client would be at odds with a central tenet of the criminal defence lawyer's role. Once a lawyer decides to practise criminal law, choosing a client based on the likelihood he is guilty or not guilty is unacceptable.

3) A lawyer's strong and genuine belief that the representation is repugnant is a legitimate consideration in deciding whether to accept a client, although as noted such a belief will usually be eclipsed by the superordinate principle that all individuals charged with a crime are entitled to a defence.

4) The repugnance felt by the lawyer should relate to concerns intimately connected to the representation at hand and not merely to the personality of the client. Provided a personality clash does not irreparably cripple the client-lawyer relationship, a client should not be rejected merely because he rubs the lawyer the wrong way.

5) A desire to avoid public condemnation for taking on a case and to skirt a real possibility of resulting economic harm to a lawyer's practice are factors that some counsel may take into account. But counsel should be slow to allow public opinion to shape her decision. In any event, lawyers whose practises are dedicated to defence work are unlikely to suffer widespread public disfavour or any consequential business loss by taking on any particular case.

6) The lawyer can take into account the likelihood that the prospective client can obtain competent representation from other counsel, that is the last-lawyer-in-town factor. This consideration is expressly mentioned in

many Canadian ethical codes, which state that a lawyer should be cautious in exercising the right to decline employment if the probable result would be to make it difficult for a person to obtain legal advice or representation, and should generally refrain from doing so merely because the client or cause is unpopular or notorious.

7) A client cannot be turned away based on a prohibited ground of discrimination.

8) As already mentioned, some criminal defence lawyers refuse to take on entire categories of representation, for example, all individuals facing sex-related charges or all individuals who wish to co-operate with the prosecution. While somewhat uncomfortable with uncompromising refusals to represent clients who fall within a particular category of case, we accept that a dedicated and highly competent criminal lawyer can have a profound moral objection to taking on certain types of representation, in which case it is acceptable to reject such briefs.

Where a lawyer decides not to accept a retainer, for whatever legitimate reason, it is advisable to take certain measures designed to protect the interests of both the lawyer and the individual whose case has been declined. A primary duty owed to the rejected individual is to help in finding a suitable lawyer.[35]

Hutchinson has a different suggestion:

Before taking on any clients, it seems ethically incumbent on lawyers to talk to them. This need not be a one-way lecture to the potential client about the lawyer's ethical values, but it might be a conversation in which lawyer and client outline their basic expectations of each other. Questions lawyers might ask before taking on a client include whether the objective of the case is worthy and whether the means that might be required will be allowed to be used. It is important that lawyers inform potential clients of the ethical limits they place on their provision of legal services — negotiation tactics or cross-examination style. In general, lawyers should treat their potential clients as moral persons who are capable of engaging in debate and changing.[36]

As we have seen, Rule 4.1-1 of the *Model Code* states that "[a] lawyer *must* make legal services available to the public efficiently and conveniently . . ." [emphasis added], but Commentary 4 adds the following:

Right to Decline Representation - A lawyer has a general right to decline a particular representation (except when assigned as counsel by a tribunal), but it is a right to be exercised prudently, particularly if the probable result would be to make it difficult for a person to obtain legal advice or representation. Generally, a lawyer should not exercise the right merely because a person seeking legal services or that person's cause is unpopular or notorious, or because powerful interests or allegations of misconduct or malfeasance are involved, or because of the lawyer's private opinion about the guilt of the accused. A lawyer declining representation

---

[35] David Layton & Michel Proulx, *Ethics and Canadian Criminal Law,* 2d ed. (Toronto: Irwin Law, 2015) at 93-95.

[36] Allan C. Hutchinson, *Legal Ethics and Professional Responsibility* (Toronto: Irwin Law, 2006) at 78.

should assist in obtaining the services of another lawyer qualified in the particular field and able to act. When a lawyer offers assistance to a client or prospective client in finding another lawyer, the assistance should be given willingly and, except where a referral fee is permitted by section 3.6-6, without charge.

NOTES AND QUESTIONS

1. Compare and contrast the proposals put forward by Layton and Proulx, and by Hutchinson, and consider whether either approach is helpful in fulfilling a lawyer's ethical obligations regarding client selection.

2. Does Commentary 4 on the right to decline representation lean more towards the "professional" or "business" model of lawyering?

3. What behaviour by a lawyer could lead to discipline pursuant to rules such as these?

4. When it comes to the question of choice of client, Canada does not follow the conventional English model. In theory, English barristers are governed by the "cab-rank" rule. Barristers are obliged to take the next person in line, wherever that person wants to go; barristers do not have a choice as to who their client might be, so long as the barrister is competent and available, and the client has the means to pay (in reality, however, it is well known that English barristers have a variety of strategies by which they can filter their clients).[37] What are the possible rationales for the English cab-rank rule? What are the possible rationales for the Canadian discretion rule? Which do you think is the better rule?

5. Not all Canadian lawyers agree with the Canadian discretion rule. In 2006, a leading Canadian advocate, Earl Cherniak, argued that lawyers have a responsibility to "take all comers" because "given the privileged position we are given in society, lawyers have a responsibility to take on those cases to which they are competent in doing".[38] Do you agree? Is Commentary 4 a real constraint on a lawyer's discretion? Whose interests does it really serve, clients' or lawyers'? Does it have any weight compared to the economic imperatives that tend to convert the profession of law into the business of law?

6. Is the general right to decline representation compatible with the Barrister's Oath in Ontario?

I accept the honour and privilege, duty and responsibility of practising law as a barrister and solicitor in the Province of Ontario. I shall protect and defend the rights and interests of such persons as may employ me. I shall conduct all cases faithfully and to the best of my ability. I shall neglect no one's interest and shall faithfully serve and diligently represent the best interests of my client. I shall not refuse causes of complaint reasonably founded, nor shall I promote suits upon frivolous pretences. I shall not pervert the law to favour or prejudice any one, but in all things I shall conduct myself honestly and with integrity and civility. I shall

---

[37] See, *e.g.*, H.H.A. Cooper, "Representation of the Unpopular: What Can the Profession Do about this Eternal Problem?" (1974) 22:10 Chitty's L.J. 333 at 338.

[38] Tim Wilbur, "Ethics", *The Lawyer's Weekly* (November 3, 2006) at 3.

seek to ensure access to justice and access to legal services. I shall seek to improve the administration of justice. I shall champion the rule of law and safeguard the rights and freedoms of all persons. I shall strictly observe and uphold the ethical standards that govern my profession. All this I do swear or affirm to observe and perform to the best of my knowledge and ability.[39]

Which one of these should prevail? Should the Ontario Barrister's Oath be rewritten or abandoned?

7. Some lawyers, particularly in the criminal law context, are leery of taking on a client because they fear that the client will lie to them, or that they will become a dupe of that client. Is one possible solution to this concern to have a potential client take a polygraph test?[40]

8. Companies that hire outside counsel often have "Outside Counsel Guidelines" - detailed, mandatory sets of terms and conditions - that impose stricter expectations on lawyers, particularly in the area of conflicts. Because of their broad definition of "conflict of interest", OC Guidelines make it much more difficult for lawyers to take on other clients at the same time. Could this threaten the lawyer's independence and compromise their ability to provide dispassionate and candid advice? Why or why not?

Assume you are approached by a deep-pocketed client who wishes to retain your services. They insist on including a conflicts of interest clause in the retainer. Identify the issues you should consider before accepting the retainer.

---

[39] Law Society of Ontario, By-law No. 4, *Licensing* (May 1, 2007, as amended April 28, 2016), s. 21(2), online (pdf): https://lawsocietyontario.azureedge.net/media/lso/media/about/governance/by-laws/by-law-4-licensing-01-15-18.pdf.

[40] Martha Neil, "Criminal defense lawyer uses polygraph test to weed out dishonest clients" (November 9, 2015), online (blog): *ABA Journal* http://www.abajournal.com/news/article/guilty_of_a_sex_crime_criminal_defense_lawyer_nixes_such_cases_using_ polygr. For a Canadian critique of a lawyer using a polygraph to limit client representation, see: *R. v. Moore,* [2002] S.J. No. 124, 2002 SKCA 30, [2002] 7 W.W.R. 424 (Sask. C.A.).

[ii] Client Selection and Discrimination

Despite the existence of a general right to decline representation, lawyers are subject to anti-discrimination norms. Please review Rule 6.3 of the *Model Code* and its Commentary.

NOTES AND QUESTIONS

In *Understanding Lawyers' Ethics in Canada*, 2d ed., Woolley identifies the following four scenarios:

1. A criminal defence lawyer is approached by an individual charged with crimes related to hate speech because of the individual's publication of pamphlets stating that homosexuality is a "sickness" and that tolerance of gays and lesbians "violates the will of God". The lawyer declines the representation because she finds the pamphlets abhorrent. The accused person alleges that he has been discriminated against because of his political and religious beliefs.

2. A criminal defence lawyer refuses to take sexual assault cases. The overwhelming majority of people charged with sexual assault are men. A man whose retainer is declined by the lawyer argues that he has suffered adverse effect discrimination on the basis of his gender.

3. A family law lawyer adopts a policy of only representing wives in divorces, and markets her practices on that basis. A man whose retainer is declined by the lawyer argues that he has been directly discriminated against on the basis of his gender.

4. A criminal defence lawyer is consulted by a man who has been charged with drunk driving. The accused is a committed Scientologist. The lawyer does not want to represent someone who is a Scientologist because the lawyer has an extremely negative view of Scientologist beliefs. The accused argues that he has been discriminated against on the basis of his religious beliefs.[41]

To what extent does Rule 6.3 and its Commentaries help us to respond to these situations?

Analyze the following scenarios based on Rule 6.3, the other Rules on client selection provided, and the general principles related to the ethics of client selection.

Scenario One

Assume you are a member of the Board of Directors of the University Legal Aid Clinic. You have been presented with a proposal from the Executive Director, staff and students at the Clinic to adopt a policy "to represent women who are victims of violence and not to represent men charged with offences of violence against their wives or intimates".

What issues does this raise for the Board? Are there any provisions in the *Model Code* that would be of assistance? Are there other legal rules, principles or norms

---

[41] Alice Woolley, *Understanding Lawyers' Ethics in Canada*, 2d ed. (Toronto: LexisNexis Canada, 2016).

that would be relevant for your analysis?[42]

Scenario Two

Assume you are a patent lawyer who has been on retainer for five years with a multinational pharmaceutical corporation.

For each of the last three years, between 15,000 and 20,000 people in South Braguay have been dying from a VIDCO virus. Throughout that time, the government of South Braguay has been negotiating with several pharmaceutical corporations, including the one you represent, to allow the manufacture of cheap generic drugs. There was no agreement.

Recently, the government of South Braguay passed a law allowing for the establishment of generic drug companies in South Braguay for the production of anti-VIDCO drugs. The stated goal of the government is to create a "high volume, no margin market".

The pharmaceutical corporation wants you to challenge the law as a breach of the World Trade Organization's Agreement on Trade Related Intellectual Property Rights (TRIPS).

What issues would you consider in deciding whether to accept this file? Having identified these issues, indicate your decision. Provide justifications for your decision.

[c]   Triggering the Lawyer-Client Relationship: First Dealings Doctrine

The foregoing discussions presume that the lawyer and client choose to enter a relationship — that there has been an offer and acceptance of the retainer contract. The *Model Code* 1.1-1 defines a client as follows:

"client" means a person who

    (a)   consults a lawyer and on whose behalf the lawyer renders or agrees to render legal services; or

    (b)   having consulted the lawyer, reasonably concludes that the lawyer has agreed to render legal services on their behalf.

and includes a client of the law firm of which the lawyer is a partner or associate, whether or not the lawyer handles the client's work.

It might be possible that the lawyer-client relationship — and the correlative ethical obligations of the lawyer — are triggered at different times in (a) and (b), and that the lawyer and client have different perspectives on whether a relationship exists at all. Consider, for example, *Descôteaux v. Mierzwinski*,[43] a case we will return to in Chapter 3. In that case, a citizen attended a legal aid office and filled in a form titled "Application for Legal Aid". Subsequently, the police presented themselves at the legal aid office and sought certain documents, including the application form. The main issue in the case was whether this form was protected by solicitor-client

---

[42] See further, Mary Jane Mossman, "'Shoulder to Shoulder': Gender and Access to Justice" (1990) 10 Windsor Y.B. Access Just. 351 at 359-63.

[43] [1982] S.C.J. No. 43, [1982] 1 S.C.R. 860 (S.C.C.).

privilege. However, this required a decision on a prior question — at what point is the solicitor-client relationship formed? The Court held:

> In the case at bar the principal issue is to determine when the solicitor-client relationship, which confers the confidentiality protected by the substantive rule and the rule of evidence, arises.

> The Superior Court judge, as we have seen, was of the view that this relationship, and consequently the right to confidentiality, did not arise until the legal aid applicant had been accepted, that is, until the retainer was established.

> When dealing with the right to confidentiality it is necessary, in my view, to distinguish between the moment when the retainer is established and the moment when the solicitor-client relationship arises. The latter arises as soon as the potential client has his first dealings with the lawyer's office in order to obtain legal advice.

> The items of information that a lawyer requires from a person in order to decide if they will agree to advise or represent them are just as much communications made in order to obtain legal advice as any information communicated to them subsequently. It has long been recognized that even if the lawyer does not agree to advise the person seeking his services, communications made by the person to the lawyer or his staff for that purpose are nonetheless privileged . . .

> Moreover, the same applies not only to information given before the retainer is perfected concerning the legal problem itself, but also to information concerning the client's ability to pay the lawyer and any other information which a lawyer is reasonably entitled to require before accepting the retainer. First, this information of an administrative nature is just as related to the establishment of the professional relationship as any other information; this is especially clear when, as in the case at bar, the legal aid applicant *"must set forth (his) financial means . . .* and the basis of his claim." In addition, information of this nature that a person gives his lawyer for that purpose may also be highly confidential and would have been kept secret by that person were it not for that person's need of the assistance of a legal adviser.[44]

NOTES AND QUESTIONS

1. Does this "first dealings" doctrine create any potential ethical problems for a lawyer?

2. Do you think that a client, having filled out an Application for Legal Aid form, could, in the words of the *Model Code*, "reasonably conclude that the lawyer has agreed to render legal services"? Or is this precluded by "having consulted the lawyer"?

3. What if, after a 15-minute discussion at the initial interview, the potential client tells the lawyer something about another current client which constitutes a conflict of interest. What should the lawyer do?

4. Assume a 16-year-old client comes into your office wanting to hire you. She is very upset. After 10 minutes, you realize that you cannot represent her because of a potential conflict of interest. You tell her you cannot

---

[44] *Descôteaux v. Mierzwinski*, [1982] S.C.J. No. 43, [1982] 1 S.C.R. 860 at 876-877 [Emphasis added] (S.C.C.).

represent her but you will help her find another lawyer. At that point she pulls a bag out of her purse, and there is a bloody knife. She bursts into tears, and flees your office, leaving the knife on your desk. What do you do?

[3] COMPETENCE, QUALITY OF SERVICE, AND CANDOUR

[a] Introduction

The Supreme Court of Canada has held that lawyers and clients have a fiduciary relationship, and the lawyer owes the client a duty of loyalty.[45] Loyalty, however, is a somewhat abstract ideal with many dimensions, including the duties to provide competent advice and representation; preserve the client's confidences; avoid conflicts of interest; and provide honest and candid advice.[46] Several of these duties will be addressed in detail in later chapters of this book; here we focus only on the issues of competence and advice.

[b] Competence and Quality of Service

The *Model Code* attempts to substantiate the principle of loyalty by, for example, mandating that lawyers should be competent and render quality service to their clients. A question can be raised however as to how seriously these obligations are pursued and enforced by the governing bodies of the legal profession. Historically, there have been relatively few cases where lawyers have been disciplined by a law society for incompetence.[47] This is the case despite the fact that empirical studies in other common law jurisdictions (*e.g.*, England and Australia) indicate that the major causes of client dissatisfaction with lawyers do not involve incidents such as stealing from the trust funds, but rather involve the perception (or reality?) that lawyers tend to provide a poor quality service for a disproportionately high price. The National Self-Represented Litigants project in Canada makes similar findings.[48] As we work our way through this section, one central question to consider is whether the Canadian legal profession does enough to ensure that lawyers are competent, and that they do in fact provide quality service.

There are three possible legal angles to address the issue of lawyers' incompetence: breach of contract, the law of lawyer malpractice (primarily negligence), and codes of professional conduct. The leading Canadian case on lawyers' negligence is

---

[45] *R. v. Neil*, [2002] S.C.J. No. 72, 3 S.C.R. 631 (S.C.C.); *Canadian National Railway Co. v. McKercher LLP*, [2013] S.C.J. No. 39, 2013 SCC 39, [2013] 2 S.C.R. 649 (S.C.C.).

[46] *R. v. Neil*, [2002] S.C.J. No. 72, 3 S.C.R. 631 (S.C.C.); *Canadian National Railway Co. v. McKercher LLP*, [2013] S.C.J. No. 39, 2013 SCC 39, [2013] 2 S.C.R. 649 (S.C.C.); See also Colin Jackson, Brent Cotter & Richard Devlin, "Of Lodestars and Lawyers: Incorporating the Duty of Loyalty into the *Model Code of Conduct*" (2016) 39:1 Dal. L.J. 37.

[47] Harry Arthurs, "The Dead Parrot: Does Professional Self-Regulation Exhibit Vital Signs?" (1995) 33:4 Alta. L. Rev. 800; Allan C. Hutchinson, *Legal Ethics and Professional Responsibility* (Toronto: Irwin Law, 2006) at 69.

[48] Julie Macfarlane, "The National Self-Represented Litigants Project: Identifying and Meeting the Needs of Self-Represented Litigants, Final Report" (May 2013), online (pdf): https://commentary.canlii.org/w/canlii/2013CanLIIDocs493.

Central Trust Co. v. Rafuse, where the Supreme Court of Canada held that the appropriate standard of care is that "of the reasonably competent solicitor".[49]

For the purposes of this chapter, we focus on competence in the *Model Code.* Traditionally, competence and quality of service were two of the least talked about issues for the legal profession, but perhaps the most significant and embarrassing. Much lip service was paid to the ideal of professionalism and inherent in that ideal was the requirement of competence, but little was done to *ensure* that lawyers were competent. The *Model Code*, adopted in 2010, attempted to respond to this criticism by didactically specifying what it means by Competence and Quality of Service.

Please review Rules 3.1 (Competence) and 3.2 (Quality of Service), and their Commentaries.

NOTES AND QUESTIONS

1. Are the *Model Code* standards for competence and quality of service too low?

2. Are the standards too high? Could it be argued that the effect of these standards is to drive up the cost of legal services thereby depriving consumers of the ability to retain a lawyer? Is this an example of what is sometimes called "the theory of negative gains", i.e. when an idea initially presumed to have a positive outcome turns out in the end to generate a negative outcome?

3. How helpful is the standard of "a competent lawyer in a like situation"? What are the strengths of such a threshold? What are the weaknesses? Does this mean that a client should have different expectations of competence and quality of service depending on whether the lawyer works in a large firm or a small firm, charges $800 per hour or $300 per hour, practises in the urban context or the rural context, is a specialist or a generalist? This question can also be asked about the concept of reasonable competence used to assess lawyer negligence, as courts have defined that concept specifically, taking into account where and in what type of firm a lawyer practises.

4. Consider how Rule 3.1-2, Commentary 15 of the *Model Code* explains the relationship between negligence and incompetence:

   Incompetence, Negligence and Mistakes - This rule does not require a standard of perfection. An error or omission, even though it might be actionable for damages in negligence or contract, will not necessarily constitute a failure to maintain the standard of professional competence described by the rule. However, evidence of gross neglect in a particular matter or a pattern of neglect or mistakes in different matters may be evidence of such a failure, regardless of tort liability. While damages may

---

[49] *Central Trust Co. v. Rafuse*, [1986] S.C.J. No. 52, [1986] 2 S.C.R. 147, 31 D.L.R. (4th) 481 at 208 (S.C.C.); Amy Salyzyn, "The Judicial Regulation of Lawyers in Canada" (2014) 37:2 Dal. L.J. 481; see also *McClenahan v. Clarke*, [2004] O.J. No. 287, 2004 CanLII 25843 (Ont. S.C.J.) and *Salomon v. Matte-Thompson*, [2019] S.C.J. No. 14, 2019 SCC 14, 1 S.C.R. 729 (S.C.C.).

be awarded for negligence, incompetence can give rise to the additional sanction of disciplinary action.

Is this the appropriate relationship? Which is the higher standard: the legal duty or the ethical duty? Which should be the higher standard?

5. The *Model Code* says little about the relationship between competence and firm management skills, merely stipulating that a lawyer should "manag[e] one's practice effectively" (Rule 3.1-1(i)) and "maintain office staff, facilities, and equipment adequate to the lawyer's practice" (Rule 3.2-1, Commentary 5(j)). Is this sufficient? For example, the old Nova Scotia *Legal Ethics and Professional Conduct Handbook* provided:

> 2.4 The duty of competence extends to practice and firm management. Practice management comprises the knowledge, skills and attributes which a lawyer applies to the organization of their work, and to resources which contribute to producing the legal services required by the client. Firm management relates to the organizational structure or environment in which a lawyer works, and may include production of correct, efficient and timely legal services by the lawyer and staff members; and development of adequate organizational systems and communications. The lawyer must ensure there are in place sufficient resources and administrative support to support the practice and the work undertaken by the lawyer, and those resources must remain current with the technology required to proficiently carry out the lawyer's area(s) of practice.

Which is the better approach? Why? Does the old Nova Scotia rule go too far? What are the likely consequences of such a requirement? What impact will this have on clients? Is it another incentive to drive up legal costs?

6. In 2019, the Federation of Law Societies of Canada (FLSC) added Commentaries 4A and 4B to the Competence Rule to ensure "technological competence". Identify the strengths and weaknesses of these Commentaries. In light of these Commentaries should law societies mandate continuing education on technological competence? Is there a connection between technological competence and enhancing access to justice? When the COVID-19 shutdown was announced, some lawyers immediately switched to Zoom to facilitate communication with their clients. Were they in compliance with the duty of technological competence? In particular, do you believe that many of the lawyers "underst[ood] the benefits and risks associated with relevant technology, recognizing the lawyers' duty to protect confidential information. . .."?

7. Should a senior lawyer be responsible for the social media activities of a junior lawyer or an articling student in their firm? See *Law Society of Ontario v. Forte*, 2019 ONLSTH 9.

The following two cases illustrate how law societies and courts have addressed incompetence. One is from the civil law context, the other from the criminal law context.

NOVA SCOTIA BARRISTERS' SOCIETY v. RICHEY

[2002] L.S.D.D. No. 30

(Nova Scotia Barristers' Society, Hearing Subcommittee: B.T. MacIntosh, Chair)

By Formal Complaint, dated October 19, 2001, the Investigative Subcommittee of the Nova Scotia Barristers' Society's Discipline Committee directed the Executive Director of the Nova Scotia Barristers' Society (hereinafter the Society) to charge Member David W. Richey (hereinafter the Member) with professional misconduct and professional incompetence . . .

* * * * *

The starting point in any analysis of the application of incompetence is the legal framework. Neither the Act nor the Regulations thereunder provide any guidance on the parameters and definition of incompetence. Regulation 39(i) merely provides a circular definition of incompetence: incompetence means professional incompetence. Section 31(3)(b) of the Act specifically empowers both an Investigative Subcommittee and a Panel to investigate allegations of professional incompetence, separate and apart from the more common allegations of professional misconduct and/or conduct unbecoming. Incompetence is accordingly distinguishable in its own right. Section 31(8) of the Act specifies that the procedural, remedial, and penal provision of the Act and Regulations are applicable to professional incompetence in the same manner as professional misconduct and conduct unbecoming.

* * * * *

Incompetence in this instance is determinable by its consistent pattern. This Panel does not have to determine whether a single act of negligence, error in judgment, or professional misconduct can, by itself, constitute incompetence. The Formal Complaint as drafted, and as argued by the Society's counsel, requires evidence beyond individual acts of disciplinary default: it is in the predictability and consistency of the pattern of such acts by the member that the finding of incompetence is based.

[The Act] identifies the mandate and objects of the Society's disciplinary process: it specifically includes protection of the public by inhibiting incompetence. The public is entitled to expect that a self governing legal profession will take reasonable measures to ensure that all lawyers who practise law will possess the minimum skill sets reasonably required of the circumstances. Repeated examples of the absence of specific skills - in this instance the skills of conscientious, diligent, and efficient service to client - will support a finding of incompetence.

The word "incompetence" has a distinctively negative connotation. When used to describe a lawyer, it evokes a strong negative mental image of a person who is unfit to practice law. In the opinion of this Hearing Committee, that is not the intent of the context in the Act. A finding of incompetence must inevitably bring with it professional embarrassment and a loss of confidence in the member found to be incompetent. Nevertheless, in finding that Member David W. Richey was guilty of incompetence, it is not the intention of this Panel to conclude that the Member is generally and generically incompetent. This specific finding of a disciplinary default of both incompetence and professional misconduct is fact and time specific, without

108

any intended inference that the Member is incapable of meeting generally accepted standards of practice. To the contrary, the evidence supports the view that Mr. Richey, when he commits to doing so, can be a most competent and conscientious practitioner of law.

* * * * *

[Mr. Richey is] a senior and experienced member of the litigation bar, [whom counsel for the Society described as] "a highly intelligent, well educated and experienced lawyer who works hard in the interests of his clients and who has a significant devotion to his clients."

. . . Based on the evidence placed before it, this Panel concurs with that description. Nevertheless, the Member has been found guilty of professional incompetence. . . . When a pattern of such poor judgment emerges, as it did in this instance, good lawyering skills on some files is no defence to incompetent lawyering on other files. When the pattern of individual acts of neglect becomes troublingly predictable, then the line is crossed from isolated acts of error in judgment to incompetence.

* * * * *

With respect to the specific allegations contained within the Formal Complaint, this Panel makes the following factual findings which contribute to the legal conclusions of professional misconduct and a pattern of conduct amounting to professional incompetence:

    a.   While representing AVW and DVW, David Richey failed to move the file to a settlement or trial, contrary to instructions of client;

    b.   While representing DVW, David Richey failed to advise his client of the reasons for not setting her case down for trial and gave frequent representations that certain commitments for moving the file forward would take place by certain dates, many of which were not met;

    c.   While representing EP, David Richey failed to file a Pre-Trial Brief in a timely manner and failed to competently obtain and disclose all relevant medical records and information to Defence counsel as required by the Civil Procedure Rules and the directions of the Court;

    d.   While representing MFB, David Richey failed to commence discoveries and related applications in a timely manner and failed to be ready for trial in accordance with conventional standards of practice;

        (i)   With respect to the allegation of being late without proper excuse, this Panel finds there is not sufficient cogent evidence to support a finding of a disciplinary default. Although an error in judgment, this Panel accepts Mr. Richey's explanation that his tardiness was unintentional and an isolated oversight. This allegation is dismissed;

        (ii)   This Panel finds that the filing of the Pre-Trial Brief on the installment plan was a deliberate and unacceptable breach of minimum standards of practice and constituted a deliberate breach of an undertaking to the Court, regardless of whether the specific word "undertaking" was used;

(iii)   This Panel does not have sufficient cogent evidence before it to make a finding with respect to the quality of Mr. Richey's Pre-Trial Brief to Justice Scanlan and accordingly this particular allegation is dismissed;

(iv)   This Panel finds David Richey failed to disclose relevant medical information on the MFB file in a timely manner and in breach of minimally acceptable standards of practice;

(v)   This Panel does not have sufficient cogent evidence before it to conclude that witness Brian Sutherland was not adequately prepared as a witness.

e.   While representing other clients during the period from January 1, 1999 up to September 13, 2001, this Panel finds that David Richey failed to serve his clients in a conscientious, diligent, and efficient manner, so as to provide a quality of service at least equal to that which lawyers generally expect of a competent lawyer in like situations, and further, that he failed to advance clients' cases and expedite litigation and/or settle matters in an expeditious manner for clients. In particular:

(i)   This Panel finds David Richey failed to respond to communications, requests for information, phone calls, and correspondence from clients, lawyers, and others in a timely manner;

(ii)   This Panel finds that David Richey failed to maintain an adequate file management and bring forward system to ensure file matters were dealt with on a timely and efficient basis, thereby significantly impeding file progress in many instances;

(iii)   This Panel finds that David Richey failed to provide full and timely disclosure of medical and other evidence by adopting an unacceptably narrow view of relevance, below the minimum generally accepted standards of practice within the profession, which failure further impeded the progress of files;

(iv)   Notwithstanding the persuasive opinion evidence of the Practice Supervisor, which this Panel accepts on its face, in the absence of more specific factual evidence from clients, this Panel does not have sufficient cogent evidence before it to conclude upon the required standard of proof that Mr. Richey's clients received little or no advice regarding outcome, or that such clients had unreasonable expectations. Accordingly, this allegation is dismissed.

Based on the foregoing evidentiary findings, this Panel concludes that Member David W. Richey is guilty of both professional incompetence and professional misconduct on the grounds set forth in the Formal Complaint, excepting only those particulars aforedescribed for which there was insufficient evidence.

[The Nova Scotia Barristers' Society went on to reprimand Mr. Richey, fined him $1,000, required him to pay costs of the proceeding (almost $30,000) and required that his practice be subject to monitoring.]

NOTES AND QUESTIONS

1.   Do you think the Nova Scotia Barristers' Society has identified the proper

balance between specific and generic incompetence? If not, has it set the threshold too high or too low? Does the test collapse incompetence into quality service?

2. At one point the panel notes that "Regulation 39(i) merely provides a circular definition of incompetence: incompetence means professional incompetence". Do the definitions in the *Model Code* resolve the circularity problem?

The second example is *R. v. Lam*, 2019 BCPC 29. In this case, Mr. Lam pleaded guilty to possessing two kilograms of cocaine for the purpose of trafficking. After pleading guilty, his then-lawyer, Larry Myers, Q.C. sought a judicial stay of proceedings, alleging an abuse of process based on derivative entrapment. Following a hearing, that application was dismissed. Before his sentencing, Mr. Lam discharged Mr. Myers and hired new lawyers. He applied to strike his guilty plea based on an allegation of ineffective assistance of counsel from Myers. Lam argued Myers was professionally incompetent.

First, Lam alleged Myers was incompetent because he did not take notes during his time representing Lam. When asked to explain, Myers testified,

> I don't usually put things in writing because I feel that they are - the notes themselves are vulnerable. If I'm having general discussions, I don't do that. And it's interesting because as you're asking me these questions, I'm revisiting that practice. I - I do it purposely as a matter of practice not to keep notes of specific instructions but I realize now that in spite of the fact that I had confidence in my relationship with Nam Lam and that he was quite happy with myself and quite happy with Ms. Paquette, never ever complained about her, that I should have gotten confirmation from him in writing so I wouldn't be having this - this discussion about this part of my evidence today.

This was not well-received by the judge:

> Aside from the self-serving nature of this comment, it did not make any sense to me. Mr. Myers did not explain how notes of his dealings with Mr. Lam would be "vulnerable". He attempted to justify his failure to take notes later in his cross-examination. He said he did not have any notes of his meetings with Mr. Lam because he did not expect Mr. Lam to testify. He went on:
>
>> As well, it - it - I - I'm going to use the term - it gives - it gives both of us some flexibility since should something else arise, I didn't want him to be in a position of having - giving me contradictory statements.
>
> Mr. Myers' evidence does not explain why he would not have notes of the following:
>
> * The dates and times of his meetings and telephone calls with Mr. Lam;
>
> * The retainer agreement;
>
> * The advice given by Mr. Myers on the various legal issues, such as the challenge to the search warrant, the guilty plea, or the argument on abuse of process;
>
> * Mr. Lam's instructions on the election to Supreme Court;
>
> * Mr. Lam's instructions on his guilty plea and re-election back down to Provincial Court; or

*   The involvement of Ms. Paquette in the file, including whether Mr. Lam agreed that she could conduct the evidentiary hearing.

Mr. Myers also failed to keep proper records of his correspondence and other communications on the file. . .

* * * * *

Mr. Myers has been a lawyer for 40 years. His failure to take notes and keep proper records of his representation of Mr. Lam has made the search for the truth much more difficult. I am left with the recollections of Mr. Myers and Mr. Lam of interactions that occurred years ago, without any objective verification. Mr. Myers failed in his duty to his client, and to the profession, when he made no notes and did not keep proper records. This failure is relevant, not only to my assessment of Mr. Myers' credibility and reliability, but also to my assessment of whether it would be a miscarriage of justice to allow Mr. Lam's guilty plea to stand.

Lam alleged Myers was incompetent for three additional reasons:

1)   Failing to challenge a search warrant for Mr. Lam's apartment;

2)   Advising Mr. Lam to enter a guilty plea under circumstances that were procedurally unfair;

3)   Substituting his representation of Mr. Lam with a junior lawyer without proper instructions.

With respect to the failure to challenge the search warrant, Lam argued Myers should have read the decision from the case related to Lam's charges:

Mr. Lam argues that Mr. Myers was incompetent when he advised Mr. Lam to plead guilty without fully exploring Judge Galati's decision and the impact it could have on a challenge to the search of Mr. Lam's apartment. . .

. . . Mr. Myers had not read the decision, or talked to defence counsel on the case. The most he could say in his cross-examination was that Judge Galati's findings "are far different than I - I would have thought would've been the findings in regard - the basis of the affiant's affirmation in regards to Ms. Tran and Mr. Lam were far different". But this was after he read from the decision in the course of his cross-examination. He had not read the decision prior to that. Furthermore, he was not aware of Judge Galati's findings regarding his residual discretion until he read the decision in the course of his cross-examination.

In my view Mr. Myers should have read the decision by Judge Galati, or at least talked to defence counsel involved in the case about the decision. He admitted as much in cross-examination. I do not believe it was reasonable for him to have simply relied upon the information provided by the Crown. If a challenge to the search warrant was, indeed, the only possible defence he had available, Mr. Myers should have taken further steps to explore the viability of this defence, before encouraging Mr. Lam to plead guilty. I agree that Mr. Myers failed to provide reasonable professional assistance when he failed [to] review Judge Galati's decision or failed to, at least, talk to defence counsel about the decision.

With respect to advising him to plead guilty, Lam said

. . . that Mr. Myers told him that the only way he could win the case was by pleading guilty and arguing entrapment. Mr. Lam said Mr. Myers was the lawyer, so he trusted him when he said that pleading guilty was the best way to win. He said

Mr. Myers did not tell him that he would lose his ability to challenge the search warrant by pleading guilty.

Myers responded that Lam could in fact challenge the search warrant despite his guilty plea. The judge was critical of this argument:

> I found it remarkable that Mr. Myers maintained [his] position in his cross-examination, but was unable to cite any authorities in support. This issue arose in the course of Mr. Myers' submissions at Mr. Lam's abuse of process application. . . The Court asked Mr. Myers if he had any authority to support his argument. Mr. Myers considered the inquiry over the break and said the following when he returned:
>
> > I wouldn't give particular weight to my suggestion of the remedy of excising the warrant or quashing the warrant, even though in effect that may be a consideration. I am not sure that we - we have no authority either way for the suggestions I am making.
>
> Mr. Myers did not have any authorities to the Court then, nor was he able to provide any authorities in his cross-examination. He advised the court then not to give any particular weight to his argument, yet he insisted in his cross-examination on this application that he was able to challenge the search warrant after a guilty plea.

The judge did not find that Myers' recommendation to plead guilty was incompetent, but he found that Myers failed to advise Lam of the consequences of pleading guilty:

> . . .Mr. Lam wanted to challenge the warrant. Mr. Myers thought he could still challenge the warrant, even after Mr. Lam pleaded guilty. He failed to inform Mr. Lam that he would lose his ability to challenge the search warrant when he pled guilty. In this regard, he failed to provide reasonable professional assistance.

With respect to having a junior lawyer, Myers was double-booked on a murder trial for the first several days of Lam's hearing and sent a junior associate, Chantal Paquette, to attend Lam's hearing in his place. Lam testified he did not know this was going to happen:

> I was wondering where Mr. Myers was. I went there — so I came to the courtroom looking for Mr. Myers and then this girl comes up to me and asked if I'm Hoang Nam Lam, and I was like, yea, and then I was like, oh, where's Mr. Myers? And then she's like, oh, he didn't have to be here for this part, the beginning part of this. He was doing a different case. A murder case. And then in my head, I was just like, I thought Mr. Myers would be here. He should be here. And — and then she introduced herself as Ms. Paquette. And I thought it - it wasn't an - same, like, as all the other times, I didn't think today is nothing special. She — it was I thought it was just like a revision — I mean, like, going over Ms. [Tran's] case before so he didn't need to be there.

Myers testified that he obtained instructions from Lam for Paquette to appear instead, but the judge did not accept this. He found this substitution established an appearance of unfairness:

> I agree with the Crown that Mr. Lam has not established any prejudice or actual unfairness to the proceedings arising from Ms. Paquette's conduct of the evidentiary hearing. He has, however, established an appearance of unfairness. Mr. Lam hired Mr. Myers and paid significant legal fees to Mr. Myers for his representation. When Mr. Myers found himself double-booked with another file, he should have applied to adjourn the evidentiary hearing. In the alternative, he should have

obtained clear and voluntary instructions from Mr. Lam that he was content to have Ms. Paquette conduct the hearing. He did neither. I do not believe this conduct falls "within the wide range of reasonable professional assistance".

Mr. Myers did not help matters when he counselled Ms. Paquette to attempt to file transcripts from Ms. Tran's 6 day hearing, without any legal authority and without the Crown's consent. It made Ms. Paquette look like she did not know what she was doing, and gave Mr. Lam reason to question her competence. In reality, her actions were driven by Mr. Myers' cavalier instructions.

Overall, despite Myers' conduct, the judge found that there was no miscarriage of justice:

I agree with the defence that, as an accused person facing serious criminal charges, Mr. Lam was in a vulnerable position. He had no legal expertise and placed complete reliance on Mr. Myers' advice. Mr. Lam was caught between a rock and a hard place when he started to have concerns about whether he was getting effective assistance from Mr. Myers; he had already given many thousands of dollars to Mr. Myers which he could not afford to simply give up and find a new lawyer, who would also require payment. He did not know that he could complain about Mr. Myers' conduct to the Law Society.

Mr. Lam paid significant legal fees to Mr. Myers and deserved much more for that investment than he received. Mr. Myers should have explored the effect that Judge Galati's decision could have on Mr. Lam's case. After 40 years of practice, Mr. Myers should have known that he could not challenge the search of Mr. Lam's residence after a guilty plea, and should have advised Mr. Lam of this before he pled guilty. Finally, Mr. Myers should not have substituted his representation with that of a newly minted lawyer without instructions from Mr. Lam. Mr. Myers' failure to make notes and keep proper records was further indication that he was not operating to the standards required of the legal profession.

Although Mr. Myers failed Mr. Lam several times, those failures did not, in my view, have a significant effect on the ultimate fairness of Mr. Lam's guilty plea. There was no evidence before me that Mr. Lam lost the opportunity to advance a viable defence. There were practical and legal difficulties with a challenge to the search of Mr. Lam's apartment. There were tactical reasons behind Mr. Lam's decision to re-elect to Provincial Court and plead guilty. Although Mr. Myers did not fully inform Mr. Lam of the consequences of pleading guilty, Mr. Lam has not shown he was prejudiced by his failure to be fully informed. Mr. Lam understood that he would be sentenced if Judge Romilly did not find Ms. Tran was entrapped. Understanding that, he still voluntarily agreed to plead guilty. He was not new to the criminal justice system. He pleaded guilty to the same offence in 2007. This time around Mr. Lam had 2 kilograms of cocaine in his apartment. Although he now clearly regrets his actions, he admitted committing the offence when he testified.

After balancing all of these considerations, I find that Mr. Lam has not established that it would be unfair, or appear to be unfair, to uphold his guilty plea. Mr. Lam has shown that Mr. Myers did not fully meet his professional obligations to him. And he has established that Mr. Myers' conduct reflects poorly on the legal profession. But, Mr. Lam has not established that the effect of this conduct was so serious that public confidence in the administration of justice would be shaken if his guilty plea is upheld. In fact, I believe the public confidence in the administration of justice would be shaken if I were to strike Mr. Lam's guilty plea.

It is understandable that Mr. Lam wishes to seek redress for Mr. Myers' failure to provide professional legal assistance. But that redress must be sought through the Law Society, not this Court. The application to strike the guilty plea is dismissed.

NOTES AND QUESTIONS

1. The Court of Appeal agreed with the trial judge on the findings of ineffective representation. However, they found that Lam's guilty plea was uninformed and there was "at least a reasonable possibility [that] the appellant would not have pleaded guilty had he been informed of the consequences of doing so." The Court ordered a new trial (R. v. Lam, [2020] B.C.J. No. 1629, 2020 BCCA 276 at paras. 87, 93 (B.C.C.A.)).

2. Should the Law Society of British Columbia have pursued disciplinary action against Mr. Myers?

Scenario Three

Roma refugees from Hungary amounted to the largest group of refugee claimants in Canada in 2010 and 2011. Between 2008 and 2012, only 7.1% of Roma claims were successful, with 59.8% being abandoned by the claimants before their completion. A study cited quality of legal representation as a major factor that hindered successful refugee claims.[50] The study found that refugee claimants whose lawyer represented 10 or fewer clients were 2.9 times more likely to succeed than claimants whose lawyer handled 200 or more clients. Unfortunately for the claimants, more than half of all Roma refugee cases were handled by eight lawyers, each with over 50 clients. 1,139 cases (34.1% of all applications) were handled by three Toronto-area lawyers.[51]

Viktor Hohots was the top lawyer for Roma refugees in terms of cases handled between 2008 and 2012. He took on 504 cases in this four-year period. 403 of those were withdrawn or abandoned. He was subsequently accused by the Law Society of failing to competently serve his clients. The Personal Information Form (PIF) is one of the most important documents for a refugee claim. The committee expressed serious concern about the level of service Mr. Hohots was able to provide to each client. The tribunal used this example to illustrate the problem: "the notes to file of the first meeting with the client and his family. . .consist of four handwritten lines, and on this basis the Lawyer's office prepared and submitted a PIF. . .Shortly before the hearing, Mr. Hohots' junior associate met with the principal claimant and took 11 pages of notes".[52] Among these lapses, the tribunal found that "in some cases random PIF narratives were relied upon that did not relate to the clients' own circumstances".[53] Mr. Hohots frequently delegated cases to a non-lawyer translator,

---

[50] Julianna Beaudoin, Jennifer Danch & Sean Rehaag, "No Refuge: Hungarian Romani Refugee Claimants in Canada" (2015) 11:3 Osgoode Hall L.J. at 45.

[51] Julianna Beaudoin, Jennifer Danch & Sean Rehaag, "No Refuge: Hungarian Romani Refugee Claimants in Canada" (2015) 11:3 Osgoode Hall L.J. at 49.

[52] *Law Society of Upper Canada v. Hohots*, [2015] L.S.D.D. No. 83, 2015 ONLSTH 72 at para. 45 (Ont. Law Society Tribunal).

[53] *Law Society of Upper Canada v. Hohots*, [2015] L.S.D.D. No. 83, 2015 ONLSTH 72 at para. 67 (Ont. Law Society Tribunal).

who would represent clients at hearings. Only 1.2% of Mr. Hohots' clients successfully claimed refugee status.

Erzsebet Jaszi took on 80 Roma refugee cases between 2008 and 2012. Ms. Jaszi would often have her clients sign blank PIFs before filling in the details herself from the client's written narrative. Ms. Jaszi occasionally delegated the task of communicating with clients to a translator, despite holding herself out as a Hungarian-speaking lawyer. In other cases, "the PIFs filed by the Lawyer on behalf of her clients reflected her lack of time and attention to detail...The PIFs were all missing significant details of persecution...The narratives were brief and general, typically six to seven paragraphs, when they should have been complete and detailed".[54] Incomplete PIFs resulted in the issuance of a Notice of Abandonment or a Notice to Appear served on Ms. Jaszi and one of her clients. Ms. Jaszi ignored both the notices and her clients' phone calls seeking assistance and explanations. When one client confronted Ms. Jaszi in her office about the Notice of Abandonment, she said she would "take care of it". The clients only learned she did not "take care of it" in the fall of 2010, when their applications to renew health coverage were denied because their refugee claims had been abandoned. When they finally were able to speak to Ms. Jaszi, she told them there was nothing she could do for them. She would not explain what happened to their file.[55] Only 1.1% of Ms. Jaszi's clients were successful in their applications.[56]

NOTES AND QUESTIONS

1. Do you think a lack of legal knowledge was the primary reason for Mr. Hohots' and Ms. Jaszi's behaviour? Were there other factors that prevented them from effectively serving their clients?

2. If you were in their position, how would you balance upholding your reputation as a prolific and experienced refugee lawyer with your obligation to provide quality service?

3. How might the identity and socio-economic circumstances of Roma refugee claimants affect the quality of service they receive?

4. Do you believe that the behaviour of Mr. Hohots and Ms. Jaszi amounted to misconduct? If so, what penalty would you impose?

5. Is it the role of the Law Society Discipline Committee to protect refugees from their lawyers? If so, how can it best accomplish that goal in these two cases?

Scenario Four

Various elements of the Roman Catholic Church in Canada are parties to the Indian

---

[54] *Law Society of Upper Canada v. Jaszi*, [2015] L.S.D.D. No. 164, 2015 ONLSTH 132 at para. 32 (Ont. Law Society Tribunal).

[55] *Law Society of Upper Canada v. Jaszi*, [2015] L.S.D.D. No. 164, 2015 ONLSTH 132 at para. 39 (Ont. Law Society Tribunal).

[56] Julianna Beaudoin, Jennifer Danch & Sean Rehaag, "No Refuge: Hungarian Romani Refugee Claimants in Canada" (2015) 11:3 Osgoode Hall L.J. at 49.

Residential Schools Settlement Agreement. As part of the settlement, the Catholic entities were required to pay $29 million in cash (deducting "reasonable administration costs"), to contribute in-kind services with a value of $25 million, and to make best efforts over seven years to raise $25 million through a Canada-wide fundraising campaign.

In 2013, Canada sought directions from the Saskatchewan Court of Queen's Bench as to whether the Catholic entities could deduct $1.6 million in legal fees as "reasonable administration costs". In June 2014, the Catholic entities' counsel, Gordon Kuski, was instructed to settle the dispute for the cash payments, as well as all other obligations arising from the settlement agreement (the in-kind services and the fundraising target). The Catholic position was that they had fulfilled the obligations for in-kind services, and had executed their best efforts to fundraise, but had come up with only $3.4 million in donations.

Mr. Kuski wrote a letter to Alexander Gay, Canada's counsel, making an offer to "settle all matters between the parties". Mr. Kuski requested that the government issue a release and indemnity for the Catholic entities, confirming that they had discharged their obligations under the agreement. In exchange, he offered $1.2 million in cash. Mr. Gay replied that the government would accept $1.2 million as payment, and that the only thing to be resolved was "the paperwork and the wording on the release documents". Mr. Gay later said that he believed he was only negotiating for the release of the cash obligation, not the in-kind services or fundraising. As the two counsel wrote back and forth on the wording, Mr. Gay realized that the Catholic entities were seeking a release of all obligations, including the fundraising target.

Negotiations broke down, and the Catholic entities sought to enforce the settlement. The Court held that a reasonable bystander would conclude that the parties had reached consensus on all essential terms, and the settlement was therefore binding. Mr. Gay had accidentally released the Catholic entities from $21.6 million in contributions to healing programs for residential school survivors, in exchange for payment of $1.2 million that was already owed by the churches.[57]

NOTES AND QUESTIONS

1. Does Mr. Gay's conduct amount to incompetence or inadequate service as defined by the *Model Code*? If yes, should he be disciplined? If yes, by whom?

2. If you were the lawyer for the Catholic entities, and it was the government who made this offer, would you have immediately accepted it? Would you simply be pursuing your duties of loyalty and commitment to your client, or might there be a hint of sharp practice?

---

[57] *Fontaine v. Canada (Attorney General)*, [2015] S.J. No. 473, 2015 SKQB 220 (Sask. Q.B.); Gloria Galloway, "Legal misstep lets Catholic Church off the hook for residential schools compensation" (April 17, 2016), online: *The Globe and Mail* http:// www.theglobeandmail.com/ news/politics/legal-misstep-lets-catholics-off-hook-for-residential-schools-compensation/article29657424/.

3. Do you think that Mr. Kuski should advise the church on their moral, as well as legal, obligations?

Scenario Five

You are a general practitioner. A potential client comes to your office asking that you draft a will for less than $700. The client has an adult daughter who is severely disabled. You know, in general terms, that there are important issues related to leaving money to a disabled person in terms of that person's ability to continue to access government services. However, you do not know how those issues are resolved, and given your hourly rate you cannot find that out and draft a will for $700. Do you take the client? Assume that they have told you that if you cannot help them for that price they will simply use a "do your own will" kit.

Scenario Six

Assume you are a Crown Attorney. Because of a lack of funding, your office is understaffed by 25% with the consequence that a significant number of lawyers are carrying approximately 500 cases at any one time. You and your colleagues have decided that because of the excess of files you cannot properly prepare for trials, especially in the context of disclosure. Considered in light of the *Model Code* are you in breach of any ethical obligations? If so, what are your options?[58]

Scenario Seven

Cally is a recent law school graduate who was the top mooter in their class. Cally also has multiple sclerosis which means that they are not physically capable of working for a full eight-hour day. Cally wants to pursue a litigation practice. Does Cally's circumstance raise questions about their competence to be a civil litigator?

Scenario Eight

Law Societies now recognize that some of the problems associated with incompetence and poor-quality service are closely connected with issues of stress, depression and perhaps substance abuse. As a consequence, Law Societies often offer "Risk and Practice Management Programs", which provide "confidential support and assistance to members", as well as "Legal Assistance Programs" to help members and their families "experiencing difficulties in their personal lives". This is clearly a positive assumption of responsibility by Law Societies. But it raises an ethical question, addressed in the following scenario:

Assume that you are a member of a Legal Assistance Program and, in the course of providing counselling to a lawyer with a substance abuse problem, you realize that the lawyer's conduct is clearly harming their client's financial interests. Do you have a duty to report such conduct to the Law Society? Does Commentary [4] to Rule 7.1-3 of the *Model Code* assist you?

Does the *Model Code* strike the appropriate balance in this Commentary?

Scenario Nine

In addition to the *Model Code* provisions on Competence and Quality of Service,

---

[58] "Crown Attorneys Help on its Way", *Canadian Lawyer* (May 2007) at 7.

section 163.2(1) of the *Income Tax Act* subjects lawyers to a regulatory sanction if they advise a client in a manner that demonstrates "indifference" to compliance with the Act or a "willful, reckless or wanton disregard for the law". Do you agree with the standard articulated in the Act? Is it too high or too low? Provide reasons for your position. Is it appropriate to confer such regulatory authority over lawyers to the Canada Revenue Agency?[59]

Scenario Ten

Deanne Sowter has proposed the following Commentary be added to Rule 3.1-2 of the *Model Code*:

> [7C] Given the variety of cases that may involve family violence . . . it is impossible to set down guidelines that would anticipate every possible circumstance in which family violence may be relevant. Training in screening for family violence is a type of knowledge relevant to many areas of practice, and it is an important skill. Family violence may be a factor for family lawyers, corporate lawyers, bankruptcy lawyers, tort lawyers, real property lawyers, employment lawyers, immigration lawyers, and criminal lawyers. Family law lawyers are most likely to encounter matters involving family violence and therefore competence in the practice of family law includes the knowledge and skill required to screen for family violence. This is an ethical consideration and is distinct from the standard of care that a tribunal would invoke for purposes of determining negligence.

Does the obligation of competent service require that Canadian lawyers screen for family violence?

Identify strengths and weaknesses of Sowter's proposal.

[c] Cultural Competence

A significant omission from traditional definitions of competence is cultural competence.[60] The provisions of the *Model Code* are quite technical in nature. They largely do not address the relational and contextual nature of legal practice. There is nothing explicit in the *Model Code* about cultural competence. Arguably the requirement of cultural competence is implicit in Rule 2.1 (Integrity) and Rule 6.3 (Harassment and Discrimination) of the *Model Code*. Please review these rules. In your opinion do they implicitly reference cultural competence?

---

[59] See *Guindon v. Canada*, [2015] S.C.J. No. 41, 2015 SCC 41, [2015] 3 S.C.R. 3 (S.C.C.).

[60] See, *e.g.*, Rose Voyvodic, "Lawyers Meet the Social Context: Understanding Cultural Competence" (2005) 84:Special Issue Can. Bar Rev. 563; Russell G. Pearce, "White Lawyering: Rethinking Race, Lawyer Identity and Rule of Law" (2005) 73:5 Fordham L. Rev. 2081; Carolyn Copps Hartley & Carrie J. Petrucci, "Practicing Culturally Competent Therapeutic Jurisprudence: A Collaboration Between Social Work and Law" (2004) 14:1 Wash. U. J.L. & Pol'y 133; Cynthia Pay, "Teaching Cultural Competency in Legal Clinics" (2014) 23:1 J.L. & Soc. Pol'y 188; Mayia Thao & Mona Tawatao, "Developing Cultural Competence in Legal Services Practice" (2004) 38 Cl. R. 244. For an insightful analysis of the creation of 'cultural information' by courts and legal processes and the critical need for avoiding simplistic approaches to 'cultural sensitivity training' for judges and lawyers see Sonia N. Lawrence, "Cultural (in)Sensitivity: The Dangers of a Simplistic Approach to Culture in the Courtroom" (2001) 13:1 C.J.W.L. 107.

There are debates over what cultural, or intercultural, competence means and how it can be attained, suggesting that perhaps what it means is best determined within particular contexts. Voyvodic argued that cultural competence has three dimensions:

> KNOWLEDGE: about how "cultural" differences affect client experiences of the legal process as well as their interactions with lawyers;

> SKILLS: through self-monitoring, to identify how assumptions and stereotypes influence their own thinking and behaviour, as well as the thinking and behaviour of others, and to work to lessen the effect of these influences;

> ATTITUDE: awareness of themselves as a cultural being and of the harmful effects of power and privilege; and the willingness and desire to practice competently in the pursuit of justice.[61]

At the very outset, this formulation invites attention to the ways in which we understand culture. Please read the following excerpt from a Canadian Bar Review article and answer the questions that follow:

POOJA PARMAR

"Reconciliation and Ethical Lawyering: Some Thoughts on Cultural Competence"

(2019) 97:3 Canadian Bar Review 526-557 [footnotes omitted]

We live in a culturally diverse world, one in which people and ideas have been traveling for centuries. And even though it is not always easy to define 'culture', we have come to understand it generally as a set of beliefs, practices, and histories that inform our assumptions about, and shape our reactions to, the world around us. Culture is also understood as a source of individual and group identity. Cultural identity, as any other identity, does not, however, represent or shape the entirety of human experience. Identities are also always contestable, even though we cannot disregard them. That is because, regardless of whether or not we can find any essence that lies at the core of an identity, being associated with a particular cultural identity has meaning for those who bear it, and even more significantly, these associations have consequences in terms of how others treat the bearer of a cultural identity. It is therefore important to acknowledge difference. It is, however, equally important to recognize that every invocation of real or perceived difference is not in pursuit of justice. Some invocations of identity and difference are shaped by a desire to be heard and seen. Others are driven by desires to maintain existing relations of power and systems of oppression.

In the context of cultural difference, it becomes necessary to ask what understanding of culture, and what approach to difference, informs attempts to be culturally competent professionals. We must ask whether, in invoking cultural difference, we are relying on, or worse, reinforcing stereotypes deployed to understand the 'other' in ways that are problematic, or whether our approach to difference acknowledges that human beings are culturally complex, and that individual and group identities are shaped by multiple social, economic, professional, and other cultures both clients and lawyers inhabit simultaneously and at different times in their lives. [. . .]

---

[61] Rose Voyvodic, "Lawyers Meet the Social Context: Understanding Cultural Competence" (2005) 84:Special Issue Can. Bar Rev. 563 at 582.

Treating cultural competence as a critical skill requires lawyers to have a deeper understanding of culture and difference and an ability to recognize the consequences of being seen as culturally different for many. It is necessary, for example, to understand how difference is deployed to justify violence. It is important to be able to recognize when and how attacks on a culture are also attacks on a peoples' self-determination. Taking cultural competence seriously also requires critical thinking on how knowledge, including knowledge about cultures, is produced and by whom. It is therefore not simply a matter of 'cultural literacy' or learning about the others' culture as part of cultural competence training.

NOTES AND QUESTIONS

1.   What knowledge of 'culture' and 'difference' do you think a culturally competent lawyer in Canada requires?

2.   To what extent do you think professional competence requires understanding racism and colonialism? Do you think a culturally competent lawyer will think critically about the culture of the legal profession? In what way?

3.   Having considered the 'knowledge' dimension of cultural competence, can you identify specific 'skills' and 'attitudes' it requires? Consider if the following proposal for lawyers to develop "five habits"[62] for culturally competent legal practice offers useful guidance:

    (1)   take note of the differences between the lawyer and the client;

    (2)   map out the case, taking into account the different cultural understandings of the lawyer and the client;

    (3)   brainstorm additional reasons for puzzling client behaviour;

    (4)   identify and solve pitfalls in lawyer-client communications to allow the lawyer to see the client's story through the client's eyes; and

    (5)   examine previous failed interactions with the client and develop proactive ways to ensure those interactions do not take place in the future.[63]

Do you agree with these suggestions? Would you add to, or subtract anything from, this list?

An issue that has come to the fore recently in the context of competence is representation of transgender (trans) and nonbinary people[64] who face unique barriers navigating the legal system. This is true both when their legal issues are

---

[62] See Sue Bryant, "The Five Habits: Building Cross-Cultural Competence in Lawyers" (2001) 8:1 Clinical L. Rev. 33.

[63] Rose Voyvodic, "Lawyers Meet the Social Context: Understanding Cultural Competence" (2005) 84:Special Issue Can. Bar Rev. 563 at 586.

[64] While nonbinary people often identify themselves as being trans, not all nonbinary people identity in this way. Furthermore, the needs of nonbinary people are also often overlooked in general conversations about trans people. The authors therefore use the phrase "trans and nonbinary" to be as inclusive as possible. For more information, see "Non-Binary

specifically related to gender and transition, as well as to more general legal matters that the wider public also encounters. There are several reasons for this: many trans and nonbinary people face severe (and often violent) harassment and discrimination because of their gender, preventing them from accessing the legal help they require. Many trans and nonbinary people who require legal services are minors with unsupportive parents, leading to sensitive dynamics between legal personnel and the child's parents. Furthermore, trans and nonbinary people often have unique needs that their lawyers may not understand due to a lack of training in the relevant laws around gender identity and expression, and appropriate education on gender issues in general. This problem is particularly pronounced for trans and nonbinary people because it is only very recently that acceptance and understanding of gender diversity has begun to take place in Canadian society. Trans and nonbinary people of colour experience even more legal challenges because they often face racist violence and harassment in addition to transphobia.

In order to properly represent trans and nonbinary clients, lawyers must educate themselves in this area of law and adopt humility and respect when it comes to learning about marginalized gender identities. Whether or not a lawyer considers themselves educated on matters of gender and transition, it is important to listen to the specific needs of their client and avoid making assumptions based on common narratives about trans people.

In his article "Trans Competent Lawyering", Samuel Singer discusses some practical steps lawyers can take to respect their trans and nonbinary clients.[65] These steps include respecting a client's privacy regarding their legal name and legal sex and, whenever possible, using the client's chosen name and true gender on documents. Client intake forms should allow people to write in their gender rather than having to select a box, as this is most inclusive. When in court, a lawyer should ensure to the best of their ability that their client is not misgendered or called by an incorrect name. Lawyers should also familiarize themselves with the legal process to changing identity documents and the impact this might have on other aspects of their client's legal circumstances, such as immigration status.

QUESTIONS

1. In light of the foregoing readings, what are some situations where the issue of cultural competency might arise? Do you have any specific suggestions as to how you might need to prepare yourself to respond to these situations?

2. Courts in British Columbia have recently adopted a policy asking lawyers and parties to state their pronouns when they are introducing themselves or their clients in court.[66] This policy decision is a first for Canadian courts. Do you think this is an adequate step in creating a more inclusive

---

Inclusion", online: *LGBT Foundation* https://lgbt.foundation/who-we-help/trans-people/non-binary.

[65] Samuel Singer, "Trans Competent Lawyering" (2019) in Joanna Radbord, ed., *LGBTQ2 + Law: Practice Issues and Analysis* (Toronto: Emond Publishing, 2019).

[66] Zena Olijnyk, "B.C. courts adopt policy of asking for preferred pronouns to encourage

environment for people of all genders? What additional measures could courts take to improve the court experience for trans and nonbinary people?

3.   Should cultural competence education be mandatory? For some lawyers? For all lawyers? For law students? For law teachers? Are arguments in favour of cultural competency education reinforced by Canada's commitment in the *Charter* to embrace equality rights and norms of multiculturalism? Does the following case influence your thinking on these questions?

R. v. FRASER

[2011] N.S.J. No. 400, 2011 NSCA 70
(N.S.C.A., J.W.S. Saunders, L.L. Oland and D.R. Beveridge JJ.A.)

J.W.S. SAUNDERS J.A.:— The appellant is a former high school teacher who was accused of various sexual improprieties by a former student.

After a trial by judge and jury he was convicted of touching for a sexual purpose contrary to s. 153(a) of the *Criminal Code of Canada*, R.S.C. 1985, c. C-46 and sentenced to nine months' incarceration followed by one year probation and 50 hours of community service work and a SOIRA order.

He asks that the verdict be overturned and a new trial ordered on the grounds that he did not receive effective assistance from his trial counsel, and that the Crown breached its obligation to provide the defence with ongoing disclosure.

For the reasons that follow I would allow the appeal, set aside the conviction and order a new trial. As to the first ground of appeal, I have reached the conclusion that the legal advice and representation Mr. Fraser received was ineffective. He was denied his constitutional right to make full answer and defence and a miscarriage of justice occurred. As to the second ground of appeal, I am satisfied the Crown met its disclosure obligations.

*   *   *   *   *

On appeal, the appellant's trial counsel [Mr. Scaravelli] was granted formal intervenor status. The scope of his participation was limited to filing a factum, and an affidavit on the fresh evidence application, and to presenting oral argument restricted to the allegation concerning his competence, but not with respect to any aspect of the merits of the appeal.

*   *   *   *   *

Issues

Mr. Fraser has identified a host of specific actions, omissions or missteps which he says proves beyond any doubt that the legal representation he received from his trial counsel was ineffective and resulted in a miscarriage of justice.

The appellant's outline of complaints is detailed and comprehensive. I wish to list

---

diversity, inclusion", *Canadian Lawyer* (January 5, 2019), online: [perma.cc/2NUX-X4CF].

them verbatim before turning to a consideration of the law, the merits of such serious allegations, and their consequences:

Omissions

(i)   failing to advise the Appellant that he had the right under *R. v. Parks* to challenge prospective jurors for cause as to whether their ability to judge the evidence without bias, prejudice or partiality would be affected by the fact that the accused is a black man and the complainant is a white teenage female - especially given the concerns expressed by the Appellant to Mr. Scaravelli during their first meeting on September 23, 2008 and again both before and after jury selection on December 7, 2009 ("the Parks issue"). . .

(iv)   failing to adequately prepare for trial, be it as a result of his failure to: (a) conduct an effective cross-examination of the complainant at the preliminary hearing for use at trial; (b) understand the case for the defence; (c) interview potential defence witnesses; (d) know the relevant law; (e) seek disclosure of the notes of Crown Attorney Alonzo Wright relating to the complainant's "new information"; and/or (f) any combination of the foregoing such that material issues relevant to the Appellant's defence at trial were either not explored sufficiently or at all;

(v)   failing to request disclosure from the Crown of Alonzo Wright's notes from his telephone conversation with the complainant and, failing production by the Crown, to make a disclosure application;

(vi)   failing to request that the Crown obtain a formal statement from the complainant with respect to the "new information";

(vii) failing to advise the Appellant of his right to request an adjournment of his trial as a result of the "new information" disclosed by the Crown;

(viii) failing to understand the importance of the time line evidence and to cross examine the complainant and adduce defence evidence at trial with respect thereto;

(ix)   failing to request a copy of the statement given by Lisa Fraser to the police on Friday, December 11, 2009. . .

Analysis

First Ground of Appeal: Ineffective Assistance of Counsel

Here again the law is well-settled. As this Court said in *West, supra*:

[268] The principles to be applied when considering a complaint of ineffective assistance of counsel, are well known. Absent a miscarriage of justice, the question of counsel's competence is a matter of professional ethics and is not normally something to be considered by the courts. Incompetence is measured by applying a reasonableness standard. There is a strong presumption that counsel's conduct falls within a wide range of reasonable, professional assistance. There is a heavy burden upon the appellant to show that counsel's acts or omissions did not meet a standard of reasonable, professional judgment. Claims of ineffective representation are approached with caution by appellate courts. Appeals are not intended to serve as a kind of forensic autopsy of defence counsel's performance at trial. [. . .]

[269] One takes a two-step approach when assessing trial counsel's competence:

first, the appellant must demonstrate that the conduct or omissions amount to incompetence, and second, that the incompetence resulted in a miscarriage of justice. As Major J., observed in *B.(G.D.), supra*, at para. 26-29, in most cases it is best to begin with an inquiry into the prejudice component. If the appellant cannot demonstrate prejudice resulting from the alleged ineffective assistance of counsel, it will be unnecessary to address the issue of the competence.

After carefully considering the totality of circumstances in this case, I am satisfied that the appellant has demonstrated that the conduct and failures of his trial counsel amount to incompetence and that the incompetence resulted in a miscarriage of justice, necessitating a new trial.

Nothing in these reasons should be taken as suggesting that any one of counsel's failures here would, independently, establish a claim of ineffective counsel in another case. Every situation is different and requires a close examination of all of the circumstances before such a finding can be made.

Rather than analyze each and every act or omission listed by the appellant in his factum, I prefer to examine the legal representation afforded the appellant in two areas. First, I will deal with challenge for cause. Then I will undertake a broader inquiry in the area of trial preparation and performance.

Challenge for Cause

The appellant complains that despite repeated and specific inquiries, he was never advised by his trial counsel that he had a statutory right to challenge potential jurors for cause on the basis that he was black, the complainant was white, and that jurors might discriminate against him on account of those circumstances. After a thorough review of the record, I am satisfied that the appellant's complaint is justified.

No informed discussion regarding challenge for cause in a potentially race-based case can occur without considering "the *Parks* issue".

*   *   *   *   *

After a careful and detailed analysis, Doherty, J.A., on behalf of the unanimous court, wrote at para. 28:

> 28 I turn now to the principles applicable to the challenge for cause process. The accused's right to challenge for cause based on partiality is essential to both the constitutional right to a fair trial and the constitutional right, in cases where the accused is liable to five or more years' imprisonment, to trial by jury. An impartial jury is a crucial first step in the conduct of a fair trial: . . . The accused's statutory right to challenge potential jurors for cause based on partiality is the only direct means an accused has to secure an impartial jury. The significance of the challenge process to both the appearance of fairness, and fairness itself, must not be underestimated.

> (Underlining mine)

Justice Doherty concluded his reasons at para. 93:

> 93 I have no reason to doubt the fairness of this trial, the impartiality of this jury or the validity of their verdict. However, the appellant was denied his statutory right to challenge for cause. That right is essential to the appearance of fairness and the integrity of the trial. The improper denial of this right necessitates the quashing of

the conviction without any demonstration of actual prejudice: [. . .]

(Underlining mine)

Parks has since been endorsed by the Supreme Court of Canada in *R. v. Williams*, [1998] 1 S.C.R. 1128 and *R. v. Spence*, 2005 SCC 71.

Against that backdrop I will consider what transpired here. Mr. Fraser was arrested and charged on September 23, 2008. He and his family then immediately proceeded to the intervenor's office where he gave his lawyer an overview of the allegations against him as they were known to him at the time.

There was never any formal contract of legal representation. The intervenor told the appellant that his fee would be "$25,000.00 up front". It took the appellant and his relatives some time to raise the money which they turned over to the intervenor in November.

The appellant expressed his profound concerns surrounding the race issue immediately and repeatedly. As he states in his affidavit:

> I explained to Mr. Scaravelli that, being black, I was concerned and nervous about a jury. . . . He also told me . . . 'don't worry about it, I got lots of black guys off with all white juries before' . . .

It is clear from the pre-trial conference report which the intervenor filed with the court that he did not consider the *Parks* issue to be an issue.

Following jury selection the appellant told the intervenor: "I don't like this" referring to the fact that the jury was all white. To this he swears that the intervenor told him that "there was nothing we can do about it" and repeated what he had told him during their initial meeting at his office on September 23, 2008, namely, that he had "gotten lots of black guys off before with all white juries".

The appellant's version of events is corroborated by his wife and his mother.

The appellant's affidavit goes on to say:

> 37. Mr. Scaravelli never told me that I had the right, as I have since been told by Mr. Arnold that I had, to challenge potential jurors for cause on the basis that I was black, the complainant was white and that they may discriminate against me because I was black; notwithstanding that I had raised this very point with Mr. Scaravelli when I met with him on the day I was charged.

> 38. Had Mr. Scaravelli told me that I had this right I would have definitely asked him to challenge each juror for cause on this basis.

(Underlining mine)

On May 31, 2010, Mr. Josh Arnold, Q.C., one of the appellant's co-appeal counsel, wrote to the intervenor and asked:

Challenge for Cause

> 11. What discussions did you have with Mr. Fraser regarding a challenge for cause?

On June 2, 2010, the intervenor responded:

> 11. Mr. Fraser and I discussed challenges for cause. He wanted to know

whether he could have or expect to have jurors who were his peers i.e. Canadians from his community or elsewhere. I told him he could not insist on that. I <u>advised him that I did not find challenges for cause particularly helpful and more of a waste of time than anything else</u>. The system was set up so that people could go up to the Judge to discuss their reasons for not wanting to be at the Trial. <u>I have my own way of selecting jurors</u>. I have been very successful in the past with jury Trials. The simple system that I use seems to work. Mr. Fraser agreed that I should do whatever I thought was best.

(Underlining mine)

At the appeal hearing, the intervenor was questioned by the panel on this issue. While acknowledging that he had read the *Parks* case, he seemed confused as to whether he had read it before or after the appellant's trial, first saying that he had not read it beforehand, and then changing his evidence to say that he had read it before the appellant's trial. In any event, he admitted that he had never discussed the procedures outlined in the case with the appellant. He also said he had only ever challenged jurors for cause in one other trial.

I have no doubt that the questions raised by the appellant in his discussions with the intervenor were related to his serious concerns about being tried by a jury for a sex related offence where the complainant was a white teenage girl and he was a black school teacher. I am satisfied that the intervenor never meaningfully explained the process or objectives in challenging for cause or reviewed with the complainant his statutory right to challenge for cause based on the principles established in *Parks*.

I find that the intervenor's failure to provide advice to the appellant in response to his client's explicit and perfectly reasonable inquiries, effectively denied him his statutory right to challenge potential jurors for cause. I accept what the appellant says in his affidavit, that had he been told he had this right, he would have asked his lawyer to challenge each juror for cause on the basis that he was black and the complainant was white and that jurors might discriminate against him for those reasons.

* * * * *

While trial counsel's failing in and of itself would justify a new trial, I think it is important to undertake a somewhat broader inquiry into the area of trial preparation and performance, with specific attention paid to certain critical features.

Trial Preparation and Performance

The criticisms that follow are not intended to grade counsel's performance or serve as a primer for best practices. Such matters are generally the preserve of the Bar. I recognize that most cases dealing with ineffective assistance claims relate to trial counsel's performance during the trial itself; whereas appeals based on an alleged failure to investigate and prepare are relatively unusual. . . .

I also recognize that busy trial lawyers have many other demands placed upon their professional and personal lives and do not have unlimited time and resources to expertly manage every case on their dockets. Their performance should never be gauged on a standard of perfection, nor subjected to a forensic audit whenever unfavourable results occur. The effectiveness of counsel is to be evaluated on an objective standard through the eyes of a reasonable person such that all an accused can expect of their defence counsel is a level of competence based on a standard of reasonableness. In other words, the lawyer is "required to bring reasonable care, skill and knowledge to the performance of the professional service which he has undertaken." (*Central Trust Co. v. Rafuse*, [1986] 2 S.C.R. 147 at para. 57.)

The appellant has met the burden of showing that the level of careful investigation and preparation one would reasonably expect of any criminal trial lawyer in such a serious matter simply did not occur in his case. Considering the variety of examples identified in these reasons, it is obvious that the legal representation afforded the appellant was largely ineffective in critical areas.

I propose to address those failings by considering several discrete examples.

First, I will review the intervenor's declared strategy. Then I will discuss his refusal to consider the importance of Antoine Fraser's wife as a material witness. Next I will comment upon his failure to effectively challenge the Crown's case on material issues, in ways that should have been obvious. Next I will describe counsel's failure to interview and call as defence witnesses persons who could be expected to seriously discredit the Crown's case. I will conclude with a discussion concerning a misguided s. 276 application, and a failure to seek an adjournment when first told the complainant had provided important last minute information to the Crown.

The intervenor described his trial strategy in his June 2, 2010, letter to Mr. Arnold as follows:

> The Trial strategy was not to question the complainant on the specific allegations of sexual assault. My strategy was to promote collateral issues, not touching her claim of specific sexual acts. In my view, you cannot win a sexual assault case that way. In addition, Antoine Fraser was denying that he had sex with the complainant so there were no new allegations to meet. . . .

I will not attempt to ascribe meaning to this statement, but if the objective were to "promote collateral issues" then surely it ought to have involved carefully identifying and prioritizing what those collateral issues were; establishing the factual basis by which they could be asserted; and then finding and properly preparing defence witnesses whose evidence would then discredit (or at the very least raise a reasonable doubt about) the key issues supporting the Crown's case.

When questioned at the appeal hearing the intervenor said that his strategy "in sexual assault cases where there's a young victim" would be to "impeach the young victim's statement" but "not necessarily" to "enhance the credibility and the believability" of his own client. When asked to explain this approach, he said that all of his efforts would be to impeach the victim of the alleged sexual assault. But because this was a case that would likely turn on the issue of credibility, he would be reluctant to produce other witnesses who might support the appellant because, to his way of thinking, the jury might conclude that the appellant "was trying to damage control" such that the jury "might dwell on damage control too much".

This was the intervenor's reason for not calling the appellant's wife, Lisa Fraser, as a defence witness. During their various meetings at the intervenor's office, the appellant's wife repeatedly told the intervenor that she could disprove parts of the complainant's allegations. When asked to explain why he refused to consider her as an important material witness the intervenor replied:

> Because I was not going to call her as a witness. There was no upside to call her as a witness, only a down side. . . . Because I talked to her enough really to know that I would not be putting her on the stand. There was no up side to it, there was no advantage to it, only a huge disadvantage, in my opinion.

Apparently the intervenor applied the same "strategy" in either not calling other witnesses who could have supported the appellant by providing evidence which could either corroborate his version of events or seriously discredit the complainant's, or failing to seriously interview persons whose names had been provided by the appellant and his family to see if their evidence would be helpful.

I cannot conceive that a defence "theory", or its application, such as I have just described would ever pass muster on a reasonableness standard. It seems clear that trial counsel's mind was made up from the very beginning that he would never call the appellant's wife as a witness at his trial. Yet that decision was taken without ever having conducted an effective interview, from which he would have discovered the host of significant facts upon which Mrs. Fraser would have been able to give material evidence which would have <u>both</u> lent credence to certain aspects of her husband's testimony, and seriously discredited the complainant's evidence.

By closing his mind to the real value of Lisa Fraser's evidence, and neglecting to take steps to effectively interview her and properly prepare her as a witness, trial counsel seriously prejudiced his client's defence. His expressed concern that Mrs. Fraser would undoubtedly be questioned by Crown counsel during cross-examination as to the times her husband <u>could</u> have been alone with the complainant (for example, in driving her home after babysitting), such that she would be forced to concede that these incidents <u>could</u> have occurred without her knowledge, can hardly be a serious "down side" given the appellant's own testimony that there were occasions when he and the complainant were alone. In my opinion the real risk would be the natural tendency for the jury to wonder why Mrs. Fraser was not being called as a witness in her husband's defence.

The appellant gave a cell phone to the complainant. The circumstances surrounding it being given to J.M.; the manner and frequency of use; and the content of messages sent from one to the other all became significant during the trial. It is likely that the appellant's wife had material evidence to give relating to the phone, its use, and its origins which could reasonably be expected to have helped her husband's case.

Had trial counsel properly interviewed the appellant's wife he would have known that her evidence would contradict and could discredit the complainant's testimony in several other material respects including: that she had met the complainant a number of times, and had invited her into their home on occasions when she babysat their children; that she was present when a photograph was taken of the complainant holding the Frasers' young baby; and that it was her idea to purchase a cell phone for the complainant and that she and her husband had given that to her as a present.

At the trial, Crown counsel recognized that Mrs. Fraser was a material witness. This was the very reason the Crown attorneys instructed a police officer to take a formal statement from Mrs. Fraser. Yet the appellant's own lawyer never took the time to interview her, or prepare her as a witness for the defence, somehow caught up in the idea that her value as a witness was negligible, that she "wouldn't be believed", and that her testimony might, in fact, harm her husband's case. After observing Mrs. Fraser testify at the appeal hearing I saw nothing to indicate that she would be anything other than an impressive witness.

Just as troubling is the fact that the intervenor never asked the Crown to produce a copy of the statement Mrs. Fraser gave to the police during the course of the trial. In fact, when questioned at the appeal hearing the intervenor said that he still had not read Mrs. Fraser's statement to the police. . . .

* * * * *

Had the appellant's trial counsel taken the trouble to interview the appellant's aunts, Ms. Viola Fraser and Ms. Rosella Fraser, he would have uncovered important evidence which could have seriously discredited the complainant. This related to evidence given by the complainant's older sister, M.M.

M.M. testified that J.M. had confided in her that she had been involved in a romantic relationship while in Grade 10. M.M. said her sister told her his name was "Ethan" "a 19-year old black guy from *". Later, when M.M. and the complainant went to their doctor's office for birth control pills she said the doctor asked her sister if she was going to go on the pill or not, and asked her if she was sexually active to which M.M. said the complainant answered in the negative. M.M. said she knew that was not the case and so she questioned her sister privately about it later. It was then that M.M. said her sister admitted that she and "Ethan" had had sex and that he had taken the complainant to a clinic in North Preston for a pap test to check for sexually transmitted diseases. The Crown's theory at trial was that "Ethan" was code for Antoine Fraser.

North Preston is a rural community on the eastern edges of the municipality with a rich and proud history as the oldest and largest black community in Canada. The area is populated mainly by African Canadians, many of whom can trace their origins to the immigration of former American slaves during the 18th and 19th centuries.

After retaining the intervenor to represent him at his trial, the appellant provided him with the names of at least 14 witnesses who could testify on his behalf. Among them were his aunts, Ms. Viola Fraser and Ms. Rosella Fraser.

Viola Fraser is 51 years of age and has been employed as a front desk administrator at the North Preston Community Centre ever since it opened in 2004. Her workstation is the focal point of the Community Centre from which she has a clear and unobstructed view of the only entrance to the Centre as well as the waiting room. Included within the facility is a walk-in medical clinic which is the only medical clinic or doctor's office in either East Preston or North Preston. To access the clinic one has to walk directly in front of Ms. Viola Fraser's workstation. Part of her duties is to keep track of the number of persons entering the Community Centre and the Wellness Centre. Her affidavit states in part:

8. Included within the Wellness Centre is a walk-in medical clinic which only operates on Thursdays from 10:00 a.m. to 12:00 noon - 1:00 p.m.

depending upon when Dr. Lorna J. Carter finishes her last patient.

. . .

15.   I have never seen a white person (male or female) attend at the Wellness Centre to see Dr. Carter since I started working at the Community Centre when it opened in 2004.

16.   I have never seen Antoine Fraser attend at the Community Centre for the purpose of seeing Dr. Carter.

17.   I have never seen Antoine Fraser at the Community Centre with a white female for the purpose of attending at the Wellness Centre or for any other purpose.

18.   I have never been told by anyone that they saw Antoine Fraser at the Community Centre with a white female for the purpose of attending at the Wellness Centre or for any other purpose.

Ms. Rosella Fraser is 48 years of age. She obtained her Bachelor of Arts degree in Sociology from St. Mary's University in 1984. She has administered all programs at the Community Centre in North Preston since it opened its doors in 2004. Her affidavit states:

10.   I know everyone who is employed at the Community Centre and they know me.

11.   The door to the Wellness Clinic is always open while the clinic is open. If the door to the Wellness Clinic is closed - the Wellness Clinic is closed.

12.   I have never seen, and I have never heard, of a white person being seen by Dr. Carter at the Wellness Clinic since the Community Centre opened in 2004.

13.   I have never seen, or been told, that Antoine Fraser has seen Dr. Carter at the Wellness Clinic.

14.   I have never seen, or been told, that Antoine Fraser has been at the Community Centre with a white girl/woman, to see Dr. Carter or for any other reason.

Ms. Viola Fraser also testified at the appeal hearing. Her *viva voce* evidence was forceful and persuasive. For example, under cross-examination by counsel for the Crown she said:

Q.   I take it then there's a possibility that you would not see a white female if she went to the Wellness Centre?

A.   If a white person came through the doors of North Preston Community Centre I would have known; everyone in the facility would have known it. . . .

Q.   Okay. But you can't say a white girl has never gone to the Wellness Centre, can you?

A.   No, yeah, I'm saying that a white girl, a white girl and Mr. Fraser did not go to the Wellness Centre. We have white students that come in that work

131

out at the Wellness Centre and they come in and they do greet me and I find out who they are and show them where they need to go. I haven't seen a white girl with Mr. Fraser.

Had sufficient thought and preparation been given to Mr. Fraser's defence, the significance of the evidence of Viola and Rosella Fraser would have been obvious. Their testimony could reasonably be expected to have struck a serious blow to the complainant's credibility based on the version of events she had recounted for her sister, M.M., and which M.M. described in her own testimony at trial. Yet trial counsel's failure to interview Viola and Rosella Fraser and realize how important their evidence would be to the defence, meant that a golden opportunity was lost.

Compounding the error was the fact that the intervenor did nothing to prepare his client for trial. As Mr. Fraser states in his affidavit:

57.   Prior to my taking the stand to testify in my own defence I never met with Mr. Scaravelli to discuss the specifics of my testimony nor did he discuss with me any of the areas of the evidence which I may be cross-examined on by the Crown.

. . .

62.   Mr. Scaravelli did not consult with me prior to making this statement in open Court nor was it my understanding that no further defence evidence would be called. To the contrary, my family and I had arranged for Reverend Desmond to be present for Mr. Scaravelli to speak to and he was, to the best of my knowledge, still in the Courthouse. I also assumed there were other defence witnesses that Mr. Scaravelli had lined up to testify from the list of witnesses I had provided to him. Moreover, I expected that Lisa would be testifying.

When questioned on his affidavit at the appeal hearing, the intervenor was asked:

Q.   You knew the Crown was going to attack him, him being Antoine Fraser, in regards to anything and everything they could . . .

A.   Oh yeah, well, he - I was convinced that Antoine Fraser would hold up because he - he's an educated man, he denied having any relations with this person. He said she was lying about everything. I had no doubt that he would hold up. . . .

The appellant entrusted his case to the care of the intervenor. Sadly, that trust was misplaced. Meaningful communications and updates never happened. During the 15 months that he acted for the appellant the intervenor sent his client *one* letter — it contained but one sentence which simply confirmed the date of trial. . .

. . .

The Notice of Application filed by the intervenor on behalf of the appellant on November 20, 2009, begins:

1.   The Applicant is charged with sexual assault contrary to s. 153(a) of the *Criminal Code* . . .

This is wrong. The appellant stood charged:

That he, between the 1st day of January 2007 and the 1st day of July 2008, at or near Eastern Passage in the County of Halifax, Province of Nova Scotia, being in a position of trust or authority towards [J.M.], a young person, did, for a sexual purpose, touch directly the body of [J.M.] with a part of his body, to wit, his penis, contrary to section 151(a) of the *Criminal Code*.

When cross-examined at the appeal hearing the intervenor admitted that he had borrowed a precedent from someone and failed to revise it to properly reflect his client's circumstances in this case. Even more startling is the fact that the intervenor had his client swear a detailed affidavit in support of the application which contained a great deal of information which could later be used (and, in fact, was used) very effectively by the Crown during its cross-examination of the appellant during the *voir dire*, and at his trial. The fact that the intervenor never prepared the appellant for trial or explained what to expect by way of cross-examination is troubling enough. Effectively forcing his client to "answer" the detailed information contained in his affidavit filed in support of the s. 276.1 application made things worse. . .

One last example will serve to illustrate the harm done by trial counsel's ineffective representation.

As noted earlier in these reasons, it was during a break in the proceedings on the first day of the appellant's trial when the intervenor told him, in the presence of his mother, father and wife, that he had just been advised by the Crown that J.M.'s story had changed. She was now making other allegations and providing further details. I am satisfied Mr. Fraser asked his lawyer whether they could get full particulars and have time to review it, but that he was told the trial had already started and there was nothing they could do about it. When pressed to explain why he had not sought an adjournment, the intervenor said his client "wanted to get this over with and behind him". I suspect that is true of anyone charged with a criminal offence who faces the prospect of a trial. But it is hardly an answer as to why an adjournment on such a serious matter was not requested, or at the very least, meaningfully discussed by the intervenor with his client. . .

*   *   *   *   *

I accept the appellant's evidence that had he been informed by the intervenor of the full extent of the allegations, and had the intervenor explained to him his options including his right to request an adjournment, the appellant would have asked the intervenor to request an adjournment of his trial.

I accept Mr. and Mrs. Fraser's evidence that they became so alarmed by the poor legal representation they were getting that Mrs. Fraser was prompted to call Mr. Josh Arnold, Q.C. to seek his advice as to what options they might have. Mr. Arnold told her that if they were to dismiss the intervenor as their lawyer in mid-trial, there was a chance the trial judge might oblige Mr. Fraser to carry on alone and without counsel. They decided the risk was too great and that they had no choice but to soldier on and see things through to the end. Following his conviction, the Fraser family retained Mr. Arnold for the sentencing hearing and to launch an appeal from conviction. Messrs. Garson and Arnold soon initiated contact with the intervenor and the Crown attorney so as to establish the facts upon which their two principal grounds of appeal could be supported.

While it has not been necessary for me to comment upon each of the complaints levelled by the appellant, the few examples I have addressed clearly establish that trial counsel's actions, omissions, and choices could not have been the result of reasonable preparation or professional judgment. Their cascading effect took away the appellant's chance for a fair trial. As in *R. v. J.B.*, 2011 ONCA 404:

> [6] . . . the cumulative effect of the failures of counsel undermined the reliability of the verdict and resulted in a miscarriage of justice.

* * * * *

Conclusion

There is no pleasure in writing a decision like this one. The reputations of the complainant, the appellant, and the intervenor have all been tarnished by the facts of this case. A new trial will once again subject the parties to the cold, impersonal scrutiny of our criminal justice system.

Mr. Fraser did not receive a fair trial. The legal representation he obtained fell far short of the mark reasonably expected of any defence counsel. His constitutional right to make full answer and defence was compromised. A miscarriage of justice occurred. The verdict is unsafe and must be set aside. I would allow the appeal, overturn the conviction and order a new trial.

* * * * *

NOTES AND QUESTIONS

1. This decision arose in the context of the accused's application for a new trial based on ineffective assistance of counsel. But do the facts also call into question Mr. Scaravelli's cultural competence in terms of knowledge, skills and attitudes?

2. In paragraph 53, Saunders J.A., quotes the *West* decision:

    There is a strong presumption that counsel's conduct falls within a wide range of reasonable, professional assistance. There is a heavy burden upon the appellant to show counsel's acts or omissions did or did not meet a standard of reasonable professional judgment. Claims of ineffective representation are approached with caution by appellate courts.

    Independent of the technical question of judicial standard of review, in a society such as Canada, where Black, Indigenous, and other people of colour are radically overrepresented in both the criminal justice system and the prisons, is such judicial deference to lawyers appropriate? If so, why? If not, why not?

3. Should the Nova Scotia Barristers' Society have investigated and laid discipline charges against Mr. Scaravelli? If so, what would be the appropriate charges and proposed penalty? If not, why not?

4. Do you think that Mr. Scaravelli's conduct may, in part, be explained by "unconscious bias"? Over the course of the last two decades, psychologists have been developing implicit association tests (IATs) to help identify how unconscious biases pervade many of our decisions. The most significant of these has been the Race IAT, which has been taken by millions of people.

It can be found at: https://implicit.harvard.edu/implicit/user/agg/blindspot/ indexrk.htm. Would you be willing to take the test? If so, why? If not, why not? If you have taken the test, would you recommend it to other law students? Do you think the test should be mandatory for law students? In light of the *Fraser* case, do you think the IAT should be mandatory for all lawyers?[67]

Scenario Eleven

You have been retained by three young Black women who have been charged with possession of stolen goods. In the course of the interviews, they tell you that they were pulled over while driving an expensive car on Highway 401, just outside of Toronto. They were not speeding or driving erratically in any way. The police conducted a search of the car and found the allegedly stolen goods in the trunk. Does this situation raise any issues of cultural competence? What sorts of questions would you raise with these clients that you would not raise with other clients? Do you have concerns about being perceived to be "playing the race card"?[68]

Scenario Twelve

Assume you are a lawyer with a credit union. You are approached by an organization called the Canadian-Islamic Housing Corp. to develop a mortgage program that is compliant with Sharia law. What issues does this raise for you? Identify the steps you would take to determine if you are competent to provide legal advice.[69]

Scenario Thirteen

You are employed at a legal aid clinic. A recent immigrant to Canada comes into your office seeking advice. They reveal that their spouse, another immigrant, was laid off from work. Now the family is under considerable financial strain and their spouse has become abusive. The potential client is staunchly against filing a

---

[67] Christine Jolls & Cass R. Sunstein, "The Law of Implicit Bias" (2006) 94 Cal. L.R. 969; R. Richard Banks, Jennifer L. Eberhardt & Lee Ross, "Discrimination and Implicit Bias in a Racially Unequal Society" (2006) 94:4 Cal. L.R. 1169. Taking an IAT causes a person to be confronted with their own implicit biases. This confrontation can change their implicit biases for at least a short period of time. Because of this, there has been interest in whether changes in implicit bias can create change in behaviour. However, a 2019 meta-analysis of 494 studies about IATs found that, while implicit bias can be changed, there was "little evidence that this translated into changes in explicit bias and behaviour." Can IATs still be valuable even if they do not change biased behaviours? See Patrick Forscher *et al.*, "A Meta-Analysis of Procedures to Change Implicit Measures" (2019) 117:3 Journal of Personality and Social Psychology 522.

[68] See *R. v. Belnavis*, [1997] S.C.J. No. 81, 3 S.C.R. 341 (S.C.C.); Kenneth B. Nunn, "'Essentially Black': Legal Theory and the Morality of Conscious Racial Identity" (2019) 97 Neb. L. Rev. 287; Angela P. Harris, "Racing Law: Legal Scholarship and the Critical Race Revolution" (2019) 52:1 Equity & Excellence in Education 12; Margaret M. Russell, "Beyond 'Sellouts' and 'Race Cards': Black Attorneys and the Straightjacket of Legal Practice" (1997) 95 Mich. L. Rev. 766.

[69] Jennifer McPhee, "Sharia mortgage comes without explicit interest" *Law Times* (June 11, 2007) at 10.

domestic abuse complaint or filing for divorce; they simply want the abuse to end.[70] What steps would you take? What cultural factors would be relevant, if any? Who, or which institutions, would you involve? What if the culture the immigrant comes from seems, from your perspective, to be more tolerant of domestic abuse? What if divorce is anathema to that culture? Does this make a difference?

Scenario Fourteen

Noor Nassar immigrated to Canada from Saudi Arabia five years ago with their spouse. They are an observant Muslim and wear the niqab. Six months ago, they were assaulted at a playground. A man saw Nassar and their child, and punched Nassar in the face and shouted "Make Canada Great Again!" He punched them again after they fell down. He then ran away but fortunately, witnesses apprehended the man and he was charged. Noor's nose was badly broken and they lost two teeth. They have to have surgery for their nose and significant dental work.

Doug Davidson is a Crown prosecutor. He met with Noor and told them that they could only pursue the case if they testified, and that they could not testify unless they remove their niqab. He told them that the ability to see a witness's face and demeanor is crucial for assessing credibility; "it's part of the Canadian system of justice".

Did Doug act improperly? In answering this question you may want to consider the judgment of the Supreme Court in *R. v. NS*, 2012 SCC 72, [2012] 3 SCR 726. Also consider the mandate of nonmedical face masks in many indoor spaces across Canada (including courtrooms) due to the COVID-19 pandemic. Does the response to the pandemic change the reasonableness of Davidson's demand? Is requiring face masks whilst banning the niqab a xenophobic decision or is there a deeper difference between the two face coverings?

Cultural Competence & Reconciliation

The Truth and Reconciliation Commission of Canada (TRC) Report published in 2015 includes Call to Action no. 27, calling upon the Federation of Law Societies of Canada (FLSC) to "ensure that lawyers receive appropriate cultural competency training, which includes the history and legacy of residential schools, the United Nations Declaration on the Rights of Indigenous Peoples, Treaties and Aboriginal rights, Indigenous law, and Aboriginal-Crown relations."[71] Call to Action no. 28 has a similar ask of all law schools in Canada. In response to these Calls, the FLSC, various provincial Law Societies, and law schools have committed to responding to the Calls to Action in various ways, including through public statements, passing resolutions, constituting advisory committees and task forces, and publishing guidelines for practitioners working with Indigenous peoples. In December 2019, the LSBC determined that "beginning in 2021, all practising lawyers in BC will be

---

[70] Antoinette Sedillo Lopez, "Making and Breaking Habits: Teaching (and Learning) Cultural Context, Self-Awareness, and Intercultural Communication Through Case Supervision in a Client-Service Legal Clinic" (2008) 28 Wash. U. J.L. & Pol'y 37 at 58-62.

[71] Truth and Reconciliation Commission of Canada, *Truth and Reconciliation Commission of Canada: Calls to Action* (2015), online (pdf): *Truth and Reconciliation Commission of Canada* trc.ca/assets/pdf/Calls_to_Action_English2.pdf.

required to take an Indigenous intercultural competency training course that will be provided online and at no cost."[72] This training will be delivered through a six-hour online course, will count towards practitioners' annual continuing professional development credit requirements, and once the training is available, lawyers will be able to complete the different modules over two years.

A recently published article by Parmar suggests that the TRC Calls to Action must be interpreted as a call to the profession to reconsider the meaning of cultural competence and rethink legal education in the specific context of reconciliation in Canada. She argues that reconciliation requires more than what traditional definitions of cultural competence include; "the task here is more than an acknowledgement of the multicultural nature of Canadian society."[73] Parmar argues for a conception of ethical and competent lawyering that makes lawyers and the profession accountable for that competence, and further suggests that competence for legal professionals must not be limited to knowledge of common/civil law traditions, but rather must include an ability to work with Indigenous laws as well.

Please read the following excerpt from the article on ethical lawyering in multi-juridical spaces and answer the questions below:

POOJA PARMAR

"Reconciliation and Ethical Lawyering: Some Thoughts on Cultural Competence" (2019) 97:3 Canadian Bar Review 526-557 [footnotes omitted]

[. . .]

Building on [the] rich and growing body of work on Indigenous laws, I suggest that the continuing disregard of Indigenous laws impoverishes not only the development of substantive law and legal principles in Canada, but also impoverishes the practice of law. The legal profession can only be enriched in seeking out ways in which Indigenous epistemologies might inform the ethical practice of law and ideas of professionalism. Existing codes or principles of ethics are shaped by old and new stories about practices of lawyering and judging in the common and civil law traditions. Absent from these are the stories of ethics that exist within Indigenous legal traditions. More research in this area is likely to reveal stories of representation, practices of advocacy, and ethical practices of responding to claims that can help us build upon, or even rethink, obligations of lawyers and judges as recognized in existing codes of professional responsibility or principles of ethics.

[. . .]

In arguing that we treat Indigenous laws and epistemologies as sources for ethical lawyering, I am neither suggesting a rejection, or replacement, of existing common or civil law principles or the Codes of Conduct, nor proposing a one-sided

---

[72] Law Society of British Columbia, *Law Society adopts Indigenous intercultural competency training* (December 6, 2019), online: *Law Society of British Columbia* https://www.lawsociety.bc.ca/about-us/news-and-publications/news/2019/law-society-adopts-indigenous-intercultural-compet/.

[73] Pooja Parmar, "Reconciliation and Ethical Lawyering: Some Thoughts on Cultural Competence" (2019) 97:3 Can. Bar Rev. 526 at 535.

appropriation of Indigenous principles. I am also not proposing an unquestioned, uncritical acceptance of Indigenous legal principles. The task instead, is that of treating Indigenous legal principles seriously and rethinking ethical practice and professionalism by drawing on more than one legal system. This work begins with humility. It must begin with recognizing the limits of traditions one is most familiar and comfortable with. Genuine commitments to reconciliation demand that legal professionals commit to unlearning colonial logics and hierarchies of legal cultures, and the disregard of particular knowledges, and approach differences with humility and respect. Instead of a cultural competence model that focuses solely on learning about the culture of particular Indigenous peoples, this alternative model would require legal professionals to consider what legal representation means within the particular Indigenous culture. It enables the professional to ask about obligations placed within that culture on a person who represents another, upon one who speaks for the other, upon one who tells the stories of another.

[. . .] Navigating multiple legal worlds is hard work, and not just in the sense of trying to figure out the rules of an unfamiliar legal system. Ideas about ethics, ethical practice as well as professional aspirations, are grounded in cultures. Figuring out ways to work with rules and aspirations that might at times be irreconcilable with ones we are familiar with cannot be easy. For example, ideas of zealous advocacy, civility, effective representation, and competence might differ not just between common law, civil law, and Indigenous laws, but even across different Indigenous laws. What the common law expects from a legal practitioner may not be what a particular Indigenous legal tradition might ask of her, or vice versa.

The difficulty of the task ahead, or even the potential of failure, are not, however, good reasons not to try, if accountability lies at the heart of the profession's response to the TRC Calls.

Ethical Translations

A commitment to ethical lawyering in multi-juridical spaces requires attention to the critical work lawyers do as translators and to questions of ethical translation. All lawyering involves translation (of complex, messy realities into focused narratives required by law) and all translations are necessarily incomplete and imperfect. But for lawyers in plural legal societies, the task is even more challenging, as they are called upon not only to translate social realities into legal facts, but are often also required to translate claims that arise from, and are shaped by, one legal system (e.g. an Indigenous legal system) into claims that will make sense within another legal system (e.g. the common law). However, legal concepts and processes are not always perfectly translatable across different legal cultures. [. . .]

Lawyers and judges often push against the perceived limits of state law in pursuit of justice. In fact, a practitioner's ability to disrupt what law is comfortable with in order to further a client's interest, is often seen as a sign of successful lawyering. And yet Indigenous peoples in Canada continue to struggle with the state law's inability to offer them a just response. The inadequacy or lack of response is because the Canadian legal system and its representatives and adherents are often unable to 'hear' what the Indigenous claimant is saying. This is not because they are not making an effort to listen (although this happens too), nor because what is being said makes them uncomfortable (which too is not uncommon), but primarily because the claim brought forward is unrecognizable within the common or civil legal system that lawyers and judges are familiar with. Sometimes the issue is mistranslation due to incompetence of the translator. Sometimes the state law does not have an equivalent category into which it can successfully translate the original claim.

Attention to the nature of work involved when working across different legal traditions therefore reveals that access to justice for Indigenous peoples is also an issue of translation. More specifically, it is about the mistranslation of their claims, sometimes by well-intentioned lawyers and judges who may otherwise be committed to ensuring justice. It is important to understand however, that the issue of mistranslation is not only one of linguistics and cross-cultural communications as emphasized in the cultural competence approach, but also of failures in conceptual translation across legal systems. The fact that a person's right to legal representation can be lost in the very process of being represented should concern those who care about access to justice for Indigenous peoples.

The practice of law that is not attentive to this translational aspect of representation in multi-juridical spaces cannot be considered ethical or competent if we are committed to undoing historical wrongs and meaningful reconciliation. A commitment to enabling access to justice for Indigenous peoples requires an acknowledgement of an obligation to engage in ethical translations. When the legal system requires claims to be rendered legible in the language of the common or civil law, a meaningful response to the TRC Calls would be training lawyers to have the skills to navigate multiple legal orders and for them to strive to be better translators for Indigenous peoples.

NOTES AND QUESTIONS

1. Do you agree with the suggestion that all lawyers and judges in Canada should have the ability to work with Indigenous laws, or should this competence requirement be limited to certain lawyers (for example those who represent Indigenous people or the government in treaty negotiations, or those representing various parties in litigation over resource extraction)?

2. What do you make of the suggestion that knowledge of Indigenous laws should not be confined to substantive legal principles only, but rather that Indigenous legal traditions should be treated as legitimate sources of professional rules and ethical principles?

3. In what other ways might the law societies and law schools respond to the TRC Calls to Action?

Scenario Fifteen

Your client is an Indigenous person who has retained you to defend against a charge for an offence relating to hunting for food. From a technical perspective, a treaty between the client's community and the government is relevant to the case. Your client wants to use the case to draw attention to the treaty issue and to facilitate greater respect between their community and the government. To accomplish this your client wants you to align the legal arguments with their community's political stance on treaty rights. In conversations about the charge, your client also repeatedly invokes Indigenous laws that you are unfamiliar with. Assume you are minimally aware of rights of Indigenous peoples under Canadian and International law, and have little knowledge of Indigenous cultures. How would you approach the case?

[d] Lawyer Wellbeing, Mental Health and Competence

An aspect of competence that has traditionally not received adequate attention within the profession is the connection between lawyers' well-being and their capacity to serve clients. While conversations about unreasonably heavy workloads and unsustainable work cultures are not new, and the profession has been aware of the prevalence of substance abuse and alcoholism among its members, the impact of these issues on competence remained unacknowledged in any meaningful way until the recent past. Part of the reason for this relates to the profession's identity, its emphasis on resilience based on one's ability to develop a "thick skin", absence or concealment of vulnerabilities, and disregard of human emotions in the work of law. In the highly competitive work environments lawyers typically inhabit, the problem is further exacerbated due to the stigma attached to mental health issues. However, a growing body of research in these areas has led to introspection, as well as new initiatives driven largely by concerns over lawyer wellbeing and the profession's obligations to provide effective and competent services to the public.[74] Mental health and wellbeing are complex and at times controversial topics, and relate to multiple regulatory issues in the legal profession ranging from admission to practice and disciplinary proceedings.[75] While many of these issues are inter-related, this section provides a brief introduction meant to draw attention to the importance of thinking about wellbeing and lawyer competence generally.

For many lawyers, repeatedly listening to accounts of violence, displacement and dispossession, and analyzing minute details of horrific crimes in their offices or in the courtroom,[76] is a part of work life. Repeated encounters with traumatic accounts and working with traumatized people over long periods of time inevitably has an impact.[77] While these encounters do not impact everyone in the same way, and lawyers in some areas of practice are more likely than others to experience what is

---

[74] See Colin James, "Towards trauma-informed legal practice: a review" (2020) 27:2 Psychiatry, Psychology and Law 275; Paula Baron & Lillian Corbin, "Lawyers, mental illness, admission and misconduct" (2019) 22:1-2 Leg. Ethics 28; Brook Greenberg, "The Enemy of the Good: Perfectionism, Self-Doubt and Mental Health in the Legal Profession" (December 17, 2019), online: https://www.canadianlawyermag.com/news/opinion/perfectionism-self-doubt-and-mental-health-in-the-legal-profession/324233.

[75] See Chapter 11. For an argument that wellbeing should also be considered in the context of neoliberalisation of legal education more broadly, see Margaret Thornton, "Law Student Wellbeing: A Neoliberal Conundrum" (2016) 58:2 Australian Universities' Review 42-50.

[76] See *R. v. Murray*, [2000] O.J. No. 2182, 48 O.R. (3d) 544 (Ont. S.C.J.), Ch. 1, s. [1][c] and Ch. 3, s. [7][b].

[77] Colin James, "Towards trauma-informed legal practice: a review" (2020) 27:2 Psychiatry, Psychology and Law 275 at 284; Myrna McCallum, "The Trauma-Informed Lawyer hosted by Myrna McCallum" (2020), online (podcast): *SimpleCast* https://thetraumainformedlawyer.simplecast.com.

recognized as 'vicarious', 'indirect' or 'secondary' trauma,[78] dealing with messy human conflicts even outside of the criminal law or refugee law contexts over long periods of time can cause serious harm to those trying to help their clients navigate such conflicts. Some of the harms identified by researchers are anxiety, extraordinary levels of stress, depression, substance abuse and PTSD.[79] Lack of well-being has also been linked to conduct such as incivility, bullying, and workplace harassment.[80] All of these have an effect on the administration of justice.[81]

In a shift from the culture of simply not acknowledging the role of trauma, a trauma-informed approach within the profession is slowly beginning to recognize the problem as well as offer ways to minimize the harm. Most importantly, researchers suggest that harms caused by the nature of the work lawyers do are not inevitable, but rather can be addressed by focusing on changing attitudes as well as workplace environments.[82] This requires attention to both structural and systemic causes underlying the problems as well as training individuals to develop better coping mechanisms.[83] As the profession in Canada and elsewhere begins to

---

[78] For definitions see Colin James, "Towards trauma-informed legal practice: a review" (2020) 27:2 Psychiatry, Psychology and Law 275 at 277-278.

[79] See Colin James, "Towards trauma-informed legal practice: a review" (2020) 27:2 Psychiatry, Psychology and Law 275 at 278; Paula Baron & Lillian Corbin, "Lawyers, mental illness, admission and misconduct" (2019) 22:1-2 Leg. Ethics 28 at 29, 31. Marie-Eve Leclerc, Jo-Anne Wemmers & Alain Brunet, "The unseen cost of justice: post-traumatic stress symptoms in Canadian lawyers" (2020) 26:1 Psychology, Crime & Law 1. Researchers note that some lawyers experience more trauma than mental health professionals.

[80] Paula Baron & Lillian Corbin, "Lawyers, mental illness, admission and misconduct" (2019) 22:1-2 Leg. Ethics 28 at 30; Anne Brafford, "Well-Being Strategies for Small Firms: Building Resilient Work Cultures" (March 2020), online: *American Bar Association* https://www.americanbar.org/groups/law_practice/publications/law_ practice_magazine/2020/ma2020/ma20ttl/.

[81] Colin James, "Towards trauma-informed legal practice: a review" (2020) 27:2 Psychiatry, Psychology and Law 275 at 280.

[82] Anne Brafford, "Well-Being Strategies for Small Firms: Building Resilient Work Cultures" (March 2020), online: *American Bar Association* https://www.americanbar.org/groups/law_practice/publications/law_practice_magazine/2020/ma2020/ma20ttl/; Colin James, "Towards trauma-informed legal practice: a review" (2020) 27:2 Psychiatry, Psychology and Law 275 at 284.

[83] Colin James, "Towards trauma-informed legal practice: a review" (2020) 27:2 Psychiatry, Psychology and Law 275; Anne Brafford, "Well-Being Strategies for Small Firms: Building Resilient Work Cultures" (March 2020), online: *American Bar Association* https://www.americanbar.org/groups/law_practice/publications/law_practice_magazine/2020/ma2020/ma20ttl/; Law Society of British Columbia, "Second Interim Report of the Mental Health Task Force" (2019), online: *Law Society of British Columbia* https://www.lawsociety.bc.ca/Website/media/Shared/docs/initiatives/MentalHealthTaskForce-SecondInterimReport2020.pdf. For a critique of the individualization and depoliticization of the issue see Margaret Thornton, "Law Student Wellbeing: A Neoliberal Conundrum" (2016) 58:2 Australian Universities' Review 42-50.

formulate responses,[84] there is a growing acknowledgement that wellbeing is a multifaceted issue and involves many legal actors. For example, in a recent sentencing decision, Justice Band of the ONCJ acknowledged both the impact of "frequent and repeated trauma" upon various participants in the justice system, and the desirability to move towards a trauma-informed approach to legal procedure and rules of evidence.[85]

Scenario Sixteen

Critical evidence in a criminal trial included voluminous records of an on-line chatroom with graphic discussions of sexual abuse of children, and 75 videos and 40 images seized from the accused person's phone containing child pornography. The videos involved children ranging in age from approximately 2 to 11 years being sexually abused by adults. During a judicial pre-trial, Crown counsel indicated that she would select a representative sample of the child pornography to show in the court. She and the defence counsel also decided to present relevant facts in court by way of a mutually agreed upon description of the contents of some of the material, with the evidence in its entirety entered as sealed exhibits. The motivation behind these decisions was to protect those present in the court from "unnecessary exposure to potentially trauma-inducing raw material".[86]

Have the crown and defence counsel in this case acted as competent professionals? Have they fulfilled their duty of loyalty to their respective clients? Which model of ethical lawyering would you associate with their conduct? Does this approach serve the goals of the criminal justice system? Why, or why not?[87]

NOTES AND QUESTIONS

1. Do you think law schools have a role in addressing mental health and wellbeing? Some Canadian law schools have begun to turn their attention to student wellbeing. Are you aware of the programs and resources offered in your law school? How would you assess the quality and accessibility of these programs and resources?

---

[84] See e.g., Canadian Bar Association, "Mental Health and Awareness Committee" (2020), online: *Canadian Bar Association* https://www.cba.org/Sections/Young-Lawyers/ Committees/Mental-Health; Canadian Bar Association, "Research" (2020), online: *Canadian Bar Association* https://www.cba.org/Sections/Wellness-Subcommittee/Resources/Research; Law Society of British Columbia, "Improving Mental Health for the Legal Profession" (2020), online: *Law Society of British Columbia* https://www.lawsociety.bc.ca/our-initiatives/ improving-mental-health/; Wellbeing at the Bar, "Vicarious trauma" (2020), online: *Wellbeing at the Bar* https://www.wellbeingatthebar.org.uk/problems/vicarious-trauma/; Tristan Jepson Memorial Foundation, "TJMF Psychological Wellbeing: Best Practice Guidelines for the Legal Profession", online (pdf): *Tristan Jepson Memorial Foundation* https://mindscount. org/wp-content/uploads/2019/09/Tristan-Jepson-Memorial-Foundation-Guidelines-1-1.pdf.

[85] *R. v. Marratt*, [2019] O.J. No. 4584, 2019 ONCJ 618 at paras. 8, 22 (Ont. C.J.).

[86] Adapted from *R. v. Marratt*, [2019] O.J. No. 4584, 2019 ONCJ 618 (Ont. C.J.).

[87] For further discussion on the subject of trauma and juries, see Bill Graveland, "Burden of isolation: Juror with PTSD urges triple-murder jury to get help", *CBC News* (February 26, 2017), online: cbc.ca/news.

2. What are some ways in which the law societies can support the larger cultural shift required to address this issue?

3. Reflecting on your answers for #1 and #2, discuss whether you believe law schools and law societies would sufficiently address these issues. Do you think it is in the interest of these institutions to embrace a cultural shift? Why or why not? What do you think about the use of content warnings by law schools? What are the upsides and downsides of doing so?

[e]   Mental Health and Diminished Capacity

Another dimension of the lawyer's competency and quality of service obligation is the lawyer's ability to serve a client who might have a mental health challenge. The *Model Code* addresses this in Rule 3.2-9. Please review this Rule and its Commentaries. A major ethical challenge for a lawyer in such a situation is to resist the impulse to over-ride the client's autonomy with the lawyer's own understanding of what would be in the client's best interest, while remaining alert to circumstances (*i.e.*, incapacity) in which the lawyer's duty shifts from respecting autonomy to protecting best interests. How does a lawyer determine if a client lacks the capacity to instruct them? Consider the following scenarios.[88]

Scenario Seventeen

Assume you are a publicly funded legal aid attorney. H is an elderly person who is seeking your help. You have represented them before in seniors and disability benefits matters. H had previously been diagnosed with a psychotic disorder and, more recently, was diagnosed with dementia consistent with Alzheimer's disease. H arrives in your office with some official-looking papers that they do not understand. A notorious real estate speculator has sent H a notice to quit their house which H has owned for 35 years. The speculator claims title of the home based on a lien contract signed by H. You know that this speculator has obtained fraudulent title to several local homes over the last few years, and it is possible that the contract was forged or H signed it without fully understanding what it was. H is distraught about losing their home, and calls you frequently, sometimes crying and sometimes angrily demanding action to solve the issue. When you propose to seek an injunction preventing the eviction, H refuses to allow any paperwork to be filed in court. They tell you that their sister and the devil are conspiring against them, and that filing a suit is likely to make the harassment worse. After unsuccessfully trying to convince H to file the suit, they accuse you of being in league with the devil and the real estate speculator. H terminates your retainer. You know that they do not have the resources to hire a private attorney, and they have no family or other support network. From prior experience, you're confident that the real estate speculator will not hesitate to

---

[88] Thanks to Sheila Wildeman for her assistance in drafting these scenarios. See also more generally, Michael L. Perlin, "Fatal Assumption: A critical evaluation of the role of counsel in mental disability cases" (1992) 16:1 Law & Human Behavior 39; and "'Too Stubborn to ever be governed by enforced insanity': some therapeutic jurisprudence dilemmas in the representation of criminal defendants in incompetency and insanity cases" (2010) 33 International Journal of Law & Psychology 475.

enforce the eviction notice. What should you do?[89]

Scenario Eighteen

In *R. v. Esseghaier*[90], the accused was alleged to have conspired to bomb passenger trains in Toronto, in connection with Al Qaeda elements in Iran. The accused self-identified as a "radical Islamist" who believed the Qur'an prophesied that he would die on December 25, 2014. At his trial in September 2015, he told a court-appointed psychiatrist: "You are lying. We are before December 2014, because I am alive. If you say it's a delusion then the Qur'an is a delusion." Suppose you are the lawyer representing Mr. Esseghaier during his trial. The Crown's case is very strong, and it's unlikely you will secure an acquittal. Should you raise a not criminally-responsible mental disorder defense (NCR-MD) in order to avoid a guilty verdict? What if Mr. Esseghaier says that he would prefer life imprisonment to a finding of NCR-MD, because such a defense will further stigmatize him and marginalize his political views?[91]

[f] Compulsory Continuing Legal Education

After several years of discussion, consultation and resistance, beginning in 2010 all provinces and territories have introduced compulsory continuing legal education. Most use the descriptor "Continuing Professional Development" (CPD). Several justifications have been advanced in support of such a program: it will help ensure the competence of members of the profession; it is necessary to maintain public confidence in the self-regulatory authority and capacity of the legal profession; other legal professions around the world have adopted continuing professional development; other analogous professions (doctors, dentists) have compulsory professional development; it will help keep lawyers abreast about ongoing developments and changes in Canadian society, technology pertinent to the practice of law, and the legal profession in general.

	Hours of CPD required	Additional requirements
AB	No minimum hours	Required Indigenous cultural competency education.
BC	12 hours/year	2 of these hours must be on practice management or professionalism and legal ethics; Required Indigenous cultural competency course.
MB	1 hour/month	At least 1.5 hours per year must be on ethics, professional responsibility, or practice management.

---

[89] Adapted from Paul Tremblay, "On Persuasion and Paternalism: Lawyer Decision Making and the Questionably Competent Client" (1987) Utah L. Rev. 515.

[90] [2015] O.J. No. 4922, 2015 ONSC 5855 (Ont. S.C.J.).

[91] This scenario is a Canadian variation of the "Unabomber dilemma" discussed by David Luban in *Legal Ethics and Human Dignity* (New York: Cambridge University Press, 2007); see also Alice Woolley, *Understanding Lawyers' Ethics in Canada*, 2d ed. (Toronto: LexisNexis Canada, 2016) at 91-92.

	Hours of CPD required	Additional requirements
NB	12 hours/year	No compulsory topics.
NL	15 hours/year	Must be approved activities. Members must report details of these activities to the Law Society.
NT	12 hours/year	2 of these hours must be on practice management or professionalism and legal ethics.
NS	12 hours/year	No compulsory topics.
NU	12 hours/year	At least 1 hour must be on professional responsibility and ethics.
ON	12 hours/year	3 of these hours must be on practice management or professionalism and ethics. New legal professionals must complete 3 hours that focus on advancing equality, diversity, and inclusion. Each year after must include 1 hour on these topics.
PE	24 hours over 2 years	At least 4 hours must be "Professionalism": ethics, client communications, professional responsibility, or practice management.
QB	30 hours over 2 years	Must be approved courses.
SK	36 hours over 3 years	6 of these hours must be "Ethics Hours".
YK	12 hours/year	These areas can be focused on substantive or professionalism content.

NOTES AND QUESTIONS

1. Do you agree with the presumption underlying these reforms that there is a causal connection between compulsory professional development and improved competence?

2. Compare and contrast these various systems. Are some better than others? Why? Do you have any suggestions on how CPD could be improved?

3. Beginning in 2021, all lawyers in BC and Alberta will be required to take a six-hour online course on Indigenous intercultural competency.[92] Would you be in favour of extending such mandatory training to the rest of Canada? In your opinion, is this training an adequate response from the legal profession to address the three dimensions of cultural competence

---

[92] Law Society of British Columbia, *Law Society adopts Indigenous intercultural competency training* (December 6, 2019), online: *Law Society of British Columbia* https://www.lawsociety.bc.ca/about-us/news-and-publications/news/2019/law-society-adopts-indigenous-intercultural-compet/; Law Society of Alberta, President's Message, "Introduction of Mandatory Indigenous Cultural Competency Training" (October 6, 2020) lawsociety.ab.ca.

(knowledge, skills and attitude)?[93]

4. Should compulsory professional development initiatives strive to go beyond merely enhancing the competency of lawyers, to strengthening their ethical character? Is such an ambition even possible?[94] What would such an initiative involve?

5. Is mere attendance sufficient to ensure that CPD is effective? Are there other assessment mechanisms available? For example, some Colleges of Physicians and Surgeons have a Peer Assessment Program where physicians are periodically selected to be reviewed by peers practising in the same area. Identify the arguments for and against adopting a similar system for lawyers. The LSO has moved towards a system of peer assessment for newly admitted members to the bar. Given that almost all of the lawyers disciplined for professional misconduct are senior lawyers, not junior, is this emphasis of the Law Society warranted? What does it say about the law societies' views about the quality of newly admitted members?

6. Should "wellness" programmes qualify as CPD?

7. In the United Kingdom, the Solicitors Regulation Authority has moved away from mandatory professional development in favour of a 'Statement of Solicitor Competence' and having solicitors declare annually: "I have reflected on my practice and addressed any identified learning and development needs." What issues might arise with a competence self-evaluation? Should Canada adopt the same model? Why or why not?[95]

8. After refusing to complete their CPD hours, and being suspended for it, a lawyer brought a legal challenge against the Law Society of Manitoba. They argued that mandatory professional development hours and the associated administrative suspension are outside the law society's statutory authority, and therefore illegal. Their argument was rejected by a majority of the Supreme Court of Canada.[96]

[g] Advising Clients: Candour and Conflicting Duties

A lawyer's duty of loyalty to their client requires that the lawyer disclose all material facts relating to the matter for which they were retained. Rule 3.2-2 of the *Model*

---

[93] See Rose Voyvodic, "Lawyers Meet the Social Context: Understanding Cultural Competence" (2005) 84:Special Issue Can. Bar Rev. 563 at 582.

[94] See Alice Woolley, "The Character of Continuing Education in Legal Ethics" (2010) 4 Can. Leg. Ed. A.R. 27.

[95] The competence statement can be found online: Solicitors Regulation Authority, "Statement of Solicitor Competence" (November 25, 2019), online: *Solicitors Regulation Authority* www.sra.org.uk/competence/.

[96] *Green v. Law Society of Manitoba*, [2017] S.C.J. No. 20, 2017 SCC 20 (S.C.C.). See also Alice Woolley, "Justice for Some" (April 13, 2017), online (blog): *ablawg.ca* http://ablawg.ca/2017/04/13/justice-for-some/.

Code requires lawyers to be "honest and candid". In *Strother v 3464920 Canada*[97] and *Canadian National Railway Co v McKercher LLP*[98], the Supreme Court of Canada discussed how candour helps to give effect to the lawyer's obligation to put their client's interests first. This duty overlaps with the standard of competence expected of lawyers – and might also engage a lawyer's duty to keep client information confidential (addressed in a later chapter) – but candour is itself a separate obligation owed by lawyers to their clients. *McKercher* illustrates particularly well how candour can be connected to issues of commitment to the client, but is also a free-standing duty. In that case, a law firm retained by CN Rail on several matters agreed to take on a class action lawsuit against their client. CN Rail didn't find out it was being sued by its own lawyer until it was served with a statement of claim. The Court held that even if McKercher could act for both clients without conflict, they had a duty to disclose to CN that they were considering taking on the class action suit.

The duty of candour supports the lawyer's long-established fiduciary duty to their clients, and allows the lawyer to disagree with the client in the interest of honest advice. However, there is a practical challenge in deciding what information is relevant. Lawyers must not hold onto information merely because it would take a long time to disclose it to the client. Lawyers must disclose material facts relating to their advice, even when the lawyer believes the client already has that information.[99] Commentators have grouped the types of information subject to candour into three categories:

1. Information on the lawyer-client relationship, such as conflicts of interest, errors, or negligence relating to the client's matter;

2. Information directly relating to the legal work for which the lawyer was retained;

3. Information that is relevant to the client's interests and relevant to the matter for which the lawyer was retained, but not directly related to the work which the lawyer was retained to perform.[100]

SALOMON v. MATTE-THOMPSON

[2019] S.C.J. No. 14, 2019 SCC 14

(S.C.C., Wagner C.J.C., Abella, Moldaver, Karakatsanis, Gascon, Côté, Brown, Rowe, Martin JJ.)

[Salomon had been the lawyer of the respondents Matte-Thompson and 166376 Canada Inc. (166) in Quebec for a long time. He introduced them to Papadopoulos,

---

[97] *Strother v. 3464920 Canada Inc.*, [2007] S.C.J. No. 24, 2007 SCC 24, [2007] 2 S.C.R. 177 (S.C.C.).

[98] *Canadian National Railway Co. v. McKercher LLP*, [2013] S.C.J. No. 39, 2013 SCC 39, [2013] 2 S.C.R. 649 (S.C.C.).

[99] *Law Society of Upper Canada v. Nguyen,* [2015] O.J. No. 6190, 2015 ONSC 7192 at para. 3 (Ont. S.C.J.).

[100] Malcolm Mercer, "Candid but unsure" (December 31, 2015), online (blog): *Slaw* www.slaw.ca/2015/12/31/candid-but-unsure/.

his personal friend and his own financial advisor, and recommended that they consult him. The respondents eventually invested over $7.5 million with Papadopoulos's investment firm, Triglobal. The funds they invested in turned out to be parts of a Ponzi scheme, and Papadopoulos and his associate, Bright, disappeared with the savings. Matte-Thompson and 166 lost more than $5 million. Although Salomon suffered a personal loss too from the fraud, he received payments by Triglobal greater than his loss. Salomon testified that these payments represented a redemption of his own investment, but in an email written by Papadopoulos at that time they were referred to as commissions.

The trial judge held Papadopoulos and Bright liable for the respondents' investment losses and for Matte-Thompson's moral injury but dismissed the claim against Salomon and SKM. The judge stressed that Salomon could not be held liable for the fraud. The trial judge also held that Salomon had committed no fault against 166, because he had not provided investment advice to the company or gone too far in reassuring it.

The Court of Appeal allowed the appeal and concluded that the judge had viewed the evidence through a distorting lens, erred by taking a restrictive approach to the evidence when considering Salomon's duty of loyalty and erred in considering the issue of causation. The Court of Appeal therefore ordered Salomon and SKM to fully compensate the respondents for their investment losses, and Matte-Thompson for her non-pecuniary loss.[101]]

The judgment of the Court was delivered by

GASCON J.:—

* * * * *

The principles articulated in *Harris [(Succession), Re*, 2016 QCCA 50] can be summarized as follows. Lawyers who refer clients to other professionals or advisors have an obligation of means, not one of result. Although lawyers do not guarantee the services rendered by professionals or advisors to whom they refer their clients, they must nevertheless act competently, prudently and diligently in making such referrals, which must be based on reasonable knowledge of the professionals or advisors in question. Referring lawyers must be convinced that the professionals or advisors to whom they refer clients are sufficiently competent to fulfill the contemplated mandates (*Harris*, at paras. 16, 20 and 22). In *Harris*, the Quebec Court of Appeal pointed out that the question of the referring lawyer's liability [TRANSLATION] "cannot be answered in the abstract. The answer necessarily depends on the facts of the case" (para. 13). The court added that "[i]n such matters, the circumstances are everything" (para. 22).

* * * * *

The question in the case at bar is not whether the initial referral of the respondents to Mr. Papadopoulos was or was not sufficient in and of itself to establish the appellants' professional liability. The focus here is instead on the entirety of Mr.

---

[101] *Salomon v. Matte-Thompson*, [2019] S.C.J. No. 14, 2019 SCC 14 (S.C.C.).

Salomon's conduct. But one thing is clear. Just as a referral is not a guarantee of the services rendered by the professional or advisor to whom the client is referred, it is also not a shield against liability for other wrongful acts committed by the referring lawyer. This is one way in which the facts in this case differ substantively from the facts in *Harris*.

Contrary to the appellants' assertion, the decision of the Court of Appeal in the instant case did not broaden the basis of liability for lawyers who refer clients to other professionals or advisors beyond the standard recently set in *Harris*: lawyers can refer their clients to other professionals or advisors so long as they discharge their professional obligations in so doing. The Court of Appeal did not find that the referral itself was determinative; rather, it assessed all of Mr. Salomon's acts in the context of his professional duties — the duty to advise and the duty of loyalty in particular — to his clients. It found that Mr. Salomon had done far more than merely make a referral. As I will explain below, Mr. Salomon also repeatedly recommended Mr. Papadopoulos, his investment firm and their in-house products, and encouraged the respondents to invest — and retain their investments — in Triglobal funds. Moreover, Mr. Salomon turned a blind eye to a conflict of interest which resulted in him serving two masters and sacrificing the respondents' interests. It was the entirety of Mr. Salomon's conduct that led the Court of Appeal to hold the appellants liable in the circumstances.

*   *   *   *   *

A lawyer's duty to advise is threefold, encompassing duties (1) to inform, (2) to explain, and (3) to advise in the strict sense. The duty to inform pertains to the disclosure of relevant facts; the duty to explain requires that the legal and economic consequences of a course of action be presented; and the duty to advise in the strict sense requires that a course of action be recommended (*Poulin c. Pilon*, [1984] C.S. 177 (C.S. Que.), at p. 180. . .

The duty to advise is inherent in the legal profession and exists regardless of the nature of the mandate (Baudouin, Deslauriers and Moore, at No. 2-138; *Labrie c. Tremblay* (1999), [2000] R.R.A. 5 (C.A. Que.), at p. 10). Its exact scope depends on the circumstances, including the object of the mandate, the client's characteristics and the expertise the lawyer claims to have in the field in question (*Côté c. Rancourt*, 2004 SCC 58, [2004] 3 S.C.R. 248 (S.C.C.), at para. 6; *Thouin*, at pp. 55-69).

As no bright lines can be drawn in this regard, the case law is replete with examples of situations in which courts have had to perform the difficult task of deciding whether lawyers should, in advising their clients, have taken the initiative to go beyond what the clients specifically asked them for (see, e.g., *Labrie*, at p. 11; *Karpinski c. Sylvestre*, 2011 QCCA 2161 (C.A. Que.), at para. 19; *Daigneault c. Lapierre*, [2003] R.R.A. 902 (C.S. Que.)). One thing is clear, however: when lawyers do provide advice, they must always act in their clients' best interests and meet the standard of the competent, prudent and diligent lawyer in the same circumstances. In this respect, I agree with the Court of Appeal that any advice lawyers give that exceeds their mandates may, if wrongful, engage their liability. Whether Mr. Salomon was acting within the limits of his mandate in providing financial advice to the respondents is therefore immaterial. He is liable for any wrongful advice he gave in that context. . .

* * * * *

[T]he Court of Appeal did not err in holding that Mr. Salomon had breached his duty to advise the respondents. Beyond the fact that Mr. Salomon often flirted with — or overstepped — the limits of his professional capabilities, the advice he provided to both of the respondents was wrongful for a number of reasons, which the Court of Appeal summarized (para. 69). To start with, Mr. Salomon should not have recommended a non-diversified investment in offshore hedge funds to clients whose primary goal was to preserve the capital. . .

Mr. Salomon also breached his duty to advise by continually recommending financial products without performing due diligence or asking any questions about them. . .

Third, the Court of Appeal did not err in holding that Mr. Salomon's faults against the respondents had commenced in 2003 and had continued until 2007. Mr. Salomon had, on the sole basis of his blind confidence in Mr. Papadopoulos, induced his clients to erroneously believe that investing in iVest and Focus was safe. From 2003 to 2007, he repeatedly reassured the respondents that their investments with Triglobal gave them security of capital. In this regard, the Court of Appeal noted the following comments made by Mr. Salomon:

* In August 2003, he stated, "iVest is an excellent vehicle whenever security of the capital is important (as with the grandchildren and yourself)". . .

* In September 2003, he suggested that the respondents "invest the Estate assets based on a conservative model, perhaps using iVest products and a mix of segregated products (for absolute security of capital)" . . .

* The following month, he added, "I would point out that [Mr.] Papadopoulos is very conservative when it comes to preservation of capital" . . .

* In July 2004, he stated, "the RBC proposal is somewhat undimensional (*sic*) and is interest rate sensitive. The Triglobal proposal is less risky and the returns are good. Let's talk" . . .

* In June 2005, he stated, referring to the iVest and Manulife funds, "I believe that both forms of investments are excellent and quite conservative, and I would have no difficulty in recommending either one to you and to your co-trustee ... (as trustees acting responsibly)" . . .

* In April 2006, he responded to concerns expressed by Ms. Matte-Thompson regarding the security of the respondents' investments (including in Focus) that he was "certain that everything [was] ok" . . .

* In November 2006, he stated, after informing Ms. Matte-Thompson that he had visited Mr. Bright in Nassau, that the latter "has become resident there in order to manage the Focus, ivest and structured products funds", concluding that "[a]ll is well" . . .

* In July 2007, he stated, "[t]he Triglobal returns continue to be excellent and I remain very happy to have my investments performing so well with such controlled risk" . . .

150

* In September 2007, he added, "I think that the two funds (iVest and Focus) are performing as predicted" . . .

* In December 2007, he stated, commenting on Mr. Papadopoulos's latest promises to worried investors, "FYI. This is good" . . .

* * * * *

This is not a case about a mere referral. It concerns a referring lawyer who, over the course of several years, recommended and endorsed a financial advisor and financial products, and encouraged his clients to retain their investments with that advisor. Further, in doing this, he failed to perform adequate due diligence, misrepresented investment information, committed breaches of confidentiality and acted despite being in a conflict of interest. In such a context, a lawyer cannot avoid liability by hiding behind the high threshold for establishing liability that applies in a case in which a lawyer has merely referred a client.

* * * * *

Consider the following scenarios.

Scenario Nineteen

Several Indigenous people are living on land that the federal government claims was never added to the reserve and is still Crown land. This Indigenous community has retained you to investigate the current legal status of the land. In order to limit costs, they have asked you to curtail your research to the current title, and don't want you to look at the impact of additions to the reserve yet. You know from work with other Indigenous communities that if the land is added to the reserve with improvements, the current residents will acquire possession rights, limiting the band's options for development. A friend of yours who works at Indigenous and Northern Affairs Canada tells you that the government has started the process to add the land to the reserve, but haven't told the Indigenous community because they don't want a building rush on the land before it is added. Would you share this information with your clients? Is there a risk that disclosure would harm your clients' interests by starting a rush on the land? Do your clients' instructions to limit your research affect your decision on whether to disclose the information?

Scenario Twenty

Provincial gambling revenues are facing increased competition from online gambling sites. Nova Scotia, being a relatively small market, wouldn't be able to create a viable online gaming service without finding customers in other provinces, which is prohibited by the *Criminal Code*.[102] The government of Nova Scotia has retained you to look into this problem, and investigate whether there is a way around the ban. While on vacation in PEI, you get into a conversation with a colleague who is working on a similar problem, and has discovered that some Indigenous people are hosting online gaming servers, but are not being prosecuted because they are asserting their right to self-government. Your colleague says that PEI likely wouldn't want to share an e-gaming platform with Nova Scotia for fear of losing

---

[102] *Criminal Code*, R.S.C. 1985, c. C-46.

revenue. He explains that the company setting up the PEI system is looking for investors, and invites you to put some money in. What should you tell the Nova Scotia government? What should you do about the investment tip?

[4] TERMINATION OF THE LAWYER-CLIENT RELATIONSHIP

Having analyzed how the lawyer-client relationship is formed and the obligations of competence and quality of service, we are now in a position to consider how the lawyer-client relationship might be terminated. First, we will consider termination in accordance with the letter of retainer, then we will assess withdrawal, both obligatory and optional.

[a]   The Retainer

The lawyer-client relationship, although saturated with fiduciary obligations, is also contractual in nature.[103] Consequently, like all contracts, the parties can anticipate the demise of the relationship. Termination may be explicit or implied. This does not normally generate any ethical concerns.

However, in recent years, as we will see in Chapter 4, Canadian courts have increasingly emphasized that lawyers have a duty of loyalty and an obligation to avoid conflicts of interest. As we shall see in *Neil*, *Strother*, and *McKercher*, the Supreme Court of Canada has made it clear that in some circumstances a business conflict can be a legal conflict, *i.e.*, that a lawyer may be retained by two clients who do not have a legal dispute with each other but may have competing business interests. Consequently, one of the clients may challenge whether the lawyer is fulfilling the duty of loyalty if the lawyer continues with both representations.

The simplest way for lawyers to avoid this potential problem would be for them to send their clients an explicit termination letter once legal services have concluded. Lawyers, however, are reluctant to do this for at least two reasons: first, it is difficult to craft such letters without giving the impression that the client is being "dumped"; second, it is in a lawyer's economic interest to maintain relationships even when the particular legal service is completed. Consequently, the economic imperatives create an ethical dilemma for lawyers: in order to avoid potential conflicts when accepting new clients, lawyers should terminate their relationships with other clients once the services have been provided; at the same time, however, some clients are likely to be repeat players, therefore it is economically unwise to alienate such clients. Can you suggest a policy that would resolve this dilemma?

Scenario Twenty-one

Draft a termination letter to a client, Pinko Enterprises, after you have helped it to purchase a small business that Pinko had just added to its three already-existing businesses.

[b]   Withdrawal: Obligatory or Optional

We have seen in section [2][b] of this chapter that lawyers have significant discretion in choosing their clients at the beginning of the relationship, and that clients (if they

---

[103] *Strother v. 3464920 Canada Inc.*, [2007] S.C.J. No. 24, 2007 SCC 24, [2007] 2 S.C.R. 177 (S.C.C.).

have the financial resources) also tend to have great choice in selecting their lawyer. This symmetry, however, does not apply when it comes to the termination of the relationship. The Commentary to Rule 3.7-1 of the *Model Code* explicitly states that "[a]lthough the client has the right to terminate the lawyer-client relationship at will, the lawyer does not enjoy the same freedom of action". In other words, if a lawyer accepts a client, the lawyer has a duty of fidelity and loyalty which limits the ability to end the relationship: "Having undertaken [representation] the lawyer should complete the task as ably as possible, unless there is justifiable cause for terminating the relationship. It is inappropriate for a lawyer to withdraw on capricious or arbitrary grounds." Rule 3.7-1 makes the same point, but negatively: "A lawyer must not withdraw from representation of a client except for good cause, and on reasonable notice to the client." The obvious questions are: What is meant by "a justifiable cause", a "good cause" and "notice appropriate in the circumstances"?

Historically, law societies have distinguished between mandatory and permissive withdrawal, although there has not always been consensus on which circumstance falls into which category. The *Model Code* has maintained this distinction. "Obligatory withdrawal" is required in the three circumstances identified in Rule 3.7-7 of the *Model Code*.

Furthermore, in the context of the Advocacy Rule, the *Model Code* provides:

> 5.1-1 When acting as an advocate, a lawyer must represent the client resolutely and honourably within the limits of the law, while treating the tribunal with candour, fairness, courtesy, and respect.

Commentary 1 of Rule 5.1-4 provides:

> If a client desires that a course be taken that would involve a breach of [the duty to disclose errors or omissions to the court], the lawyer must refuse and do everything reasonably possible to prevent it. If that cannot be done, the lawyer should, subject to rule 3.7-1 (Withdrawal from Representation), withdraw or seek leave to do so.

Optional withdrawal is governed by Rules 3.7-2 (Optional Withdrawal), 3.7-3 (Non-payment of Fees), and their Commentaries.

NOTES AND QUESTIONS

1. Do you agree with the distinction between "obligatory" and "optional" withdrawal? If yes, do you also agree with the circumstances that would put a lawyer in each category?

2. In *Brace v. Canada (Customs and Revenue Agency)*,[104] a client swore at an employee of the law firm and accused the firm of unfitness. The lawyer sought to withdraw on the basis of a "serious loss of confidence between the lawyer and client". Chief Justice Green denied the request because of possible prejudice to the client's case. He also analogized the lawyer-client relationship to a marriage. Do you agree with Green C.J.'s decision? Is the marriage analogy helpful or confusing? Should it make a difference if the lawyer works for a large firm or is a sole practitioner?

---

[104] [2004] N.J. No. 46, 2004 NLSCTD 26, 234 Nfld & P.E.I.R. 335 (N.L.T.D.).

3.   In terms of non-payment of fees, is the "serious prejudice to the client" test the appropriate test? Does it give proper weight to the interests of the lawyer? Does it properly acknowledge the different economic circumstances of different lawyers and their different clienteles: corporate lawyers versus family lawyers versus criminal lawyers?

4.   Rule 1.16(b)(6) of the American Bar Association's *Model Rules of Professional Conduct* also permits withdrawal where continued representation "will result in an unreasonable financial burden on the lawyer". Should we adopt such a rule in Canada?

5.   In 2001, Robert William Pickton was charged with murder in the case of 15 missing women in Vancouver. Pickton retained Peter Ritchie as his lawyer. While Pickton and his siblings had reportedly disposed of property worth upwards of $6 million in the mid-1990s, and while his own land was worth upwards of $3 million,[105] his liquid assets left him both ineligible for legal aid and unable to afford private counsel. The police conducted one of the biggest investigations in the history of Canada relating to the 15 murder charges faced by Pickton, uncovering volumes of forensic evidence. Pickton's attempts to negotiate government funding for his counsel stalled immediately before the preliminary inquiry. Ritchie threatened to withdraw on the basis of Pickton's inability to pay the overwhelming costs of defending the case. Is this sufficient reason to withdraw?[106]

6.   The classic example of the ethics of withdrawal is the perjury problem. The first situation can be described as anticipated perjury, where the client indicates to the lawyer an intent to lie when put on the stand.

7.   The second situation is described as "surprise perjury", where the client says something on the stand which the lawyer knows to be false. The *Model Code* attempts to respond to this situation in Rule 5.1-4 and its Commentary. Does this Rule provide adequate guidance for lawyers? What is the impact of the phrase, "subject to section 3.3 (Confidentiality)"? If the lawyer's knowledge of the truth is based on both what the client told them and another source, would the lawyer's duty differ?

8.   Gavin MacKenzie argues that it is no part of the lawyer's duty to assist the client in misleading the court. He advances five useful suggestions that run the gamut from a duty to remonstrate to obligatory withdrawal:

    (1)   The lawyer should bear in mind the fact that clients are entitled to

---

[105] This land was, however, essentially valueless as the site of the ongoing forensic investigation: Jane Armstrong, "Pickton's lawyer says he'll quit over bills" (October 5, 2002), online: *The Globe and Mail* https://www.theglobeandmail.com/news/national/picktons-lawyer-says-hell-quit-over-bills/article25423085/.

[106] See Robert Matas, "Pickton's lawyer quits in fee battle" (October 16, 2002), online: *The Globe and Mail* https://www.theglobeandmail.com/news/national/picktons-lawyer-quits-in-fee-battle/article4140005/. Pickton (through Ritchie) eventually negotiated an agreement with the British Columbia government to cover his legal fees: Jane Armstrong, "Pickton lawyer in private talks" *The Globe and Mail* (November 7, 2002).

have issues of credibility assessed by a duty-constituted court or tribunal. Lawyers have no professional duty to refuse to call evidence except where they have actual knowledge of its falsity.

(2) Where lawyers have actual knowledge of the falsity of evidence favourable to their client's position that their client or a witness proposes to give, lawyers should remonstrate with their client or the witness for the purpose of dissuading the client or witness from testifying falsely. The fundamental importance to our system of justice of evidence that is adduced being truthful, the possibility of criminal prosecution for perjury, the likelihood that the falsity of the evidence will be exposed on cross-examination or otherwise, possible cost consequences, and the duties of lawyers to refrain from calling false evidence and to expose perjury in many circumstances, should all form part of the remonstrance.

(3) The effects of remonstrating for this purpose are likely to include the termination of the lawyer's retainer if the client or witness is not convinced. Withdrawal may be necessary, if permitted by the court, even though it may accomplish little except to shift the problem to another lawyer or to encourage the client or witness to be less candid with the next lawyer, and to disclose the witness's perjury to the court and other parties in many cases.

(4) Lawyers acting as counsel in civil cases should not call witnesses who, to the lawyers' knowledge, will testify falsely. Lawyers may, however, call witnesses who will testify truthfully on some points but falsely on others if the lawyers' questions are confined to the evidence in the former category.

(5) If false evidence is introduced unexpectedly, or if the lawyer learns of the falsity of evidence after it is introduced, the lawyer should take reasonable steps to correct it. This should be done by urging the client or witness to correct the evidence if possible, either privately or by asking questions designed to enable the truth to emerge. If the client or witness does not correct the evidence, the lawyer should do so. This may be accomplished by informing the court or tribunal in argument, without explanation, that the evidence in question cannot be relied upon. Anything short of that, including silence, is inadequate, as lawyers cannot know what weight a court or tribunal will place on the false evidence even if lawyers make no use of it.[107]

Do you agree with these suggestions? Does (5) not convert lawyers from "trusted counsel" to snitches? Recommendation (3) counsels withdrawal for anticipated perjury, but (5) only suggests disclosure, not withdrawal, for surprise perjury. Are there any justifications for this distinction? Are MacKenzie's suggestions

---

[107] Gavin MacKenzie, *Lawyers and Ethics: Professional Responsibility and Discipline*, 6th ed. (Scarborough, ON: Carswell, 2018) at 4, 35-36.

consistent with the requirements of the *Model Code*?

Scenario Twenty-two

In a maintenance dispute, your client makes it clear that they are not willing to reveal the full extent of income received. Identify the various courses of action that you should consider. Do any of the above provisions on mandatory or optional withdrawal apply?

Scenario Twenty-three

What should a lawyer do if a client misrepresents to the judge that they have no prior criminal record, when the lawyer knows that such a statement is false? Would it make a difference if the lawyer's knowledge of the client's criminal record came from someone other than the client?

Scenario Twenty-four

Assume you are a senior partner in a law firm. Prior to this you served as a minister in a government that was defeated a few years ago. The political party in which you were, and still are, a member retains you to provide legal advice on a bill it is proposing to the House of Commons that will prohibit same-sex marriage. In particular, the party anticipates a constitutional challenge, and requests you to prepare a constitutional defence of the bill.

When this retainer becomes public, there is intense criticism of your firm, especially from the two-spirit, gay, lesbian, bisexual, transgender, and queer (2SLGBTQ+) community, which attracts significant media attention. Simultaneously, potential recruits to your firm, both law students and lateral hires, decline offers because of the firm's involvement in the case. The other partners in the firm request that you terminate the retainer by the political party. What are your options?[108]

Scenario Twenty-five

Solomon Porter is a young criminal defense lawyer in Toronto with a substantial online presence. He was hired by the Toronto Police Service to represent Jeremy Caputo, a police officer who shot and killed Serkan Nasser. Nasser was an 18-year-old man who was shot by police on a streetcar after threatening passengers with a knife. Community members and activists called for a full enquiry, and for Cpl. Caputo to be charged with murder. Shortly after being hired, Solomon made a statement to the media that "once the community hears all the facts of this shooting, they'll have a better understanding of the circumstances surrounding this investigation". Days later, a bystander's cell phone video surfaced that cast doubt on the officer's version of events. Solomon withdrew as counsel the same day and issued a press release that called the shooting "a terrible tragedy for our community". The next day, a local paper published an interview with Solomon, in which the interviewer asked him the reason for his withdrawal, and whether Solomon knew

---

[108] Michael D Shear & John Schwartz, "Law firm won't defend Marriage Act" (April 25, 2011), online: *The New York Times* www.nytimes.com/2011/04/26/us/politics/26marriage. html?_r=0; Adam Liptak, "The Case Against Gay Marriage: Top Law Firms Won't Touch It" (April 11, 2015), online: *The New York Times* www.nytimes.com/2015/04/12/us/the-case-against-gay-marriage-top-law-firms-wont-touch-it.html.

about the video: "All I can say is that the same day of the discovery of the video that was disclosed publicly, I withdrew as counsel immediately. Whatever factors people want to take from that and conclusions they want to make, they have the right to do that. But I can't confirm from an attorney-client standpoint what the reason is." Do you think Solomon had a just cause for withdrawing his representation? Was Solomon still obligated to protect Cpl. Caputo's interests after his withdrawal? Did he do so?[109]

Scenario Twenty-six

LP is a highly respected senior lawyer with a large practice. She is well known in the legal profession for her integrity, and for her support and mentorship of many junior lawyers. Over her long career, LP has regularly taken up *pro bono* legal representation of vulnerable members of society. She has also represented several persons who were sexually harassed or sexually assaulted, and she is regularly invited to comment on the low rates of conviction in cases involving sexual assault and harassment.

In August 2019 LP began representing AB, an anti-police brutality activist who was arrested while filming three police officers as they used excessive force while arresting a young Black man. AB alleges that he (AB) was physically assaulted while in custody on more than one occasion. AB's arrest, his allegations of assault, and the fact that LP was representing him were reported widely in newspapers. On February 21, 2020 LP posted the following on Twitter:

> A lawyer is not a hired spokesperson of a client but must uphold public interest #MeToo

LP's tweet was liked and retweeted by thousands of people. The tweet included a link to her longer statement published online on LAWBLOGS that stated that she would no longer represent AB because her "social commitment to the #MeToo movement overrides [her] professional engagement". Her statement explained that her decision was a result of allegations of sexual assault against her client by a university student. These allegations against her client were made in an article published in an online news source on February 17, 2020. Although the article did not name the student or AB, many people on social media noted that the "obvious reference" was to AB. Following the publication of the article, several people publicly criticized LP's representation of AB, and questioned her commitments to justice. Several hundred people retweeted a tweet that stated that lawyers like LP were "a big part of the problem". In her published statement LP stated that she is "committed to the #MeToo movement and stand[s] with the student's right to speak in the public domain without fear of reprisals." Her continued representation of AB, she stated, was "inconsistent" with her "support of the #MeToo movement". Many prominent news sources reported LP's decision. You are an articling student. Your principal JS is the President of the Criminal Lawyers' Association. JS has received several emails from members of the Association asking that a formal complaint be made against LP for "professional misconduct" and "conduct unbecoming a

---

[109] Scott Greenfield, "Memo to David Aylor: Shut Up" (April 9, 2015), online (blog): *Mimesis Law* http://mimesislaw.com/the-business-of-law/memo-to-david-aylor-shut-up/793.

lawyer". JS holds LP in high regard and is troubled by these allegations. JS has asked you to look into the matter and prepare a memo addressing the following two questions:

1. Whether LP's actions amount to "professional misconduct" and/or "conduct unbecoming a lawyer"?

2. Is LP an ethical lawyer?

[c] Court Approval of Withdrawal

The ethical dilemmas generated by withdrawal are not just "private" matters between a client and a lawyer. One key question in this regard is whether, and to what extent, a lawyer must give reasons to the court to justify their withdrawal. The Supreme Court of Canada addressed this question in the case of *R. v. Cunningham*.[110] Prior to *Cunningham*, some courts regulated withdrawal because of their inherent jurisdiction over the orderly administration of justice. Other courts did not require lawyers to seek approval before withdrawing. This resulted in some checkerboard jurisprudence across Canada. In the context of withdrawal by criminal defence lawyers, for example, the Supreme Court noted divergent lines of authority. In British Columbia, courts did not appear to invoke a supervisory power, but in Alberta, Quebec and Ontario they did.

R. V. CUNNINGHAM

[2010] S.C.J. No. 10, 2010 SCC 10
(S.C.C., McLachlin C.J.C. and Binnie, LeBel
Deschamps, Fish, Abella, Charron, Rothstein, Cromwell JJ.)

[Ms. Cunningham was an employee of the Yukon Legal Services Society ("Legal Aid"). Through Legal Aid she was retained as defence counsel for an accused, Mr. Morgan, charged with three sexual offences against a young child. In order for Mr. Morgan to continue receiving Legal Aid funding, Legal Aid instructed him to update his financial information. He failed to do so. After two weeks Ms. Cunningham applied to the Territorial Court of Yukon to withdraw from the case as counsel. She provided one reason for her withdrawal: Mr. Morgan, because of the suspension from legal aid and own limited resources, was unable to pay for legal services.]

The judgment of the Court was delivered by

ROTHSTEIN J. —

* * * * *

4. <u>Issue</u>

The issue in the present appeal is whether, in a criminal matter, a court has the authority to refuse to grant defence counsel's request to withdraw because the accused has not complied with the financial terms of the retainer. The reasons use the phrase "non-payment of legal fees" to refer to situations where, for example, an accused has actually defaulted on payment, where an accused has failed to provide

---

[110] [2010] S.C.J. No. 10, 2010 SCC 10, [2010] 1 S.C.R. 331 at para. 10.

funds on account at the agreed upon time, or where a legal aid certificate has been suspended or revoked.

5. Analysis

. . . The fiduciary nature of the solicitor-client relationship means that counsel is constrained in their ability to withdraw from a case once they have chosen to represent an accused. These constraints are thoroughly outlined in the rules of professional conduct issued by the provincial or territorial law societies (e.g. Law Society of Yukon, *Code of Professional Conduct*, Part One, r. 21) . . . This appeal raises the issue of whether a court's jurisdiction to control its own process imposes a further constraint on counsel's ability to withdraw.

A. *Divergent Lines of Authority*

There are two lines of provincial and territorial appellate court reasoning on this issue. The British Columbia and Yukon Courts of Appeal have determined that a court has no authority to prevent criminal defence counsel from withdrawing for non-payment of legal fees. The Alberta, Saskatchewan, Manitoba, Ontario, and Quebec Courts of Appeal have taken the opposite position — a court may refuse counsel's request to withdraw. . . .

* * * * *

For the following reasons, I conclude that a court does have the authority to refuse criminal defence counsel's request to withdraw for non-payment of legal fees.

B. *Jurisdiction of the Court*

[Justice Rothstein determined that superior courts have the authority, inherent and necessarily implied, to both remove counsel from cases and to refuse an application of withdrawal from a case submitted by counsel in order to protect the administration of justice.]

C. *Exercise of Jurisdiction*

[Ms. Cunningham argued that the Court should always decline to exercise jurisdiction over withdrawal applications because of solicitor-client privilege, the role of law societies, and a conflict of interest. Justice Rothstein addressed each of Ms. Cunningham's arguments. In the end he determined that none of the arguments, alone or combined, were sufficient to prevent a court from exercising its jurisdiction over applications for withdrawal based on non-fee payments.]

(1) Solicitor-Client Privilege

[Justice Rothstein noted that fee information is only *prima facie* privileged. Whether or not it is, in fact, privileged is determined by the Court. Withdrawal for non-payment of legal fees was, in this context, not privileged because it was impossible to use the fact of non-payment to speculate about the accused's activities. Even so, the Court cautioned that in other contexts, payments, or lack of, are pertinent to the case and will be protected under solicitor-client privilege. . .]

(2) Exclusive Law Society Oversight

I am also unable to accept the argument of Ms. Cunningham and the interveners that oversight of lawyer withdrawal falls exclusively to the law societies. The law societies play an essential role in disciplining lawyers for unprofessional conduct; however, the purpose of the court overseeing withdrawal is not disciplinary. The court's authority is *preventative* — to protect the administration of justice and ensure trial fairness. The disciplinary role of the law society is *reactive*. Both roles are necessary to ensure effective regulation of the profession and protect the process of the court.

[Justice Rothstein listed a number of rules and approaches different Law Societies take to withdrawal for non-payment of fees.]

While the court is not bound to apply law society or Canadian Bar Association codes of professional conduct, these codes "should be considered an important statement of public policy" (*MacDonald Estate*, at p. 1246). These standards complement the court's discretion to refuse withdrawal where the effects on the administration of justice will be severe. For example, the Canadian Bar Association rules recognize the distinct, yet complementary, nature of the functions served by the court and law societies:

> Where withdrawal is required or permitted by this Rule the lawyer must comply with all applicable rules of court as well as local rules and practice. [c. XII, commentary 3]

* * * * *

Ms. Cunningham and the interveners submit that court supervision over withdrawal threatens the independence of the bar. . . . I do not agree that an exceptional constraint on counsel, necessary to protect the integrity of the administration of justice, threatens counsel's independence . . .

(3) Conflict of Interest

I am also unpersuaded by the Law Society of British Columbia's point that forcing unwilling counsel to continue may create a conflict between the client's and lawyer's interests. It is argued that where counsel is compelled to work for free, they may be tempted to give legal advice which will expedite the process in order to cut counsel's financial losses even though wrapping up a criminal matter as quickly as possible may not be in the best interests of the accused. This argument, however, is inconsistent with the Law Society's position — with which I agree — that the court should presume that lawyers act ethically. There are many situations where counsel's personal or professional interests may be in tension with an individual client's interest, for example where counsel acquires an interesting new file that requires immediate attention, or has vacation plans that conflict with the timing of court proceedings affecting the client. Counsel is obligated to be diligent, thorough and to act in the client's best interest. Similarly, if counsel agrees to be retained *pro bono*, they must act just as professionally as if acting for the client on a paid retainer of the same nature. Where the court requires counsel to continue to represent an accused, counsel must do so competently and diligently. Both the integrity of the profession and the administration of justice require nothing less.

* * * * *

(5) Remedy of Last Resort

Ms. Cunningham's arguments do not, therefore, support a wholesale denial of the court's jurisdiction to refuse counsel's request to withdraw.

That being said, ordering counsel to work for free is not a decision that should be made lightly. . . . Refusing to allow counsel to withdraw should truly be a remedy of last resort and should only be relied upon where it is necessary to prevent serious harm to the administration of justice.

D. *Refusing Withdrawal*

The court's exercise of discretion to decide counsel's application for withdrawal should be guided by the following principles.

If counsel seeks to withdraw far enough in advance of any scheduled proceedings and an adjournment will not be necessary, then the court should allow the withdrawal. In this situation, there is no need for the court to enquire into counsel's reasons for seeking to withdraw or require counsel to continue to act.

Assuming that timing is an issue, the court is entitled to enquire further. Counsel may reveal that he or she seeks to withdraw for ethical reasons, non-payment of fees, or another specific reason (e.g. workload of counsel) if solicitor-client privilege is not engaged. Counsel seeking to withdraw for ethical reasons means that an issue has arisen in the solicitor-client relationship where it is now impossible for counsel to continue in good conscience to represent the accused. Counsel may cite "ethical reasons" as the reason for withdrawal if, for example, the accused is requesting that counsel act in violation of his or her professional obligations (see, *e.g.*, Law Society of Upper Canada, r. 2.09(7)(b), (d) . . .), or if the accused refuses to accept counsel's advice on an important trial issue (see, *e.g.*, Law Society of Upper Canada, r. 2.09(2) . . .). If the real reason for withdrawal is non-payment of legal fees, then counsel cannot represent to the court that he or she seeks to withdraw for "ethical reasons". However, in either the case of ethical reasons or non-payment of fees, the court must accept counsel's answer at face value and not enquire further so as to avoid trenching on potential issues of solicitor-client privilege.

If withdrawal is sought for an ethical reason, then the court must grant withdrawal (see *C. (D.D.)*, at p. 328, and *Deschamps*, at para. 23). Where an ethical issue has arisen in the relationship, counsel may be *required* to withdraw in order to comply with their professional obligations. It would be inappropriate for a court to require counsel to continue to act when to do so would put him or her in violation of professional responsibilities.

If withdrawal is sought because of non-payment of legal fees, the court may exercise its discretion to refuse counsel's request. The court's order refusing counsel's request to withdraw may be enforced by the court's contempt power (*C. (D.D.)*, at p. 327). In exercising its discretion on the withdrawal request, the court should consider the following non-exhaustive list of factors:

- whether it is feasible for the accused to represent himself or herself;
- other means of obtaining representation;
- impact on the accused from delay in proceedings, particularly if the accused is in custody;

- conduct of counsel, *e.g.* if counsel gave reasonable notice to the accused to allow the accused to seek other means of representation, or if counsel sought leave of the court to withdraw at the earliest possible time;

- impact on the Crown and any co-accused;

- impact on complainants, witnesses and jurors;

- fairness to defence counsel, including consideration of the expected length and complexity of the proceedings;

- the history of the proceedings, *e.g.* if the accused has changed lawyers repeatedly.

As these factors are all independent of the solicitor-client relationship, there is no risk of violating solicitor-client privilege when engaging in this analysis. On the basis of these factors, the court must determine whether allowing withdrawal would cause serious harm to the administration of justice. If the answer is yes, withdrawal may be refused. . .

* * * * *

The question of whether this case meets the high threshold that must be met to refuse leave to withdraw is now moot. . . . I simply emphasize that the threshold for refusing leave to withdraw is a high one and requires a proper basis in the record for its exercise.

* * * * *

6. Conclusion

In sum, a court has the authority to control its own process and to supervise counsel who are officers of the court. The Supreme Court of the Yukon Territory correctly concluded that the Territorial Court had the jurisdiction to refuse to grant counsel's request to withdraw. This jurisdiction, however, should be exercised exceedingly sparingly. It is not appropriate for the court to refuse withdrawal where an adjournment will not be necessary, nor where counsel seeks withdrawal for ethical reasons. Where counsel seeks untimely withdrawal for non-payment of fees, the court must weigh the relevant factors and determine whether withdrawal would cause serious harm to the administration of justice.

7. Disposition

I would allow the appeal. I would decline to grant an order as to costs.

NOTES AND QUESTIONS

1. Do you agree with how the Supreme Court of Canada characterizes the relationship between the courts and the law societies?

2. Has the Court been precise enough in explaining the circumstances in which lawyers can withdraw because of non-payment of legal fees?

3. What is the point of a court asserting supervisory authority over a lawyer who seeks to withdraw if the lawyer can simply announce that there is an ethical issue, which the court must accept at "face value"?

4. Both the Supreme Court of Canada (in *Cunningham*) and the *Model Code* (in Rule 3.7-4) explicitly address court supervision of withdrawal in the criminal law context. What about the non-criminal context? Do different rules, principles and policies apply? Should they?[111]

5. Lawyers working for organizations who discover that the organization has acted, or intends to act, dishonestly, fraudulently, criminally or illegally must engage in "upward reporting" within the organization. If the organization continues with the wrongful conduct, the lawyer must withdraw. These obligations are discussed further in Chapter 9. Is the duty to withdraw practically different for lawyers who are also employees of their clients? How, if at all, do you think that might affect those lawyers' discharge of their ethical obligations?

[d] Supplementary Obligations on Withdrawal

Rule 3.7-1 of the *Model Code* provides that if a lawyer withdraws they must give "reasonable notice". This obligation to avoid expense or harm to the client is reinforced by the Commentaries to this Rule, as well as Rule 3.7-8 (Manner of Withdrawal). Do these provisions provide sufficient protection for the client? Do they provide sufficient guidance for a lawyer?

There are also a series of more particular obligations in Rule 3.7-9 which Smith characterizes as being guided by "cooperation and generosity".[112] Are these supplementary obligations on withdrawal sufficient to protect the interests of the client?

One inherently conflictual situation arises when the client fails to pay after withdrawal by the lawyer. Can a lawyer take lien on the client's property? The Commentary to Rule 3.7-9 suggests that a lawyer ought not to do so where it would be prejudicial to the client's legal interests. If it is permissible for a lawyer to breach confidentiality in order to recover their fees (as we shall see in Chapter 3), why are lawyers discouraged from taking a lien when they withdraw, especially if it is mandatory withdrawal caused by inappropriate client conduct?

---

[111] There is still debate as to whether the *Cunningham* test applies in non-criminal cases. The judges in *Seaway Consultants Inc. v. J.D. Irving Ltd.*, [2013] N.B.J. No. 450, 2013 NBQB 234 (N.B.Q.B.), and *Sandhu v. Household Realty Corp.*, [2013] B.C.J. No. 244, 2013 BCSC 192 (B.C.S.C.), considered and applied the *Cunningham* factors to withdrawal applications in civil proceedings. In *Tri-Link Consultants Inc. v. Saskatchewan Financial Services Commission*, [2012] S.J. No. 225, 2012 SKCA 41, leave to appeal refused [2012] S.C.C.A. No. 252 (S.C.C.), the judge noted that Cunningham's application to administrative proceedings was "questionable". In *Children's Aid Society of the Region of Halton v. D.K.*, [2012] O.J. No. 3644, 2012 ONCJ 502 (Ont. C.J.), the Court held that it may exercise its jurisdiction to deny withdrawal in all 'high-stakes' cases, not just criminal ones, pointing to the application of *Cunningham* in a case about child protection: *Catholic Children's Aid Society of Toronto v. H (F)*, [2011] O.J. No. 4107 (Ont. C.J.). See also Michel Proulx & David Layton, *Ethics and Criminal Law*, 2nd ed. (Toronto: Irwin Law, 2015) at 559.

[112] Beverley G. Smith, *Professional Conduct for Lawyers and Judges*, 4th ed. (Fredericton: Maritime Law Book, 2011), ch. 7 at 51.

Complications might also arise on the dissolution of a law firm.

On termination of the lawyer-client relationship, the question arises as to what "property" the lawyer is obliged to return to the client. See 3.5-2 Commentary 3 *Model Code*. In Canada, the only guidance is to be found in Rule 3.5-1, which includes "money, securities, original documents. . .and all other papers. . .as well as personal property.. . ." At first blush this might seem clear but consider the following situation.

Scenario Twenty-seven

You have represented a local municipality for 10 years under a term contract for legal services. The contract has now expired, and the municipality has chosen a different lawyer to provide legal services. The municipality requests that you send their new counsel all files — both open and closed. You have been paid in full for your work. How can you distinguish between 'end-product' documents and documents created for administrative purposes or to assist in the work? Which of the following items would you send?

- A contract with a water utility company for service to the municipality. The contract is ongoing.

- A draft version of the water contract, with handwritten notes and edits.

- A finalized contract with a different water utility that has now expired.

- Personnel files and employment contracts (produced by their previous lawyer) that the municipality sent to you in relation to a wrongful dismissal suit.

- Memos to your office staff assigning tasks for the municipality's file.

- Research notes, articles, and case reports relating to public-private partnership contracts.

- A memo created by your junior associate on a potential conflict of interest between the municipality and another of your clients.

Scenario Twenty-eight

A client approaches you with a scheme to obtain money from lenders through fake documents in which he represents that he owns assets which he does not. You refuse and withdraw. You find out that he has gone to lawyer B. In conversations with lawyer B, it becomes clear that she has not been told, and does not realize, that the documents are false and is assisting the client to obtain financing on the basis that they are accurate. What, if anything, do you tell lawyer B?

Finally, successor lawyers also have some obligations to balance the interests of the former lawyer with the interests of the client under Rule 3.7-10 and its Commentary. Please review this Rule and its Commentary.

[5] FURTHER READING

Canadian Bar Association, *Futures: Transforming the Delivery of Legal Services in Canada* (August 2014), online (pdf): http://www.cba.org/CBAMediaLibrary/cba_na/PDFs/CBA%20Legal%20Futures%20PDFS/Futures-Final-eng.pdf.

Hutchinson, Allan, *Legal Ethics and Professional Responsibility*, 2d ed., (Toronto: Irwin Law, 2006).

MacKenzie, Gavin, *Lawyers and Ethics: Professional Responsibility and Discipline*, loose-leaf (Scarborough, ON: Carswell, 1993).

Proulx, Michel & David Layton, *Ethics and Criminal Law*, 2d ed. (Toronto: Irwin Law, 2015).

Smith, Abbe & Monroe Freedman, eds., *How Can You Represent Those People?* (New York: Palgrave MacMillan, 2013).

Smith, Beverley, *Professional Conduct for Lawyers and Judges*, 4th ed. (Fredericton: Maritime Law Book, 2011).

Woolley, Alice, *Understanding Lawyers Ethics in Canada*, 2d ed, (Toronto: LexisNexis Canada, 2016).

CHAPTER 3

THE LAWYER'S DUTY TO PRESERVE CLIENT CONFIDENCES

[1] INTRODUCTION

A lawyer's duty to preserve the confidences of their client is at the heart of the lawyer-client relationship. From the lawyer's point of view, comprehensive and candid information about the client's situation is often critical to the lawyer's ability to adequately advise the client and provide appropriate representation of the client's interests. From the client's perspective, it is difficult to share information — which is often highly personal and capable of exposing a client to significant vulnerability — without great confidence that the information will be closely guarded and not disclosed without the client's permission. From the perspective of the legal profession as a whole, and the justice system itself, it is essential not only that any individual be able to trust in the confidentiality of a particular lawyer but more generally — systemically — that the general public knows that information shared with lawyers within the lawyer-client relationship will be vigorously protected.

For these reasons, communications and information covered by a lawyer's duty of confidentiality and the common law doctrine of solicitor-client privilege are among the most highly-protected communications and information in law.

From the perspective of the public, however, the lawyer's preservation of a client's confidences is often at the heart of criticisms of lawyers for their disregard of a larger public interest in favour of the specific interests of their clients. Attempting to identify the circumstances when a public interest value should take precedence over a foundational dimension of client representation — the preservation of client confidences — is one of the most provocative and challenging aspects of legal ethics. As we shall also see, in limited but important circumstances, the protection of client confidences does yield to a greater public interest. An exploration of these exceptions to confidentiality and privilege, and the overriding public interest values imbedded in them, will show that lawyer-client confidentiality holds a very high place within the constellation of public policy values in our society. This exploration also identifies values seen to be of greater importance, as well as the evolution of confidentiality and privilege over time.

The opportunity to explore these questions has been assisted by a rapidly-growing jurisprudence in Canada on the subject of solicitor-client privilege and confidentiality. As Adam Dodek observes in his text on solicitor-client privilege:

> [p]rivilege is one of the oldest and most venerated doctrines under the common law.

Over the past three decades, Canadian courts have elevated this limited evidentiary privilege into a quasi-constitutional right. Between 1999-2013, the Supreme Court of Canada rendered no less than thirteen decisions in cases directly involving the privilege. In 2010, the Supreme Court described the privilege as "one of the most ancient and powerful privileges known to our jurisprudence". . .[1]

In the course of this chapter you should give consideration to the following questions:

(a) In the jurisprudence, academic commentaries and codes of professional conduct, are the justifications for lawyer-client confidentiality and privilege sufficiently made out? Are they overstated? Understated?

(b) Is there a conceptual framework for the limited number of exceptions to confidentiality and privilege? Is this framework sound? Is it applicable to the right sort of circumstances?

(c) What are the differences between confidentiality and the various forms of privilege? What is the legal significance of these differences?

(d) To what extent ought the obligations associated with confidentiality and privilege be "discretionary" in the sense that an individual lawyer may choose to preserve confidences, or choose to disclose, according to the lawyer's judgment of the circumstances and his or her own ethical perspectives?

[2] A LAWYER'S DUTY NOT TO DISCLOSE CLIENT CONFIDENCES

A lawyer's obligation not to disclose client confidences is grounded in both the common law doctrine of solicitor-client privilege and the duty of confidentiality found in lawyer codes of professional conduct. Although many lawyers and, indeed, sometimes judges in court decisions, use the terms "confidentiality" and "privilege" interchangeably, it is important to note that these are two similar but legally distinct concepts. While each concept is based upon the principle that a lawyer owes a duty of loyalty to a client, including a duty to maintain a client's confidences, the source, scope and enforcement of the respective duties are distinct.

[a] Solicitor-Client Privilege

Courts are the source of the law of solicitor-client privilege. Historically, the common law on solicitor-client privilege tended to arise in relation to evidentiary questions (like, for example, whether a particular communication between a lawyer and their client could be tendered as evidence in court). More recently, however, solicitor-client privilege has come to be featured in case law as a substantive legal principle and, moreover, has now achieved constitutional status as a "principle of fundamental justice" for the purposes of section 7 of the *Canadian Charter of Rights and Freedoms*.[2]

---

[1] Adam M. Dodek, *Solicitor-Client Privilege* (Markham, ON: LexisNexis Canada, 2014) at 15 (footnotes omitted).

[2] Part I of the *Constitution Act, 1982*, being Schedule B to the *Canada Act 1982* (U.K.), 1982, c. 11.

As observed by Adam Dodek, the following definition set out by John Henry Wigmore "continues to remain the touchstone or the framework for privilege analysis in Canada":

> [w]here legal advice of any kind is sought from a professional legal adviser, in his capacity as such, the communications relating to that purpose, made in confidence by the client, are at his instance permanently protected from disclosure by himself or by the legal adviser, except the privilege be waived.[3]

[b] The Duty of Confidentiality

Professional conduct rules established by law societies and their interpretation by law society tribunals determine the parameters of a lawyer's professional obligation to preserve client confidences. Breaches of the professional conduct rules governing client confidentiality can result in a lawyer being investigated and potentially disciplined by the law society of which they are a member.

The scope of the duty of confidentiality is quite broad, as reflected in the wording contained in lawyers' professional codes of conduct. For example, the Federation of Law Societies of Canada's *Model Code of Professional Conduct* ("FLSC *Model Code*") provides:

Confidential Information

3.3-1 A lawyer at all times must hold in strict confidence all information concerning the business and affairs of a client acquired in the course of the professional relationship and must not divulge any such information unless:

    (a)   expressly or impliedly authorized by the client;

    (b)   required by law or a court to do so;

    (c)   required to deliver the information to the Law Society; or

    (d)   otherwise permitted by this rule.

[c] Differences between Solicitor-Client Privilege and the Duty of Confidentiality

A number of differences in scope can be gleaned from the above definitions. Two of the most important differences – each of which make the scope of the duty of confidentiality broader than the scope of the solicitor-client privilege – are highlighted below.

One difference between solicitor-client privilege and the duty of confidentiality relates to the nature of the communication. To be privileged, a lawyer-client communication must be made for the purpose of providing legal advice. In contrast,

---

[3] Adam M. Dodek, *Solicitor-Client Privilege* (Markham, ON: LexisNexis Canada, 2014) at lii, citing John H. Wigmore, *Wigmore on Evidence,* McNaughton rev. ed. (Boston: Little Brown, 1961) vol. 8 at s. 2292. As Dodek notes, *infra*, this definition has been repeatedly adopted by the Supreme Court of Canada. Recent examples include: *Canada (Attorney General) v. Chambre des notaires du Québec*, [2016] S.C.J. No. 20, [2016] 1 S.C.R. 336, 2016 SCC 20 at para. 72 (S.C.C.); *R. v. McClure*, [2001] S.C.J. No. 13, [2001] 1 S.C.R. 445, 2001 SCC 14 at para. 29 (S.C.C.) and *R. v. Campbell*, [1999] S.C.J. No. 16, [1999] 1 S.C.R. 565 at para. 49 (S.C.C.).

"all information concerning the business and affairs of a client acquired in the course of the professional relationship" attracts the lawyer's professional duty of confidentiality.[4]

In considering the impact of this first distinction, it is important to note that courts in practice have taken a relatively broad approach to what is covered by solicitor-client privilege, applying a presumption "that all communications between lawyer and client are privileged" and "increasingly moving to protecting the solicitor-client *relationship* under the heading of solicitor-client privilege."[5] For example, in *Cusson v. Quan*,[6] the court held that a draft newspaper article was privileged on the basis that article was a part of a "continuum of communications" between a reporter and his lawyer in relation to legal advice sought regarding potential exposure to a defamation claim.

A second important difference relates to the source of the information or communication. Solicitor-client privilege attaches only to information that comes from the client or, in some cases, an agent of the client.[7] In contrast, "[u]nder the codes of conduct it is clear that the lawyer's obligation of confidentiality applies irrespective of where information came from."[8]

An example of how this second distinction could make a practical difference can be found in provisions of provincial and territorial child protection legislation that require lawyers to make a report to the relevant authorities if they have a reasonable suspicion that a child is need of protection due to abuse or other enumerated harms and potential risks. In general, this legislation specifies that it does not abrogate solicitor-client privilege.[9] However, the legislation does not specify any protections for information that falls under a lawyer's duty of confidentiality, but which is not privileged.[10] As Deanne Sowter has observed, the effect of this legislation, whether intentional or not, is to require a lawyer to report information (received in the course of a lawyer-client relationship) about a child in need of protection if such information was received from a third party:

> [I]f a lawyer learns about a situation from a third party (who is not the lawyer's agent) the information will be confidential but not privileged, so a lawyer is

---

[4] For further discussion of this distinction, see Alice Woolley, *Understanding Lawyers' Ethics in Canada* 2d ed. (Toronto: LexisNexis Canada, 2016) at 179-182.

[5] Adam M. Dodek, *Solicitor-Client Privilege* (Markham, ON: LexisNexis Canada, 2014) at 49 and 117.

[6] *Cusson v. Quan*, [2004] O.J. No. 3466, 10 C.P.C. (6th) 308 (Ont. S.C.J.).

[7] For further discussion of when privilege will attach to communications from agents of a client, see Adam M. Dodek, *Solicitor-Client Privilege* (Markham, ON: LexisNexis Canada, 2014) at 49 and 117.38-39.

[8] For further discussion of this distinction, see Alice Woolley, *Understanding Lawyers' Ethics in Canada* 2d ed. (Toronto: LexisNexis Canada, 2016) at 188.

[9] See, for example, *Child, Youth and Family Services Act, 2017*, S.O. 2017, c. 14, Sched. 1, s. 125(11).

[10] See, for example, *Child, Youth and Family Services Act, 2017*, S.O. 2017, c. 14, Sched. 1, s. 125(11).

required to report what she knows. In other words, if a lawyer learns something directly from [a client's] child, or her client's spouse, she is required to report her concern.[11]

As this example demonstrates, although there is "significant overlap" between solicitor-client privilege and the duty of confidentiality, it is important that lawyers understand that these two concepts are not equivalent and that their differing scopes can result in distinct legal consequences and obligations in certain circumstances.[12]

[3] WHAT IS THE RATIONALE FOR PRESERVING CLIENT CONFIDENCES?

The introduction to this chapter discusses individual and systemic rationales that have been used to justify the lawyer's duty to preserve client confidences. The following excerpt discusses these rationales in further detail.

D. LAYTON & M. PROULX

Ethics and Criminal Law
(Toronto: Irwin Law, 2015)*

A. INTRODUCTION

The lawyer's duty to keep confidential all information received as a result of representing a client is a core obligation of the professional relationship. The scope of this duty is exceptionally broad, demanding that counsel take great care in handling all information pertaining to or affecting a client. At the same time, there are exceptions to the duty of confidentiality that permit, and sometimes even demand, disclosure of such information by the lawyer. Determining the instances where exceptions should apply raises some of the most controversial and daunting ethical problems facing the criminal bar today. . . .

The standard justification for imposing a duty of confidentiality on lawyers is that the client who is assured of complete secrecy is more likely to reveal to his counsel all information pertaining to the case. The lawyer who is in possession of all relevant information is better able to advise the client and hence provide competent service, furthering both the client's legal rights and the truth-finding function of the adversarial system. The obligation to maintain confidentiality also protects the client's privacy, as well as promoting autonomy and dignity by facilitating her control over personal information and the conduct of the defence. And the duty of confidentiality is closely connected to the overarching duty of loyalty owed by a lawyer to the client. The obligation to be loyal would be compromised if a lawyer could use information so as to adversely impact the client. A complete bar on the unauthorized use of confidential information by counsel, even where no adverse impact is possible, accordingly serves a prophylactic function that helps to ensure undivided loyalty.

---

[11] For further discussion of this distinction, see Alice Woolley, *Understanding Lawyers' Ethics in Canada*, 2d ed., (Toronto: LexisNexis Canada, 2016) at 179-182.

[12] The characterization of "significant overlap" is taken from Adam M. Dodek, *Solicitor-Client Privilege* (Markham, ON: LexisNexis Canada, 2014) at 21.

* Reproduced with permission. [footnotes omitted]

What is more, solicitor-client privilege and thus by implication the ethical duty of confidentiality acquires "an added dimension" where the client is the subject of a criminal investigation. The "promise of confidentiality" engaged by the privilege is particularly vital, because the client is facing the state as a "singular antagonist". More specifically, maintaining client confidences is especially important in the criminal context because doing so substantially furthers the client's ability to exercise constitutional rights against the state.

In promoting effective legal advice, the duty of confidentiality not only benefits the individual client but also serves a broader societal interest. As already noted, a client who is able to rely on the assurance of confidentiality is more likely to receive sound legal counsel. As a result, he is more likely to obey the law and if charged with a crime is better able to mount a defence. It is in the public interest that these ends be encouraged, and the duty of confidentiality thus advances fundamental systemic goals.

[4] WHEN DOES THE DUTY TO PRESERVE CLIENT CONFIDENCES ARISE?

Both solicitor-client privilege and the duty of confidentiality apply in the context of a lawyer-client relationship. Chapter 2 discusses when a lawyer-client relationship is formed. In the context of whether information disclosed to a lawyer is protected from disclosure, it is important to emphasize that the law protects not only information received from actual clients but also information received from prospective clients. The Supreme Court of Canada has stated that the protections of solicitor-client privilege arise "as soon as the potential client has his first dealings with the lawyer's office in order to obtain legal advice."[13] Similarly, the FLSC *Model Code* states "[a] lawyer also owes a duty of confidentiality to anyone seeking advice or assistance on a matter invoking a lawyer's professional knowledge, although the lawyer may not render an account or agree to represent that person."[14]

The receipt of confidential information from a prospective client can be relevant in the context of proceedings to disqualify a lawyer on the basis of a conflict of interest. For example, if a wife contacts a family law lawyer for an initial consultation about a divorce but never retains the lawyer, the lawyer may be later disqualified from representing her husband if the lawyer had received confidential information from the wife. A detailed discussion of the law on conflicts of interest can be found in Chapter 4. The topic is raised here for the purposes of noting that a lawyer's duty to preserve client confidences can arise at an early stage and have important practical consequences. For this reason, when screening potential clients, lawyers should take care to avoid receiving any confidential information before first checking for conflicts of interest. Lawyers should also caution prospective clients

---

[13] *Descôteaux v. Mierzwinski*, [1982] S.C.J. No. 43, [1982] 1 S.C.R. 8690 at 893 (S.C.C.).

[14] Federation of Law Societies of Canada, *Model Code of Professional Conduct* at Rules 3.3-1, Commentary [4], online: *Federation of Law Societies of Canada* https://flsc.ca/ interactivecode/.

against leaving confidential information on the lawyer's voicemail, or sending unsolicited information or material to the lawyer over email.

The question of when a duty to preserve client confidences arises is particularly salient in the context of lawyers who are employed by organizations, such as in-house counsel and government lawyers. Employed lawyers often serve a variety of functions within their employer organizations, not all of which involve providing legal advice. For example, "[g]overnment lawyers who have spent years with a particular client department may be called upon to offer policy advice that has nothing to do with their legal training or expertise, but draws on departmental know-how."[15] Likewise, in-house counsel often provide business advice in addition to legal advice. The Supreme Court of Canada has been clear that "[a]dvice given by lawyers on matters outside the solicitor-client relationship is not protected."[16] In some cases, drawing the distinction between which communications constitute legal advice, and those which can be fairly said to arise outside the solicitor-client relationship, will be relatively straightforward. For example, an in-house lawyer's report on whether their employer corporation is in compliance with a securities regulator's reporting obligations relating to gender diversity would generally be considered legal advice and privileged. In contrast, if the same lawyer, while acting as a member of the corporation's diversity and inclusion committee, offered suggestions for improving the corporation's record for retaining women in leadership positions, such comments would not generally be considered legal advice and would not be protected by solicitor-client privilege. Ultimately, lawyers who are employed by organizations and their employers need to be alert to the fact that not all communications produced by such lawyers will be protected under solicitor-client privilege. Adopting best practices – like, for example, drafting legal and policy or business advice in separate documents and keeping separate files – can help avoid confusion and may be helpful in defending against challenges to an organization's claims to solicitor-client privilege.[17]

Just as business advice is not protected by solicitor-client privilege, neither are criminal communications. This issue is most commonly referred to under the label of the "crime/fraud" exclusion to solicitor-client privilege. As observed by Adam Dodek, "[t]he rationale for the crime-fraud exclusion is straightforward: communications in furtherance of a crime or fraud do not form part of the legal professional relationship and hence no privilege can apply."[18]

This exclusion applies to both (1) communications that can be considered, in and of themselves, to be criminal and (2) communications that were made in order to facilitate a crime. An example of the first type of situation can be found in the

---

[15] *R. v. Campbell*, [1999] S.C.J. No. 16, [1999] 1 S.C.R. 565 at para. 50.

[16] *R. v. Campbell*, [1999] S.C.J. No. 16, [1999] 1 S.C.R. 565 at para. 50.

[17] Markus Koehnen, "Privilege primer: Best practices for internal counsel" (August 2011), online: mcmillian.ca, https://www.martindale.com/legal-news/article_mcmillan-llp_1331400.htm.

[18] Adam M. Dodek, *Solicitor-Client Privilege* (Markham, ON: LexisNexis Canada, 2014) at 54.

Descôteaux v. Mierzwinski case excerpted below. An example that would fall under the second type of situation would be advice given by a lawyer to an individual about how to launder money.[19] It is important to note that "merely seeking advice on an unlawful or criminal scheme does not trigger the criminal communications exclusion" and, thus, for example, if a person "asks a lawyer whether a particular activity constitutes money laundering and the lawyers advises. . .that it does, then that communication is privileged, even if [the person] later engage[s] in money laundering."[20]

DESCOTEAUX v. MIERZWINSKI

[1982] S.C.J. No. 43, [1982] 1 S.C.R. 860, 141 D.L.R. (3d) 590
(S.C.C., Martland, Ritchie, Dickson, Beetz, Estey, Chouinard and Lamer JJ.)

[In order to obtain proof that Ledoux, an applicant for legal aid, had committed an indictable offence by fraudulently reporting a lower income in order to be eligible for such services, two peace officers presented themselves at a legal aid bureau with a search warrant. This warrant related to certain documents, including an "Application for Legal Aid" form which contained, inter alia, information on the applicant's financial situation. The search was made in the presence of the syndic of the Bar and the police officers agreed to receive the documents in a sealed envelope without examining them. Appellants' application for certiorari to quash the seizure on the ground that the documents seized were protected by solicitor-client privilege was dismissed both in the Superior Court and in the Court of Appeal.

At trial and on appeal to the Quebec Court of Appeal, the documents were found not to attract the protection of lawyer-client confidentiality or privilege. The decision was appealed to the Supreme Court of Canada.

As we saw in Chapter 2, the Supreme Court of Canada found that the lawyer-client relationship commences "as soon as the potential client has his first dealings with the lawyer's office in order to obtain legal advice". The remaining part of the case, considered here, focused on whether the circumstances meant that the client did not have an entitlement to confidentiality or privilege in relation to the documents in question.]

LAMER J.:— A citizen who lies about his financial means in order to obtain legal aid is committing a crime. This appeal concerns the right of the police to be authorized by a search warrant to search a legal aid bureau and seize the form filled out by the citizen at his interview, for purposes of proving that this crime was committed. This issue raises several others, including, in particular, the scope of and procedures for exercising the authority to search lawyers' offices, in view of the confidential nature of their clients' files. This appeal will also give everyone an opportunity to note the deficiencies in the law in this area and the limited ability of the courts to compensate for them since their role is not primarily legislative.

---

[19] See, e.g. the situation in *R. v. Rosenfeld*, [2009] O.J. No. 1478, 2009 ONCA 307 (Ont. C.A.).

[20] Alice Woolley, *Understanding Lawyers' Ethics in Canada*, 2d ed. (Toronto: LexisNexis Canada, 2016) at 184-185.

. . . . .

I do not intend to repeat here everything that others have said, on numerous occasions and very clearly and completely, about solicitor-client privilege, or about the issuance and execution of search warrants.

I think, however, that I should make a few remarks about the existence and effects of a person's right to have his communications with his lawyer kept confidential; I shall then deal more particularly with the search power provided for in the *Criminal Code*.

THE RIGHT TO CONFIDENTIALITY

It is not necessary to demonstrate the existence of a person's right to have communications with his lawyer kept confidential. Its existence has been affirmed numerous times and was recently reconfirmed by this court in *Solosky v. The Queen*, [1980] 1 S.C.R. 821, where Dickson J. stated (at p. 839):

> One may depart from the current concept of privilege and approach the case on the broader basis that (i) *the right to communicate in confidence with one's legal adviser is a fundamental civil and legal right, founded upon the unique relationship of solicitor and client,* and (ii) a person confined to prison retains all of his civil rights, other than those expressly or impliedly taken from him by law. (Emphasis added)

There is no denying that a person has a right to communicate with a legal adviser in all confidence, a right that is "founded upon the unique relationship of solicitor and client" (*Solosky, supra*). It is a personal and extra-patrimonial right which follows a citizen throughout his dealings with others. Like other personal, extra-patrimonial rights, it gives rise to preventive or curative remedies provided for by law, depending on the nature of the aggression threatening it or of which it was the object. Thus a lawyer who communicates a confidential communication to others without his client's authorization could be sued by his client for damages; or a third party who had accidentally seen the contents of a lawyer's file could be prohibited by injunction from disclosing them.

. . . . .

THE SUBSTANTIVE RULE

Although the right to confidentiality first took the form of a rule of evidence, it is now recognized as having a much broader scope, as can be seen from the manner in which this court dealt with the issues raised in *Solosky*.

Solosky was an inmate at Millhaven Penitentiary. He was seeking a declaration that henceforth all properly identified items of solicitor-client correspondence would be forwarded to their respective destinations unopened.

The inmates' right to confidentiality conflicted with the *Penitentiaries Act*, . . . and more particularly with s. 2.18 of the *Penitentiary Service Regulations*, allowing the director of the institution to order censorship of correspondence to the extent considered necessary or desirable for the security of the institution.

[On behalf of the Supreme Court, Dickson J. found that the solicitor-client privilege existed and that the communications between solicitor and client were to be treated as confidential subject to certain articulated exceptions or qualifications related to the safety and security of the penitentiary.]

. . . . .

It is quite apparent that the court in that case applied a standard that has nothing to do with the rule of evidence, the privilege, since there was never any question of testimony before a tribunal or court. The court in fact, in my view, applied a substantive rule, without actually formulating it, and, consequently, recognized implicitly that the right to confidentiality, which had long ago given rise to a rule of evidence, had also since given rise to a substantive rule.

It would, I think, be useful for us to formulate this substantive rule, as the judges formerly did with the rule of evidence; it could, in my view, be stated as follows:

1. The confidentiality of communications between solicitor and client may be raised in any circumstances where such communications are likely to be disclosed without the client's consent.

2. Unless the law provides otherwise, when and to the extent that the legitimate exercise of a right would interfere with another person's right to have his communications with his lawyer kept confidential, the resulting conflict should be resolved in favour of protecting the confidentiality.

3. When the law gives someone the authority to do something which, in the circumstances of the case, might interfere with that confidentiality, the decision to do so and the choice of means of exercising that authority should be determined with a view to not interfering with it except to the extent absolutely necessary in order to achieve the ends sought by the enabling legislation.

4. Acts providing otherwise in situations under para. 2 and enabling legislation referred to in para. 3 must be interpreted restrictively.

. . . . .

CONFIDENTIALITY IN THE CASE AT BAR

. . . . .

The items of information that a lawyer requires from a person in order to decide if he will agree to advise or represent him are just as much communications made in order to obtain legal advice as any information communicated to him subsequently. It has long been recognized that even if the lawyer does not agree to advise the person seeking his services, communications made by the person to the lawyer or his staff for that purpose are none the less privileged . . .

Moreover, the same applies not only to information given before the retainer is perfected concerning the legal problem itself, but also to information concerning the client's ability to pay the lawyer and any other information which a lawyer is reasonably entitled to require before accepting the retainer. First, this information of an administrative nature is just as related to the establishment of the professional relationship as any other information; this is especially clear when, as in the case at bar, the legal aid applicant "*must set forth (his) financial means . . . and the basis of his claim*". In addition, information of this nature that a person gives his lawyer

176

for that purpose may also be highly confidential and would have been kept secret by that person were it not for that person's need of the assistance of a legal adviser.

. . . . .

I therefore do not think that a distinction should be made between information that must be given in order to establish the probable existence of a valid claim and that given to establish eligibility from the point of view of financial means, since, on the one hand, information concerning the person's financial situation may be just as highly confidential as any other information and since, on the other hand, the fact of being unable to meet the eligibility requirements respecting financial means is no less fatal to the ability to obtain the services sought.

. . . . .

Confidential communications, whether they relate to financial means or to the legal problem itself, lose that character if and to the extent that they were made for the purpose of obtaining legal advice to facilitate the commission of a crime.

The same is true a *fortiori* where, as in the case at bar, the communication itself is the material element (*actus reus*) of the crime; this is all the more evident where the victim of the crime is precisely the office of the lawyer to whom the communication was made.

[Justice Lamer concluded that this "criminal communication" purpose prevented the communication from attracting lawyer-client privilege.]

NOTES AND QUESTIONS

1. The Supreme Court of Canada in this case confirms the elevation of solicitor-client privilege to a "substantive right", and not just a rule of evidence. It will be important to observe the ways in which the Court builds upon this right in subsequent cases.

2. The Court established that this right, grounded in the lawyer-client relationship, takes effect at a very early stage. Indeed, the obligations related to client confidences are among the most significant consequences of a lawyer-client relationship commencing at such an early point. Is this appropriate? Is it manageable for lawyers who actually intend to decline to represent a person and never enter into an arrangement where they are retained by the client? What consequences for the lawyer may flow from this?

3. *Descôteaux* is an example of the "crime/fraud" or "criminal communications" exclusion from solicitor-client privilege. As observed by Adam Dodek, "[w]hile this rule is often referred to as the crime-fraud 'exception' it is in fact an 'exclusion' from [solicitor-client] privilege in the same way that non-legal advice is excluded by or not covered by the privilege".[21] There is little doubt that the same exclusion applies to the ethical duty of confidentiality. The *Model Code*, however, does not explicitly address the

---

[21] Adam M. Dodek, *Solicitor-Client Privilege* (Markham, ON: LexisNexis Canada, 2014) at 54.

relationship between criminal communications and the ethical duty of confidentiality. Is this lack of guidance a problem?

4. Understandably, lawyers are not pleased to be used by clients to facilitate the commission of crimes, and the existence of a "crime/fraud" exclusion from confidentiality protections is widely accepted. At the same time, clients may use the instrumentality of a lawyer's services to facilitate crime without the actual communication constituting a part of the crime itself. Lying to one's lawyer in order to get the lawyer to prepare a false document would be one example. Would this be caught by Lamer J.'s articulation of the crime/fraud exclusion? Should it be?

5. If a client sought legal advice on whether a particular course of action was "illegal", acted on the advice and it was subsequently determined that the activity was illegal, could the information regarding the advice be required to be disclosed on the basis that it came within the "criminal communications" exclusion? If one part of the person's defence to the allegation of criminal misconduct was that he relied on legal advice that the actions were lawful, could the legal advice be required to be disclosed?[22]

6. As is commonly the case, the nature and importance of lawyer-client confidences is usually articulated when the right is challenged, or an exception to the right is under consideration. You will have noted that Lamer J. set out a framework for dealing with challenges and exceptions to confidentiality and privilege. Would you agree that a strong element of this framework is the expression of support for the importance of protecting client confidences and that, consequently, any interference with clients' rights in this respect should be kept to a minimum? Do you agree with this perspective? It will be important to familiarize yourself with Lamer J.'s framework, since it will make a regular appearance in subsequent cases when exceptions to confidentiality and privilege arise.

[5] WAIVER

Solicitor-client privilege belongs to the client, not their lawyer.[23] One consequence of this principle is that the common law recognizes that a client can instruct their lawyer to waive privilege in respect of a communication. Professional conduct rules permit lawyers to disclose confidential client communication "if expressly or impliedly authorized by the client."[24]

Although the issue of waiver might seem to involve a simple question – does the client want to disclose the information at issue? – it can, in fact, also involve tricky

---

[22] See *R. v. Campbell*, [1999] S.C.J. No. 16, [1999] 1 S.C.R. 565 (S.C.C.), especially paras. 55-62 and 67-71.

[23] *Lavallee, Rackel & Heintz v. Canada (Attorney General); White, Ottenheimer & Baker v. Canada (Attorney General); R. v. Fink*, [2002] S.C.J. No. 61, 2002 SCC 61, [2002] 3 S.C.R. 209 at para.39 (S.C.C.).

[24] Federation of Law Societies of Canada, *Model Code of Professional Conduct* at Rule 3.3-1(a), online: *Federation of Law Societies of Canada* https://flsc.ca/interactivecode/.

factual and legal questions for the lawyer to consider. For example, if the client is an organization, who has the authority in the organization to waive the protections provided by solicitor-client privilege and the duty of confidentiality? Another issue that commonly arises involves determining the scope of the waiver. It is essential for a lawyer to understand, for example, that while a client can choose what information they would like to disclose, the law surrounding "partial waiver prevents a party from engaging in selective and self-serving disclosure on a particular topic, disclosing only those privileged documents that support the position of the party and not disclosing those communications that do not".[25]

The fact that a waiver can be implied, in addition to expressly authorized by a client, also adds complexity. The issue of implied waiver most commonly arises in circumstances where a litigant relies on legal advice sought or received as part of their claim or defence. An example of such a situation can be found in *R. v. Campbell* in which the RCMP defended a sting operation that it had conducted on the grounds that it had been relying on legal advice received from the federal Department of Justice.[26] The Supreme Court of Canada held that, in so doing, "the RCMP waived the right to shelter behind solicitor-client privilege the contents of the advice thus exposed and relied upon."[27]

Additional issues arise in the context of mistaken or "inadvertent" disclosures. An inadvertent disclosure of privileged material to opposing counsel or a third party will not automatically result in a loss of privilege. Indeed, courts will generally not find a waiver in those circumstances. As Adam Dodek has observed, "court are generally very forgiving of inadvertent disclosure."[28] In determining whether an inadvertent disclosure amounts to a waiver of privilege, courts have looked at a variety of factors such as the conduct of the disclosing party (e.g. was the disclosure the result of "reckless conduct"?[29]), any acquiescence on the part of the privilege-holder[30], and the "fairness" implications in maintaining the privilege both in relation to the opposing party and in relation to "the processes of the court."[31]

It should also be noted that inadvertent disclosure triggers obligations for lawyers under professional conduct rules. Rule 7.2-10 of the *Model Code* states that "[a] lawyer who receives a document relating to the representation of the lawyer's client and knows or reasonably should know that the document was inadvertently sent

---

[25] Adam M. Dodek, *Solicitor-Client Privilege* (Markham, ON: LexisNexis Canada, 2014) at 209.

[26] *R. v. Campbell*, [1999] S.C.J. No. 16, [1999] 1 SCR 565 (S.C.C.).

[27] *R. v. Campbell*, [1999] S.C.J. No. 16, [1999] 1 SCR 565 at 67 (S.C.C.).

[28] Adam M. Dodek, *Solicitor-Client Privilege* (Markham, ON: LexisNexis Canada, 2014) at 209.

[29] See, e.g. *Eisses v. CPL Systems Canada Inc.*, [2009] O.J. No. 3628, 77 C.P.C. (6th) 335 (Ont. S.C.J.).

[30] See, e.g. *Federation of Newfoundland Indians Inc. v. Benoit*, [2020] N.J. No. 87, 2020 NLCA 16 (N.L.C.A.).

[31] See, e.g. *R. v. Ward*, [2016] O.J. No. 3816, 2016 ONCA 568 (Ont. C.A.).

must promptly notify the sender."[32] This is one area, however, in which not all jurisdictions have adopted the exact wording of the *Model Code*. For example, Rule 7.2-13 of the Law Society of Alberta's *Code of Conduct* states "[a] lawyer who comes into possession of a privileged communication of an opposing party must not make use of it and must immediately advise the opposing lawyer or opposing party."[33] The corresponding rule in the Law Society of British Columbia's *Code of Professional Conduct* directs, among other things, a lawyer who has read "part or all of the document before realizing that it was not intended for him or her, cease reading the document and promptly return it or delete it, uncopied, to the party to whom it belongs, advising that party: (i) of the extent to which the lawyer is aware of the contents, and (ii) what use the lawyer intends to make of the contents of the document."[34]

[6] EXCEPTIONS TO CONFIDENTIALITY AND PRIVILEGE

The scope of and justifications for confidentiality and privilege are most commonly articulated in circumstances in which someone seeks to set aside an individual's right to have confidences preserved or the privilege maintained, or where it is argued that a law requires disclosure of the information. This section examines exceptions to lawyer confidentiality and privilege as found in case law, statutes and the *Model Code*.

[a] The "Public Safety" Exception

SMITH v. JONES

[1999] S.C.J. No. 15, [1999] 1 S.C.R. 455
(S.C.C., Lamer C.J.C. and L'Heureux-Dubé, Gonthier, Cory, McLachlin,
Iacobucci, Major, Bastarache and Binnie JJ.)

CORY J. [for the majority]:— The solicitor-client privilege permits a client to talk freely to his or her lawyer secure in the knowledge that the words and documents which fall within the scope of the privilege will not be disclosed. It has long been recognized that this principle is of fundamental importance to the administration of justice and, to the extent it is feasible, it should be maintained. Yet when public safety is involved and death or serious bodily harm is imminent, the privilege should be set aside. This appeal must determine what circumstances and factors should be set aside in the interest of protecting the safety of the public.

I. Factual Background

Solicitor-client privilege is claimed for a doctor's report. Pending the resolution of that claim the names of the parties involved have been replaced by pseudonyms. The appellant, "James Jones", was charged with aggravated sexual assault of a prostitute. His counsel referred him to a psychiatrist, the respondent, "John Smith", for a forensic psychiatric assessment. It was hoped that it would be of assistance in the

---

[32] Federation of Law Societies of Canada, *Model Code of Professional Conduct* at Rule 7.2-10, online: *Federation of Law Societies of Canada* https://flsc.ca/interactivecode/.

[33] Law Society of Alberta, *Code of Conduct,* Rule 7.2-13.

[34] Law Society of British Columbia, *Code of Professional Conduct,* Rule 7.2-10.

preparation of the defence or with submissions on sentencing in the event of a guilty plea. His counsel advised Mr. Jones that the consultation was privileged in the same way as a consultation with him would be. Dr. Smith interviewed Mr. Jones for 90 minutes on July 30, 1997. His findings are contained in an affidavit he submitted to the judge of first instance. They set out the basis for his belief that Mr. Jones poses a continuing danger to the public.

Dr. Smith reported that Mr. Jones described in considerable detail his plan for the crime to which he subsequently pled guilty. It involved deliberately choosing as a victim a small prostitute who could be readily overwhelmed. He planned to have sex with her and then to kidnap her. He took duct tape and rope with him, as well as a small blue ball that he tried to force into the woman's mouth. Because he planned to kill her after the sexual assault he made no attempt to hide his identity.

Mr. Jones planned to strangle the victim and to dispose of her body in the bush area near Hope, British Columbia. He was going to shoot the woman in the face before burying her to impede identification. He had arranged time off from his work and had carefully prepared his basement apartment to facilitate his planned sexual assault and murder. He had told people he would be going away on vacation so that no one would visit him and he had fixed dead bolts on all the doors so that a key alone would not open them.

Mr. Jones told Dr. Smith that his first victim would be a "trial run" to see if he could "live with" what he had done. If he could, he planned to seek out similar victims. He stated that, by the time he had kidnapped his first victim, he expected that he would be "in so deep" that he would have no choice but to carry out his plans.

On July 31, Dr. Smith telephoned Mr. Jones's counsel and informed him that in his opinion Mr. Jones was a dangerous individual who would, more likely than not, commit future offences unless he received sufficient treatment.

On September 24, 1997, Mr. Jones pled guilty to aggravated assault and the matter was put over for sentencing. Sometime after November 19, Dr. Smith phoned Mr. Jones's counsel to inquire about the proceedings. On learning that the judge would not be advised of his concerns, Dr. Smith indicated that he intended to seek legal advice and shortly thereafter commenced this action.

The *in camera* hearing took place in December 1997. Dr. Smith filed an affidavit describing his interview with Mr. Jones and his opinion based upon the interview. Mr. Jones filed an affidavit in response. On December 12, 1997, Henderson J. ruled that the public safety exception to the law of solicitor-client privilege and doctor-patient confidentiality released Dr. Smith from his duties of confidentiality. He went on to rule that Dr. Smith was under a duty to disclose to the police and the Crown both the statements made by Mr. Jones and his opinion based upon them. Henderson J. ordered a stay of his order to allow for an appeal and Mr. Jones promptly appealed the decision.

The Court of Appeal allowed the appeal but only to the extent that the mandatory order was changed to one permitting Dr. Smith to disclose the information to the Crown and police . . ..

II. Analysis

A. The Nature of the Solicitor-Client Privilege

Both parties made their submissions on the basis that the psychiatrist's report was protected by solicitor-client privilege, and it should be considered on that basis. It is the highest privilege recognized by the courts. By necessary implication, if a public safety exception applies to solicitor-client privilege, it applies to all classifications of privileges and duties of confidentiality. It follows that, in these reasons, it is not necessary to consider any distinction that may exist between a solicitor-client privilege and a litigation privilege.

The solicitor-client privilege has long been regarded as fundamentally important to our judicial system. Well over a century ago in *Anderson v. Bank of British Columbia* (1876), 2 Ch. D. 644 (C.A.), at p. 649, the importance of the rule was recognized:

> The object and meaning of the rule is this: that as, by reason of the complexity and difficulty of our law, litigation can only be properly conducted by professional men, it is absolutely necessary that a man, in order to prosecute his rights or to defend himself from an improper claim, should have recourse to the assistance of professional lawyers . . . .. to use a vulgar phrase, that he should be able to make a clean breast of it to the gentleman whom he consults with a view to the prosecution of his claim, or the substantiating of his defence. . . . . that he should be able to place unrestricted and unbounded confidence in the professional agent, and that the communication he so makes to him should be kept secret, unless with his consent (for it is his privilege, and not the privilege of the confidential agent), that he should be enabled properly to conduct his litigation.

Clients seeking advice must be able to speak freely to their lawyers secure in the knowledge that what they say will not be divulged without their consent. It cannot be forgotten that the privilege is that of the client, not the lawyer. The privilege is essential if sound legal advice is to be given in every field. It has a deep significance in almost every situation where legal advice is sought whether it be with regard to corporate and commercial transactions, to family relationships, to civil litigation or to criminal charges. Family secrets, company secrets, personal foibles and indiscretions all must on occasion be revealed to the lawyer by the client. Without this privilege, a client could never be candid and furnish all the relevant information that must be provided to lawyers if they are to properly advise their clients. It is an element that is both integral and extremely important to the functioning of the legal system. It is because of the fundamental importance of the privilege that the onus properly rests upon those seeking to set aside the privilege to justify taking such a significant step.

. . . . .

As the British Columbia Court of Appeal observed, solicitor-client privilege is the privilege "which the law has been most zealous to protect and most reluctant to water down by exceptions". Quite simply it is a principle of fundamental importance to the administration of justice.

B. Limitations on Solicitor-Client Privilege

Just as no right is absolute so too the privilege, even that between solicitor and client, is subject to clearly defined exceptions. The decision to exclude evidence that would be both relevant and of substantial probative value because it is protected by the solicitor-client privilege represents a policy decision. It is based upon the importance to our legal system in general of the solicitor-client privilege. In certain circumstances, however, other societal values must prevail.

. . . . .

(3) The Public Safety Exception

In *Solosky* [1980] 1 S.C.R. 821] . . . an inmate in a federal penitentiary asked this Court to make a declaration that all properly identified correspondence between solicitors and clients would be forwarded to their destinations without being opened. The inmate's privilege was in conflict with the *Penitentiary Act* . . . and with Regulation 2.18 of the Penitentiary Services Regulations, which allowed the institution's director to censor any correspondence to the extent the censor considered necessary.

In his decision, Dickson J. ruled that the inmate's privilege must yield when the safety of members of the institution is at risk. In his reason at p. 840, he implicitly limited the solicitor-client privilege. He wrote:

> The result, as I see it, is that the Court is placed in the position of having to balance the public interest in maintaining the safety and security of a penal institution, its staff and its inmates, with the interest represented by insulating the solicitor-client relationship. Even giving full recognition to the right of an inmate to correspond freely with his legal adviser, and the need for minimum derogation therefrom, the scale must ultimately come down in favour of the public interest.

In certain circumstances, therefore, when the safety of the public is at risk the solicitor-client privilege may be set aside.

. . . . .

C. The Public Safety Exception and Solicitor-Client Privilege

The foregoing review makes it clear that even the fundamentally important right to confidentiality is not absolute in doctor-patient relationships, and it cannot be absolute in solicitor-client relationships . . . When the interest in the protection of the innocent accused and the safety of members of the public is engaged, the privilege will have to be balanced against these other compelling public needs. In rare circumstances, these public interests may be so compelling that the privilege must be displaced. Yet the right to privacy in a solicitor-client relationship is so fundamentally important that only a compelling public interest may justify setting aside solicitor-client privilege.

Danger to public safety can, in appropriate circumstances, provide the requisite justification. It is significant that public safety exceptions to the solicitor-client privilege are recognized by all professional legal bodies within Canada. See, for example, Chapter 5, s. 12, of the British Columbia Professional Conduct Handbook:

> Disclosure to prevent a crime

> 12. A lawyer may disclose information received as a result of a solicitor-client relationship if the lawyer has reasonable grounds to believe that the disclosure is necessary to prevent a crime involving death or serious bodily harm to any person.

183

See as well the even broader Rule 4.11 of the Law Society of Upper Canada's Professional Conduct Handbook.

Quite simply, society recognizes that the safety of the public is of such importance that in appropriate circumstances, it will warrant setting aside solicitor-client privilege. What factors should be taken into consideration in determining whether that privilege should be displaced?

(1) Determining When Public Safety Outweighs Solicitor-Client Privilege

There are three factors to be considered: First, is there a clear risk to an identifiable person or group of persons? Second, is there a risk of serious bodily harm or death? Third, is the danger imminent? Clearly if the risk is imminent, the danger is serious.

These factors will often overlap and vary in their importance and significance. The weight to be attached to each will vary with the circumstances presented by each case, but they all must be considered. As well, each factor is composed of various aspects, and, like the factors themselves, these aspects may overlap and the weight to be given to them will vary depending on the circumstances of each case. Yet as a general rule, if the privilege is to be set aside the court must find that there is an imminent risk of serious bodily harm or death to an identifiable person or group.

(a) Clarity

What should be considered in determining if there is a clear risk to an identifiable group or person? It will be appropriate and relevant to consider the answers a particular case may provide to the following questions: Is there evidence of long-range planning? Has a method for effecting the specific attack been suggested? Is there a prior history of violence or threats of violence? Are the prior assaults or threats of violence similar to that which was planned? If there is a history of violence, has the violence increased in severity? Is the violence directed to an identifiable person or group of persons? This is not an all-encompassing list. It is important to note, however, that as a general rule a group or person must be ascertainable. The requisite specificity of that identification will vary depending on the other factors discussed here.

The specific questions to be considered under this heading will vary with the particular circumstances of each case. Great significance might, in some situations, be given to the particularly clear identification of a particular individual or group of intended victims. Even if the group of intended victims is large, considerable significance can be given to the threat if the identification of the group is clear and forceful. For example, a threat, put forward with chilling detail, to kill or seriously injure children five years of age and under would have to be given very careful consideration. In certain circumstances, it might be that a threat of death directed toward single women living in apartment buildings could in combination with other factors be sufficient in the particular circumstances to justify setting aside the privilege. At the same time, a general threat of death or violence directed to everyone in a city or community, or anyone with whom the person may come into contact, may be too vague to warrant setting aside the privilege. However, if the threatened harm to the members of the public was particularly compelling, extremely serious and imminent, it might well be appropriate to lift the privilege.
. . .

. . . . .

(b) Seriousness

The "seriousness" factor requires that the threat be such that the intended victim is in danger of being killed or of suffering serious bodily harm. Many persons involved in criminal justice proceedings will have committed prior crimes or may be planning to commit crimes in the future. The disclosure of planning future crimes without an element of violence would be an insufficient reason to set aside solicitor-client privilege because of fears for public safety. For the public safety interest to be of sufficient importance to displace solicitor-client privilege, the threat must be to occasion serious bodily harm or death.

It should be observed that serious psychological harm may constitute serious bodily harm, as this Court held in *R. v. McCraw*, [1991] 3 S.C.R. 72, at p. 81:

> So long as the psychological harm substantially interferes with the health or well-being of the complainant, it properly comes within the scope of the phrase "serious bodily harm". There can be no doubt that psychological harm may often be more pervasive and permanent in its effect than any physical harm.

(c) Imminence

The risk of serious bodily harm or death must be imminent if solicitor-client communications are to be disclosed. That is, the risk itself must be serious: a serious risk of serious bodily harm. The nature of the threat must be such that it creates a sense of urgency. This sense of urgency may be applicable to some time in the future. Depending on the seriousness and clarity of the threat, it will not always be necessary to impose a particular time limit on the risk. It is sufficient if there is a clear and imminent threat of serious bodily harm to an identifiable group, and if this threat is made in such a manner that a sense of urgency is created. A statement made in a fleeting fit of anger will usually be insufficient to disturb the solicitor-client privilege. On the other hand, imminence as a factor may be satisfied if a person makes a clear threat to kill someone that he vows to carry out three years hence when he is released from prison. If that threat is made with such chilling intensity and graphic detail that a reasonable bystander would be convinced that the killing would be carried out the threat could be considered to be imminent. Imminence, like the other two criteria, must be defined in the context of each situation.

. . . . .

(2) Extent of Disclosure

The disclosure of the privileged communication should generally be limited as much as possible. The judge setting aside the solicitor-client privilege should strive to strictly limit disclosure to those aspects of the report or document which indicate that there is an imminent risk of serious bodily harm or death to an identifiable person or group. In undertaking this task consideration should be given to those portions of the report which refer to the risk or serious harm to an identifiable group, that the risk is serious in that it involves a danger of death or serious bodily harm; and that the serious risk is imminent in the sense given to that word in para. 84 above. The requirement that the disclosure be limited must be emphasized. For example, if a report contained references to criminal behaviour that did not have an imminent risk of serious bodily harm but disclosed, for example, the commission of crimes of fraud, counterfeiting or the sale of stolen goods, those references would necessarily be deleted.

D. Application of the Public Safety Exception to Solicitor-Client Privilege to the Case at Bar

(1) Clarity

Would a reasonable observer, given all the facts for which solicitor-client privilege is sought, consider the potential danger posed by Mr. Jones to be clear, serious, and imminent? The answer must, I think, be in the affirmative. According to Dr. Smith's affidavit, the plan described by Mr. Jones demonstrated a number of the factors that should be considered in determining the clarity of the potential danger. They are the clear identification of the victim group, the specificity of method, the evidence of planning, and the prior attempted or actual acts that mirror the potential act of threatened future harm.

. . . . .

(2) Seriousness

The seriousness of the potential harm, a sexually sadistic murder, is clearly sufficient. The fact that Mr. Jones has after careful and detailed planning already committed an assault upon a prostitute supports the finding that the potential harm caused would be extremely serious.

(3) Imminence

The most difficult issue to resolve is whether the risk of serious bodily harm can be termed "imminent". . . .

. . . . .

There are two important factors that indicate that the threat of serious bodily harm was indeed imminent. First, Mr. Jones admitted that he had breached his bail conditions by continuing to visit the Downtown Eastside where he knew prostitutes could be found. Second, common sense would indicate that after Mr. Jones was arrested, and while he was awaiting sentence, he would have been acutely aware of the consequences of his actions. This is of particular significance in light of his fear of being attacked while he was in jail.

Let us assume that the evidence as to imminence of the danger may not be as clear as might be desired. Nonetheless, there is some evidence of imminence. Furthermore, the other factors pertaining to clarity, the identifiable group of victims, and the chilling evidence of careful planning, when taken together, indicate that the solicitor-client privilege must be set aside for the protection of members of the public.

. . . . .

III. Disposition

The file will be unsealed and the ban on the publication of the contents of the file is removed, except for those parts of the affidavit of the doctor which do not fall within the public safety exception. Subject to this direction the order of the British

Columbia Court of Appeal is affirmed and this appeal is dismissed without costs.
The reasons of Lamer C.J.C. and Major and Binnie JJ. were delivered by
MAJOR J. [dissenting in part]:—

. . . . .

The chilling effect of completely breaching the privilege would have the undesired effect of discouraging those individuals in need of treatment for serious and dangerous conditions from consulting professional help. In this case the interests of the appellant and more importantly the interests of society would be better served by his obtaining treatment. This Court has recognized that mental health, including those suffering from potentially dangerous illnesses, is an important public good: see *M. (A.) v. Ryan*, [1997] 1 S.C.R. 157 . . ..

Although the appellant did not go to Dr. Smith to seek treatment, it is obvious that he is more likely to get treatment when his condition is diagnosed than someone who keeps the secret of their illness to themselves. It seems apparent that society will suffer by imposing a disincentive for patients and criminally accused persons to speak frankly with counsel and medical experts retained on their behalf.

As appealing as it may be to ensure that Mr. Jones does not slip back into the community without treatment for his condition, completely lifting the privilege and allowing his confidential communications to his legal advisor to be used against him in the most detrimental ways will not promote public safety, only silence. For this doubtful gain, the Court will have imposed a veil of secrecy between criminal accused and their counsel which the solicitor-client privilege was developed to prevent. Sanctioning a breach of privilege too hastily erodes the workings of the system of law in exchange for an illusory gain in public safety.

VI. Application to the Facts

While I agree with Cory J. that the danger in this case is sufficiently clear, serious and imminent to justify some warning to the relevant authorities, I find that the balance between the public interests in safety and the proper administration of justice is best struck by a more limited disclosure than the broader abrogation of privilege he proposes. In particular, Cory J. endorses the trial judge's limitation of Dr. Smith's affidavit to those portions which indicate an imminent risk of serious harm or death. In the result, conscriptive evidence such as the accused's confession can be disclosed. In my opinion, the danger posed by the accused can be adequately addressed by the expression of that opinion by Dr. Smith without disclosing the confession.

Two principles should guide the analysis of the scope of this disclosure. First, the breach of privilege must be as narrow as possible; *Descôteaux v. Mierzwinski* . . . Disclosure is justified only when it can actually accomplish something in the public interest, such as preventing injury or death. . . .

. . . . .

Second, an accused's right to consult counsel without fear of having his words used against him at trial is vital to our conception of justice. . . .

The public interest in cases such as this is twofold, and requires not only that the dangerous individual is prevented from harming anyone, but that they obtain treatment if needed. Appealing as it might be to force individuals in Mr. Jones's position into treatment through the criminal process, it is unlikely to happen. If there is a risk that conscriptive evidence from the mouth of the accused can be used against him, the defence bar is going to be reluctant to refer dangerous clients to the care of experts. Disclosure will be discouraged and treatment will not occur.

As the facts of this case illustrate, Mr. Jones was only diagnosed and made aware of the possibility of treatment because he felt secure in confiding to Dr. Smith. If that confidence is undermined, then these individuals will not disclose the danger they pose, they will not be identified, and public safety will suffer.

. . . . .

Accordingly, I would allow the appeal without costs, confirm the entirety of Mr. Jones's communications to Dr. Smith to be privileged, but permit Dr. Smith to give his opinion and diagnosis of the danger posed by Mr. Jones.

NOTES AND QUESTIONS

1. To what extent do the Cory J. and Major J. judgments coincide? To what extent do they diverge? To what extent do they represent fundamentally different conceptions of solicitor-client privilege and different conceptions of the lawyer's role in representing clients in criminal proceedings? Do you think that Major J. is right in his argument that greater protection accorded to solicitor-client privilege would be more likely to cause lawyers to refer their clients for professional help?

2. This case is in many ways a balancing act between (a) the public interest values inherent in the criminal justice system and the defence lawyer's role within that system in relation to their client; and (b) the public interest value of protecting the public from potentially dangerous people, even at the sacrifice of a privacy right. Has the Supreme Court struck the right balance?

3. This decision authorized the psychiatrist to disclose information that would otherwise have been protected by solicitor-client privilege. Does it impose an obligation upon anyone possessed of such information (lawyer, doctor, counsellor, citizen) to make such disclosure? Should it?

4. What would have been the outcome if Mr. Jones' intentions had only been disclosed to the lawyer? The FLSC *Model Code* provision on the future harm/public safety exception appears to reflect the outcome in the case. It provides:

   > 3.3-3 A lawyer may disclose confidential information, but must not disclose more information than is required, when the lawyer believes on reasonable grounds that there is an imminent risk of death or serious bodily harm, and disclosure is necessary to prevent the death or harm.

   Do you agree that this provision corresponds with the principle enunciated in *Smith v. Jones*? What criteria should guide the lawyer in determining whether to exercise their discretion to disclose client confidences or keep them secret? Is the deference to lawyer discretion, set out in the language of the Court that the lawyer is "authorized" to disclose or in the *Model Code* that the "lawyer *may* disclose", justified in such situations? Despite the desire for a national consensus on contentious issues such as the public safety/future crime exception, some law societies have declined to follow the *Model Code*. For example, the opening language of the comparable provision in Rule 3.3-3 of the Saskatchewan *Code of Professional Conduct* provides that "[a] lawyer *must* disclose confidential information . . ." Is this provision inconsistent with *Smith v. Jones*? How does it align with your own values?

5. You will notice that the *Model Code* provision speaks of "harm" rather than "crime". Should the exception be limited to future "crimes" rather than other potentially harmful behaviour that a client may be planning, and which intention the client communicates to their lawyer, but which does not meet the definition of a crime? Should the primary focus be on the potential legal consequences for the client, and the protection afforded the client in those circumstances, or should we focus instead on the consequences upon others of the client's potential actions? In some cases, a third party may be devastated by "financial harm". However, the Law Society of New Brunswick has been the only Canadian law society to date which has included an exception that allows a lawyer to disclose confidential information in relation to "an imminent risk of substantial financial injury to an individual caused by an unlawful act that is likely to be committed" (see Rule 3.3-3B for full details). If the objective is to protect the public interest from serious harm, should more law societies include "financial harm" within their future harm exceptions? What do the profession's choices among the options discussed in this note imply with respect to the balance between a duty to clients and a duty to the wider public interest?

6. In 2016, the Ontario Securities Commission introduced a whistle-blowing policy under which individuals, including in-house counsel, are eligible for financial rewards of up to five million dollars upon disclosure of serious securities or derivative-related misconduct (OSC Policy 15-601). Originally, the policy excluded any reward for the disclosure of information subject to solicitor-client privilege, but explicitly included disclosures that would violate a lawyer's ethical duty of confidentiality under the rules of professional conduct in certain limited circumstances, including where "the whistleblower has a reasonable basis to believe that disclosure of the information to the Commission is necessary to prevent the subject of the whistleblower submission from engaging in conduct that is likely to cause or continue to cause substantial injury to the financial interest or property of the entity or investors".[35] In 2018, the Ontario Securities Commission amended the policy to exclude any disclosures from in-house counsel where such disclosures would be in violation of law society professional conduct rules. What are some of the potential benefits and risks to amending the policy in this way?

---

[35] OSC Policy 15-601, *Whistleblower Program,* section 15(2)(a).

7. As a general rule, citizens, including those acting in a professional capacity in relation to children, are under a positive duty to report situations of child abuse or neglect pursuant to the provisions of provincial child protection legislation. Failure to report constitutes an offence under the legislation. Consider, however, the following legislative provisions as they relate to lawyers representing clients, and try to assess your obligations as a lawyer, and your own personal sentiments, in the two differing situations. In Ontario, the reporting obligations are set out in section 125 of the *Child, Youth and Family Services Act, 2017*.[36] In the more general "reporting obligation" provision a "lawyer" is included.[37] However, section 125(11) provides: "Nothing in this section abrogates any privilege that may exist between a lawyer and the lawyer's client." By contrast, the comparable provision in the Newfoundland and Labrador legislation, section 11 of the *Children, Youth and Families Act*,[38] imposes upon citizens, including "solicitors" (s. 11(5)(d)), a duty to report where a child is or may be in need of protective intervention, and provides in section 11(6) that "[t]his section applies notwithstanding that the information is confidential or privileged . . . .". What are the competing public policy motivations behind these two conflicting approaches? How would you deal with information from your client that relates to child abuse or neglect in the two different jurisdictions? How would you feel about it?

8. *Canada v. Solosky*[39] was a case in which penitentiary officials were found to be justified in opening an inmate's letters to his lawyer on the grounds of public safety, even though there appears to have been no evidence that the inmate was communicating to his lawyer about an intention to cause serious harm to anyone. Does *Smith v. Jones* suggest that the entitlement of penitentiary officials to open inmates' mail to their lawyers is circumscribed? Does the general framework for the application of legislated exceptions to confidentiality and privilege cover the situation?

9. You will have noted that the courts and the legal profession place an extremely high value on lawyer-client confidentiality, to the extent that the risk of harm to others is often a secondary concern. Now consider Rule 3.3-5 of the *Model Code*:

> A lawyer may disclose confidential information in order to establish or collect the lawyer's fees, but must not disclose more information than is required.

In view of the very high value of lawyer-client confidentiality, where important public interest values are often given secondary consideration, how can this exception be justified?

---

[36] S.O. 2017, c. 14, Sched. 1.

[37] S.O. 2017, c. 14, Sched. 1 s. 72(5).

[38] S.N.L. 2018, c. C-12.3.

[39] [1979] S.C.J. No. 130, [1980] 1 S.C.R. 821 (S.C.C.).

Scenario One

You are a criminal defence lawyer. Last week, your client pled guilty to a charge of sexual assault and was sentenced to one year in prison. The Crown has informed you that they will be appealing the sentence. You learned today that your client is HIV positive. Out of a concern for the victim, you have asked your client for permission to disclose their HIV positive status to the Crown but your client has refused. What would you do? On what basis would you justify your course of action?[40]

Scenario Two

A client advises you, in the course of discussions about their legal matters, that for a variety of reasons (financially and personally) their life holds no future use, and that they intend to commit suicide. In discussing the matter with them, you conclude that they are quite serious with respect to their intentions. What, if anything, would you do with this information?

Scenario Three

A client advises you that his elderly mother is terminally ill and is constantly in great pain. There is no hope of recovery and virtually no prospect that his mother's pain can be moderated. She wishes to end her life but is too weak to do so, and does not qualify for medical assistance in dying. She has asked her son (who is your client) for assistance and he has agreed to assist her in committing suicide. He has come to you for advice on his potential liability. You are satisfied that the son intends to assist his mother in this way and you are equally satisfied that his mother is mentally alert and clear in her own intentions. What, if anything, would you do in this situation?

[b]   The "Innocence at Stake" Exception

R. v. McCLURE

[2001] S.C.J. No. 13, [2001] 1 S.C.R. 445
(S.C.C., McLachlin C.J.C. and L'Heureux-Dubé, Gonthier, Iacobucci, Major,
Bastarache, Binnie, Arbour and LeBel JJ.)

[McClure was charged with a number of sexual offences against former students. Another person, J.C., learned of the charges and came forward with further allegations, including that J.C. himself had been sexually assaulted. J.C. also commenced a civil action against McClure. McClure sought production of J.C.'s civil litigation file to "determine the nature of [J.C.'s] allegations first made by J.C. to his solicitor and to assess the extent of [J.C.'s] motive to fabricate or exaggerate the incidents of abuse". The trial judge allowed limited access to J.C.'s litigation file to enable McClure to make full answer and defence. The matter was ultimately appealed to the Supreme Court of Canada.]

MAJOR J.:— This appeal revisits the reach of solicitor-client privilege. This

---

[40] In 2012, an Ontario lawyer was confronted with a similar scenario, see "Can lawyers reveal clients' HIV status?" (August 6, 2012) online: lawtimesnews.com,: https://www.lawtimesnews.com/news/general/can-lawyers-reveal-clients-hiv-status/259741 For a broader context on issues related to HIV disclosure, see Kyle Kirkup, "The Gross Indecency of Criminalizing HIV Non-Disclosure" (2020) 70:3 U.T.L.J. 263-282.

privilege comes with a long history. Its value has been tested since early in the common law. Its importance has not diminished.

Solicitor-client privilege describes the privilege that exists between a client and his or her lawyer. This privilege is fundamental to the justice system in Canada. The law is a complex web of interests, relationships and rules. The integrity of the administration of justice depends upon the unique role of the solicitor who provides legal advice to clients within this complex system. At the heart of this privilege lies the concept that people must be able to speak candidly with their lawyers and so enable their interests to be fully represented.

Interests compete within our legal system. The policy justifying the existence of solicitor-client privilege might clash with an accused's right under s. 7 of the *Canadian Charter of Rights and Freedoms* to make full answer and defence. This appeal raises the issue of whether the solicitor-client privilege of a third person should yield to permit an accused to make full answer and defence to a criminal charge, and, if so, when.

Solicitor-client privilege and the right to make full answer and defence are integral to our system of justice. Solicitor-client privilege is not absolute so, in rare circumstances, it will be subordinated to an individual's right to make full answer and defence. The problem is when and under what circumstances the right to full answer and defence will override the solicitor-client privilege. . . .

. . . . .

III. Issues

   1.   Should the solicitor-client privilege ever give way to an accused's right to full answer and defence and if so in what circumstances?

   2.   If solicitor-client privilege should yield, what is the appropriate test?

   3.   Should the trial judge have ordered the litigation file to be disclosed in the circumstances of this case?

IV. Analysis

A. Evolution of Solicitor-Client Privilege

Solicitor-client privilege is part of and fundamental to the Canadian legal system. While its historical roots are a rule of evidence, it has evolved into a fundamental and substantive rule of law.

. . . . .

. . . The debate surrounding the origin of solicitor-client privilege while of some interest need not be resolved here. Whatever the origin of the privilege, it has clearly evolved into a substantive rule of law in Canada.

. . . . .

The existence of solicitor-client privilege as a fundamental legal right answers little. The solicitor-client privilege must be examined in the context of other types of privileges to demonstrate its unique status within the legal system.

B. Types of Privilege

The law recognizes a number of communications as worthy of confidentiality. The protection of these communications serves a public interest and they are generally referred to as privileged.

There are currently two recognized categories of privilege: relationships that are protected by a "class privilege" and relationships that are not protected by a class privilege but may still be protected on a "case-by-case" basis. See *R. v. Gruenke*, [1991] 3 S.C.R. 263, per Lamer C.J., at p. 286, for a description of "class privilege":

> The parties have tended to distinguish between two categories: a "blanket", *prima facie*, common law, or "class" privilege on the one hand, and a "case-by-case" privilege on the other. The first four terms are used to refer to a privilege which was recognized at common law and one for which there is a *prima facie* presumption of inadmissibility (once it has been established that the relationship fits within the class) unless the party urging admission can show why the communications should not be privileged (i.e., why they should be admitted into evidence as an exception to the general rule). Such communications are excluded not because the evidence is not relevant, but rather because, there are overriding policy reasons to exclude this relevant evidence. Solicitor-client communications appear to fall within this first category . . . . [Emphasis in original]

For a relationship to be protected by a class privilege, thereby warranting a *prima facie* presumption of inadmissibility, the relationship must fall within a traditionally protected class. Solicitor-client privilege, because of its unique position in our legal fabric, is the most notable example of a class privilege. Other examples of class privileges are spousal privilege . . . and informer privilege (which is a subset of public interest immunity).

Other confidential relationships are not protected by a class privilege, but may be protected on a case-by-case basis. Examples of such relationships include doctor-patient, psychologist-patient, journalist-informant and religious communications. . . .

. . . . .

C. Rationale of Solicitor-Client Privilege

The foregoing privileges, such as communication between a doctor and his patient, do not occupy the unique position of solicitor-client privilege or resonate with the same concerns. This privilege, by itself, commands a unique status within the legal system. The important relationship between a client and his or her lawyer stretches beyond the parties and is integral to the workings of the legal system itself. The solicitor-client relationship is a part of that system, not ancillary to it. See *Gruenke* . . .:

> The *prima facie* protection for solicitor-client communications is based on the fact that the relationship and the communications between solicitor and client are essential to the effective operation of the legal system. Such communications are inextricably linked with the very system which desires the disclosure of the communication [. . .] In my view, religious communications, notwithstanding their social importance, are not inextricably linked with the justice system in the way that solicitor-client communications surely are.

It is this distinctive status within the justice system that characterizes the solicitor-client privilege as a class privilege, and the protection is available to all who fall within the class.

The importance of solicitor-client privilege to both the legal system and society as a whole assists in determining whether and in what circumstances the privilege should yield to an individual's right to make full answer and defence. The law is complex. Lawyers have a unique role. Free and candid communication between the lawyer and client protects the legal rights of the citizen. It is essential for the lawyer to know all of the facts of the client's position. The existence of a fundamental right to privilege between the two encourages disclosure within the confines of the relationship. The danger in eroding solicitor-client privilege is the potential to stifle communication between the lawyer and client. The need to protect the privilege determines its immunity to attack.

D. Scope of Solicitor-Client Privilege

Despite its importance, solicitor-client privilege is not absolute. It is subject to exceptions in certain circumstances. *Jones, supra,* examined whether the privilege should be displaced in the interest of protecting the safety of the public . . .

However, solicitor-client privilege must be as close to absolute as possible to ensure public confidence and retain relevance. As such, it will only yield in certain clearly defined circumstances, and does not involve a balancing of interests on a case-by-case basis.

Not all communications between a lawyer and her client are privileged. In order for the communication to be privileged, it must arise from communication between a lawyer and the client where the latter seeks lawful legal advice. *Wigmore* . . . sets out a statement of the broad rule . . .:

> Where legal advice of any kind is sought from a professional legal adviser in his capacity as such, the communications relating to that purpose, made in confidence by the client, are at his instance permanently protected from disclosure by himself or by the legal adviser, except the protection be waived.

As stated, only communications made for the legitimate purpose of obtaining lawful professional advice or assistance are privileged. The privilege may only be waived by the client. See M. M. Orkin, *Legal Ethics: A Study of Professional Conduct* (1957), at p. 84:

> It is the duty of a solicitor to insist upon this privilege which extends to "all communication by a client to his solicitor or counsel for the purpose of obtaining professional advice or assistance in a pending action, or in any other proper matter for professional assistance" [. . .] The privilege is that of the client and can only be waived by the client.

E. Full Answer and Defence

While solicitor-client privilege is almost absolute, the question here is whether the privilege should be set aside to permit the accused his right to full answer and defence by permitting him access to a complainant's civil litigation file. It is agreed that the file in this case qualifies for solicitor-client privilege. The solicitor-client privilege and the accused's Charter right to full answer and defence are both protected by law. Which prevails when they clash?

R. v. Seaboyer, [1991] 2 S.C.R. 577, at p. 607, opened this question:

> The right of the innocent not to be convicted is reflected in our society's fundamental commitment to a fair trial, a commitment expressly embodied in s. 11(d) of the Charter. It has long been recognized that an essential facet of a fair hearing is the "opportunity adequately to state [one's] case" . . . . This applies with particular force to the accused, who may not have the resources of the state at his or her disposal. Thus . . . our courts have held that even informer privilege and solicitor-client privilege may yield to the accused's right to defend himself on a criminal charge: . . . . [. . .]

Rules and privileges will yield to the Charter guarantee of a fair trial where they stand in the way of an innocent person establishing his or her innocence . . . This Court has held that informer privilege will yield in circumstances where to fail to do so will result in a wrongful conviction. Our system will not tolerate conviction of the innocent. However, an accused's right to make full answer and defence in our system, while broad, is understandably not perfect. Section 7 of the Charter entitles an accused to a fair hearing but not always to the most favourable procedures that could possibly be imagined . . .

F. Solicitor-Client Privilege vs. Full Answer and Defence

Solicitor-client privilege and the right to make full answer and defence are principles of fundamental justice. The right of an accused to full answer and defence is personal to him or her and engages the right to life, liberty, security of the person and the right of the innocent not to be convicted. Solicitor-client privilege while also personal is broader and is important to the administration of justice as a whole. It exists whether or not there is the immediacy of a trial or of a client seeking advice.

The importance of both of these rights means that neither can always prevail. In some limited circumstances, the solicitor-client privilege may yield to allow an accused to make full answer and defence. What are those circumstances?

. . . . .

H. The Innocence at Stake Test for Solicitor-Client Privilege

. . . The appropriate test by which to determine whether to set aside solicitor-client privilege is the innocence at stake test, set out below. Solicitor-client privilege should be set aside only in the most unusual cases. Unless individuals can be certain that their communications with their solicitors will remain entirely confidential, their ability to speak freely will be undermined.

In recognition of the central place of solicitor-client privilege within the administration of justice, the innocence at stake test should be stringent. The privilege should be infringed only where core issues going to the guilt of the accused are involved and there is a genuine risk of a wrongful conviction.

Before the test is even considered, the accused must establish that the information he is seeking in the solicitor-client file is not available from any other source and he is otherwise unable to raise a reasonable doubt as to his guilt in any other way.

By way of illustration, if the accused could raise a reasonable doubt at his trial on the question of *mens rea* by access to the solicitor-client file but could also raise a reasonable doubt with the defence of alibi and/or identification, then it would be unnecessary to use the solicitor-client file. The innocence of the accused would not be at stake but instead it is his wish to mount a more complete defence that would be affected. On the surface it may appear harsh to deny access as the particular privileged evidence might raise a reasonable doubt, nonetheless, the policy reasons favouring the protection of the confidentiality of solicitor-client communications must prevail unless there is a genuine danger of wrongful conviction.

The innocence at stake test is applied in two stages in order to reflect the dual nature of the judge's inquiry. At the first stage, the accused seeking production of a solicitor-client communication must provide some evidentiary basis upon which to conclude that there exists a communication that could raise a reasonable doubt as to his guilt. At this stage, the judge has to decide whether she will review the evidence.

If the trial judge is satisfied that such an evidentiary basis exists, then she should proceed to stage two. At that stage, the trial judge must examine the solicitor-client file to determine whether, in fact, there is a communication that is likely to raise a reasonable doubt as to the guilt of the accused. It is evident that the test in the first stage (could raise a reasonable doubt) is different than that of the second stage (likely to raise a reasonable doubt). If the second stage of the test is met, then the trial judge should order the production but only of that portion of the solicitor-client file that is necessary to raise the defence claimed.

(1) Stage #1

The first stage of the innocence at stake test for invading the solicitor-client privilege requires production of the material to the trial judge for review. There has to be some evidentiary basis for the request. This is a threshold requirement designed to prevent "fishing expeditions". Without it, it would be too easy for the accused to demand examination of solicitor-client privileged communications by the trial judge. As this request constitutes a significant invasion of solicitor-client privilege, it should not be entered into lightly. On the other hand, the bar cannot be set so high that it can never be met. The trial judge must ask: "Is there some evidentiary basis for the claim that a solicitor-client communication exists that could raise a reasonable doubt about the guilt of the accused?"

. . . . .

That is then followed by a requirement that the communication sought by the accused could raise a reasonable doubt as to his guilt. This must be considered in light of what the accused knows. It is likely that the accused who, it must be remembered, has had no access to the file sought, may only provide a description of a possible communication. It would be difficult to produce and unfair to demand anything more precise. It is only at stage two that a court determines conclusively that such a communication actually exists.

. . . . .

(2) Stage #2

Once the first stage of the innocence at stake test for setting aside the solicitor-client privilege has been met, the trial judge must examine that record to determine whether, in fact, there exists a communication that is likely to raise a reasonable doubt as to the accused's guilt. The trial judge must ask herself the following question: "Is there something in the solicitor-client communication that is likely to raise a reasonable doubt about the accused's guilt?"

. . . . .

The trial judge does not have to conclude that the information definitely will raise a reasonable doubt. If this were the case, the trial would effectively be over as soon as the trial judge ordered the solicitor-client file to be produced. There would be nothing left to decide. Instead, the information must likely raise a reasonable doubt as to the accused's guilt. Also, upon reviewing the evidence, if the trial judge finds material that will likely raise a reasonable doubt, stage two of the test is satisfied and the information should be produced to the defence even if this information was not argued as a basis for production by the defence at stage one.

I. Application to the Case at Bar

In this case, the litigation file should not have been produced to the defence.

. . . . .

The first stage of the innocence at stake test for solicitor-client privilege was not met. There was no evidence that the information sought by the respondent McClure could raise a reasonable doubt as to his guilt. Even if the chronology of events in this case — *i.e.*, lawyer, police, therapist, civil suit — was unusual, it does not justify overriding solicitor-client privilege. . . .

. . . . .

V. Disposition

The appeal is allowed and the order for production by Hawkins J. is set aside.

NOTES AND QUESTIONS

1. In 2002, the Supreme Court again considered the "innocence at stake" exception. In *R. v. Brown*[41] the accused sought information from a lawyer who he alleged may have received information from the lawyer's client suggesting that the client had admitted to having committed the murder for which Brown was charged. In dismissing this application, the Court reaffirmed the *McClure* tests but added four features. First, the Court held that despite the risk that after the fact, it may be discovered that an innocent person was convicted of a crime, the most appropriate mechanism for addressing such an injustice lay with the traditional procedure of appealing to royal prerogative, as codified in section 690 of the *Criminal Code*,[42] and not by relaxing lawyer client privilege. Second, the Court was of the opinion that *McClure* applications are applicable to both oral and written communications between lawyer and client. Third, in those cases where disclosure is mandated, disclosure is to be made to the accused but not the Crown. Fourth, disclosure must be limited to the purpose of adducing information that would avoid a wrongful conviction, and cannot be used to incriminate the privilege holder, who is entitled to "immunity

---

[41] [2002] S.C.J. No. 35, [2002] 2 S.C.R. 185 (S.C.C.).
[42] R.S.C. 1985, c. C-46.

regarding the subsequent use of his privileged communications which would have been protected but for the operation of *McClure*".[43]

2. As the courts note, the disclosure of client confidences will only be facilitated if the information it generates is highly relevant and likely to affect a decision with respect to charges against the "innocent party". *McClure* deals with the situation where the lawyer for an accused has some awareness of the existence of confidential client information that might assist the defence. The judgments articulate the process by which the quality of this information, and its significance to the defence, is to be determined. This is the most typical situation in which confidences are sought to be disclosed to assist a defendant in a potential "innocence at risk" situation. Does this restrictive approach to access to this information further signal the priority given by the courts and the justice system to the preservation of client confidences, except in the most compelling situations? Is this the right choice?

3. *Brown* reinforces the limited application of this exception. In two more recent cases, the Ontario Court of Appeal has emphasized the very rare applicability of this exception and its stature as a "last resort" mechanism.[44] Indeed, there appears to be only one reported case in which a court has applied the exception (*R. v. Nuttall*, [2015] B.C.J. No. 2472, 2015 BCSC 2012 (B.C.S.C.)). Are you satisfied with Major J.'s invitation that resort be had to "wrongful conviction processes" and "moderations in the rules of evidence" as alternatives to setting aside lawyer-client confidences?

4. What about circumstances where this information is completely unknown to the accused or their counsel? Consider the following situation: A client discloses to you that they are the perpetrator of a serious crime. They share with you information that confirms for you that they are telling you the truth. They do not want this information disclosed. They are not in any way a suspect. Someone else is believed to have committed this crime and the circumstantial evidence against this person is strong.

    Woolley suggests that this

    > demonstrates one of the challenges of the distinction between the lawyer's ethical duty of confidentiality and the solicitor-client privilege. Specifically, there may be circumstances where a lawyer knows that her client committed a crime of which another person has been convicted. Under the current ethical rules, a lawyer in that situation cannot disclose the existence of such information, even to trigger counsel for the accused bringing an application under the "innocence at stake" exception. The lawyer may be compelled to produce the information if there is a successful application to invoke the "innocence at stake" exception, but

---

[43] *R. v. Brown*, [2002] S.C.J. No. 35, [2002] 2 S.C.R. 185 at paras. 88-89 (S.C.C.).

[44] *R. v. Ward*, [2016] O.J. No. 3816, 2016 ONCA 568 (Ont. C.A.), and *R. v. Rutigliano*, [2015] O.J. No. 3273, 2015 ONCA 452, 126 O.R. (3d) 161 (Ont. C.A.).

cannot voluntarily disclose that the information exists. As often as not this will mean that even if the "innocence at stake" exception could be invoked, the accused will not even be aware that the information exists and that he could bring a court application to obtain it.[45]

How would you deal with such information in your possession? Would it make any difference to your decision if the innocent person was on trial but not yet convicted? Convicted and now incarcerated? Convicted, served his sentence and is now released? Would it make a difference in any of these situations if your client is now deceased? Should any of these decisions be up to you? Is there any way that the issue of your obligations with respect to this information, or your discretion, could be "litigated" in some way? Note that, in some American states, professional conduct rules have been amended to address the issue of wrongful convictions. For example, in Massachusetts, there is an exemption to lawyer confidentiality rules which states that "a lawyer may reveal confidential information relating to the representation of a client to the extent the lawyer reasonably believes necessary . . . to prevent the wrongful execution or incarceration of another." Would you be in favour of Canadian jurisdictions adopting similar rules? If not, why not?

[c] Statutory Exceptions

As we have seen, there exists a fairly clear body of law and ethics reinforcing the lawyer's obligation to preserve client confidentiality (including confidentiality with respect to documents). From time to time, however, Parliament or a provincial legislature has introduced provisions that circumscribe or set aside the client's right to confidentiality.

In the last several decades, the Supreme Court of Canada has considered multiple cases relating to the question of when and how legislatures may statutorily interfere with solicitor-client privilege. Among other things, the Court has confirmed that any statutory abrogation of solicitor-client privilege must be expressly authorized.[46] Additionally, in cases where legislation creates a discretionary statutory authority to abrogate solicitor-client privilege, the Court has ruled that such discretion must be exercised only to the extent "absolutely necessary in order to achieve the ends sought by the enabling legislation."[47]

In the early 2000s, the Court classified solicitor-client privilege as a principle of fundamental justice under section 7 of the Charter and recognized that a client has a reasonable expectation of privacy of "the highest order" in relation to documents

---

[45] Alice Woolley, *Understanding Lawyers' Ethics in Canada*, 2d ed. (Toronto: LexisNexis Canada, 2016) at 213.

[46] *Canada (Privacy Commissioner) v. Blood Tribe Department of Health*, [2008] S.C.J. No. 45, [2008] 2 S.C.R. 574 (S.C.C.).

[47] *Descôteaux v. Mierzwinski*, [1982] S.C.J. No. 43, [1982] 1 S.C.R. 860 at 875 (S.C.C.), *Alberta (Information and Privacy Commissioner) v. University of Calgary*, [2016] S.C.J. No. 53, [2016] 2 S.C.R. 555, 2016 SCC 53 at para. 121 (S.C.C.).

protected by solicitor-client privilege for the purpose of section 8 of the Charter.[48] This development has been referred to as the "constitutionalization" of solicitor-client privilege.[49] In cases where statutory interferences with solicitor-client privilege implicate Charter rights, the court will consider the interferences in the context of the language of the Charter and applicable constitutional case law. This issue mostly commonly arises in the context of law office searches pursuant to the police investigation of crimes.

The three cases excerpted below – *Goodis v. Ontario (Ministry of Correctional Services)*,[50] *Law Society of Saskatchewan v. E.F.A. Merchant*,[51] and *Canada (Attorney General) v. Federation of Law Societies of Canada*[52] – demonstrate the courts' approach to analyzing statutory restrictions on solicitor-client privilege in both non-constitutional (*Goodis* and *Merchant*) and constitutional cases (*Federation of Law Societies*).

GOODIS v. ONTARIO (MINISTRY OF CORRECTIONAL SERVICES)

[2006] S.C.J. No. 31, 2006 SCC 31
(S.C.C., McLachlin C.J.C. and Bastarache, Binnie, LeBel, Deschamps, Fish, Abella, Charron and Rothstein JJ.)

[A journalist applied pursuant to the Ontario *Freedom of Information and Protection of Privacy Act*[53] for access to all records pertaining to allegations of sexual abuse of offenders by probation officers of the Ontario Ministry of Correctional Services in Cornwall, Ontario. The Ministry claimed solicitor-client privilege with respect to virtually all relevant documents. A Freedom of Information adjudicator ordered that 19 pages be disclosed. On appeal, Blair J. ordered that the entire private record be disclosed to the journalist's counsel to enable counsel to argue Ontario's application for judicial review, subject to an undertaking that counsel not disclose the information to his journalist client. In further appeals, the matter was argued as a question of whether the court had jurisdiction to control its own process on this issue, one part of which would be the authority to order limited disclosure and thereby "ensure procedural fairness to all parties". On this basis the Ontario courts upheld the order of Blair J. On appeal to the Supreme Court of Canada, the main

---

[48] See *R. v. McClure*, [2001] S.C.J. No. 13, [2001] 1 S.C.R. 445, 151 C.C.C. (3d) 321 (S.C.C.) (section 7) and *Lavallee, Rackel & Heintz v. Canada (Attorney General); White, Ottenheimer & Baker v. Canada (Attorney General); R. v. Fink*, [2002] S.C.J. No. 61, 2002 SCC 61, 167 C.C.C. (3d) 1 (S.C.C.) (section 8).

[49] For further discussion of the "constitutionalization" of solicitor-client privilege, see, for example, Mamhud Jamal & Brian Morgan, "The Constitutionalization of Solicitor-Client Privilege" (2003), 20 S.C.L.R. (2d) 213; Adam Dodek, "Reconceiving Solicitor-Client Privilege" (2010), 35 Queen's L.J. 493, and Amy Salyzyn "Another One Bites the Dust! Bolstered Law Offices and a Blocked Taxman in Chambre des notaires du Québec" (2017) 81 S.C.L.R. (2d) 173.

[50] [2006] S.C.J. No. 31, 2006 SCC 31 (S.C.C.);

[51] [2008] S.J. No. 623, 2008 SKCA 128, [2009] 3 W.W.R. 279 (Sask. C.A.).

[52] [2015] S.C.J. No. 7, [2015] 1 S.C.R. 401 (S.C.C.)

[53] R.S.O. 1990, c. F.31.

issue was framed differently by Rothstein J., who wrote the unanimous decision of the Court.]

ROTHSTEIN J.:—

. . . . .

There are two issues in this appeal:

(a) Can the records in issue be disclosed to counsel for the requester notwithstanding the Ministry's claim of solicitor-client privilege?

(b) Is the Divisional Court bound by the provisions of the *Access Act* such that the prohibition on the Commissioner's disclosing records applies to the court?

. . . . .

The substantive rule laid down in *Descôteaux* is that a judge must not interfere with the confidentiality of communications between solicitor and client "except to the extent absolutely necessary in order to achieve the ends sought by the enabling legislation". . . .

. . . . .

(3) Meaning of Absolute Necessity

Absolute necessity is as restrictive a test as may be formulated short of an absolute prohibition in every case. The circumstances in which the test has been met exemplify its restrictive nature. In *Solosky* . . . for example, it was found that subject to strict safeguards, mail received by an inmate at a penitentiary could be inspected to maintain the safety and security of the penitentiary. Similarly, in *McClure*, it was found that documents subject to privilege could be disclosed where there was a genuine danger of wrongful conviction because the information was not available from other sources and the accused could not otherwise raise a reasonable doubt as to his guilt.

While I cannot rule out the possibility, it is difficult to envisage circumstances where the absolute necessity test could be met if the sole purpose of disclosure is to facilitate argument by the requester's counsel on the question of whether privilege is properly claimed. Hearing from both sides of an issue is a principle to be departed from only in exceptional circumstances. However, privilege is a subject with which judges are acquainted. They are well equipped in the ordinary case to determine whether a record is subject to privilege. There is no evidence in this case that disclosure of records to counsel for the purpose of arguing whether or not they are privileged is absolutely necessary.

. . . . .

(5) Conclusion on Solicitor-Client Privilege

In sum, I agree with the Ministry that there is no justification for establishing a new or different test for disclosure of records subject to a claim for solicitor-client privilege in an access to information case.

I am of the respectful opinion that the Ontario courts were in error in permitting disclosure of all the documents in this case. The appropriate test for any document claimed to be subject to solicitor-client privilege is "absolute necessity". That test was not applied. Had it been, disclosure of all the records would not have been ordered.

I am mindful that openness of the court's process is a recognized principle. However, as with all general principles, there are exceptions. Records that are subject to a claim of solicitor-client privilege in an access to information case are such an exception. Absent absolute necessity in order to achieve the end sought by the enabling legislation, such records may not be disclosed. As stated, the evidence disclosed no such absolute necessity in this case.

LAW SOCIETY OF SASKATCHEWAN V. E.F.A. MERCHANT, Q.C.

[2008] S.J. No. 623, 2008 SKCA 128, [2009] 3 W.W.R. 279
(Sask. C.A., J. Klebuc C.J.S., R.G. Richards and Y.G.K. Wilkinson JJ.A.
Leave to appeal refused: [2008] S.C.C.A. No. 538 (S.C.C.).)

[The Law Society was investigating a complaint that Merchant, a lawyer, disobeyed a court order requiring Merchant to pay into court any funds that his client, Hunter, received from a residential school claim to secure his child support obligations. Pending Merchant's appeal from the order, the client's former wife received information that Hunter had received a settlement six months earlier. The former wife obtained court documentation to this effect. She wrote to the Law Society, indicating that Merchant had refused to discuss whether or not he had paid the funds into court as required by the order, or to her former husband, on the basis of solicitor-client privilege. She advised the Law Society that Merchant had made two payments from the settlement funds to her former husband, apparently in violation of the order. The Society began investigating the wife's complaint and requested from Merchant information about his dealings with his client. It applied for an order authorizing it to enter Merchant's offices and take possession of the records relevant to the wife's complaint. The application was refused and the Law Society appealed, arguing (i) that disclosure of privileged information to the Law Society did not constitute a breach of the privilege; and (ii) that the disclosure was "absolutely necessary" for the Law Society to fulfill its statutory responsibilities.]

R.G. RICHARDS J.A.:—

. . . . .

V. Analysis

A. Basic Principles

The essential contours of the law of solicitor-client privilege are well established and are not contested by the parties.

[The Court of Appeal rejected the Law Society's first argument to the effect that "the common law extends the envelope of solicitor-client privilege to include the Law Society".]

. . . . .

The Law Society's second submission is more conventional than its first. It contends the Chambers judge misapplied or misinterpreted the "absolutely necessary" requirement referred to in *Descôteaux v. Mierzwinski*. The Society says it has a statutory obligation to investigate Ms. Wolfe's complaint and has narrowly tailored its request for documents with the result that all the records being sought are required for its investigation. It emphasizes there is no other way of obtaining these records and, in the result, submits the absolute necessity test is satisfied.

The respondents reject this line of analysis. They say the "absolutely necessary" consideration cannot be satisfied on the facts at hand because the operation of the *Act* and the Rules does not fully ensure the records sought by the Law Society will be kept confidential and, in particular, do not ensure they will be kept confidential from Ms. Wolfe. This line of argument parallels the reasoning of the Chambers judge who concluded that the "absolutely necessary" standard had not been met because the *Act* and the Rules allowed "too much discretion to adequately address the protection of the solicitor-client privilege".

In my respectful view, the respondents' submissions on this aspect of the appeal are misdirected. In the present context, the "absolutely necessary" concept is concerned not with whether or how effectively the Law Society will protect the confidentiality of privileged records after they are produced. It is concerned with whether those records should be produced at all. The respondents' position, particularly in oral argument, was to the effect that solicitor-client privilege could not be overcome unless the *Act* and the Rules guaranteed the privileged information would be kept strictly confidential. However, this misconceives the "absolutely necessary" concept.

. . . . .

What then is the proper line of analysis in relation to this aspect of the appeal? It seems to me that it is ultimately quite straightforward. First, it must be determined whether the Law Society has the authority to demand the production of records subject to solicitor-client privilege. Second, if the Society has such powers, consideration must be given to whether that authority has been exercised so as not to interfere with privilege except to the extent absolutely necessary. I will examine each of these points in turn.

In assessing the nature of the Law Society's authority to demand access to privileged records, it is useful to begin with the admonishment in *Descôteaux v. Mierzwinski* that legislation which enables incursions on privilege should be interpreted restrictively. More particularly, it is important to note the Supreme Court's caution about inferring powers to abrogate privilege. Most recently, in *Privacy Commissioner of Canada v. Blood Tribe Department of Health*, [2008 SCC 44] Binnie J. wrote as follows at para. 11:

> To give effect to this fundamental policy of the law [i.e. solicitor-client privilege], our Court has held that legislative language that may (if broadly construed) allow incursions on solicitor-client privilege must be interpreted restrictively. The privilege cannot be abrogated by inference. Open-textured language governing production of documents will be read *not* to include solicitor-client documents: *Lavallee*, at para. 18; *Pritchard*, at para. 33 . . . . [Emphasis in original]

In the present case, the Law Society's demand for records was made pursuant to s.

63(1) of the *Act*. As noted above, it reads as follows:

> 63(1) Every member and every person who keeps any of a member's records or other property shall comply with a demand of a person designated by the benchers to produce <u>any of the member's records or other property</u> that the person designated by the benchers reasonably believes are required for the purposes of an investigation pursuant to this Act. [Emphasis added]

This provision does not authorize the Law Society, in so many words, to demand privileged documents. However, in my view, an authority to require production of "*any* of the member's records", found in the unique context of a statute dealing with the regulation of the legal profession, must be taken as referring to documents subject to solicitor-client privilege. . . .

It can be readily seen that s. 63(1) stands on quite different ground than the legislation considered by the Supreme Court in the cases where it said the power to limit solicitor-client privilege should not be inferred. . . .

. . . . .

. . . The wording of s. 63(1) of *The Legal Profession Act, 1990*, considered in its statutory context, clearly reveals a legislative intention that the Law Society be empowered to demand access to material subject to solicitor-client privilege. The phrase ". . . any of a member's records or other property . . .", when used in reference to the professional activities of a lawyer, must necessarily include privileged material.

It is clear, therefore, that the Law Society has the authority to demand the production of privileged records. Indeed, the respondents have taken no issue with that notion.
. . .

As noted above, given the existence of an authority to demand privileged records, the next step in the analysis is to consider the "absolutely necessary" principle. As indicated, the question here is whether the Law Society exercised its power to request records from Mr. Merchant and his firm in a fashion which avoided interfering with privilege except, to use Lamer J.'s words, "to the extent absolutely necessary in order to achieve the end sought by the enabling legislation".

The first point to underline in this regard is that the *Act* gives the Law Society the significant responsibility of governing the legal profession in Saskatchewan and of ensuring the profession's ongoing integrity. Lebel J. explained the importance of this self-governance function in *Finney v. Barreau du Québec*, 2004 SCC 36, [2004] 2 S.C.R. 17 at para. 1:

> An independent bar composed of lawyers who are free of influence by public authorities is an important component of the fundamental legal framework of Canadian society. In Canada, our tradition of allowing the legal profession to regulate itself can largely be attributed to a concern for protecting that independence and to lawyers' own staunch defence of their autonomy. In return, the delegation of powers by the State imposes obligations on the governing bodies of the profession, which are then responsible for ensuring the competence and honesty of their members in their dealings with the public.

In order to facilitate and ensure the execution of these responsibilities, the *Act*, in Part IV, lays out a comprehensive regime dealing with issues of competency and discipline. One feature of that regime places a positive obligation on the Society to investigate complaints. Section 40(1) of the *Act* states:

40(1) Where the society:

(a)   receives a complaint with respect to a member, alleging conduct unbecoming; . . .

a person designated by the benchers shall review the conduct of the member.

As a result, the Society must delve into complaints in order to satisfy the objectives of the *Act*.

The scope of the demand for records made by the Law Society in this case is also significant. On this front, it is important to note that the Society has carefully framed the demand so as to limit it to matters directly related to Ms. Wolfe's complaint. It has abandoned the original, more general, request for all file material relating to Mr. Hunter's residential school claim and his matrimonial dispute with Ms. Wolfe.

In light of these circumstances, the respondents quite properly concede both that the Law Society has reasonable and probable grounds for requesting the records in question and, significantly, that those records are required for purposes of the investigation which the *Act* obliges the Law Society to conduct.

In my opinion, these concessions effectively determine the result of this appeal. The Law Society has a duty to investigate complaints and the authority to demand privileged records in the course of discharging that duty. It has framed a request which is as narrow as reasonably possible and is thus seeking only those documents necessary to investigate Ms. Wolfe's complaint. It is self-evident that there is no other way to obtain those records or to pursue the investigation. Thus, in my view, this is a clear example of what *Descôteaux v. Mierzwinski* described as ". . . not interfering with [privilege] except to the extent absolutely necessary in order to achieve the ends sought by the enabling legislation".

[The Appeal was allowed on this basis.]

CANADA (ATTORNEY GENERAL) v. FEDERATION OF LAW SOCIETIES OF CANADA

[2015] S.C.J. No. 7, [2015] 1 S.C.R. 401 (S.C.C.)

[In 2001, the Government of Canada established a "Regime" intended to prevent or detect proceeds of crime that might be laundered to assist in criminal activities, in particular the financing of terrorist activities. The legislation and regulations require certain businesses and professions to collect and maintain personal and financial information in relation to their clients or customers that can in some cases be obtained by federal authorities. Prior to being judicially challenged, most aspects of the Regime were applicable to lawyers, and imposed on them new client identification and record-keeping obligations. It also gave government authorities (specifically, the Financial Transactions and Reports Analysis Centre of Canada, commonly referred to by its acronym "FINTRAC") new powers to conduct warrantless searches and seizures of lawyers' offices. The Federation of Law Societies of Canada commenced a constitutional challenge to the legislation as it applied to the legal profession, alleging that the Regime breached both section 7 and section 8 of the Charter and that the infringement was not saved under section 1 of the Charter. The application judge of the Supreme Court of British Columbia held that the challenged provisions violated section 7, and that the infringement was not saved under section 1. She did not address whether the provisions infringed section 8. The British Columbia Court of Appeal dismissed an appeal.

At first instance, the application judge identified and applied "solicitor-client privilege" as the relevant principle of fundamental justice for the section 7 analysis. On appeal, the British Columbia Court of Appeal held that a new principle of fundamental justice – "independence of the bar" — was engaged, as opposed to solicitor-client privilege. As you will see in the excerpt below, the majority of the Supreme Court of Canada identified and applied yet another new principle of fundamental justice in its section 7 analysis: "commitment to a client's cause". This aspect of the case was also discussed in the excerpt included in chapter 1.]

CROMWELL J.:—

I. Introduction

Lawyers must keep their clients' confidences and act with commitment to serving and protecting their clients' legitimate interests. Both of these duties are essential to the due administration of justice. However, some provisions of Canada's anti-money laundering and anti-terrorist financing legislation are repugnant to these duties. They require lawyers, on pain of imprisonment, to obtain and retain information that is not necessary for ethical legal representation, and provide inadequate protection for the client's confidences subject to solicitor-client privilege. I agree with the British Columbia courts that these provisions are therefore unconstitutional. They unjustifiably limit the right to be free of unreasonable searches and seizures under s. 8 of the *Canadian Charter of Rights and Freedoms*, and the right under s. 7 of the Charter not to be deprived of liberty otherwise than in accordance with the principles of fundamental justice.

II. Overview and Background

A. Overview

There is a risk that financial intermediaries — those who handle funds on behalf of others — may facilitate money laundering or terrorist financing. To reduce that risk, Canada's anti-money laundering and anti-terrorist financing legislation imposes duties on financial intermediaries, including lawyers, accountants, life insurance brokers, securities dealers and others. They must collect information in order to verify the identity of those on whose behalf they pay or receive money, keep records of the transactions, and establish internal programs to ensure compliance. The legislation also subjects financial intermediaries, including lawyers, to searches and seizures of the material that they are required to collect, record and retain.

Lawyers object to these provisions, and the Federation of Law Societies of Canada ("Federation"), supported by several interveners, challenges them on constitutional grounds. The Federation says that the scheme makes lawyers unwilling state agents. They are required to obtain and retain information about their clients. They must do this within a scheme that authorizes unreasonable searches and seizures, and provides inadequate protections for solicitor-client privilege. This, the Federation argues, turns law offices into archives for use by the police and prosecution. The provisions, therefore, violate both s. 7 and s. 8 of the Charter.

. . . . .

III. Analysis

A. Do the Provisions Infringe Section 8 of the Charter?

[Although the courts below did not engage in a section 8 analysis, Justice Cromwell considered whether the Regime's search and seizure provisions infringed section 8 and concluded that there was an infringement largely on the basis that the Regime did not comply with the Court's guidance on law office searches in *Lavallee, Rackel & Heintz v. Canada (Attorney General)*, [2002] S.C.J. No. 61, [2002] 3 S.C.R. 209 (S.C.C.)

In the context of this analysis, Justice Cromwell rejects the Attorney General's submission that the principles discussed in *Lavallee* should not apply, because the Regime involves an "administrative law regulatory compliance regime", as opposed to a situation in "where law enforcement officials are seeking evidence of criminal wrongdoing". This part of the section 8 analysis is excerpted below.]

. . ..[T]he reasonable expectation of privacy in relation to communications subject to solicitor-client privilege is invariably high, regardless of the context. The main driver of that elevated expectation of privacy is the specially-protected nature of the solicitor-client relationship, not the context in which the state seeks to intrude into that specially protected zone. I do not accept the proposition that there is a reduced expectation of privacy in relation to solicitor-client privileged communication when a FINTRAC official searches a law office rather than when a police officer does so in the course of investigating a possible criminal offence. . ..

. . . . .

I see no basis for thinking that solicitor-client communications should be more vulnerable to non-consensual disclosure in the course of a search and seizure by FINTRAC officials than they would be in the course of any other search by other law enforcement authorities.

The Attorney General submits that the information here is sought in aid of monitoring the lawyer's activities, not the client's, and that there is protection against derivative use. But these factors are entitled to little weight here. As discussed earlier, the overriding purposes of this scheme are the prevention and detection of serious, criminal offences. It has little in common with, for example, the competition legislation at issue in *Thomson Newspapers* [[1990] 1 SCR 425], or the fisheries legislation in *Fitzpatrick* [[1995] 4 SCR 154]. Moreover, I do not accept the Attorney General's submission that the broad scope of this search power is somehow limited by what the "regulator" is "interested in reviewing": A.F., at para. 107. The Act on its face purports to give the authorized person licence to troll through vast amounts of information in the possession of lawyers. As the intervener Criminal Lawyers' Association fairly put it, the Act gives authorized persons the power "to roam at large within law offices, and . . . to examine and seize any record or data found therein": factum, at para. 23. The exercise of these powers in relation to records in possession of lawyers creates a very high risk that solicitor-client privilege will be lost.

In short, there is nothing about the regulatory context here or the interests of the regulator which in any way takes this regime out of the field of criminal law or diminishes in any way the very high reasonable expectation of privacy in relation to material subject to solicitor-client privilege. In my view, the *Lavallee* standard applies to this regime.

. . . . .

[The Court concluded that the Regime's search and seizure provisions could not be saved under section 1 of the *Charter*.]

B. Do the Provisions Violate Section 7 of the Charter?

There are two steps to the analysis under s. 7 of the Charter. The first is to determine whether the challenged provisions limit the right to life, liberty or security of the person. If they do, the analysis moves to the second step of determining whether that limitation is in accordance with the principles of fundamental justice: *Canada (Attorney General) v. Bedford*, [2013] S.C.J. No. 72, 2013 SCC 72, [2013] 3 S.C.R. 1101, at para. 57 (S.C.C.); *Blencoe v. British Columbia (Human Rights Commission)*, [2000] S.C.J. No. 43, 2000 SCC 44, [2000] 2 S.C.R. 307 at para. 47 (S.C.C.). The Attorney General maintains that there is no s. 7 violation here, but I respectfully disagree. These provisions limit the liberty of lawyers in a way that is not in accordance with the principle of fundamental justice in relation to the lawyer's duty of commitment to the client's cause.

(1) Do the Provisions Limit Lawyers' and/or Clients' Right to Life, Liberty or Security of the Person?

There is no dispute that these provisions engage the liberty interests of lawyers. . . .

Both the application judge and a majority of the Court of Appeal found that this regime also limited the liberty of clients. However, I do not find it necessary to decide this point. I have already concluded that lawyers' liberty interests are engaged by the challenged provisions, and it has not been suggested that the s. 7 analysis would be different in relation to clients' as compared to lawyers' liberty interests.

(2) Is the Limitation Contrary to the Principle of Fundamental Justice in Relation to Solicitor-Client Privilege?

I have already concluded that the search provisions of the Act offend the s. 8 right to be free from unreasonable searches and seizures, and that they are unconstitutional and of no force and effect as they apply to records in the possession of lawyers. This conclusion makes it unnecessary to undertake an independent s. 7 analysis based on a principle of fundamental justice in relation to solicitor-client privilege in this case: see, *e.g.*, *Lavallee*, at para. 34; *R. v. Rodgers*, 2006 SCC 15 (CanLII), [2006] 1 S.C.R. 554, at para. 23; and *R. v. Mills*, 1999 CanLII 637 (SCC), [1999] 3 S.C.R. 668, at para. 88.

(3) Is the Limitation Contrary to the Principle of Fundamental Justice Relating to the Independence of the Bar?

. . . . .

The Federation, supported by several interveners, maintains that the independence of the bar is a principle of fundamental justice, and that the scheme is contrary to that principle in two respects. First, the scheme directly interferes with how lawyers deliver legal services to clients because it requires lawyers, by threat of imprisonment, to prepare records of the clients' activities, relationships and details of their transactions as part of a regime whose overall purpose is predominantly criminal. This, it is argued, is direct government intervention in the way in which the lawyer delivers legal services. Second, the lawyer is required to retain that information so the lawyer's office, as the Federation puts it, becomes an archive for the use of the prosecution. This undermines the trust between lawyer and client that is and must be at the foundation of the solicitor-client relationship. The argument goes that the lawyer is being conscripted against his or her clients by being required to obtain information from a client that is not required in order to provide legal services and to act as a government repository for that information .

As I understand these submissions, there are really two versions of the principle that are being advanced, a broad one and a narrow one.

According to the broad version, the independence of the bar means that lawyers "are free from incursions from any source, including from public authorities": Court of Appeal reasons, at para. 113. The narrower, more focused version, is anchored in concern about state interference with the lawyer's commitment to the client's cause. This narrower version, as I see it, boils down to the proposition that the state cannot impose duties on lawyers that interfere with their duty of commitment to advancing their clients' legitimate interests. In my view, the narrower principle is the one that is most relevant to this case: the central contention is that this scheme substantially interferes with the lawyers' duty of commitment to their clients' cause because it imposes duties on lawyers to the state to act in ways that are contrary to their clients' legitimate interests and may, in effect, turn lawyers into state agents for that purpose.

. . . . .

The narrower understanding of the independence of the bar, which relates it to the lawyer's duty of commitment to the client's cause is the aspect of the lawyer's special duty to his or her client that is most relevant to this appeal.

The duty of lawyers to avoid conflicting interests is at the heart of both the general legal framework defining the fiduciary duties of lawyers to their clients and of the ethical principles governing lawyers' professional conduct. This duty aims to avoid two types of risks of harm to clients: the risk of misuse of confidential information, and the risk of impairment of the lawyer's representation of the client (see, *e.g., Canadian National Railway Co. v. McKercher LLP*, 2013 SCC 39, [2013] 2 S.C.R. 649 at para. 23).

The Court has recognized that aspects of these fiduciary and ethical duties have a constitutional dimension. I have already discussed at length one important example. The centrality to the administration of justice of preventing misuse of the client's confidential information, reflected in solicitor-client privilege, led the Court to conclude that the privilege required constitutional protection in the context of law office searches and seizures: see *Lavallee*. Solicitor-client privilege is "essential to the effective operation of the legal system": *R. v. Gruenke*, [1991] 3 S.C.R. 263, at p. 289. As Major J. put it in *R. v. McClure*, 2001 SCC 14, [2001] 1 S.C.R. 445, at para. 31: "The important relationship between a client and his or her lawyer stretches beyond the parties and is *integral to the workings of the legal system itself*." (Emphasis added).

The question now is whether another central dimension of the solicitor-client relationship — the lawyer's duty of commitment to the client's cause — also requires some measure of constitutional protection against government intrusion. In my view it does, for many of the same reasons that support constitutional protection for solicitor-client privilege. "The law is a complex web of interests, relationships and rules. The integrity of the administration of justice depends upon the unique role of the solicitor who provides legal advice to clients within this complex system": *McClure*, at para. 2. These words, written in the context of solicitor-client privilege, are equally apt to describe the centrality to the administration of justice of the lawyer's duty of commitment to the client's cause. A client must be able to place "unrestricted and unbounded confidence" in his or her lawyer; that confidence which is at the core of the solicitor-client relationship is a part of the legal system itself, not merely ancillary to it: *Smith v. Jones*, [1999] 1 S.C.R. 455 at para. 45, citing with approval, *Anderson v. Bank of British Columbia* (1876), 2 Ch. D. 644 (C.A.); *McClure*. The lawyer's duty of commitment to the client's cause, along with the protection of the client's confidences, is central to the lawyer's role in the administration of justice.

We should, in my view, recognize as a principle of fundamental justice that the state cannot impose duties on lawyers that undermine their duty of commitment to their clients' causes. Subject to justification being established, it follows that the state cannot deprive someone of life, liberty or security of the person otherwise than in accordance with this principle.

. . . . .

Of course the duty of commitment to the client's cause must not be confused with being the client's dupe or accomplice. It does not countenance a lawyer's involvement in, or facilitation of, a client's illegal activities. Committed representation does not, for example, permit let alone require a lawyer to assert claims that he or she knows are unfounded, or to present evidence that he or she knows to be false or to help the client to commit a crime. The duty is perfectly consistent with the lawyer taking appropriate steps with a view to ensuring that his or her services are not being used for improper ends.

. . . . .

Clients — and the broader public — must justifiably feel confident that lawyers are committed to serving their clients' legitimate interests free of other obligations that might interfere with that duty. Otherwise, the lawyer's ability to do so may be compromised, and the trust and confidence necessary for the solicitor-client relationship may be undermined. This duty of commitment to the client's cause is an enduring principle that is essential to the integrity of the administration of justice. In *Neil*, the Court underlined the fundamental importance of the duty of loyalty to the administration of justice. The duty of commitment to the client's cause is an essential component of that broader fiduciary obligation. On behalf of the Court, Binnie J. emphasized the ancient pedigree of the duty and wrote that it endures "because it is essential to the integrity of the administration of justice and it is of high public importance that public confidence in that integrity be maintained": para. 12 (emphasis added). This unequivocal and recent affirmation seems to me to demonstrate that the duty of commitment to the client's cause is both generally accepted and fundamental to the administration of justice as we understand it.

The duty of commitment to the client's cause is thus not only concerned with justice for individual clients but is also deemed essential to maintaining public confidence in the administration of justice. Public confidence depends not only on fact but also on reasonable perception. It follows that we must be concerned not only with whether the duty is in fact interfered with but also with the perception of a reasonable person, fully apprised of the relevant circumstances and having thought the matter through. The fundamentality of this duty of commitment is supported by many more general and broadly expressed pronouncements about the central importance to the legal system of lawyers being free from government interference in discharging their duties to their clients. . .

. . . . .

The duty of commitment to the client's cause ensures that "divided loyalty does not cause the lawyer to 'soft peddle' his or her [representation]" and prevents the solicitor-client relationship from being undermined: *Neil*, at para. 19; *McKercher*, at paras. 43-44. In the context of state action engaging s. 7 of the Charter, this means at least that (subject to justification) the state cannot impose duties on lawyers that undermine the lawyer's compliance with that duty, either in fact or in the perception of a reasonable person, fully apprised of all of the relevant circumstances and having thought the matter through. The paradigm case of such interference would be state-imposed duties on lawyers that conflict with or otherwise undermine compliance with the lawyer's duty of commitment to serving the client's legitimate interests.

(e) Is the Scheme Consistent With This Principle?

. . . . .

The scheme requires lawyers to make and retain records that the profession does not think are necessary for effective and ethical representation of clients. The Federation's *Model Rule on Client Identification and Verification Requirements* (online), which has been adopted by all law societies in Canada, contains a number of verification and record-keeping provisions similar to the requirements of the Act and Regulations. However, the Model Rule is narrower in scope.

. . . ..

Professional ethical standards such as these cannot dictate to Parliament what the public interest requires or set the constitutional parameters for legislation. But these ethical standards do provide evidence of a strong consensus in the profession as to what ethical practice in relation to these issues requires. Viewed in this light, the legislation requires lawyers to gather and retain considerably more information than the profession thinks is needed for ethical and effective client representation. This, coupled with the inadequate protection of solicitor-client privilege, undermines the lawyer's ability to comply with his or her duty of commitment to the client's cause.

The lawyer is required to create and preserve records which are not required for ethical and effective representation. The lawyer is required to do this in the knowledge that any solicitor-client confidences contained in these records are not adequately-protected against searches and seizures authorized by the scheme. This may, in the lawyer's correctly formed opinion, be contrary to the client's legitimate interests and therefore these duties imposed by the scheme may directly conflict with the lawyer's duty of committed representation.

I also conclude that a reasonable and informed person, thinking the matter through, would perceive that these provisions in combination significantly undermine the capacity of lawyers to provide committed representation. The reasonable and well-informed client would see his or her lawyer being required by the state to collect and retain information that, in the view of the legal profession, is not required for effective and ethical representation and with respect to which there are inadequate protections for solicitor-client privilege. Clients would thus reasonably perceive that lawyers were, at least in part, acting on behalf of the state in collecting and retaining this information in circumstances in which privileged information might well be disclosed to the state without the client's consent. This would reduce confidence to an unacceptable degree in the lawyer's ability to provide committed representation.

I conclude that the scheme taken as a whole limits the liberty of lawyers in a manner that is not in accordance with the principle of fundamental justice relating to the lawyer's duty of committed representation.

I emphasize, however, that this holding does not place lawyers above the law. It is only when the state's imposition of duties on lawyers undermines, in fact or in the perception of a reasonable person, the lawyer's ability to comply with his or her duty of commitment to the client's cause that there will be a departure from what is required by this principle of fundamental justice.

. . . . .

McLACHLIN C.J. and MOLDAVER J.:— We have read the decision of Cromwell J. and we agree with his reasons insofar as they relate to s. 8 of the *Canadian Charter of Rights and Freedoms.*

However, we respectfully disagree with the approach taken by our colleague in his analysis of s. 7 of the Charter. To the extent that the s. 7 interests of the lawyer are engaged, we do not share our colleague's view that the principle of fundamental justice that would be offended is the lawyer's commitment to the client's cause. In our view, this "principle" lacks sufficient certainty to constitute a principle of fundamental justice: see *R. v. Malmo-Levine*, 2003 SCC 74, [2003] 3 S.C.R. 571, at para. 113. The lawyer's commitment to the client's interest will vary with the nature of the retainer between the lawyer and client, as well as with other circumstances. It does not, in our respectful opinion, provide a workable constitutional standard.

Rather, we are inclined to the view that the s. 7 analysis would be better resolved relying on the principle of fundamental justice, which recognizes that the lawyer is required to keep the client's confidences — solicitor-client privilege. This duty, as our colleague explains in his discussion of s. 8, has already been recognized as a constitutional norm. We note that in applying the norm of commitment to the client's cause, our colleague relies on breach of solicitor-client privilege. In our view, breach of this principle is sufficient to establish that the potential deprivation of liberty would violate s. 7.

For these reasons, we would allow the appeal in part in accordance with the disposition of our colleague.

. . . . .

NOTES AND QUESTIONS

1.   One aspect of *Goodis* included the lower court decision that confidential information be disclosed to the lawyer for the other side's counsel, subject to an undertaking that the information not be disclosed to that lawyer's client. To what extent is this justified? To what extent does it compromise the ability of the lawyer to obtain instructions from the client and for the lawyer to give frank and honest advice to the client if the lawyer cannot disclose any of the information on which that advice is based?

2.   *Goodis* reminds us of the importance of the "disclosure of confidences" framework articulated by Lamer J. in *Descôteaux*. The reassertion of the principle corresponds with recent court statements of the increasing significance and legal status of confidentiality and privilege. Does this signal a restatement of more conventional lawyering values that are seen to be central to the administration of justice? In *Goodis* the "search for truth" is rendered more difficult as a result. Nevertheless, courts have historically placed some "systemic" values on a higher plane than an unrestricted search for the truth in the individual case. Does this case, as well as *McClure*, suggest that the entitlement to have one's confidences preserved is a higher value than the search for truth in the litigation process?

3.   In Canada (Privacy Commissioner) v. Blood Tribe Department of Health,[54] the Privacy Commissioner for Canada sought access to documents with respect to which solicitor-client privilege was asserted. The Commissioner sought the right to examine the documents in order to assess the privilege assertion and complete an investigation, pursuant to her jurisdiction and responsibilities under the Personal Information Protection and Electronic Documents Act.[55] The initial dispute related to the dismissal of a person from employment with the Blood Tribe. In its decision, the Supreme Court of Canada noted *Pritchard v. Ontario (Human Rights Commission)*[56] and the importance of the prohibition against abrogation of solicitor-client privilege "by inference". The Court found that the Privacy Commissioner did not have status equivalent to a court with respect to access to privileged documents, and that the Privacy Commissioner's assertion that privilege be set aside must meet the same criteria established in *Descôteaux v.*

---

[54] [2008] S.C.J. No. 45, [2008] 2 S.C.R. 574 (S.C.C.).

[55] S.C. 2000, c. 5.

[56] [2004] S.C.J. No. 16, [2004] 1 S.C.R. 809 (S.C.C.).

Mierzwinski and *R. v. McClure*. The Court found that access to solicitor client confidences was not "absolutely necessary" to the achievement of the goals of the PIPEDA.

More recently, in *Alberta (Information and Privacy Commissioner) v. University of Calgary*,[57] the Supreme Court considered a similar situation in relation to provincial privacy legislation. In this case, a delegate of the Information and Privacy Commissioner of Alberta had sought documents with respect to which solicitor-client privilege had been asserted by the University of Calgary in the context of a request for access to information under the provincial *Freedom of Information and Protection of Privacy Act* in order to determine if the University was properly asserting privilege. The initial dispute in this case also related to the dismissal of an individual from employment. Although the legislative provision in this case did explicitly mention "privilege" specifically (*i.e.*, it required a public body to produce required records "[d]espite . . . any privilege of the law of evidence"), a majority of the Supreme Court held that the language of the provision did not "evince a clear and unambiguous legislative intent to [pierce solicitor-client privilege by statute]".

Do these cases represent a preservation of client rights at the expense of the legitimate ability of government officials to carry out legislated public duties? Does it represent a choice to preserve the privilege at the expense of "the truth"?

4. What explains the willingness of the Saskatchewan Court of Appeal in *Merchant* to essentially read into the *Legal Profession Act, 1990*[58] a requirement of disclosure of client confidences, and find it to be absolutely necessary to the administration of the Act?

5. Merchant was subsequently disciplined by the Law Society of Saskatchewan for breaching the court order and for "counselling and/or assisting his client to act in defiance of" the court order.[59]

6. Subsequent to the *FLSC* decision, the Supreme Court of Canada released its decision in *Canada (Attorney General) v. Chambre des notaires du Québec*,[60] wherein it held that provisions of the *Income Tax Act*,[61] which required lawyers or notaries to provide information or documents relating

---

[57] [2016] S.C.J. No. 53, 2016 SCC 53 (S.C.C.).

[58] S.S. 1990-91, c. L-10.1.

[59] Mr. Merchant was disciplined again in 2014 for breach of a court order, and for "counselling and/or assisting his client to act in defiance of" a court order (*Merchant v. Law Society of Saskatchewan* [2014] S.J. No. 245, 2014 SKCA 56 (Sask. C.A.)) and in 2020 for inducing a client to provide a prohibited assignment under the Indian Residential Schools Settlement Agreement and acting on the improper assignment (Online: https://www.lawsociety. sk.ca/wp-content/uploads/2021/01/2020-SKLSS-6-Merchant.pdf) although that suspension has been stayed pending appeal (Online: https://www.lawsociety.sk.ca/wp-content/uploads/2021/01/Stay-Order-issued-January-11-2021.pdf).

[60] [2016] S.C.J. No. 20, 2016 SCC 20, [2016] 1 S.C.R. 336 (S.C.C.).

to their clients to the tax authorities for tax collection or audit purposes, infringed section 8 of the Charter, and the infringement could not be saved under section 1 of the Charter. In reaching this conclusion, the Court emphasized several ways in which the regime failed to provide sufficient protections for solicitor-client privilege, including the fact that the Regime did not require notice to clients when their legal professionals were asked to produce information or documents. Among other things, providing notice to client would allow for clients to decide if they wished to consent to production or challenge the request in court.

In the *FLSC* decision and in the *Chambre des Notaires* decision, the Court expressed concerns that lawyers not be turned into "state agents", and that law firms not be turned into "archives" for government authorities. What do these statements tell us about how the courts view the role of lawyers in relation to the administration of justice?

7. In the *FLSC* decision, the majority identified and applied a new principle of fundamental justice – "commitment to a client's cause" – when conducting its section 7 analysis, while in their concurring reasons then Chief Justice McLachlin and Justice Moldaver took the position that "the s. 7 analysis would be better resolved relying on the principle of fundamental justice which recognizes that the lawyer is required to keep the client's confidences — solicitor-client privilege". Which analysis do you prefer? In what ways do the concepts of "solicitor-client privilege" and "commitment to a client's cause" overlap? In what ways might the latter concept be broader than the former?

[d]   Law Society Investigations and Disciplinary Proceedings

As a general matter, law societies have explicit statutory authority to require a lawyer to provide information or produce documents in the context of a law society investigation or proceeding notwithstanding that confidentiality or solicitor-client privilege may attach to such documents.[62] These statutory regimes also often contain protections against broader disclosure of confidential or privileged information. For example, Ontario's *Law Society Act* stipulates that a lawyer, by providing privileged or confidential information or documents to the Law Society pursuant to its statutory authority, does "not negate or constitute a waiver of any privilege" and affirms that "the privilege continues for all other purposes."[63]

Even in circumstances where law societies do not have explicit statutory authority to override claims of confidentiality and privilege, courts have been willing to find that law societies must be given access in order to carry out their regulatory

---

[61] R.S.C. 1985, c. 1 (5th Supp.).

[62] It should be noted that the nature of this authorization does vary between jurisdictions. For further discussion, see Adam M. Dodek, *Solicitor-Client Privilege* (Markham, ON: LexisNexis Canada, 2014) at 287-292 (noting, among other things, that there is no explicit authorization in the relevant New Brunswick statute).

[63] R.S.O. 1990, c. L.8, s. 49.8(3).

functions. The case of *Law Society of Saskatchewan v. E.F.A. Merchant*,[64] excerpted above, is an example of a court finding implicit authority to breach solicitor-client privilege in the absence of an explicit legislative clause. A similar judicial approach has been taken more recently in relation to reporting trust account data to the law society.[65]

Professional conduct rules also permit lawyers, on their own accord, to disclose confidential client information for the purpose of defending themselves in law society proceedings against allegations of professional misconduct or conduct unbecoming.[66] Equivalent permissions exist in relation to a lawyer's defence in relation to criminal or civil proceedings involving a client's affairs.[67] In such cases, the lawyer must take care to not to disclose more information than is required.[68]

[7] SPECIAL CASES

[a] Lawyer-Client Confidentiality and Privilege in the Context of Withdrawal from Representation

When withdrawing from representation, issues arise with respect to the lawyer's duty of confidentiality to the client. An obligation of confidentiality does not cease when the representation of the client ceases. However, in some circumstances, the need for the lawyer to withdraw from the representation can create challenges for the lawyer's ability to protect the client's confidentiality — the lawyer must withdraw, but must do so in a way that does not jeopardize the client's right to confidentiality. This point was addressed by the Supreme Court in the following case.

R. v. CUNNINGHAM

[2010] S.C.J. No. 10, [2010] 1 S.C.R. 331
(S.C.C., McLachlin C.J.C. and Binnie, LeBel, Deschamps, Fish,
Abella, Charron, Rothstein and Cromwell JJ.)

[As we saw in Chapter 2, "The Lawyer-Client Relationship", section [4][c], "Court Approval of Withdrawal", in *R. v. Cunningham* the Supreme Court of Canada articulated the scope of a court's authority to refuse counsel's application for withdrawal from the representation of a client in court proceedings. Associated with this question is the degree to which the lawyer may, or must, disclose the reasons for the application to withdraw, and the degree to which such disclosure might compromise confidentiality or privilege. In *Cunningham* it will be recalled that the lawyer sought to withdraw because of non-payment of fees. The Court also offered

---

[64] [2008] S.J. No. 623, 2008 SKCA 128, [2009] 3 W.W.R. 279 (Sask. C.A.).

[65] *Morris v. Law Society of Alberta (Trust Safety Committee)*, [2020] A.J. No. 231, 2020 ABQB 137 (Alta. Q.B.).

[66] Federation of Law Societies of Canada, *Model Code of Professional Conduct* at Rule 3.3-4(d), online: *Federation of Law Societies of Canada* https://flsc.ca/interactivecode/.

[67] Federation of Law Societies of Canada, *Model Code of Professional Conduct* at Rule 3.3-4(a)-(c), online: *Federation of Law Societies of Canada* https://flsc.ca/interactivecode/.

[68] Federation of Law Societies of Canada, *Model Code of Professional Conduct* at Rule 3.3-4(a)-(c), online: *Federation of Law Societies of Canada* https://flsc.ca/interactivecode/.

views with respect to the lawyer's obligations of disclosure of his or her reason for withdrawal.]

ROTHSTEIN J.:—

. . . . .

Ms. Cunningham and the interveners argue that solicitor-client privilege could be violated in one of two ways: simply by disclosure of the mere fact that the accused has not paid his or her fees, or inadvertent disclosure of privileged information when engaging in a discussion with the court about the reasons for withdrawal.

Concern regarding the protection of solicitor-client privilege is warranted. It need hardly be said that solicitor-client privilege is a fundamental tenet of our legal system. The solicitor-client relationship is integral to the administration of justice; privilege encourages the free and full disclosure by the client required to ensure effective legal representation (see *Smith v. Jones*, . . ., at para. 45, *per* Cory J. for the majority, and *R. v. McClure*, . . ., at paras. 31 and 33, *per* Major J.).

However, revealing that an accused has not paid his or her fees does not normally touch on the *rationale* for solicitor-client privilege in the criminal context. A client must be able to rely on the confidentiality of the communications made between lawyer and client because only then can there be full and frank discussion of the facts of the case, and the giving and receiving of soundly based legal advice (see *Anderson v. Bank of British Columbia* (1876), 2 Ch. D. 644 (C.A.), at p. 649; relied on in *Smith v. Jones*, at para. 45, and *McClure*, at para. 32). There has been no explanation as to why an accused would be any more inclined to withhold information from counsel, where the court has discretion over withdrawal, than where counsel can unilaterally withdraw.

In arguing that disclosure of the mere fact that an accused has not paid or will not be paying his or her legal fees is protected by solicitor-client privilege, the Law Societies of British Columbia and Yukon rely on this Court's decisions in *Descôteaux v. Mierzwinski*, . . ., and *Maranda v. Richer*, . . ., where this Court held that, in the context of a law office search, an accused's financial and fee information may be privileged. In *Maranda*, the Court was concerned that fee information, specifically the amount of fees and disbursements, may appear to be "neutral" when in fact disclosure of the information could be prejudicial to the accused. In particular, LeBel J. stated that fee information

> might enable an intelligent investigator to reconstruct some of the client's comings and goings, and to assemble evidence concerning his presence at various locations based on the documentation relating to his meetings with his lawyer. [para. 24]

This information could then be used to charge and/or convict the client. Because of the potentially detrimental effect of disclosure on the client, fee information is considered *prima facie* privileged for the purposes of the search. If the Crown seeks disclosure, the ultimate decision of whether the fee information is *in fact* privileged is made by the court, not the police.

Counsel seeking to withdraw for non-payment of legal fees is a decidedly different context from a police search of counsel's accounts and records. The most significant difference is the content of the information being disclosed. The only information revealed by counsel seeking to withdraw is the sliver of information that the accused has not paid or will not be paying fees. It has not been explained how, in this case, this sliver of information could be prejudicial to the accused. Indeed, it is hard to see how this simple fact alone could be used against the accused on the merits of the criminal proceeding: it is unrelated to the information given by the client to the lawyer, and unrelated to the advice given by the lawyer to the client. It would not be possible to infer from the bare fact of non-payment of fees any particular activities of the accused that pertain to the criminal charges against him.

To be sure, this is the case where non-payment of fees is not linked to the merits of the matter and disclosure of non-payment will not cause prejudice to the accused. However, in other legal contexts, payment or non-payment of fees may be relevant to the merits of the case, for example, in a family law dispute where support payments are at issue and a client is alleging inability to pay. Or disclosure of non-payment of fees may cause prejudice to the client, for example, where the opposing party may be prompted to bring a motion for security for costs after finding out that the other party is unable to pay its legal fees. Where payment or non-payment of fees is relevant to the merits of the case, or disclosure of such information may cause prejudice to the client, solicitor-client privilege may attach.

Disclosure of non-payment of fees in cases where it is unrelated to the merits and will not cause prejudice to the accused is not an exception to privilege, such as the innocence at stake or public safety exceptions (see generally *McClure* and *Smith v. Jones*). Rather, non-payment of legal fees in this context does not attract the protection of solicitor-client privilege in the first place. However, nothing in these reasons, which address the application, or non-application, of solicitor-client privilege in disclosures to a court, should be taken as affecting counsel's ethical duty of confidentiality with respect to payment or non-payment of fees in other contexts.

In the alternative, Ms. Cunningham and the interveners argue that counsel may inadvertently disclose privileged information when explaining the reasons for withdrawing and answering questions from the judge. They argue that this risk is so unacceptable that it requires the court to decline to exercise any discretion to refuse counsel's request to withdraw. They point to *Leask* where counsel sought withdrawal due to irreconcilable differences between counsel and the accused. The provincial court judge wanted specific details to determine if the differences could be resolved (*Leask*, at pp. 318-19). The accused in *Leask* was drawn into the conversation with the judge as well. They argue that this is dangerous because the accused may unknowingly waive his or her right to privilege and disclose information that is otherwise protected.

I agree that the exchange initiated by the provincial court judge in *Leask* was inappropriate. The judge repeatedly pressed counsel for detailed reasons for withdrawal, and continued to press even when counsel attempted to rely on the professional rules of conduct. The judge bluntly asked the accused if he objected to counsel disclosing the specific reason for withdrawal. I think it is fair to say that what occurred in *Leask* was unacceptable.

. . . . The remote possibility that a judge will inappropriately attempt to elicit privileged information in hearing the application does not justify leaving the decision to withdraw exclusively to counsel.

. . . . .

The court's exercise of discretion to decide counsel's application for withdrawal should be guided by the following principles.

If counsel seeks to withdraw far enough in advance of any scheduled proceedings and an adjournment will not be necessary, then the court should allow the withdrawal. In this situation, there is no need for the court to enquire into counsel's reasons for seeking to withdraw or require counsel to continue to act.

Assuming that timing is an issue, the court is entitled to enquire further. Counsel may reveal that he or she seeks to withdraw for ethical reasons, non-payment of fees, or another specific reason (e.g. workload of counsel) if solicitor-client privilege is not engaged. Counsel seeking to withdraw for ethical reasons means that an issue has arisen in the solicitor-client relationship where it is now impossible for counsel to continue in good conscience to represent the accused. Counsel may cite "ethical reasons" as the reason for withdrawal if, for example, the accused is requesting that counsel act in violation of his or her professional obligations (see, e.g., Law Society of Upper Canada, r. 2.09(7)(b), (d); Law Society of Alberta, c. 14, r. 2; Law Society of British Columbia, c. 10, r. 1), or if the accused refuses to accept counsel's advice on an important trial issue (see, e.g., Law Society of Upper Canada, r. 2.09(2); Law Society of Alberta, c. 14, r. 1; Law Society of British Columbia, c. 10, r. 2). If the real reason for withdrawal is non-payment of legal fees, then counsel cannot represent to the court that he or she seeks to withdraw for "ethical reasons". However, in either the case of ethical reasons or non-payment of fees, the court must accept counsel's answer at face value and not enquire further so as to avoid trenching on potential issues of solicitor-client privilege.

If withdrawal is sought for an ethical reason, then the court must grant withdrawal (see *C. (D.D.)*, at p. 328 . . . .). Where an ethical issue has arisen in the relationship, counsel may be required to withdraw in order to comply with his or her professional obligations. It would be inappropriate for a court to require counsel to continue to act when to do so would put him or her in violation of professional responsibilities.

. . . . .

NOTES AND QUESTIONS

1. In *Cunningham*, the Court stated that information regarding a client's non-payment of legal fees, at least in relation to a lawyer's application for withdrawal, is not privileged information. Yet the client's financial information was found to be covered by privilege in *Descôteaux*. Does this suggest that privilege is "contextual"? Or was it a matter of the Court wishing to avoid the consequences of (i) creating a new exception to privilege; or (ii) having to deal with the consequences of allowing a lawyer to "hide behind" privilege when they wished to get out of a case due to a dispute over fees? Is the outcome sound in light of the general language regarding the almost "absolute" sanctity of lawyer-client communications? You will recall that privilege is lost when the information comes to be known to a third party. In cases where a legal aid certificate is the basis upon which a legal aid tariff is paid (or not paid) to a lawyer, there is always "third party knowledge". Does this mean that *Cunningham* is not

really about privilege but about the lawyer's overriding ethical duty of confidentiality?

[b] Taking Custody and Control of Physical Evidence

Defence counsel's taking custody or control of physical evidence associated with the commission of a crime raises issues concerning the scope of a criminal defence lawyer's zealous advocacy on behalf of a client, along with a lawyer's duty to the court and to the administration of justice generally. This tension is different from the nature of client communications to their lawyer, and therefore invites different policy and ethical considerations.

R. v. MURRAY

[2000] O.J. No. 2182, 144 C.C.C. (3d) 289
(Ont. S.C.J., Gravely J.)

[The relevant facts are excerpted in Chapter 1, "Introduction to Legal Ethics" at pages X to X]

GRAVELY J.:—

. . . . .

THE INDICTMENT

Kenneth Murray is charged:

> That from May 6th, 1993 to September 12th, 1994 inclusive in the Regional Municipality of Niagara, Central South Region, and elsewhere in the Province of Ontario, did wilfully obstruct or attempt to obstruct the course of justice by concealing certain video tapes for approximately seventeen months which are the products and/or instrumentalities of crime, those video tapes containing scenes depicting the unlawful confinement of Leslie Erin Mahaffy, unlawful confinement of Kristen Dawn French, aggravated sexual assault of Leslie Erin Mahaffy, aggravated sexual assault of Kristen Dawn French, aggravated sexual assault of Tammy Lynn Homolka, aggravated sexual assault of Jane Doe by Paul Bernardo and Karla Homolka, contrary to section 139(2) of the *Criminal Code.*

CRIME AND ETHICS

I have been supplied by counsel with voluminous material on legal ethics.

I want to make clear that my function in this case is limited to deciding if Murray has committed the crime of attempting to obstruct justice, not to judge his ethics. While ethics may integrate with the issue of *mens rea*, ethical duties do not automatically translate into legal obligations.

. . . . .

Ontario courts have uniformly applied the tendency test [as to the *actus reus* for obstruction of justice]. In *R. v. May* . . ., Martin J.A. said . . . that the gist of the offence:

> . . . is the doing of an act which has a tendency to pervert or obstruct the course of justice and which is done for that purpose . . .

. . . . .

The *actus reus* issue, therefore, is whether Murray's action in secreting the videotapes had a tendency to obstruct the course of justice.

The word "wilfully" denotes the *mens rea* of the section. This is a specific intent offence and the onus is on the Crown to prove that Murray, when he secreted the tapes, intended to obstruct the course of justice . . .

. . . . .

The effect of section 139(2) is to prohibit improper interference with the functioning of any part of the justice system.

APPLICATION OF THE TENDENCY TEST

On the face of the evidence Murray's action in secreting the critical tapes had the tendency to obstruct the course of justice at several stages of the proceedings.

The tapes were put beyond the reach of the police who had unsuccessfully attempted to locate them. Secreting them had the tendency to obstruct the police in their duty to investigate the crimes of Bernardo and Homolka.

. . . . .

It would be difficult to over-estimate the evidentiary significance of these tapes. The making of them formed an integral part of the crimes. The victims were forced to participate not just in perverse sexual acts, but also actively in the videotaping of them. The resulting images amounted to the basest kind of forced child pornography. The tapes were the products and instrumentalities of crime and were far more potent "hard evidence" than the often-mentioned "smoking gun" and "bloody shirt." Once it possessed either of those items, the prosecution would still have to connect them to the accused and the accused would have room to raise issues such as self-defence. Here, jurors became eyewitnesses to Bernardo committing most of the crimes with which he was charged. Once the jury viewed the tapes, Bernardo was left with no defence to anything but the murder charges and little chance of a successful defence on those.

While Murray's conduct had a tendency to obstruct the course of justice in relation to the police and the Crown, it also influenced the way new defence counsel, Rosen, approached the conduct of Bernardo's defence. It had the further potential for a jury to be deprived of admissible evidence.

Concealment of the tapes had the potential to infect all aspects of the criminal justice system.

JUSTIFICATION

Prima facie, Murray's action in concealing the tapes is caught by the tendency test. He cannot, however, be said to attempt to obstruct justice if he had legal justification for his conduct.

There is no obligation on a citizen to help the police, but taking positive steps to conceal evidence is unlawful . . .

While Mr. Cooper conceded a lay person may not conceal evidence, he argued that defence counsel's obligations to the client dictate a special status that provides reasonable justification in some cases for concealment of evidence, and while the tapes could not be permanently suppressed, these tapes had some exculpatory value and counsel was entitled to temporarily conceal them for defence purposes.

Mr. Cooper did not suggest that confidentiality of the tapes is protected under the umbrella of solicitor-client privilege and no privilege, in my opinion, attaches to this evidence. Solicitor-client privilege protects *communications* between solicitor and client . . . These videotapes are not communications. They are, rather, dramatic evidence of crime and pre-existed the solicitor-client relationship. They are not similar, for example, to a sketch, which might be prepared by a client to help explain a point to his counsel, or even a videotape prepared for that purpose. Murray's discussions with his client about the tapes are covered by the privilege; the physical objects, the tapes are not. Hiding them from the police on behalf of the client cannot be said to be an aspect of solicitor-client communication.

The point is expressed well in the "bloody shirt" case. There, a lawyer was confronted with a client, wanted for murder, whose shirt was soaked in blood. Before surrendering the client to the police, the lawyer took possession of the shirt. Having some misgivings about his conduct, he retained counsel who approached the Professional Conduct Committee of the Law Society of Upper Canada for advice. He was told:

> You should not have taken the shirt. It is a piece of physical evidence. Not only that, what you saw with your eyes as opposed to what you heard with your ears, is not privileged so that you may be a witness now in this case. Our advice to you is that you must withdraw from the case and you must turn the shirt over forthwith to the Crown Attorney.

Although Murray had a duty of confidentiality to Bernardo, absent solicitor-client privilege there was no legal basis permitting concealment of the tapes. In this sense Murray had no higher right than any other citizen. Nor, in my opinion, can it be said that concealing the critical tapes was permissible because they may have had some exculpatory value. They were overwhelmingly inculpatory. Some of the United States authorities, including *The American Bar Association; Standards for Criminal Justice, Prosecution Function and Defence Function, Third Edition*, suggest counsel may retain incriminating physical evidence for a reasonable time for examination and testing. There was no testing contemplated here and, by some time in June 1993, Murray had examined the tapes and knew their contents. He chose to continue to conceal them.

In a line of United States cases . . . not only is there recognition that solicitor-client privilege does not protect physical evidence, but there is a suggested obligation on counsel to turn over incriminating physical evidence to a prosecutor.

That position appears to have been supported by Canadian commentators, at least with reference to instrumentalities of crime.

I am not entirely clear why there exists this almost universal view that incriminating physical evidence must go to the prosecution. In my opinion it does not follow that because concealment of incriminating physical evidence is forbidden there is always a corresponding positive obligation to disclose. In *R. v. P. (M.B.)* (1994) . . . Lamer C.J.C. said . . .: "With respect to disclosure, the defence in Canada is under no legal obligation to cooperate with or assist the Crown by announcing any special defence, such as an alibi, or by producing documentary or *physical evidence*". [Emphasis of Gravely J.]

Perhaps the general view that there is a turn-over obligation to the prosecution arises from the dilemma counsel faces once improperly in possession of incriminating physical evidence. At that point, almost any step involves potential risk of criminal liability. For example, in Mr. Martin's address . . . he recounts the difficulty created when the murder weapon is dropped on the lawyer's desk.

> What should the lawyer do?

> If he says, "Take the gun and come back after you have disposed of it," he has committed a criminal offence unless, of course, he can persuade a jury at his own trial that his intention was merely to instruct the client that he should leave the pistol at his residence so that it would be available to the police under a search warrant. If he takes possession of the pistol and puts it in his desk or vault a serious problem is created. Obviously, if he buried the pistol in his backyard he would be an accessory after the fact. If he puts it in his desk or vault, may it not be argued that he has just as effectively concealed it?

The American Bar Association Standards, supra, provide generally that defence counsel should return an incriminating physical item to the source after a reasonable period to allow for testing, etc.

Even if that were permissible it was not an option open to Murray. While he had no obligation to assist the police in their investigation or the Crown in its prosecution, Murray could not be a party to concealing this evidence. Having removed the tapes from their hiding place, he could not hide them again. Nor could he implement any instructions from Bernardo that would result in their continued concealment.

Once he had discovered the overwhelming significance of the critical tapes, Murray, in my opinion, was left with but three legally justifiable options:

    (a)   Immediately turn over the tapes to the prosecution, either directly or anonymously;

    (b)   Deposit them with the trial judge; or,

    (c)   Disclose their existence to the prosecution and prepare to do battle to retain them.

I am satisfied that Murray's concealment of the critical tapes was an act that had a tendency to pervert or obstruct the course of justice.

MENS REA

The onus is on the Crown to prove beyond a reasonable doubt that it was Murray's intention to obstruct the course of justice.

By putting the tapes beyond the reach of the police and the Crown, Murray clearly intended to impede the prosecution of the case against Bernardo. Defence strategy was based upon concealment of the tapes.

If Murray was aware concealment was unlawful, then the only reasonable inference would be, that by doing so, he intended to obstruct the course of justice.

Murray knew it was unlawful to permanently suppress the tapes. Asked by Mr. Cooper for his reaction to Bernardo's August 30, 1994 direction not to disclose the tapes, Murray said:

> It put me in a position that I was being asked to suppress evidence. I was being

asked to do something that was improper, *unlawful*, unethical and something that I couldn't either under the rules of conduct or professional ethics do. [Emphasis added]

The factual questions of intent then are:

1. Did Murray intend to conceal the tapes permanently or only up to the point of resolution discussions or trial?

2. If the latter, was it his honest belief he was entitled to do so?

MURRAY'S INTENTION

Murray testified he intended to use the tapes in the defence. With the tapes he could prove Homolka to be a liar and pave the way for Bernardo to give evidence that it was Homolka who committed the murders. The tapes would be used to cross-examine her at trial or in resolution discussions with the Crown.

Mr. Scott [for the Crown] argued that Murray's evidence was a tissue of lies, that his intention was to permanently suppress the tapes and he went to Mr. Cooper for advice only when the case was so ill-prepared for trial that Rosen had to be brought in to take over and Murray was faced with giving evidence by affidavit as to his reasons for ceasing to act.

Murray was an enthusiastic witness and his answers at times on cross-examination were more combative than responsive. Perhaps that is natural for an advocate. He was casual with the truth in selling the case to Rosen. I cannot conclude from his demeanour alone that he was untruthful in his evidence. Substantial character evidence was given as to his excellent reputation for integrity and truthfulness.

I am sceptical of Murray's evidence of his intention. I am troubled by the following:

1. Murray's evidence was inconsistent as to his tactical plans to use the tapes. His primary plan seems to have been that, without disclosing them to the Crown, he would surprise Homolka with them on cross-examination at trial. Another plan was that the Crown would get the tapes as soon as serious plea negotiations occurred, or perhaps, he said, negotiations could be concluded without the Crown knowing the contents of the tapes.

2. Murray failed to disclose the existence of the tapes to Rosen.

3. Rosen testified there was nothing in the file when he took over that suggested any use of tapes in the defence.

4. In Murray's summaries of the tapes, he suggested how the non-critical tapes might be used at trial. He had no similar suggestions for the critical tapes.

5. In his resolution discussions with the Crown, Murray made no mention of the tapes.

6. The tapes were not used to tie down Homolka in cross-examination at the Kingston Prison for Women. Nor was there any mention of use of the tapes in the file prepared for that cross-examination. MacDonald conducted the cross-examination without having seen the critical tapes.

7. As of September 1, 1994, 11 days before trial motions were to begin,

Doyle and MacDonald (who were said to have spent hundreds of hours preparing the case for trial) had not seen the critical tapes. The absence of consultation with co-counsel MacDonald is bizarre. In a case of this nature, one would normally expect that extensive preparation be conducted with co-counsel and very careful strategies and plans developed as to how the defence is to be approached. There was nothing of that nature apparent here in relation to the critical tapes.

If the tapes were inevitably going to come out and probably be used at trial, MacDonald eventually had to see them. That would occur in spite of all Murray's efforts to "protect" her.

8. Murray received authorization from Legal Aid to retain not only MacDonald and Doyle, but also numbers of other individuals to assist in the defence. . . . There is no evidence that any of these individuals ever saw the tapes or were briefed on their contents.

   Dr. Ben-Aron was expected to develop a psychiatric profile of Homolka without knowing videotapes existed that showed her apparently revelling in sexual perversions.

   Professor Yarmi no doubt would have been assisted in his analysis of the psychology of the case by viewing Bernardo and Homolka engaged in these crimes.

   In spite of all this preparation and all the experts and other individuals assisting in preparation for trial without knowledge of the tapes, Murray's evidence was that "the trial was the tapes" and their existence made the case a simple one.

9. Murray on August 30, 1994 had Bernardo sign a series of directions that, if followed, would result in continued concealment of the tapes.

10. It is difficult to conceive how the critical tapes were useful to Bernardo's case. They were damning evidence against him. Murray agreed that once shown the tapes "any jury would have convicted him of sinking the Titanic". While they provided scope for the cross-examination of Homolka, as Rosen said, "the client would have been in a substantially better position if the tapes had never surfaced".

11. When asked by Mr. Cooper why he failed on September 1, 1994 to mention his ethical dilemma to LeSage A.C.J.O.C., Murray said:

    > Because, as much as I was in a jackpot, the client's interests are paramount to protect. There may be an ethical issue, there may be something that I had to straighten out, but if I had gone to that meeting and said, well My Lord, the reason I want to get off is there are these video tapes that, you know, *bury his defence*, that the Crown doesn't have and he's told me to hold on to them. Well I couldn't do that . . .
    > [Emphasis added]

    This hardly sounds as if Murray, at least at that point, was viewing the tapes as a defence "bonanza".

Mr. Cooper submitted that Murray's explanations should deal with my concerns. While Murray's plans to use the critical tapes at trial were unfocused, it was clear they were to be employed in some way at some stage. Much is explained, he said, by Murray's belief he had to keep the tapes strictly secret in order to retain their tactical value. Rosen could not be told because he was only conditionally on the record for Bernardo. None of the four directions was in fact followed. The tapes were not specifically used in the Homolka cross-examination because of the difficulties mentioned in the evidence and the choice was made to hold back the tapes for their surprise value in cross-examination.

Mr. Cooper argued that Murray should be believed when he says he planned to use the critical tapes for defence purposes. In a careful and detailed review of the evidence, Mr. Cooper examined the position of the defence had the tapes not existed compared to the position with the tapes available.

Without the tapes, he suggested, the evidence against Bernardo was overwhelming. In addition to other pieces of circumstantial evidence, the DNA placed Bernardo in the house and having had sexual connection with one of the victims. The defence would then be faced with Homolka, an eyewitness, who would play her role as innocent, savagely beaten wife, coerced into helping Bernardo commit his crimes. There was little potential for a successful cross-examination of her. It was a "he did it" – "she did it" case, and, with the Scarborough Rapes going in as similar fact evidence, "Bernardo the Stalker" had no chance.

The tapes, suggested Mr. Cooper, gave Bernardo a slim chance. While they show Bernardo in a terrible light, Homolka turns out to be almost as bad. The benefit to the defence was not just that Homolka could be shown as a liar, but also as a person capable of committing murder. She is shown on the tapes administering halothane to her sister and to Jane Doe, and participating in sexual assaults on both of them. The tapes also show her using items of her dead sister's clothing to sexually stimulate Bernardo. For the same purpose she employs a rose which she was then going to put on her sister's grave. Mr. Cooper conceded the tapes were "an atomic bomb" for Bernardo, but, he suggested, "it bombed both ways."

In spite of all the inferences I am tempted to draw against the credibility of Murray based on his actions as I have enumerated them, I am satisfied on the basis of Mr. Cooper's argument that a defence strategy of use of the tapes at trial was reasonably feasible. That lends support to Murray's evidence that he did not intend to permanently suppress them. In this context, I have warned myself about the dangers of hindsight.

. . . . .

Murray's evidence that he would at some time disclose the tapes is supported by the fact that MacDonald and Doyle knew they existed. Murray would know that the pact of silence, no matter how solemn, would be unlikely to survive the Bernardo trial if the tapes were ultimately suppressed.

I conclude, therefore, that Murray's explanation as to his use of the critical tapes in the defence of his client is one that might reasonably be true.

MURRAY'S BELIEF

Assuming he intended to use the tapes for defence purposes, did Murray believe he had a right to conceal them to the extent he did?

Murray testified he believed his conduct was lawful.

C.c. 139(2) casts a broad net. It does not specifically isolate as criminal the conduct Murray engaged in.

The only official guide given to lawyers in Ontario on this issue is contained in rule 10 of the Law Society of Upper Canada Professional Conduct handbook. It reads in part:

> 2. The lawyer must discharge this duty by fair and honourable means, without illegality and in a manner consistent with the lawyer's duty to treat the tribunal with candour, fairness, courtesy and respect.

> The lawyer must not, for example:

> (e) knowingly attempt to deceive a tribunal or influence the course of justice by offering false evidence, misstating facts or law, presenting or relying upon a false or deceptive affidavit, *suppressing what ought to be disclosed*, or otherwise assisting in any fraud, crime or illegal conduct . . ." [Emphasis of Gravely J.]

The rule provides no guidance as to the nature of evidence that "ought to be disclosed". It is of small help either to counsel or to clients who may believe that both their secrets and their evidence are safe with their lawyers.

While Murray made only a token effort to find out what his obligations were, had he done careful research he might have remained confused. The weight of legal opinion in Ontario is to the effect that lawyers may not conceal material physical evidence of crime, but how this rule applies to particular facts has been the subject of extensive discussion. . . .

. . . . .

If I make the assumption Murray intended to use the tapes in the defence, I have no difficulty with the proposition that he may well have believed under the circumstances he had no legal duty to disclose the tapes until resolution discussions or trial.

PART FOUR – CONCLUSION

In summary, I find;

1. Murray's concealment of the critical tapes had the tendency to obstruct justice.

2. Murray knew it would be obstructing justice to permanently suppress the tapes.

3. He may not have intended to permanently suppress them.

4. He may have believed he had no obligation to disclose them before trial.

. . . . .

In the context of the whole of the evidence, Murray's testimony I find raises a reasonable doubt as to his intention to obstruct justice.

I find him not guilty.

NOTES AND QUESTIONS

1. Though he found that Murray's concealment of the tapes "had a tendency to pervert or obstruct the course of justice", Gravely J. also observed:

   > The weight of legal opinion in Ontario is to the effect that lawyers may not conceal material physical evidence of crime, but how this rule applies to particular facts has been the subject of extensive discussion. . . .

   Is the effect of this decision that a lawyer in possession of relevant physical evidence that could implicate their client must make disclosure of some sort with respect to this evidence? Does this amount to a qualification, or exception, to a lawyer's obligation of confidentiality to one's client? What factors would you take into account in determining whether and how you would make disclosure in "real evidence" situations?

2. You will have noted that, following his recitation of the professional conduct rule applicable to this situation, Gravely J. stated that the rule provided "no guidance as to the nature of evidence that 'ought to be disclosed'". Following the *Murray* decision, the Law Society of Ontario and others struggled with the issue and attempted to formulate a workable rule with respect to relevant physical evidence that comes into the possession of a lawyer. In 2014, the Federation of Law Societies amended its *Model Code* to provide greater clarity regarding lawyers' obligations in relation to incriminating physical evidence, and adopted Rule 5.1-2A. Review Rule 5.1-2A now.

   In what ways do Rule 5.1-2A and its associated Commentary provide more clarity than the historic Rule mentioned in *Murray*? What questions might a lawyer in possession of physical evidence still have about the appropriate course of action when consulting Rule 5.1-2A?

3. Should professional conduct rules about handling client property apply to all property having evidentiary value? For example, if your client were to bring to you the bottle of whisky from which he claims that he had only two drinks before driving his car (thus putting into dispute a breathalyzer reading, but constituting evidence that he had been drinking), what, if anything, must you do with the whisky bottle? What about hard copies of e-mails that he sent to a former lover that had potential value as evidence of harassment or stalking? Would you be required to disclose the information? Do the copies of the e-mails constitute physical evidence? If so, is there a basis for distinguishing this type of evidence from the conventional types of physical evidence? Does it make any difference that the authorities probably have access to the e-mail trail from the alleged victim's end of the e-mail chain?

4. The situation where a lawyer ends up in possession of physical evidence potentially related to a crime is relatively rare. But consider the following situation: A British Columbia man seized two motion-activated surveillance cameras he says the RCMP had hidden in trees near his trailer home, and they are full of images from crime scenes and investigations, as well as pictures of himself and his friends coming and going from his home.

The man believed the RCMP installed the cameras in the trees because he is a graffiti artist and they wanted to track his movements.

They are now in his lawyer's possession. The lawyer said he is keeping the cameras until he gets an explanation from police. The RCMP want their cameras returned. "The fact that someone has committed a criminal act and stolen our cameras certainly is, I guess, a concern for RCMP and for our investigators", said the RCMP spokesperson.

What are the lawyer's legal and ethical duties in these circumstances?

[8] CONFIDENTIALITY RISKS ARISING FROM THE USE OF TECHNOLOGY

Increasing use of technology in the practice of law has given rise to new risks that confidential and privileged client information will be either inadvertently disclosed or maliciously compromised. The failure to understand and guard against confidentiality risks posed by the use of technology can result in significant harms to both lawyers and their clients. In 2019, the *Model Code* was amended to recognize that a lawyer's failure to understand risks associated with technology that is relevant to their practice amounts to incompetence under professional conduct rules. Commentary [4A] to rule 3.1-2 "Competence" now reads:

> [4A] To maintain the required level of competence, a lawyer should develop an understanding of, and ability to use, technology relevant to the nature and area of the lawyer's practice and responsibilities. A lawyer should understand the benefits and risks associated with relevant technology, recognizing the lawyer's duty to protect confidential information set out in section 3.3.[69]

Lawyers need to be aware that the use of even relatively simple technology like email can give rise to major hazards for an unsuspecting user. For example, in recent years, multiple Canadian law firms have been targets of cyber-criminals using "ransomware", which can infiltrate a law firm's computer system through infected email attachments and which operates by encrypting the system's files and requiring a fee to be paid in order for access to be restored.[70] More innocently, features built into some email programs can result in inadvertent disclosures of confidential client information. For example, the use of the "AutoComplete" function, which automatically populates email addresses after a few letters are typed in, has led some Canadian lawyers to accidentally email confidential information to incorrect

---

[69] Federation of Law Societies of Canada, *Model Code of Professional Conduct* at Rule 3.1-2, Commentary [4A], online: *Federation of Law Societies of Canada* https://flsc.ca/interactivecode/.

[70] For discussion of some of these attacks, see, for example, Sean Kavanagh, "Ransomware attacks lock 2 Manitoba law firms out of computer systems" *CBC News* (April 14, 2020), online: https://www.cbc.ca/news/canada/manitoba/winnipeg-law-firms-computer-virus-ransomware-1.5530825; Jason Proctor, "Ransomware hackers pose threat to B.C. law firms" *CBC News* (January 12, 2015), online: http://www.cbc.ca/news/canada/british-columbia/ransomware-hackers-pose-threat-to-b-c-law-firms-1.2898490; and LawPRO, "Cybercrime and Law Firms: The Risks and Dangers are Real" LawPRO Magazine, Vol. 12, Issue 4 (December 2013).

recipients, and has led to malpractice claims.[71]

Additionally, some activities that Canadian lawyers did in the past with relatively little regard for their obligations to protect client confidences are now fraught with significant risks, due to the increased use of technology in practice. Crossing international borders with electronic devices is one such activity. When crossing borders, lawyers should be aware of what policies and procedures may apply to searches of their electronic devices and any safeguards in place (or lack thereof) in relation to confidential and privileged client information. Both the Canadian Bar Association and Federation of Law Societies of Canada have now published guidance for Canadian lawyers on crossing borders with electronic devices.[72] Among other things, these documents suggest several practical steps for lawyers to take to mitigate the risk that confidential and privileged client information will be exposed, including crossing the border with "clean" or "blank slate" devices that do not contain any client information, putting the device in "airplane mode" and then accessing any needed information or files once crossed through a secure remote connection.[73] It is also recommended that, if lawyers do travel with confidential or privileged client information, they carry identification that indicates that they are a licensed lawyer.[74]

To date, Canadian law societies have not issued any rules or regulations which mandate specific precautions or technical standards for lawyers to adopt in order to safeguard confidential client information. However, several Canadian law societies, professional indemnity insurers and lawyer professional organizations have published guidance to help lawyers navigate these new and emerging risks.[75]

NOTES AND QUESTIONS

1. In light of the risks identified in this section, do you think law schools

---

[71] See, for example, discussion in Nova Scotia Barristers' Society, "Beware of Auto Complete", online: https://www.lians.ca/resources/technology/beware-auto-complete.

[72] Canadian Bar Association, *A Toolkit for Canadian Lawyers who Travel to the United States* (May 2019) and Federation of Law Societies of Canada, *Crossing the Border with Electronic Devices: What Canadian Legal Professionals Should Know* (January 2019).

[73] Canadian Bar Association, *A Toolkit for Canadian Lawyers who Travel to the United States* (May 2019) and Federation of Law Societies of Canada, *Crossing the Border with Electronic Devices: What Canadian Legal Professionals Should Know* (January 2019).

[74] Canadian Bar Association, *A Toolkit for Canadian Lawyers who Travel to the United States* (May 2019) and Federation of Law Societies of Canada, *Crossing the Border with Electronic Devices: What Canadian Legal Professionals Should Know* (January 2019).

[75] See, for example, The Law Society of British Columbia, "Cloud computing checklist" (January 2013), Law Society of British Columbia, online: www.lawsociety.bc.ca/docs/practice/resources/checklist-cloud.pdf; The Law Society of British Columbia, "Cloud computing due diligence guidelines" (January 27, 2012), Law Society of British Columbia, online: www.lawsociety.bc.ca/docs/practice/resources/guidelines-cloud.pdf; The Law Society of Upper Canada, "Technology Practice Tips – Podcasts", The Law Society of Upper Canada, online: lsuc.on.ca/technology-practice-tips-podcasts-list/; and The Law Society of Upper Canada, "Technology Practice Management Guideline", Law Society of Upper Canada, online: https://lso.ca/lawyers/practice-supports-and-resources/practice-management-guidelines/technology.

should do more to inform and prepare students about the potential risks that the use of technology poses to client confidentiality?

[9] FURTHER READING

Dodek, Adam, *Solicitor-Client Privilege* (Markham, ON: LexisNexis Canada 2014).

Dodek, Adam, "The Public Safety Exception to Solicitor-Client Privilege" (2000–2001) 34 U.B.C. L. Rev. 293.

Frankel, Simon, "The Attorney-Client Privilege After the Death of the Client" (1992) 6 Geo. J. Leg. Ethics 45.

Freedman, Munroe, "Getting Honest About Client Perjury" (2008) 21 Geo. J. Leg. Ethics 133.

Freedman, Munroe, "The Professional Responsibility of the Criminal Defense Lawyer: The Three Hardest Questions" (1966) 64 Mich. L. Rev. 1469.

Ho, Hock Lai, "Legal Professional Privilege and the Integrity of Legal Representation" (2006) 9 Leg. Ethics 163.

Hutchinson, Allan, *Legal Ethics and Professional Responsibility*, 2d ed. (Toronto: Irwin Law, 2007), ch. 7.

Jamal, Mahmud, "The Supreme Court of Canada on Solicitor-Client Privilege: What Every Practitioner Needs To Know" (Canadian Bar Association: November 2006).

Layton, David, "*R. v. Jenkins*: Client Perjury and Disclosure by Defence Counsel" (2001) C.R. (5th) 259.

Layton, David, "The Public Safety Exception: Confusing Confidentiality, Privilege and Ethics" (2002) 6 Can. Crim. L. Rev. 209.

Layton, David & Michel Proulx, *Ethics and Criminal Law*, 2d ed. (Toronto: Irwin Law, 2015), chs. 4, 5.

MacKenzie, Gavin, *Lawyers and Ethics: Professional Responsibility and Discipline* (Toronto: Thomson Carswell, 2018), Chapter 3, "Confidentiality" and Chapter 7.2, "Confidentiality and Truth".

Maher, Kathleen, "May vs. Must" (2005) 91 A.B.A. J. 30.

Mercer, Malcolm, "Professional Conduct Rules and Confidential Information Versus Solicitor-Client Privilege: Lawyers' Dispute and the Use of Client Information" (2013) 92 Can. Bar Rev. 596.

Noonan, John T., Jr., "The Purposes of Advocacy and the Limits of Confidentiality" (1966) 64 Mich. L. Rev. 1485.

Paton, Paul, "The Independence of the Bar and the Public Interest Imperative: Lawyers as Gatekeepers, Whistleblowers, or Instruments of State Enforcement?" in Lorne Sossin, ed., *The Independence of the Bar* (Toronto: Irwin Law, 2007).

Pitel, Stephen & Jordan McKie, "Solicitor-Client Privilege for Ethics Counsel: Lessons for Canada from the United States" (2013) 91 Can. Bar Rev. 313.

Salyzyn, Amy, "A False Start in Constitutionalizing Lawyer Loyalty in *Canada (Attorney General) v. Federation of Law Societies of Canada*" (2016) 76 S.C.L.R. (2d) 169.

Simon, William, "The Confidentiality Fetish" *Atlantic Monthly* (November 2004) 112.

Simon, William, "Attorney-Client Confidentiality: A Critical Analysis" (2017) 30 Geo. J. Leg. Ethics 447.

Sowter, Deanne, "A Lawyer's Duty to (Sometimes) Report a Child in Need of Protection" (February 26, 2020) online: http://www.slaw.ca/2020/02/26/a-lawyers-duty-to-sometimes-report-a-child-in-need-of-protection/.

Woolley, Alice, "Volkswagen, Legal Advice and the Criminal-Communication Exclusion to Confidentiality and Privilege" (October 30, 2015) online: slaw.ca, http://www.slaw.ca/2015/10/30/volkswagen-legal-advice-and-the-criminal-communication-exclusion-to-confidentiality-and-privilege/.

Woolley, Alice, *Understanding Lawyers' Ethics in Canada*, 2d ed. (Toronto: LexisNexis Canada 2016), Chapter 5, "Lawyer-Client Trust and Confidence".

CHAPTER 4

THE DUTY OF LOYALTY AND CONFLICTS OF INTEREST

[1] INTRODUCTION

We saw in the previous chapter that a lawyer's duty of confidentiality is complex and sometimes morally problematic. In this chapter we shall see that lawyers are presented with similar and equally complex obligations in relation to conflicts of interest. These obligations arise generally from the same source — the various dimensions of the duty of loyalty owed to clients. At the same time, however, a number of other public policy values are implicated in the regulation of conflicts. For example, it is reasonable to expect lawyers to try to limit the total cost of legal services to clients, to make services available as widely as possible, especially in areas where legal services are not readily attainable, and, to the greatest extent possible, to enable a client to retain the lawyer of their choice. In other words, these public policy values invite us to take into account other requirements of the administration of justice even when doing so creates a tension with a more pristine environment where conflicts of interest are to be avoided at all costs.

Added to this is the evolving shape of the legal profession, including the concentration of many lawyers in large law firms, the evolution of "national" and "international" law firms who serve a multitude of clients across many jurisdictions, and the development of "multi-disciplinary" firms in which lawyers and other professionals practice side by side. The lawyer's ability to provide legal representation to a client with undivided loyalty has become a much more complex enterprise in the modern-day practice of law. In her textbook on lawyers' ethics, Alice Woolley suggests "[p]erhaps no area of the law governing lawyers consumes more time, creates more confusion and frustration, or causes lawyers more difficulty in their practices, than the rules governing conflicts of interest"[1].

Further, the lawyer personally may have interests that are not perfectly aligned with those of their client. These interests may be related to the issues at stake in the representation. For example, the lawyer's financial interests may be served to a greater degree by one outcome than another, outcomes over which the lawyer may have influence, but which may be at odds with the most beneficial outcome for the client. The lawyer may have an interest in entering into a potentially lucrative business relationship with a client. Or a lawyer may develop or have a pre-existing personal or family relationship that places "extra-legal" loyalties in tension with

---

[1] Alice Woolley, *Understanding Lawyers' Ethics in Canada*, 2d ed (Toronto: LexisNexis Canada, 2016) at 241.

accomplishment of the client's ends. Sometimes a lawyer will develop a romantic interest in a client.

While some of these circumstances lend themselves to "black and white" prescriptions, most have subtleties generated by the values embedded in the rich and complex environment in which lawyers provide legal services. Richard Devlin has described these challenges in a way that invites consideration of the issue at a more fundamental level:

> The issues generated by conflicts of interest and the duty of loyalty are multiple and complex. On one level, they raise key questions about the role morality and ethical identity of individual lawyers, and how to manage and reconcile their own interests, those of their (various) clients and the public good. At the level of law firms, conflicts of interest and the duty of loyalty generate important issues of governance, accountability and responsibility. . . .When we move to the level of regulatory authority – and legitimacy – the challenges become even more pronounced. In many jurisdictions the regulation of conflicts of interest and the duty of loyalty falls within the jurisdiction of both the courts and law societies. If both institutions are reading from the same script and pursuing the same objectives then the challenges are likely to be minor. But if courts and legislatures are whistling different tunes, and motivated by different goals, then there are likely to be some deep structural tensions – if not contradictions. Finally, the duty of loyalty and conflicts of interests shine a spotlight on the capabilities of regulators – be they law societies or oversight bodies – to regulate in the public interest. As the business model for the practice of law gains ascendency, the temptations to maximize the economic interests of lawyers and law firms necessarily intensify. The duty of loyalty – and the correlative obligations to avoid conflicts of interest – serve as a potential bulwark against the hegemony of the business model. If that bulwark does not remain strong, the claim that regulators' primary responsibility is to serve the public interest is cast into doubt.[2]

This chapter examines the circumstances that can pull lawyers in different, and often conflicting, directions. The chapter is organized to address the two central dimensions of lawyers' conflicts of interest: those arising between or among clients ('client-client' conflicts), and those arising due to a potential conflict between the lawyer's own interests and those of the client ('lawyer-client' conflicts). However, as we shall see, these categories are not mutually exclusive; as some cases illustrate, client-client and lawyer-client conflicts can often converge and collide with unfortunate results for all involved.

Even a modest consideration of this topic will lead the reader to appreciate that conflicts of interest can arise in any aspect of the practice of law. Whether a person practices law in a solo practice in a small community, in a large firm with offices in multiple locations, as a lawyer in government service or as in-house counsel, it will be common for the lawyer's loyalty to be subject to competing claims. More than platitudes are required to deal with these issues in a professionally appropriate and principled way.

Historically, this area of lawyers' obligations was the subject of a set of ethical

---

[2] Richard Devlin, "Guest Editorial: Governance, Regulation and Legitimacy: Conflicts of Interest and the Duty of Loyalty" (2011) 14:2 Leg. Ethics iii.

guidelines and little else. Codes of conduct focused on a set of general principles, perhaps honoured as much in the breach as in the observance, to guide lawyer conduct. In the last few decades, however, as has been the case with lawyer-client confidentiality and privilege, courts and disciplinary authorities have been asked to articulate standards for lawyer conduct in conflict of interest situations in more precise and meaningful ways. As a consequence, and led by the Supreme Court of Canada, a significant jurisprudence has developed in relation to lawyers' conflicts of interest. This work has been grounded in large measure on the fundamental principles and obligations owed to clients by lawyers, and informed by the expectation that a lawyer's behaviour is (and appears to be) beyond reproach. It has given deeper meaning to concepts such as loyalty. Indeed, in recent Supreme Court decisions the duty of loyalty owed to clients has been enriched and expanded, to the point where, some authors argue, that the duty is a primary duty – a 'lodestar' – in the lawyer's ethical world.[3]

Controversies regarding the scope of the lawyer's duty to avoid conflicts of interest have also generated legalistic interpretations of lawyers' obligations. In some circumstances the concept of a disqualifying conflict of interest - where a lawyer is disqualified from representing a specific client - has been turned from an honourable principle into a tool of litigation, often for less than honourable purposes. As well, these more recent developments have motivated efforts by the legal profession to articulate, or modify, the degree to which certain behaviours constitute conflicts of interest, resulting in dramatic changes to lawyers' understandings of their obligations. The materials in this chapter invite you to build an understanding of the legal and ethical dimensions of conflict of interest and to reflect on the courts' and the legal profession's efforts to breathe life into, and build precision around, such a concept. As well, you will have the opportunity to consider whether, in their efforts to balance the various competing public and professional values and interests at stake, the decision-makers have succeeded. Or have the profession's own interests been privileged in an area where lawyers themselves have a great deal at stake?

---

[3] See e.g. Colin Jackson, Brent Cotter & Richard Devlin, "Of Lodestars and Lawyers: Incorporating the Duty of Loyalty into the Model Code of Conduct" (2016) 39:1 Dal. L.J. 37.

[2] CLIENT-CLIENT CONFLICTS

[a] Introduction

Beginning in 1990, the Supreme Court of Canada has rendered four major judgments in the field of lawyers and conflicts of interest, often referred to as its "conflicts quartet". In these cases, arising from widely disparate practice settings, the Court has attempted to articulate a clear set of expectations of lawyer behaviour in the face of conflicting demands. In two of the cases, the central issue was whether a law firm could continue to act for a client in a context where another person involved in the litigation asserted that the law firm's continued involvement in the case could jeopardize its interests. In two cases, a person asserted that the ways in which a lawyer or law firm acted – in an alleged conflict of interest – damaged the legal rights of that person. In each case, as we shall see, the behaviour of the lawyer in question fell short of the standard set by the Supreme Court.

What is more significant, however, is the work of the Court to articulate the appropriate standards and its effort to ground these standards in fundamentally important values. Combined with the Court's decisions in other cases, a picture is emerging of the nature of lawyers' duties to their clients. But this work is not uncontroversial. The emerging jurisprudence has generated disagreements within the legal profession and has required the leaders of the profession to restate the nature of lawyers' ethical duties in this area. Indeed, the tensions surrounding the scope of a lawyer's duty to avoid conflicts of interest has been one of the most hotly contested areas of legal ethics and professional regulation in the history of the self-regulation of lawyers.

[b] Duties to Former Clients

The first significant decision of the Supreme Court of Canada in the modern era of conflicts of interest was *Re Macdonald Estate*, or *MacDonald Estate v.Martin*.[4] It is the quintessential "transferring lawyer" case, in which there is a conflict between the transferring lawyer's duty to his or her former client and the duties of the lawyer's new firm to its current client. In this case, Sopinka J. wrote for a bare majority of four. Cory J. wrote a concurring opinion which includes an uncompromising critique of the majority decision, perhaps the most powerful such commentary he ever wrote. These diverging judgments signal the difficulty presented by these cases, and the division of opinion that exists within the Court, and within the legal profession itself, over the standard of behaviour required of lawyers, and the principles that should be applied. As we shall see, this decision generated a great deal of work within the legal profession to establish professional standards aimed at implementing the majority's decision.

---

[4] *MacDonald Estate v. Martin*, [1990] S.C.J. No. 41, [1990] 3 S.C.R. 1235 (S.C.C.).

MacDONALD ESTATE v. MARTIN

[1990] S.C.J. No. 41, [1990] 3 S.C.R. 1235
(S.C.C., Dickson C.J., Wilson, La Forest, L'Heureux-Dubé,
Sopinka, Gonthier and Cory JJ.)

[Dangerfield, a lawyer in a law firm in Winnipeg, was involved in the representation of Martin, the plaintiff in a lawsuit related to the MacDonald estate. She was privy to confidential information related to the plaintiff's case. Her law firm dissolved and Ms. Dangerfield joined another law firm which eventually merged with the Thompson Dorfman Sweatman (TDS) law firm. TDS represented the defendant in the lawsuit initiated by Martin. That litigation was continuing when Dangerfield joined the firm. Dangerfield was not assigned to the case and was not in any way involved in the representation of the defendant.

The plaintiff brought an application to have the TDS firm disqualified from continuing to represent the defendant in the litigation. Dangerfield and other TDS lawyers provided sworn statements that no confidential information related to the plaintiff had been shared between Dangerfield and the law firm, and gave undertakings that nothing would be shared in the future.

At the lower courts the application was dismissed. Martin appealed to the Supreme Court.]

SOPINKA J.:— This appeal is concerned with the standard to be applied in the legal profession in determining what constitutes a disqualifying conflict of interest. The issue arose in the context of a lawsuit in which a former junior solicitor for the appellant transferred her employment to the law firm acting for the respondent.

. . . . .

The Issue

The sole issue in this appeal is the appropriate standard to be applied in determining whether Thompson, Dorfman, Sweatman are disqualified from continuing to act in this litigation by reason of a conflict of interest.

Legal Ethics — Policy Considerations

In resolving this issue, the Court is concerned with at least three competing values. There is first of all the concern to maintain the high standards of the legal profession and the integrity of our system of justice. Furthermore, there is the countervailing value that a litigant should not be deprived of his or her choice of counsel without good cause. Finally, there is the desirability of permitting reasonable mobility in the legal profession. The review of the cases which follows will show that different standards have been adopted from time to time to resolve the issue.

The legal profession has changed with the changes in society. One of the changes that is most evident in large urban centers is the virtual disappearance of the sole practitioner and the tendency to larger and larger firms. This is a product of a number of factors including a response to the demands of large corporate clients whose multi-faceted activities require an all-purpose firm with sufficient numbers in every area of expertise to serve their needs. With increase in size come increasing demands for management of a law firm in accordance with the corporate model. These changes in the composition and management practices of law firms are reflected in changes to ethical practices of the profession. Some of the old practices have been swept aside as anachronistic, perhaps with justification. Advertising to inform the public in a tasteful way of the services provided by a firm and of its fee schedule is but one example.

Merger, partial merger and the movement of lawyers from one firm to another are familiar features of the modern practice of law. They bring with them the thorny problem of conflicts of interest. When one of these events is planned, consideration must be given to the consequences which will flow from loss of clients through conflicts of interest. To facilitate this process some would urge a slackening of the standard with respect to what constitutes a conflict of interest. In my view, to do so at the present time would serve the interest of neither the public nor the profession. The legal profession has historically struggled to maintain the respect of the public. This has been so notwithstanding the high standards that, generally, have been maintained. When the management, size of law firms and many of the practices of the legal profession are indistinguishable from those of business, it is important that the fundamental professional standards be maintained and indeed improved. This is essential if the confidence of the public that the law is a profession is to be preserved and hopefully strengthened. Nothing is more important to the preservation of this relationship than the confidentiality of information passing between a solicitor and his or her client. The legal profession has distinguished itself from other professions by the sanctity with which these communications are treated. The law, too, perhaps unduly, has protected solicitor and client exchanges while denying the same protection to others. This tradition assumes particular importance when a client bares his or her soul in civil or criminal litigation. Clients do this in the justifiable belief that nothing they say will be used against them and to the advantage of the adversary. Loss of this confidence would deliver a serious blow to the integrity of the profession and to the public's confidence in the administration of justice.

An important statement of public policy with respect to the conduct of barrister and solicitor is contained in the professional ethics codes of the governing bodies of the profession. The legal profession is self-governing. In each province there is a governing body usually elected by the lawyers practising in the province. The governing body enacts rules of professional conduct on behalf of those it represents. These rules must be taken as expressing the collective views of the profession as to the appropriate standards to which the profession should adhere.

While there exists no national law society, the Canadian Bar Association, a national society representing lawyers across the country, adopted a Code of Professional Conduct in 1974. The Code has been adopted by the Law Society of Manitoba and by the Law Societies of other provinces. Chapter V, entitled "Impartiality and Conflict of Interest", commences with the following rule:

> The lawyer must not advise or represent both sides of a dispute and, save after adequate disclosure to and with the consent of the client or prospective client concerned, he should not act or continue to act in a matter when there is or there is likely to be a conflicting interest. A conflicting interest is one which would be likely to affect adversely the judgment of the lawyer on behalf of or his loyalty to a client or prospective client or which the lawyer might be prompted to prefer to the interests of a client or prospective client.

The rule is followed by thirteen commentaries. The most relevant of these are Commentaries 11 and 12, which state:

> 11. A lawyer who has acted for a client in a matter should not thereafter act against him (or against persons who were involved in or associated with him in that matter) in the same or any related matter, or place himself in a position where he might be tempted or appear to be tempted to breach the Rule relating to Confidential Information. It is not, however, improper for the lawyer to act against a former client in a fresh and independent matter wholly unrelated to any work he has previously done for that person.

> 12. For the sake of clarity the foregoing paragraphs are expressed in terms of the individual lawyer and his client. However, it will be appreciated that the term "client" includes a client of the law firm of which the lawyer is a partner or associate whether or not he handles the client's work.

A code of professional conduct is designed to serve as a guide to lawyers and typically it is enforced in disciplinary proceedings. . . . The courts, which have inherent jurisdiction to remove from the record solicitors who have a conflict of interest, are not bound to apply a code of ethics. Their jurisdiction stems from the fact that lawyers are officers of the court and their conduct in legal proceedings which may affect the administration of justice is subject to this supervisory jurisdiction. Nonetheless, an expression of a professional standard in a code of ethics relating to a matter before the court should be considered an important statement of public policy. The statement in Chapter V should therefore be accepted as the expression by the profession in Canada that it wishes to impose a very high standard on a lawyer who finds himself or herself in a position where confidential information may be used against a former client. The statement reflects the principle that has been accepted by the profession that even an appearance of impropriety should be avoided.

The Law

The law in Canada and in other jurisdictions has adopted one of two basic approaches in determining whether a disqualifying conflict of interest exists: (1) the probability of real mischief, or (2) the possibility of real mischief. The term "mischief" refers to the misuse of confidential information by a lawyer against a former client. The first approach requires proof that the lawyer was actually possessed of confidential information and that there is a probability of its disclosure to the detriment of the client. The second is based on the precept that justice must not only be done but must manifestly be seen to be done. If, therefore, it reasonably appears that disclosure might occur, this test for determining the presence of a disqualifying conflict of interest is satisfied.

. . . . .

[I]t is evident from this review of authorities that the clear trend is in favour of a stricter test. This trend is the product of a strong policy in favour of ensuring not only that there be no actual conflict but that there be no appearance of conflict.

A number of cases have specifically addressed the question as to whether possession of confidential information on the part of one member of a firm should be imputed to the rest of the firm. The strict application of the appearance principle has led some courts to apply it so that the presumption that "the knowledge of one is the knowledge of all" is irrebuttable.

. . . . .

The Appropriate Test

What then should be the correct approach? Is the "probability of mischief" standard sufficiently high to satisfy the public requirement that there be an appearance of justice? In my opinion, it is not. This is borne out by the judicial statements to which I have referred and to the desire of the legal profession for strict rules of professional conduct as its adoption of the Canadian Code of Professional Conduct demonstrates. The probability of mischief test is very much the same as the standard of proof in a civil case. We act on probabilities. This is the basis of *Rakusen [v. Ellis, Munday & Clarke*, [1912] 1 Ch. 831]. I am, however, driven to the conclusion that the public, and indeed lawyers and judges, have found that standard wanting. In dealing with the question of the use of confidential information we are dealing with a matter that is usually not susceptible of proof. Since, however, it is not susceptible of proof, the test must be such that the public represented by the reasonably informed person would be satisfied that no use of confidential information would occur. That, in my opinion, is the overriding policy that applies and must inform the court in answering the question: Is there a disqualifying conflict of interest?

Typically, these cases require two questions to be answered: (1) Did the lawyer receive confidential information attributable to a solicitor and client relationship relevant to the matter at hand? (2) Is there a risk that it will be used to the prejudice of the client?

. . .

In my opinion, once it is shown by the client that there existed a previous relationship which is sufficiently related to the retainer from which it is sought to remove the solicitor, the court should infer that confidential information was imparted unless the solicitor satisfies the court that no information was imparted which could be relevant. This will be a difficult burden to discharge. Not only must the court's degree of satisfaction be such that it would withstand the scrutiny of the reasonably informed member of the public that no such information passed, but the burden must be discharged without revealing the specifics of the privileged communication. Nonetheless, I am of the opinion that the door should not be shut completely on a solicitor who wishes to discharge this heavy burden.

The second question is whether the confidential information will be misused. A lawyer who has relevant confidential information cannot act against his client or former client. In such a case the disqualification is automatic. No assurances or undertakings not to use the information will avail. The lawyer cannot compartmentalize his or her mind so as to screen out what has been gleaned from the client and what was acquired elsewhere. Furthermore, there would be a danger that the lawyer would avoid use of information acquired legitimately because it might be perceived to have come from the client. This would prevent the lawyer from adequately representing the new client. Moreover, the former client would feel at a disadvantage. Questions put in cross-examination about personal matters, for example, would create the uneasy feeling that they had their genesis in the previous relationship.

The answer is less clear with respect to the partners or associates in the firm. Some courts have applied the concept of imputed knowledge. This assumes that the knowledge of one member of the firm is the knowledge of all. If one lawyer cannot act, no member of the firm can act. This is a rule that has been applied by some law firms as their particular brand of ethics. While this is commendable and is to be encouraged, it is, in my opinion, an assumption which is unrealistic in the era of the mega-firm. Furthermore, if the presumption that the knowledge of one is the knowledge of all is to be applied, it must be applied with respect to both the former firm and the firm which the moving lawyer joins. Thus there is a conflict with respect to every matter handled by the old firm that has a substantial relationship with any matter handled by the new firm irrespective of whether the moving lawyer had any involvement with it. This is the "overkill" which has drawn so much criticism in the United States to which I have referred above.

Moreover, I am not convinced that a reasonable member of the public would necessarily conclude that confidences are likely to be disclosed in every case despite institutional efforts to prevent it. There is, however, a strong inference that lawyers who work together share confidences. In answering this question, the court should therefore draw the inference, unless satisfied on the basis of clear and convincing evidence, that all reasonable measures have been taken to ensure that no disclosure will occur by the "tainted" lawyer to the member or members of the firm who are engaged against the former client. Such reasonable measures would include institutional mechanisms such as Chinese Walls and cones of silence. These concepts are not familiar to Canadian courts and indeed do not seem to have been adopted by the governing bodies of the legal profession. It can be expected that the Canadian Bar Association, which took the lead in adopting a Code of Professional Conduct in 1974, will again take the lead to determine whether institutional devices are effective and develop standards for the use of institutional devices which will be uniform throughout Canada. . . . In this regard, it must be borne in mind that the legal profession is a self-governing profession. The Legislature has entrusted to it and not to the court the responsibility of developing standards. The court's role is merely supervisory, and its jurisdiction extends to this aspect of ethics only in connection with legal proceedings. The governing bodies, however, are concerned with the application of conflict of interest standards not only in respect of litigation but in other fields which constitute the greater part of the practice of law. It would be wrong, therefore, to shut out the governing body of a self-regulating profession from the whole of the practice by the imposition of an inflexible and immutable standard in the exercise of a supervisory jurisdiction over part of it.

A *fortiori* undertakings and conclusory statements in affidavits without more are not acceptable. These can be expected in every case of this kind that comes before the court. It is no more than the lawyer saying "trust me". This puts the court in the invidious position of deciding which lawyers are to be trusted and which are not. Furthermore, even if the courts found this acceptable, the public is not likely to be satisfied without some additional guarantees that confidential information will under no circumstances be used. . . .

These standards will, in my opinion, strike the appropriate balance among the three interests to which I have referred. In giving precedence to the preservation of the confidentiality of information imparted to a solicitor, the confidence of the public in the integrity of the profession and in the administration of justice will be maintained and strengthened. On the other hand, reflecting the interest of a member of the public in retaining counsel of her choice and the interest of the profession in permitting lawyers to move from one firm to another, the standards are sufficiently flexible to permit a solicitor to act against a former client provided that a reasonable member of the public who is in possession of the facts would conclude that no unauthorized disclosure of confidential information had occurred or would occur.

Application to this Case

The answer to the first question in this case presents no problem. It is acknowledged that Kristin Dangerfield actively worked on the very case in respect of which her new firm is acting against her former client. She is therefore in possession of relevant confidential information.

With respect to the second question, there is nothing beyond the sworn statements of Sweatman and Dangerfield that no discussions of the case have occurred and undertaking that none will occur. In my opinion, while, as stated by the courts below, there is no reason not to accept the affidavits of apparently reputable counsel, this is not sufficient to demonstrate that all reasonable measures have been taken to rebut the strong inference of disclosure. Indeed, there is nothing in the affidavits to indicate that any independently verifiable steps were taken by the firm to implement any kind of screening. There is nothing to indicate that when Ms. Dangerfield joined the firm, instructions were issued that there were to be no communications directly or indirectly between Ms. Dangerfield and the four members of the firm working on the case. While these measures would not necessarily have been sufficient, I refer to them in order to illustrate the kinds of independently verifiable steps which, along with other measures, are indispensable if the firm intends to continue to act.

I would therefore allow the appeal . . ..

. . . . .

CORY J.:— I have read with interest the reasons of my colleague, Justice Sopinka. Although I agree with his disposition of the appeal, I would impose a stricter duty upon lawyers than that which he proposes. He puts his position in this way . . .:

> In my opinion, once it is shown by the client that there existed a previous relationship which is sufficiently related to the retainer from which it is sought to remove the solicitor, the court should infer that confidential information was imparted unless the solicitor satisfies the court that no information was imparted which could be relevant.

He observes that it will be difficult for a solicitor to meet that onus. He states that the position, taken by some courts, that if one lawyer in the firm cannot act, then no member of the law firm can act, is unreasonable in this era of mega-firms and mergers. Thus, he reasons that it should be open for a solicitor to show "that no information was imparted which could be relevant."

With respect, I disagree. Neither the merger of law firms nor the mobility of lawyers can be permitted to affect adversely the public's confidence in the judicial system. At this time, when the work of the courts is having a very significant impact upon the lives and affairs of all Canadians, it is fundamentally important that justice not only be done, but appear to be done in the eyes of the public.

My colleague stated that this appeal called for the balancing of three competing values, namely: the maintenance and integrity of our system of justice; the right of litigants not to be lightly deprived of their chosen counsel; and the desirability of permitting reasonable mobility in the legal profession.

Of these factors, the most important and compelling is the preservation of the integrity of our system of justice. The necessity of selecting new counsel will certainly be inconvenient, unsettling and worrisome to clients. Reasonable mobility may well be important to lawyers. However, the integrity of the judicial system is of such fundamental importance to our country and, indeed, to all free and democratic societies that it must be the predominant consideration in any balancing of these three factors.

Lawyers are an integral and vitally important part of our system of justice. It is they who prepare and put their clients' cases before courts and tribunals. In preparing for the hearing of a contentious matter, a client will often be required to reveal to the lawyer retained highly confidential information. The client's most secret devices and desires, the client's most frightening fears will often, of necessity, be revealed. The client must be secure in the knowledge that the lawyer will neither disclose nor take advantage of these revelations.

Our judicial system could not operate if this were not the case. It cannot function properly if doubt or suspicion exists in the mind of the public that the confidential information disclosed by a client to a lawyer might be revealed.

There can be no question that such a doubt would certainly be instilled if the public were to gather the perception that lawyers, by their actions, such as changing firms, create situations where the possibility of a conflict of interest exists.

Imagine a situation where a client involved in a contentious matter has divulged confidential information to a lawyer. If that lawyer practised with one partner, it would be perceived by the public as unfair and completely unacceptable if the partner were to act for the client's adversary. Similarly, if the lawyer moved to another firm which had been retained by those in opposition to the client, the most reasonable and fair-minded member of the public would find it intolerable for that firm to continue to act for those who opposed the client. In both situations the perception of unfairness would arise from the ease with which confidential information received from clients could be privately communicated between lawyers who are working together in the same firm.

Fortunately, partners rarely attempt to act for clients on both sides of a lawsuit. However, the problem more frequently arises when a lawyer, who has received confidential information, joins a firm that is acting for those opposing the interests of the former client. In such a situation there should be an irrebuttable presumption that lawyers who work together share each other's confidences with the result that a knowledge of confidential matters is imputed to other members of the firm. This presumption must apply to the members of the new firm the lawyer joins if public confidence in the administration of justice is to be maintained.

. . .

243

It is contended that it is too demanding to hold that the knowledge of one member of a law firm constitutes knowledge of all members of the firm in situations where there has been a merger of large firms or a lawyer has joined a "mega-firm". I cannot agree. It is the appearance of fairness in the eyes of the public that is fundamentally important. No matter how large the mega-firm, there will be innumerable occasions when a lawyer with a possible conflict of interest will be meeting with those lawyers in the firm who are in opposition to that lawyer's former client. Whether at partners' meetings or committee meetings, at lunches or the office golf tournament, in the boardroom or the washroom, the lawyer of the former client will be meeting with and talking to those who are on the other side of the client's case. To those who are not members of the legal profession, it must appear that the opportunities for private discussion are so numerous that the disclosure of confidential information, even if completely inadvertent, would be inevitable. Nor is it likely that disclosures of confidential information will ever be discovered. Further, if a lawyer even inadvertently discloses those weaknesses of the client that have been divulged to him or her, this may be sufficient to give the client's opponents an unfair advantage. This, I think, would be the inevitable conclusion of reasonable people.

That same conclusion would be drawn by the public no matter what form of restrictions were sought to be imposed on individual lawyers and law firms involved. No matter how carefully the Chinese Wall might be constructed, it could be breached without anyone but the lawyers involved knowing of that breach. Law has, after all, the historical precedent of Genghis Khan who, by subterfuge, breached the Great Wall of China, the greatest of Chinese walls. Nor would any system of cones of silence change the public's perception of unfairness. They do not change the reality that lawyers in the same firm meet frequently nor do they reduce the opportunities for the private exchange of confidential information. The public would, quite properly, remain skeptical of the efficacy of the most sophisticated protective scheme.

Let us consider again the two factors which are said to be the competing values to be weighed against the maintenance of the integrity of our system of justice. One of these was the desirability of permitting reasonable mobility in the legal profession. Yet, no matter how strong may be the current rage for mergers or how desirous the mega-firms may be to acquire additional lawyers, neither the large firms nor the lawyers who wish to join them or amalgamate with them should dictate the course of legal ethics. The latest available statistics (as of May 1990) from the Law Society of Upper Canada for the province of Ontario, where the greatest concentration of large law firms might be expected, demonstrate that lawyers in large firms do not comprise the majority of lawyers in that province. . . .

[Justice Cory presented a table showing the number of lawyers practicing in Ontario in 1990, divided between those practicing law in small firms and those practicing in large law firms; the table indicates 64.3 per cent of lawyers in Ontario work in firms of 10 lawyers or less, and that outside of Toronto 82.7 per cent of lawyers work in firms of 10 lawyers or less.]

This indicates that, although the large firms may be the movers and shakers on Bay Street, they do not represent the majority of lawyers soldiering on in the cause of justice.

. . .

This conclusion should not be taken as an impediment to the mobility of lawyers, the merger of law firms or the growth of very large firms; rather, it is a recognition of a professional responsibility owed by lawyers to the litigation process so that the process may retain the respect of the public. It is a small price to pay for mobility of lawyers, mergers of law firms and the increasing size of law firms. It is no more than the fulfilment of a duty owed by members of the legal profession to the public to preserve the integrity of, and public confidence in, the judicial system.

The other factor to be weighed against maintaining the integrity of the justice system was that litigants ought not to be lightly deprived of their chosen counsel. It seems to me that to give undue weight to this factor would unduly benefit the large corporate clients who are said by my colleague to be the raison d'être of the larger firms. It is they who would retain counsel of their choice and primarily benefit from a change in the irrebuttable presumption of shared knowledge. I can see no reason for extending any special benefit or privilege to such clients of large firms. They, like any client who must seek new counsel, will suffer from inconvenience, loss of time and the inevitable worry and concern over such a change. However, the legal profession has many able counsel. The requirement of change imposed on a client is, on balance, a small price to pay for maintaining the integrity of our system of justice.

Conclusion

Where a lawyer who has had a substantial involvement with a client in an ongoing contentious matter joins another law firm which is acting for an opposing party, there is an irrebuttable presumption that the knowledge of such lawyer, including confidential information disclosed to him or her by the former client, has become the knowledge of the new firm. Such an irrebuttable presumption is essential to preserve public confidence in the administration of justice.

. . . . .

NOTES AND QUESTIONS

1. Did the Supreme Court select the appropriate factors for consideration in its decision? Did it evaluate them appropriately? This will become an important question for the Supreme Court in the subsequent cases of *R.v.Neil* and *Strotherv.Monarch Entertainment Ltd.*, below.

2. In many other circumstances courts accept the word of a lawyer, even when given in an unsworn statement. For example, courts will accept a lawyer's word with respect to undertakings, the reasons for delay in bringing a matter to trial and other questions related to the conduct of litigation. Here the Supreme Court of Canada took the view that even a sworn statement from the lawyers stating that they acted with propriety was insufficient. Why? What is at stake here that seems to require a more rigorous approach? Is the Court concerned about the trustworthiness of lawyers when their own interests are implicated? The public's perception of the trustworthiness of lawyers?

3. What is Sopinka J.'s justification for leaving the development of the

conflict of interest regime essentially in the hands of lawyers and the legal profession? Is this an appropriate resolution of the matter? It should be noted that Sopinka J. refers to the Canadian Bar Association for anticipate guidance on the question but the actual regulatory authority resides with provincial and territorial law societies, not the CBA.

4. Cory J.'s stinging concurrence includes what appears to be his own research on the distribution of lawyers in Ontario, a curious reference considering that the case is from Manitoba. Does this suggest that he was unusually troubled by the apparent "big law firm orientation" of the majority? Is he right to criticize the majority on the basis that the decision is unprincipled and too "lawyer-sympathetic"? Or is his judgment a desperate attempt to cling to the ideals of a bygone era, ideals now out of step with the modern day practice of law?

5. On the other hand, perhaps the majority, and Sopinka J. himself, saw that too rigorous a standard would create a powerful and dangerous tool in the hands of highly zealous lawyers, who would be only too willing to threaten or proceed with disqualification motions to gain a tactical advantage in litigation. It will be important to be attentive to the ways in which the Court deals with this 'tactical' weapon in subsequent cases Another interpretation is that too rigorous a standard would work an unnecessary hardship on both lawyers and clients and would not significantly serve the public interest.

6. The *Model Code* contemplates that a lawyer's duty to preserve client confidences continues after the representation ends (See, *e.g.*, Rule 3.4-1, Commentary 7). Does this case suggest that there may be other duties that continue after a lawyer-client relationship ends, including the duty not to place oneself in a position of perceived conflict of interest, or in some other situation that would be perceived to be disloyal to that former client?

7. There is no explicit reference in the judgment to Ms. Dangerfield's obligation of loyalty to her original, now former, client. Is this an oversight on the part of the court? What are the dimensions of a lawyer's duty to a former client?

8. Subsequent to *MacDonald Estate*, Canada's law societies established elaborate screening mechanisms to guide law firms so that they could: (1) minimize the risk that a client's confidential information, in the possession of their former lawyer, will be made known to the lawyers representing the client's adversary; and (2) at the same time enable the former lawyer to join the new oppositional law firm. The *Model Code* sets out these mechanisms in Rules 3.4-17 to 3.4-23 and their Commentaries. Review those provisions. Do the Rules and Commentaries satisfactorily resolve the issues and respect the values identified by the majority in *MacDonald Estate*? The following case identifies some of the issues that remain. As you read it, consider: (i) the interplay between the role of the courts and the law society on conflicts questions; (ii) whether the guidelines in the Code solve the problem; and (iii) whether the standard established in this case

brings us closer to the standard sought by Cory J in his minority concurrence in *MacDonald Estate*.

ONTARIO v. CHARTIS INSURANCE CO. OF CANADA

[2017] O.J. No. 332; 2017 ONCA 59

The judgment of the Court was delivered by S.E. Pepall J.A.:—

A. INTRODUCTION

This appeal concerns the disqualification of counsel due to an alleged conflict of interest. At issue is the possibility of inadvertent disclosure of confidential information arising from the close working relationship between two lawyers after one transferred law firms to work with the other. The integrity of counsel involved is unchallenged and there is no suggestion of any actual impropriety.

. . .

B. BACKGROUND FACTS

Ontario was a defendant in four class actions. Ontario carried insurance, however a dispute arose over its insurance coverage with AIG and three other insurers. Ontario retained Laurence Theall of TG to act on its behalf. In 2012, Theall commenced an action against the insurers to compel coverage.

Foulds was an associate at TG and began working with Theall on the insurance dispute in November 2010. Foulds' involvement included work on the actions and settlement negotiations with the insurers. These negotiations were successful with respect to all of the insurers except AIG. The settlements were finalized in August 2013. The action against AIG continues.

As a result of his involvement, Foulds is in possession of privileged and confidential information relating to the class actions, the coverage action, the negotiations, and the settlements. During the time he was with TG, Foulds docketed more than 160 hours on the coverage proceedings.

McInnis of LBM is opposing counsel and acts for AIG in the coverage dispute. He was retained in June 2009 and has been actively and directly involved in both defending AIG in the action brought by Ontario and in the unsuccessful settlement negotiations. McInnis has docketed more than 400 hours on matters relating to the coverage action.

McInnis has worked for AIG as coverage advisor and counsel since 1986. Since the early 1990s, he has represented AIG on more than 50 separate coverage files relating to the Ontario Insurance Program.

In the summer of 2013, McInnis approached Foulds to join LBM, a 14 member Toronto litigation boutique, as a partner. . . .

In early December 2013, McInnis contacted Theall by telephone to discuss the establishment of an ethical screen. On January 2, 2013, McInnis sent an e-mail outlining the safeguards to be put in place upon Foulds' arrival at LBM. These would include:

    (a)   Foulds would have no involvement in LBM's representation of AIG in the coverage action;

(b)   Foulds would not discuss any Ontario-AIG matters with anyone at LBM or AIG;

(c)   no one from LBM would discuss any Ontario-AIG matters with Foulds;

(d)   immediately upon arriving at LBM, Foulds would sign an undertaking confirming that he understood, and would adhere to, all elements of the ethical screen;

(e)   all LBM lawyers and staff involved in Ontario-AIG matters would sign a similar undertaking;

(f)   LBM would inform all personnel in writing of the ethical screen, of the requirement to adhere to it, and of the possible sanctions for failing to abide by the terms of the ethical screen, which sanctions could include dismissal;

(g)   Foulds' office would be located several offices away from those LBM personnel working on Ontario-AIG matters; and

(h)   the ethical screen would be monitored and enforced by a senior partner with no personal involvement in Ontario-AIG matters.

Subsequently, as an extra precaution, LBM decided that Foulds would not work with McInnis' assistant.

Foulds commenced work at LBM on January 6, 2014. Foulds estimates that one-half of his time is spent doing work for AIG and that 50 to 60 percent of his time is spent working with McInnis.

On February 7, 2014, Theall advised McInnis of Ontario's objection to LBM continuing to act on the coverage dispute because of the serious conflict of interest that arose from Foulds' move to LBM. Theall wrote that Foulds had docketed over 160 hours on the case between Ontario and AIG and was "privy to not only privileged information, but the entire litigation strategy". . . .

Since he joined LBM, Foulds has not been involved in the class actions, the coverage action, the Ontario Insurance Program, or any Ontario-AIG matters. He does work on AIG files not involving Ontario.

[In the lower courts, the disqualification application was initially dismissed by the applications judge. This decision was reversed by the Divisional Court, leading to the insurance company's law firm being disqualified. The insurance company appealed to the Ontario Court of Appeal.]

. . .

The applicable test to determine whether a disqualifying conflict exists was set out in MacDonald Estate. Sopinka J. stated, at pp. 1259-60:

> The test must be such that the public represented by the reasonably informed person would be satisfied that no use of confidential information would occur.

According to Sopinka J., that is the overriding policy and has to inform the court in answering whether there is a disqualifying conflict of interest. The questions to be answered are: (i) did the lawyer receive confidential information attributable to a solicitor and client relationship relevant to the matter at hand, and (ii) is there a risk that it would be used to the prejudice of the client?: MacDonald Estate, at p. 1260.

There is no issue in this appeal with respect to the answer to the first question. It is conceded that Foulds is in possession of such confidential information. The appeal therefore turns on the answer to the second question.

In assessing risk of prejudice to the client, the court is to infer that Foulds will impart confidential information to his new colleagues at LBM. However, as Sopinka J. explained in MacDonald Estate, that inference is rebuttable:

> There is, however, a strong inference that lawyers who work together share confidences. In answering this question, the court should therefore draw the inference, unless satisfied on the basis of clear and convincing evidence, that all reasonable measures have been taken to ensure that no disclosure will occur by the "tainted" lawyer to the member or members of the firm who are engaged against the former client: p. 1262.

In this appeal, the inference is rebuttable if the measures instituted by LBM would satisfy a reasonably informed person that use of confidential information had not occurred or would not occur: MacDonald Estate, pp. 1259-60.

In MacDonald Estate, Sopinka J. invited lawyers' professional regulatory bodies to address appropriate measures to prevent the disclosure of confidential information in circumstances where a lawyer transfers firms. He also noted that, since the legal profession is self-governing, the codes of conduct of lawyers' governing bodies are "an important statement of public policy with respect to the conduct of a barrister and solicitor": p. 1244.

. . .

At the relevant time, the LSUC's approach to what constitutes adequate measures to prevent the disclosure of confidential information was set out in r. 2.05 of the LSUC's Rules of Professional Conduct under the heading 'Conflicts from Transfer between Law Firms', and more specifically in subsection (4) on Law Firm Disqualification:

> Where the transferring lawyer actually possesses relevant information respecting the former client that is confidential and that, if disclosed to a member of the new law firm, may prejudice the former client, the new law firm shall cease its representation of its client in that matter unless
>
> (a) the former client consents to the new law firm's continued representation of its client, or
>
> (b) the new law firm establishes that it is in the interests of justice that it act in the matter, having regard to all relevant circumstances, including,
>
> (i) the adequacy and timing of the measures taken to ensure that no disclosure to any member of the new law firm of the former client's confidential information will occur,
>
> (ii) the extent of prejudice to any party,
>
> (iii) the good faith of the parties,
>
> (iv) the availability of suitable alternative counsel, and
>
> (v) issues affecting the public interest.

Guidelines to protect confidential information are set out in the commentary to r. 2.05. In particular, guidelines 1, 10,11 and 12 state:

1. The screened lawyer should have no involvement in the new law firm's representation of its client.

. . . . .

10. The screened lawyer's office or work station and that of the lawyer's support staff should be located away from the offices or work stations of lawyers and support staff working on the matter.

11. The screened lawyer should use associates and support staff different from those working on the current matter.

12. In the case of law firms with multiple law offices, consideration should be given to referring conduct of the matter to counsel in another office.

In Robertson v. Slater Vecchio, 2008 BCCA 306, 81 B.C.L.R. (4th) 46, the British Columbia Court of Appeal held that not every guideline must be followed to the letter

. . . . .

However, implementation of the guidelines is a significant factor to consider when an application judge is exercising his or her discretion. Canadian courts have typically held that compliance with the guidelines provides sufficient protection for the migrating lawyer's former client: . . .That said, while highly persuasive, compliance is not determinative.

. . . . .

F. ANALYSIS

. . . . .

(i)   LSUC Guidelines not Dispositive in Circumstances of this Case

First, having identified the proper test as described in MacDonald Estate, the application judge proceeded to treat the guidelines as an exhaustive answer and effectively reversed the onus of proof. The application judge acknowledged the applicable presumption that lawyers who work together share confidences. But, in considering whether that presumption had been rebutted, at para. 41, he asked the wrong question.: "What more could be done to protect the confidentiality of [Ontario's] information?"

To ask this question precludes the possibility that no measure could be sufficient to address the degree of professional contact between the two lawyers. The application judge assumed that every conflict could be successfully met by the imposition of the guidelines. This was in error.

As an example, as Mr. MacKenzie for AIG candidly acknowledged, no screen would effectively screen a firm of two lawyers having a familial relationship. Post-MacDonald Estate jurisprudence does not uniformly provide that compliance with regulatory guidelines precludes disqualification.

Further, in the province of Ontario, the legal profession has expressly recognized that compliance with the rules and guidelines may not be adequate in every case. In the commentary to its Rules of Professional Conduct, the LSUC writes:

> It is not possible to offer a set of "reasonable measures" that will be appropriate or adequate in every case. Instead, the new law firm that seeks to implement reasonable measures must exercise professional judgment in determining what steps must be taken "to ensure that no disclosure will occur to any member of the new law firm of the former client's confidential information".
>
> . . . . .
>
> Adoption of only some of the guidelines may be adequate in some cases, while adoption of them all may not be sufficient in others.

Sopinka J. observed, at p. 1262 of MacDonald Estate, that it is not for the court to develop standards; that is the role of the governing bodies of the self-governing legal profession. The court's role is merely supervisory. But neither MacDonald Estate, nor the guidelines themselves, suggest that the court should abdicate its supervisory responsibility. In fact, the Supreme Court recently reiterated the supervisory role of the courts in resolving conflicts of interest. In Canadian National Railway Co. v. McKercher LLP, 2013 SCC 39, [2013] 2 S.C.R. 649, McLachlin C.J. stated, at para. 16:

> Both the courts and law societies are involved in resolving issues relating to conflicts of interest — the courts from the perspective of the proper administration of justice, the law societies from the perspective of good governance of the profession. [Citations omitted.]

I would also add that this decision is not about small firms versus large firms. Admittedly, by Toronto standards, LBM is a small firm. It is a litigation boutique and consists of 14 lawyers. But, in this case, the size of the firm is irrelevant. What is relevant is the integrated nature of Foulds' and McInnis' practices. Foulds works with McInnis 50 to 60 percent of the time. While technology, such as e-mail, might serve to diminish face-to-face interaction, the potential for inadvertent disclosure is significant. Indeed, LBM recognized the potential for such disclosure by imposing a safeguard that Foulds' office would be located several offices away from those LBM personnel working on Ontario-AIG matters. However, this precaution does little to address Foulds' actual working relationship with McInnis. In addition, Foulds also continues to spend 50 percent of his time working for AIG, and AIG is a client he shares in common with McInnis.

Moreover, any disclosure of the subject matter of the confidential information held by Foulds has the potential to be very prejudicial to Ontario. The dispute between AIG and Ontario relates to coverage. Significantly, Foulds was privy to the failed negotiations with AIG and is in possession of the terms of the confidential settlements entered into between Ontario and the other insurers who were originally disputing coverage along with AIG.

While the appellants may have achieved technical compliance with the r. 2.05 guidelines, in my view, compliance with the spirit of those guidelines is absent.

The objective of the guidelines is to limit or screen interaction. This is particularly evident from guidelines 10, 11 and 12. The most striking feature of this case is that Foulds spends 50 to 60 percent of his time working with McInnis In the face of that fact, it cannot be said that there is clear and convincing evidence that all reasonable measures are being taken to ensure that no disclosure would occur by Foulds to AIG's counsel. The public, represented by the reasonably informed person, could not be satisfied that no use of confidential information would occur between two people with such an intense working relationship.

(ii) Paramountcy of the Integrity of Legal Profession

Secondly, the application judge treated the examination of the conflict issue as a balancing exercise between the three competing interests: protecting Ontario's confidential information, the integrity of the legal system, and the right to choose one's own counsel. In my view, he erred is so doing.

Although the right to one's choice of counsel is one of the three values identified in MacDonald Estate as bearing on the issue of conflict, it is not paramount. As noted in that case, and as rephrased by the Saskatchewan Court of Appeal in Wallace v. Canadian National Railroad, 2011 SKCA 108, 340 D.L.R. (4th) 402, rev'd on other grounds (sub nom. Canadian National Railway Co. v. McKercher LLP) 2013 SCC 39, [2013] 2 S.C.R. 649) at para. 55, "primacy [is] given to the integrity of both the legal profession and the administration of justice over. . .a client's choice of lawyer and lawyer mobility."

H. DISPOSITION

For these reasons, the appeal is dismissed.

. . . . .

NOTES AND QUESTIONS

1. In finding that the presumption that lawyers share information was not rebutted, the Court here said "in this case the size of the firm is irrelevant" – *i.e.*, the issue was not that he transferred to a firm of 14 lawyers working on the opposite side of the file on which he had worked, but was rather the integrated nature of the work he would be doing. Do you agree that the size of the firm should be irrelevant in this case? What about in different circumstances? If he had moved to a firm of 14 lawyers but had ostensibly been shielded from both the lawyer and the client on the opposite side of the file, do you think a reasonable person would have been as comfortable that information would not be shared as if it were a 200- lawyer firm?

2. Do you think that, given the lawyer's duty of loyalty, it should ever be permissible for a lawyer to "switch sides" and move to the firm on the opposite side of litigation, absent the client's consent? Consider this question, and the facts of *Chartis*, in light of the principles set out in *Neil* below, and in particular this statement: "Unless a litigant is assured of the undivided loyalty of the lawyer, neither the public nor the litigant will have confidence that the legal system, which may appear to them to be a hostile and hideously complicated environment, is a reliable and trustworthy means of resolving their disputes and controversies".

3. The Court asserts that while a client's choice of counsel is important, "A court is to give primacy to the integrity of the legal profession and the administration of justice". Do you agree? Why is a client's choice of counsel in any way relevant in assesing conflicts of interest?

4. Having considered these issues, in your view is this the right decision? The analysis focuses on the interests of the complaining client. Does it take sufficient account of the persepctive of the lawyers. The lawyers identified the concerns and made efforts to address them, and to follow the law society-mandated rules for dealing with such situations – rules that the Supreme Court of Canada itself called for. In this way, they acted with integrity. Was it fair for the Court to, after the fact, tell them that this was insufficient?

[c] Duties to Current Clients

In *MacDonald Estate*, the complaint came from Ms. Dangerfield's former client. In that instance, as is clear from the judgment, the primary concern of the court was that no confidential information with respect to the former client would pass to the current client. A different – indeed additional – problem arises where the conflict involves two clients that a lawyer or firm is representing at essentially the same time. Even if confidential information can be protected in such a situation (for example, by protective screens placed between the two lawyers in a firm who are acting for the respective clients) a significant question arises as to whether the law firm can represent both clients and still fulfill its legal and ethical obligations to both. The following case, among the most controversial and important in the field of lawyers' professional duties, analyzes this problem.

R. v. NEIL

[2002] S.C.J. No. 72, [2002] 3 S.C.R. 631

[Neil operated a business as an independent paralegal in Edmonton. Lambert was his assistant. On occasion, Neil would refer clients to the Venkatraman law firm or seek the law firm's assistance. During the relevant time Lazin was a lawyer working either as an employee of the Venkatraman law firm or associated with the firm — associated in the sense that he had his own independent law practice but shared office space and some facilities with the Venkatraman firm. Neil did some work that the Law Society of Alberta regarded as the unauthorized practice of law — essentially practicing law without a license — and a complaint led to a police investigation. Two criminal charges against Neil ultimately brought the case to the Supreme Court of Canada.

In one indictment — referred to as the "*Canada Trust*" matter — Neil and ultimately Lambert were alleged to have defrauded Canada Trust by arranging for mortgages to be signed up in Lambert's name for some of Neil's clients who did not qualify financially for a mortgage. Lazin took on the representation of Lambert in this matter at approximately the same time that the Venkatraman firm was representing Neil. Lazin attended some consultations with Neil, essentially to obtain information that would enable him to run a so-called "cut-throat" defence, blaming Neil and portraying Lambert as an innocent dupe. The Venkatraman law firm eventually withdrew from the representation of Neil due to Lazin's representation of Lambert.

In the second indictment, the "*Doblanko*" matter, Lazin learned through the representation of one of his clients, Darren Doblanko, that Mrs. Doblanko had obtained a divorce with the assistance of Neil, allegedly on the basis of false affidavits prepared by Neil. Lazin arranged for Doblanko to report this information to the police – specifically the officer investigating Neil on the Canada Trust matter. This was said to have been done to "multiply the allegations of dishonesty" against Neil and thereby assist in Lazin's defence of Lambert. Ultimately, the charges against Lambert were dropped in exchange for her testimony against Neil.

Neil sought to have these charges stayed on the basis of abuse of process. He argued that Lazin, in substance a member of the law firm representing him, had failed to adequately represent him and had effectively sold him out to the interests of Lambert and Doblanko, other clients of the law firm.]

BINNIE J.:— What are the proper limits of a lawyer's "duty of loyalty" to a current client in a case where the lawyer did not receive any confidential information that was (or is) relevant to the matter in which he proposes to act against the current client's interest?

. . . . .

In my view, the law firm did owe a duty of loyalty to the appellant at the material time, and the law firm ought not to have taken up the cause of one of the appellant's alleged victims (Darren Doblanko) in proceedings before a civil court at the same time as it maintained a solicitor-client relationship with the appellant in respect of other matters simultaneously pending before the criminal court (the "*Canada Trust*" matters). The *Doblanko* mandate, though factually and legally unrelated to the *Canada Trust* matters, was adverse to the appellant's interest. The law firm, as fiduciary, could not serve two masters at the same time. Having said that, the appellant falls short on the issue of remedy. He may (and perhaps did) choose to take his complaint to the Law Society of Alberta, but he is not entitled to a stay of proceedings. The law firm's conduct did not affect the fairness of the *Doblanko* trial. Its involvement predated the laying of charges by the police. There was no issue of confidential information. The *Doblanko* charges were serious and would almost certainly have been laid in any event. In my view, the prosecution of the *Doblanko* charge was not an abuse of process.

. . . . .

II. Analysis

I make three preliminary observations. The first is that while misuse of confidential information is not an issue in the *Doblanko* case, in which the stay was entered, it is an issue in the *Canada Trust* matter where Lazin, acting against the appellant's interest, sat in on part of the solicitor-client interview on April 18, 1995, described above. Secondly these cases do not require the imputation of confidential knowledge from one partner of the firm to another. Here the same member of the firm (Lazin) had a finger in each of the conflict situations. Thirdly, we are not being asked to intervene based merely on an "appearance" of conflict. The conflicts were actual.

. . . . .

A. The Lawyer's Duty of Loyalty

Appellant's counsel reminds us of the declaration of an advocate's duty of loyalty made by Henry Brougham, later Lord Chancellor, in his defence of Queen Caroline against the charge of adultery brought against her by her husband, King George IV. He thus addressed the House of Lords:

[A]n advocate, in the discharge of his duty, knows but one person in all the world, and that person is his client. To save that client by all means and expedients, and at all hazards and costs to other persons, and, among them, to himself, is his first and only duty; and in performing this duty he must not regard the alarm, the torments, the destruction which he may bring upon others. Separating the duty of a patriot from that of an advocate, he must go on reckless of consequences, though it should be his unhappy fate to involve his country in confusion.

(*Trial of Queen Caroline* (1821), by J. Nightingale, vol. II, The Defence, Part 1, at p. 8)

These words are far removed in time and place from the legal world in which the Venkatraman law firm carried on its practice, but the defining principle — the duty of loyalty — is with us still. It endures because it is essential to the integrity of the administration of justice and it is of high public importance that public confidence in that integrity be maintained . . .. Unless a litigant is assured of the undivided loyalty of the lawyer, neither the public nor the litigant will have confidence that the legal system, which may appear to them to be a hostile and hideously complicated environment, is a reliable and trustworthy means of resolving their disputes and controversies . . .. As O'Connor J.A. (now A.C.J.O.) observed in *R. v. McCallen* [(1999) 116 OAC 308]:

. . . the relationship of counsel and client requires clients, typically untrained in the law and lacking the skills of advocates, to entrust the management and conduct of their cases to the counsel who act on their behalf. There should be no room for doubt about counsel's loyalty and dedication to the client's case.

The value of an independent bar is diminished unless the lawyer is free from conflicting interests. Loyalty, in that sense, promotes effective representation, on which the problem-solving capability of an adversarial system rests.

. . . . .

The duty of loyalty is intertwined with the fiduciary nature of the lawyer-client relationship. One of the roots of the word fiduciary is *fides*, or loyalty, and loyalty is often cited as one of the defining characteristics of a fiduciary

. . . . .

Fiduciary duties are often called into existence to protect relationships of importance to the public including, as here, solicitor and client. Disloyalty is destructive of that relationship.

B. More Than Just Confidential Information

While the Court is most often preoccupied with uses and abuses of confidential information in cases where it is sought to disqualify a lawyer from further acting in a matter, as in *MacDonald Estate, supra*, the duty of loyalty to current clients includes a much broader principle of avoidance of conflicts of interest, in which confidential information may or may not play a role . . ..

. . . . .

The aspects of the duty of loyalty relevant to this appeal do include issues of confidentiality in the *Canada Trust* matters, but engage more particularly three other dimensions:

(i)   the duty to avoid conflicting interests . . .

(ii)   a duty of commitment to the client's cause (sometimes referred to as "zealous representation") from the time counsel is retained, not just at trial, i.e. ensuring that a divided loyalty does not cause the lawyer to "soft peddle" his or her defence of a client out of concern for another client . . . and

(iii)   a duty of candour with the client on matters relevant to the retainer.

C. The Venkatraman Law Firm's Breach of Professional Obligations

. . . . .

(2) The Duty of Loyalty to an Existing Client

The Law Society of Alberta's *Code of Professional Conduct* provides that "[i]n each matter, a lawyer's judgment and fidelity to the client's interests must be free from compromising influences" (c. 6, Statement of Principle, p. 50). The facts of this case illustrate a number of important objectives served by this principle. Loyalty required the Venkatraman law firm to focus on the interest of the appellant without being distracted by other interests including personal interests. Part of the problem here seems to have been Lazin's determination to hang onto a piece of litigation. When Lazin was asked about "the ethical issue" in acting for Lambert, he said maybe "it was a question of not wanting to give up the file". Loyalty includes putting the client's business ahead of the lawyer's business. The appellant was entitled to a level of commitment from his lawyer that whatever could properly be done on his behalf would be done as surely as it would have been done if the appellant had had the skills and training to do the job personally. On learning that his own lawyer had put before the divorce court evidence of his further wrongdoing, the appellant understandably felt betrayed. Equally, the public in Edmonton, where the prosecution of the appellant had attracted considerable notoriety, required assurance that the truth had been ascertained by an adversarial system that functioned clearly and without hidden agendas.

The general duty of loyalty has frequently been stated. In *Ramrakha v. Zinner* (1994) 157 A.R. 279 (C.A.), Harradence J.A., concurring, observed at para 73:

> A solicitor is in a fiduciary relationship to his client and must avoid situations where he has, or potentially may, develop a conflict of interests . . . . The logic behind this is cogent in that a solicitor must be able to provide his client with complete and undivided loyalty, dedication, full disclosure, and good faith, all of which may be jeopardized if more than one interest is represented.

The duty of loyalty was similarly expressed by Wilson J.A. (as she then was) in *Davey v. Woolley, Hames, Dale & Dingwall* [(1982) 35 O.R. (2d) 599 (C.A.)] at p. 602:

> The underlying premise . . . is that, human nature being what it is, the solicitor cannot give his exclusive, undivided attention to the interests of his client if he is torn between his client's interests and his own or his client's interests and those of another client to whom he owes the self-same duty of loyalty, dedication and good faith.

More recently in England, in a case dealing with the duties of accountants, the

House of Lords observed that "[t]he duties of an accountant cannot be greater than those of a solicitor, and may be less" and went on to compare the duty owed by accountants to *former* clients (where the concern is largely with confidential information) and the duty owed to *current* clients (where the duty of loyalty prevails irrespective of whether or not there is a risk of disclosure of confidential information). Lord Millett stated:

> My Lords, I would affirm [possession of confidential information] as the basis of the court's jurisdiction to intervene on behalf of a *former* client. *It is otherwise where the court's intervention is sought by an existing client,* for a fiduciary cannot act at the same time both for and against the same client, and his firm is in no better position. A man cannot without the consent of both clients act for one client while his partner is acting for another in the opposite interest. His disqualification has nothing to do with the confidentiality of client information. It is based on the inescapable conflict of interest which is inherent in the situation. [Emphasis added]
>
> *Bolkiah* v. *KPMG*, [1999] 2 A.C. 222 (H.L.)

. . . . .

In exceptional cases, consent of the client may be inferred. For example, governments generally accept that private practitioners who do their civil or criminal work will act against them in unrelated matters, and a contrary position in a particular case may, depending on the circumstances, be seen as tactical rather than principled. Chartered banks and entities that could be described as professional litigants may have a similarly broad-minded attitude where the matters are sufficiently unrelated that there is no danger of confidential information being abused. These exceptional cases are explained by the notion of informed consent, express or implied.

The general prohibition is undoubtedly a major inconvenience to large law partnerships and especially to national firms with their proliferating offices in major centres across Canada. Conflict searches in the firm's records may belatedly turn up files in another office a lawyer may not have been aware of. Indeed, he or she may not even be acquainted with the partner on the other side of the country who is in charge of the file. Conflict search procedures are often inefficient. Nevertheless it is the firm not just the individual lawyer, that owes a fiduciary duty to its clients, and a bright line is required. The bright line is provided by the general rule that a lawyer may not represent one client whose interests are directly adverse to the immediate interests of another current client — *even if the two mandates are unrelated* — unless both clients consent after receiving full disclosure (and preferably independent legal advice), and the lawyer reasonably believes that he or she is able to represent each client without adversely affecting the other.

The Venkatraman law firm was bound by this general prohibition to avoid acting contrary to the interest of the appellant, a current client, who was a highly vulnerable litigant in need of all the help and reassurance he could legitimately get.

(3) Breaches of the Duty of Loyalty

In my view the Venkatraman law firm, and Lazin in particular, put themselves in a position where the duties they undertook to other clients conflicted with the duty of loyalty which they owed to the appellant. I adopt, in this respect, the notion of a "conflict" in s. 121 of the *Restatement Third, The Law Governing Lawyers* (2000), vol. 2, at pp. 244-45, as a "substantial risk that the lawyer's representation of the client would be materially and adversely affected by the lawyer's own interests or by the lawyer's duties to another current client, a former client, or a third person".

The initial conflict was to attempt to act simultaneously for both the appellant and his eventual co-accused in the *Canada Trust* charges, Helen Lambert. They were clearly adverse in interest. It is true that at the time Lazin and his colleague from the firm met the appellant in the Remand Centre on April 18, 1995 Lazin had not been retained by Lambert on the criminal charges. He was acting only with respect to her divorce. It is also true that in the end the appellant was eventually represented by other counsel. Nevertheless the trial judge found that on April 18, 1995, Lazin was *in fact* (if not yet officially) acting on Lambert's behalf in the criminal proceedings. Her indictment was reasonably anticipated (given her involvement in the subject matter of the *Canada Trust* charge) and, most importantly, the trial judge held that the purpose of Lazin's attendance at the Remand Centre was to get evidence to run a "cut-throat" defence against the appellant who, he found, was an ongoing client of the Venkatraman law firm. The fact that the appellant eventually looked elsewhere for a lawyer in the *Canada Trust* case, whether as a result of his choice or theirs, did not diminish their duty of loyalty. Nor does it make a difference that no professional fee was charged for that particular consultation. The Venkatraman firm (Lazin) appreciated that the appellant having been arrested, the long arm of the law would soon be laid on Helen Lambert. In fact, Helen Lambert was arrested less than two months later, on June 6, 1995.

The second conflict relates to the *Doblanko* charges. As mentioned, both Doblanko and his former wife (who had by now remarried and produced children of her second "marriage") needed their earlier divorce to be regularized. The Venkatraman firm breached their duty to the appellant in accepting a retainer that required them to put before the divorce court judge evidence of the illegal conduct of their client, the appellant, at a time when they knew he was facing other criminal charges related to his paralegal practice, in which their firm had had a long-standing involvement. It was contended that the *Doblanko* and *Canada Trust* cases were wholly unrelated in the sense that Lazin could not have obtained in the *Doblanko* mandate confidential information that would be relevant in the *Canada Trust* mandate. This, as stated, is not the test of loyalty to an *existing* client, and it is not entirely true either. While the two cases were wholly independent of each other in terms of their facts, the Lambert's cut-throat defence was helped by piling up the allegations of dishonest conduct in different matters by different complainants in a way that would make it easier for the jury to consider her a victim rather than a perpetrator. The linkage was thus strategic. The *Doblanko* application was initiated in July 1995. The Crown advised us that the *Canada Trust* criminal charges against Helen Lambert were not resolved until the spring of 1996.

In the course of the *Doblanko* application, the divorce court judge expressed the view (according to Lazin) that Lazin should report the appellant's apparent falsification of documents to the police. I think at that point that Lazin, as an officer of the court, was obliged to do so. Lazin then called the Law Society (without disclosing that the appellant was a client of his firm) who advised that Lazin *could* advise his divorce court client to report the matter to the police but he was not bound to. Lazin advised neither the trial judge nor the Law Society that the suspected forger (the appellant) was a client of his firm. Further, Lazin made a point of having the matter reported to the police officer who was responsible for investigating the appellant in connection with the *Canada Trust* and other matters.

It was the Venkatraman firm that put the cat among the pigeons by bringing the *Doblanko* application before the divorce court. Mr. Doblanko would likely have found another lawyer to make the application, and the facts might equally have eventually made their way to the police, but it was in violation of the firm's duty of loyalty to the appellant to contribute in this way to the appellant's downfall.

(4) Remedies for Breach of the Duty of Loyalty

It is one thing to demonstrate a breach of loyalty. It is quite another to arrive at an appropriate remedy.

A client whose lawyer is in breach of his or her fiduciary duty has various avenues of redress. A complaint to the relevant governing body, in this case the Law Society of Alberta, may result in disciplinary action. A conflict of interest may also be the subject matter of an action against the lawyer for compensation, as in *Szarfer v. Chodos, supra* [excerpted in Chapter 1]. Breach of the ethical rules that could raise concerns at the Law Society does not necessarily give grounds in a malpractice action or justify a constitutional remedy.

. . . . .

The appellant's argument that the purity of the waters of the fountain of justice was irredeemably polluted in these cases by the action of the Venkatraman law firm (to borrow a metaphor from Lord Brougham's era) is very difficult to sustain on the facts.

[Justice Binnie ultimately declined to enter a judicial stay of proceedings.]

NOTES AND QUESTIONS

1. To some extent the *"Canada Trust"* aspects of this case are straightforward, involving as they do a concurrent conflict (the Venkatraman law firm, including Lazin, representing both Neil and Lambert at the same time) with Lazin obtaining and making inappropriate use of confidential information from Neil in the course of his representation of Lambert. Recall the presumption, articulated in *Re MacDonald Estate* and reinforced in *R. v. Neil*, that confidential information known to one lawyer in a law firm is attributed to all members of the firm. Assuming that there were no 'screens' in place to adequately protect this information, would not the law firm normally have been disqualified anyway, whether or not Lazin had attended the interview with Neil? Does this matter in this case?

2. Conflicts of interest usually revolve around the possibility of a client's (or former client's) confidential information being shared with lawyers in opposition to that client's interests. In the *"Doblanko"* matter, however, the information was obtained in ways not associated with a client or former client whose interests were at stake. How does the Supreme Court of Canada deal with this aspect of the alleged conflict? Does this represent a

significant departure from the way that conflicts of interest were viewed in *MacDonald Estate*, not only in terms of the ultimate scope of the conflict, but, more importantly, in terms of the principles applied by the Court in reaching its conclusion? Does this constitute a reconsideration or reformulation of the principles upon which the lawyer's ethical duties to a client are based? It will be important to watch the way in which the Supreme Court addresses conflicting intersts that do not involve the compromise of confidential information.

3. Was the part of the bright line rule that was highlighted by Binnie J. to the effect that it applies *'even where the matters are unrelated'* necessary to the decision? Recall that part of Lazin's disloyalty to Neil was his use of the 'Doblanko divorce' information against Neil, information that he obtained in the 'unrelated' representation of Doblanko. But was it really 'unrelated'? Woolley argues:

> The representation that drove the disclosure [by Lazin of the falsified documents in the Doblanko divorce] was, instead, Lazin's representation of [his client] Lambert; it was to benefit Helen Lambert that Lazin disclosed the information in the way he did. The wrongful conduct was acting in a manner that was injurious to Neils' interest *on the very matter for which the Ventrakaman firm had been retained.*[5]

4. In his text *Professional Conduct for Lawyers and Judges*[6] written shortly before the Supreme Court of Canada's decision in *R. v. Neil*, Beverley Smith wrote at Chapter 2, pp. 3-4 that:

> [T]he lawyer will be required to act in the utmost good faith toward the person for whom and on whose behalf he/she has undertaken to act. The Latin phrase *"uberrimae fidei"* aptly sums up the requirement that the lawyer act in the most trustworthy fashion. It is the existence of this duty of good faith and trustworthiness which colours all that the lawyer does during *and following* the term as the client's legal advisor and advocate.
> [Emphasis added]

This concept of utmost good faith seems to capture something deeper and not limited to, a specific incident of the lawyer-client relationship, such as the sharing of confidential information. Is this what the Supreme Court of Canada was trying to articulate or revive as a principle? If so, does the decision achieve this?

[d] The Aftermath of R. v. Neil

The *Neil* decision, and its articulation of a "bright line" rule restricting representation of current clients whose interests are directly adverse to those of other current clients, even in unrelated matters, became the most hotly debated topic in legal ethics in Canada in recent memory. We begin with some academic commentary on the matter. Shortly after the *Neil* decision, Richard F. Devlin and Victoria Rees

---

[5] Alice Woolley, *Understanding Lawyers' Ethics in Canada*, 2d ed. (Toronto: LexisNexis Canada, 2016) at 313-314.

[6] Beverley Smith, *Professional Conduct for Lawyers and Judges*, 3rd ed (Fredericton: Maritime LawBook, 2007).

examined the topic and came to this conclusion:

> [W]hile some commentators have dismissed the *Neil* case as an example of egregious conflict in the area of criminal law and, therefore, not of great significance, revisionists argue that this is a mistake because Binnie J. went out of his way to articulate quite carefully the Court's reflections on the duty of loyalty, echoing the biblical homily that "No man can serve two masters: either he will hate the one and love the other; or else he will hold to the one and despise the other."
>
> Consequently . . . Binnie J. makes it clear that a business conflict can now be a legal conflict because "[l]oyalty includes putting the client's business ahead of the lawyer's business." A lawyer's desire to "hang onto a piece of litigation" is insufficient justification. As a result, retainers will have to be declined because of business conflicts. Moreover, "Chinese walls" and "cones of silence" do not apply in the context of a breach of loyalty because their concern is confidentiality, not loyalty.[7]

This passage is significant in at least two respects. First, it highlights the point that in some respects the duty of loyalty is of greater import than the duty of confidentiality since it cannot easily be addressed through the use of prophylactic devices like "Chinese walls" and "cones of silence" or other lawyer screening mechanisms. Second, the Devlin and Rees observation about business conflicts capable of becoming legal conflicts was prescient, as we will see in *Strother*, the third case in the Supreme Court trilogy.

Of equal significance to those observations, however, is the degree to which *Neil* changed the standard against which 'loyalty to current clients' is measured, and the degree to which previously allowed representations of clients are now allegedly disallowed. This issue largely revolved around the 'bright line' prohibition against the representation of a current client whose interests are directly adverse to the interests of another client, even if the matter on which that other client is being represented is unrelated to the subject matter of the adverse representation.

This became the centrepiece of the conflicts debate.[8] Both the Canadian Bar Association (CBA) and the Federation of Law Societies of Canada (FLSC) developed interpretations of the case. In its Task Force Report on Conflicts of Interest, the CBA concluded that the bright line rule was 'obiter' and therefore not germane to the resolution of *Neil*, asserting that current client conflicts of interest should be resolved on the basis of whether a 'substantial risk' to client representation was liable to occur. At the same time, the FLSC in the finalization of the *Model Code*, concluded that the test for the resolution of current client conflicts should focus on whether there was a risk to loyalty or representation – a position closer to the literal statement of the bright line rule in *Neil*.

The third case in the "conflicts quartet", *Strother v. 3464920 Canada Inc.*[9] offered

---

[7] Richard F. Devlin & Victoria Rees, "Beyond Conflicts of Interest to the Duty of Loyalty" (2005) 48:1 Can. Bar Rev. 433 at 443-444.

[8] A comprehensive account of the debate may be found in Adam Dodek's article, "Conflicted Identities: The Battle over the Duty of Loyalty in Canada" (2011) 14:2 Leg. Ethics 193.

[9] *Strother v. 3464920 Canada Inc.*, [2007] S.C.J. No. 24, [2007] 2 S.C.R. 177 (S.C.C.).

some insights into the Supreme Court's view about the scope and application of the 'bright line rule'. However, as we shall see below, the case was ultimately decided on other grounds, themselves contentious within the Court, and did not fully resolve the debate over the application of *Neil*.

STROTHER v. 3464920 CANADA INC.

[2007] S.C.J. No. 24, [2007] 2 S.C.R. 177

[Monarch Entertainment (3464920 Canada Inc.) was a film development and financing company. It was actively involved in this business through much of the 1990s, arranging the financing of Hollywood films made in Canada through the use of attractive tax advantages available to investors under Canada's income tax system. Monarch retained Davis and Company, a Vancouver law firm, to handle much of its legal business, including the film financing arrangements. Strother was a senior tax partner at Davis and Company and was responsible for much of the tax advice provided to Monarch. For the calendar years 1996 and 1997 Davis and Company entered into an arrangement whereby the firm would represent Monarch exclusively on matters related to movie financing.

During this period the Government of Canada moved to eliminate the tax deduction regime that had made Monarch's business extremely lucrative. These changes took effect in late 1997. Strother advised Monarch that there were no options available to it and Monarch began to wind down its business. Additional legal work was done for Monarch by Davis and Company and Strother in 1998 but no longer under the exclusive representation arrangement of the previous two years. In late 1997 or early 1998, Darc, formerly a senior employee of Monarch, approached Strother. They agreed to apply for an advance tax ruling (a standard arrangement that essentially can provide a pre-authorization by the government for the specific tax treatment of a proposed financing arrangement). A favourable ruling would establish that certain dimensions of the 'loophole' remained open. Strother agreed to develop the submission without a fee on the understanding that if the ruling was favourable he would become a partner with Darc in the new business. Strother did not communicate any of this to Monarch. Nor did he disclose the full particulars of his arrangement to Davis and Company. Davis and Company had policies that forbade such arrangements between its lawyers and the firm's clients. Late in 1998 Darc (and Strother) received a favourable advance tax ruling. Shortly afterward, as planned, Strother left Davis and Company and joined Darc and others in the venture. The venture was extremely lucrative, and the two partners earned over $60-million over the next two to three years, until the 'loophole' was closed completely.

When Monarch learned of the tax ruling, and of Strother having joined Darc in their movie financing business, it commenced proceedings against Darc for violations of his obligations as a former employee, and against Strother and Davis and Company for breach of fiduciary obligations owed to Monarch as their client. The proceedings against Darc were dismissed at trial and on appeal. The proceedings against Strother and Davis and Company were dismissed at trial but reversed on appeal. Strother and Davis and Company appealed to the Supreme Court of Canada.]

BINNIE J. [for the majority].:

. . . . .

When a lawyer is retained by a client, the scope of the retainer is governed by contract. It is for the parties to determine how many, or how few, services the lawyer is to perform, and other contractual terms of the engagement. The solicitor-client relationship thus created is however overlaid with certain fiduciary responsibilities, which are imposed as a matter of law. The Davis factum puts it well:

> The source of the duty is not the retainer itself, but all the circumstances (including the retainer) creating a relationship of trust and confidence from which flow obligations of loyalty and transparency. [para. 95]

Not every breach of the contract of retainer is a breach of a fiduciary duty. On the other hand, fiduciary duties provide a framework within which the lawyer performs the work and may include obligations that go beyond what the parties expressly bargained for. The foundation of this branch of the law is the need to protect the integrity of the administration of justice: *MacDonald Estate v. Martin* . . . .. "[I]t is of high public importance that public confidence in that integrity be maintained"
. . ..

Fiduciary responsibilities include the duty of loyalty, of which an element is the avoidance of conflicts of interest, as set out in the jurisprudence and reflected in the *Rules of Practice of The Law Society of British Columbia*. As the late Hon. Michel Proulx and David Layton state, "[t]he leitmotif of conflict of interest is the broader duty of loyalty", *Ethics and Canadian Criminal Law* (2001) . . .:

In recent years as law firms have grown in size and shrunk in numbers, the courts have increasingly been required to deal with claims by clients arising out of alleged conflicts of interest on the part of their lawyers. Occasionally, a law firm is caught innocently in crossfire between two or more clients. Sometimes the claim of conflict is asserted for purely tactical reasons, an objectionable practice criticized in *Neil* at paras. 14-15, and a factor to be taken into account by a court in determining what relief if any is to be accorded. . .. Sometimes, however, the dilemma is of the lawyer's own making. Here the firm's position was compromised by the personal conflict of a lawyer (Strother) who, contrary to the instructions of Davis's managing partner, contracted for a personal financial interest in one client (Sentinel) whose interest he then preferred over another client (Monarch) who now sues for compensation. In that regard, Monarch relies upon the well-known proposition endorsed by Professors Waters that:

> The other (the beneficiary) is entitled to expect that the fiduciary will be concerned solely for the beneficiary's interests, never the fiduciary's own.

. . . . .

A. The Scope of the 1998 Retainer

A critical issue in this case is the scope of Monarch's contractual retainer with Davis in 1998. Davis acknowledges "that a solicitor's duty of single-minded loyalty to his client's interest had its roots in the fiduciary nature of the solicitor-client relationship but that duty . . . 'may have to be moulded and informed by the terms of the contractual relationship'" (Davis factum, at para. 80, citing *Hilton v. Barker Booth and Eastwood*, [2005] 1 All E.R. 651 (H.L.)). At para. 30 of the *Hilton* case, Lord Walker elaborated:

> On this issue of liability both sides have been content for the case to be dealt with as a claim for breach of contract. However, the content of BBE's contractual duty,

so far as relevant to this case, has roots in the parties' relationship of trust and confidence.

Here, too, the claim arises out of "the parties' relationship of trust and confidence" but the case is pleaded as a breach of the fiduciary duty of loyalty rather than breach of contract . . .

. . . . .

Where a retainer has not been reduced to writing (as was the case with the 1998 retainer here) and no exclusions are agreed upon, as here, the scope of the retainer may be unclear. The court should not in such a case strain to resolve the ambiguities in favour of the lawyer over the client. The subject matter of the retainer here was, as it had been for years, "tax-assisted business opportunities". It was not to sell an office building, draft an informatics contract or perform other legal services unrelated to the subject matter of the earlier advice. The trial judge exonerated Strother by placing the emphasis on Monarch's interest in "alternative" tax opportunities, but of course Monarch only considered "alternative" tax opportunities because Strother had given categorical advice that the tax-assisted film production services business in which Strother had profitably been advising Monarch since 1993 was unequivocally dead.

I believe, as did the Court of Appeal, that the trial judge erred in drawing so narrowly the *legal* effect of his *factual* finding that the retainer dealt with tax-assisted business opportunities, alternative or otherwise. (In fact Strother's position is that what he pursued on behalf of Sentinel in 1998 *was* an alternative tax-assisted business opportunity and not the same TAPSF scheme as he had pronounced dead in 1997.) Monarch was a major Davis client of long standing. It had been Strother's biggest source of billings for years. It was in the business of marketing tax schemes whose success turned on Strother's expertise in finding a "way [to get] around the rules" . . . .. Strother's factum emphasizes nice distinctions between tax credits, tax shelters and so on but I do not think this oral retainer can or ought to be parsed so closely.

Nor can I agree with the Chief Justice when she characterizes the legal obligation arising out of the 1998 retainer as follows:

> Only if Monarch had specifically asked Strother for advice on new film tax- shelter opportunities and Strother had agreed to give that advice, could Strother have been under any duty to provide Monarch with such advice, placing him in a conflict of interest with Sentinel Hill.

Monarch's tax business was in a jam. Strother was still its tax lawyer. There was a continuing "relationship of trust and confidence". Monarch was dealing with professional advisors, not used car salesmen or pawnbrokers whom the public may expect to operate on the basis of "didn't ask, didn't tell", and who collectively suffer a corresponding deficit in trust and confidence. Therein lies one of the differences between a profession and some businesses.

In my view, subject to confidentiality considerations for other clients, if Strother knew there was still a way to continue to syndicate U.S. studio film production expenses to Canadian investors on a tax-efficient basis, the 1998 retainer entitled Monarch to be told that Strother's previous negative advice was now subject to reconsideration.

It is this contractual duty that came into conflict with Strother's personal financial interest when he took a major stake in Sentinel which was, as Newbury J.A. pointed out, a competitor in a small market where experience showed that, even limited, competition could lead to a rapid erosion of market share.

B. Breach of the 1998 Retainer

The trial judgment, as stated, was premised on the finding that Monarch did not specifically ask about the possible revival of TAPSF-type shelters in 1998. I agree with the trial judge that *generally* a lawyer does not have a duty to alter a past opinion in light of a subsequent change of circumstances.

. . .

There are, however, exceptions to the general rule. As Deschamps J. stated in *Côté v. Rancourt* 2004 SCC 58. . . the "boundaries of [a lawyer's] duty to advise will depend on the circumstances" (para. 6). The issue here was not so much a duty to alter a past opinion, as it was part of Strother's duty to provide candid advice on all matters relevant to the 1998 retainer . . . It appears that Lowry J. turned his mind to this exception to the general rule when he stated that a lawyer is not obligated to "alter advice given under a *concluded* retainer" (para. 121 (emphasis added)). Here Monarch's retainer of Davis was *not* a concluded retainer. The written 1997 retainer had come to an end but the solicitor-client relationship based on a continuing (if more limited) retainer carried on into 1998 and 1999. As Deschamps J. further observed in *Côté*, "the obligational content of the lawyer-client relationship is not necessarily circumscribed by the object of the mandate" . . .. The *Côté* approach is not consistent with the "didn't ask, didn't tell" approach taken by the trial judge. Strother was meeting with Monarch to brainstorm tax schemes and knew perfectly well Monarch would be vitally interested in Strother's re-evaluation of the tax potential of the MER. The duty to advise Monarch required Strother and Davis, as a term of the 1998 retainer, if not expressed (as claimed by Monarch) then certainly implied, to explain to Monarch that Strother's earlier advice had been overtaken by events and would have to be revisited. Indeed, Strother discussed this concern with another partner at Davis, Rowland K. McLeod who testified in cross-examination as follows:

> A. I did consider whether or not Monarch *could* be told and I guess that would include *should* be told . . . And my recollection is that Mr. Strother came to me before a meeting that he was going to have with Mr. Knutson [a principal of Monarch] and we discussed and considered whether or not Monarch could be told [that the previous advice about "no fix" had been premature], and my, my recollection was that we didn't reach a consensus on what could be done and he was going to play it by ear . . . . *He was afraid Mr. Knutson was going to ask him.*
>
> Q. When was that?
>
> A. It was in, I think it was June of 1998 . . . We discussed it, came to no conclusion. He went to the meeting, told me either later that day or the next day, that the issue had not arisen. [Emphasis added]
>
> (Davis's A.R., at p. 196)

McLeod continued:

> A. The nature of the, the, the nature of the discussion was, he was going to meet

with Monarch. He was concerned that Mr. Knutson would raise the question of *is there a way around the, whatever the change in the law was.* [Emphasis added]

(Davis's A.R., at p. 198)

The fact that Strother and McLeod discussed what should be said if Monarch put the right question ("is there a way around . . .?") recognized that Strother appreciated that his modified view about the potential of the s. 18.1(15)(*b*) exception would likely be of continuing interest and importance to Monarch because Monarch was still looking to him for advice in rebuilding its shattered tax-related business. At that point, of course, Strother had every interest in keeping Monarch in the dark. In June of 1998, under the January 1998 agreement, he was entitled to 55 percent of the first $2 million in profits and 50 percent of Sentinel's profits on the revival of tax-assisted film production services deals, which constituted a small and select marketplace. The fewer competitors faced by Sentinel the more money Strother would make and the faster he would pocket it.

Of course, it was not open to Strother to share with Monarch any *confidential* information received from Darc. He could nevertheless have advised Monarch that his earlier view was too emphatic, that there may yet be life in a modified form of syndicating film production services expenses for tax benefits, but that because his change of view was based at least in part on information confidential to another client on a transaction unrelated to Monarch, he could not advise further except to suggest that Monarch consult another law firm. Moreover, there is no excuse at all for Strother not advising Monarch of the successful tax ruling when it was made public in October 1998. As it turned out, Monarch did not find out about it until February or March 1999. I therefore conclude that Davis (and Strother) failed to provide candid and proper legal advice in breach of the 1998 retainer.

. . . . .

1. Davis was Free to Take on Darc and Sentinel as New Clients

Monarch claims (and the Court of Appeal agreed) that even after the expiry of the "exclusive" retainer in 1997, Davis was conflicted out of acting for Darc and Sentinel by reason of its ongoing solicitor-client relationship with Monarch. As the House of Lords recently noted in relation to conflicting *contractual* duties, "a solicitor who has conflicting duties to two clients may not prefer one to another . . . . [T]he fact that he [the lawyer] has chosen to put himself in an impossible position does not exonerate him from liability" (*Hilton.* . .). The same principle applies to a lawyer getting into a position of conflicting *fiduciary* duties. . . . The general rule is of long standing but I do not think it applied here to prevent Davis and Strother from acting for Sentinel. As stated in *Neil* . . .:

> An unnecessary expansion of the duty may be as inimical to the proper functioning of the legal system as would its attenuation. The issue is always to determine what rules are sensible and necessary and how best to achieve an appropriate balance among the competing interests.

This is not to say that in *Neil* the Court advocated the resolution of conflict issues on a case-by-case basis through a general balancing of interests, the outcome of which would be difficult to predict in advance. . . . The "bright line" rule is the product of the balancing of interests not the gateway to further internal balancing. In *Neil*, the Court stated . . .:

> The bright line is provided by the general rule that a lawyer may not represent one client whose interests are directly adverse to the immediate interests of another current client — *even if the two mandates are unrelated* — unless both clients consent after receiving full disclosure (and preferably independent legal advice), and the lawyers reasonably believes [*sic*] that he or she is able to represent each client without adversely affecting the other. [Emphasis in original.]

I agree with Strother's counsel when he writes that "[t]he retainer by Sentinel Hill was . . . not 'directly adverse' to any 'immediate interest' of Monarch". On the contrary, as Strother argues, "Sentinel Hill created a business opportunity which Monarch could have sought to exploit" (Strother factum, at para. 66). A Sentinel ruling that revived the TAPSF business even in modified form would indirectly help any firm whose tax syndication business had been ruined by the *ITA* amendments, including Monarch. Representation of Sentinel was thus not "directly adverse" to representation of Monarch by Davis/Strother even though both mandates related to tax-assisted business opportunities in the film production services field. Strother's problem arose because despite his duty to an existing client, Monarch, he acquired a major personal financial interest (unknown to Davis) in another client, Sentinel, in circumstances where his prospects of personal profit were enhanced by keeping Monarch on the sidelines. . . .

(a) Monarch Was a Current Client

I agree with Newbury J.A. that too much was made in argument about the shift from the 1997 written retainer to the 1998 oral retainer. The trial judge in places referred to a *concluded* retainer. However, this is not a case where *a former* client alleges breach of the duty of loyalty . . .. Monarch was a *current* client and was unquestionably entitled to the continuing loyalty of Strother and Davis.

. . .

(b) Acting for Clients with Competing Commercial Interests

As recognized by both the trial judge and Newbury J.A., the conflict of interest principles do not generally preclude a law firm or lawyer from acting concurrently for different clients who are in the same line of business, or who compete with each other for business. There was no *legal* dispute between Monarch and Sentinel. Monarch relies on the "bright line" rule set out in *Neil* but (leaving aside, for the moment, Strother's personal financial stake) there is no convincing case for its application here.

The clients' respective "interests" that require the protection of the duty of loyalty have to do with the practice of law, not commercial prosperity. Here the alleged "adversity" between concurrent clients related to business matters. This is not to say that commercial interests can *never* be relevant. The *American Restatement* offers the example of two business competitors who seek to retain a single law firm in respect of competing applications for a single broadcast licence, i.e. a unique opportunity. The *Restatement* suggests that acting for both without disclosure and consent would be improper because the subject matter of both retainers is the same licence (*Restatement (Third) of the Law Governing Lawyers*, vol. 2, at § 121 (2000)). The lawyer's ability to provide even-handed representation is put in issue. However, commercial conflicts between clients that do *not* impair a lawyer's ability to properly represent the legal interests of both clients will not generally present a conflict problem. Whether or not a real risk of impairment exists will be a question of fact. In my judgment, the risk did not exist here provided the necessary even-handed representation had not been skewed by Strother's personal undisclosed financial interest. Condominium lawyers act with undiminished vigour for numerous entrepreneurs competing in the same housing market; oil and gas lawyers advise without hesitation exploration firms competing in the oil patch, provided, of course, that information confidential to a particular client is kept confidential. There is no reason in general why a tax practitioner such as Strother should not take on different clients syndicating tax schemes to the same investor community, notwithstanding the restricted market for these services in a business in which Sentinel and Monarch competed. In fact, in the case of some areas of high specialization, or in small communities or other situations of scarce legal resources, clients may be taken to have consented to a degree of overlapping representation inherent in such law practices, depending on the evidence . . .. The more sophisticated the client, the more readily the inference of implied consent may be drawn. The thing the lawyer must *not* do is keep the client in the dark about matters he or she knows to be relevant to the retainer . . .

. . . . .

(c) The Duty of Loyalty is Concerned with Client Representation

While the duty of loyalty is focussed on the lawyer's ability to provide proper client representation, it is not fully exhausted by the obligation to avoid conflicts of interest with other concurrent clients. A "conflict of interest" was defined in *Neil* as an interest that gives rise to a

> substantial risk that the lawyer's representation of the client would be materially and adversely affected by the lawyer's own interests or by the lawyer's duties to another current client, a former client, or a third person.
>
> (*Neil*, at para. 31, adopting § 121 of the *Restatement (Third) of Law Governing Lawyers*, vol. 2, at pp. 244-45).

. . .

(d) The Impact on the Representation of Monarch Was "Material and Adverse"

There is no doubt that at all material times there was a "current meaningful" solicitor-client relationship between Monarch and Davis/Strother to ground the duty of loyalty . . .. The availability of Strother's ongoing tax advice was important to Monarch and is the cornerstone of its claim.

Strother is dismissive of the impact his breach had on Monarch's interest (i.e. in obtaining proper legal advice). He is correct that the test requires that the impact must be "material and adverse" (as set out in the definition of conflict adopted in *Neil*, previously cited). While it is sufficient to show a possibility (rather than a probability) of adverse impact, the possibility must be more than speculation . . .. That test is met here, for the reasons already discussed. Once the existence of Strother's personal financial interest in Sentinel was established, it was for Strother, not Monarch, to demonstrate the absence of any material adverse effect on Monarch's interest in receiving proper and timely legal advice . . ..

(e) Sentinel's Desire to Secure the Counsel of its Choice Was Also an Important Consideration

The evidence showed that Strother's special expertise was available from few other firms. Sentinel's Paul Darc had worked successfully with Davis and Strother for years. Our legal system, the complexity of which perhaps reaches its apex in the ITA, depends on people with legal needs obtaining access to what they think is the best legal advice they can get. Sentinel's ability to secure the advice of Davis and Strother as counsel of choice is an important consideration . . . .. It does not trump the requirement to avoid conflicts of interest but it is nevertheless an important consideration.

2. The Difficulty in Representing Monarch Arose from a Strother Conflict not a Davis Conflict

Davis did not appreciate what Strother was up to and had no reason to think the Sentinel retainer would interfere with the proper representation of Monarch.

. . . . .

. . . In general, Davis and Strother were free to take on Darc and Sentinel as new clients once the "exclusivity" arrangement with Monarch expired at the end of 1997. Issues of confidentiality are routinely dealt with successfully in law firms. Strother could have managed the relationship with the two clients as other specialist practitioners do, by being candid with their legal advice while protecting from disclosure the confidential details of the other client's business. If the two are so inextricably bound together that legal advice is impossible, then of course the duty to respect confidentiality prevails, but there is nothing here to justify Strother's artful silence. Strother accepted Sentinel as a new client and the Davis firm was given no reason to think that he and his colleagues could not provide proper legal advice to both clients.

3. Strother was not Free to Take a Personal Financial Interest in the Darc/Sentinel Venture

The trial judge found that Strother agreed to pursue the tax ruling on behalf of Sentinel in return for an interest in the profits that would be realized by Sentinel if the ruling was granted. . .

Strother had *at least* an "option" interest in Sentinel from January 30th until at least August 1998 (when he was told by Davis to give up *any* interest). This was during a critical period when Monarch was looking to Strother for advice about what tax-assisted business opportunities were open. The precise nature of Strother's continuing financial interest in Sentinel between August 1998 and March 31, 1999 (when Strother left Davis) is unclear, but whatever it was it came to highly profitable fruition in the months that followed. The difficulty is not that Sentinel and Monarch were potential competitors. The difficulty is that Strother aligned his personal financial interest with the former's success. By acquiring a substantial and direct financial interest in one client (Sentinel) seeking to enter a very restricted market related to film production services in which another client (Monarch) previously had a major presence, Strother put his personal financial interest into conflict with his duty to Monarch. The conflict compromised Strother's duty to "zealously" represent Monarch's interest . . . a delinquency compounded by his lack of "candour" with

Monarch "on matters relevant to the retainer" . . . i.e. his own competing financial interest.

. . . . .

In these circumstances, taking a direct and significant interest in the potential profits of Monarch's "commercial competito[r]" . . . created a substantial risk that [Strother's] representation of Monarch would be materially and adversely affected by consideration of his own interests. . .. As Newbury J.A. stated, "Strother . . . *was* 'the competition'" . . .. It gave Strother a reason to keep the principals of Monarch "in the dark" (*ibid.*), in breach of his duty to provide candid advice on his changing views of the potential for film production services tax shelters. I agree with Newbury J.A. that Monarch was "*entitled* to candid and complete advice from a lawyer who was not in a position of conflict" . . . (emphasis in original).

Strother could not with equal loyalty serve Monarch and pursue his own financial interest which stood in obvious conflict with Monarch making a quick re-entry into the tax-assisted film financing business. As stated in *Neil*, at para. 24, "[l]oyalty includes putting the client's business ahead of the lawyer's business". It is therefore my view that Strother's failure to revisit his 1997 advice in 1998 at a time when he had a personal, undisclosed financial interest in Sentinel Hill breached his duty of loyalty to Monarch. The duty was further breached when he did not advise Monarch of the successful tax ruling when it became public on October 6, 1998. Why would a rainmaker like Strother not make rain with as many clients (or potential clients) as possible when the opportunity presented itself (whether or not existing retainers required him to do so)? The unfortunate inference is that Strother did not tell Monarch because he did not think it was in his personal financial interest to do so.

4. Davis Did Not Participate in Strother's Disabling Conflict of Interest

[Binnie J. found that, as Davis was unaware of Strother's financial interest in Sentinel, it was 'as much an innocent victim of Strother's financial conflict as was Monarch'. Binnie J. concluded that Strother was liable for the monies he earned from the beginning of the venture until March 31, 1999, when other business developments influenced the direction of the venture, and by which time the information on the tax ruling was fully known and Strother's links with Monarch and with Davis and Company has been severed. He found Davis and Company were innocently duped by a "rogue partner" but that Strother was nevertheless acting in the ordinary course of business", making Davis vicariously liable for Strother's actions pursuant to the Partnership Act.]

THE CHIEF JUSTICE [dissenting in part]:

. . . . .

Insistence on actual conflicting duties or interests based on what the lawyer has contracted to do in the retainer is vital. If the duty of loyalty is described as a general, free-floating duty owed by a lawyer or law firm to every client, the potential for conflicts is vast. Indeed, it is difficult to see how a lawyer or law firm could ever act for two competitors. Consider, as in this case, a specialized tax lawyer who acts for client A and B, where A and B are competitors. Client A may ask for help in minimizing capital gains tax. Client B may seek advice on a tax shelter. The lawyer owes both A and B contractual and associated fiduciary duties. If the duty that the lawyer owes to each client is conceived in broad general terms, it may well preclude the lawyer from acting for each of them; at the very least, it will create uncertainty. If the duty is referenced to the retainer, by contrast, these difficulties do not arise. The lawyer is nonetheless free to act for both, provided the duties the lawyer owes to client A do not conflict with the duties he owes to client B.

This manner of viewing a lawyer's duties conforms to the realities of the legal profession and the needs of clients. Modern commerce, taxation and regulation flow together in complex, sometimes murky streams. To navigate these waters, clients require specialized lawyers. The more specialized the field, the more likely that the lawyer will act for clients who are in competition with each other. Complicating this reality is the fact that particular types of economic activity may be concentrated in particular regions. The obligation of the legal profession is to provide the required services. Yet in doing so, lawyers and law firms must inevitably act for competitors.

Practical considerations such as these cannot be used to dilute the rigor of the fiduciary duties that the law rightly demands of lawyers. Rather, they explain why the law has developed a precise conception of the lawyer's duty grounded in the contract of retainer. Our law rightly imposes rigorous fiduciary duties on lawyers, but it also recognizes the need to ensure that fiduciary obligations remain realistic and meaningful in the face of the realities of modern practice.

. . . . .

[Chief Justice McLachlin, writing for a minority of four, would have adopted a more limited interpretation of Strother's obligations, bounded by the terms of the retainer. The result would have been that Strother was not found to have been in violation of his fiduciary duties. On this basis she would have dismissed the claims against Strother and Davis .]

NOTES AND QUESTIONS

1. To what extent, if any, does *Strother* moderate the lawyer's obligation of loyalty to a client that is articulated in *R.v. Neil*? Had the dissenting view prevailed, would this have further moderated the lawyer's loyalty obligation to clients? Is McLachlin C.J. correct in her concern that the more open-ended approach of the majority will generate uncertainty for lawyers and the legal profession on the issue of conflicts of interest?

2. The minority in *Strother* would have upheld the trial judge's decision that the contract of retainer delineated the core of the lawyer's responsibilities, and that Strother's conduct was not actionable. To what extent might the majority have viewed the case as highlighting opportunistic behaviour on the lawyer's part, behaviour that might have been an embarrassment to the legal profession? As such, did the majority seek to ensure that the fiduciary net, by going beyond the mere particulars of the retainer, was cast wide enough to prevent and, in this case to some extent at least, sanction such behaviour?

3. Chief Justice McLachlin appears to assume that a law firm's representation of two competitors is acceptable, unless there is some specific constraint

imposed by the clients themselves. This argument is remarkably similar to that of Sopinka J. in *MacDonald Estate*, advancing as it does the business reality of client and law firm needs. Yet this argument does not carry the day in *Strother*. Does this suggest that the majority decision of Binnie J. constitutes a noticeable, though highly contested, shift in the Court's thinking, or re-statement, that lawyer's duty of loyalty to their client's interests is still the paramount principle?

4. In what other ways is the situation in *Strother* different from the conflicts of interest in the earlier cases? Consider, for example, that Monarch Entertainment and Darc (and Strother in his capacity as Darc's business partner) were not in a dispute with one another, so much as they were competing for the same business? Does this make a difference to the resolution of the conflict?

5. Note as well that *Strother* is different from the other cases in that the lawyer and the lawyer's personal interests are at the centre of the controversy. The British Columbia Court of Appeal referred to Strother as "the competition" for Monarch. This complicates the issue of conflicts of interest, but in ways that correspond with everyday reality. In many aspects of law practice, business opportunities regularly present themselves to lawyers in ways that are associated with work on behalf of clients. Is the lawyer required to decline these opportunities? What principles should be used to distinguish the types of opportunities that could be taken up by lawyers from the ones that are off limits? These questions are addressed when we examine the second general type of conflict – lawyer-client conflicts of interest - later in this chapter.

The debate about 'current client' conflicts, and the scope and application of *Neil's* 'bright line rule' eventually came to be addressed by the Supreme Court in another case involving an application to have a law firm disqualified from a client representation. The case had been followed with interest in the legal profession as it made its way through the courts. It presented an opportunity for the Supreme Court to directly address both the contested interpretations of *Neil* and the apparent conflicts within the Court as to the extent of lawyers' obligations in this area of law and ethics. Unlike the previous cases in the 'conflicts quartet', both the Federation of Law Societies of Canada and the Canadian Bar Association sought and received intervenor status and advanced contrary positions as to the scope and application of *Neil*.

CANADIAN NATIONAL RAILWAY CO. v. McKERCHER LLP

[2013] S.C.J. No. 39, [2013] 2 S.C.R. 649

The judgment of the Court was delivered by

McLACHLIN C.J.:— Can a law firm accept a retainer to act against a current client on a matter unrelated to the client's existing files? More specifically, can a firm bring a lawsuit against a current client on behalf of another client? If not, what remedies are available to the client whose lawyer has brought suit against it? These are the questions raised by this appeal.

I. Background

McKercher LLP ("McKercher") is a large law firm in Saskatchewan. The Canadian National Railway Company ("CN") retained McKercher to act for it on a variety of matters. In late 2008, McKercher was acting for CN on three ongoing matters: a personal injury claim concerning a rail yard incident in which children had been injured; the purchase of real estate; and the representation of CN's interests as a creditor in a receivership. As well, two of its partners held power of attorney from CN for service of process in Saskatchewan.

At the same time, the McKercher firm accepted a retainer from Gordon Wallace ("Wallace") to act against CN in a $1.75 billion class action based on allegations that CN had illegally overcharged Western Canadian farmers for grain transportation. It is not contested on appeal that the Wallace action was legally and factually unrelated to the ongoing CN retainers.

The McKercher firm did not advise CN that it intended to accept the Wallace retainer. CN learned this only when it was served with the statement of claim on January 9, 2009. Between December 5, 2008, and January 15, 2009, various McKercher partners hastily terminated their retainers with CN, except on the real estate file, which was terminated by CN.

Following receipt of the statement of claim, CN applied for an order removing McKercher as solicitor of record for Wallace in the class action against it, on the grounds that the McKercher firm had breached its duty of loyalty to CN by placing itself in a conflict of interest, had improperly terminated its existing CN retainers, and might misuse confidential information gained in the course of the solicitor-client relationship.

The motion judge granted the application, and disqualified McKercher from acting on the Wallace litigation: *Wallace v. Canadian Pacific Railway*, [2009] S.J. No. 549, 2009 SKQB 369, 344 Sask. R. 3 (Sask. Q.B.). He found that the firm had breached the duty of loyalty it owed CN, placing itself in a conflict of interest by accepting the Wallace retainer while acting for CN on other matters. In his view, CN felt an understandable sense of betrayal, which substantially impaired the McKercher firm's ability to represent CN in the ongoing retainers. Moreover, McKercher had received a unique understanding of the litigation strengths, weaknesses and attitudes of CN; this understanding constituted relevant confidential information. The motion judge concluded that McKercher's violation of the duty of loyalty, in addition to the possession of relevant confidential information, made disqualification of McKercher as counsel on the Wallace action an appropriate remedy.

The Court of Appeal overturned the motion judge's order disqualifying McKercher: [2011] S.J. No. 589, 2011 SKCA 108, 375 Sask. R. 218 (Sask. C.A.), revd [2013] S.C.J. No. 39 (S.C.C.). The Court of Appeal found that a general understanding of CN's litigation strengths and weaknesses did not constitute relevant confidential information warranting disqualification. Moreover, it found that McKercher had not breached its duty of loyalty by accepting to act concurrently for Wallace. CN was a large corporate client that was not in a position of vulnerability or dependency with respect to McKercher. As such, its implied consent to McKercher acting for an opposing party in unrelated legal matters could be inferred. However, the Court of

Appeal found that McKercher had breached its duty of loyalty towards CN by peremptorily terminating the solicitor-client relationship on its existing files for CN. Nevertheless, disqualification was not an appropriate remedy in this case, since McKercher's continued representation of Wallace created no risk of prejudice to CN. Indeed, the termination of the lawyer-client relationship had effectively put an end to any possibility of prejudice.

The case at hand requires this Court to examine the lawyer's duty of loyalty to his client, and in particular the requirement that a lawyer avoid conflicts of interest. As we held in *R. v. Neil*, [2002] S.C.J. No. 72, 2002 SCC 70, [2002] 3 S.C.R. 631 (S.C.C.), the general "bright line" rule is that a lawyer, and by extension a law firm, may not concurrently represent clients adverse in interest without obtaining their consent — regardless of whether the client matters are related or unrelated: para. 29. However, when the bright line rule is inapplicable, the question becomes whether the concurrent representation of clients creates a "substantial risk that the lawyer's representation of the client would be materially and adversely affected by the lawyer's own interests or by the lawyer's duties to another current client, a former client, or a third person": *Neil*, at para. 31. This appeal turns on the scope of the bright line rule: Did it apply to McKercher's concurrent representation of CN and Wallace? Or is the applicable test instead whether the concurrent representation of CN and Wallace created a substantial risk of impaired representation?

In these reasons, I conclude that McKercher's concurrent representation of CN and Wallace fell squarely within the scope of the bright line rule. The bright line rule was engaged by the facts of this case: CN and Wallace were adverse in legal interests; CN has not attempted to tactically abuse the bright line rule; and it was reasonable in the circumstances for CN to expect that McKercher would not concurrently represent a party suing it for $1.75 billion. McKercher failed to obtain CN's consent to the concurrent representation of Wallace, and consequently breached the bright line rule when it accepted the Wallace retainer.

In addition to its duty to avoid conflicts of interest, a law firm is under a duty of commitment to the client's cause which prevents it from summarily and unexpectedly dropping a client in order to circumvent conflict of interest rules, and a duty of candour which requires the law firm to advise its existing client of all matters relevant to the retainer. I conclude that McKercher's termination of its existing retainers with CN breached its duty of commitment to its client's cause, and its failure to advise CN of its intention to accept the Wallace retainer breached its duty of candour to its client. However, McKercher possessed no relevant confidential information that could be used to prejudice CN.

As regards the appropriate remedy to McKercher's breaches, I conclude that the only concern that would warrant disqualification in this case is the protection of the repute of the administration of justice. A breach of the bright line rule normally attracts the remedy of disqualification. This remains true even if the lawyer-client relationship is terminated subsequent to the breach. However, certain factors may militate against disqualification, and they must be taken into consideration. As the motion judge did not have the benefit of these reasons, I would remit the matter to the Queen's Bench for redetermination in accordance with them.

II. Issues

The appeal raises the following issues:

A. The Role of the Courts in Resolving Conflicts Issues

B. The Governing Principles

C. Application of the Principles

D. The Appropriate Remedy

III. Analysis

A. The Role of the Courts in Resolving Conflicts Issues

Courts of inherent jurisdiction have supervisory power over litigation brought before them. Lawyers are officers of the court and are bound to conduct their business as the court directs. When issues arise as to whether a lawyer may act for a particular client in litigation, it falls to the court to resolve those issues. The courts' purpose in exercising their supervisory powers over lawyers has traditionally been to protect clients from prejudice and to preserve the repute of the administration of justice, not to discipline or punish lawyers.

In addition to their supervisory role over court proceedings, courts develop the fiduciary principles that govern lawyers in their duties to clients. Solicitor-client privilege has been a frequent subject of court consideration, for example.

The inherent power of courts to resolve issues of conflicts in cases that may come before them is not to be confused with the powers that the legislatures confer on law societies to establish regulations for their members, who form a self-governing profession: *MacDonald Estate v. Martin*, [1990] S.C.J. No. 41, [1990] 3 S.C.R. 1235, at 1244 (S.C.C.). The purpose of law society regulation is to establish general rules applicable to all members to ensure ethical conduct, protect the public and discipline lawyers who breach the rules — in short, the good governance of the profession.

Both the courts and law societies are involved in resolving issues relating to conflicts of interest — the courts from the perspective of the proper administration of justice, the law societies from the perspective of good governance of the profession: see *R. v. Cunningham*, [2010] S.C.J. No. 10, 2010 SCC 10, [2010] 1 S.C.R. 331 (S.C.C.). In exercising their respective powers, each may properly have regard for the other's views. Yet each must discharge its unique role. Law societies are not prevented from adopting stricter rules than those applied by the courts in their supervisory role. Nor are courts in their supervisory role bound by the letter of law society rules, although "an expression of a professional standard in a code of ethics . . . should be considered an important statement of public policy": *Martin*, at 1246.

In recent years, the Canadian Bar Association and the Federation of Law Societies of Canada have worked toward common conflict rules applicable across Canada. However, they have been unable to agree on their precise form: see, for example, A. Dodek, "Conflicted Identities: The Battle over the Duty of Loyalty in Canada" (2011), 14 Legal Ethics 193. That debate was transported into the proceedings before us, each of these interveners asking this Court to endorse their approach.

275

While the court is properly informed by views put forward, the role of this Court is not to mediate the debate. Ours is the more modest task of determining which principles should apply in a case such as this, from the perspective of what is required for the proper administration of justice.

Against this backdrop, I now turn to examine the principles that govern this appeal.

B. The Governing Principles

A lawyer, and by extension a law firm, owes a duty of loyalty to clients. This duty has three salient dimensions: (1) a duty to avoid conflicting interests; (2) a duty of commitment to the client's cause; and (3) a duty of candour: *Neil*, at para. 19. I will consider each in turn.

1. Avoiding Conflicts of Interest

(a) English Origins

Canada's law of conflicts as administered by the courts is based on precedents rooted in the English jurisprudence. Traditionally, the main concern was that clients not suffer prejudice from a lawyer's representation — at the same time or sequentially — of parties adverse in interest. Disqualification of a lawyer from a case was reserved for situations where there was a real risk of harm to the client, as opposed to a theoretical possibility of harm. . .

(b) The *Martin* Test: A Focus on Risk of Prejudice and Balancing of Values

In the *Martin* case, this Court (*per* Sopinka J.) adopted the English common law's focus on protecting the client from real risks of harm, although it diverged from some of the English case law with respect to the exact level of risk that should attract the conflicts rule. The issue in *Martin* was whether a law firm should be disqualified from acting against a party because a lawyer in the firm had received relevant confidential information in the course of her prior work for that party. As will be discussed further below, the Court held that a firm cannot be disqualified unless there is a risk of prejudice to the client, although in some cases the client benefits from a presumption of risk of prejudice: pp. 1260-61.

In addition to retaining an emphasis on risk of prejudice to the client, the Court concluded in *Martin* that an effective and fair conflicts rule must strike an appropriate balance between conflicting values. On the one hand stands the high repute of the legal profession and the administration of justice. On the other hand stand the values of allowing the client's choice of counsel and permitting reasonable mobility in the legal profession. The realities of large law firms and litigants who pick and choose between them must be factored into the balance. As was the case in the English common law, the Court declined to endorse broad rules that are not context-sensitive.

(c) Types of Prejudice Addressed by Conflict of Interest Rules

The law of conflicts is mainly concerned with two types of prejudice: prejudice as a result of the lawyer's misuse of confidential information obtained from a client; and prejudice arising where the lawyer "soft peddles" his representation of a client in order to serve his own interests, those of another client, or those of a third person. As regards these concerns, the law distinguishes between former clients and current clients. The lawyer's main duty to a former client is to refrain from misusing confidential information. With respect to a current client, for whom representation is ongoing, the lawyer must neither misuse confidential information, nor place himself in a situation that jeopardizes effective representation. I will examine each of these aspects of the conflicts rule in turn.

(d) Confidential Information

The first major concern addressed by the duty to avoid conflicting interests is the misuse of confidential information. The duty to avoid conflicts reinforces the lawyer's duty of confidentiality — which is a distinct duty — by preventing situations that carry a heightened risk of a breach of confidentiality. A lawyer cannot act in a matter where he may use confidential information obtained from a former or current client to the detriment of that client. A two-part test is applied to determine whether the new matter will place the lawyer in a conflict of interest: (1) Did the lawyer receive confidential information attributable to a solicitor and client relationship relevant to the matter at hand? (2) Is there a risk that it will be used to the prejudice of that client?: *Martin*, at 1260. If the lawyer's new retainer is "sufficiently related" to the matters on which he or she worked for the former client, a rebuttable presumption arises that the lawyer possesses confidential information that raises a risk of prejudice: p. 1260.

(e) Effective Representation

The second main concern, which arises with respect to current clients, is that the lawyer be an effective representative — that he serve as a zealous advocate for the interests of his client. The lawyer must refrain "from being in a position where it will be systematically unclear whether he performed his fiduciary duty to act in what he perceived to be the best interests" of his client: D. W.M. Waters, M.R. Gillen and L.D. Smith, eds., *Waters' Law of Trusts in Canada* (4th ed. 2012), at p. 968. As the oft-cited Lord Brougham said, "an advocate, in the discharge of his duty, knows but one person in all the world, and that person is his client": Trial of Queen Caroline (1821), by J. Nightingale, vol. II, The Defence, Part I, at p. 8.

Effective representation may be threatened in situations where the lawyer is tempted to prefer other interests over those of his client: the lawyer's own interests, those of a current client, of a former client, or of a third person: Neil, at para. 31. This appeal concerns the risk to effective representation that arises when a lawyer acts concurrently in different matters for clients whose immediate interests in those matters are directly adverse. This Court has held that concurrent representation of clients directly adverse in interest attracts a clear prohibition: the bright line rule.

(f) The Bright Line Rule

In *Neil*, this Court (*per* Binnie J.) stated that a lawyer may not represent a client in one matter while representing that client's adversary in another matter, unless both clients provide their informed consent. Binnie J. articulated the rule thus:

> The bright line is provided by the general rule that a lawyer may not represent one client whose interests are directly adverse to the immediate interests of another current client — even if the two mandates are unrelated — unless both clients consent after receiving full disclosure (and preferably independent legal advice), and the lawyer reasonably believes that he or she is able to represent each client

without adversely affecting the other. [Emphasis in original] (*Neil*, at para. 29)

The rule expressly applies to both related and unrelated matters. It is possible to argue that a blanket prohibition against concurrent representation is not warranted with respect to unrelated matters, where the concrete duties owed by the lawyer to each client may not actually enter into conflict. However, the rule provides a number of advantages. It is clear. It recognizes that it is difficult — often impossible — for a lawyer or law firm to neatly compartmentalize the interests of different clients when those interests are fundamentally adverse. Finally, it reflects the fact that the lawyer-client relationship is a relationship based on trust. The reality is that "the client's faith in the lawyer's loyalty to the client's interests will be severely tried whenever the lawyer must be loyal to another client whose interests are materially adverse": *Restatement of the Law Third: The Law Governing Lawyers* (2000), vol. 2, s. 128(2), at 339.

The parties and interveners to this appeal disagreed over the substance of the bright line rule. It was variously suggested that the bright line rule is only a rebuttable presumption of conflict, that it does not apply to unrelated matters, and that it attracts a balancing of various circumstantial factors that may give rise to a conflict. These suggestions must be rejected. Where applicable, the bright line rule prohibits concurrent representation. It does not invite further considerations. As Binnie J. stated in *Strother v. 3464920 Canada Inc.*, 2007 SCC 24, [2007] 2 S.C.R. 177, "[t]he 'bright line' rule is the product of the balancing of interests not the gateway to further internal balancing": para. 51. To turn the rule into a rebuttable presumption or a balancing exercise would be tantamount to overruling *Neil* and *Strother*. I am not persuaded that it would be appropriate here to depart from the rule of precedent.

However, the bright line rule is not a rule of unlimited application. The real issue raised by this appeal is the scope of the rule. I now turn to this issue.

(g) The Scope of the Bright Line Rule

The bright line rule holds that a law firm cannot act for a client whose interests are adverse to those of another existing client, unless both clients consent. It applies regardless of whether the client matters are related or unrelated. The rule is based on "the inescapable conflict of interest which is inherent" in some situations of concurrent representation: *Bolkiah v. KPMG*, [1999] 2 A.C. 222 (H.L.), at p. 235, cited in *Neil*, at para. 27. It reflects the essence of the fiduciary's duty of loyalty: ". . . a fiduciary cannot act at the same time both for and against the same client, and his firm is in no better position": *Bolkiah*, at p. 234.

However, *Neil* and *Strother* make it clear that the scope of the rule is not unlimited. The rule applies where the immediate legal interests of clients are directly adverse. It does not apply to condone tactical abuses. And it does not apply in circumstances where it is unreasonable to expect that the lawyer will not concurrently represent adverse parties in unrelated legal matters. The limited scope of application of the rule is illustrated by *Neil* and *Strother*. This Court found the bright line rule to be inapplicable to the facts of both of those cases, and instead examined whether there was a substantial risk of impaired representation: *Neil*, at para. 31; *Strother*, at para. 54.

First, the bright line rule applies only where the immediate interests of clients are directly adverse in the matters on which the lawyer is acting. In *Neil*, a law firm was concurrently representing Mr. Neil in criminal proceedings and Ms. Lambert in divorce proceedings, when it was foreseeable that Lambert would eventually become Neil's co-accused in the criminal proceedings. The lawyer representing Lambert in the divorce proceedings began to gather information that he could eventually use against Neil. The law firm also encouraged another one of its clients, Mr. Doblanko, to report criminal actions by Neil to the police. The goal was to mount a "cut-throat" defence for Lambert in the criminal case, painting her as an innocent dupe who had been manipulated by Neil.

This Court did not apply the bright line rule to the facts in *Neil*, because of the nature of the conflict. Neither Neil and Lambert, nor Neil and Doblanko, were directly adverse to one another in the legal matters on which the law firm represented them. Neil was not a party to Lambert's divorce, nor to any action in which Doblanko was involved. The adversity of interests was indirect: it stemmed from the strategic linkage between the matters, rather than from Neil being directly pitted against Lambert or Doblanko in either of the matters.

Second, the bright line rule applies only when clients are adverse in legal interest. The main area of application of the bright line rule is in civil and criminal proceedings. *Neil* and *Strother* illustrate this limitation. The interests in *Neil* were not legal, but rather strategic. In *Strother*, they were commercial:

> . . . the conflict of interest principles do not generally preclude a law firm or lawyer from acting concurrently for different clients who are in the same line of business, or who compete with each other for business. . .

> The clients' respective "interests" that require the protection of the duty of loyalty have to do with the practice of law, not commercial prosperity. Here the alleged "adversity" between concurrent clients related to business matters. [paras. 54-55, *per* Binnie J.]

Third, the bright line rule cannot be successfully raised by a party who seeks to abuse it. In some circumstances, a party may seek to rely on the bright line rule in a manner that is "tactical rather than principled": *Neil*, at para. 28. The possibility of tactical abuse is especially high in the case of institutional clients dealing with large national law firms. Indeed, institutional clients have the resources to retain a significant number of firms, and the retention of a single partner in any Canadian city can disqualify all other lawyers within the firm nation-wide from acting against that client. As Binnie J. remarked,

> In an era of national firms and a rising turnover of lawyers, especially at the less senior levels, the imposition of exaggerated and unnecessary client loyalty demands, spread across many offices and lawyers who in fact have no knowledge whatsoever of the client or its particular affairs, may promote form at the expense of substance, and tactical advantage instead of legitimate protection. [Emphasis added] (*Neil*, at para. 15)

Thus, clients who intentionally create situations that will engage the bright line rule, as a means of depriving adversaries of their choice of counsel, forfeit the benefit of the rule. Indeed, institutional clients should not spread their retainers among scores of leading law firms in a purposeful attempt to create potential conflicts.

Finally, the bright line rule does not apply in circumstances where it is unreasonable for a client to expect that its law firm will not act against it in unrelated matters. In *Neil*, Binnie J. gave the example of "professional litigants" whose consent to concurrent representation of adverse legal interests can be inferred:

> In exceptional cases, consent of the client may be inferred. For example, governments generally accept that private practitioners who do their civil or criminal work will act against them in unrelated matters, and a contrary position in a particular case may, depending on the circumstances, be seen as tactical rather than principled. Chartered banks and entities that could be described as professional litigants may have a similarly broad-minded attitude where the matters are sufficiently unrelated that there is no danger of confidential information being abused. These exceptional cases are explained by the notion of informed consent, express or implied. [para. 28]

In some cases, it is simply not reasonable for a client to claim that it expected a law firm to owe it exclusive loyalty and to refrain from acting against it in unrelated matters. As Binnie J. stated in Neil, these cases are the exception, rather than the norm. Factors such as the nature of the relationship between the law firm and the client, the terms of the retainer, as well as the types of matters involved, may be relevant to consider when determining whether there was a reasonable expectation that the law firm would not act against the client in unrelated matters. Ultimately, courts must conduct a case-by-case assessment, and set aside the bright line rule when it appears that a client could not reasonably expect its application.

(h) The Substantial Risk Principle

When a situation falls outside the scope of the bright line rule for any of the reasons discussed above, the question becomes whether the concurrent representation of clients creates a substantial risk that the lawyer's representation of the client would be materially and adversely affected. The determination of whether there exists a conflict becomes more contextual, and looks to whether the situation is "liable to create conflicting pressures on judgment" as a result of "the presence of factors which may reasonably be perceived as affecting judgment": Waters, Gillen and Smith, at 968. In addition, the onus falls upon the client to establish, on a balance of probabilities, the existence of a conflict — there is only a deemed conflict of interest if the bright line rule applies.

(i) Practical Implications

When a law firm is asked to act against an existing client on an unrelated matter, it must determine whether accepting the retainer will breach the bright line rule. It must ask itself whether (i) the immediate legal interests of the new client are directly adverse to those of the existing client, (ii) the existing client has sought to exploit the bright line rule in a tactical manner; and (iii) the existing client can reasonably expect that the law firm will not act against it in unrelated matters. In most cases, simultaneously acting for and against a client in legal matters will result in a breach of the bright line rule, with the result that the law firm cannot accept the new retainer unless the clients involved grant their informed consent.

If the law firm concludes that the bright line rule is inapplicable, it must then ask itself whether accepting the new retainer will create a substantial risk of impaired representation. If the answer is no, then the law firm may accept the retainer. In the event that the existing client disagrees with the law firm's assessment, the client may bring a motion before the courts to prevent the firm from continuing to represent the adverse party. In this manner, the courts will be called upon to further develop the contours of the bright line rule, and to ensure that lawyers do not act in matters where they cannot exercise their professional judgment free of conflicting pressures.

(j) Summary

The bright line rule is precisely what its name implies: a bright line rule. It cannot be rebutted or otherwise attenuated. It applies to concurrent representation in both related and unrelated matters. However, the rule is limited in scope. It applies only where the immediate interests of clients are directly adverse in the matters on which the lawyer is acting. It applies only to legal — as opposed to commercial or strategic — interests. It cannot be raised tactically. And it does not apply in circumstances where it is unreasonable for a client to expect that a law firm will not act against it in unrelated matters. If a situation falls outside the scope of the rule, the applicable test is whether there is a substantial risk that the lawyer's representation of the client would be materially and adversely affected.

I now turn to the other dimensions of the duty of loyalty which are relevant to the present appeal.

2. The Duty of Commitment to the Client's Cause

The duty of commitment is closely-related to the duty to avoid conflicting interests. In fact, the lawyer must avoid conflicting interests precisely so that he can remain committed to the client. Together, these duties ensure that "a divided loyalty does not cause the lawyer to 'soft peddle' his or her representation "of a client out of concern for another client": *Neil*, at para. 19.

The duty of commitment prevents the lawyer from undermining the lawyer-client relationship. As a general rule, a lawyer or law firm should not summarily and unexpectedly drop a client simply in order to avoid conflicts of interest with existing or future clients. This is subject to law society rules, which may, for example, allow law firms to end their involvement in a case under the terms of a limited scope retainer. . .

3. The Duty of Candour

A lawyer or law firm owes a duty of candour to the client. This requires the law firm to disclose any factors relevant to the lawyer's ability to provide effective representation. As Binnie J. stated in *Strother*, at para. 55: "The thing the lawyer must not do is keep the client in the dark about matters he or she knows to be relevant to the retainer." (Emphasis deleted)

It follows that as a general rule a lawyer should advise an existing client before accepting a retainer that will require him to act against the client, even if he considers the situation to fall outside the scope of the bright line rule. At the very least, the existing client may feel that the personal relationship with the lawyer has been damaged and may wish to take its business elsewhere.

I add this. The lawyer's duty of candour towards the existing client must be reconciled with the lawyer's obligation of confidentiality towards his new client. In order to provide full disclosure to the existing client, the lawyer must first obtain the consent of the new client to disclose the existence, nature and scope of the new retainer. If the new client refuses to grant this consent, the lawyer will be unable to fulfil his duty of candour and, consequently, must decline to act for the new client.

C. Application of the Principles

All three of the duties that flow from the lawyer's duty of loyalty are engaged in this case: the duty to avoid conflicting interests; the duty of commitment to the client's cause; and the duty of candour to the client. I will deal with each in turn.

1. Duty to Avoid Conflicting Interests

The question here is whether McKercher's concurrent representation of CN and Wallace fell within the scope of the bright line rule. I conclude that it did.

The bright line rule prevents the concurrent representation of clients whose immediate legal interests are directly adverse, subject to the limitations discussed in these reasons. The fact that the Wallace and CN retainers were legally and factually unrelated does not prevent the application of the bright line rule.

Here, the bright line rule is applicable. The immediate interests of CN and Wallace were directly adverse, and those interests were legal in nature. Indeed, McKercher helped Wallace bring a class action directly against CN. In addition, there is no evidence on the record that CN is seeking to use the bright line rule tactically. Nothing suggests that CN has been purposefully spreading out its legal work across Saskatchewan law firms in an attempt to prevent Wallace or other litigants from retaining effective legal counsel. The motion judge accepted the testimony of CN's general counsel and concluded that CN was acting "on a principled basis, and not merely for tactical reasons": para. 62. I find no palpable and overriding error in this conclusion.

Finally, it was reasonable in these circumstances for CN to expect that McKercher would not act for Wallace. I agree with the motion judge's findings on this point:

> The solicitor and client had a longstanding relationship. CN used the McKercher Firm as the "go to" firm. Although there were at least two other firms in Saskatchewan that also did CN's legal work, I accept the testimony of Mr. Chouc, that the McKercher Firm was its primary firm within this province. . . . The lawsuit commenced seeks huge damages against CN and alleges both aggravated and punitive damages, which connote a degree of moral turpitude on the part of CN. Simply put, it is hard to imagine a situation that would strike more deeply at the loyalty component of the solicitor-client relationship. [para. 56]

In other words, it was reasonable for CN to be surprised and dismayed when its primary legal counsel in the province of Saskatchewan sued it for $1.75 billion.

Consequently, the facts of this appeal fall within the scope of the bright line rule. McKercher breached the rule, and by extension its duty to avoid conflicting interests, when it accepted to represent Wallace without first obtaining CN's informed consent.

However, I cannot agree that this is a situation where there also exists a risk of misuse of confidential information. CN's contention that McKercher obtained confidential information that might assist it on the Wallace matter — namely, a general understanding of CN's litigation philosophy — does not withstand scrutiny.

"[M]erely . . . making a bald assertion that the past relationship has provided the solicitor with access to . . . litigation philosophy" does not suffice: *Moffat v. Wetstein* (1996), 29 O.R. (3d) 371 (Gen. Div.), at p. 401. "There is a distinction between possessing information that is relevant to the matter at issue and having an understanding of the corporate philosophy" of a previous client: *Canadian Pacific Railway v. Aikins, MacAulay & Thorvaldson* (1998), 23 C.P.C. (4th) 55 (Man. C.A.), at para. 26. The information must be capable of being used against the client in some tangible manner. In the present case, the real estate, insolvency, and personal injury files on which McKercher worked were entirely unrelated to the Wallace action, and CN has failed to show how they or other matters on which McKercher acted could have yielded relevant confidential information that could be used against it.

2. The Duty of Commitment to the Client's Cause

The duty of commitment to the client's cause suggests that a law firm should not summarily and unexpectedly terminate a retainer as a means of circumventing conflict of interest rules. The McKercher firm had committed itself to act loyally for CN on the personal injury, real estate and receivership matters. McKercher was bound to complete those retainers, unless the client discharged it or acted in a way that gave McKercher cause to terminate the retainers. McKercher breached its duty of commitment to CN's causes when it terminated its retainer with CN on two of these files. It is clear that a law firm cannot terminate a client relationship purely in an attempt to circumvent its duty of loyalty to that client. . .

The conclusion on this point is supported by the obligation imposed on McKercher by its Law Society that it not withdraw its services from a client without good cause and appropriate notice: see the ethical rules applicable at the relevant time, Law Society of Saskatchewan Code of Professional Conduct (1991), chapter XII, at p. 47. The desire to accept a new, potentially lucrative client did not provide good cause to withdraw services from CN.

3. The Duty of Candour

The McKercher firm breached its duty of candour to CN by failing to disclose to CN its intention to accept the Wallace retainer.

It bears repeating: a lawyer must not "keep the client in the dark about matters he or she knows to be relevant to the retainer": Strother, at para. 55. As discussed, this rule must be broadly construed to give the client an opportunity to judge for itself whether the proposed concurrent representation risks prejudicing its interests and if so, to take appropriate action.

CN should have been given the opportunity to assess McKercher's intention to represent Wallace and to make an appropriate decision in response — whether to terminate its existing retainers, continue those retainers, or take other action. Instead, CN only learned that it was being sued by its own lawyer when it received a statement of claim. This is precisely the type of situation that the duty of candour is meant to prevent.

D. The Remedy

I have concluded that accepting the Wallace retainer placed McKercher in a conflict of interest, and that McKercher breached its duties of commitment and candour to

CN. The question is whether McKercher should be disqualified from representing the Wallace plaintiffs because its acceptance of the Wallace retainer breached the duty of loyalty it owed CN.

As discussed, the courts in the exercise of their supervisory jurisdiction over the administration of justice in the courts have inherent jurisdiction to remove law firms from pending litigation. Disqualification may be required: (1) to avoid the risk of improper use of confidential information; (2) to avoid the risk of impaired representation; and/or (3) to maintain the repute of the administration of justice.

Where there is a need to prevent misuse of confidential information, as set out in Martin, disqualification is generally the only appropriate remedy, subject to the use of mechanisms that alleviate this risk as permitted by law society rules. Similarly, where the concern is risk of impaired representation as set out in these reasons, disqualification will normally be required if the law firm continues to concurrently act for both clients.

The third purpose that may be served by disqualification is to protect the integrity and repute of the administration of justice. Disqualification may be required to send a message that the disloyal conduct involved in the law firm's breach is not condoned by the courts, thereby protecting public confidence in lawyers and deterring other law firms from similar practices.

In assessing whether disqualification is required on this ground alone, all relevant circumstances should be considered. On the one hand, acting for a client in breach of the bright line rule is always a serious matter that on its face supports disqualification. The termination of the client retainers — whether through lawyer withdrawal or through a client firing his lawyer after learning of a breach — does not necessarily suffice to remove all concerns that the lawyer's conduct has harmed the repute of the administration of justice.

On the other hand, it must be acknowledged that in circumstances where the lawyer-client relationship has been terminated and there is no risk of misuse of confidential information, there is generally no longer a concern of ongoing prejudice to the complaining party. In light of this reality, courts faced with a motion for disqualification on this third ground should consider certain factors that may point the other way. Such factors may include: (i) behaviour disentitling the complaining party from seeking the removal of counsel, such as delay in bringing the motion for disqualification; (ii) significant prejudice to the new client's interest in retaining its counsel of choice, and that party's ability to retain new counsel; and (iii) the fact that the law firm accepted the conflicting retainer in good faith, reasonably believing that the concurrent representation fell beyond the scope of the bright line rule and applicable law society restrictions.

Against this background, I return to this appeal. The motion judge concluded that the appropriate remedy was to disqualify McKercher from the *Wallace* action. He based this conclusion on a variety of factors — in particular, he focused on what he perceived to be CN's justified sense of betrayal, the impairment of McKercher's ability to continue to represent CN on the ongoing retainers, and the risk of misuse of confidential information. Some of these considerations were not relevant. Here, disqualification is not required to prevent the misuse of confidential information.

Nor is it required to avoid the risk of impaired representation. Indeed, the termination of the CN retainers that McKercher was working on ended the representation. The only question, therefore, is whether disqualification is required to maintain public confidence in the justice system.

As discussed, a violation of the bright line rule on its face supports disqualification, even where the lawyer-client relationship has been terminated as a result of the breach. However, it is also necessary to weigh the factors identified above, which may suggest that disqualification is inappropriate in the circumstances. The motion judge did not have the benefit of these reasons, and obviously could not consider all of the factors just discussed that are relevant to the issue of disqualification. These reasons recast the legal framework for judging McKercher's conduct and determining the appropriate remedy. Fairness suggests that the issue of remedy should be remitted to the court for consideration in accordance with them.

IV. Conclusion

I would allow the appeal and remit the matter to the Queen's Bench to be decided in accordance with these reasons. I would award costs to the appellant, CN.

NOTES AND QUESTIONS

1. You will recall the deference shown by the Supreme Court of Canada to the Canadian Bar Association and law societies in relation to the prospective resolution of conflicts of interest like the one that arose in *MacDonald Estate*. As noted, in this case both the Federation of Law Societies of Canada and the Canadian Bar Association intervened to advance competing interpretations of *Neil* and different views about the scope of the 'bright line rule'. In its judgment the Court is moderately critical of the contested views of the CBA and the Federation. Why did the Court opt to comment on this aspect of the case? What if anything does it tell you about the relevance of "an expression of a professional standard in a code of ethics . . . should be considered an important statement of public policy" - in the process of judicial decision-making. Is this an accurate characterization of the legal significance of law society Codes of Professional Conduct?

2. In the Court of Queen's Bench, Popescul J. (as he then was) found that the law firm's possession of information related to CN's negotiation and settlement strategies constituted confidential information. Do you agree with the Court's interpretation that this is not relevant confidential information relevant to the law firm's representation of Wallace against CN? Given that there was no compromise of confidential information in the case, but the Court finds that McKercher breached its duty of loyalty in three different ways, does this not endorse the larger idea – that the duty of loyalty is much broader principle that the mere preservation of client confidences - that Binnie J. was trying to establish in *Neil*?

3. In the Saskatchewan Court of Appeal, Ottenbreit J.A. found CN to be a 'professional litigant', which had impliedly consented to the McKercher law firm acting against it in the class action. Furthermore, CN was disentitled from withdrawing this implied consent. The Supreme Court has

changed this formulation, substituting for it the concept of a client 'unreasonably withholding its consent' to have its law firm act against it in a matter, though it found that CN was not unreasonable in the withholding its consent in the circumstances of the Wallace action against it. Why do you think that the Court introduced the concept of 'unreasonably withholding consent'? Why was CN's withholding of consent 'not unreasonable'? In what circumstances do you think a client's withholding of consent would be unreasonable?

4. The Supreme Court found that the McKercher law firm had violated three aspects of the duty of loyalty. In "Three Strikes and You're Out . . . . Or Maybe Not: A Comment on *Canadian National Railway Co. v. McKercher*",[10] Brent Cotter and Richard Devlin review the Court's findings. They note the finding that the law firm breached three aspects of the duty of loyalty and express 'concern' that the law firm was not disqualified by the Court from continuing its representation of Wallace. Why was the matter referred back to the trial court for a determination? Was this appropriate in the circumstances?[11]

5. In "Of Lodestars and Lawyers: Incorporating the Duty of Loyalty into the Model Code of Conduct"[12], Colin Jackson, Brent Cotter and Richard Devlin argue that a central message from *Wallace,* reinforced by the Supreme Court's decision in *Federation of Law Societies of Canada v. Canada,* (discussed in Chapter 3) is that the key organizing principle for lawyer's ethical and legal duties is loyalty to the client. Do you agree? If loyalty to client is the lawyer's central orientation, are other orientations (such as justice or integrity, discussed in Chapter 1) liable to be diminished? Is this a good or bad thing?

6. *McKercher* was relied upon in *Federation of Law Societies of Canada v. Canada,* as well as in a more recent case, *Salomon v. Matte-Thomson,* [2019] 1S.C.R. 729, 2019 S.C.J. No. 14. Salomon, a lawyer, referred a client, Matte-Thomson, to an investment firm. He recommended the investment as ''an excellent vehicle where security of capital was important.' He repeatedly provided assurances to Matte-Thomson, though without 'due diligence'. As well, the lawyer received, periodically, cash payments from the investment firm. It turned out that the investment firm was operating fraudulently, and Matte-Thomson lost essentially all of her approximately $1,000,000 investment. The Supreme Court relied on *McKercher* in concluding that the lawyer was in a conflict of interest,

---

[10] Brent Cotter & Richard Devlin, "Three Strikes and You're Out . . . Or Maybe Not: A Comment on *Canadian National Railway Co. v. McKercher*" (2013) 92:1 Can. Bar Rev. 1 at 21.

[11] On referral of the matter back to the trial court, the McKercher firm withdrew from its representation of Wallace and Popescul C.J. was not required to decide on the issue of disqualification.

[12] Colin Jackson, Brent Cotter & Richard Devlin, "Of Lodestars and Lawyers: Incorporating the Duty of Loyalty into the Model Code of Conduct" (2016) 39:1 Dal. L.J. 37.

having had a close personal and financial interest in the investment firm and having shared the client's confidential information with the investment firm, including information regarding the client's concerns that her investments were in jeopardy. The Court found that the duty not to 'soft-peddle' the client's interests, and the duty to preserve client confidentiality, components of the duty of loyalty, were violated by the lawyer.

7.   As we saw in *Neil*, the duty to avoid conflicting interests also operates in the context of criminal law. *McKercher* was applied in *R. v. Baharloo* 2017 ONCA 362, 348 CCC (3d) 64. A lawyer was defending one client, Baharloo, and at the same time representing a third party who was also a suspect, though not charged. Given that a defence was available to Baharloo, but not pursued, that would have implicated the third party, the Ontario Court of Appeal concluded that the lawyer had a conflict of interest. The bright line rule and the 'substantial risk' principle were violated, impairing the lawyer's representation of the defendant.

8.   One consequence of this quartet of Supreme Court of Canada cases is that the potential for law firm disqualification is noticeably heightened. One negative consequence is that a lawyer, willing to offer a limited range of legal services or pro bono legal services to clients could, despite the best of intentions, generate a significant and disqualifying conflict for their law firm. Imagine a lawyer offering limited services or pro bono services to a client who, in an unrelated matter, faces a mortgage foreclosure by a lender who is a major client of the lawyer's law firm. Is the law firm disqualified from representing the lender? Would such a consequence discourage lawyers from providing public spirited representation to clients in need? Might law firms discourage, or even prohibit, their lawyers from providing such service? To attempt to address this situation the *Model Code* was amended in the following way.

Short-term Summary Legal Services

3.4-2A   In rules 3.4-2B to 3.4-2D "Short-term summary legal services" means advice or representation to a client under the auspices of a pro bono or not-for-profit legal services provider with the expectation by the lawyer and the client that the lawyer will not provide continuing legal services in the matter.

3.4-2B   A lawyer may provide short-term summary legal services without taking steps to determine whether there is a conflict of interest.

3.4-2C   Except with consent of the clients as provided in rule 3.4-2, a lawyer must not provide, or must cease providing short-term summary legal services to a client where the lawyer knows or becomes aware that there is a conflict of interest.

Commentary

[1]   Short-term summary legal service and duty counsel programs are usually offered in circumstances in which it may be difficult to systematically screen for conflicts of interest in a timely way, despite the best efforts and existing practices and procedures of the not-for-profit legal services provider and the lawyers and law firms who provide these services. Performing a full conflicts screening in circumstances in which the short-term summary services described in these rules are being

offered can be very challenging given the timelines, volume and logistics of the setting in which the services are provided.

[2]   The limited nature of short-term summary legal services significantly reduces the risk of conflicts of interest with other matters being handled by the lawyer's firm. Accordingly, the lawyer is disqualified from acting for a client receiving short-term summary legal services only if the lawyer has actual knowledge of a conflict of interest between the client receiving short-term summary legal services and an existing client of the lawyer or an existing client of the *pro bono* or not-for-profit legal services provider or between the lawyer and the client receiving short-term summary legal services.

[3]   Confidential information obtained by a lawyer providing the services described in Rules 3.42A-2D will not be imputed to the lawyers in the lawyer's firm or to non-lawyer partners or associates in a multi-discipline partnership. . . .

9.   You will have observed that aspects of the *Neil*, *Strother* and *Wallace* decisions acknowledge the possibility of a law firm concurrently representing clients with opposing interests. In what contexts can this occur? Recognizing this, the *Model Code* provides:

Concurrent Representation with protection of confidential client information

3.4-4   Where there is no dispute among the clients about the matter that is the subject of the proposed representation, two or more lawyers in a law firm may act for current clients with competing interests and may treat information received from each client as confidential and not disclose it to the other clients, provided that:

(a)   disclosure of the risks of the lawyers so acting has been made to each client;

(b)   the lawyer recommends each client consents after having received independent legal advice, including on the risks of concurrent representation;

(c)   the clients each determine that it is in their best interests that the lawyers so act; and consent to the concurrent representation;

(d)   each client is represented by a different lawyer in the firm;

(e)   appropriate screening mechanisms are in place to protect confidential information; and

(f)   all lawyers in the law firm withdraw from the representation of all clients in respect of the matter if a dispute that cannot be resolved develops among the clients.

Is this consistent with the leading cases? Is it sufficient to ensure that the lawyers' obligation of loyalty to the respective clients is met?

Scenario One

Lawyers at law firm ABC have been retained to represent Client X in its bid to acquire property in order to undertake a resort condominium development. Shortly thereafter, Client Y approaches a lawyer at the same law firm seeking to have him represent the client in an effort to acquire the same property for the purpose of pursuing an oil exploration project. Under what circumstances, if any, may the law firm accept client Y as a client? How do you work through the analysis of this question, both in terms of the legal and ethical requirements and the dealings with the clients in question?

Scenario Two

In a three-lawyer firm, two lawyers represent separately client A and client B in unrelated refugee (or any other unrelated) matters. Is the third lawyer in the firm barred by the bright line rule from representing client A in a criminal matter in which client A is the accused and client B is the complainant and chief witness for the prosecution? When it comes to lawyers in the same firm representing different persons who are adverse in interest, the bright line rule only applies where the clients are adverse in legal interest . For the purpose of the bright line rule, are the legal interests of the accused and the complainant in a criminal case adverse? Alternatively, does the mere possibility of a civil suit mean their legal interests are adverse? What about the application of the substantial risk principle)

[e]   Former Client Conflicts: Other Issues

As the following sections describe, conflicts of interest can arise in relation to a lawyer or law firm's former clients. *MacDonald Estate* addressed this type of conflict. Codes of conduct do so as well, reflecting the principles set out in *MacDonald Estate* but also the regulatory perspective of the provincial law societies.

The *Model Code*, and the general understanding of lawyers' obligations to clients, identifies a continuing but moderated duty of loyalty to former clients. The *Model Code*, in identifying the scope of this moderated duty of loyalty, also seeks to accommodate the access to legal services. For example, unlike with 'current client conflicts', lawyers are not precluded from acting against former clients in *unrelated* matters.

Essentially, the *Model Code* provisions seek to protect the vulnerability of former clients in two respects. First, lawyers may not act against former clients in matters related to the previous representation. Second, lawyers may not act against former clients when they possess confidential information relevant to the matter, and that was acquired by virtue of the previous representation. Recognizing that even these proscriptions could limit client access to lawyers, particularly in small or remote communities, the *Model Code* also sets out in Rule 3.4-10 and 3.4-11 an additional 'access to justice' exception.

The *Model Code* provides:

Acting Against Former Clients

3.4-10 Unless the former client consents, a lawyer must not act against a former client in:

(a)   the same matter,

(b)   any related matter, or

(c)   any other matter if the lawyer has relevant confidential information arising from the representation of the former client that may prejudice that client.

3.4-11 When a lawyer has acted for a former client and obtained confidential information relevant to a new matter, another lawyer ("the other lawyer") in the lawyer's firm may act in the new matter against the former client if:

    (a)   the former client consents to the other lawyer acting; or

    (b)   the law firm has:

        (i)   taken reasonable measures to ensure that there will be no disclosure of the former client's confidential information by the lawyer to any other lawyer, any other member or employee of the law firm, or any other person whose services the lawyer or the law firm has retained in the new matter; and

        (ii)   advised the lawyer's former client, if requested by the client, of the measures taken.

Are these provisions sufficiently flexible to accommodate meaningful access to legal services? Do they 'water down' the lawyer's duty of loyalty to former clients to too great a degree? For example, we have seen that lawyer client confidentiality is strongly protected in law and in legal ethics. *MacDonald Estate* and *R.* v. *Neil* made it clear that, with rare exceptions, when one lawyer in the firm is in possession of confidential information, that knowledge is imputed to the other lawyers in the firm. Does Rule 3.4-11 put this principle at risk?

Another dimension of the dilemma regarding acting against former clients is the situation that arises when, perfectly legitimately, a lawyer has acted for a group of clients at the same time, either in what are known as joint or concurrent representation and one of that group of clients is a longstanding client of the lawyer. If a falling out or controversy arises, it is common for the longstanding client, and the lawyer as well, to want to continue the representation of that client, one consequence of which could be acting against the other previously represented clients. The *Model Code* sets out the duties of lawyers when acting on behalf of multiple clients [See Rules 3.4-4 and 3-4-5, and related Commentaries]. But is not uncommon for lawyers, often out of misguided loyalty to the longstanding client, to cross the line. Consider and assess the following scenario which raises these issues:

Scenario Three

A lawyer had acted for a longstanding client NW. He was retained to represent NW as well as GA and WW in a renovation project and its financing. He got an oral commitment from GA and WW that they would get alternative representation in the event of a conflict. Issues arose in the project and its financing and the lawyer championed NW's interests in relation to these issues.

As well, after they parted company with the lawyer, GA and WW sued NW in small claims court in relation to alleged deficiencies in the renovations. The lawyer continued the representation of NW. A settlement was negotiated, one part of which released the law firm from any liability.

Did the lawyer cross the line in this matter? If so, what possible sanctions might be imposed on the lawyer? See *Re Suberlak and the Law Society of Alberta*, LSA 2020 HE20200081[13]

[3] LAWYER-CLIENT CONFLICTS

[a] Introduction

While in every lawyer-client relationship there is inherent tension between the interests of the lawyer and those of the client — for example, in the financial success of their law practice — "lawyer-client conflicts" tend to arise in more problematic situations. These conflicts of interest have the potential to undermine the lawyer's ability or perceived ability to represent the client properly. The fundamental question is whether the conflict which has arisen interferes with the lawyer's duty of loyalty to the client or constitutes a substantial risk that the representation of the client's interests will be compromised.

The most obvious example is where a lawyer takes possession of client assets. Lawyers maintain trust accounts to hold clients' money for client needs. They have significant fiduciary obligations to take special care of client assets and to account appropriately for them. Indeed, clients' ability to place a high degree of confidence in lawyers with respect to their financial assets facilitates transactions for clients in many aspects of their lives, from business takeovers to buying a house to settling an account. It is not surprising, therefore, that lawyers who abuse this trust by misappropriating clients' money for their personal use are dealt with harshly by law societies and the courts. Aside from the injury to an individual client, such behaviour damages the reputation of the legal profession and has the potential to compromise the ease with which transactions are facilitated through lawyers.

Troubling conflicts between lawyers and their clients are not, however, limited to financial matters. In some cases they arise where a lawyer is not sufficiently respectful of their client's circumstances and reputation when the lawyer is engaged in other activities, sometimes advancing their own reputation through those activities. Such cases are rarely litigated, but *Stewart v. CBC*, set out below, is such a case.

Lawyer-client conflicts can also arise in the context of personal relationships that may develop between a lawyer and their client. We have already seen a few of these situations. Recall *Szarfer v. Chodos*[14], a case that we considered in Chapter 1. In that case Chodos had an affair with his client's wife and was sued by the client in negligence and for breach of fiduciary obligation for the harm he suffered. This case on the surface is a case of professional negligence. But at its centre was the conflict between the lawyer's duty to his client and his own selfish interests. In rare cases the matter may come before a court. More often these cases arise in the context of law society discipline proceedings against the lawyer for professional misconduct. These proceedings may lead to sanctions that jeopardize the lawyer's career. A close

---

[13] Law Society of Alberta, "Anton Suberlak" (December 11, 2020), online (pdf): *Law Society of Alberta* https://documents.lawsociety.ab.ca/wp-content/uploads/2020/12/18163328/Suberlak-Anton-HE20200081-Order-Public.pdf.

[14] *Szarfer v. Chodos*, [1986] O.J. No. 256, 54 O.R. (2d) 663 (Ont. H.C.J.).

parallel to *Szarfer v. Chodos*, and perhaps a more egregious failure by a lawyer, is *Law Society of Upper Canada v. Daboll*[15]. In *Daboll*, a lawyer while representing a client in a family law matter, became romantically and sexually involved with his client's wife.

One of those types of cases, *Law Society of Upper Canada v. Hunter*, is excerpted below. When reading it consider the nexus between the sexual relationship and the lawyer's ability to be loyal to their client as required by cases such as *Neil*, the obligation to act consistently with the duty of integrity, and the duty to ensure the proper administration of justice. Is loyalty the only ethical obligation undermined by this conflict, or are other ethical obligations or values also at play? In what ways?

Another problematic situation can arise when a lawyer's financial interests become intertwined with the financial interests of a client. Law societies have put in place strict rules to guide lawyers and provide protection for clients. Nevertheless, as some lawyer discipline cases at the end of this chapter highlight, it is not uncommon for lawyers, as a result of self-interest or bad judgment, to 'cross the line'. The question of whether a lawyer's involvement in this sort of problematic behaviour "crosses the line" is addressed in the following excerpts.

STEWART v. CANADIAN BROADCASTING CORP.

[1997] O.J. No. 2271, 150 D.L.R. (4th) 24

(Gen. Div., J. Macdonald J.)

[This case involves a claim by Stewart, a former client of Edward Greenspan, a prominent criminal defence lawyer. Stewart had retained Greenspan to represent him on his sentencing, after Stewart had been convicted of criminal negligence causing death. The case was gruesome. An intoxicated Stewart had run over Judy Jordan and dragged her beneath his car for a considerable distance. His counsel at trial presented a number of defences suggesting that unknown others were responsible for her death and in the course of doing so sought to impugn Jordan's reputation. These defences were unsuccessful and, given the notoriety of the case, placed Stewart in a bad light among the public. At the sentencing, Greenspan did excellent work in rehabilitating Steward, including distancing him from his trial counsel's tactics and arranging for Stewart to make a public apology, with the hope and expectation that it would assist in sentencing and in Stewart's return to society after having served his sentence. Stewart was sentenced to three years imprisonment.

A decade later the Canadian television program, Scales of Justice, presented a re-enactment of Stewart's case as one of its episodes. The show was broadcast by the Canadian Broadcasting Corporation (CBC). Greenspan was, with George Jonas, co-creator of the television program and played a role in development of the Stewart episode. Stewart was of the view that the ways in which he was depicted in the episode damaged his reputation, and that Greenspan had violated duties owed to Stewart as his former lawyer in participating in the episode and allowing Stewart to

---

[15] *Law Society of Upper Canada v. Daboll*, [2006] L.S.D.D. No. 82, 2006 ONLSHP 79 (L.S.U.C.).

be portrayed in inaccurate ways. He sued Greenspan, the company that produced the show and the CBC. The violations alleged against Greenspan included breaches of contract, breach of the duty of confidentiality and breach of fiduciary duties.

The judge dismissed against the CBC. The judge also dismissed, in emphatic terms, the aspect of Stewart's claim that Greenspan had made use of confidential information obtained from Stewart in his contributions to the episode.]

J. MACDONALD J.: —

. . . . .

b) Mr. Greenspan's role in scripting the broadcast.

Draft scripts for the television broadcast prepared by Messrs. Tait and Jonas were forwarded to Mr. Greenspan for his review.

. . . . .

As a result, according to Messrs. Greenspan and Jonas, Mr. Greenspan succeeded in moderating some aspects of the portrayal of Mr. Stewart, his crime and his trial. For example, Mr. Greenspan's intervention caused the deletion of a reference to the "bizarre callousness" of Mr. Stewart's crime, and the substitution of a reference to Mr. Stewart's conviction. Mr. Greenspan also intervened during filming because he found that the portrayal of Mr. Stewart on his arrival home, minutes after running over Mrs. Jordan, created a strong impression of guilt. The scene was therefore changed to give a different visual impression.

I find there is compelling evidence which proves the assertions that Mr. Greenspan had substantial control over script contents. Mr. Greenspan's impact upon the way in which Mr. Stewart's first counsel was depicted demonstrates the ability he had to determine the script contents which would be broadcast.

. . . . .

[A]t no point in the broadcast was it mentioned that Mr. Stewart was not complicit in these unsavoury actions by his counsel, that he had apologized publicly for these actions or that [the judge in the criminal trial] had accepted Mr. Stewart's apology as genuine, by relying on it in his reasons for sentence. In my opinion, explaining counsel's excesses and describing the benefit which Mr. Stewart could obtain from them without any reference to Mr. Stewart's lack of complicity in these unsavoury tactics and his genuine apology for them was neither sympathetic nor fair to Mr. Stewart.

. . . . .

In 1979, Mr. Greenspan knew that a significant part of the negative public perceptions of Mr. Stewart resulted from media reports about his first counsel's trial tactics. He knew that Mr. Stewart was seen as involved in what counsel did in his name. Mr. Greenspan therefore took steps to protect Mr. Stewart from those perceptions. Mr. Greenspan spoke to the public objectives of sentencing. He also spoke during sentencing to his objective of protecting Mr. Stewart from the effects of public revulsion in the post-sentencing period. In 1991, as part of the media, Mr. Greenspan left out of this nationally broadcast portrayal of his former client and his case the very things he had put before the public in 1979, as Mr. Stewart's counsel, to guard against public revulsion and repercussions in the years to come.

. . . . .

In addition, I find that Mr. Greenspan's narration exaggerated the distance that Mrs. Jordan was dragged screaming, and thereby exaggerated the length of time that Mr. Stewart drove on knowing that a living human being was in agony beneath his vehicle. In this fashion, Mr. Greenspan's narration portrayed his former client's conduct more negatively than the court had found it to be.

. . . . .

Mr. Stewart's Position Respecting the Broadcast

. . . . .

Mr. Stewart became aware of Scales' intentions when fliers explaining their filming in the area of 6010 Bathurst Street came to his attention.

. . . . .

I find as follows. On June 14, 1991, one week before filming or recording of Mr. Greenspan's role in the broadcast began, Mr. Stewart told Mr. Greenspan that he objected to the broadcast in issue. The precise nature of his objections is determined most reliably by the contents of his letter June 17, 1991. . . . I find that Mr. Greenspan was told on June 14, 1991 that Mr. Stewart objected to any portrayal of the conduct for which he had been found guilty of criminal negligence causing death.

. . . . .

. . . . Mr. Greenspan considered withdrawing from the production and broadcast after speaking with Mr. Stewart, to avoid a headache. However, he concluded that Mr. Stewart's lack of consent and objections posed no problem for him. He testified that he wanted to do this program because of its educational value.

If Mr. Greenspan Had Refrained From Any Involvement

. . . I find that if he had withdrawn, Mr. Jonas probably would have found another lawyer to appear on screen as host/narrator.

. . . . .

This leads to an important point. The Scales of Justice concept was educational. . . . I find that the educational content of the *Regina v. Stewart* broadcast was fully independent of Mr. Greenspan because, if Mr. Greenspan had chosen to refrain from participation, the educational content of any broadcast of Mr. Stewart's crime and trial was nonetheless assured.

. . . . .

[T]hen the small script changes for Mr. Stewart's benefit upon which Mr. Greenspan places such heavy reliance may not have been included. However, I find them to be of very little significance in terms of the overall portrayal of Mr. Stewart and his conduct which was broadcast with Mr. Greenspan's participation.

Mr. Greenspan's Loyalty to Former Counsel.

The decency and civility which are apparent in the way Mr. Greenspan portrayed former counsel are a form of loyalty to a fellow professional and to ideals based on respect for personal dignity and reputation. Mr. Greenspan chose to give that to former counsel. He could have given his former client similar benefits and protections in the broadcast, of the type I have addressed. This leads to the central questions. Did Mr. Greenspan owe a duty of loyalty to his former client in the circumstances which existed in 1991? What are the nature and extent of any such duty? Are his involvement in this broadcast and the omissions and the exaggeration in the portrayal of his former client breaches of a duty of loyalty which Mr. Greenspan owed? I will begin my analysis by considering the role of counsel.

The Role of Counsel

. . . . .

(d) The Duties of Former Counsel.

(i) The evidence of Messrs. Greenspan and Sandler.

In considering the question of post-retainer obligations to Mr. Stewart resting on Mr. Greenspan, I return to the evidence of both Mr. Greenspan and Mr. Mark Sandler that counsel has the discretion to publicize information in the public domain respecting the case of a former client, barring contractual constraint upon such conduct.

. . . . .

I accept that there is an important benefit to society in knowing about cases before the courts, as Mr. Sandler testified. However, I reject his conclusion that counsel have the right to refer publicly to any non-confidential information respecting former clients and their cases.

. . . . .

I find as follows. Careful, competent and responsible criminal defence counsel should and do take into account the risk of harm to a former client in deciding whether to discuss publicly a former client or the former client's case, when all relevant information is in the public domain. That is because counsel do not wish to injure a former client by public discussion of information. If the former client may be harmed, counsel may well exercise caution and not talk about the former client or the case. Since the rules of professional conduct are not an exhaustive code of lawyer's professional obligations, and there is no rule or other standard in the profession which invariably prohibits all counsel from any mention of any information in the public domain after any retainer is over, each counsel is in the position of having to decide whether he or she will speak or write publicly about the type of information being considered. However, in my opinion, it does not follow from the need for each counsel to make decisions about his or her professional conduct in these circumstances that such decisions are never subject to legal or equitable principles and are solely personal choices.

. . . . .

[Greenspan argued that the Rules of Professional conduct define the scope of his fiduciary obligations to a former client.]

. . . . .

In my opinion, the rules and commentaries have two limiting features which are significant here:

1. The Law Society Act R.S.O. 1990, c. L. 8 gives the Law Society through Convocation the power to regulate lawyers' conduct. The Act does not give Convocation the power to regulate clients or their rights. In any event, in the rules and commentaries relevant to the issues herein, Convocation has not attempted to regulate clients or their rights.

2. The rules and commentaries are not an all inclusive code governing lawyers' conduct in every circumstance which may arise in professional life. They address only specific issues, and do so in a variety of ways ranging from mandatory to advisory.

[A]s of the broadcast in issue, the regulations made by Convocation did not, by their language, purport to affect the rights or protections which law and equity afford to clients. Consequently, I am of the opinion that both the Law Society Act and the regulations pursuant to it should not be interpreted so as to diminish by implication the rights and protections afforded to clients by law or equity. . . . In my opinion, the intention of the Legislature manifest in the Law Society Act is to regulate the legal profession for the protection of clients. Occasionally, that enhances of [*sic*] client's rights in order to afford greater protection: see for example s. 51 respecting the compensation fund. In my opinion, the Legislature's intention was that Convocation not have the power to diminish or dissolve the legal or equitable rights or protections of clients.

. . . . .

Rule 21

I turn now to rule 21, paragraph 5. It is raised indirectly and partially in the pleading that one way in which Mr. Greenspan breached his fiduciary duty of loyalty to Mr. Stewart was by putting "his own self promotion or self aggrandizement before the interests of the plaintiff". This is an allegation of duty to the former client which conflicted with self interest in the form of self promotion or self aggrandizement. Rule 21, paragraph 5 contains two separate directions, not obligations. First, a public communication should not be used for the purpose of publicizing the lawyer. Second, a public communication should be free from any suggestion that the lawyers' real purpose is self promotion or self aggrandizement.

I find the facts to be as follows. Mr. Greenspan identified himself in the broadcast as Mr. Stewart's counsel during sentencing. He spoke of his work as counsel. He referred indirectly to his success on Mr. Stewart's behalf, in that he was sentenced to three years in prison when another person convicted of the same offence by the same Judge was sentenced to five years. There is also Mr. Greenspan's broadcast presence. To the viewer, he explained the case and its legal issues. He was thus seen by close to one million people in the role of knowledgeable professional adviser. His image and his voice were prominent throughout. His name was mentioned and displayed. In my opinion, this broadcast was not just education about the justice system. It was also education about Edward Greenspan, his role in the justice system, and his effectiveness as counsel. I find that Mr. Greenspan's primary purpose in involving himself in this production and broadcast, in which educational content was otherwise assured, was to publicize himself and his services as counsel to a national audience.

[J. Macdonald J. found that a violation of the second aspect of Rule 21, paragraph

5 - that Mr. Greenspan's primary purpose was 'self-promotion or self-aggrandisement - was not established.]

. . . . .

Contractual Allegations.

There are two aspects to these allegations. The first is the claim of breach of implied terms of the retainer. The second is the part which the retainer plays in the determination of fiduciary issues.

. . . . .

In my opinion, the terms of the retainer do not prevent the existence of a fiduciary duty of loyalty. The retainer term which permitted Mr. Greenspan to act as he saw it put in place certain circumstances which are fundamental to the existence of such a duty.

Fiduciary Issues.

(a) General.

Mr. Stewart's crime, trial and sentence were the subject of public controversy and widely known in 1978 and 1979. This extensive information, made known through the justice system and published by the media, was public knowledge. This information remained public knowledge in 1991 even if, with the passage of time, it had faded to the fringes of public awareness.

In 1991, Mr. Stewart did not have the legal right to preserve any decreased public awareness of this public knowledge. The law did not shield him from what he had done, or from the public's right to know how its justice system had dealt with him and his conduct, or from the media's right to remind the public about this public information. . ..

Mr. Stewart's claim is narrower and more specific than an attack on media re-publication of public information. Mr. Stewart takes the position that, regardless of the public nature of information about his crime, trial and sentencing, and regardless of the media's right to re-broadcast it, Mr. Greenspan owed him a fiduciary duty of loyalty which arose from their concluded counsel and client relationship, which duty did not allow Mr. Greenspan to participate as he did in this broadcast.

[J. Macdonald J. concluded that a fiduciary relationship existed between Mr. Greenspan and Mr. Stewart.]

(c) The duty which arises from this relationship.

It is trite but necessary, I think, to begin by noting that Mr. Greenspan was not bound to be Mr. Stewart's advocate forever. This is consistent with rule 5, commentary 13 of the rules of professional conduct which does not prohibit a lawyer from acting against a former client. It advises when a lawyer may not act, and when it is "not improper" for a lawyer to act. This standard of the profession demonstrates that a lawyer is not bound indefinitely to serve the former client's interests which were the subject of the earlier retainer. In my opinion, that obligation ends when the retainer ends. However, the end of the lawyer and client relationship as such does not end the fiduciary relationship. Duties arising from that fiduciary relationship may well restrain the lawyer from speaking about the former client's issues or business which were the subject of the concluded retainer, or from taking steps which affect them.

In my opinion, the fundamental principles which Dubin, J.A. re-stated in *R. v. Speid* [(1983) 43 O.R. (2d) 596 (C.A.)] included the nature of a lawyer's ongoing fiduciary duties to a former client. This was done through quoting part of Gale, J.'s reasons in *Tombill Gold Mines Ltd. v. Hamilton (City)* [[1954] O.R. 871 (S.C.)] Gale, J. did not just speak of an existing principal and agent relationship such as an existing lawyer and client relationship, he spoke of an existing fiduciary relationship. That fiduciary relationship survives the termination of the lawyer and client relationship and the end of the duties which are solely part of it. Paraphrasing Gale, J., in a fiduciary relationship, the agent (read lawyer) is:

- obliged to obey instructions.

- obliged to act solely for the benefit of the principal (read client of former client) in all matters connected with the agency (read subject matter of the retainer).

- prohibited from competing with his principal (read client or former client).

- prohibited from taking unfair advantage of his position either:

  - in the use of the things acquired by him because of the agency (read retainer) or

  - in the use of the opportunities which his position affords.

- prohibited from acting disloyally in matters which are related to the agency (read subject matter of the retainer).

In my opinion, this authoritative and helpful listing of duties was not intended to be all inclusive, and the separate headings were not intended to be regarded as mutually exclusive. If regarded as all-inclusive, this list would close the categories of fiduciary obligations and stifle the ability of the fiduciary remedy to meet new fact situations. As Laskin, J. observed in *Canadian Aero Service Ltd. v. O'Malley* [(1973) 40 D.L.R. (3d) 371 (SCC)] "new fact situations may require a reformulation of existing principle to maintain its vigour in the new setting." . . . Further, Gale, J.'s prohibition against disloyalty is frequently expressed as a positive obligation of loyalty. A positive obligation of loyalty is more consistent with the positive obligation to act solely for the benefit of the principal. Consequently, in my view, these categories are best regarded as authoritative examples of underlying principle.

. . .

Mr. Greenspan has raised in his defence the public benefit derived from the *Regina v. Stewart* broadcast and from his involvement. I understand the argument also to rely upon his role in developing the Scales of Justice concept and bringing it to fruition on television. A public policy purpose is said to arise from this public benefit. Mr. Jack put it this way in his written outline of argument:

> There is a very significant public policy purpose to be served by ensuring that lawyers continue to feel at liberty to take part in educational presentations which enhance the public's understanding of the legal process, and thus enhance the administration of justice in Canada.

Some evidence also addressed the advantage to the legal profession and to the public when lawyers and law students are able to learn from lawyers discussing their professional experiences.

. . .

It is clear that Mr. Greenspan played a substantial role in developing the Scales of Justice concept and the defendant Scales as a vehicle for providing both education and information to the public about the justice system. It is also clear the Scales radio and T.V. programs other than *Regina v. Stewart* impressed various members of the bench and the bar with the quality of the information they imparted about the justice system, and I accept the evidence in this regard, filed in letter form on consent, as establishing the public benefit of these programs. The *Regina v. Stewart* episode also provided a public benefit through education about the justice system. Nonetheless, . . . Mr. Greenspan's involvement in the *Regina v. Stewart* episode was not necessary to provide the public benefit which is the focus of the public policy argument he raises is a significant consideration. As well, it is clear that Mr. Greenspan could have withdrawn from his involvement in the episode without any difficulty. No aspect of prior commitment or overarching duty affected his decision. He chose to carry on. In addition, Mr. Greenspan's work in preparing and presenting the *Regina v. Stewart* episode was in fact primarily self-promotion, not public education. Public education was assured without this work of Mr. Greenspan's.

What then is to be said in support of attaching a fiduciary duty to Mr. Greenspan's broadcast involvement? . . . It was when he acted as Mr. Stewart's counsel that a fiduciary duty attached to Mr. Greenspan in respect of Mr. Stewart and his case. That duty was alive but inoperative through the years that Mr. Greenspan and Mr. Stewart were independent of each other. Mr. Greenspan brought himself within the sphere of that duty when, in 1991, he chose to involve himself again in the public aspects of Mr. Stewart's case. Involving himself again in the subject matter of his concluded retainer triggered the fiduciary obligation of loyalty. Mr. Greenspan's duty was to be loyal to Mr. Stewart to the extent of firstly, not taking advantage of him, and the information and issues which had been the subject of his professional services and secondly, to the extent of not undoing the benefits and protections provided by those professional services. In my opinion, the duty of loyalty itself is sufficient to ensure public confidence in the legal profession, in its relevant activities. Loyalty reciprocates the faith the client had in the lawyer respecting the information and issues which were the subject of the professional services.

In my opinion, the public policy issues raised by Mr. Greenspan do not materially alter these loyalty obligations and do not dissolve them, in the circumstances. . . . Mr. Greenspan simply didn't understand his duty and, in the presence of self-interest, didn't ascertain it despite Mr. Stewart's objection to his intended conduct. I see no public benefit in holding that incidental public education resulting from counsel's inattention to fiduciary obligations should alter, dilute or destroy those obligations to a former client. That is particularly so when the incidental benefit to the public resulted from a substantial breach of duty to the former client.

. . . Since this counsel and client relationship included professional services consisting of publication of information about Mr. Stewart and public appearance on Mr. Stewart's behalf in a public forum to address public interest issues and public perceptions attended by substantial publicity, counsel's fiduciary obligation attaches to these professional services and in particular, to the information which was the subject of them. This fiduciary obligation of loyalty is not materially altered, diluted or dissolved by the public nature of Mr. Greenspan's work or by the public nature of the information with which he worked, as it might have been if the fiduciary duty depended on confidentiality.

. . . . .

. . . In a sensational case like Mr. Stewart's, particularly one involving flight to avoid prosecution, much information is public knowledge before the accused is identified and charged and often, before counsel is retained. It is noteworthy that such public information probably would not prevent the existence of a fiduciary duty based on confidentiality. Rule 4 of the rules of professional conduct indicates that a duty of confidentiality on the part of counsel may apply to information which is widely known. When the fiduciary duty is one of loyalty, unrelated to confidentiality, and in respect of the public disclosure and use of information by counsel, pre-retainer publication is of very little significance. . . . The fiduciary duty in issue therefore arises in part from what Mr. Greenspan said and did in public as counsel, it applies to what he said and did in public as broadcaster and, in my opinion, it is not defeated by what others said and did publicly before that fiduciary duty of loyalty arose.

(d) Breach of Fiduciary Duty.

For the above reasons, Mr. Greenspan breached his fiduciary duty of loyalty to Mr. Stewart in the following ways:

- He favoured his financial interests over the plaintiff's interests as alleged in sub-paragraph 25(h) of the statement of claim.

- He put his own self promotion before the plaintiff's interests as alleged in sub-paragraph 25(i) of the statement of claim.

- By the way he publicized his former client and his former client's case in 1991, he undercut the benefits and protections he had provided as counsel, and therefore, increased the adverse public effect on the plaintiff of his crime, trial and sentencing, which falls within sub-paragraph 25(j) of the statement of claim.

Summary.

I assess the compensation which Mr. Stewart is entitled to recover from Mr. Greenspan in the amount of $2,500.00. The amount of profit which Mr. Greenspan is obliged to disgorge to Mr. Stewart is $3,250.00.

NOTES AND QUESTIONS

1. Do you agree with the decision in the case? In particular, do you agree that Greenspan should owe a continuing fiduciary obligation to his former client, and that he breached that obligation by discussing the former client's case for the purpose of self-promotion? What are the arguments in favour of Macdonald J.'s decision? What are the arguments against his decision?

2. How significant is the fact that Greenspan misrepresented certain facts with respect to Stewart's case? If the broadcast had been completely accurate would/should Greenspan still be liable??

3. Is the remedy imposed by Macdonald J. appropriate? What penalty would you impose?

4. Should the Law Society of Upper Canada have commenced an investigation into Greenspan's conduct? Would you encourage the Law Society to impose a penalty? If so, what penalty would you recommend?

5. What if Greenspan had published an academic article discussing the issues of legal strategy raised by Stewart's case? Should Stewart be able successfully to bring a similar claim? What reasons of law or policy would make such a claim distinguishable (or not)?

LAW SOCIETY OF UPPER CANADA v. HUNTER

[2007] L.S.D.D. No. 8; 2007 ONLSHP 27

[A complaint of professional misconduct came before the Law Society of Upper Canada. George Hunter a senior lawyer, a partner at a large Ottawa law firm, a prominent family lawyer, Treasurer of the Law Society of Upper Canada and a President of the Federation of Law Societies of Canada, represented XY in acrimonious custody, access and related matters for a number of years. In During his representation of XY, Hunter and XY commenced a 'sexual/romantic' relationship. Both Hunter and XY agreed that the relationship was consensual, though XY claimed that Hunter made use of confidential information to take advantage of her. Hunter denied this. Both the relationship and Hunter's representation of XY continued for approximately two and one-half more years. He arranged in November of 2005 to meet with XY to have her review and initial a copy of Rule 2.04 of the Rules of Professional Conduct and get her to sign an Acknowledgement that he had complied with Rule 2.04 at the commencement of their sexual/romantic relationship regarding the existence of a conflict and that she had been advised by him to obtain independent legal advice. Hunter admitted that he had not actually done so. At this meeting with XY, Hunter ended the relationship, also informing her that he had been involved romantically with two other women during the period of his relationship with XY. XY left the meeting disappointed and shocked. Subsequently Hunter e-mailed and tried to telephone XY on numerous occasions. He attended XY's home with his lawyer, unannounced, to seek to get her to confirm to his lawyer that the sexual/romantic relationship was as he had described, causing XY concern and emotional distress. Though other facts related to the Hunter/XY relationship were disputed, the Law Society 'placed no reliance upon any allegations made by XY that were not admitted to by the member'.

Hunter informed his law firm of the situation. The firm and Hunter referred the matter to the Law Society and Hunter resigned as Treasurer. Hunter was charged with, and admitted to, professional misconduct in having placed himself in a 'conflict of interest in relation to his client, XY, and in so doing he failed to maintain the integrity of the profession'. He co-operated fully with the Society in its subsequent investigation, Counsel for Hunter submitted extensive evidence of Hunter's status in the legal profession, the contributions he has made to the profession, and the devastating effect that the proceedings had upon him, his family and his practice. Counsel for the Law Society submitted evidence showing the effect of his behaviour on the complainants.]

. . . . .

Analysis

Rule 2.04 of the *Rules of Professional Conduct* provides, in part:

2.04 AVOIDANCE OF CONFLICTS OF INTEREST

Definition

2.04 (1) In this rule,

a *"conflict of interest"* or a *"conflicting interest"* means an interest that

     (a)   that would be likely to affect adversely a lawyer's judgment on behalf of, or loyalty to, a client or prospective client . . .

. . . . .

Commentary

. . .

Where a lawyer is acting for a friend or family member, the lawyer may have a conflict of interest because the personal relationship may interfere with the lawyer's duty to provide objective, disinterested professional advice to the client.

. . . . .

2.04 (3) A lawyer shall not act or continue to act in a matter when there is or is likely to be a conflicting interest unless, after disclosure adequate to make an informed decision, the client or prospective client consents.

. . . . .

A client or the client's affairs may be seriously prejudiced unless the lawyer's judgment and freedom of action on the client's behalf are as free as possible from conflict of interest.

A lawyer should examine whether a conflict of interest exists not only from the outset but throughout the duration of a retainer because new circumstances or information may establish or reveal a conflict of interest.

...

If a lawyer has a sexual or intimate personal relationship with a client, this may conflict with the lawyer's duty to provide objective, disinterested professional advice to the client. Before accepting a retainer from or continuing a retainer with a person with whom the lawyer has such a relationship, a lawyer should consider the following factors:

     a.   The vulnerability of the client, both emotional and economic;

     b.   The fact that the lawyer and client relationship may create a power imbalance in favour of the lawyer or, in some circumstances, in favour of the client;

     c.   Whether the sexual or intimate personal relationship will jeopardize the client's right to have all information concerning the client's business and

302

affairs held in strict confidence. For example, the existence of the relationship may obscure whether certain information was acquired in the course of the lawyer and client relationship;

d. Whether such a relationship may require the lawyer to act as a witness in the proceedings;

e. Whether such a relationship will interfere in any way with the lawyer's fiduciary obligations to the client, his or her ability to exercise independent professional judgment, or his or her ability to fulfill obligations owed as an officer of the court and to the administration of justice.

There is no conflict of interest if another lawyer of the firm who does not have a sexual or intimate personal relationship with the client is the lawyer handling the client's work.

While subrule 2.04(3) does not require that a lawyer advise the client to obtain independent legal advice about the conflicting interest, in some cases, especially those in which the client is not sophisticated or is vulnerable, the lawyer should recommend such advice to ensure that the client's consent is informed, genuine, and uncoerced.

. . . . .

The gravamen of the misconduct in this case is the conflict of interest arising out of the intimate relationship between the member and his client XY, the member's failure to appropriately recognize and address the issues surrounding that conflict of interest and the complainant's vulnerability, and his conduct on November 21, 2005 and thereafter to attempt to rectify the situation by pressing the complainant to confirm the member's position.

There is no doubt (and the member admitted) that the sexual/romantic relationship between the member and XY created a conflict of interest. The member had a duty to provide objective, disinterested professional advice to XY. The sexual/romantic relationship had the significant potential of jeopardizing the member's ability to provide such advice. It also had the significant potential of inhibiting the client from challenging or even questioning the advice being given by someone who was not only her lawyer, but an intimate partner. The fact that XY viewed the relationship as serious and committed reinforced this potential danger. As well, the nature of the work being performed by the member on XY's behalf — involving a dispute with XY's former husband and access issues — further underscores that danger.

The *Rules of Professional Conduct* do not create an absolute prohibition against initiating or continuing a sexual/romantic relationship with a client. This is not the case or the forum to debate whether the existing Rule is sufficiently broad or inclusive. However, it can fairly be said that any sexual/romantic relationship with a client, at the very least, raises serious questions about whether the lawyer is thereby placed in a conflict of interest or is otherwise jeopardizing the solicitor-client relationship. (In many cases, it also invites concern over whether the sexual/romantic relationship is truly consensual.)

Given the conflict of interest, the member was obligated to discuss with his client at the outset of their sexual/romantic relationship whether he should continue to act on her behalf. The member should have referred, at a minimum, to the circumstances that created the conflict of interest, and the dangers associated with that conflict of interest. The factors articulated in the Commentary to subrule 2.04(3) should have figured prominently in such a discussion.

Subrule 2.04(3) does not compel a lawyer to advise the client to obtain independent legal advice about the conflicting interest in all cases. However, where the client is unsophisticated or is vulnerable, the lawyer should recommend such advice to ensure that the client's consent is informed, genuine and uncoerced. Here, the client was emotionally vulnerable (whether as a result of the family law dispute, her new, intimate relationship with the member or both), and the member should have recommended independent legal advice. Any uncertainty on the member's part as to whether the circumstances compelled him to recommend independent legal advice should have been resolved in favour of such a recommendation.

It should be noted that, in some circumstances, the conflict of interest created by the existence of a sexual/romantic relationship will be so profound and irreconcilable with the lawyer's ability to provide objective, disinterested professional advice that the lawyer simply cannot continue to act, and must recommend that the client retain a different lawyer.

As is made clear by Rule 2.04, the member's obligation did not cease at the outset of his sexual/romantic relationship with XY. Even had an informed consent been obtained by the member at the outset of that relationship, circumstances during the relationship may have compelled the member to revisit the issue with his client.

In November 2005, the member had the client review and initial a copy of Rule 2.04 and had her sign an Acknowledgement to the effect that the member had complied with Rule 2.04. There remains some disagreement (as reflected in the agreed statement of facts) over the accuracy of some aspects of the Acknowledgement, or of the contents of the e-mails which the member subsequently sent to XY. We need not resolve that disagreement, and we draw no inference against the member in that regard. But several things are clear. First, the Acknowledgement was inaccurate in asserting that the member had complied with his obligations under Rule 2.04. As he has admitted, he did not. Second, the circumstances surrounding the initialing of a copy of Rule 2.04 and the signing of the Acknowledgement did not permit an informed decision on the part of the client. On the contrary, the circumstances advanced the interests of the member, but not those of the client. Third, the member's conduct in pressing XY to confirm the member's position to his former lawyer and law partners through e-mails and telephone calls, and through an attendance at her home without prior notification was inappropriate, contributed to the client's concern and emotional distress, and attempted to advance the member's interests, rather than those of the client.

This is a serious matter, as correctly acknowledged by some of those who acted as character references on behalf of the member. Nonetheless, the Hearing Panel recognizes the existence of a number of mitigating factors that must inform the appropriate penalty.

The member co-operated fully with the Society. He acknowledged his wrongdoing at the earliest opportunity. He self-reported to the Society. Through his counsel, an agreed statement of facts was created that spared the complainant the ordeal of testifying at these proceedings. The complainant's privacy was respected through the introduction of a summary of her psychologist's findings. A victim impact statement was filed, again on consent. The member spoke positively about the complainant's attributes. As earlier indicated, he was deeply remorseful, and did not seek to minimize, justify or excuse his misconduct.

There is no evidence before us that the member's legal work was actually affected by the conflict of interest, despite the dangers earlier articulated.

The misconduct has already taken a significant toll upon the member. We have observed his considerable fall from grace, culminating in his resignation as Treasurer of the Society. He has been unable to practise law (albeit on paid leave) since December 2005 for health and other reasons related, in large measure if not entirely, to this matter. This underscores the impact of these proceedings upon him, and is a significant factor in setting the appropriate penalty in this case.

The Society conceded that the member is in no need of specific deterrence. Its proposed disposition was based upon the need for general deterrence: in other words, to dissuade like-minded lawyers from similar misconduct.

This Hearing Panel must remain mindful of the impact of this and other decisions on the profession as a whole, and upon the confidence of the public in the profession. However, the member should not be treated more harshly as a result of his former status as Treasurer and as a bencher. Nor, of course, should he receive favoured treatment, although he is entitled to make the important point that his entire career is incompatible with this misconduct and that, therefore, this misconduct can be regarded as "out of character." We have no difficulty in so finding.

The letters filed on behalf of the member were impressive, and spoke to the member's character, integrity, and commitment to the profession. They demonstrate, in our view, that the member remains capable of serving in the future as a valuable member of his firm, and of the profession.

. . . . .

[Hunter received a 60-day suspension and a fine of $2,500. The portion of the judgment dealing with the basis for this penalty is excerpted in Chapter 12.]

NOTES AND QUESTIONS

1. Are there any circumstances in which a sexual relationship between a lawyer and a client, and the lawyer's continued representation of a client, would be appropriate? What if, for example, the client was a corporation and the relationship was between the lawyer and the corporation's Chief Executive Officer? Its in-house counsel? Consider Scenario Four below.

2. Some professions have established a zero tolerance approach to professional-client (or patient) sexual relations. What should be the approach of the legal profession? The FLSC's Model Code of Professional Conduct has chosen to deal with this issue as part of the general 'conflict of interest' provisions:

A **"conflict of interest"** means the existence of a substantial risk that a lawyer's

305

loyalty to or representation of a client would be materially and adversely affected by the lawyer's own interest or the lawyer's duties to another client, a former client, or a third person.

Rule 3.4-1, Commentary 11 identifies the following example of a conflict of interest:

. . . . .

(d) A lawyer has a sexual or close personal relationship with a client.

    i. Such a relationship may conflict with the lawyer's duty to provide objective, disinterested professional advice to the client. The relationship may obscure whether certain information was acquired in the course of the lawyer and client relationship and may jeopardize the client's right to have all information concerning his or her affairs held in strict confidence. The relationship may in some circumstances permit exploitation of the client by his or her lawyer. If the lawyer is a member of a firm and concludes that a conflict exists, the conflict is not imputed to the lawyer's firm, but would be cured if another lawyer in the firm who is not involved in such a relationship with the client handled the client's work.

Do you agree with this Rule? What are its strengths and weaknesses?

3. What do you think the appropriate penalty should be for a lawyer who takes advantage of the lawyer-client relationship and initiates sexual relations with that client? Do you think Hunter's penalty might have been different had he been a solo practitioner with no association with the Law Society?

4. The judgment may imply that if Hunter had referred the file to another lawyer in the firm no Law Society discipline would have resulted. Would such a result be appropriate? Can you think of situations where it would not be appropriate (*e.g.*, where professional discipline would be warranted for the sexual relationship even if there was no continued representation of the client)?

5. What other kinds of relationships might cause serious lawyer-client conflicts? *Strother* demonstrates that conflicting financial interests between the lawyer and client might be one such conflict. Can you think of any others?

Civil litigation is only occasionally the route by which lawyers are held accountable for conflicts of interest that involve conflicting financial interests. More commonly, law societies, informed of the issue, usually through a client complaint, will institute formal discipline proceedings against the lawyer. Sometimes both a law suit and discipline proceedings against the lawyer are commenced, as happened to Strother[16]. Consider the following case of a lawyer who faced discipline proceedings in relation to a conflict between himself and a client in a business transaction.

---

[16] *Law Society of British Columbia v. Strother*, [2015] L.S.D.D. No. 43, 2015 LSBC 7 (B.C. Law Society Panel).

LAW SOCIETY OF SASKATCHEWAN V. BALON

2016 SKLSS 8

The lawyer, Balon [the 'member'], had represented S.D. in the past, primarily on real estate transactions. In the spring of 2012, Balon offered to sell his office building to S.D. for $565,000.00. The office building included the Member's law office and a bar. The Member drafted the Offer to Purchase which included a provision that a $40,000.00 deposit would be forfeited should the sale not proceed. The $40,000.00 deposit was paid by trust funds held by the Member on deposit for S.D. At some point S.D. learned that there were questions about the ability of the tenant of the bar to be able to make its rent payments due to the bar license being in jeopardy. Balon asserted that the payments were not in jeopardy and as a consequence he was not obliged to disclose this information to S.D. S.D. declined to proceed with the transaction and Balon treated the $40,000 deposit as forfeited by S.D. Throughout the transaction, S.D. did not obtain independent legal advice.

Balon pleaded guilty to charges that he:

1) Did enter into and continued in a business transaction with his client, S.D., when his interests and the interests of his client were in conflict;

2) Did prepare and sign an Offer to Purchase his property with his client, S.D., on terms beneficial to him without ensuring his client had independent legal advice;

3) Did prefer his own interests over those of his client, S.D., in receiving a $40,000 payment under the terms of the Offer to Purchase to the detriment of his client.

Hearing Committee:

. . . . .

The Member is 68 years of age and has practiced law for over 40 years, primarily in Prince Albert. He has no prior discipline history with the Law Society. Counsel for the Member advised that the Member has significant health problems that affected his ability to practice law. His health problems began in the late 1990's and over the years his health has increasingly deteriorated.

The Member resigned as a member of the Law Society of Saskatchewan in November 2014. The Member remains subject to disciplinary proceedings as a "former member" given section 34.2 of The Legal Profession Act, 1990.

. . . . .

In examining the cases:

(a) *Halford* – the member entered into a business relationship with his clients in order to purchase a commercial building. A company was created with the shares being held equally by the member and the clients. The member drafted a Shareholders Agreement. Conflict between the parties and litigation followed. No independent legal advice was obtained by the clients. The decision states: "There also does not appear to be any evidence of a commercial advantage gained by the member as a result of

307

the conflict of interest situation." A joint submission consisting of a reprimand, a $500 fine, and costs in the amount of $2,195 was accepted.

(b) *Howe* – the member provided a mortgage loan to his secretary's parents who were in difficult circumstances. The mortgage had a 0 per cent interest rate, but it provided for a $10,500 lending fee. The property was sold and the member received the $10,500 lending fee. The end result of the transaction arranged by the member was to place the clients in a better financial position, although the $10,500 lending fee represented a significant return on investment for the member. A joint submission consisting of a reprimand and costs of $1,645 was accepted.

(c) *Johnston* – the member failed to disclose he had an interest in a corporation while acting for a client purchasing a condominium. The corporation owned the condominium development. The client did not obtain independent legal advice regarding the risks in purchasing the property. The client and others brought litigation against the member and other members of the corporation because of aspects of the development. A joint submission consisting of a reprimand and payment of costs in the amount of $1,955 was accepted.

(d) *Simaluk* – the member's client was unable to secure credit anywhere. The member entered into a mortgage agreement against the client's primary residence. The client did not have the benefit of independent legal advice. The client did not suffer any financial loss and the decision notes that in fact the client "was extended credit that she might not otherwise have been able to secure". The matter came to light when the member reported the loan as part of the annual trust review. A joint submission consisting of a reprimand and a fine of $500 was accepted. Costs were not agreed to. The hearing committee assessed costs in the amount of $1,495.

(e) *Braun* – the member entered into a farming operation with a client. The member financed the operation. The farming operation was not success-ful, and the client was unable to repay the moneys. The member prepared and registered a transfer of the land into his name. In a letter, the member encouraged the client to obtain independent legal advice, which the client did not do. The member acted on the transfer. . . . The Committee imposed a reprimand, a $500 fine, and payment of costs.

. . . . .

Overall and in considering the relevant legal factors and the Member's personal circumstances, the Hearing Committee is prepared to endorse the joint submission. The Hearing Committee therefore orders:

(i) The Member shall receive a formal reprimand;

(ii) The Member shall pay a fine of $500.00 . . .and

(iii) The Member shall pay costs in the amount of $4,000.00.

NOTES AND QUESTIONS

1. This can be dangerous terrain, even for lawyers who do not have a

particular desire to pursue a business opportunity. In some cases the lawyer's engagement in the business transaction may initially be motivated by a genuine desire to assist the client. In *Law Society of Saskatchewan v. Ferraton*[17], a lawyer entered into an arrangement to finance the purchase of a property on behalf of a client who could not afford to effect the purchase. Eventually, as the circumstances of her 'investment' spun out of control and in an effort to protect her investment in the property, the lawyer prepared false documents and submitted them to the land registration authorities. Ferraton had no previous discipline history with the Law Society. She was suspended for one month and required to pay the costs of the discipline proceedings.

2   The ethical guidance provided by the *Model Code* imposes some requirements, but does not prohibit lawyers from going into business with their clients. At Rules 3.4-27 to 3.4-41, the Code sets out general cautions in relation to "doing business with a client", and then provides specific guidance in the case of six specific scenarios: borrowing from clients; lending to clients; providing guarantees; payment for fees through an interest in the client's business; receipt of gifts and bequests in clients' wills; acting as a surety to obtain a client's bail.

The general statement appears in Rules 3.4-28 and 3.4-29:

Transactions With Clients

3.4-28 A lawyer must not enter into a transaction with a client unless the transaction with the client is fair and reasonable to the client.

3.4-29 Subject to Rules 3.4-30 to 3.4-36, where a transaction involves: lending or borrowing money, buying or selling property or services having other than nominal value, giving or acquiring ownership, security or other pecuniary interest in a company or other entity, recommending an investment, or entering into a common business venture, a lawyer must, in sequence,

   (a)   disclose the nature of any conflicting interest or how a conflict might develop later;

   (b)   consider whether the circumstances reasonably require that the client receive independent legal advice with respect to the transaction; and

   (c)   obtain the client's consent to the transaction after the client receives such disclosure and legal advice.

Prior to a set of amendments to the *Model Code* in 2014, Rule 3.4-28 provided:

Transactions With Clients

3.4-28 Subject to this rule, a lawyer must not enter into a transaction with a client unless the transaction with the client is fair and reasonable to the client, the client consents to the transaction and the client has independent legal representation with respect to the transaction.

Since this Rule precluded lawyers from entering into transactions with clients unless

---

[17] *Law Society of Saskatchewan v. Ferraton*, [2013] L.S.D.D. No. 207, 2014 SKLSS 2 (Sask. Law Society Discipline).

the client had received independent legal representation, it was necessary, in the 2014 amendments, to add the provision, in Rule 3.4-29(b), requiring the lawyer to "consider whether the circumstances reasonably require that the client receive independent legal advice".

These amendments provide more flexibility for lawyers to enter into transactions with clients without: (a) the requirement of ensuring in every instance that the client has independent representation or advice; and (b) places the question of the client's acquisition of independent legal advice (not representation) at the discretion of the lawyer.

Are these modifications to the *Model Code* justified? Might this reduced cautionary standard invite the kinds of problems that arose in *Balon* or *Ferraton*? Keeping in mind that the improper conduct of the lawyer in each case occurred before the 2014 amendments to the *Model Code*, might it not matter?

Scenario Four

Tom Thomas is the President and Chief Executive Officer of Thomas Manufacturing Ltd. His company has retained ABC law firm to handle its legal business. In the course of representing Thomas Manufacturing, one of the ABC lawyers, Gerry Gordon, becomes romantically involved with Thomas. Advise Gordon as to his ethical obligations in light of the relationship. Does your answer depend on how many other ABC lawyers are involved? Or whether Gordon is an associate at ABC or a partner? Or whether Gordon has disclosed his relationship to other lawyers at ABC? What if Gordon is not "out" at his law firm and does not wish to disclose the existence of the relationship to his law firm colleagues?

Scenario Five

J.J. is a lawyer in Calgary. A few years ago she persuaded a client to enter into a business transaction with her. She continued to provide legal services for the client. Ultimately the business venture collapsed, with J.J. and the client ending up in litigation for breach of contract and breach of fiduciary duty. J.J. failed to advise her client to obtain independent legal advice and should not have continued to act for him. The Law Society found, however, that the reasons for the business venture failing were largely related to the client's unreasonable behaviour. In addition, the client was sophisticated and experienced in business matters. J.J. has never been disciplined previously and has cooperated fully with the Law Society. The litigation has been settled out of court on terms that have not been disclosed. Is J.J.'s behaviour sanctionable?

[4] FURTHER READING

Brenner, Susan & James Durham, "Towards Resolving Prosecutor Conflicts of Interest" (1993) 6:1 Geo. J. Leg. Ethics 415.

Buhai, Sarah, "Emotional Conflicts: Impaired Dispassionate Representation of Family Members" (2008) 21:1 Geo. J. Leg. Ethics 1159.

Cotter, Brent & Richard Devlin, "Three Strikes and You're Out . . . Or Maybe Not: A Comment on *Canadian National Railway Co. v. McKercher*" (2013) 92:1 Can. Bar Rev. 1.

Devlin, Richard "Governance, Regulation and Legitimacy: Conflicts of Interest and the Duty of Loyalty", *Guest Editorial*, (2011) 14:2 Leg. Ethics iii.

Devlin, Richard & Victoria Rees, "Beyond Conflicts of Interest to the Duty of Loyalty: From *Martin v. Gray* to *R. v. Neil*" (2005) 84:1 Can. Bar Rev. 433.

DiLernia, Michael, "Advance Waivers of Conflicts of Interest in Large Law Firm Practice" (2009) 22:1 Geo. J. Leg. Ethics 97.

Dodek, Adam, "Conflicted Identities: The Battle Over the Duty of Loyalty in Canada" (2011) 14:1 Leg. Ethics 193.

Duggan, Anthony, "Solicitors' Conflict of Interest and the Wider Fiduciary Question" (2007) 45:1 Can. Bus. L.J. 414.

Graham, Randal, *Legal Ethics: Theories, Cases, and Professional Regulation*, 2d ed (Toronto: Emond Montgomery, 2011) at ch. 6.

Hume, Gavin, "Current Client Conflicts: Finally Resolved? *Canadian National Railway Co v McKercher LLP*" (2014) 72:3 Advocate 349.

Hutchinson, Allan C., *Legal Ethics and Professional Responsibility*, 2d ed (Toronto: Irwin Law, 2006) at ch. 8.

Jackson, Colin, Brent Cotter & Richard Devlin, "Of Lodestars and Lawyers: Incorporating the Duty of Loyalty into the Model Code of Conduct" (2016) 39:1 Dal. L.J. 37.

Loughrey, Joan, "Large Law Firms, Sophisticated Clients and the Regulation of Conflicts of Interest in England and Wales" (2011) 14:1 Leg. Ethics 215.

Mackenzie, Brooke "The Not-So-Bright Line Rule: Lingering Questions About Lawyer's Duty to Avoid Conflicting Interests – *CN Railway v. McKercher*", Case Comment, (2014) 42:4 Adv. Q. 422.

MacKenzie, Gavin, *Lawyers and Ethics: Professional Responsibility and Discipline*, (Toronto: Thomson Carswell, 2007) at ch. 5.

MacKenzie, Gavin, "Clarity brought to conflicts of interest but grey areas remain" (May 1, 2014), online: *LExpert* https://www.lexpert.ca/article/clarity-brought-to-conflicts-of-interest-but-grey-areas-remain/?p=%7C273&sitecode=DIR.

Moore, Nancy, "Regulating Law Firm Conflicts in the 21st Century: Implications of the Globalization of Legal Services and the Growth of the 'Mega Firm'" (2005) 18:1 Geo. J. Leg. Ethics 521.

Morrison, Harvey, "Conflicts of Interest and the Concept of Loyalty" (2008) 87:1 Can. Bar Rev. 565.

O'Sullivan, Terrence & Paul Michell, "Analyzing Conflicts of Interest After *Strother*: Has Anything Changed?" *Canadian Bar Association* (November, 2007).

Perell, Paul, *Conflict of Interest in the Legal Profession* (Markham, ON: Butterworths, 1995).

Proulx, Michel & David Layton, *Ethics and Canadian Criminal Law*, (Toronto: Irwin Law, 2001) at ch. 6.

Smith, Beverley G., *Professional Conduct for Lawyers and Judges*, 3rd ed

(Fredericton: Maritime Law Book, 2010).

Stagg-Taylor, Joanne, "Lawyers' Business: Conflicts of Duties Arising from Lawyers' Business Models" (2011) 14:1 Leg. Ethics 173.

Wolfram, Charles, *Modern Legal Ethics* (St. Paul, MN: West, 1986) at ch. 7.

Woolley, Alice, *Understanding Lawyers' Ethics in Canada*, 2d ed (Toronto: LexisNexis Canada, 2017) at ch. 8.

CHAPTER 5

ETHICS IN ADVOCACY

[1] INTRODUCTION

There are many opportunities to act as an advocate in the practice of law: as a business lawyer negotiating a deal on behalf of a corporate client; as a legal aid lawyer advocating for the return to school or the safe housing of a young person in custody; as a labour lawyer negotiating the terms of a collective bargaining agreement; as an Indigenous rights lawyer working with government representatives on a land claim settlement; as a public interest lawyer holding a press conference to raise support for a client's opposition to the creation of a nuclear waste facility; as a collaborative lawyer seeking to work out the solution to a conflict involving the breakdown of a family relationship; marching in a street protest; or as a litigator arguing on behalf of a client in a virtual or in-person hearing before a tribunal or court. All of these examples are moments of advocacy. Each one involves making choices: some legal, some practical, most strategic, and essentially all ethical and professional. For a code-based definition of "advocacy", see Rule 5.1-1 and Commentary of the *Model Code*.

What this chapter deals with, specifically, is the latter example: advocacy in litigation and, in particular, advocacy in civil litigation. Because advocacy engages many other aspects of lawyers' ethics and professional regulation, it is important to connect the issues and discussions raised in this chapter with related issues and discussions elsewhere in this book, including, for example, the introduction to legal ethics (Chapter 1), the professional and ethical discussions involving confidentiality (Chapter 3), competence and the lawyer-client relationship (Chapter 2), conflicts of interest (Chapter 4), counselling and negotiation (Chapter 6), criminal law advocacy (Chapter 7), and access to justice (Chapter 11).

[2] VISIONS OF THE ADVOCATE

The basic role of the legal advocate is to engage in advocacy on behalf of someone else, typically a client. And while the client plays a role in all visions of litigation advocacy, the centrality of their interests varies depending on the vision of the advocate to which one subscribes. As was discussed in Chapter 1, the role of the lawyer as advocate can be defined in various ways, including by loyalty (the "standard conception" model), by pursuit of the public interest (the "moral agent" model), or by seeing the lawyer as required to pursue and balance a variety of competing interests (described in Chapter 1 in the context of "integrity"). The advocacy context provides opportunities, mandates and requirements for, and places restraints on, the lawyer's ability to accomplish this difficult balancing act. It is the context in which the lawyer is most strongly urged to act zealously for a client's interests but where, as well, the lawyer can be seen as having the greatest responsibility to protect and ensure the proper functioning of the justice system. Regardless of which vision of the advocate one prefers, lawyers have power – primarily as a result of their training and membership in the legal profession – to influence and shape the world of those around them (those for whom they act, those against whom they act, and others not represented at all). How that power is exercised is primarily up to the lawyer.

On the one hand, modern codes of conduct, as supported by academic literature, while noting lawyers' obligations towards the administration of justice in general, continue primarily to define the litigation lawyer's role largely in terms of the zealous advocate. For example, according to Rule 5.1-1 of the *Model Code*, when "acting as an advocate", the lawyer must:

> . . . represent the client resolutely and honourably within the limits of the law, while treating the tribunal with candour, fairness, courtesy and respect . . . [and]

> **Commentary [1]**

> . . . raise fearlessly every issue, advance every argument and ask every question, however distasteful, that the lawyer thinks will help the client's case and to endeavour to obtain for the client the benefit of every remedy and defence authorized by law.

This vision of the zealous advocate not only requires lawyers to emphasize their clients' views, it also requires that they de-emphasize their own views. According to Commentary [5] to Rule 5.1-1, when acting as an advocate, a "lawyer should refrain from expressing the lawyer's personal opinions on the merits of a client's case . . . .".

On the other hand, the former Chief Justice of Ontario, speaking on the topic of "advocacy in the 21st century", emphasized the various competing interests to which advocates must be faithful:

> Lawyers are not solely professional advocates or "hired guns". And while they do not surrender their free speech rights upon admission to the bar, they are also officers of the court with fundamental obligations to uphold the integrity of the judicial process, both inside and outside the courtroom. It is the duty of counsel to be faithful both to their client and to the administration of justice.[1]

Similarly, according to Lord Denning M.R., an advocate

> . . . is a minister of justice equally with the judge. He has a monopoly of audience in the higher courts. No one save he can address the judge, unless it be a litigant in person. This carries with it a corresponding responsibility. . . . He must . . . do all he honourably can on behalf of his client. I say "all he honourably can" because his duty is not only to his client. He has a duty to the court which is paramount. It is a mistake to suppose that he is the mouthpiece of his client to say what he wants: or his tool to do what he directs. He is none of these things. He owes allegiance to a higher cause. It is the cause of truth and justice. He must not consciously misstate the facts. He must not knowingly conceal the truth. He must not unjustly make a charge of fraud, that is, without evidence to support it. He must produce all the

---

[1] The Honourable Chief Justice R. Roy McMurtry, "Role of the Courts and Counsel in Justice", The Advocates' Society Spring Symposium 2000, *Advocacy in the 21st Century* (June 6, 2000).

relevant authorities, even those that are against him. He must see that his client discloses, if ordered, the relevant documents, even those that are fatal to his case. He must disregard the most specific instructions of his client, if they conflict with his duty to the court. The code which requires a barrister to do all this is not a code of law. It is a code of honour. If he breaks it, he is offending against the rules of the profession and is subject to its discipline. . . . Such being his duty to the court, the barrister must be able to do it fearlessly. He has time and time again to choose between his duty to his client and his duty to the court. This is a conflict often difficult to resolve. . . .[2]

Complicating things further is the modern reality that typical visions of the adversary system – a system in which all litigants are fairly and fully represented by an advocate – do not adequately account for the fact that many people cannot access a lawyer.

Standard visions of the advocate often rely on, or in some instances amplify, visions of and assumptions about the role of the lawyer and advocate that do not always include or reflect the diversity, needs and interests of modern society.[3]

The challenges, then, when thinking about ethics in advocacy, are first to identify the various and often competing interests to which a litigator must be faithful; and, second, to try to sort out how to balance and resolve those potentially competing interests in a particular case, which is an exercise — as recognized by Lord Denning — that is "often difficult".

For the purposes of this chapter, we will look at a number of these competing interests and how to resolve them in the everyday contexts in which they typically arise during the many pre-trial and trial stages of the litigation process.

NOTES AND QUESTIONS

1.   What do the above phrases "officers of the court", "minister of justice" and "code of honour" specifically mean? What is the "cause of truth and justice"? What is the relevance of advocates having a "monopoly of

---

[2] *Rondel v. Worsley*, [1967] 1 Q.B. 443 (H.L. Eng) (following note 27 and surrounding text), affd [1969] 1 A.C. 191.

[3] See e.g. David B. Wilkins, "Identities and Roles: Race, Recognition, and Professional Responsibility" (1998) Maryland L. Rev. 1502. See generally Canadian Association of Black Lawyers (CABL), Open Letter to Prime Minister and Minister Lametti (June 25, 2020), online: *CABL* https://cabl.ca/wp-content/uploads/2020/06/CABL-Letter-to-Prime-Minister-and-Minister-Lametti-June-25-2020.pdf; Trevor C.W. Farrow, "What is Access to Justice?" (2014) 51:3 Osgoode Hall L.J. 957, online: *Osgoode Digital Commons* https://digitalcommons.osgoode.yorku.ca/ohlj/vol51/iss3/10/; Truth and Reconciliation Commission of Canada, *Honouring the Truth, Reconciling the Future: Summary of the Final Report of the Truth and Reconciliation Commission of Canada* (2015), online: Truth and Reconciliation Commission of Canada http://www.trc.ca/assets/pdf/Honouring_the_Truth_Reconciling_for_the_Future_July_23_2015.pdf; the Advocates' Society, the Indigenous Bar Association, the Law Society of Ontario, *Guide for Lawyers Working with Indigenous Peoples* (Toronto: Advocates' Society May 8, 2018), online: Advocates' Society https://www.advocates.ca/Upload/Files/PDF/Advocacy/BestPracticesPublications/Guide_for_Lawyers_Working_with_Indigenous_Peoples_may16.pdf.

audience"? How do lawyers act faithfully "both to their client and to the administration of justice"? How can lawyers "disregard" client instructions that conflict with a "duty to the court"? How is an advocate ethical "both inside and outside the courtroom"? Can you think of examples? Do these phrases provide adequate guidance to the advocate? Does Lord Denning M.R. in *Rondel v. Worsley* provide enough guidance to assist the lawyer in making advocacy choices?

2. What about Chapter 5 of the *Model Code*? How should lawyers balance Rule 5.1-1, Commentary [1] (above) with Rule 5.1-2(b), mandating that an advocate must not ". . .assist or permit a client to do anything that the lawyer considers to be dishonest or dishonourable"? When thinking about these questions, recall the different visions of the advocate discussed in Chapter 1.

3. *Model Code*, Rule 5.1-1, Commentary [1] contemplates the lawyer's role in "adversarial proceedings". Commentary [2], which sets out the contexts to which the rule applies, acknowledges that the role of the advocate extends to various contexts beyond the courtroom. Does advocacy need to be adversarial? Can you think of circumstances – in which lawyers are called upon to be advocates – that are not, or should not be, adversarial? Should the same professional obligations apply? For a recent discussion, see Deanne Sowter, "What Is Non-Adversarial Advocacy?" (24 April 2020), online: *Slaw* https://www.slaw.ca/2020/04/24/what-is-non-adversarial-advocacy/. See further section [3][c], "Negotiation", below, and Chapter 6.

4. What about contexts in which the adversarial model, and the role of lawyer as advocate, caused significant harm – or, worse, much greater harm than good? For several discussions, particularly with respect to the role of lawyers and the justice system in disputes involving the tragic legacy of Canada's Residential Schools, see Trevor C.W. Farrow, "Truth, Reconciliation, and the Cost of Adversarial Justice" in Trevor C.W. Farrow and Lesley A. Jacobs, eds., *The Justice Crisis: The Cost and Value of Accessing Law* (Vancouver: University of British Columbia Press, 2020) at c. 6; Trevor C.W. Farrow, "Residential Schools Litigation and the Legal Profession" (2014) 64:4 U.T.L.J. 596.

[3] ETHICS IN PRE-TRIAL PROCEDURES

Many, if not most, of the challenging ethical and professional issues in the context of civil litigation arise well before trial. During an initial meeting with a client ethical issues arise related to competence, conflicts of interest, fees (and access to the legal system for that particular client) and confidentiality. In addition, pre-trial steps in the litigation process present specific ethical dilemmas for the lawyer to identiy and resolve.

[a] Pleadings

Once a lawyer is retained and the matter has progressed to the stage of pleadings the lawyer must make many difficult advocacy decisions. What is my client's case? How can I best plead the case in order to "raise fearlessly every issue" and "advance every argument"? (*Model Code*, Rule 5.1-1, Commentary [1]) By doing so, am I overstating the merits of the case? Is this client simply using the system to extract a settlement or to "get" the other side, and if so, am I participating as an advocate in an abuse of process?[4]

Most of these considerations are the subject of pleadings rules in the various provincial rules of court. For example, a pleading may be struck out on motion by the other party to the litigation if an advocate pushes zealousness too far. This includes putting in a client's pleading allegations that: are "unnecessary", "scandalous", "frivolous" or "vexatious"; may "prejudice" or "delay" the "fair trial of the action"; or, are otherwise "an abuse of the process of the court".[5] Indeed, pursuit of an action without legal merit can place a client at risk of liability in an action for abuse of process.[6] Plus, if the matter proceeds to trial and – as is highly likely– the client loses, the client may be at risk of an elevated costs award.

In addition, however, and regardless of whether or not a procedural motion is brought to strike out a pleading, all of these considerations are also at the core of professional rules governing the advocate's role. For example, according to Rule 5.1-2(a) of the *Model Code*, when acting as an advocate, including when drafting a client's pleading, a lawyer shall not:

> abuse the process of the tribunal by instituting or prosecuting proceedings that, although legal in themselves, are clearly motivated by malice on the part of the client and are brought solely for the purpose of injuring the other party . . ..

These specific pleadings requirements fit within broader professional rules that prohibit the lawyer-as-advocate from pursuing unmeritorious or improper steps in the litigation process. For example, according to Rule 5.1-1 of the *Model Code*, when acting as an advocate, a lawyer:

> . . . must discharge [their duty as an advocate in adversarial proceedings] by fair and honourable means, without illegality and in a manner that is consistent with the lawyer's duty to treat the tribunal with candour, fairness, courtesy and respect and in a way that promotes the parties' right to a fair hearing in which justice can be done. . . . (Rule 5.1-1, Commentary [1])

and:

> . . . should avoid and discourage the client from resorting to frivolous or vexatious objections, attempts to gain advantage from slips or oversights not going to the merits or tactics that will merely delay or harass the other side. . . . (Rule 5.1-1, Commentary [8])

In addition, Rule 5.1-2(b) (mentioned above) states that a lawyer must not

---

[4] For a discussion of abuse of process in the context of pleadings, see, *e.g.*, *National Trust Co. v. Furbacher*, [1994] O.J. No. 2385, 50 A.C.W.S (3d) 1196 (Ont. Gen. Div.), as further discussed in Trevor C.W. Farrow, "Five Pleadings Cases Everyone Should Read" (2009) 35(4) Advocates' Q. 466 at 467-473.

[5] See, *e.g.*, British Columbia's *Supreme Court Civil Rules*, B.C. Reg. 168/2009, Rule 9-5(1); Ontario's *Rules of Civil Procedure*, R.R.O. 1990, Reg. 194, Rules 21 and 25.11.

[6] See, *e.g.*, *Colborne Capital Corp. v. 542775 Alberta Ltd.*, [1995] A.J. No. 538, 30 Alta. L.R. (3d) 127 at paras. 375-378 (Alta. Q.B.), affd [2000] A.J. No. 161, 250 A.R. 352 (Alta. C.A.).

"knowingly assist or permit a client to do anything that the lawyer considers to be dishonest or dishonourable", and clarifies in Commentary [1] that this includes "a duty not to mislead the tribunal about the position of the client in the adversarial process".

Consider the ethical duties related to pleadings, and instigating a cause of action, through the following case.

D.C.B. v. ZELLERS INC.

[1996] M.J. No. 362, 138 D.L.R. (4th) 309 (Man. Q.B.),
affd [1996] M.J. No. 499, 10 W.W.R. 689 (Man. C.A.)
(Man. Q.B., Jewers J.)

JEWERS J.:— In this small claim appeal, the plaintiff sues the defendants for money she paid to them as compensation for damages the defendant Zellers (Zellers) sustained resulting from thefts committed by her young son. The issue is whether in the particular circumstances of this case having paid over the money, the plaintiff can recover it on the ground that Zellers never had a valid claim against her personally. The proceedings against the defendant Arkin have been discontinued.

A hearing officer dismissed the claim and the plaintiff appeals.

The parties filed the following agreed statement of facts. . . .

[The statement of facts indicated that the plaintiff's son had been arrested for shoplifting. The goods were recovered and had a value of around $50. No damage was done to the items and they were returned for sale. After the shoplifting incident the following letter was sent to the plaintiff by Mr. Arkin, counsel for Zellers:]

"I act for Zellers to recover their damages in civil court. The civil recovery process is SEPARATE AND DISTINCT from any criminal action and the two must not be confused.

"It is alleged that on May 26, 1956 [sic] J.R.B., a young person for whose supervision my client holds you legally responsible, took unlawful possession of merchandise from Zellers, located at 969 Henderson Highway, Winnipeg, Manitoba, to the value of $59.95.

"In accordance with the Court of Queen's Bench Act of Manitoba and/or The Court of Queen's Bench Small Claims Practices Act of Manitoba, Zellers has a legal right to claim Civil Restitution from you.

"In order to eliminate additional expense to you, Zellers is willing to settle THE CIVIL CASE ONLY out of court, providing you pay the following amount by August 25, 1995:

"Restitution for cost of incident including damages and costs: $225.00

"Should you elect to ignore this demand, refuse or fail to pay the amount of the proposed out of Court settlement, Zellers will take the case before a Civil Court and claim damages, including legal costs and interest pursuant to The Court of Queen's Bench Act of Manitoba and/or The Court of Queen's Bench Small Claims Practices Act of Manitoba. Administration charges will continue to increase until the matter is concluded. Payment of the total amount demanded will be deemed full restitution and will halt the civil court action only. Any criminal court action which is, or has been undertaken, remains under the jurisdiction of the criminal prosecutor and is separate from this particular court action. Payment should be by cheque or money order made payable to CIVIL RECOVERY and sent via the enclosed postage paid envelope. Include your NAME and the CASE NUMBER, shown above.

"Any questions with regard to this matter are to be made in writing and addressed to this office. You may call (416) 234-0000 for payment enquiries only. Phone calls will be accepted between 9:00 a.m. and 4:00 p.m. Monday through Friday. (No collect calls.) NOTE; My telephone staff will not discuss the circumstances of the case.

(signed)

Harold J. Arkin 22325"

This claim is part of a loss recovery programme or policy which Zellers initiated several years ago and which commenced in their Manitoba Division in or about February 1995. Zellers wanted to recover what they called their "incremental" costs of shoplifting. These would be the costs of employing loss prevention officers and purchasing their equipment for the purpose of detecting losses (presumably mostly from theft) attributable to their customers and their employees. They concluded that the cost per incident would be approximately $310.00. They conceived the idea of claiming against the parents of children involved in thefts — obviously because it would be futile to pursue the children.

Zellers decided not to use, or hire, their own employees to process these claims but, instead, gave the job to an independent organization called Aclaim Civil Loss Recovery System. That organization reviewed the incident reports regarding the various claims and then engaged lawyers to prosecute them. If there was recovery, Aclaim would get a portion of the recovery and the balance would go to Zellers. Typically, a recovery of $325.00 would result in a fee of $125.00 to Aclaim and $200.00 to Zellers.

If necessary, the lawyers would write two demand letters and the amount claimed in the second letter would be increased somewhat over the amount claimed in the first.

In this case, because two boys were involved, the amount claimed was reduced to $225.00.

There is no general rule that parents are liable for the torts of their children by virtue of their status as parents per se. . . . The parents would only be liable if they, themselves, were in some way negligent or had engaged in tortious conduct in relation to the activities of their children. There is no suggestion in this case that the plaintiff was negligent or had committed any tort in her personal capacity.

Nevertheless, counsel for Zellers submits that, whatever the validity of the underlying claim, the plaintiff voluntarily paid the compensation sought and, in effect, entered into a valid and enforceable contract with Zellers: there was consideration moving both ways; in exchange for Zellers' forbearance to bring suit against her, the plaintiff voluntarily paid to them the sum of $225.00.

Counsel for the plaintiff submits that, in the circumstances, the law will not countenance such a contract; that Zellers was never entitled to claim or get any money from the plaintiff; and that the sum in question should be returned to her on equitable principles.

It is well settled that a forbearance to sue is good consideration and that monies paid in exchange for a promise not to sue is a valid and enforceable legal contract. There are qualifications to this general rule and they are well summed up in *Chitty on Contracts*, 27th ed., vol. 1, General Principles, Articles 3-041 to 3-04-5 which are as follows:

> "3-041 *Claims known to be invalid.* A promise is not binding if the sole consideration for it is a forbearance to enforce (or a promise to forbear from enforcing) a claim which is invalid and which is either known by the party forbearing to be invalid or not believed by him to be valid.
>
> . . . . .
>
> "3-043 Two further conditions must be satisfied by a party who relies on his forbearance to enforce an invalid claim as the consideration for a promise made to him. He must not deliberately conceal from the other party (i.e. the promisor) facts which, if known to the latter, would enable him to defeat the claim. *And he must show that he seriously intended to pursue the claim.* (Emphasis mine)
>
> . . . . .

In my opinion, the defendant's claim was not merely a doubtful claim — it was an invalid claim.

However, the matter is not quite so simple as that because the plaintiff has actually voluntarily paid the money over to Zellers. There was thus an executed compromise and so, ordinarily, the plaintiff would not be entitled to the return of the money. . . . To establish a claim for the return of the money, the plaintiff would have to rely on other grounds.

The ground advanced by counsel for the plaintiff is under the rubric of unjust enrichment: that the money was paid over by reason of a mistake in fact or law or both.

The plaintiff testified that when she got Mr. Arkin's letter, of course she had to decide what to do about it. She thought about it and discussed the matter with her husband. It was decided that the best course would be to simply pay the claim rather than to incur the loss of time and money and the aggravation involved in defending it. Hence, the claim was paid and her son was disciplined by "grounding" him and deducting a portion of the settlement monies from his regular allowance.

The plaintiff honestly believed that the claim was a serious one and that if she did not pay it the defendant would sue her.

. . . . .

I accept this evidence. After all, the plaintiff had received a letter from a lawyer who should know something about the law and who was making an apparently serious threat of legal action if the claim was not paid. And she paid. She would not have done so if she had not believed that there was something to it.

In this belief, the plaintiff was mistaken. Whatever legal opinion or opinions Zellers might have had regarding their claims generally, I cannot believe that they seriously thought that this claim could succeed or that they seriously intended to pursue it to court if it was not paid. Mr. Arkin was not called as a witness at the trial and so we do not have the benefit of what his opinion of the claim was. But I assume that as a competent and responsible lawyer, he knew or ought to have known that the claim had no prospect whatsoever of succeeding in court and that it would be futile to pursue it.

The plaintiff subsequently took legal advice, learned of her mistake and now wants her money back.

. . . . .

The plaintiff was certainly mislead [sic] by the tone and content of the lawyer's letter. In my opinion, in the particular circumstances of this case, the plaintiff is entitled to a refund on the ground of monies paid under a mistake.

The appeal is allowed and the plaintiff's claim is allowed with interest and costs. Although the claim is a small one, and was dealt with in the small claims procedure, it appeared to have been treated as a sort of "test" case which will have a bearing on Zellers entire recovery programme. Senior counsel were engaged and I received well-researched arguments on both sides. In the circumstances, I will allow the plaintiff her costs to be assessed as if this were a Class 2 action.

NOTES AND QUESTIONS

1. Do you think the defendant's lawyer should have been disciplined by the Law Society of Manitoba? Does it matter that no pleadings were filed? Does it matter that he was (presumably) instructed to write the demand letter by his client? What if, instead, he convinced Zellers to create the recovery programme? For a further discussion, see Amy Salzyn, "Zealous Advocacy or Exploitative Shakedown?: The Ethics of Shoplifting Civil Recovery Letters" (2015) 36 Windsor Rev. of Legal and Soc. Issues 1.

2. Should the costs of this action awarded to the mother have been awarded against Zellers or against its lawyer? Further, would it make a difference if Mr. Arkin, at trial, gave evidence that he believed — mistakenly — that the claims for recovery were somehow valid? For a discussion, see *Best v. Ranking*, [2016] O.J. No. 3284, 2016 ONCA 492 (Ont. C.A.), leave to appeal refused [2016] S.C.C.A. No. 372 (S.C.C.).

3. When evaluating the conduct of the defendant's lawyer, the judge in this case mentioned the notion of a "competent and responsible lawyer". For judicial commentary on what amounts to a lawyer's "duty of competence", see, *e.g.*, *R. v. McKenzie*, [2007] O.J. No. 3222 (Ont. C.A.). See further, *R. v. Meer*, [2016] S.C.J. No. 5, 2016 SCC 5, [2016] 1 S.C.R. 23 (S.C.C.).

4. How weak a case should a client have before counsel is criticized or sanctioned for pursuing it? What if the case were novel — for example, the pursuit of an action in tort where, previously, liability would have only arisen in contract law (that is, the classic case of *Donoghue v. Stevenson*, [1932] A.C. 562 (H.L.))? Traditionally, codes of conduct give some latitude to the right of lawyers to pursue novel or test cases. (See, *e.g.*, *Model Code*, Rule 3.2-7 and Commentary [4].) Consider the ethics of the following scenario:

Scenario One

In the residential schools litigation, damages were sought for harm done to the culture and community of former students who had been compelled to attend the schools. This was a novel cause of action. Based on principles governing pleadings set out here, how would you advise a client who approached you with this or a similarly novel claim? For similar novelty pleading issues being raised in a different legal context, see *Jane Doe v. Metropolitan Toronto (Municipality) Comissioners of Police*, [1990] O.J. No. 1584, 74 O.R. (2d) 225 (Ont. H.C.J.). For a further discussion of *Jane Doe*, see Trevor C.W. Farrow, "Five Pleadings Cases Everyone Should Read" (2009) 35(4) Advocates' Q. 466 at 478-480. Could counsel for Zellers have relied on the "novel" case argument, raised above, as a defence to the ethics of their conduct in writing the demand letter?

5. These letters, which typically include a basic articulation of an issue or dispute and a request or demand for some kind of action or resolution, essentially involve lawyers advocating on behalf of their clients. When thinking about the ethics of these letters, consider also the decision in *Law Society of British Columbia v. Laarakker*, [2011] L.S.D.D. No. 175, 2011 LSBC 29 (L.S.B.C.), which is included in section [5], "Advocacy and Civility", near the end of this chapter. In that case, the Law Society of British Columbia was faced with a complaint about the conduct of a lawyer who acted for a client who received a demand letter very similar to the demand letter that was at issue in *D.C.B. v. Zellers Inc.*

6. In the context of drafting a pleading, at what point does an advocate's effort to "raise fearlessly every issue [and] advance every argument" (*Model Code*, Rule 5.1-1 (Commentary [1])) through vigorous advocacy on behalf of a client turn into an exercise of using the litigation process for purposes that are "scandalous", "frivolous" or "vexatious" (see, *e.g.*, British Columbia's *Supreme Court Civil Rules*, B.C. Reg. 168/2009, Rule 9-5(1)) or that are "dishonourable" (*Model Code*, Rule 5.1-2(b))? Consider the following scenario:

Scenario Two

You are an employment law lawyer. You act for a small business. Your client would like to fire one of its employees and has asked you to draft the termination paperwork. The employee is not a particularly nice person, and some of their co-workers have complained that they do not help to create a particularly friendly or productive work environment. Having said that, their work is solid and all of their performance reviews have been positive. You are of the view that, although technically possible, justifying termination for cause would be a long shot (at best) in this situation. Your client, however, is strongly of the view that you should proceed to assist with the termination. Further, your client instructs you to make your termination letter as tough as possible, with a view to "wrangling" the best possible settlement out of the employee if the employee asks for something in return. What do you do? Do the rules of professional conduct assist you with that determination? For some guidance on this issue, see, *e.g.*, *Model Code*, Rules 5.1-2(a) and (b), 7.2-1, together with Rule 5.1-1.

7. Acting for clients in cases in which the other side is not represented by a lawyer — self-represented litigants (SRLs) — involves specific challenges and concerns (both before and during trial). While these circumstances may have at one time been rare, given the cost and general inaccessibility

of legal representation, SRLs are part of modern court and tribunal work (see further Chapter 11). In some jurisdictions and contexts (*e.g.*, family law), SRLs are more the rule than the exception. Given basic loyalty and conflict of interest obligations (see further Chapter 4), the lawyer acts only for their client (the "represented client") and not for the SRL. That should be made explicit and clear at the outset, to avoid any mistaken belief that somehow the lawyer acts for both parties in the litigation. According to the Court of Appeal for Ontario in *Girao v. Cunningham*, [2020] O.J. No. 1729, 2020 ONCA 260 at para. 152 (Ont. C.A.)(footnote omitted),

> [T]he professional ethical obligations of a lawyer toward a self-represented litigant is fairly limited under the Law Society of Ontario's *Rules of Professional Conduct*: see Law Society of Ontario, *Rules of Professional Conduct*, Toronto: Law Society of Ontario, 2000, (as amended), ch. 7, s. 7.2-9. I would further note that lawyers have more general ethical obligations when acting as an advocate, such as the duty to bring to the court's attention any binding authority that the lawyer considers to be directly on point that has not been mentioned by an opponent: see generally, *Rules of Professional Conduct*, ch. 5, s. 5.1-2. [For corresponding provisions, see *Model Code*, Rules 5.1-2(i), 7.2-9.]

8. In some circumstances, the represented client may want the lawyer to "take advantage" of the SRL. That is unethical and unprofessional. It is one thing to provide robust client advocacy; it is another to take unethical advantage of the other side. From time to time, the Court — and in some limited circumstances the lawyer for the represented client — may be asked to provide some basic information to the SRL in terms of accessing the legal system (for example, where to ask for help, what office to file materials, *etc.*). Having said that, the lawyer for the represented client must make sure not to cross the line and provide the SRL with legal advice.

9. As indicated above, the *Model Code* provides some guidance for lawyers who act for represented clients in cases involving SRLs. See, for example, Rule 7.2-9 and Commentary [1]. For further guidance, particularly (although not exclusively) in the context of online hearings, see the joint E-Hearings Task Force of The Advocates' Society, the Ontario Bar Association, the Federation of Ontario Law Associations, and the Ontario Trial Lawyers Association, *Best Practices for Remote Hearings* (May 13, 2020) at paras. 24-27, online: Advocates' Society https://www.advocates. ca/Upload/Files/PDF/Advocacy/BestPracticesPublications/BestPractices-RemoteHearings/Best_Practices_for_Remote_Hearings_13_May_2020_FINAL_may13.pdf. For further judicial comments, see, *e.g.*, *Pintea v. Johns*, [2017] S.C.J. No. 23, 2017 SCC 23 (S.C.C.); *Girao v. Cunningham*, [2020] O.J. No. 1729, 2020 ONCA 260 at paras. 148-157 (Ont. C.A.) (mentioned above). See also Jennifer A. Leitch, "Lawyers and Self-Represented Litigants an Ethical Change of Role?" (2017) 95:3 Can. Bar Rev. 669.

10. Would your thinking in Scenario Two above be any different if you knew that the employee did not have access to a lawyer to assist them with this matter? For further discussions and materials on self-represented liti-

gants, see National Self-Represented Litigants Project (NSRLP), online: //representingyourselfcanada.com/; Trevor C.W. Farrow, *et al.*, "Addressing the Needs of Self-Represented Litigants in the Canadian Justice System", A White Paper Prepared for the Association of Canadian Court Administrators (Toronto and Edmonton: 2012), online: Canadian Forum on Civil Justice //www.cfcj-fcjc.org/sites/default/files/docs/2012/Addressing% 20the%20Needs%20of%20SRLs%20ACCA%20White%20Paper%20March% 202012%20Final%20Revised%20Version.pdf.

[b]   Discovery

Perhaps one of the thorniest areas for advocacy dilemmas, arising typically after the pleadings stage, is the discovery process. This is one of the few areas of the litigation process where parties are asked essentially to open up their offices, homes, personal files, trade secrets, and other sensitive materials to the scrutiny of the other side. It is a moment of apparent cooperation in an otherwise largely combative system. Clients typically do not understand the discovery process and almost invariably do not like it.

Again, as a matter of civil procedure, discovery is subject to significant regulation. Provincial rules of court provide relatively detailed guidelines for the kinds of information that may be subject to discovery and the methods by which that information may or must be provided to the other side. Further, the same rules also typically provide litigants and the court with various remedial options for dealing with non- or improper conduct at all stages of the discovery process.[7]

However, notwithstanding these rules of civil procedure, the actual day-to-day process of discovery is largely conducted either (at the document production stage) in the privacy of the office or boardroom of a lawyer or client without the other side being present, or (when examinations for discovery are taking place) in a boardroom or court reporter's office without a judge being present. It is, therefore, largely in the hands of the parties and their lawyers, leaving significant need for rigorous ethical behaviour and significant room for unethical conduct.

Although many of the same ethical considerations apply, discovery involving electronically stored information has dramatically expanded the amount and sources of information that are potentially part of the discovery process. Advocates must be increasingly aware of new types of information and how that information can become part of the evidentiary process. Working with clients to uncover, access and disclose such information has become an increasingly central part of the advocate's role in the context of discovery. For general information, discussions and principles, see the Sedona Conference, online: Sedona Conference https://thesedonaconference. org/. For commentary, see e.g. Anatoliy Vlasov, "Judicial Treatment of the Sedona Canada Principles in Canadian Courts" (October 2020) CanLIIDocs 2615, online: CanLII https://canlii.ca/t/sxp3; Lisa A. Silver, "The Unclear Picture of Social Media Evidence" (2020) 43:3 Man L.J. 111; Gideon Christian, "Predictive Coding: Adopting and Adapting Artificial Intelligence in Civil Litigation" (2019) 97:3 Can.

---

[7]   See, *e.g.*, Ontario's Rules of Civil Procedure, R.R.O. 1990, Reg. 194, Rules 30.08, 31.07, 34.14-15, 35.05.

Bar Rev. 486; Gideon Christian, "Ethical and Legal Issues in E-Discovery of Facebook Evidence in Civil Litigation" (2017) 15:2 C.J.L.T. 335; Dana Remus, "The Uncertain Promise of Predictive Coding" (2014) 99 Iowa L. Rev. 101.

The following case highlights some of the professional, procedural and ethical challenges of discovery, in the context of the document production process. Although focusing primarily on the rules of court, the Court's strong language in this case applies equally to — and in fact directly engages — the professional and ethical obligations of an advocate actively to participate in the proper conduct of the discovery process (obligations that Lord Denning identified in *Rondel v. Worsley* as being part of the "difficult" balancing act of the advocacy role).[8]

GROSSMAN ET AL. V. TORONTO GENERAL HOSPITAL ET AL.

[1983] O.J. No. 3001, 41 O.R. (2d) 457
(Ont. H.C.J., Reid J.)

REID J.:— The action arises out of the death of Howard Grossman who is claimed to have been lost while a patient in the Toronto General Hospital ("the Hospital"). It is alleged that his body was discovered after 12 days in an air-duct shaft in the hospital.

The defence entered by the Hospital for itself and its staff amounts to a general traverse. Not even the death was directly admitted.

That document gave a hint of what was in store for plaintiffs. The Hospital's affidavit on production (the affidavit) revealed only one thing the Hospital had no objection to producing: the deceased's hospital record. That was the only entry made in the first part of the first schedule of the form . . . required by the Rules of Practice.

· · · · ·

I now turn to consider the attack made on the order requiring a better affidavit on production.

Defendants' position is essentially this: plaintiffs have failed to establish that any documents exist that should be produced other than the deceased's medical record and those now described in paras. 1(a) and (b) of the master's order. When I expressed surprise that a 12-day search for a missing patient in a hospital would not have produced one scrap of paper relevant to the issues in this lawsuit Mrs. Farrer replied that any such piece of paper would be privileged, the Hospital having retained solicitors at a very early point.

That may be so. It may be a proper basis for a claim of privilege for any and all documents other than the one thing produced voluntarily and the others forced out of defendants' hands by reason of the motion before the master . . .. However, no one could have told from reading defendants' original affidavit whether or not that claim was justified. The answer made in the second part of the first schedule is a mere boiler-plate calculated to conceal all and any documents from inspection. The

---

[8] *Rondel v. Worsley*, [1967] 1 Q.B. 443 (H.L.) (following note 27 and surrounding text), affd [1969] 1 A.C. 191.

result was to deprive opposing counsel of any basis for challenging the privilege claimed. Equally, if a challenge had been made, no court could have decided it, without resorting to ordering production to the court of all the documents referred to in the second part of the first schedule. Since no one could have known from reading the schedule what documents are referred to, that would have been an order made in the dark.

The Rules of Practice are designed to facilitate production, not frustrate it.

. . . . .

Honest differences of opinion might arise over the question whether a given document should or must be produced. If that occurs, the court has power to decide the issue . . . .

Notwithstanding [the rules of court] . . . it becomes quickly clear to anyone setting out to practise in the courts that "production" is open to serious abuse. The integrity of the system depends upon the willingness of lawyers to require full and fair discovery of their clients. The system is, in a sense, in the hands of the lawyers. The opportunity for stonewalling and improper concealment is there. Some solicitors grasp it. They will make only such production as can be forced from them. That is bad practice. It can work real injustice. It causes delay and expense while the other side struggles to see that which they had a right to see from the first. In such a contest the advantage is to the long purse. The worst consequence is that the strategy is sometimes successful, giving its perpetrators a disreputable advantage. The practice must be condemned. If it were widespread it would undermine the trial system.

Master Sandler has written of the susceptibility of the system to abuse. . . .

> I also observe that under our present system of documentary discovery, the choice as to what documents that are in a party's possession are relevant is, in the first instance, left up to the party itself, and my experience and observations have taught me that nowhere is the abuse of our rules of procedure greater than in this area of documentary production and in the failure of each party to fairly and reasonably disclose and produce to the opposite party all relevant documents, and to disclose the existence of all relevant but privileged documents. . . .

The duty upon a solicitor is now, and always has been, to make full, fair and prompt discovery. Williston and Rolls, in *The Law Of Civil Procedure* (1970), vol. 2, put it this way, at pp. 892-4:

> A party giving discovery is under a duty to make a careful search for all relevant documents in his possession and to make diligent inquiries about other material documents which may be in the possession of others for him. A solicitor has a duty of careful investigation and supervision and of advising his client as to what documents should be included in the affidavit, because a client cannot be expected to know the whole scope of his obligation without legal assistance. In *Myers v. Elman* [[1940] A.C. 282] a solicitor was ordered to pay the costs of the proceedings because his managing clerk was guilty of misconduct in the preparation and filing of an incorrect and inadequate affidavit. Lord Atkin said:

> "What is the duty of the solicitor? He is at an early stage of the proceedings engaged in putting before the Court on the oath of his client information which may afford evidence at the trial. Obviously he must explain to his client what is the meaning

of relevance: and equally obviously he must not necessarily be satisfied by the statement of his client that he has no documents or no more than he chooses to disclose. If he has reasonable ground for supposing that there are others he must investigate the matter; but he need not go beyond taking reasonable steps to ascertain the truth. He is not the ultimate judge, and if he reasonably decides to believe his client, criticism cannot be directed to him. But I may add that the duty is specially incumbent on the solicitor where there is a charge of fraud; for a wilful omission to perform his duty in such a case may well amount to conduct which is aiding and abetting a criminal in concealing his crime, and in preventing restitution."

Lord Wright put the matter even more bluntly:

"The order of discovery requires the client to give information in writing and on oath of all documents which are or have been in his corporeal possession or power, whether he is bound to produce them or not. A client cannot be expected to realize the whole scope of that obligation without the aid and advice of his solicitor, who therefore has a peculiar duty in these matters as an officer of the Court carefully to investigate the position and as far as possible see that the order is complied with. A client left to himself could not know what is relevant, nor is he likely to realize that it is his obligation to disclose every relevant document, even a document which would establish, or go far to establish, against him his opponent's case. The solicitor cannot simply allow the client to make whatever affidavit of documents he thinks fit nor can he escape the responsibility of careful investigation or supervision. If the client will not give him the information he is entitled to require or if he insists on swearing an affidavit which the solicitor knows to be imperfect or which he has every reason to think is imperfect, then the solicitor's proper course is to withdraw from the case. He does not discharge his duty in such a case by requesting the client to make a proper affidavit and then filing whatever affidavit the client thinks fit to swear to."

In the same case, there was a discussion of the duty to make further disclosure when subsequent to filing the affidavit other relevant documents were found. Viscount Maugham said:

"A solicitor who has innocently put on the file an affidavit by his client which he has subsequently discovered to be certainly false owes it to the Court to put the matter right at the earliest date if he continues to act as solicitor upon the record. The duty of the client is equally plain. I wish to say with emphasis that I reject the notion that it is justifiable in such a case to keep silence and to wait and wait till the plaintiff succeeds, if he can, in obtaining an order for a further and better affidavit. To do so is, in the language of Singleton J., to obstruct the interests of justice, to occasion unnecessary costs, and — even if disclosure is ultimately obtained — to delay the hearing of the action in a case where an early hearing may be of great importance."

Those pronouncements are clear and unequivocal. Anyone familiar with them, or with many others to the same effect, would not require a master's motion to know that the exhibits filed at the coroner's inquest would have to be produced in this case.

It has equally always been the case that sufficient information must be given of documents for which privilege is claimed to enable a party opposed in interest to be able to identify them. It is not, however, necessary to go so far as to give an indirect discovery. . . ..

327

. . . . .

The order made by Master Sandler is exactly in accord with the prevailing law as I understand it. I see no risk of an "indirect discovery" if defendants comply with reasonable common sense. It should be possible to describe a document sufficiently without revealing its contents.

The whole course of defendants' conduct has been to refuse to disclose anything on the ground that unless plaintiffs can prove something exists they have no right to know of its existence. The unfairness of that attitude is described by Master Sandler in *Bow Helicopters v. Textron Canada Ltd. et al.; Rocky Mountain Helicopters Inc. et al., Third Parties* (1981), 23 C.P.C. 212, he said at p. 214-15:

> I observe that in modern litigation, one of the most important tools in the pre-trial process is documentary discovery. . .and in no case is the proper use of this tool by the plaintiff more important than in a products liability case where the plaintiff must establish negligence in design or manufacture, or both, on the part of the defendant. In such a case, the defendant knows everything and usually has a large volume of documentary records, whereas the plaintiff has little or no information, except the product itself, and often, even that has been destroyed in the mishap. In this type of case, the plaintiff must try to penetrate the defendant's operation to see if it can discover records to indicate negligence in design or manufacture, and one tool to gain entry is the affidavit on production. . . .

This action is in a real sense the same as the action in *Bow Helicopters* so far as discovery is concerned, for most, if not all, of the relevant information is within the scope of defendants' knowledge, not plaintiffs'. That is what makes fair compliance with discovery obligations so acutely necessary.

Modern courts strongly favour disclosure.

. . . . .

The rule is, therefore, that a party must candidly describe in an affidavit on production not only documents for which no privilege is claimed but also those for which a privilege is claimed. It is not enough to do the one but not the other.

Litigation is, after all, a search for truth. Its processes are, we all know, imperfect. To permit advantage to be taken of its weaknesses to the point of injustice and unfairness would be wrong. Defendants' strategy in this case must not be tolerated. The appeal must be dismissed.

Plaintiffs ask for costs on a solicitor and his own client scale. That is a punitive award. Yet it was the disposition made by Master Sandler in both orders under appeal. It reveals his view of defendants' course of action.

That course of action may reflect merely excessive concern for the protection of his clients' rights or it may reveal simple stonewalling. My concern that it may be the latter is deepened by the decision of my brother Carruthers in *Fiege v. Cornwall General Hospital et al.* (1980), 30 O.R. (2d) 691 (S.C.), 117 D.L.R. (3d) 152. I am informed by counsel that the solicitor responsible for the defence in that case up to the point of trial is the solicitor responsible for the conduct of the defence herein. (That is not, I must add, Mrs. Farrer, whose lot it was to seek to justify someone else's conduct, and who did so with much skill and fortitude.) The failure in *Fiege* to produce an important document was strongly condemned by Carruthers J. He awarded costs on a solicitor and his own client scale against the defendant in that case because of the waste of time and money that resulted. The same may be said of this case. Time has been wasted and money thrown away. There is no merit in defendants' position.

. . . . .

Defendants' conduct in this case amounts to a deliberate refusal to comply with the notice to produce and is subject to . . . sanction. But in the absence of any indication that defendants' conduct was other than as advised by their solicitor, the responsibility for it must fall on the solicitor.

The consequences for a solicitor can be severe. In *Myers v. Elman*, [1940] A.C. 282, [1939] 4 All E.R. 484 (H.L.), the solicitor was ordered to pay the costs. If the course of action followed in this case were shown to be widespread an order to that effect would be appropriate as a general deterrent.

It could be argued that because this case is a repetition of conduct that has already been deplored that order should be made here. Although I have some doubt, I am satisfied to treat this case as an example of excessive zeal and to adopt Master Sandler's order. His order shall stand. The costs of the appeal shall be to plaintiffs in any event of the cause as between a solicitor and his own client. However, because this is a repetition of the same error found in *Fiege, supra*, the costs may be taxed forthwith and shall be payable forthwith thereafter.

The further affidavit, or affidavits, shall be delivered forthwith subject to any extension allowed by Master Sandler.

Appeal dismissed.

NOTES AND QUESTIONS

1. In *Grossman*, Justice Reid, after discussing the apparent discovery abuse that occurred on the part of the defendants (as apparently "advised by their solicitor", which was also apparently not the first time this kind of conduct involving the defendants' solicitor had occurred), was satisfied (although with "some doubt") that the discovery conduct by the defendants' counsel was "an example of excessive zeal". Justice Reid, therefore, although making a punitive solicitor-client (substantial indemnity) costs award, did not order the solicitor to pay those costs personally. Do you think Justice Reid was right? If subsequent proceedings before a law society discipline panel were brought against the defendants' lawyer, do you think the lawyer's conduct that was found to amount to "excessive zeal" would have offended against code of conduct provisions that regulate lawyers' actions when acting as advocates? Why or why not?

One of the primary areas for potential difficulty in the documentary production stage is confidentiality. Consider the following scenario:

Scenario Three

Suppose you act for a plaintiff in a products liability case against an automobile manufacturer involving a defective seatbelt. You have been seeking information on discovery concerning unrelated litigation in which the other side is involved regarding similar problematic issues with their seatbelt manufacturing processes (that you think are relevant to the issues in your litigation). Counsel for the other side indicates that such information is irrelevant, and that in any event, if it exists, it would also be privileged. You disagree but are unable to obtain the information. Four weeks before trial, counsel for the other side's assistant sends to you — by accident — the information that you have been seeking (it was sent to you instead of their client's auditors, for whom it was intended). You still think the material is relevant. You also question the claim that it is privileged. What should you do? On what professional basis will you make your decision? In answering this question you can take into account the fact that under the *Model Code* lawyers are obliged to advise the disclosing party that they have obtained inadvertently disclosed privileged documents and, depending on the circumstances, may then need either to destroy or return them (*Model Code*, Rules 7.2-2 and 7.2-10 and Commentaries [1]-[2]). For some commentary and potential guidance on the topic, see, *e.g.*, *Firemaster Oilfield Services Ltd. v. Safety Boss (Canada) (1993) Ltd.*, [2000] A.J. No. 1466, 285 A.R. 141 at paras. 23 and 29 (Alta. Q.B.), *per* Marceau J., affd [2001] A.J. No. 1317, 293 A.R. 366 (Alta. C.A.).

[c] Negotiation

Key to Reid J.'s reasoning in *Grossman* is the fact that the discovery process — because it occurs in private and out of court, and is therefore "open to serious abuse" — is "in the hands of the lawyers". Another advocacy process, again typically occurring prior to trial, which is similarly private and often in the hands of lawyers is settlement negotiation. As Armstrong J.A. has stated, "[s]ettlement discussion is something which pervades, and should pervade, almost every lawsuit".[9] And given the mounting costs and delays that are typical in the public court system, settlement negotiation is being actively encouraged not only by the courts,[10] but also by rules of civil procedure[11] and by litigants themselves.[12]

Settlement negotiations are also increasingly being encouraged by litigation lawyers and the professional code provisions that govern them. For example, according to *Model Code*, Rule 3.2-4, in the specific context of "encouraging compromise or settlement":

> Rule 3.2-4
>
> A lawyer must advise and encourage a client to compromise or settle a dispute whenever it is possible to do so on a reasonable basis and must discourage the client from commencing or continuing useless legal proceedings.
>
> Commentary

---

[9] *Ristimaki v. Cooper*, [2006] O.J. No. 1559, 79 O.R. (3d) 648 at para. 76 (Ont. C.A.).

[10] See *Ristimaki v. Cooper*, [2006] O.J. No. 1559, 79 O.R. (3d) 648 at para. 76 (Ont. C.A.).

[11] See, *e.g.*, Ontario's *Rules of Civil Procedure*, R.R.O. 1990, Reg. 194, Rule 49.

[12] For a general discussion on settlement preferences in the context of the civil process, see Trevor C.W. Farrow, *Civil Justice, Privatization, and Democracy* (Toronto: University of Toronto Press, 2014) at ch. 5.

[1] A lawyer should consider the use of alternative dispute resolution (ADR) when appropriate, inform the client of ADR options and, if so instructed, take steps to pursue those options.

Most codes of professional conduct, including the *Model Code*, are still relatively silent on the professional obligations of lawyers during the conduct of a negotiation. However, the Law Society of Alberta has included some further provisions in its *Code of Conduct* that govern an advocate's conduct during the negotiation process. For example, according to Rule 7.2-2, a lawyer "must not lie to or mislead another lawyer". According to the commentary to that Rule:

This rule expresses an obvious aspect of integrity and a fundamental principle. In no situation, including negotiation, is a lawyer entitled to deliberately mislead a colleague. When a lawyer (in response to a question, for example) is prevented by rules of confidentiality from actively disclosing the truth, a falsehood is not justified. The lawyer has other alternatives, such as declining to answer. If this approach would in itself be misleading, the lawyer must seek the client's consent to such disclosure of confidential information as is necessary to prevent the other lawyer from being misled. The concept of "misleading" includes creating a misconception through oral or written statements, other communications, actions or conduct, failure to act, or silence . . . .

Further, according to Rule 7.2-5 ("correcting misinformation") of Alberta's *Code of Conduct*:

If a lawyer becomes aware during the course of a representation that:

(a)   the lawyer has inadvertently misled an opposing party, or

(b)   the client, or someone allied with the client or the client's matter, has misled an opposing party, intentionally or otherwise, or

(c)   the lawyer or the client, or someone allied with the client or the client's matter, has made a material representation to an opposing party that was accurate when made but has since become inaccurate,

then, subject to confidentiality, the lawyer must immediately correct the resulting misapprehension on the part of the opposing party.

Because settlement negotiation is discussed elsewhere in this book (see Chapter 6), it will not be significantly further developed in this section. However, because a lawyer's vigorous settlement negotiation on behalf of a client is part of an advocate's role in the adversary system, the duties that apply to the conduct of such negotiations are part of ethics in advocacy. Consider the following scenario in light of the *Model Code* and Alberta's *Code of Conduct* provisions regarding negotiation and, as well, in light of the general ethical duties of an advocate that include both zealous advocacy and fidelity to the justice system.

Scenario Four

Suppose, in the employment law scenario discussed previously, the employee agrees to leave your client's company in return for a cash settlement. Your client authorizes you to settle the matter on the basis that it would pay the other side a lump sum of no more than $55,000 (the approximate equivalent of 10 months' salary). With that information in hand, are you ethically permitted to make the following statement at the settlement negotiation meeting with the lawyer on the other side: "Although my client would like to settle this matter, my sense is that it is not willing to pay a penny more than $35,000"? What if the other side does not have a lawyer – would that make any difference? In Alberta, does it matter that Rule 7.2-2 of the *Code of Conduct* prohibits lawyers from lying to or misleading another "lawyer", as opposed to another "party"? Is Rule 7.2-5 of Alberta's *Code of Conduct* more broadly framed?

[4] ETHICS AT TRIAL

Once the pre-trial procedures are complete and the trial process has started, a new opportunity begins for ethical issues to arise (not always with much time to think about or prepare for them). As was the case with the pre-trial stage, most of the ethical issues that arise in the context of trials engage the "difficult" balance that Lord Denning identified in *Rondel v. Worsley* between an advocate's "duty to his client and his duty to the court" (or more broadly to the overall administration of justice).[13]

According to the Supreme Court of Canada, the trial process "is one of the cornerstones of our constitutional democracy. It is essential to the maintenance of a civilized society. Trials are the primary mechanism whereby disputes are resolved in a just, peaceful, and orderly way."[14] At all times in the trial process, lawyers must balance their obligations to represent their client "fearlessly" and to "advance every argument . . . that . . . will help the client's case" (*Model Code*, Rule 5.1-1 (Commentary [1])) with their similarly strong obligation not to "knowingly assist or permit a client to do anything that the lawyer considers to be dishonest or dishonourable" (*Model Code*, Rule 5.1-2(b)). This balance is further articulated in *Model Code*, Rule 5.1-1:

> When acting as an advocate, a lawyer must represent the client resolutely and honourably within the limits of the law, while treating the tribunal with candour, fairness, courtesy and respect.

An advocate must, therefore, establish all trial conduct on the ethical side of that difficult balance. Respecting that boundary — where resolute advocacy must give way to respect for the limits of the law and the tribunal — requires the lawyer both to advocate and recognize advocacy's limits. Typically — as will be seen in the *Lyttle* case excerpted below — the basis of these determinations, in addition to rules of evidence and rules of professional conduct, is simply the conscience and good faith beliefs of the lawyer personally. But regardless of whether that line is sometimes difficult to see, it must not be crossed.

There are many aspects to the trial process that engage this balance, including representing facts and evidence to a jury in an opening statement, preparing your own witness for testimony and then taking the witness through their direct evidence, objecting to an opponent's line of questioning during the cross-examination of your

---

[13] *Rondel v. Worsley*, [1967] 1 Q.B. 443 (H.L.) (following note 27 and surrounding text), affd [1969] 1 A.C. 191.

[14] *Groia v. Law Society of Upper Canada*, [2018] S.C.J. No. 27, 2018 SCC 27 at para. 1 (S.C.C.). See generally Trevor C.W. Farrow, *Civil Justice, Privatization, and Democracy* (Toronto: University of Toronto Press, 2014).

client, calling reply evidence, cross-examining your opponent's witnesses, or summarizing the law in a closing argument before a judge or jury. All of these examples (several of which are discussed below) are moments when advocates must resist the urge to cross the line from vigorous adversarial representation to unethical conduct. They are also addressed by various rules of professional conduct (see, *e.g.*, *Model Code*, Rules 5.1-1-5.1-4).

[a]   Witness Preparation

Witness preparation is a particularly important but ethically thorny aspect of the trial process. It is well accepted that, as part of trial preparation, lawyers are expected to prepare their witnesses. Witness preparation often starts with a blanket instruction "always to tell the truth". Lawyers will then discuss a number of further issues, including: a review of the various parties' theories of the case; some of the basic issues and materials in the case; a review of the issues that the witness may be asked to speak about; specific areas of questioning; areas of particular interest to the other side; what the examination process will look like; what the judge might say; and other information about the experience of being a witness . Further, lawyers may also conduct some mock examinations and cross-examinations (to give the witness a feel for the process). All of that, when conducted properly and in good faith, is ethically acceptable and part of the trial preparation process.

It is also well-accepted that there is an important difference between witness "preparation" and witness "coaching". The distinction between the two is not always clear. However, unlike witness preparation, witness coaching (or "wood-shedding") is unethical and unprofessional. It is also illegal. Witness coaching takes preparation beyond the purpose of getting the witness comfortable with the process and with their own knowledge of the facts of the case, and into the terrain of evidence and witness tampering and obstruction of justice. Lawyers have a clear obligation not to assist their own client (or any witness) in the giving of false or misleading evidence. The rules of conduct forbid this kind of unethical behaviour. For example, according to *Model Code*, Rules 5.1-2(b) and (k), a lawyer shall not "knowingly assist or permit a client to do anything that the lawyer considers to be dishonest or dishonourable" [or] "knowingly permit a witness or party to be presented in a false or misleading way . . .". Further, according to *Model Code*, Rule 5.4-1(b), a lawyer must not "encourage the witness to suppress evidence or to refrain from providing information to other parties. . .". Similar rules and principles apply for witness preparation in the context of examinations for discovery and other examinations out of court (see, *e.g.*, *Model Code*, Rule 5.4-3, Commentary [8]).

In *R. v. Sweezey*,[15] the Newfoundland Court of Appeal considered an appeal by a lawyer of 14 years' standing from his sentence on a conviction for attempted obstruction of justice. The lawyer had counselled a witness to be forgetful and evasive when testifying. In its majority judgment (upholding the conviction but reducing the lawyer's sentence from 18 months to 12 months), the court — in the context of protecting the integrity of the evidentiary system and the administration of justice — cited the following excerpt from the trial judgment:

---

[15] [1987] N.J. No. 295, 66 Nfld. & P.E.I.R. 29 (Nfld. C.A.).

> The Canadian justice system relies on the honesty and integrity of counsel who practise within it. To that end, every lawyer is made an officer of the Courts in which he will practise. Cases before such Courts are in pursuit of justice through truthful evidence. A lawyer who attempts to obstruct justice by wilfully counselling evasive evidence not only commits an offence contrary to . . . the Criminal Code but also breaches his solemn duty as an officer of the Court.

This passage from *Sweezey* highlights some of the various potential avenues for sanction for misconduct on the part of an advocate, which can include: costs against a client; costs against a lawyer personally; a negative order under a given rule of civil procedure; a law society disciplinary order; and criminal sanctions. Further, and perhaps equally important, is the resulting negative reputation that will obtain in the eyes of an advocate's partners, fellow members of the bar, judges and current and future clients. Put simply, such conduct is just not worth it, for any case or any client.

The Court in *R. v. Spence*[16] provided a useful set of witness preparation guidelines for Crown prosecutors, which — with appropriate adaptation — could apply generally to most if not all witness preparation contexts. According to P.H. Howden J. at para. 28 (references omitted):

(a) Counsel should generally not discuss evidence with witnesses collectively.

(b) A witness's memory should be exhausted, through questioning and through, for example, the use of the witness' own statements or notes, before any reference is made (if at all) to conflicting evidence.

(c) The witness' recollection should be recorded by counsel in writing. It is sometimes advisable that the interview be conducted in the presence of an officer or other person, depending on the circumstances.

(d) Questioning the witness should be non-suggestive.

(e) Counsel *may* then choose to alert the witness to conflicting evidence and invite comment.

(f) In doing so, counsel should be mindful of the dangers associated with this practice.

(g) It is wise to advise the witness that it is his or her own evidence that is desired, that the witness is not simply to adopt the conflicting evidence in preference to the witness' own honest and independent recollection and that he or she is, of course, free to reject the other evidence. This is no less true if several other witnesses have given conflicting evidence.

(h) Under no circumstances should counsel tell the witness that he or she is wrong.

(i) Where the witness changes his or her anticipated evidence, the new evidence should be recorded in writing.

(j) Where a witness is patently impressionable or highly suggestible, counsel

---

[16] [2011] O.J. No. 2051, 2011 ONSC 2406 (Ont. S.C.J.).

may be well-advised not to put conflicting evidence to the witness, in the exercise of discretion.

(k)   Facts which are obviously uncontested or uncontestable may be approached in another way. This accords with common sense.

In light of the requirements set out in the *Model Code* and the warnings and guidelines provided in *R. v. Sweezey* and *R. v. Spence*, which of the following questions or statements likely amount to proper witness preparation and which amount to witness coaching? Why? Can you think of other examples?

(a)   "When you say you saw someone that night, wouldn't it be better to say that in fact you are pretty sure the person you saw was the defendant?"

(b)   "If you are asked that question on cross-examination, I think it would be better if you were to leave out the part about having been at a bar and drinking that night. I'm worried that, by saying you were drinking, you will be less credible to the judge or jury. Instead, just say you were out with friends — that's still true, isn't it?"

(c)   "When you testify tomorrow, in addition to always telling the truth, make sure that you typically only answer the question you are asked."

(d)   "When answering questions, don't just look at me. You should also from time to time look at the judge, and most importantly, don't forget the jury. They are the people who ultimately need to believe you."

(e)   "I think you should wear business attire when you come to court — you will look more professional and maybe more credible."

(f)   "I will be asking questions, the other side's lawyer will be asking questions, and from time to time the judge might ask you questions."

(g)   "I think you should go down to the courthouse before your trial next week — just to get a sense of the process."

(h)   "Remember that your theory of the case, as we set out in your pleading, is that the other side never agreed to the terms of the contract. So when you are asked about that on cross-examination, what are you going to say?"

(i)   "Let's go through some practice questions. I have brought in one of my law partners to play the role of opposing counsel, OK?"

(j)   "When the other side's lawyer asks you about the night in question, don't forget to say that it was raining."

(k)   "Based on the time and date stamp on the security camera video, your recollection of the timing of the events cannot be right, can it?"

(l)   "You just told me that you entered the store at 3:30 pm. You also just watched the video from the store security camera, which indicated that you entered the store at 4:30 pm (after the events in question). What do you have to say about all that?"

(m)   "The trial next week will be conducted by video. The judge, the lawyers and everyone else will be on a computer screen. So we should practice having you answer questions by video. When we do, make sure you look at your video camera. It's important to have eye contact, so that you don't look like you are avoiding something – OK?"

(n) "During the online hearing next week, documents will be shared on everyone's screen. If you don't know what the document is, or what to say, don't worry – just send me a text or use the private online 'chat' function and I'll let you know what it is."

For general discussions on the practice and ethics of witness preparation, see Bryan Finlay, Q.C., Honourable Justice Thomas A. Cromwell, Nikiforos Iatrou, *Witness Preparation: A Practical Guide* (Aurora, ON: Canada Law Book, 2010).

For recent guidance on witness preparation in the context of remote hearings, see the joint E-Hearings Task Force of The Advocates' Society, the Ontario Bar Association, the Federation of Ontario Law Associations, and the Ontario Trial Lawyers Association, *Best Practices for Remote Hearings* (13 May 2020) at paras. 60-64. For further materials and resources, see Canadian Bar Association, "Virtual Hearings".[17]

The *Best Practices for Remote Hearings* guide, and the CBA resources, provide some tips and commentary for remote hearings, specifically including recommendations involving the use and competence around remote technologies, e-documents and hearings. For example, although specific considerations and recommendations apply to the context of remote hearings, the *Best Practices for Remote Hearings* guide also provides that: "The applicable Rules of Professional Conduct and rules of practice and procedure should be referred to in all dealings with witnesses. Counsel's obligations and responsibilities remain the same regardless of the technology used to communicate with witnesses." See Canadian Bar Association, "Virtual Hearings".[18] For further commentary, see Gideon Christian, "Lawyer Ethics in the Virtual Courtroom"[19]; *Law Society of Alberta v. Adelowokan*, L.S.D.D. No. 10, 2020 ABLS 3 (cited in "Lawyer Ethics in the Virtual Courtroom".[20]

[b] Cross-Examination

In the following two cases, the issue of ethics in the context of cross-examination is discussed. In the first case, *R. v. Lyttle*, the Supreme Court of Canada articulates the scope of an advocate's ethical conduct in the context of cross-examination of an opposing witness. Although the case deals with a criminal matter, the Court's

---

[17] Online: CBA https://www.cba.org/Membership/COVID-19/Resources/Virtual-Hearings.

[18] Online: CBA https://www.cba.org/Membership/COVID-19/Resources/Virtual-Hearings.

[19] Gideon Christian, "Lawyer Ethics in the Virtual Courtroom" (June 3, 2020), online: ABlawg.ca, *University of Calgary, Faculty of Law* https://ablawg.ca/2020/06/03/lawyer-ethics-in-the-virtual-courtroom/#more-11618.

[20] Gideon Christian, "Lawyer Ethics in the Virtual Courtroom" (June 3, 2020), online: ABlawg.ca, *University of Calgary, Faculty of Law* https://ablawg.ca/2020/06/03/lawyer-ethics-in-the-virtual-courtroom/#more-11618).

statements regarding the appropriate scope of cross-examination at trial are relevant in the civil context as well. In the second case, *R. v. R. (A.J.)*, the Court of Appeal for Ontario examines the issue of Crown counsel's ethics in the context of cross-examining an accused. The comments of the court in *R. v. R. (A.J.)* on the need for counsel to be respectful of a witness during cross-examination are, again, also relevant to the civil context (see Chapter 7 for a general discussion of ethics in the criminal law context).

R. v. LYTTLE

[2004] S.C.J. No. 8, [2004] 1 S.C.R. 193
(S.C.C., McLachlin C.J.C., Major, Binnie, Arbour, LeBel,
Deschamps and Fish JJ.)

[Stephen Barnaby was beaten by five men with baseball bats, four of whom were masked. The fifth — the accused — was said to be unmasked. According to Barnaby, he was attacked over a gold chain. According to the police (in separate reports from two officers), the attack was related to a drug debt. Barnaby identified the accused in a photographic line-up. The theory of the defence's case was that Barnaby identified the accused as the man who attacked him in order to shield Barnaby's associates in a drug ring — the real assailants — from prosecution. The Crown did not plan to call the police who made the reports as witnesses. At trial, the judge ruled that counsel for the defence could only cross-examine the Crown's witnesses if she furnished "substantive evidence" of her "drug-debt" theory of the case. The defence called the officers as witnesses and, as a consequence, the accused lost his statutory right to address the jury last. No other evidence was called by the defence. The accused was convicted of robbery, assault, kidnapping and possession of a weapon. On appeal to the Ontario Court of Appeal, the Court found that the trial judge erred in allowing counsel for the accused to cross-examine only on matters for which she had a "substantive" evidentiary basis. However, the Court upheld the convictions and dismissed the appeal by resorting to the harmless error provision of s. 686(1)(b)(iii) of the *Criminal Code*. The accused appealed to the Supreme Court of Canada.]

The judgment of the Court was delivered by **MAJOR** and **FISH JJ.**:—

Cross-examination may often be futile and sometimes prove fatal, but it remains nonetheless a faithful friend in the pursuit of justice and an indispensable ally in the search for truth. At times, there will be no other way to expose falsehood, to rectify error, to correct distortion or to elicit vital information that would otherwise remain forever concealed.

. . . . .

In *R. v. Osolin*, [1993] 4 S.C.R. 595, Cory J. reviewed the relevant authorities and . . . explained why cross-examination plays such an important role in the adversarial process, particularly, though of course not exclusively, in the context of a criminal trial:

> There can be no question of the importance of cross-examination. It is of essential importance in determining whether a witness is credible. Even with the most honest witness cross-examination can provide the means to explore the frailties of the testimony. For example, it can demonstrate a witness's weakness of sight or

hearing. It can establish that the existing weather conditions may have limited the ability of a witness to observe, or that medication taken by the witness would have distorted vision or hearing. Its importance cannot be denied. It is the ultimate means of demonstrating truth and of testing veracity. Cross-examination must be permitted so that an accused can make full answer and defence. The opportunity to cross-examine witnesses is fundamental to providing a fair trial to an accused. This is an old and well established principle that is closely linked to the presumption of innocence. . . .

Commensurate with its importance, the right to cross-examine is now recognized as being protected by ss. 7 and 11(d) of the *Canadian Charter of Rights and Freedoms*. . . .

The right of cross-examination must therefore be jealously protected and broadly construed. But it must not be abused. Counsel are bound by the rules of relevancy and barred from resorting to harassment, misrepresentation, repetitiousness or, more generally, from putting questions whose prejudicial effect outweighs their probative value. . . .

Just as the right of cross-examination itself is not absolute, so too are its limitations. Trial judges enjoy, in this as in other aspects of the conduct of a trial, a broad discretion to ensure fairness and to see that justice is done — and seen to be done. In the exercise of that discretion, they may sometimes think it right to relax the rules of relevancy somewhat, or to tolerate a degree of repetition that would in other circumstances be unacceptable. . . .

This appeal concerns the constraint on cross-examination arising from the ethical and legal duties of counsel when they allude in their questions to disputed and unproven facts. Is a good faith basis sufficient or is counsel bound, as the trial judge held in this case, to provide an evidentiary foundation for the assertion?

Unlike the trial judge, and with respect, we believe that a question can be put to a witness in cross-examination regarding matters that need not be proved independently, provided that counsel has a good faith basis for putting the question. It is not uncommon for counsel to believe what is in fact true, without being able to prove it <u>otherwise than by cross-examination</u>; nor is it uncommon for reticent witnesses to concede suggested facts — in the mistaken belief that they are already known to the cross-examiner and will therefore, in any event, emerge. [Emphasis in original]

In this context, a "good faith basis" is a function of the information available to the cross-examiner, his or her belief in its likely accuracy, and the purpose for which it is used. Information falling short of admissible evidence may be put to the witness. In fact, the information may be incomplete or uncertain, provided the cross-examiner does not put suggestions to the witness recklessly or that he or she knows to be false. The cross-examiner may pursue any hypothesis that is honestly advanced on the strength of reasonable inference, experience or intuition. The purpose of the question must be consistent with the **lawyer's** role as an officer of the court: to suggest what counsel genuinely thinks possible on known facts or reasonable assumptions is in our view permissible; to assert or to imply in a manner that is calculated to mislead is in our view improper and prohibited.

. . . . .

[In] *R. v. Shearing*, [2002] 3 S.C.R. 33 . . . while recognizing the need for exceptional restraint in sexual assault cases, Binnie J. reaffirmed . . . the general rule that "in most instances the adversarial process allows wide latitude to cross-examiners to resort to unproven assumptions and innuendo in an effort to crack the untruthful witness." As suggested at the outset, however, wide latitude does not mean unbridled licence, and cross-examination remains subject to the requirements of good faith, professional integrity and the other limitations set out above. . . .

A trial judge must balance the rights of an accused to receive a fair trial with the need to prevent unethical cross-examination. There will thus be instances where a trial judge will want to ensure that "counsel [is] not merely taking a random shot at a reputation imprudently exposed or asking a groundless question to waft an unwarranted innuendo into the jury box". See *Michelson v. United States*, 335 U.S. 469 (1948), at p. 481, *per* Jackson J.

Where a question implies the existence of a disputed factual predicate that is manifestly tenuous or suspect, a trial judge may properly take appropriate steps, by conducting a *voir dire* or otherwise, to seek and obtain counsel's assurance that a good faith basis exists for putting the question. If the judge is satisfied in this regard and the question is not otherwise prohibited, counsel should be permitted to put the question to the witness.

. . . . .

The trial judge also made reference to the case of *Browne v. Dunn* . . ., as support for the proposition that an evidentiary foundation is required for questions put in cross-examination. He was mistaken. The rule in *Browne v. Dunn* requires counsel to give notice to those witnesses whom the cross-examiner intends later to impeach. The rationale for the rule was explained by Lord Herschell . . .:

> Now, my Lords, I cannot help saying that it seems to me to be absolutely essential to the proper conduct of a cause, where it is intended to suggest that a witness is not speaking the truth on a particular point, to direct his attention to the fact by some questions put in cross-examination showing that that imputation is intended to be made, and not to take his evidence and pass it by as a matter altogether unchallenged, and then, when it is impossible for him to explain, as perhaps he might have been able to do if such questions had been put to him, the circumstances which it is suggested indicate that the story he tells ought not to be believed, to argue that he is a witness unworthy of credit. My Lords, I have always understood that if you intend to impeach a witness you are bound, whilst he is in the box, to give him an opportunity of making any explanation which is open to him; and, as it seems to me, that is not only a rule of professional practice in the conduct of a case, but is essential to fair play and fair dealing with witnesses. Sometimes reflections have been made upon excessive cross-examination of witnesses, and it has been complained of as undue; but it seems to me that a cross-examination of a witness which errs in the direction of excess may be far more fair to him than to leave him without cross-examination, and afterwards to suggest that he is not a witness of truth, I mean upon a point on which it is not otherwise perfectly clear that he has had full notice beforehand that there is an intention to impeach the credibility of the story which he is telling.

The rule, although designed to provide fairness to witnesses and the parties, is not fixed. The extent of its application is within the discretion of the trial judge after taking into account all the circumstances of the case. . . . In any event, the foregoing rule in *Browne v. Dunn* remains a sound principle of general application, though irrelevant to the issue before the trial judge in this case.

As long as counsel has a good faith basis for asking an otherwise permissible question in cross-examination, the question should be allowed. In our view, no distinction need be made between expert and lay witnesses within the broad scope of this general principle. Counsel, however, bear important professional duties and ethical responsibilities, not just at trial, but on appeal as well. This point was emphasized by Lord Reid in *Rondel v. Worsley* . . . when he said:

> Every counsel has a duty to his client fearlessly to raise every issue, advance every argument, and ask every question, however distasteful, which he thinks will help his client's case. But, as an officer of the court concerned in the administration of justice, he has an overriding duty to the court, to the standards of his profession, and to the public, which may and often does lead to a conflict with his client's wishes or with what the client thinks are his personal interests. <u>Counsel must not mislead the court, he must not lend himself to casting aspersions on the other party or witnesses for which there is no sufficient basis in the information in his possession,</u> he must not withhold authorities or documents which may tell against his clients but which the law or the standards of his profession require him to produce. . . . [Emphasis added]

. . . . .

R. v. R. (A.J.)

[1994] O.J. No. 2309, 94 C.C.C. (3d) 168
(Ont. C.A., Osborne, Doherty and Laskin JJ.A.)

[The accused was charged with multiple counts of incest and sexual assault in relation to his daughter T. and his granddaughter J. The daughter T. had been given up for adoption at birth and had later sought out and found her father, the accused. When she was 20 years old, T. moved in with the accused, together with her own daughter, J. It was alleged that the sexual abuse of both T. and J. took place over the ensuing years until T. eventually went to the police. The accused was convicted at trial and appealed.]

DOHERTY J.A.:—

. . . . .

Counsel for the appellant submits that Crown counsel's cross-examination of the appellant resulted in a miscarriage of justice. He does not base this contention on any isolated feature of the cross-examination or any specific line of questioning, but contends that the overall conduct and tenor of the cross-examination was so improper and prejudicial to the appellant, that it rendered the trial unfair and resulted in a miscarriage of justice. This argument is becoming a familiar one in this court . . . [Doherty J.A. then cites four recent decisions of the Court.]

Crown counsel conducted an aggressive and exhaustive 141-page cross-examination of the appellant. She was well prepared and well armed for that cross-examination. Crown counsel is entitled, indeed, in some cases expected, to conduct a vigorous cross-examination of an accused. Effective cross-examination of an accused serves the truth-finding function as much as does effective cross-examination of a complainant.

There are, however, well-established limits on cross-examination. Some apply to all witnesses, others only to the accused. Isolated transgressions of those limits may be of little consequence on appeal. Repeated improprieties during the cross-examination of an accused are, however, a very different matter. As the improprieties mount, the cross-examination may cross over the line from the aggressive to the abusive. When that line is crossed, the danger of a miscarriage of justice is very real. If improper cross-examination of an accused prejudices that accused in his defence or is so improper as to bring the administration of justice into disrepute, an appellate court must intervene . . ..

After careful consideration of the entire cross-examination of the appellant in the context of the issues raised by his examination-in-chief and the conduct of the entire trial, I am satisfied that the cross-examination must be characterized as abusive and unfair.

From the outset of the cross-examination, Crown counsel adopted a sarcastic tone with the accused and repeatedly inserted editorial commentary into her questions. I count at least eight such comments in the first eight pages of the cross-examination. During that part of the cross-examination, Crown counsel referred to one answer given by the appellant as "incredible". She repeatedly asked the appellant if he "wanted the jury to believe that one too". When questioned as to how he met T., the appellant said he was told by a friend that a relative would be coming to see him, whereupon Crown counsel remarked "so I guess you were expecting some long lost cousin in the old country". After the appellant had described his reaction to being told by T. that she was his daughter, Crown counsel sarcastically said "gee, I guess everybody would react the way you did".

Crown counsel's approach from the very beginning of the cross-examination was calculated to demean and humiliate the appellant. She persisted in that approach throughout. For example, after the appellant said that he had allowed T. to move in with him shortly after they had met, Crown counsel said "you are just a really nice guy". At another point, she said "tell me sir, do fathers usually have sexual intercourse with their daughters". Still later, after the appellant had testified that his girlfriend had left him but had told him that she wished to come back, Crown counsel said "you just have all these women running after you wanting to come back".

These are but a few of a great many instances where Crown counsel used the pretence of questioning the appellant to demonstrate her contempt for him and the evidence he was giving before the jury. No counsel can abuse any witness. This self-evident interdiction applies with particular force to Crown counsel engaged in the cross-examination of an accused.

The tone adopted by Crown counsel is not the only problem with her cross-examination. Crown counsel repeatedly gave evidence and stated her opinion during cross-examination. She also engaged in extensive argument with the appellant. For example, when the appellant gave contradictory explanations in the course of cross-examination, Crown counsel announced "you were lying", and when the appellant questioned Crown counsel's description of T. as "your victim" Crown counsel replied "certainly she is". Still later, after Crown counsel had very effectively cross-examined the appellant as to when he had learned that T. was his daughter, she proclaimed "you are playing games with me, with this jury". She followed that comment with the admonition "let's try and be honest". In several instances, the cross-examination degenerated into pure argument between the appellant and Crown counsel. After one lengthy exchange, Crown counsel announced: "it is hard to keep up with you sir because you keep changing your story".

Statements of counsel's personal opinion have no place in a cross-examination. Nor is cross-examination of the appellant the time or place for argument.

. . . . .

Cases like this, where the allegations are particularly sordid, the complainants particularly sympathetic and the accused particularly disreputable, provide a severe test of our criminal justice system. It is very difficult in such cases to hold the scales of justice in balance and to provide the accused with the fair trial to which he or she is entitled. By her cross-examination, Crown counsel skewed that delicate balance. The cross-examination, considered in its totality and in the context of the entire trial, prejudiced the appellant in his defence and significantly undermined the appearance of the fairness of the trial.

. . . . .

[Appeal allowed.]

NOTES AND QUESTIONS

1. Is an advocate's assurance of their "good faith basis" for conducting a given line of cross-examination, as required by the Supreme Court of Canada in *Lyttle*, adequate to protect potential witnesses? Does it answer the concern of Jackson J. in the *Michelson* case, of a "random shot at a reputation imprudently exposed or asking a groundless question to waft an unwarranted innuendo into the jury box"? Does *Lyttle* strike the right balance between the rights of the accused, the rights of a witness and the overall protection of the administration of justice? Can the decision of the court in *R. v. R. (A.J.)* be used in conjunction with *Lyttle* to make it clear what a lawyer is to do, or do the cases together simply make the lawyer's exercise of discretion more complicated?

2. As discussed above in the context of witness preparation, rules of professional conduct typically provide some guidance to advocates in the context of their participation in the evidentiary process (see, *e.g.*, *Model Code*, Rule 5.1-2). Do these ethical requirements fit with the wide latitude given to advocates by the Supreme Court of Canada in *Lyttle* in the context of the cross-examination of an opposing witness?

3. How should lawyers balance the various obligations set out in *Lyttle* and *R. v. R. (A.J.)*? How are they similar and how are they different? Did Crown counsel in *R. v. R. (A.J.)* conduct themself in the manner explicitly permitted by *Model Code*, Rule 5.1-3, which provides that: "When acting as a prosecutor, a lawyer must act for the public and the administration of

justice resolutely and honourably within the limits of the law while treating the tribunal with candour, fairness, courtesy and respect"? Does the nature of the allegations have any relevance to your thinking? Does it make a difference if an accused is represented by counsel?

4. The high profile trial of Jian Ghomeshi — *R. v. Ghomeshi*, [2016] O.J. No. 1487, 2016 ONCJ 155 (Ont. C.J.) — raised in the public mind questions about the scope of cross-examination in criminal trials (particularly involving sexual assault allegations). The Supreme Court of Canada, in *Lyttle*, cited comments from Binnie J. in *R. v. Shearing*, which noted – notwithstanding "the general rule" that "in most instances the adversarial process allows wide latitude to cross-examiners" – a "need for exceptional restraint in sexual assault cases". For a discussion of lawyers' ethics and sexual assault trials, see Elaine Craig, *Putting Trials on Trial: Sexual Assault and the Failure of the Legal Profession* (Montreal and Kingston: McGill-Queen's University Press, 2018); Alice Woolley, "Defending Rapists" (December 30, 2016), online: *ABlawg. ca*, University of Calgary, Faculty of Law //ablawg.ca/wp-content/uploads/2016/12/Blog_AW_DefendingRapists.pdf.

[c] Representations about the Law

The *Sweezey, Spence, Lyttle* and *R. v. R. (A.J.)* cases deal with an advocate's ethical role in the evidentiary process. Equally important are ethical considerations regarding an advocate's obligation to inform the court about governing authorities, both positive and negative, an obligation to which Lord Denning M.R. referred in *Rondel v. Worsley*[21] as being part of an advocate's role as a "minister of justice".

Codes of conduct are typically sources of this obligation. See, for example, *Model Code*, Rule 5.1-2(i), which provides that a lawyer shall not

> deliberately refrain from informing a tribunal of any binding authority that the lawyer considers to be directly on point and that has not been mentioned by another party.

The following case provides judicial treatment of this important ethical obligation of an advocate.

GENERAL MOTORS ACCEPTANCE CORP. OF CANADA v. ISAAC ESTATE

[1992] A.J. No. 1083, 7 Alta. L.R. (3d) 230
(Alta. Q.B., Master Funduk)

MASTER FUNDUK:— These are competing applications for summary judgment.

In June 1991 Frank and Jean Isaac, who are husband and wife, bought a car from Ken Beauchamp Chevrolet Oldsmobile Ltd. under a conditional sale contract. The dealer assigned the contract to the Plaintiff.

The evidence by a son of the Isaacs is that the father has been in an auxiliary hospital since February 1989 (so he would obviously not need a car) and the mother was

---

[21] [1967] 1 Q.B. 443 (H.L.).

diagnosed with an incurable malignant brain tumor in August, 1991, was hospitalized and later passed away.

After the mother's condition became known the family discussed what to do with the car.

[The family then decided to give up the car and indicated that they had done so by surrendering it through the dealer and the plaintiff. However, the plaintiff subsequently successfully moved to a Master for possession of the car, not by accepting the family's surrender of it or by seizure, but rather pursuant to the preservation rules of Alberta's Rules of Court. The plaintiff then sold the car.]

Counsel cited a number of cases in their written briefs and their oral submissions. Although I have read the cases I need not dwell on them. The matter can be properly disposed of based on a case not cited by either counsel in their briefs, but which was brought forward by me at the end of the application: *G.M.A.C. v. Sherwood* . . . . An appeal to the Court of Appeal was dismissed from the Bench; C.A. Calgary 12743, Sept. 29, 1992.

Sherwood is also a case of a conditional sale contract assigned by the vendor to the same financier.

. . . . .

The Plaintiff in this action and the plaintiff in the *Sherwood* action are the same. In addition, counsel for the Plaintiff was also the counsel for the plaintiff in *Sherwood*.

There is a remarkable similarity between the order in *Sherwood* and the order in this action.

. . . . .

I am satisfied that here, as in *Sherwood*, that the Plaintiff attempts to go against the car and also to sue for the purchase price. The law is seize or sue, not seize and sue or sue and seize.

What happened here is just an attempt to get around s. 49(4) [of the Alberta *Law of Property Act*]. As in *Sherwood*, the attempt fails. In *Sherwood* the Court of Appeal uses the word "scheme" to describe what the plaintiff did. The same can be said here. This is all just a scheme by the Plaintiff to exercise its rights against the car without the limitation imposed by s. 49(4).

Decision

One

The application by the Plaintiff for summary judgment is dismissed. There will be summary judgment [for the defendant] dismissing the action.

Two

This is a case which calls for solicitor and client costs because of exceptional circumstances.

This application was heard as a special afternoon application.

Mr. Weldon, counsel for the Plaintiff, filed a written brief on October 20, 1992.

Mr. Vipond, counsel for the Defendants, filed a written brief on October 26, 1992.

Neither written brief refers to Sherwood although both are over a year after the chambers judge's decision and, as it turns out — over a short time after the Court of Appeal's decision.

When I read the briefs I noticed that neither referred to Sherwood. I was aware of the two Queen's Bench decisions in Sherwood but I was not aware of the Court of Appeal's decision.

I eagerly awaited to see if either counsel would bring up Sherwood in their oral submissions. Neither did. I assumed, wrongly as it turns out, that neither was aware of it.

At the end of the day, after I had heard the submissions of both counsel, I told them that I was reserving my decision and that I would give a written decision.

I then told counsel that there was a remarkably similar case where there was a written decision by Master Alberstat which was upheld by a written decision by a chambers judge. (I had not had the time to run down the case and I did not offhand know its name or who counsel were on it.)

My disclosure at the end of the day of my knowledge of the two Queen's Bench decisions in Sherwood prompted a sudden revelation by Mr. Weldon of his knowledge of the case. He quickly told me the name of the case, that he was counsel for GMAC on it and that he had been rejected by the Court of Appeal a few weeks before.

When I disclosed my knowledge of Sherwood it became obvious that I intended to run it down (when I got back to Edmonton) and that I would then see that Mr. Weldon was counsel for GMAC on it. The jig was up. Better a belated disclosure than not one at all.

It was Mr. Weldon's responsibility as an officer of the Court to bring Sherwood to my attention. Silence about a relevant decision, especially a binding one, is not acceptable.

I am satisfied that only my fortuitous knowledge of the Queen's Bench decisions in Sherwood and my disclosure of that knowledge were the events which triggered Mr. Weldon's disclosure of his knowledge of Sherwood. It is not supposed to be that way.

It would not be an answer to say that Sherwood is distinguishable so it need not be disclosed. That also does not work that way. The fallacy in that argument should be obvious. That would leave it to counsel to decide if a case is distinguishable. Counsel do not make that decision. The Court does.

It is proper for counsel to bring forward a relevant case and then submit that it is distinguishable for whatever reason. That is fair play. It is improper to not bring forward a relevant case on the ground that it is distinguishable. That is not fair play.

Mr. Vipond, counsel for the Defendants, did not refer to *Sherwood* in either his written brief or his oral submissions. I have no doubt he simply was not aware of Sherwood.

I will close my comments under this heading by a quote from *Lougheed Enterprises v. Armbruster* [[1992] B.C.J. No. 712 (C.A.)]:

There is here an apparent conflict between two principles:

1. This is an adversarial system. That being so, every judge is generally in the hands of counsel, or where a party is not represented by counsel, in the hands of that party, on the points to be raised and decided. A judge, as has often been said, must not "descend into the arena".

2. A judge has an overriding duty, in the words of the old judicial oath, "to administer justice without fear or favour, affection or ill-will according to the laws and usages of this realm." To this extent, the judge has a duty to ensure that the law is applied, even though the litigants may not be aware of its requirements.

The concept of judicial self-restraint, to which we adhere, is founded, if not wholly, at least in part, upon the assumption that counsel will do their duty, which is to do right by their clients and right by the court, and that all parties will be represented by counsel. In this context, "right" includes taking all legal points deserving of consideration and not taking points not so deserving. The reason is simple. Counsel must assist the court in doing justice according to law. When a point is deserving of consideration, the judge must have regard to all the relevant authorities.

As Lord Birkenhead, then Lord Chancellor, said in *Glebe Sugar Refining Co. v. Greenock Port & Harbours Trustees . . .*:

It was not, of course, in cases of complication possible for their Lordships to be aware of all the authorities, statutory or other, which might be relevant to the issues requiring decision in the particular case. Their Lordships were therefore very much in the hands of counsel and those who instructed counsel in these matters, and the House expected, and indeed insisted, that authorities which bore one way or the other upon the matters under debate should be brought to the attention of their Lordships by those who were aware of those authorities. That observation was irrespective of whether or not the particular authority assisted the party which was aware of it.

The Lord Chancellor's remarks arose in the following circumstance. An appeal was argued before the House of Lords in which neither party referred to a provision in an 1847 Act incorporated by reference in the 1913 statute under consideration. After argument Lord Atkinson looked at the 1847 Act and drew one of its sections, which bore on the issue, to the attention of his colleagues. A second hearing was ordered before the same panel confined to the effect of the 1847 provision. It was held to dispose of the issues before the court. In allowing the appeal ([1921] 2 A.C. 66 at 76 (H.L.)), Lord Birkenhead concluded [written judgment]:

The appeal succeeds, not, however, upon the grounds put forward by the appellants, but upon grounds never put forward by the appellants (though they should have been); never alluded to by either of the parties in any court. It may be that this omission has brought about the entire litigation, certainly I should think it has brought about this appeal. I therefore think that both parties should bear their own costs here and below.

The term "relevant" in the context of the case before us means that counsel has a duty to be aware of all cases in point decided within the judicial hierarchy of British Columbia which consists of the Supreme Court of Canada, this Court and the Supreme Court of British Columbia, and where applicable, one of its predecessor courts, the County Court and to refer the Court to any on which the case might turn.

It is not necessary in these reasons to go into the exceptions to this duty. It is not the same as the duty to one's client to be persuasive which often requires counsel to produce authorities outside the hierarchy of British Columbia.

But these points must be made:

1. We do not expect counsel to search out unreported cases, although if counsel knows of an unreported case in point, he must bring it to the court's attention.

2. "On point" does not mean cases whose resemblance to the case at bar is in the facts. It means cases which decide a point of law.

3. Counsel cannot discharge his duty by not bothering to determine whether there is a relevant authority. In this context, ignorance is no excuse.

In the case at bar, there was a relevant authority which went to the very root of these proceedings. It said that the order sought in the petition could not be granted as a matter of law.

. . . . .

The duty to bring relevant law to the attention of the court is founded upon the proposition that counsel has an obligation to the court to assist in duly administering the law, as well as a duty to his client and that, in some circumstances, the former duty may override the latter.

In these special circumstances the Defendants will have costs of the action against the Plaintiff on a solicitor and client basis.

NOTES AND QUESTIONS

1. Notwithstanding counsel's failure to bring the *Sherwood* case to the attention of the court in *Isaac Estate*, Master Funduk ordered costs against the plaintiff, but not the lawyer, on the solicitor and client scale. Was that the correct order? If disciplinary proceedings were brought against the lawyer by the law society in your jurisdiction, what would the result be? What are the competing arguments that counsel for the law society and counsel for the lawyer would make at that disciplinary hearing? Which do you prefer? Why?

2. For a particularly colourful judgment regarding a lawyer's duty to bring controlling precedents to the court's attention, see *Gonzalez-Servin v. Ford Motor Co.*, 662 F.3d 931 (7th Cir. 2011).

3. *Lougheed Enterprises v. Armbruster*, cited by Master Funduk in *Isaac Estate*, noted that the "concept of judicial self-restraint" is premised on, among other things, "the assumption that . . . all parties will be represented by counsel". Given the prevalence of SRLs in modern litigation, should there be special obligations on counsel to search for and provide authorities, particularly including negative authorities, in cases involving SRLs? When acting in a case involving an SRL, does the balance change in the context of the following two *Model Code* provisions: "The lawyer's function as advocate is openly and necessarily partisan. Accordingly, the lawyer is not obliged (except as required by law or under these rules . . . to assist an adversary or advance matters harmful to the client's case"

(Rule 5.1-1, Commentary [3]); and "When acting as an advocate, a lawyer must not . . . deliberately refrain from informing a tribunal of any binding authority that the lawyer considers to be directly on point and that has not been mentioned by another party" (Rule 5.1-2(i)). Are these provisions easily reconcilable, particularly given the decision in *Isaac Estate*, in the context of cases involving SRLs? What about cases in which all parties are self-represented? For recent judicial commentary, see *Girao v. Cunningham*, [2020] O.J. No. 1729, 2020 ONCA 260 at para. 152 (Ont. C.A.), mentioned earlier in this chapter (at section [3][a], "Pleadings", note 7).

4.   In addition to informing the court about negative legal authorities that are on point, counsel must also make sure to avoid misleading the court and the other side during the course of litigation about facts or issues relevant to the case. Further, counsel must, subject to rules of confidentiality, take steps to correct misapprehensions. For a further treatment of this issue, see *Law Society of Alberta v. Piragoff*, [2005] L.S.D.D. No. 47 (L.S.A.).

Consider the competing legal, personal and professional obligations in the following scenario:

Scenario Five

Assume that your practice focuses primarily on construction law, real estate and municipal regulatory matters. You are contacted by a potential client who owns a home just outside a relatively small town. She has begun renovating her home and a small cabin on her property using a local contractor. Specifically, in the cabin, which she uses as part of her bed-and-breakfast business, she is upgrading the kitchen and bathroom facilities, replacing the roof, moving some interior walls, replacing the electrical service and adding a new set of windows. The renovations to her house are smaller and simply involve painting and some plumbing repairs and upgrades to existing fixtures. At the planning stage, she asked her contractor about the need for building permits. The contractor said that, because the renovations are in the nature of "repairs" instead of "improvements", local by-laws did not require permits for the project. The contractor also indicated that the local member of town council is a friend of his with whom he regularly socializes and goes on fishing trips. With all of this, the contractor told your client "not to worry" about permits. Part way through the renovation process, your client was visited by the local building inspector (because of some complaints from the neighbours). The inspector asked to see the building permit, which of course did not exist. Shortly after the inspector's visit, your client received a "stop work" order as well as a letter indicating that if work did not stop and if a permit were not obtained, the town would consider its legal options including taking her to court. Your client is very concerned about the situation. Specifically, in order to obtain a permit, there is at least the potential concern that some of the renovation work will need to be undone and, in any event, a significant fine will likely be imposed. More importantly, however, because other work over the years has been done on the property for which permits were also not obtained, your client is concerned about the possibility of having inspectors combing the balance of the property on a re-inspection visit. Last week, the contractor was at a party with the member of council. After hearing about the situation from the contractor, the member of council indicated that your client "should just ignore the inspector. He is simply trying to flex his muscles and has no authority to be threatening lawsuits. The council would have to approve that kind of action, which it rarely does. And in any event, the council has no money at the moment to pursue these kinds of issues. So she has nothing to worry about". Based on your experience, you happen to know that the member of council is likely correct: although litigation is possible (particularly given the apparent multiple permit-related infractions on the property), at the moment it is unlikely that the council would pursue litigation against your client. Your client is very concerned about potential litigation. When thinking about whether to take the retainer, you look at Rule 5.1-1 (and Commentaries [1], [3] and [5]) and Rule 5.1-2(b) of the *Model Code.* You are of the view that land use and municipal planning matters are important public policy initiatives. Your practice also involves a significant amount of ongoing work and contact with the local authorities. However, because you are a lawyer, you are aware that all clients deserve adequate representation. Do you take this case? On what basis? If you do, subject to rules of confidentiality and conflict of interest (discussed further in Chapters 3 and 4 of this book), which *Model Code* provisions set out above, or others from your jurisdiction, will influence or determine the way you approach your advice or the way you will proceed to advocate on behalf of your client? Whose interests are at stake in this case? Do you have obligations to balance those interests?

[5] ADVOCACY AND CIVILITY

"Civility" amongst lawyers is a term that can mean many things. According to Alice Woolley, "Does Civility Matter?" (2008) 46 Osgoode Hall L.J. 175 at 177-179,[22] civility, as applied by law societies and as expressed in "civility" provisions, has two central meanings. First, it includes a requirement that lawyers treat each other, and those participating in the justice system, with a degree of politeness. Second, it has been defined to include obligations — which are also enshrined independently in provisions of law society codes of conduct — on lawyers to act fairly, honestly and with integrity in their dealings with other lawyers and with members of the court. Civility is said to help ensure that lawyers uphold their duties as officers of the court and maintain and improve the standing of the administration of justice in the eyes of the public. Sources for this obligation are at least fourfold:

(1) The court's inherent jurisdiction to govern proceedings in the courtroom, including lawyers' conduct within those proceedings, includes obligations for lawyer civility. This jurisdiction is exercised in the *Schreiber* case that follows.

(2) Codes of conduct contemplate a high level of lawyer civility. In addition to *Model Code*, Rule 5.1-5, dealing specifically with "courtesy" in the context of the lawyer's role as "advocate", *Model Code*, Rules 7.2-1 (and Commentaries [1]-[4]), 7.2-2 and 7.2-4 (dealing with "courtesy and good

---

[22] See also Alice Woolley, "'Uncivil by too much civility'?: Critiquing Five More Years of Civility Regulation in Canada" (2013) 36:1 Dal. L.J. 239; Amy Salyzyn, (2013) "John Rambo v. Atticus Finch: Gender, Diversity and the Civility Movement" (2013) 16:1 Leg. Ethics 97.

faith") set out specific obligations on lawyers to act with civility and courtesy, to "agree to reasonable requests" and to "avoid sharp practice".

(3) Best practice civility codes have been developed that, although not formally binding, provide guidance for courts, lawyers and regulators in the area of civility. See, *e.g.*, the Advocates' Society, *Principles of Civility and Professionalism for Advocates* (20 February 2020), an earlier version of which was referred to, for example, by Newbould J. in *Schreiber*, below.

(4) Regardless of judicial or professional sources, lawyers' own personal ethics play an important and positive self-regulating role in the area of civility.

Although these various sources promote its importance, civility is not an uncontroversial principle. Well-intentioned lawyers sometimes balk at civility, on the theory that it can at times chip away at their role as a zealous advocate. Those in favour respond that just because a lawyer decides to be civil to the other side does not mean that the lawyer is necessarily prejudicing the client's case — judges and juries can in fact derive negative impressions of bad conduct which may impair the clients' interests.[23] Clearly, there is a balance that must ultimately be struck, a balance that was directly addressed by the Supreme Court of Canada in *Groia*, below.

GROIA V. LAW SOCIETY OF UPPER CANADA

[2018] S.C.J. No. 27, 2018 SCC 27
[footnotes and some case references omitted]

Reasons for judgment delivered by Moldaver J., concurred in by McLachlin C.J. and Abella, Wagner and Brown JJ. Concurring reasons delivered by Côté J. Dissenting reasons delivered by Karakatsanis, Gascon and Rowe JJ.

Moldaver J.:—

I. Overview

The trial process in Canada is one of the cornerstones of our constitutional democracy. It is essential to the maintenance of a civilized society. Trials are the primary mechanism whereby disputes are resolved in a just, peaceful, and orderly way.

To achieve their purpose, it is essential that trials be conducted in a civilized manner. Trials marked by strife, belligerent behaviour, unwarranted personal attacks, and other forms of disruptive and discourteous conduct are antithetical to the peaceful and orderly resolution of disputes we strive to achieve.

By the same token, trials are not — nor are they meant to be — tea parties. A lawyer's duty to act with civility does not exist in a vacuum. Rather, it exists in concert with a series of professional obligations that both constrain and compel a lawyer's behaviour. Care must be taken to ensure that free expression, resolute

---

[23] See, *e.g.*, Robert F. Reid & Richard E. Holland, *Advocacy: Views from the Bench* (Aurora, ON: Canada Law Book, 1984) at 28-30.

advocacy and the right of an accused to make full answer and defence are not sacrificed at the altar of civility.

The proceedings against the appellant, Joseph Groia, highlight the delicate interplay that these considerations give rise to. At issue is whether Mr. Groia's courtroom conduct in the case of *R. v. Felderhof*, 2007 ONCJ 345, 224 C.C.C. (3d) 97, warranted a finding of professional misconduct by the Law Society of Upper Canada. To be precise, was the Law Society Appeal Panel's finding of professional misconduct against Mr. Groia reasonable in the circumstances? For the reasons that follow, I am respectfully of the view that it was not.

The Appeal Panel developed an approach for assessing whether a lawyer's uncivil behaviour crosses the line into professional misconduct. The approach, with which I take no issue, targets the type of conduct that can compromise trial fairness and diminish public confidence in the administration of justice. It allows for a proportionate balancing of the Law Society's mandate to set and enforce standards of civility in the legal profession with a lawyer's right to free speech. It is also sensitive to the lawyer's duty of resolute advocacy and the client's constitutional right to make full answer and defence.

Moreover, the Appeal Panel's approach is flexible enough to capture the broad array of situations in which lawyers may slip into uncivil behaviour, yet precise enough to guide lawyers and law societies on the scope of permissible conduct.

That said, the Appeal Panel's finding of professional misconduct against Mr. Groia on the basis of incivility was, in my respectful view, unreasonable. Even though the Appeal Panel accepted that Mr. Groia's allegations of prosecutorial misconduct were made in good faith, it used his honest but erroneous views as to the disclosure and admissibility of documents to conclude that his allegations lacked a reasonable basis. However, as I will explain, Mr. Groia's allegations were made in good faith and they were reasonably based. As such, the allegations themselves could not reasonably support a finding of professional misconduct.

Nor could the other contextual factors in this case reasonably support a finding of professional misconduct against Mr. Groia on the basis of incivility. The evolving abuse of process law at the time accounts, at least in part, for the frequency of Mr. Groia's allegations; the presiding judge took a passive approach in the face of Mr. Groia's allegations; and when the presiding judge and reviewing courts did direct Mr. Groia, apart from a few slips, he listened. The Appeal Panel failed to account for these contextual factors in its analysis. In my view, the only conclusion that was reasonably open to the Appeal Panel on the record before it was a finding that Mr. Groia was not guilty of professional misconduct.

Accordingly, I would allow Mr. Groia's appeal.

[Moldaver J. proceeded to set out the factual background in the case. For an excerpt of those facts, see Chapter 1]

. . . . .

IV. <u>Analysis</u>

. . . . .

B. *Was the Appeal Panel's Decision Reasonable?*

(1) <u>The Appeal Panel's Approach</u>

To determine whether the Appeal Panel's decision was reasonable, i.e. whether it fell within a range of reasonable outcomes, it is necessary to explore how the Appeal Panel reached its result. In this case, as is apparent from its reasons, the Appeal Panel first developed an approach for assessing whether a lawyer's behaviour crosses the line into professional misconduct on the basis of incivility. Having done so, it then evaluated whether Mr. Groia was guilty of professional misconduct.

The Appeal Panel took a context-specific approach to evaluating a lawyer's in-court behaviour. In particular, it considered whether Mr. Groia's allegations were made in good faith and had a reasonable basis. It also identified the frequency and manner in which Mr. Groia made his submissions and the trial judge's reaction to Mr. Groia's behaviour as relevant considerations.

Mr. Groia maintains that the Appeal Panel's approach led to an unreasonable result. Several interveners join him, pointing to perceived weaknesses in different aspects of the Appeal Panel's approach and urging this Court to adopt their preferred approaches for evaluating a lawyer's conduct.

These arguments can be broadly grouped into four categories. First, the Appeal Panel's approach does not appropriately balance civility and resolute advocacy. Second, it does not provide enough guidance to lawyers. Third, it does not properly account for the presiding judge's reaction to the lawyer's behaviour and judicial independence. Fourth, it disproportionately balances the Law Society's statutory mandate with the lawyer's right to free expression.

For the reasons that follow, I would reject these submissions. When developing an approach for assessing whether incivility amounts to professional misconduct, the Appeal Panel recognized the importance of civility while remaining sensitive to the lawyer's duty of resolute advocacy — a duty of particular importance in the criminal context because of the client's constitutional right to make full answer and defence. Its context-specific approach is flexible enough to assess allegedly uncivil behaviour arising out of the diverse array of situations in which courtroom lawyers find themselves. At the same time, the Appeal Panel set a reasonably precise benchmark that instructs lawyers as to the permissible bounds of ethical courtroom behaviour, articulating a series of factors that ought generally to be considered when evaluating a lawyer's conduct and describing how those factors operate when assessing a lawyer's behaviour. Finally, the Appeal Panel's approach allows law society disciplinary tribunals to proportionately balance the lawyer's expressive freedom with its statutory mandate in any given case.

(a) *The Appeal Panel Recognized the Importance of Civility*

To begin, when developing its approach, the Appeal Panel recognized the importance of civility to the legal profession and the corresponding need to target behaviour that detrimentally affects the administration of justice and the fairness of a particular proceeding. The duty to practice with civility has long been embodied in the legal profession's collective conscience — and for good reason. Civility has been described as "the glue that holds the adversary system together, that keeps it from imploding": Morden A.C.J.O., "Notes for Convocation Address — Law Society of Upper Canada, February 22, 2001", in Law Society of Upper Canada, ed., *Plea Negotiations: Achieving a "Win-Win" Result* (2003), at pp. 1-10 to 1-11. Practicing law with civility brings with it a host of benefits, both personal and to the profession as a whole. Conversely, incivility is damaging to trial fairness and the administration of justice in a number of ways.

First, incivility can prejudice a client's cause. Overly aggressive, sarcastic, or demeaning courtroom language may lead triers of fact, be they judge or jury, to view the lawyer — and therefore the client's case — unfavourably. Uncivil communications with opposing counsel can cause a breakdown in the relationship, eliminating any prospect of settlement and increasing the client's legal costs by forcing unnecessary court proceedings to adjudicate disputes that could have been resolved with a simple phone call.

. . . . .

Second, incivility is distracting. A lawyer forced to defend against constant allegations of impropriety will naturally be less focused on arguing the case. Uncivil behaviour also distracts the triers of fact by diverting their attention away from the substantive merits of the case.

. . . . .

Third, incivility adversely impacts other justice system participants. Disparaging personal attacks from lawyers — whether or not they are directed at a witness — can exacerbate the already stressful task of testifying at trial.

Finally, incivility can erode public confidence in the administration of justice — a vital component of an effective justice system: *Valente v. The Queen*, 1985 CanLII 25 (SCC), [1985] 2 S.C.R. 673, at p. 689. Inappropriate vitriol, sarcasm and baseless allegations of impropriety in a courtroom can cause the parties, and the public at large, to question the reliability of the result: see *Felderhof ONCA*, at para. 83; *Marchand (Litigation Guardian of) v. Public General Hospital Society of Chatham* (2000), 2000 CanLII 16946 (ON CA), 51 O.R. (3d) 97, at para. 148. Incivility thus diminishes the public's perception of the justice system as a fair dispute-resolution and truth-seeking mechanism.

The Appeal Panel was alive to the profound importance of civility in the legal profession when developing its approach. It recognized that "'civility' protects and enhances the administration of justice" (para. 211), targeting behaviour that could call into question trial fairness and the public's perception of the administration of justice (paras. 228 and 230-31).

Mr. Groia and various interveners argue that the Appeal Panel should have gone further. Like the Divisional Court, they would require that before a lawyer can be found guilty of professional misconduct, the lawyer's behaviour must bring the administration of justice into disrepute or impact trial fairness. With respect, I would not give effect to their arguments. I echo the comments of Cronk J.A. that such a requirement is "unnecessary and unduly restrictive": *Groia ONCA*, para. 169. The Appeal Panel's approach targets conduct that tends to compromise trial fairness and bring the administration of justice into disrepute, making an explicit requirement unnecessary. Moreover, uncivil behaviour worthy of sanction may not have a perceptible impact on the fairness of the particular proceeding. Finally, in my view, requiring the Law Society to evaluate the fairness of a proceeding would shift the focus away from the lawyer's behaviour and inappropriately imbue the Law Society with a judicial function.

(b) *The Appeal Panel Accounted for the Relationship Between Civility and Reso-lute Advocacy*

Second, in developing its approach, the Appeal Panel was sensitive to the lawyer's duty of resolute advocacy and the client's constitutional right to make full answer and defence. It held that "the word 'civility' should not be used to discourage fearless advocacy" (par. 211) and was careful to create an approach which ensured "that the vicissitudes that confront courtroom advocates are fairly accounted for so as not to create a chilling effect on zealous advocacy" (para. 232).

Although of doubtless importance, the duty to practice with civility is not a lawyer's sole ethical mandate. Rather, it exists in concert with a series of professional obligations that both constrain and compel a lawyer's behaviour. The duty of civility must be understood in light of these other obligations. In particular, standards of civility cannot compromise the lawyer's duty of resolute advocacy.

The importance of resolute advocacy cannot be overstated. It is a vital ingredient in our adversarial justice system — a system premised on the idea that forceful partisan advocacy facilitates truth-seeking: see e.g. *Phillips v. Ford Motor Co.* (1971), 1971 CanLII 389 (ON CA), 18 D.L.R. (3d) 641, at p. 661. Moreover, resolute advocacy is a key component of the lawyer's commitment to the client's cause, a principle of fundamental justice under s. 7 of the Canadian Charter of Rights and Freedoms: *Canada (Attorney General) v. Federation of Law Societies of Canada*, 2015 SCC 7, [2015] 1 S.C.R. 401, at paras. 83-84.

Resolute advocacy requires lawyers to "raise fearlessly every issue, advance every argument and ask every question, however distasteful, that the lawyer thinks will help the client's case": Federation of Law Societies of Canada, *Model Code of Professional Conduct* (online), r. 5.1-1 commentary 1. This is no small order. Lawyers are regularly called on to make submissions on behalf of their clients that are unpopular and at times uncomfortable. These submissions can be met with harsh criticism — from the public, the bar, and even the court. Lawyers must stand resolute in the face of this adversity by continuing to advocate on their clients' behalf, despite popular opinion to the contrary.

The duty of resolute advocacy takes on particular salience in the criminal law context. Criminal defence lawyers are the final frontier between the accused and the power of the state.

. . . . .

For criminal defence lawyers, fearless advocacy extends beyond ethical obligations into the realm of constitutional imperatives.. . . . Defence lawyers must have sufficient latitude to advance their clients' right to make full answer and defence by raising arguments about the propriety of state actors' conduct without fear of reprisal.

In saying this, I should not be taken as endorsing incivility in the name of resolute advocacy. In this regard, I agree with both Cronk J.A. and Rosenberg J.A. that civility and resolute advocacy are not incompatible: see *Groia ONCA*, at paras. 131-39; *Felderhof ONCA*, at paras. 83 and 94. To the contrary, civility is often the most effective form of advocacy. Nevertheless, when defining incivility and assessing whether a lawyer's behaviour crosses the line, care must be taken to set a sufficiently high threshold that will not chill the kind of fearless advocacy that is at times necessary to advance a client's cause. The Appeal Panel recognized the need to develop an approach that would avoid such a chilling effect.

(c) *The Appeal Panel's Approach Is Both Flexible and Precise*

The Appeal Panel developed an approach that is both flexible and precise. A rigid definition of when incivility amounts to professional misconduct in the courtroom is neither attainable nor desirable. Rather, determining whether a lawyer's behaviour warrants a finding of professional misconduct must remain a context-specific inquiry that is flexible enough to assess behaviour arising from the diverse array of situations in which lawyers find themselves.

And yet standards of civility must be articulated with a reasonable degree of precision. An overly vague or open-ended test for incivility risks eroding resolute advocacy. Prudent lawyers will steer clear of a blurry boundary to avoid a potential misconduct finding for advancing arguments that may rightly be critical of other justice system participants. In contrast, a standard that is reasonably ascertainable gives lawyers a workable definition which they can use to guide their behaviour. It also guides law society disciplinary tribunals in their task of determining whether a lawyer's behaviour amounts to professional misconduct.

The Appeal Panel's approach strikes a reasonable balance between flexibility and precision. The Appeal Panel described its approach to assessing whether a lawyer's uncivil behaviour warrants professional sanction as "fundamentally contextual and fact specific", noting the importance of "consider[ing] the dynamics, complexity and particular burdens and stakes of the trial or other proceeding": paras. 7 and 232. By focussing on the particular factual matrix before it, the Appeal Panel's approach is flexible enough to accommodate the diverse array of situations in which courtroom lawyers find themselves.

At the same time, the Appeal Panel's approach is sufficiently precise to delineate an appropriate boundary past which behaviour warrants a professional misconduct finding. The Appeal Panel identified a set of factors that a disciplinary panel ought generally to consider when evaluating a lawyer's conduct. It then provided guidance on how those factors operate when assessing a lawyer's behaviour. Importantly, as the Appeal Panel recognized, this list is not closed and the weight assigned to each factor will vary case-by-case. I turn to those factors now.

(i) Factors to Consider When Assessing a Lawyer's Behaviour

1. *What the Lawyer Said*

First, the Appeal Panel looked to *what* the lawyer said. Mr. Groia alleged prosecutorial misconduct throughout Phase One of the Felderhof trial. As such, the Appeal Panel had to determine when these kinds of allegations amount to professional misconduct. It concluded that prosecutorial misconduct allegations, or other challenges to opposing counsel's integrity, cross the line into professional misconduct unless they are made in good faith *and* have a reasonable basis: A.P. reasons, at paras. 9 and 235. In other words, allegations that are *either* made in bad faith *or* without a reasonable basis amount to professional misconduct.

. . . . .

I share the interveners' concerns that law societies should not sanction lawyers for sincerely held but mistaken legal positions or questionable litigation strategies. Nonetheless, in my view, the Appeal Panel's standard withstands scrutiny. Allegations that impugn opposing counsel's integrity must not be made lightly. A reputation for integrity is a lawyer's most important professional asset. It generally takes a long time to build up and it can be lost overnight.

. . . . .

Maintaining a reputation for practicing with integrity is a lifelong challenge. Once sullied, a lawyer's reputation may never be fully restored. As such, allegations of prosecutorial misconduct must have a reasonable foundation.

. . . . .

Finally, the Appeal Panel's reasonable basis requirement will not chill resolute advocacy. . . .. Unreasonable allegations, therefore, do nothing to advance the client's case. An ethical standard prohibiting such allegations does not impair resolute advocacy.

. . . . .

[I]t is not professional misconduct to challenge opposing counsel's integrity based on a sincerely held but incorrect legal position so long as the challenge has a sufficient factual foundation, such that if the legal position were correct, the challenge would be warranted.

Nor is it professional misconduct to advance a novel legal argument that is ultimately rejected by the court. Many legal principles we now consider foundational were once controversial ideas that were fearlessly raised by lawyers. Such innovative advocacy ought to be encouraged — not stymied by the threat of being labelled, after the fact, as "unreasonable".

. . . . .

When a lawyer alleges prosecutorial misconduct based on a legal mistake, law societies are perfectly entitled to look to the reasonableness of the mistake when assessing whether it is sincerely held, and hence, whether the allegations were made in good faith.. . . The more egregious the legal mistake, the less likely it will have been sincerely held, making it less likely the allegation will have been made in good

356

faith. And if the law society concludes that the allegation was not made in good faith, the second question — whether there was a reasonable basis for the allegation — falls away.

I pause here to note that there is good reason why a law society can look to the reasonableness of a legal mistake when assessing whether allegations of impropriety are made in good faith, but not when assessing whether they are reasonably based. The "good faith" inquiry asks what the lawyer *actually* believed when making the allegations. The reasonableness of the lawyer's legal mistake is one piece of circumstantial evidence that may help a law society in this exercise. However, it is not determinative. Even the most unreasonable mistakes can be sincerely held.

In contrast, the "reasonable basis" inquiry requires a law society to look beyond what the lawyer believed, and examine the foundation underpinning the allegations. Looking at the reasonableness of a lawyer's legal position at this stage would, in effect, impose a mandatory minimum standard of legal competence in the incivility context. In other words, it would allow a law society to find a lawyer guilty of professional misconduct on the basis of incivility for something the lawyer, in the law society's opinion, *ought to have known* or *ought to have done*. And, as I have already explained, this would risk unjustifiably tarnishing a lawyer's reputation and chilling resolute advocacy.

That, however, does not end the matter. As my colleagues correctly observe, "the Law Society rules govern civility *and* competence". . .. A lawyer who bases allegations on "outrageous" or "egregious" legal errors may be incompetent. My point is simply that he or she should not be punished for *incivility* on that basis alone. As such, any concern that law societies are "effectively dispossess[ed]" of their regulatory authority misstates my position.

. . . . .

2. *The Manner and Frequency of the Lawyer's Behaviour*

The Appeal Panel also considered the frequency of what was said and the manner in which it was said to be relevant factors. A single outburst would not usually attract sanction. In contrast, repetitive attacks on opposing counsel would be more likely to cross the line into professional misconduct. The Appeal Panel also found that challenges to opposing counsel's integrity made in a "repetitive stream of invective", or with a "sarcastic and biting" tone were inappropriate. Finally, the Appeal Panel held that whether the lawyer was provoked was a relevant factor: paras. 233 and 236.

Considering the manner and frequency of the lawyer's behaviour was reasonable. Trials are often hard fought. The stakes are high — especially so in a criminal trial where the accused faces a loss of liberty. Emotions can sometimes get the better of even the most stoic litigators. Punishing a lawyer for "a few ill-chosen, sarcastic, or even nasty comments" (A.P. reasons, at para. 7) ignores these realities.

This does not mean that a solitary bout of incivility is beyond reproach. A single, scathing attack on the integrity of another justice system participant can and has warranted disciplinary action

. . . . .

3. *The Trial Judge's Reaction*

The third factor the Appeal Panel identified is the presiding judge's reaction to the lawyer's behaviour: para. 225. I agree that when the impugned behaviour occurs in a courtroom, what, if anything, the judge does about it becomes relevant. Unlike the law society, the presiding judge observes the lawyer's behaviour firsthand. This offers the judge a comparatively advantageous position to evaluate the lawyer's conduct relative to the law society, who only enters the equation once all is said and done.

. . . . .

These observations underscore the importance of considering the presiding judge's response to the lawyer's conduct. The question then becomes: how important is that response?

. . . . .

It follows that the judge's reaction is not conclusive of the propriety of the lawyer's conduct. Rather, as the Appeal Panel concluded, it is simply one piece of the contextual analysis. Its weight will vary depending on the circumstances of the case.

Part and parcel of the presiding judge's response is how the lawyer modified his or her behaviour thereafter. The lawyer who crosses the line, but pays heed to the judge's direction and behaves appropriately from then on is less likely to have engaged in professional misconduct than the same lawyer who continues to behave inappropriately despite the judge's instructions.

(d) *The Appeal Panel's Approach Allows for a Proportionate Balancing of Lawyers' Expressive Rights and the Law Society's Statutory Mandate*

An administrative decision that engages the Charter by limiting its protections will only be reasonable if it reflects a proportionate balancing of the Charter protections at play with the decision maker's statutory mandate.

. . . . .

Law society decisions that discipline lawyers for what they say may engage lawyers' expressive freedom under s. 2(*b*) of the Charter: *Doré*, at paras. 59, 63 and 65-68. This is true regardless of whether the impugned speech occurs inside or outside a courtroom. Courtroom lawyers are engaged in expressive activity, the method and location of the speech do not remove the expressive activity from the scope of protected expression, and law society decisions sanctioning lawyers for what they say in the courtroom have the effect of restricting their expression.

. . . . .

As such, a particular professional misconduct finding that engages a lawyer's expressive freedom will only be reasonable if it reflects a proportionate balancing of the law society's statutory objective with the lawyer's expressive freedom. Similarly, an approach to assessing whether a lawyer's uncivil communications warrant law society discipline must allow for such a proportionate balancing to occur.

Under its statutory mandate, the Law Society has a duty to advance the public interest, the cause of justice and the rule of law by regulating the legal profession: Law Society Act, s. 4.2. Disciplinary tribunals fulfill an integral subset of this function by setting and enforcing standards of professional conduct — in this case civility. Performing this mandate can engage lawyers' expressive rights under the Charter: *Doré*, at para. 63.

Allowing lawyers to freely express themselves serves an important function in our legal system. As Steel J.A. noted in *Histed*, at para. 71:

> The lawyer, as an intimate part of the legal system, plays a pivotal role in ensuring the accountability and transparency of the judiciary. To play that role effectively, he/she must feel free to act and speak without inhibition and with courage when the circumstances demand it.

. . . I would go further and add that lawyers play an integral role in holding *all* justice system participants accountable. Reasonable criticism enhances the transparency and fairness of the system as a whole, thereby serving the interests of justice. Overemphasizing civility has the potential to thwart this good by chilling well-founded criticism: A. Woolley, "Does Civility Matter?" (2008), 46 *Osgoode Hall L.J.*, 175, at p. 180. Proportionately balancing lawyers' expressive rights, therefore, "may involve disciplinary bodies tolerating a degree of discordant criticism": *Doré*, at para. 65.

When the impugned behaviour occurs in a courtroom, lawyers' expressive freedom takes on additional significance. In that arena, the lawyer's primary function is to resolutely advocate on his or her client's behalf.

. . . . .

That said, speech is not sacrosanct simply because it is uttered by a lawyer. Certain communications will be far removed from the core values s. 2(*b*) seeks to protect: the search for truth and the common good. . . .. The protection afforded to expressive freedom diminishes the further the speech lies from the core values of s. 2(*b*). . . .. As such, a finding of professional misconduct is more likely to represent a proportionate balance of the Law Society's statutory objective with the lawyer's expressive rights where the impugned speech lies far from the core values of lawyers' expressive freedom.

. . . . .

The flexibility built into the Appeal Panel's context-specific approach to assessing a lawyer's behaviour allows for a proportionate balancing in any given case. Considering the unique circumstances in each case — such as what the lawyer said, the context in which he or she said it and the reason it was said — enables law society disciplinary tribunals to accurately gauge the value of the impugned speech. This, in turn, allows for a decision, both with respect to a finding of professional misconduct and any penalty imposed, that reflects a proportionate balancing of the lawyer's expressive rights and the Law Society's statutory mandate.In addition, the Appeal Panel's reasonable basis standard allows for a proportionate balancing between expressive freedom and the Law Society's statutory mandate.

. . . . .

In contrast, sanctioning a lawyer for good faith, reasonably based allegations that are grounded in legal error does not reflect a proportionate balancing. Advancing good faith, reasonable allegations — even those based on legal error — helps maintain the integrity of the justice system by holding other participants accountable. Well-founded arguments exposing misconduct on the part of opposing counsel thus lie close to the core of the s. 2(*b*) values underpinning a lawyer's expressive freedom. Discouraging lawyers from bringing forward such allegations does nothing to further the Law Society's statutory mandate of advancing the cause of justice and the rule of law. If anything, silencing lawyers in this manner undercuts the rule of law and the cause of justice by making it more likely that misconduct will go unchecked.

(e) *Conclusion*

. . .The Appeal Panel appreciated the need to guard against the consequences of incivility, and remained sensitive to the lawyer's duty of resolute advocacy. Its contextual analysis accommodates the diversity of modern legal practice. At the same time, the Appeal Panel articulated a series of factors — what the lawyer said, the manner and frequency in which it was said, and the presiding judge's reaction to the lawyer's behaviour — and explained how those factors operate in a way that is sufficiently precise to guide lawyers' conduct and instruct disciplinary tribunals in future cases. Finally, the Appeal Panel's approach allows for a proportionate balancing of lawyers' expressive rights and the Law Society's statutory mandate.

[Moldaver J. then proceeded to apply the Court of Appeals' approach to Mr. Groia's conduct.]

. . . . .

V. Conclusion and Disposition

The Appeal Panel's finding of professional misconduct against Mr. Groia was unreasonable. The Appeal Panel used Mr. Groia's sincerely held but mistaken legal beliefs to conclude that his allegations of prosecutorial misconduct lacked a reasonable basis. But, as I have explained, Mr. Groia's legal errors — in conjunction with the OSC prosecutor's conduct — *formed* the reasonable basis upon which his allegations rested. In these circumstances, it was not open to the Appeal Panel to conclude that Mr. Groia's allegations lacked a reasonable basis. And because the Appeal Panel accepted that the allegations were made in good faith, it was not reasonably open for it to find Mr. Groia guilty of professional misconduct based on what he said. The Appeal Panel also failed to account for the evolving abuse of process law, the trial judge's reaction to Mr. Groia's behaviour, and Mr. Groia's response — all factors which suggest Mr. Groia's behaviour was not worthy of professional discipline on account of incivility. The finding of professional misconduct against him was therefore unreasonable.

. . . . .

I would allow the appeal and set aside the decision of the Appeal Panel with respect to the finding of professional misconduct against Mr. Groia and the penalty imposed. I would award costs to Mr. Groia in this Court and in the courts below, as well as in the proceedings before the Law Society. Because Mr. Groia, in the circumstances of this case, could not reasonably be found guilty of professional misconduct, the complaints against him are dismissed and there is no need to remit the matter back to the Law Society

. . . . .

NOTES AND QUESTIONS

1. Do you agree with the majority's decision – both its approach and the result? If so, why? If not, why not?

2. By raising the theme of resolute advocacy numerous times, it seems that the Court was concerned about limiting a lawyer's ability fully to advocate on behalf of their client. Did the court strike the right balance between protecting advocacy, protecting speech, and limiting incivility? Does the Court's "contextual approach" give too much latitude to the lawyer?

    For recent commentary on oral advocacy and the importance of trials, see the Advocates' Society, "The Right to be Heard: The Future of Advocacy in Canada, Final Report of the Modern Advocacy Task Force" (Toronto, The Advocates' Society, June 2021).

3. When introducing its decision, the Court stated that "trials are not . . . tea parties." Do you agree with this characterization? Why or why not? What is the implicit or explicit message to counsel from this characterization?

4. What did the Court mean when it said that the "contextual analysis [of whether a lawyer has been uncivil] accommodates the diversity of modern legal practice"? Do you think adding context is sufficient to ensure that civility regulation encompasses and encourages diversity within the profession and in its practice norms?

5. When considering professional obligations of civility and resolute advocacy, the Court in *Groia* described resolute advocacy as "a duty of particular importance in the criminal context" (para. 62). Does the kind of practice area matter when it comes to civility? Should it? When reading the following two cases — *Schreiber* and *Laarakker* — consider whether and if so how context matters in those cases. Further, consider whether the decision in *Groia* would have any influence on their outcomes?

SCHREIBER v. MULRONEY

[2007] O.J. No. 3040

(Ont. S.C.J., F.J.C. Newbould J.)

F.J.C. NEWBOULD J.:— This is a motion by the defendant Brian Mulroney to set aside a default judgment obtained by Karlheinz Schreiber on July 24, 2007. Mr. Schreiber's counsel noted Mr. Mulroney in default and obtained a default judgment without any judicial intervention during litigation that was being hotly contested. For the reasons that follow, the noting of Mr. Mulroney in default and the default judgment are set aside. The actions taken to obtain the default judgment were egregious and wrong. I regret to say that counsel for Mr. Schreiber breached his obligations to the court and to counsel for Mr. Mulroney. No litigant deserves to be treated in the way that Mr. Mulroney was treated that led to the default judgment.

[Justice F.J.C. Newbould reviewed the background facts. Mr. Mulroney had been served with a statement of claim. He disputed the jurisdiction of Ontario to decide the litigation. Counsel for Mr. Schreiber agreed that while the jurisdictional issue was being resolved Mr. Mulroney would not file a statement of defence and would not be noted in default. The parties subsequently had a disagreement about whether Mr. Mulroney could be compelled to testify on an affidavit filed with respect to the jurisdictional issue. As part of that disagreement counsel for Mr. Mulroney obtained relief from Master Haberman in relation to the attempt of counsel for Mr. Schreiber to obtain a certificate of non-attendance with respect to Mr. Mulroney. Counsel for Mr. Schreiber then obtained a default judgment with respect to the original action.]

. . . . .

On July 20, 2007, Mr. Anka had a discussion with his client Mr. Schreiber. This is referred to in Mr. Sennecke's affidavit who participated in the call with Mr. Schreiber. Thus privilege was waived. Mr. Sennecke states that the options available to Mr. Schreiber at that stage were (i) they do nothing; (ii) they seek a timetable to be set for the defendant's motion or (iii) they note the defendant in default. Mr. Sennecke states that Mr. Schreiber instructed them to note Mr. Mulroney in default because Mr. Schreiber owed Mr. Mulroney no courtesy in light of the manner in which Mr. Mulroney's counsel went about obtaining the order from Master Haberman without his counsel being offered the opportunity to be present and make submissions to Master Haberman on his behalf.

This remarkable evidence is as important for what it does not say as for what it does say. There is no indication that Mr. Anka or Mr. Sennecke told Mr. Schreiber that they had an agreement in place with Mr. Prehogan [counsel for Mr. Mulroney] that Mr. Mulroney would not be noted in default. The statement that they were not offered an opportunity to be present before Master Haberman was not true. Nor was there any indication that Mr. Schreiber was told that there was a pending motion by Mr. Mulroney to extend the time to file a statement of defence.

In these circumstances it does not lie in Mr. Anka's mouth to seek to put the blame entirely upon his client for the steps that were taken. No doubt his client was more than willing to proceed with the noting of Mr. Mulroney in default and to proceed to a default judgment, but that does not excuse the matter.

On July 20, 2007, the same day that the conversation with Mr. Schreiber took place, a requisition to have the defendant noted in default was made and Mr. Mulroney was noted in default by the registrar. The memorandum of instructions given by Mr. Tingley makes clear that the court was not told of the agreement not to note Mr. Mulroney in default or of the outstanding jurisdictional motion or the motion to extend the time for filing a statement of defence.

On July 24, 2004, a requisition for default judgment was filed in which it was stated that default judgment could properly be signed because the claim was for a debt or liquidated demand in money. The default judgment was signed that day by an official in the registrar's office.

On the same day that the default judgment was signed, Mr. Anka wrote to Mr. Prehogan taking issue with the right of Master Haberman to settle the form of the order made by Master Haberman on July 5, 2007. He also took issue with what had occurred on that day in Master Haberman's office. He suggested he would be available before the registrar in the next day or two to discuss settling the order of Master Haberman. Mr. Anka did not inform Mr. Prehogan that the default judgment had been obtained that day. He said this morning that he did not know whether the default judgment had been obtained at the time he wrote the letter. He acknowledged, however, that four days earlier he had instructed people in his office to note Mr. Mulroney in default and obtain a default judgment. He ought to have given notice to Mr. Prehogan of his intention, and he ought not in his letter of July 2, 2007 have suggested that there were steps to be taken with respect to the order of Master Haberman without disclosing the true state of affairs. By that time a default judgment would render moot whatever procedural issues there were with respect to a prior interlocutory order. The letter to Mr. Prehogan was misleading in the extreme.

. . . . .

It is clear in my view that the noting of Mr. Mulroney in default and the default judgment must be set aside. I say this for a number of reasons:

(1) Throughout the litigation Mr. Mulroney indicated a clear intention to defend the action by taking the position that Ontario lacked jurisdiction over the matter. When Mr. Prehogan first learned of the default from the press on July 26, 2007, the motion to set aside the default judgment was served on the following day. There was no delay.

(2) The outstanding motion at the time of the default judgment to set aside the statement of claim on jurisdictional grounds is sufficient reason for the default proceedings to be set aside even if it could not be said that the defendant had a reasonable defensive position in the action. . . .

(3) There is authority that if a plaintiff obtains default judgment to which he is not entitled, the default judgment is to be [set] aside *ex debito justitiae*. . . .

. . . . .

(5) Mr. Anka breached his agreement with Mr. Prehogan when he sought default judgment. It was an egregious breach that Mr. Anka had no right to commit and Mr. Schreiber had no right to instruct his solicitor to commit.

(6) Mr. Anka did not give any advance notice to Mr. Prehogan that he was going to note the defendant in default or take default judgment proceedings. In the circumstances of this case it is quite obvious that he should have done so. It constituted sharp practice that should not be condoned. While the "Principles of Civility for Advocates" published by the Advocates' Society are not the force of law, the lack of notice to Mr. Prehogan breached those principles of civility. Incredibly, even after instructions had been given by Mr. Anka to obtain a default judgment, he wrote on July 24, 2007 suggesting that there were still interlocutory matters to be dealt with without disclosing the default proceedings. Mr. Anka conceded that his client had not told him not to provide advance or post notice to Mr. Prehogan, so this is something that Mr. Anka took on his own behalf. This lack of frankness should not be condoned.

. . . . .

(9) Mr. Anka in his material and in argument contended that Mr. Mulroney's actions

363

in this case have been motivated by an attempt to delay the case until Mr. Schreiber is extradited to Germany. There is nothing however in the record to substantiate this allegation. To the contrary, it is quite clear from the record that Mr. Prehogan and Mr. Holland continuously tried to move matters along in an agreeable way and that when that could not be achieved they sought unsuccessfully to have Mr. Anka agree to case management. Contrary to Mr. Anka's assertions, neither Mr. Prehogan nor Mr. Holland acted in a way other than professionally and with courtesy. The same cannot be said with respect to Mr. Anka. Mr. Prehogan was forceful in defence of his client's interests, as he was required to be, but civil. It should not be forgotten that the allegations of delay on Mr. Anka's part are on behalf of a client who waited 13 years to commence this action towards the end of his fight to avoid extradition.

Mr. Prehogan asked that if the default proceedings are set aside, there be an order restraining Mr. Schreiber or his counsel from noting Mr. Mulroney in default without express court order brought on proper notice. This request in the circumstances in this case is reasonable.

Mr. Anka on behalf of Mr. Schreiber requested that in the event that the default proceedings are set aside there be an order that Mr. Mulroney pay into court the amount of the judgment. He relies upon Rule 19.03(1) [of the Ontario Rules of Civil Procedure] that provides that the noting of default may be set aside by the court on such terms as are just. In my view it would be entirely unjust to make the order sought by Mr. Schreiber. He and his counsel are the author of the misfortune that has occurred. Mr. Anka also asked on behalf of Mr. Schreiber that he be paid the costs of the abandoned motion that was returnable on July 17, 2007. I make no such order. The motion was not abandoned nor is there any reason to be awarding Mr. Schreiber costs.

Mr. Prehogan on behalf of Mr. Mulroney has been trying for some time without success to have Mr. Anka agree to this case being case managed. It is obvious that this case cries out for case management. Mr. Anka has avoided that. However, Mr. Anka this morning agreed that the case should be case managed and he was content that there be such an order. In the circumstances I will make that order.

NOTES AND QUESTIONS

1. Is the primary issue with counsel for Mr. Schreiber one of civility, or is it a more fundamental violation of his multi-faceted ethical duties as an advocate? Further to the judge's comments, do you think counsel for Mr. Schreiber should have been subjected to professional discipline? Would the validity of his instructions from Mr. Schreiber (which the court questioned) be relevant to the determination of whether his conduct was sanctionable? Do the rules of professional conduct in your jurisdiction assist with this question? See further *Mcleod (Re)*, 2019 LSBC 33.

2. If dealing with counsel for Mr. Schreiber in the future, how might counsel for Mr. Mulroney conduct themself? Do you think the adage "what goes around comes around" might come into play in circumstances like this? Is the conduct of counsel for Mr. Schreiber in this matter consistent with duties of resolute advocacy (discussed in *Groia*) — which arise from the lawyer's obligation of loyalty and require the lawyer to act in the best

interests of the client — or are they inconsistent with those duties? Do the rules of civility add anything further to those (or other) existing professional obligations? Do the professionalism and civility principles articulated in *Groia* provide any assistance to these questions?

3. Is it legitimate for the court to note that the "allegations of delay on Mr. Anka's part are on behalf of a client who waited 13 years to commence this action towards the end of his fight to avoid extradition"? What relevance, if any, would this fact have for Mr. Anka's identification of his ethical obligations to Mr. Schreiber and more generally?

4. Misleading conduct need not be limited to the merits or procedural outcome of a case. In *Ahuja (Re)*, 2017 LSBC 26 (paragraph numbers omitted), a lawyer was disciplined for misleading the court and a client with respect to the reason for being unable to attend a hearing. According to an agreed statement of facts: "On the night before the Respondent was to travel to Kelowna to attend a contested hearing, he attended a firm event (Canucks Hockey Game). As a result, he was out later than planned and, in addition, consumed some alcohol. He slept through his alarm. When he woke, realizing that he was not going to get to Kelowna in time, he embarked on a series of initiatives aimed at 'damage control.' He spoke to his assistant and asked her to send a memo to the court in Kelowna advising that he had missed his plane because the flight had been overbooked. He provided a similar explanation in a call to his client in Kelowna." When considering the lawyer's conduct, the panel noted an earlier admission made by the lawyer in the course of the lawyer's law society admission application that "while driving under suspension, he was stopped by the police and provided a false name to the officer. This compounded the problem of driving while under suspension." When imposing a one month suspension, the panel found that the "similarities between this matter and the issue considered by the Credentials Committee are too stark to be ignored. It is apparent that the necessary lesson was not conveyed by the letter requested in support of this Respondent's initial admission to the Law Society. A reinforcement of the importance of honesty in all our dealings as a lawyer is necessary." The lawyer was also ordered to pay costs in the amount of $3,500 plus disbursements. Do you agree with this result? Does it matter that, according to the panel's decision, the lawyer apologized to the court and the client? The decision is silent as to whether the lawyer also apologized to the assistant, who was asked to send the initial memo to the court.

Law Society of British Columbia v. Laarakker

[2011] L.S.D.D. No. 175, 2011 LSBC 29
(Law Society of British Columbia, Hearing Panel: Leon Getz, Q.C., Chair,
Nancy Merrill and Alan Ross)

. . . . .

BACKGROUND

This matter arises out of allegedly discourteous and personal remarks made by the

Respondent about a lawyer in Ontario (the "Ontario Lawyer").

The citation alleges:

(a) On or about November 20, 2009 the Respondent posted comments on the internet that contained discourteous and personal remarks about the Ontario Lawyer; and

(b) In the course of representing a client, the Respondent sent a fax on or about November 22, 2009 to the Ontario Lawyer which contained discourteous and personal remarks about the Ontario Lawyer.

The Respondent has admitted the evidence in the Agreed Statement of Facts. The Respondent's position is that his conduct in respect of the posting on the internet and the correspondence with the Ontario Lawyer was justified given the correspondence that the Respondent's client had received from the Ontario Lawyer.

. . . . .

FACTS

The Respondent is a sole-practitioner in Vernon, British Columbia. In or about November, 2009, a client approached the Respondent regarding a letter that she had received from the Ontario Lawyer (the "Demand Letter").

The Demand Letter sought payment of $521.97 (the "Settlement Amount") as damages from the client. The client's teenage daughter had been caught shoplifting at a retail outlet. The Demand Letter stated that the retailer took the position that it had a right to claim damages against the parent or guardian of a young person who had been caught shoplifting on the basis that the parent had failed to provide reasonable supervision.

The Demand Letter threatened that if the client did not pay the Settlement Amount, the Ontario Lawyer may receive instructions to file a civil suit against the client seeking an amount greater than the Settlement Amount.

The Respondent, for personal reasons, felt strongly about the Demand Letter.

After consulting with the client, the Respondent sent a one page fax letter to the Ontario Lawyer. The Respondent's letter read:

> I have been approached by [the client] with respect to your letter of October 30, 2009. Suffice it to say that I have instructed her not to pay a penny and to put your insulting and frankly stupid letter to the only use for which it might be suitable, however uncomfortably.

> It is disappointing when members of our profession lend themselves to this kind of thing. You must know that you are on the thinnest of legal grounds and would be highly unlikely to get a civil judgment against my client. That is aside from the logistics in bringing this matter to court in BC. I am also well aware that by preying on people's embarrassment and naiveté you will unfortunately be able to pry some money out of the pockets of some of the humiliated parents.

> I have notified the local paper of this scam. Save the postage in the future and become a real lawyer instead! You must have harboured dreams of being a good lawyer at one point. Surely bullying people into paying some small amount of money is not what you went into law for.

But then again, someone has to be at the bottom of his class, practising with a restricted license as you appear to be.

Good luck.

Two days before sending the letter, on November 20, 2009, the Respondent posted a comment on the "Canadian Money Advisor" internet blog. The Respondent posted the comment in response to two postings made by an individual who had received a letter similar in nature to the Demand Letter. The Respondent posted on the blog as follows:

> I am a lawyer.
>
> This guy is the kind of lawyer that gives lawyers a bad name. He is relying on intimidation and blackmail to get the lousy $500. Don't pay him. I hate these sleazy operators.
>
> Speaking as a lawyer, he would have little chance of collecting in court. He would have rto [sic] prove that a chiold [sic] was a habitual criminal. As far as an adult is concerned, he has to prove the loss.
>
> Also remember this, he has to bring the action in a court near to where the incident took place (at least in BC) Gueuss [sic] what — that ain't going to happen.

The Respondent identified himself as a lawyer on this posting. He testified that he later received telephone calls from potential clients who read the posting.

The Ontario Lawyer made a complaint to the Law Society of British Columbia (the "Law Society") about the Respondent's remarks contained in the letter.

It is unclear when, but the Ontario Lawyer also made a complaint to the Law Society about the Respondent's blog posting.

There was a series of correspondence between the Law Society and the Respondent between February 1, 2010 and March 18, 2010. This Panel acknowledges that the Respondent was assiduous in his responses to the Law Society. When it was suggested that he should remove the blog posting, he immediately wrote to the operator of the blog and requested that the posting be removed.

In his substantive response to the Law Society's letter, the Respondent took the position that the real issue in this case was the conduct of the Ontario Lawyer. He raised several issues regarding the conduct of the Ontario Lawyer. The Respondent did concede that, if the Ontario Lawyer was found to have conducted himself professionally and ethically according to Law Society standards, then the Respondent's actions in denouncing the Ontario Lawyer were wrong and, in that case, he advised that he regretted his remarks and apologized unequivocally.

However, the entire tone of the Respondent's substantive response to the Law Society was that his letter to the Ontario Lawyer and his blog-posting were justified because the actions of the Ontario Lawyer were blameworthy.

In his oral submissions before this Panel, the Respondent indicated that he believed that he was allowed to do what he did in the face of a "rogue lawyer". He submits that none of his actions constitute professional misconduct or conduct unbecoming.

The Respondent further submitted that, if he is found to be wrong, then he would apologize.

Finally, the Respondent argued that if his conduct warranted sanction, then the Ontario Lawyer's letter constituted provocation and should be a mitigating factor.

. . . . .

The allegation of the Law Society is that the Respondent's incivility constitutes professional misconduct and/or conduct unbecoming.

TEST FOR PROFESSIONAL MISCONDUCT

"Professional misconduct" is not defined in the *Legal Profession Act*, the Law Society Rules or the *Professional Conduct Handbook*. We rely on the decisions of prior panels for the definition. In *Law Society of British Columbia v. Martin*, 2005 LSBC 16, the panel considered the question of what constitutes professional misconduct and concluded that the test is as follows:

> Whether the facts as made out disclose a marked departure from that conduct the Law Society expects of its members; if so, it is professional misconduct. (para. [171])

The reasoning in *Martin* was revised in *Re: Lawyer 10*, 2010 LSBC 02, in which the panel decided that, in addition to the test developed in *Martin*, the conduct of the respondent must also be "culpable or blameworthy". In our opinion, the reasoning in *Re: Lawyer 10* simply provides a category of conduct that may fit within the "marked departure test", but requires a degree of personal responsibility or culpability in order to reach a finding of professional misconduct.

TEST FOR CONDUCT UNBECOMING A LAWYER

"Conduct unbecoming a lawyer" is defined in Section 1(1) of the *Legal Profession Act* LSBC 1998 c. 9. That section defines "conduct unbecoming a lawyer" as conduct that is considered in the judgment of the benchers or a panel:

(a)   to be contrary to the best interest of the public or of the legal profession, or

(b)   to harm the standing of the legal profession.

The Benchers adopted a "useful working distinction" between professional misconduct and conduct unbecoming a lawyer (see *Law Society of British Columbia v. Berge*, 2005 LSBC 28 (upheld on Review, 2007 LSBC 07), *Law Society of British Columbia v. Watt*, [2001] LSBC 16). In *Watt* the Benchers stated:

> In this case the Benchers are dealing with conduct unbecoming a Member of the Law Society of British Columbia. We adopt, as a useful working distinction, that professional misconduct refers to conduct occurring in the course of a lawyer's practice while conduct unbecoming refers to conduct in the lawyer's private life.

Hence, on the facts of this case, we are of the opinion that the letter to the Ontario Lawyer cannot be considered to be conduct unbecoming a lawyer because it was undertaken within the Respondent's practice.

The blog posting, however, could be considered a mixture of conduct in the Respondent's private life and in the course of the lawyer's practice. As noted above, the blog posting was made on November 20, 2009 before the letter was sent to the Ontario Lawyer. The Respondent identified himself as a lawyer and received potential file referrals as a result of his blog posting.

Therefore, in our opinion, if it warrants sanction, the blog posting must be considered either professional misconduct or conduct unbecoming a lawyer. It was an action performed, at least in part, in the course of the lawyer's practice.

INCIVILITY

The Canons of Legal Ethics, *Professional Conduct Handbook* Chapter 1 [see now Chapter 2], provide the following instruction regarding a lawyer's obligations in communicating with other parties:

> A lawyer is a minister of justice, an officer of the courts, a client's advocate, and a member of an ancient, honourable and learned profession.
>
> In these several capacities it is a lawyer's duty to promote the interests of the state, serve the cause of justice, maintain the authority and dignity of the courts, be faithful to clients, be candid and courteous in relations with other lawyers and demonstrate personal integrity.
>
> . . .
>
> 3. To the client
>
> (4) A lawyer should treat adverse witnesses, litigants, and counsel with fairness and courtesy, refraining from all offensive personalities. The lawyer must not allow a client's personal feelings and prejudices to detract from the lawyer's professional duties. At the same time the lawyer should represent the client's interests resolutely and without fear of judicial disfavour or public unpopularity.
>
> . . .
>
> 4. To other lawyers
>
> (1) A lawyer's conduct toward other lawyers should be characterized by courtesy and good faith. Any ill feeling that may exist between clients or lawyers, particularly during litigation, should never be allowed to influence lawyers in their conduct and demeanour toward each other or the parties. Personal remarks or references between lawyers should be scrupulously avoided, as should quarrels between lawyers which cause delay and promote unseemly wrangling.

In prior decisions, the Law Society has enforced the Canons with respect to correspondence. In *Law Society of British Columbia v. Lanning*, 2008 LSBC 31, it was held:

> A lawyer's communications must be courteous, fair, and respectful. A lawyer is to refrain from personal remarks or references, and to maintain objectivity and dignity. The purpose of a lawyer's communication is to properly advance the client's matter to a conclusion.

Further, in *Law Society of British Columbia v. Greene* [2003] LSBC 30, the Respondent had made comments about another lawyer and members of the judiciary. The panel held (at paras. 34 and 35):

> Our occupation is one where we often deal in difficult circumstances with difficult people, and emotions often run high. It is not in the best interests of the justice system, our clients, and ourselves to express ourselves in a fashion which promotes acrimony or intensifies the stressfulness or the difficulty of those already stressful and difficult circumstances.
>
> Public writings or comments which promote such acrimony or denigrate others in the justice system have a negative effect upon the system as a whole. This is

particularly true where it appears that the comments are made for no purposeful reason.

In both the *Lanning* and *Greene* cases, the respondent's uncivil conduct was found to be professional misconduct.

. . . . .

DISCUSSION

We set out earlier in these reasons the portions of the Canons of Legal Ethics dealing with civility. The duties described in those Canons are not restricted to situations where the lawyer agrees with the position, or the practice style, of the opposing lawyer or party. The duty of courtesy and good faith applies to all counsel, regardless of one's feelings about them. The Canons specifically note that "personal remarks or references between lawyers should be scrupulously avoided, as should quarrels between lawyers which cause delay and promote unseemly wrangling."

We accept that the Respondent may have been upset by the legal position and the allegations set out in the Ontario Lawyer's Demand Letter. However, those feelings do not justify the correspondence and blog posting drafted by the Respondent.

As noted above, the Respondent takes the position that he was allowed, perhaps even compelled, to do what he did in the face of a "rogue lawyer". Even if the Ontario Lawyer can be considered to be a "rogue", it is not the Respondent's place to pursue some form of vigilante justice against that lawyer by posting intemperate personal remarks or by writing letters that do not promote any possibility of resolution of the client's legal dispute.

Clearly, the appropriate avenue for the Respondent to take would have been to file a complaint either with the Law Society of Upper Canada or the Law Society of British Columbia. Obviously, the Respondent did not take those steps. Thus, by taking actions that he felt were protecting the integrity of the profession, he was achieving the opposite result.

The Respondent's actions were a marked departure from the conduct the Law Society expects of its members. The Respondent's belief in the correctness of his position does not relieve him of culpability.

DETERMINATION

On the basis of the reasoning set out above, we find that the Respondent's letter to the Ontario Lawyer and the blog posting constitute professional misconduct in respect of the allegations in the citation.

NOTES AND QUESTIONS

1. In its follow-up discipline hearing decision, the Law Society of British Columbia fined Mr. Laarakker $1,500 (plus costs in the amount of $3,000) for what the panel described as "professional misconduct" that was "not of the most serious nature". See *Law Society of British Columbia v. Laarakker*, [2012] L.S.D.D. No. 8, 2012 LSBC 2 at paras. 2, 10 and 15 (L.S.B.C.). Do you agree with this result?

2. Does the Law Society of British Columbia's decision in *Laarakker* fit with the court's decision in *D.C.B. v. Zellers Inc.* (set out earlier in this chapter)?

Is one case saying that it is unethical for a lawyer to send a demand letter based on a dubious cause of action, and the other saying that it is unethical or uncivil for a lawyer to claim that another lawyer is doing just that? Can they be reconciled? Do you agree? Does *Groia* help with your thinking?

3. If law societies are not regularly going to police unprofessional demand letters (unless called upon to do so), should lawyers be allowed to play that role? If so, to what extent? Is the public's perception of civil communication the most important professional concern here? What other professional considerations are at stake?

4. For discussions of the *Laarakker* case, see Alice Woolley, "Lawyers regulating lawyers?" (November 3, 2011), online: *ABlawg.ca*, University of Calgary, Faculty of Law //ablawg.ca/2011/11/03/lawyers-regulating-lawyers/. See also Micah Rankin, "Gerry Laarakker: From Rustic Rambo to Rebel With a Cause" in *In Search of the Ethical Lawyer*, Adam Dodek and Alice Woolley eds. (Vancouver: UBC Press, 2016).

In light of all of these discussions, consider what might be some considerations associated with requiring lawyers to be civil in the context of the following scenarios.

Scenario Six

Shae Kumar is defending her client in securities fraud litigation. The allegations involve claims that Kumar's client knowingly produced inaccurate geological reports inflating the amount of oil that was apparently found in a newly-discovered off-shore oil field. Kumar's client publicized the reports. Shares in her client's company shot up dramatically and were then sold at a vastly overvalued price. As it turns out, there is very little oil in that area of the seabed. The legal team for the Securities Commission, including two experienced lawyers and a team of law students, experts and other assistants, has been vigorously pursuing this litigation in a lengthy hearing. Kumar has a summer student assisting her with the case. Part of her strategy has been to raise every procedural challenge they can imagine in order to keep the Government's team working overtime, which Kumar thinks will help their client's case. Further, Kumar has been extremely tough with every Government witness, keeping them in the witness box for as long as possible (in order to wear them down and, hopefully, to elicit some useful testimony). Finally, during Kumar's closing — in response to some of the Government's complaints about Kumar's conduct and also about some of the Government's handling of evidence at trial — Kumar stated, among other things:

> *So you are now hearing the Government say we have changed our mind. Kumar doesn't want to play by our rules, so we're going to take our ball and go home. And so essentially I can't prove this document because the Government isn't prepared to stand by its representations to this Court. They promised to provide the background to this document only days ago. Well, the Government's promises aren't worth the transcript that they appear to be written on. Since they don't live up to their promises, then I don't think I have a basis to tender the document.*
>
> *When is the Crown going to accept the fact that they are prosecuting a case? Why do they stand before this Court and continually whine about how unfair it is that the law in this country says if you want to prosecute my client you must do so in*

accordance with certain fundamental rules of basic fairness, honesty and trial advocacy. They didn't care about those rules when they stood in front of this courthouse and said they were simply here to seek a conviction. I mean it's the most nonsensical proposal from a Government prosecutor that one could imagine. What do you make of that? What kind of proposal is that from a prosecutor who claims at least that they want to conduct this trial in a responsible fashion?

I am heartened to see that Your Honour is no more able to get a straight answer out of the prosecutor than the defence has been.

In your view, do any of these comments — individually or taken as a whole — amount to conduct that should be sanctioned? If so, on what basis? If not, why not?[24]

Scenario Seven

A Crown is prosecuting an individual for sexual assault. The alleged victim is HIV-positive. On learning this fact, the judge in the case directs the Crown to have the witness testify wearing a mask, electronically from another courtroom, or from a table situated 30 feet from the judge. In submissions, the Crown loses his temper and states that the judge has "the intelligence of a goat" and the "moral sensitivity of a member of the KKK". Do you think the Crown should be subject to professional discipline? Why or why not?[25]

Scenario Eight

Quinn Smith represents a client in a real estate purchase. Alex Jones, the lawyer for the vendor, suggests that her client condition the sale of the property on the purchaser's ability to assume the mortgage on the property. Smith declines to do so. Nonetheless, on the closing of the transaction, Jones places this condition in the trust obligations. Smith objects, and ultimately Jones backs down. However, by this point the closing is delayed. Jones then seeks to require Smith's client to pay daily interest on the funds owed as a result of the delay in closing. Smith writes a letter to Jones, with whom they went to law school, stating: "I regret to say this, Jonesie, but you are clueless. I would hope that the other solicitors in your firm are not similarly clueless." Jones brings a complaint to the law society. What should the law society do?[26]

Scenario Nine

During the recent Covid-19 pandemic, a motion that was scheduled to be heard in person was rescheduled to be heard by video conference. The lawyer for the moving party was having difficulty with his internet connection on the morning of the

---

[24] The statements by counsel in this scenario are based on partly revised comments made by counsel as reported in the *Groia* hearings.

[25] The conduct of the judge in this scenario is based on "Case reveals judge's court his domain: Judge steps down amid worries over HIV-positive witness" *Law Times* (January 14, 2008).

[26] See *Law Society of Alberta v. Pozniak*, [2002] L.S.D.D. No. 55 (Law Society of Alberta.), discussed further in Alice Woolley, "Does Civility Matter?" (2008) 46 Osgoode Hall L.J. 175 at 181-182.

motion. He texted the lawyer for the responding party to inform her of the problem, indicating that: "My internet seems really bad today. Not sure why. As such, I might be a bit slow joining the motion today. However, I will either fix the problem or change locations. Either way I'll be there." The lawyer for the responding party joined the judge on the video conference at the scheduled motion time. The moving lawyer was absent. The lawyer for the responding party did not say anything about the moving lawyer's internet problems. After four minutes of silent waiting, the judge said: "I have a busy docket today. I can't wait any longer. I will dismiss the motion, with costs, but without prejudice to it being brought back on. Have a good day." The judge then promptly left the video conference. Should the lawyer for the responding party have said anything to the judge? Was it her responsibility? Does it matter that the moving lawyer did not contact the judge themselves? If this matter were brought to a law society discipline panel, what, if any, penalty should be imposed? On what basis? For recent discussions, see the joint E-Hearings Task Force of The Advocates' Society, the Ontario Bar Association, the Federation of Ontario Law Associations, and the Ontario Trial Lawyers Association, *Best Practices for Remote Hearings* (May 13, 2020) at paras. 21-23, online: Advocates' Society https://www.advocates.ca/Upload/Files/PDF/Advocacy/BestPracticesPublications/ BestPracticesRemoteHearings/Best_Practices_for_Remote_Hearings_13_May_2020_ FINAL_may13.pdf; Gideon Christian, "Lawyer Ethics in the Virtual Courtroom" (June 3, 2020), online: *ABlawg.ca*, University of Calgary, Faculty of Law https:// ablawg.ca/2020/06/03/lawyer-ethics-in-the-virtual-courtroom/#more-11618.

[6] FURTHER READING

The Advocates' Society, "The Right to be Heard: The Future of Advocacy in Canada, Final Report of the Modern Advocacy Task Force" (Toronto, The Advocates' Society, June 2021).

Code, Michael, "Counsel's Duty of Civility: An Essential Component of Fair Trials and an Effective Justice System" (2007) 11 Can. Crim. L.R. 97.

Farrow, Trevor C.W., "Sustainable Professionalism" (2008) 46 Osgoode Hall L.J. 51.

Graham, Randal N.M., *Legal Ethics: Theories, Cases, and Professional Regulation*, 3d ed. (Toronto: Emond Montgomery, 2014), cc. 3 and 7.

Hanycz, Colleen M., Trevor C.W. Farrow & Frederick H. Zemans, *The Theory and Practice of Representative Negotiation* (Toronto: Emond Montgomery, 2008), cc. 2 and 5.

Lubet, Steven, adapted for Canada by Cynthia L. Tape, Julie Rosenthal & Lisa K. Talbot, *Modern Trial Advocacy: Analysis & Practice*, 4th ed. (Boulder, CO: National Institute for Trial Advocacy, 2019).

McKenzie, Gavin, *Lawyers and Ethics: Professional Responsibility and Discipline*, 6th ed. (Toronto: Carswell, 2018).

Reid, Robert F. & Richard E. Holland, *Advocacy: Views from the Bench* (Aurora, ON: Canada Law Book, 1984).

Smith, Beverley G., *Professional Conduct for Lawyers and Judges*, 4th ed. (Fredericton: Maritime Law Book, 2011), chs. 6-7.

White, Q.C., Robert B., *The Art of Trial* (Aurora, ON: Canada Law Book, 1993).

Woolley, Alice, *Understanding Lawyers' Ethics in Canada*, 2d ed. (Toronto: LexisNexis Canada, 2016).

CHAPTER 6

COUNSELLING AND NEGOTIATION

[1] INTRODUCTION

This chapter looks at the ethical rules governing two tasks frequently performed by a lawyer. The first is providing counsel by giving the client information, opinion and advice. The second is acting as a negotiator on behalf of the client. These tasks span all areas of legal practice and, in particular, are not restricted to a litigation context.

As you read this chapter, bear in mind that, unlike many other tasks lawyers perform, counselling and negotiation often take place in a relatively private setting. You should consider what impact that should have on the need for ethical rules and the content of those rules. You should also consider the potential for conflict between rules governing these activities and other rules of professional conduct such as the duty of loyalty to the client.

[2] COUNSELLING

It is vital that members of the public know the law, and so one of the most important services lawyers provide is telling them what the law is. The client often lacks the means of accessing the law, so the lawyer provides that access. Sometimes the law is clear and the lawyer simply communicates its content. Other times there may be doubt as to what the law is. There may be ambiguity in the wording of a statute or conflicting decisions in the reported cases. Here, the lawyer not only provides information but must also offer an opinion as to the law's true content. Further, the lawyer is frequently asked to apply the law to the client's factual situation. This too can be straightforward in some cases and more difficult in others. Finally, the client may ask the lawyer for an opinion on how the client should proceed.

There can be tension in the counselling process. On the one hand, lawyers should be concerned about client autonomy and respect the client's desires and decisions. On the other hand, the client is frequently looking to the lawyer for advice and guidance, which can result in lawyers expressly or implicitly making the actual decision about what is best for the client.

Counselling clients raises several important ethical issues. One is whether a lawyer can ever advise the client to break the law. Another is the extent to which a lawyer can provide advice that could be used by the client as a basis for a subsequent decision to break the law. These and other issues will be addressed in the material that follows.

In counselling clients, lawyers are not permitted to simply tell them what they want to hear. Rather, lawyers are obliged to be honest and candid. The advice must

375

be clear and communicated in language that their clients can understand.

[a]   Central Aspects of Counselling

FEDERATION OF LAW SOCIETIES OF CANADA

Model Code of Professional Conduct, Rule 3

3.1-2 A lawyer must perform all legal services undertaken on a client's behalf to the standard of a competent lawyer.

. . . . .

Commentary

[8] A lawyer should clearly specify the facts, circumstances and assumptions on which an opinion is based, particularly when the circumstances do not justify an exhaustive investigation and the resultant expense to the client. However, unless the client instructs otherwise, the lawyer should investigate the matter in sufficient detail to be able to express an opinion rather than mere comments with many qualifications. A lawyer should only express his or her legal opinion when it is genuinely held and is provided to the standard of a competent lawyer.

[9] A lawyer should be wary of providing unreasonable or over-confident assurances to the client, especially when the lawyer's employment or retainer may depend upon advising in a particular way.

[10] In addition to opinions on legal questions, a lawyer may be asked for or may be expected to give advice on non-legal matters such as the business, economic, policy or social complications involved in the question or the course the client should choose. In many instances the lawyer's experience will be such that the lawyer's views on non-legal matters will be of real benefit to the client. The lawyer who expresses views on such matters should, if necessary and to the extent necessary, point out any lack of experience or other qualification in the particular field and should clearly distinguish legal advice from other advice.

. . . . .

3.2-2 When advising a client, a lawyer must be honest and candid and must inform the client of all information known to the lawyer that may affect the interests of the client in the matter.

. . . . .

Commentary

[2] A lawyer's duty to a client who seeks legal advice is to give the client a competent opinion based on a sufficient knowledge of the relevant facts, an adequate consideration of the applicable law and the lawyer's own experience and expertise. The advice must be open and undisguised and must clearly disclose what the lawyer honestly thinks about the merits and probable results.

[3] Occasionally, a lawyer must be firm with a client. Firmness, without rudeness, is not a violation of the rule. In communicating with the client, the lawyer may disagree with the client's perspective, or may have concerns about the client's position on a matter, and may give advice that will not please the client. This may

legitimately require firm and animated discussion with the client.

NOTES AND QUESTIONS

1. As this extract indicates, issues relating to counselling clients are addressed in the *Model Code*'s commentaries to both the duty of competence and the duty to be honest and candid with the client. After reviewing these provisions, how would you explain these obligations to an unsophisticated client?

2. Despite rules like these, an anecdotal study of American lawyers concluded that "[l]awyers deceive their clients more than is generally acknowledged by the ethics codes or by the bar".[1] Common lies relate to the amount of work done for the client, whether certain work has been completed, the lawyer's availability to meet with the client or work on the matter, and the lawyer's degree of experience and competence. While there is a lack of empirical data, in the words of one commentator, "we all suspect strongly that many lawyers misrepresent their knowledge and experience to gain a client's confidence [and] exaggerate the complexity of work or the demands of skill to justify their fees".[2]

3. Lawyers sometimes deceive their clients to avoid admitting that they have made a mistake. In *Law Society of British Columbia v. Ahuja* a lawyer missed a flight to attend a hearing.[3] He told the client this was because the flight was overbooked but actually he had overslept. He was found to have committed professional misconduct for failing to be honest and candid with the client and suspended for one month. As discussed in Chapter 5 in the notes following *Schreiber v. Mulroney*, [2007] O.J. No. 3040 (S.C.J.), this discipline reflected the fact that he misled not only his client but also the court.

4. In *Law Society of Saskatchewan v. Bachynski* a lawyer argued a summary judgment motion.[4] The court rendered an unfavourable judgment and commented negatively on the material the lawyer had filed. However, for four months the lawyer told the client that the judgment had not yet been rendered. This lack of honesty and candour was held to be conduct unbecoming a lawyer.

5. The duty under *Model Code* Rule 3.2-2 to be honest and candid in advising

---

[1] Lisa G. Lerman, "Lying to Clients" (1990) 138 U. Pa. L. Rev. 659 at 663.

[2] Richard Uviller, "The Lawyer as Liar" (1994) 13(2) Crim. Justice Ethics 2 at 102.

[3] [2017] L.S.D.D. No. 185, 2017 LSBC 26 (Law Soc. B.C. Hearing Panel). See also *Law Society of British Columbia v. Simons*, [2012] L.S.D.D. No. 94, 2012 LSBC 23 (Law Soc. B.C. Hearing Panel); *Law Society of British Columbia v. Kim*, [2019] L.S.D.D. No. 241, 2019 LSBC 43 (Law Soc. B.C. Hearing Panel).

[4] [2018] L.S.D.D. No. 103, 2018 SKLSS 5 (Law Soc. Sask. Hearing Comm.). See also *Law Society of Saskatchewan v. Wolfe*, [2015] L.S.D.D. No. 183, 2015 SKLSS 5 (Law Soc. Sask. Hearing Comm.); *Luft v. Taylor, Zinkhofer & Conway*, [2017] A.J. No. 692, 2017 ABCA 228 at paras. 13, 15 (Alta. C.A.).

clients covers not only candour in the advice itself but also candour about the relationship between the lawyer and client. This aspect of candour is analyzed with the material on conflicts of interest and the duty of loyalty, discussed in Chapter 4. See *Canadian National Railway Co. v. McKercher LLP*, in which the court stated "A lawyer or law firm owes a duty of candour to the client. This requires the law firm to disclose any factors relevant to the lawyer's ability to provide effective representation".[5]

6.   Lawyers are sometimes asked to provide business, financial or strategic advice. If they choose to do so, they should clearly differentiate between this advice and their legal advice. They should make sure the client is aware of any limitations on their ability to provide non-legal advice, such as not having financial or accounting training. If a lawyer provides non-legal advice, this opens up the possibility of the client suing the lawyer in negligence if the advice turns out to be incorrect. Such a claim would not likely be covered by the lawyer's professional insurance which covers claims based on providing legal services.

7.   Why might you as a lawyer ever choose to provide non-legal advice to a client? How could you do so in a way that would best protect you from subsequent legal liability for the advice?

8.   Some other specific ethical obligations relate to counselling clients and so should be noted. If a lawyer discovers that they have made an error that could damage the client's position, the lawyer should promptly notify the client and discuss how to proceed, including candidly discussing the possibility of a claim against the lawyer. The lawyer should insist that the client obtain independent legal advice (from another lawyer) before making a decision. Similarly, the lawyer should insist on independent legal advice in connection with any of the client's transactions in which the lawyer has an interest. See, for example, the *Model Code*'s Rule 3.4-29 and Rule 7.8-1.

FEDERATION OF LAW SOCIETIES OF CANADA
Model Code of Professional Conduct, Rule 3

3.2-4 A lawyer must advise and encourage a client to compromise or settle a dispute whenever it is possible to do so on a reasonable basis and must discourage the client from commencing or continuing useless legal proceedings.

. . . . .

Commentary

[1] A lawyer should consider the use of alternative dispute resolution (ADR) when appropriate, inform the client of ADR options and, if so instructed, take steps to pursue those options.

---

[5] [2013] S.C.J. No. 39, 2013 SCC 39 at para. 45 (S.C.C.). See also *MTM Commercial Trust. v. Statesman Riverside Quays Ltd.*, [2015] A.J. No. 415, 2015 ABCA 142 at paras. 29-30 (Alta. C.A.).

QUESTIONS

1. How does *Model Code* Rule 3.2-4 restrict lawyers in the counsel they can provide to their clients? What justifies these restrictions?

[b] The Lawyer as Gatekeeper

Clients frequently want to pursue a particular course of action but, for a variety of reasons, are unable or unwilling to do so without first receiving favourable legal advice. The client requires or desires the protection of a legal opinion before, for example, entering into the transaction or claiming various deductions on the tax return. A striking example of this phenomenon is the "torture memos" situation discussed below. Another striking example is the United Kingdom's decision to invade Iraq in March 2003 (the legal advice on the invasion is analyzed in detail in Section 5 of *The Report of the Iraq Inquiry* (2016)[6]). Moreover, in many of these cases the accuracy of the advice will never come to be tested in court, because no dispute will arise. In these cases, the lawyer is the gatekeeper for the course of action.

These situations can put the lawyer under considerable pressure to provide a favourable opinion. They test the lawyer's ability to resist simply telling the client what they want to hear. But these situations also raise questions about when it would be appropriate for a lawyer to refuse to provide a favourable opinion, even when correct as a matter of law, because doing so enables the client's course of action. Even if the lawyer is morally opposed to the course of action, refusing to provide the opinion solely on that basis would seem to violate core duties to the client, such as loyalty.

This leads to the questions of whether a lawyer can separate legal advice and moral advice, and whether the lawyer can or should offer both to the client. It is possible that the client, in the face of the lawyer's moral advice, might decline to pursue the otherwise legal course of action. However, clients are likely to vary dramatically in their willingness to receive and heed moral advice from their lawyers.

DAVID LUBAN

"Tales of Terror: Lessons for Lawyers from the 'War on Terrorism'" in Kieran Tranter *et al.*, eds., *Reaffirming Legal Ethics: Taking Stock and New Ideas*(New York: Routledge, 2010) 56 at 60-61[*]
[footnotes omitted]

[A dramatic example of the ethical obligation related to the advice a lawyer gives to the client arose in the context of the United States government's dealings with detainees following the September 11, 2001 terrorist attacks. The government wanted to interrogate the detainees in as forceful and effective a way as possible without violating international law related to torture. It sought opinions from senior lawyers in the Office of Legal Counsel of the Justice Department. These opinions

---

[6] Online: https://www.gov.uk/government/publications/the-report-of-the-iraq-inquiry.

[*] Reproduced with permission.

concluded that interrogative techniques did not amount to torture unless they posed a threat of organ failure to the detainee.

The opinions were provided to a client that presumably wanted as much leeway as possible in obtaining information from detainees in order to prevent further terrorist attacks and to capture the perpetrators of terrorist attacks. The opinions have since been discredited as having significantly overreached the legitimate interpretations of what constitutes torture and they were ultimately disavowed by the Office of Legal Counsel in 2009.

David Luban was one of the most vocal critics of these "torture memos", partly because of their content, but also because, in his view, the lawyers who provided the advice to their client failed in their ethical duties as counsellors and advisors.]

Are there lessons that lawyers can learn from this episode? The crucial question has to do with the ethical obligations of lawyers in their role as confidential counsellors, or legal advisors, to their clients. Let me set aside for the moment the most fundamental criticism of the Bybee memo, namely, that it enabled torture. The more general criticisms of the memo are two: first, it stretched and distorted the law to reach the outcome that the client wanted; and second, it nowhere indicated that its interpretations were outside the mainstream. The principles behind these criticisms apply to lawyers in private practice as well as government lawyers.

They are noteworthy criticisms, because they highlight the ethical distortion that results when lawyers bring the neutral partisan role morality of courtroom advocates into the counselling role. After all, stretching the law to reach the client's desired outcome, and disguising the fact that stretching is going on, are exactly what advocates do every day in litigation and brief-writing. The major point, then, is that the role of the counsellor and that of the advocate are fundamentally different. In the words of current U.S. ethics rules, the counsellor is supposed to provide clients with independent and candid advice — telling the client what the law requires even if that is not what the client wants. The reason for sharply distinguishing the advocate's pro-client tilt in stating the law from the counsellor's more objective stance is straightforward. In adversary litigation, whatever exaggerations a lawyer introduces in presenting the law can be countered by the lawyer on the other side, and an impartial decision-maker will choose between the arguments. In a counselling situation, it is just the lawyers and their clients, with no adversary and no impartial adjudicator. The institutional setting that justifies an advocate's one-sided partisanship in setting forth the law is absent in the counselling role.

For that reason, the counsellor's rule of thumb should be different from the one-sided partisanship of the advocate. It is to make your description of the law more or less the same as it would be if your client wanted the opposite result from the one you know your client wants. That should be the litmus test of whether your advice is truly independent, rather than result-driven by what you know your client wants. It seems clear that the torture memos failed this test.

What should legal opinion writers do when they believe they have the law right and the mainstream has it wrong? Here, it seems to me, the rule of thumb should be this: if your view of the law is out of the mainstream, but you believe you're right, you have the responsibility to tell your client both those things: what the law, on your own best understanding, requires; *and* the fact that your own best understanding is not one that the legal interpretive community would accept.

KATHERINE R. KRUSE

"The Jurisprudential Turn in Legal Ethics" (2011) 53
Arizona Law Review 493 at 494-95 and 504-05*
[footnotes omitted]

Clients come to lawyers to find out what the law requires, prohibits, or allows them to do. However, the limits of the law are often unclear, and lawyers must exercise professional judgment in choosing how to explain the law to their clients. . . . [I]n counseling and advising their clients, lawyers are not merely transmitting information about law but are playing a quasi-official role in shaping the "bounds of the law" within which their clients operate. Although each lawyer-client consultation affects the life and affairs of only one client, legal ethicists argue, the aggregate of these consultations determines the shape of law as it exists in society. Lawyers thus play a lawmaking or law-interpreting role that is different from, but no less important than, the role that legislatures and judges play in creating and interpreting law.

. . . . .

Legal ethicists have long recognized that the choices lawyers make in characterizing the law to their clients have jurisprudential implications, but have only recently focused attention on theoretical analysis of lawyers' duties to interpret the law correctly or appropriately.

. . . . .

The reliance on lawyers' moral judgments to supplement and limit the professional duty of partisan advocacy creates significant tension with lawyers' role in the legal system. The permission given to lawyers to pursue client objectives all the way to the "bounds of the law" is grounded in rule-of-law values that individuals should be free to pursue their projects and objectives within limits set through open, public, and democratic processes. When lawyers supplement these legal boundaries and curtail or withhold legal representation based on their private and personal judgments about whether clients' projects or objectives are morally worthy, society runs the risk of substituting the rule of law with the rule of an "oligarchy of lawyers". The tension becomes especially acute in the context of a morally pluralistic society, where the promotion of a robust role for morality in the lawyer-client relationship can become a license for lawyers to impose their personal resolution of contested moral issues on their clients' life choices.

Although lawyers are not ethically prevented from providing moral advice to their clients, attempts to fashion a professional duty to incorporate moral judgment into legal representation strain against the nature and purpose of the lawyer-client relationship. . . . [C]lients have only limited ability to assess their lawyers' competence and diligence and very little information from which to ascertain the lawyer's personal, moral, or political views. . . . When a lawyer takes on the goal

---

* Reproduced with permission.

of morally educating the client or making the client a better person through moral conversation, the problems of lack of moral expertise, risk of moral overreaching, and threat to rule-of-law values arise.

. . . Moreover, the incorporation of moral judgment into legal representation has the paradoxical quality of being least effective in shaping moral outcomes in the situations in which it is acknowledged to be most appropriate. Legal ethicists across the spectrum agree that the lawyer's moral management of legal representation is least appropriate for clients who are vulnerable to moral overreaching by their lawyers due to their relative lack of power, sophistication, and capacity to seek a second opinion from another lawyer. Yet they acknowledge that more sophisticated and powerful clients are less likely to tolerate a lawyer's moral maneuvering, either by brushing off moral advice as irrelevant or by seeking legal representation from a lawyer who will provide representation free of moral challenge.

NOTES AND QUESTIONS

1. One of Luban's concerns is with advice that "stretched and distorted the law to reach the outcome that the client wanted". Does *Model Code* Rule 3.2-2, which requires lawyers to be honest and candid in providing advice, prevent such stretching?

2. The obligation to give honest and candid advice can, in certain circumstances, include an obligation to advise a client against a legal transaction the client is otherwise committed to doing. *Neushul v. Mellish & Harkavy*[7] is routinely cited as a case in which a lawyer appears to have been held liable for failing to advise a client against a transaction on general commercial grounds. The plaintiff became romantically involved with a rogue and, when the rogue asked her for a loan, she was willing to lend him money. The plaintiff borrowed the money she needed to lend to the rogue, securing the loan with her house. For these transactions she retained a lawyer who was also the rogue's lawyer and thus knew something of his business and affairs. The rogue absconded with the money and the plaintiff sued the lawyer. The court held that a lawyer should not refrain from expressing an opinion where it is plain that the client is rushing into an unwise or disastrous transaction. The rogue's unreliability was known to the lawyer and he owed the plaintiff a duty to advise her so that she could decide what arrangements she wanted in order to protect her position.

3. Might lawyers take the duty of honesty and candour too far? In Donald C. Langevoort and Robert Rasmussen, "Skewing the Results: The Role of Lawyers in Transmitting Legal Rules" (1997) 5 S. Cal. Interdisciplinary L.J. 375, the authors argue that lawyers systematically tend to overstate legal risks. They suggest that this can be explained in economic terms, in that the overstatement can lead to lawyers being paid more for their services by their clients. They also suggest other contributing factors such as a lawyer's concern for their reputation in the event a transaction the lawyer opines is legal is subsequently found to be illegal.

---

[7] (1967), 203 EG 27, 111 Sol. Jo. 399 (C.A.).

4. Do you agree with the approach to counselling outlined by Luban? Are there problems with requiring a lawyer to tell a client that the lawyer's views differ from the mainstream approach? How might this affect the client's confidence in the lawyer? Would it be preferable to insist that advice satisfy two requirements: the lawyer must subjectively believe it to be accurate and it must be objectively reasonable? See Alice Woolley, "The Lawyer as Advisor and the Practice of the Rule of Law" (2014) 47 U.B.C.L. Rev. 743.

5. Are lawyers limited in providing favourable advice to clients by a "fidelity to law" such that the law must be interpreted respectfully and with due regard for its intended meaning? Should they be? See W. Bradley Wendel, *Lawyers and Fidelity to Law* (Princeton: Princeton University Press, 2010) at 59, 131 and 196. See also Tim Dare, *The Counsel of Rogues? A Defence of the Standard Conception of the Lawyer's Role* (Farnham, UK: Ashgate Publishing Limited, 2009) at 76.

6. Consider the way the common law evolves. The law on a particular issue can change with a single judicial decision, sometimes quite dramatically, and this usually happens at the urging of one of the parties to a dispute. For this process to function, does the system require at least some lawyers with unorthodox opinions as to the law, who in turn provide those opinions to clients?

7. How comfortable would you be in providing moral advice to a client who had not requested it? How comfortable would you be in giving a favourable opinion to a client about a course of conduct to which you morally objected?

[c] Counselling and Illegal Conduct

LAW SOCIETY OF UPPER CANADA v. SUSSMAN

[1995] L.S.D.D. No. 17
(Law Soc. Upper Canada, Discipline Comm.: D.W. Scott,
V.C. Krishna and N. Graham)

. . . . .

Background

The solicitor, Frederick Bernard Sussmann, was called to the Bar of the Province of Ontario on the 15th of June 1973. Prior to that date he was a member of the Bar of the State of New York, U.S.A., and had been since March 1944. He came to Canada to join the Faculty of Law at the University of Ottawa and upon his retirement took up practice in the City of Ottawa. The complaint in the case arises out of his representation of Jaqueline Joubarne. The solicitor is charged that:

> while acting for a wife in a matrimonial proceeding, he counselled his client to breach the terms of the Court Order respecting access.

The Facts

On November 14, 1991 the Honourable Mr. Justice McWilliam of the Ontario Court (General Division) at Ottawa issued an Order in a proceeding in which one Daniel

Joubarne, the husband, was the Applicant and Jacqueline Joubarne, the wife, the Respondent. The Order was to the effect, *inter alia*, that the wife would have custody of the two children of the marriage, Jessie St. Anne Joubarne born February 29, 1980 (the child of the wife's previous marriage) and Jill Samantha Joubarne born December 28, 1983, and that the husband would have, in effect, weekend access to both children in accordance with the specific terms of the Order. . . .

In accordance with the terms of the Order for access the children were with their father on Saturday and Sunday, November [30] and December 1, 1991. On Tuesday, December 3, the solicitor wrote to Richard B. Bowles, the solicitor for the husband . . ., remonstrating with him with respect to his client's behaviour during access and concluded that:

> The further consequence is that, as soon as I can get the necessary affidavit from my client, I will prepare a motion for an interim restraining order barring your client's access to both children.

Some ten days later on December 13, 1991 the solicitor again wrote to Richard B. Bowles. . . . His letter contained the following statement:

> The purpose of this letter is to tell you that I have instructed my client not to permit your client access to the children this coming weekend, or at any time until I can make my application for a temporary restraining order, and that you had better advise your client accordingly, since originally he was to have had access this coming weekend.

The solicitor for the husband responded . . . on the same day, which was a Friday, complaining about the propriety of the position adopted by the solicitor having in mind his obligations as an officer of the Court and the terms of the existing Order. It is clear from the evidence that was tendered at the Hearing that, as a result of the position adopted by the solicitor and the advice which he gave to his client, the husband was denied access to his two children on the weekend in question, that is to say the weekend of December 14 and 15, 1991.

. . . . .

. . . Far from complying, or even suggesting some viable alternative, the solicitor, on August 24, 1992, wrote to Mr. Bowles . . . and again made it quite clear that he was advising his client to ignore the terms of the outstanding access Order of November 14, 1991. Specifically, in this letter he notes at Point 4:

> Be advised that my client's position is that your client will be granted no further access to either child, and no further support payments for either will be accepted. This position was adopted by my client in consultation with me following consideration of your client's behaviour. . . .

As a result of this communication Mr. Bowles . . . reported the solicitor to the Law Society. . . .

Certain matters are clear from a factual standpoint. In the first place it is conceded that the solicitor counselled his client to disobey the terms of the Order of the Honourable Mr. Justice McWilliam of November 14, 1991. Not only is this apparent from his written communications, but he admitted the same in evidence. Furthermore, it is equally clear that his client followed his advice, as she might well have done, it having been proffered by an officer of the Court. Mr. Bowles testified that access was denied during the weekend of December 14 and 15, 1991. Furthermore, Judge Desmarais concluded that access had been denied, as threatened, on [a] second occasion in August 1992.

. . . . .

. . . [T]he solicitor argued that he had always intended to bring a variation application and had simply never done so. This position is equally untenable. He first denied access to the children on his client's behalf on December 13, 1991. The first (and apparently only) document which he filed in support of a variation of the Order was filed some seven months later on July 17, 1992. His explanations as to why he did not make a variation application are groundless. Whether they were based on his being overburdened with work or his somewhat convoluted theory as to the onus being on the husband to apply to the Court, they provide no escape. The circumstances in which a solicitor may counsel his client to ignore the terms of a mandatory order are, not surprisingly, extremely confined. In a decision of a Discipline Committee of the Law Society in the matter of Carole Curtis (decided December 29, 1993) the Committee noted the following on the subject at page 19:

> The principle appears to be reasonably, clearly established, and we emphasize that the circumstances in which the counselling of the disobedience of a court order can be countenanced are extremely narrow, have implicit in them the elements of reasonable and honest belief of there being imminent risk or danger to a child, and co-exist with the requirement that there be an immediate application to a court to have the issues determined forthwith. Once that application is made and the facts have been presented before a court of competent jurisdiction however briefly, if that court refuses to act to change an outstanding order, then the obligation of the client is to 'trust in the efficacy of the legal system' and adhere to the court order, and then if so advised, to seek a full hearing for a permanent change. . . .

The solicitor did not suggest that there was any imminent risk or danger to the child which might have justified his behaviour. Furthermore, as pointed out by counsel for the Law Society, not only was there no immediate application to vary, there was no application by the solicitor at all. Indeed, the Committee is of the view that . . . the solicitor never really intended to make an application so long as his assertions with respect to his client's decision not to follow the dictates of the Order had the intended effect upon the husband.

The complaint has accordingly been established. There will be a finding of professional misconduct against the solicitor. In particular, we find that, while acting for the wife in a matrimonial proceeding, the solicitor counselled his client to breach the terms of a Court Order respecting access.

. . . . .

. . . There can be no behaviour more disruptive to our system of justice and more likely to bring its administration into disrepute than a lawyer, while representing a party to a dispute, counselling his or her client to disobey the clear, unequivocal terms of a Court Order. To do so is to undermine the Court's effectiveness, contaminate the esteem with which it is held in the eyes of the citizenry and foment the law of the jungle. Behaviour of this kind is particularly troubling by reason of the highly undesirable example which it provides to ordinary citizens, lawyers and indeed law students. . . .

[Mr. Sussman had an otherwise clean disciplinary record, a lengthy record of service as a lawyer, and was in ill health. He was suspended from practice for one month.]

FEDERATION OF LAW SOCIETIES OF CANADA

Model Code of Professional Conduct, Rule 3

3.2-7 A lawyer must never: a) knowingly assist in or encourage any dishonesty, fraud, crime or illegal conduct, b) do or omit to do anything that the lawyer ought to know assists in or encourages any dishonesty, fraud, crime, or illegal conduct by a client or others, or c) instruct a client or others on how to violate the law and avoid punishment.

. . . . .

3.2-8 A lawyer who is employed or retained by an organization to act in a matter in which the lawyer knows that the organization has acted, is acting or intends to act dishonestly, fraudulently, criminally, or illegally, must do the following, in addition to his or her obligations under rule 3.2-7:

(a) advise the person from whom the lawyer takes instructions and the chief legal officer, or both the chief legal officer and the chief executive officer, that the proposed conduct is, was or would be dishonest, fraudulent, criminal, or illegal and should be stopped;

(b) if necessary because the person from whom the lawyer takes instructions, the chief legal officer or the chief executive officer refuses to cause the proposed conduct to be stopped, advise progressively the next highest persons or groups, including ultimately, the board of directors, the board of trustees, or the appropriate committee of the board, that the proposed conduct was, is or would be dishonest, fraudulent, criminal, or illegal and should be stopped; and

(c) if the organization, despite the lawyer's advice, continues with or intends to pursue the proposed wrongful conduct, withdraw from acting in the matter in accordance with the rules in section 3.7.

NOTES AND QUESTIONS

1. What rules of professional conduct did Mr. Sussman violate? How relevant is it to the analysis that his client followed his advice? For an American case with similar facts, see *In re Scionti*.[8]

2. Why might Mr. Sussman have advised his client to violate the court order concerning access to the children? In what circumstances would such advice not be unethical?

3. If a client acts illegally based on advice received from the client's lawyer, can the client rely on the advice as a defence if charged with an offence or with contempt of court?

4. In addition to prohibiting lawyers from encouraging their clients to act illegally, provincial codes of professional conduct also prohibit lawyers

---

[8] 630 N.E.2d 1358 (Sup. Ct. Ind. 1994).

from actually taking part in the illegal conduct. This is an even more serious ethical violation and can also expose the lawyer to criminal and civil sanctions as a party to the conduct.[9]

5. The same conduct can engage several professional conduct rules. In *Merchant v. Law Society of Saskatchewan*, a lawyer was found to have violated a court order and to have assisted a client to violate the same order, but not to have counselled the client to violate the order.[10]

6. Notwithstanding their duty of loyalty to the client, lawyers need to be vigilant to avoid becoming the "tool or dupe" of an unscrupulous client. The commentary to the *Model Code*'s Rule 3.2-7 tells lawyers that "[i]f a lawyer has suspicions or doubts about whether he or she might be assisting a client or others in dishonesty, fraud, crime or illegal conduct, the lawyer should make reasonable inquiries to obtain information about the client or others and, in the case of the client, about the subject matter and objectives of the retainer". See also American Bar Association Informal Ethics Opinion 1470 (1981) and New York City Bar Ethics Formal Opinion 2018-4 (2018) which specifically address when a lawyer should inquire further about a client's reasons for seeking advice. Lawyers are particularly susceptible to being involved in activities like mortgage fraud and money laundering because these activities typically use commercial transactions which lawyers commonly arrange.

7. What is the difference between a lawyer advising the client to dispose of a weapon used to commit a recent crime and advising the client that if the weapon was not found by the police it would be harder for the client to be convicted? For one view, see *In re Bullowa*.[11] See also Joel S. Newman, "Legal Advice Towards Illegal Ends" (1994) 28 U. Rich. L. Rev. 287 at 291.

8. Is there a way in which Mr. Sussman could have ethically advised his client that would have led to the same actions by the client?

9. Would it be acceptable for a lawyer to advise a client to breach a contract? A client might, for example, be much better off financially by breaking a contract, even after paying damages for the breach, because of alternative arrangements the client could make. Is this different from advice about breaching a court order? In *Law Society of Upper Canada v. Chojnacki* the majority stated that the Ontario equivalent of Rule 3.2-7 "on its plain reading encompasses, and was intended to encompass, both civil and criminal misconduct".[12] However, the dissent stated that "[a]ssuming . . . a thorough examination of the facts and proper advice on the adverse

---

[9] See, for example, *Criminal Code*, R.S.C. 1985, c. C-46, s. 21.

[10] [2014] S.J. No. 245, 2014 SKCA 56 (Sask. C.A.). At para. 124, the court refers to *Law Society of Upper Canada v. Sussman*.

[11] 229 N.Y.S. 145 (Sup. Ct. N.Y. 1928).

[12] [2010] L.S.D.D. No. 89, 2010 ONLSHP 74 at para. 82 (Law Soc. Upper Canada Discipline Comm.).

consequences, advice that a client's best course of action is to break a contract is not, in my opinion, professional misconduct. . . . To deprive the lawyer of the right to advise a client on the client's best course of action in any of these circumstances is not good public policy because it prevents the lawyer from giving any practical advice in a situation where the only advice available may be a choice between the lesser of two evils."[13]

10. Commentary 4 to the *Model Code*'s Rule 3.2-7 provides that "so long as no injury to a person or violence is involved, a lawyer may properly advise and represent a client who, in good faith and on reasonable grounds, desires to challenge or test a law and the test can most effectively be made by means of a technical breach giving rise to a test case". What is a "technical" breach of the law? Do you support this exception for test cases? For more on test cases see American Bar Association Formal Opinion 85-352.

11. Until 2017, Rule 3.2-7 provided that "[w]hen acting for a client, a lawyer must never knowingly assist in or encourage any dishonesty, fraud, crime or illegal conduct, or instruct the client on how to violate the law and avoid punishment". The rule was changed to expand the relationships to which the rule can apply (beyond only clients) and to increase the level of knowledge or awareness expected of a lawyer. The change followed similar changes made in British Columbia and Ontario.

12. Law societies developed rules like Rule 3.2-8 to address the role that lawyers should play in proper corporate governance. These were drafted in the wake of several high-profile corporate scandals in Canada and the United States. What do these rules require of lawyers? Do these rules strike a proper balance between the public interest in having corporations act legally and the lawyer's duty of loyalty? These rules are discussed in more detail in Chapter 9.

13. Rule 1.2(d) of the American Bar Association's *Model Rules of Professional Conduct* provides that "[a] lawyer shall not counsel a client to engage, or assist a client, in conduct that the lawyer knows is criminal or fraudulent, but a lawyer may discuss the legal consequences of any proposed course of conduct with a client". While the *Model Code*'s Rule 3.2-7 refers to illegal conduct, Rule 1.2(d) refers to criminal or fraudulent conduct. For an argument that this allows lawyers wide latitude with respect to conduct that is illegal but not criminal or fraudulent see Paul R. Tremblay, "At Your Service: Lawyer Discretion to Assist Clients in Unlawful Conduct" (2018) 70:2 Fla. L. Rev. 251.

14. The commentary to Rule 1.2(d) provides that there is "a critical distinction between presenting an analysis of legal aspects of questionable conduct and recommending the means by which a crime or fraud might be committed with impunity". Can you explain this distinction?

---

[13] [2010] L.S.D.D. No. 89, 2010 ONLSHP 74 at paras. 144 and 154 (Law Soc. Upper Canada Discipline Comm.).

15. The Alberta equivalent to *Model Code* Rule 3.2-7, which is Rule 3.2-13[6], contains the following commentary not found in the *Model Code*: "The mere provision of legal information must be distinguished from rendering legal advice or providing active assistance to a client. . . . merely providing legal information that could be used to commit a crime or fraud is not improper since everyone has a right to know and understand the law. Indeed, a lawyer has a positive obligation to provide such information or ensure that alternative competent legal advice is available to the client. Only if there is reason to believe beyond a reasonable doubt, based on familiarity with the client or information received from other reliable sources, that a client intends to use legal information to commit a crime should a lawyer decline to provide the information sought." Do you accept this distinction between advice and information? Should this commentary be added to the *Model Code*?

16. To what extent is it acceptable for a lawyer to provide advice about a client's likelihood of being caught in any violation of the law, such as the chances of police apprehension or of a tax audit? Might not this information lead the client to choose to violate the law? See Stephen L. Pepper, "Counseling at the Limits of the Law: An Exercise in the Jurisprudence and Ethics of Lawyering" (1995) 104 Yale L.J. 1545 at 1551-52. See also American Law Institute, *Restatement of the Law Third: The Law Governing Lawyers* (St. Paul, MN: American Law Institute, 2000) at para. 94, comment c.

17. To what extent should limitations on advising clients depend on whether the client has requested particular advice from the lawyer or whether the lawyer volunteers it without a specific request? Would this give an advantage to more sophisticated or creative clients?

18. Pepper identifies several factors a lawyer should consider in determining whether to provide certain legal information to a client. They include: (i) whether the law truly prohibits the conduct or only provides conse-quences for it; (ii) the degree to which the law is enforced (never? rarely?); (iii) the extent to which the information is public or private; and (iv) the likelihood the client will use the information to assist in unlawful conduct. Is this sort of analysis consistent with the obligation to be honest and candid? Does it undercut the lawyer's duty of loyalty to the client?

19. For further discussion of counselling and unlawful activity see Alice Woolley, *Understanding Lawyers' Ethics in Canada*, 2d ed. (Toronto: LexisNexis Canada, 2016) at 93-105.

Scenario One

Your client is charged with fraud and is alleged to have millions of dollars in accounts in offshore banking havens. Your client asks you to identify countries from which extradition to Canada would be impossible or very difficult. Can you ethically comply with the client's request? How does your answer take account of the *Model Code*'s Rules 3.2-2 and 3.2-7?

Scenario Two

Your client in an ongoing divorce dispute asks you to explain the law in Canada on automatism as a defence to a murder charge. Would you do so? Would you insist on knowing why the client wanted this information before providing an answer? Would you confine your answer to the strict legal test for the defence, or would you also advise as to the relative strength of alternative defences?

Scenario Three

Sam Smith and Jane Jones are criminal defence lawyers. They routinely retain you for advice on legal ethics issues. You have a reputation in the legal community for advancing the cause of the wrongfully convicted. Sam and Jane represent a client, Frank Forani, who has confessed to them that he is responsible for a murder for which Alex Adams was convicted. Alex is currently serving a life sentence. Sam and Jane very much want to assist Alex. They would like you to provide them with an opinion that the rules of professional conduct implicitly allow them to disclose Frank's confession to Alex, so that a lawyer for Alex can bring an application to compel Frank, under the innocence at stake exception to privilege, to reveal the truth. Can you provide that opinion?

Scenario Four

A client comes to you for tax advice. Based on its situation, you can identify steps that would save the client $100,000 in taxes but would cost it the same amount in legal fees (paid to you). What advice do you give the client?

[3] NEGOTIATION

One way for people to resolve disputes between them is to negotiate a solution. The process of negotiation has been extensively studied and there are many different approaches people can take to it. Books abound proposing various ways to negotiate. These books frequently discuss negotiation ethics, but very much in a non-binding sense, looking at morality and what might be perceived by others as inappropriate. See, for example, Roy Lewicki, Bruce Barry & David Saunders, *Negotiation*, 8th ed. (New York: McGraw-Hill Education, 2020) at 1.12-1.13; Colleen M. Hanycz, Trevor C.W. Farrow and Frederick H. Zemans, *The Theory and Practice of Representative Negotiation* (Toronto: Emond Montgomery, 2008) at ch. 5. Subject to some relatively minimal legal restrictions imposed by the law on fiduciary duties, deceit and misrepresentation, people can act in their own best interests and are free to negotiate unethically if they so choose.

In general, negotiating parties can withhold material facts from each other[14] and make untruthful statements. This frequently happens when a party sets out a bottom-line position. For example, a party may state that it will not accept anything less than $100,000, knowing, at that time, that it would accept less. Under many approaches to negotiation this is not unethical, even in a moral or personal sense. Negotiation is frequently seen as a kind of "game" in which deception and bluffing

---

[14] This can be modified by specific disclosure requirements in certain contexts. For example, under the *Family Law Act*, R.S.O. 1990, c. F.3, s. 56(4)(a) a domestic contract can be set aside if one party did not make full financial disclosure to the other. Additionally, parties might agree, by contract, to make full disclosure of all relevant facts, as can happen in some family law disputes resolved using collaborative practice.

are key tactics. Indeed, one commentator has claimed that "the critical difference between those who are successful negotiators and those who are not lies in [the] capacity both to mislead and not to be misled".[15] This view of negotiation has been endorsed by the courts. For example, in *Westcom TV Group Ltd. v. CanWest Global Broadcasting Inc.* the court noted that "[p]arties involved in arm's length negotiations commonly conceal their true intentions. It is part of the negotiating process that positions are advanced that do not represent what a party truly expects or is prepared to agree to in the end."[16] Other cases make it clear, despite the occasional argument to the contrary, that "there is no recognized pre-contractual duty to bargain in good faith".[17]

Negotiating parties often employ lawyers to negotiate on their behalf. This raises two questions which will be addressed in the material that follows. The first is the extent to which the lawyer must be skilled in the process of negotiation. Lawyers are required to be competent. What does it mean to be competent to negotiate? The second question is whether the general rule about truth in negotiations, outlined above, is different when lawyers are the ones negotiating. For example, can lawyers knowingly misrepresent their clients' bottom-line position?

[a] Competence to Negotiate

FEDERATION OF LAW SOCIETIES OF CANADA

Model Code of Professional Conduct, Rule 3

3.1-1 In this section, "Competent lawyer" means a lawyer who has and applies relevant knowledge, skills and attributes in a manner appropriate to each matter undertaken on behalf of a client and the nature and terms of the lawyer's engagement, including . . .

    (c)   implementing as each matter requires, the chosen course of action through the application of appropriate skills, including: . . .

        (v)   negotiation; . . .

3.1-2 A lawyer must perform all legal services undertaken on a client's behalf to the standard of a competent lawyer.

NOTES AND QUESTIONS

1.   Why do ethical rules make express reference to negotiation skills in defining competence?

2.   Is a lawyer a competent negotiator just by virtue of being a lawyer? How

---

[15] James J. White, "Machiavelli and the Bar: Ethical Limitations on Lying in Negotiation" [1980] Am. B. Found. Res. J. 926 at 927. See also Raymond A. Friedman & Debra Shapiro, "Deception and Mutual Gains Bargaining: Are They Mutually Exclusive?" (1995) 11 Neg. J. 243.

[16] [1996] B.C.J. No. 1638, 26 B.C.L.R. (3d) 311 at para. 18 (B.C.S.C.).

[17] *Doucet v. Spielo Manufacturing Inc.*, [2011] N.B.J. No. 153, 2011 NBCA 44 at para. 31 (N.B.C.A.). See also *Bank of Montreal v. No. 249 Seabright Holdings Ltd.*, [2014] B.C.J. No. 1319, 2014 BCSC 1094 at paras. 109-117 (B.C.S.C.).

many lawyers do you think would consider themselves incompetent negotiators?

3.   What have you done to develop your skill at negotiation? Do you consider it sufficient?

4.   Law schools offer specialized courses in negotiation, as do other educational institutions. If the people who take these courses know more about the process of negotiation than those who do not, should all lawyers be required to take such a course? Why or why not?

5.   Does competency to negotiate only refer to the procedural skills involved in performing the negotiations or does it also include a certain level of awareness about the substance of the dispute, including the client's position on various issues?

[b]   Regulation of Negotiations

Most provincial codes of ethics contain a requirement that lawyers must, in their dealings with other lawyers and self-represented opposing parties, act with integrity and in good faith. For example, Rule 7.2-1 of the *Model Code* provides that a "lawyer must be courteous and civil and act in good faith with all persons with whom the lawyer has dealings in the course of his or her practice". This differentiates lawyers from the negotiating parties. However, it is debatable whether these general requirements impose on lawyers an obligation not to misrepresent or conceal information in negotiations. The orthodoxy in many provinces is that the usual degree of deception involved in negotiations is not altered by having lawyers involved. Being untruthful in negotiations, it would seem, is not a failure to act in "good faith".

This may seem surprising, but there are several reasons supporting a lack of more aggressive regulation of lawyer negotiation. One is the need to respect the lawyer's obligation to promote the interests of the client. The lawyer is acting for the client, trying to achieve the most favourable result, rather than acting with a view to the interests of both sides and the most reasonable bargain. A second reason is that if lawyers are more restricted in their negotiation tactics, clients will be tempted to forego the use of lawyers and either conduct the negotiations themselves or hire other professionals. Third, concerns about misrepresentations and non-disclosure are already covered by, and better left to, other areas of law such as the torts of deceit and misrepresentation, and the doctrine of mistake in contract. Finally, even if these other reasons could be overcome, drafting a rule about what is and is not permissible in negotiations would be a difficult exercise and it would be hard to achieve consensus among lawyers.[18]

Proponents of greater regulation reject each of these reasons. They argue it is too simplistic to fall back on the lawyer's fundamental duties to the client's interests. The modern regulation of lawyers involves many areas in which those duties have to be balanced against duties to the court, the fairness of the process and the public

---

[18] See Gavin MacKenzie, *Lawyers and Ethics: Professional Responsibility and Discipline*, 6th ed. (Toronto: Thomson Reuters, 2018) at 15-1 to 15-2.

interest. There are no compelling reasons why a similar balancing could not happen in the context of negotiations. There is no evidence that clients would either choose to negotiate themselves or hire other professionals to avoid any restrictions on what lawyers could say or do. Other areas of law at best only cover some of the conduct in negotiations which is seen as problematic and are impractical as remedies in many cases given the difficulties of litigating such claims through to a successful conclusion.[19] As to whether a workable rule about negotiation can be drafted, the examples in the material below will allow you to judge that for yourself. Accordingly, there is scope for a considerable debate about whether, and to what extent, lawyers should be regulated in their conduct in negotiations.

As is the case for many aspects of the regulation of lawyer conduct, the assumption is generally that the lawyer is negotiating within an adversarial context. This assumption is increasingly being challenged as lawyers operate in more non-adversarial situations. Any rules about lawyer negotiations based on this assumption might not be appropriate for these situations. Our view of what constitutes ethical negotiations could differ depending on the context.

LAW SOCIETY OF NEWFOUNDLAND AND LABRADOR v. REGULAR

[2005] N.J. No. 372, 252 Nfld. & P.E.I.R. 91
(N.L.C.A., C.K. Wells C.J.N.L., B.G. Welsh and M. Rowe JJ.A.)

[Robert Regular represented Petroleum Services Ltd. and Barrie James, who held 75 per cent of the shares of Petroleum Services Ltd. James Hughes represented Randy Spurrell, an individual who held 25 per cent of the shares of Petroleum Services Ltd. Mr. Regular and Mr. Hughes were in negotiations on behalf of their clients to ascertain the value of Mr. Spurrell's shares.]

B.G. WELSH J.A.:—

. . . . .

. . . Mr. Hughes wrote to Mr. Regular on December 12, 2000:

> Re: Petroleum Services Ltd.
>
> Further to the above, please be advised that we have heard that "Petroleum Services Ltd." is being sold.
>
> Rumour or not, please remind your client of Section 19 of their agreement and that Mr. Spurrell is a 25% shareholder and, even as a minority shareholder, should have input.

The letter did not request confirmation regarding the rumour. It was open to Mr. Regular simply to acknowledge receipt, and perhaps confirm that section 19 of their agreement had been drawn to his client's attention. However, Mr. Regular chose to respond on December 13, 2000, by telecopier transmittal:

> Re: Petroleum Services Ltd.
>
> Your Fax of Dec. 12/00

---

[19] See Gavin MacKenzie, *Lawyers and Ethics: Professional Responsibility and Discipline*, 6th ed. (Toronto: Thomson Reuters, 2018) at 15-2 to 15-3.

Jim: I apologize for the delay in getting back to you. The "rumour" that Petroleum Services Ltd. is being sold is untrue. My client is committed to resolving the issues between your client and the co. (sic) As soon as I get a reply to your last correspondence I'll be back to you.

The Benchers [in the discipline proceedings below] noted that:

[11] . . . On December 14, 2000, by way of a notice of Directors dated December 12, 2000, filed by Regular as solicitor for [Petroleum Services Ltd.], Randy Spurrell was removed as a Director of [Petroleum Services Ltd.]. This was done without actual notice to Spurrell and without following the process for removal of directors set out in the Corporations Act. This was acknowledged by Regular in the hearing before the Adjudication Panel. The effective date of the removal of Spurrell as a Director pursuant to the notice of Directors was March 17, 2000. On the same date (Dec. 12/00), Regular filed a Notice with the Registry of Companies changing the registered office address of [Petroleum Services Ltd.], and Articles of Amendment changing the name of [Petroleum Services Ltd.] to Bar-Jam Holdings Limited.

This was followed, on December 19, 2000, by a sale of Petroleum Services Ltd. assets to Comstock Canada Ltd. Mr. Regular testified at the adjudication panel hearing that he was of the opinion that substantially all the assets of Petroleum Services Ltd. were not being sold. He said 50 to 60 percent of the assets were sold, while he considered 90 percent would constitute "all or substantially all the assets". However, Mr. Regular's position depended solely on a monetary calculation, without regard to the business as a going concern.

. . . . .

In a situation where less than all the assets of a company are sold, the distinction between a qualitative and a quantitative description of the sale is significant. A failure to specify which description is being relied upon is an open invitation to misunderstanding.

Accordingly, if Mr. Regular was relying on a quantitative assessment of the sale of the assets, in light of . . . judicial authority which favours a qualitative analysis, it was necessary for him to identify that fact in his December 13th response to Mr. Hughes' letter. In the absence of such an explanation, it could be expected that Mr. Hughes would, in fact, be misled by Mr. Regular's blanket statement that the rumour that Petroleum Services Ltd. was being sold was untrue.

Indeed, a review of the evidence, applying a qualitative analysis to the sale of assets, leads inexorably to the conclusion that Petroleum Services Ltd. was being sold.

Commenting on this issue, the Benchers stated:

[26] Without doubt a substantial portion of the assets of [Petroleum Services Ltd.] were disposed of, as indicated in the documentary evidence placed before the Adjudication Panel. They included contracts assigned, tools, equipment, office equipment and furniture, the company name and acronym, and the building from which [Petroleum Services Ltd.] had carried on business. While the real estate was leased rather than sold outright, we attach no particular significance to this — it was disposed of to Comstock [with an option to purchase at fair market value]. . . . We agree with counsel for the Law Society that following the transaction with Comstock the company ([Petroleum Services Ltd.]) for practical purposes ceased to exist. . . .

. . . I am satisfied that there was ample evidence to establish that substantially all the assets of Petroleum Services Ltd. were sold. Given the evidence, the members of the adjudication panel could reasonably have concluded, as two of the three members specifically did, that substantially all the assets of Petroleum Services Ltd. were sold.

. . . . .

. . . The question, then, is why did Mr. Regular respond with such absolute clarity that: "The 'rumour' that Petroleum Services Ltd. is being sold is untrue"? The answer to this question must be considered within the framework of all the evidence, including: the instructions from Mr. Regular's client that Mr. Hughes was not to be told about the sale of assets to Comstock in case Mr. Hughes' client would somehow interfere with the sale; the steps taken by Mr. Regular, coincidental to the time of the sale, to retroactively, and without notice, remove Mr. Hughes' client as a director of the company; confirmation by Mr. Regular to the solicitor for Comstock, on closing the sale, that Mr. Hughes' client was not a shareholder of Petroleum Services Ltd.; the recital in the Escrow Agreement, one of the documents closing the sale, signed by Mr. Regular, stating, "AND WHEREAS the Assets and Contracts comprise all or a significant portion of the assets of [Petroleum Services Ltd.]"; and the inclusion of a "non-competition" clause as part of the sale agreement.

Considering this evidence as a whole, the inescapable inference is that Mr. Regular's response to Mr. Hughes' letter was deliberately intended to mislead Mr. Hughes. It is in this sense that the Benchers concluded that it was not critical to deciding the complaint to establish that substantially all the assets of Petroleum Services Ltd. were sold. The evidence supports the conclusion that Mr. Regular's response was calculated to deceive and to conceal the sale of the assets. On this basis it follows that Mr. Regular failed to act with integrity, failed in his responsibility to an individual lawyer, James D. Hughes, and failed to avoid questionable conduct.

. . . . .

NOTES AND QUESTIONS

1. How would Mr. Regular's conduct be analyzed under the rules of professional conduct of your jurisdiction?

2. Does this decision undermine Mr. Regular's obligations of confidentiality and loyalty to his clients?

3. Mr. Regular and Mr. Hughes were in negotiations about the value of Mr. Hughes' client's shares in the company. Can you make an argument that Mr. Regular's December 13 statement did not relate to the value of the shares? If it did not, is this a case about ethics in negotiations? If it is not, why was Mr. Regular disciplined?

4. How strongly does this case support the argument that law societies do not need to specifically regulate lawyer negotiation, and can instead rely on more general provisions? Consider also The Advocates' Society, "Principles of Civility and Professionalism for Advocates", which provides that

"[a]dvocates should always be honest and truthful with opposing counsel".[20]

5. It is well-accepted that settlements of disputes are to be encouraged and represent a better outcome than would be produced through litigation or arbitration. To what extent does this view depend on appropriate regulation of negotiation by lawyers?

6. Even if not considered to be unethical, deceptive or misleading conduct during a negotiation may increase the risk that a settlement will be legally invalid. See, for example, *Spaulding v. Zimmerman*,[21] excerpted in Chapter 1. Does this change your analysis with respect to Question 2 above?

LAW SOCIETY OF ALBERTA

Code of Conduct, Chapter 7

7.2-2 A lawyer must not lie to or mislead another lawyer.

Commentary

[1] This rule expresses an obvious aspect of integrity and a fundamental principle. In no situation, including negotiation, is a lawyer entitled to deliberately mislead a colleague. When a lawyer (in response to a question, for example) is prevented by rules of confidentiality from actively disclosing the truth, a falsehood is not justified. The lawyer has other alternatives, such as declining to answer. If this approach would in itself be misleading, the lawyer must seek the client's consent to such disclosure of confidential information as is necessary to prevent the other lawyer from being misled. The concept of "misleading" includes creating a misconception through oral or written statements, other communications, actions or conduct, failure to act, or silence (See Rule 7.2-5, Correcting Misinformation).

. . . . .

7.2-5 If a lawyer becomes aware during the course of a representation that:

    (a)   the lawyer has inadvertently misled an opposing party, or

    (b)   the client, or someone allied with the client or the client's matter, has misled an opposing party, intentionally or otherwise, or

    (c)   the lawyer or the client, or someone allied with the client or the client's matter, has made a material representation to an opposing party that was accurate when made but has since become inaccurate,

then, subject to confidentiality, the lawyer must immediately correct the resulting misapprehension on the part of the opposing party.

Commentary

"Subject to confidentiality" (see Rule 3.3, Confidentiality)

[1] Briefly, if correction of the misrepresentation requires disclosure of confidential

---

[20] Online: https://www.advocates.ca/Upload/Files/PDF/Advocacy/InstituteforCivilityand-Professionalism/Principles_of_Civility_and_Professionalism_for_AdvocatesFeb28.pdf.

[21] 263 Minn. 346 (1962).

information, the lawyer must seek the client's consent to such disclosure. If the client withholds consent, the lawyer is obliged to withdraw. The terminology used in this rule is to be broadly interpreted. A lawyer may have provided technically accurate information that is rendered misleading by the withholding of other information; in such a case, there is an obligation to correct the situation. In paragraph (c), the concept of an inaccurate representation is not limited to a misrepresentation that would be actionable at law.

NOTES AND QUESTIONS

1. To what extent do these rules impose different obligations from the rules of your province on lawyers as negotiators? Reflecting on the debate, outlined earlier, about the appropriateness of such regulation, do you prefer the Alberta rules, the rule in your province or an alternative rule? Are you concerned that the *Model Code* does not explicitly address the obligation to be truthful in negotiations?

2. Do the Alberta rules make negotiation conducted by Alberta lawyers different from that conducted by other Canadian lawyers? What are the consequences of requiring lawyers not to lie? Are there potential problems if an Alberta lawyer enters into negotiations with a lawyer from another jurisdiction in which lawyers are not prohibited from lying in negotiations? In such a case would a client in Alberta be better off with no lawyer at all?

3. Prior to November 2011, the Alberta rules addressed negotiations even more explicitly in a chapter entitled "The Lawyer as Negotiator". The predecessor of Rule 7.2-2 stated that "[a] lawyer must not lie to or mislead an opposing party". Why has Alberta changed this provision? The commentary to the earlier rule contained some quite detailed statements about negotiating, including the following: "The process of negotiation often involves representations as to the extent of a lawyer's authority. For example, a client may authorize a lawyer to settle an action for no more than $100,000.00. The lawyer may not pretend a lack of authority to offer more than $50,000.00 or $75,000.00 or any other amount under $100,000.00. In response to a direct question about the monetary limits of the lawyer's authority, the alternatives of the lawyer are to respond truthfully or simply decline to answer. The lawyer is not entitled to offer a response intended or likely to create a misleading impression, which would be tantamount to lying." Does removing this language in any way change the lawyer's obligations?

4. Negotiation is employed to attempt to resolve a very wide range of disputes. Should the same ethical standards for negotiation apply in all contexts? As a lawyer for the government, are there important differences between negotiating with a minority rights group and negotiating with terrorists? See James J. White, "Machiavelli and the Bar: Ethical Limitations on Lying in Negotiation" [1980] Am. B. Found. Res. J. 926 at 927. Does the Alberta rule address this issue?

5. Is it unethical for a lawyer in negotiations to represent the client's legal position as being stronger than the lawyer knows it to be? Could a lawyer

claim the client's position "has recently been confirmed by the Court of Appeal" without mentioning that the case was then reversed on appeal to the Supreme Court of Canada?

6. How context-sensitive should any obligations to be truthful be? Should they depend on the client? The client on the other side of the negotiations? The community of lawyers both negotiators are from? Whether the negotiations are proceeding on an "integrative" (cooperative) or a "distributive" (win-lose/competitive) basis? For an interesting discussion of the circumstantial reasons that might be offered for lying in negotiation, see Gerald B. Wetlaufer, "The Ethics of Lying in Negotiations" (1990) 75 Iowa L. Rev. 1219.

AMERICAN BAR ASSOCIATION

Model Rules of Professional Conduct, Rule 4.1,
"Transactions with Persons Other Than Clients"

Rule 4.1 Truthfulness In Statements To Others

In the course of representing a client a lawyer shall not knowingly:

(a)   make a false statement of material fact or law to a third person; . . .

[2] This Rule refers to statements of fact. Whether a particular statement should be regarded as one of fact can depend on the circumstances. Under generally accepted conventions in negotiation, certain types of statements ordinarily are not taken as statements of material fact. Estimates of price or value placed on the subject of a transaction and a party's intentions as to an acceptable settlement of a claim are ordinarily in this category, and so is the existence of an undisclosed principal except where nondisclosure of the principal would constitute fraud. Lawyers should be mindful of their obligations under applicable law to avoid criminal and tortious misrepresentation.

NOTES AND QUESTIONS

1. How high is the threshold under this rule? See American Bar Association Formal Opinion 06-439. It provides, in part, "Under Model Rule 4.1, in the context of a negotiation, including a caucused mediation, a lawyer representing a client may not make a false statement of material fact to a third person. However, statements regarding a party's negotiating goals or its willingness to compromise, as well as statements that can fairly be characterized as negotiation 'puffing', ordinarily are not considered 'false statements of material fact' within the meaning of the Model Rules." To similar effect is The State Bar of California Standing Committee on Professional Responsibility and Conduct Formal Opinion No. 2015-194.

2. What is the difference between a false statement of a material fact and the torts of deceit and fraudulent misrepresentation? Is this rule imposing a higher standard on lawyers than on other people? See E. Cliff Martin & T. Karena Dees, "The Truth about Truthfulness: The Proposed Commentary to Rule 4.1 of the Model Rules of Professional Conduct" (2002) 15 Geo. J. Leg. Ethics 777.

3. To what extent does the commentary to this rule sanction misrepresentation in negotiations?

4. Model Rule 8.4(c) provides that it is professional misconduct for a lawyer to "engage in conduct involving dishonesty, fraud, deceit or misrepresentation". How does this interact with the provisions extracted above?

5. In *Virzi v. Grand Trunk Warehouse and Cold Storage Co.*,[22] the court stated, somewhat generally, that "The handling of a lawsuit and its progress is not a game. There is an absolute duty of candour and fairness on the part of counsel to both the Court and opposing counsel." Is this duty reflected in the *Model Rules*? Is it reflected in the rules in your province? Should it be? See John A. Humbach, "Shifting Paradigms of Lawyer Honesty" (2009) 76 Tenn. L. Rev. 993.

6. Is it immoral for a lawyer to make false statements during negotiations? Does it indicate a lack of respect for the person to whom the statements are made? What impact could this have on the lawyer's reputation?

7. It has been argued that requiring lawyers to be truthful in negotiations reduces the transaction costs of the negotiation process. Do you agree with this argument? See Geoffrey C. Hazard, Jr., "The Lawyer's Obligation to be Trustworthy when Dealing with Opposing Parties" (1981) 33 S.C.L. Rev. 181 at 183.

8. In *Fire Insurance Exchange v. Bell*[23] the lawyers for the defendant insurer offered to pay the plaintiff the full amount available under the policy, which they said was $100,000. This was incorrect: the policy covered losses up to $300,000. The plaintiff accepted the offer, even though he had suffered losses of more than $100,000. It was open to the plaintiff to obtain a copy of the policy and determine its limits for himself. Did the defendant's lawyers violate the ethical rules of: (a) Alberta; (b) the American Bar Association; or (c) your province? See also *In re McGrath*.[24]

9. Is it ethically acceptable for a lawyer to raise a series of demands about issues which the client does not really care about, so that concessions can be made later which make the client look reasonable?

10. There are different styles of being a negotiator. To what extent do the rules of professional conduct bear on negotiation style? Can a lawyer, as a tactical decision, choose to be brusque and aggressive? See, for example, the *Model Code*'s Rule 5.1-5, which provides that "[a] lawyer must be courteous and civil and act in good faith to the tribunal and all persons with whom the lawyer has dealings".

11. There is empirical evidence indicating that unethical negotiating is considered ineffective. Andrea Kupfer Schneider, "Shattering Negotiation

---

[22] 571 F. Supp. 507 at 512 (E.D. Mich. 1983). See also the concurring opinion of Kite J. in *Lavatai v. Wyoming (State)*, 121 P. 3d 121 (Wyo. S.C., 2005).

[23] 643 N.E.2d 310 (Sup. Ct. Ind. 1994).

[24] 96 A.D.2d 267 (N.Y. App. Div. 1983).

Myths: Empirical Evidence on the Effectiveness of Negotiation Style" (2007) 7 Harv. Negot. L. Rev. 143 at 196 concludes that the "myth of the effective hard bargainer should be destroyed" and that "75% of the unethical adversarial bargainers . . . were considered ineffective".

12.   Lawyers need to appreciate that they need to be concerned with more than just how the ethical rules impact their own conduct in negotiations. They also need to be concerned with the conduct of the lawyer with whom they are negotiating. A lawyer who chooses to always tell the truth may be less likely to violate the ethical rules. However, depending on what the rules allow, such a lawyer is vulnerable to being deceived by a less truthful lawyer, and so must be on guard to protect the client. One way to do this is by insisting that the other party confirm, in writing, the material facts underlying the settlement and by making the settlement conditional on the truth of those facts.

[c]   Other Issues in Negotiations

Most of a lawyer's general professional obligations apply equally in a negotiation context, such as the duties to avoid conflict of interest and to preserve confidentiality. But there are some such obligations that specifically refer to or concern negotiation. For example, most provincial rules of professional conduct expressly require lawyers to work towards achieving a settlement of a dispute. Since this will most likely be attempted through negotiation, these rules are in a sense compelling lawyers to engage in negotiation in certain circumstances. See, for example, the *Model Code*'s Rule 3.2-4, which states that "a lawyer must advise and encourage a client to compromise or settle a dispute whenever it is possible to do so on a reasonable basis". The rules may also require that lawyers must have their client's instructions before proposing any settlement. In their provisions on tasks which may not be delegated by lawyers to non-lawyers, or which can only be so delegated with the client's consent, some provinces include negotiations: see, for example, the *Model Code*'s Rule 6.1-3(i). See also the Law Society of Upper Canada's By-Law 7.1, *Operational Obligations and Responsibilities*, sections 5(2) and 6(1)(c). Finally, lawyers are typically restricted in the use they can make, in negotiations, of threats of starting or stopping criminal or quasi-criminal proceedings: see, for example, the *Model Code*'s Rule 3.2-5.

Negotiations often lead to settlements, and the terms of such settlements are often confidential. This lack of public disclosure raises ethical considerations for the negotiating lawyers. Is confidentiality appropriate, for example, in a case of an alleged sexual battery or manufacture of a defective product?

Scenario Five

Jennifer acts for the defendant in litigation. The defendant tells her that it wants to settle and will pay up to $300,000 to do so. The plaintiff's lawyer tells Jennifer that he thinks his client would settle for $250,000 and asks Jennifer whether the defendant is willing to pay that amount. This is the first time the plaintiff's lawyer has mentioned a specific settlement amount. Could Jennifer ethically reply that: (a) her client would not pay that amount; (b) her client would not pay more than $200,000; or (c) she has no instructions on this issue from her client?

Scenario Six

You are defending Shinji, a client charged with impaired driving. There is no evidence of Shinji's blood alcohol level. Since being arrested, he has insisted, to the police and others, that he had had nothing to drink but he tells you that he had two large drinks immediately before driving. In attempting to negotiate the withdrawal of the charges, can your position with the Crown be that: (a) Shinji had nothing to drink; (b) he was not impaired; or (c) there is no evidence that he was impaired?

Scenario Seven

You act for the plaintiff in personal injury litigation. The plaintiff's injuries are very severe. You are quite close to negotiating a substantial settlement with the defendant's lawyers when the plaintiff dies. The plaintiff had provided you with instructions to accept any offer of $6 million or more. Three days later, the defendant's lawyer offers $6 million. Can you accept? Do you have any obligation to tell the defendant's lawyer that your client has died? Would it change your answer if instead of dying, the plaintiff made a sudden and dramatic recovery?

Scenario Eight

You act for the defendant in corporate finance litigation. In settlement negotiations, you tell the plaintiff's lawyer that if your client loses it intends to declare bankruptcy, so that the plaintiff will be unable to recover on the judgment. In fact you do not know whether or not that is something the defendant intends to do, and do not know whether a bankruptcy declaration would prevent the plaintiff from recovering. Have you acted ethically?

[4] FURTHER READING

Counselling

American Law Institute, *Restatement of the Law Third: The Law Governing Lawyers* (St. Paul, MN: American Law Institute, 2000), para. 94.

Binder, David A., *et al.*, *Lawyers as Counselors: A Client-Centered Approach*, 4th ed. (St. Paul, MN: West Academic Publishing, 2019).

Bubany, Charles P., "Counseling Clients to Do the Right Thing in Child Custody Cases" (1996) 16 Child. Legal Rts. J. 22.

Dare, Tim, *The Counsel of Rogues? A Defence of the Standard Conception of the Lawyer's Role* (Farnham, UK: Ashgate Publishing Limited, 2009).

Hazard, Geoffrey C., Jr., "Lawyers and Client Fraud: They Still Don't Get It" (1993) 6 Geo. J. Leg. Ethics 701.

Lallouz, Sasha, "A Call for Ethical Accountability: The Necessity for Lawyer-Client Ethical Dialogue in a One-Sided Adversarial System" (2016) 37 Windsor Rev. Legal & Soc. Issues 45.

Langevoort, Donald C. & Robert Rasmussen, "Skewing the Results: The Role of Lawyers in Transmitting Legal Rules" (1997) 5 S. Cal. Interdisciplinary L.J. 375.

Lerman, Lisa G., "Lying to Clients" (1990) 138 U. Pa. L. Rev. 659.

Luban, David, "Paternalism and the Legal Profession" (1981) Wis. L. Rev. 454.

MacKenzie, Gavin, *Lawyers and Ethics: Professional Responsibility and Discipline*, 6th ed. (Toronto: Thomson Reuters, 2018), ch. 14.

Newman, Joel S., "Legal Advice Towards Illegal Ends" (1994) 28 U. Rich. L. Rev. 287.

Pepper, Stephen L., "Counseling at the Limits of the Law: An Exercise in the Jurisprudence and Ethics of Lawyering" (1995) 104 Yale L.J. 1545.

Roiphe, Rebecca, "The Ethics of Willful Ignorance" (2011) 24 Geo. J. Leg. Ethics 187.

Tremblay, Paul R., "At Your Service: Lawyer Discretion to Assist Clients in Unlawful Conduct" (2018) 70:2 Fla. L. Rev. 251.

Uviller, Richard, "The Lawyer as Liar" (1994) 13(2) Crim. Justice Ethics 2.

Wendel, Bradley W., *Lawyers and Fidelity to Law* (Princeton: Princeton University Press, 2010).

Woolley, Alice, "The Lawyer as Advisor and the Practice of the Rule of Law" (2014) 47 U.B.C.L. Rev. 743.

Woolley, Alice, *Understanding Lawyers' Ethics in Canada*, 2d ed. (Toronto: LexisNexis Canada, 2016), 93-105.

Negotiation

Benson, Marjorie L., *The Skills and Ethics of Negotiation: Wisdom and Reflections of Western Canadian Civil Practitioners* (Saskatoon: College of Law, University of Saskatchewan, 2007).

Boon, Andrew, *The Ethics and Conduct of Lawyers in England and Wales*, 3d ed. (Oxford: Hart Publishing, 2014), 653-656 and 671-680.

Cohen, Jonathan R., "When People are the Means: Negotiating with Respect" (2001) 14 Geo. J. Leg. Ethics 739.

Craver, Charles B., "Negotiation Ethics: How to be Deceptive Without Being Dishonest/How to be Assertive Without Being Offensive" (1997) 38 S. Texas L. Rev. 713.

Craver, Charles B., "Negotiation Ethics for Real World Interactions" (2010) 25 Ohio St. J. on Disp. Resol. 299.

Folberg, Jay & Dwight Golann, *Lawyer Negotiation: Theory, Practice, and Law*, 3d ed. (New York: Aspen Publishers, 2016), ch. 10.

Friedman, Raymond A. & Debra Shapiro, "Deception and Mutual Gains Bargaining: Are They Mutually Exclusive?" (1995) 11 Neg. J. 243.

Hanycz, Colleen M., Trevor C.W. Farrow & Frederick H. Zemans, *The Theory and Practice of Representative Negotiation* (Toronto: Emond Montgomery, 2008), ch. 5.

Hazard, Geoffrey C., Jr., "The Lawyer's Obligation to be Trustworthy when Dealing with Opposing Parties" (1981) 33 S.C.L.R. 181.

Holmes, Eleanor Norton, "Bargaining and the Ethic of Process" (1989) 64 N.Y.U.L. Rev. 493.

Humbach, John A., "Shifting Paradigms of Lawyer Honesty" (2009) 76 Tenn. L. Rev. 993.

Jarvis, Peter R. & Bradley F. Tellam, "A Negotiation Ethics Primer for Lawyers" (1996) 31 Gonz. L. Rev. 549.

Kleefeld, John, *et al.*, *Dispute Resolution: Readings and Case Studies*, 4th ed. (Toronto: Emond Montgomery, 2016), 266-285.

Lewicki, Roy, Bruce Barry & David Saunders, *Negotiation*, 8th ed. (New York: McGraw-Hill Education, 2020), 1.12-1.13.

Longan, Patrick Emery, "Ethics in Settlement Negotiations: Foreword" (2001) 52 Mercer L. Rev. 807.

Lowenthal, Gary Tobias, "The Bar's Failure to Require Truthful Bargaining by Lawyers" (1988) 2 Geo. J. Leg. Ethics 411.

MacKenzie, Gavin, *Lawyers and Ethics: Professional Responsibility and Discipline*, 6th ed. (Toronto: Thomson Reuters, 2018), ch. 15.

Martin, E. Cliff & T. Karena Dees, "The Truth about Truthfulness: The Proposed Commentary to Rule 4.1 of the Model Rules of Professional Conduct" (2002) 15 Geo. J. Leg. Ethics 777.

McGinniss, Michael S., "Breaking Faith: Machiavelli and Moral Risks in Lawyer Negotiation" (2015) 91 N.D. L. Rev. 247.

Menkel-Meadow, Carrie, "The Evolving Complexity of Dispute Resolution Ethics" (2017) 30:3 Geo. J. Leg. Ethics 389.

Rubin, Alvin B., "A Causerie on Lawyers' Ethics in Negotiation" (1975) 35 La. L. Rev. 577.

Schneider, Andrea Kupfer, "Shattering Negotiation Myths: Empirical Evidence on the Effectiveness of Negotiation Style" (2007) 7 Harv. Negot. L. Rev. 143.

Wetlaufer, Gerald B., "The Ethics of Lying in Negotiations" (1990) 75 Iowa L. Rev. 1219.

White, James J., "Machiavelli and the Bar: Ethical Limitations on Lying in Negotiation" [1980] Am. B. Found. Res. J. 926.

Zahnd, Mel David, "Who's Afraid of the Light? Product Liability Cases, Confidential Settlements, and Defense Attorneys' Ethical Obligations" (2015) 28 Geo. J. Leg. Ethics 1005.

CHAPTER 7

ETHICS IN CRIMINAL LAW PRACTICE

[1] INTRODUCTION

In earlier chapters, you have been exposed to core ethical principles such as cultural competence, confidentiality and privilege, conflicts of interest, production of physical evidence of a crime, and withdrawal. Many of the leading cases arose in the criminal law context,[1] and are not to be discussed in detail here, although you should bear in mind the duties and principles they set out when considering the issues discussed here. In this chapter, we explore the more general, and arguably distinct, ethical obligations of those who practice criminal law either as defence lawyers or prosecutors. As you read this chapter, you should ask yourself whether you are satisfied with the justifications offered for the ethical rules that we have carved out for defence lawyers and prosecutors in this context, and whether you think we have achieved the right balance.

To assist you in thinking about the modern-day ethical roles of criminal lawyers, we begin with two historic cases, one from England and the other from Quebec, which frame the obligations in arguably extreme terms – defence lawyers justified in unbridled zealousness within the bounds of the law on the one hand, and the prosecutor as a "minister of justice" on the other. In reading the descriptions of the cases, consider whether you think the duties of defence lawyers and prosecutors should be so different. What would justify that sort of difference? What common framing for the duties of defence lawyers and prosecutors might be available?

Queen Caroline's Case

In 1820, George IV brought proceedings against his estranged wife Queen Caroline that led to a trial before the House of Lords. As described by Professor Deborah Rhode:

> The bill before the House alleged her involvement in an 'unbecoming and degrading' adulterous liaison with one of her couriers while she was Princess of

---

[1] See for example, *R. v. Murray*, [2000] O.J. No. 2182, 48 O.R. (3d) 544 (Ont. S.C.J.) (Chapters 1 and 3) (production of physical evidence of a crime); *R. v. Neil*, [2002] S.C.J. No. 72, [2002] 3 S.C.R. 631 (S.C.C.) (Chapters 1 and 4) (resolute advocacy & conflicts); *R. v. Fraser*, [2011] N.S.J. No. 400, 2011 NSCA 70 (N.S.C.A.) (cultural competence) (Chapter 2); *R. v. Cunningham*, [2010] S.C.J. No. 10, 2010 SCC 10 (S.C.C.) (Chapter 2) (withdrawal for non-payment of fees); *Smith v. Jones*, [1999] S.C.J. No. 15, [1999] 1 S.C.R. 455 (Chapter 3) (privilege and public safety); and, *R. v. McClure*, [2001] S.C.J. No. 13, 2001 SCC 14 (S.C.C.) (Chapter 3) (privilege and "innocence at stake").

Wales. The proposed legislation sought a divorce on behalf of George IV, who was known for a few scandals of his own, including the abusive treatment of his wife. Shortly after Caroline became pregnant with an heir, he insisted on a separation. He subsequently banished her from the royal court and denied her access to their daughter.[2]

Queen Caroline's lawyer before the House of Lords was Henry Brougham, who would later become Lord Chancellor. He had evidence of George IV's affairs and earlier marriage to a Catholic woman. However, if he introduced this evidence in defence of his client, it would have potentially thrown the monarchy into chaos.[3] As a result, it was suggested to Brougham "that his duty to be a good citizen and promote the welfare of his country required him to 'pull his punches', and not assert the right of recrimination against the king".[4] Brougham responded with the now infamous speech:

> An advocate, in the discharge of his duty, knows but one person in all the world, and that person is his client. To save that client by all means and expedients, and at all hazards and costs to other persons, and, amongst them, to himself, is his first and only duty; and in performing this duty he must not regard the alarm, the torments, the destruction which he may bring upon others. Separating the duty of a patriot from that of an advocate, he must go on reckless of consequences, though it should be his unhappy fate to involve his country in confusion.[5]

The bill was withdrawn by the government. Queen Caroline died a year later.

NOTES AND QUESTIONS

1.   In his speech, Brougham suggested that an advocate's only duty is that to their client. Do you agree with him? In contemporary times, the strongest proponents of this approach include Monroe Freedman[6] and Abbe Smith. As Smith strongly puts it:

> My own view of criminal defense lawyering owes much to Monroe Freedman. I agree with his "traditionalist view" of criminal defense

---

[2]   Deborah L. Rhode, "An Adversarial Exchange on Adversarial Ethics: Text, Subtext, and Context" (1991) J. Leg. Educ. 29 at 30-31.

[3]   Gerald F. Uelman, "Lord Brougham's Bromide: Good Lawyers as Bad Citizens" (1996) 30 Loy. L.A.L. Rev. 119 at 119-120. Professor Uelman was one of O.J. Simpson's lawyers.

[4]   Gerald F. Uelman, "Lord Brougham's Bromide: Good Lawyers as Bad Citizens" (1996) 30 Loy. L.A.L. Rev. 119 at 120.

[5]   As quoted by Justice Binnie in *R. v. Neil*, [2002] S.C.J. No. 72, 2002 SCC 70 at para. 12 (S.C.C.). See also *Groia v. Law Society of Upper Canada*, [2018] S.C.J. No. 27, 2018 SCC 27 at paras. 74-76 (S.C.C.); *Canadian National Railway Co. v. McKercher LLP*, [2013] S.C.J. No. 39, 2013 SCC 39 at para. 25 (S.C.C.).

[6]   See Monroe H. Freedman, "Henry Lord Brougham and Resolute Lawyering" (2011) 37 Advoc. Q. 403 and Monroe H. Freedman, "How Lawyers Act in the Interests of Justice" (2002) 70 Fordham L. Rev. 1717. According to Freedman, Lord Brougham brought this same zeal to his human rights advocacy: see "Henry Lord Brougham – Advocating at the Edge for Human Rights" (2007) 36 Hofstra L. Rev. 311. Freedman also has challenged assertions that Brougham later came to regret his famous speech. See Monroe H. Freedman, "Henry Lord Brougham, Written by Himself" (2006) 19 Geo. J. Leg. Ethics 1213.

ethics as a lawyering paradigm in which zealous advocacy and the maintenance of client confidence and trust are paramount. Simply put, zeal and confidentiality trump most other rules, principles, or values. When there is tension between these "fundamental principles" and other ethical rules, criminal defense lawyers must uphold the principles, even in the face of public or professional outcry. Although a defender must act within the bounds of the law, he or she should engage in advocacy that is as close to the line as possible, and, indeed, should test the line, if it is in the client's interest in doing so.[7]

2. In Chapter 1, you were exposed to a number of different theoretical approaches to what it means to be an ethical lawyer. How does Brougham's view fit in with those approaches? How would Tim Dare, David Luban or Tom Shaffer respond to Brougham's view of the role of the advocate in the context of criminal law?

3. Based on what you have read so far, can you identify what other duties defence lawyers owe?

R. v. Boucher, [1955] S.C.R. 16 (S.C.C.)

Ovila Boucher was charged with murder. In his closing address, Crown counsel said this:

> The doctor spoke to us about blood, – we were taken to task gentlemen because we had an analysis of the blood made. But the Crown is not here for the pleasure of having innocent people convicted. It is the duty of the Crown, when an affair like that happens, no matter what affair, and still more in a serious affair, to make every possible investigation, and if in the course of these investigations with our experts, the conclusion is come to that the accused is not guilty or that there is a reasonable doubt, it is the duty of the Crown, gentlemen, to say so or if the conclusion is come to that he is not guilty, not to make an arrest. That is what was done here.

> When the Crown put in that evidence, it is not with the intention of bearing down on the accused, it was with the intention of rendering justice to him. [. . .]

> Every day we see more and more crimes than ever, thefts and many other things, at least one who commits armed robbery does not make his victim suffer as Boucher made Jabour suffer. It is a revolting crime for a man with all the strength of his age, of an athlete against an old man of 77, who is not capable of defending himself. I have a little respect for those who steal when they at least have given their victim a chance to defend himself, but I have no sympathy, none, and I tell you not to have any sympathy for these dastards who strike men, friends. Jabour was perhaps not a friend, but he was a neighbour, at least they knew each other. In a cowardly manner, with blows of an ax. – And, if you bring in verdict of guilty, for once it will almost be a pleasure to me to ask for the death penalty for him.[8]

In the Supreme Court of Canada, Boucher argued that the closing was inflammatory

---

[7] Abbe Smith, "The Difference in Criminal Defense and the Difference It Makes" (2003) 11 Wash Univ. J.L. & Pol'y 83 at 89-91. See also Abbe Smith, "Defending Defending: The Case for Unmitigated Zeal On Behalf of People Who Do Terrible Things" (2010) 28 Hofstra L. Rev. 925.

[8] *R. v. Boucher*, [1954] S.C.J. No. 54, [1955] S.C.R. 16 at 23, 26-27; 30-31 (S.C.C.) (translation).

and inconsistent with the professional responsibilities of a prosecutor. The Supreme Court agreed and ordered a new trial. In his opinion, Justice Rand delivered one of the most oft-quoted statements describing the role of the Crown:

> It cannot be over-emphasized that the purpose of a criminal prosecution is not to obtain a conviction, it is to lay before a jury what the Crown considers to be credible evidence relevant to what is alleged to be a crime. Counsel have a duty to see that all available legal proof of the facts is presented: it should be done firmly and pressed to its legitimate strength but it must also be done fairly. The role of prosecutor excludes any notion of winning or losing; his function is a matter of public duty than which in civil life there can be none charged with greater personal responsibility. It is to be efficiently performed with an ingrained sense of the dignity, the seriousness and the justness of judicial proceedings.[9]

NOTES AND QUESTIONS

1. What was wrong with the Crown's closing address?

[2] CRIMINAL DEFENCE COUNSEL

Criminal defence lawyers play a fundamental role in our constitutionalized system of adversarial justice. However, the work of defence lawyers is often misunderstood, with many assuming the lawyer is the alter-ego of the client who either shares their client's morals, or who is prepared to do their bidding regardless of the harm caused. We see this in popular culture with movies like "The Devil's Advocate". We also saw this vividly, a few years ago, when Stockwell Day wrote a letter to a Red Deer newspaper suggesting that a defence lawyer who brought a constitutional argument in relation to our child pornography law was validating child pornography.[10] And so, any discussion of the ethics of criminal defence work must begin with an identification of the various justifications for the work of criminal defence lawyers, including for the defence of the guilty.

[a] Justification

All law students who have expressed an interest in criminal law have likely faced THE questions at some point: Why do you want to be a criminal lawyer? How can you defend a person you know is guilty? David Layton provides the following response:

> How I live with myself starts with the standard justification that as a lawyer I take on particular ethical responsibilities by virtue of my special role in the justice system. We have an adversarial system in which litigants are responsible for presenting their own case in court. Yet this system is highly complex, replete with complicated rules of procedure and substance, thereby necessitating that an accused person must have the help of a lawyer to present the case effectively. It follows, I think, that the lawyer must loyally advance the client's position in the litigation. By playing this partisan role the lawyer respects the client's autonomy while furthering his or her legal rights, and ensures that the adversarial system functions properly. Consequently, the lawyer does good simply by fighting for his or her clients. The

---

[9] *R. v. Boucher*, [1954] S.C.J. No. 54, [1955] S.C.R. 16 at 23-24 (S.C.C.).

[10] See Scott Anderson, "Stockwell Day Ruined My Life" *Now Magazine* (November 16, 2000). Day eventually settled a defamation suit brought by the lawyer.

virtues of their causes are usually of little significance because it is the responsibility of others in the system to present opposing views and to decide each case on the merits. [. . .]

The idea that a lawyer must resolutely advance the client's position is particularly potent in the criminal context. To begin with, the adversarial system, including the right of an accused to control his or her own defence, is a fundamental principle of justice protected by the *Charter*, with a rationale closely related to the dominant view of lawyering. Solicitor-client privilege also has constitutional protection which, as we have seen, is based on the rationale underlying the dominant view. An accused's rights to state-funded counsel, counsel of choice and the effective assistance of counsel are likewise guaranteed by s. 7 of the *Charter* based on similar reasoning. Defence counsel's ethical duty to act resolutely is thus inextricably linked with constitutional rights related to the client's representation at trial.

Just as important in defining defence counsel's role are due process rights that shape the very meaning of justice in the criminal law setting. Every accused person is presumed innocent, which means that the Crown has the onus of proving guilt beyond a reasonable doubt. This constitutional guarantee goes hand-in-hand with the right to make full answer and defence, which includes the right to test the reliability of the Crown case by cross-examining Crown witnesses. There is also the principle against self-incrimination, which precludes the state from coercing an accused person to aid in building the prosecution case and operates so that the accused generally need not disclose any information to the prosecution. Conversely, the accused has the right to obtain full disclosure from the Crown of all information relevant to the matter. Finally, individuals charged with crimes sometimes have the right to exclude evidence, even reliable evidence pointing to guilt, as a remedy for a violation of *Charter* rights.

The central concern underlying these and other constitutional rights is that people must be protected from a powerful and sometimes overweening state. We want to limit the ability of the state to exercise power over us. We fear that absent these rights, including the assistance of loyal counsel, the state's representatives (in particular the police) will abuse their power. So we "over-protect" accused persons in order to keep the state in check. This means that truth-finding is not the only goal of the criminal justice system. It means that a pivotal aspect of defence counsel's job, as all ethical codes expressly recognize, is to ensure that the state does not obtain a conviction in the absence of proof beyond a reasonable doubt based on admissible and reliable evidence. Ethical advocacy in the criminal context is thus heavily influenced by a conception of justice that includes due process rights and their underlying values.[11]

In her classic article "Defending the Guilty", Professor Barbara Babcock offers a number of additional justifications for criminal defence work:

- *"The Garbage Collector's Reason.* Yes it is dirty work, but someone must do it. We cannot have a functioning adversary system without a partisan for both sides.". . .

- *"The Legalistic or Positivist's Reason.* Truth cannot be known. Facts are indeterminate, contingent, and, in criminal cases, often evanescent. A

---

[11] David Layton, "The Criminal Lawyer's Role" (2004) 27 Dal L.J. 379 at 380-383 [footnotes omitted]. Reproduced with permission.

finding of guilt is not necessarily the truth, but a legal conclusion arrived at after the role of the defense lawyer has been fully played.". . .

- *"The Political Activist's Reason.* Most people who commit crimes are themselves the victims of horrible injustice. [. . .] Moreover, the conditions of imprisonment may impose violence far worse than that inflicted on the victim. A lawyer performs good work when he helps to prevent the imprisonment of the poor, the outcast, and minorities in shameful conditions."

- *"The Social Worker's Reason.* [. . .] Those accused of crime, as the most visible representatives of the disadvantaged underclass in America, will actually be helped by having a defender, notwithstanding the outcome of their cases. Being treated as a real person in our society [. . .] and accorded the full panoply of rights and the measure of concern afforded by a lawyer can promote rehabilitation.". . ..

- *"The Egotist's Reason.* Defending criminal cases is more interesting than the routine and repetitive work done by most lawyers [.]"[12]

NOTES AND QUESTIONS

1. Which, if any, of these reasons do you find persuasive? Are there other justifications that can be advanced for defending the guilty?[13] Is this, as Professor Babcock asks later in her article, even the right question to be asking? What might she mean by that?

2. How does the defence of the guilty advance Charter rights for all of us?

3. Former prosecutor Paul Butler has argued that the classic question – "How Can You Represent Those People?" – should be asked of prosecutors, and that systemic injustices in the United States mean that American prosecutors cannot provide a satisfactory answer, that prosecutors necessarily perpetuate those injustices.[14] Do you think that prosecutors should be asked the question? What answer could Canadian prosecutors give? In answering that question, consider incarceration rates for Black[15] and Indigenous peoples in Canada. As of January 2020, 30% of the federal inmate population in Canada was Indigenous (and 43% of the female federal inmate population was Indigenous).[16] Consider in particular these

---

[12] Barbara Allen Babcock, "Defending the Guilty" (1983-84) 32 Clev. St. L. Rev. 175 at 177-178.

[13] See, for example, the discussion in Abbe Smith, "The Difference in Criminal Defense and the Difference It Makes" (2003) 11 Wash. U. J.L. & Pol'y 83.

[14] Paul Butler, *How Can You Prosecute Those People?, in* HOW CAN YOU REPRESENT THOSE PEOPLE? 15-27 (Abbe Smith & Monroe H. Freedman eds., New York: Palgrave Macmillan, 2013).

[15] Catherine McIntyre, "Canada Has a Black Incarceration Problem" *Torontoist* (April 21, 2016), online: http://torontoist.com/2016/04/african-canadian-prison-population/.

[16] Office of the Correctional Investigator, Online: https://www.oci-bec.gc.ca/cnt/comm/press/press20200121-eng.aspx.

comments from a Press Release of the Office of the Correctional Investigator:

> While accounting for 5% of the general Canadian population, the number of federally sentenced Indigenous people has been steadily increasing for decades. More recently, custody rates for Indigenous people have accelerated, despite an overall decline in the inmate population. In fact, since April 2010 the Indigenous inmate population has increased by 43.4% (or 1,265), whereas the non-Indigenous incarcerated population has declined over the same period by 13.7% (or 1,549). The rising numbers of Indigenous people behind bars offsets declines in other groups, giving the impression that the system is operating at a normal or steady state. As Dr. Zinger noted, nothing could be farther from the truth.

> The Correctional Investigator suggests that surpassing the 30% mark indicates a deepening "Indigenization" of Canada's correctional system. Dr. Zinger referred to these trends as "disturbing and entrenched imbalances," noting that the numbers are even more troubling for Indigenous women, who now account for 42% of the women inmate population in Canada. The Correctional Investigator drew attention to the fact that federal corrections seems impervious to change and unresponsive to the needs, histories and social realities behind high rates of Indigenous offending.

> Dr. Zinger stated, "On this trajectory, the pace is now set for Indigenous people to comprise 33% of the total federal inmate population in the next three years. Over the longer term, and for the better part of three decades now, despite findings of Royal Commissions and National Inquiries, intervention of the courts, promises and commitments of previous and current political leaders, no government of any stripe has managed to reverse the trend of Indigenous over-representation in Canadian jails and prisons. The Indigenization of Canada's prison population is nothing short of a national travesty."[17]

[b] General Ethical Limits on Criminal Defence

In his defence of Queen Caroline, Henry Brougham argued that advocates owe only one duty, and that is to the client. There is no question that criminal lawyers' primary duty is to their client, and they owe an ethical duty to resolutely advance their client's case. As the Ontario Court of Appeal recognized in *R. v. Delchev*:[18]

> The relationship between accused persons and their counsel is essential to the proper and fair administration of criminal justice. [. . .]

> It is essential that an accused person have confidence in his or her representation, and that defence counsel be free to further the accused's interests as much as possible. [. . .]

> . . . . .

> Defence counsel is therefore permitted to argue a weak defence and call the accused

---

[17] Office of the Correctional Investigator, Online: https://www.oci-bec.gc.ca/cnt/comm/press/press20200121-eng.aspx.

[18] [2015] O.J. No. 2710, 2015 ONCA 381 at paras. 58-59, 61-62 (Ont. C.A.).

to testify even if the lawyer's private opinion is that the client will be disbelieved. [. . .]

> If accused persons have reason to doubt the ability and faithfulness of their counsel, their defence is likely to suffer. If counsel has reason to hold back in the defence to protect their own interests, or even allows personal doubt about the merits to cloud their pursuit of the defence, the defence is also likely to suffer. Without a relationship of faith and confidence between an accused and his or her counsel, the obligations placed on defence counsel [. . .] to defend the guarantees of the presumption of innocence and the burden of proof beyond a reasonable doubt — are put at risk.[19]

However, the duty to the client is not absolute. Criminal lawyers, like all lawyers, owe other, sometimes competing, duties. The Supreme Court in *R. v. Lyttle*, excerpted in Chapter 5 with respect to ethics and cross-examination, described the criminal lawyer's responsibilities in this way:

> The cross-examiner may pursue any hypothesis that is honestly advanced on the strength of reasonable inference, experience or intuition. The purpose of the question must be consistent with the lawyer's role as an officer of the court: to suggest what counsel genuinely thinks possible on known facts or reasonable assumptions is in our view permissible; to assert or to imply in a manner that is calculated to mislead is in our view improper and prohibited.
>
> [. . . . .]
>
> As long as counsel has a good faith basis for asking an otherwise permissible question in cross-examination, the question should be allowed. [. . .] Counsel, however, bear important professional duties and ethical responsibilities, not just at trial, but on appeal as well. This point was emphasized by Lord Reid in *Rondel v. Worsley*, [1969] 1 A.C. 191 (H.L.), at pp. 227-28, when he said:
>
> Every counsel has a duty to his client fearlessly to raise every issue, advance every argument, and ask every question, however distasteful, which he thinks will help his client's case. But, as an officer of the court concerned in the administration of justice, he has an overriding duty to the court, to the standards of his profession, and to the public, which may and often does lead to a conflict with his client's wishes or with what the client thinks are his personal interests. Counsel must not mislead the court, he must not lend himself to casting aspersions on the other party or witnesses for which there is no sufficient basis in the information in his possession, he must not withhold authorities or documents which may tell against his clients but which the law or the standards of his profession require him to produce... .[20]

NOTES AND QUESTIONS

1. Does *Lyttle* create a "good faith" minimum ethical standard against which to measure the conduct of all lawyers? If not, should the courts create such a standard?

2. Is "good faith" different from the classic "officer of the court" standard set out in the first paragraph of the excerpt, and in *Rondel v Worsley*? If so, how?

---

[19] [2015] O.J. No. 2710, 2015 ONCA 381 at paras. 58-59, 61-62 (Ont. C.A.).

[20] [2004] S.C.J. No. 8, 2004 SCC 5 at paras. 48, 66 (S.C.C.) [Emphasis added].

3. How could a court assess a lawyer's good faith? How should it?

We will examine this "good faith" and "officer of the court" obligation in the context of guilty pleas, making submissions to the court and client perjury. There are also other limits on the conduct of defence lawyers including the duty not to discriminate (see Model Rule 6.3-5). We will examine this obligation in the context of defending sexual assault cases.

[i] Pleading Innocents Guilty

Most criminal charges are resolved by guilty pleas. And so, we start our look at the general ethical limits on criminal defence with the ethical responsibilities of a lawyer in relation to guilty pleas. As a general rule, the decision about whether to plead guilty or have a trial belongs solely to the client.[21] The other decisions regarded as those of the client include whether to have a jury or judge-alone trial;[22] to testify;[23] or, to raise a not criminally responsible defence.[24]

What ethical limits are there on the role defence counsel can play in plea bargaining and in-court guilty pleas? In a number of cases that reached the Ontario Court of Appeal, factually-innocent clients pleaded guilty because of the plea deal offered by the Crown and a belief that an acquittal was unlikely.[25] Surprisingly, in none of these cases was the Court of Appeal critical of defence counsel for their participation in the guilty pleas. Indeed, in *R. v. Hanemaayer*,[26] a case involving a guilty plea to a crime later discovered to have been committed by Paul Bernardo, Justice Rosenberg held:

> [T]o constitute a valid guilty plea, the plea must be voluntary, unequivocal and informed. There is no suggestion in this case that the appellant's plea almost twenty years ago did not meet these requirements. While the appellant speaks of advice from his lawyer to plead guilty, the fresh evidence makes clear that in the end the appellant came to his own decision. His plea was unequivocal and he understood the nature of the charges he faced as well as the consequences of his plea.

> On the other hand, the court cannot ignore the terrible dilemma facing the appellant. He had spent eight months in jail awaiting trial and was facing the prospect of a further six years in the penitentiary if he was convicted. The estimate of six years was not unrealistic given the seriousness of the offence. The justice system held out

---

[21] See generally, Arthur Martin, "The Role and Responsibility of the Defence Advocate" (1969-1970) 12 Crim L.Q. 376 at 387-388.

[22] *R. v. Stark*, [2017] O.J. No. 834, 2017 ONCA 148 at paras. 17-18 (Ont. C.A.).

[23] *R. v. Moore*, [2002] S.J. No. 124, 1 C.R. (6th) 97 (Sask. C.A.).

[24] *R. v. Swain*, [1991] S.C.J. No. 32, [1991] 1 S.C.R. 933 at paras. 35-36 (S.C.C.).

[25] See, for example, *R. v. Hanemaayer*, [2008] O.J. No. 3087, 2008 ONCA 580 (Ont. C.A.); *R. v. Brant*, [2011] O.J. No. 2062, 2011 ONCA 362 (Ont. C.A.); *R. v. Kumar*, [2011] O.J. No. 618, 2011 ONCA 120 (Ont. C.A.). For a recent and comprehensive discussion of the problem of false guilty pleas see: *R. v. McIlvride-Lister*, [2019] O.J. No. 1489, 2019 ONSC 1869 (Ont. S.C.J.). See further, Amanda Carling, "A Way to Reduce Indigenous Overrepresentation: Prevent False Guilty Plea Wrongful Convictions" (2017) 64 Crim L.Q. 415.

[26] [2008] O.J. No. 3087, 2008 ONCA 580 (Ont. C.A.).

to the appellant a powerful inducement that by pleading guilty he would not receive a penitentiary sentence.[27]

Scenario One

Imagine that you have a client who is desperate to get out of jail because of child care responsibilities. She has been denied bail. She is charged with causing a disturbance and assaulting a police officer. She vehemently maintains her innocence. You believe that she has a strong Charter racial profiling application but that with the assigned judge, it is unlikely to succeed. You are also concerned about racial bias in sentencing by this trial judge, particularly as your client is a member of Black Lives Matters. Your client wants to plead guilty and take the Crown offer of time served. Can you ethically participate in the guilty plea? What other options are available to you?

The Federation of Law Societies' *Model Code of Professional Conduct* provides guidance about the role of defence counsel in plea bargaining in Rule 5.1-7 and 5.1-8. Review those rules before considering the following Notes and Questions.

NOTES AND QUESTIONS

1. Do those rules assist you in thinking about what you would do in the Scenario? Is there anything in this Rule that explicitly prohibits you from participating in a guilty plea for the client where the client is prepared to "admit the necessary factual and mental elements"?

2. In *R. v. S.K.*,[28] the accused did not voluntarily admit the necessary factual and mental elements of the offences himself in court. Rather, his lawyer stood up and pled his client guilty. The trial judge accepted the pleas. On appeal, SK sought to strike the pleas on the grounds that he had always maintained his innocence, including in his pre-sentence report. The Ontario Court of Appeal ordered a new trial. Justice Carthy held:

    > This is not an appeal where one need be suspicious of the motives of the appellant in seeking to set aside a plea of guilty. It was not prompted by dissatisfaction with the disposition, although I have no doubt the appellant was disappointed. It was prompted rather by the fact that the continued denial of guilt made performance of a term of probation impossible. The appellant was unaware of the contradiction between a plea of guilty and denial until he received advice from his probation officer. His state of mind was induced by his trial counsel and perpetuated by the trial judge who failed to intervene and make inquiry as to the validity of the guilty pleas when he read the pre-sentence reports. The trial judge went in the opposite direction from a review of the plea and refused to accept the joint submission for a non-custodial sentence. The system was tilted askew by the simple fact that a person protesting innocence became engaged in plea bargaining. [. . .]

    > [. . . . .]

    > I have no hesitation in concluding that the guilty pleas should be set

---

[27] *Hanemaayer* [2008] O.J. No. 3087, 2008 ONCA 580 at 17-18 (Ont. C.A.).

[28] [1995] O.J. No. 1627, 99 C.C.C. (3d) 376 (Ont. C.A.).

aside. This case presents a graphic example of why it is essential to the plea bargaining process that the accused person is prepared to admit to the facts that support the conviction. The court should not be in the position of convicting and sentencing individuals, who fall short of admitting the facts to support the conviction unless that guilt is proved beyond a reasonable doubt. Nor should sentencing proceed on the false assumption of contrition. That did not happen here, but worse, the sentence became impossible to perform. Plea bargaining is an accepted and integral part of our criminal justice system but must be conducted with sensitivity to its vulnerabilities. A court that is misled, or allows itself to be misled, cannot serve the interests of justice.[29]

3. Was the problem in *S.K.* that the accused did not himself voluntarily agree to the facts in court, or that there was a guilty plea in circumstances where the accused maintained his innocence to his probation officer?

R. v. JOHNSON

[2014] O.J. No. 2290, 2014 ONSC 2093 (Ont. S.C.J.)

McMAHON J.

The applicant, Cameron Johnson, applies to strike his pleas of guilty to one count of trafficking in cocaine and the charge of common assault. . . . The pleas were entered, and the Crown Attorney read in the facts. After the facts were read in, there was the following exchange:

THE COURT:	Okay, Counsel, are those facts substantially correct?
COUNSEL:	Mr. Johnson instructs me that those facts are substantially correct, Your Honour.
THE COURT:	Okay, is that correct, sir?
[MR.] JOHNSON:	Yes. . . .

It is the position of Mr. Johnson that from the time he retained Mr. Christie as his counsel, he never told Counsel that he was guilty of the charges alleged. On the contrary, Mr. Johnson asserts that he made it clear to his lawyer that he was not guilty and wanted the matter to proceed to trial. He was told by Counsel . . . that he had little likelihood of successfully defending the charges and that counsel had worked out a very good deal for him. It is the applicant's evidence – both in his affidavit and at the hearing – that he felt pressure from his lawyer to plead guilty. His evidence is that they had a heated exchange over whether he should accept the resolution negotiated by his counsel. He lost confidence in Counsel and felt pressured into making a decision to plead guilty.

It is the applicant's evidence that Counsel specifically told him that during his guilty plea, Mr. Johnson should listen carefully to what I asked him and simply answer in the affirmative. The applicant acknowledges that he in fact lied to the court in his answers to these questions during the plea inquiry. However, he indicates that he did so because he was following the instructions of his lawyer. The applicant continues to maintain his innocence and his wish to have the matter decided through a trial.
. . .

---

[29] [1995] O.J. No. 1627, 99 C.C.C. (3d) 376 at 380-382 (Ont. C.A.).

In both his affidavit and his *viva voce* evidence, Counsel's evidence is that he never conducted a plea comprehension review with his client prior to Mr. Johnson pleading guilty. This position is completely inconsistent with my question to counsel on the day of the guilty plea:

THE COURT:	Okay, and Counsel, you've ha[d] an opportunity to conduct a plea inquiry with Mr. Johnson?
COUNSEL:	I have, Your Honour.

Further, after the facts were read in during the guilty plea proceeding, there was the following exchange:

THE COURT:	Okay, Counsel, are those facts substantially correct?
COUNSEL:	Mr. Johnson instructs me that those facts are substantially correct, Your Honour.

Based upon Counsel's affidavit and *viva voce* evidence, I find that Mr. Johnson never admitted that he committed the offences. I accept Counsel's evidence that at no time did his client ever indicate he was guilty or admit the facts to support the plea. Counsel assessed the evidence, advised his client his chances were slim, and worked out the best deal he could for the client. I accept former counsel's evidence in his affidavit that Mr. Johnson maintained he was not guilty but agreed to the resolution.

. . . . .

Based upon my findings of fact, I am satisfied on a balance of probability that the applicant did not enter his plea voluntarily. Further, I am satisfied that he neither believed at any time that he was guilty nor was he prepared to admit the facts in support.

Sadly, what transpired on November 5, 2013, was a fraud on the court. Mr. Johnson pled guilty to offences that he believes he did not commit and lied to the court during the plea inquiry.

What is most troubling is the role played by trial counsel. A defence counsel cannot represent a client entering a plea of guilty to an offence that the client does not admit he committed. To do so is to assist the client in perpetrating a fraud on the court. Such fraud leads to a miscarriage of justice and brings the administration of justice into disrepute.

In the *Defending a Criminal Case: Special Lectures of the Law Society of Upper Canada 1969* (Toronto: Richard De Boo Ltd., 1969), at p. 318, this issue was addressed in the following exchange between Chief Justice Gale and Mr. G. Arthur Martin:

> *Chief Justice Gale*: Mr. Martin I'm going to ask you to continue with it. What is the position of counsel where his client has informed him that he is not guilty but he wishes to plead guilty . . . because he thinks he will get a lighter sentence. . .?

> *Mr. Martin*: To permit a client to plead guilty who is innocent and who informs you that he is innocent is really in the nature of a fraud on the administration of justice and is improper . . . I think . . . that so long as the client persists in maintaining his innocence after you have confronted him with the evidence against him, and have explained the relevant law, that it is preferable not to represent him for the purpose of entering a plea of guilty.

The duty and expectations of defence counsel as described more than 45 years ago by Mr. G. Arthur Martin are still the same today.

The *Rules of Professional Conduct* support this proposition. . . . [They state] "a lawyer shall not . . . (b) knowingly assist or permit the client to do anything that the lawyer considers to be dishonest".

. . . . .

Defence counsel cannot assist a client in entering a plea of guilty unless the client is prepared to admit his guilt and admit the facts required on the essential elements. If the client insists on proceeding with the guilty plea without satisfying these prerequisites, counsel must seek to be removed as counsel without breaching solicitor-client privilege. Counsel cannot participate in or be a party to an accused pleading guilty to an offence for which the accused maintains his innocence.

Regrettably, I must find that trial counsel did not meet his professional or ethical obligations to the court. He breached his duty to both his client and the court in several ways. First, he knowingly participated in a guilty plea with a client who consistently maintained his innocence. Second, he advised the client how to answer the plea inquiry questions to avoid the plea being struck. Third, he advised the court he conducted a plea inquiry when he had not. Fourth, he advised the court his client had advised him the facts were substantially correct when he had received no such instruction. Fifth, he advised the Court he does not conduct plea inquires with a client in advance if he thinks the Judge will conduct a plea inquiry.

The courts of this province must be able to rely on defence counsel – who is an officer of the court – to do his or her job professionally and ethically. In this case, counsel's failure to do so has created the risk of a miscarriage of justice. To remedy the risk of a miscarriage of justice, I am ordering the pleas of guilty to be struck.

NOTES AND QUESTIONS

1. In England and the United States, lawyers can participate in pleading clients guilty who privately maintain their innocence. What are the policy reasons for the *Johnson* approach even where the client's decision is an informed one?[30]

2. What if, upon investigation, you determine that the Crown's case is overwhelming and there is no viable defence. You come to believe that the client simply cannot admit his guilt to you. How would *Johnson* apply here?[31]

Scenario Two

Your client is Indigenous. The police were patrolling an area identified as a high-crime area and were conducting street checks. They stopped your client because he looked "suspicious". After conducting a computer check, the police

---

[30] See Chris Sherrin, "Guilty Pleas from the Innocent" (2011) 30 Windsor Rev. Leg. Soc. Issues 1.

[31] See David Layton and Michel Proulx, *Ethics and Criminal Law*, 2d ed. (Toronto: Irwin Law, 2015) at 455-473.

conducted a pat-down and found a small amount of cocaine. You meet with your client on the first appearance, and he advises you that he wants to plead guilty: "I had the drugs on me, so let's get this over with." You agree and arrange for a plea for a conditional discharge. Have you acted ethically?

[ii]   Misleading the Court

Criminal lawyers, like all advocates, have a duty to not mislead the court. In this section, we will consider a number of different examples to determine the scope of this duty including allowing your client to use a false name, using glasses to alter your client's appearance, failing to correct the record, failing to disclose your client's prior criminal convictions and client perjury. In thinking about the issue of misleading the court, lawyers must always be mindful of their duty of confidentiality, particularly as it relates to possible disclosure or rectification.

The general obligations of a lawyer acting as an advocate were discussed in Chapter 6 and are, as noted there, set out in part in the rules of professional conduct. Of particular relevance here is *Model Code* Rule 5.1-2, which clearly prohibits a lawyer from misleading the Court in any respect:

5.1-2 When acting as an advocate, a lawyer must not:

(b)   knowingly assist or permit a client to do anything that the lawyer considers to be dishonest or dishonourable;

(e)   knowingly attempt to deceive a tribunal or influence the course of justice by offering false evidence, misstating facts or law, presenting or relying upon a false or deceptive affidavit, suppressing what ought to be disclosed or otherwise assisting in any fraud, crime or illegal conduct;

(f)   knowingly misstate the contents of a document, the testimony of a witness, the substance of an argument or the provisions of a statute or like authority;

(g)   knowingly assert as true a fact when its truth cannot reasonably be supported by the evidence or as a matter of which notice may be taken by the tribunal;

(h)   make suggestions to a witness recklessly or knowing them to be false;

(i)   deliberately refrain from informing a tribunal of any binding authority that the lawyer considers to be directly on point and that has not been mentioned by another party;

(k)   knowingly permit a witness or party to be presented in a false or misleading way or to impersonate another;

(l)   knowingly misrepresent the client's position in the litigation or the issues to be determined in the litigation . . .

R. v. LEGEBOKOFF

[2016] B.C.J. No. 1999, 2016 BCCA 386 (B.C.C.A.),
leave to appeal refused
[2016] S.C.C.A. No. 508 (S.C.C.)

[The accused was charged with four counts of first degree murder. Defence counsel brought a change of venue application. In support of the motion, he hired a market researcher. The motion was dismissed. In his reasons, the trial judge criticized defence counsel for conducting the application in an "unprofessional and unethical manner". The purported basis for this conclusion was the trial judge's view that defence counsel had engaged in "the selective preparation and presentation of their material" in such a manner as to "distort the process".]

FRANKEL, J.A.

The trial judge was highly critical of Ms. Blok's affidavits. He described the affidavits as having been "selectiv[ly] prepar[ed] and present[ed]" because they did not contain information with respect to searches of non-newspaper websites in the Vancouver area: para. 43. This criticism appears to be based on the erroneous assumption that, in our adversarial system of criminal justice, defence lawyers are required to present their client's case in an impartial manner. To the contrary, while lawyers cannot knowingly present false or misleading evidence, they are entitled to fairly and forcefully attempt to place their client's case in the best light possible. There is no suggestion that the information Ms. Blok presented in the affidavits was factually incorrect. In this regard, it is important to note that Mr. Heller did not advance the application on the basis that the case had not received media attention outside the Prince George area, but on the basis that the risk of prejudice to a fair trial was greater in Prince George than it would be in a larger urban centre such as Vancouver.

. . . . .

In summary, I would categorically reject the trial judge's conclusion that defence counsel engaged in "the selective preparation and presentation of their material" in such a way as to "distort the process" and, in so doing, conducted the application in an unprofessional and unethical manner. The judge's criticism of counsel's conduct was entirely without merit.

NOTES AND QUESTIONS

1. How should a trial judge respond when they believe that defence counsel have acted unethically? This was an issue addressed in *Legebokoff*:

    Unprofessional or unethical conduct can manifest itself in countless ways, some far more serious than others. Not every judge will have the same opinion as to whether counsel has "crossed the line". The issues of whether, how, and when to voice concerns about counsel are difficult and delicate ones for judges. There are no "bright line" answers. Rather, these are matters that must be left for each judge to determine based on the circumstances in which they arise. Judges can be expected to move cautiously.

    . . . . .

    While repeated instances of unprofessional or unethical conduct may lead a judge to intervene during the course of the proceedings, such action should be taken only when the judge is firmly of the view that counsel's continued involvement will imperil trial fairness or undermine public confidence in the administration of justice.

    . . . . .

    That a judge is not obligated to immediately advise an accused of his or her concerns with respect to the conduct of defence counsel is further evinced by the 1997 protocol between the Law Society of British Columbia and the three levels of court in this province "respecting concerns that arise in ongoing proceedings". Under that protocol judges can seek to have their concerns addressed informally by senior members of the bar without the client being made aware of those concerns. The complete text of the protocol is attached as an appendix to these reasons.[32]

Scenario Three

Susan Jones comes into your office and retains you for an upcoming impaired driving trial. When you receive the disclosure, you learn the name of the individual charged is Sarah Jones. When you confront your client, she tells you she has three other impaired driving convictions, and that she gave the police her twin sister's name so that she wouldn't be detained. She wants you to arrange a quick guilty plea before the error is detected. What do you do? What if your client decides to represent herself?[33]

Scenario Four

Your client is charged with manslaughter. While on bail, your client did some research and uncovered a study that revealed that juries are more likely to acquit accused who testify wearing glasses as compared to those who didn't wear glasses.[34] Apparently, the seriousness of the offence did not change the results. Your client does not require prescription lens. However, he buys a pair of glasses to wear while testifying. Do you allow him to wear them?

Scenario Five

Your client is convicted of possession of cocaine. You know from previous representation that the client has two previous cocaine possession convictions. During sentencing, the Crown does not allege a prior record. Are you obligated to reveal your client's record to the Court? What will you say in your sentencing submissions? What if the trial judge asks you to confirm that your client is a first offender?

Scenario Six

Your client is charged with murder. He tells you that he witnessed the shooting, but was not involved. In his examination-in-chief, your client begins to testify about shooting the deceased in self-defence. What do you do? Consider the following case, which is one of the only Canadian cases to address this situation.

R. v. JENKINS

[2001] O.J. No. 760, 152 C.C.C. (3d) 426 (Ont. S.C.J.)

[The accused was charged with first degree murder. During the accused's cross-examination, a lawyer (Clay Powell) retained by the accused's defence lawyer

---

[32] *R. v. Legebokoff*, [2016] B.C.J. No. 1999, 2016 BCCA 386 at paras. 52, 54, 59 (B.C.C.A.).

[33] See *Law Society of Upper Canada v. Brown*, [1997] L.S.D.D. No. 93 (Ont. Law Soc. Disc. Comm.).

[34] See Kevin Deutsch, "'Nerd defense' as popular as ever" *Daily News* (February 13, 2011), online: http://www.nydailynews.com/news/crime/defense-lawyers-swear-gimmick-defendants-wearing-glasses-trial-article-1.138930.

brought an application to permit defence counsel to withdraw from the case to avoid being involved in the misleading of the court.]

ABBEY J.:

Mr. Powell and Mr. Peel are both very experienced trial counsel. In his submissions, Mr. Peel recalled that in neither of their long careers had a situation such as this presented itself. Indeed, neither counsel were able to present to me any authority directly addressing the circumstances of this case. The jury in this trial, to the point that the application was made, had heard, as I said, approximately eight weeks of testimony. Mr. Powell, as counsel for the accused, had conducted the trial on behalf of the accused with a particular plan consistent with his being able to advance, at the end of the trial, that the Crown had failed to prove, beyond reasonable doubt, the guilt of the accused.

Mr. Peel, in his submissions to me, emphasized that the information which the accused had conveyed to Mr. Powell was such that it was fundamentally inconsistent with the very essence of the case which had been advanced to the jury on behalf of the accused. It was his view that, should Mr. Powell be required to continue his representation of the accused, any active participation whatsoever would raise the potential of Mr. Powell misleading the court. In fact, Mr. Peel submitted that, as counsel to Mr. Powell, should Mr. Powell be required to continue, he would advise, in order to comply with his duty to the court, that he not actively participate:

- in the presentation of further evidence for the defence,
- in the cross-examination of any reply witness called by the Crown, or
- in the presentation of a closing address except to advance the most basic of principles.

Further than that, the position advanced by Mr. Peel was that even without active participation in the continuation of the trial there would be a serious risk of Mr. Powell being seen to deceive the court.

Mr. Peel was in the awkward position of being unable to set forward the precise factual underpinning for the application. He could go no further than to say to me that the information communicated by the accused was such that any involvement by Mr. Powell in the continuation of this trial would raise the hazard of a deception of the court.

Whatever, therefore, may have been the information conveyed by the accused to his counsel, I am convinced that it was contrary to the very core of the case which had been presented on behalf of the accused through the cross-examinations of Crown witnesses and the testimony of the accused himself.

There are, as far as I have been made aware, few authorities that have addressed the subject of silence, in relation to deception, although I note that . . . [the *Rules of Professional Conduct*] prohibit a counsel from knowingly attempting to deceive a tribunal by suppressing what ought to be disclosed.

. . . . .

I have before me no guidance as to the interpretation which the Law Society of Upper Canada may place upon its *Rules of Professional Conduct* in relation to the obligation of counsel in continuing to represent the accused in the circumstances presented in this case. Of course, the *Rules of Professional Conduct* are not, in any event, the sole basis by which to determine the duty owed by counsel to the court.

It was the position of the Crown that, even should the accused, in the continuation of this trial, testify contrary to the disclosure made to Mr. Powell, the duty which Mr. Powell owes to the court would be fulfilled provided he did not, to use the Crown's words, advance the lie. As I understood his position, it was that as long as Mr. Powell remained silent it would not matter that silence in the face of what had gone before would have the effect of deceiving the court nor would it matter that even further testimony would have that effect, so long as Mr. Powell did not actively do anything to advance the deception.

Respectfully, I disagree. It is important to note that this was not a case where the application was made before trial so that deception might be avoided by counsel, to borrow the Crown's words, not advancing the lie in the way in which the case was then presented. Rather, the deception in this case would arise from silence alone on the part of counsel in the face of what had already been presented to the court.

My view is that, quite apart from the obvious prejudicial inferences that might be taken by the jury as a result of Mr. Powell continuing as counsel while virtually tied to his chair, even silence on the part of Mr. Powell would have the potential of placing him in jeopardy in respect to his duty to the court, remembering that the communication made to Mr. Powell cuts to the very core and essence of the defence that had been presented in the trial. Silence on the part of counsel may not in all circumstances be deception, but in these circumstances, I believe that it would be. Limited representation on the part of Mr. Powell would not be an acceptable alternative. To borrow the words of Mr. Martin (as he then was) from 1969, the application has been made in good faith, there is a serious problem and counsel has acted promptly. I am, therefore, reluctantly compelled to the conclusion that the application must be granted.

NOTES AND QUESTIONS

1. Years later, the *Model Code* still provides no guidance to defence counsel in dealing with completed perjury. What do you think of the following approach that used to be in force in New Brunswick before they adopted the *Model Code*:

   Chapter 8 - False testimony

   12 (a) The lawyer who as an advocate for the client becomes aware of intentional false testimony participated in by the client or by a witness called by the lawyer that is material to the matter before the court shall

       (i)   make immediate disclosure to the court and to other counsel, or

       (ii)   continue in the proceedings without making reference to the intentional false testimony and in argument without explanation advise the court that such testimony should not be relied on, or

      (iiii) seek leave of the court to withdraw from the matter

   (b) In the event that the client for whom the lawyer is acting as an advocate insists that a course of action in a matter be pursued that would

423

occasion a breach of the Rule or of a Commentary in this chapter the lawyer shall refuse to follow the course of action, shall do everything reasonable to prevent it being pursued and shall withdraw from the matter.

2. After *Jenkins*, it would appear that a lawyer's only recourse to the completed perjury dilemma in Canada is to withdraw if the client refuses to correct the lie. What are some other alternatives? Are any of them more workable?[35]

3. One of the concerns with withdrawal in the middle of the trial is that the jury will inevitably use withdrawal against the accused. The Court of Appeal in *R. v. Jenkins* was unconvinced by this argument:

> We agree with the way that the trial judge handled this difficult situation, including his firm and fair instruction to the jury. The appellant's principal submission is that the jury would have concluded his lawyer no longer believed in him. This submission is no more than speculative and, moreover, would require us to accept the untenable proposition that jurors do not follow a trial judge's directions. Accordingly, the appeal is dismissed.[36]

[iii]   Defending Sexual Assault Cases

The treatment of sexual assault complainants at trial, including by defence counsel, raises questions of access to justice, fairness and equality. In 1988, a senior Ottawa defence lawyer gave a talk about defending sexual assault cases at a continuing education event. He said this about the role of defence counsel:

> Generally, if you destroy the complainant in a prosecution . . . you destroy the head. *You cut off the head of the Crown's case and the case is dead.* My own experience is the preliminary inquiry is the ideal place in a sexual assault trial to try and win it all. You can do things [. . .] with a complainant at a preliminary inquiry in front of a judge which you would never try to do for tactical, strategic reasons – sympathy of the witness, etcetera – in front of a jury . . . *You have to go in there as defence counsel and whack the complainant hard* . . . You have . . . to get all the medical evidence, get all the Children's Aid Society reports, and *you've got to attack the complainant with all you've got*, so that he or she will say "I'm not coming back in front of 12 good citizens to repeat this bullshit story that I've just told the judge." [Emphasis added][37]

11 years later, the Supreme Court of Canada heard the following case, which dealt with the constitutionality of a provision of the *Criminal Code* that created an exclusionary rule for the kinds of records referred by the lawyer in his talk. The Court also specifically addressed his "whack the complainant" exhortation.

---

[35] See David Layton, "*R v. Jenkins*: Client Perjury and Disclosure by Defence Counsel" (2001) 44 C.R. (5th) 259.

[36] [2005] O.J. No. 282 at para. 1 (Ont. C.A.).

[37] Cristin Schmitz, "'Whack' Sex Assault Complainant at Preliminary Inquiry" *The Lawyers Weekly* (May 27, 1988) at 22.

R. v. MILLS

[1999] S.C.J. No. 68, [1999] 3 S.C.R. 668

[In *Mills*, the accused challenged the constitutionality of provisions of the *Criminal Code* governing the production of a sexual assault complainant's private records.]

McLACHLIN AND IACOBUCCI, J.J.

Equality concerns must also inform the contextual circumstances in which the rights of full answer and defence and privacy will come into play. In this respect, an appreciation of myths and stereotypes in the context of sexual violence is essential to delineate properly the boundaries of full answer and defence. As we have already discussed, the right to make full answer and defence does not include the right to information that would only distort the truth-seeking goal of the trial process. In *R. v. Osolin*, [1993] 4 S.C.R. 595, Cory J., for the majority on this issue, stated, at pp. 669-70:

> The provisions of ss. 15 and 28 of the *Charter* guaranteeing equality to men and women, although not determinative should be taken into account in determining the reasonable limitations that should be placed upon the cross-examination of a complainant... . A complainant should not be unduly harassed and pilloried to the extent of becoming a victim of an insensitive judicial system... .

> The reasons in *Seaboyer* make it clear that eliciting evidence from a complainant for the purpose of encouraging inferences pertaining to consent or the credibility of rape victims which are based on groundless myths and fantasized stereotypes is improper.

The accused is not permitted to "whack the complainant" through the use of stereotypes regarding victims of sexual assault.

NOTES AND QUESTIONS

1. "Whacking" has been defined as "tactics that seek to exploit the stereotypes and vulnerabilities inherent in sexual assault cases to secure a favourable outcome". See David Tanovich and Elaine Craig, "Whacking the Complainant: A Real and Current Systemic Problem," *The Globe and Mail* (February 10, 2016). What are some examples of "whacking"?

2. What *Model Code* rules could be used to control "whacking"?

3. Three years later, in *R. v. Shearing*,[38] the Supreme Court reaffirmed that defence counsel do not have the same latitude in cross-examining sexual assault complainants given the equality and privacy interests at stake. Justice Binnie held:

> While in most instances the adversarial process allows wide latitude to cross-examiners to resort to unproven assumptions and innuendo in an effort to crack the untruthful witness, sexual assault cases pose particular dangers. *Seaboyer*, *Osolin* and *Mills* all make the point that these cases should be decided without resort to folk tales about how abuse victims are expected by people who have never suffered abuse to react to the trauma [. . .] This does not turn persons accused of sexual abuse into

---

[38] [2002] S.C.J. No. 59, [2002] 3 S.C.R. 33 (S.C.C.).

second-class litigants. It simply means that the defence has to work with facts rather than rely on innuendoes and wishful assumptions.[39]

More recently, in *R. v. Barton*,[40] the Supreme Court issued the following call to action:

> We live in a time where myths, stereotypes, and sexual violence against women — particularly Indigenous women and sex workers — are tragically common. Our society has yet to come to grips with just how deep-rooted these issues truly are and just how devastating their consequences can be. Without a doubt, eliminating myths, stereotypes, and sexual violence against women is one of the more pressing challenges we face as a society. While serious efforts are being made by a range of actors to address and remedy these failings both within the criminal justice system and throughout Canadian society more broadly, this case attests to the fact that more needs to be done. Put simply, we can — and *must* — do better.
>
> . . . . .
>
> With this in mind, in my view, our criminal justice system and all participants within it should take reasonable steps to address systemic biases, prejudices, and stereotypes against Indigenous persons — and in particular Indigenous women and sex workers — head-on. Turning a blind eye to these biases, prejudices, and stereotypes is not an answer. Accordingly, as an additional safeguard going forward, in sexual assault cases where the complainant is an Indigenous woman or girl, trial judges would be well advised to provide an express instruction aimed at countering prejudice against Indigenous women and girls.

4. Do you agree with these limits on the advocacy of a criminal defence lawyer? A well-known and thoughtful American legal ethicist does not. In "Defending Defending: The Case For Unmitigated Zeal On Behalf Of People Who Do Terrible Things",[41] Abbe Smith argues:

> It is difficult, if not impossible, to zealously represent the criminally accused and simultaneously tend to the feelings of others. This is so in any political climate, but even more so in a time when criminal punishment is regarded as the answer to almost all of our social problems. We cannot seem to build prisons fast enough, and we are on the road to the virtual banishment of young African American men from society. It is simply wrong to place an additional burden on criminal defense lawyers to make the world a better place as they labor to represent individuals facing loss of liberty or life.
>
> . . . . .
>
> I came to criminal defense work out of a desire to fight for the underdog

---

[39] [2002] S.C.J. No. 59, [2002] 3 S.C.R. 33 at paras. 121-122 (S.C.C.). See further, *R. v. V(R)* [2019] S.C.J. No. 41, 2019 SCC 41 at para. 133 (S.C.C.) and *R. v. Goldfinch* [2019] S.C.J. No. 38, 2019 SCC 38 at 33-37 (S.C.C.).

[40] [2019] S.C.J. No. 33, 2019 SCC 33 (S.C.C.).

[41] (1999-2000) 28 Hofstra L. Rev. 925 at 951-954; 956-957.

and participate in a larger movement for social change. There are times when my concern for individual justice, for the rights and interests of an individual accused of crime, are at odds with my concern for the rights and interests of some larger community. I do not enjoy stirring up or manipulating homophobia or race, gender, or ethnic prejudice in the course of representing a client. However, my own ideological values cannot be the determining factor. A lawyer ought not undertake the representation of a client if he or she will be hobbled by personal or ideological conflicts. . . .

It is the prosecutor's responsibility to anticipate and counter defense strategies – even those that play into juror prejudice. If they fail to do so, why blame the defense?

There is nothing unethical about using racial, gender, ethnic, or sexual stereotypes in criminal defense. It is simply an aspect of zealous advocacy. Prejudice exists in the community and in the courthouse, and criminal defense lawyers would be foolhardy not to recognize this as a fact of life. Of course, most bias and prejudice works *against* the accused, disproportionate numbers of whom are poor and nonwhite. Defence lawyers must incorporate this knowledge, as well as knowledge about the stereotypes that might apply, to the prosecution and defense witnesses in all their trial decisions.

. . . . .

A good criminal lawyer – one with sound judgment – would recognize a weak and potentially offensive strategy and carefully assess the benefits and hazards before raising it. It may be that the lawyer has nothing else and most go forward because the client insists on a trial.[42]

[c]   Additional Ethical Limits on Defending the Guilty

So far, we have examined the general ethical limitations on the conduct of criminal defence work. There are some additional limitations that arise when you know that your client is guilty. We begin with an examination of the difficult issue of when you have sufficient knowledge of your client's guilt to trigger those limitations.

[i]   Acquiring Knowledge of Your Client's Guilt

Commentary 10 to *Model Code* Rule 5.1-1 states:

Admissions made by the accused to a lawyer may impose strict limitations on the conduct of the defence, and the accused should be made aware of this. For example, if the accused clearly admits to the lawyer the factual and mental elements necessary to constitute the offence, the lawyer, if convinced that the admissions are true and voluntary . . .

Scenario Seven

Your client is charged with possession of drugs for the purposes of trafficking. You meet him in the cells before his bail hearing. He admits he was in possession of the drugs for sale, and wants to plead guilty. He has a criminal record for drug trafficking. You are able to secure his bail. You meet with him one month later. He

---

[42]   (1999-2000) 28 Hofstra L. Rev. 925 at 951-954, 956-957.

now insists that the drugs were planted, and that he is innocent. He informs you that he read about one of the officers involved in his case in the newspaper. That officer is facing an internal disciplinary hearing for allegedly planting drugs in another case. Can you run a "plant" defence? Do you need to conduct any further inquiries?

Scenario Eight

Your client is charged with killing her abusive partner. In your initial meeting with her, you gather some basic background information. She turns to you and asks, "Don't you want to know what happened?" You reply "no", and then explain that there are limits on your ability to run a defence if she admits to having killed him. She states "Oh, I didn't realize that." Has counsel acted ethically? What are the dangers in avoiding the facts?

Defence counsel enter dangerous waters when they allow their private opinion of guilt to trump the client's assertion of innocence, as exemplified by the following case:

R. v. DELISLE

[1999] J.Q. no. 18, 133 C.C.C. (3d) 541 (Que. C.A.)

PROULX, J.A. (translation)

In the case at bar, it was established, on the basis of the fresh evidence introduced into the record, that the appellant, because of the sudden illness of his lawyer, had to retain the services of another lawyer who had been practising for at most a year. It was also established that the appellant always maintained to his lawyer that he was innocent, that he wanted to testify in his defence and that he even identified Kevin Carl to his lawyer as one of the assailants. I would mention here that the victim had been attacked by a group of individuals and that the main issue the trial judge had to resolve was the identity of the aggressors. The second lawyer, undoubtedly because of his lack of experience, relied on his impressions rather than undertaking the steps required for effective representation.

Because he did not believe his client's story, he did not even attempt to meet the witness Carl and determined that his client should not testify in his own defence. Following the verdict of guilty but before sentencing, Carl communicated with the lawyer, confiding to him that he was in fact the person responsible for the acts attributed to the appellant. The lawyer then attempted, but in vain, to get the trial judge to reopen the case. In the context of this appeal, Carl gave an affidavit in which he reiterated his participation in the events which led to the conviction of the appellant. He could not be reached, however, to give testimony at the request of the appellant in the context of his motion to call fresh evidence. Furthermore, the transcript of the appellant's and of his lawyer's testimony, which confirms the foregoing, was filed in this Court's record.

It is not astonishing that the Crown here conceded that the appeal must be granted. The appellant always maintained that he was innocent. He had indicated to his lawyer the identity of the guilty party and, is it necessary to mention, wanted to testify in his own defence. These instructions of the client were never respected by the lawyer. He thereby imposed on his client his decision not to call him and not to attempt to meet the witness Carl. The lawyer committed a first significant error. The lawyer's explanation that he did not believe his client's story is also totally unacceptable. *The lawyer cannot set himself up as the judge of his client. . . .*

ii) When one sets himself up as the judge of one's own client

If there is a universal rule of ethics in criminal law which has existed for centuries, it is the rule which provides that counsel must not set himself up as the judge of his own client before the trial begins and then leave it to the trier of fact to decide guilt or innocence. [. . .] In the case at bar, counsel for the appellant totally misunderstood the role which was his, by setting himself up as the judge of his client instead of respecting his client's instructions and truly defending his client's interests. Taking into account what we know now as a result of the fresh evidence, this demonstrates even more the danger for counsel of relying upon his impressions.

In conclusion therefore, taking into account the two serious errors committed by counsel for the appellant, each of which is proof of flagrant incompetence and fundamentally violates the appellant's right to make full answer and defence, I am of the view, as the Crown moreover conceded, that irreparable prejudice resulted therefrom justifying the quashing of the judgment and the ordering of a new trial. For these reasons, I am of the view that the appeal must be granted and a new trial ordered.

NOTES AND QUESTIONS

1. But what about a client who maintains innocence in the face of a compelling and reliable Crown case? David Layton and Michel Proulx in *Ethics and Criminal Law*[43] argue that in some cases, defence counsel will have an "irresistible knowledge of guilt" which should constitute deemed knowledge:

    > In the very great majority of cases, a lawyer is not justified in restricting the conduct of the defence based merely on a personal view of a client's guilt. Occasionally, however, after careful investigation and thorough assessment, a lawyer may reach such a level of certainty with respect to the client's culpability that she "will have as much reason to feel confidence in concluding that a client is guilty as charged as to feel confidence about anything else". Indeed, we sometimes forget that the lawyer's special position as a recipient of confidential information that must not be shared with third parties may make her *better* able to determine what is true or false than is the prosecutor, judge or jury. In these unusual cases, the lawyer is surely restricted in the conduct of the defence by the ethical codes' prohibition against *knowingly* assisting in dishonest action, presenting false evidence, or otherwise misleading the court.

    > . . . . .

    > The standard that must be met before counsel can be said to have knowledge of guilt must be very demanding, however, given the lawyer's special role as partisan in an adversarial system that seeks not only the truth but also to protect the client's constitutional rights. In our view,

---

[43] 2d ed. (Toronto: Irwin Law, 2015).

knowledge of guilt within the meaning of the ethical rules can only be said to exist where counsel reaches an *irresistible conclusion* that the client is culpable on the criminal standard, by which we mean a conclusion that not even a zealous but honest partisan could deny. Our standard, which has been endorsed by the Supreme Court of Canada, will be easy to meet where the client provides counsel with a clear and convincing admission that fully jibes with the rest of the evidence in the case. But it will be very difficult to satisfy, and only rarely be met, where the client has not admitted guilty. Absent such an admission, it will not be enough for the lawyer simply to conclude that he would find the client guilty beyond a reasonable doubt if deciding the case as judge or jury member. Rather, the lawyer must irresistibly come to this conclusion while adopting a very different mindset – that of the zealous but honest partisan.

Some defence lawyers may view the position that a lawyer can ethically "know" the client is guilty in the absence of a confession as a heresy. Yet in our view it is unacceptable for counsel to put up a defence she irresistibly concludes is false, for instance by calling evidence that someone else committed the crime, regardless of how she comes to know the client is undoubtedly the culprit. The justification for prohibiting a lawyer from knowingly misleading the court should apply whether the knowledge of falsity originates from the client's confession or from other reliable sources of information. Consequently, although a lawyer must in the vast majority of cases resist passing judgment on a client, there will be exceptional situations where he cannot escape the irresistible conclusion and where the attendant ethical constraints will therefore apply. Counsel is precluded from reaching such a conclusion, however, absent a careful investigation of all relevant aspects of the case.[44]

2.   Layton and Proulx refer to their "irresistible inference" being accepted by the Supreme Court. In *R. v. Youvarajah*,[45] the Court said this:

> Furthermore, the involvement of defence counsel provides no meaningful check on the danger of an accused acknowledging false allegations against a third party in order to obtain a favourable plea bargain. Counsel have an ethical duty to not knowingly mislead the court. However, it does not require them to verify or investigate the truth of information they present; and the duty is triggered only where counsel has information leading to the "irresistible conclusion" that something is false. See M. Proulx and D. Layton, *Ethics and Canadian Criminal Law* (2001), at pp. 40-47 and 460.[46]

3.   Do you agree with the Layton and Proulx approach? Does it provide sufficient guidance to lawyers? What is a "zealous but honest partisan"?

Scenario Nine

Your client is charged with killing his business partner. The deceased is found dead

---

[44]   *Ethics and Criminal Law* 2d ed. (Toronto: Irwin Law, 2015) at 33-34.

[45]   [2013] S.C.J. No. 41, 2013 SCC 41 at para. 61 (S.C.C.).

[46]   [2013] S.C.J. No. 41, 2013 SCC 41 at para. 61 (S.C.C.).

in his car with his throat slit. The condition of the car suggests that the deceased struggled with his assailant. At the preliminary inquiry, the Crown leads evidence that DNA found at the crime scene matches your client's DNA. Hair and fibre evidence in the car is also linked to your client. Your expert confirms the reliability of this evidence in his report to you. The Crown also calls a witness who one month earlier, overheard your client threaten to kill the deceased. Your client maintains his innocence. He tells you that he was with his wife and children at the time the deceased was killed. Do you have an irresistible inference of guilt on these facts?

[ii] The Additional Limitations

When you "know" that your client is guilty, Commentary 10 of *Model Code* Rule 5.1-1 makes it clear that you are not obligated to plead your client guilty. According to Commentary 10, you can "properly take objection to the jurisdiction of the court, the form of the indictment or the admissibility or sufficiency of the evidence [. . .]" However, you cannot "suggest that some other person committed the offence or call any evidence that, by reason of the admissions, the lawyer believes to be false. Nor may the lawyer set up an affirmative case inconsistent with such admissions, for example, by calling evidence in support of an alibi intended to show that the accused could not have done or, in fact, has not done the act". The nature of the limits will depend, of course, on the content of the admission. If the client admits that he intentionally killed the victim, defence counsel cannot call an alibi defence, or allow the client to testify that it was an accident. However, even with that admission, defence counsel might still, depending on the other evidence, be able to pursue a self-defence or provocation defence.

Finally, Commentary 10 states that an admission "will also impose a limit on the extent to which the lawyer may attack the evidence for the prosecution. The lawyer is entitled to test the evidence given by each individual witness for the prosecution and argue that the evidence taken as a whole is insufficient to amount to proof that the accused is guilty of the offence charged, but the lawyer should go no further than that". So even with knowledge of your client's guilt, you are ethically obligated, if the client so instructs, to vigorously challenge the admissibility of the evidence and the sufficiency of the Crown's case. Did defence counsel meet that standard in the following case?

R. v. TUCKIAR

(1934), 52 C.L.R. 335 (Aust. H.C.)

[Dhakiyarr (Tuckiar) Wirrpanda, a Yolngu elder from northeast Arnhem, was charged with killing a white police officer (Constable McColl) with his spear. He was tried by an all-white jury. The facts of the case and trial process are summarized by Justice Virginia Bell in her 2008 Law and Justice Address:

> In 1933 a small party of police were despatched to Woodah Island in the Gulf of Carpentaria to investigate the murder of several Japanese fishermen. Constable McColl was one of the party. The police came upon a group of Aboriginal women whom they took into custody, handcuffing them together, and taking them back to their camp so as to interrogate them. A group of Aboriginal men were observed setting off in a boat and the main body of the police party headed off in pursuit; leaving Constable McColl to superintend the Aboriginal women. On their return,

the police found that Constable McColl and the women were missing. His body was found the next day not far from the camp. His pistol was lying nearby. Three shots had been fired from it, the third a misfire. He had been speared through the heart. Tuckiar and another Yolgnu man named Parriner and some others were persuaded by a white fisherman with whom they were on good terms to go to Darwin to sort the matter out. Three of the aboriginal women whom the police had seized were said to have been "Tuckiar's women". He was charged with the murder of Constable McColl.

The only evidence against him presented at his trial was of confessions which he was alleged to have made. One was to Parriner, and the other to an Aboriginal boy named Harry. Tuckiar spoke no English and the evidence was given through an interpreter, who relayed it to the court in pidgin. Tuckiar was alleged to have told Parriner that he had hidden in the bushes and given a signal to the woman handcuffed to Constable McColl to move away and that when she did so he had speared him. Harry's evidence was that Tuckiar said he had seen Constable McColl having sexual intercourse with his wife and that, after this, McColl had seen Tuckiar and fired at him. It was against this background that Tuckiar had thrown the spear.

The Protector of Aborigines arranged for counsel to appear for Tuckiar. Unfortunately both the trial judge and Tuckiar's counsel appeared more concerned to protect Constable McColl's reputation than to ensure that Tuckiar had a fair trial. Evidence was led to show that Constable McColl was a man of good moral character who had been known to behave with decorum including when he was in the company of half-caste girls. At the conclusion of Parriner's evidence, the judge asked counsel in front of the jury whether he had obtained instructions from Tuckiar about what Parriner had to say. Counsel said that he had not. The judge adjourned the trial so that counsel could speak with Tuckiar. On the resumption of the trial, counsel asked if he could speak with the judge in chambers because he had been placed in the most difficult predicament of his life. There followed a further adjournment during which counsel and the Protector of Aborigines conferred with the judge in chambers. The trial resumed. No evidence was called on Tuckiar's behalf.

The jury was troubled by the lack of evidence and they sent a note asking, "if we are satisfied that there is not enough evidence, what is our position?" The judge answered their question, saying among other things, that they should not be swayed if they thought the Crown had not done its duty, he reminded them that if they brought in a verdict of not guilty Tuckiar would be freed and could not be tried again no matter what evidence may be discovered in the future. In his summing up the judge told the jury, "you have before you two different stories, one of which sounds highly probable, and fits in with all the known facts, and the other is so utterly ridiculous as to be an obvious fabrication". He went on to comment that Tuckiar had not given evidence and that the jury could draw any inference that they cared to draw from that circumstance. Tuckiar was convicted and sentenced to death. After the jury returned their verdict, Tuckiar's counsel informed the Court that he had spoken with Tuckiar, with the assistance of the interpreter, putting to him that he had told two different stories and asking him which was true. Tuckiar had said that the true account was the one he had told Parriner.[47]

---

[47] Online: http://www.lawfoundation.net.au/ljf/app/C19B9386B33532B3CA257 4F1008285A9.html.

The conduct of his defence counsel and the trial judge were the focus of the Australian High Court decision.]

GAVAN DUFFY C.J., DIXON, EVATT and McTIERNAN, J.J.

Upon the jury's finding a verdict of guilty, the Judge postponed pronouncing sentence, which, in the case of an aboriginal, is not necessarily death. The prisoner's counsel then made the following statement:

> I have a matter which I desire to mention before the Court rises. I would like to state publicly that I had an interview with the convicted prisoner Tuckiar in the presence of an interpreter. I pointed out to him that he had told these two different stories and that one could not be true. I asked him to tell the interpreter which was the true story. He told him that the first story told to Parriner was the true one. I asked him why he told the other story. He told me that he was too much worried so he told a different story and that story was a lie. I think this fact clears Constable McColl. As an advocate I did not deem it advisable to put the accused in the box.

. . . When the Court resumed his Honor added:

> It did not occur to me at the time, but I think I should have stated publicly that immediately that confession had been made to you, you and Dr. Cook (the Protector of Aborigines) consulted me about the matter and asked my opinion as to the proper course for you, as counsel, to take, and I then told you that if your client had been a white man and had made a confession of guilt to you I thought your proper course would have been to withdraw from the case; but as your client was an aboriginal, and there might be some remnant of doubt as to whether his confession to you was any more reliable than any other confession he had made, the better course would be for you to continue to appear for him, because if you had retired from the case it would have left it open to ignorant, malicious and irresponsible persons to say that this aboriginal had been abandoned and left without any proper defence.

After hearing some evidence upon the subject of punishment, the learned Judge pronounced sentence of death. We think that this narrative of the proceedings shows that for more than one reason the conviction cannot stand. In the first place, we think the observations made by the learned Judge upon the failure of the prisoner to give evidence amounted to a clear misdirection, and one which in the circumstances was calculated gravely to prejudice the prisoner. Sec. 1 of Act No. 245 of South Australia, which enables persons accused of offences to give evidence on their own behalf and is in force in the Northern Territory, contains a proviso that no presumption of guilt shall be made from the fact of such person electing not to give evidence.

In the present case, the jury witnessed the spectacle of the prisoner's counsel, at the suggestion of the Judge, retiring to discuss with the prisoner the evidence of the principal witness against him and see whether it was correct, and of his saying after doing so, that he wished to discuss with the Judge a specially important matter, which put him in the worst predicament that he had encountered in his legal career. Afterwards, the Judge, who had to their knowledge heard counsel's communication, directed them that for some reason the prisoner had not gone into the witness box and told them which of the stories was true and that they were entitled to take that fact into consideration and draw any inference from it they liked. He thus authorized them to make a presumption of guilt from the prisoner's failure to give evidence and the circumstances which had occurred before them were likely to reinforce the presumption with a well-founded surmise of what the Judge had been told by the prisoner's counsel.

In the next place, although the evidence of McColl's good character and moral tendencies was not objected to, it clearly should have been disallowed. The purpose of the trial was not to vindicate the deceased constable, but to inquire into the guilt of the living aboriginal. Before he could be found guilty it was necessary that by admissible evidence the jury should be finally satisfied to the exclusion of reasonable doubt that he had killed Constable McColl in circumstances which amounted to murder. By leading evidence that the prisoner told a story that he killed the deceased in circumstances supporting a plea of self-defence and involving a reflection upon the moral conduct of the dead man, the prosecution could not make relevant the latter's reputation and moral tendencies. The prisoner should not have been exposed to the danger of the jury's regarding the matter as a dilemma between an imputation on the dead and the conviction of the aboriginal. That danger is likely to have been much increased by the manner in which the Judge expressed himself when the jury asked what was their position if they were satisfied that the evidence was not sufficient and afterwards in his summing up in the first passage therefrom which we have set out. Notwithstanding the direction which accompanied them, the observations as to the slander upon a dead man and the possibility of a miscarriage of justice by the escape of a guilty man were calculated to do anything but fix the jury's attention on the necessity of being satisfied beyond reasonable doubt of the guilt of the accused. No doubt, his Honor was in the best position to interpret the jury's question, but it cannot be certain that it did not mean what the foreman's words appear literally to imply, namely, what were they to do if the evidence appeared to them to fall short of establishing guilt? If they did mean this, the answer and subsequent treatment of the matter must have had a still greater tendency to prejudice the prisoner.

It would be difficult for anyone in the position of the learned Judge to receive the communication made to him by counsel for the prisoner and yet retain the same view of the dangers involved in the weakness of the Crown evidence. This may, perhaps, explain his Honor's evident anxiety that the jury should not under-estimate the force of the evidence the Crown did adduce. Indeed counsel seems to have taken a course calculated to transfer to the Judge the embarrassment which he appears so much to have felt. Why he should have conceived himself to have been in so great a predicament, it is not easy for those experienced in advocacy to understand. He had a plain duty, both to his client and to the Court, to press such rational considerations as the evidence fairly gave rise to in favour of complete acquittal or conviction of manslaughter only. No doubt he was satisfied that through Paddy he obtained the uncoloured product of his client's mind, although misgiving on this point would have been pardonable; but, even if the result was that the correctness of Parriner's version was conceded, it was by no means a hopeless contention of fact that the homicide should be found to amount only to manslaughter.

Whether he be in fact guilty or not, a prisoner is, in point of law, entitled to acquittal from any charge which the evidence fails to establish that he committed, and it is not incumbent on his counsel by abandoning his defence to deprive him of the benefit of such rational arguments as fairly arise on the proofs submitted. The subsequent action of the prisoner's counsel in openly disclosing the privileged communication of his client and acknowledging the correctness of the more serious testimony against him is wholly indefensible. It was his paramount duty to respect the privilege attaching to the communication made to him as counsel, a duty the obligation of which was by no means weakened by the character of his client, or the moment at which he chose to make the disclosure. No doubt he was actuated by a desire to remove any imputation on Constable McColl. But he was not entitled to divulge what he had learnt from the prisoner as his counsel. Our system of administering justice necessarily imposes upon those who practice advocacy duties which have no analogies, and the system cannot dispense with their strict observance.

In the present case, what occurred is productive of much difficulty. We have reached the conclusion, as we have already stated, that the verdict found against the prisoner must be set aside. Ordinarily the question would next arise whether a new trial should be had. But upon this question we are confronted with the following statements made by the learned trial Judge in his report—"After the verdict, counsel — for reasons that may have been good — made a public statement of this fact which has been published in the local press and otherwise broadcasted throughout the whole area from which jurymen are drawn. If a new trial were granted and another jury were asked to choose between Parriner's story, Harry's story, and some third story which might possibly be put before them it would be practically impossible for them to put out of their minds the fact of this confession by the accused to his own counsel, which would certainly be known to most, if not all, of them. ... Counsel for the defence ... after verdict made, entirely of his own motion, a public statement which would make a new trial almost certainly a futility."

In face of this opinion, the correctness of which we cannot doubt, we think the prisoner cannot justly be subjected to another trial at Darwin, and no other venue is practicable. We therefore allow the appeal, and quash the conviction and judgment and direct that a verdict and judgment of acquittal be entered.

NOTES AND QUESTIONS

1. How did the defence lawyer fail his client in this case?

2. After Tuckiar was released, he disappeared, and his fate remains unknown, although many suspect that he was murdered by those who disagreed with the Court's decision. In June of 2003:

   > . . . On Saturday 29 June, a Wukidi ceremony was held for Dhakiyarr Wirrpanda at the Darwin Supreme Court. This historical act of reconciliation was attended by Chief Justice of Australia Murray Gleeson, Chief Justice of the Northern Territory Brian Martin, Solicitor General, Tom Pauling QC, and a healthy contingent of the local legal profession and the general public. . . .. The aim of the Wukidi ceremony was to lay the spirit of Dhakiyarr to rest. The ceremony stems from Garrawan (Woodah Island) in north east Arnham Land.[48]

3. To what extent do you think racism played a role in the conduct of the defence lawyer and the trial judge?

---

[48] "Wukidi ceremony for Dhakiyarr Wirpanda", online: http://www.austlii.edu.au/au/journals/BalJlNTLawSoc/2003/119.pdf.

4. How is the case similar to the Nova Scotia case of *R. v. Fraser*[49] discussed in Chapter 2?

5. *Tuckiar* is considered a landmark case in Australia, both for what it reveals about the role of defence counsel, and the treatment of Aboriginals in the criminal justice system.[50]

One of the more difficult issues for criminal lawyers is how resolute you can be in defending the guilty. Recall that Commentary [10] provides that defence counsel is "entitled to test the evidence given by each individual witness for the prosecution and argue that the evidence taken as a whole is insufficient to amount to proof that the accused is guilty of the offence charged, but the lawyer should go no further than that". What is the "go no further than that"? Does it mean you can't suggest that the primary Crown witness is lying, or their evidence is unreliable in your closing submissions? Does it mean you can't impeach a truthful witness through cross-examination or by calling truthful evidence? These are issues that divide legal ethics scholars.[51]

In the following case, the accused admitted to his lawyer that he committed the robbery. However, the Crown witnesses were mistaken in their descriptions of the accused's appearance at the time of the robbery. The issue on appeal was whether defence counsel had acted inappropriately in calling truthful evidence to contradict their evidence.

R. v. LI

[1993] B.C.J. No. 2312 (B.C.C.A.)

McEACHERN, CJBC:

Having received an admission from the accused that he robbed the store, Mr. Brooks was required to refrain from setting up any inconsistent defence. He was entitled, however, indeed under a duty, to test the proof of the case in every proper way. Thus, in my view, it was not improper for Mr. Brooks to call two independent witnesses who gave uncontroversial evidence about the hairstyle of the accused, and about his fluency in English. Those matters might have raised a doubt about the reliability of the identification evidence given by the jewellery store clerks.

On this point, I agree with Mr. Crossin's argument that if the evidence of the Crown was that an assailant was about 6 feet in height, a counsel defending an accused who

[49] [2011] N.S.J. No. 400, 2011 NSCA 60 (N.S.C.A.).

[50] The following documentary aired a few years ago and provides additional insights into the case: *Hindsight* (July 7, 2013), online: http://www.abc.net.au/radionational/programs/hindsight/hindsight-sunday-july-7th2c013/4760586.

[51] See for example, Harry I. Subin, "The Criminal Lawyer's 'Different Mission': Reflections on the 'Right' to Present a False Case" (1987) 1 Geo. J. Leg. Ethics 125; and John B. Mitchell, "Reasonable Doubts Are Where You Find Them: A Response to Professor Subin's Position on the Criminal Lawyer's 'Different Mission'" (1987) 1 Geo. J. Leg. Ethics 339. See also the thoughtful discussion in David Layton and Michel Proulx, *Ethics and Criminal Law*, 2d ed. (Toronto: Irwin Law, 2015) at 48-70.

has privately admitted guilt, could properly call evidence to prove the real height of the accused was less or more than that.

Thus, it does not appear that Mr. Brooks breached any ethical rule by continuing to act after the accused admitted he participated in the Burnaby robbery. He cross-examined the witnesses and sought to raise a doubt about identification (which was the only hope the accused had). He did not call the accused or put up any defence inconsistent with the facts believed by him to be true.

NOTES AND QUESTIONS

1. Do you agree with the Court of Appeal? Is there a discernable difference between challenging the credibility (*i.e.*, truthfulness) of a witness and their reliability when you know your client is guilty? Is the latter more consistent with testing the evidence and ensuring that the state can prove its case on the basis of reliable evidence? How does the *Li* position protect against wrongful convictions?

2. Is the Supreme Court decision in *R. v. Lyttle* discussed earlier (and excerpted in Chapter 5) relevant here? Recall that in that case, the Court held that lawyers need a good faith basis as to the truthfulness of a suggestion before putting it to a witness in cross-examination. As the Court put it, "to suggest what counsel genuinely thinks possible on known facts or reasonable assumptions is in our view permissible; to assert or to imply in a manner that is calculated to mislead is in our view improper and prohibited".[52]

3. As you work through the following scenarios, what factors would you identify as relevant as you think about how you would navigate this grey area? Think back to the earlier discussion of *Mills* and Abbe Smith in her article "Defending Defending".[53]

Scenario Ten

Your client is charged with sexual assault. The issue is consent. Your client has admitted that there was no consent. You learn that the complainant has a criminal record for fraud. Can you ethically cross-examine them on this conviction? How would you use their answer in your closing address? What would you do?[54]

Scenario Eleven

Your client, a young Black male, is charged with assaulting a police officer by pushing him off the sidewalk. He admits that he did assault the officer because he was tired of being regularly carded and racially profiled. Your *Charter* application alleging unlawful detention and racial profiling is dismissed. Two years ago, the officer was found guilty of a disciplinary offence for excessive force in an arrest of

---

[52] [2004] S.C.J. No. 8, 2004 SCC 5 (S.C.C.).

[53] See also: "A Difficult Case: Cross-Examination of the Truthful Witness" in David Layton, "The Criminal Defence Lawyer's Role" (2004) 27 Dal. L.J. 379 at 389-400.

[54] See David M. Tanovich, "Whack No More: Infusing Equality into the Ethics of Defence Lawyering in Sexual Assault Cases" (2015) 45(3) Ottawa L. Rev. 495 at 510-511.

a Black man. Can you ethically cross-examine the officer on this offence? How would you use his answer in your closing address? What would you do?

[3] THE PROSECUTOR

[a] Role Of?

The prosecutor occupies a unique role in our criminal justice system. First, they do not have a client in the traditional sense of an aggrieved party or defendant. Their client is the "Crown". Second, through the exercise of discretion, the prosecutor serves, in many respects, as a gatekeeper. She decides whether charges should be laid or withdrawn; whether to consent to bail; whether to agree to a guilty plea; whether to agree to a joint submission on sentencing; or whether to appeal an acquittal or sentence. Prosecutors are also advocates who must provide advance notice of their case through disclosure, present sufficient evidence to move the case forward, and, test any evidence called by the defence.

In carrying out these dual functions of gatekeeper and advocate, the oft-cited *Boucher* case instructs us that the role of the prosecutor is not to "obtain a conviction" but to ensure that these functions are carried out with fairness, efficiency and "an ingrained sense of dignity".[55] Are these standards sufficient to guide prosecutors? We also see frequent reference to prosecutors as "ministers of justice".[56] In *Boucher*, Justice Locke, speaking for himself, referred to the leading English evidence text that observed that "prosecuting counsel should regard themselves rather as ministers of justice assisting in its administration than as advocates".[57]

In *R. v. Regan*,[58] Justice Binnie described the "minister of justice" function as

---

[55] *R. v. Boucher*, [1954] S.C.J. No. 54, [1955] S.C.R. 16 at 23, 26-27, 30-31 (translation), at 24 (S.C.C.). See also *R. v. Stinchcombe*, [1991] S.C.J. No. 83, [1991] 3 S.C.R. 326 at 333 (S.C.C.).

[56] The phrase appears to date back to 1865, and *R. v. Puddick* (1865), 176 E.R. 662. *Puddick* was a sexual assault case where in his closing address, the prosecutor adversely commented on the failure of the defence to call any witnesses and, observed that an acquittal would be tantamount to convicting the complainant of perjury. Puddick was acquitted. In his reasons, Justice Crompton observed that in exercising their recently granted right to summing up the evidence where the defence calls no evidence (see section 2, *Criminal Procedure Act 1865* (28 & 29 Vict., c. 18)) prosecutors will "regard themselves as ministers of justice, and not to struggle for a conviction [. . .] nor be betrayed by feelings of professional superiority, and a contest for skill and pre-eminence." *R. v. Puddick* (1865), 176 E.R. 662 at 663.

[57] *R. v. Boucher*, [1954] S.C.J. No. 54, [1955] S.C.R. 16 at 23, 26-27, 30-31 (translation) at 26 (S.C.C.). See further: *R. v. Quesnelle*, [2014] S.C.J. No. 46, 2014 SCC 46 at para. 18 (S.C.C.); *R. v. Davey*, [2012] S.C.J. No. 75, 2012 SCC 75 at para. 32 (S.C.C.); *R. v. McNeil*, [2009] S.C.J. No. 3, 2009 SCC 3 at para. 49 (S.C.C.); *R. v. Regan*, [2002] S.C.J. No. 14, 2002 SCC 12 at paras. 64-65 (as per LeBel J.) (S.C.C.); *R. v. Stinchcombe*, [1991] S.C.J. No. 83, [1991] 3 S.C.R. 326 at 341 (S.C.C.); and *Nelles v. Ontario*, [1989] S.C.J. No. 86, [1989] 2 S.C.R. 170 at 191 (S.C.C.). In *Miazga v. Kvello Estate*, [2009] S.C.J. No. 51, 2009 SCC 51 at para. 47 (S.C.C.), Justice Charron suggested that the Crown plays a "*quasi*-judicial role as 'ministers of justice'".

[58] [2002] S.C.J. No. 14, 2002 SCC 12 at 155-156 (S.C.C.).

follows:

> The "Minister of Justice" responsibility is not confined to the courtroom and attaches to the Crown Attorney in all dealings in relation to an accused person whether before or after charges are laid. It is a responsibility "that should be conducted without feeling or animus on the part of the prosecution" . . .
>
> [There are] at least three related but somewhat distinct components to the "Minister of Justice" concept. The first is objectivity, that is to say, the duty to deal dispassionately with the facts as they are, uncoloured by subjective emotions or prejudices. The second is independence from other interests that may have a bearing on the prosecution, including the police and the defence. The third, related to the first, is lack of animus – either negative or positive – towards the suspect or accused. The Crown Attorney is expected to act in an even-handed way.[59]

The Supreme Court has also recognized that the prosecutor's "minister of justice" function does not prevent vigorous Crown advocacy which the Court in *R. v. Cook*[60] recognized as "a critical element of this country's criminal law mechanism".[61] As Justice L'Heureux-Dube held:

> Nevertheless, while it is without question that the Crown performs a special function in ensuring that justice is served and cannot adopt a purely adversarial role towards the defence [. . .] it is well recognized that the adversarial process is an important part of our judicial system and an accepted tool in our search for the truth [...] Nor should it be assumed that the Crown cannot act as a strong advocate within this adversarial process. In that regard, it is both permissible and desirable that it vigorously pursue a legitimate result to the best of its ability. [. . .] In this sense, within the boundaries outlined above, the Crown must be allowed to perform the function with which it has been entrusted; discretion in pursuing justice remains an important part of that function.[62]

In *Ethics and Criminal Law*,[63] David Layton and Michel Proulx, relying on *Cook*, argue that:

> Consequently, there is nothing wrong with Crown counsel's adopting adversarial strategies and tactics best calculated to advance the state's case, asking the trier of fact to convict where such a result is justified on the evidence, or declining to act so as to assist the accused in presenting the best possible defence. The prosecutor's distinct mission requires competent, vigorous, and thorough advocacy provided nothing is done to undermine the truth-seeking and fairness functions of the criminal justice process. One should perhaps therefore speak of a prosecutor as exercising "controlled zeal", a modified version of the traditional advocate's zeal.[64]

NOTES AND QUESTIONS

1. Do you find these various general articulations of the role of the Crown to

---

[59] [2002] S.C.J. No. 14, 2002 SCC 12 at 155-156 (S.C.C.).

[60] [1997] S.C.J. No. 22, [1997] 1 S.C.R. 1113 at para. 21 (S.C.C.).

[61] [1997] S.C.J. No. 22, [1997] 1 S.C.R. 1113 at para. 21 (S.C.C.).

[62] [1997] S.C.J. No. 22, [1997] 1 S.C.R. 1113 at para. 21 (S.C.C.). [Emphasis added].

[63] (2d ed) (Toronto: Irwin Law, 2015).

[64] David Layton and Michel Proulx, *Ethics and Criminal Law*, 2d ed. (Toronto: Irwin Law, 2015) at 586-587. (footnotes omitted).

be useful in navigating the myriad of ethical issues that arise in the course of a criminal trial?[65] Alice Woolley has argued that:

> In my view, directing prosecutors to do justice does not, in and of itself, provide useful guidance. Courts do [. . .] provide concrete direction to prosecutors as to their obligations in exercising discretion, providing disclosure to an accused, and in the conduct of a matter before and at trial. There are things that prosecutors must not do, and things that they are required to do, in the conduct of a prosecution. But those obligations follow from the demands of fairness in an adversarial trial, and from judicial determinations of what will and will not prejudice an accused or risk a miscarriage of justice, not from the highly abstract observation that a prosecutor eschews ideas of winning or losing. Principles can have content, but to do so they have to have *some* degree of specificity or something to which they refer; an entirely abstract exhortation to "do justice" is no more helpful than telling prosecutors that they ought to "be good" or "be ethical". It may be true, but it does not say much of use or interest.
>
> Further, there is some reason to be concerned about unintended negative consequences arising from telling prosecutors they are "ministers of justice". . . . lawyers have many duties with which they must comply. A prosecutor must not: abuse a witness in cross-examination; seek irrelevant or inadmissible testimony; make inflammatory opening or closing remarks; pursue trial strategies that undermine trial fairness; or fail to disclose all relevant information in their possession or control. Prosecutors who violate these obligations risk having a guilty verdict overturned, costs or damages awarded against the Crown or, in serious cases, a stay of proceedings entered. Telling prosecutors that their duty requires doing justice risks diminishing the importance of their more concrete ethical responsibilities. It implicitly encourages the prosecutor to do what seems just, even if that means ignoring her legal and ethical obligations. A prosecutor focused on "justice" might, for example, rationalize the inflammatory statement in her opening that "this trial is about . . . the difference between reasonable human beings and animals" through her own certainty of the accused's factual guilt and consequent belief that justice requires conviction, however obtained.[66]

Do you agree?

2.   Earlier in the Chapter, we asked whether the *Lyttle* "good faith" obligation

---

[65] For further discussion, see Abbe Smith, "Can You be a Good Person and a Good Prosecutor" (2001) 14 Geo. J. Leg. Ethics 355; Bruce A. Green, "Why Should Prosecutors 'Seek Justice'" (1999) 26 Fordham Urb. L.J. 607; and Fred C. Zacharias, "Structuring the Ethics of Prosecutorial Trial Practice: Can Prosecutors Do Justice?" (1991), 44 Vand. L. Rev. 45.

[66] Alice Woolley, *Understanding Lawyers' Ethics in Canada*, 2d ed. (Toronto: LexisNexis Canada, 2016) at 402-403. For a more detailed articulation of this position, and her identification of how the prosecutor's ethical obligations ought to be understood, see: Alice Woolley, "Reconceiving the Standard Conception of the Prosecutor's Role" (2017) 95:3 Cdn. Bar Rev. 795.

is a more operational ethical standard than "officer of the court" for defence counsel. Is this a more workable standard for prosecutors?

Scenario Twelve

One of the issues raised following *R. v. Ghomeshi*[67] is the proper role of the Crown in preparing witnesses in sexual assault cases. Many believed that the Crown had taken too passive a role in preparing the complainants for cross-examination. Others argued that the role of the Crown is to only present their witnesses as they find them.[68] What do you think based on the dual role of the Crown? Assume you are a Crown assigned to sexual assault prosecutions. You decide to adopt a policy of conducting mock cross-examinations to prepare the complainant for the trial in the presence of a social worker. Of course, any new information obtained during this preparation sessions will be disclosed to the defence. Have you acted ethically? In answering this question, consider *Model Code* Rules 5.4-2 and 5.4-3.

---

[67] [2016] O.J. No. 1487, 2016 ONCJ 155 (Ont. C.J.).

[68] See Alice Woolley, "What Ought Crown Counsel to do in Prosecuting Sexual Assault Charges? Some Post-Ghomeshi Reflections" (March 29, 2016), online: http://ablawg.ca/2016/03/29/ what-ought-crown-counsel-to-do-in-prosecuting-sexual-assault-charges-some-post-ghomeshi- reflections/.

[b] Who Regulates?

[i] The Law Societies

KRIEGER v. LAW SOCIETY OF ALBERTA

[2002] S.C.J. No. 45, 2002 SCC 65 (S.C.C.)

[In 1993, Douglas Ward was charged with murder. The prosecutor in the case was Craig Krieger. Prior to the preliminary inquiry, Krieger informed Ward's defence counsel that the forensic evidence results would not be available for the hearing. After the first day of the inquiry, defence counsel learned that Krieger was in possession of exculpatory test results that implicated a different person in the homicide. A complaint was filed to the Deputy Attorney General. Krieger asserted that he had no intent to withhold the results, but had delayed disclosure pending confirmation and the full results. An internal investigation concluded that the delay was unjustified. Krieger was reprimanded for making an error in judgment and removed from the case. Six months later, Ward himself filed a complaint with the Law Society of Alberta. Krieger challenged the jurisdiction of the Law Society to review the exercise of prosecutorial discretion by a Crown prosecutor or to discipline him or her for any breach of the Rules.]

IACOBUCCI AND MAJOR, J.J.

It is a constitutional principle in this country that the Attorney General must act independently of partisan concerns when supervising prosecutorial decisions. . . .

This side of the Attorney General's independence finds further form in the principle that courts will not interfere with his exercise of executive authority, as reflected in the prosecutorial decision-making process. . . .

The quasi-judicial function of the Attorney General cannot be subjected to interference from parties who are not as competent to consider the various factors involved in making a decision to prosecute. To subject such decisions to political interference, or to judicial supervision, could erode the integrity of our system of prosecution. Clearly drawn constitutional lines are necessary in areas subject to such grave potential conflict. . . .

The Law Society's Jurisdiction

We agree with the Court of Appeal that the Law Society has the jurisdiction to regulate the conduct of all Alberta lawyers. [. . .] To be a Crown prosecutor in Alberta, there are two requirements: (1) employment as such by the Attorney General's office and (2) membership in the Law Society of Alberta. To keep his or her job, a Crown prosecutor must perform to the standards of the employer, the Attorney General's office, and must remain in good standing by complying with the ethical requirements of the Law Society. All Alberta lawyers are subject to the rules of the Law Society — Crown prosecutors are no exception.

Prosecutorial Discretion

In making independent decisions on prosecutions, the Attorney General and his agents exercise what is known as prosecutorial discretion. This discretion is generally exercised directly by agents, the Crown attorneys, as it is uncommon for

442

a single prosecution to attract the Attorney General's personal attention.

"Prosecutorial discretion" is a term of art. It does not simply refer to any discretionary decision made by a Crown prosecutor. Prosecutorial discretion refers to the use of those powers that constitute the core of the Attorney General's office and which are protected from the influence of improper political and other vitiating factors by the principle of independence. . . .

. . . . .

As discussed above, these powers emanate from the office holder's role as legal advisor of and officer to the Crown. In our theory of government, it is the sovereign who holds the power to prosecute his or her subjects. A decision of the Attorney General, or of his or her agents, within the authority delegated to him or her by the sovereign is not subject to interference by other arms of government. An exercise of prosecutorial discretion will, therefore, be treated with deference by the courts and by other members of the executive, as well as statutory bodies like provincial law societies.

Without being exhaustive, we believe the core elements of prosecutorial discretion encompass the following: (a) the discretion whether to bring the prosecution of a charge laid by police; (b) the discretion to enter a stay of proceedings in either a private or public prosecution, as codified in the *Criminal Code*, R.S.C. 1985, c. C-46, ss. 579 and 579.1; (c) the discretion to accept a guilty plea to a lesser charge; (d) the discretion to withdraw from criminal proceedings altogether: *R. v. Osborne* (1975), 25 C.C.C. (2d) 405 (N.B.C.A.); and (e) the discretion to take control of a private prosecution: *R. v. Osiowy* (1989), 50 C.C.C. (3d) 189 (Sask. C.A.). While there are other discretionary decisions, these are the core of the delegated sovereign authority peculiar to the office of the Attorney General.

Significantly, what is common to the various elements of prosecutorial discretion is that they involve the ultimate decisions as to whether a prosecution should be brought, continued or ceased, and what the prosecution ought to be for. Put differently, prosecutorial discretion refers to decisions regarding the nature and extent of the prosecution and the Attorney General's participation in it. Decisions that do not go to the nature and extent of the prosecution, *i.e.*, the decisions that govern a Crown prosecutor's tactics or conduct before the court, do not fall within the scope of prosecutorial discretion. Rather, such decisions are governed by the inherent jurisdiction of the court to control its own processes once the Attorney General has elected to enter into that forum. . . .

. . . . .

Prosecutorial Discretion vs. Professional Conduct

There is a clear distinction between prosecutorial and professional conduct. It is only the latter that can be regulated by the Law Society. The Law Society has the jurisdiction to investigate any alleged breach of its ethical standards, even those committed by Crown prosecutors in connection with their prosecutory discretion. This is important as the interests of the Attorney General in promoting the administration of justice may differ from those of the Law Society in regulating the legal profession and maintaining public confidence. The remedies available to each entity differ according to their respective function. The Attorney General's office has the ability to discipline a prosecutor for failing to meet the standards set by the Attorney General's office for prosecutors but that is a different function from the ability to discipline the same prosecutor in his or her capacity as a member of the Law Society of Alberta. It may be that in some instances the conduct required by the Attorney General to retain employment will exceed the standards of the Law Society but of necessity that conduct will never be lower than that required by the Law Society. In addition, the Attorney General, after finding that a Crown prosecutor has acted in bad faith, does not have the power to restrict a member's practice or disbar a member. An Attorney General can do nothing to prevent a Crown prosecutor from practising law in another area.

Review by the Law Society for bad faith or improper purpose by a prosecutor does not constitute a review of the exercise of prosecutorial discretion *per se*, since an official action which is undertaken in bad faith or for improper motives is not within the scope of the powers of the Attorney General. As stated by McIntyre J. in his concurrence in *Nelles, supra*, at p. 211: "public officers are entitled to no special immunities or privileges when they act beyond the powers which are accorded to them by law in their official capacities". We agree with the observation of MacKenzie J. that "conduct amounting to bad faith or dishonesty is beyond the pale of prosecutorial discretion" (para. 55). A finding that the Law Society does not have the jurisdiction to review or sanction conduct which arises out of the exercise of prosecutorial discretion would mean that prosecutors who act in bad faith or dishonestly could not be disciplined for such conduct. A prosecutor who laid charges as a result of bribery or racism or revenge could be discharged from his or her office but, in spite of such malfeasance, would be immune to review of that conduct by the Law Society. . . .

. . . . .

G. *Crown Prosecutor's Failure to Disclose Relevant Exculpatory Evidence Not Within Prosecutorial Discretion*

In *Stinchcombe, supra*, the Court held that the Crown has an obligation to disclose all relevant information to the defence. While the Crown Attorney retains the discretion not to disclose irrelevant information, disclosure of relevant evidence is not, therefore, a matter of prosecutorial discretion but, rather, is a prosecutorial duty. Absent an explanation demonstrating that the Crown Attorney did not act dishonestly or in bad faith, it is settled law, *per* Sopinka J. for the Court in *Stinchcombe, supra*, at p. 339, that "[t]ransgressions with respect to this duty constitute a very serious breach of legal ethics". This is reflected in para. (d) of the Rule which applies only to breaches of the duty to disclose which involve dishonesty or bad faith.

In this case, it would appear that the respondent Krieger failed to disclose all relevant information to the defence, but later offered an explanation. If true, the failure to disclose would constitute a violation of the duty expressed in *Stinchcombe*. The explanation would help to determine if the respondent Krieger had acted dishonestly or in bad faith. If so, this would be an ethical breach and would fall within the jurisdiction of the Law Society. The Law Society in the fulfillment of their duties will determine whether the respondent acted in conformity with the professional ethics of the Law Society of Alberta. . . . The Law Society's

444

jurisdiction to review the respondent's failure to disclose relevant evidence to the defendant is limited to examining whether it was an ethical violation. As explained by M. Proulx and D. Layton in *Ethics and Canadian Criminal Law* (2001), at p. 657:

> It is worth underlining that not every breach of the legal and constitutional duty to disclose constitutes a violation of an ethical duty. Non-disclosure can result, for instance, from mere inadvertence, a misunderstanding of the nature of the evidence, or even a questionable strategy adopted in good faith. These lapses may represent a denial of the accused's constitutional rights, but an ethical violation often requires more. A finding of professional misconduct must be based upon an act or omission revealing an intentional departure from the fundamental duty to act in fairness. Thus, a judicial determination that disclosure has wrongfully been withheld will not necessarily reveal a breach of ethics. Conversely, an egregious breach of ethics may in some cases have no appreciable effect on the fairness of the trial, when appropriate remedies can cure any harm suffered by the accused.

In light of the foregoing analysis, we answer the issues in this appeal as follows. The Rule is *intra vires* the Act and the Legislature of Alberta. The Law Society has jurisdiction to review the conduct of a prosecutor to determine whether the prosecutor acted dishonestly or in bad faith in failing to disclose relevant information to an accused in a timely manner, notwithstanding that his employer, the Attorney General, has reviewed it from the perspective of an employer.

NOTES AND QUESTIONS

1.   The *Model Code* provides the following with respect to prosecutors:

Duty as Prosecutor

5.1-3 When acting as a prosecutor, a lawyer must act for the public and the administration of justice resolutely and honourably within the limits of the law while treating the tribunal with candour, fairness, courtesy and respect.

Commentary

[1] When engaged as a prosecutor, the lawyer's primary duty is not to seek to convict but to see that justice is done through a fair trial on the merits. The prosecutor exercises a public function involving much discretion and power and must act fairly and dispassionately. The prosecutor should not do anything that might prevent the accused from being represented by counsel or communicating with counsel and, to the extent required by law and accepted practice, should make timely disclosure to defence counsel or directly to an unrepresented accused of all relevant and known facts and witnesses, whether tending to show guilt or innocence.

2.   As both *Krieger* and Commentary 1 make clear, there is an ethical duty and constitutional obligation on the Crown to disclose all relevant evidence to the defence that is not privileged or subject to another legal disclosure/ production regime. Indeed, a Director of Crown Operations in Toronto once advised his staff "If in doubt, give it out".[69] Why is Crown disclosure so important?

---

[69] Christine McGoey, "The "Good" Criminal Law Barrister – A Crown Perspective" (Second Colloquia on the Legal Profession, 2004) at 4-11.

3. In what circumstances should the law societies investigate or discipline prosecutors who have been sanctioned by the provincial or federal Attorney General's office? What should the standard be – bad faith, dishonesty or negligence?

4. Do you think there is a systemic problem of a lack of accountability for prosecutorial misconduct by the law societies? Alice Woolley observes that:

> Law societies have, however, shown themselves extremely reluctant to discipline prosecutors on any grounds at all; in 2014, the *Toronto Star* reported that, of 2,200 disciplinary hearings held by the Law Society of Upper Canada in the preceding 23 years, only nine involved prosecutors.[70]

Scenario Thirteen

The accused is charged with attempted murder. The Crown and defence agree on a plea to aggravated assault and a joint submission on sentencing of two years. The day before court proceedings, the victim dies in an unrelated car accident. You are the Crown. Do you advise defence counsel of the victim's death?

Scenario Fourteen

The accused is charged with multiple drug offences. Before trial, defence counsel learns that the lead investigator was involved in drug-related misconduct that led to both internal discipline proceedings under the *Police Services Act*[71] and criminal charges. Defence counsel writes to the Crown and asks for disclosure of all materials relating to the misconduct. The Crown writes back: "Look, we both have read *Stinchcombe*. I am only required to disclose material in my possession. The records you are seeking are not in my possession." Has the Crown acted ethically?[72]

[ii] Attorney General

Regulation of the conduct of prosecutors also occurs internally by the Attorney General. As the British Columbia Court of Appeal noted in *British Columbia (Attorney General) v. Davies*[73]:

> Prosecutorial discretion, ultimately, rests with the Attorney General. As the Attorney General concedes on this appeal, he is entitled to establish a system to review exercises of prosecutorial discretion, and for improving the policies that govern its exercise. He is also entitled to take steps to satisfy the public that prosecutorial discretion is being exercised in a principled way. The Attorney General is in a unique position to gauge the necessity for a public airing of issues

---

[70] *Understanding Lawyers' Ethics in Canada*, 2d ed. (Toronto: LexisNexis Canada, 2016) at 418, referring to Jennifer Paglioro, Jayme Poisson, "Ontario fails to track complaints against Crown Attorneys", *The Toronto Star* (December 16, 2014).

[71] R.S.O. 1990, c. P.15.

[72] See *R. v. McNeil*, [2009] S.C.J. No. 3, 2009 SCC 3 at paras. 23-25, 48-51 (S.C.C.).

[73] [2009] B.C.J. No. 1469, 2009 BCCA 337 at para. 77 (B.C.C.A.), leave to appeal refused [2009] S.C.C.A. No. 421 (S.C.C.).

surrounding prosecutorial discretion, and to balance the need for prosecutorial independence with public accountability.[74]

To assist prosecutors in the exercise of their discretion and to promote ethical decision-making as advocates, we have begun to see the publication of guidelines for prosecutors. In Ontario, for example, the Ministry of the Attorney General in 2005 created a Crown Policy Manual, now available online.[75] Federally, the Director of Public Prosecutions has published the following guidelines:[76]

PUBLIC PROSECUTION SERVICE OF CANADA DESKBOOK

Department of Justice Canada, March 1, 2014

2.1 Duties and Responsibilities of Crown Counsel

2.2. The duty to ensure that the mandate of the Director is carried out with integrity and dignity

Counsel fulfill this duty by:

- complying with their bar association's applicable rules of ethics;
- complying with the Public Prosecution Service of Canada (PPSC) Code of Conduct;
- exercising careful judgment in presenting the case for the Crown, in deciding whether or not to oppose bail, in deciding what witnesses to call, and what evidence to tender;
- acting with moderation, fairness, and impartiality;
- conducting oneself with civility;
- not discriminating on any basis prohibited by s. 15 of the *Canadian Charter of Rights and Freedoms* (Charter);
- adequately preparing for each case;
- remaining independent of the police or investigative agency while working closely with it; and
- conducting resolution discussions in a manner consistent with the DPP guideline. [. . .]

2.3. The duty to be fair and to maintain public confidence in prosecutorial fairness

In order to maintain public confidence in the administration of justice, Crown counsel must not only act fairly; their conduct must be seen to be fair. One can act fairly while unintentionally leaving an impression of secrecy, bias or unfairness.

---

[74] [2009] B.C.J. No. 1469, 2009 BCCA 337 at para. 77 (B.C.C.A.), leave to appeal refused [2009] S.C.C.A. No. 421 (S.C.C.).

[75] Available online: https://www.attorneygeneral.jus.gov.on.ca/english/crim/cpm/.

[76] Department of Justice Canada, *The Public Prosecution Service of Canada Deskbook* (Ottawa: Department of Justice, 2014), (March 1, 2014), online: http://www.ppsc.gc.ca/eng/pub/fpsd-sfpg/index.html (footnotes omitted).

Counsel fulfil this duty by:

- making disclosure in accordance with the law;

- bringing all relevant cases and authorities known to counsel to the attention of the court, even if they may be contrary to the Crown's position;

- not misleading the court;

- not expressing personal opinions on the evidence, including the credibility of witnesses or on the guilt or innocence of the accused in court or in public. Such expressions of opinion are improper;

- not adverting to any unproven facts, even if they are material and could have been admitted as evidence;

- asking relevant and proper questions during the examination of a witness and not asking questions designed solely to embarrass, insult, abuse, belittle, or demean the witness. Cross examination can be skilful and probing, yet still show respect for the witness The law distinguishes between a cross-examination that is "persistent and exhaustive", which is proper, and a cross-examination that is "abusive";

- stating the law accurately in oral pleadings;

- respecting defence counsel, the accused, and the proceedings while vigorously asserting the Crown's position, and not publicly and improperly criticizing defence strategy;

- respecting the court and judicial decisions and not publicly disparaging judgments; and

- avoiding themselves engaging in active "judge shopping".

2.4. The duty to maintain objectivity

Counsel fulfill this duty by:

- being aware of the dangers of tunnel vision and ensure they review the evidence in an objective, rigorous and thorough manner in assessing the strength of the evidence emanating from the police investigation throughout the proceedings;

- exercising particular care regarding actual and perceived objectivity when involved in an investigation at the pre-charge stage;

- making all necessary inquiries regarding potentially relevant evidence;

- never permitting personal interests or partisan political considerations to interfere with the proper exercise of prosecutorial discretion; and

- not exceeding the scope of appropriate opening remarks, for example elevating the role of Crown counsel in the eyes of the jury to the custodian of the public interest.

2.4.1. Inflammatory remarks and conduct

As part of the Crown's duty to be fair, counsel are obliged to ensure that any comments made during jury addresses are not "inflammatory". Whether an address will be considered to be inflammatory is determined by looking at the number and nature of the comments, the specific language used and the overall tone of counsel's address. Inflammatory conduct or comments could render a trial unfair.

The kinds of comments and conduct that the courts have found to be "inflammatory" (and thus could render the trial unfair) can be divided into six categories:

- Expressions of personal opinion
    - These include opinions on the honesty and integrity of police witnesses; that Crown counsel does not believe the accused; or on the guilt of the accused.

- Inappropriately negative comments about the accused's or a witness's credibility or character
    - Such comments include characterizations of the accused as a liar, excessive use of sarcasm, ridicule, derision or exaggeration in referring to the accused or defence witnesses, excessive reference to the accused's criminal record, native country.

- Observations or statements of fact not supported by the evidence
    - These situations include ones in which Crown counsel misstates the evidence in a way which impugns the accused's character.

- Appeals to fear, emotion or prejudice
    - These comments are often *in terrorem* arguments in which Crown counsel urges the jury to protect society from the accused, who is portrayed in very unflattering terms.

- Negative comments about defence counsel or defence strategy
    - Crown counsel shall not suggest that defence counsel have used improper tactics, presented illegal evidence or made other comments designed solely to portray defence counsel as being untrustworthy.

- Inappropriate language, tactics, and conduct in general
    - Inappropriate tactics include:
        - not placing before the court all the circumstances surrounding the obtaining of statements from the accused;
        - in cross-examination of the accused, while professing to test his credibility, bringing various matters before the jury which have no relevance to the issues at trial;
        - at the conclusion of the evidence given by the accused in his defence, stating in the presence of the jury that the accused will be arrested for perjury;
        - improperly presenting evidence to the jury through the device of reading from reports of judgments of the Supreme Court of Canada and other courts;
        - raising a "concoction theory" based on Crown disclosure for the first time in the closing address.

NOTES AND QUESTIONS

1. Should internal discipline of prosecutors be made public?[77]

2. Do you think that guidelines like these provide more guidance to prosecutors than the exhortation to act as a "minister of justice"?

3. Do these guidelines constitute "law" that can be relied upon in court?[78] Can they be used by the Law Society in disciplinary proceedings?

4. As we work through the problems in the rest of this Chapter consider the extent to which these guidelines were useful.

[iii] Courts

The Courts and our common law (*i.e.*, tort of malicious prosecution) also have a role to play in regulating the conduct of prosecutors. In the following case, the issue was whether prosecutors are constitutionally obligated to take into account an accused's Aboriginal status when deciding whether to seek a mandatory minimum sentence.

R. v. ANDERSON

[2014] S.C.J. No. 41, 2014 SCC 41 (S.C.C.)

MOLDAVER, J.

There are two distinct avenues for judicial review of Crown decision making. The analysis will differ depending on which of the following is at issue: (1) exercises of prosecutorial discretion; or (2) tactics and conduct before the court.

All Crown decision making is reviewable for abuse of process. However, as I will explain, exercises of prosecutorial discretion are *only* reviewable for abuse of process. In contrast, tactics and conduct before the court are subject to a wider range of review. The court may exercise its inherent jurisdiction to control its own processes even in the absence of abuse of process.

(a) *Prosecutorial Discretion*

This Court has repeatedly affirmed that prosecutorial discretion is a necessary part of a properly functioning criminal justice system . . . In *Miazga v. Kvello Estate*, [2009] 3 S.C.R. 339, at para. 47, the fundamental importance of prosecutorial discretion was said to lie, "not in protecting the interests of individual Crown attorneys, but in advancing the public interest by enabling prosecutors to make discretionary decisions in fulfilment of their professional obligations without fear of judicial or political interference, thus fulfilling their *quasi*-judicial role as 'ministers of justice'". . . .

Unfortunately, subsequent to this Court's decision in *Krieger v. Law Society of Alberta*, [2002] 3 S.C.R. 372, confusion has arisen as to what is meant by "prosecutorial discretion" and the law has become cloudy. The present appeal provides an opportunity for clarification.

---

[77] See Jacques Gallant, "Critics decry secretive discipline system for Crown Attorneys" *The Toronto Star* (September 24, 2016).

[78] See *R. v. Stobbe*, [2011] M.J. No. 457, 2011 MBQB 280 at para. 47 (Man. Q.B.).

. . . . .

Since *Krieger*, courts have struggled with the distinction between prosecutorial discretion, and tactics and conduct. The use of the word "core" in *Krieger* has led to a narrow definition of prosecutorial discretion, notwithstanding the expansive language used in *Krieger* to define the term, namely: ". . . decisions regarding the nature and extent of the prosecution and the Attorney General's participation in it" (para. 47). Difficulty in defining the term has also led to confusion regarding the standard of review by which particular Crown decisions are to be assessed.

. . . . .

In an effort to clarify, I think we should start by recognizing that the term "prosecutorial discretion" is an expansive term that covers all "decisions regarding the nature and extent of the prosecution and the Attorney General's participation in it" (*Krieger*, at para. 47). As this Court has repeatedly noted, "[p]rosecutorial discretion refers to the discretion exercised by the Attorney-General <u>in matters within his authority</u> in relation to the prosecution of criminal offences" (*Krieger*, at para. 44, citing *Power*, at p. 622, quoting D. Vanek, "Prosecutorial Discretion" (1988), 30 *Crim. L.Q.* 219, at p. 219 (Emphasis added)). While it is likely impossible to create an exhaustive list of the decisions that fall within the nature and extent of a prosecution, further examples to those in *Krieger* include: the decision to repudiate a plea agreement (as in *R. v. Nixon*, [2011] 2 S.C.R. 566); the decision to pursue a dangerous offender application; the decision to prefer a direct indictment; the decision to charge multiple offences; the decision to negotiate a plea; the decision to proceed summarily or by indictment; and the decision to initiate an appeal. All pertain to the nature and extent of the prosecution. As can be seen, many stem from the provisions of the *Code* itself, including the decision in this case to tender the Notice.

In sum, prosecutorial discretion applies to a wide range of prosecutorial decision making. That said, care must be taken to distinguish matters of prosecutorial discretion from constitutional obligations. The distinction between prosecutorial discretion and the constitutional obligations of the Crown was made in *Krieger*, where the prosecutor's duty to disclose relevant evidence to the accused was at issue

. . .

Manifestly, the Crown possesses no discretion to breach the *Charter* rights of an accused. In other words, prosecutorial discretion provides no shield to a Crown prosecutor who has failed to fulfill his or her constitutional obligations such as the duty to provide proper disclosure to the defence.

(i) The Standard of Review for Prosecutorial Discretion

The many decisions that Crown prosecutors are called upon to make in the exercise of their prosecutorial discretion must not be subjected to routine second-guessing by the courts. The courts have long recognized that decisions involving prosecutorial discretion are unlike other decisions made by the executive: see M. Code, "Judicial Review of Prosecutorial Decisions: A Short History of Costs and Benefits, in Response to Justice Rosenberg" (2009), 34 *Queen's L.J.* 863, at p. 867. Judicial non-interference with prosecutorial discretion has been referred to as a "matter of principle based on the doctrine of separation of powers as well as a matter of policy

451

founded on the efficiency of the system of criminal justice" which also recognizes that prosecutorial discretion is "especially ill-suited to judicial review": *Power*, at p. 623 . . .

. . . . .

Manifestly, prosecutorial discretion is entitled to considerable deference. It is not, however, immune from all judicial oversight. This Court has repeatedly affirmed that prosecutorial discretion is reviewable for abuse of process: *Krieger*, at para. 32; *Nixon*, at para. 31; *Miazga*, at para. 46.

The jurisprudence pertaining to the review of prosecutorial discretion has employed a range of terminology to describe the type of prosecutorial conduct that constitutes abuse of process. In *Krieger*, this Court used the term "flagrant impropriety" (para. 49). In *Nixon*, the Court held that the abuse of process doctrine is available where there is evidence that the Crown's decision "undermines the integrity of the judicial process" or "results in trial unfairness" (para. 64). The Court also referred to "improper motive[s]" and "bad faith" in its discussion (para. 68).

Regardless of the precise language used, the key point is this: abuse of process refers to Crown conduct that is egregious and seriously compromises trial fairness and/or the integrity of the justice system. Crown decisions motivated by prejudice against Aboriginal persons would certainly meet this standard.

In sum, prosecutorial discretion is reviewable solely for abuse of process. . . .

(ii) The Threshold Evidentiary Burden

The burden of proof for establishing abuse of process lies on the claimant, who must prove it on a balance of probabilities: *Cook*, at para. 62; *R. v. O'Connor*, [1995] 4 S.C.R. 411, at para. 69, *per* L'Heureux-Dubé J.; *R. v. Jolivet*, [2000] 1 S.C.R. 751, at para. 19. However, given the unique nature of prosecutorial discretion — specifically, the fact that the Crown will typically (if not always) be the only party who will know *why* a particular decision was made — this Court in *Nixon* recognized that where prosecutorial discretion is challenged, the Crown may be required to provide reasons justifying its decision where the claimant establishes a proper evidentiary foundation: para. 60.

In *Nixon*, this Court noted the following reasons as to why there must be a "proper evidentiary foundation" before the abuse of process claim should proceed:

> Quite apart from any such pragmatic considerations, there is good reason to impose a threshold burden on the applicant who alleges that an act of prosecutorial discretion constitutes an abuse of process. Given that such decisions are generally beyond the reach of the court, it is not sufficient to launch an inquiry for an applicant to make a bare allegation of abuse of process... paras. 61-62] . . .

. . . . .

Requiring the claimant to establish a proper evidentiary foundation before embarking on an inquiry into the reasons behind the exercise of prosecutorial discretion respects the presumption that prosecutorial discretion is exercised in good faith: *Application under s. 83.28 of the Criminal Code (Re)*, [2004] 2 S.C.R. 248, at para. 95. It also accords with this Court's statement in *Sriskandarajah*, at para. 27, that "prosecutorial authorities are not bound to provide reasons for their decisions,

<u>absent evidence</u> of bad faith or improper motives" (Emphasis added).

Finally, I note that the content of a Crown policy or guideline may be relevant when a court is considering a challenge to the exercise of prosecutorial discretion. Policy statements or guidelines are capable of informing the debate as to whether a Crown prosecutor's conduct was appropriate in the particular circumstances. See R. J. Frater, *Prosecutorial Misconduct* (2009), at p. 259. For example, a decision by a Crown prosecutor that appears to contravene a Crown policy or guideline may provide some evidence that assists the claimant in establishing the threshold evidentiary foundation. However, as the intervener the Director of Public Prosecutions of Canada submits, Crown policies and guidelines do not have the force of law, and cannot themselves be subjected to *Charter* scrutiny in the abstract: see *R. v. Beaudry*, [2007] 1 S.C.R. 190, at para. 45 (discussing police practices manuals).

(b) *Tactics and Conduct Before the Court*

The second category in the framework for review of Crown activity was referred to in *Krieger* as "tactics or conduct before the court": para. 47. As stated in *Krieger*, "such decisions are governed by the inherent jurisdiction of the court to control its own processes once the Attorney General has elected to enter into that forum" (para. 47).

Superior courts possess inherent jurisdiction to ensure that the machinery of the court functions in an orderly and effective manner . . . Similarly, in order to function as courts of law, statutory courts have implicit powers that derive from the court's authority to control its own process . . . This jurisdiction includes the power to penalize counsel for ignoring rulings or orders, or for inappropriate behaviour such as tardiness, incivility, abusive cross-examination, improper opening or closing addresses or inappropriate attire. Sanctions may include orders to comply, adjournments, extensions of time, warnings, cost awards, dismissals, and contempt proceedings.

While deference is not owed to counsel who are behaving inappropriately in the courtroom, our adversarial system *does* accord a high degree of deference to the tactical decisions of counsel. In other words, while courts may sanction the conduct of the *litigants*, they should generally refrain from interfering with the conduct of the *litigation* itself. In *R. v. S.G.T.*, [2010] 1 S.C.R. 688, at paras. 36-37, this Court explained why judges should be very cautious before interfering with tactical decisions:

> In an adversarial system of criminal trials, trial judges must, barring exceptional circumstances, defer to the tactical decisions of counsel . . . . [C]ounsel will generally be in a better position to assess the wisdom, in light of their overall trial strategy, of a particular tactical decision than is the trial judge. By contrast, trial judges are expected to be impartial arbiters of the dispute before them; the more a trial judge second-guesses or overrides the decisions of counsel, the greater is the risk that the trial judge will, in either appearance or reality, cease being a neutral arbiter and instead become an advocate for one party. . . .

The corollary of the preceding is that trial judges should seldom take it upon themselves, let alone be required, to second-guess the tactical decisions of counsel. Of course, trial judges are still required to "make sure that [the trial] remains fair and is conducted in accordance with the relevant laws and the principles of fundamental justice" . . .

Crown counsel is entitled to have a trial strategy and to modify it as the trial unfolds, provided that the modification does not result in unfairness to the accused: *Jolivet*, at para. 21. Likewise, as this Court recently held in *R. v. Auclair*, [2014] 1 S.C.R. 83, a judge may exceptionally override a Crown tactical decision in order to prevent a Charter violation.

Finally, as with all Crown decision making, courtroom tactics or conduct may amount to abuse of process, but abuse of process is not a precondition for judicial intervention as it is for matters of prosecutorial discretion.

VI. Conclusion

. . . . .

For these reasons, I conclude that [the decision whether to seek a mandatory minimum sentence] is a matter of prosecutorial discretion. As a result, it is reviewable only for abuse of process. In the complete absence of any evidence to support it, Mr. Anderson's abuse of process argument must fail.

As a final matter, I note that the s. 15(1) *Charter* challenge to the constitutionality of the statutory scheme was not pursued before this Court. These reasons should not be taken as endorsing the trial judge's analysis or conclusion with respect to that issue.

NOTES AND QUESTIONS

1. The Court in this case held that an "abuse of process refers to Crown conduct that is egregious and seriously compromises trial fairness and/or the integrity of the justice system". Do you think that standard is appropriate? Too rigorous? Insufficiently rigorous?

2. The Court in this case was considering how to review prosecutorial discretion in relation to sentencing decisions. Courts will also, as noted earlier, review exercises of prosecutorial discretion where there are allegations that a prior criminal prosecution constituted "malicious prosecution". The Court has imposed a stringent standard for reviewing decisions by prosecutors in those cases as well, holding that the prosecutor must have acted for some improper purpose in bringing forward the prosecution — that they must have "deliberately intended to subvert or abuse the office of the Attorney General or the process of criminal justice".[79] The prosecutor must have done more than demonstrate "incompetence, inexperience, poor judgment, lack of professionalism, laziness, recklessness, honest mistake, negligence, or even gross negligence".[80] Actual malfeasance must be shown. Do you think that standard is appropriate? Ought there to be different considerations in reviewing an exercise of discretion after an acquittal than are at play prior to trial?

---

[79] *Miazga v. Kvello Estate*, [2009] S.C.J. No. 51, 2009 SCC 51 at para. 89 (S.C.C.).

[80] *Miazga v. Kvello Estate*, [2009] S.C.J. No. 51, 2009 SCC 51 at para. 81 (S.C.C.).

3.   Which body do you think is best suited to restrain improper exercises of prosecutorial discretion or abusive trial conduct: law societies, the Attorney General or the courts? Does the answer depend on whether you are considering prosecutorial discretion or abusive trial conduct?

[c]   Exercising Prosecutorial Discretion

[i]   Charging/Screening Decisions

Outside of British Columbia, Quebec and New Brunswick, prosecutors in Canada are generally not involved in the decision whether to lay a charge. Once a charge is laid by the police, the Crown is responsible for screening the charge(s) and deciding whether there should be a trial. It is well-established that a prosecutor should only prosecute an offence where there is a reasonable prospect of conviction;[81] and, it is in the public interest to do so.[82] Are mandatory charge/prosecution policies that remove prosecutorial discretion in the public interest? Consider the following case.

R. v. K. (M.)

[1992] M.J. No. 334, 74 C.C.C. (3d) 108 (Man. C.A.)

O'SULLIVAN, J.A.

The crime rate in Winnipeg has been rising dramatically. The situation has got so bad that many women are afraid to walk the streets at night without being accompanied. Houses are broken into with great regularity. There are street muggings and sexual assaults. An overburdened police force is having trouble coping with all the complaints of violence and crime. The case now before us is an example of why the state authorities are unable to cope with burgeoning crime. Instead of going after real criminals, men and women who wantonly attack innocent

---

[81] See *Henry v. British Columbia (Attorney General)*, [2015] S.C.J. No. 24, 2015 SCC 24 at para. 61 (S.C.C.). The test for reasonable prospect of conviction is higher than the test used at a preliminary inquiry or at trial (at the end of the Crown's case) to determine whether there is sufficient evidence to move the case forward. That sufficiency test simply looks at whether there is some evidence on all of the essential elements of the offence. As noted by the Public Prosecution Deskbook, (Department of Justice Canada, *The Public Prosecution Service of Canada Deskbook* (Ottawa: Department of Justice, March 1, 2014), online: http://www.ppsc. gc.ca/eng/pub/fpsd-sfpg/index.html (footnotes omitted)) at 2.3:

> A proper assessment of the evidence will take into account such matters as the availability, competence and compellability of witnesses and their likely impression on the trier of fact, as well as the admissibility of evidence implicating the accused. Crown counsel should also consider any defences that are plainly open to or have been indicated by the accused [. . .] Crown counsel must also zealously guard against the possibility that they have been afflicted by "tunnel vision", through close contact with the police or investigative agency, or victims, such that the assessment is insufficiently rigorous and objective.

[82] Relevant considerations in determining public interest include the nature of the alleged offence; the nature of the harm caused by or the consequences of the alleged offence; the circumstances, consequences to and attitude of victims; the level of culpability and circumstances of the accused; the need to protect sources of information; and confidence in the administration of justice. See Public Prosecution Deskbook, note 79, at 2.3.

neighbours, the whole engine of the state has been concentrated in this case on the prosecution of a citizen who has been accused of using excessive force in the disciplining of his children.

K. (M.) was charged with assaulting his two boys, aged eight and six. He was acquitted of the charge of assaulting the younger of the boys. With respect to the eight-year-old, he was acquitted of the charge of assault occasioning bodily harm, but was convicted of simple assault. He was given a conditional discharge by Meyers Prov. Ct. J. and ordered to take counselling courses in an effort to control his anger. He appeals to this court.

In my opinion, this is a case which should never have come to the courts. I do not understand the policy of the Ministry of Justice which apparently believes that the full force of the criminal law should be brought to bear against a father who in good faith administers punishment to his son in a manner which the trial judge deemed to be excessive, but which was well within the range of what has been generally accepted by parents in this province over the years. It sounds nice to say we will have zero tolerance for domestic violence, but the result of such a policy is a case such as we have here where a family is torn apart by judicial proceedings.

I shudder to think what would have happened to my father or my mother if they had got caught in the toils of the law enforcement authorities as administered by the current Department of Justice. The discipline administered to the boy in question in these proceedings was mild indeed compared to the discipline I received in my home. There were times when I thought my parents were too strict, but in retrospect I am glad that my parents were not subjected to prosecution or persecution for attempting to keep the children in my family in line.

The incident out of which the main charge arose happened on a Sunday afternoon. The accused decided to take a nap because he had been called out to work that weekend by the city as a power engineer on emergency calls. His wife took the three children to a school tea. While having the nap, the accused received a phone call from a co-worker wondering why the accused's name had been in the newspaper. On inquiry the accused was told to look at a certain page of the newspaper and there, behold, the accused saw that his house was up for mortgage sale. When his wife came home with the kids he confronted her, but she said it was all due to a mistake. In actual fact what had happened was that she had made off with six mortgage payments each of over $500 which he had given her to pay. She spent the money instead of paying the mortgage, but she was afraid to own up to her defalcation.

In this setting, the eight-year-old child decided to open a packet of sunflower seeds which he had brought back from the tea. Both father and mother told him not to do so for fear of spilling the seeds on the carpet in the way of the two-year-old child playing nearby. But the boy decided to open the packet of sunflower seeds notwithstanding his parents' admonition. Sure enough the seeds fell on the carpet. While the eight-year-old was attempting to pick up the fallen seeds, the two-year-old got hold of some of the seeds and started to choke. There was a great outcry as the little boy was saved from choking. Then the father decided the boy should be punished for his actions and in the process he administered more force than the judge thought reasonable in the circumstances.

The judge could understand spanking and even hitting, but he felt he could not condone kicking of the child. The kick was described by the father as a "coup de grace". It was administered with his stockinged foot as a prelude to sending the boy to bed. The wife took the children to Osborne House (a hostel for abused families) where she complained her husband was a child abuser. Police were called, statements taken, an arrest was made. She attempted to reconcile, writing an apology to her husband but it was of no avail. The full force of the criminal law was used against the accused and the policy of the Minister of Justice appears to be that, once set in motion, the law cannot be stopped.

In my opinion, it is not sound policy to mandate that every violation of the law requires the laying of charges. That policy has the undesirable effect of nullifying prosecutorial discretion; such discretion should be exercised in favour of values in society such as family life. In my opinion, such prosecutorial discretion is subject to judicial review. . . .

We are invited by counsel to determine in this case what degree of force in disciplining a child is reasonable. It is said that allowing the appeal means we are saying that a father may kick his child as he pleases. On the other hand, it is said that by dismissing the appeal we will be protecting children from being kicked by their parents or anyone else. I do not regard my task as one of determining whether a child may be kicked or not. A case of this kind cannot be judged by a nice calculation of the degree of force used in this particular case. The answer to this appeal is, in my opinion, that this case should never have been proceeded with. That being the case, I would favour granting leave to appeal and ordering a stay of the proceedings.

Appeal allowed; stay of proceedings entered.

NOTES AND QUESTIONS

1. If you were the prosecutor would you have withdrawn the charge? Please explain.

2. Are you more troubled by the prosecution or the comments of the Court of Appeal?

3. From the perspective of fulfilling their ethical obligations, what are the pros and cons of mandatory policies? In his article "The Attorney General and the Administration of Criminal Justice", Justice Marc Rosenberg observed, in the context, of Crown guidelines, more generally, that:

> On the one hand, making the policies more transparent can help avoid abuses caused by idiosyncratic decision-making where discretion is exercised on the basis of stereotypes and prejudice. Decisions made on the basis of clear and fair guidelines promote equality within the criminal justice system. On the other hand, some of the desirable flexibility has left the system, leaving prosecutors uncertain about the degree to which they can exercise discretion in accordance with compassion and the particular case. Highly publicized zero-tolerance policies can have unforeseen and potentially disastrous consequences, not only for individuals, but also for the public interest as complainants flee the criminal justice system for fear that it will overreact to their complaints.[83]

---

[83] (2009) 34 Queen's L.J. 813 at 851.

In the context of exercising discretion at the bail stage, Justice Casey Hill held in *R. v. Brooks*:[84]

> Crown counsel are expected to exercise discretion to consent to bail in appropriate cases and to oppose release where justified. That discretion must be informed, fairly exercised, and respectful of prevailing jurisprudential authorities. Opposing bail in every case, or without exception where a particular crime is charged, or because of a victim's wishes without regard to individual liberty concerns of the arrestee, derogates from the prosecutor's role as a minister of justice and as a guardian of the civil rights of all persons.[85]

Scenario Fifteen

On a cold winter night, the police took an Indigenous man into custody. Earlier in the day, he had been held in their "drunk tank" for a few hours. That night, however, a decision was made to not keep him. The police drove him to an alleyway and left him there. Within a few hours, he died of hypothermia. Acute alcohol intoxication was determined to be one factor in his death. The police have approached you whether to prosecute the two officers who left him in the alleyway for criminal negligence causing death.[86] What factors will you take into consideration?[87]

Scenario Sixteen

In an effort to address the high rates of "unfounded" determinations by police in sexual assault cases,[88] a province is considering assigning a Crown to each police station to assist in the interview of sexual assault complainants. Do you think that this is a good idea?[89] Is there a difference between deciding whether charges should be laid and interviewing witnesses?

Scenario Seventeen

The police charge the accused with robbery. You are the trial Crown. You have reviewed the file and believe that there is sufficient evidence to convict. However, the case involves cross-racial identification evidence and you wouldn't be convinced beyond a reasonable doubt if you were the judge. Are you ethically obligated to withdraw the charge?[90] What would you do?

---

[84] [2001] O.J. No. 1563, 153 C.C.C. (3d) 533 (Ont. S.C.J.).

[85] [2001] O.J. No. 1563, 153 C.C.C. (3d) 533 at para. 22 (Ont. S.C.J.).

[86] Criminal negligence is defined in section 219 of the *Criminal Code* as "doing anything" that "shows wanton or reckless disregard for the lives or safety of other persons". The fault requirement is marked and substantial departure from the conduct expected of a reasonable person in the circumstances.

[87] See Davies Commission, "Alone and Cold: Criminal Justice Branch Response" (2011), online: http://www2.gov.bc.ca/assets/gov/law-crime-and-justice/about-bc-justice-system/inquiries/daviescommission-finalreport.pdf.

[88] Robyn Doolittle, "Why Police Dismiss 1 In 5 Sexual Assault Claims As Baseless" The *Globe and Mail* (February 3, 2017), online: http://www.theglobeandmail.com/news/investigations/unfounded-sexual-assault-canada-main/article33891309/.

[89] See *R. v. Regan*, [2002] S.C.J. No. 14, 2002 SCC 12 at paras. 67-86 (S.C.C.).

[90] See *R. v. Proulx*, [2001] S.C.J. No. 65, 2001 SCC 66 at para. 31 (S.C.C.).

Scenario Eighteen

The accused is charged with weapons offences. The defence alleged that the accused was compelled to store the contraband by another person who threatened him with physical harm. On the Charter motion to exclude his statements to the police, the accused testified about threats made by this person. The Charter application is dismissed. Prior to the commencement of the trial, a resolution meeting is held. At the meeting, the Crown indicates that if the accused were to provide an induced statement in which he would admit that his evidence on the Charter application was false, and that his counsel knew it to be false, the Crown would recommend a conditional sentence. Has the Crown acted ethically? What are the concerns raised?[91]

[ii]   Plea bargaining

R. v. NIXON

[2011] S.C.J. No. 34, 2011 SCC 34 (S.C.C.)

CHARRON, J.

The appellant, Ms. Nixon, was charged with several *Criminal Code*, R.S.C. 1985, c. C-46, offences, including dangerous driving causing death, dangerous driving causing bodily harm, and parallel charges for impaired driving. The charges arose as a result of a motor vehicle accident which occurred on September 2, 2006. The Crown alleged that Ms. Nixon drove her motor home through an intersection without stopping and struck another vehicle, killing a husband and wife and injuring their young son. A roadside screening test was administered at the scene, followed by breath samples which resulted in readings of 200 mg of alcohol in 100 mL of blood. Expert extrapolation concluded that Ms. Nixon's blood alcohol level would have been between 225 and 250 mg per 100 mL at the time of the accident.

Given that Ms. Nixon elected trial by judge and jury, the matter proceeded to a preliminary inquiry on March 1, 2007. Crown counsel who had carriage of the case at the time had concerns about some of the evidence, in particular the admissibility of the breathalyzer results and the probative value of the eyewitness evidence that a motor home had been seen driving erratically some time before the accident. Based on his assessment, Crown counsel did not adduce the breath sample results at the preliminary hearing, although he specifically reserved the right to call this evidence at trial. He also informed the presiding judge that the Crown would not be seeking a committal on any charge other than the dangerous driving counts. Ms. Nixon consented to a committal order on the dangerous driving charges.

Following the preliminary inquiry, additional discussions were held between counsel during the first weeks of May 2007 regarding a plea to a charge of careless driving under the *Traffic Safety Act*, R.S.A. 2000, c. T-6, with a joint sentence recommendation for a $1,800 fine. Counsel ultimately entered into a written agreement to that effect on May 22, and Ms. Nixon re-elected her mode of trial in anticipation of entering a guilty plea to the lesser charge on June 5.

---

[91] See *R. v. Delchev*, [2015] O.J. No. 2710, 2015 ONCA 381 (Ont. C.A.). See further, *R. v. Nixon*, [2011] S.C.J. No. 34, 2011 SCC 34 (S.C.C.).

Before making the offer for a plea resolution, Crown counsel had discussed the matter in general terms with some of his colleagues in the Crown's office, including his immediate supervisor who reluctantly agreed with the terms of the proposed agreement. Due to the sensitive nature of the case, a report was also prepared for senior officials in the justice department. When the Acting Assistant Deputy Minister ("ADM") of the Criminal Justice Division of the office of the Attorney General saw the report and the proposed resolution scheduled to be perfected a few days later, he became concerned and initiated an inquiry. This in turn prompted an adjournment of the June 5 date to June 26. The defence was not informed of the reason for the adjournment at the time.

The ADM obtained additional legal opinions about the merits of the Nixon prosecution and about the repudiation of plea agreements. Based on the results of this research, the ADM concluded that Crown counsel's assessment of the strength of the case was flawed as he had failed to consider the totality of the evidence. In his view, a plea to careless driving in the circumstances was contrary to the interests of justice and would bring the administration of justice into disrepute. The ADM also concluded that Ms. Nixon could be restored without prejudice to the position she had been in prior to entering into the plea agreement. Thus, it was resolved that the decision by Crown counsel at the preliminary hearing not to proceed on the impaired driving counts would be maintained. However, the ADM instructed Crown counsel to withdraw the May 22 resolution agreement and to proceed to trial on the dangerous driving charges in accordance with the committal order. . . .

. . . . .

Clearly, the ADM's decision to repudiate the plea agreement also constitutes an act of prosecutorial discretion. Prosecutorial discretion was not spent with the decision to initiate the proceedings, nor did it terminate with the plea agreement. So long as the proceedings are ongoing, the Crown may be required to make further decisions about whether the prosecution should be continued and, if so, in respect of what charges.

Thus, it follows that the Crown's ultimate decision to resile from the plea agreement and to continue the prosecution is subject to the principles set out in *Krieger*: it is *only* subject to judicial review for abuse of process.

The more difficult question in this appeal is how the initial exercise of prosecutorial discretion — Crown counsel's offer to resolve the matter on the basis of a plea to a lesser charge — should figure in the analysis regarding abuse of process. . . .

. . . . .

In this case, I agree with the Court of Appeal that there is no evidence to support a finding of abuse of process. . . . In rejecting Ms. Nixon's claim that the ADM's decision was made for an improper motive, [the application judge] concluded that "there is absolutely no evidence" of political interference (para. 22) and "nothing to suggest that [the ADM's] action was taken in bad faith or to accommodate a real or perceived political stance of his Minister of Justice" (para. 25). There was also nothing improper in the considerations that informed the ADM's decision to resile from the agreement. The application judge described these considerations as follows (at para. 26):

Those who influenced [the ADM's] decision to repudiate the resolution agreement took exception to a pair of [Crown counsel's] conclusions: first, that the analyses of the breath samples provided by Ms. Nixon would be inadmissible at trial and second, that the evidence of Ryan Galloway, who had earlier observed erratic driving by a van with the same licence plate as hers, was too remote in the circumstances to be relevant to the prosecution. In view of those two mistakes, the Assistant Deputy Minister was persuaded that any agreement which permitted Ms. Nixon to escape *Criminal Code* convictions was contrary to the public interest, especially considering that two people had died and another had been orphaned as the result of her driving. He therefore concluded that to honour it would bring the administration of justice into disrepute. [Emphasis added]

. . . As discussed earlier, the ADM's decision to resile from the plea agreement falls within the scope of prosecutorial discretion. In the absence of any prosecutorial misconduct, improper motive or bad faith in the approach, circumstances, or ultimate decision to repudiate, the decision to proceed with the prosecution is the Crown's alone to make. Reasonable counsel may indeed, and often do, differ on whether a particular disposition is in the public interest in the circumstances of the case. The ADM, in good faith, determined that Crown counsel's assessment of the strength of the evidence was erroneous and, on that basis, having regard to the seriousness of the offences, concluded that it would not be in the public interest to terminate the prosecution on the criminal charges. This can hardly be regarded as evidence of misconduct.

This does not mean that plea agreements can be overturned on a whim. The method by which the decision was reached can itself reveal misconduct of a sufficient degree to amount to abuse of process. But that is not what occurred here. The act of repudiation was indeed a rare and exceptional occurrence. The evidence revealed that there have been only two prior occurrences in Alberta, "one in the 1980s and one within the year prior to the trial in this matter" (Court of Appeal decision, at para. 48). There was also no evidence of abusive conduct in the process leading to the decision to repudiate. I agree with the analysis of Paperny J.A. in this regard (at para. 50):

> Further, this is not a case where the repudiation was done "unfairly" or when the discretion of the Attorney General was exercised "irrationally, unreasonably or oppressively". The ADM carefully reviewed the evidence that was the subject of concern and relied on legal opinions and took guidance from the Ontario Attorney General's policy to instruct himself on the relevant considerations. Having satisfied himself that the original view of the trial prosecutor was incorrect and that the resulting plea resolution agreement would bring the administration of justice into disrepute, he acted expeditiously in communicating the decision to withdraw the plea resolution agreement to the respondent. He also considered possible prejudice to the respondent and concluded that there would be no such prejudice. The ADM's conduct, viewed in its totality, cannot be characterized as unfair, unreasonable, oppressive or irrational. The high threshold to find abuse of process has not been met here.

Finally, Ms. Nixon was returned to the position she was in at the conclusion of the preliminary hearing before the plea agreement was entered into. There is no merit to the contention that she suffered prejudice as a result of the repudiation.

[iii] Calling Witnesses

The decision of whether or not to call a witness by the Crown can have an important impact on the conduct of the defence at trial. If the Crown decides not to call the witness, the defence may have to call them, and potentially lose their right to cross-examination or address the jury last if it is a jury trial (this latter statutory right (section 651(3) of the *Criminal Code*) is dependent on the defence calling no evidence). In *R. v. Cook*, the Supreme Court of Canada held that there is no obligation, generally speaking, on the Crown to call a witness. *Cook* involved the failure of the Crown to call one of the complainants. In the following case, the defence argued that there is an obligation on the prosecution to call particular witnesses in some cases.

R. v. HILLIS

[2016] O.J. No. 818, 2016 ONSC 451 (Ont. S.C.J.)

[The accused was charged with murder and aggravated assault. The parties agreed that the accused was not the aggressor, and that he was entitled to use force to defend himself. The central issue was whether the force used was reasonable. Earlier in the trial, the trial judge ruled that the defence could elicit exculpatory evidence from two Crown witnesses. Two days after that ruling, the Crown announced that it was not going to call these witnesses. The Crown acknowledged that that decision was made because the evidence would be exculpatory. It further suggested that this was an acceptable strategy because full disclosure had been made and the witnesses were available to be called by the defence. The defence sought an order from the trial judge directing the Crown to call these witnesses.]

POMERANCE, J.

As a general rule, the Crown is entitled to choose the witnesses that it will and will not call. The prosecution is not required to assist the defence strategy. However, in exceptional cases, the court may direct that certain witnesses be called by the Crown. This is one of those exceptional cases. ...

. . . . .

In R. v. Cook, [1997] 1 S.C.R. 1113, 114 C.C.C. (3d) 481 [Cook], the Supreme Court of Canada held that, as a general rule, the Crown is entitled to decide how it will present its case. It is at liberty to choose the witnesses that it will and will not call. Because these types of decisions involve the exercise of prosecutorial discretion, they are not generally subject to judicial review.

While the Cook decision advocates judicial restraint, it does not allow for unlimited prosecutorial power. The courts have consistently recognized that, while prosecutorial decision making is generally immune from scrutiny, the courts shall interfere where it is shown that a decision was based on an oblique or improper motive. This is akin to saying that prosecutorial discretion may be reviewed when it is alleged to give rise to an abuse of process. . . .

. . . . .

Is the Crown entitled to refrain from calling reliable evidence on the basis that it could assist the accused? I find that this is not a permissible Crown strategy. The desire to withhold reliable exculpatory evidence during the case for the Crown is inconsistent with the role of Crown counsel as a quasi-minister of justice, and custodian of the public interest. The Crown argues that the evidence is not concealed because there has been full disclosure to the defence. That may be so, but the effect of not calling the evidence is to conceal it from the jury unless the defence decides that it has to call it, thereby giving up procedural protections. The Crown may decide not to call a witness for any number of legitimate reasons. It should not omit reliable evidence from its case solely because it might help the accused.

This is borne out by the authorities. In Cook, at para. 28, the court, citing earlier Supreme Court authority, affirmed that: "the Crown must not hold back evidence because it would assist the accused". Similarly, at para. 39, the Court in Cook affirmed the following statements of Lebel J.A. in R. v. V. (J.) (1994), 91 C.C.C. (3d) 284, [1994] J.Q. No. 347 (Que. C.A.):

> Once [crown counsel] has satisfied the obligation to disclose the evidence, it is for him, in principle, to choose the witnesses necessary to establish the factual basis of his case...if improper motives cannot be imputed to him, such as the desire, for example to hide exculpatory evidence, as a general rule [crown counsel] will be considered to have properly executed this part of his function in the criminal trial.

This is not a startling proposition. It flows quite naturally from the conception of the Crown as a quasi-minister of justice, and the implications of that role. . . .

. . . . .

In other words, the Crown is not at liberty to curate the evidence, excising anything that might be exculpatory. To do so is to place too high a premium on "winning". It is to lose sight of the Crown's primary duty to present the case fairly, and in a manner that will secure a just result.

This is not to say that Crown counsel is foreclosed from being a strong and vigorous advocate. That is expected in our adversarial system. It is only to say that Crown counsel cannot adopt a *purely* adversarial role toward the defence. . . . This balance between advocacy and fairness is reflected in several places in the Ontario Crown Policy Manual. The Preamble includes the following statement at p. 2:

> A prosecutor's responsibilities are public in nature. As a prosecutor and public representative, Crown counsel's demeanour and actions should be fair, dispassionate and moderate; show no signs of partisanship; open to the possibility of the innocence of the accused person and avoid "tunnel vision".

. . . . .

The Crown does not have to call evidence merely because it assists the defence, but the Crown cannot categorically exclude all evidence that might have that effect.

It is against this backdrop that I must assess the Crown strategy in this case. As I understand it, the Crown acknowledges that it decided not to call the witnesses because they have exculpatory evidence to offer. This is confirmed by the chronology of events. The Crown told the defence that it would not decide on a witness list until it received the court's ruling on the admissibility of evidence. I ruled against the Crown on certain issues. Two days later the Crown excluded the witnesses whose evidence was admitted over the Crown's objection.

Apart from the exculpating nature of the evidence, it is hard to imagine why else the

Crown would decline to call these witnesses. Their evidence is directly relevant to the issues the jury must determine. The evidence purports to be reliable. Three of the witnesses are police officers. Two of them arrived at the scene just minutes after the 911 call was placed. The third is the blood spatter expert retained by the Crown and called by the Crown at the preliminary hearing. This is the very type of evidence that is ordinarily called by the Crown in a homicide prosecution. The Crown does not take issue with the accuracy of the evidence offered by these witnesses in this case.

. . . . .

It is true that the defence has full disclosure of the witnesses' evidence, and could call them to testify at trial. However, this would disadvantage the defence. The defence cannot cross-examine its own witnesses, and by calling evidence it forfeits the right to address the jury last. These tactical disadvantages are a natural incident of the trial process, but should not be forced upon the defence by an unfair prosecution strategy.

While I disagree with the Crown's position in this case, I need not determine whether it amounts to an oblique motive, or results in an abuse of process. I am satisfied that it is open to the court to intervene on a lower standard of review.

In Cook, the Supreme Court of Canada perceived that the identification of Crown witnesses is an exercise of prosecutorial discretion. Since Cook, the Supreme Court of Canada has refined what it means by "prosecutorial discretion". Recent authority suggests that the choice of witnesses is more a question of trial tactics than prosecutorial discretion. While Crown tactics are entitled to deference, they are reviewable on a standard below that of prosecutorial discretion, which only warrants judicial intervention in cases of an abuse of process.

. . . . .

Decisions relating to trial strategy are outside of the realm of true prosecutorial discretion, falling into the category of crown conduct or tactics. [. . .]

Relying on Felderhof, Krieger, and Anderson, I find that the decision of the prosecution to call or not call certain witnesses at trial is a matter of Crown tactics, reviewable under the court's trial management authority. These decisions are, like all prosecutorial decisions, subject to review where the product of oblique motive. But they are also subject to judicial review on a lesser standard relating to the fairness of trial.

I am concerned that the Crown strategy in this case could adversely affect trial fairness. This justifies the court's intervention, whether or not the conduct amounts to an abuse of process. The Crown proposes to call evidence of certain observations and events at the crime scene, but not others. The jurors will hear about certain things that happened during the case for the prosecution. But they will not hear Daniel Gobeil's evidence about the accused's statements at or around the time of the victim's death, in which he apologized and said he "didn't mean it". They will not hear PC Kettlewell's evidence that the accused was trying to staunch the victim's bleeding, by holding his neck when the police arrived (though this evidence might be available from PC D'Alimonte, which is being called by the Crown). They will not hear that the blood spatter evidence is consistent with the accused having been punched with significant impact. In short, the narrative will be missing several critical pieces.

In some cases, the Crown is motivated to call all relevant evidence because it needs to prove its case. If it leaves out certain evidence, it may not discharge its onus of proof. At para. 30 of Cook, Justice L'Heureux-Dubé cited with approval the following passage from Yebes:

> While the Crown may not be required to call a given witness, the failure of the Crown to call a witness may leave a gap in the Crown's case which will leave the Crown's burden of proof undischarged and entitle the accused to an acquittal. It is in this sense that the Crown may be expected to call all witnesses essential to the unfolding of the narrative of events upon which the Crown's case is based.

This "self policing" rationale does not apply here. The missing evidence does not expose gaps in the Crown's case. It leaves the erroneous impression that no such gaps exist. The Crown insists that the evidence could be called by the defence. The defence could, indeed, call the evidence. This would ensure that the evidence is heard by the jury. It might even afford the defence a tactical advantage. The jury, realizing that important information was withheld by the Crown, might lose faith in the prosecution. Be that as it may, it is for Mr. Gordner, as the accused's counsel, to weigh the pros and cons of these alternatives. It was not unreasonable for him to conclude that the benefits of calling the evidence are outweighed by the disadvantages, such as losing the ability to cross-examine, and the possibility of addressing the jury last.

For the reasons discussed above, . . . I direct that the Crown call these witnesses during the case for the prosecution. I leave it to the Crown to determine when it calls these witnesses and what, if any, evidence it chooses to elicit in-chief.

NOTES AND QUESTIONS

1. Do you think that the trial judge came to the correct conclusion? If the Crown is truly a "minister of justice" whose role is not to secure a conviction, why would they refuse to call exculpatory evidence, especially when that evidence is from police officers?

[d] Presenting Its Case

[i] Cross-Examination and Closing Submissions

Cross-examining an accused and making closing submissions pose particular fairness challenges to the prosecutor, especially in cases involving sympathetic or vulnerable witnesses. As Justice Doherty noted in *R. v. R. (A.J.)*[92] (Chapter 5), a sexual assault case: "[c]ases like this, where the allegations are particularly sordid, the complainants particularly sympathetic and the accused particularly disreputable, provide a severe test of our criminal justice system". With respect to cross-examination, we continue to see the following concerns raised in the cases:

> the expression of personal opinion; requiring the accused to comment on the veracity of other witnesses or to provide a motive for them to fabricate; asking the

---

[92] [1994] O.J. No. 2309, 20 O.R. (3d) 405 at para. 30 (Ont. C.A.).

accused to explain why a witness was not called by the defence; using the accused's constitutional right to disclosure as a trap to suggest he has scripted his evidence to meet the case against him; making baseless and prejudicial suggestions to witnesses or the accused; and cross-examinations riddled with sarcasm, irrelevancies, or crafted to demean and humiliate.[93]

As for the Crown's closing submissions to the jury, recall *Boucher* from the beginning of this Chapter. Were you able to identify why it was problematic when you read it? Almost fifty years later, the *Boucher* issue arose in the following case:

R. v. LEVERT

[2001] O.J. No. 3907, 159 C.C.C. (3d) 71 (Ont. C.A.)

ROSENBERG, J.A.

The appellant appeals from his conviction and sentence for sexual interference. . . .

. . . . .

(ii) Cross-examination and jury address concerning the "perfect victim"

Counsel for the appellant submits that it was improper for Crown counsel to cross-examine the appellant to suggest that the complainant was the "perfect victim". After receiving a denial from the appellant that he sexually assaulted the complainant, Crown counsel suggested to the appellant that P.G. was the perfect victim because he would have a problem remembering things. Crown counsel repeated this theme in his jury address in the following terms:

. . . well, wasn't P.G. just perfect for Gerald Levert? Young, intellectually challenged, not much family support . . .

A conclusion, ladies and gentleman of the jury, as I have already indicated, the Crown's theory is that P.G. was the ideal victim for Gerald Levert. And that P. was in fact sexually abused as he described. Is there any other logical and reasonable conclusion?

I agree with counsel for the appellant that these parts of the cross-examination and jury address were improper. This line of argument is based on the inadmissible theory that the appellant had a propensity to sexually assault young boys and was just looking for the "perfect victim". The substantial attack on the credibility and reliability of the complainant by the defence because of the complainant's learning and other disabilities did not justify this attack on the appellant's character. I will consider the impact of these improper comments after discussing the other alleged improprieties.

. . . . .

(iv) Crown counsel does not "win or lose"

This trial took place in the small community of L'Orignal. Perhaps in a misguided effort to make use of the home field advantage, Crown counsel at trial referred on several occasions to counsel for the defence (who is from Ottawa) as a "very learned lawyer". He referred to his own role in the following terms:

---

[93] Christine McGoey, *The Good Criminal Law Barrister A Crown Perspective*, at 4-13.

> As Crown prosecutor I'm not in this to win or lose. The concept of winning is foreign to the Crown prosecutor. So, don't do it for me. Do it only if you're satisfied beyond a reasonable doubt that this gentleman is guilty.

At trial, defence counsel complained to the trial judge that the remarks by Crown counsel about defence counsel's skill were disingenuous and designed to denigrate defence counsel and thus his client. It would seem that the trial judge did not draw the same inference from Crown counsel's conduct. I think in this area an appellate court should ordinarily defer to the trial judge's view. We can only rely upon the transcript and, subject to some comments I wish to make about the role of the Crown, I cannot say that Crown counsel's comments were improper.

I am concerned about Crown counsel explicitly setting out his view of the role of the Crown. There is a danger that it invites an invidious comparison with defence counsel's role. In other words, the jury may give more weight to the submissions of Crown counsel because of the impression that they are objective whereas the submissions of defence counsel should be discounted because they are biased and driven by loyalty to the client.

As well, such comments come perilously close to the conduct criticized by the court in *Boucher v. The King* (1954), 110 C.C.C. 263 (S.C.C.). In that case, Crown counsel said the following:

> It is the duty of the Crown, when an affair like that happens, no matter what affair, and still more in a serious affair, to make every possible investigation, and if in the course of these investigations with our experts, the conclusion is come to that the accused is not guilty or that there is a reasonable doubt, it is the duty of the Crown, gentlemen, to say so, or if the conclusion is come to that he is not guilty, not to make an arrest. That is what was done here.

> When the Crown put in that evidence, it is not with the intention of bearing down on the accused, it was with the intention of rendering justice to him.

Rand J. was highly critical of these remarks at pp. 269-70:

> Many, if not the majority of, jurors acting, it may be, for the first time, unacquainted with the language and proceedings of Courts, and with no precise appreciation of the role of the prosecution other than as being associated with Government, would be extremely susceptible to the implications of such remarks. So to emphasize a neutral attitude on the part of Crown representatives in the investigation of the facts of a crime is to put the matter to unsophisticated minds as if there had already been an impartial determination of guilt by persons in authority. Little more likely to colour the consideration of the evidence by jurors could be suggested. It is the antithesis of the impression that should be given to them: they only are to pass on the issue and to do so only on what has been properly exhibited to them in the course of the proceedings. [Emphasis added]

Later at p. 270, Rand J. made the comments that were the source of Crown counsel's statement to the jury in this case: "The role of prosecutor excludes any notion of winning or losing; his function is a matter of public duty than which in civil life there can be none charged with greater personal responsibility."

If Crown counsel conduct themselves in a fair and even-handed manner, this will be apparent to the trier of fact. They need not take unfair advantage of their important role in the administration of justice by wrapping themselves in the *Boucher* flag.

That said, I cannot think that the jury in this case was so naïve as to accept at face value Crown counsel's description of his role or that they would unfairly discount the defence submissions. Unlike *Boucher*, Crown counsel did not expressly or implicitly suggest that he had investigated the case and determined the appellant was guilty. Thus, while I think comments like those made by Crown counsel are best avoided, I am satisfied that they did not affect the fairness of the trial.

(v) Conclusion

Of the many allegations of misconduct against the Crown, I have found that those concerning the "perfect victim" were improper. In *R. v. R. (A.J.)*, [1994] O.J. No. 2309, 94 C.C.C. (3d) 168 at 176 (Ont. C.A.), Doherty J.A. described the test to be applied when an appellate court is faced with allegations of Crown impropriety:

> There are, however, well-established limits on cross-examination. Some apply to all witnesses, others only to the accused. Isolated transgressions of those limits may be of little consequence on appeal. Repeated improprieties during the cross-examination of an accused are, however, a very different matter. As the improprieties mount, the cross-examination may cross over the line from the aggressive to the abusive. When that line is crossed, the danger of a miscarriage of justice is very real. If improper cross-examination of an accused prejudices that accused in his defence or is so improper as to bring the administration of justice into disrepute, an appellate court must intervene . . . [Emphasis added]

Crown counsel's conduct of this case was not a model of propriety even if the "perfect victim" remark is the only one that has the capacity to undermine a fair trial. I have not, however, been persuaded that this conduct was so improper as to bring the administration of justice into disrepute. I am also not satisfied that there is a danger of a miscarriage of justice from the "perfect victim" comments. The defence was able to present its case. The cross-examination was not abusive. The appellant handled himself well in the face of a vigorous cross-examination. Although credibility was the crucial factor in this case, I am satisfied that the improper remarks by Crown counsel did not prejudice a fair trial. The appellant dealt well with the "perfect victim" cross-examination and there was no evidence at all before the jury to suggest the appellant had any disposition to sexually assault young boys. The trial judge, apparently in response to some of defence counsel's complaints about Crown counsel's jury address, gave the jury a "very special caution" not to speculate and, rather, to base their conclusions on the trial evidence and nothing else. It follows that I would not give effect to this ground of appeal.

. . . . .

Scenario Nineteen

LP and F planned to break into a home. While they were at the house, the housekeeper was strangled to death. Both men were charged with first degree murder. At trial, LP said he had nothing to do with the killing, but was sitting outside in his van when it happened. In contrast, F said he unexpectedly came upon LP in the basement, in the act of killing the deceased. The Crown argued the killing was a two-man job, and that both were guilty of first degree murder on the basis that the death was caused while they committed or attempted to commit the offence of unlawful confinement. They were convicted. Part of F's cross-examination included the following:

Q: So you went from the three car garage stairs direct to the kitchen?

A: Yes.

Q: And you arrived at a time that suits your evidence perfectly. And I'm going to suggest something. You arrived just in time for her to scratch you before she goes unconscious, correct?

A: She didn't scratch me. She tried to hang on me.

Q: Okay. And you arrive just in – just a little late to stop him killing her, correct?

A: Yes.

Q: So you arrive at a perfect time for you.

A: I wouldn't say was a perfect time for me, it was the worst of my life.

. . .

Q: The two of you stole three [computers], correct? Correct?

A: There's three computers, yes.

Q: How many did you sell? Pick a number.

A: Two.

Q: Two. Where's the other one?

A: I told them, is in Ecuador.

Q: You sent it to Ecuador?

A: Yes.

Q: Did you send the dead girl's computer to Ecuador?

A: I don't know. I just don't know how to use those things. I took one of them. It was the white one.

Q: Did you dare sell the dead girl's computer?

The Crown's closing address in relation to F included the following:

Another way, to get right to the truth zone easy, you take Christian's implausible rescuer story – no, no, not implausible, his ridiculous rescuer story, and you just change it a hair. . . .

How are you going to save somebody without even touching them? And you say, how could a guy be so stupid in his evidence? Because to lie you've got to remember the truth, the lie and the difference. . . .

He's inventing an arrival within seconds. And that's what happens when you start messing with the truth. The truth bites you because people like you can see that that is just too convenient, too coincidental, too much of a chance, and along with the rescuer story, is absolutely unbelievable.

And here's what I urge you to do, when you're looking at evidence, look at the whole package because this belongs in with the rescuer story, the timing. It's not, not just what he doesn't do, it's when he gets there. And both are fakes. Both are big outrageous lies, and they are an insult to the actual truth of what happened, namely, that he was hands-on involved in the murder of Jocelyn. . . .

469

And now you have a clear picture of two men guilty of first degree murder beyond a reasonable doubt. Like drowning men, they have reached out that last remaining life jacket to take it for themselves. Each one wants that life jacket. Neither one deserves it.

On appeal, F argues that the Crown's conduct was improper. Do you agree?[94]

[4] FURTHER READING

Carling, Amanda, "A Way to Reduce Indigenous Overrepresentation: Prevent False Guilty Plea Wrongful Convictions" (2017) 64 Crim L.Q. 415.

Craig, Elaine, "The Ethical Identity of Sexual Assault Lawyers" (2016) 47 Ottawa L. Rev. 73.

Craig, Elaine, "The Ethical Obligations of Defence Counsel in Sexual Assault Cases" (2014) 51 Osgoode Hall L.J. 427.

Craig, Elaine, "The Inhospitable Court" (2016) 66 U.T.L.J. 197.

Freedman, Monroe, "Getting Honest about Client Perjury" (2008) 21 Geo. J. Leg. Ethics 133.

Freedman, Monroe, "Professional Responsibility of the Criminal Defense Lawyer: The Three Hardest Questions" (1966) 64 Mich. L. Rev. 1469.

Hutchinson, Allan C., "Putting Up a Defence: Sex, Murder, and Videotapes" (Chapter 3) in Dodek, Adam and Woolley, Alice, *In Search of the Ethical Lawyer* (Vancouver: UBC Press, 2016).

Kennedy, Jerome, "Crown Culture and Wrongful Convictions" (2016) 63 Crim. L.Q. 415.

Layton, David, "*R v. Jenkins*: Client Perjury and Disclosure by Defence Counsel" (2001) 44 C.R. (5th) 259.

Layton, David and Proulx, Michel, *Ethics and Criminal Law*, 2d ed. (Toronto: Irwin Law 2015).

Luban, David, "Are Criminal Defenders Different" (1993) 91 Mich. L. Rev. 1729.

Manikis, Marie, "Towards Accountability and Fairness For Aboriginal People: The Recognition of Gladue as a Principle of Fundamental Justice That Applies to Prosecutors" (2016) 21 Can. Crim. L. Rev. 173.

Mitchell, John B., "Reasonable Doubts Are Where You Find Them: A Response to Professor Subin's Position on the Criminal Lawyer's 'Different Mission'" (1987) 1 Geo. J. Leg. Ethics 339.

Sherrin, Chris, "Guilty Pleas from the Innocent" (2011) 30 Windsor Rev. Leg. Soc. Issues 1.

Simon, William, "The Ethics of Criminal Defense" (1993) 91 Mich. L. Rev. 1703.

Smith, Abbe, "Can You Be a Good Person and a Good Prosecutor?" (2001) 14 Geo. J. Leg. Ethics 355.

---

[94] See *R. v. Figueroa*, [2016] O.J. No. 4491, 2016 ONCA 645 (Ont. C.A.).

Smith, Abbe, "Defending Defending: The Case for Unmitigated Zeal on Behalf of People Who Do Terrible Things" (2000) 28 Hofstra L. Rev. 925.

Smith, Abbe, "Defending Those People" (2012) 10 Ohio State J. Crim Law 277.

Smith, Abbe, "Nice Work If You Can Get It: "Ethical" Jury Selection in Criminal Defense" (1998) 67 Fordham L. Rev. 523.

Smith, Abbe, "Representing Rapists: The Cruelty of Cross Examination and Other Challenges For A Feminist Criminal Lawyer" (2016) 55 Am. Crim L. Rev. 255.

Subin, Harry I, "Is This Lie Necessary? Further Reflections on the Right to Present a False Defense" (1988) 1 Geo. J. Leg. Ethics 689.

Subin, Harry I., "The Criminal Lawyer's "Different Mission": Reflections on the "Right" to Present a False Case" (1987) 1 Geo. J. Leg. Ethics 125.

Tanovich, David M, "*Taillefer*: Disclosure, Guilty Pleas and Ethics" (2004) 17 C.R. (6th) 149.

Tanovich, David M, "Whack No More: Infusing Equality into the Ethics of Defence Lawyering in Sexual Assault Cases" (2015) 45 Ottawa L. Rev. 495.

Thrower, Susan, "Neither Reasonable nor Remedial: The Hopeless Contradictions of the Legal Ethics Measures to Prevent Perjury" (2010) 58 Clev. St. L. Rev. 781.

Woolley, Alice "Reconceiving the Standard Conception of the Prosecutor's Role" (2017) 95:3 Can. Bar Rev. 795.

Woolley, Alice, "Hard Questions and Innocent Clients: The Normative Framework of *The Three Hardest Questions*, and the Plea Bargaining Problem" (2016) 44(4) Hofstra L. Rev. 1179.

Woolley, Alice, "Lawyers' Ethics In The Context of Criminal Law" (Chapter 9) *Understanding Lawyers' Ethics in Canada*, 2d ed. (Toronto: LexisNexis Canada, 2016).

Zacharias, Fred & Green Bruce A., "The Uniqueness of Federal Prosecutors" (2000) 88 Geo. L.J. 1030.

CHAPTER 8

GOVERNMENT LAWYERS

[1] INTRODUCTION

The dominant model of the Canadian lawyer is the lawyer in private practice, specifically the advocate, representing the client against the state or another adversary. We have raised generations of lawyers on Lord Brougham's model of lawyers as zealous advocates focused exclusively on the interests of their clients.[1]

This model is problematic in various ways. As set out in Chapter 1, many critics, such as David Luban, criticize the ethical foundations of this approach. Further, on a descriptive level, it does not accurately reflect what most Canadian lawyers actually do. The model of the lawyer as a strongly zealous advocate tends to be invoked most frequently in relation to the criminal defence lawyer yet, as the prior chapter discussed, it does not capture the range of duties such lawyers owe; and, importantly, only a small percentage of Canadian lawyers can be described as engaging in criminal defence work. The dominant model fits only poorly when applied to public sector lawyers.

Public sector lawyers include lawyers who work for one of the three levels of government or for one of the many public entities that have been created with the rise of the administrative state in Canada since the 1960s. These include lawyers for hospitals, school boards, public utilities, securities commissions, Crown corporations, human rights commissions, legal aid clinics and like bodies. In 1961, 6.7% of all Canadian lawyers worked in the public sector. By 1986, that figure had increased to 10.8%[2] and by 2008–2009, an estimated 15-25% of Canadian lawyers worked in the public sector, depending on the jurisdiction.[3] Think about that for a moment: if you are an aspiring lawyer in Nova Scotia, one in four of you will likely work in the public sector.[4] In British Columbia or Ontario, that figure is about one in six. Yet, until recently, references to public sector lawyers were almost entirely absent from

---

[1] Lord Brougham's perspective on the lawyer, and the circumstances that gave rise to his characterization of lawyers in this way, are excerpted in Chapter 7. More generally see: J. Nightingale, ed., *Trial of Queen Caroline*, vol. 2 (London: J. Robins & Co., 1821).

[2] David A.A. Stager with Harry W. Arthurs, *Lawyers in Canada* (Toronto: University of Toronto Press, 1990) at 158 (Table 6.12).

[3] There are no available comprehensive figures but the range of 15-25% is taken from statistics from the individual Law Societies.

[4] See Nova Scotia Barristers' Society, "Statistical Snapshot – Fall/Winter 2019/20", online: https://nsbs.org/wp-content/uploads/2020/01/2019-statsnapshot.pdf (25% of lawyers in Government/Legal Aid).

most codes of conduct and discussions of legal ethics in Canada. For these reasons, Allan Hutchinson rightly called government lawyers "the orphans of legal ethics" because so "little energy has been directed towards defining and defending the role and duties of government lawyers".[5]

In this chapter, we are concerned with a subset of public sector lawyers: the government lawyer. As former Assistant Deputy Attorney General of Canada Elizabeth Sanderson has explained, "Government lawyers are public servants practising law in the service of the Crown within the federal Department of Justice or within provincial or territorial counterparts or within client departments."[6] In fact, we might consider the federal Department of Justice to be Canada's largest law firm, although they do not describe themselves as such. In 2020, the "DOJ" or "Justice" employed around 5,000 persons, about half of whom are lawyers. With approximately 2,500 lawyers, Justice is more than twice the size of the largest Canadian law firm.[7] It has offices in cities across Canada and has practice groups specializing in tax, Aboriginal law, transportation, immigration, civil litigation, terrorism, international law and many other areas. It is the most frequent litigator in the Supreme Court of Canada, and it advises cabinet ministers and government agencies.

In this chapter, we explore some of the unique ethical issues relating to and experienced by government lawyers. In the first part, we examine the issue of whether government lawyers owe "special obligations" that would lead to those lawyers being held to higher ethical duties. In the second part, we examine what the nature of such special obligations would be. Then in the third part we examine some of the organizational pressures faced by government lawyers.

[2] SPECIAL OBLIGATIONS?

Canadian lawyers who work for the government do so in a wide variety of contexts, just a few of which include: advising government on the legality of public policy; bringing or defending civil actions to which the government is a party; prosecuting criminal or regulatory offences; working for regulatory agencies or tribunals; negotiating government contracts; advising government on foreign affairs and international law; and designing and drafting legislation.

The question considered here is this: to what extent does the fact that a lawyer's client is "the Crown" affect the nature of the lawyer's ethical obligations? Is the lawyer required to be more critical of what they are being asked to do? Do they have broader and deeper ethical obligations to the administration of justice and/or the

---

[5] Allan C. Hutchinson, "'In the Public Interest': The Responsibilities and Rights of Government Lawyers" (2008) 46 Osgoode Hall L.J. 105 at 106. For notable exceptions, see the references at the end of this chapter. The paucity of attention to government lawyers in Canada compares poorly with the attention given to the subject in the United States.

[6] Elizabeth Sanderson, *Government Lawyering: Duties and Ethical Challenges of Government Lawyers* (Lexis Nexis, 2018) xxiii.

[7] See Canada, Department of Justice, *Canada's Department of Justice*, online: https://www.justice.gc.ca/eng/abt-apd/org.html. See also Canada, Department of Justice, *Report on Plans and Priorities 2020-21*, online: https://www.justice.gc.ca/eng/rp-pr/cp-pm/rpp/2020_2021/rep-rap/dp-pm.pdf.

protection of the public interest? Some of these questions were touched upon in Chapter 7 with respect to Crown counsel prosecuting criminal trials, but they arise more generally for all lawyers working for federal or provincial governments. In Canada, there has been very little discussion of whether government lawyers owe a "higher" ethical duty than other lawyers. The *Everingham* case below provides one of the few judicial considerations of this issue. Consider the contrasting perspectives of Borins J. and the Divisional Court.

EVERINGHAM v. ONTARIO

[1991] O.J. No. 3578, 84 D.L.R. (4th) 354, 3 C.P.C. (3d) 87
(Ont. Gen. Div., Borins J.)

[Denis LePage was a patient in the Social Behaviour Program at the Oak Ridge division of the Mental Health Centre in Penetanguishene, Ontario. He and other patients had brought an application alleging that they had been subject to Charter rights violations and were entitled to relief pursuant to section 24(2) of the Charter. Mr. LePage was due to be cross-examined by attorneys for the Crown. The day before his cross-examination he had a conversation with Thomas Haldane Wickett, the lawyer for the Crown who was to cross-examine Mr. LePage the following day. Mr. LePage's own counsel was not present when the conversation took place. The content of that conversation was disputed. However, it was found by Borins J. that Mr. Wickett did tell Mr. LePage that he was the lawyer who was going to cross-examine him the next day, that Mr. LePage stated that he understood that his lawyer was going to be present during the cross-examination, that Mr. Wickett "did not obtain any information from Mr. LePage which he could use in questioning him the next day" but that "Mr. LePage was sufficiently concerned and upset . . . that he reported the incident to his lawyer, Mr. Taman". Mr. LePage and the other applicants brought a motion seeking to have the Attorney General for Ontario removed as solicitor of record.]

BORINS J. (orally):—

. . . . .

The starting point is Rule 10, Commentary 14, of the Rules of Professional Conduct of The Law Society of Upper Canada. Rule 10 states:

> When acting as an advocate the lawyer, while treating the tribunal with courtesy and respect, must represent the client resolutely and honourably within the limits of the law.

The relevant portion of Commentary 14 reads:

> An opposite party who is professionally represented should not be approached or dealt with save through or with the consent of that party's lawyer.

I have no doubt that what occurred in this case represented a breach of the rule and the commentary by Mr. Wickett. The consequences which should flow from this breach represent a more difficult question. In this regard, the obvious alternatives which I have are to dismiss or allow the motion. A further alternative would be to disqualify Mr. Wickett from any further involvement in the case as solicitor for the respondents. This alternative arises from the inherent jurisdiction which this court has to control and supervise barristers and solicitors who are, of course, officers of the court in respect of their conduct in legal proceedings. Should it be necessary to cite authority for this proposition, I would rely upon the decision of the Supreme Court of Canada in *MacDonald Estate v. Martin*, [1990] 3 S.C.R. 1235.

Notwithstanding the comprehensive submissions of Mr. Taman, I am of the view that it would not be appropriate in the circumstances of his case to remove the Attorney General for Ontario as solicitor of record for the respondents. I base this conclusion on a number of grounds. First, this is not a case in which a lawyer deliberately sought out and spoke to a party behind the back of the party's lawyer. The meeting of Mr. LePage by Mr. Wickett was purely coincidental. Second, in speaking to Mr. LePage, Mr. Wickett had no oblique motive. He simply wanted to alleviate Mr. LePage's concern with respect to his identity and why he was there and what was to occur in respect to his cross-examination the next day. Third, nothing concerning the application was discussed and Mr. Wickett obtained no information confidential, or otherwise, from Mr. LePage. Fourth, this is not a case - being a *Charter* application - in which there are conflicting interests in the usual sense of that term as encountered in private litigation. Fifth, the meeting was brief and innocent in its nature. Sixth, other than the loss of confidence which Mr. LePage may now have if Mr. Wickett is to be permitted to continue as counsel for the respondents, and I do not minimize this, no prejudice was caused to Mr. LePage by the interview.

It remains to be decided, however, whether in the circumstances Mr. Wickett should be permitted to continue as counsel for the respondents. In my view, he should not. Although the spirit of Rule 10, Commentary 14, was not breached because Mr. Wickett did not obtain any advantage in the conduct of the litigation by talking to Mr. LePage, nevertheless what he did constituted a serious indiscretion on his part. He should have been more sensitive to the circumstances and the situation in which he found himself. In this regard, I trust it goes without saying that Ms. Regenstreif committed no indiscretion. Being aware of the litigation and the pending cross-examination of Mr. LePage and the other applicants, Mr. Wickett should not have toured the hospital. However, he did. When he came into contact with Mr. LePage he should not have talked to him. If it was necessary for Mr. Wickett to explain his presence in the ward to Mr. LePage, he should have asked Dr. Jones or somebody else to do so. However well motivated he was, it is now obvious that what he did seriously affected Mr. LePage and has so undermined his confidence in the system that I feel that I must, to restore that confidence, disqualify Mr. Wickett from any further participation in this litigation.

Although the Rules of Professional Conduct of The Law Society of Upper Canada must necessarily apply to all lawyers, it is my view that one who is a lawyer employed by the government must be particularly sensitive to the rules which govern his or her professional conduct. Such a lawyer may be said to have a higher obligation than lawyers generally. The government lawyer, to use the expression employed by counsel, is usually one who is a principal legal officer of a department, ministry, agency or other legal entity of the government, or a member of the legal staff of the department, ministry, agency or entity. This lawyer assumes a public trust because the government in all of its parts, is responsible to the people in our democracy with its representative form of government. Each part of the government has the obligation of carrying out, in the public interest, its assigned responsibility in a manner consistent with the applicable laws and regulations and the Charter of Rights. While the private lawyer represents the client's personal or private interest, the government lawyer represents the public interest. Although it may not be accurate to suggest the public is the client of the government lawyer as the client concept is generally understood, the government lawyer is required to observe in the performance of his or her professional responsibility the public interest sought to be served by the government department, ministry or agency of which he or she is a part. That is why I believe there is a special responsibility on the part of government lawyers to be particularly sensitive to the Rules of Professional Conduct, a responsibility which, regrettably, Mr. Wickett overlooked in this case.

Therefore, there will be an order disqualifying Mr. Wickett from any further involvement directly, or indirectly, in the conduct of this litigation on behalf of the respondents.

EVERINGHAM v. ONTARIO

[1992] O.J. No. 304, 88 D.L.R. (4th) 755
(Ont. Gen. Div., Callaghan C.J.O.C., Hartt and Campbell JJ.)

THE COURT:—

The application

The Attorney General for Ontario appeals, with leave, against an order disqualifying a Crown solicitor from any further involvement in a lawsuit brought against the Ontario government by a number of patients at the Oak Ridge Mental Health Centre.

The issue

Should a solicitor acting against a patient confined in a mental hospital be disqualified from continuing because he met privately with the patient in the institution without the presence or knowledge of the patient's counsel?

The facts

[The court reiterated the facts and findings of the motions court judge, and quoted Rule 10, Commentary 14 of the *Rules of Professional Conduct* of the Law Society of Upper Canada.]

The legal findings

Because the solicitor did not intend or obtain any advantage in the conduct of the litigation by talking to the patient, the learned judge found that the solicitor had not breached "the spirit" of Rule 10, Commentary 14 of the Law Society of Upper Canada.

The judge, however, concluded that the solicitor had breached Rule 10, Commentary 14, that lawyers employed by the government have a higher professional obligation to observe the Rules of Professional Conduct than other lawyers and that the solicitor's conduct in breaching the rule had so seriously undermined the patient's confidence in the system that it was necessary to disqualify the solicitor from further participation in the litigation.

Was the rule breached?

The judge erred in law in concluding that the solicitor had breached Rule 10, Commentary 14. Having found the meeting coincidental, innocent, unprejudicial, motivated solely out of concern to alleviate the patient's concern, having additionally found that the solicitor did not discuss the lawsuit or obtain any information, confidential or otherwise, and having further found that the spirit of the rule was not breached, there was no basis for the motions court judge to conclude that the rule was breached.

A purposive interpretation of the rule requires consideration of the purpose, intent, content and setting of the contact between the solicitor and the opposite party. No lawyer can completely avoid all contact, casual or otherwise, with every party against whom he or she acts. The words "approached or dealt with" must mean approached or dealt with in relation to the subject-matter or process of the litigation itself.

Having regard to the findings above and the fact that the solicitor did not approach or deal with the client in relation to the subject-matter or process of the litigation, there is no basis for a finding that the rule was breached and it cannot fairly be said that the solicitor breached the rule in this case.

The professional standard of Crown solicitors

Central to the conclusion of the learned judge was his view that lawyers employed by the government have a higher professional obligation than other lawyers to observe the Rules of Professional Conduct. There is no basis for this conclusion in the laws or traditions that govern the bar of this province.

All lawyers in Ontario are subject to the same single high standard of professional conduct. It is not flattering to the lawyers of Ontario to say that most of them are held to a lower standard of professional conduct than government lawyers.

The Ministry of the Attorney General Act, R.S.O. 1990, c. M.17, and the *Law Society Act*, R.S.O. 1990, c. L.8, codify some of the special public obligations of the Attorney General in relation to the public interest in the legal profession and the conduct of government business according to law. The unique obligations of Crown counsel in the conduct of public prosecutions are well known. Because of these public obligations and the traditions associated with the Crown office in this province, the courts have come to expect a particular level of conduct and expertise from Crown counsel in various types of judicial business.

It is one thing to say that a particular branch of the Crown law office or a particular law firm or lawyer has earned a reputation for a high standard of professional conduct. It is quite different to say that any lawyer or group of lawyers is subject to a higher standard of liability than that required of every lawyer under the Rules of Professional Conduct.

In respect of their liability under the Rules of Professional Conduct, as opposed to the public interest duties associated with their office, Crown counsel stand on exactly the same footing as every member of the bar.

It is therefore an error of law to exact from government lawyers a higher standard under the Rules of Professional Conduct than that required of lawyers in private practice.

Subjective or objective standard

The standard for the removal of counsel is objective. The standard is that of a reasonably informed member of the public: *MacDonald Estate v. Martin*, [1990] 3 S.C.R. 1235, . . . at pp. 1259-60 S.C.R. . . . . The personal feelings of the litigant are only one element in the application of an objective standard.

The motions court judge applied a subjective standard by requiring the solicitor's removal on the grounds that his conduct "seriously affected the patient and undermined his confidence in the process". By applying a subjective rather than an objective standard, the motions court judge erred in law.

Should the removal order stand?

Notwithstanding the error in finding a breach of the rule, the error in requiring a higher standard of professional conduct from government lawyers and the error in applying a subjective standard, should the removal be upheld?

In our view, it should.

It is within the inherent jurisdiction of a superior court to deny the right of audience to counsel when the interests of justice so require by reason of conflict or otherwise. This power does not depend on the rules of professional conduct made by the legal profession and is not limited to cases where the rules are breached.

The issue here is not whether or not the rule was breached or whether the solicitor worked for the government. Nor is it solely whether the patient lost confidence in the process.

The issue is whether a fair-minded reasonably informed member of the public would conclude that the proper administration of justice required the removal of the solicitor.

It is simply a matter of common sense that mental patients confined in institutions are in a vulnerable position. The administration of justice requires not only that confined mental patients be treated fairly in the legal process, but that they also be seen to be treated fairly in the legal process.

There is an obvious appearance of unfairness when a lawyer acting against a confined mental patient conducts a private meeting with the patient in an interview room in the institution without the presence or even the knowledge of the patient's counsel. This is particularly so when the meeting takes place at the arrangement and authority of the very custodians whose authority is challenged by the patient in the legal proceeding.

There is an obvious appearance of compulsion and an obvious apprehension of oppression in the very fact of such a meeting. The patient, with no notice to his counsel or access to legal or other advice or assistance, was under a custodial compulsion to meet privately with his legal opponent in an interview room in a closed institution hidden away from any public or judicial scrutiny, with no record kept of what was said. There is an obvious appearance that the patient's right to counsel is being undermined.

It is irrelevant that the solicitor's innocent version of the meeting is eventually found by a court to be preferable to the patient's version of the meeting. Apart from the obvious appearance of compulsion, oppression and deprivation of counsel, it is inevitable that such a meeting will produce different versions of the conversation. That is the mischief to be avoided, yet that is the very mischief that occurred here in the patient's version of what happened and the impression left with him that the meeting was pre-arranged with a view to gaining an advantage over him.

The public interest in the administration of justice requires an unqualified perception of its fairness in the eyes of the general public. This is particularly so when the rights are at stake of powerless and vulnerable litigants like detained mental patients. The appearance of unfairness, oppression and deprivation of counsel is not, as noted above, cured by an eventual finding that a court prefers the evidence of the solicitor to the evidence of the detained mental patient. The goal is not just to protect the interests of the individual litigant but even more importantly to protect public confidence in the administration of justice: *Goldberg v. Goldberg* (1982), 141 D.L.R. (3d) 133 . . . (Ont. Div. Ct.), per Callaghan J., at pp. 135-36 D.L.R. . . . The sine qua non of the justice system is that there be an unqualified perception of its fairness in the eyes of the public: *MacDonald Estate, supra*, at p. 1256 S.C.R., . . . quoting *O'Dea v. O'Dea* (1987), 68 Nfld. & P.E.I.R. 67, . . . (Nfld. U.F.C.), aff'd Nfld. C.A., June 6, 1988.

No reasonably informed member of the public would think it fair for any lawyer, about to cross-examine a detained mental patient, to take the patient into a closed institutional interview room under the authority of the very custodians whose legal authority over the patient is challenged, and conduct a private unrecorded conversation without any notice to the patient's counsel either before or after the interview.

The objective appearance of unfairness, oppression and deprivation of counsel is too blatant to be tolerated.

Notwithstanding the errors of law in the judgment appealed from, the order removing the lawyer must be upheld for the reasons stated above. The appeal is dismissed.

NOTES AND QUESTIONS

1. What did the lawyer for the Government do wrong according to Borins J.? Are there any circumstances in which it would be acceptable for a lawyer to speak with the opposing client without their counsel present? What features would such circumstances have in common?

2. How would you describe the key differences in the approaches of Borins J. and the Divisional Court to the question of whether government lawyers have special ethical duties? Which approach is preferable? Why?

3. If the Divisional Court found there was no conflict, why did it confirm the order of Borins J. to remove the lawyer? In answering this question consider in particular the court's statement that "no reasonably informed member of the public would think it fair" to act as the Crown did when examining Mr. LePage. If no reasonably informed member of the public would think it fair, does it make sense to describe the Crown's conduct as nonetheless ethically satisfactory?

4. In Chapter 4, dealing with conflicts of interest, you read in *MacDonald*

Estate v. Martin[8] that where one lawyer is found to be in a conflict of interest, that lawyer's firm is also disqualified. Does this apply when a Government lawyer is found to be in a conflict of interest? Can it? Should it? What rule should apply when an individual government lawyer is found to be in a conflict of interest?

5. The heart of the debate in *Everingham* is whether government lawyers owe "a higher duty". The readings that follow take different approaches to this issue. In reading each excerpt recall the facts and judgments in the two *Everingham* cases. Which approach would best resolve the problem that case presented?

ADAM DODEK

"Lawyering at the Intersection of Public Law and Legal Ethics: Government Lawyers as Custodians of the Rule of Law" (2010) 33 Dal. L.J. 1 at 18-28 [footnotes omitted]

. . . . .

As a matter of public law, government lawyers should owe higher ethical duties than private lawyers because they exercise public power . . .

. . . . .

[Exercising public power] is what it means to be lawyers for the Crown because the Crown is the concept that personifies the exercise of state power. As discussed below, government lawyers are not just passive vessels implementing the instructions of their political masters. Government lawyers interpret, advise and advocate on the powers and duties of the Crown. In so doing, government lawyers exercise public power. This exercise of public power is therefore the key distinction between government lawyers and all other lawyers. This is why it is an oversimplification, an understatement and is misleading to characterize government lawyers as lawyers for an organization. The source of this heightened ethical duty is therefore to be found in public law, specifically in the constitutional responsibilities of the Attorneys General.

All government Lawyers are agents of the Attorney General and under the *Carltona* doctrine, it is recognized that the Attorney General can only fulfill the duties of the office through delegation to his or her agents. Government lawyers' higher duty therefore derives from the duties and responsibilities of the Attorney General. That office has a unique constitutional status in Canada. It has been described as "the guardian of the public interest" or "the defender of the Rule of Law." . . . [In *Secession Reference*, [1998] 2 S.C.R. 217 at para. 70, the Supreme Court of Canada held that] "At [its] most basic level, the rule of law vouchsafes to the citizens and residents of the country a stable, predictable and ordered society in which to conduct their affairs. It provides a shield for individuals from arbitrary state action."

With this understanding of the rule of law, the case for the Attorney General as its

---

[8] [1990] S.C.J. No. 41, [1990] 3 S.C.R. 1235 (S.C.C.).

defender becomes more straightforward. The Attorney General has a statutory duty to "see that the administration of public affairs is in accordance with the law." As former Ontario Attorney General Ian Scott explained,

> the Attorney General has a positive duty to ensure that the administration of public affairs complies with the law. Any discussion of the Attorney General's responsibilities must keep this fundamental obligation in mind.

In the landmark 1968 McRuer Report into Civil Liberties in Ontario, Commissioner McRuer explained that

> [t]he duty of the Attorney General to supervise legislation imposes on him a responsibility to the public that transcends his responsibility to his colleagues in the Cabinet. It requires him to exercise constant vigilance to sustain and defend the Rule of Law against departmental attempts to grasp unhampered arbitrary powers, which may be done in many ways.

Government lawyers operate within a matrix of a rule of law triangle. Their higher duties are a result of operating at the intersection of three axes: as delegates of the Attorney General, as public servants and as members of the legal profession.

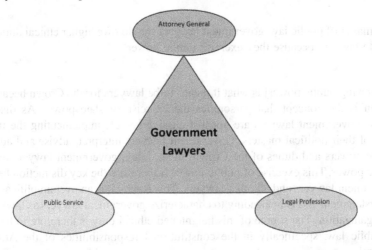

The Attorney General has a clear duty to uphold the rule of law. At its most basic level, this requires the Attorney General to ensure that all government action complies with the law. The Attorney General can only fulfill this duty through his or her agents, government lawyers. Government lawyers therefore have a delegated responsibility for fulfilling this public law duty. This is a critical point which distinguishes government lawyers from other lawyers who do not have such an express duty to ensure that their client complies with the law. While ethical codes prohibit lawyers from actively assisting or facilitating their client's commission of illegal conduct, they do not generally require lawyers to prevent their client from committing illegal acts. As delegates of the Attorney General, government lawyers have an affirmative duty that extends far beyond this minimal general duty of all lawyers. Government lawyers must ensure that all actions of government comply with all laws: civil, criminal and administrative. The ramifications of this duty are discussed below.

As public servants, government lawyers also have a duty to uphold the rule of law.

As Chair of the Task Force on Public Service Values and Ethics, former Deputy Minister of Justice John Tait, Q.C. explained:

> One of the defining features of public service organizations, especially in Canada, is that they are established under law and have as one of their chief roles the administration and upholding of the laws of Canada. In order to do this well, the public service and individual public servants should be animated by an unshakable conviction about the importance and primacy of law, and about the need to uphold it with integrity, impartiality and judgement.

Elsewhere Tait asserted that public servants must remember some of the basic purposes of government "such as democratic accountability, the rule of law, and fairness and equity." In short, all public servants have a duty to uphold the rule of law and government lawyers *qua* public servants share in this duty.

As lawyers, government lawyers are part of a profession devoted to the Rule of Law, but the perspectives of the profession and of Government are different. As the Law Society of Upper Canada's Task Force on the Rule of Law and the Independence of the Bar asserted, "[a]n independent Bar works in tandem with an independent judiciary in the implementation of the Rule of Law." The conceptual problem for government lawyers is that at first glance their position as lawyers for the government is inimical to most conceptions of an independent bar. These include the notion that lawyers are able to put their clients' interest first without fear of constraint *especially by the state*. It also includes the asserted "right of the public who need legal assistance to obtain it from someone who is independent of the state and can thereby provide independent representation." The other element of independence of the bar that is problematic for government lawyers is the idea of independence from client control: lawyers "should have autonomy to decide which clients and causes to represent and how to conduct that representation." As members of the legal profession, government lawyers are part of a profession dedicated to preserving the rule of law; however in the work that they do as government lawyers, the bar's conception of independence does not accurately describe their work.

When the three elements of government lawyers' identity — public servants, lawyers and delegates of the Attorney General — are combined, the unique relationship between government lawyers and the rule of law begins to appear. The core meanings of independence for the bar involve independence from the state, either in terms of interference with the lawyer-client relationship by the state or in terms of regulation by the state. For government lawyers, their client is the state. And as lawyers for the state, government lawyers are not only tasked with ensuring that the state and its officials comply with the law, but they are also involved in creating law in a way that private sector lawyers are not. Government lawyers are involved in protecting the rule of law from the inside. Moreover, what fundamentally distinguishes government lawyers from their non-government counterparts is that they exercise state power.

Government lawyers exercise state power in everything they do. There are some who will challenge this assertion and claim that government lawyers do not exercise state power but rather they represent the interests of those who do. This assertion fails to adequately capture the nature of government lawyers' work. We no longer live in a legal culture dominated by formalism where we believe that legal reasoning is the process of finding one true "correct" answer. Rather, we have come to acknowledge the indeterminacy of law and to acknowledge that there are subjective influences on legal interpretation. Government lawyers who are advising their clients on the law exercise power given to them under law. In many cases, they exercise significant discretion in providing legal advice. The act of giving legal advice, of interpreting the law, is itself an exercise of power. It can have a broad impact on people's lives – sometimes equal to or exceeding that of a Crown counsel in a criminal prosecution. Nowhere is this more the case nor more important than in the area of human rights and constitutional law.

The American example of the torture memos is the best example of the powerful impact that legal advice can have on people's lives. The act of legal interpretation can be used to constrain or to authorize power. In this instance, government lawyers used the law not as a constraint on power, but as "the handmaiden of unconscionable abuse." In the words of legal ethicist David Luban, the government lawyers spun their legal advice because they knew that "spun advice" is what their clients wanted. Lawyers in the Office of Legal Counsel in the Department of Justice interpreted law to authorize a host of heightened interrogation methods which most people would identify as torture. Moreover, lawyers in the Office of Legal Counsel used legal interpretation to create an entire category of persons who would not be protected by the rule of law (enemy combatants) and their advice supported the attempt to create a rule of law-free zone (Guantánamo). While this American example may be extreme, an important Canadian example demonstrates how the act of legal interpretation is itself an exercise of state power.

Under the *Canadian Bill of Rights*, the Minister of Justice is required to examine every draft regulation and every government bill introduced in the House of Commons "in order to ascertain whether any of the provisions thereof are inconsistent with the purposes and provisions" of the *Bill of Rights* and the Minister "shall report any such inconsistency to the House of Commons at the first convenient opportunity." An analogous provision of the *Department of Justice Act* requires the Minister to examine every draft regulation and every Government Bill introduced in the House of Commons

> in order to ascertain whether any of the provisions thereof are inconsistent with the purposes and provisions of the *Canadian Charter of Rights and Freedoms* and the Minister shall report any such inconsistency to the House of Commons at the first convenient opportunity.

Since 1960 when the *Canadian Bill of Rights* was enacted and since 1982 when the *Charter* was enacted, there has never been a single report made to the House of Commons by any Minister of Justice. Some think this is negative while other are less concerned about it. Here my point is that every time a decision is made not to make a report to the House of Commons, there has obviously been an act of interpretation. Indeed, this was made clear when a Department of Justice lawyer disclosed at a house committee that the standard used to trigger the reporting requirement was "manifestly unconstitutional." This phrase is itself an act of legal interpretation and a highly discretionary one at that. If lawyers in the Department had chosen a standard of "arguably unconstitutional," it is likely that many more bills would have been reported as under these provisions. This could have had a very different effect on legislation and the relationship between the courts, the legislature and the executive, to say the least of the potential impact of such legislation on affected groups.

These arguments for the higher duty of government lawyers as custodians of the rule of law are supported by existing duties of the Crown in other areas, government statements and some judicial pronouncements. In fact, if we examine the conduct expected of government lawyers, we find that they are already subject to a higher duty than private lawyers. The standards of conduct expected of government lawyers in areas outside of criminal law demonstrate that there are a whole host of areas where a higher duty is expected of government lawyers. Outside of criminal law, there are other areas where the Attorney General is expected to act independently, that is without political considerations or involvement. These include public interest injunctions and interventions. Other areas where the Attorney General represents the public interest include *parens patriae* jurisdiction, child protection, expropriation and charities. In Aboriginal Law, the honour of the Crown doctrine requires the Crown to consider Aboriginal interests in dealings with Aboriginal peoples.

When government lawyers are dealing with vulnerable parties who are represented by counsel, a higher standard of conduct may be expected of them than if the case simply involved two private parties. Thus, in the public inquiry into wrongful conviction of Donald Marshall, the Commission was critical of how the government handled the negotiations with Mr. Marshall's counsel over compensation. Counsel for Nova Scotia negotiated what would objectively be considered a good deal for the government to settle Mr. Marshall's claims for the sum of $270,000. However, the public inquiry did not view it in this manner. The Commissioners did not analyze government counsel's actions through the traditional paradigm of the adversarial model of litigation. Instead, the Commission stated that the Deputy Attorney General "should have realized that the Donald Marshall, Jr. compensation question was not merely a routine piece of civil litigation and the question of fairness needed to be considered. It was not." No further explanation was given as to why this was not an ordinary piece of civil litigation. If it was because of Crown wrongdoing, then the Commission did not make clear why counsel for the Crown owed a higher duty than in other cases of Crown wrongdoing.

In essence, when we put aside the situations where it is recognized that government lawyers do owe higher duties, we are left with two types of government lawyering activities: civil litigation against a non-vulnerable party and advisory functions, including legislative drafting and policy development. In ordinary civil litigation, government lawyers often do not behave like their private counterparts. For example, in the area of costs, the Crown routinely foregoes its right to seek costs against the losing party in litigation or seeks significantly less in indemnification than what a private party would.

A more recent decision addressing the conduct of government lawyers against a non-vulnerable party is perhaps more illuminating than the Hickman Inquiry's statements regarding government counsel's conduct *vis à vis* Donald Marshall. In a decision unsealed in 2010 involving the disclosure of a privileged report, Justice Michael Code of the Ontario Superior Court of Justice made the express connection between counsel's conduct and the government's duty under the rule of law. According to Justice Code, it is not enough for a public sector lawyer to take an adversarial stance in litigation because opposing counsel's argument is not well-framed. The government lawyer has a duty to ensure that the government complies with the law: "the importance of the rule of law as constitutional precept in Canada does not permit this approach to public administration at any level of government." Justice Code's statements involved the conduct of a lawyer for the City of Toronto. They have stronger force in the case of lawyers for the provincial or federal government because of the constitutional responsibilities of the federal and provincial Attorneys General.

If the statements of Justice Code are representative of a wider judicial attitude towards government lawyers, it is likely that many judges expect more from government counsel — even in ordinary civil litigation cases where the adversary is a well-resourced private lawyer. I would suspect that many government lawyers similarly hold themselves to a higher standard and take very seriously the moniker that they are lawyers for the Crown. In fact, the mandate, mission and values of the Department of Justice provide that its lawyers should "provide high-quality legal services" while "upholding the highest standards of integrity and fairness." Thus, the official policy of the Department of Justice would seem to support the idea of a higher duty. In policy and in practice, government lawyers are committed to a higher duty and not simply to the minimal standards of ethical conduct prescribed in law society rules.

MALLIHA WILSON, TAIA WONG & KEVIN HILLE

"Professionalism and the Public Interest"
(2011) 38 Advocates' Q. 1 at 14-17*
[footnotes omitted]

Dodek argues that government lawyers are subject to a higher ethical duty because they operate at the intersection of three axes . . .

But the fact of operating within that matrix does not necessarily or easily translate into higher ethical standards for government lawyers. In litigation against major corporate or institutional litigants, for example, wouldn't the public interest be best served by government lawyers who avail themselves of whatever arguments they can within the bounds of the law in order to achieve the government's goals? The matrix within which government lawyers operate may indeed be unique, but it is not monolithic. Instead, government lawyers advise on and litigate a wide range of matters involving a broad spectrum of litigants. Imposing higher ethical duties on government lawyers without regard to the diversity of their practice and the needs and obligations of the ministries and agencies they serve would impede the delivery of legal services in government.

Moreover, Dodek's suggestion that government lawyers owe a higher ethical duty as a result of their exercise of public power is difficult to reconcile with government decision-making processes involving significant matters, in which only certain public officials have the legal authority to decide matters on behalf of the Crown.

---

* Reproduced with permission.

These public officials wield and exercise public power, not the government lawyers who advise them. The government lawyer provides legal advice on proposed courses of action that government officials may wish to take, but he or she does not have decision making authority either directly or indirectly, as legal considerations are only one factor, along with policy and political considerations, that influence official decision-making.

While it may be true that, as Dodek suggests, government lawyers exercise discretion in providing legal advice and that the act of giving legal advice, of interpreting the law, is itself an exercise of power, that discretion and power is circumscribed by the institutional and constitutional confines within which the government lawyer works. The role of the government lawyer is to state what the law is, thereby enabling the Attorney General to discharge his or her obligations to defend the rule of law and safeguard the public interest. In a democratic, post-Charter society, government lawyers cannot decide what constitutes the public interest and enforce the rule of law themselves by pre-emptively acting inconsistently with the legitimate goals of a democratically-elected government, particularly when their advice is cloaked in secrecy and protected by solicitor-client privilege. Rather, government lawyers are responsible for empowering the Attorney General to discharge his or her responsibilities of upholding the rule of law and protecting the public interest by providing advice that is thorough, balanced and independent of partisan political consideration. The suggestion that government lawyers owe higher ethical duties because they exercise public power therefore collapses the roles of the government lawyer and the Attorney General, when in fact constitutional norms, the institutional hierarchy of government and democratic ideals require their separation. The government lawyer's job is fundamentally to give the best legal advice about what is required by the rule of law. There is no need for a higher ethical obligation for that to occur.

Some legal theorists have taken the fact that regulatory codes are silent on the difference between government lawyers and private counsel as an indication that the expectations of the former are not substantially different than those of the latter. Other theorists have suggested, however, that even where a higher standard of conduct is not contained in extrinsic codes of conduct, it is nevertheless derived intrinsically from the position of a government lawyer as a public official. They argue that the oath of loyalty taken by government lawyers, to the Crown and to the public interest, along with the public interest obligations inherent in their office, is enough to elevate the standards of ethical and professional conduct by which government lawyers must govern themselves.

These theorists reason, as did the motions judge in *Everingham*, that there is a positive obligation on government lawyers to advance the public interest in litigation and to seek a fair result beyond the interests of their government client. As representatives of a sovereign whose interest is to seek justice, these theorists reason that government lawyers must also seek justice. This mandate could require a government lawyer to not bring forth unmeritorious or undeserving cases, exploit legal or factual errors made by the court or the opposing party, call attention to mistakes or take advantage of procedural lapses without regard to the actual merits of a party's position. For such theorists, seeking justice could also mean disclosing confidential information if it were in the democratic interests of preserving open and transparent government.

According to these commentators, the key difference between the government lawyer and the private lawyer is that the government lawyer serves the public interest exclusively, if indirectly and derivatively, over and above any private interests. The public interest, however, is a concept that is itself amorphous, representing a plurality of interests and conflicting values. It is therefore difficult to translate the service of such dynamic interests into clear ethical obligations. Moreover, some commentators suggest that the way in which government lawyers ultimately interpret their role with respect to these obligations to the public will no doubt influence the types of arguments that they make and the litigation strategies that they employ, such as asserting technical defences to defeat meritorious claims, accepting erroneous court decisions and pursuing costly litigation of questionable merit for political purposes. For instance, Catherine Lanctot has argued that the public interest is sufficiently served by government lawyers advocating the interests of their agency clients with the same zeal as private counsel:

> If the bar truly believes its own rhetoric that zealous advocacy on behalf of a client serves the highest purposes of the American justice system, and if the bar expects government lawyers to "seek justice," then logically the bar should demand of government lawyers that they be at least as zealous as their private counterparts, if not more so.

Accordingly, there is no need for additional, elevated standards of ethical conduct in order for the public interest to be served. Government lawyers serve the public interest by representing "their clients to the best of their ability, asserting whatever arguments they can in order to achieve their clients' goals."

NOTES AND QUESTIONS

1. What do you think of Dodek's argument that government lawyers exercise public power? If you agree, do you think this necessarily imposes a higher obligation on government lawyers?

2. How do Wilson, Wong & Hille respond to Dodek? Which account of the work of government lawyers do you prefer and why? Which account would best explain the reasonable person's reaction that the Crown's conduct in *Everingham* was not "fair"? Does the answer to that question affect your assessment of which account is preferable?

3. What is at stake in the debate over whether government lawyers owe a higher duty? Two government lawyers have asserted that the debate is "academic" because in practice government lawyers are held to a higher standard than other lawyers, by themselves and by courts. See Michael H. Morris & Sandra Nishikawa, "The Orphans of Legal Ethics: Why Government Lawyers are Different – And How We Protect and Promote that Difference in Service of the Rule of Law and the Public Interest."[9] See also how former Assistant Deputy Attorney General of Canada Elizabeth Sanderson addresses this issue: See Elizabeth Sanderson, *Government*

---

[9] (2013) 26 Can. J. Admin. L. & Prac. 171.

Lawyering: Duties and Ethical Challenges of Government Lawyers.[10]

[3] NATURE OF THE GOVERNMENT LAWYER'S DUTY

As noted by Dodek, developments in the United States in the first decade of the 21st century brought the issue of the ethical obligations of government lawyers to the fore. Specifically, the question of whether government lawyers have particular ethical obligations, and as to the nature of those obligations, became the subject of considerable discussion in response to the participation of lawyers in designing and authorizing the Bush administration's use of torture in its pursuit of the "War on Terror". The Bush administration used a variety of methods of torture to obtain information from detainees and terrorism suspects, including waterboarding, which has been described as "slow motion suffocation with enough time to contemplate the inevitability of black out and expiration — usually the person goes into hysterics on the board".[11]

As discussed in detail by David Luban, amongst others, the lawyers advising the Bush administration and the Central Intelligence Agency (CIA) were willing to go to extraordinary lengths to justify torture of this type. Not only were numerous legal opinions provided by government lawyers in support of the use of torture, the opinions provided were notable for their willingness to stretch legal doctrine and analysis in order to endorse the government's goals. Luban, in analyzing the various opinions, goes so far as to describe one memo's conclusions as ranging "from the doubtful to the loony".[12] This was the "Bybee" memo, in which Jay Bybee and John Yoo, lawyers at the Office of Legal Counsel, advised the CIA on how far it could go in abusing detainees. In the memo, Bybee and Yoo concluded that "inflicting physical pain does not count as torture until the pain reaches the level associated with organ failure or death" and that "utilizing techniques known to be painful is not torture unless the interrogator specifically intends the pain to be equivalent to the pain accompanying organ failure or death".[13] As described by Luban, Bybee and Yoo relied in defending this conclusion on a domestic Medicare statute:

> The statute defines an emergency medical condition as one in which someone experiences symptoms that "a prudent lay person . . . could reasonably expect" might indicate "serious impairment to bodily functions, or serious dysfunction of any bodily organ or part." The statute specifies that severe pain is one such symptom. In an exquisite exercise of legal formalism run amok, the Memo infers that pain is severe only if it is at the level indicating an emergency medical condition. The authors solemnly cite a Supreme Court decision to show that Congress's use of a phrase in one statute should be used to interpret its meaning in

---

[10] (LexisNexis, 2018) 15

[11] W. Bradley Wendel, "Executive Branch Lawyers in a Time of Terror" (2008) 31 Dal. L.J. 247, citing an article by Malcolm Nance from *Small Wars Journal*.

[12] David Luban, *Legal Ethics and Human Dignity* (New York: Cambridge University Press, 2007) at 175.

[13] David Luban, *Legal Ethics and Human Dignity* (New York: Cambridge University Press, 2007) at 175.

another.[14]

Luban goes on to argue that this and other memos written in justification of torture violated the ethical standards that should apply to lawyers providing advice to government or, indeed, to anyone. The lawyers were not candid or independent, they simply acted to provide "cover" to the agencies receiving the advice, and their conduct in writing the memos did not represent an act of good faith legal interpretation.

In this analysis, Luban focuses primarily on the way in which the torture lawyers violated basic and common norms of legal ethics; in the main he argues that the torture lawyers were unethical because they were bad lawyers as measured against the normal standard which applies to lawyers, not because they were government lawyers pursuing a wicked end. Luban does go on, however, to argue that the fact that the violation of the lawyer's ethical obligations was in pursuit of state-sanctioned torture is itself significant:

> I have focused on . . . the procedural side of the subject: the requirements of honesty, objectivity, and non-frivolous argument regardless of the subject-matter on which lawyers tender their advice. But that does not mean the subject-matter is irrelevant. It is one thing for boy-wonder lawyers to loophole tax laws and write opinions legitimizing financial shenanigans. It is another thing entirely to loophole laws against torture and cruelty. Lawyers should approach laws defending basic human dignity with fear and trembling.[15]

Luban does not generalize from this argument to conclude that government lawyers have a heightened or different ethical obligation. As discussed in the previous section, however, it is certainly arguable that government lawyers do have such an ethical obligation. As Luban notes, there is a difference between the sorts of legal matters addressed by government lawyers and those addressed by lawyers in private practice. Government lawyers have the power — inescapably — to facilitate and endorse the exercise of state power against individuals. A government lawyer may be asked to provide an opinion on the ethics of, for example, using surveillance against participants in a regulatory proceeding; this is simply not an ethical issue likely to be faced by a lawyer in private practice. It is also, of course, not an ethical issue that raises the same moral and legal stakes as advising on the legality of torture. Nonetheless, like opining on the legality of torture, it places the government lawyer at the intersection between the rights of the citizenry and the power of the state, and raises moral, political and ethical dimensions to the lawyer's conduct that are not obviously present for the lawyer in private practice. It is for this reason that, as Dodek suggests, government lawyers can reasonably be understood to be ethically distinct from the profession in general.

Assuming that that is correct, of what would government's special ethical obligation consist? What, ethically speaking, would be the difference between being a government lawyer and not? In the following excerpt Brent Cotter argues that

---

[14] David Luban, *Legal Ethics and Human Dignity* (New York: Cambridge University Press, 2007) at 178-179.

[15] David Luban, *Legal Ethics and Human Dignity* (New York: Cambridge University Press, 2007) at 205.

government lawyers have a special "duty of fair dealing" which should inform their conduct.

In reading this excerpt, consider how a duty of fair dealing would apply to a lawyer such as Jay Bybee. Or consider how it would apply to being a lawyer in President Trump's administration.[16] Consider as well how the existence of such a duty might have changed the conduct of the government lawyer in *Everingham*, or changed the Court's response to that conduct.

BRENT COTTER

"Lawyers Representing Public Government and a Duty of 'Fair Dealing'"
Canadian Bar Association, Alberta Law Conference (March 2008)

Introduction

The aim of this short paper is to give broad brush consideration to the ethical framework of lawyers in government service, and those retained to represent governments, and to suggest that this framework differs in one significant respect from that of lawyers in private practice. This difference is based on the nature of the client — public government — and on certain unique responsibilities of that client. I argue that these unique responsibilities inform the ethical obligations of lawyers in their representation of government interests and impose upon those lawyers "public interest" responsibilities in ways that are noticeably different from those of lawyers with private sector clients.

Some commentators have claimed that lawyers retained to represent government are required to serve the "public interest"; or that their client is "the public". I argue that while there is a set of public interest obligations imposed upon these lawyers, the idea that one "serves the public interest" is a vacuous concept, and a potentially dangerous one if "public interest" obligations are not given a clear framework. Equally, the idea that the government lawyer's client is "the public" amounts to an operational impossibility in any conventional understanding of a lawyer's role and responsibilities. As a lawyer, try to imagine taking instructions from "the public", or honouring one's obligations of confidentiality to "the public". Just stating the circumstance exposes the absurdity of the concept.

Rather, I argue that such a lawyer does have a client in the conventional way, but in the representing public government, the lawyer owes obligations to the community of interest in opposition to the government — obligations that are not owed by lawyers for private clients. These greater obligations derive their shape from the duties owed by the government itself to the public interest. They can be articulated in general ways, though I readily concede that it may not always be easy to fulfill them perfectly. I shall call this set of responsibilities the "duty of fair dealing", and try to give it some preliminary shape.

The Conventional Paradigm

The standard conception of a lawyer's representation of a client is that this

---

[16] See W. Bradley Wendel, "Government Lawyers in the Trump Administration", Cornell Legal Studies Research Paper No. 17-04, online: https://papers.ssrn.com/sol3/papers.cfm?abstract_id=2906422.

representation is significantly "client-centred". This orientation, and the lawyer's concomitant duty of loyalty, is certainly the governing paradigm in the representation of private clients. This orientation reinforces the entitlement of the client to pursue actions favourable to himself or herself, with the aid of a lawyer, despite the consequences for others. Indeed, the only limitations suggested to qualify this pursuit of self-interest are that the objective and the means used to pursue it not be unlawful or require the lawyer to engage in unethical conduct. Indeed, from a lawyer's perspective, the adversary system — a civilized conflict between adversaries in the pursuit of interests at odds with one another — relies on this contest of self-interest to justify conventional lawyering roles in many of our legal and judicial processes. In large measure this approach is based on the sense that the individual entity owes a duty only to himself or herself or itself. The lawful pursuit of enlightened self-interest is a central tenet of our society and of the consequent design of our legal system.

The Nature of "Representational Entities"

Is this orientation appropriate for "representational entities"? By representational entities, I mean those organizations with a different purpose than the pursuit of self-interest. Organizations that seek to "represent" the interests of a larger community with one or many objectives related to the community of interest it seeks to represent.

There are many types of "representational" entities. In certain respects corporations are representational. Many organizations designed to advance the interests of their members have a "representational" dimension. And it is surely the case that public government has a representational dimension. Indeed, one might argue that its "representational" role — the representation of the interests of its citizens — is the raison d'être for public government to exist. To get at the question of the role and responsibilities for a government lawyer, it is necessary to consider the question of who exactly does the 'representational' entity, government, represent.

This appears to be a straightforward question. The conventional understanding is that public government represents all of its citizens. As a consequence the conventional understanding of the ambit of legal and ethical duties naturally extends to "all citizens" — the public, from which it is argued that lawyers representing public government therefore represent "the public" or "the public interest". This concept presents two significant problems. One is practical. It is pretty much impossible to consult or take instructions from "the public" or "the public interest", except through some legally authorized representative of "the public". It also goes without saying that some of the standard understandings of a lawyer's duties would be rendered meaningless if one is required to consider "the public" to be the client. It also renders meaningless the significance of "representative government", as the entity which actuates the public's wishes. To assume that the lawyer owes client-like duties to "the public" or "the public interest" makes a mockery of representative government and invites the lawyer to determine what the public interest is. Surely no one contemplates this outcome.

A second difficulty is the one related to the complicated nature of government itself. One of the critical responsibilities of governments is to make choices among scarce public resources in pursuit of public policy objectives. By definition, this involves a choice between or among competing interests, as a consequence of which not all of the citizens will be satisfied all of the time. Similarly, governments have a duty to protect taxpayers' resources, in the form of government revenues and government assets, from claims upon them, even from their own citizens. This may require a choice on the part of government to protect the collective interests of citizens against the claims of one individual citizen. These situations will often lead to conflict between the government and its representatives, on the one hand, and one or more of the citizens it exists to represent. These conflicts may arise in a variety of forms and forums. Legislators may be required to choose among conflicting legislative approaches. Decisions will be made to use the financial resources of the government in ways that embrace some policy choices and that reject other choices. The government will choose to acknowledge some citizens' claims and resist the claims of others. The representatives of public government will be called upon to make these choices and to direct their agents, including lawyers, to pursue the choices, resist the claims, as the representatives deem appropriate.

From this set of examples it is clear that the government in its representative capacities will of necessity place itself in conflict with individual citizens or groups of citizens. This happens to individuals and private actors all the time. When it does occur, within the limits of law and the moral choices of the private actor, self-interest is entitled to prevail without any special consideration of the interests of the "other". Is this the case with public government in terms of duties owed to the "other" — citizens with whom it is in conflict? Is there a particular set of obligations owed to those who are part of the collective, representational interest of government but who are also its adversaries in one or other context?

I argue that governments do owe duties to that "other". To take a different view would require us to accept the proposition that a citizen in conflict with his or her government is somehow diminished in his citizenship by virtue of the conflict. This does not mean that government is somehow required to accede to the claims of citizens in conflict with government. Rather, the real question is the nature of the duties owed by the government, as a "representational" entity, to the members of its "representational" community with whom it might be in disagreement or conflict. It is here that I believe the roles and responsibilities of a lawyer representing public government diverge from those of a lawyer representing a private interest.

The Dimensions of this "Representational" Duty

I propose to examine the nature of this duty from the perspective of a citizen in a legal conflict with his or her government. It is often the case that citizens make claims upon governments that are not well founded in law, or that are in direct conflict with the policy direction that the government wishes to pursue. In these situations governments are surely entitled, on behalf of the collective interest of their citizens, to resist these claims, to stay the course. Sometimes, however, citizens make claims that are entirely or at least partly well founded. Is government entitled, in advancing the collective interest of their citizens, to resist the legitimate claims of its citizens? The answer in my view is "no". I make this assertion from two perspectives; first, from analogies drawn from the criminal law and the responsibilities owed by public prosecutors to defendants in criminal proceedings; second,

493

from the perspective of a set of duties owed by representative governments to it citizens.

(a) The Public Prosecutions Analogy

Prosecutors represent the state in criminal proceedings. They are legally styled as "agents of the Crown". Their role is to review and prosecute allegations of criminal conduct. They are required to do so in the pursuit of fair and just outcomes. This requires an assessment of whether there is sufficient evidence in a case to justify laying charges or proceeding with them, and an assessment of whether the public interest is served in pursuing the charges. As a matter of policy, and perhaps law, prosecutors are not entitled to proceed with charges that do not meet this standard. As well, as a matter of good policy and law [*R. v. Stinchcombe*] prosecutors are required to disclose to the defence all relevant information in relation to the criminal proceedings, whether it helps or hurts the prosecution's case. This is intended to ensure that a person who is the subject of a prosecution gets a fair trial. It is part of the obligation placed upon the Crown of 'fair dealing' with its citizens in criminal proceedings. This has the consequence of ensuring full disclosure of everything relevant to a prosecution, and of ensuring that, as far as a system can do so, the Crown acknowledges and concedes everything in an accused person's favour that should legitimately be acknowledged or conceded in a proceeding, to ensure that justice is done.

Criminal cases have potentially serious implications for those who are accused of crimes, and in that sense may require certain values — including constitutional values — to be given priority; values that are not directly implicated in other proceedings between the Crown and its citizens. However, the consequences for citizens of a wide variety of non-criminal dealings with government are likely as profound as many criminal matters. Is a citizen any less entitled to this standard of fair dealing because the matter does not involve criminal proceedings against him or her? Or because the conflict between a citizen and the government does not involve a court proceeding?

(b) A Duty of "Fair Dealing"

The government serves in a "representational" capacity with respect to all of its citizens. Indeed, we often refer to our form of government as "representative government". This "representativeness" includes those who support its policies and those who oppose them. It includes those who may benefit from the political choices politicians and governments make, and those who are adversely affected. And it includes those who may be in legal conflicts with the government. A "representational" entity, and particularly government, understandably owes a duty to the collective interest of all of its citizens. With respect to government, this may require the government to do its best to ensure that chosen public policies are not derailed, or that illegitimate claims upon the public purse are resisted, or that other actions or claims seen to be contrary to the public interest are opposed. These are all perfectly legitimate, even required, roles for a government to undertake. And as a general rule they benefit the public interest as defined at the time.

But what duty is owed to the claimant in opposition to the government. In this respect the government, as a "representational entity", is in a different position from others. One aspect of that "representativeness" includes a duty to the very citizen who brings the challenge, or makes the claim, against his or her own government. What is the nature of that duty?

I argue that at the very least it requires a standard of "fair dealing" with its citizens in these positions, a standard that exceeds the requirements of private persons. This governmental standard of fair dealing should, for example, exceed the minimum requirements one finds in legal proceedings. Aside from making the disclosures required by law to claimants, it should include admitting what should reasonably be admitted, conceding what should reasonably be conceded, accommodating what should reasonably be accommodated. In its "representational" duties to one of its citizens with whom it is in conflict, a duty of fair dealing requires nothing less. This requires the accommodation of the legitimate interests of citizens whenever those interests are reasonably known to be legitimate.

This does not mean that governments must accede to any allegation made by a claimant, or acquiesce in the face of every challenge to its policies. To do so would subjugate, illegitimately, the representative responsibilities of government to its larger public interest. I concede that in some cases the role of a government's legal representative will be difficult in trying to ensure a fair outcome without giving away too much, and being constrained in the use of certain legal tools available to the private litigant. It does require however, that in the interests of legitimate claimants the larger public interest defers to and accommodates these legitimate claims. Not grudgingly, but in a fair and timely way. In this way, "fair dealing" with its citizens does not detract from the representative nature of public government. Rather, it advances and enriches it for all.

Conclusion

There is a fundamental "public" value at stake here that does not have the same resonance when conflict arises between private claimants. Simply put, largely un-moderated self-interest — justified within our systems of dispute resolution for private disputants — has no place in where a government finds itself in conflict with its citizens. Governments owe "just" outcomes to all of their citizens, including the ones with whom they are in conflict. This can only be achieved through a moderation of zealous advocacy, in much the same way that this moderation is required in criminal prosecutions in order to achieve just outcomes. Governments, and their lawyers, owe to their citizens a duty of fair dealing.

NOTES AND QUESTIONS

1. Do you find Cotter's argument that a general duty to the public interest is not an appropriate obligation to place on a government lawyer, but that a duty of fair dealing is, compelling?

2. How significant a constraint on government conduct is a duty of "fair dealing"?

3. Dodek is sympathetic to Cotter's argument but ultimately finds it difficult to translate on a practical level as to what lawyers should do. Instead, Dodek falls back on the explanation offered by former Deputy Minister of Justice of Canada, John Tait, who asserted that government lawyers owed

a number of unique duties including being "guardians of the rule of law as it applies within government in a parliamentary democracy".[17] Tait asserted that government lawyers have a higher duty to the law and to the Constitution.[18] In practical terms, this means that government lawyers must provide objective and independent advice. Tait explained:

> The duty to promote and uphold the rule of law means that there is a quality of objectivity in the interpretation of the law that is important to the public service lawyer. There must be a fair inquiry into what the law actually is. The rule of law is not protected by unduly stretching the interpretation to fit the client's wishes. And it is not protected by giving one interpretation to one client and another to another department.[19]

Dodek asserts that in advising the Crown, government lawyers must provide a fair interpretation of the law: "Moreover, as custodians of the Rule of Law, they cannot use the law as a sword to batter their opponents, for the Rule of Law is intended as a shield against arbitrary government action not as a weapon in the Government's arsenal. Thus, unlike private sector lawyers, government lawyers should not exploit loopholes in the law in sanctioning government action or rely on technicalities in litigation." Dodek also argues that being custodians of the Rule of Law imposes a special obligation on government lawyers to support other institutions crucial to the maintenance of the Rule of Law like the independence of the judiciary and the independence of the bar.

Do you find conceptual or practical differences between Cotter's and Dodek's approaches? Which do you find more helpful?

4. What would the effect of an obligation of fair dealing be on lawyers asked to provide an opinion on the legality of waterboarding or on a ban on Muslim immigrants? Or, to put it slightly differently, would Cotter provide a different explanation for the ethical failure of the torture lawyers than that provided by Luban?

5. As noted prior to the Cotter excerpt, the presidency of Donald J. Trump raised questions about the ethics of the conduct of lawyers representing him personally, but also of lawyers working within the Department of Justice under then Attorney General Bill Barr. Rebecca Roiphe noted the following about the issues that arose from the Trump presidency, and also articulated how the ethical duties of government lawyers ought to be understood:

> There is value in using examples from the Trump administration to illustrate the different roles of government lawyers, because the Presi-

[17] John C. Tait, "The Public Service Lawyer, Service to the Client and the Rule of Law" (1997) 23 Commonwealth L. Bull. 542 at 543.

[18] John C. Tait, "The Public Service Lawyer, Service to the Client and the Rule of Law" (1997) 23 Commonwealth L. Bull. 542 at 548.

[19] John C. Tait, "The Public Service Lawyer, Service to the Client and the Rule of Law" (1997) 23 Commonwealth L. Bull. 542 at 543-544.

dent's repeated assaults on legal institutions has highlighted how central lawyers' ethical obligations are to the rule of law. He has, in essence, exposed the fault lines. Without a neutral mechanism to apply and interpret the law, this vital aspect of American democracy is in jeopardy. In some respects, the rule of law is a game of trust. If the public loses faith in the institutions that implement the law, then the group with the greatest power to enforce its will always wins. The President's statements, on Twitter and elsewhere, have the power to undermine this trust. When the President criticizes the Federal Bureau of Investigation ("FBI"), DOJ, or Special Counsel Robert Mueller's investigation, he undermines the law as a serious constraint on power. When he accuses courts of being captive to one party or another, once again he threatens to collapse law into power. When he orders the investigation and prosecution of political enemies, he tramples on an essential democratic principle. When President Trump mischaracterizes facts, like the content of the Mueller Report, he destabilizes the law itself, which is dependent on faith in a discernible reality. In politics, discernible reality itself is based on a basic faith in the institutions whose job is to ascertain that reality.

The premise for my argument about each type of government lawyer is that government lawyers ought to approach their job in a way that supports an institution designed to implement and interpret the law in an evenhanded way, in light of administration priorities. While seemingly simple, the assertion of presidential priorities can, at times, impede the fair interpretation and evenhanded enforcement of the law. The government should define lawyers' roles so as to preserve the law as a neutral and legitimate mechanism for resolving disputes and as a real check on power without undermining the ability of elected officials to articulate and implement the administration's policy objectives. Interpreting government lawyers' obligations with this larger goal in mind leads to a view of government lawyers' ethics that varies given the role the particular lawyer plays.[20]

Do you think it is possible for a Canadian politician or political party to unsettle the ethics of government lawyers in the way that the Trump presidency arguably did? How does Roiphe's articulation of the government lawyer's ethical duties compare to that of Cotter or Dodek? What are its strengths and weaknesses, normatively or practically?

6. Who should fall within the category of government lawyers? Would the lawyers who acted for the Toronto General Hospital in *Grossman v. Toronto General Hospital*, [1983] O.J. No. 3001 (Ont. H.C.J.), excerpted in Chapter 5, count? If so, would you describe their conduct as consistent with the obligation of fair dealing? What would fair dealing have looked like in a case like that one?

---

[20] Rebecca Roiphe, "A Typology of Justice Department Lawyers' Role and Responsibilities" (2020) 98 N.C. Law Rev. 1077 at 1080-1082. For an overview of the articles on the special issue of the North Carolina Law Review on legal ethics and the Trump presidency see: Michael J. Gerhard, "Introduction: Legal Ethics in the Age of Trump" (2020) 98 N.C. Law Rev. 1029 at 1029-1030.

7. Former Assistant Deputy Attorney General of Canada and Deputy Minister of Justice of Nunavut Elizabeth Sanderson provides a different explanation of the "layers" of government lawyers' duties. She explains that in private practice, lawyers owe professional and common law duties to clients. In house corporate lawyers additionally owe additional obligations to the Law Society and also have to follow in-house/corporate rules. Government lawyers owe professional obligations as members of law societies but also have public law duties and public service duties. See Elizabeth Sanderson, *Government Lawyering: Duties and Ethical Challenges of Government Lawyers* (Lexis Nexis, 2018) c. 1.

Scenario One

You act for the government in litigation brought by an Aboriginal band alleging that the government violated its fiduciary obligations in relation to natural resources on reserve lands. The band alleges that the government failed to maximize the value of the resources, and profited at the band's expense. In substance your assessment of the claim is that the band is likely correct — the conduct of the government did breach its fiduciary obligations. However, a significant portion of the band's claim likely falls outside the applicable limitation periods and is, as a consequence, statute barred. Is it ethical for you to apply for the claim to be struck on that basis? Is doing so consistent with your obligation of fair dealing or your duty as a custodian of the Rule of Law? See: *Canada (Attorney General) v. Lameman*[21] *and Wewaykum Indian Band v. Canada.*[22]

[4] GOVERNMENT LAWYERS AND RECONCILIATION

[a] The Truth and Reconciliation Commission's Report

As part of its report into Canada's residential schools, the Truth and Reconciliation Commission (TRC) issued 94 Calls to Action.[23] These include the following:

Justice

26. We call upon the federal, provincial, and territorial governments to review and amend their respective statutes of limitations to ensure that they conform to the principle that governments and other entities cannot rely on limitation defences to defend legal actions of historical abuse brought by Aboriginal people. . . ..

42. We call upon the federal, provincial, and territorial governments to commit to the recognition and implementation of Aboriginal justice systems in a manner consistent with the Treaty and Aboriginal rights of Aboriginal peoples, the *Constitution Act, 1982*, and the *United Nations Declaration on the Rights of Indigenous Peoples*, endorsed by Canada in November 2012. . . ..

---

[21] [2008] S.C.J. No. 14, 2008 SCC 14 (S.C.C.).

[22] [2002] S.C.J. No. 79, [2002] 4 S.C.R. 245 (S.C.C.).

[23] Truth and Reconciliation Commission of Canada, *Calls to Action*, online: http://www.trc.ca/assets/pdf/Honouring_the_Truth_Reconciling_for_the_Future_July_23_2015.pdf.

Equity for Aboriginal People in the Legal System

51. We call upon the Government of Canada, as an obligation of its fiduciary responsibility, to develop a policy of transparency by publishing legal opinions it develops and upon which it acts or intends to act, in regard to the scope and extent of Aboriginal and Treaty rights.

52. We call upon the Government of Canada, provincial and territorial governments, and the courts to adopt the following legal principles:

   i.   Aboriginal title claims are accepted once the Aboriginal claimant has established occupation over a particular territory at a particular point in time.

   ii. Once Aboriginal title has been established, the burden of proving any limitation on any rights arising from the existence of that title shifts to the party asserting such a limitation. . ..

Professional Development and Training for Public Servants

57. We call upon federal, provincial, territorial, and municipal governments to provide education to public servants on the history of Aboriginal peoples, including the history and legacy of residential schools, the *United Nations Declaration on the Rights of Indigenous Peoples*, Treaties and Aboriginal rights, Indigenous law, and Aboriginal–Crown relations. This will require skills based training in intercultural competency, conflict resolution, human rights, and anti-racism.

[b] Implementing the Truth and Reconciliation Commission's Report

The government of Prime Minister Justin Trudeau committed to implement the recommendations of the Truth and Reconciliation Commission. In 2017, the Government of Canada published *Principles Respecting the Government of Canada's Relationship with Indigenous Peoples*.[24] The principles provide:

The Government of Canada recognizes that:

1. All relations with Indigenous peoples need to be based on the recognition and implementation of their right to self-determination, including the inherent right of self-government.

2. Reconciliation is a fundamental purpose of section 35 of the *Constitution Act, 1982.*

3. The honour of the Crown guides the conduct of the Crown in all of its dealings with Indigenous peoples.

4. Indigenous self-government is part of Canada's evolving system of cooperative federalism and distinct orders of government.

5. Treaties, agreements, and other constructive arrangements between Indigenous peoples and the Crown have been and are intended to be acts of

---

[24] Canada, Department of Justice, "Principles Respecting the Government of Canada's Relationship with Indigenous Peoples", online: https://www.justice.gc.ca/eng/csj-sjc/principles-principes.html.

reconciliation based on mutual recognition and respect.

6. Meaningful engagement with Indigenous peoples aims to secure their free, prior, and informed consent when Canada proposes to take actions which impact them and their rights on their lands, territories, and resources.

7. Respecting and implementing rights is essential and that any infringement of section 35 rights must by law meet a high threshold of justification which includes Indigenous perspectives and satisfies the Crown's fiduciary obligations.

8. Reconciliation and self-government require a renewed fiscal relationship, developed in collaboration with Indigenous nations, that promotes a mutually supportive climate for economic partnership and resource development.

9. Reconciliation is an ongoing process that occurs in the context of evolving Indigenous-Crown relationships.

10. A distinctions-based approach is needed to ensure that the unique rights, interests and circumstances of the First Nations, the Métis Nation and Inuit are acknowledged, affirmed, and implemented.

In 2019, Attorney General Jody Wilson-Raybould issued a directive on Civil Litigation involving Indigenous Peoples.[25] This was intended to change how the Crown, and by extension federal government lawyers, approach civil litigation with Indigenous Peoples. There are 20 litigation guidelines. Review them online.

NOTES AND QUESTIONS

1. How do the approaches of Dodek, Wilson, Wong & Hille and Cotter inform how government lawyers should deal with Indigenous persons in a legal context? How should the government's adoption of the TRC's recommendations and its Calls to Action affect government lawyers' interaction with Indigenous persons?

2. Does the context of Government lawyers' legal interaction with Indigenous persons matter? I.e. is there a difference between criminal prosecutions, regulator proceedings, civil litigation, negotiation, etc.

3. Litigation is adversarial. As a general matter, lawyers have "a duty to the client to raise fearlessly every issue, advance every argument and ask every question, however distasteful, that the lawyer thinks will help the client's case and to endeavour to obtain for the client the benefit of every remedy and defence authorized by law." *Model Code*, Rule 5.1-1, Commentary [1]. Does this apply to government lawyers' dealing with Indigenous litigants? Should it? Does it matter whether the Indigenous litigant is an Indigenous group pursuing or defending a claim on behalf of that group as opposed to an Indigenous person in a simple commercial dispute with the Crown?

---

[25] Canada, Department of Justice, *Directive on Civil Litigation Involving Indigenous Peoples*, online: https://www.justice.gc.ca/eng/csj-sjc/ijr-dja/dclip-dlcpa/litigation-litiges.html.

4. What training should government lawyers be provided with in accordance with Call to Action 57? How might this impact how government lawyers deal with Indigenous litigants?

5. Go back and review Scenario One in the last section. Does your answer change after reading the material in this section?

6. Review the Attorney General of Canada's *Directive on Civil Litigation Involving Indigenous Peoples*. Are there any guidelines that are at odds with a lawyer's duties under the *Model Code*? How should such inconsistencies be reconciled? Are there any guidelines that should be applied more generally to all government lawyers in civil litigation? Why or why not? Should any of these guidelines apply beyond civil litigation or to lawyers regardless of who their client or their employer is?

[5] ORGANIZATIONAL PRESSURES

Another significant ethical issue for government lawyers arises from the fact that they, like corporate counsel, are employees in organizations. Working within an organization can heighten the risk that lawyers engage in cognitive dissonance, and as a consequence cease to be independent and candid in the advice they provide. They can also become socially and culturally embedded in the norms of their organization, regardless of whether those norms are consistent with their broader ethical obligations as lawyers. In addition, and again like corporate counsel, because "withdrawal" for a government lawyer means quitting their job, it can seem costly and perhaps impossible for a lawyer to dissent from the positions being taken by their organization more generally.

One particular manifestation of these organizational pressures can be excessive commitment to the client's goals. This arguably was one factor at work for the "torture lawyers" — that those lawyers simply became psychologically committed to the policy goals of the government entities with which they were organizationally associated. Consider whether organizational pressures — such as, for example, ensuring that goals of taxation authorities are realized — provide a possible explanation for the ethical violations of the Crown lawyer in his conduct of the tax case excerpted below.

In addition, in reading the case consider whether the Crown lawyer acted consistently with a duty of "fair dealing" outlined previously by Cotter or a duty as "custodian of the Rule of Law" outlined by Dodek and whether his conduct would be considered unethical regardless of whether he is a Crown, and, alternatively, whether the fact that he is renders the conduct more offensive.

GENERAL MOTORS OF CANADA LTD. v. CANADA

[2008] T.C.J. No. 80, 2008 TCC 117 (T.C.C.),
affd [2009] F.C.J. No. 447 (F.C.A.)
(Tax Court of Canada, Campbell T.C.J.)

[General Motors (GM) appealed a Goods and Services Tax assessment made pursuant to the *Excise Tax Act*, R.S.C. 1985, c. E-15. One issue in the case was whether the respondent Crown had acted improperly in pleading that, in making its assessment of GM, it had assumed a particular fact. In tax litigation cases if the

Minister of National Revenue, at the time of making an assessment, relies on an assumption of fact then the onus is on the taxpayer to demonstrate that the fact is not true. Conversely, if the Minister of National Revenue does *not* make an assumption of fact then the Crown bears the onus of proving that the fact is true. In this case the respondent Crown stated in its pleadings that the Minister of National Revenue had assumed a particular fact: that the "investment management services", which were part of the matters in dispute, were not a "service" as defined by the legislation. The Appellant GM argued that the Minister of National Revenue (the Respondent) had never made any such assumption. It argued that the Crown had wrongfully and inaccurately pled the assumption which it had not made in order to obtain a tactical advantage about the burden of proof.]

CAMPBELL T.C.J.:—

. . . . .

Preliminary Matter #2 — Improper Pleading of Assumption 5(f) . . .

Paragraph 5(f) of the Reply states:

> 5. In assessing the Appellant . . . the Minister of National Revenue (the "Minister") relied on, *inter alia*, the following assumptions or findings of fact . . .
>
> (f) the investment management services were not a service listed in paragraphs (a) to (m) of the definition of a financial service under the *Act*; . . .

This is not the first time I have considered this assumption of fact. In a pre-hearing Motion, the Appellant [GM] requested the Court to either instruct the auditor, Aaron Wong, to answer questions posed to him during the examination for discovery concerning paragraph 5(f) or to strike paragraph 5(f). Although I concluded that it would be premature to strike the paragraph, I ruled that those questions posed to Mr. Wong by Appellant counsel had been properly put to him and that the examination for discovery should be continued to give Mr. Wong an opportunity to respond. I also concluded that Respondent counsel's objections were inappropriate and amounted to interference by counselling and cuing the witness to give essentially the same response of "the services are taxable" to all of those questions.

It was the Appellant that called Mr. Wong as a witness. It is clear from his evidence that the voluntary disclosure provided by [GM] to CRA was the sole basis of the initial assessment. However, this disclosure made no reference to whether the supply of Investment Management Services was a financial service as referenced in paragraph 5(f) of the Reply. Instead it dealt only with the subsection 169(1) issue. In response to questioning by both Appellant and Respondent counsel, it is evident that Mr. Wong never considered or addressed in any manner whether these services were exempt financial services under the *Act*. His repeated parroting of the response that "the services were taxable" was entirely non-responsive. It comes nowhere close to a consideration of whether those Investment Management Services fell within each of the paragraphs (a) through (m) of subsection 123(1) of the *Act*. It was apparent that Appellant counsel was frustrated with this response, and with good reason, particularly given my directions subsequent to the hearing of the Motion. What is conspicuously offensive here is the approach which Respondent counsel took with this issue. After hearing the Motion, I concluded that counsel's actions were tantamount to cuing and coaching Mr. Wong to state that "the services were taxable". Mr. Wong was true to this response and kept to his script during the hearing of the appeal.

Respondent counsel argued that the Appellant's position [that the Respondent filed improper pleadings] is both "irrelevant and wrong" . . . I am quite frankly shocked by the Respondent's position. Essentially the position of the Respondent was that since sufficient evidence was adduced during the hearing, issues of assumptions and burden of proof became merely academic. While this, on its face, is true, it cannot transform the Crown's actions, which I consider to be intrinsically appalling, into something that is right and therefore acceptable.

Respondent counsel argued that the cross-examination of Mr. Phillips elicited sufficient facts pertaining to the specifics of the Investment Management Services to enable the Court to determine whether those services are a financial service as contemplated by subsection 123(1). While this may be true, it does not assist the Respondent in defending its position that in fact this assumption was made.

In reviewing the transcripts, I believe I have sufficient testimony together with documentary evidence to make a determination on whether the supply was a financial service. However, this line of reasoning does not negate the fact that the Crown was wrong in pleading assumption 5(f) in the first place which became more blatantly evident after the Motion and the continuation of the examination for discovery.

[Tax Court Justice Campbell then addressed the Respondent Crown's argument that the assumption was pled legitimately because the assumption was implicit in the tax assessment. Justice Campbell held that the evidence given by Mr. Wong in discovery demonstrated that this argument was not supportable.]

. . . . .

Paragraph 5(f) of the Reply explicitly refers to the various sub-provisions of the definition of financial services. This undoubtedly gives the impression that the Minister had put his mind to the various components of the definition, going through each and every subparagraph, before finally concluding that the service in question did not fall under each individual subcomponent of that definition. Although Mr. Wong's testimony for the most part was simply of no assistance, he did admit that he did not review each of the paragraphs (a) through (m) of subsection 123(1) and therefore did not consider whether the Investment Management Services fit under any of them. At page 113 of the Transcript, the following exchange occurred between Appellant counsel and Mr. Wong:

> Q: . . . I am putting to you [you] did not ask yourself that question. I want you to answer the precise question I am asking. Not that you thought it was taxable. I know you thought it was taxable. That is not what the assumption says. The assumption doesn't say it is taxable. The assumption speaks specifically as to whether it is a financial service under (a) to (m). You did not ask yourself that question, did you, sir?
>
> A: No.
>
> Q: Your answer was no, I think?

A: No.

Q: In fact, sir, you did not open the sections, the definition in 123, and say to yourself, what is the investment management service and then ask yourself does it fit in (a)? What is the investment management service, does it fit into (b)? You didn't do that because your audit was only about the input tax credit. Would you agree with me, sir?

A: Yes.

I believe that my directions were very clear in the Order issued in the pre-hearing Motion and as a result the Respondent should have been on notice of the impugned assumption.

At the subsequent examination of Mr. Wong, it should also have been abundantly clear to Respondent counsel, if it was not previously, that Mr. Wong never considered in any manner the financial service issue. The proper next step was to amend the Reply to delete this assumption of fact. This step was not taken and I consider this to be a very serious matter.

The Respondent cannot be permitted to trivialize the inclusion of assumption 5(f) in its pleadings and I am not persuaded by any of its arguments. There were ample warning signs along the way. They were all ignored. The fact that there is sufficient evidence before me to make a factual determination of the issue does not negate the Respondent's duty to honestly plead assumptions at the outset or to amend the pleadings once it becomes abundantly clear that an assumption had not been made. Assumptions relied upon in pleadings must be stated fairly, honestly and accurately. That was not done here.

So what is the appropriate remedy where the Minister improperly pleads an assumption of fact, but where there is sufficient evidence before the Court to make a determination of the issue? . . .

. . . . .

Although this may be a case akin to what Justice Bowman in *Holm* described as "flagrant and reprehensible behavior," I believe that I can and should address this issue pleaded in the alternative, based on the evidence adduced through Mr. Phillips, and that I can best deal with the seriousness of the Respondent's actions and the attempt to trivialize this issue through an award of elevated costs . . . .

NOTES AND QUESTIONS

1. Tax Court Justice Campbell thus found that the Crown in this case had improperly pled an assumption of fact where the assumption was not made; improperly coached his witness on discovery in order to avoid the Respondent finding out unfavourable information; and maintained the pleading even once it was clear that it was false. Would this conduct be ethical in any advocate, whether Crown counsel or otherwise? Is it more egregious because the counsel in question was a Crown?

2. What would a duty of fair dealing have required of the Crown here? At what point would such a duty have required the Crown to amend the pleading, or otherwise admit that no such assumption had been made? What would Dodek's theory of government lawyers as "custodians of the Rule of Law" have required here?

3. Is an order of costs against the Crown a sufficient sanction? Why or why not?

4. Would you advise the Law Society to bring disciplinary proceedings against this Crown? On what basis? Note in analyzing this question, Campbell T.C.J.'s statements that the Crown's conduct was akin to "flagrant and reprehensible", was "intrinsically appalling" and that the Crown was "counselling and cuing" his witness during discoveries.

Scenario Two

You are a lawyer at a provincial regulatory agency. The agency is conducting a hearing into the proposed construction of a 500 kV electricity transmission line. The provincial government has publicly stated its commitment to developing the transmission grid in the province, and congestion on the transmission grid has been a significant problem since at least 1999. Landowners who may be affected by the line are, however, strongly opposed to its construction, and the hearing into the construction of the facility can fairly be said to have gone badly. In a report filed with the provincial Privacy Commission about what happened at the hearing the following information was provided:

> In the first incident . . . an individual approached one . . . [agency] employee and swung twice at the employee's head with a closed fist. The . . . employee was able to duck and none of the punches landed . . . [A] news video . . . showed a second incident involving an individual raising his hand close to another . . . [agency] employee's neck and then grabbing the employee's arm and pushing the employee aside. The . . . third incident occurred later that same day when a group of landowners attempted to prevent a lawyer from approaching the podium to give evidence by physically standing between the lawyer and the podium.[26]

The agency has adjourned the hearing while it considers how to respond. After some discussion it is suggested that it would be appropriate to segregate the landowners and other interveners in a separate facility where they can watch the proceedings through closed circuit televisions. It is also suggested that private investigators be retained to observe the interveners and report back on any suspicious activities.

You are asked to advise as to the legality of these suggestions. It is clear to you that the agency wants you to affirm this proposal. And it is also clear to you that by relying on a very doctrinal analysis of the law on procedural fairness you can probably do so. In reading the law, however, you are also of the view that the proposed steps are in substance unfair, and may well later be found by a court to have been problematic at best. How do you advise the agency? If you advise the agency not to take these steps, and they do so anyway, what are your ethical obligations, if any? (See Alice Woolley, "Enemies of the State? — The Alberta Energy and Utilities Board, Landowners, Spies, a 500 kV Transmission Line and Why Procedure Matters"[27]).

Scenario Three

As lawyers, government lawyers have an ethical duty to keep confidential "all

---

[26] Alberta Information and Privacy Commissioner, Investigation Report F2007-IR-005 at 3.

[27] (2008) Journal of Energy and Natural Resources Law 234.

information concerning the business and affairs of a client acquired in the course of the professional relationship" (*Model Code*, Rule 3-3-1). Each Law Society has a limited public safety exception which permits or requires lawyers to disclose confidential information in certain circumstances. For example, the *Model Code* provides:

Future Harm / Public Safety Exception

3.3-3 A lawyer may disclose confidential information, but must not disclose more information than is required, when the lawyer believes on reasonable grounds that there is an imminent risk of death or serious bodily harm, and disclosure is necessary to prevent the death or harm.

This does not necessarily accord with federal public servants' whistleblowing provisions. Under the *Public Servants Disclosure Protection Act*, a public servant may make a public disclosure if there is not sufficient time to make a report to the relevant official and:

. . . the public servant believes on reasonable grounds that the subject-matter of the disclosure is an act or omission that

> (a) constitutes a serious offence under an Act of Parliament or of the legislature of a province; or
>
> (b) constitutes an imminent risk of a substantial and specific danger to the life, health and safety of persons, or to the environment . . .[28]

Imagine that you are a lawyer working for the federal government and you discover that a public official has been defrauding the government of millions of dollars. If you exercise your whistleblowing rights as a public servant, would you be violating your ethical duties under the *Model Code* (as adopted by the provincial law societies)? Could a federal justice lawyer be disciplined by a law society for breaching their duty of confidentiality in such circumstances? Conversely, if a lawyer complied with the ethical duty of disclosure under Law Society rules, would they be violating their oath of confidentiality as a public servant and be subject to discipline by their Government employers?

Consider the same scenario if the government lawyer discovered that a government agency or official was ignoring the dumping of hazardous waste into a river which was likely to cause serious damage to the surrounding ecosystem.

Scenario Four

The *Canadian Charter of Rights and Freedoms Examination Regulations*, SOR/85-781 requires the Minister of Justice to examine every government bill that is introduced in the House of Commons "in order to determine whether any of the provisions thereof are inconsistent with the purposes and provisions of the Canadian Charter of Rights and Freedoms." The regulations further provide that if the Minister does determine that any provision of a bill is inconsistent with the Charter, the Minister "shall make a report in writing of the inconsistency" to the House of Commons.

---

[28] S.C. 2005, c. 46, s. 16(1).

No Minister of Justice has ever made a report of an inconsistency of a provision of a government bill with the Charter. In 2012, Edgar Schmidt, a lawyer with the Department of Justice, filed a lawsuit against the Minister of Justice alleging that the Minister was in violation of the above regulation. Schmidt revealed that the government had interpreted the provision to mean that a report was only required where there was "no credible argument" to support the provision. If there was a five percent chance of success, the argument was deemed credible. The Department of Justice fired Schmidt.

Do you think Schmidt should have "blown the whistle" on his employer? Do you think the government was right to fire Schmidt? What do you think the standard means? How do you think the Minister should apply it?

Schmidt lost his case in the Federal Court, and the Federal Court of Appeal dismissed his appeal. See *Schmidt v. Canada (Attorney General)*, 2016 FC 269; 2018 FCA 55. For commentary about the Schmidt case see: Roderick Macdonnell, "The Whistleblower" *The National* (Nov-Dec 2013). http://www.nationalmagazine. ca/Articles/November/The-whistleblower.aspx. See also Andrew Flavelle Martin, "The Government Lawyer as Activist: A Legal Ethics Analysis" (2020) 41 Windsor Review of Legal & Social Issues 28, Available at SSRN: https://ssrn.com/abstract= 3625992 and Andrew Flavelle Martin, "The Attorney General's Forgotten Role as Legal Advisor to the Legislature: A Comment on *Schmidt v. Canada (Attorney General)*".(2019) 52:1 U.B.C. L. Rev. 201, Available at SSRN: https://ssrn.com/ abstract=3329670.

[6] FURTHER READING

Perhaps the most comprehensive treatment is found in Elizabeth Sanderson, *Government Lawyering: Duties and Ethical Challenges of Government Lawyers* (Lexis Nexis, 2018). Professor Sanderson has also proposed a "code" of government lawyering and "Advice on Giving the Best Possible Advice."

Other useful articles include:

Berenson, Steven K., "Hard Bargaining on Behalf of the Government Tortfeasor: A Study in Governmental Lawyer Ethics" (2005) 56(2) Case W. Res. L. Rev. 345.

Dodek, Adam M., "The 'Unique Role' of Government Lawyers in Canada" (2016) 49 Israel L.R. 23.

Edwards, John L.I.L., *The Attorney General, Politics and the Public Interest* (London: Sweet & Maxwell, 1984).

Hammond, Kristina, "Plugging the Leaks: Applying the Model Rules to Leaks Made by Government Lawyers" (2005) 18(3) Geo. J. Leg. Ethics 783.

Hutchinson, Allan C., "'In the Public Interest': The Responsibilities and Rights of Government Lawyers" (2008) 46 Osgoode Hall L.J. 105.

Keyes, John Mark, "The Professional Responsibilities of Legislative Counsel" (2009) 3 J.P.P.L. 453.

Luban, David, *Legal Ethics and Human Dignity* (New York: Cambridge University Press, 2007).

Martin, Andrew Flavelle, "From Attorney General to Backbencher or Opposition

Legislator: The Lawyer's Continuing Duty of Confidentiality to the Former Client" (2020) 43 Man. L.J. 247.

Martin, Andrew Flavelle, "Legal Ethics and Canada's Military Lawyers" (2019) 97:1 Can. Bar Rev. 727.

Martin, Andrew Flavelle, "The Minister's Office Lawyer: A Challenge to the Role of the Attorney General?" (2019) 12:3 J.P.P.L. 641.

Martin, Andrew Flavelle, "Legal Ethics and the Political Activity of Government Lawyers" (2018) 49:2 Ottawa L.R. 263.

Martin, Andrew Flavelle, "Consequences for Broken Political Promises: Lawyer-Politicians and the Rules of Professional Conduct" (2016) 10:2 J.P.P.L. 337.

Martin, Andrew Flavelle, "Legal Ethics versus Political Practices: The Application of the Rules of Professional Conduct to Lawyer-Politicians" (2013) 91:1 Can. Bar Rev. 1.

MacNair, Deborah, "The Role of the Federal Public Sector Lawyer: From Polyester to Silk" (2001) 50 U.N.B.L.J. 125.

MacNair, Deborah, "In the Service of the Crown: Are Ethical Obligations Different for Government Counsel?" (2005) 84 Can. Bar Rev. 501.

Paulson, M.S., "Hell, Handbaskets and Government Lawyers: the Duty of Loyalty and its Limits" (1998) 61 Law & Contemp. Probs. 83.

Schmitt, Edgar, "Lawyers Serving the State: Ethical Issues When Administrative Directions Conflict with the Client-State's Interests" (2020) 43 Man. L.J. 115.

Scott, Ian, "Law, Policy and the Role of the Attorney General: Constancy and Change in the 1980s" (1989) 39 U.T.L.J. 109.

Shpall, Jessica, "A Shakeup for the Duty of Confidentiality: The Competing Priorities of a Government Attorney in California" (2008) 41(2) Loy. L.A. L. Rev. 701.

Symposium, "Legal Ethics for Government Lawyers: Straight Talk for Tough Times" (2000) 9 Widener J. Pub. L. 199.

Tait, John C., "The Public Service Lawyer, Service to the Client and the Rule of Law" (1997) 23 Commonwealth L. Bull. 542.

Webb, Duncan, "Keeping the Crown's Conscience: A Theory of Lawyering for Public Sector Counsel" (2007) 5(2) N. Z. J. Pub. & I. L. 243.

Wendel, W. Bradley, "Executive Branch Lawyers in a Time of Terror" (2008) 31 Dal. L.J. 247.

Wendel, W. Bradley, "Government Lawyers, Democracy, and the Rule of Law" (2009) 77(4) Fordham L. Rev. 1333.

Wilner, Joshua, "Service to the Nation: A Living Legal Value for Justice Lawyers in Canada" (2009) 32 Dal. L.J. 177.

Woolley, Alice, "Enemies of the State? The Alberta Energy and Utilities Board, Landowners, Spies, a 500 kV Transmission Line and Why Procedure Matters" (2008) 26(2) Journal of Energy & Natural Resources Law 234.

Note, "Government Counsel and their obligations" (2008) 121(5) Harv. L. Rev. 1409.

Note, "Rethinking the Professional Responsibilities of Federal Agency Lawyers" (2002) 115(4) Harv. L. Rev. 1170.

CHAPTER 9

IN-HOUSE COUNSEL AND THEIR UNIQUE CONSIDERATIONS

[1] Introduction

Instead of relying always or solely on external law firms, organizations often employ lawyers within the organization. These positions adopt a variety of names, such as in-house counsel, general counsel, corporate counsel, or Chief Legal Officer, which this chapter uses interchangeably. If they find it beneficial, business corporations, governments, public agencies, commissions, tribunals, and any other organization can employ in-house counsel.[1] In-house counsel accordingly may work alone, as part of a larger internal department, or in conjunction with external lawyers. Specific in-house counsel roles and duties depend on the organization, its context, and its needs.

Despite this inherent diversity, many of the ethical issues that in-house counsel face overlap with issues faced by lawyers in general and are covered by the *Model Code of Professional Conduct*. For example, confidentiality and its exceptions,[2] loyalty and conflicts of interest,[3] understanding who your client is,[4] providing business/policy advice in addition to legal advice,[5] communicating with the public (including unrepresented people),[6] advocating for legislative or administrative change,[7] and the complications of working with organizations[8] are all issues dealt with by lawyers both inside and outside organizations. However, the ongoing presence of an organization's context and its pressures, including the fact that the organization is the sole or predominate client for the lawyer who pays their salary, raise ethical and professionalism issues unique for in-house counsel. This reality makes the lawyer's general challenges of "(1) compliance and risk management; (2) gatekeeper autonomy and moral sources; (3) the scope of representation and ethics;

---

[1] See e.g. *Pritchard v. Ontario (Human Rights Commission)*, [2004] S.C.J. No. 16, 2004 SCC 31 at paras. 19-21 (S.C.C.).

[2] See e.g. *Model Code*, r. 3.3.

[3] See e.g. *Model Code*, rs. 3.4, 7.3-2.

[4] See e.g. *Model Code*, r. 1.1-1 sub verbo "client".

[5] See e.g. *Model Code*, r. 3.1-2[10].

[6] See e.g. *Model Code*, rs 7.5-1, 7.2-9.

[7] See e.g. *Model Code*, r. 5.6-2.

[8] See e.g. *Model Code*, rs. 3.2-3, 3.2-8.

(4) ethics and the limits of agency; and (5) the lawyer as a social/moral agent"[9] particularly important for in-house counsel.

This chapter provides an overview of several key considerations relevant to in-house counsel regardless of organizational context, particularly from an ethical and professionalism perspective. The chapter begins by examining how in-house counsel arose and what they generally do today. It then focuses on issues related to maintaining professionalism and avoiding client tunnel vision, especially since an in-house counsel is dependent on their employer as their main client. The chapter then reviews common ethical and professionalism issues that in-house counsel often encounter: 1) confidentiality/privilege considerations for Canadian and common law jurisdictions versus the European Union; 2) multiple client conflict considerations, particularly with respect to subsidiaries; 3) loyalty issues that arise from potential gatekeeping and reporting roles; and 4) potential advisor issues arising from providing business and policy advice in addition to legal advice as part of risk/crisis assessment and management as well as in corporate sustainability and diversity contexts.

[2] How In-House Counsel Arose and What They Do

To understand the unique ethical and professional issues that in-house counsel face, one first needs to have a basic understanding of how they came to be and what they do. The first piece by Gunz & Jennings provides a brief history of in-house counsel and how they developed over time. The second piece by Veasey & Di Guglielmo provides detailed insight into the roles that in-house counsel have within organizations and the stakeholders with whom they work.

As you read these two excerpts, consider the following questions:

- Why would organizations want to hire in-house counsel rather than simply rely on external private lawyers? What are the pros and cons? How do these different types of lawyers compare?

- How has the role of counsel in organizational settings changed and developed over time?

- What professional roles and duties can be engaged, particularly compared to a lawyer in private practice? How are they the same or different?

- What considerations do in-house counsel need to keep in mind when providing corresponding advice and solutions to problems?

Sally Gunz & Marianne M. Jennings

"University Legal Counsel: The Role and Its Challenges" (2019) 33:1 Notre Dame J.L. Ethics & Pub. Pol'y 177 at 179-181 [footnotes omitted]

I. THE HISTORY OF THE CORPORATE COUNSEL FUNCTION

A. Early Developments in Corporate Counsel Growth

The corporate counsel profession has a long but not always proud history. For many

---

[9] Larry Catá Backer, "Lawyers Are Not Algorithms: Sustainability, Corruption, and the Role of the Lawyer in Institutional Frameworks and Corporate Transactions" (2021) 24 Leg. Ethics (forthcoming).

years it was routine to describe the early profession as having been rather feeble and certainly a poor relation to that of private practice. Whether in fact this was ever the case or this categorization was merely a useful foil by which to explain an enlightened "present," it became (and continues to be) the accepted wisdom that real change to the status of the profession occurred somewhere in the late 1970s or early 1980s. The [Abram Chayes & Antonia H Chayes] article ["Corporate Counsel and the Elite Law Firm" (1985) 37:2 Stan. L. Rev. 277] that perhaps more than any other laid the groundwork for scholarly studies of the in-house legal profession, stated in its opening paragraph:

> The traditional [in-]house counsel was a relatively minor management figure, stereotypically, a lawyer from the corporation's principal outside law firm who had not quite made the grade as partner. The responsibilities of general (corporate) counsel were confined to corporate housekeeping and other routine matters and to acting as liaison (perhaps a euphemism for channeling business) to his former firm.

What interested the Chayes and others in the early 1980s was not only the growth of in-house law departments but also their impact on private law firms. The allocation of legal work was seen as something of a zero-sum game: "whatever the future form of the elite law firm, its relation to big business will have been profoundly altered. The vast bulk of the legal work for America's leading corporations will be performed in corporate law departments." While work for big law firms has undoubtedly been reduced at times by growth in the in-house delivery of legal services, firms have, perhaps not surprisingly, proven remarkably agile in withstanding the dire predictions from earlier times.

. . .

B. The Corporate Counsel Growth and Shift in Roles

Despite the lack of academic attention, the role of corporate counsel was evolving. What we do know about in-house law departments in their early years (1970s/1980s) is that while some had been very large for a long time, the majority were reasonably small and remain so today. This statement will appear to be counterintuitive to many since it is, almost by definition, the large departments that attract most of the attention in the literature and popular press. In 1981, close to seventy percent of law departments had five or fewer lawyers and while this reported size had shrunk to around sixty percent by 1990, there was minimal increase in the percentage of large departments (generously defined as twenty-plus lawyers). A good deal of the growth in this period would be likely attributed to changing economic conditions. By the end of the decade (1980s) it appeared, at least in the United States, that growth in overall numbers of corporate counsel was slowing.

However, two simultaneous developments were taking hold that resulted in a trend toward corporate counsel, a trend that has been called "irreversible." There was increasing government regulation and increasing growth in the size of corporations. [American-based] [c]orporations needed to talk to the Securities and Exchange Commission ("SEC"), the Occupational Safety and Health Administration ("OSHA"), the Department of Energy ("DOE"), and the Federal Trade Commission ("FTC") daily, and it made more sense to "pay an attorney on your payroll $20 [per] hour and have him work all day instead of phoning your outside counsel and paying him $60 an hour for the same work." The prediction of irreversibility was accurate. The 2013 survey of the Association of Corporate Counsel ("ACC") found that there were 33,000 in-house counsel in eighty-five countries. The ACC survey netted responses from 10,000 corporate counsel in Fortune 500 and other U.S. firms. The survey also found increased salaries for corporate counsel and their staffs as well as increased budgets for general counsel staff. Since 2013, actual data suggest only incremental growth. However, one of the most commonly expressed beliefs is that growth in overall numbers of corporate counsel (and likely size of departments) is at least just around the corner if not likely already occurring." Certainly while numbers of corporate counsel have obviously increased, so also have those for the legal profession as a whole. Presently, it is unlikely that the proportion of in-house counsel has itself increased significantly." To repeat, the majority of corporate counsel have and continue to practice their art in the company of relatively few colleagues.

Why are the observations about the size of the in-house counsel profession important? This feature alone helps determine what role the average law department and the individuals within it can fulfill. For many, their role will be that of a generalist. Outside legal services will continue to be essential. The effectiveness of the in-house counsel will be as much (likely more) a result of how corporate counsel integrate into the business and manage legal risk and legal services, as how they practice the art of law itself.

Undoubtedly more significant than the numbers themselves is that "today's" (as of the time of the [1985] Chayes writing) counsel were described in much more glowing fashion: "[t]he new breed of general counsel has left this stereotype far behind. Not only have the offices grown in size, but in importance as well. The General Counsel sits close to the top of the corporate hierarchy as a member of senior management."

NOTES AND QUESTIONS

1. How could the nature of an in-house counsel's position change based on the size of the company? The field in which the company operates? Changes in the regulatory context? One's role with respect to the company's senior management team? The size of the legal department? Other factors?

2. Despite the various ways that in-house counsel can manifest, what roles, perceptions, and issues may arise for in-house counsel regardless of context?

E. Norman Veasey & Christine T. Di Guglielmo

Indispensable Counsel: The Chief Legal Officer in the New Reality (Oxford: Oxford University Press, 2012) at 34, 39-46 [emphasis in original, footnotes omitted]

Chapter 2 – Evolution of the Role of General Counsel

C. Key Takeaways on the Evolution of the Role of General Counsel

. . .

The [Chief Legal Officer ("CLO")] of today as partner/guardian is normally positioned within the highest ranks of senior management, while also serving as a legal advisor to the board of directors. The quintessential general counsel of today is the archetypical persuasive counselor—part gatekeeper, part enabler, part advocate, and (perhaps most of all) wise advisor.

How to live up to the expectations for the chief legal officer of today is "job one" for the incumbent in that position. And it is all about expectations.

The CEO may wish for and expect primarily an enabler. The CLO of today is part enabler. Otherwise, she would not last long in the position. The question is, what kind of enabler? The expectation should be that her skills at enabling will be leavened by a balanced mix of legal skills, responsibility, business knowledge, a dash of gatekeeping, and a heaping helping of integrity, independence, and common sense.

The board may wish for and expect primarily a legal and ethical guardian. This expectation is self-evident. With the shift from outside counsel to the CLO as the font of legal wisdom in the boardroom, the expectation is very high. The in-house general counsel must be able persuasively to communicate to the directors the confidence and security that she and her staff either (a) know the legal answer as applied to a business strategy or brewing trouble or (b) have the depth of knowledge of the outside practicing bar to obtain the best advice for the board.

The challenges arise in striking the right balance between the role of partner and of guardian, between the CEO's expectations and the board's expectations, in order to pursue the best interests of the corporate entity-client. . . .

Chapter 3 – The General Counsel on the Balance Beam

A. The Many Hats Worn by the Modern General Counsel

A major factor contributing to the variety and complexity inherent in the general counsel position is the multiplicity of roles inherent in the office. In a broad view, the general counsel's roles within the corporation may be divided into four general categories:

- legal advisor
- corporate officer and member of the senior executive team
- administrator of the in-house legal department; and
- corporate agent in dealings with third parties, including outside counsel.

Each of these categories encompasses numerous important functions. The general counsel's roles are not limited to purely legal functions—companies frequently assign functions other than legal to the CLO and the legal department. As Bruce Sewell, Senior Vice President and General Counsel, Apple Inc., explained:

> The general counsel's role has really expanded to encompass a portfolio that is not just legal, but includes matters such as government affairs, corporate social responsibility, reputational matters, and compliance. These all play into the reputational value of the corporate brand. More and more companies are organizing so that these functions are under the general counsel. For example, at Intel, the general counsel's role had four pillars: law, public policy, government relations, and corporate social responsibility. At Apple, the legal department includes law,

government affairs, global security, and all of the compliance functions. I think companies are increasingly recognizing the relationship, the synergies, between a law function and the government affairs and compliance functions.

Whatever the organizational structure of the legal department within the overall corporate organization may be, the wide range of more specific functions that the general counsel often fulfills reflects the breadth and depth of the general counsel's roles. Indeed, the broad scope of the job may even be key to enabling the general counsel "to address the myriad business-in-society issues facing modern corporations," as well as enhancing the general counsel's job satisfaction and personal fulfillment. As Daniel Desjardins, Senior Vice President, General Counsel and Assistant Secretary of Bombardier, described:

> It is important for the fulfillment of the role of the general counsel to go outside of the strong legal responsibility and take on more functions such as corporate social responsibility, because doing so enhances the scope of the daily life of the general counsel and serves them well in their personal fulfillment.

The general counsel's functions often include:

- *Business as well as legal advisor.* The general counsel's position in the top levels of the corporation's management structure gives the general counsel a broad impact on strategic business planning. This may often affect the style of lawyering that a *general* counsel brings to the table. . . .

- *Manager.* The general counsel must devote substantial time to managing or directing the management of the work and employees of the corporation's legal department, as well as the corporation's procurement and monitoring of outside legal services. . . .

- *Promoter of values and ethics.* The CLO has a pivotal role in framing, implementing, and overseeing the company's values and ethical standards. . . .

- *Problem solver.* As a trusted member of senior management, with specialized skills and a strong dose of independence, the general counsel is often a problem solver on a wide range of issues. . . .

- *Mediator among corporate constituencies.* The general counsel often acts as a middleman, ferrying between two groups, such as the board and senior management, in an effort to reach a solution to a problematic issue. . . . Some corporations also call upon the general counsel or in-house counsel in a more formal way to help resolve disputes or issues among individuals or groups within the corporation.

- *Compliance program designer and implementer.* As the complexity of corporate compliance programs has increased, so too has the general counsel's involvement in the planning or management of those programs. . . . Moreover, the whistleblower rules adopted by the SEC, pursuant to the Dodd-Frank Act, present a new layer of challenges to the management of the corporation's compliance program, and, thus, to the general counsel's role in the program.

- *Manager of legal and reputational risk* and *educator.* General counsel perform the increasingly important function of assessing legal risks and translating those risks into business terms in order to facilitate decision-making concerning those risks. The CLO's role in risk assessment and risk management may be akin to her role in respect to compliance issues. . . .

- *Public Policy Advisor.* The general counsel may also be in charge of or have a major role in government affairs for the company. Public policy is an area of varied functions, including broad public policy activity as well as more targeted lobbying or other government affairs.

- *Corporate advocate, gatekeeper to the securities markets,* or *persuasive counselor.* General counsel's role with respect to the corporation's access to the securities markets has been the subject of significant recent debate. . . . [Our preferred model is] as persuasive counselors, [which] can serve to protect the firm by guiding its constituents to the right course, without compromising their ability to provide to the corporation excellent and independent legal advice, service, and advocacy. Moreover, the general counsel often sets the standards and tone for the professional services to be rendered to the corporation by outside counsel.

- *Corporate secretary.* Although the duties of general counsel and corporate secretary are discrete and these positions are often held by different persons, the general counsel sometimes acts as or supervises the corporate secretary in carrying out that increasingly complex and important role. Indeed, one of the key functions of the CLO and/or the corporate secretary relates to documenting board decision-making and oversight in minutes and other corporate records. The corporate secretary is also an important bridge between management and the board, assisting in effective governance of the organization.

In short, general counsel "function in a strategic capacity . . . at the intersection of most corporate activity," which affords them "(i) access to information and institutional knowledge, (ii) the power to promote internal action, (iii) responsibility for outside counsel, and (iv) the capacity to engage in preventive law."

. . . [T]he general counsel's deep and daily understanding of, and involvement in, the corporation's business brings different value to the organization than is brought by outside counsel, who does not have the same familiarity with the business. General counsel's business involvement can also work, paradoxically, to increase both her professional fulfillment and the tensions she experiences. Greater knowledge and familiarity often leads to greater recognition of problems (for example, the ability to ascertain the accuracy or inaccuracy of corporate disclosures), which in turn can lead to increased exposure to ethical dilemmas.

The many and varied roles and functions of the general counsel are impacted from company to company by such widely divergent matters as corporate culture and risk tolerance, individual personalities of executives and directors, the business and regulatory environment of a particular company and its industry, the general counsel's personal and professional experiences, and many others. Thus, there can be no "one-size-fits-all" approach to handling the multifaceted responsibilities and expectations of the lawyer for the corporation.

NOTES AND QUESTIONS

1. How does the potential nature and focuses of an in-house counsel's role differ from other legal professionals? How are they the same? How would the needed skills, knowledge, and abilities be different or the same? What is potentially transferable and what would need to be learned? And how could they be picked up?

2. How can the organization and structure of the legal department affect these issues and the organization's "culture of integrity"?[10] For example, centralized vs decentralized; what functions/services are central to the department; resources available and their management; the role of the top lawyer; how an organization's in-house lawyers interact with groups/units in the organization; etc.?[11] What potential issues arise from the incentives used (e.g. cost-savings/efficiency or profit-making in for-profit businesses)? How could these concerns be addressed?

3. How can an in-house lawyer affect how an organization approaches and considers its "role as a corporate citizen"?[12] For example, what considerations are potentially engaged when trying to balance a company's own private interests with the interests of the general public or specific groups affected by the company's actions?[13]

4. When dealing with outside counsel selection and compensation, what considerations could come into play?[14]

[3] Maintaining Professionalism and Avoiding Client Tunnel Vision

Given the unique contexts that in-house counsel work in, their varied roles, their payment structures, and the relationships they have within organizations, there is a risk that in-house counsel may over-identify with their clients' perspectives and wants. While such client loyalty may be initially seen as a positive, the resulting professional concern is that a lawyer's professional independence and perspective can become compromised when providing advice, especially if it is something the client does not want to hear. However, the nature of in-house counsel roles also provides opportunities for such lawyers to use their inside understanding, influence, and professional background to affect such decisions in different ways than traditional outside lawyers.

To better understand how such issues play out in practice, the following two

---

[10] See e.g. E. Norman Veasey & Christine T. Di Guglielmo, *Indispensable Counsel: The Chief Legal Officer in the New Reality* (Oxford: Oxford University Press, 2012) at 41.

[11] E. Norman Veasey & Christine T. Di Guglielmo, *Indispensable Counsel: The Chief Legal Officer in the New Reality* (Oxford: Oxford University Press, 2012) at 189, 41-42.

[12] E. Norman Veasey & Christine T. Di Guglielmo, *Indispensable Counsel: The Chief Legal Officer in the New Reality* (Oxford: Oxford University Press, 2012) at 42.

[13] E. Norman Veasey & Christine T. Di Guglielmo, *Indispensable Counsel: The Chief Legal Officer in the New Reality* (Oxford: Oxford University Press, 2012) at 42.

[14] E. Norman Veasey & Christine T. Di Guglielmo, *Indispensable Counsel: The Chief Legal Officer in the New Reality* (Oxford: Oxford University Press, 2012) at 189-190.

pieces summarize some key results from two empirical research studies regarding such potential organizational-professional conflicts and influences. As you read these pieces, consider the factors, influences, and processes that affect how in-house counsel come to make decisions and recommendations, as well as how that differs from traditional practice. Consider also what steps one can and should take to maintain one's professionalism and avoid the tunnel vision of only your client's intentions and expectations in different contexts.

Richard Moorhead, Steven Vaughan, & Christina Godinho

In-House Lawyers' Ethics: Institutional Logics, Legal Risk and the Tournament of Influence (Oxford: Hart, 2019) at 211-213.

The Place of In-Housers in the Network of Influences

Traditionally, lawyers were brought in-house because they were cheaper, but as their status has risen, their role has broadened to include more strategic and managerial functions, such as the management of legal risk. In-house lawyers are no longer merely cheaper; they are different. Personal motivations for moving in-house reflect some of these differences. Our interviewees spoke of having a more embedded, varied role; less legally specialised, but involving a broader set of skills. Importantly, their in-house roles involved a closer engagement with organisational imperatives (be they business or policy). Elements of private practice were also rejected: the 'moral bankruptcy' of timesheets; hyper-specialisation; and the business model of big law, in particular.

In this way, lawyers who have moved in-house are cognitively and affectively open to being more business-like or policy-focused. Plausibly, they thought this enabled them to do a better job. [Ken] Grady describes what happens when a client comes to a new in-house lawyer asking for a contract:

> Those lawyers who had recently joined the law department from a law firm and those lawyers still in a law firm . . . would jump into action, gathering data for the document and plotting the path to victory.

> A lawyer experienced with the in-house client and environment would take a different path. She would ask about the situation giving rise to the request. She would probe the context, the parties involved, the existence of other legal instruments, and the risks. A really good lawyer would ask questions trying to get at the situation from the client's perspective. By the time she was done, the client and lawyer might have concluded that no legal instrument was needed, a short amendment to an existing document would suffice, and that the client needed something different from what he first requested.

Here, the ecology of the organisation trains the in-house lawyer to better understand the organisation's needs. It strikes us as a good description of the pragmatic, results-oriented dimensions to what we call being commercially oriented. And as well as the better fitness for purpose that Grady describes, we saw ways in which greater cognitive openness to an organisation's needs might lead to more ethical approaches to practice: in-house lawyers could, through wider and earlier exposure to the organisation's decision-making, be more tuned into, and influential on, the long-term interests of their organisation that are shaped by legal and reputational risk. They could spot problems early and respond, at least in theory.

Embedding professional expertise in this way involves the everyday grounding of legal work in the organisation's values. The reason the job is being done, and the outcome that the job delivers, are influential on how the job is done. For many, this meant being asked to be 'value adding': integrating in-house lawyers into business development and planning functions, and away from 'pure' legal advice towards risk management and commercial input. Value-adding was a concept which sometimes unsettled, rather than worked with the grain of, the legal thinking of our in-housers. It destabilised professional norms. We would surmise they felt themselves rubbing up against a genuine incommensurability between legal and commercial ways of thinking. Value-adding very likely encourages cognitive dissonance which, by design or accident, encourages professional neuroticism. Imagine being faced with a legal question to which one is not sure of the legal answer, but to which the *commercial* answer is clear. Here, consciously or unconsciously, the incentive is to adjust one's view of the legal uncertainties to accommodate the organisational imperatives. In parallel, in-house lawyers worked within a negative stereotype: often, *very* often, assuming they were seen as deal-blockers or costly nit-pickers.

The extent of such dissonance was varied. A clear understanding of the in-house legal team's role in organisations was sometimes strong, but more often tentative or absent. It could also be hierarchical, with interviewees suggesting that understanding of the need for independent in-house legal functions was stronger at the apex of organisations. Unevenness of relationships within the business were common, as was criticism of in-house lawyers for being obstructive . . . . That such dissonance was important is suggested by almost half of our respondents who reported that their organisations acted *against* legal advice on important matters. Furthermore, about 10 per cent of our respondents reported being asked to advise on ethically or legally debatable actions frequently or very frequently, and 40 per cent were asked to so advise on such actions at least sometimes. About 10–15 per cent agreed or strongly agreed that they were asked to advise on things that made them uncomfortable, or in ways which suggested the business took a different view on whether and/or how to uphold the rule of law. About a quarter to a third agreed at least somewhat with these concerns.

We can be depressed by such findings, but recognition of the problem may also be a healthy sign. Our work stands in contrast to other work on occupational professional conflict in law, which has tended to suggest that such conflict is muted, absent, or well-managed. We see clearly here that conflict does arise. The key thing is whether it is recognized and how it is dealt with. . . . [O]ur in-house lawyers varied in their moral attentiveness and engagement. To give two examples, those we called the 'Champions' were more morally engaged and attentive in the face of ethical pressure, whereas the 'Troubled' show signs of having succumbed to pressure through greater disengagement. Conversely, in describing the in-house lawyer's place in the organisational network, we can see how engagements with the organisation are part of a tournament of influence which in-house lawyers sometimes (perhaps often) expect to lose. There is a trading of helpfulness with any legal question or task for acceptance from their non-legal colleagues. Organisational scepticism, where it exists, is tackled by adopting a cultivated posture of flexibility. The need for independence and difficult advice is camouflaged, restrained, or diluted. The question is not whether to compromise, but how much, when, and in what circumstances.

NOTES AND QUESTIONS

1. If you were to become an in-house counsel, what are things you would need to learn about the organization? What are things you should be careful of? What things should you be willing to change or protect over time? How would you go about doing and assessing that?

2. Moorhead, Vaughan, & Godinho later note at 216 with respect to independence that:

> [W]e do not think that independence is a trope, but there is a danger that independence is a less useful concept if it is not allied with an intrinsic value. . . . Professional rules are clear that in-house lawyers (and those in private practice) must protect the rule of law and the administration of justice. This provides an intrinsic value that in-house lawyers should be thinking about explicitly. Another way of thinking about this is that the influence model of independence is prone to temporal and social vulnerability. If a [general counsel] had to say 'No' in uncomfortable circumstances three times, the fourth time they will be less inclined to say 'No' simply as a result of the three previous decisions rather than because of the actual risk posed by not saying 'No' to the fourth question. This is socially intelligible, but dangerous. Put another way, independence does not simply mean not being prone to influence, or being one's own person. It means independently and, insofar as it is possible, objectively assessing what the rule of law and the administration of justice really requires when one is advising or assisting an organisational client.

3. What steps or processes could you take to ensure independence and be a "Champion" rather than the "Troubled" when faced with ethical pressure? For example, what values should be kept in mind? How could you approach things differently if you had processes/principles/approaches set up beforehand versus dealing with issues on an emergency issue as they arise? What supports or structures may be helpful or a barrier?

In addition to the questions posed at the beginning of this section, consider for the next piece how in-house counsel identifies their role and how one views their work can impact the approach to the legal and ethical problems they face as well as the recommendations they ultimately make.

Hugh Gunz & Sally Gunz

"Ethical Challenges in the Role of In-House Counsel" (2019) 69:4 Case W. Res. L. Rev. 953 at 968-972 [footnotes omitted].

III. LESSONS LEARNED FOR THE ETHICAL ROLE OF PROFESSION-ALS

The study we draw on surveyed Canadian corporate counsel, who were asked to respond to vignettes putting them in the position of having to decide how to respond to situations drawn from practice (albeit anonymized). Based on the precept noted above, that these professionals aim to act professionally, the study set out to see whether organizational influences could be identified that might affect the lawyers' judgement, quite possibly, in ways that they are entirely unaware. The study drew on identity theory to structure its argument.

We discussed above the concept of [organizational-professional conflict ("OPC")] and noted that, while it might be expected as a consequence of working as a lawyer for an employer with different aims than those of a law firm, a number of studies have established that in-house counsel and other professionals in similar situations report surprisingly low levels of OPC. The study we draw on here suggests an explanation for this well-established finding, based on identity theory. Identity is a widely used concept in organization studies. It has been described as a "relatively stable and enduring constellation of attributes, beliefs, values, motives, and experiences in terms of which people define themselves in a professional role." Individuals have multiple identities that come into play under differing circum- stances and are organized into a salience hierarchy. Identity salience is "the probability that an identity will be invoked across a variety of situations, or alternatively across persons in a given situation . . . commitment shapes identity salience shapes role choice behavior." Earlier research had shown that in-house counsel vary in the identities they adopt, between two poles labelled "technician" and "organization person." In the more recent study, these were relabeled "profes- sional" and "organizational."

> The 'professional' identity is adopted by someone who sees him or herself as, for example, a lawyer, accountant or engineer who just happens to be working for the NPO in question . . . The 'organizational' identity is that of a professional who has taken on some of the characteristics of a non-professional employee of the NPO, in the limit, seeing him- or herself as an employee who just happens to have, for example, a law, accounting or engineering degree."

To put it another way:

> [S]omeone enacting a professional identity will ask him- or herself: *how does my profession require me to deal with this ethical dilemma?* By contrast, someone adopting an organizational identity will ask him- or herself: *how should I, as an employee of this [non-professional organization], deal with this ethical dilemma?*

Drawing on the "logic of appropriateness" the individual is, in effect, asking themselves: "What does a person like me do in a situation like this?"

In order to establish the identity that respondents regarded as most salient, they were asked to say where they fell on a scale that ranged from "[l]awyer with captive client" at one end and "[e]mployee of organization who happens to have law degree" at the other." While half of the respondents put themselves at the midpoint of the scale, a third put themselves at the professional end and the remaining 17 percent at the organizational end.

The respondents were also presented with several vignettes drawn from professional practice in three cases and, in the fourth, from the famous Texaco boardroom imbroglio.[15] Each vignette represented an ethical dilemma in the sense that it

---

[15] During a recorded meeting of three Texaco executives, they used racist terms to refer

raised issues of professional ethics, but there was no ideal solution; however, one participant in the study responded that any decision would have a downside for someone. The vignettes were anonymized and carefully tested on a pilot group of subjects for their realism and their lack of bias, the latter in the sense that it was important not to bias the wording in favor of one type of response or the other. In each case, the respondents were given two possible courses of action for them to take, each based on one of the identities. The courses of action were carefully worded to ensure that they represented reasonable actions for an in-house counsel to take without breaking any laws or rules of professional practice. For example, in the (disguised) Texaco case the respondent is general counsel and compliance officer for a large corporation with a major public profile. "[T]he top management team (TMT) is almost uniformly WASP (White Anglo-Saxon Protestant)," and it is common for its members to inject racist comments into their conversation. On the one hand, the subject is told that they are aware that if these comments became public it would be a public relations disaster for the company, and there was a risk that a disaffected employee might well make this happen. On the other, the executives in question are the subject's friends and colleagues and have already reacted to mild attempts to change their behavior with derision. The respondents were given two choices, one organizational—an in-camera, non-minuted discussion in which the risks are pointed out and it is suggested that the executives keep their behavior strictly private; and the other professional—a formal note that goes to the TMT explaining that if the situation does not change it will have to be reported to the board.

There were two main findings from the study. First, the identity claimed by the respondent predicted well the approach they said they would take with each of the vignettes: those with organizational identities preferred organizational responses, and those with professional identities preferred professional responses. Second, it was possible to explain some of the reasons for adopting one identity over the other based on information the respondents provided about themselves. They were given a list of ten items drawn from research on the work of corporate counsel and asked to describe the allocation of their time between the items." Some (e.g. routine legal matters and caseload, legal counselling) were clearly professional, while others (e.g. management outside the legal department, government liaison) were more obviously non-professional. The greater the proportion of their time was spent on non-professional work, the more likely they were to say that they had organizational identities. Furthermore, a workload biased towards non-professional work was also associated with a feeling of isolation from the organization's strategic decision-making process. In other words, the more involved the counsel were in the strategic management of the organization and the more time they spent on non-professional work, the more likely they were to adopt an organizational identity and to resolve

---

to minority employees and discussed potentially destroying documents to protect themselves from an active discrimination class action (see e.g. "Racism at Texaco", *The New York Times* (November 6, 1996) A-26, online: https://www.nytimes.com/1996/11/06/opinion/racism-at-texaco.html; but see Sharon Walsh, "Tape Analysis Disproves Racial Slurs, Texaco Says" *The Washington Post* (November 12, 1996), online: https://www.washingtonpost.com/archive/politics/1996/11/12/tape-analysis-disproves-racial-slurs-texaco-says/47094dbf-c0be-47a0-a3ab-36e30545771e/).

the ethical dilemmas they were presented with in an organizational, as opposed to professional, manner.

Other features of their work situation also appeared to play a part in deciding how they handled the dilemmas. The most interesting involved the vulnerability the respondents felt towards their work being outsourced, an outcome commonly faced by in-house counsel. The more vulnerable they felt, the more likely they were to adopt an organizational identity and choose organizational solutions to the dilemmas.

To summarize, then, this study produced disquieting findings with respect to the way in which in-house counsel might be expected to respond to ethical dilemmas. Nothing in the study addressed the individual ethical standards of the counsel. There may or may not have been some bad apples in the 484 counsel who responded, but the study's authors had no way of knowing whether this was the case. On the other hand, it was possible to predict something of the way that each respondent would respond to the dilemmas by knowing something of their situation in the organization: how involved they felt themselves to be in the firm's strategic leadership, and whether they felt their work to be at risk of outsourcing. Firms hire in-house counsel in order to have legal expertise at hand. But this expertise risks being subject to a phenomenon known as "client capture." Normally used to reference the client's power to "capture" the professional by "undermin[ing] professional prerogatives and status"; in the case of corporate counsel, the risk that is evident in this study's findings is that, consciously or otherwise, the professional advice that corporations get from their in-house counsel may be less "professional" than they realize, and the more closely they involve their counsel in the operations of the company, the less "professional" it may be. But it is a frequent recommendation that in-house counsel *should* be involved in the corporation's management; otherwise, so goes the argument, why have in-house counsel at all? Why not just outsource legal work to law firms specializing in corporate law? So a paradox emerges—the arguments favoring the use of in-house counsel and its effective deployment also result in the legal advice being potentially less useful to the firm, or, at least, not as disinterested and unbiased as expected. On the other hand, as pointed out above, a legal department that isolates itself from the firm's management may be seen to be not earning its keep.

NOTES AND QUESTIONS

1. How can organizational context and professional identity influence how one makes decisions? What are the potential implications and consequences (such as with respect to perceived conflicts with the organization)? Should one act as a "professional" or an "organization person"? "A cop, counsel, or entrepreneur"? A mix? In what contexts? Have you used such approaches when making decisions or providing advice? What were the results or effects?

2. In a previous article, Hugh Gunz and Sally Gunz characterized the potential roles as "lawyer", "technician", "organization person", and

"advisor" to address organization-professional conflicts.[16] They particularly noted for the "advisor" that "the in-house lawyer . . . handles ethical dilemmas by using his or her professional social capital to try to influence the behavior of senior non-legal colleagues without playing the role of 'cop.' In other words, they use their legal identity at a social, rather than a technical, level."[17] What are the potential uses and implications of the "advisor" approach for in-house counsel?

3. Are there other potential reasons for why in-house counsel report low levels of organizational-professional conflict? How much weight should be assigned to the various factors?

4. How could one structure an in-house counsel position and their work to get the benefits of an in-house counsel without potential corrupting influences? For example, what are the potential implications for and what steps should one take to ensure ethical and professional decision-making? And what structures and processes may need to be in place?

5. How would you respond if you faced the "(disguised) Texaco scenario" that Gunz & Gunz used in this study? What other approaches or options could an in-house counsel do in the moment? Could previously adopted principles, policies, or processes potentially assist? How?

[4] Ethical/Professionalism Complications Commonly Encountered

Given the range of positions, roles, and organizational contexts, it is impossible to review all of the complicated ethical and professional issues that in-house counsel experience. But certain key issues often arise that in-house counsel must consider from their unique perspective of working primarily for and within an organization. These include: confidentiality/privilege issues for their discussions and advice; potential multiple client conflicts when doing work for subsidiaries or others within the organization; loyalty concerns arising from gatekeeping and reporting requirements; and issues associated with providing policy or business advice, particularly in risk management or crisis situations and when acting as a conscience for the organization. The subsections below provide introductions to each of these complications.

[a] Confidentiality/Privilege Considerations

Confidentiality initially appears straightforward since the *Model Code's* wide-ranging confidentiality provisions also apply to in-house counsel (e.g. "*all* information concerning the business and affairs of a client" is kept confidential).[18] But in-house counsel must also keep in mind that this basic broad confidentiality

---

[16] Hugh P. Gunz & Sally P. Gunz, "The Lawyer's Response to Organizational Professional Conflict: An Empirical Study of the Ethical Decision Making of In-House Counsel" (2002) 39:2 Am. Bus. L.J. 241 at 253-257, 278-280.

[17] Hugh P. Gunz & Sally P. Gunz, "The Lawyer's Response to Organizational Professional Conflict: An Empirical Study of the Ethical Decision Making of In-House Counsel" (2002) 39:2 Am. Bus. L.J. 241 at 274, 278, 279-280.

[18] *Model Code*, r. 3.3-1 [emphasis added].

provision is subject to disclosures "required by law or a court",[19] and such requirements can vary significantly among the jurisdictions an organization operates in. An in-house counsel must thus be aware of the effects of this exception, particularly in the context of privilege.

Privilege is a complicated area that has its original roots in evidentiary law regarding what questions must be answered or materials disclosed as part of a court process, and there are various types of privilege that can apply (e.g. solicitor-client (or legal professional), litigation, settlement, 3rd party, "deal teams" for complicated financial transactions, etc.).[20] However, these forms are usually narrower and more nuanced than the *Model Code's* default and wide confidentiality provision (e.g. privilege only applies to certain communications or it can be lost). In-house counsel thus need to understand how privilege may apply and affect the confidentiality of their discussions and advice.

The following cases explain how courts apply privilege to an in-house counsel's legal and other advice and discussions in the Canadian context, which reflects the general approach in other common law jurisdictions, versus the European Union. As you read these excerpts, keep in mind how the courts view in-house counsel compared to lawyers who practice more traditionally. As well, even if courts determine that privilege generally applies to in-house counsel, consider the extent to which the privilege applies or not. As a result, what general considerations should in-house counsel keep in mind given the resulting potential disclosure of their work in litigation, investigations, and other matters involving the organization? And can this affect how organizations interact with their in-house counsel?

[i] Canada (and Other Common Law Countries)

The following two excerpts are from the leading cases on how Canadian courts view the work and advice of in-house counsel and how that affects privilege. Other common law jurisdictions often have an analogous approach.[21]

Alfred Crompton Amusement Machines Ltd. v. Customs and Excise Commissioners (No. 2)

[1972] 2 Q.B. 102 at 129, 136, 138, [1972] 2 All E.R. 353 (C.A.), aff'd on other grounds (1973), [1974] A.C. 405, [1973] 2 All E.R. 1169 (H.L. (Eng.)).

[The amusement company claimed that the assessed tax it was paying on its machines was too high and requested an arbitration under the applicable statutory

---

[19] *Model Code*, r. 3.3-1(b).

[20] See e.g. *Canada v. Solosky*, (1979), [1980] 1 S.C.R. 821 at 833-837 (S.C.C.); *Barrick Gold Corp. v. Goldcorp Inc.*, [2011] O.J. No. 3530, 2011 ONSC 1325 at para. 19 (Ont. S.C.J.); *Mutual Life Assurance Co. of Canada v. The Deputy Attorney General of Canada* (1988), 88 D.T.C. 6511 at 6512-6513 (T.C.C.); *Toronto-Dominion Bank v. Leigh Instruments Ltd. (Trustee of)*, [1997] O.J. No. 1117, 32 O.R. (3d) 575 at 581-582, 585-588 (Ont. Gen. Div.).

[21] See e.g. *Upjohn Co. v. United States*, 449 U.S. 383 at 383, 392-395 (1981) (U.S.S.C.); *Akzo Nobel Chemicals Ltd. and Akcros Chemicals Ltd. v. European Commission*, C-550/07 P, Opinion of Advocate General Kokott at para. 103 & n. 87.

process, which included discovery. Discovery is a pre-hearing process by which each side can obtain evidence and documents in the possession of the other side. The Commissioners claimed: legal professional privilege on documents consisting of communications between themselves and their legal department (both in the course of their general work and in preparation for the arbitration (i.e. litigation privilege)); and Crown privilege as it would be injurious to the public interest since disclosing certain documents would reveal investigatory methods and confidential information provided by third parties both voluntarily and pursuant to the Commissioners' statutory powers. The company applied to a court for discovery of these documents before the arbitration, which a Master initially denied. However, a judge overturned the Master's decision on the basis that legal professional privilege does not apply to: communications within an organization with its own legal department; documents created before litigation was anticipated; nor documents whose primary purpose was to levy the tax. The judge also found that Crown privilege did not apply as the "damage to the public interest" was "trifling" compared to the "damage to the administration of justice" by withholding the documents.[22] The matter was appealed to the Court of Appeal.][23]

Lord Denning M.R.:

4. Salaried legal advisers

The law relating to discovery was developed by the Chancery Courts in the first half of the 19th century. At that time nearly all legal advisers were in independent practice on their own account. Nowadays it is very different. Many barristers and solicitors are employed as legal advisers, whole time, by a single employer. Sometimes the employer is a great commercial concern. At other times it is a government department or a local authority. It may even be the government itself, like the Treasury Solicitor and his staff. In every case these legal advisers do legal work for their employer and for no one else. They are paid, not by fees for each piece of work, but by a fixed annual salary. They are, no doubt, servants or agents of the employer. For that reason [the motion judge] thought they were in a different position from other legal advisers who are in private practice. I do not think this is correct. They are regarded by the law as in every respect in the same position as those who practise on their own account. The only difference is that they act for one client only, and not for several clients. They must uphold the same standards of honour and of etiquette. They are subject to the same duties to their client and to the court. They must respect the same confidences. They and their clients have the same privileges. I have myself in my early days settled scores of affidavits of documents for the employers of such legal advisers. I have always proceeded on the footing that the communications between the legal advisers and their employer (who is their client) are the subject of legal professional privilege: and I have never known it questioned. There are many cases in the books of actions against railway companies

---

[22] *Alfred Crompton Amusement Machines Ltd. v. Customs and Excise Commissioners (No. 2)*, [1972] 2 Q.B. 102 at 103, [1972] 2 All E.R. 353 (C.A.), aff'd on other grounds (1973), [1974] A.C. 405, [1973] 2 All E.R. 1169 (H.L. (Eng.)).

[23] *Alfred Crompton Amusement Machines Ltd. v. Customs and Excise Commissioners (No. 2)*, [1972] 2 Q.B. at 102-103, [1972] 2 All E.R. 353 (C.A.).

where privilege has been claimed in this way. The validity of it has never been doubted.

I speak, of course, of their communications in the capacity of legal advisers. It does sometimes happen that such a legal adviser does work for his employer in another capacity, perhaps of an executive nature. Their communications in that capacity would not be the subject of legal professional privilege. So the legal adviser must be scrupulous to make the distinction. Being a servant or agent too, he may be under more pressure from his client. So he must be careful to resist it. He must be as independent in the doing of right as any other legal adviser. It is true, as the Law Reform Committee said in their report in 1967 on *Privilege in Civil Procedure* (Cmd. 3472) that the "system is susceptible to abuse," but I have never known it abused. So much so that I do not think the law should be changed in the way that [the motion judge] would have it. There is a safeguard against abuse. It is ready to hand. If there is any doubt as to the propriety or validity of a claim for privilege, the master or the judge should without hesitation inspect the documents himself so as to see if the claim is well-founded, or not. He has ample power under R.S.C. Ord. 24, r. 12. The affidavit should not be treated as conclusive, nor anything like it. A party cannot use the affidavit as a taboo or spell to prevent anyone looking at the documents. When the master or judge sees the documents, he will see if the privilege is rightly claimed—or not—and make an order accordingly.

Karminisky L.J.: . . . On the issue of legal professional privilege I have come to the clear conclusion that there can be no difference between the position of a full-time salaried solicitor employed by a government department or by an industrial or commercial board, on the one hand, and that of a solicitor who practices his profession independently and is rewarded for his services by fees. In both cases the solicitor is consulted as a legal adviser by the lay client and the purpose of being consulted is to enable him to advise the lay client on legal matters. . . .

Orr L.J.: . . . As to the application of the rules of privilege to salaried lawyers, there is little I wish to add to what Lord Denning M.R. has said. There is no doubt that the privilege which [the motion judge] would withhold in such cases has been allowed in practice over a very long period of time and I can see no ground on which this court could hold it to be inapplicable.

[After inspecting the documents, the Court found that legal professional privilege and litigation privilege applied to various documents. With respect to the claimed Crown privilege, the Court found that the public interest did not require those documents to be withheld given their nature, but they were still privileged as "they were obtained in confidence for the purposes of the litigation".[24] Appeal allowed with costs.][25]

R. v. Campbell

[1999] 1 S.C.R. 565 at paras. 1-3, 49-51, 171 DLR (4th) 193 (S.C.C.).

BINNIE J. [for a unanimous Court] – . . . Here the police were alleged to have

---

[24] *Alfred Crompton Amusement Machines Ltd. v. Customs and Excise Commissioners (No. 2)*, [1972] 2 Q.B. 102 at 135, [1972] 2 All E.R. 353 (C.A.).

[25] *Alfred Crompton Amusement Machines Ltd. v. Customs and Excise Commissioners (No. 2)*, [1972] 2 Q.B. 102 at 131-136, 137, 139, [1972] 2 All E.R. 353 (C.A.).

violated the *Narcotic Control Act* . . . by selling a large quantity of hashish (cannabis resin) to senior "executives" in a drug trafficking organization as part of what counsel called a "reverse sting" operation. The appellants [Campbell and his co-defendant], as purchasers, were charged with conspiracy to traffic in cannabis resin and conspiracy to possess cannabis resin for that purpose. The trial judge found the appellants guilty as charged but, before sentencing, heard the appellants' motion for a stay of any further steps in the proceeding. The appellants argued that the reverse sting constituted illegal police conduct which "shocks the conscience of the community and is so detrimental to the proper administration of justice that it warrants judicial intervention" [citation omitted]. The stay was refused by the courts below.

As part of their case for a stay the appellants sought, but were denied, access to the legal advice provided to the police by the Department of Justice on which the police claimed to have placed good faith reliance. The Crown indicated that the undisclosed advice assured the police, rightly or wrongly, that sale of cannabis resin in the circumstances of a reverse sting was lawful. The appellants argue that the truth of this assertion can only be tested by a review of the otherwise privileged communications.

We are therefore required to consider in the context of the "war on drugs", the effect of alleged police illegality on the grant of a judicial stay of proceedings, and related issues regarding the solicitor-client privilege invoked by the RCMP and pre-trial disclosure of solicitor-client communications to which privilege has been waived.

. . .

(a) Existence of a Solicitor-Client Relationship between the RCMP Officers and Lawyers in the Department of Justice

The solicitor-client privilege is based on the functional needs of the administration of justice. The legal system, complicated as it is, calls for professional expertise. Access to justice is compromised where legal advice is unavailable. It is of great importance, therefore, that the RCMP be able to obtain professional legal advice in connection with criminal investigations without the chilling effect of potential disclosure of their confidences in subsequent proceedings. As Lamer C.J. stated in *R. v. Gruenke*, [1991] 3 S.C.R. 263, at p. 289:

> The *prima facie* protection for solicitor-client communications is based on the fact that the relationship and the communications between solicitor and client are essential to the effective operation of the legal system. Such communications are inextricably linked with the very system which desires the disclosure of the communication . . ..

. . . This Court had previously, in *Descôteaux v. Mierzwinski*, [1982] 1 S.C.R. 860, at p. 872, adopted Wigmore's formulation of the substantive conditions precedent to the existence of the right of the lawyer's client to confidentiality (Wigmore on Evidence, vol. 8 (McNaughton rev. 1961), § 2292, at p. 554):

> Where legal advice of any kind is sought from a professional legal adviser in his capacity as such, the communications relating to that purpose, made in confidence by the client, are at his instance permanently protected from disclosure by himself or by the legal adviser, except the protection be waived. [Emphasis and numerotation deleted.]

Cpl. Reynolds' consultation with Mr. Leising of the Department of Justice falls squarely within this functional definition, and the fact that Mr. Leising works for an "in-house" government legal service does not affect the creation or character of the privilege.

It is, of course, not everything done by a government (or other) lawyer that attracts solicitor-client privilege. While some of what government lawyers do is indistinguishable from the work of private practitioners, they may and frequently do have multiple responsibilities including, for example, participation in various operating committees of their respective departments. Government lawyers who have spent years with a particular client department may be called upon to offer policy advice that has nothing to do with their legal training or expertise, but draws on departmental know-how. Advice given by lawyers on matters outside the solicitor-client relationship is not protected. A comparable range of functions is exhibited by salaried corporate counsel employed by business organizations. Solicitor-client communications by corporate employees with in-house counsel enjoy the privilege, although (as in government) the corporate context creates special problems: see, for example, the in-house inquiry into "questionable payments" to foreign governments at issue in *Upjohn Co. v. United States*, 449 U.S. 383 (1981), *per* Rehnquist J. (as he then was), at pp. 394-95. In private practice some lawyers are valued as much (or more) for raw business sense as for legal acumen. No solicitor-client privilege attaches to advice on purely business matters even where it is provided by a lawyer. As Lord Hanworth, M.R., stated in *Minter v. Priest*, [1929] 1 K.B. 655 (C.A.), at pp. 668-69:

> [I]t is not sufficient for the witness to say, "I went to a solicitor's office." ...
> Questions are admissible to reveal and determine for what purpose and under what
> circumstances the intending client went to the office.

Whether or not solicitor-client privilege attaches in any of these situations depends on the nature of the relationship, the subject matter of the advice and the circumstances in which it is sought and rendered. One thing is clear: the fact that Mr. Leising is a salaried employee did not prevent the formation of a solicitor-client relationship and the attendant duties, responsibilities and privileges. This rule is well established, as set out in *Crompton (Alfred) Amusement Machines Ltd. v. Comrs. of Customs and Excise (No. 2)*, [1972] 2 All E.R. 353 (C.A.), *per* Lord Denning, M.R., at p. 376:

> [Many barristers and solicitors are employed . . . They and their clients have the
> same privileges. . . .
>
> I have always proceeded on the footing that the communications between the legal
> advisers and their employer (who is their client) are the subject of legal professional
> privilege: and I have never known it questioned.]

[The Court ultimately determined that the RCMP waived solicitor-client privilege as the RCMP put in issue a good faith belief in the reverse sting's legality, including pertinent Department of Justice consultations. The relevant documents thus could not be fairly withheld. As the appellants sought a stay of proceedings, the Court granted the appeal in part, ordered the disclosure of the particular advice put in issue by the RCMP's witness that related to live issues at this stage of the case, and ordered a new trial limited to whether abuse of process exists for a stay of proceedings.][26]

NOTES AND QUESTIONS FOR BOTH CASES

1. In *Pritchard v. Ontario (Human Rights Commission)*, 2004 SCC 31, the Court summarized the key issues as follows:

   > 20   Owing to the nature of the work of in-house counsel, often having both legal and non-legal responsibilities, *each situation must be assessed on a case-by-case basis* to determine if the circumstances were such that the privilege arose. Whether or not the privilege will attach *depends on the nature of the relationship, the subject matter of the advice, and the circumstances in which it is sought and rendered*: [citation omitted]

   > 21   Where solicitor-client privilege is found, it applies to a broad range of communications between lawyer and client . . . . It will apply with equal force in the context of advice given to an administrative board by in-house counsel as it does to advice given in the realm of private law. *If an in-house lawyer is conveying advice that would be characterized as privileged, the fact that he or she is "in-house" does not remove the privilege, or change its nature.* [emphasis added]

2. As a more detailed example of the relevant solicitor-client privilege considerations, Alberta courts used the following questions as a framework:

   1) Is there a communication between a solicitor and a client?

   2) Does the communication entail the seeking, giving or receiving of legal advice?

   3) Is the communication intended by the parties to be confidential?

   4) Is the lawyer acting as a lawyer?

   5) What was the purpose for which the record came into existence?

   6) Is the particular communication part of a continuum in which legal advice is given?

   7) Does the particular communication reveal that legal advice has been sought or given?

   8) If there is any privileged information, can it be reasonably severed from the rest of the record, without revealing the privilege?[27]

3. What are the resulting implications for in-house counsel? For example:

---

[26] *R. v. Campbell*, [1999] S.C.J. No. 16, [1999] 1 S.C.R. 565 at paras. 67, 71, 74, 79, 171 (S.C.C.).

[27] *Alberta (Municipal Affairs) v. Alberta (Information and Privacy Commissioner)*, [2019] A.J. No. 466, 2019 ABQB 274 at para. 11 (Alta. Q.B.); *Calgary (Police Service) v. Alberta (Information and Privacy Commissioner)*, [2019] A.J. No. 188, 2019 ABQB 109 at para. 6 (Alta. Q.B.).

a. Is it sufficient to say that the in-house counsel is a lawyer?[28] Can someone who is legally trained but doing another role claim privilege?[29]

b. What if the materials are simply copied to the in-house counsel?[30] What if the in-house counsel makes notes on the copied materials?[31] What if the in-house counsel gathered the materials for the purpose of litigation?[32]

c. What if an in-house counsel holds multiple roles and positions and there is a lack of clarity regarding in what role person prepared the materials?[33] Which roles/advice are covered by privilege and which are not?[34]

d. To what extent do the documents need to indicate that they are confidential or privileged?[35] What if they are circulated broadly within an organization?[36]

e. What if an organization puts its state of mind at issue?[37] How could an organization do this?

f. What happens when an organization merges with another organiza-

---

[28] See e.g. *Blough v. Busy Music Inc.*, [2018] A.J. No. 924, 2018 ABQB 560 at paras. 83-87, 96 (Alta. Q.B.).

[29] See e.g. *Blough v. Busy Music Inc.*, [2018] A.J. No. 924, 2018 ABQB 560 at paras. 83-87, 96 (Alta. Q.B.); *Re Ontario Securities Commission and Greymac Credit Corp*, 41 O.R. (2d) 328, 146 D.L.R. (3d) 73 (Ont. H.C.J.); *Husky Oil Operations Ltd. v. MacKimmie Matthews*, [1999] A.J. No. 604, 1999 ABQB 54 (Alta. Q.B.); *Canary v. Vested Estates Ltd.*, 1930 CanLII 252 (B.C.S.C.).

[30] See e.g. *Mutual Life Assurance Co. of Canada v. The Deputy Attorney General of Canada* (1988), 88 D.T.C. 6511 at 6513 (T.C.C.).

[31] *Mutual Life Assurance Co. of Canada v. The Deputy Attorney General of Canada* (1988), 88 D.T.C. 6511 at 6513 (T.C.C.).

[32] See e.g. *Toronto-Dominion Bank v. Leigh Instruments Ltd. (Trustee of)*, [1997] O.J. No. 1177, 32 O.R. (3d) 575 at 585-588 (Ont. Gen. Div.).

[33] See e.g. *Barton v. Potash Corporation of Saskatchewan*, [2011] S.J. No. 502, 2011 SKCA 96 at paras. 51-53 (Sask. C.A.); *Toronto-Dominion Bank v. Leigh Instruments Ltd. (Trustee of)*, [1997] O.J. No. 1177, 32 O.R. (3d) 575 at 583-584 (Ont. Gen. Div.); *IBM Canada Limited v. Xerox Canada Limited*, [1978] 1 F.C. 513 at 516-517 (F.C.A.).

[34] See e.g. *Mutual Life Assurance Co. of Canada v. The Deputy Attorney General of Canada* (1988), 88 D.T.C. 6511 at 6513 (T.C.C.).

[35] See e.g. *Toronto-Dominion Bank v. Leigh Instruments Ltd. (Trustee of)*, [1997] O.J. No. 1177, 32 O.R. (3d) 575 at 584 (Ont. Gen. Div.).

[36] See e.g. *Toronto-Dominion Bank v. Leigh Instruments Ltd. (Trustee of)*, [1997] O.J. No. 1177, 32 O.R. (3d) 575 at 582-585 (Ont. Gen. Div.).

[37] See e.g. *Toronto-Dominion Bank v. Leigh Instruments Ltd. (Trustee of)*, [1997] O.J. No. 1177, 32 O.R. (3d) 575 at 588-594 (Ont. Gen. Div.).

tion?[38] Or organizational control otherwise changes?[39]

    g.   What happens if an in-house counsel wishes to investigate a potential impropriety or illegality by questioning an organization's employees?[40] Should there be any difference between those who provide the in-house counsel instructions versus those who simply work for the organization? What if the investigation is to provide a basis for the in-house counsel to provide legal advice? Non-legal advice?

4.   What are the potential implications of privilege and the likelihood of disclosure for how in-house counsel works with an organization and ensuring the organization's best interests? For example, could an organization's agents choose to not fully and candidly communicate with its in-house counsel? Why or why not?

[ii] The European Union's Different Approach to In-House Counsel and Privilege

In contrast to common law jurisdictions, the European Union takes a different perspective on whether privilege should apply to an in-house counsel's work and instructions, which is largely based on professional independence concerns. Review the following European Court of Justice decision, which was in the context of a European Commission investigation, and consider how the Court's view and approach to privilege for in-house counsel contrasts with that of common law jurisdictions.

Akzo Nobel Chemicals Ltd. and Akcros Chemicals Ltd. v. European Commission

C-550/07 P, [2010] ECR I-8360 at paras. 30-61
[citations omitted]

[During an investigation into the companies (Akcros was a subsidiary of Akzo during the relevant times, and both companies were based in the United Kingdom), the European Commission used its powers to seek evidence of possible anti-competitive practices. Disputes arose regarding whether legal professional privilege covered certain documents, including two emails between Akcros' general manager and Akzo's coordinator for competition law, who was a Netherlands lawyer and a member of Akzo's legal department. Despite the companies being based in the

---

[38] See e.g. *NEP Canada ULC v. MEC OP LLC*, [2013] A.J. No. 984, 2013 ABQB 540 at paras. 26, 36, 42-44 (Alta. Q.B.).

[39] See e.g. *NEP Canada ULC v. MEC OP LLC*, [2013] A.J. No. 984, 2013 ABQB 540 at para. 36 (Alta. Q.B.). See also *Commodity Futures Trading Commission v. Weintraub*, 471 US 343 (1985) at 349 (U.S.S.C.); Adam M. Dodek, *Solicitor-Client Privilege* (Markham, ON: LexisNexis, 2014) at §§ 6.35-6.36 (example of new Hollinger Board waiving privilege to co-operate with SEC and US Attorney, which allowed prosecutors to use privileged materials, even though the communications were by Conrad Black and his allies before their removal from the Hollinger Board).

[40] See e.g. *Upjohn Co. v. United States*, 449 U.S. 383 at 383, 392-395 (U.S.S.C.).

common law United Kingdom, the Netherlands legislature seeking to treat in-house lawyers in the same way as external lawyers, and the person being subject to the Netherlands Bar's professional obligations, code of conduct, and supervision, the head of the Commission's investigation team determined that the documents were not privileged and took copies of the documents. The European Commission and the European Court of First Instance upheld this determination. The companies appealed these decisions to the European Court of Justice, specifically on excluding and returning the two emails.][41]

1. The first ground of appeal

Akzo and Akcros base the first ground of appeal on two arguments. They submit, first of all, that the General Court incorrectly interpreted the second condition for legal professional privilege, which concerns the professional status of the lawyer with whom communications are exchanged, as laid down in the *AM & S Europe* v *Commission* judgment, and, second, that by that interpretation the General Court breached the principle of equality.

The Commission submits that that ground of appeal is unfounded.

(a) The first argument

. . .

(ii) Findings of the Court

It must be recalled that, in *AM & S Europe* v *Commission*, the Court, taking account of the common criteria and similar circumstances existing at the time in the national laws of the Member States, held, in paragraph 21 of that judgment, that the confidentiality of written communications between lawyers and clients should be protected at [the European] Community level. However, the Court stated that that protection was subject to two cumulative conditions.

In that connection, the Court stated, first, that the exchange with the lawyer must be connected to 'the client's rights of defence' and, second, that the exchange must emanate from 'independent lawyers', that is to say 'lawyers who are not bound to the client by a relationship of employment'.

As to the second condition, the Court observed, . . . in *AM & S Europe* v *Commission*, that the requirement as to the position and status as an independent lawyer, which must be fulfilled by the legal adviser from whom the written communications which may be protected emanate, is based on a conception of the lawyer's role as collaborating in the administration of justice and as being required to provide, in full independence and in the overriding interests of that cause, such legal assistance as the client needs. The counterpart to that protection lies in the rules of professional ethics and discipline which are laid down and enforced in the general interest. The Court also held . . . that such a conception reflects the legal traditions common to the Member States and is also to be found in the legal order of the European Union, as is demonstrated by the provisions of Article 19 of the Statute of the Court of Justice.

---

[41] *Akzo Nobel Chemicals Ltd. and Akcros Chemicals Ltd. v. European Commission*, C-550/07 P, [2010] ECR I-8360 at paras. 3-5, 14, 35-36, 57.

The Court repeated those findings in . . . that judgment, according to which written communications which may be protected by legal professional privilege must be exchanged with 'an independent lawyer, that is to say one who is not bound to his client by a relationship of employment'.

It follows that the requirement of independence means the absence of any employment relationship between the lawyer and his client, so that legal professional privilege does not cover exchanges within a company or group with in-house lawyers.

As the Advocate General observed . . ., the concept of the independence of lawyers is determined not only positively, that is by reference to professional ethical obligations, but also negatively, by the absence of an employment relationship. An in-house lawyer, despite his enrolment with a Bar or Law Society and the professional ethical obligations to which he is, as a result, subject, does not enjoy the same degree of independence from his employer as a lawyer working in an external law firm does in relation to his client. Consequently, an in-house lawyer is less able to deal effectively with any conflicts between his professional obligations and the aims of his client.

As regards the professional ethical obligations relied on by the appellants in order to demonstrate Mr S.'s independence, it must be observed that, while the rules of professional organisation in Dutch law mentioned by Akzo and Akcros may strengthen the position of an in-house lawyer within the company, the fact remains that they are not able to ensure a degree of independence comparable to that of an external lawyer.

Notwithstanding the professional regime applicable in the present case in accordance with the specific provisions of Dutch law, an in-house lawyer cannot, whatever guarantees he has in the exercise of his profession, be treated in the same way as an external lawyer, because he occupies the position of an employee which, by its very nature, does not allow him to ignore the commercial strategies pursued by his employer, and thereby affects his ability to exercise professional independence.

It must be added that, under the terms of his contract of employment, an in-house lawyer may be required to carry out other tasks, namely, as in the present case, the task of competition law coordinator, which may have an effect on the commercial policy of the undertaking. Such functions cannot but reinforce the close ties between the lawyer and his employer.

It follows, both from the in-house lawyer's economic dependence and the close ties with his employer, that he does not enjoy a level of professional independence comparable to that of an external lawyer.

Therefore, the General Court correctly applied the second condition for legal professional privilege laid down in the judgment in *AM & S Europe* v *Commission*.

Accordingly, the first argument put forward by Akzo and Ackros under the first ground of appeal cannot be accepted.

(b) The second argument

. . .

(iii) Findings of the Court

It must be recalled that the principle of equal treatment is a general principle of European Union law, enshrined in Articles 20 and 21 of the Charter of Fundamental Rights of the European Union.

According to settled case-law, that principle requires that comparable situations must not be treated differently and that different situations must not be treated in the same way unless such treatment is objectively justified [citations omitted].

As to the essential characteristics of those two categories of lawyer, namely their respective professional status, it is clear from paragraphs 45 to 49 of this judgment that, despite the fact that he may be enrolled with a Bar or Law Society and that he is subject to a certain number of professional ethical obligations, an in-house lawyer does not enjoy a level of professional independence equal to that of external lawyers.

As the Advocate General stated, . . . that difference in terms of independence is still significant, even though the national legislature, the Netherlands legislature in this case, seeks to treat in-house lawyers in the same way as external lawyers. After all, such equal treatment relates only to the formal act of admitting an in-house lawyer to a Bar or Law Society and the professional ethical obligations incumbent on him as a result of such admission. On the other hand, that legislative framework does not alter the economic dependence and personal identification of a lawyer in an employment relationship with his undertaking.

It follows from those considerations that in-house lawyers are in a fundamentally different position from external lawyers, so that their respective circumstances are not comparable for the purposes of the case-law set out in paragraph 55 of this judgment.

Therefore, the General Court rightly held that there was no breach of the principle of equal treatment.

Consequently, the second argument put forward as part of the first ground of appeal must also be rejected.

Therefore, [the first] ground of appeal must be rejected in its entirety.

[The Court also rejected the second and third grounds of appeal, which essentially were that the law of member states or the European Union had evolved or that the European Union's law should be changed to recognize the privilege for various reasons.[42] The Court rejected these grounds of appeal, and it included a finding that "the legal situation in the Member States of the European Union has not evolved . . . to an extent which would justify a change in the . . . recognition for in-house lawyers of the benefit of legal professional privilege" as a "a large number of Member States still exclude correspondence with in-house lawyers from protection

---

[42] See generally *Akzo Nobel Chemicals Ltd. and Akcros Chemicals Ltd. v. European Commission*, C-550/07 P, [2010] ECR I-8360 at paras. 62-121.

under legal professional privilege" nor allowed them to be admitted as lawyers.[43]

The Court thus dismissed the entire appeal, with the companies paying the Commission's costs.[44]]

NOTES AND QUESTIONS

1. How does the European Union's approach to in-house counsel and privilege compare with that of common law jurisdictions?

2. Do you agree with the Court's rationale and concerns about an in-house counsel's professional independence to deny them and their clients the benefit of solicitor-client privilege? Why or why not? Does this approach account for potential nuances with respect to in-house counsel maintaining professionalism and avoiding client tunnel vision discussed in Section [3] above?

3. Suppose you are an in-house counsel for a major publicly-listed corporation that has offices in Canada, the United States, the United Kingdom, and the European Union. Due to a proposed takeover of a significant competitor, competition regulators in all four jurisdictions are conducting analyses and investigations into your company and the proposed takeover target. As both companies are listed on stock exchanges in all four areas, you are also responsible for preparing and advising your company on related stock filings.

   a. What are the potential practical implications of the different privilege approaches for you and your company? How may that affect who does what work?

   b. What issues or factors should in-house counsel and organizations consider as result?

   c. What potential complications may arise if the company operated in the United Kingdom both before and after it withdrew from the European Union?

4. Suppose your corporation wishes to operate in South America (i.e. a jurisdiction not covered by this section) by taking over a complementary company there. Given the concerns and issues about privilege and potential disclosure for your in-house counsel work raised in the common law and European Union jurisdictions, what issues would you want to explore and be aware of? How would that affect how you and your corporation approach your work regarding this takeover?

[b] Multiple Clients and Conflicts Complications

Given the nature of organizations and their constituent parts, in-house counsel must be particularly alive to potential conflict situations and the relevant rules. For

---

[43] *Akzo Nobel Chemicals Ltd. and Akcros Chemicals Ltd. v. European Commission*, C-550/07 P, [2010] ECR I-8360 at paras. 72, 76.

[44] *Akzo Nobel Chemicals Ltd. and Akcros Chemicals Ltd. v. European Commission*, C-550/07 P, [2010] ECR I-8360 at paras. 122-123.

example, while their ultimate duty is to the organization as whole,[45] this duty can become clouded given the various roles and impacts of directors, senior officers, employees, and majority/minority shareholders. As a result, in-house lawyers need to be careful about potentially working for and providing advice to multiple clients. If such work still proceeds, it engages the conflicts rules regarding joint retainers and ensuring appropriate consent.[46] Even if these requirements are met, an in-house counsel may have to stop working on a matter if the organization and other client develop an irresolvable conflict, and confidentiality for the organization would not be exclusive, at least for the joint matter.[47] As well, once an in-house lawyer works for a client outside of their primary organization, the in-house counsel must be alive to the issues of working against such former clients and their interests (e.g. same or related matter? have confidential information that may prejudice that client?).[48]

Since companies often have wholly- or partially-owned subsidiaries for legal, tax, and other reasons, another key example is when an organization asks an in-house counsel to work with and provide advice to both itself and its subsidiaries on key projects or other work. While such issues may be less of an issue if the subsidiary is and remains wholly-owned, what happens if the parent organization decides to no longer be affiliated with its subsidiary? What is or is not confidential between the parent and the subsidiary before and after that point? What are the duties and loyalties that the parent's in-house counsel has to the parent and the subsidiary? How do privilege and other issues play out if the subsidiary sues the former parent for actions of the subsidiary done at the parent's directions?

Consider such issues and complications when reading the following excerpt from the decision of the United States Court of Appeals for the Third Circuit regarding bankrupt US subsidiaries of some major Canadian telecommunication companies.[49]

In Re Teleglobe Communications Corporation

493 F (3d) 345 at 352-353, 359-360, 369, 370-372, 373-374 (3rd Cir. 2007) [citations/ footnotes omitted]

Ambro, Circuit Judge [for the Court]: This is a twist on a classic corporate divorce story. It begins much as Judge Richard Cudahy's "classic corporate love story": "Company A meets Company B. They are attracted to each other and after a brief courtship, they merge." . . . Sadly, it does not last. Not long after Company A acquires Company B, they start taking risks together, some of which go terribly wrong. After only a year or so, Company B is steeped in debt, and, not surprisingly,

---

[45] See e.g. *Model Code*, r. 3.2-3.

[46] *Model Code*, rs. 3.4-5 to 3.4-9 and 3.4-2.

[47] *Model Code*, r. 3.4-5(c).

[48] *Model Code*, rs. 3.4-10 to 3.4-11. See also *Strother v. 3464920 Canada Inc.*, [2007] S.C.J. No. 24, 2007 SCC 24 at paras. 40-43, 46-47 (S.C.C.).

[49] According to Adam M. Dodek, this decision "is likely to influence the development of Canadian law because of the thoroughness of its consideration of the issues, because it involved a Canadian company ("BCE")[,] and because it assumed that there was no difference between Canadian and American law on the issues before the Court" (Adam M. Dodek, Solicitor-Client Privilege (Markham: LexisNexis, 2014) at § 11.49).

Company A begins to "los[e] that lovin' feelin'." It leaves Company B, explaining that it simply must do so in order to save itself. Jilted and out of money, Company B promptly turns to that shelter for abandoned corporations, the bankruptcy system.

In bankruptcy, Company B's children (subsidiaries), also in the shelter of bankruptcy, become indignant, and they sue Company A for all manner of ills relating to the break-up. Here, we deal not with the merits of the action, but with a pretrial dispute over corporate documents. Everyone agrees that the attorney-client privilege protects these documents against third parties. The wrinkle is that they were produced by and in communication with attorneys who represented the entire corporate family back when they all got along.

The question, then, is whether Company A may assert the privilege against its former family members. Because we conclude that the District Court's factual findings do not support setting aside the parent company's privilege in this case, we vacate its order compelling production and remand for further proceedings.

. . .

[For this case, Bell Canada Enterprises, Inc. ("BCE") is Company A, and Teleglobe Inc. ("Teleglobe") is Company B. In 2000, BCE increased its previous minority stake in Teleglobe by purchasing all of Teleglobe's remaining shares and taking control. BCE then directed Teleglobe to accelerate development of its GlobeSystem fiberoptic network. BCE pledged financial support and caused Teleglobe and its subsidiaries to borrow $2.4 billion. Teleglobe exhausted its funding in 2001, and BCE approved an additional $850 million equity infusion in November 2001 (which was to be disbursed at the sole discretion of BCE's Chairman and CEO, who was also Teleglobe's Chairman and CEO). BCE also announced in December 2001 its intention to continue funding. However, in April 2001, BCE began and announced a comprehensive reassessment of its plans for Teleglobe, and BCE ceased its funding a few weeks later. With Teleglobe effectively abandoned, it had no means of paying its debt, and it and its subsidiaries began bankruptcy/insolvency proceedings in Canada and the United States.

Teleglobe's US subsidiaries sued BCE for its role in funding and abandoning the GlobeSystem project, and privilege disputes arose as part of the discovery process. BCE asserted that it produced all documents covered by common interest / joint representation with Teleglobe and its US subsidiaries, but BCE refused to produce reassessment documents that were legal advice only for BCE and no one else. In the end, a Special Master determined that all of the documents were discoverable and ordered production as BCE's in-house counsel "were jointly representing Teleglobe [and its subsidiaries] and could not, therefore, withhold the documents", and "[h]e applied this reasoning even to documents produced by outside counsel hired only to work for BCE."[50] The District Court affirmed the Special Master's decision and ordered production for three reasons: "(1) BCE made a binding agreement to disclose all communications generated as part of a BCE/Teleglobe joint representation . . .; (2) the Debtors, as wholly owned subsidiaries of Teleglobe, were parties to the joint representation as a matter of law; and (3) even the documents that fell

---

[50] *In Re Teleglobe Communications Corporation*, 493 F (3d) 345 at 357 (3rd Cir. 2007).

outside of the joint representation (*i.e.* were produced by outside counsel) must be disclosed because they were shared with BCE's in-house attorneys, who jointly represented Teleglobe."[51] BCE appealed this interlocutory order to the United States Court of Appeals for the Third Circuit.][52]

A. The Attorney-Client Privilege

The attorney-client privilege protects communications between attorneys and clients from compelled disclosure. . . . "Privileged persons" include the client, the attorney(s), and any of their agents that help facilitate attorney-client communications or the legal representation. . . .

As common-law courts developed the privilege in an age in which clients were almost exclusively natural persons, more modern courts sought to adapt it to the now ubiquitous corporate client. For more than a century, common-law courts have recognized that communications between corporate clients and their attorneys are indeed privileged. . . .

Because corporations act through human agents, the question of whose communications with the corporation's attorneys are entitled to protection comes up often. In *Upjohn* the Supreme Court [of the United States]. . . held that when a corporation's managers require its employees to give information to its attorneys in the course of providing legal advice, those communications also are protected. . . . This serves the policy goals of the privilege—to enhance compliance with the law and facilitate the administration of justice—by encouraging open communication between attorneys and clients. . . .

F. Putting It All Together: Parents, Subsidiaries, and the Modern Corporate Counsel's Office

"A striking development in the legal profession . . . has been the rapid growth in both importance and size of in-house, or corporate, counsel." . . . The roles of in-house counsel are many, *e.g.*, overseeing the corporation's compliance with myriad regulatory regimes. The primary advantages of in-house (rather than outside) counsel are the breadth of their knowledge of the corporation and their ability to begin advising senior management on important transactions at the earliest possible stage, often well before anyone would think to hire a law firm. . . . While there is much debate over how corporate counsel should go about promoting compliance with law . . ., both sides of the debate seem to see in-house counsel as the "front lines" of the battle to ensure that compliance while preserving confidential communications. . . . Because in-house counsel are crucial and clear rules are needed to sort out attorney-client privilege problems (particularly for corporate groups), this section sets out how the various principles we have discussed apply to a parent company's in-house counsel.

1. Intra-group Information Sharing: Parents and Subsidiaries as Joint Clients

Because parent companies often centralize the provision of legal services to the

---

[51] *In Re Teleglobe Communications Corporation*, 493 F (3d) 345 at 357 (3rd Cir. 2007).

[52] *In Re Teleglobe Communications Corporation*, 493 F (3d) 345 at 353-357 (3rd Cir. 2007).

entire corporate group in one in-house legal department, it is important to consider how the disclosure rule affects the sharing of information among corporate affiliates. Recognizing that any other result would wreak havoc on corporate counsel offices, courts almost universally hold that intra-group information sharing does not implicate the disclosure rule. This result is unquestionably correct. . . .

Within the wholly owned corporate family, it superficially makes sense to hold, as BCE urges, that the family is really one client for purposes of the privilege and that the privilege is held exclusively by the parent because all fiduciary duties flow to the parent. . . .

On the other hand, treating members of a corporate family as one client fails to respect the corporate form. It is a bedrock principle of corporate law . . . that courts must respect entity separateness unless doing so would work inordinate inequity. . . . By structuring its various activities by forming separate corporations, a parent company realizes numerous benefits, not the least of which are the liability shields. With that structure comes the responsibility to treat the various corporations as separate entities. . . .

Put simply, BCE wants to have it both ways: it wants us to view the corporate group as a single client, and it wants the controlling entity to own the privilege in perpetuity. But the Supreme Court held in *Commodity Futures Trading Comm'n v. Weintraub*, . . . that control of the privilege passes with control of the corporation, so it is unclear (even accepting BCE's theory) that it is the initial corporate parent who should control the privilege unilaterally once the group breaks up. In any event, absent some compelling reason to disregard entity separateness, in the typical case courts should treat the various members of the corporate group as the separate corporations they are and not as one client.

. . .

It makes the most sense, then, to rest not applying the disclosure rule to many intra-group disclosures on the ground that the members of the corporate family are joint clients. This reflects both the separateness of each entity and the reality that they are all represented by the same in-house counsel (whether that counsel typically takes up office with the parent or with a subsidiary).

. . .

3. When Conflicts Arise

It is inevitable that on occasion parents and subsidiaries will see their interests diverge, particularly in spin-off, sale, and insolvency situations. When this happens, it is wise for the parent to secure for the subsidiary outside representation. Maintaining a joint representation for the spin-off transaction too long risks the outcome of . . . parent companies . . . forced to turn over documents to their former subsidiaries in adverse litigation—not to mention the attorneys' potential for running afoul of conflict rules. That the companies should have separate counsel on the matter of the spin-off transaction, however, does not mean that the parent's in-house counsel must cease representing the subsidiary on all other matters. After all, spin-off transactions can be in the works for months (or even years), and during that time it is proper (and obviously efficient) for in-house counsel to continue to

541

represent the subsidiary (jointly or alone) on other matters.

Once conflicts begin coming to the surface, the question of when to acquire separate counsel is often difficult. . . . [F]rom the perspective of protecting the privilege[,] the best answer is that once the parties' interests become sufficiently adverse that the parent does not want future controllers of the subsidiary to be able to invade the parent's privilege, it should end any joint representation on the matter of the relevant transaction. . . . This standard is, of course, only relevant if the parties have already begun a joint representation on that transaction; if they have not, then the parent has nothing to fear as far as the privilege goes (though other concerns, such as their fiduciary duties to their subsidiaries, may argue in favor of separating counsel).

In sum, in-house counsel have available numerous means to protect a parent company's privilege. By taking care not to begin joint representations except when necessary, to limit the scope of joint representations, and seasonably to separate counsel on matters in which subsidiaries are adverse to the parent, in-house counsel can maintain sufficient control over the parent's privileged communications.

[As there was no factual finding that joint representations actually occurred and to what extent (i.e. were Teleglobe's US subsidiaries included or not), the Court remanded the case back to the District Court to determine what joint representation occurred. "[W]hat matters is the scope of any joint representation: documents within the scope are discoverable; documents outside of it are not [e.g. documents produced by outside counsel only for BCE], irrespective of whether they were improperly funneled through joint attorneys."][53]

NOTES AND QUESTIONS

1. What are the implications and considerations (e.g. advantages and disadvantages) of an in-house counsel being in a joint retainer relationship when working with subsidiaries, parent companies, their employees, or others?[54] What if the subsidiary is wholly-owned? Majority-owned? Minority-owned? When should in-house counsel be careful and what steps should they take? In what situations would consent likely not cure a conflict?

2. Assume that you are in-house counsel for a large public-listed corporation that focuses on resource extraction. As a result of the corporation's mining activities in South America through a wholly-owned subsidiary (which has some overlapping officers with the parent), local Indigenous peoples are bringing a claim regarding the overly aggressive actions of security forces contracted by the subsidiary to protect access to the tract the mining permit covers, which includes undeveloped historic territories of the Indigenous peoples. As a result of previous representations to the shareholders and public by senior officers (but not you) denying these claims, and these security actions coming to light, the minority shareholders also begin

---

[53] *In Re Teleglobe Communications Corporation*, 493 F (3d) 345 at 387 (3rd Cir. 2007).

[54] See e.g. *Mutual Life Assurance Co. of Canada v. The Deputy Attorney General of Canada* (1988), 88 D.T.C. 6511 at 6512 (T.C.C.).

proceedings against the publicly listed corporation.

    a.   What issues and considerations arise if you enter into joint retainers with and provide advice to directors, senior officers, employees, majority shareholders, or minority shareholders in preparation for or as part of these proceedings?[55] What if the in-house counsel had acted in a joint capacity for some of these parties before? When should in-house counsel be careful and what steps should they take? In what situations are the parties' interests more likely to diverge? Would consent cure a conflict?

   3.   If an in-house counsel leaves their organization for another organization or private law firm, what concerns and issues may arise if they litigate directly against their former client(s) or their interests?[56] What information could they have that may now pose a conflict, even if they are not litigating directly against their former client?

[c] Loyalty Issues That Can Arise From Potential Gatekeeping and Reporting Roles

Over the years, there have been significant securities, financial, and other scandals that had major impacts on the economy and society as a whole. Some of the most well known cases include:

- Exploding Ford Pintos that the engineers knew about, but Ford did not inform the public nor issue a recall due to analyses based on a cost-benefit analysis;[57]

- Bre-X Minerals falsifying claims indicating that it had found one of the richest gold deposits in the world, resulting in a $3-6 billion hoax on investors;[58]

- Livent Entertainment's officers convicted of fraud and forgery related to kickbacks and accounting irregularities, including charges of falsifying financial statements over nine years that resulted in "bilking investors and creditors of $500 million";[59]

---

[55] See e.g. *Model Code*, rs. 3.4-5 to 3.4-9, 3.4-2, 3.2-3.

[56] See e.g. *ATCO Gas and Pipelines Ltd. v. Sheard*, [2003] A.J. No. 235, 2003 ABCA 61 at paras. 2-3, 12, 25-30 (Alta. C.A.); *R. v. Sandhu*, [2011] B.C.J. No. 1600, 2011 BCSC 1137 at paras. 54-70, 73, 91, 101-102, 109-115 (B.C.S.C.); *Valeant Canada LP v. Canada (Health)*, [2014] F.C.J. No. 178, 2014 FCA 50 at paras. 15-16, 20-27 (F.C.A.); *Strother v. 3464920 Canada Inc*, [2007] S.C.J. No. 24, 2007 SCC 24 at paras. 40-43, 46-47 (S.C.C.). See also *Model Code*, rs. 3.4-10 to 3.4-11.

[57] See e.g. David Luban, *Lawyers and Justice: An Ethical Study* (Princeton: Princeton University Press, 1988) at 206-213.

[58] "Bre-X: The Real Story and Scandal that Inspired the Movie Gold" *Calgary Herald* (January 27, 2017), online: https://calgaryherald.com/news/local-news/bre-x-the-real-story-and-scandal-that-inspired-the-movie-gold.

[59] The Canadian Press, "Curtain Call: A Look at Key Events in the Livent Entertainment Fraud Scandal" *CityNews* (February 22, 2017), online: https://toronto.citynews.ca/2017/02/

- Enron and Arthur Andersen (their accountants) "fool[ing] regulators with fake holdings and off-the-books accounting practices" as well as "hid[ing] mountains of debt and toxic assets from investors and creditors", resulting in the loss of $74 billion to shareholders in the four years prior to Enron's bankruptcy and Enron's employees losing "billions in pension benefits";[60]

- The WorldCom accounting scandal (which involved Arthur Andersen again), resulting in inflating earnings by nearly four billion dollars in one year, with an eventual $11 billion total in accounting errors;

- The General Motors faulty ignition switch scandal, which GM knew about as early as 2003, but the recall of nearly 30 million cars only occurred in 2014, with at least 97 related deaths occurring between 2005 and 2015;[61]

- The Volkswagen/Audi/Porsche diesel emission scandal, where up to 11 million vehicles worldwide would enter a "cheat" mode when administered emissions tests to appear to comply with required standards;[62] and

- Potential corruption, hiding ownership identities, and other issues through offshore corporations, as illustrated through the Panama Papers (with governments recouping $1.36 billion so far as of April 2021).[63]

Given the organizations' size and the public effects of these and other scandals, including criminal charges and large-scale bankruptcies, questions arise about the role of lawyers in such situations, particularly for their in-house counsel. The *Model Code* contains relevant provisions that apply to in-house counsel, such as: not assisting in, encouraging, or omitting things that are dishonest, fraudulent, criminal, or illegal;[64] not being a tool or dupe and what steps to take if one suspects such problematic activities;[65] "reporting up the ladder" within an organization if it does

---

22/curtain-call-a-look-at-key-events-in-the-livent-entertainment-fraud-scandal/.

[60] Troy Segal, "Enron Scandal: The Fall of a Wall Street Darling" (January 19, 2021), online: *Investopedia* https://www.investopedia.com/updates/enron-scandal-summary/.

[61] Brad Plumer, "The GM Recall Scandal of 2014" (May 11, 2015), online: *Vox* https://www.vox.com/2014/10/3/18073458/gm-car-recall.

[62] See e.g. Jeff S. Bartlett, Michelle Naranjo, & Jeff Plungis, "Guide to the Volkswagen Emissions Recall: [A] FAQ with Everything You Need to Know About the VW 'Dieselgate'" (October 23, 2017), online: *Consumer Reports* https://www.consumerreports.org/cars-guide-to-the-volkswagen-dieselgate-emissions-recall/.

[63] See e.g. Will Fitzgibbon & Michael Hudson, "Five years later, Panama Papers still having a big impact" (April 3, 2021), online: *International Consortium of Investigative Journalists* https://www.icij.org/investigations/panama-papers/five-years-later-panama-papers-still-having-a-big-impact/; Sean McGoey, "Panama Papers revenue recovery reaches $1.36 billion as investigations continue" (April 6, 2021), online: *International Consortium of Investigative Journalists* https://www.icij.org/investigations/panama-papers/panama-papers-revenue-recovery-reaches-1-36-billion-as-investigations-continue/. See also generally "Panama Papers: The Secrets of Dirty Money", online: *Süddeutsche Zeitung* https://panamapapers.sueddeutsche.de/en/.

[64] *Model Code*, r. 3.2-7.

[65] *Model Code*, rs. 3.2-7[1], [3].

such things, to the point of the lawyer withdrawing if necessary;[66] and being honest and candid when giving advice, including firmness when needed.[67] But are these approaches sufficient protection for the public?

These questions have led to debates about whether in-house counsel should take a greater gatekeeping and "whistleblowing" (i.e. mandatory/discretionary disclosure) role in such circumstances. For example, in addition to "reporting" and "reporting up" requirements,[68] the US Securities and Exchange Commission considered whether to implement a "noisy withdrawal" requirement with notifications to the Commission if the final authority in the "reporting up" process did not respond to the lawyer's concerns.[69] Lawyers can also disclose otherwise confidential information if the future harm or public safety exception is met;[70] and lawyers can disclose information to defend themselves from criminal, civil, or professional allegations.[71]

So in what circumstances should in-house counsel be able to warn others, both inside and outside the organization? If whistleblowing is discretionary, when should you blow the whistle? How does that potentially interact with other professional obligations and considerations, including the lawyer's role and client interactions? And even if whistleblowing is not applicable, in what circumstances would you withdraw as in-house counsel? The following piece generally introduces some of the competing considerations and issues for gatekeeping, whistleblowing, and related professional obligations and roles that one needs to keep in mind, including loyalty and related confidentiality.

Gerry Ferguson

Global Corruption: Law, Theory & Practice, 3rd ed. (Victoria, BC: University of Victoria, 2018) at 775-778 [footnotes omitted]

2.4 The Lawyer as a Corporate Gatekeeper

The term gatekeeper in the world of business generally refers to an outside or independent monitor or watchdog. A corporate gatekeeper is someone who

---

[66] *Model Code*, r. 3.2-8.

[67] *Model Code*, r. 3.2-2.

[68] See e.g. *Sarbanes-Oxley Act of 2002*, Pub. L. No. 107–204, § 307, 116 Stat. 745 [US Securities and Exchange Commission can set "minimum standards of professional conduct" for lawyers representing issuers]; 17 C.F.R. §§ 205.1–205.7 [lawyer reporting requirements, including "reporting up", which applies to foreign lawyers as well].

[69] In such situations, lawyers would withdraw and inform the SEC that the withdrawal was due to "professional considerations" and would disaffirm any "tainted submissions" they may have made to the SEC. However, this rule was ultimately not included due to various objections during the feedback period (see generally Paul D Paton, "Corporate Counsel as Corporate Conscience: Ethics and Integrity in the Post-Enron Era" (2005) 84 Can. Bar Rev. 533 at 549-551).

[70] *Model Code,* r. 3.3-3; *Smith v. Jones*, [1999] S.C.J. No. 15, [1999] 1 S.C.R. 455 at paras. 74-86 (S.C.C.). Lawyers must also provide particulars to ensure court security when they have reasonable grounds that a dangerous situation is likely to develop (r. 5.6-3).

[71] *Model Code*, r. 3.3-4.

"screen[s] out flaws or defects or who verifies compliance with standards or procedures." A corporate gatekeeper will normally have at least one of two roles: (1) prevention of a corporate client's wrongdoing by withholding their legal approval from actions that appear illegal and/or disclosing such actions if the client does not desist from those actions; and (2) acting as a "reputational intermediary" who assures investors of the quality of the message or signal sent out by the corporation. It has been suggested that there are four elements involved in gatekeepers' responsibilities:

(1)   independence from the client;

(2)   professional skepticism of the client's representations;

(3)   a duty to the public investor; and

(4)   a duty to resign when the [gatekeeper's] integrity would otherwise be compromised.

Gatekeeping is "premised on the ability of professionals to monitor and control their client's conduct." Failure to do so can result in gatekeeper liability. Some scholars consider auditors, attorneys and securities analysts to be the primary gatekeeping professions. However, the legal profession generally seeks to distance itself from the view that lawyers are gatekeepers, promoting instead the view that the lawyer's role is to facilitate transactions. Since legal liability may extend to gatekeepers for their failure to advise a corporation appropriately or to disclose illegal dealings, the legal profession resists the label of gatekeeper. Being a gatekeeper, with the attached obligation of protecting the public from potential harm caused by clients, runs contrary to the traditional role of the lawyer as a committed and loyal advocate for the client's interests and a guardian of the confidentiality between lawyer and client. Regulators and the legal profession disagree over whether lawyers should play a gatekeeping role in certain large corporate affairs. On the one hand, the government has an obligation to regulate the corporate arena to prevent widespread public harm and, on the other hand, the legal profession has an interest in upholding the legal duties of confidentiality and loyalty to their clients.

Nonetheless, in some contexts lawyers are considered gatekeepers. The strongest argument for the lawyer's role as a gatekeeper has arisen in the context of the securities and banking sectors in the US, in which lawyers facilitated the questionable or illegal behaviour that lead to major stock market collapses and harm to the economy and public. The US Congress described lawyers as gatekeepers in the sense of "[p]rivate intermediaries who can prevent harm to the securities markets by disrupting the misconduct of their client representatives." If corporate lawyers are seen as transaction engineers rather than advocates for their clients, this strengthens the argument that (some) corporate lawyers may have a gatekeeping role. Litigators are not generally in the same position; they are approached on an *ex post* basis, i.e., after trouble has arisen, and are by definition advocates for their clients. However, corporate lawyers that provide services on an *ex ante* basis are described as "wise counselors who gently guide their clients toward law compliance." In that sense, they may be seen as having a role to play in ensuring that all transactions they assist and advise comply with the law.

The key debate centers on the question of whether corporate lawyers have or should have a duty to report their client or employer to market regulators when that client or employer refuses to comply with the law. As noted, the primary arguments against assigning lawyers the role of corporate gatekeeper (i.e., requiring disclosure of client wrongdoing) are that (1) the role of gatekeeper destroys the duty of confidentiality and loyalty owed by a lawyer to his or her client, and (2) it will tend to have a chilling effect on full and open solicitor-client communications. These risks exist where gatekeepers must report wrongdoing externally rather than simply withhold their consent and withdraw from representation. Critics of the imposition of gatekeeper obligations on lawyers also oppose the idea that lawyers owe a duty to anyone aside from their clients and the courts, since additional duties may be at odds with the interests of clients. Acting as a gatekeeper, the lawyer is put in a potentially adversarial position with their client. This diminishes the lawyer's ability to effectively fulfill his or her essential role of "promoting the corporation's compliance with law." The American Bar Association Task Force on Corporate Responsibility found that lawyers are not gatekeepers in the same way that auditors are:

> Accounting firms' responsibilities require them to express a formal public opinion, based upon an independent audit, that the corporation's financial statements fairly present the corporation's financial condition and results of operations in conformity with generally accepted accounting principles. The auditor is subject to standards designed to assure an arm's length perspective relative to the firms they audit. In contrast . . . corporate lawyers are first and foremost counselors to their clients.

The American Bar Association also asserts that lawyers do not have an obligation or a right to disclose reasonable doubts concerning their clients' disclosures to the Securities and Exchange Commission.

If corporate lawyers are considered gatekeepers, or at least partial gatekeepers, it should be recognized that the extent of influence they can or will practically exert on a corporation can vary. The employment relationship between in-house counsel and their client dampens the lawyer's independence from their client. The practical ability of in-house counsel to give unwelcome but objective advice may be lessened by the existence of internal reviews of counsel and pressure from senior managers, as well as reprisals if lawyers refuse to provide legal approval for a transaction. Since the legality of certain conduct may be grey, rather than black or white, in-house counsel may consciously or unconsciously tend to approve grey areas in circumstances where an external counsel may not.

However, external counsel may also feel pressure to approve grey-area transactions due to the desire to maintain the corporation as a client, especially if that corporation comprises a significant portion of their billing. Additionally, as the role of in-house counsel expands and less transactional business goes through external counsel, external counsel may have less opportunity to discover and put a stop to corrupt or unlawful practices. Although in-house counsel arguably have less professional independence than external counsel, they may be able to exert greater influence over corporate officers and directors because of their working relationship and the ability of corporations to shop for another law firm if unhappy with the advice or lack of cooperation of their current external law firm.

A different aspect of a gatekeeper's role is the use of their reputation to assure the marketplace that the corporation is abiding by various rules and regulations.

External law firms are arguably better suited to this role than in-house counsel. In-house counsel will generally have less credibility in acting as a reputational intermediary, since they are seen as too closely associated with their company to provide an objective and impartial assurance to the marketplace.

At present, it seems that corporate lawyers in the US, UK and Canada are not gatekeepers in the same way auditors are, since lawyers generally do not have a duty to report a client's past wrongdoing or a duty to report a client's planned crimes unless death or serious bodily harm to others is reasonably imminent. . . . They do, however, have a duty not to assist in breaching the law. If asked to engage in illegal transactions, they are under a duty to withdraw as counsel.

Even if lawyers are not gatekeepers in the sense that auditors are, counsel often have the influence and ability to alter an organization's direction and propose a plan of action that achieves a client's objective without illegality. While both in-house and external counsel must say no to illegal methods of achieving the client's objectives, they are entitled and expected to attempt to accomplish the client's objectives through alternative legal means.

NOTES AND QUESTIONS

1. What are the potential complications of in-house counsel being gatekeepers or whistleblowers? How would it affect their decision-making and their involvement and role in organizations? How are lawyers different or the same as other professions that can act as gatekeepers or whisteblowers (e.g. accountants)?

2. Rule 3.2-8 of the *Model Code*, which is in place across most of Canada, provides the steps and considerations for progressively "reporting up" dishonesty, fraud, criminality, and illegality within an organization when the client is the organization. However, this rule does not allow for disclosure or reporting outside the organization as confidentiality remains in place, unless the stringent requirements of the "Future Harm / Public Safety Exception" are met.[72]

3. In contrast, the Law Society of New Brunswick's *Code of Professional Conduct* includes an additional Rule 3.3-3B:

    > A lawyer may disclose confidential information, but must not disclose more information than is required, when the lawyer believes on reasonable grounds that there is an imminent risk of substantial financial injury to an individual caused by an unlawful act that is likely to be committed, and disclosure is necessary to prevent the injury.

4. The American Bar Association also includes a comparable provision in Rule 1.6 of its *Model Rules of Professional Conduct*:

    > (b) A lawyer may reveal information relating to the representation of a client to the extent the lawyer reasonably believes necessary: . . .

---

[72] *Model Code*, r. 3.3-3. Even if met, disclosure is permissive and not mandatory under the *Model Code*. While other confidentiality exceptions exist, they are unlikely to assist in preventing the dishonesty, fraud, criminality, or illegality.

(2) to prevent the client from committing a crime or fraud that is reasonably certain to result in substantial injury to the financial interests or property of another and in furtherance of which the client has used or is using the lawyer's services;

(3) to prevent, mitigate or rectify substantial injury to the financial interests or property of another that is reasonably certain to result or has resulted from the client's commission of a crime or fraud in furtherance of which the client has used the lawyer's services; . . .

5. Rule 1.13(c) of the American Bar Association's *Model Rules of Professional Conduct* also allows for potential disclosure "to the extent the lawyer believes reasonably necessary to prevent substantial injury to the organization" if "reporting up the ladder" is unsuccessful in a timely and appropriate manner.[73]

6. What are the potential benefits and issues associated with the New Brunswick and American approaches for in-house counsel? What requirements are needed for those rules to apply? What complications may arise? What are the implications if you are a Canadian lawyer who practices in New Brunswick or the United States? Do you think that the New Brunswick and American approaches should be more broadly adopted in Canada? Why or why not?

7. The US Securities and Exchange Commission proposed a "noisy withdrawal" process for securities violations if lawyers did not receive a response from the highest level at the end of the "reporting up" process (which was ultimately not adopted due to objections raised during the feedback process).[74] In such situations, instead of the lawyer simply withdrawing and maintaining client confidentiality, the lawyer would withdraw and inform the SEC that the withdrawal was due to "professional considerations" and would disaffirm any "tainted submissions" they may have made to the SEC. What are the pros and cons of such an approach? How would this proposal interact with and potentially complicate the lawyer's professional role and relationship with the client?

8. Suppose you are in-house counsel with a major multi-national based in Canada that provides engineering and construction services around the world through various divisions and subsidiaries.[75] A supervisor notices that the subsidiary for northern Africa seems to have and be using a lot more cash than typical, and upon investigation, you determine that the

---

[73] Rule 1.13(d) specifies that "[p]aragraph (c) shall not apply with respect to information relating to a lawyer's representation of an organization to investigate an alleged violation of law, or to defend the organization or an officer, employee or other constituent associated with the organization against a claim arising out of an alleged violation of law."

[74] See generally Paul D. Paton, "Corporate Counsel as Corporate Conscience: Ethics and Integrity in the Post-Enron Era" (2005) 84 Can. Bar Rev. 533 at 549-551.

[75] This scenario and the linked scenario in Section [4][d] are inspired by the SNC-Lavalin affair (see e.g. Canada, Conflict of Interest and Ethics Commissioner, Trudeau II Report (Ottawa: Office of the Conflict of Interest and Ethics Commissioner, 2019)).

subsidiary was using the cash to bribe government officials to obtain contracts and is continuing to do so. That particular regime is notorious for corruption, but your company asserted in securities filings that it does not bribe government or other officials. What professional issues are engaged and what do you do?

    a.   In Canada, the company often participates in tenders for major engineering and construction activities for federal, provincial, and municipal governments as well as for private parties, which makes up a substantial amount of the company's business. However, the federal government has anti-bribery laws to prevent the bribery of foreign officials,[76] which is in accordance with Canada's obligations under the *United Nations Convention Against Corruption*.[77] If found guilty, penalties include fines and imprisonment up to 14 years. The company could also be banned from federal contracts for up to 10 years.[78] What professional issues are engaged and what do you do?

[d] Providing Non-Legal Advice In Addition to Legal Advice

One of the potential major differences between in-house and traditional counsel is the greater responsibility of in-house to often provide non-legal advice in conjunction with or in addition to legal advice. Such a difference makes sense given the varied roles associated with in-house counsel (discussed in Section [2] above), and non-legal advice can relate to business, economic, policy/political, and social issues. While such an approach may initially feel counter-intuitive, providing such advice is consistent with the *Model Code* since "[i]n many instances the lawyer's experience will be such that the lawyer's views on non-legal matters will be of real benefit", and the key is "to clearly distinguish legal from non-legal advice" and "point out any lack of experience or other qualification".[79] However, lawyers still need to be "wary of providing unreasonable or over-confident assurances", especially given the nature of the employment relationship between in-house counsel and their client.[80]

This section examines in-house counsel providing such non-legal advice in two particular circumstances: 1) risk/crisis assessment and management, and 2) potential conscience and leadership roles. As you go through these subsections, reflect on the skills needed to make such broader roles effective, and consider your potential willingness to take on such roles.

[i] Risk/Crisis Assessment and Management Issues

In-house counsel normally have to be aware of and advise organizations on

---

[76] *Corruption of Foreign Public Officials Act*, S.C. 1998, c. 34.

[77] *United Nations Convention Against Corruption*, (December 9, 2003) 2349 U.N.T.S. 41 (entered into force 14 December 2005).

[78] Public Services and Procurement Canada, "Guide to the *Ineligibility and Suspension Policy*" (December 16, 2020), online: https://www.tpsgc-pwgsc.gc.ca/ci-if/guide-eng.html.

[79] *Model Code*, r. 3.1-2[10].

[80] *Model Code*, r. 3.1-2[9].

numerous issues. For example, they often provide advice on: regulatory issues; the fiduciary and other duties of directors and officers to the organization, shareholders/ members, and others; potential director and other liability; and the frameworks for analyzing other laws and issues, particularly in a global context.[81] Given the varied roles that in-house counsel can play as well as jurisdiction-specific nuances, it is difficult to provide introductory advice and materials applicable for all contexts and situations. But two issues that most in-house counsel take large roles in are risk and crisis assessment and management, particularly since those issues involve both preventative and reactionary reviews and actions from both legal and non-legal viewpoints. The following passages discuss the different contexts, perspectives, and approaches that in-house counsel should include when addressing such issues. How can such questions help an in-house counsel act professionally and ethically for both the legal and non-legal advice they may provide as a result?

E. Norman Veasey & Christine T. Di Guglielmo

Indispensable Counsel: The Chief Legal Officer in the New Reality (Oxford: Oxford University Press, 2012) at 150-154 [footnotes omitted].

Chapter 5 – Advising the Board on Corporate Law and Other Laws

B. The CLO's Advice on Other . . . Issues

b. Risk Assessment and Management

In the area of evaluating the corporation's appetite for, and management of, risk, the general counsel might be well advised to encourage the directors to ask management and each other these kinds of questions:

1. What are we aiming to accomplish, and how (corporate strategy)?

2. What alternative strategies have been considered/explored?

3. Do the directors receive risk material which adequately distills vast quantities of risk information into prioritized, actionable summaries?

4. Are the risks associated with business units presented to the board in a comprehensive, holistic manner?

5. How do the losses which have occurred compare to the risks which have been identified? Are the losses consistent in magnitude and frequency with what one could expect given the risk profile presented to the board?

6. Can management and the board tie profits, as well as losses, to the presented risk profile?

7. How actively are resources—capital, balance sheet, talent—redeployed? Does the organization consistently, and on a timely basis, feed its winners and starve its losers?

8. What could go wrong or derail our strategy? For example, could multiple problems arise simultaneously or sequentially (the "perfect storm")?

---

[81] See e.g. E. Norman Veasey & Christine T. Di Guglielmo, *Indispensable Counsel: The Chief Legal Officer in the New Reality* (Oxford: Oxford University Press, 2012) at 11-12, 154-158, 164-165.

9. Has management been forthcoming about any differences among senior leadership regarding material strategic recommendations and decisions?

10. What assumptions underlie our strategy, and which of those assumptions could change/be wrong?

11. What processes did management use to develop strategy and identify risk?

12. Have we achieved a common understanding of what triggers bring an issue to the board's attention?

13. What capabilities are required to address risks? Where do we have capability gaps?

14. Is there a common understanding among management, the board, and board committees about their respective roles, responsibilities, and accountabilities on strategy and risk oversight?

15. Does the board have a clear understanding of where strategy and risk oversight are delegated and what processes are used within management and among business units?

16. Do the board and committees discuss risk appetite with management?

17. How can this discussion become a part of the board's regular routine?

18. Is the board and are the appropriate committees meeting regularly with a chief risk officer (CRO)?

19. If there is a CRO, has the board ensured that the CRO and general counsel have adequate resources and appropriate reporting lines to bring any changes in material risks to the board's attention?

20. Does the board have the appropriate committee structure for its significant oversight obligations in the risk area?

21. Does the board have sufficient personnel (including advisors) and financial resources in place to enable it to fulfill its risk engagement responsibilities?

22. Has the board adopted a board leadership structure that ensures that the independent directors have a clearly defined leader?

23. Do the board and appropriate committees have access to the information they need to provide oversight in troubled financial times?

24. Has the board and have the appropriate committees reviewed the incentive structure with strategy and risks in mind?

25. Has the board and have the appropriate committees reviewed board composition and director skill sets in relation to up-to-date competencies for oversight of the company's strategy, business lines, and material risks?

These kinds of questions and the robust process inherent in the kind of discussion, consideration, and analysis that they will prompt will help not only the optics of the company's process but also will enhance the quality of board decisions and oversight.

c. Crisis Preparation, Management, and Internal Investigation

. . .

As a matter of crisis management preparation, the general counsel is the key player in ensuring that on a "clear day" a crisis management plan is in place. When the crisis hits, the general counsel should normally be intimately involved in executing that plan, absent a potential conflict of interest. Then, if, despite corporate counsel's best preventive efforts, the specter of corporate misconduct arises, an internal investigation may be necessary in order to uncover and deal with wrongdoing within the corporation, ensure compliance with the law or the public interest, or minimize the long-term criminal and civil liability of the corporation.

The pursuit of these goals brings many conflicting forces to bear on counsel. A lawyer must deal with management, governmental agencies, employees, and other third parties while acting in the best interests of the corporation. Most significantly, in this context counsel may take on the role of corporate "cop," effectively acting as internal law enforcement agents. Also, there are many occasions when conflicts or allegations of misconduct at high levels of the corporation require that the board undertake its own investigation through a standing committee (such as the audit committee) or a special committee of independent directors who must hire its own counsel.

An internal investigation may advance the objective of minimizing corporate liability, but it also presents risks. It may lead to unintended adverse consequences, corral facts supporting corporate liability, or chill employees' willingness to disclose problems. Furthermore, the results of an internal investigation might ultimately be disclosed to third parties. These issues may affect the attorney-client privilege as well as airing the corporation's "dirty laundry," thus enhancing liability or reputational risk. As a result, a general counsel who is considering an internal investigation faces a complex risk/benefit calculus.

In certain cases, the decision to undertake an internal investigation is not difficult. A whistleblower, an impending government investigation, a conflict transaction, or a private lawsuit often compels an internal investigation. Close questions place counsel in a more difficult position. Prosecutors increasingly expect counsel to be proactive in ferreting out "culture problems," even when no clear triggering event has occurred. To accomplish this, in-house counsel must leverage their familiarity with corporate culture to make a legal judgment that may put them at odds with their close colleagues.

Once the decision to undertake an investigation is made, corporate counsel must decide or recommend who should conduct the investigation. In-house counsel's superior familiarity with corporate operations and culture are an asset in the management of an internal investigation. But reliance on insiders may undermine the real or perceived independence of the investigation, thereby leading the general counsel or a special board committee to consider whether outside counsel should be engaged to conduct the investigation.

The use of outside counsel does not, by itself, guarantee that law enforcement (nor, certainly, public opinion) will credit an internal investigation with independence, however. Prior relationships between the company and outside counsel may limit the extent to which the investigation is perceived as independent. Moreover, outside counsel's mandate must afford a sufficiently broad scope of review, and management must not exert control on the investigation while it is in progress.

NOTES AND QUESTIONS

1. How can taking more holistic than strictly legal approaches to potential risks and crises assist in-house counsel with acting professionally and ethically? What pitfalls and dangers exist? For example, what if your non-legal advice is given more weight because of your professional accreditation?

2. When crises arise, time and other pressures to act may increase significantly for in-house counsel and others. What steps and approaches can in-house counsel take to ensure they continue to act ethically and professionally given such pressures? What should you do if you make a mistake in your advice? Or if the organization's actions in such time-sensitive situations turn out to be wrong or have unintended consequences in retrospect?

3. How do these issues relate to and overlap with decision-making influences and considerations discussed in Section [3], such as maintaining professionalism and avoiding client tunnel vision?

[ii] Potential Conscience and Leadership Roles

If an in-house counsel's role is not necessarily that of a gatekeeper (see Section [4][c] above), what other normative and influencing perspectives can and do they provide to assist and lead their organizations? The *Model Code* "recognizes that lawyers as the legal advisers to organizations are in a central position to encourage organizations to comply with the law and to advise that it is in the organization's and the public's interest that organizations do not violate the law".[82] It further notes that in-house counsel "may guide organizations to act in ways that are legal, ethical, reputable and consistent with the organization's responsibilities to its constituents and to the public."[83] But how can an in-house counsel act in such an influencing manner?

One approach is for an in-house counsel's responsibilities to include acting as a persuasive counsellor and conscience, as well as providing leadership so that organizations go above and beyond complying with legal minimums for various reasons. But such a role cannot occur without an appropriate foundation. For example, "[w]hat authority does the conscience [or persuasive counsellor] have? [W]hat training does the lawyer have to be a conscience [or persuasive counsellor]? [W]ho or what is the conscience of the conscience [or persuasive counsellor]? . . . Does a conscience [or persuasive counsellor] have to be listened to?"[84] But if properly supported, such a role and corresponding leadership can manifest in a

---

[82] *Model Code*, r. 3.2-8[6].

[83] *Model Code*, r. 3.2-8[6].

[84] H.P. Gunz & S.P. Gunz, "Ethical Implications of the Employment Relationship for Professional Lawyers" (1994) 28:1 U.B.C. L. Rev. 123 at 128.

variety of ways that benefit both the organization and society as a whole.

The first piece below briefly discusses some of the factors, skills, and approaches that can help an in-house counsel be a successful "persuasive counsellor". The second piece uses corporate social responsibility and diversity as two examples of how an in-house counsel can act as a conscience and provide leadership within and potentially outside the organization on major issues that reflect and impact societal concerns. As you read these pieces, consider what insights and lessons you can learn as well as what an in-house counsel could do if the context does not allow them to act in these ways or if the organization does not follow their advice.

Sally Gunz & Marianne M. Jennings

"University Legal Counsel: The Role and Its Challenges" (2019) 33:1 Notre Dame J.L. Ethics & Pub. Pol'y 177 at 193 [footnotes omitted].

The word "gatekeeper" is sometimes used to define what we might expect of professionals; "[i]nherently, gatekeepers are reputational intermediaries who provide verification and certification services to investors." Yet it is argued, for the most part this does not reflect the role of the in-house lawyer and, indeed, lawyers in general have resisted the use of this term. Rather, [Deborah A.] DeMott argues [in "The Stages of Scandal and the Roles of General Counsel" 2012 Wis. L. Rev. 463] a role for the lawyer (general counsel) that can clearly enhance their own reputation and indeed add real value to the institution that they serve. She says their advantage comes from the dual source of their authority; "as a member of senior management depends, as noted above, both on counsel's membership in the corporation's cohort at the top of its managerial hierarchy, as well as on counsel's credibility as a holder of specialized expertise, arguably grounded in technique and knowledge that are distinctive and separable from skills in business management per se." She says "[o]nly the 'nimble' and strong-willed succeed in a position grounded in two potentially inconsistent sources of authority, which are proximity to senior management and the capacity to exercise judgment as a professional in a detached manner."

> Scandal, that is, undergirds general counsel's capacity to serve, not precisely as a "gatekeeper" comparable to a financial auditor, but as a "persuasive counselor" who "go[es] further than simply describing the law and suggesting ways to comply with it. . . . [but] [i]nstead . . . affirmatively, proactively, and courageously tr[ies] to persuade their client," as represented by the CEO, to comply with the law and, beyond literal compliance, to act to minimize jeopardy to the corporation. Essential to this role is a capacity for prediction beyond the immediate specifics, that is, to "see around the corners" using many angles of vision. And, as discussed at length in connection with Salomon Bros. and its rogue trading incident, remaining a bystander to fumbling by other members of senior management is unlikely to be an adequate response.

NOTES AND QUESTIONS

1. What factors and skills would help an in-house counsel be a successful "persuasive counsellor"? What parts of their professional responsibilities, skills, and role would assist and are transferrable from traditional legal practice? What are the potential difficulties that one should be aware of?

2. How would such an approach fit with the decision-making influences and

considerations discussed in Sections [3] and [4][c] above? How can one maintain professionalism and avoid client tunnel vision? Can one be both a "gatekeeper" and a "persuasive counsellor"?

E. Norman Veasey & Christine T. Di Guglielmo

Indispensable Counsel: The Chief Legal Officer in the New Reality (Oxford: Oxford University Press, 2012) at 117-119, 121-123, 125-126 [footnotes omitted].

Chapter 4 – The General Counsel Leading the Charge

C. Demonstrating Openness and Community Involvement

1. Corporate Citizenship

As part of the general counsel's role in creating and fostering an ethical corporate culture, she may also be called upon to contribute to, or even oversee, the company's efforts regarding corporate citizenship (also known as "corporate social responsibility" or "CSR"). As a general matter, corporate citizenship or CSR "is a business concept pursuant to which companies seek to address social and environmental issues through support for international legal norms and sustainable business practices."

One of the goals of a corporate citizenship program is to ensure that the company follows internationally-adopted standards relating to such issues as labor conditions and environmental practices, which may not be adequately implemented by regulators in certain locales. Thus, corporate citizenship efforts bolster the rule of law through self-enforcement of international standards that may be in place but not enforced in some areas. Because these issues lie at the intersection of law, business, public relations, and risk management, the general counsel is well situated to be a leader among the key players in a company's corporate social responsibility initiatives.

Corporations have a variety of social responsibilities as participants in, and beneficiaries of, society. As articulated by John G. Ruggie, Special Representative of the UN Secretary-General on Business and Human Rights, "in addition to compliance with national laws, the baseline responsibility of companies is to respect human rights. . . .. The responsibility exists even where national laws are absent or not enforced because respecting rights is the very foundation of a company's social license to operate."

In addition to a general duty to behave as socially responsible participants in society, conducting corporate affairs in a socially responsible manner makes good business sense and may even be a matter of compliance or liability. The Report of Weil, Gotshal & Manges LLP for the U.N. Corporate Law Project of the Special Representative of the Secretary-General (SRSG) on the Issue of Human Rights and Transnational Corporations and Other Business Enterprises explains:

> Apart from abiding by laws and regulations, corporations owe no specific duty to society. However, they are permitted to use corporate resources for public welfare, humanitarian, educational or philanthropic purposes where consistent with the interests of the company and its shareholders. They are encouraged by a variety of forces to act ethically and in socially and environmentally responsible ways above the requirements of law and regulation. It is common for corporations in the U.S.

to engage in such activities because, in part due to reputational interests, it is often good business sense to do so.

Joe W. (Chip) Pitts III, former chief legal officer of Nokia, Inc. and Chair of Amnesty International USA, has identified the key business-related drivers of corporate social responsibility efforts as "brand/reputation assurance, business productivity, risk management, [and] employee recruitment and retention." The practical, business- and reputation-driven effects are likely to be enhanced as technology rapidly increases the public visibility and transparency of corporate actions around the world.

. . .

The key focus of directors and officers must be the best interests of the corporate entity, and compliance with statutory or regulatory requirements is an essential component of determining those best interests. The point here, however, is that corporate social responsibility efforts often far exceed any obligations imposed by law or regulation, and the general counsel often is one of the leaders of those efforts.

A CSR initiative tends to fit well within the framework of existing corporate efforts surrounding compliance and ethics. The steps, as a general matter, are

- assembling the appropriate team, which often includes the general counsel, ethics and compliance officers, and corporate-citizenship-dedicated officers;

- identifying potential trouble spots and the company's most significant corporate citizenship risks and opportunities;

- setting the tone at the top by communicating to (and training, as applicable) employees, suppliers, investors, and customers the company's corporate citizenship commitments;

- tracking global standards and verifying the company's conformance to those standards and the effectiveness of the corporate citizenship efforts; [and]

- reporting results to stakeholders.

. . .

2. Diversity

General counsel have also taken the lead in fostering diversity and inclusion efforts within their corporations. U.S. public companies must disclose whether and the extent to which their nominating committees consider diversity in selecting director candidates. But "[m]ost corporate boards recognize the value that diverse experiences and skill sets bring to board decision making, and many recognize the specific value in diversity reflective of customers and employees." Therefore, many companies are designing and implementing diversity programs and efforts that far exceed—in both scope and quality—this reporting requirement. In a recent article in Metropolitan Corporate Counsel, Tom Sager, General Counsel of DuPont, articulated some of the value derived from promoting diversity:

> From DuPont's perspective, to succeed in today's highly competitive global marketplace our company must have an employee base and a law firm network that is as diverse as the customers who buy our products, the shareholders who purchase

our stock, the vendors who supply us with goods and services, and the judges and juries who hear our cases. It long ago became clear to us that juries, judges, regulators and policy makers were becoming increasingly diverse and this trend impacted our ability to connect with these segments of the legal and business world. So besides valuing people of all races, ethnicities, and genders, diversity efforts also became a business imperative. It has proven critically important in a number of cases. One of them allowed us to find an alternative solution to a lawsuit against former lead pigment and paint manufacturers.

. . .

Similarly, in May 2011, a group of general counsel in Canada launched Legal Leaders for Diversity, an initiative that aims to focus general counsel on encouraging diversity and inclusion throughout the legal profession and the Canadian business community. In a "Statement of Support for Diversity and Inclusion by General Counsel in Canada," the Legal Leaders for Diversity signatories "undertake to practice and advance diversity and inclusion by":

- Promoting diversity within our own departments;
- Considering diversity in our hiring and purchasing practices;
- Encouraging Canadian law firms to follow our example;
- Promoting diversity initiatives at all levels in the legal and business community;
- Measuring the effectiveness of our efforts.

. . .

Including the legal department at the helm of a company's diversity efforts makes sense. In-house counsel are well positioned to understand the effects of discriminatory employment practices, and they have the analytical and persuasive skills to improve diversity and inclusiveness throughout the corporation. . . .

Many law departments are also recognizing the importance of "pipeline" efforts. Through pipeline programs, lawyers are "address[ing] diversity by reaching out to minority and low-income students throughout their educations. The idea is that by working with kids in their communities, lawyers are also investing in the profession with the hope that some of the young people will go on to law school and become lawyers where previously that might have been a distant goal—if it appeared on their radar screens at all." Pipeline programs include mentoring, programs through which lawyers engage with elementary through high school students about legal subjects such as constitutional rights or intellectual property law, and academic-and career-choice programs.

NOTES AND QUESTIONS

1. As part of CSR, key sources can provide guidance on how organizations can be better corporate citizens. For example, according to John F Sherman III:

   Global soft law (notably the 2011 UN Guiding Principles on Business and Human Rights ('UNGPs')),[85] multistakeholder norms, the business practices and policies of leading companies, the expectations of investors and stakeholders, and hard law in a growing number of jurisdictions, all expect that businesses should respect human rights in their operations and in their value chains.[86]

He also provides a number of "[p]ractical steps that general counsel can take to support a rights respecting culture":[87]

    a. Integrating human rights due diligence into environmental and social due diligence processes;

    b. Seeing human rights risks thorough the eyes of the stakeholder;

    c. Fostering an open and learning culture;

    d. Ensuring that external representatives act consistently with the company's commitment to respect human rights; and

    e. Structuring supply chain contracts to respect human rights [by]:

        i. Challenging the procurement business model;

        ii. Setting human rights performance standards in the contract and assessing supplier capacity to perform;

        iii. Mapping the entire supply chain [not just the first tier or two] to identify involvement in human rights risks;

        iv. Supporting supplier's efforts to meet its human rights performance responsibilities;

        v. Providing for remedy of involvement of harm where appropriate; and

        vi. Mitigating the human rights impact of terminating a supplier.[88]

  2. Brigit Spiesshofer lists other potential CSR sources,[89] which include *The Ten Principles of the UN Global Compact*,[90] the *OECD Guidelines for*

---

[85] OHCHR, *Guiding Principles on Business and Human Rights: Implementing the United Nations "Protect, Respect and Remedy Framework"*, UN Doc. HR/Pub/11/04 (2011), online (pdf): https://www.ohchr.org/documents/publications/guidingprinciplesbusinesshr_en.pdf.

[86] John F. Sherman III, "The Corporate General Counsel Who Respects Human Rights" (2021) 24 Leg. Ethics (forthcoming).

[87] John F. Sherman III, "The Corporate General Counsel Who Respects Human Rights" (2021) 24 Leg. Ethics (forthcoming).

[88] John F. Sherman III, "The Corporate General Counsel Who Respects Human Rights" (2021) 24 Leg. Ethics (forthcoming).

[89] Brigit Spiesshover, "Be Careful What You Wish For: A European Perspective on the Limits of CSR in the Legal Profession" (2021) 24 Leg. Ethics (forthcoming).

[90] United Nations Global Compact, *The Ten Principles of the UN Global Compact*, online: https://www.unglobalcompact.org/what-is-gc/mission/principles.

    Multinational Enterprises,[91] and *the ISO 26000 Guidance on Social Responsibility*.[92] Gerry Ferguson also notes international sources to help prevent corruption, including key conventions and compliance guidelines.[93] Domestic sources can also be helpful, as illustrated by *The Attorney General of Canada's Directive on Civil Litigation Involving Indigenous Peoples*.[94] Such sources illustrate how an in-house counsel can provide broader leadership, and they are not exhaustive.

3. Suzanne Le Mire & Christine Parker also note "the possibility that ethically aware in-house counsel can influence the actions of the external lawyers they hire in positive ways."[95] For example, the tender process and negotiations can extend beyond cost and other outcomes to firms' "equal opportunity and work-life balance practices and policies".[96] Work can also be removed from firms who do not meet expectations.[97]

4. How effective do you think the above approaches can be? Why? What additional roles, steps, or processes could an in-house counsel do to assist with these areas? What other areas could an in-house counsel provide analogous leadership on? How and what issues may arise?

---

[91] OECD, *OECD Guidelines for Multinational Enterprises* (2011), online (pdf): https://www.ohchr.org/documents/publications/guidingprinciplesbusinesshr_en.pdf. See also OECD, *OECD Due Diligence Guidance for Responsible Business Conduct* (2018), online (pdf): http://mneguidelines.oecd.org/OECD-Due-Diligence-Guidance-for-Responsible-Business-Conduct.pdf.

[92] See e.g. International Organization for Standardization, *ISO 26000: Social Responsibility* (last visited March 19, 2021), online: https://www.iso.org/iso-26000-social-responsibility.html.

[93] Gerry Ferguson, *Global Corruption: Law, Theory & Practice*, 3rd ed. (Victoria, BC: University of Victoria, 2018) at 804-808.

[94] Canada, Department of Justice, *The Attorney General of Canada's Directive on Civil Litigation Involving Indigenous Peoples* (Ottawa: Minister of Justice and Attorney General of Canada, 2018), online (pdf): https://www.justice.gc.ca/eng/csj-sjc/ijr-dja/dclip-dlcpa/litigation-litiges.pdf. Amy Salyzyn and Penelope Simons note that the *Directive* "takes into account the unique context of this type of civil litigation", particularly given reconciliation and renewing the Crown-Indigenous relationship, and the *"Directive* mandates that government lawyers adopt a different approach to lawyering [instead of the traditional adversarial process]" ("Professional Responsibility and the Defence of Extractive Corporations in Transnational Human Rights and Environmental Litigation in Canadian Courts" (2021) 24 Leg. Ethics (forthcoming)).

[95] Suzanne Le Mire & Christine Parker, "Keeping It In-House: Ethics in the Relationship Between Large Law Firm Lawyers and Their Corporate Clients Through the Eyes of In-House Counsel" (2008) 11:2 Leg. Ethics 201 at 208.

[96] Suzanne Le Mire & Christine Parker, "Keeping It in-House: Ethics in the Relationship between Large Law Firm Lawyers and Their Corporate Clients through the Eyes of in-House Counsel" (2008) 11:2 Leg. Ethics 201 at 208.

[97] Suzanne Le Mire & Christine Parker, "Keeping It in-House: Ethics in the Relationship between Large Law Firm Lawyers and Their Corporate Clients through the Eyes of in-House Counsel" (2008) 11:2 Leg. Ethics 201 at 208.

5. The above assumes one can successfully use these approaches to provide legal or non-legal arguments and advice for specific actions that organizations are willing to accept, which many organizations may be amenable to since it would be good business or fit with organizational purposes and policies. However, what if an organization is not willing to take such actions or listen to the in-house counsel on such matters? How could perspectives and arguments change if one is considering the organization's past actions instead of future actions? What considerations and choices would one need to account for to act professionally and ethically? And what other interacting professional duties would one need to consider (e.g., confidentiality; loyalty/conflicts)?

6. For example, let us continue the engineering and construction company foreign bribery example discussed in Section[4][c] above. Suppose your company begins high-level discussions with prosecutors to resolve the issues in a way that does not result in a ban from federal tendering. As those discussions are not proceeding well, the company also has discussions with high-level Canadian politicians and their staff, including lobbying for the creation of a "deferred prosecution agreement" ("DPA") system found in other countries to avoid being found guilty of formal charges in exchange for fines and complying with other conditions. Such an approach would allow the company to continue competing for contracts since they would not be formally convicted. The government ultimately decides to implement such a system as part of its next omnibus budget legislation, but the legislation provides that the "national economic interest" (i.e. the potential impact of your company being convicted) is not a consideration for whether to grant a DPA, which is also a standard provision in other jurisdictions. As a result, discussions with prosecutors continue to go poorly. Discussions continue with high-level politicians and their staff, who in turn try to repeatedly discuss with and indirectly pressure the Attorney-General regarding why your company should get a DPA (which are normally decisions made solely by prosecutors). In the meantime, your company has put you in charge of a new CSR initiative, which includes researching and implementing best practices to avoid such situations in the future.

   a. What professional and ethical issues and considerations are raised as in-house counsel? How do the corporation's in-progress changes and its past actions complicate issues, your potential role, and your advice? What should you be involved in and to what extent? And what ultimately do you feel comfortable and willing to do and why?

   b. If you were an in-house lawyer advising the politicians instead, what professional and ethical considerations are raised? How would you approach this situation?

7. Suppose you are a lawyer who is leading major CSR and diversity initiatives for a multi-national corporation. The board of directors is very supportive of these approaches, particularly since the corporation's customers reflect all parts of society. Corresponding policies and guidelines

are in the process of being developed and implemented, particularly since the corporation gets a lot of its products made overseas. However, certain officers would prefer for such things to be more symbolic than substantive. They are used to business as usual, and do not see the point of changing, especially since their incentives and bonuses are based strictly on profits and the corporation's costs will be higher in the short-term. What do you do? And what professional and ethical concerns would you need to deal with?

    a.   While continuing to work on these initiatives, a class action is launched by minority-female workers alleging pay discrimination. You work with litigation counsel and retain experts to find out what is happening on the ground, which reveals that the corporation was engaged in systemic pay discrimination for decades. What do you? What if the corporation directs that it wants to take a highly adversarial approach to the litigation instead of a conciliatory approach?

    b.   Let's say you are also a minority-female in-house counsel and those studies reveal that you are also experiencing pay discrimination.[98] What do you do? What if the corporation is unwilling to address even your personal pay discrimination over time? Could you join the class action? Why or why not? What professional and ethical issues would be engaged? Could things be different if there were other such persons in the organization's leadership versus just you?

[5] Conclusion – Key Role Issues and Decision-Making Influences

To fully understand the professional and ethical issues that face in-house counsel, this chapter closes by summarizing the key issues associated with such roles as well as examining how their decisions can be influenced by various factors, including task definition.

    Given the different roles, opportunities, and challenges that face in-house counsel compared to traditional practice, Veasey & Di Guglielmo characterize such positions as having "interesting", "multifaceted", "lonely", and "perilous" aspects.[99] As a result, they require "a thorough immersion in, and understanding of, the nature of the [organization]'s business, its people, its culture, and its competitive environment";[100] they must be a persuasive counselor and problem solver;[101] they need to be able to deal with the inherent tensions of their role, including resisting pressure

---

[98] The last two parts of this scenario are inspired by the Delulio pay discrimination situation (see e.g., David Luban, *Lawyers and Justice: An Ethical Study* (Princeton: Princeton University Press, 1988) at 177-180).

[99] E. Norman Veasey & Christine T. Di Guglielmo, *Indispensable Counsel: The Chief Legal Officer in the New Reality* (Oxford: Oxford University Press, 2012) at 6-14.

[100] E. Norman Veasey & Christine T. Di Guglielmo, *Indispensable Counsel: The Chief Legal Officer in the New Reality* (Oxford: Oxford University Press, 2012) at 6.

[101] E. Norman Veasey & Christine T. Di Guglielmo, *Indispensable Counsel: The Chief Legal Officer in the New Reality* (Oxford: Oxford University Press, 2012) at 7-8.

"to compromise [their] professional judgment and moral standards to fit into, or "go along with," a problematic business decision";[102] and they must also be able to deal with outside scrutiny as well as "balance [their] need for self-preservation [including a continued livelihood] with [their] need to serve [their] client . . . with skill, integrity, and zeal".[103]

Some resulting overall questions one should consider for in-house counsel roles thus include:

1. What are the advantages and disadvantages of being an in-house counsel compared to traditional practice? How can one develop the needed skills and knowledge? How could someone address and mitigate some of the concerns (such as those discussed in this chapter)? What options are available if one is unable to do so?

2. Are you interested in becoming an in-house counsel? Why or why not?

3. How could one design a compensation plan so that it rewards "exceptional professionally independent legal work" rather than "pure financial performance"?[104] What arguments support the use of such incentives?

As well, to ensure that in-house counsel make professional and ethical decisions, one needs to be aware of factors that may influence their decision-making and advice. For example, according to Moorhead, Vaughan, & Godinho, broad influences include the organization (such as the nature/culture of its field (e.g. banking vs government vs extractive industries) and relevant markets/competition), the legal team, legal regulators, and society (including media, legislatures, the public, and other regulators).[105] Due to their interrelations, one must realize that such factors influence each other rather than being independent,[106] and they can thus affect what an in-house counsel considers appropriate at any particular time.

The type and degree of effect on ethical and professional decision making can be explicit or implicit depending on the key policies, task definitions, decision-making approaches, and supporting structures in place. In particular, task definition, expectations, and structure can be key influences:

> How those tasks are framed, what the scope of the task is (is an investigation narrow or wide-ranging, for instance), what the resources available are, whether

---

[102] E. Norman Veasey & Christine T. Di Guglielmo, *Indispensable Counsel: The Chief Legal Officer in the New Reality* (Oxford: Oxford University Press, 2012) at 10.

[103] E. Norman Veasey & Christine T. Di Guglielmo, *Indispensable Counsel: The Chief Legal Officer in the New Reality* (Oxford: Oxford University Press, 2012) at 10-11.

[104] See e.g. E. Norman Veasey & Christine T. Di Guglielmo, *Indispensable Counsel: The Chief Legal Officer in the New Reality* (Oxford: Oxford University Press, 2012) at 13-14.

[105] Richard Moorhead, Steven Vaughan, & Christina Godinho, *In-House Lawyers' Ethics: Institutional Logics, Legal Risk and the Tournament of Influence* (Oxford: Hart, 2019) at 218-219.

[106] Richard Moorhead, Steven Vaughan, & Christina Godinho, *In-House Lawyers' Ethics: Institutional Logics, Legal Risk and the Tournament of Influence* (Oxford: Hart, 2019) at 219.

legal is engaged early or late in any process, and what expectations all parties have of what constitutes delivery might all influence the how individual sees their role on that task (and over time on tasks more generally). It might also influence their willingness to draw on particular orientations: a task which is framed in strongly commercial terms might lead to an in-houser more strongly drawing upon commercial orientations.[107]

How can these issues effect ethicality? Moorhead, Vaughan, & Godinho note that an institutional logics perspective (particularly regarding how such different systems interact) is "crucial to understanding the *embeddedness of in-house ethicality. Ways of thinking and speaking* about problems *are an essential component* of the interaction between the different value systems".[108] Given the "wide range of competing ideas", as well as the "counter-logics and tensions" present, such systems and methods influence ethical decision-making processes by what individuals intentionally choose to focus on and what they "are subconsciously influenced by".[109] Accordingly, "increasing the extent to which in-house teams think about and support appropriate professional role orientations is important."[110]

As an illustration of the importance of task definition and discussions to ensure ethical and professional decision making, Gerry Ferguson notes that there are six categories for success that arise from the anti-corruption guidelines: "(1) clear policy from the top; (2) communication and training; (3) developing and implementing an anti-corruption program; (4) incentivizing and promoting compliance; (5) detecting and reporting violations; and (6) continual testing and improvement."[111] He also notes the potential critiques of increased enforcement and over-enforcement resulting in over- or excessive compliance and compliance fatigue rather than actually reducing corruption.[112] He further notes potential issues with program design, particularly if the person is not the one who will be implementing the program.[113] For example, designers may have a different background than the

---

[107] Richard Moorhead, Steven Vaughan, & Christina Godinho, *In-House Lawyers' Ethics: Institutional Logics, Legal Risk and the Tournament of Influence* (Oxford: Hart, 2019) at 219 [footnote omitted].

[108] Richard Moorhead, Steven Vaughan, & Christina Godinho, *In-House Lawyers' Ethics: Institutional Logics, Legal Risk and the Tournament of Influence* (Oxford: Hart, 2019) at 221 [emphasis added].

[109] Richard Moorhead, Steven Vaughan, & Christina Godinho, *In-House Lawyers' Ethics: Institutional Logics, Legal Risk and the Tournament of Influence* (Oxford: Hart, 2019) at 221.

[110] Richard Moorhead, Steven Vaughan, & Christina Godinho, *In-House Lawyers' Ethics: Institutional Logics, Legal Risk and the Tournament of Influence* (Oxford: Hart, 2019) at 221.

[111] Gerry Ferguson, *Global Corruption: Law, Theory & Practice*, 3rd ed. (Victoria, BC: University of Victoria, 2018) at 809, 809-814.

[112] Gerry Ferguson, *Global Corruption: Law, Theory & Practice*, 3rd ed. (Victoria, BC: University of Victoria, 2018) at 824-825.

[113] Gerry Ferguson, *Global Corruption: Law, Theory & Practice*, 3rd ed. (Victoria, BC: University of Victoria, 2018) at 825.

implementers (e.g. education, departmental culture, or different "language") or are from a different country (e.g. the design is incompatible with the country's political, social, and economic conditions).[114]

All of the above reinforces the need for and usefulness of deliberative decision-making to ensure ethicality and professionalism, as well as the best outcome for the client organization. According to Evan Peterson:

> [D]eliberation involves a more structured, systematic approach to decision-making [than intuitive decision-making]. . . . [T]he decision maker: (1) frames the problem needing resolution; (2) identifies and prioritizes pertinent interests and objectives that may span a wide variety of perspectives; (3) develops possible courses of action; (4) assesses the consequences of each course of action and the resulting effect on the previously identified interests and objectives; and (5) chooses and implements the course of action that optimizes the interests and objective.[115]

While intuitive decision-making still has an important role and part in the process, the use of deliberate decision-making processes can assist with considering "the full range of possible outcomes".[116] Given that in-house counsel are also often involved in group decision-making, such an approach can help overcome cognitive, social, personal, and other barriers to creative group problem-solving.[117] Such an approach can also assist with bringing an in-house counsel's ethical and professional considerations to the front of decision-making rather than being potentially overlooked or not being given appropriate consideration and weight.

As a result, there are certain questions and issues that in-house counsel ought to keep in mind to ensure that their decision-making processes are ethical and professional.

1. How can one stay up to date on current and emerging systems, influences, issues, and their implications for in-house counsel, their organization, decision-making processes, and ensuring ethicality and professionalism?

2. If a task is not defined or discussions do not occur in a way that allow someone to act ethically or professionally, what tangible steps could the person take? What skills and context are needed for success?

---

[114] Gerry Ferguson, *Global Corruption: Law, Theory & Practice*, 3rd ed. (Victoria, BC: University of Victoria, 2018) at 825.

[115] Evan A. Peterson, "Enhancing Legal Decision-Making in Organizational Crisis Management" (2018) 10 S.J. Bus. & Ethics 115 at 117.

[116] Evan A. Peterson, "Enhancing Legal Decision-Making in Organizational Crisis Management" (2018) 10 S.J. Bus. & Ethics 115 at 117-118. But see Jonathan Haidt, "The Emotional Dog and Its Rational Tail: A Social Intuitionist Approach to Moral Judgment" (2001) 108:4 Psychol. Rev. 814.

[117] Evan A. Peterson, "Enhancing Legal Decision-Making in Organizational Crisis Management" (2018) 10 S.J. Bus. & Ethics 115 at 120-121. Peterson, at p. 121, describes three barriers as: "[c]ognitive barriers – people have a tendency to embrace the first solution that comes to mind[;] [s]ocial barriers – people often converge on a 'safe' solution quickly to avoid proposing untested ideas that will leave them looking foolish in front of others[; and] [p]ersonal barriers – people have different creative aptitudes".

3. How useful and applicable are Ferguson's comments to other contexts and issues? Why?

4. How can one use deliberate decision-making or analogous processes to help ensure that ethicality and professionalism are considered explicitly as part of an in-house counsel's work and advice?

This chapter's issues, readings, and discussions thus illustrate how the lawyer-client relationships between in-house counsel and their organizations are "contingent, shifting, complex, and constantly negotiated" given the nature and variety of in-house counsel roles and issues, as well as how in-house counsel "negotiate multiple tensions and questions. [For example,] [s]hould [they] be involved in a particular business decision? What should [their] role be? Should [they] act as a cop, counsel, or entrepreneur?".[118] There are no simple answers, particularly since in-house counsel bring their unique professional background and insights to key questions facing organizations, and traditional practice approaches are not necessarily transferable. However, since "[a] lawyer's behavior is shaped by past experiences in the [organization]",[119] it is important for in-house counsel to continually monitor and engage with potential ethical and professional issues from the beginning. In-house counsel and their organizations should accordingly build and reinforce appropriate approaches, policies, and structures to deal with such issues appropriately and to recognize the distinctive background, context, roles, and contributions of in-house counsel in organizations.

[6] Further Materials

Canada, Department of Justice, *The Attorney General of Canada's Directive on Civil Litigation Involving Indigenous Peoples* (Ottawa: Minister of Justice and Attorney General of Canada, 2018), online (pdf): https://www.justice.gc.ca/eng/csj-sjc/ijr-dja/dclip-dlcpa/litigation-litiges.pdf.

Dodek, Adam M., *Solicitor-Client Privilege* (Markham: LexisNexis, 2014), ch. 11.

Dodek, Adam M., *Canadian Legal Practice: A Guide for the 21st Century* (Markham: LexisNexis, 2009) (loose-leaf), §§ 1.16-1.18, 7.72-7.85, & ch. 21.

Ferguson, Gerry, *Global Corruption: Law, Theory & Practice*, 3rd ed. (Victoria, BC: University of Victoria, 2018), ch. 8.

In-House Counsel Worldwide, "ICW Universal Competency Profile for In-House

---

[118] Robert L. Nelson & Laura Beth Nielsen, "Cops, Counsel, and Entrepreneurs: Constructing the Role of Inside Counsel in Large Corporations" (2000) 34 L. & Soc'y Rev. 457 at 489. See also Sally Gunz & Marianne M. Jennings, "University Legal Counsel: The Role and Its Challenges" (2019) 33:1 Notre Dame J.L. Ethics & Pub. Pol'y 177 at 188-189.

[119] Robert L. Nelson & Laura Beth Nielsen, "Cops, Counsel, and Entrepreneurs: Constructing the Role of Inside Counsel in Large Corporations" (2000) 34 L. & Soc'y Rev. 457 at 490. Nelson and Nielsen further note that "[w]hen lawyers are criticized by businesspeople or when businesspeople resist legal advice in various ways (by not going to lawyers at all, or by choosing to go to a different lawyer within the corporation, or by complaining to higher ups that the lawyers are not 'team players')[,] it affects how the lawyer will behave the next time".

Counsel: Transcending Geographical and Jurisdictional Boundaries", online (pdf): https://icwweb.files.wordpress.com/2018/09/icw_ucp2018.pdf.

International Organization for Standardization, *ISO 26000: Social Responsibility*, online: https://www.iso.org/iso-26000-social-responsibility.html.

Lexis Practical Guidance, *In-House Counsel*, online: https://advance.lexis.com/api/permalink/8efd05c5-6327-4f74-b6e1-7a44070c2493/?context=1518425.

MacKenzie, Gavin, *Lawyers & Ethics: Professional Responsibility and Discipline* (Toronto: Thomson Reuters, 1993) (loose-leaf), ch. 20.

MacNair, M Deborah, *Conflicts of Interest: Principles for the Legal Profession* (Toronto: Thomson Reuters, 2019) (loose-leaf), chs. 9, 14.

Moorhead, Richard, Steven Vaughan, & Christina Godinho, *In-House Lawyers' Ethics: Institutional Logics, Legal Risk and the Tournament of Influence* (Oxford: Hart, 2019).

OECD, *OECD Guidelines for Multinational Enterprises* (2011), online (pdf): https://www.ohchr.org/documents/publications/guidingprinciplesbusinesshr_en.pdf.

OECD, *OECD Due Diligence Guidance for Responsible Business Conduct* (2018) online (pdf): http://mneguidelines.oecd.org/OECD-Due-Diligence-Guidance-for-Responsible-Business-Conduct.pdf.

OHCHR, *Guiding Principles on Business and Human Rights: Implementing the United Nations "Protect, Respect and Remedy" Framework*, UN Doc HR/Pub/11/04 (2011), online (pdf): https://www.ohchr.org/documents/publications/guidingprinciplesbusinesshr_en.pdf.

Practical Law Canada Law Department, "Crisis Management for In-House Counsel", online: *Practical Law* https://ca.practicallaw.thomsonreuters.com/w-026-0714.

Practical Law Canada Law Department, "Ethical Considerations for In-House Counsel", online: *Practical Law* https://ca.practicallaw.thomsonreuters.com/w-002-7188.

Practical Law Canada Law Department, "Informal Roles of General Counsel", online: *Practical Law* https://ca.practicallaw.thomsonreuters.com/w-026-7228.

Practical Law Canada Law Department, "Practical Tips for New General Counsel", online: *Practical Law* https://ca.practicallaw.thomsonreuters.com/w-020-5286.

Practical Law Canada Law Department, "Practical Tips for New In-House Counsel", online: *Practical Law* https://ca.practicallaw.thomsonreuters.com/w-020-5287.

Practical Law Canada Law Department, "Role of the General Counsel in Executive Leadership", online: *Practical Law* https://ca.practicallaw.thomsonreuters.com/w-022-1729.

Practical Law Canada Law Department, "Serving as Corporate Secretary: Considerations for In-House Counsel", online: *Practical Law* https://ca.practicallaw.thomsonreuters.com/w-023-8929.

Practical Law Canada Law Department, "Soft Skills for In-House Counsel", online: *Practical Law* https://ca.practicallaw.thomsonreuters.com/w-022-1730.

United Nations Global Compact, *The Ten Principles of the UN Global Compact*, online: https://www.unglobalcompact.org/what-is-gc/mission/principles.

Veasey, E. Norman & Christine T Di Guglielmo, *Indispensable Counsel: The Chief Legal Officer in the New Reality* (Oxford: Oxford University Press, 2012).

CHAPTER 10

CHALLENGES FOR LAWYER REGULATION: ENSURING LAWYERS' ETHICS

[1] INTRODUCTION

Regulation involves the consistent and sustained effort to create particular behaviour and to achieve particular outcomes.[1] It can involve traditional mechanisms of the regulatory state – where governing legislation empowers a regulatory body to control admission to a profession, to set standards of conduct, and to discipline those who violate those standards. It can also involve less direct mechanisms and more informal systems. In addition to the traditional form of regulation by provincial law societies, regulation of the legal profession includes norms flowing from case law, the actions of non-governmental bodies that shape and direct lawyer behaviour, the expectations and practices of law firms, and even cultural and social forces that set norms and standards of acceptable conduct by lawyers.

This book has to this point considered a range of sources that direct and shape lawyer conduct, including law society rules of professional conduct, case law, academic articles, and guidelines from government departments and the Canadian Bar Association. It has considered those sources in relation to particular ethical questions: how a lawyer should think about questions of ethical difficulty such as, for example, when to terminate a representation or what 'civility' requires in representing a client. In this chapter, and the two that follow it, the book shifts to considering the question of regulation itself – the challenges of creating effective mechanisms to encourage and ensure ethical conduct by Canadian lawyers.

This chapter outlines the traditional regulatory mechanisms governing Canadian lawyers, specifically the regulatory power and scope of authority of the provincial law societies. As it does so it considers some challenges faced by law societies when exercising their regulatory authority:

- What is the public interest in the practice of law and does regulation by lawyers – in particular, lawyers elected by lawyers – allow for identification of the public interest?

- How should law societies regulate admission to the practice of law? In particular, how if at all should they regulate legal education? Should they

---

[1] Julia Black, "Critical Reflections on Regulation" (2002) 27 Australian J. Leg. Phil. 1 at 26.

assess the "good character" of prospective lawyers and, if so, what form should that assessment take?

- What is the appropriate scope for lawyer regulation? In particular:

  - How, if at all, should law societies regulate the unauthorized practice of law?

  - How, if at all, should law societies regulate extra-professional misconduct by lawyers?

  - How can law societies effectively regulate sexual harassment by lawyers?

  - How, if at all, should law societies regulate the fees charged by lawyers?

  - How, if at all, should law societies provide more specific regulatory guidance to family law practitioners? If provided, should that guidance depart from what is expected of lawyers in other areas of practice?

  - How, if at all, should law societies regulate diversity and inclusion in the practice of law?

Chapter 11 considers the challenging public policy problem of deficient access to justice, and various responses to that public policy problem, including regulatory responses. Chapter 12 considers reforms to regulation, including regulatory innovation and possible shifts away from a self-regulatory model.

[2] LAW SOCIETY MANDATES AND GOVERNANCE

Provincial law societies have exclusive jurisdiction to issue licenses permitting a person to practice law, to set requirements for admission, to establish rules of practice and conduct, to investigate and adjudicate complaints of misconduct, and to sanction lawyers found to have committed such misconduct. As noted, other bodies play a role in setting and enforcing standards of conduct; however, the provincial law societies alone have the authority to admit and exclude people from the practice of law.

The provincial law societies have played a role in the regulation of the legal profession from before the establishment of Canada as an independent nation. The Law Society of Upper Canada was established by statute in 1797, the Barreau du Québec in 1849 (with its predecessor body established in the late 1770s), the Law Society of New Brunswick and the Nova Scotia Barristers' Society in 1825, the Law Society of British Columbia in 1874 and the Law Society of Alberta in 1898.[2]

The authority of the law societies, then and now, derives from legislation. The specific powers of each law society varies by province; however, all have an obligation to regulate in the public interest, and have authority related to standards of admission and conduct. An example of the mandate typical of the law societies

---

[2] William H. Hurlburt, *The Self-Regulation of the Legal Profession in Canada and in England and Wales* (Edmonton: Alberta Law Reform Institute and the Law Society of Alberta, 2000).

can be seen in the "Purpose" provision of the Nova Scotia *Legal Professions Act,* 2004, c. 28, s. 4:

(1) The purpose of the Society is to uphold and protect the public interest in the practice of law.

(2) In pursuing its purpose, the Society shall

  (a) establish standards for the qualifications of those seeking the privilege of membership in the Society;

  (b) establish standards for the professional responsibility and competence of members in the Society;

  (c) regulate the practice of law in the Province by

    (i) regularly consulting with organizations and communities in the province having an interest in the Society's purpose, including, but not limited to, organizations and communities reflecting the economic, ethnic, racial, sexual and linguistic diversity of the Province, and

    (ii) engaging in such other relevant activities as approved by the Council.

In the common law provinces, legislation grants governance of law societies primarily to the societies' members – that is, lawyers and (in some provinces) paralegals. That is why we describe lawyers as "self-regulated"; the majority of the members of each law society's governing body, often known as "benchers", are lawyers elected by other lawyers to serve in that role. Other people are appointed to the governing body, but control remains with the lawyers elected by other lawyers. A typical provision can be found in s. 7 of the Nova Scotia *Legal Professions Act*:

(1) The Council consists of:

  (a) such number of members of the Society elected or appointed as prescribed by the regulations;

  (b) the Attorney General of the province for the time being or a representative appointed by the Attorney General;

  (c) the President, First Vice-President and Second Vice-President of the Society;

  (d) the Dean of the Faculty of Law of Dalhousie University; and

  (e) at least three persons who are not members of the Society and who are appointed in the manner prescribed by the regulations.

(2) The Executive Director is a non-voting member of the Council.

Consider the public interest mandate of the law societies, and the structure of the law society governing bodies, through the following excerpt:

ALICE WOOLLEY

"Bencher Elections – the Challenge of Self Regulation's Legitimacy"
Slaw.ca, April 30, 2015
[citations omitted]

Prior to the election of Law Society of Upper Canada benchers on April 30, 2015, the Ontario Trial Lawyers' Association posted on its website a list of benchers who opposed the introduction of Alternative Business Structures. The website stated: "OTLA urges all association members and other eligible licensed lawyer to vote for the following candidates opposed to ABS". At the time some commentators, including me, were quite critical of the OTLA for this approach.

In this column I want to expand on those criticisms. Not because I want to further criticize the OTLA. But rather because I think politicizing this election, and the focus on the single issue of ABS, creates some risks and concerns about the viability of our current regulatory model. Specifically, can a regulatory system in which control rests with elected lawyers be trusted to regulate in the public interest?

[Woolley explains that ABS creates potential risks and rewards for lawyers that are distinct from the risks and rewards it creates for the public – e.g. even if ABS benefits the public, it might hurt lawyers]

A lawyer voting in a bencher election, or running as a bencher, is likely to be influenced as much by lawyer concerns as by those of the public interest. This is not an indictment of those lawyers. Human beings are always influenced by our own interests; even when we try not to be, our cognitive biases and weaknesses make true abandonment of self-interest impossible (as Malcolm Mercer discussed on SLAW, http://www.slaw.ca/2014/09/17/independence-and-self-regulation-im-ok-but-im-not-so-sure-about-you/). A lawyer voting or running may also use the public interest concerns simply for effective advocacy in relation to lawyer-focused concerns. And – worst of all – it will be impossible to know whether a lawyer voting or running for bencher is in fact motivated by lawyer-based concerns or public-based ones. That may mean that even a largely public-interest focused candidate or voter will appear as lawyer-interested.

Not all regulatory issues raise this concern. On questions of, for example, the maintenance of solicitor-client privilege, to a great extent the public interest and lawyer interests will be aligned. But with ABS the distinction between public interests and lawyer interests is significant, and making this the focus of the election, and encouraging people to vote on the basis of prospective bencher's position on ABS, focuses attention on the difference between the interests of the regulators and those on whose behalf they are supposed to act. It has the potential to make the whole election as driven towards protection of lawyer concerns, rather than as attentive to who will do the best job of regulating in the public interest.

It creates other legitimacy problems as well. . . . the question of whether ABS is a good idea or a bad idea . . . is largely an empirical and practical question, not a philosophical one. To turn this issue into a moral benchmark – like the "Emily's List" PAC used to help elect pro-choice democrats in the US – is to ensure that it cannot be considered in the way that it must be to satisfy the public interest. ABS isn't decided based on a person's values and beliefs. It's something that may or may not be a desirable regulatory change based on available evidence and regulatory mechanisms for successfully implementing that change. Elected benchers need to assess it on that basis, and forcing them to declare a position prior to election – and the actual consideration of the issue as a regulator – is to ensure that the public interest will not be properly assessed, whatever the outcome.

An "OTLA List" election may also inhibit regulatory courage. With this precedent as a backdrop will an elected bencher be willing to take a stand unpopular with lawyers in an effort to protect the public interest? Or will she decline to do so because she is fully aware that such a stand will make her a target next time around.

Finally, and most importantly, focus on ABS detracts from the issues that people who are not lawyers actually care about. A google search for "alternative business structures Canada" revealed two stories in the first three pages of hits from non-lawyer publications. Yet in the last year the Toronto Star alone has had numerous stories in relation to the conduct and regulation of Ontario lawyers. Members of the public do care about effective lawyer regulation, and the issues of concern to them ought to be the focus when electing the benchers charged with protecting the public interest.

NOTES AND QUESTIONS

1. Do you believe that lawyers can regulate the legal profession in the public interest? Why or why not?

2. What is the "public interest" in the practice of law? What advantages might a lawyer have in identifying the public interest in the practice of law? What disadvantages?

3. When you become a member of a provincial law society, you will be entitled to vote in elections for the law society's governing body. What factors will be important to you in voting for a lawyer to play that role? Would you want to play that role yourself? Why or why not?

4. In the 2019 election for the Law Society of Ontario, a number of prospective benchers ran as a slate in opposition to the adoption of the statement of principles requirement. The requirement, discussed below, was for lawyers and paralegals to "create and abide by an individual Statement of Principles that acknowledges your obligation to promote equality, diversity and inclusion generally, and in your behaviour towards colleagues, employees, clients and the public." The slate, called "Stop-SOP", elected 22 members in the 2019 election. Do you think Woolley's analysis would apply to the Statement of Principles issue? What are the interests of lawyers related to the requirement that lawyers submit a Statement of Principles? What are the interests of the public? Do they align?

5. 16,156 voters submitted ballots in the 2019 election, out of a possible 53,899, a 29.97% voter turnout. It was the lowest voter turnout in any Law Society of Ontario election since 1999.[3] Of eligible ballots, some 28% went to StopSOP candidates (approximately 4524 votes). Does this affect your analysis of whether the governance structure of the law societies can ensure regulation in the public interest?

[3] REGULATION OF ADMISSIONS

A traditional emphasis in regulating the legal profession has been on "inputs" — on

---

[3] The Law Society of Ontario has data on bencher elections on its website: https://lso.ca/about-lso/governance/bencher-election-2019.

determining whether applicants for law society admission are suitably qualified for the practice of law. The main input requirements imposed by provincial law societies relate to questions of competence: whether the applicant has achieved the prescribed educational and licensing requirements. These requirements normally include that applicants have graduated from an approved Canadian law school, have passed their bar examinations or training programs required by the law society, and have completed a period of articles or an alternative such as Ontario's Law Practice Program.

The authority of the law societies to determine the competence requirements for admission is established (and constrained) by legislation. For example, s. 24 of Saskatchewan's *Legal Profession Act* provides:

> 24(1) Any person may apply to the society to be admitted as a lawyer, and the society may admit that person as a member if that person:
>
> (a) produces evidence satisfactory to the society of service as a student-at-law or practice as a lawyer;
>
> (b) produces evidence that the person has completed a legal education program that is prescribed in the rules;
>
> (c) complies with the rules; and
>
> (d) fulfils any other requirement that the society may prescribe.

Some – although not most – provincial statutes grant the law society explicit authority to regulate legal education. Thus, s. 62(23) of the Ontario *Legal Profession Act* gives the Law Society of Ontario authority to enact by-laws "respecting legal education, including programs of pre-licensing education".

In addition to the power to regulate the competence of prospective members of the law society, legislation grants the law society the power to assess their "character" and, in some cases, their fitness. Thus, for example, s. 19(1) of the British Columbia *Legal Profession Act* provides that "No person may be enrolled as an articled student, called and admitted or reinstated as a member unless the benchers are satisfied that the person is of good character and repute and is fit to become a barrister and a solicitor of the Supreme Court."

The following two sections will consider issues and challenges related to each of these aspects of the law societies' regulation of the suitability of candidates for admission, beginning with the good character requirement.

[a] The Good Character Requirement

The "good character" requirement exists in many professions and trades. The requirement does not actually involve a regulator determining whether an applicant is of "good character" – if, for example, they have done volunteering, good works or otherwise lived a morally upright life. Rather, it requires applicants to demonstrate an absence of conduct thought to indicate bad character such as prior criminal convictions, academic dishonesty or attempting to deceive the law society; then, if such behaviour has occurred, it requires those applicants to demonstrate repentance and rehabilitation. Applicants must have recovered from the conduct which gives rise to a negative inference about their character.

The stated purposes of the good character requirement are to protect the public, maintain high ethical standards and maintain public confidence in the legal profession.[4] Its ability to accomplish these purposes rests, however, on the truth of two specific underlying assumptions: First, that we can identify the conduct that indicates bad character and, second, that character determines conduct, such that an applicant of bad character who becomes a lawyer is more likely to act unethically and more likely to pose a risk to an unsuspecting public.

In reading the next two cases consider the following questions:

(1)   How plausible is the assertion that character determines conduct?

(2)   Assuming character does determine conduct, how likely is it that a law society panel will be able to gauge accurately an applicant's character based on evidence of past conduct, rehabilitation or remorse?

(3)   Does the conduct which led to the character inquiry in each of these cases justify the law society's concern and attention?

(4)   Does it matter that good character is determined through an absence of bad character, as opposed to a positive determination that the applicant's character is good?

PREYRA v. LAW SOCIETY OF UPPER CANADA
[2000] L.S.D.D. No. 60
(Law Society of Upper Canada, Hearing Panel: C. Curtis, Chair,
B. Wright and A. Coffey)
[footnotes omitted]

Introduction

The purpose of this hearing is to determine whether the applicant is of good character (under section 27(2) of the *Law Society Act*, R.S.O. 1990, c. L.8, as amended), and should now be admitted to the Bar. The applicant is Alan Preyra, a 33-year-old student-at-law who has completed the Bar Admission Course and his articles.

The applicant completed law school at Queen's University in 1994 and completed Phase One of the Bar Admission Course in June 1994. He was unable to find an articling job and in August 1994, in his attempt to find an articling job, the applicant intentionally falsified his law school marks and other academic credentials and pursuits to prospective employers, as follows:

- He altered 11 grades on the transcript.

- He sent the altered transcript to at least five law firms.

- His resume falsely indicated he was a candidate for the Rhodes scholarship.

- The cover letter falsely indicated he intended to pursue a Master of Laws degree at Harvard but could not do so because of financial reasons.

- He misrepresented that he had submitted two lengthy research papers in

---

[4] *Rajnauth v. Law Society of Upper Canada*, [1993] O.J. No. 999, 13 O.R. (3d) 381 (Ont. Div. Ct.).

various different areas to several law journals for publication (including papers on international taxation and intellectual property, competition law and intellectual property, competition law and liability in tort, mergers and monopolies and law and economics).

- He falsely stated that he had been offered five or six articling interviews during articling week.

- He falsely told one law firm that another law firm had told him they would rank him if he ranked their firm.

These misrepresentations were uncovered in August 1994. . . . Even after his misrepresentations were exposed, the applicant continued to misrepresent what had happened in significant ways.

- He told the Dean of his law school that he sent false transcripts to only one or two firms.

- He did not disclose the full extent of the misrepresentations to the mentor assigned him by the Law Society (Chuck Magerman), and told the mentor that he had reported it to the Law Society himself.

- In a document prepared by him to be given to prospective employers in January 1998, he did not disclose the full extent of the misrepresentations, but continued to claim that he self-reported, not that he had been caught.

- He continued to misrepresent the extent of his behaviour, even to his own lawyer (Derek Freeman), and his articling employer (David Diamond) until November 1998, when he was finally honest with them about the details of his misrepresentations.

The Test for Admission

The applicant's counsel acknowledged that all of the applicant's behaviour . . . dealt directly with honesty and integrity.

These misrepresentations go to the very heart of who lawyers are and what lawyers do. Integrity is fundamental to the competence of a lawyer; competence necessarily includes integrity. The applicant was not of good character from at least 1994 through to at least late 1998. The question for the admissions panel is whether the applicant has changed since November 1998 and is now of good character.

The purpose of the good character requirement is to ensure that the Law Society can protect the public and maintain high ethical standards in the lawyers the Law Society admits to practice. Any decision about this Application must serve to protect the public and maintain high public confidence in the Law Society's self-governance.

The definition of good character is set out in previous decisions of Law Society admissions panels, and is an evolving definition. The definition is not exhaustive, and refers to a bundle of attributes which, when taken together, amount to good character:

> Character is that combination of qualities or features distinguishing one person from another. Good character connotes moral or ethical strength, distinguishable as an amalgam of virtuous attributes or traits which would include, among others, integrity, candour, empathy and honesty.

The onus is on the applicant to prove that he is of good character at the time of the hearing of the application. The standard of proof is the balance of probabilities. The relevant test is not whether there is too great a risk of future abuse by the applicant of the public trust, but whether the applicant has established his good character at the time of the hearing on a balance of probabilities. The test does not require perfection of certainty. The applicant need not provide a warranty or assurance that he will never again breach the public trust. The issue is his character today, not the risk of his re-offending.

It is important not to confuse the good character requirement for admission with notions about forgiveness or about giving an applicant a second chance. The admissions panel is not in the forgiveness business, the test to be applied is clear, and the admissions panel is to determine if the applicant is of good character today. The Law Society Act does not permit an admissions panel to apply any test other than that relating to the applicant's good character at the time of the hearing.

The Evidence

The Applicant's Evidence

The applicant comes from a success-oriented family of ten children, all of whom have achieved significant academic and vocational success. He explained his behaviour in altering his transcript as motivated by his belief that "some of my grades weren't competitive, I wasn't competitive". He described himself as without a safety net in 1994, and having no one he could turn to and rely on when he felt out of control (although his brother was at law school with him in the same class at law school).

The applicant described a healing process for himself that began in September 1994 with a breakthrough at the end of 1998, when he says he fully accepted the extent of his wrongdoing. The applicant says that until the end of 1998 he was still running away from the other details of his wrongdoing. The applicant says that he became an honest person with the Law Society in late 1998, and that he became an honest person before that in other aspects of his life.

The applicant entered therapy from December 1998 to March 1999 with a psychologist, Dr. Leon Steiner. Dr. Steiner treated the applicant with a technique known as brief dynamic psychotherapy during six sessions over a three-month period. There is no therapy, although there is ongoing therapeutic contact (telephone calls). It is the position of the applicant and Dr. Steiner that the applicant's behavioural patterns of misrepresentation and deception, which lasted for at least four years, have now been treated in the six sessions.

The applicant has had some very good things happen to him in the last few years. He married in May 1999, and had two very positive work relationships with the lawyers who acted as his articling principals (Winfield Corcoran and David Diamond). In two major areas of his life (home and work), the applicant has some very good supportive relations.

The Articling Principals' Evidence

Both Winfield Corcoran and David Diamond gave evidence on the applicant's behalf. They were each his articling principals (one after the other) and are now his

577

friends. They were straightforward and supportive. They testified that he had demonstrated honesty and integrity in their offices and in the handling of his files, and that he was a very competent articling student. The applicant was still working for David Diamond at the time of the hearing.

Competence, however, does not prove good character. As well, even his articling principals didn't learn all the details of the applicant's misbehaviour and misrepresentations when they hired him. The applicant was not entirely honest with either of them about what he had done. Both articling principals admitted that they learned of some of the details of the applicant's behaviour for the first time at the hearing.

The Medical Evidence

The medical evidence was detailed, complicated, extremely technical, often contradictory, and in some respects inconclusive. There were five medical reports prepared by three different doctors: Two psychologists (Dr. Leon Steiner and Dr. Percy Wright) and a psychiatrist (Dr. Philip Klassen). All three doctors were present when the applicant gave his evidence, and all three doctors gave evidence.

. . . . .

Evidence of Dr. Klassen

Dr. Klassen is a forensic psychiatrist, who works with issues dealing with the legal process, and conducts assessments and prepares reports for the Law Society and other professional disciplinary bodies. Both his report and his oral testimony were extremely detailed. He found no mental illness in the applicant, but described him as experiencing, in 1994, grandiosity, a sense of being special or unique, with a need for admiration and, perhaps most significantly, a sense of entitlement. The medical evidence established that the applicant had been very angry throughout law school and in the period immediately after law school.

The fact that the applicant came from a high-achieving, and success-oriented family, coupled with the fact that he struggled at law school, resulted in anger, a sense of injustice, and a sense of entitlement in the applicant. He felt that others had an easier time, and that he was being treated unfairly. The sense of failure was a blow to his self-esteem, which resulted in a counterattack. Dr. Klassen described the applicant in 1994 as an angry man who was going to take control of the profession that had treated him badly.

Dr. Klassen's analysis was that the applicant had been involved with serious transgressions in 1994 and had continued behaving in duplicitous and fraudulent ways for a number of years after that.

Only in late 1998 or early 1999 did the applicant decide to discontinue his struggle with the Law Society. Dr. Klassen expressed doubt that this was the result of his therapy. He noted that the therapeutic contacts had been brief. He noted that of the six sessions with Dr. Steiner, it was not clear how many sessions were assessment sessions. He described the result of the sessions as more confession than treatment. Dr. Klassen's skepticism about Dr. Steiner's therapy was related to the applicant's history of duplicity over a long period of time, which appeared to be caused by a personality of character deviation which, in turn, was a foundation of lying.

Dr. Klassen described the relationship between character and behaviour, stating that behaviour flows from character. In 1994, the applicant displayed bad behaviour from which an inference could be drawn about bad character. In 1999, the applicant displayed good behaviour. The question for Dr. Klassen was whether this was the result of a conscious decision on the part of the applicant to change his behaviour without an underlying change in character (in which case, his earlier behaviour was related to transient factors), or whether that good behaviour flowed from the applicant's bad character as yet unchanged.

. . . . .

Decision

Being a lawyer is a great privilege; it is a gift, not a right. It is not automatic, and does not necessarily follow from passing law school and the Bar Admission Course. More than simply meeting the academic standards, the statutory scheme is clear that an applicant must also be of good character.

The applicant engaged in duplicitous behaviour over a long period. He failed to be entirely honest about it for four years. This was not a single lapse of judgment resulting from a stressful situation. Even after being caught, the applicant had several opportunities to admit his misrepresentations to all that he should have. He did not do so. As recently as one year before the hearing, the applicant was still misrepresenting the truth to people close to him, and was still failing to be honest with his articling principal, and even with his own lawyer.

The transition from being a person not of good character to one of good character is a process, not an event. It may or may not happen to someone who was not of good character. It may or may not happen to this applicant. The applicant asserts that he has been in the process of change since 1994. Central to the task of the admissions panel is to determine whether that process is concluded. . . .

The applicant has not satisfied the onus of proof, on the balance of probabilities, that he is now of good character.

LAW SOCIETY OF UPPER CANADA v. BURGESS

[2006] L.S.D.D. No. 81
(Law Society of Upper Canada, Hearing Panel: P. Copeland, Chair,
A.F. Coffey and J.M. Potter)

. . . The purpose of this hearing was to determine whether the applicant is of good character and should now be admitted to the bar. The applicant is Aidan Christine Burgess, a 27-year-old law student who has completed the Bar Admission Course and her articles.

. . . . .

As revealed in the Agreed Statement of Facts, Ms. Burgess was found to have committed plagiarism in regard to an essay she handed in during her fourth year at the University of Toronto. That event, which occurred in the spring of 2001, standing alone, would not have precluded us from making a finding five years later that Ms. Burgess was of good character.

What is of much more serious weight are the ongoing and persistent lies told by Ms. Burgess to the Law Society of Upper Canada and to various persons who provided her with character references.

As revealed in the [University] Discipline Case Report . . . received by the Law Society, Ms. Burgess was caught having submitted an essay for credit that was substantially based on material taken verbatim from an internet source without appropriate sourcing.

In her letter to the Law Society, dated November 11, 2003, Ms. Burgess gave a false account of the U of T incident:

> While attending the University of Toronto, there was a claim made against me for academic misconduct in PHL382 "Death and Dying," for handing in a paper that was deemed to be too similar to a paper that I had handed in for another course. Although the claim was the result of a misunderstanding, I did not proceed with a hearing because I was graduating. I failed the course and was cautioned for academic misconduct.
>
> . . . . .

By letter dated January 4, 2005 Ms. Burgess provided a 2 1/2 page letter to the Law Society. In that letter, in great detail, Ms. Burgess in effect repeated her original lie to the Law Society, the same lie that she had given to her two personal character references and to her two professional references. In that letter (a portion is reproduced below) Ms. Burgess explained why she had not obtained the requested letter from her Articling Principal.

Reproduced below is a significant portion of the letter (with footnotes omitted.) The letter was addressed to Kim Bailey, an investigator at the Law Society.

> This is in response to your letter dated November 29, 2004 in which you requested that I provide a written explanation of the circumstances surrounding my academic record at the University of Toronto and at Queen's University.
>
> 1. University of Toronto
>
> At the University of Toronto I was cautioned for academic misconduct under the University's Code of Behaviour on Academic Matters. This Code states in section B.I.1 that it "shall be an offence for a student knowingly: e) to submit, without the knowledge and approval of the instructor to whom it is submitted, any academic work for which credit has previously been obtained or is being sought in another course or program of study in the University or elsewhere." I was enrolled in both PHL 382 — Death and Dying, and PHL 407 — Seminar in Ethics. I wrote a paper for both courses.
>
> For the Ethics course, I wrote a paper regarding the use of "slippery slope" arguments within ethical debates. I maintained that such arguments are not valid and should not be used to substantiate ethical norms. I received an A- in this course, and there was no issue with respect to the authorship or proper referencing of any materials. In the course on Death and Dying, I wrote a paper on the euthanasia debate which incorporated the illegitimate use of slippery slope arguments when arguing against euthanasia. This paper was focused on arguments for and against euthanasia, and only used slippery slope arguments as one example. I did, however, use portions of my paper from the Ethics course. I did not think this would be a problem since I was only using a portion of the paper and they were significantly different papers with different substantive arguments using different philosophers. Because I did not think it would be a problem to use sections of a paper that I had written when writing another paper, I did not ask for permission from my instructor to use my previous paper.

The instructor in my Death and Dying course believed that I had committed an academic offence by submitting similar academic work for two courses, and reported the matter to the department chair and the Dean. The Dean called me in for a meeting where we discussed the situation and the various options available to me. The Dean advised me that if I did not admit the alleged offence, my case would proceed to a tribunal for decision. He stated that the University tried to avoid such costly and lengthy proceedings, and indicated that if I were to be found guilty at such a proceeding, the penalty could range from suspension to expulsion from the University. The Dean said that if I were to admit to the offence, I would fail the course with 40% and would have a notation on my transcript for 6 months. This notation would say that I had been cautioned for academic misconduct. After the 6 months, the notation would be removed.

I decided to admit to the offence even though I did not think I had violated the University's policy. Despite my certainty that the papers were substantially and significantly different and did not constitute the same academic work, I was not sure how a tribunal would respond, especially if it included members who were not familiar with philosophical papers and arguments. I was about to graduate and did not want to risk facing suspension or expulsion from the University. At the time, I thought that since I had already been accepted into law school, having one failed course on my transcript was better than risking my entire degree. After coming to this conclusion, I admitted to the offence, failed the course and was cautioned for academic misconduct with a six month notation on my transcript.

[The portion of the letter addressing her alleged plagiarism at Queen's University is redacted.]

3. My Thoughts on Plagiarism and My Actions

I recognize that plagiarism is a very serious academic offence and appreciate that the functioning of the academic system relies on students properly referencing materials. I think that it is dishonest to attempt intentionally to pass off someone else's work as your own, and that stealing ideas is just as wrong as stealing anything else. Although there is a lot of pressure on students to get good marks, I think that grades must be earned and be an accurate reflection of a student's ability. Students should not receive grades for work that they did not do.

I would definitely handle my situation at the University of Toronto differently today.

. . . . .

On April 21, 2005 the Law Society Investigator, Yvonne Skilton telephoned Ms. Burgess to enquire about the apparent discrepancy between the explanation contained in Ms. Burgess' letter dated November 11, 2003 and the Discipline Case Report that had been received from the University of Toronto. That Discipline Case Report had been received by the Law Society on September 30, 2004.

In oral evidence, Ms. Burgess said that at the time of the incident she had been given a handbook and Rules regarding the situation at the University of Toronto. From reading the handbook and Rules she knew that handing in a paper that was too similar to another paper that had been handed in was treated as plagiarism. She testified that as a result of gathering that knowledge she created her original (false) story. She was aware that she had to give some explanation to the Law Society about the nature of the plagiarism.

It was only when confronted with the discrepancy that Ms. Burgess acknowledged to the Law Society the correct facts concerning the plagiarism incident at the University of Toronto.

. . . . .

On April 25, 2005 Ms. Burgess had spoken with Lorne Abugov and Patricia Brady [her professional references] and explained what actually happened in the plagiarism incident at the University of Toronto.

By letter dated May 4, 2005 Mr. Abugov and Ms. Brady advised the Law Society that notwithstanding the lie told to them by Ms. Burgess about the U of T plagiarism incident, they continue to stand by her in support of her as a person of good character.

By letter dated August 9, 2005, Ms. Burgess advised Professors Pardy and Baines [her academic references] of the U of T incident.

By e-mail dated August 12, 2005 Professor Baines acknowledged receipt of the letter from Ms. Burgess and indicated "I have no intention of amending the character reference that I provided".

By letter dated September 30, 2005, Professor Pardy stated, in part, to Ms. Skilton as follows:

> At the time I wrote my January 2005 letter, I was not aware of this incident of plagiarism. The fact that Ms. Burgess was found guilty of plagiarism at the University of Toronto does not change the observations that I made in my letter. However, I am surprised and disappointed that Ms. Burgess did not communicate this fact to me earlier. I would have expected, in a request for a reference letter, complete disclosure of circumstances surrounding the investigation.

Ms. Burgess' August 9, 2005 letter to Professors Pardy and Baines acknowledged a plagiarism incident at the U of T but did not, in any way, reveal to those Professors that Ms. Burgess had lied to the Law Society about the nature of that plagiarism incident.

The oral evidence of good character given by Blair Williams and by Lorne Abugov was very thoughtful and impressive. Lorne Abugov, in particular, had taken very seriously his responsibilities in regard to providing a letter of character reference for Ms. Burgess.

He testified that Ms. Burgess had made disclosure (albeit a false disclosure) of the U of T plagiarism incident to Mr. Abugov on April 1st. Mr. Abugov indicated that his initial view of Ms. Burgess had been that she was one of the best articling students he had seen.

Mr. Abugov testified that he had come to the Law Society and talked to them about his responsibilities and to help him figure out his responsibilities to all of the various stakeholders. Mr. Abugov testified that it took him 18 days to write the first character letter for Ms. Burgess. He said he was stunned and shocked by the first disclosure.

Even after the second disclosure, Mr. Abugov continued to support Ms. Burgess and to regard her as a person of good character. Both Mr. Abugov and Ms. Burgess testified that Ms. Burgess withdrew her name from consideration for hire-back by Osler, Hoskin and Harcourt.

Ms. Burgess testified as to the six counselling sessions that she had taken through the Osler, Hoskin & Harcourt Employee Assistance Program which paid for counselling services at Warren Shepell Consultants Corp. Mr. Abugov testified that he was aware Ms. Burgess had attended those counselling sessions.

The Panel was provided with the counselling note from those six sessions. They were quite minimal and of little to no assistance to the Panel.

Ms. Burgess testified that both for economic reasons and because in the counselling session she had dealt with the issue of putting forward the false account of plagiarism, that she felt the six counselling sessions were sufficient.

There was evidence presented to us of many varied positive things that Ms. Burgess had done in the community, including volunteer work for Amnesty International, extensive coaching of soccer, and assistance to other students.

It is also of significance to the Panel that Melanie Polowin, the counsel for Ms. Burgess was from the Ottawa branch of Osler, Haskin & Harcourt. We regard that as another indication of the support that firm is giving to Ms. Burgess.

The issue for the Panel is whether or not, on a balance of probabilities, Ms. Burgess has established that she is of good character today.

It is very clear that she was not of good character up until August 25, 2005. Ms. Burgess lied to the Law Society over an extended period of time and lied to her references. The sophistication of the lie, describing a very different type of activity that still fit within the definition of plagiarism at the University of Toronto, is of great significance to this Panel.

We note that there was no psychiatric or psychological evidence called at this hearing. Such evidence was called in the second *Preyra* case and was called in the *Miller* character hearing. . . .

. . . . .

In Ms. Burgess' case we do not think that there has been sufficient passage of time for us to be able to conclude that Ms. Burgess has established that she is a person of good character and suitable for admission as a member of the Law Society.

Given the serious nature of the deception engaged in by Ms. Burgess, the Panel would have found it helpful if we had had some psychiatric and/or psychological evidence presented to us concerning Ms. Burgess and concerning the behaviour that she engaged in, up until as recently as 17 months ago.

The Panel references the comments from paragraph 42 of the first *Preyra* decision.

> The transition from being a person not of good character to one of good character is a process, not an event. It may or may not happen to someone who was not of good character. It may or may not happen to this applicant. The applicant asserts that he has been in the process of change since 1994. Central to the task of the admissions panel is to determine whether that process is concluded.

It is urged before us that the applicant's serious deception resulted from her embarrassment and shame over the plagiarism incident at the University of Toronto.

As noted above, the deceptions to the Law Society and Ms. Burgess' references continued until April 25, 2005.

Central to the task of this Panel it is to determine whether the process of change since April 2005 has concluded. We do not believe that there has been sufficient passage of time for us to find that the bad character exhibited by Ms. Burgess up until April 2005 has changed.

In our view the applicant has not satisfied the onus of proof on the balance of probabilities that she is now of good character.

It gives us no pleasure to make this decision. From the references it appears that Ms. Burgess is a very intelligent and competent individual. Perhaps in future she will be able to establish to the satisfaction of a Panel that she is of good character and a suitable person to be admitted to the Law Society.

NOTES AND QUESTIONS

1. Preyra was ultimately admitted to the Law Society of Upper Canada: *Law Society of Upper Canada v. Preyra*, [2003] L.S.D.D. No. 25 (L.S.U.C.). In the subsequent decision, the panel noted the improved evidence of rehabilitation. It also noted the evidence of Preyra's law firm employers under whose supervision he worked in an essentially legal capacity (these lawyers also gave evidence in the first hearing).

2. In *Preyra* and *Burgess*, the bad conduct of the applicants concerned misrepresentations to the Law Society and to prospective employers as well as, in Burgess' case, academic misconduct. How significant should the nature of the applicant's misconduct be in determining whether or not the applicant is of good character? In answering the question, consider the following three cases from the Law Society of Upper Canada.

   In *Law Society of Upper Canada v. Manilla*, [2011] L.S.D.D. No. 39, 2011 ONLSAP 10 (L.S.U.C.), the Law Society rejected Manilla's application for admission on the basis that he was not of good character. Manilla had engaged in a protracted dispute with his condo board and had shouted, made ethnic slurs, written and posted defamatory letters about board members purportedly written by someone else, and engaged in other offensive conduct. He was charged criminally but the charges were withdrawn after he agreed to sell his condominium unit, refrain from any further statements about the board and made a charitable contribution in the names of the complainants.

   In *Law Society of Upper Canada v. Bornmann*, [2011] L.S.D.D. No. 141, 2011 ONLSHP 130 (L.S.U.C.), the Law Society accepted Bornmann's application for admission on the basis that he was of good character. In 2004 Bornmann had admitted to paying bribes to government officials in British Columbia and had agreed to provide evidence against the government officials in a criminal investigation in exchange for immunity from prosecution. When applying for articles Bornmann only told the law firm that he was going to be a witness in a criminal trial; when the firm found out about his admission of bribery they requested that Bornmann resign.

   In *Law Society of Upper Canada v. Melnick*, [2013] L.S.D.D. No. 210, 2013 ONLSAP 27 at para. 23 (Law Soc. Hearing Panel), the Law Society admitted Melnick on the basis of his current good character. In 2006, Melnick had been criminally convicted of sexually exploiting a 14-year-old student whom he had taught during her seventh and eight grade years. The sexual exploitation included "sexual contact such as kissing, oral sex and mutual sexual touching, including to ejaculation.". Melnick was incarcerated and his teaching license was removed.

3. Manilla was eventually admitted to the Law Society in 2013: *Manilla v. Law Society of Upper Canada*, 2013 ONLSHP 93 (L.S.U.C.). On January 28, 2021 the Law Society Tribunal found that Manilla engaged in professional misconduct for, amongst other things, "signing Client A's name on . . . Documents without such client's knowledge or consent".

4. Another applicant admitted despite character concerns who later committed related misconduct was Ahuja, who was sanctioned for misleading the court and a client, and whose case was discussed in Chapters 5 and 6: *Ahuja (Re)*, 2017 LSBC 26. Do the *Manilla* and *Ahuja* cases give you more or less faith in the good character process?

5. In *Preyra* the applicant argued that he should be admitted subject to conditions. The Law Society held that it had no power to impose conditions on an applicant for admission. Most law societies now have such power. Had it been in place when *Preyra* was decided what kind of conditions do you think should have been imposed?

6. The Law Society of Ontario's licensing bylaw (Bylaw 4) provides "An applicant who makes any false or misleading representation or declaration on or in connection with an application for a licence, by commission or omission, is deemed thereafter not to meet, and not to have met, the requirements for the issuance of any licence under the Act." In a 2020 decision, *Sohail v. Law Society of Ontario*, 2020 ONLSTH 38 the Law Society denied admission to an applicant who it found had made deliberate misrepresentations in filling out her good character form. In your view, should deceit of the law society be automatically exclusive? What other types of behaviour should preclude admission?

7. In an early case on the good character requirement, the Law Society of Ontario rejected the relevance of evidence of future good conduct to the decision. The panel said that the applicant in that case "did not need to demonstrate good character beyond a reasonable doubt, nor was he obligated to provide a warranty or assurance that in the future he would not breach the public trust".[5] This position was also noted in *Preyra*. Is this limitation on the consideration of character consistent with the accomplishment of the requirement's stated purpose of protecting the public and ensuring the maintenance of ethical standards?

8. How appropriate is the weight given by the panel to the psychological evidence filed in the *Preyra* case and to the absence of such evidence in the *Burgess* case?

9. In good character cases applicants generally provide positive character

---

[5] *In the Matter of an Application for Admission to the Law Society of Upper Canada by Joseph Rizzotto*, Reasons of Convocation (September 14, 1992) at para. 32.

evidence. Indeed, in the first published case of a person denied admission to the Law Society of Upper Canada — whose character was at issue because of his conviction for crimes related to his sexual assault of two children — one witness testified that it would be "a tragedy for him and the legal profession if such a talented person were to be shut out".[6] What weight should the Law Society give such evidence?

10.   A study of 1343 applicants to the Connecticut bar and their subsequent disciplinary records discovered that the predictive power of pre-admission misconduct is extremely low; applicants with a criminal conviction only had a 1.2% greater likelihood of being subject to regulatory discipline.[7] How does this affect your analysis of the merits of the good character requirement?

Historically, an extraordinarily small number of applicants have been excluded from admission to the law society based on allegations of character. That does not mean, however, that the good character requirement imposes no costs on applicants. Consider the following account from an Ontario lawyer who satisfied the good character requirement, but only after an investigation by the Law Society.

NAOMI SAYERS
"The Trauma of proving my good character"
Canadian Lawyer, September 4, 2018
[citations omitted]

In July 2017, I stood on my sister's balcony. I looked out and over the balcony. I then asked her if it would be OK if I could call her for safety. I had images of me jumping over the 23rd-floor balcony. I felt guilty putting my family through what I was experiencing; they had been here before. At the time, I was under a good character investigation by the Law Society of Ontario.

Applicants to the LSO must be of good character and they indicate such by filling out a form. The form asks questions about past convictions or findings of guilt, among other things. The applicant must answer yes or no. Positive answers require supporting or relevant documentations. While I asked for clarification, nobody could provide answers to my simple question: What are supporting or relevant documentations? The LSO does not provide any information about what these are.

At the time, I also attached a letter detailing my history of surviving gender-based violence and exploitation to now becoming an expert on these issues. I thought the letter was sufficient; it was not.

In June 2017, I received a call from an investigator, nearly six months after I applied.

---

[6] *Re P. (D.M.)*, [1989] L.S.D.D. No. 1 (L.S.U.C.).

[7] Leslie Levin, Christine Zozula & Peter Siegelman, "The Questionable Character of the Bar's Character and Fitness Inquiry" (2015) 40 Law & Soc. Inquiry 51-85; Alice Woolley, "Can Good Character Be Made Better? Assessing the Federation of Law Societies' Proposed Reform of the Good Character Requirement for Law Society Admission" 26 C.J.A.L.P. 29 at 47.

The investigator described the letter she was sending and told me to not "stress." She said the LSO requires more information. She outlined that I would also need to meet with her in person at some point.

I was unable to follow her advice to not "stress" after seeing nearly 20 disclosure requests. At the time, I was in the process of moving to Toronto to begin my articles, completing the lawyer licensing examinations and overcoming grief after the recent passing of my father in February 2017.

The first time I tried to commit suicide, I was a young person. After my first attempt, I ended up in the intensive care unit. I was in my early twenties in my final attempt. In the past, I did not have the appropriate supports. When I read the LSO's letter, I felt this way again because I felt guilt and sadness for simply surviving as a young Indigenous woman. I also witnessed the LSO laud its equity, diversity and inclusion initiatives, including its statement of principles, which requires all members to acknowledge their obligation to promote equality, diversity and inclusion. As the debate raged about whether the statement of principles was "compelled speech," I was advised that it was best that I wait until I was called to the bar before I wrote about my experiences.

The investigator received my reply to the LSO's June 2017 request in January 2018. This was after a nearly three-month delay for one document disclosure (these delays were not caused by me or my lawyers).

It was not until February 2018 that I could find some time to meet with the investigator as I was working on major projects as part of my articles. I asked my lawyers, Ian Smith and Amy Ohler, if they could be present because I was scared to return to a time in my life filled with violence and exploitation. Having just turned 31 in October 2017, I thought I could leave that part of my life behind.

The purpose of the good character requirement is to protect the public, maintain high ethical standards and to maintain public confidence, among other things. One must be honest and forthright, regardless of the required disclosures. These disclosures required me to highlight two exploitative situations, one when I was 18 years old and another when I was in my early twenties. Both situations also involved police. During one instance, I tried to kill myself while in police custody. When the police brought me to the hospital, the doctor recommended I stay at the hospital for further care but agreed to my release back to the police if I was placed on suicide watch and followed up with a psychiatrist. For the first set of charges, I received an absolute discharge. In the second, the charges were withdrawn.

When I met with the investigator, some of the questions related to suicide and drug/alcohol counselling. I have never been to such counselling; rather, I have been to counselling to address the trauma I have experienced throughout my life. Ironically, I also had to return to counselling because of the investigation. I requested a copy of the recording made during this interview with the LSO investigator to ensure I accurately captured what was discussed, but the LSO would not release the recording.

Before meeting the investigator, I sat at a board room table at my lawyers' office. We talked about my first letter, the process and the questions the investigator might ask. I recall Ian asking about why I wrote my first letter. He stated, "It makes you seem worse than you actually are." I paused for a second, to think about my response, and I replied, "Because it is the truth." The truth is, and from my perspective, the LSO needs to do better.

NOTES AND QUESTIONS

1. How does Sayers' account of her experience affect your analysis of the merits of the good character requirement as a method for ensuring ethical lawyers?

2. In several papers Alice Woolley argued that the good character requirement "is based on falsifiable empirical premises, improperly shielded from public scrutiny, characterized by inconsistent and incoherent decisions, and in general imposes costs without producing measurable benefits." She argued that the requirement should be abolished or, if not, should be replaced by specific exclusionary rules (see, for example, Alice Woolley (2013) 26 Cdn Journal Admin Law and Practice 115-139; "Tending the Bar: The Good Character Requirement for Law Society Admission" (2007) 30 Dal. L.J. 27-78). Based on what you have read here, and your own knowledge and experience, what do you think? Is regulating applicant character worth it? What are the downsides of abolishing good character regulation? The benefits?

[b] Education

As noted, under their enabling legislation, provincial law societies exercise authority over the educational standards that must be achieved by people seeking admission to the bar. Some even have the express authority to regulate pre-licensing education.

The specific authority granted to the law societies varies between provinces, but together, through the Federation of Law Societies, the law societies have identified "competencies" that each Canadian law school must ensure its students achieve in order for the school's degree to be an "approved" law degree for admission to the profession. These include competencies in substantive areas of law, along with competencies in practical skills such as research, writing and problem-solving. In addition, in order to achieve approval of its degree, the academic program provided by a law school must include a stand-alone course in lawyers' ethics and professionalism:

> The Federation will accept a. . . J.D. degree from a Canadian law school [where] the law school meets the following criteria:. . . The academic program includes instruction in ethics and professionalism in a course dedicated to those subjects and addressing the required competencies.[8]

Further, the law societies have established a common process for the admission of foreign trained lawyers.

A further issue confronted by the law societies relates to what power or responsibility the law societies have, if any, in relation to non-academic aspects of a law school seeking approval of its law degree. Specifically, can a law society

---

[8] Federation of Law Societies, National Requirement, Approved Law Degree, 2018, online: https://flsc.ca/wp-content/uploads/2018/01/National-Requirement-Jan-2018-FIN.pdf.

refuse to approve a law degree because the law school engages in what the law society views as discriminatory practices?

This issue came to the front of the regulatory agenda of the provincial law societies because a private religious university in British Columbia, Trinity Western University, sought to open a law school. Trinity Western requires students to sign a Community Covenant Agreement, under which they commit not to engage in sex outside of marriage between a man and a woman.

After Trinity Western received approval from British Columbia's Minister of Advanced Education to open a law school in December 2013, it sought to have its law degree approved by the Federation of Law Societies. The Federation struck an Approval Committee to consider Trinity Western's request. The Approval Committee was originally made up of four members of the profession and three law school deans, but the three law school deans recused themselves after the Canadian Council of Law Deans formally opposed Trinity Western's application. Ultimately the Committee — now with only four members, and only three of the original members — granted preliminary approval to Trinity Western's law degree. The Committee noted concerns with Trinity Western's ability to teach ethics and constitutional law in light of the fact that its Covenant "effectively bans LGBT students". It concluded, however, that Trinity Western had given sufficient assurances to satisfy the Committee that it would "ensure that students understand the full scope of [human rights and constitutional] protections in the public and private spheres of Canadian life".[9]

The Federation's position was ultimately accepted in all of the provinces except British Columbia, Ontario and Nova Scotia. The accepting law societies did not necessarily embrace Trinity Western enthusiastically. The Law Society of Alberta, for example, stated that while it had delegated the decision to the Federation and accepted the outcome, it had advised the Federation that "a review of the existing criteria [for law school approval] by the Federation is advisable. . . consistent with the recommendation. . . that the possibility of a non-discrimination provision should be discussed".[10]

In British Columbia, Ontario and Nova Scotia, the law societies all declined to accept the Federation's approach. The law societies used varying processes and took different approaches, in part because of the differences in their enabling statutes, but the result in all three provinces was effectively to preclude Trinity Western graduates from being admitted to the law societies of those provinces while the Community Covenant was used. Following the decisions of the law societies, British Columbia's Minister of Advanced Education revoked its approval of the law school due to the

---

[9] Alice Woolley & Jennifer Koshan, "Trinity Western Law School: Equality Rights, Freedom of Religion and the Training of Canadian Lawyers" (2015) 40(2) Law Matters 9 at 9-10.

[10] Letter from the Law Society of Alberta to the Faculties of Law, University of Calgary and University of Alberta (February 21, 2014), online: http://ablawg.ca/wp-content/uploads/2014/03/LSA_TWU_Feb_21_2014_Letter.pdf.

"current level of legal uncertainty".[11] He said, however, that Trinity Western could renew its request for approval if it successfully resolved its legal issues.

Trinity Western sought judicial review of the decisions of each law society, and was successful in British Columbia and Nova Scotia, and unsuccessful in Ontario.[12] It sought leave to appeal to the Supreme Court in the Ontario case, and the Law Society of British Columbia sought leave to appeal to the Supreme Court in the British Columbia case. The Nova Scotia Barristers' Society did not seek leave to appeal The Supreme Court granted leave in both cases, and on June 15, 2018 allowed the appeal of the Law Society of British Columbia and dismissed Trinity Western's appeal of the decision of the Law Society of Upper Canada.

On August 14, 2018, following the Supreme Court of Canada's decision, Trinity Western dropped its requirement that students adhere to the community covenant forbidding sex outside of heterosexual marriage; it also said, however, that it would not revive its proposal to start a law school.[13]

The following excerpt from the judgments of the majority and dissent in the British Columbia case focuses on the Supreme Court's consideration of the regulatory scope of the law societies in relation to the public interest, legal education and discrimination. In reading the excerpts consider the following questions:

(1)   What are the key differences between the majority and the dissent in framing the nature of the Law Society of British Columbia's decision denying approval to Trinity Western's law school?

(2)   Should law societies determine questions of equality and human rights?

(3)   What concept of the public interest in the practice of law does each judgment reflect? Which do you find more persuasive?

LAW SOCIETY OF BRITISH COLUMBIA v. TRINITY WESTERN UNIVERSITY

[2018] S.C.J. No. 32; [2018] 2 S.C.R. 293; 2018 SCC 32

Per Abella, Moldaver, Karakatsanis, Wagner and Gascon JJ:

I. Overview

Trinity Western University (TWU), an evangelical Christian postsecondary institu-

---

[11] CBC News, "Trinity Western Law School: BC advanced education minister revokes approval" (December 11, 2014), online: *CBCNews*, http://www.cbc.ca/news/canada/british-columbia/trinity-western-law-school-b-c-advanced-education-minister-revokes-approval-1. 2870640.

[12] *Trinity Western University v. Law Society of Upper Canada*, [2016] O.J. No. 3472, 2016 ONCA 518 (Ont. C.A.), leave to appeal granted [2016] S.C.C.A. No. 418 (S.C.C.); *Trinity Western University v. Law Society of British Columbia*, [2016] B.C.J. No. 2252, 2016 BCCA 423 (B.C.C.A.), lave to appeal granted [2016] S.C.C.A. No. 510 (S.C.C.); *Nova Scotia Barristers' Society v. Trinity Western University*, [2016] N.S.J. No. 292, 2016 NSCA 59 (N.S.C.A.).

[13] Wendy Stueck & Sunny Dhillon, "B.C.'s Trinity Western University drops mandatory covenant forbidding sex outside heterosexual marriage" *Globe and Mail*, (August 14, 2018).

tion, seeks to open a law school that requires its students and faculty to adhere to a religiously based code of conduct prohibiting "sexual intimacy that violates the sacredness of marriage between a man and a woman".

At issue in this appeal is a decision of the Law Society of British Columbia (LSBC) not to recognize TWU's proposed law school. TWU and Brayden Volkenant, a graduate of TWU's undergraduate program who would have chosen to attend TWU's proposed law school, successfully brought judicial review proceedings to the Supreme Court of British Columbia, arguing that the LSBC's decision violated religious rights protected by s. 2(a) of the *Canadian Charter of Rights and Freedoms*. The Court of Appeal for British Columbia found that the LSBC should have approved the law school.

In our respectful view, the LSBC's decision not to recognize TWU's proposed law school represents a proportionate balance between the limitation on the Charter right at issue and the statutory objectives governing the LSBC. The LSBC's decision was therefore reasonable. The balance between these interests has been considered previously in the context of professional regulation, but that consideration does not eliminate uncertainty about the appropriate legal and policy response to TWU law school.

. . . . .

II. Background

A. *The Parties*

TWU is a privately funded evangelical Christian university located in Langley, British Columbia. It offers around 40 undergraduate majors and 17 graduate programs spanning an array of academic disciplines and subjects, all taught from a Christian perspective.

. . . . .

Its approach to Christian education is set out in its mission statement:

> The mission of Trinity Western University, as an arm of the Church, is to develop godly Christian leaders: positive, goal-oriented university graduates with thoroughly Christian minds; growing disciples of Christ who glorify God through fulfilling the Great Commission, serving God and people in the various marketplaces of life: (A.R., vol. I, at p. 119)

Evangelical Christians believe in the authority of the Bible, the commitment to sharing the Christian message through evangelism, and sexual moral purity which requires sexual abstention outside marriage between a man and a woman. TWU's curriculum is developed and taught in a manner consistent with its religious worldview. The foundational beliefs of evangelical Christianity are also reflected in TWU's Community Covenant Agreement (Covenant). The Covenant requires TWU community members to "voluntarily abstain" from a number of actions, including harassment, lying, cheating, plagiarism, and the use or possession of alcohol on campus. At the heart of this appeal, however, is the Covenant's prohibition on "sexual intimacy that violates the sacredness of marriage between a man and a woman" (A.R., vol. III, at p. 403).

All TWU students and faculty must sign and abide by the Covenant as a condition of attendance or employment. The behavioural expectations set out in the Covenant apply to conduct both on and off campus. A student's failure to comply with the Covenant may result in disciplinary measures including suspension or permanent expulsion.

. . . . .

While a large proportion of the students who enroll at TWU identify as Christian, TWU says that its students may, and in fact do, hold and express diverse opinions on moral, ethical and religious issues and are encouraged to debate different viewpoints inside and outside the classroom.

. . . . .

B. *TWU's Proposed Law School*

[The Court then reviewed the history of TWU's law school and of the process and decision of the Law Society of British Columbia, and the lower court decisions reviewing the Law Society's decision]

IV. Analysis

A. *Questions on Appeal*

At the outset, it is important to identify what the LSBC actually decided when denying approval to TWU's proposed law school. The LSBC did not deny graduates from TWU's proposed law school admission to the LSBC; rather, the LSBC denied TWU's proposed law school with a mandatory covenant.

. . . . .

B. *The Scope of the LSBC's Statutory Mandate*

This appeal requires us to address the scope of the LSBC's statutory mandate. At issue in this case is the LSBC's decision not to approve TWU's proposed law school as a route of entry to the legal profession in British Columbia -- a decision that falls within the core of the LSBC's role as the gatekeeper to the profession. A question that arises is whether the LSBC was entitled to consider factors apart from the academic qualifications and competence of individual graduates in making this decision to deny approval to TWU's proposed law school.

TWU argues that the LSBC is only entitled to consider a law school's academic program, rather than its admissions policies, in deciding whether to approve it.

. . . . .

In our view, the *LPA* requires the Benchers to consider the overarching objective of protecting the public interest in determining the requirements for admission to the profession, including whether to approve a particular law school.

The legal profession in British Columbia, as in other Canadian jurisdictions, has been granted the privilege of self-regulation. In exchange, the profession must exercise this privilege in the public interest (*Law Society of New Brunswick v. Ryan*), 2003 SCC 20, at para. 36, . . . The statutory object of the LSBC is, broadly, to uphold and protect the public interest in the administration of justice.

. . . . .

As the governing body of a self-regulating profession, the LSBC's determination of the manner in which its broad public interest mandate will best be furthered is entitled to deference. The public interest is a broad concept and what it requires will depend on the particular context.

. . . . .

In sum, where legislatures delegate regulation of the legal profession to a law society, the law society's interpretation of the public interest is owed deference. This deference properly reflects legislative intent, acknowledges the law society's institutional expertise, follows from the breadth of the "public interest", and promotes the independence of the bar.

The LSBC in this case interpreted its duty to uphold and protect the public interest in the administration of justice as precluding the approval of TWU's proposed law school because the requirement that students sign the Covenant as a condition of admission effectively imposes inequitable barriers on entry to the school. The LSBC was entitled to be concerned that inequitable barriers on entry to law schools would effectively impose inequitable barriers on entry to the profession and risk decreasing diversity within the bar. Ultimately, the LSBC determined that the approval of TWU's proposed law school with a mandatory covenant would negatively impact equitable access to and diversity within the legal profession and would harm LGBTQ individuals, and would therefore undermine the public interest in the administration of justice.

In our view, it was reasonable for the LSBC to conclude that promoting equality by ensuring equal access to the legal profession, supporting diversity within the bar, and preventing harm to LGBTQ law students were valid means by which the LSBC could pursue its overarching statutory duty: upholding and maintaining the public interest in the administration of justice, which necessarily includes upholding a positive public perception of the legal profession. We arrive at this conclusion for the following reasons.

Limiting access to membership in the legal profession on the basis of personal characteristics, unrelated to merit, is inherently inimical to the integrity of the legal profession. This is especially so in light of the societal trust placed in the legal profession and the explicit statutory direction that the LSBC should be concerned with "preserving and protecting the rights and freedoms of all persons" as a means to upholding the public interest in the administration of justice (*LPA*, s. 3(a)). Indeed, the LSBC, as a public actor, has an overarching interest in protecting the values of equality and human rights in carrying out its functions.

. . . . .

Eliminating inequitable barriers to legal education, and thereby, to membership in the legal profession, also promotes the competence of the bar and improves the quality of legal services available to the public. The LSBC is statutorily mandated to ensure the competence of lawyers as a means of upholding and protecting the public interest in the administration of justice (LPA, s. 3(b)). The LSBC is not limited to enforcing minimum standards of competence for the individual lawyers it licenses; it is also entitled to consider how to promote the competence of the bar as a whole.

As well, the LSBC was entitled to interpret the public interest in the administration of justice as being furthered by promoting diversity in the legal profession -- or, more accurately, by avoiding the imposition of additional impediments to diversity in the profession in the form of inequitable barriers to entry. A bar that reflects the diversity of the public it serves undeniably promotes the administration of justice and the public's confidence in the same. A diverse bar is more responsive to the needs of the public it serves. A diverse bar is a more competent bar (see *LPA*, s. 3(b)).

The LSBC's statutory objective of "protect[ing] the public interest in the adminis-tration of justice by ... preserving and protecting the rights and freedoms of all persons" entitles the LSBC to consider harms to some communities in making a decision it is otherwise entitled to make, including a decision whether to approve a new law school for the purposes of lawyer licensing. In the context of its decision whether to approve TWU's proposed law school, the LPA's direction that the LSBC should be concerned with the rights and freedoms of all persons in our view permitted the LSBC to consider potential harm to the LGBTQ community as a factor in its decision making.

That the LSBC considered TWU's admissions policies in deciding whether to approve its proposed law school does not amount to the LSBC regulating law schools or confusing its mandate for that of a human rights tribunal. As explained above, the LSBC considered TWU's admissions policies in the context of its decision whether to approve the proposed law school for the purposes of lawyer licensing in British Columbia, in exercising its authority as the gatekeeper to the legal profession in that province. The LSBC did not purport to make any other decision governing TWU's proposed law school or how it should operate.

Respectfully, we disagree with the suggestion that in making a decision about whether to approve a law school for the purposes of lawyer licensing in British Columbia, the LSBC was purporting to exercise a free-standing power to seek out conduct which it finds objectionable. Nor did the LSBC usurp the role of a human rights tribunal in considering the inequitable barriers to entry posed by the Covenant in making its decision: the LSBC did not purport to declare that TWU was in breach of any human rights legislation or issue a remedy for any such breach.

. . . . .

Thus, there can be no question that the LSBC was entitled to consider an inequitable admissions policy in determining whether to approve the proposed law school. Its mandate is broad. In promoting the public interest in the administration of justice and, relatedly, public confidence in the legal profession, the LSBC was entitled to consider an admissions policy that imposes inequitable and harmful barriers to entry. Approving or facilitating inequitable barriers to the profession could undermine public confidence in the LSBC's ability to self-regulate in the public interest.

[The majority went on to hold that the procedure followed by the Law Society was acceptable, and that its decision did not violate the Charter.]

Côté and Brown JJ (dissenting):

[Côté and Brown JJ., took the position that the Law Society of British Columbia exercised its discretion improperly, and relying on irrelevant considerations. In their view, the only question properly considered by the Law Society was whether a "law school's graduates, as individual applicants to the LSBC, meet the standards of competence and conduct required to become licensed. The dissent also took issue with the procedure used by the Law Society. The following paragraphs address the scope of the LSBC's public interest mandate]

. . . . .

In our view, the majority's broad interpretation of the LSBC's public interest mandate eschews this prudent, rights-conscious methodology. It is completely untethered from the express limits to the LSBC's statutory authority found in the *Legal Profession Act*, S.B.C. 1998, c. 9 (*"LPA"*). The LSBC's mandate is limited to the governance of "the society, lawyers, law firms, articled students and applicants" (s. 11). It does not extend to the governance of law schools, which lie outside its statutory authority. It may only act with a view to upholding and protecting the "public interest" within the bounds of this mandate. These express limits to the LSBC's mandate cannot be disregarded in order to justify the infringement of Charter rights. A careful reading of the *LPA* leads us to conclude that the only proper purpose of an approval decision by the LSBC is to ensure that individual licensing applicants are fit for licensing. Given the absence of any concerns relating to the fitness of prospective TWU graduates, the only defensible exercise of the LSBC's statutory discretion for a proper purpose in this case would have been for it to approve TWU's proposed law school.

. . . . .

A plain reading of the Rule, in its entirety, leads to the obvious conclusion that its purpose is to ensure that individual applicants are fit for licensing. . . . It is readily apparent that the approval of law faculties is tied to the purpose of assessing the fitness of an individual applicant for licensing. . . . Read in its entire context, the LSBC's authority to approve law schools acts only as a proxy for determining whether a law school's graduates, as individual applicants to the LSBC, meet the standards of competence and conduct required to become licensed.

. . . . .

A careful reading of the *LPA* reveals that the scope of the LSBC's mandate is limited to the governance of the practice of law. The *LPA*'s provisions only relate to matters relevant to the governance of the legal profession and its constituent parts (the LSBC, lawyers, law firms, articled students and applicants). Even its farthest-reaching provisions confirm its limited mandate. For example, Part 3 of the *LPA* (ss. 26 to 35), concerned with the protection of the public, is limited to allegations regarding the conduct or competence of a law firm, lawyer, former lawyer or articled student (s. 26). Similarly, s. 28, which, under the heading of "Education", empowers benchers to establish and maintain or otherwise support a system of legal education, grant scholarships, bursaries and loans, establish or maintain law libraries, and to provide for publication of court and other legal decisions, expressly confines these actions to those taken "to promote and improve the standard of practice by lawyers". The LSBC's object, duties and powers are, in short, limited to regulating the legal profession, starting at (but not before) the licensing process -- that is, starting at the doorway to the profession.

Section 3 of the *LPA* states the LSBC's overarching object and duty, which includes upholding and protecting the public interest in the administration of justice by "preserving and protecting the rights and freedoms of all persons". It is on this basis that the majority concludes that the LSBC's decision to refuse to approve TWU's proposed law school because of its admissions policy was a valid exercise of its statutory authority. In doing so, it is our respectful view that it misconstrues the purpose underlying the LSBC's discretionary power to approve a law school under the Rule and extends the Rule's scope beyond the limits of the LSBC's mandate.

. . . . .

This is not to say that public interest considerations are irrelevant to the exercise of the LSBC's discretionary power. The LSBC's duty is to uphold and protect the public interest; however, this duty may only be exercised within the scope of its statutory mandate. The *LPA* does not empower the LSBC to police human rights standards in law schools. . . . The LSBC does not enjoy a free-standing power under its "public interest" mandate to seek out conduct which it finds objectionable, howsoever much the "public interest" might thereby be served. Under the Rule, the LSBC can act in the public interest only for the purpose of ascertaining whether individual applicants are fit for licensing.

While ensuring the competence of licensing applicants clearly falls within the LSBC's mandate, this purpose does not rationally extend to guaranteeing equal access to law schools. The fact that the Rule sets out minimum requirements for licensing confirms that the LSBC is properly concerned with competence, not with merit. Setting admissions criteria to select the "best of the best" is up to law schools. To be clear, the selection of law students does not in any way fall within the LSBC's mandate, which is confined to the narrow task of ensuring that those who have graduated from law school and who apply for licensing meet minimum standards of competence and ethical conduct. Whether or not law schools have themselves selected the "best of the best" has no bearing on the LSBC's task of determining who is fit to practise law in British Columbia. Contrary to what the majority concludes at paras. 42 and 43 of their reasons, equal access to the legal profession and diversity in the legal profession are distinct from the duty to ensure competent practice. Indeed, the facts of this appeal are an example. Despite the unequal access effected by the requirement that applicants to TWU commit to a community covenant, the LSBC concedes its lack of concern regarding the competence or ethical conduct of TWU graduates. Relatedly, and while the majority notes (at para. 45) that "[t]he LSBC did not purport to make any other decision governing TWU's proposed law school or how it should operate", the majority's statement (at para. 39) that "[t]he LSBC was entitled to be concerned that inequitable barriers on entry to law schools would effectively impose inequitable barriers on entry to the profession and risk decreasing diversity within the bar" would logically apply to other aspects of law school admissions which might be said to create inequitable barriers to legal education, such as tuition fees. By the majority's logic, then, the LSBC would be entitled (or indeed, required) to consider such barriers in accrediting law schools in order to promote the competence of the bar as a whole.

. . . . .

The majority's overextension of the LSBC's mandate is equally apparent in discussing the LSBC's duty to "preven[t] harm to LGBTQ law students" (para. 40). The majority correctly notes that any risk of harm falls on "LGBTQ people who attend TWU's proposed law school" (para. 96 (emphasis added); see also paras. 98 and 103); in other words, the harm occurs in the context of legal education rather than the legal profession. Again, it is conceded by the LSBC that it has no basis for doubting that the graduates of TWU's proposed law school will be competent lawyers that will practise in accordance with human rights codes prohibiting discrimination against LGBTQ persons. There is, therefore, no basis upon which to find that such harms will manifest in the legal profession. Any harms to marginalized communities in the context of legal education must be considered by provincial human rights tribunals, by legislatures, and by members of the executive, which grant such institutions the power to confer degrees. The LSBC is not a roving, free-floating agent of the state. It cannot take it upon itself to police such matters when they lie beyond its mandate.

. . . . .

NOTES AND QUESTIONS

1. Which reasons do you find more persuasive? Why?

2. What other admissions standards ought law societies to consider from a regulatory perspective? Should law schools be permitted to rely on the Law School Admissions Test for admission purposes if it is discriminatory? In answering that question consider the lawsuit brought against the Law School Admissions Council on the grounds that the analytical reasoning test unlawfully discriminates against the blind (see, "LSAT will change for all would-be lawyers as a result of blind man's lawsuit settlement", ABA Journal, October 9, 2019).

3. Should law societies regulate the level of law school tuition?

4. The process followed by the Law Society of British Columbia with respect to TWU was unusual. The Law Society initially approved the law school; only later, following member initiated proceedings, and a referendum of its members, did it deny TWU approval of its proposed law school. What do you think of the process used by the Law Society of British Columbia? Do you think a referendum is an effective way of identifying what the public interest requires? What might motivate a lawyer in British Columbia to vote against the approval of a new law school? Will the lawyer focus primarily on the issue of the community covenant or might other factors come into play?

Scenario One

Look up the legislation governing your provincial law society and identify the statutory provisions that set out its purposes and/or regulatory objectives. Revise and rewrite the legislative objectives or regulatory mandate given to the law society to provide appropriate guidance to the law society about how to regulate the public interest in the practice of law.

Scenario Two

Create a process for a law society to consider an issue like that presented by TWU's proposed law school. In particular, design a process which will ensure a) the law society acts within its legislative mandate; b) the parties directly affected by the decision will have the ability to be heard; c) the reason for the decision will be clear; d) the decision reflects the nature of the law society governing body – that is, that it is made up of elected representatives of the law society membership.

[4] PRACTICE REGULATION

Once lawyers have been admitted to the legal profession, law societies set out rules and requirements to govern their behaviour, and to ensure ethical conduct.

Most obviously, law societies create standards for practice in the form of codes of conduct. They also receive and investigate complaints about lawyer conduct. If investigations show that those complaints have some apparent foundation, law societies adjudicate the complaints through a hearing, and sanction lawyers who are found to have engaged in unprofessional conduct.

Law societies also regulate the mode and form of lawyer practice. They have, for example, rules governing trust accounting, record keeping and the structure and names of law firms They conduct audits and practice reviews of lawyers and law firms to review compliance with these requirements.

The focus of legal regulation in this respect is to a significant extent reactive – it reacts to, and seeks to identify instances of, lawyer misconduct. It also focuses primarily on individual lawyers rather than on the structure and form of legal practice. The final chapter of this book considers the structure of the current approach to regulation – whether, for example, it is possible to regulate more effectively through compliance regulation, or in moving away from self-regulation. Here, our focus is on the effectiveness of practice regulation by law societies and, in particular, on whether law society regulation does enough to encourage ethical practice by lawyers. It considers these questions through some issues regarding the nature and extent of law society regulation, while also providing examples and discussion topics to allow you to reflect on these questions in relation to the ethical issues discussed in other chapters of the book.

In reading these materials ask yourself the following questions:

1.   One common metric for assessing regulation is whether it is efficient (considered from a cost/benefit perspective) and whether it is effective (does it achieve what it sets out to achieve?). What are the costs of regulating these areas of practice? What are the benefits? Are they – or are they likely to be – effective in achieving their desired outcomes?

2.   Consider the other chapters of the book and topics that you have studied such as civility, termination of the lawyer-client relationship, conflicts of interest and confidentiality. Which areas of lawyers' ethics discussed in the book do you think it is most important that lawyers comply with? From whose point of view? What do you think a regulator could best do to ensure lawyers act consistently with those ethical norms and principles?

3.   Do the cases and materials you read elsewhere in the book raise concerns for you about whether law society regulation is efficient and effective? How might those concerns be addressed? What other methods of regula-

tion might be as or more efficient and effective?

4.   How would a member of the public define a "good" lawyer? How would another lawyer do so? A client? A judge? Given those definitions, on what areas of practice should a law society focus its regulatory activities?

5.   In considering the topics here, and the ethical norms and principles discussed elsewhere, who is best situated to regulate lawyer conduct?

6.   Do the law societies do a good job? Who else might ensure the proper outcome – for example, the courts, law firms or lawyer associations? Who is most likely to be the most efficient and effective?

[a] Unauthorized Practice of Law

Legislation in almost every Canadian province confers a virtual monopoly on lawyers to practise law, although some other legal service providers, such as paralegals or notaries public, have permission to perform particular legal tasks or work in specific legal areas. In conjunction with lawyers' monopoly, provincial law societies have the power to police the unauthorized practice of law. The following case illustrates this issue and provides an example of the sort of penalty that might be imposed by a law society, and ultimately by a court, in such a case. When reading the case consider whether this regulation protects the public interest, particularly in relation to ensuring access to justice and competence.

LAW SOCIETY OF UPPER CANADA v. BOLDT

[2006] O.J. No. 1142
(Ont. S.C.J., P.C. Hennessy J.)

P.C. HENNESSY J.:— The Law Society of Upper Canada (LSUC) brings a motion for contempt against Maureen Boldt for breaching the injunction Order of Bolan J. dated September 1, 2000.

History

Ms. Boldt is not and has never been a member of the LSUC or licensed to practice law in Ontario. At the time these proceedings were initiated, she carried on business as a paralegal and mediator.

The LSUC prosecuted Ms. Boldt in 1995 and 1998 for the unauthorized practice of law contrary to s. 50 of the *Law Society Act*. The 1995 proceedings ended following a successful motion for non-suit. That decision was appealed and a new trial was ordered. Just prior to trial, which was scheduled for April 1998, the parties entered into an agreement. As a result of the pre-trial agreement, Maureen Boldt pleaded guilty to one count of unlawfully acting or practicing as a barrister and solicitor. The agreement included the following additional terms:

1.   An admission that Maureen Boldt had unlawfully offered legal services in the areas of wills, divorces and incorporations.

2.   An admission that Maureen Boldt had represented clients in Ontario Court (General Division) including the preparation of court documents and pleadings.

3. An admission that Maureen Boldt had provided legal advice when preparing wills and separation agreements.

4. An acknowledgement by Maureen Boldt that her actions constituted a breach of s. 50 of the *Law Society Act*.

5. A fine of $100.00.

6. An undertaking by Maureen Boldt not to engage in the offering or delivering of legal services of any kind except those specifically authorized by statute and not to commit further breaches of s. 50 of the *Law Society Act.*

7. An agreement by the LSUC to drop the balance of the charges.

In 1999, the LSUC made an application for an injunction against Maureen Boldt to prohibit her from practicing law. After a five-day hearing, Bolan J. issued a permanent injunction.

In October 2003, the Labbe incident, which is central to this case, came to the attention of the LSUC. In September 2004, the LSUC initiated these contempt proceedings. They were adjourned once before this hearing.

The Issue

The LSUC argues that Ms. Boldt has violated the injunction and has carried on the unauthorized practice of law. In particular, the LSUC claims that Ms. Boldt has prepared separation agreements, provided legal advice for the separation agreement and offered to institute and complete divorce proceedings.

Ms. Boldt's response to the motion was that she engaged in the mediation of memoranda of understanding between parties in domestic relationships. She submits that neither mediators nor mediation are regulated by the LSUC and that therefore she has not violated the terms of the injunction or her undertaking to the court.

The first issue in this case is whether Ms. Boldt's conduct constitutes the unauthorized practice of law as prohibited by the injunction. If this question is answered in the affirmative, the next question is: "What is the remedy"?

. . . . .

Analysis

The practice of law in Ontario is regulated by the governing body of the LSUC, the *Law Society Act* and regulations as administered. When a government provides a profession with exclusive use of a particular title, for example, barrister and solicitor, and provides that profession with the exclusive right to perform specific professional services for members of the public, the return obligation of those professionals is to govern themselves in the public interest.

Among other things, the LSUC requires its members to carry professional liability insurance and it administers an indemnity fund for victims of a lawyer's dishonest conduct. In addition, in order to deal with public complaints, the LSUC operates a rigorous complaints and discipline process in which members of the public participate. These processes are designed to ensure that lawyers who have the exclusive right to practice law also have the heavy and costly burden of doing so in a manner that is in the public's interest.

On the other hand, if an individual who is not a member of the LSUC and is not entitled to practice law in Ontario provides legal advice to members of the public and prepares documents that purport to define legal entitlements and obligations, the members of the public are not protected in any way from service which is below standard.

. . . .

Counsel for Maureen Boldt, who did not give evidence, argued that the Labbe-Lowney Memorandum of Understanding [and others] are the results of mediations and that they are not separation agreements. This argument is based largely on the title of the document. Counsel for Ms. Boldt argued that the title "Memorandum of Understanding" demonstrates that the document was the product of mediation and was not intended to be binding. However, it is the substance of the document that must be considered in determining the central issue in this case.

I find that these documents, notwithstanding their title, were prepared with the intention of affecting the legal rights and obligations of the parties who signed them. The evidence of Ms. Labbe is uncontradicted. She sought and believed she obtained an agreement which would finally resolve the issues of exclusive possession, division of property and spousal support.

I am of the view that, in substance, the documents in the Labbe-Lowney case [and other] case are separation agreements. In these documents, the parties agree to grant one another certain rights to property, support, exclusive possession and parenting. Equally, they waive rights to these things. They also make these agreements acknowledging the intended legal effect by incorporating releases into the appropriate clauses, putting a final catch-all release paragraph at the end of the agreement, and signing their names.

. . . . .

The problems with access to justice are the subject of current comment within the profession and the community generally. It is a well-known fact that low and middle income persons often find the cost of legal services beyond their means. There are alternatives to the legal process for the resolution of disputes. Mediation is one of these alternatives. However, mediators should not be seen as a low-priced alternative to lawyers. The mediation process cannot be a shield for those who are illegally providing legal advice and leading clients to believe that their legal rights and entitlements are fixed. Where individuals seek advice about creating documents that are legally binding and enforceable and will have an impact on their rights and entitlements, they are entitled to that advice only from lawyers who are regulated in the public interest.

Ms. Boldt did not call any evidence in her defence. The evidence of the LSUC is uncontradicted. Drafting separation agreements was a lucrative enterprise for Ms. Boldt, who carried on her practice as if there had been no injunction at all. In substance, her practice did not change from 1993-2003, notwithstanding the significant injunction proceedings where she was wholly unsuccessful in advancing her positions.

Maureen Boldt was fully aware of the terms of the injunction Order made by Bolan

J. She had every opportunity to observe the restrictions. Although there was some suggestion that there is a blurring of the line between mediating and giving legal advice or drawing up separation agreements, there was no evidence to support it. This position does not have the air of reality. In any event, it is a moot point, because Maureen Boldt did not engage in mediation as it is commonly understood. Her practice was not consistent with the *Code of Ethics* of the OAFM, of which she was a member.

I find that Maureen Boldt breached the terms of the injunction dated September 1, 2000 by engaging in the unauthorized practice of law contrary to s. 50 of the *Law Society Act* and more particularly, that she dispensed legal advice, prepared separation agreements and offered to undertake divorce proceedings. I, therefore, find that Maureen Boldt carried on the unauthorized practice of law in direct contradiction to the clear and plain terms of the injunction. It is obvious from the transcript of the discovery, read in for these proceedings, that she fully understood the terms of the injunction. It is regrettable that she thought she could ignore the injunction simply by changing the title on her document. This is a flagrant breach of the Order of Bolan J.

I find Maureen Boldt to be in contempt of court. The trial coordinator, in consultation with the parties, will set a date for further submissions on penalty and costs.

NOTES AND QUESTIONS

1. In a separate proceeding, Boldt was sentenced to four months of house arrest, was prohibited from working as a paralegal, and was ordered to pay costs of $35,000. The Court noted past issues with Boldt and the fact that "Ms. Boldt showed deliberate and wilful contempt of the court's Order. She profited from her continued violations of the court Order. Her unauthorized practice of law has had serious and prejudicial consequences for some of her clients."[14] To what extent is the sanction justified by the fact that she was in contempt of court? To what extent is it justified by the fact that she was engaged in unauthorized practice of law?

The regulation of unauthorized practice raises significant issues of public policy. Specifically, how should we appropriately balance the need to protect people from the harm that may be done by a person providing legal services who is unqualified to do so, while at the same time ensuring access to justice. In the decision, P.C. Hennessy J. notes (at para. 70) that "[i]t is a well-known fact that low and middle income persons often find the cost of legal services beyond their means" but emphasizes the need for protection of the public and the statutory monopoly that lawyers enjoy. Is this the right balance? Consider that question in light of the following case. In particular, note the role played by lawyers in controlling unauthorized practice. Do you think that non-lawyers would approach the issue in the same way?

---

[14] *Law Society of Upper Canada v. Boldt*, [2007] O.J. No. 3757 at para. 5 (Ont. S.C.J.).

LAMEMAN v. ALBERTA

[2011] A.J. No. 966, 2011 ABQB 396

(Alta. Q.B., K.D. Yamauchi J.)

K.D. YAMAUCHI J.:—

I. Introduction

The Plaintiffs apply on behalf of certain lawyers from Tooks Chambers, UK (the "Tooks barristers") for a right of audience to assist the Plaintiffs in their case against Defendants. The Plaintiffs claim to be impecunious and unable to prosecute the case without substantial *pro bono* assistance. The Tooks barristers have agreed to provide this assistance.

. . . .

The Plaintiffs first broached with this Court the prospect of retaining the Tooks barristers during their adjournment application. During that application, the Plaintiffs advised this Court that their request was restricted to obtaining the Tooks barristers' assistance in the preparation of their briefs, which they would file to challenge the Applications to Strike. Since then, the Plaintiffs have expanded their request to include Tooks barristers' assistance in other capacities, including a request for the right of audience, and questioning of witnesses in the absence of Canadian counsel of record.

No one takes exception to Tooks barristers participating "behind the scenes," such that they would assist the Plaintiffs' counsel of record in the conduct of research and preparation of briefs, provided any documents that the Plaintiffs place before the court are under the signature of the Plaintiffs' counsel of record. However, the Law Society of Alberta ("Law Society") and the Defendants argue that questioning witnesses and otherwise having a right of audience constitute "practising law." For the Tooks barristers to undertake the practise of law in this case, they must comply with s. 106 of the *Legal Profession Act*, R.S.A. 2000, c. L-8 (the "LPA").

. . . . .

III. Background

The Plaintiffs claim that the federal and provincial Crowns have infringed their treaty rights by taking up so much of their traditional territory that no meaningful right to hunt, trap or fish remains.

Garry Benson, instructing counsel for the Plaintiffs, in his affidavit that he affirmed on November 3, 2010, deposes that the Beaver Lake Cree Nation does not have sufficient funds to cover the cost of completing this litigation.

. . .

Tooks barristers have offered to provide services on a purely voluntary and completely *pro bono* basis, as indicated in an exhibit attached to Garry Benson's affidavit. All of the lawyers in question are trained as barristers in England, have been called to the bar of England and Wales, and are experienced. None is a member of the Law Society.

. . .

VIII. Analysis

The Alberta Court of Appeal in *Pacer Enterprises*, held that whether a non-lawyer is practising law is a question of degree. . . .

Significant time was spent in oral argument on what constitutes the "practice of law". It is not the task of this Court to delineate the limits of the practice of law; nor would it be desirable so to do. The law, as a profession, evolves along with societal needs and desires.

However, we are dealing here with represented Plaintiffs proposing to engage trained foreign lawyers who are non-members. This Court finds that the proposed involvement of Tooks barristers, including questioning of witnesses, preparation of argument, and advocacy before the Court, clearly encompasses matters in respect of which law students receive training and which the public understands to form part of a litigator's stock and trade. It involves acts which in the usual course, if performed improperly, might appropriately draw comment or sanction from the Law Society. If these tasks do not form part of the practice of law, what does?

The Alberta Legislature has chosen to grant the privilege of self-regulation to the legal profession in Alberta. The Alberta Legislature enacted LPA, s. 106(1) for the purpose of ensuring, among other things, that lawyers practising in Alberta be competent and proficient, adequately insured by the Alberta Lawyers' Insurance Association, and bound by the CPC. While Tooks barristers may well be competent and proficient, there was no evidence before this Court that they are insured, nor did the Plaintiffs present evidence to establish that Tooks barristers would be bound by the CPC.

. . . . .

Having considered all of the arguments presented, this Court can come to no other conclusion but that under the current circumstances the proposed participation of Tooks barristers, beyond the supporting role conceded by the Law Society and the Defendants, are prohibited by LPA, ss. 102 and 106. Further, this Court declines to exercise its inherent jurisdiction to grant an order for expanded participation beyond that to which the parties have agreed.

. . . . .

NOTES AND QUESTIONS

1. The judgment was upheld on appeal: See *Lameman v. Alberta*, [2012] A.J. No. 180, 2012 ABCA 59 (Alta. C.A.).

2. In "Unauthorized Practice and Access to Justice", *ABlawg.ca* (August 3, 2011), online: University of Calgary, Faculty of Law, http://ablawg.ca/wp-content/uploads/2011/08/blog_aw_tooks_aug2011.pdf, Alice Woolley said the following:

   > Justice Yamauchi's reasons seem compelling given the clear terms of the *LPA*, and the constrained language of the Rules of Court. The case does raise, though, the question of whether lawyers in Alberta should be given a monopoly over the provision of legal services as extensive as the one they enjoy.
   >
   > It is true that the lawyers from Took Chambers may not carry Canadian insurance, and may not be technically bound by the Code of Professional Conduct. It is also true that they have not been trained — at law school,

through articles or otherwise — in the substantive content of Canadian law. However, these barriers do not seem especially substantial, or to undermine the point that the firm's services would provide real and tangible benefits to the Nation in the prosecution of their action at little cost. The terms of English codes of conduct are in substance similar to those that apply in Canada. In the event that their services prove to be negligent or in breach of contract, it seems likely that the firm has resources to cover claims made against them by their clients. Further, those clients are not unsophisticated, and could make the decision themselves as to whether to be represented by an uninsured firm. After all, most American lawyers are not legally required to carry insurance, and yet the US legal services market seems to carry on regardless. Lawyers are rarely sued successfully for their conduct of litigation.

Further, what information I could obtain on them from the web suggests that lawyers from Took Chambers are likely to provide outstanding service to their clients, whether in Canada or elsewhere. They have a practice that they describe as "unashamedly political" and have been involved in a wide variety of domestic and international matters raising questions of access to justice and civil rights. . . .

On the specific facts of this case it seems likely that the benefits of the Took Chambers representing the Nation significantly outweigh the costs and risks with their doing so.

The arguments against the representation are likely to operate at the level of generality and policy — that even if it might be a good thing for the Took Chambers to act for the Nation, it is nonetheless a bad thing to allow people who are not members of the Law Society of Alberta (or, given our new mobility rules, another Canadian law society) to practice law here. Non-members may not be competent, and their practice cannot be regulated by the law society; they may inflict costs on their clients and the functioning of the administration of justice while not meaningfully improving access to justice.

These general arguments undoubtedly have considerable weight. One of the reasons why we license certain activities and restrict who may participate in them is to protect the public against incompetent or unscrupulous persons to whom they might otherwise be vulnerable. But their weakness in the particular case of Took Chambers does suggest that we should be careful in simply assuming that those arguments are sufficient to justify the blanket prohibitions contained in the *LPA*. Can there not be a more nuanced or careful approach to the provision of legal services, in which consumer and public interests are protected, but the availability of competent and helpful legal advice is not irrationally restricted? I have to think that there could be; the facts of this case invite us to try.

Do you agree with this analysis? What, in your view, would a more careful and nuanced approach to these issues look like?

3.   In 2016, an Edmonton lawyer was temporarily suspended, pending Law Society resolution of allegations that he had committed professional misconduct. Soon thereafter he had begun working as a legal agent, and the

Law Society of Alberta sought and obtained an injunction against him. In upholding the injunction, the Court of Appeal stated:

> There are strong public policy reasons for concluding that a suspended member, as with an active member, cannot simultaneously be an "agent", shedding his or her role as a barrister and solicitor while seemingly maintaining it. When a member of the public retains a barrister and solicitor on a matter with legal implications, the member of the public would reasonably assume that the person is acting in that role. It cannot be that for some matters, the person is a barrister and solicitor and for others, he or she is merely an agent. This would potentially expose members of the public — not to mention the LSA itself — to jeopardy and perhaps loss, especially in circumstances involving the transfer of funds to the person in question. One can readily imagine the problems that would arise if barristers and solicitors were entitled to pick and choose when acting as a barrister and solicitor or agent only. The reality is that, no matter the disclaimers given (and irrespective of their content and notification to the public), members of the public cannot reasonably be expected to understand the subtleties and nuances of the distinction between acting as a barrister and solicitor and as an agent and still less as a "legal agent".

Law Society of Alberta v. Beaver, [2016] A.J. No. 994, 2016 ABCA 290 at para. 21 (Alta. C.A.). Do you agree? What work should a suspended or disbarred lawyer be permitted to do? In February 2017, Beaver was disbarred; online: https://documents.lawsociety.ab.ca/wp-content/uploads/2019/10/Beaver_Shawn_HE20160048_HCR_Sanction_Public.pdf. In May 2020 Beaver was convicted of contempt of court for breaching the injunction, and in February 2021 he was sentenced to one year imprisonment. The Court of Appeal has stayed his sentence pending appeal: *Law Society of Alberta v. Beaver*, [2021] A.J. No. 303, 2021 ABCA 83 (Alta. C.A.).

4. Do you think regulating unauthorized practice of law is a good use of limited law society resources? Consider, for example, that law societies generally only investigate lawyer misconduct in response to complaints. If a judge makes a negative comment about a lawyer's behaviour, but that comment is not reported to the law society, no investigation or discipline of that conduct is likely to occur.[15] Such investigations would cost much more than regulation of unauthorized practice which is only an issue from time to time; however, consider the relative merits of each as a subject of regulatory attention.

[b] Extra-Professional Misconduct

In addition to disciplining lawyers for misconduct in the practice of law, law societies also assert jurisdiction over misconduct by lawyers outside of legal practice. At its narrowest, this jurisdiction allows a law society to regulate ethical

---

[15] Alice Woolley, "Regulation in Practice: The 'Ethical Economy' of Lawyer Regulation in Canada and a Case Study in Lawyer Deviance" (2015) 15(2) Leg. Ethics 243-275.

misconduct which is substantially, but not technically, related to the lawyer's practice conduct. The power of the law societies to discipline for extra-professional misconduct ensures that a technical argument that the misconduct occurred outside of the lawyer's legal practice is unavailable to lawyers who have behaved unethically in this way.

At its broadest, however, the power of the law societies to regulate for extra-professional misconduct extends much further. It allows the law societies to discipline a lawyer for any behaviour which the law society identifies as "conduct unbecoming" a member of the law society. Canadian lawyers have been disciplined (albeit in some cases mildly) for "conduct unbecoming" as varied as public nudity, failing to care for animals at the lawyer's farm, writing a bad cheque to a landlord, and trying to conceal evidence of impaired driving with mouthwash.

The lawyer in the following excerpt was disciplined by the law society for a far more serious incident of extra-professional misconduct: murder. In reading the excerpt, consider the following questions:

(1) Is it legitimate to take away someone's ability to practice their profession because failing to do so would "compromise the public's respect for the law and the legal profession"?

(2) Where there is no evidence to indicate that the lawyer has acted unethically within the confines of their legal practice, is it nonetheless reasonable to conclude that lawyer's unethical behaviour outside of their practice casts doubt on that lawyer's future ability to practice law ethically?

(3) What types of extra-professional misconduct should concern law societies? What types of extra-professional misconduct should not?

(4) At what point should we view a lawyer who committed extra-professional misconduct as rehabilitated? Are there some types of misconduct from which a lawyer cannot recover?

LAW SOCIETY OF ALBERTA v. SYCHUK

[1999] L.S.D.D. No. 15
(Law Society of Alberta, Hearing Committee: A.D. Macleod,
F. Swanson and W. Willier)

This is an application for reinstatement pursuant to the above sections of the Legal Profession Act and the Law Society Rules. The Applicant was disbarred on October 18, 1990 following his conviction of Second Degree Murder for which he was sentenced to life imprisonment without eligibility for parole for ten years.

. . . . .

On October 13th, 1998, the Applicant applied for reinstatement as a member of the Law Society of Alberta. Under the Legal Profession Act, a person who has been disbarred shall not be reinstated as a member except by an Order of the Benchers.

. . . . .

Events Leading up to Disbarment

One only has to read Mr. Sychuk's curriculum vitae as of October, 1986 . . . to appreciate how tragic and dramatic was his fall from grace. He was a very well known professor of law at the University of Alberta. He was frequently consulted by other lawyers, companies and individuals because of his reputation as an expert in oil and gas law and land titles matters. He was a Bencher of the Law Society of Alberta.

However, while the Applicant was a very high achiever, signs of a troubled person emerged. He was a heavy drinker. On November 10th, 1985, the Applicant became inebriated and quarrelled with his wife. When he went down to the basement, she locked the basement door and he subsequently blew the lock off the door with a shotgun. He entered a plea of guilty to a charge of using a firearm without lawful excuse and without reasonable precautions for the safety of other persons and received a conditional discharge. One of the conditions was to continue therapy for alcohol abuse.

On December 31st, 1987, Mr. Sychuk and his wife, Claudia, went out with friends to a New Years Eve Party. They quarrelled. The Applicant was intoxicated and when they returned home, the quarrel continued. The following is a quote taken from the Reasons for Judgment of the Honourable Mr. Justice MacKenzie delivered on January 27th, 1989 in the case of *Her Majesty the Queen vs. Maurice Sychuk*:

> On the early morning of January 1st, 1988, a total of twenty-two stabs wounds were inflicted upon the wife of the accused. In addition, her left arm had been broken by a twisting motion requiring considerable force coupled with blunt trauma. Her hands had cuts indicating efforts to defend herself from a knife attack. She was also struck with considerable force on the mouth and on the left eye. Of the twenty-two stab wounds, nine of them were life-threatening and, indeed, the wounds caused her death. There is no question but that the accused inflicted the injuries and caused her death.

On behalf of the Applicant, it was argued that because of his intoxication, a conviction of manslaughter was appropriate, but the Applicant was convicted of second degree murder and this conviction was upheld by the Alberta Court of Appeal on January 9th, 1990. Leave to appeal to the Supreme Court of Canada was refused on June 14th, 1990. Although he sought to resign, the Applicant was disbarred on October 18th, 1990.

Applicant's Testimony at the Hearing

. . . . .

As one might expect, the events of January 1st, 1988 were devastating to the entire Sychuk family. The Applicant attempted suicide following the murder and deep feelings of agony, guilt, remorse, self-loathing, and depression plagued him for years. Of the three children, the two older ones do not have a relationship with the Applicant. Fortunately, the Applicant and his youngest son Bruce have developed a close relationship and early on, he promised Bruce that he would not take his own life. Since then he has embarked upon a long and difficult journey of rehabilitation. His progress has been remarkable and admirable. He has received a lot of psychiatric and psychological treatment and counselling. He is a recovering alcoholic and has not had a drink since that fateful evening. He states that he has gotten in touch with his feelings and has developed coping mechanisms and methods of monitoring which are designed to enable him to manage his anger and remain sober. Whereas before the tragedy, he was unable to get in touch with his feelings including his deep-seated hatred of his father, he is now sensitive to his feelings and is able to deal with them without drinking or venting his feelings in the form of anger.

While in prison, he participated in a number of programs and indeed, he has designed and led programs dealing with rehabilitation from addictions.

The Applicant acknowledges the enormity of the crime he has committed and states that over the last eleven years he has grown as a person and believes that he has a great deal to contribute as a member of the Law Society of Alberta. He says that the prime motivation for his wanting to be reinstated is not to practice his specialty which is oil and gas law, but to help others who have problems with respect to addictions and related problems.

. . . . .

While the practice of law is part of it, he made it very clear that it was not his prime motivation.

The Applicant has developed a new relationship with a lady friend and is presently living in Calgary with her. She was one of the witnesses interviewed by Mr. Busch and her interview is contained in Exhibit D. She is, of course, supportive and it appears that their relationship is excellent.

. . . . .

Responses to the Law Society's Notice

This application is controversial. Letters were received from over ninety people, most of them members, and they were still coming in during the course of the hearing. All but a handful expressed opposition to the Applicant's reinstatement. The opposition had a common theme, which was unrelated to the issue of rehabilitation. It had to do with the public's perception of the Law Society and public respect for the law and the rule of law. Typical of the responses is the following:

> I read with concern the Notice in this matter dated June 2nd, 1999. Although I do not have any evidence relating to Mr. Sychuk's application for reinstatement, I do know of a reason why he should not be reinstated, and that is simply this: As lawyers, we are sworn to uphold the law. The rule of law is so vital to a civil society, yet so fragile, and under so much attack in today's world. Violent responses to emotionally charged situations are becoming more commonplace. Many people (especially our young people) are being bombarded with influences against the law and the rule of law in society. Assuming for the moment that Mr. Sychuk has completely reformed himself and has overcome his psychological problems, it would still be problematic to allow reinstatement of his membership in the Law Society because of the mixed message we would be sending to the general public. By allowing Mr. Sychuk, a convicted killer, to again practise law, the importance of the rule of law to lawyers and the importance of keeping oaths is minimized, and this will erode the confidence of the public in our profession. As a former high profile member of the legal community, Mr. Sychuk and his criminal conduct have already reflected badly on lawyers in this province: let us not make the mistake of throwing aside justice, integrity, and morality, and allow him to once again be reinstated as a certified member of our profession.

A response was received from eleven members of the Faculty of Law of the University of Alberta. The letter said in part:

> Thirdly, an exercise of self-governance cannot be proper if it brings the entire practice and philosophy of self-governance into disrepute. In our view, a decision to readmit Mr. Sychuk would work just such a result. The public whom we serve and on whose trust we finally depend would loudly and widely condemn the decision and the independence which made it possible, and this response would be entirely justified. Quite simply, there exists no defensible theory of self-governance or of legal ethics which would ground a decision to re-admit a person under a life sentence or a person who has been proven, in a court of law, guilty of committing an act in violation of the most basic human right, morally and at law, namely, the right to life.

. . . . .

Discussion

The textbook, *Lawyers and Ethics*, by Gavin MacKenzie of the Ontario Bar was cited to us. At page 23-2, it states:

> The purposes of the good character requirement are the same as the purposes of professional discipline: to protect the public, to maintain high ethical standards, to maintain public confidence in the legal profession and its ability to regulate itself, and to deal fairly with persons whose livelihood and reputations are affected.

. . . . .

Understandably, counsel for the Applicant stressed three cases in which individuals convicted of homicide were admitted to the bar.

. . . . .

It must be noted that in none of these cases was the crime committed while the Applicant was a member of the bar. Indeed, in *Manville*, the Court made it clear that had the crime been committed while the Applicant was a member, the disbarment would be permanent. Moreover, in at least two of the cases, the crimes were committed by the Applicants when they were young. While the age of Mr. Brousseau is not revealed in the decision, it seems likely that he too was young. In only one of the cases (the English case) was the Applicant on parole. With respect to the Brousseau case, it would appear that there may be mitigating factors of which we are not aware because the sentence of fifty-eight months was a light one, given the nature of the crime, and the Applicant only served one year of that sentence.

We agree with counsel for the Applicant that as a Committee of Inquiry, we must carry out our mandate and make our recommendation in accordance with the law. In our view, however, the lists of criteria contained in the textbooks and cases cited on behalf of the Applicant are not very helpful in this particular case. In a case such as this, certain principles come to the forefront making other considerations pale in significance. We agree with counsel for the Law Society that rehabilitation cannot be the paramount factor at the expense of the standing of the legal profession.

As a starting point, Section 47 of the *Legal Profession Act* defines "conduct deserving of sanction" as:

> any conduct of a member, arising from incompetence or otherwise, that:

(a) is incompatible with the best interests of the public or of the members of the Society, or

(b) tends to harm the standing of the legal professional generally.

Clearly, then, the statute under which the Applicant applies for reinstatement recognizes the importance of the standing of the legal profession. Moreover, under Section 39, people are not admitted as students at law unless they are "of good character and reputation". Good character without a good reputation is insufficient.

An independent legal profession is an important part of a democratic society. Along with an independent judiciary, it serves the Rule of Law. More than that, each of our members takes an oath which includes the following:

> I will not pervert the law to favour or prejudice anyone, but in all things will conduct myself truly and with integrity. I will uphold and maintain the Sovereign's interest and that of my fellow citizens according to the law in force in Alberta.

While he was not there dealing with reinstatement, it is useful to read the words of Stevenson, J.A. [in] *Achtem v. Law Society of Alberta* [1981 ABCA 145]

> Indeed, it may be thought to be unseemly to permit someone to practise law who has been found guilty of a serious violation of the law which he is bound to uphold. The legislature may have recognized the undesirability of permitting a serving prisoner the privilege of membership in the Law Society.

Then, later on at the same page:

> The status of convict is *prima facie* inconsistent with the privileged office a lawyer occupies.

Fundamental to the role of lawyers in society and the administration of justice is the need to uphold the law. In our view, this principle becomes even more critical when the legal profession is self-governing and independent from the state. In Alberta, unlike some other jurisdictions throughout the world, the legal profession is not supervised directly by the courts or by the state. As a self-governing profession, we are all too aware that the public sometimes sees us as self-serving rather than fulfilling our mandate which is to govern in the public interest and to protect the public interest.

. . . . .

In our view, an application for reinstatement is much different from an application for admission to the Bar. The Applicant in this case, in addition to committing the most serious of crimes, has broken faith with his oath, his role as an officer of the court, and as a member of our Law Society.

. . . . .

Mr. Sychuk was convicted of a brutal crime, one of the most serious crimes one can commit. It was not a product of youthful indiscretion. Two years prior to killing his wife, he discharged a shotgun in his own home in the presence of his wife and children while drunk. This case has achieved widespread notoriety. For the crime of murder, he was sentenced to life imprisonment. We have received a great deal of evidence as to Mr. Sychuk's difficult journey to rehabilitation. However, rehabilitation is not the only principle at play here.

. . . . .

The life sentence imposed upon the Applicant reflected society's denunciation of the crime he committed. Moreover, at the time, he was an officer of the court sworn to uphold the law and this exacerbating factor calls for increased denunciation by the Law Society which governs the legal profession in the public interest. In our opinion, this denunciation by the public and the Law Society would be compromised or undermined if the Law Society were to reinstate him. One of the main reasons he seeks reinstatement is to improve his acceptability; in other words, his respectability in the community. Implicit in that is that membership in the Law Society and the Bar of Alberta carries with it a badge of respect, but that brings us full circle. In our view, the Applicant's admission to the Bar of Alberta would tarnish that badge, not because he is a bad person, but because of the enormity of the crime he committed while a member of the bar. In reaching this view, we are not rejecting the principle of rehabilitation or the qualities of forgiveness and mercy. Indeed, we recognize them as valid considerations. In the circumstances of this case, however, it is our view that these considerations cannot prevail where reinstatement may compromise the public's respect for the law and the legal profession.

Even if we are wrong, however, and rehabilitation is the controlling factor, we would not have recommended that the Applicant be admitted to the bar. We concede that the evidence of rehabilitation is substantial, and we concede that the Applicant has developed new ways to deal with his anger and his addiction. Nevertheless, he has only been out on full parole since January 1, 1998, and in our view, insufficient time has passed to provide us with sufficient comfort of complete rehabilitation.

Conclusion:

We are all of the opinion that the application for reinstatement should not be granted.

. . . . .

. . . While our recommendation is against his reinstatement, we wish to assure Mr. Sychuk that we very much admire the inner strength he has demonstrated on his continuing journey to personal redemption and rehabilitation. We wish him well.

. . . . .

NOTES AND QUESTIONS

1. The 2007 Calendar of Seminars for the Canadian Association of Petroleum Landmen contained the following entry for one of its instructors:

   Maurice J. Sychuk, B.A.; LL.B.; M.C.L.; Q.C.

   Mr. Sychuk taught Oil and Gas Law for 22 years at the Universities of Alberta and Saskatchewan. He also taught Land Titles, Company Law, Real Property Law and Contracts.

   Mr. Sychuk practised law for 24 years and was a member of the Law Societies of Alberta, Saskatchewan and the Northwest Territories. His principal area of expertise was the negotiation, drafting, interpretation and litigation of contracts used in the oil and gas industry, but he acted as Counsel, Advisor, Consultant, Expert Witness and Arbitrator on a myriad of oil and gas law issues. His expertise in oil and gas law has been recognized internationally. . . .

Mr. Sychuk is now semi-retired and has been working part-time as a Consulting Landman where his work has involved him in all aspects of the oil and gas business. He teaches in the Canadian Association of Petroleum Production Accounting Program at Mount Royal College and teaches the CAPL seminars on The Law of Pooling: Voluntary and Compulsory and The *Alberta Limitations Act.*

Was it acceptable for Sychuk to be permitted to teach and to work as a Consulting Landman? If not, then what prospect is there for someone convicted of a serious offence to re-establish a life after imprisonment? If so, then what is the distinction that warrants excluding him from the practice of law but permitting him to work as a Landman?

2. Is it a legitimate regulatory function of a law society to "denounce" the immoral conduct of a lawyer where that immorality occurs outside of the context of the lawyer's legal practice? Does this denunciation potentially duplicate the denunciatory effect of the legal sanctions imposed on Sychuk elsewhere in the legal system?

3. Sychuk was convicted of a crime involving serious moral turpitude. What is more relevant in determining whether they should be allowed to continue to practise law: the immorality of their actions or the closeness of their misconduct to the practice of law? What if, for example, a lawyer through negligence — as a result of being overcommitted — fails to keep proper accounts for the high-level amateur sports team she coaches and operates? As a result, there are funds unaccounted for and the team has financial difficulties, which result in it being placed on probation by its league. The lawyer is not charged criminally but she is fired. Is this a matter which should concern the law society?

4. In allocating law society resources, do you think reviewing lawyers' extra-professional misconduct is a more or less effective and efficient in creating ethical conduct than expanding regulation of conduct directly related to a lawyer's legal practice? In answering this question, consider your analysis of the allocation of law society resources in relation to the regulation of unauthorized practice.

Scenario Three

John Jones, a lawyer, is a white supremacist. He has published materials casting aspersions on racialized minorities. Specifically, he has published pamphlets that identify certain activist groups and accused them of conspiratorial activities to "infiltrate" the "corridors of power" in government and business. Jones has not been charged with any crime. However, his local law society has asked you for guidance as to whether they should nonetheless prosecute him for conduct unbecoming. What would you advise?

Scenario Four

Frank Fox practices real estate law in Hamilton. He also owns a local pub and craft brewery. In 2018, a number of women who had worked at the pub accused Frank of persistent sexual harassment. They said that he regularly commented on their clothes and bodies, suggested that women weren't "suited" to working in the kitchen or in the brewery operations, and made sexual advances to women who worked for him. In one case it was alleged that he terminated the employment of Beth Brown, who worked at the pub as a brewmaster, after she refused to have a sexual relationship with him. Ms. Brown has made a complaint about Mr. Fox to the Law Society of Ontario. Advise the Law Society of Ontario whether they should investigate Mr. Fox and, if so, whether their investigation should be limited to his conduct of his legal practice, or whether it should include Mr. Fox's restaurant and brewery.

[c] Sexual Harassment

Rule 6.3 of the *Model Code* explicitly prohibits lawyers from sexually harassing, or discriminating against, any person.

Lawyers have been sanctioned for sexual misconduct in relation to their clients, including being suspended or disbarred.[16] Critics argue, however, that regulation of harassment, including sexual harassment, does not reflect its significance as an issue in the profession, especially for junior lawyers and, in particular, junior lawyers who are female or racialized. The first two excerpts consider one specific change: a mandatory reporting requirement for lawyers aware of harassing behaviour by other lawyers. The final excerpt is one lawyer's experience of sexual harassment. In reading these excerpts consider the following questions:

(1) What does the public interest in the practice of law require in relation to the regulation of sexual harassment by lawyers?

(2) Should discipline of sexual harassment focus on redress for the specific victim or victims of the harassment, or should it focus on regulatory concerns related to the perpetrator's suitability for practice?

(3) Should there be a mandatory reporting requirement with respect to sexual harassment?

ELAINE GRAIG & JOCELYN DOWNIE

"Everyone turns to lawyers for #MeToo advice, but the legal community needs its own reckoning"
Globe & Mail, December 23, 2019

The legal profession must change the way it responds to sexual misconduct within its own ranks. The culture of the profession – with its social power, history of elitism and male dominance – makes it harder for women to speak out and easier for men to stay silent.

Take the example of Gerald Regan, perhaps the Nova Scotia legal profession's most infamous sexual predator. More than three dozen women – babysitters, family friends, dates, secretaries, a journalist and a legislative page – came forward alleging that the former premier violated their sexual integrity over the course of 40 years. These women reported detailed, and often similar, experiences of sexual harassment and sexual assault. Did a single lawyer report the open secret of Mr. Regan's alleged sexual misconduct to the law society over the course of his six decades as a lawyer?

---

[16] *Adams v. Law Society of Alberta*, [2000] A.J. 1031, 2000 ABCA 240 (Alta. C.A.); *Law Society of Upper Canada v. Hunter,* [2007] L.S.D.D. No. 8, 2007 ONLSHP 27 (L.S.U.C.).

Did the law society ever investigate? We know of no record of reports or investigations.

Instead, in 2006, Mr. Regan was celebrated. The province's law society awarded him a "special gold pin" and a certificate for having been a member of the Nova Scotia bar for 50 years. It feted him again at a reception in 2015. Why wasn't he disbarred, instead of celebrated? Some argue that Mr. Regan was acquitted of eight charges of rape and other sexual offences, but the evidence from dozens of other women was not before the jury and charges involving numerous other women were, according to the Supreme Court of Canada, wrongly stayed. The profession had a duty to respond through its own processes to Mr. Regan's sexual misconduct.

· · · · · ·

A professional culture that tolerates, even celebrates, men who engage in harmful sexual behaviour makes it almost impossible for women to speak out about their experiences. Law societies need to be part of the solution, not part of the problem.

Law societies permit, but do not require, their members to report known sexual misconduct by other lawyers. The Codes of Conduct for lawyers state that "A lawyer must not sexually harass any person" and notes that "A lawyer has a special responsibility to respect the requirements of human rights laws in Canada." This approach is not enough. Law societies need to change their rules to require lawyers to report other lawyers whom they have reasonable grounds to believe have engaged in sexual harassment or sexual assault. Lawyers who are the victims of another lawyer's sexual misconduct should not be required to report. Third-party reporting should anonymize the name of the victim, unless they request otherwise. Lawyers can't report privileged information. But, otherwise, lawyers should be required to notify their law society of improper sexual behaviour rather than merely ignoring it, dealing with it internally or passing the problem forward to other firms by enabling lawyers to transfer. Law societies should discipline, not celebrate, those who engage in this misconduct.

A mandatory-reporting rule for professionals is not unprecedented. In Alberta, doctors must report unprofessional conduct. In Nova Scotia, doctors must report unethical behaviour. Lawyers across Canada are already required to report other types of unethical and unprofessional behaviour. Sexual harassment and sexual assault should be added to this list.

Journalists, performing artists, chefs and others have turned to the legal profession for help, to push for a just response to their #MeToo ... moments. When will the legal profession respond appropriately to sexual misconduct within its own ranks?

AMY SALYZYN
"Reporting Sexual Harassment: A New Professional Duty for Lawyers?"
slaw.ca, June 3, 2020
[Citations Omitted]

Sexual harassment in the legal profession is a serious problem. Anecdotal accounts abound, and empirical data reveals sexual harassment among lawyers to be a significant issue. While the experiences of those subjected to sexual harassment are diverse, there is no doubt that, collectively, the impact on the wellbeing and careers of victims is profound.

Professional conduct rules explicitly prohibiting sexual harassment have been in place for roughly 30 years. The enforcement of these rules has led, in some instances, to lawyer discipline, but has not, obviously, stopped sexual harassment in the legal profession. So, what more should law societies do?

. . . . .

A mandatory reporting rule was proposed by Professors Elaine Craig and Jocelyn Downie in a December 2019 Globe and Mail op ed, where they make the compelling argument that "[l]aw societies need to change their rules to report other lawyers whom they have reasonable grounds to believe have engaged in sexual harassment or sexual assault." Changing professional conduct rules to require sexual harassment to be reported was also discussed as part of a panel on professional conduct codes at the CBA-FLSC Ethics Forum in March 2020. Outside of Canada, in 2018, a New Zealand Law Society Working Group report recommended "enhancing lawyer reporting obligations" vis-à-vis sexual harassment, bullying, discrimination and other inappropriate workplace behaviour.

There's much that is appealing about a mandatory reporting requirement. Not least, it signals that the legal profession views sexual harassment as serious misconduct. Presumably, more incidents of sexual harassment would be reported and stopped if a mandatory reporting rule was in place. Would-be harassers might be deterred if they knew their colleagues had a duty to report harassing behaviour. Lawyers are already obligated to report other lawyers who engage in bad behaviour like misappropriating trust funds or engaging in serious criminal activity related to their practice; why not add sexual harassment to this list?

While I wholeheartedly agree with the intent behind a mandatory reporting rule – we need to force the legal profession to take sexual harassment more seriously and better hold sexual harassers to account – I worry about the possible unintended consequences of mandatory reporting. For victims of sexual harassment, mandatory reporting may limit their ability to decide for themselves how best to respond to instances of harassment, and instead force them into a possibly invasive regulatory process. Although lawyers already have the option to report other lawyers for sexual harassment, requiring, rather than simply allowing, reporting meaningfully impacts victim autonomy. Mandatory reporting may also place undue burdens on vulnerable bystanders, including new calls and those in precarious employment situations, by enlisting them as a de facto investigatory arm of the law society. . . .

Take, for example, a first-year associate at a large law firm who works with a partner who repeatedly makes sexually suggestive comments in her presence. Right now, the associate has several options available to her. She could, do nothing, confront the harasser herself, report the harassment to the firm's HR department or a mentor at the law firm, seek confidential advice and comfort from friends or make a complaint to her law society.

There are many reasons why the associate may not want to report the matter to the law society. . . . There is research that indicates "that sexual harassment litiga-tion. . .appear[s] to exacerbate or perpetuate symptoms developed as a result of the original harassment" and can trigger "demoralization, anxious arousal, fear and self-blame." Making a report about sexual harassment to a regulator is not the same as initiating a civil lawsuit, but it is certainly plausible that, for some, engaging with the law society about an experience of sexual harassment could be re-traumatizing.

To be sure, some victims who report sexual harassment to their law societies might have a positive experience. It is also possible that some victims will experience the harms and costs discussed above but still believe that reporting to the law society was the best choice for them. To be clear, I do not think that any of the potential harms or costs that I detail above mean that victims of sexual harassment should not report the harassment or that we, as a profession, are not obligated to mitigate these harms and costs. My concern is about trying to preserve, as much as possible, the victim's ability to make an informed decision for herself about what course of action is in her best interests.

· · · · ·

One response to the above concerns is to exempt those who experience sexual harassment from the mandatory reporting rule. Indeed, this is exactly what Professors Craig and Downie propose. The New Zealand Working Group report also recommends that victims be exempted from mandatory reporting obligations.

A victim-exemption would allow the associate in the above example to avoid discipline for not, herself, reporting the behaviour, but many concerns remain. If she engages the law firm's internal processes or talks about the harassment with her friends who are lawyers, would the law firm or those lawyer-friends be required to report what happened to the law society against the associate's wishes? One could graft on another exemption to the mandatory rule for lawyers who are contacted by victims of sexual harassment for advice or support. Indeed, the New Zealand Working Group recommends "an exception for lawyers providing confidential guidance and support about ethical and professional concerns." Such an exemption may give the victim more options, but requires her to engage in an interpretative exercise: is the person she is talking to "providing confidential guidance and support about ethical and professional concerns"? More pressingly, others falling outside of this "guidance and support" exception would still be required to report to the law society. If another lawyer in the firm – who is not approached for advice or guidance – witnesses the behaviour, this lawyer would be required to report and the law society would be involved notwithstanding the associate's desire to deal with the issue in another way. No one has suggested, to my knowledge, that bystanders could be exempted from reporting and it is hard to think of how a bystander exemption could be implemented without robbing a mandatory reporting rule of meaningful effect.

In their op ed, Professors Craig and Downie suggest anonymization as an additional measure, writing "[t]hird-party reporting should anonymize the name of the victim, unless they request otherwise." Here, I wonder if it is possible to generally provide for anonymity. What about cases where the facts in the report would easily reveal the identity of the victim? Moreover, at least some of these reports will presumably lead to law society investigations in which the victim would be contacted. As a general matter, lawyers have a duty to cooperate with law society inquiries and investigations. The New Zealand Working Group report acknowledges: "ensuring confidentiality may not be possible. One example is when a matter proceeds to a disciplinary process that requires witness testimony." In these types of cases, anonymization might shield the victim's identity from the public-at-large, but she still risks being identified to others – the law society, the offending lawyer and possibly others at her law firm. The stress and potential harms associated with being enveloped in a regulatory process still exist, too.

In relation to bystanders, part of my concern is rooted in the fact that sexual harassment – quite properly – is understood to encompass a broad range of behaviours, including:

- Displaying sexualized or other demeaning or derogatory images;
- Sexually suggestive, intimidating or obscene, comments, gestures or threats;
- Jokes that cause awkwardness, humiliation, embarrassment or offence, or which by their nature are clearly embarrassing, humiliating or offensive;
- Innuendoes or leering;
- Gender-based insults or sexist remarks;
- Communications with sexual overtones;
- Inquiries or comments about a person's sex life;
- Sexual flirtations, advances, propositions, invitations or requests;
- Unsolicited or unwelcome physical contact or touching;
- Sexual violence; or
- Persistent unwanted contact or attention after the end of a consensual relationship.

Does mandatory reporting in the context of such a broad, context-specific definition require bystanders to be in a constant state of vigilance and assessment as to whether their colleagues, opposing counsel or any other lawyers they encounter are misconducting themselves? Some potential bystanders will be new calls or others in precarious employment situations. Is it too much of a burden to require these lawyers to make a formal report to the law society any time they see something that might constitute sexual harassment, under threat that they themselves would face discipline if they do not make such a call? Is a new disciplinary rule the best response to bystanders who make incorrect judgements or who are, indeed, fearful of contacting their regulator about lawyers who exercise supervisory roles over them or make employment decisions that impact them?

There might be a few ways to reduce any undue burdens on bystanders. One option would be to allow for anonymous third-party reporting so a bystander doesn't have to identify himself or herself. Once again, I'm not sure if anonymity could actually be preserved in many cases once surrounding facts are provided. Perhaps identifying facts could be stripped out of reports, but then procedural fairness issues would seem to arise if the result is requiring lawyers to respond to anonymous and vague complaints about their behaviour.

· · · · ·

A further option might be to add a threshold so only particularly bad behaviour must be reported. The reporting requirement could stipulate that lawyers have to a duty to report only "serious" or "very serious" sexual harassment, with seriousness being defined in relation to instances of conduct, harmfulness of the behaviour or some combination thereof. There will be, no doubt, some cases where it is relatively easy to assess if this threshold is met. But, as a general matter, there will still be a significant self-adjudication burden on the lawyer to assess what constitutes "serious" or "very serious" sexual harassment in a given context. The stakes are high for the lawyer to "get it right" given that "to get it wrong" means that the lawyer him or herself is then breaching a professional conduct rule. And, of course, even if only "serious" or "very serious" harassment is formally subject to mandatory reporting, there will still be instances where the victims involved do not want the law society engaged.

It may be that I am overthinking all of this. Professors Craig and Downie correctly note that doctors and other medical professionals already have a duty to report their colleagues for sexual misconduct, including sexual harassment, although I wonder if there are ways in which the two practice contexts are meaningfully distinct in relation to the issue of mandatory reporting.

It may also be that some accept that a degree of harm, or a risk of some harm, to victims and bystanders of sexual harassment is a necessary cost of fighting a culture of silence in the legal profession. Some might argue that the public interest in mandatory reporting outweighs whatever harm some individuals might experience as a result.

Ultimately, I'm left wondering if there are options other than a mandatory reporting rule that might pose less risk of harm to the most vulnerable in the legal profession but still achieve the same goals of advancing the public interest and reducing sexual harassment in the legal profession. I tend to favour focussing on measures to improve law society capacity to respond better to voluntary reports by victims.

. . . . .

Law societies can and should do more to respond to sexual harassment in the legal profession; I'm just not sure that a mandatory reporting rule is the best answer.

ALICE WOOLLEY

"#yesallwomen/#Notallmen: Sexual Harassment in the Legal Profession"
slaw.ca June 10, 2014
[Citations Omitted]

How do we understand bad things done to women by men? Through the few men who do them (#Notallmen)? Through misogyny in our culture as a whole? Through the experience of all women living with the risk that such bad things can happen (#Yesallwomen)? The ferocity of recent internet debate on this topic clouds the possibility that harm done by men to women should be understood as about all these things: the men who inflict it, the society in which it occurs and the lives of the women who live with the possibility of that threat.

In this column I explore the thought that sexual harassment and sexual discrimination in the legal profession must be understood with this sort of breadth of perspective: it is conduct reflecting the pathologies of the specific men who do it; it in no way reflects the conduct of all – or even that many – men in the profession;

yet it is conduct that reflects aspects of our professional culture, aspects that we need to address to achieve gender equity and fairness.

I make my case through recounting a story from which I make some general observations, the story being my own experience of sexual harassment and assault (i.e., unconsented to sexual touching) by a senior lawyer early in my career. By doing so I will endeavor not to over claim. I know my story is only my own. It is necessarily a story that I tell from my own perspective. But the number of personal stories told publicly by women lawyers about sexual harassment is small; I am privileged to be senior enough and tenured enough and removed enough from the emotional turmoil of that time to take the risk of telling it. It may not be the best evidence, but it may nonetheless be evidence of something.

I began practicing law as an articling student in Calgary in 1996; I had graduated from the University of Toronto law school in 1994 but had gone on to complete my LLM at Yale and to clerk for Chief Justice Lamer. After my call to the bar I was working at a boutique litigation firm in the city; the firm did high end corporate-commercial cases, and was led by a very senior and eminent lawyer, "XY", and a few much younger partners and associates whose work was primarily through him. Calgary was blessed by a number of very strong corporate-commercial litigators whose careers began in the 1960s – former Supreme Court justice Jack Major and current Alberta Court of Appeal justice Cliff O'Brien amongst them; XY was part of that group. He had a brilliant legal mind and a willingness to do whatever work was required to be fully prepared for his cases. He was a fierce advocate for his clients. XY was also generous with the pay and benefits that he offered to his partners and associates. The work he gave them was excellent.

Yet the conditions for doing that work were complicated by XY's remarkably volatile personality – his temper was legend, and I later learned that one of XY's opposing counsel said that he used to feel growing stress as he flew into Calgary for meetings or discoveries in which XY would be involved. When he shouted at me, XY would sometimes shake with rage.

As I discovered soon after joining the firm, XY was also willing to make derogatory comments about women, using the c-word in reference to a judge who had decided against his client, and commenting on the attractiveness – or not – of other women. He expressed surprise that a woman at his former firm did not have a boyfriend because she was very pretty, and wondered if she was a lesbian. He commented on how one of the legal assistants was "a little girl with big boobs" (this is a paraphrase based on my recollection). Eventually I became one of the people that he made comments about. I remember in particular one incident, where the topic of Princess Diana's 1997 Vanity Fair cover had come up, and I had observed that people sometimes said that I resembled her. He responded, "except for your boobs" and then followed with "but it's OK, you've got great legs" (again, a paraphrase).

I found this remarkably difficult to deal with. I did not feel like it would be remotely acceptable to say anything negative in response to his comments about other women. I very much wanted XY to think well of me; I wanted his approval and praise. And I did not know how to create a relationship with him where he would consider the quality of my professional work, without considering the quality of my appearance. I did not know how to discourage one sort of reaction while generating the other, and I generally just tried to be positive with him, even while feeling that this was almost certainly not helping the situation.

Things became much worse at firm social events when XY was drinking. At the firm dinner to celebrate my call to the bar, he put his hand on my leg under the table as we were eating. And at a firm retreat, as we sat around a campfire after dinner, he put his hand up the back of my shirt and undid my bra.

After that incident it was obvious that I had to do something – that the situation was out of hand. I spoke to the two male partners who worked on litigation with XY and to my husband (who had known about the earlier incidents as well); the more senior of the partners talked to XY, and XY apologized to me.

After the apology XY did not sexually touch me again, and I do not remember him commenting on my appearance. But his outbursts and temper continued; they were not directed just at me, but for the next year I was the lawyer working most closely with him, and so internally to our firm I bore the brunt of it. I found that almost as difficult and upsetting as his sexual harassment, although in some ways it was difficult to separate the two experiences. They felt like different versions of the same behaviour. The two partners did what they could to protect me. One began working on the file I was on, and tried to create space for me from XY. When we were away for the arbitration, he made sure that I was able to go home for a break. I was also protected by the in-house lawyer at the client, who observed XY's behaviour and did what he could to ameliorate it, and to protect me from it.

Nonetheless, after a year, I had to leave. My departure was greatly assisted by the lawyer at the client, who worked to have his company consent to my joining a firm where there would otherwise have been a serious conflicts problem; I know he understood why I was leaving, and I know he had to make real efforts internally to get that result.

I never had another experience like that in legal practice, although I worked almost entirely with senior male lawyers over the next 5 years.

In the 16 years since, in thinking about what happened to me, it is obvious to me that XY's behaviour was very much reflective of his own personality and issues. In the words that I would use now as a parent, he seemed to me to lack self-regulation: if he wanted something he took it; if he felt something he expressed it. He had no grasp of the difference between professional and personal space, of the effect of his degrading comments about women on the women he worked with, of the effect of his angry outbursts on others.

It is also equally obvious to me that most male lawyers do not act as he did. Even the male lawyers at his own firm and who worked at his client did not follow XY's example or endorse his behaviour. In addition, incidents of sexual harassment would not normally include actual physical touching. His behaviour was – and is – the exception.

But it also seems to me that his actions are not divorced from the professional culture of lawyers – a culture I am part of. After all, his behaviour – at least his comments about women and his rage – was tolerated for over 30 years and had little real effect on his professional success (although it certainly had some). At the end of the day, I took no steps to derail that success. And while it was clearly not normal,

621

XY's behaviour was also not entirely aberrational; excess drinking, angry outbursts and sexist comments are things that lawyers other than XY engage in, albeit to a lesser degree. I drank to excess at more than one firm event, and I've said sexist things. Even the harassment is something that more than one of my friends experienced in legal practice (and once you have more than one close friend who something has happened to, the law of probabilities suggests that there are an awful lot of women it has happened to). Some general statistics on complaints about harassment and discrimination by Ontario lawyers [indicate] 132 complaints about sexual harassment between 2003 and 2011.

Yet even if I'm right, what to do about it is not obvious. Our professional culture reflects our broader society; the insistent requirement that women be sexually attractive even if professionally accomplished, the verbal and physical aggression directed at women, the blasé attitude towards derogatory discussion of women, are things that occur across Canada, not just across the legal profession.

I am also not inclined to think that sanctions or discipline are the answer. I never seriously considered complaining about XY's conduct to the law society – the personal exposure and costs of being a complainant to my career and life were not something I wanted to bear. My guess is that my reaction is the typical one. I also do not think post-facto reactions are the most effective tool in relation to any ethical issue.

Yet I cannot suggest that we give up – I will not suggest that. My niece is entering this profession and one day my daughter may do so. I never want them to experience what I did, or to live their professional lives making an effort to avoid it happening – going along with sexist banter in fear of being an outsider or a target. I refuse to believe that we cannot do better. If we can learn to call each other learned friends, and express our most hostile thoughts with respect, then surely we can try to create a culture where the subject of our colleagues' "hotness" is not discussed, where we create appropriate separation between professional and sexual interactions, where senior lawyers embrace the limits on personal interactions that come with seniority and power, and where drinking much too much is not a normal condition of social interactions between lawyers.

That learning comes through acculturation. And I have told this story as much as anything in the hopes that it will begin productive conversations and – hopefully – further progress towards that kind of change.

NOTES AND QUESTIONS

1. What do you think the goal of the regulator should be in regulating harassment? What is the public interest that this sort of regulation ought to be directed at?

2. Craig, Downie and Salyzyn set out some of the advantages and risks associated with mandatory reporting obligations, and some of the ways in which a mandatory reporting rule could be drafted. In light of Woolley's experience of harassment as a young lawyer, which regulatory approach to you see as most promising? What are the risks and benefits of each?

Scenario Five

Your provincial law society has decided to adopt a mandatory reporting obligation.

They are trying to decide, however, whether that obligation ought to apply only to sexual harassment or whether it should apply to all types of lawyer misconduct – for example, acting in a conflict of interest or violating confidentiality. Based on these excerpts, and on the other topics you have covered in the course, advise the law society on the scope the mandatory reporting obligation ought to have.

Scenario Six

Draft a mandatory reporting obligation with respect to sexual harassment, taking into account the issues, concerns and objectives identified in these excerpts.

[d] Lawyers' Fees

As discussed in Chapter 2, the Federation of Law Societies' Model Code governs lawyers' fees. Lawyers' fees must be fair and reasonable, and the basis for charging those fees must be disclosed in a timely fashion. What is fair and reasonable depends on a number of factors, including the lawyers' time and effort, the difficulty and importance of the matter, and the results obtained.

Lawyers' fees are also regulated through the assessment process created by the rules of court in different provinces (often called taxation). That process helps lawyers collect their accounts, but also gives clients the opportunity to have their bills reviewed and reduced by a judicial officer.

In a 2004 paper, Alice Woolley reviewed law society disciplinary decisions and taxation cases and argued that unethical billing practices are a problem in the Canadian legal profession. She identified issues related to lawyers overworking files through overstaffing and excessive research, deficient recording of time and dishonesty. She proposed various regulatory reforms.[17] The following excerpt provides a more recent articulation of the issues with lawyer billing and how to improve fee regulation. In reading this excerpt consider the following questions:

- What does the public interest require in relation to the regulation of lawyers' fees?

- Lawyers' fees places lawyers and clients' interests in conflict (lawyers want to earn more; clients to pay less). How does that conflict relate to the general principles against lawyers acting in circumstances where their interests conflict with those of their clients?

- What regulatory mechanism is most likely to be efficient and effective in regulating fees: law society regulation of individual lawyers, law society regulation of law firms, assessment processes, civil litigation?

NOEL SEMPLE

"Shady Billing: Closing the Hall of Shame"
slaw.ca January 30, 2018
[Citations Omitted]

Only "fair and reasonable" fees and disbursements can be charged by lawyers to

---

[17] Alice Woolley, "Time for Change: Unethical Hourly Billing and How to Fix It" (2004) 83 Can. Bar Rev. 859.

their clients. This rule is uncontroversial, and applies across the country. Nevertheless, the following billing practices are used by some Canadian firms, and not clearly forbidden by regulation:

- a retainer contract lists current hourly rates but also provides that the firm can increase those rates as much as it wants, at any point in the future without the client's further consent

- a retainer can also allow a firm to both charge for each hour docketed, and charge the client whatever bonus the firm decides is appropriate based on results obtained

- a partner may perform a task personally, despite knowing that an associate or clerk within the firm with a lower hourly rate could do it just as well and just as quickly

- disbursements create profit for some firms, because they are charged to clients at rates well in excess of cost (e.g. 25 or 50 cents per page of printing)

(Please add your own hall of shame billing practices in the comments, without naming names.)

Here, I will suggest that regulators should be much more specific about what is and is not fair and reasonable. Unethical billing undermines the reputation of all legal professionals, including the majority who abjure such practices. The ethical pitfalls of time-based billing are perhaps best known. However, contingency billing creates its own temptations.

A fair and reasonable legal fee isn't necessarily a low fee or one that's easy for the client to afford. But a fair and reasonable fee must be clearly comprehensible to the average client at the time the client retains the lawyer. It must also reflect the reasonable expectations of the client at the conclusion of the matter. A fair and reasonable fee must be consonant with legal professionals' fiduciary obligation to not take advantage of superior knowledge to enrich themselves at clients' expense.

The Rules we Need

Here are a few ideas for putting regulatory meat on the bones of "fair and reasonable:"

- Every minute that a client pays for should actually have been worked on the client's matter. . . . Regulation could require a one-minute billing increment, or allow increments of no more than six minutes but require tasks taking less than 3 minutes to be rounded down to 0.

- Billable hour rates should not change during a retainer. ...

- Every decision or recommendation that costs a client money should be made with exclusive regard to the best interest of the client, and with no regard to the profitability of the firm. . .

- This "best interest of the client" rule would also apply in non-time-billed retainers. Some contingency and fixed-fee retainers entitle the firm to an increased percentage of recovery, or a new fixed fee, if a matter proceeds beyond a certain point. . . . ..

624

- Referrals should be made with exclusive reference to the best interest of the client, and no regard to the referral fee or other incentives available to the referring firm.

- Disbursements charged to clients should never be a source of profit or other benefit for law firms. . . .

- In many provinces, Commentary in the Code says that "what is a fair and reasonable fee will depend on such factors" as "results obtained" and "whether special skill or service has been required and provided." The Rules should stipulate that these factors do not mean that a bill can be increased beyond the amount explicitly authorized by the initial retainer. Similarly, if a retainer entitles a firm to bill for time spent but also to a success fee, the method of calculation for the success fee must be explicit.

Prohibiting billing practices that are clearly unfair and unreasonable would improve the trustworthiness of all legal professionals. It would also make legal services more affordable, at least for the unfortunate clients who are currently exposed to these practices.

. . . . .

NOTES AND QUESTIONS

1. Do you think we need active regulation of lawyers' fees, or will the market take care of it? In answering this question consider the nature of the market for legal services and the excerpts included in the chapter on access to justice.

2. Having read these excerpts, how would you identify the public interest in relation to the regulation of lawyers' fees? In answering this question consider it from the perspective of clients, lawyers, the judiciary, the state and the general public.

Scenario Seven

The Federation of Law Societies wants to revise the *Model Code* rules governing legal fees and has asked you to advise it as to which of the recommendations from Semple it should adopt. Provide that advice to the Federation, and then draft an amended version of Rule 3.6-1 of the *Model Code* to incorporate that advice.

(e) Family Law Practice

With the exception of lawyers practicing in the area of criminal law, law society regulation generally treats all areas of legal practice in the same way. Commentary to the rules will sometimes identify ethical issues specific to one type of practice, but more often the codes articulate the rules as applicable to all lawyers in more or less the same way.

Doing so can create a problem, insofar as some areas of practice raise distinct ethical issues. Lawyers representing a party with insurance, for example, have ethical issues arising with respect to the fact that the party paying the fees (the insurance company) is not the same as the party being represented (the insured).[18]

Family law raises unique ethical issues. The lawyers' clients are the separating parents; however, the representation has the capacity to affect the interests of the children, and the legal test governing many family law decisions is the "best interests of the child".[19] In that case, should the ethical duties of the lawyer have to take into account the child who is not the lawyer's client? Commentary 4 to Rule 5.1-1 of the *Model Code* says that when a child's interests might be affected by litigation, "a lawyer should advise the client to take into account the best interests of the child, if this can be done without prejudicing the legitimate interests of the client". But is that enough?

Another distinct feature of family law is that the litigants often have to continue to deal with each other after the litigation concludes (if the litigation ever concludes). They need to continue to parent the children of the marriage. Clients or lawyers in family law litigation may be attracted to the traditional adversarial model of dispute resolution; however, that model may be unsuitable for achieving the interests of parties who may need to deal with each other on a long-term basis.

The following excerpts are non-mandatory guidelines from the Law Society of British Columbia for family law lawyers and a blog arguing for further regulation for family law lawyers. In reviewing these excerpts, consider the following questions:

- What does the public interest require in relation to the regulation of specific areas of legal practice, including family law lawyers?

- What is the relevance to regulating family law lawyers of the fact that a large number (as many as 70%) of family law litigants are self-represented?

- Would it be better for law society codes of conduct to regulate specific areas of practice, rather than regulating all lawyers in a similar way?

LAW SOCIETY OF BRITISH COLUMBIA

"Common-sense guidelines for family law lawyers"
May 1, 2013

. . . . .

Best practice guidelines for lawyers practising family law

Lawyers involved in a family law dispute should strive to ensure it is conducted in the following manner:

1. Lawyers should be constructive, respectful and seek to minimize conflict and should encourage clients to do likewise.*

2. Lawyers should strive to remain objective at all times, and not to

---

[18] Case law addresses this issue, and generally provides that the lawyer "owes a duty to fully represent and protect the interst of the insured": *Pembridge Insurance Co. v. Parlee*, [2005] N.B.J. No. 174, 2005 NBCA 49 at para. 17 (N.B.C.A.).

[19] *Divorce Act* R.S.C. 1985 c.3 s. 16(8).

over-identify with clients or be unduly influenced by the emotions of the moment.

3. Lawyers should avoid using inflammatory language in spoken or written communications, and should encourage clients to do likewise.

4. Lawyers should caution clients about the limited relevance of allegations or evidence of conduct.

5. Lawyers should avoid actions that have the sole or predominant purpose of hindering, delaying or bullying an opposing party, and should encourage clients to do likewise.

6. Lawyers cannot participate in, and should caution clients against, any actions that are dishonest, misleading or undertaken for an improper purpose.

7. Lawyers should keep clients advised of, and encourage clients to consider, at all stages of the dispute:

   (a) the risks and costs of any proposed actions or communications;

   (b) both short and long term consequences;

   (c) the consequences for any children involved; and

   (d) the importance of court orders or agreements.

8. Lawyers should advise clients that clients are in a position of trust in relation to their children, and that:

   (a) it is important for clients to put their children's interests before their own; and

   (b) failing to do so may have a significant impact on both the children's well-being and the client's case.

9. At all stages of the dispute, lawyers should advise and encourage their clients to consider all available and suitable resources for resolving the dispute, in or out of court.

* Lawyers are not obliged to assist persons who are being disrespectful or abusive.

JOHN-PAUL BOYD

"The Need for a Code of Conduct for Family Law Disputes"
slaw.ca April 29, 2016
[Citations Omitted]

The Codes of Conduct of Canada's various law societies set the standards of conduct expected of members of the profession. . . .

The Codes of Conduct require us to find a balance between our obligations as advocates and the general duty to uphold the rule of law and practice with honour and integrity. It seems to me, however, that bar admission courses, intending to simultaneously instill a healthy respect for practice standards and a dread fear of complaints, often emphasize the former at the expense of the latter. We are taught that we owe an undivided fealty to our clients.

. . . . .

It occurs to me that this vision of advocacy – the lawyer as champion, resolutely engaged in battle within the confines of an obscure chivalric code – is perhaps incompatible with the broader duties owed by counsel in the context of family law disputes. With the greatest of respect to my licensing bodies, the Codes of Conduct ill serve both our clients and their children.

. . . . .

There are. . . a number of critical differences between non-family disputes and family disputes:

1. family law disputes concern adults engaged in the most non-arm's-length relationship imaginable, whose personal relationship is ongoing and will continue after trial;

2. the dispute affects people other than the parties, as the parties' children, extended family members and new partners may all be impacted by the conduct of the dispute and its outcome;

3. the issues involved are often intangible and insusceptible to quantification — rather than dealing with the cost of a collapsed deal or the speed and state of repair of a car involved in an accident, family law disputes often concern parenting capacity, employability, personality disorders and well-being;

4. the conclusion of the trial, and the expiry of the appeal period, does not signal the end of litigation, as family law disputes may continue into the indefinite future where support and children are at issue;

5. the evidence at trial does not concern a closed event occurring in the past, but an ongoing series of events which continues to the present; and,

6. the object of the litigation is not an award of damages to address the consequences of the past event but securing the best possible future for the separated family, with respect to both finances and the care of any children.

In other words, family law disputes concern the indiscernible future, not the known past, and have repercussions affecting the day to day wellbeing of children. As a result, and except for specific issues such as the imputation of income or the payment of arrears, the resolution of family law disputes rarely involves "winning" and "losing" and such should not be the goal of counsel.

. . . .

We need, I suggest, a new code for family law matters, or at least amendments to the old, which:

1. directs counsel to critically assess clients' instructions, and discuss those instructions with the client, in light of the circumstances of the case and the range of probable outcomes;

2. directs counsel to develop strategy taking into account the impact that the strategy will likely have on any children, the degree of conflict the strategy will likely entail, the complexity of the case and the need to promote future family functioning;

3. directs counsel to give equal priority to the interests and needs of the children and the interests and objectives of the client when developing strategy and advocating on behalf of the client;

4. allows counsel to refuse instructions which, if followed, are likely to unreasonably or unnecessarily inflame conflict, negatively affect the health, welfare or security of the children or commence a useless process;

5. directs counsel to consider settlement opportunities, and discuss those opportunities with the client, at each stage of a family law proceeding; and,

6. directs counsel to promote the rights of children under art. 12 of the UN Convention on the Rights of the Child in any family law process, judicial or otherwise, affecting their interests.

NOTES AND QUESTIONS

1. How might a lawyer, as Boyd suggests, "give equal priority to the interests and needs of the children"? How would the lawyer identify those interests and needs? On what basis would the lawyer disagree with a client's assessment of those interests and needs, given that it is the client who is the child's parent? If the lawyer did so, would the parent be receiving advocacy? If the lawyer did not, would the lawyer be acting with respect for the law given the legal recognition of the "best interests of the child"? Do you prefer Boyd's articulation of the Rule, or that contained in *Model Code* Rule 5.1-1, Commentary 4?

2. Boyd suggests that the Code should allow "counsel to refuse instructions which, if followed, are likely to unreasonably or unnecessarily inflame conflict, negatively affect the health, welfare or security of the children or commence a useless process". Do you think this is a desirable change? What would it do to the balance of power between a lawyer and a family law litigant? Do you see any heightened risks where the client is a woman or racialized? On what basis should a lawyer decide that a process is "useless" or will "unreasonably or unnecessarily inflame conflict"?

3. Should the BC Guidelines be mandatory? Why or why not?

4. Neither the BC Guidelines nor Boyd address the relationship between family law lawyers and self-represented litigants. Should they? What sort of guidelines should lawyers have when dealing with self-represented litigants? See: Karen Dyck "Lawyers and Self-Represented Litigants", slaw.ca (April 20, 2016); Malcolm Mercer, "Self-Represented Parties and Sharp Practice by Counsel – Should We Be Thinking Differently?" slaw.ca (November 22, 2018).

5. What benefits and what risks do you see from identifying distinct ethical duties for family law lawyers? Should codes or law societies provide rules or guidance directed at other specific practice areas?

Scenario Eight

Review Boyd's recommendations for a new code for family law matters, or amendments to the *Model code*. Assess which three recommendations you think are most likely to promote the public interest in the practice of law and articulate the basis for that opinion. Then, draft new provisions to the *Model Code* (or amendments to current provisions of the *Model Code*) to incorporate those three recommendations.

[f] Diversity

A significant challenge for the legal profession, including for legal regulators, has been ensuring the legal profession reflects the diversity of the general population. The profession does not reflect the racial diversity of Canadian society:

> Since 2001, the proportion of racialized lawyers in the Ontario legal profession has doubled, rising from 9% of the profession in 2001 to 18% in 2014 This is compared to 23% of the Ontario population who indicated in the 2006 Canada Census that they are racialized and 26% of the Ontario population who indicated in the 2011 National Household Survey that they are racialized.[20]

The profession has also not achieved racial equality. An engagement process by the Law Society of Ontario identified "widespread barriers experienced by racialized licensees within the professions at all stages of their careers".[21] It also found that "racialized licensees have a lower success rate in securing job placements, finding first jobs and securing suitable practice environments. Moreover, racialized licensees felt that they were disadvantaged in law school and that they had not advanced in their careers at the same rate as their non-racialized colleague".[22]

The Trinity Western case, discussed earlier, shows some of the challenges faced by 2SLBTQ+ people in ensuring equal status and acceptance in the profession.

The profession has also struggled to achieve gender equality; while women have made enormous progress relative to their almost complete absence from the profession in the 1960s, they remain under-represented in many spheres of professional life, particularly law firm partnership, and have had less success relative to women in other traditionally male-dominated professions.[23] Women lawyers of colour face additional barriers to achieving professional success.[24]

---

[20] Law Society of Upper Canada, Challenges Faced by Racialized Licensees Working Group Final Report, "Working Together for Change: Strategies to Address Systemic Racism in the Legal Professions" September 22, 2016.

[21] Working Group Final Report, Appendix A.

[22] Working Group Final Report, Appendix A. See also, Joshua Sealy-Harrington, "(Dis)proving Racism: A Rebuttal to Klippenstein's Critical Review of the Law Society of Ontario's Report on Challenges Facing Racialized Licensees", ablawg.ca (February 20, 2020).

[23] See Alice Woolley & Elysa Darling, "Nasty Women and the Rule of Law" (2017) 51 U.S.F. L. Rev. 479; Christine Dobby, "At Bay Street's Top Law Firms, Pay and Power Gaps are Well-Kept Secrets – But Women are Struggling Toward Equity", *Globe and Mail* (February 6, 2021); Robyn Doolittle & Christine Dobby, "Female partners earned nearly 25 per cent less than male colleagues at a major Toronto law firm, document shows", *Globe and Mail* (February 9, 2021).

[24] See Tsedale M. Melaku, "Why Women and People of Color in Law Still Hear: 'You Don't Look Like a Lawyer" *Harvard Business Review* (August 7, 2019), online: https://hbr.

While the reasons and solutions for the profession's failure to achieve diversity extend beyond lawyer regulation, law societies have recognized the need and opportunity for regulatory responses to facilitate the accomplishment of a more diverse profession. In 2016, the Law Society of Upper Canada's "Challenges Faced by Racialized Licensees Working Group" published a Report with 13 recommendations intended to help it achieve three key objectives: ensuring inclusive workplaces, "reducing the barriers created by racism, unconscious bias and discrimination" and achieving better representation of racialized lawyers in the profession. Those recommendations were approved by Convocation — the governing body of the Law Society. The following excerpt sets out those recommendations.[25] In reading them, consider: which of these recommendations do you believe would be the most effective? What other recommendations do you think the Working Group could have identified?

LAW SOCIETY OF UPPER CANADA

"Working Together for Change: Strategies to Address Systemic Racism in the Legal Professions"
December, 2016[*]

Recommendation 1 — Reinforcing Professional Obligations

The Law Society will review and amend, where appropriate, the Rules of Professional Conduct, the Paralegal Rules of Conduct, and Commentaries to reinforce the professional obligations of all licensees to recognize, acknowledge and promote principles of equality, diversity and inclusion consistent with the requirements under human rights legislation and the special responsibilities of licensees in the legal and paralegal professions.

Recommendation 2 — Diversity and Inclusion Project

The Law Society will work with stakeholders, such as interested legal workplaces, legal associations, law schools and paralegal colleges to develop model policies and resources to address the challenges faced by racialized licensees.

Recommendation 3 — The Adoption of Equality, Diversity and Inclusion Principles and Practices

The Law Society will:

1) require every licensee to adopt and to abide by a statement of principles acknowledging their obligation to promote equality, diversity and inclusion generally, and in their behaviour towards colleagues, employees, clients and the public;

2) require a licensee representative of each legal workplace of at least 10 licensees in Ontario to develop, implement and maintain a human

---

org/2019/08/why-women-and-people-of-color-in-law-still-hear-you-dont-look-like-a-lawyer.

[25] The excerpt has been edited to incorporate one small change between the document as submitted and as approved by Convocation.

[*] © 2016, The Law Society of Upper Canada. Reproduced with permission of The Law Society of Upper Canada.

rights/diversity policy for their legal workplace addressing at the very least fair recruitment, retention and advancement, which will be available to members of the professions and the public upon request;

3) require a licensee representative of each legal workplace of at least 10 licensees in Ontario to complete, every two years, an equality, diversity and inclusion self-assessment for their legal workplace, to be provided to the Law Society; and

4) encourage legal workplaces to conduct inclusion surveys by providing them with sample templates.

Recommendation 4 — Measuring Progress through Quantitative Analysis

Each year, the Law Society will measure progress quantitatively by providing legal workplaces of at least 25 licensees in Ontario with the quantitative self-identification data of their licensees compiled from the Lawyers Annual Report and the Paralegal Annual Report in a manner consistent with the best practices established to protect licensees vulnerable to harm that may flow from this disclosure, so they can compare their data with the aggregate demographic data gathered from the profession as a whole through the annual reports.

Recommendation 5 — Measuring Progress through Qualitative Analysis

The Law Society will measure progress by:

1) asking licensees to voluntarily answer inclusion questions, provided by the Law Society, about their legal workplace, every four years; and

2) compiling the results of the inclusion questions for each legal workplace of at least 25 licensees in Ontario and providing the legal workplace with a summary of the information gathered.

Recommendation 6 — Inclusion Index

Every four years, the Law Society will develop and publish an inclusion index that reflects the following information, including, for each legal workplace of at least 25 licensees: the legal workplace's self-assessment information (Recommendation 3(3)), demographic data obtained from the Lawyer Annual Report and Paralegal Annual Report (Recommendation 4) and information gathered from the inclusion questions provided by the Law Society (Recommendation 5).

Recommendation 7 — Repeat Challenges Faced by Racialized Licensees Project Inclusion Survey

The Law Society will conduct inclusion surveys with questions similar to those asked in Appendix F of the Stratcom Challenges Faced by Racialized Licensees Final Report (March 11, 2014) (available online . . .). The first inclusion survey will be conducted within one year of the adoption of these recommendations, and thereafter every four years, subject to any recommendation by the Equity and Aboriginal Issues Committee to Convocation.

Recommendation 8 — Progressive Compliance Measures

The Law Society will consider and enact, as appropriate, progressive compliance measures for legal workplaces that do not comply with the requirements proposed in Recommendation 3 and/or legal workplaces that are identified as having systemic barriers to diversity and inclusion.

Recommendation 9 — Continuing Professional Development (CPD) Programs on Topics of Equality and Inclusion in the Professions

The Law Society will:

1) launch a three-hour accredited program focused on advancing equality and inclusion in the professions;

2) develop resources to assist legal workplaces in designing and delivering their own three-hour program focused on advancing equality and inclusion in the professions, to be accredited by the Law Society; and

3) require each licensee to complete three hours of an accredited program focused on equality and inclusion within the first three years following the adoption of these recommendations and one hour per year every year thereafter, which will count towards the licensee's professionalism hours for that year.

Recommendation 10 — The Licensing Process

The Law Society will include the topics of cultural competency, equality and inclusion in the professions as competencies to be acquired in the Licensing Process.

Recommendation 11 — Building Communities of Support

The Law Society, in collaboration with legal associations where appropriate, will provide support to racialized licensees in need of direction and assistance through mentoring and networking initiatives.

Recommendation 12 — Addressing Complaints of Systemic Discrimination

The Law Society, in light of the findings of this project and emerging issues in the professions, will:

1) review the function, processes and structure of the Discrimination and Harassment Counsel Program (DHC), including considering effective ways for the DHC to address issues of systemic discrimination;

2) revise the Rules of Professional Conduct and the Paralegal Rules of Conduct, where appropriate, so that systemic discrimination and reprisal for complaints of discrimination and harassment are clearly identified as breaches of professional conduct requirements;

3) create effective ways for the Professional Regulation Division to address complaints of systemic discrimination; and

4) create a specialized and trained team to address complaints of discrimination.

Recommendation 13 — Leading by Example

1) The Law Society will continue to monitor and assess internal policies, practices and programs, to promote diversity, inclusion and equality within the workplace and in the provision of services by:

    a) as required, adopting, implementing and maintaining a human rights/diversity policy addressing at the very least fair recruitment, retention and advancement;

b) measuring quantitative progress through a census of the workforce or other method;

c) measuring qualitative progress by conducting inclusion surveys;

d) conducting regular equality, diversity and inclusion self-assessments; and

e) based on the results from b), c) and d), identifying gaps and barriers and adopting measures to address the gaps and barriers;

f) publishing relevant findings from b), c), d) and e); and

g) providing equality and inclusion education programs for staff at the Law Society on a regular basis.

2) The Law Society will:

a) conduct an internal diversity assessment of the bencher composition and publicize the results;

b) provide equality and inclusion education programs for Convocation on a regular basis.

NOTES AND QUESTIONS

1. The Recommendations emphasize the importance of principles of equality, diversity and inclusion. The Report does not define inclusion, but includes a quotation saying "Inclusion is not about bringing people into what already exists; it is making a new space, a better space for everyone". What do you see as the key attributes of an inclusive profession? What do you think are the principles of equality, diversity and inclusion? Do you think the Recommendations will contribute to the creation of an inclusive profession as you understand it? Why or why not? What recommendations would assist in accomplishing that goal?

2. Recommendation 3 requires law firms with 10 or more lawyers to develop, implement and maintain a human rights/diversity policy, and to complete an equality, diversity and inclusion self-assessment every two years. This recommendation gives flexibility and autonomy to law firms about what such a policy would include, although Recommendation 8 does permit the Law Society to address workplaces that have not prepared such polies or self-assessments. Do you think that is the right approach? Why or why not?

3. Recommendations 4 through 7 focus on the collection of data about inclusion. Do you think the collection of data will have a positive effect on the hiring and retention of racialized lawyers? Will it have other positive effects on diversity and inclusion? Could it have negative effects? What might those be?

4. Recommendation 9 requires lawyers to complete Continuing Professional Development on equality and inclusion every year. What do you think the

CPD should address? What do you think law schools could do to enhance diversity and inclusion in the legal profession?

Recommendation 3(1) directed the Law Society to "require every licensee to adopt and to abide by a statement of principles acknowledging their obligation to promote equality, diversity and inclusion generally, and in their behaviour towards colleagues, employees, clients and the public". In 2017, the Law Society began implementation of this requirement, notifying its members in September 2017 that they would be required to confirm that they had adopted a Statement of Principles in their annual report.[26] In November 2017, it published a Guide for Law Society members as to how to complete the Statement of Principles.[27] It also advised them that for the 2017 Annual Report there would be no sanctions for non-compliance.[28]

The requirement that lawyers provide a Statement of Principles proved controversial. Opponents claimed that it violated lawyers' freedom of conscience and expression. Surprisingly, some also challenged the premise underlying the requirement, that systemic racism is a significant issue in the legal profession that undermines the inclusion, advancement and success of racialized lawyers.[29] Two opponents, Professor Ryan Alford of Lakehead University and Toronto lawyer Murray Klippenstein, commenced a legal challenge to the validity of the requirement (excerpted below). Some supported the Statement of Principles but argued that it did not go far enough to address racism in the profession.[30]

The opposition to the Statement of Principles culminated in members of the Law Society running as a "StopSOP" slate in the bencher election of that year. 22 of the slate's members were elected to office.

Following the election, the Law Society's governing body, Convocation, had difficult and divisive discussions about the future of the Statement of Principles. Ultimately, on September 11, 2019 after a majority of Convocation voted to repeal the mandatory Statement of Principles requirement, Convocation approved a motion stating:

> **That**: the Law Society shall require every lawyer licensee to acknowledge in the
> lawyer annual report that, in accordance with the Rules of Professional Conduct,
> the lawyer has a special responsibility to respect the requirements of human rights

---

[26] *Alford v. The Law Society of Upper Canada*, [2018] O.J. No. 3653, 2018 ONSC 4269 at para. 9 (Ont. S.C.J.).

[27] *Alford v. The Law Society of Upper Canada*, [2018] O.J. No. 3653, 2018 ONSC 4269 at para. 10 (Ont. S.C.J.).

[28] *Alford v. The Law Society of Upper Canada*, [2018] O.J. No. 3653, 2018 ONSC 4269 at para. 11 (Ont. S.C.J.).

[29] See discussion in Malcolm Mercer, "The Statement of Principles and Inter-Bubble Communication about Racism", slaw.ca (January 17, 2018) and Joshua Sealy-Harrington, "(Dis)proving Racism: A Rebuttal to Klippenstein's Critical Review of the Law Society of Ontario's Report on Challenges Facing Racialized Licensees", ablawg.ca (February 20, 2020).

[30] Atrisha Lewis, "A personal reflection on the statement of principles resistance", *Canadian Lawyer* (January 15, 2018) (Ms. Lewis is a bencher of the Law Society of Ontario).

laws in force in Ontario and, specifically, to honour the obligation not to discriminate on the grounds of race, ancestry, place of origin, colour, ethnic origin, citizenship, creed, sex, sexual orientation, gender identity, gender expression, age, record of offences (as defined in the Ontario Human Rights Code), marital status, family status, or disability with respect to professional employment of other lawyers, articled students, or any other person or in professional dealings with other licensees or any other person: and

That: the Law Society shall require every paralegal licensee to acknowledge in the paralegal annual report that, in accordance with the Paralegal Rules of Professional Conduct, the paralegal has the obligation to respect the requirements of human rights laws in force in Ontario and without restricting the generality of the foregoing, a paralegal shall not discriminate on the grounds of race, ancestry, place of origin, colour, ethnic origin, citizenship, creed, sex, sexual orientation, gender identity, gender expression, age, record of offences, marital status, family status or disability with respect to the employment of others or in dealings with other licensees or any other person.

The motion passed 27-18 with five abstentions.

The Statement of Principles requirement, and reactions to it, raise questions about how and to what extent law societies ought to ameliorate racism and foster diversity and inclusion in the practice of law. The following excerpts allow further consideration of these questions.

The first is from the Application of Alford and Klippenstein to the Ontario Superior Court of Justice (Divisional Court) seeking judicial review of the enactment of the Statement of Principles. The second is from an article by Joshua Sealy-Harrington challenging the premises and analysis of critics of the Statement of Principles, including Alford and Klippenstein.

Much of the focus in the discussion of the Statement of Principles in the excerpts (and elsewhere), especially in parts not included here, is with respect to the constitutional validity of the Statement of Principles requirement. In reading the excerpts, however, you should focus on the regulatory questions and, in particular:

1. Is a statement of principles requirement, as it was or as it is now, an efficient and effective exercise of a regulator's mandate to protect the public interest in the practice of law?

2. How can the law society contribute to ameliorating systemic racism that undermines the opportunities and advancement of Indigenous, Black and other lawyers of colour? Consider this question in light of the existence of racism in the practice of law, in the legal system and in society generally.

3. Recommendation 3(1) is one of numerous recommendations made by the Working Group. Which Recommendation (or Recommendations) do you think would best address systemic racism and barriers to equality in the legal profession?

ALFORD AND KLIPPENSTEIN v. LAW SOCIETY OF UPPER CANADA

Notice of Application for Judicial Review (as amended)
November 6, 2016
[Citations Omitted][31]

THE APPLICANTS MAKE AN APPLICATON FOR:

A Declaration that the Law Society of Upper Canada's requirement that licensees are required to create and abide by an individual Statement of Principles. . . is not supported by the *Rules of Professional Conduct* or the *Paralegal Rules of Conduct*.

A declaration that licensees do not have an obligation under the *Rules of Professional Conduct*. . . or otherwise to promote equality, diversity and inclusion generally and in licensees' behaviour towards colleagues, employees, clients and the public.

In addition and in the alternative, a Declaration that the requirement to complete the Statement of Principles, and the obligation on the part of licensees to promote equality, diversity and inclusion generally and in licensees' behaviour towards colleagues, employees, clients and the public, to the extent that there exists such an obligation under the *Rules of Professional Conduct*. . .are each *ultra vires* the *Law Society Act*, R.S.O. 1990, c. L-8 (the "LSA").

. . . . .

In the alternative, a Declaration that the requirement to complete the Statement of Principles shall be interpreted as follows:

a) The requirement requires licenses to affirm existing obligations under the *Rules of Professional Conduct*. . . to comply with human rights laws.

b) The requirement shall not be interpreted to mean that licensees have an obligation to endorse, demonstrate a personal valuing of, or profess any specific belief or value, or that licensees have an obligation to persuade anyone about anything or be persuaded by anyone about anything.

c) The requirement applies only to the professional conduct of licensees with each other, with employees, with clients and with the public.

d) The requirement shall not be interpreted as imposing any new obligation that licensees will or must take, or any specific actions that licensees will or must take.

e) The requirement shall not be interpreted as derogating from or impinging upon licensees' rights of free thought, opinion and expression, including, but not limited to, the right to hold and express the opinion that licensees should not be compelled to complete a Statement of Principles or promote or adopt any value, or a particular interpretation of a value.

THE GROUNDS FOR THE APPLICATION ARE

. . . . .

Pursuant to s. 4.1 of the LSA, it is a function of the Law Society to ensure that all

---

[31] Available online at: https://theccf.ca/wp-content/uploads/Fresh-As-Amended-Notice-of-Application-MATTHEWS-Alford-v-LSUC-Asher.pdf.

persons who practise law in Ontario or provide legal services in Ontario meet standards of learning, professional competence and professional conduct that are appropriate for the legal services they provide.

Pursuant to s. 4.2 of the LSA, in carrying out its functions, duties and powers under the LSA, the Law Society has a duty to protect the public interest, to maintain and advance the cause of justice and the rule of law, to facilitate access to justice for the people of Ontario, and to act in a timely, open and efficient manner.

[The application then references Rules 2.1-1, 5.6-1, 6.3.1-1 and 6.3.1-2 of the Law Society of Ontario Rules of Conduct, along with the *Human Rights Code* R.S.O. 1990, c. H.19]

At the December 2, 2016 meeting of convocation the Law Society adopted a new Statement of Principles requirement . . . The Statement of Principles requirement was one of 13 recommendations before Convocation on that date. Some of the recommendations also had numerous sub-recommendations. In total, there were 23 individual recommendations or sub-recommendations before Convocation.

The Law Society adopted the requirement for a Statement of Principles based entirely upon *Recommendation 3(1) in the Challenges Faced by Racialized Licensees Working Group's Final Report*, which was prepared by the Equity Initiatives Department.

On December 2, 2016, Convocation first heard a preliminary motion that the 13 recommendations should each be voted on separately. This motion was dismissed, and the Statement of Principles requirement was therefore voted on together with all of the other recommendations before Convocation.

During the meeting of Convocation on December 2, 2016, certain benchers who were in favour of the new Statement of Principles requirement articulated the view that the purpose of the Statement of Principles requirement was to change the "mentality" and "culture" of the bar, so that all licensees would "come to the same understanding and belief system."

Convocation did not invite any licensee to make submissions before it on or before December 2, 2016 regarding the proposed adoption of the Statement of Principles. . .

The Law Society does not require licensees to submit their Statement of Principles to the Law Society or distribute them to other lawyers, to clients, or to any other member of the legal community or the public. Licensees are required to keep a copy of their Statement of Principles on file.

. . . . .

The deadline to create and abide by an individual Statement of Principles was December 31, 2017. The Law Society stated publicly that it would not sanction licensees who failed to do so by December 31, 2017. However, should licensees fail to create and abide by an individual Statement of Principles going forward, they may be subject to disciplinary sanction, including administrative suspension, by the Law Society.

The Law Society has not moved to amend the *Rules of Professional Conduct*. . .

The Law Society has created a page to accompany the requirement to complete the Statement of Principles entitled "Key Concepts of a Statement of Principles." It states: "The **intention** of the statement of principles is to demonstrate a personal valuing of equality, diversity, and inclusion with respect to the employment of others, or in professional dealings with other licensees or any other person" [emphasis in original]. The Statement of Principles is therefore intended to be more than simply a reporting requirement. The requirement to complete the Statement of Principles is a requirement to "demonstrate a personal valuing" of certain values and the underlying obligation to promote equality, diversity and inclusion, to the extent one exists, which is denied, is an obligation to personally value equality, diversity and inclusion. The intent of the Statement of Principles requirement and the supposed underlying obligation to promote equality, diversity and inclusion is therefore to compel the expression of, the adherence to, and the belief in certain values.

The Law Society's Requirement is *ultra vires*

The Statement of Principles requires licensees to acknowledge and abide by an obligation that does not exist and has no legal foundation. The *Rules of Professional Conduct. . .* and the *[Human Rights] Code* do not currently impose an obligation upon licensees to "promote" diversity, equality or inclusion. The Statement of Principles therefore relies upon an incorrect or, alternatively, an unreasonable interpretation of the *Rules of Professional Conduct* and the *Code*.

The requirement that licensees complete the Statement of Principles, and the obligation to promote equality, inclusion and diversity generally and in a licensees' behaviour towards colleagues, employees, clients and the public, to the extent that such an obligation exists under the *Rules of Professional Conduct. . .*which is denied, each constitute an incorrect or, alternatively, an unreasonable interpretation of the Law Society's function to ensure an appropriate standard of learning, competence and professional conduct, and/or the Law Society's duties under s. 4.2 of the LSA.

[The Application then sets out the position that the Statement of Principles requirement violates s. 2(a) and (b) of the *Charter* and cannot be saved under s. 1]

The Adoption of the Statement of Principles is a Breach of Natural Justice

The applicants plead, and the fact is, that they and other licensees in the Province of Ontario were not afforded a reasonable opportunity to be heard prior to the adoption of the Statement of Principles Requirement, and that the decision to adopt the Statement of Principles, which affects the liberty of all Ontario licensees, was made without sufficient input from or consultation with Ontario licensees, including but not limited to the applicants.

In addition, the Law Society adopted the Statement of Principles in conjunction with 13 other recommendations and without considering the merits of the Statement of Principles in isolation. This further frustrated the ability of licensees to be heard on the merits of whether the Statement of Principles should be adopted. The applicants plead that the conduct of the Law Society amounts to a breach of natural justice.

. . . . .

An *Intra Vires* and *Charter*-Compliant Interpretation

In the alternative, the applicants submit that the requirement to complete the Statement of Principles must be interpreted in the manner that allows it to remain *intra vires* and in compliance with the *Charter*. In particular,

a.   The requirement requires licensees to affirm existing obligations under the *Rules of Professional Conduct. . .*to comply with human rights law.

b.   The requirement shall not be interpreted to mean that licensees have an obligation to endorse, demonstrate a personal valuing of, or profess any specific belief or value, or that licensees have an obligation to persuade anyone about anything or be persuaded by anyone about anything;

c.   The requirement applies only to the professional conduct of licensees with each other, with employees, with clients and with the public.

d.   The requirement shall not be interpreted as imposing any new obligation that licensees will or must take, or any specific actions that licensees will or must take.

e.   The requirement shall not be interpreted as derogating from or impinging upon licensees' rights of free thought, opinion and expression, including, but not limited to, the right to hold and express the opinion that licensees should not be compelled to complete a Statement of Principles or promote or adopt any value, or a particular interpretation of value.

. . . . .

JOSHUA SEALY-HARRINGTON

"Twelve Angry (White) Men: The Constitutionality of the Statement of Principles" (2020) 51 Ottawa L. Rev. 195
[Citations Omitted]

The other thing that disturbs me about this, and I suppose this is a consequence of my experience with delving deeply into the history of places like the Soviet Union in its early stages of development is that there's a class-based guilt phenomena that's lurking at the bottom of this, which is also absolutely, I would say, terrifying. — Jordan Peterson

My first instinct was to check my passport. Was I still in Canada, or had someone whisked me away to North Korea, where people must say what officials want to hear? —Bruce Pardy

This is the cultural enemy that has arisen within, after Western civilization routed the largely external and outright evils of Nazism and international Communism ... the law society is conferring capricious dictatorial powers on its own administration ... —Conrad Black

The chilling Orwellian language bears repeating ... Forcing lawyers to subscribe to a particular worldview for regulatory purposes is an unacceptable intrusion into a lawyer's liberty and promotes significant harm to the public. —Arthur Cockfield

[A] breed of hyper-progressive social activists who feel justified in co- opting the prerogatives of a regulatory monopoly as a means to force white-collar workers to lip-sync doctrinaire liberalism. It's creepy. It's coercive. It's presumably unconstitutional. And it's an embarrassment to the law society. — Jonathan Kay

Now the Law Society is demanding that I openly state that I am adopting, and will promote, and will implement "generally" in my daily life, two specific and pretty significant words or "principles," words that are quite vague but sound important. When I first read that a year ago I was completely floored. What is going on here? This sounds like I'm supposed to sign up to some newly discovered religion, or some newfangled political cult. — Murray Klippenstein

[T]here is one reason above all others why Ontario lawyers should not only refuse to sign on to the Law Society's "progressive agenda" but they should send the current Society's head office packing. That is the principle of "merit." Because most lawyers believe that a person should be hired, evaluated, and promoted solely on merit, and not on superficial criteria like ethnic origin, race, or gender, this view places these professionals in contravention to the "progressive agenda" of their professional association. To the Society, everything is about race and gender. That is simply wrong. — Brian Giesbrecht

Special interest groups have gained a foothold in convocation. They seek to erase our history, mandate ideological training and implement discriminatory race and sex-based quotas. I will stand up to special interest groups to defend our profession's proud traditions and values. — Nicholas Wright

[T]his Initiative by the LSO is profoundly disturbing ... It has certainly awoken the spirit of vigilance in me. In my view, it requires all lawyers of conscience to oppose this initiative in order to maintain and protect the cherished independence and liberties lawyers have inherited and to which they have been entrusted. — Michael Menear

If the requirement that I hold and promote values chosen by the Law Society is not repealed or invalidated, I will cease being a member of the legal profession in Ontario. This is not an outcome I desire ... However, I simply cannot remain a member of the legal profession in Ontario if to do so would violate some of my most deeply held conscientious beliefs. —Leonid Sirota

The requirement is ... the result of political ideology, rather than any evidence-based process, and ... deeply offensive to me personally in terms of its clear implication that I and my profession and society are racist. —Alec Bildy

As Shawn Richard, one of the architects of the Law Society's policy, asked: "What are you conscientiously objecting to?" ... It's easy to forget that decades of progress can be wiped out in an instant. Citizens who belong to religious groups subjected to significant persecution — especially those who have recently arrived as refugees from totalitarian states — can easily imagine the dangerous consequences of a values test compelled by forced speech ... I hope that as a *cranky old white man* I can make myself useful by defending their rights. —Ryan Alford

I. INTRODUCTION

The twelve impassioned quotes above concern a requirement that Ontario lawyers annually draft a statement reflecting on their professional and human rights obligations pertaining to diversity. Equality, it seems, is a divisive ideal; so divisive, in fact, that while the requirement was in force during the drafting and peer-review of this article, it was repealed on the same day my final revisions were due to the *Ottawa Law Review*. The evasive rationale behind opposition to this requirement was, most often, freedom of speech. I explain below, principally, how the requirement does not violate freedom of speech, and secondarily, how its opposition was not really about freedom of speech in any event.

The Law Society of Ontario (LSO) previously required all lawyers to "adopt and to abide by a statement of principles." The sole requirement of any Statement of Principles (SOP) was that it must acknowledge the lawyer's "obligation to promote equality, diversity and inclusion." Two lawyers — Ryan Alford and Murray Klippenstein — applied to judicially review the SOP requirement (Application). That Application alleged that the SOP requirement, among other things, violated lawyers' constitutional right to free speech by "compel[ling] licensees to communicate political expression." This paper explains why, to the contrary, the SOP requirement does no such thing. . . .

My analysis proceeds in three parts. First, I conduct a statutory analysis, including an explanation of the background to the SOP requirement. This statutory analysis is an essential antecedent inquiry to interpreting and resolving the SOP controversy. Two ships cross paths in this dispute as to the proper statutory interpretation of the SOP requirement: a right-bound ship requiring that lawyers *value* equality (SOP opponents) and a left-bound ship requiring that lawyers *acknowledge* existing equality law obligations (SOP proponents). We cannot assess the SOP critically or constitutionally without first choosing which ship best reflects the enacted text. And as I explain below, the left-bound ship better reflects the text, context, and purpose of the SOP requirement. Second, having chosen the left-bound ship, I then interpret the SOP controversy through a critical race theory lens. I explain how liberty claims — here, "free speech" — obscure the apparent motivation for sustained resistance to the modest SOP requirement, namely, opposition to diversity and denial of systemic racism. Third, I assess the SOP requirement's constitutionality

. . . . . .

II. STATUTORY ANALYSIS

A. Why the SOP Was Adopted

Systemic racism is a problem in Canada, despite views to the contrary. Articles abound illustrating systemic racism's reach within Canada's justice system, and similarly, the legal profession. With this concern in mind, the LSO established a Working Group on Challenges Faced by Racialized Licensees (Working Group), which "studied the experience of racialized licensees" and found they faced "widespread barriers."

[Sealy-Harrington reviews the history of the Working Group and adoption of the SOP]

B. What the SOP Required

According to the LSO's materials, the SOP was simply an *acknowledgement* of extant *obligations* — that "[t]he requirement will be satisfied by licensees acknowledging their ... existing legal and professional obligations." In stark contrast, the Applicants characterize the SOP as a *creator* of *novel obligations*. In my view, the former characterization best reflects the text, context, and purpose of the SOP requirement. In turn, as the SOP was anchored in extant legal obligations, analogizing it with values tests divorced from such obligations is inapt. It was, however, strategic for SOP opponents to mischaracterize the SOP's regulatory scope to advance a narrative of regulatory overreach. Indeed, a quirk of the SOP controversy is how both sides never reached agreement on the scope of the SOP, and thus, never meaningfully engaged with each other on the SOP's constitutionality. As I explain below, I interpret the SOP to be a mere regulatory acknowledgment. Accordingly, anti-SOP advocates, it seems, manufactured a phantom SOP requirement, and then leveraged that mythology for rhetorical purposes. In my understanding, *no one* argued in favour of regulating licensees' thoughts about equality; yet *most*, if not *all* anti-SOP advocates, presupposed such thought regulation to justify their constitutional posturing. They were thus, ironically, the architects of their own contrived oppression.

To interpret the SOP requirement, we must begin, of course, with its text, described by Cockfield as "chilling Orwellian language." In his analysis, Cockfield isolates the phrase "statement of principles" when interpreting the scope of the SOP requirement. This truncated analysis, however, deviates from established principles of statutory interpretation. The *full* text of the requirement reads as follows: "The Law Society will ... require every licensee to adopt and to abide by a statement of principles acknowledging their obligation to promote equality, diversity and inclusion generally, and in their behaviour towards colleagues, employees, clients and the public." Three points follow from the plain text of the SOP requirement: (1) it was mandatory, not optional ("require"); (2) it was an ongoing, not intermittent, obligation ("adopt" and "abide"); and (3) it was an acknowledgement of extant obligations, rather than a creator of novel obligations ("acknowledging their obligation").

That the SOP requirement was explicitly framed as an "acknowledgement" does not end the discussion. For example, if the SOP requirement mandated lawyers to conduct activities clearly outside existing obligations — *e.g.* to "acknowledge their obligation to discriminate against female articling students" — few scholars would respond that it is simply administrative. Indeed, such an acknowledgment would run directly counter to lawyers' obligations *not* to discriminate in their employment practices. But, on a textual basis, the SOP requirement appears to have been an acknowledgment of extant legal obligations.

. . . . .

The Guide reinforces the characterization of the SOP requirement as a mere acknowledgment. While I recognize that the Guide, unlike the SOP requirement, is not the product of Convocation, it is cited extensively by the Applicants and their supporters and thus warrants some discussion. The Guide repeatedly affirms the view that the SOP requirement created no new obligations, but instead, acknowledged existing ones: that it "reinforces existing obligations in the *Rules of Professional Conduct*"; that it pertains to "human rights laws in force in Ontario"; that it "does not create any obligation ... [but] will be satisfied by licensees acknowledging their obligation to take reasonable steps to cease or avoid conduct that creates and/or maintains barriers for racialized licensees or other equality-seeking groups"; that "[t]he reference to the obligation to promote equality, diversity and inclusion generally refers to existing legal and professional obligations in respect of human rights"; and that "[t]he content of the Statement of Principles does not create or derogate from, but rather reflects, professional obligations." This remains, of course, the LSO's framing. However, it is difficult to fathom the LSO seeking to impose novel obligations originating with the SOP — the Applicants' central concern — when the LSO has repeatedly and expressly opined to the contrary, and in a manner that could presumably be used in legal defense against the imposition of any such novel requirements in the future.

That the SOP requirement pertained to licensees' obligations in terms of *conduct*, not *thought*, follows from the requirement's phrasing. It referred to an "obligation to promote equality, diversity and inclusion generally, and *in* their *behaviour* towards colleagues, employees, clients and the public." On a truncated reading, one could argue that requiring lawyers to "promote equality" *per se*, demanded that they advocate for equality in their free time. But, when read as a whole, the emphasized language above — "in their behaviour" — suggests that the requirement to "promote equality" referred to ways in which one's "behaviour" (*e.g.* sexually harassing female colleagues) can impede (*i.e.* not promote) equality.

In this sense, the SOP requirement was more performative than declaratory; it required an acknowledgment of each licensees' obligation to *act* in accordance with extant obligations (in the hiring and treatment of employees, the provision of legal services, *etc.*), not that licensees *think* anything preordained about those obligations.

Lastly, the principle that absurd interpretations should be rejected favours an interpretation of the SOP requirement that does not extend to proselytizing equality. For example, Leonid Sirota writes that, on his interpretation of the SOP requirement, he is obligated to "devote [his] scholarship to the promotion of equality." But it would be absurd to think that the LSO — with a view to serving the "public interest" — created the SOP requirement, not only to ensure that all academic writing on equality adopted a homogenous position, but further, that all academic writing on any topic was directed exclusively towards advancing progressive equality principles. Surely the public interest is best served through diverse academic discourse on a range of topics, including those that have nothing to do with equality.

. . . . .

In sum, the SOP requirement mandated nothing more than "acknowledging" one's extant professional and human rights obligations. The following, then, would have met the requirement: "I acknowledge my existing professional and human rights obligations." That is what this controversy boils down to — the textual equivalent of checking a box next to an identical administrative phrase in an annual reporting form. However, one could go even further. While the SOP "need not include any statement of thought, belief or opinion," it certainly *could* — and that statement could have been as critical of the SOP, or equality rights generally, as the author desired. As noted, the SOP requirement only demanded that every SOP include an acknowledgment of existing regulatory obligations, not that it exclude any other content. Accordingly, the following statement would have also met the SOP requirement:

> I hate equality. I hate diversity. And I hate inclusion. The only thing our legal profession should care about is merit. And reverse discrimination initiatives that are founded on the Statement of Principles' ideology tokenize minorities, alienate

broad coalitions, and punish white men (including Jewish men) for the sole fact of their birth.

The tyrannical Statement of Principles is a useless half-assed attempt at PC thought control that is intolerable in a liberal society. The Law Society of Ontario should be ashamed for buying into the misguided far-left zeitgeist.

I begrudgingly acknowledge my existing professional and human rights obligations, but only because I am compelled to, and in no way out of a sincere belief that diversity — whatever that means — is important, or something the Law Society has any business concerning itself with in any event.

It follows that near limitless protest can be built into any given SOP should its author — in "good conscience" — so desire. In the words of Annamaria Enenajor, even a "closet neo-nazi" could draft an acceptable SOP. Further, the LSO does not scrutinize SOPs. There is no obligation on any lawyer to publicize their SOP, or to even disclose it to the LSO; lawyers need only "confirm its existence." Therefore, while the SOP had a modest requirement (*i.e.* acknowledging extant obligations), the LSO provided no substantive oversight. The Applicants claimed that meeting the SOP requirement — drafting virtually whatever statement they wanted, which no one would ever read — forced them "to cease practicing law." Given the wide latitude afforded to licensees in meeting this modest requirement, abandoning legal practice strikes me as disproportionate. At a minimum, if this dispute had ever reached the justification stage of the constitutional analysis — which, as I argue below, it should not — I strain to think of a more trivial incursion on free expression (which, in turn, strongly favours that incursion's demonstrable justification in a free and democratic society). In Ha-Redeye's words: "[i]f that's not minimal impairment, I'm not sure what is."

C. Whether the SOP Reflected Extant Obligations

[Sealy Harrington explained the narrow content of the SOP requirement to "promote" equality, and then reviewed the Rules and other provisions to show the existence of an obligation to promote equality]

. . . . .

D. Conclusion: The SOP Is a Regulatory Reminder

The foregoing discussion clarifies the true nature of the SOP. It is not a "Loyalty Oath" enforced by the "thought police"; it is not a "quota"; it does not "mak[e] it harder for members of the public to identify impartial and independent-minded lawyers and judges"; or force lawyers to violate their ethical "duty of loyalty" to their clients; it does not mandate that Canadian law professors endorse current equality jurisprudence; and it *certainly* does not "place[] vulnerable and marginalized people at risk." Rather, the SOP is a modest step towards enhancing regulatory compliance. It "calls on licensees to reflect on their professional context and on how they will uphold and observe human rights laws" to "ensure that licensees do not lose sight of regulatory obligations in the scramble of keeping a practice running." In this sense, I agree with Cockfield regarding the intent of the SOP requirement to promote "reflect[ion] on racism within law practice."

By reminding lawyers of their professional and public obligations — but not creating novel obligations — the LSO seeks to combat systemic discrimination *proactively*, which existing instruments are already directed towards addressing *reactively*; "shift[ing] the focus from individuals to systems and from ad hoc human rights liability to the promotion of an inclusive and diverse professional culture." A proactive approach is, indeed, particularly critical in the context of racial discrimination given how difficult it is to detect its "subtle" scent — a critical point for those who view the SOP requirement as an unnecessary redundancy. Indeed, as critical race theorist Alan Freeman instructs, "affirmative efforts" directed towards changing the "conditions" of systemic hierarchy are a necessary ingredient in combatting racial discrimination. In then Professor (now Justice) Woolley's words:

> Compliance-based regulation depends on regulated parties — and in particular on regulated entities — acknowledging regulatory obligations, creating strategies for accomplishing those obligations and reporting on the success of those strategies. Compliance-based regulation aims not to punish lawyers for doing things wrong, but to help lawyers create structures and strategies for getting it right. Doing that requires lawyers acknowledging what they need to do, creating strategies for doing it, and monitoring how those strategies work ... It aims to achieve and support good practices, rather than occasionally and haphazardly punishing the bad.

I acknowledge that the SOP is not immune to critique. One might criticize whether such acknowledgments are effective at improving compliance with regulatory obligations, whether they should target institutions rather than individuals, whether they should be optional, or whether they go far enough. One might also criticize the name of the requirement — Statement of Principles — which, I will readily concede, connotes aspects of speech ("statement") and conscience ("principles"), although "Reminder of Regulatory Obligations" has less ring to it. One could doubt that anyone will actually reflect on their equality obligations, though there is anecdotal evidence to the contrary. Lastly, one might note that certain non-binding explanatory materials disseminated by the LSO — though not formally enacted by it — supported the Applicants' interpretation of the SOP as violating freedom of conscience. Specifically, an earlier version of a "Key Concepts" document explained that the SOP's intention "is to demonstrate *a personal valuing of* equality, diversity, and inclusion," which would extend the SOP beyond a simple "reporting requirement." However, that document was revised — wisely — and then simply provided what a statement of principles "may consist of." Notably, none of these critiques establish that the SOP *as enacted* created new equality promotion obligations or violated free speech. Further, none of these critiques offer an alternative as to how to better promote pro- active compliance with human rights obligations.

III. CRITICAL ANALYSIS: LIBERTY VEILS AND EQUALITY TALES

Having clarified the SOP requirement's modest imposition of annual self- directed journaling, I now take a theoretical detour from my doctrinal analysis to make a brief observation in the tradition of critical race theory. In my view, free speech is a "smokescreen" in this case

. . . . .

There has been significant debate surrounding whether the SOP opponents are "good faith constitutional objectors." Of course, I cannot divine whether each of the objectors is subjectively acting in good faith, and, following the wise words of W.E.B. Du Bois, do not want to "inveigh indiscriminately" against the mass of SOP opponents who, publicly or privately, range from apprehension to antipathy. But the circumstances surrounding the SOP controversy strongly call into question the extent to which it is accurately characterized, on the whole, as a debate pertaining to free speech, not equality. Limited criticism has been levied at the more obtrusive Required Oath, which has existed for over a century, or the LSO's other speech regulations, such as those pertaining to lawyer advertising. In comparison, the SOP has received significant and sustained resistance. . . Of course, the incongruity between opposition against the Required Oath and the SOP requirement does not directly respond to any substantive concerns regarding the latter. But when a public state-drafted oath demanding that licensees "champion" (*i.e.* publicly and militantly support) the "rule of law" goes virtually unchallenged for over a century, and a private self-drafted journal entry alluding to "diversity" raises instant fury, it is suspect to claim that this controversy has nothing to do with diversity. In fact, by the final stages of peer-review for this article, the anti-SOP benchers twice voted *against* making the SOP a voluntary requirement, instead seeking its outright repeal. Those benchers shifted from seeking to prevent compelled speech (which is satisfied by a voluntary SOP), to seeking to prevent "virtue signalling" and "political correctness" (only satisfied by a repealed SOP). It seems, therefore, that their opposition was not motivated by speech, but rather, diversity.

That this controversy is "pro speech *in form*, but anti-diversity *in substance*," is corroborated by two further considerations: the demographics of the SOP debate, and many of its opponents' openly admitted disdain for diversity. The homogeneity of those who oppose the SOP requirement is anecdotally notable; they are predominantly — though not exclusively — white men. And, as multiple racialized commentators have observed, such a demographic may "misunderstand the issues because they cannot see them from the perspective of minority lawyers" and "may not experience the same kind of discrimination that some of us in the profession who are racialized ... experience." More perniciously, their motivation to deny the existence of systemic racism may be its corollary — that they, as white people, are unjustly enriched by the racial privileges systemic racism bestows on them (especially, perhaps, for those individuals whose positive perceptions of themselves were more fragile"). Just as "[i]t is instructive that the chief proponents for sanctioning people who inflict [racist speech] injuries are women and people of colour," it is instructive that the chief proponents of diversity in the legal profession are, similarly, women and people of colour. In my view, it is difficult — if not wilfully blind — to disregard the optics of this demographic divide, and to not interrogate whether the real target of this fury is diversity, not speech. In other words, the *content*, not *compulsion*, of the SOP is its real controversy.

But why speculate? Sure, overwhelmingly white resistance to the SOP and hotably racialized support for it can support the inference that this controversy was triggered by disagreement over equality, not speech. Thankfully, though, no such inference is needed in this case. Indeed, many SOP opponents have, by open admission, made their disdain for equality initiatives clear: that diversity is vacuous ("whatever that means"); is a misguided trend ("faddish and jargonistic concepts" or "fashionable ideological causes"); overlooks how racialized people are simply disinterested in the law ("[w]hat if there are many reasons why different groups of people choose different paths?"); is a fiction predicated on the myth of "systemic racism"; and even

647

is anti-Semitic ("the Law Society is telling us that there are, in effect, too many white Jewish lawyers"). Bencher Goldstein went even further, quoting — with admitted "common sense" approval — an online comment claiming that the underrepresentation of racial minorities in law is, in "large part," credited to their lack of "a culture of learning" (a tweet he has since deleted). This admitted contempt for equality, diversity, and inclusion (or worse, this open admission of racist beliefs) in publications specifically directed towards resisting the SOP requirement illustrates that the *real* reason for the forceful opposition to the SOP is precisely the rationale for its imposition: insufficient awareness of systemic discrimination in Canadian legal practice, which, in turn, can meaningfully impair the profession's ability to proactively redress that discrimination. The protest against the SOP, ironically, illustrates its importance.

So what is the SOP controversy *really* about? It's about a system of oppression that certain largely privileged licensees are unwilling to acknowledge, and who, through their rejection of that system, demonstrate its sustained force.

NOTES AND QUESTIONS

1. As was the case with the majority and dissent in *Trinity Western*, part of the difference between opponents and proponents of the Statement of Principles requirements relates to how broadly they define the scope of a law society's authority. Proponents view law societies as having a mandate broad enough to incorporate the promotion of diversity and inclusion in the legal profession. Opponents view the mandate as limited, as the Alford and Klippenstein application puts it, to ensuring "an appropriate standard of learning, competence and professional conduct,". Which concept of the law society's mandate do you think as most consistent with ensuring the public interest in the practice of law? Is the promotion of diversity distinct from competence and professional conduct, or necessary for it?

2. In the spring of 2020, subsequent to the Statement of Principles debate, public awareness of systemic racism and injustice, including in the legal system, increased after the killing of George Floyd and Breonna Taylor by American police officers and subsequent international protests. Do you think that shift in public perception, if it persists, would change how future initiatives to address systemic racism in the legal profession are received?

3. Compare the interpretation of the Statement of Principles sought by Alford and Klippenstein to the "regulatory reminder" interpretation of the Statement of Principles offered by Sealy-Harrington. Are those interpretations consistent or inconsistent? To the extent they are consistent, why do you think it was so difficult for proponents and opponents of the Statement of Principles to find common ground as to what the requirement imposes on lawyers?

4. Sealy-Harrington argues that the reliance of opponents on freedom of speech and conscience concerns was to a significant extent a smoke screen for the actual concern, which was with promoting of diversity. He notes in particular the opposition to initiatives to make the Statement of Principles voluntary not mandatory. What do you think of Sealy-Harrington's

argument? Are you persuaded? To the extent he is correct, and the real concern is with diversity, where do you think that concern comes from? Is there an argument that promoting diversity does not promote the public interest in the practice of law? What arguments could be advanced to persuade a person opposed to such initiatives that promoting diversity furthers the public interest in the practice of law?

5. In thinking about diversity, equality and the public interest in the practice of law, both lawyers and clients might have interests and concerns. What issues of diversity and equality in the practice of law might be of the greatest concern to a client? To a person practicing law? What initiatives of a law society would best address the concerns of clients? What initiatives of a law society would best address the concerns of lawyers?

The final excerpt in this section is an essay written by Hadiya Roderique about her experience as a Black woman lawyer on Bay Street. As you read this essay, consider what Roderique's essay says about issues of diversity and equality in the legal profession, and also what Recommendations of the Working Group would be most important for the Law Society of Ontario – or other law societies – to implement.

HADIYA RODERIQUE

"Black on Bay Street: Hadiya Roderique had it all. But still could not fit in" Globe and Mail, November 4, 2017

As a kid, I was proud of my name. Ha-DEE-ya. I always loved the rhythmical quality of it, the middle syllable emphasized, almost a "ta-da" in its phrasing alone. I was Hadiya, or, in Arabic, "a gift," the only one in the world, or at least in mine.

Twenty-six years after my parents gave me my beautiful name, I sat in front of a screen in my brightly lit Toronto apartment trying to figure out whether to use it on applications for jobs at Bay Street law firms. Should I use my anglicized middle name Joleene, evoking the white, auburn-haired, green-eyed temptress trying to steal Dolly Parton's man? Or do I choose to show my blackness, own my name and my heritage, knowing what it may invite? Do I include my membership in the Black Law Students Association and point out that I won the Harry Jerome Scholarship? Or do I leave the content more meagre, but whiter? It seemed ridiculous that this was something I needed to consider. My parents, Joseph and Judith, almost named me Jody. Joe and Judy could be a nice white couple from Mississauga, and Jody their equally white-bread daughter. But they chose instead to honour my African and Indian heritage.

My dilemma wasn't unique – these are considerations for many minority applicants at the gates of professional careers. In a recent study, a third of Asian and black participants reported whitening their resumé or covering their minority status. And though it may pain the soul to do so, it works. Black students who whiten resumés get 2.5 times more callbacks. For Jamal to be considered equal to Greg, he needs eight more years of experience. Companies say they want diverse candidates, but the numbers don't bear the claims out. Whitening is just one of the many ways we try to fit into these worlds when we would rather they expand to include us.

I sighed and typed my name in large, bold letters at the top of the page. H-A-D-I-Y-A.

I desperately wanted a big law job. As the black daughter of low-income Caribbean immigrants, a cab driver and a customer service representative, such a job had a special allure. First year lawyers on Bay Street make about $100,000, a figure that puts them in the top 8 per cent of Canadians earners. Make partner and you're a solid 1 per center. It's a way to leap, instantly, into a different social and economic category. For first-generation children, the weight of our parents' sacrifice is heavy, even when unspoken. That burden can influence our choices. I got a science degree from McGill University instead of pursuing dance. I quit my band to go to law school. I didn't want to struggle like they did. I owed it to them not to.

My parents moved here to offer me the promise of the North American dream, the promise that if I had the brains and the willingness to work hard, I would get what I deserve. But pure merit is a myth. Even in the legal profession, and maybe especially so there, as much as merit may be about working hard, it is more accurately about opportunity, belonging and fit. And as a person of colour, these are roadblocks at every step along the way. Do you fit in as a law student? Can you even go to law school in the first place? Do you get an interview? Do you choose not to apply because you don't see yourself represented? Do you fit enough to get the job? And if you get the job, can you fit enough to remain? These are questions we all ask, black or white, male or female, but the answers are harder for some of us than others.

After firms review applications, each law school hosts interview days for its students in late September and October. Every year, each firm chooses about 40 students from my school, the University of Toronto, to meet with over two days at the Metro Convention Centre. Then, a few candidates are invited to the firms, meeting with lawyers in one-on-ones and small groups during November Interview Week. Finally, that same week, the offers are made.

Because U of T's Faculty of Law is considered one of the best in the country, almost everyone in my 190-person class got an interview with at least one firm. My intellect was sufficient and my activities suitably interesting that I made it past the resumé screen for about 10 firms. The only remaining question was: Did I fit the firm culture? Was I someone the associates and partners would want to spend 16 hours with in a boardroom? . . .

I hate malls. But on an early fall day in 2006, I shuffled reluctantly after class to the Eaton Centre, braving the dreaded crowds to outfit myself. As I ascended the escalator from the subway, the air smelled of popcorn and teenage sweat. I walked quickly, ducking around slower stragglers to make my first visit to a Banana Republic

I prefer clothes that don't look like anyone else's, acquired from vintage stores and thrift shops, complemented with high-end pieces. But here, the suits all looked the same: slim pencil skirt, fitted jacket, three buttons. I filled my arms with two colours – black to blend and the more daring light grey. I added a glittery aqua stiletto heel from Aldo. If I had to look like everyone else, I was going to be a slightly more sparkly version.

Later, a fellow law student, a white woman, asked me if I was going to wear my natural hair to interviews. I hadn't thought of that. I'd worn it naturally since I started university. But how black is black enough, and how black is too much? Should I straighten my hair, which I hadn't done in seven years? I didn't want to work for a firm that wouldn't want me as I am. But I knew this principle might come at a cost. After all, I'd never met a black lawyer with natural hair.

At 7:30 a.m. on interview day at the Metro Convention Centre, it seemed like my entire law school class was surrounding me, a sea of black and grey suits.

. . .

The interviews were all similar: 20 minutes of unstructured pleasantries about things on my resumé. But anything was fair game. I was keen, for instance, on Cassels Brock, a large firm with a strong entertainment-law department. I arrived at their booth just in time, out of breath and somewhat exhausted, only to have the grey curtains give way more easily than I expected: I catapulted into the company of my would-be employers like an overeager gymnast. "Graceful swan," I muttered to myself, instantly channelling my ballet training to stand up straight, head tall, shoulders back – and quipped that I was so excited to be interviewing with them that I'd changed my shoes. "You're cool enough to get the snakeskin," I said, pointing one toe forward. The head of the student committee tilted her head back and laughed. Ten minutes of discussion about footwear ensued, followed by an analysis of the Leafs. Having never watched an NHL hockey game to completion on TV, I brought up my fledgling career as a rec-league hockey player in university.

Another partner noticed a cappella and jazz in my extracurriculars and asked me to sing, so I launched into George Gershwin's Summertime. I could tell instantly if I was headed to the in-firm round based on my rapport with the interviewer.

I made it through to the November stage for five firms, but Fasken Martineau was one of the highest on my list. It was a down-to-earth firm, and more like me – scrappy up and coming, fighting for a place at the establishment's table. Just before my interview with Faskens, I noticed a tear in my pantyhose. I panicked, only to find a basket of hosiery in the washroom. The interview went well and ended at noon. I attended lunch in a boardroom with other interviewees and articling students. We all ate slowly, to avoid spills – a no-no in the legal profession. Monday concluded with a dinner at a Queen West restaurant with Cassels Brock lawyers, and I tried to maintain my energy and excitement.

On Tuesday, after more meetings, lunches, and breaks in the safety of coffee shops, I attended two cocktail parties. . . .

I planned to nurse one glass of wine and had a small sip before joining a conversation with a male partner and two other interviewees, all white men. After the usual exchanges of names, the partner began asking questions. "Where did you go to school?" he asked the young man farthest to my left. After listening to a detailed reply about the student's undergraduate and law school education, the partner's eyes panned to the man immediately beside me. "What about you?" He took a sip of wine and nodded along patiently. But his scan stopped shy of me and he launched into a story about his alma mater, the same as one of the men.

For a while I stood there, dumbfounded by his lack of interest in me. He was clean-shaven in a well-fitting grey suit. He had white hair and blue eyes that ignored

651

me as if I were under a Romulan cloaking device. We were so close I could see the small light blue diamonds on his navy tie and smell his cologne. This wasn't a case of that awkwardness because someone doesn't know what to say. He knew I was there. I just wasn't worthy of his attention. I stepped back, put my full wine glass down on the nearest table, and walked out of the building into the November wind. It was cold out, but I didn't notice. I was hot with indignation. Screw being buttoned up, screw smiling and nodding. I wanted to have real fun

Ten minutes later at Faskens, I decided I would do this on my terms. I indulged in a full glass of chardonnay, and fluidly joined and exited groups, refusing to be excluded again. I laughed when I found things funny. I approached the chocolate fountain next to a tall, tiered platter piled with strawberries, banana slices and other fruit. Most students were too afraid of spilling, but I speared a toothpick into the largest strawberry, turned it three times to coat it with a respectable amount of chocolate, and ate it in one triumphant swoop. "I don't think I've seen any other student brave the chocolate," said the head of the hiring committee. "Well done."

At 5 p.m. the next day, standing in my underwear in my apartment, tired of being penned in by clothing I would otherwise not have bought, I received a phone call with an offer from Faskens, my first choice. I accepted immediately. I was excited to get the summer position. I felt free at the cocktail party. And it seemed like a place where I wouldn't have to change to fit in.

I had a great first summer and articling year at the firm. I felt accepted. They loved that I was well-rounded. They applauded my participation in extracurriculars and, my other life as an elite ultimate Frisbee player. When prospective students visited, the partners routinely asked me to speak. "This is Hadiya, one of our students," they'd beam. "She's able to balance her work here at the firm, and compete at the national level in her sport."

I worked hard, at times sleeping four hours a night so I wouldn't say no to any projects. The market crash of 2008 meant that the chance of being hired as an associate was no longer as high as it used to be. I was scared. I still had student loans to pay. Had I worked hard enough? When the hiring committee members sat across from my desk in May and offered me an associate position, I teared up with happiness and relief.

People gravitate toward people who are like them. Social scientists call this homophily. We consciously and unconsciously surround ourselves with others like us, who in turn validate our own choices and values. "You are trying to pick candidates from a very, very qualified group of people," a management consultant named Amit explains in Pedigree, a book by sociologist Dr. Lauren Rivera that explores professional hiring. "And what separates them ends up being some of your preferences and if you have shared experiences." We end up defining fit, and thus merit, in our own image.

But when a firm is mostly white, who do you have to be and what experiences do you have to have to belong? What does it mean to be like them? The website of any major downtown Toronto firm shows an ocean of mostly white faces, especially at the partnership level.

. . . . .

To their credit, firms are aware of their lack of diversity. They plaster their websites, publications and speeches with diversity statements. Brochures often feature a variety of hues of smiling faces, even though they represent a mere fraction of the lawyers. The firms give the appearance of being hungry for qualified and diverse candidates, but their attempts fumble because of a fundamentally flawed process. They hire people who fit into the firm as it already exists.

. . . . .

When I was a child, my father told me I could be anything I wanted if I put my mind to it. He always added a reminder that as a black person, I would have to be twice as good to be considered equal. But I learned that other people don't like it when I'm twice as good and am the colour I am. They didn't like my confidence, and they didn't like when I overshadowed their daughters and outperformed their sons without the tutors and the lessons my parents couldn't afford. Invariably, these people would take steps to try to put me in my place. And so, I learned to excel, for me, for my father, but to keep it hidden.

I mastered fitting into places, mostly white spaces. I boxed myself in just enough so others were comfortable. I did it when I was in grade school, growing up in the heart of Mississauga, the only black child in my enhanced class. I struggled with it in high school, one of about 20 black students, the only one in my year in the dance program at my performing arts high school; and again, as the only black student in my 40-person psychology honours program at McGill; as the only black female competitive ultimate Frisbee player in my city, let alone on my team; and as one of five black law students in my class of 190.

I called my dad a while ago and asked him if he ever worried about me fitting in. He told me that there was a nice young lady in his cab, but answered anyway. "I always worried about that," he replied. He explained that this was part of the reason he put me in arts and sports.

"Did you do anything else to help me fit in?" I asked. I don't remember this part of our relationship, but I knew I must have gotten my chameleon abilities from somewhere.

"I talked to you, about exposing your intellect appropriately and not just randomly. And when you were older, I could see that you were very good at manipulating yourself to the situations that you wanted to participate in."

"Great parenting, Joe!" I said. It was a joke, but I meant every word. Born the same, but to different parents, my life could have ended up quite different.

Sociologist Annette Lareau distinguishes between the approaches of working-class parents and privileged parents. The former tend to adopt a natural-growth parenting strategy, where kids are free to develop without interference in their school lives and extracurriculars. Conversely, privileged parents engage in "concerted cultivation," playing integral and operative roles in their children's schooling and activities.

. . . . .

No matter what firms claim, the hiring process is just not set up to test how good a lawyer you might be, whether you'll craft that memo just so, or be willing to work 18-hour days on a pressing transaction. Instead gut feelings and underlying similarity seem prized over all else, a significant disadvantage for those from less privileged backgrounds.

653

Partners fawn over hockey players and people who've travelled extensively and volunteered in foreign countries – all signs of affluence and privilege. Unstructured chats and cocktail parties test whether you belong with the people that are already there. How can asking me about types of Scotch and shoes be anything but a test of belonging in an upper-class white world?

Firms get excited about black people when they seem like they fit. I can tell when they get the gleam in their eye, when they see me as one of them, but with the bonus of brown skin. At times, it can feel like that's all they see. An acquaintance who recently left law for academia is blunt about the excitement. "They were thrilled to have me. I was the white black person, the lawyer in the firm with slightly different skin who could be trotted out as an example of diversity." Like him, I was the acceptable Negro. I was to be visible yet invisible. I had to make them believe that I was a black girl they could spend two hours in a car with on the way to a hearing in Barrie, Ont., listening and humming to Bob Dylan and talking about summer vacations, when I wanted to sing along with Nina Simone and talk about inequality.

. . . . .

As an associate, things started out well for me. I chose Brian, a white partner, as my senior mentor. He was refreshingly frank, a trait appreciated by both his clients and me. He didn't care what I looked like, just that I was smart. I had two informal black mentors, both named Andrew, that I affectionately called the Andrews. (They were both in the corporate law department, and shared an assistant, which I imagine led to much confusion. "Hello, can I speak to Andrew?" "Which one?" "Uh, the black one?" "Right, which one?") We regularly had what I called black lunch at a nearby restaurant. Another mentor from my articling days, Paul, was someone I could always be myself with – a brilliant, incredibly social lawyer who also loved to dance.

Meanwhile, I was able to balance my work at the firm with my commitment to ultimate Frisbee, dedicating my weekends to tournaments and training sessions. On weekdays, I stepped out of the office at 6 p.m. twice a week for practice, often picking up where I left off when I was done at 9.

I got excellent first-year reviews. As a second-year associate, I brought a client to the firm. I developed a reputation for being smart, creative and for anticipating people's needs. I was told that I worked at a level beyond my years.

But slowly, fitting in became harder and harder, especially when I was no longer in front of the lawyers chosen for the student-hiring process because of their strong social skills. The pressure to belong intensifies as you get closer to the summit, and away from kindred spirits such as the Andrews, Paul and Brian; each raised eyebrow, each slight, each difference felt like a message that I didn't fit. There were two barriers: One was the colour of my skin, the other was my values.

A week into my time as an associate, I wore my new black pinstriped Holt Renfrew suit to work. Two assistants joined me in the elevator. One of them, attempting to be friendly, said "You're new. Who do you work for?"

"I'm in the labour and employment group," I responded.

"I mean, which lawyer?" she replied. I realized that despite my suit, she thought I was an assistant. She hadn't even bothered to look down past my face, hadn't noticed my outfit or the sharp leather briefcase I had rewarded myself with for getting the job.

"I'm an associate," I said, pointedly. She blushed beet red, finally seeing my clothes. Finally seeing me.

Another day, I was in a client meeting getting the background of a case against the company. A senior partner, a white woman, and I were questioning the manager about a series of firings being grieved by the union, partly based on racial discrimination. The senior partner asked about the racial makeup of the workers. The manager said, "Well, they're mostly black," and pointed at me. The white partner froze. I could see the internal struggle on her face.

What I really wanted to say was, "Thanks, I know what colour I am," in the most sarcastic voice I could channel. But I knew it was my job to make people comfortable with my otherness. I asked another question, moving the meeting along, thankful I was wearing black as sweat seeped through my shirt.

Later in the car ride, the "mostly black" moment lingered in my mind. Should I have brought it up? Discussed with the partner what to do in that situation? Would she have even understood how I felt? Or would I have received the stock, "That's probably not what they meant" or "Are you sure you're not being too sensitive?" – the subtle yet constant gaslighting of my experience? I said nothing. I did nothing.

Nowadays in Canada, overt acts of racism are rare. Instead, the subtle ones tire you out and wear your sense of belonging. They happen more often, more insidiously. These acts of discrimination can be more detrimental than blatant racism or sexism. It's easier to point out prejudice when someone is overtly racist. Organizations have policies and procedures for reporting explicit racism and sexism. Others, hearing your story, are suitably outraged. But the underground cracks, passive-aggressive dismissals, the ghostly put downs, are harder to mark.

Yet, each drop in the bucket adds up. How do you report the frosty reaction or the startled pause you got when you were introduced as the associate on file? The confusing silence when you walk over to the corporate defence team, and turn out not to be the black woman bringing the human-rights claim? The assumption that you'd have no interest in a ski trip, when someone "jokingly" says, "I thought black people don't ski?" How do you not internalize these quiet messages that you don't really belong?

I was not alone in these feelings. Ritu Bhasin, a diversity consultant and former legal talent director at Stikeman Elliott, and author of The Authenticity Principle says, "People feel they have to change who they are, move away from their authentic self to get ahead. But there's only so much conforming and masking we can do. It eats away at your spirit. And after a while, you'll either be pushed out or self-select out, because it's exhausting to be someone you're not." No wonder so many of us leave.

I was a lawyer and I belonged there. But it felt like I had to prove it more, while others got the benefit of the doubt. Two different fonts on a document would get nary a mention for a white, male associate. When I did it, I earned a sit-down, closed-door conversation about my commitment and dedication. Everyone makes mistakes. But it feels like some of us can make more mistakes than others, a feeling borne out by research that shows that black women leaders are more harshly evaluated for failure compared to white men, white women, and even black men. While black men and white women receive lower evaluations than white men, they both benefit from the primary aspects of their identities: being white or being male. I was neither.

. . . . .

By mid-December of 2011, I'd finally had enough. Big law could not accommodate the person and the colour I was. I searched for a life line. Four months later, I received an offer from a smaller boutique law firm, and was accepted to the University of Toronto to do my Ph.D. in Organizational Behaviour, where I would be able to study diversity and retention. I had considered academia before law school, having been accepted to Stanford's psychology Ph.D. program. School was always a safe haven. I was drawn to the latter, but I had put so much time and effort into my law career I couldn't just walk away. I accepted the offer from the other firm and tendered my resignation. Later that day, another partner who had questioned my commitment to ultimate [Frisbee] and the firm called me from the airport and pleaded with me to stay.

I called my dad. He was at a cab stand and I could hear sirens in the background. I asked him what he thought about me leaving the law.

"I didn't think law was it for you," he said.

"Why not?" This was not the answer I expected.

"I wanted you to be your own boss. I was worried you wouldn't be able to move up the ladder because you're a woman or because you're black." He recounted the racism he experienced as an engineer in Canada in the early eighties with a sad tinge in his voice.

I asked my dad what makes him proud of me. This answer surprised me, too. "It's not your academic achievements. It's your tenacity, the confidence you have in yourself. Your character."

"I got that from you," I responded. I could feel his black Santa smile through the phone.

"You never give up, and the most important thing for you is your happiness."

It relieves some of my first-generation guilt to know that my dad would rather I be happy than wealthy.

. . . . .

Firms should want to be diverse. This isn't political correctness, it's business. Even the mere presence of minorities adds a competitive advantage. Companies in the highest quartile of racial or ethnic diversity are 35 per cent more likely to outperform those in the bottom quartile. But firms still cannot reconcile excellence with making diversity a priority, even though recent research has found that increasing diversity weeds out mediocrity.

The Law Society of Upper Canada, the body responsible for the self-regulation of lawyers and paralegals in Ontario, recently conducted a study of the challenges facing racialized lawyers. The research culminated in series of recommendations to address issues of systemic racism within the profession. Among these is a requirement to write and abide by a statement of principles "acknowledging their obligation to promote equity, diversity and inclusion," which has already received some push-back in the legal community.

And, while these recommendations, noble in their aspirations, may move the needle somewhat, I find it hard to believe that they will have much real sway until there is a clear impact on the bottom line. A statement is great in theory, but how do you objectively measure compliance? What company or person is going to say that they don't currently follow those guidelines? But when clients start demanding change, ears will perk up.

Walwyn believes the number of clients taking diversity seriously is increasing daily. Organizations such as BMO are starting to ask law firms for diversity numbers and how they've changed, who's spending time on files, and who's leading the legal team. When clients start to demand that their cases and deals be staffed by equal numbers of men and women, with female partners and minority involvement, and only 25 per cent of partners are women, with even fewer minorities, firms will lose money. And, in turn, they'll lose talent, which will lead to losing more money. Companies have been toppled by lesser things. How will firms meet these targets, when they can't even keep people like me, the ones who are ostensibly closer to fitting in? For starters, they will need to talk honestly about it. Real diversity acknowledges, celebrates and actually talks about differences as much as it tries to render them invisible in other ways.

. . . . .

I still feel some discomfort, guilt and shame about my time at the firm. Uncomfortable that I kept myself boxed in. Shame that I didn't stand up for myself and my values and push the needle on what constituted a good associate. Guilt that I didn't do more to stick around to be there for the next black woman to come up the ranks. I tried to return to the firm, after discovering that the small firm wasn't for me – I missed my friends and colleagues, the bigger files. The same partner who'd asked me to stay argued against my return.

Sometimes I imagine what it could have been like if I had stayed and become the partner sitting with the young black lawyer the client pointed at. "We are all aware of what black looks like, thank you," I say, as I gently push down her arm. I turn to the associate and mouth, "I'm sorry." I return to the interview.

As we walk to my BMW – I like German engineering – I ask the associate if she's okay. "Unfortunately, some people are idiots. Are you okay with how I handled it? Is there anything else you would have liked me to do?" We talk about the incident and she feels supported. Like she belongs

. . . . .

But that will never happen for me. That belonging remains out of reach for so many. It's been five years since I left private practice – I eventually left the small firm and have been working on my Ph.D. at U of T since then – and even now I still feel on edge when I find myself at the intersection of Bay and Adelaide, staring up at Fasken's windows. No one slows down or engages with anyone else, motoring forward in a form of Bay Street chicken and dodging only when faced with an equally determined person. I engaged in that battle, noting how often the white person expected me to be the one who moved out of the way, and was surprised when I didn't.

It's a subtle assertion of power here on the sidewalk, same as the right bowtie, a flashy sock, the name-brand purse, the determined march while making a deal on the phone. The assumption that I should be the one to make way is a means of stating that I don't belong down here in the world of power and money. I notice a black man in a sharp suit, and then a black woman talking on her cellphone. We catch eyes, almost as if to say, "I see you," and "We belong here, too."

I do miss some things about being a lawyer: power outfits; coffees with my fellow associates to decompress after a busy morning; nailing a legal argument for a case; Brian taking me to a grocery store in Rosedale to buy my first soft-shell crab after our hearing ended early; the confidence of handing my business card to people and seeing them look suitably impressed. But I don't miss the isolation and the nagging sense that other people didn't feel I belonged. Or the sense that I was once again play-acting at another life, putting on a mask and the body armour of a sharp pin-striped suit to go to work, steeling myself against the discomfort I might face. And, then, when I returned home, unzipping my skirt as quickly as possible, massaging my aching feet after eight hours in heels, sinking into the comfort of my couch and changing back into myself.

. . . . .

[5] FURTHER READING

American Bar Association Commission on Professionalism, *In the Spirit of Public Service: A Blueprint for the Rekindling of Lawyer Professionalism* (Chicago: American Bar Association, 1986).

Arthurs, Harry, Richard Weisman & Fredrick Zemans, "The Canadian Legal Profession" (1986) Am. Bar Assoc. Res. J. 447.

Barton, Benjamin H., "Why Do We Regulate Lawyers?: An Economic Analysis of the Justifications for Entry and Conduct Regulation" (2001) 33 Ariz. St. L.J. 429.

Boon, Andrew & Avis Whyte, "Lawyer Disciplinary Processes: An Empirical Study of Solicitors' Misconduct Cases in England and Wales in 2015" (2019) 39:3 L.S. 455-478.

Canadian Bar Association, *Futures: Transforming the Delivery of Legal Services in Canada* (Toronto: Canadian Bar Association, 2014).

Chambliss, Elizabeth, "Evidence-Based Lawyer Regulation" (2019) 97:2 Wash. Univ. L. Rev. 297.

Levin, Leslie "The Politics of Lawyer Regulation: The Case of Malpractice Insurance" (2020) 33 Geo. J. Leg. Ethics 969.

Levin, Leslie, Christine Zozula & Peter Siegelman, "The Questionable Character of the Bar's Character and Fitness Inquiry" (2015) 40 Law & Soc. Inquiry 51.

MacKenzie, Brooke, "Why do We Regugulate Lawyers?" (January 14, 2021) *slaw.ca*, online: http://www.slaw.ca/2021/01/14/why-do-we-regulate-lawyers/.

Orkin, Mark, *Legal Ethics* (Toronto: Cartwright & Sons, 1957).

Rhode, Deborah, "Moral Character as Professional Credential" (1985) 44 Yale L.J. 491.

Roiphe, Rebecca, "The Decline of Professionalism" (2016) 29 Geo. J. Leg. Ethics 649.

Sheey, Elizabeth & Sheila McIntyre, *Calling for Change: Women, Law and the Legal Profession* (Ottawa: University of Ottawa Press, 2006).

Smith, Beverley G., *Professional Conduct for Lawyers and Judges*, 2d ed. (Fredericton: Maritime Law Book, 2002).

Webb, Duncan, "Are Lawyers Regulatable?" (2008) 45 Alta. L. Rev. 233.

Woolley, Alice, "Lawyers and the Rule of Law: Independence of the Bar, the Canadian Constitution and the Law Governing Lawyers" (2015) 34 N.J.C.L. 49-74.

Woolley, Alice, "Rhetoric and Realities: What Independence of the Bar Requires of Lawyer Regulation" (2011) 45 U.B.C. L. Rev. 145.

Woolley, Alice, "Tending the Bar: The Good Character Requirement for Law Society Admission" (2007) 30 Dal. L.J. 28.

Woolley, Alice & Amy Salyzyn, "Protecting the Public Interest: Law Society Decision-Making After Trinity Western" (2019) 97 Can. Bar Rev. 70.

Woolley, Alice & Trevor W.C. Farrow, "Addressing Access to Justice Through New Legal Service Providers: Opportunities and Challenges" (2016) 3 Texas A & M L. Rev. 549-579.

CHAPTER 11

CHALLENGES FOR LAWYER REGULATION: ACCESS TO JUSTICE

[1] INTRODUCTION

It seems uncontroversial to say that Canada is a country committed to the rule of law. To the extent that we can measure such concepts, comparative data seem to support this claim. According to the World Justice Project's *2020 Rule of Law Index*, Canada ranks among the top 10 countries globally on aggregate legal system indicators such as fundamental rights, open government, and order and security.

And yet, our best evidence suggests that many of the 3.8 million Canadians who experience one or more legal problems each year are unable to resolve their problems fairly, effectively or affordably.[1] Looking more closely at the data comprising the *Rule of Law Index*, Canada lags behind on several indicators of civil justice in particular, ranking an abysmal 52nd out of 128 countries based on the public's ability to "access and afford civil justice"; 54th based on "unreasonable delay" in the civil justice system; and 64th based on civil justice being "free from discrimination".[2] The most recent data collected from national legal needs surveys in Canada confirm Canadians' widespread dissatisfaction with the options available to address their problems.[3] After years of denying, ignoring or underestimating the scale and distribution of these challenges, lawyers, judges, governments, law societies and other key actors now widely recognize—in name, if not always by their actions—that access to justice in Canada is at a point of national crisis.[4]

The consequences of this crisis for individuals and communities already experiencing forms of social exclusion are especially severe. As the Canadian Bar Association concluded in its report on equal access to justice, "[s]ocially excluded groups are more vulnerable and this vulnerability compounds the effects of

---

[1] Ab Currie, *Nudging the Paradigm Shift, Everyday Legal Problems in Canada* (Toronto: Canadian Forum on Civil Justice, 2016) at 4.

[2] World Justice Project Rule of Law Index, *Canada 2020*, online: *World Justice Project* https://worldjusticeproject.org/rule-of-law-index/country/2020/Canada/Civil%20Justice.

[3] Ab Currie, *Nudging the Paradigm Shift, Everyday Legal Problems in Canada* (Toronto: Canadian Forum on Civil Justice, 2016) at 21 (reporting that almost 50% of respondents felt that the outcome of resolved problems was unfair).

[4] Trevor C.W. Farrow & Lesley A. Jacobs, eds., *The Justice Crisis: The Cost and Value of Accessing Law* (Vancouver: University of British Columbia Press, 2020).

unresolved legal problems. It also makes it more challenging to navigate the justice system".[5] For example, the Truth and Reconciliation Commission of Canada, which released its final report in 2015 on the legacy of the Canadian residential schools for Aboriginal children, drew attention to the ongoing barriers to access to justice faced by Indigenous peoples, both individually and collectively — including their overrepresentation in the criminal justice system, their struggles for recognition of land and resource rights, and impediments to accessing justice through Indigenous systems of law.[6] Likewise, research has begun to expose the challenges experienced by refugees and other new Canadians who regularly confront justice systems and processes that are designed without attention to their needs, resources or cultural contexts.[7]

There are of course several different possible "pathways" to achieving justice, including hiring a lawyer, going to a court or tribunal, engaging in mediation, consulting with friends, family and neighbours, and/or taking up various forms of self-help. Among those who proceed through the formal court system, the number of litigants who are self-represented in complex civil and criminal cases is alarming.[8] For example, a study of legal representation in Ontario family law cases found that 64% of applications and only 30% of respondents had acquired legal representation.[9] And while some people may elect to self-represent for various reasons, self-represented litigants tend to experience higher levels of stress, anxiety and other forms of ill-health, and they generally have poorer legal outcomes than those who are represented by a lawyer.[10] The limited social supports in place to address the public's lack of legal representation are also under increasing strain. While rates of funding legal aid applications for full legal representation have

---

[5] Canadian Bar Association, *Reaching Equal Justice Report: An Invitation to Envision and Act* (Ottawa: Canadian Bar Association, November 2013) at 34.

[6] Truth and Reconciliation Commission of Canada, *Honouring the Truth, Reconciling for the Future: Summary of the Final Report of the Truth and Reconciliation Commission of Canada* (Winnipeg: Truth and Reconciliation Commission of Canada, 2015), online: http://www.trc.ca/assets/pdf/Honouring_the_Truth_Reconciling_for_the_Future_July_23_2015.pdf. *See also* Hadley Friedland, "Different Stories: Aboriginal Peoples, Order, and the Failure of the Criminal Justice System" (2009) 72 Sask. L. Rev. 105.

[7] Emily Bates, Jennifer Bond & David Wiseman, "Troubling Signs: Mapping Access to Justice in Canada's Refugee System Reform" (2015) 47 Ottawa L. Rev. 1.

[8] Julie MacFarlane, *The National Self-Represented Litigants Project: Identifying and Meeting the Needs of Self-Represented Litigants* (Windsor: The National Self-Represented Litigants Project, May 2013), online: https://representingyourselfcanada.files.wordpress.com/2014/02/reportm15-2.pdf.

[9] Michael Saini *et al.*, "Understanding Pathways to Family Dispute Resolution and Justice Reforms: Ontario Court File Analysis & Survey of Professionals" (2016) 54 *Family Court Review* 382 at 387 (these statistics describe individual cases at the end of the litigation process).

[10] Jo Miles, Nigel Balmer & Marisol Smith, "When Exceptional Is the Rule: Mental Health, Family Problems and the Reform of Legal Aid in England and Wales" (2012) 24 Child & Family Law Quarterly 320.

increased considerably in recent years,[11] only those facing the most acute financial need meet the criteria for financial assistance, and there is considerable regional disparity in eligibility. In Ontario, for example, as of 2020 a single applicant who makes more than $18,795 in annual gross income is ineligible for legal aid, while that threshold in Quebec is $23,842.[12] As Justice Nordheimer of the Ontario Superior Court remarked in the context of a recent criminal law proceeding: "[i]t should be obvious to any outside observer that the income thresholds being used by Legal Aid Ontario do not bear any reasonable relationship to what constitutes poverty in this country."[13] That same sentiment extends to most legal aid assistance thresholds across Canada.

The current crisis in access to justice raises difficult questions about the obligations of lawyers, the sustainability of lawyers' self-regulatory regimes, and the respective roles of the state and market in the provision of legal services. At a fundamental level, the inequality of access to justice in Canada calls into question the very legitimacy of claims that we live together in a society governed by the rule of law. In a speech marking "Canada's Legal System at 150", Chief Justice Beverly McLachlin observed:

> I believe we must meet the challenge of providing access to justice to ordinary Canadians, if we are to maintain public confidence in the justice system. If people are excluded from the system, if they conclude it exists only to serve the interests of the elites, they will turn away. Respect for the rule of law will diminish. Our society will be the poorer.[14]

In this chapter, we approach the questions and challenges of improving access to justice from the standpoint of both social and professional obligation. To understand those obligations and how we can or should meet them, three essential questions need to be answered:

1. What is "access to justice", and what does this broad term mean from the

---

[11] Aggregated nationally, the percentage of legal aid applications approved for full legal representation increased from roughly 65% in 2013-2014 to 81% in 2018-2019. Statistics Canada, *Table 1: Legal Aid in Canada 2013/14*, online: *Statistics Canada* http://www.statcan. gc.ca/pub/85-002-x/2015001/article/14159/tbl/tbl01-eng.htm. Government of Canada, *Legal Aid in Canada, 2018-2019*, online: *Department of Justice* https://www.justice.gc.ca/eng/rp-pr/jr/aid-aide/1819/p1.html#table6.

[12] These base thresholds are higher in some jurisdictions for certain types of claims (such as domestic abuse cases) and for some locations (such as remote communities). Legal Aid Ontario, Details on Legal Aid Ontario's financial eligibility increase for 2020, online: *Legal Aid Ontario* https://www.legalaid.on.ca/news/details-on-legal-aid-ontarios-financial-eligibility-increase-for-2020/; Commission des Services Juridiques, *Legal Aid – Am I Financially Eligible?*, online: *Commission des Services Juridiques* http://www.csj.qc.ca/commission-des-services-juridiques/aide-juridique/volet-gratuit-aj/en. Some provinces have more complex eligibly criteria—for example, individuals in Nova Scotia who qualify to receive provincial income assistance or are in an equivalent position qualify to receive legal aid.

[13] *R. v. Moodie*, [2016] O.J. No. 2727, 2016 ONSC 3469 at para. 6 (Ont. S.C.J.).

[14] "Remarks of the Right Honourable Beverley McLachlin, P.C. Chief Justice of Canada" (June 3, 2016) (S.C.C.), online: https://www.scc-csc.ca/judges-juges/spe-dis/bm-2016-06-03-eng.aspx.

perspective of different participants in the justice system?

2. Who is responsible for addressing and fostering access to justice, and on what foundation are these obligations built? Are current barriers to accessing justice due to failures of the state to provide adequate resources to its citizens; failures in the market for legal services to operate effectively and thereby set the "right price" for clients and providers; failures of individual lawyers to temper their economic interests in order to ensure that their services are broadly affordable; or failures of the profession as a whole to regulate in the public interest?

3. Given the nature of access to justice and the web of social and professional obligations that motivate action, which solutions are most likely to improve access for those in need?

Each of these questions is taken up in turn in the remaining sections below.

[2] DESCRIBING AND DEFINING THE CRISIS

According to Trevor Farrow, "[a]ccess to justice is the most pressing justice issue today."[15] But despite growing public, political and professional attention to the barriers people face when trying to access justice, there is still much that we do not know about the nature of peoples' legal needs, and about their own perspectives on what it means to have adequate access. Nor do we fully understand individuals' reasons for acting or their patterns of response when they are confronted with a problem that they might—though often do not—bring to law.

[a] Understanding "Legal" Need

In order to understand why barriers to access to justice persist, it is first important to be clear about what access to justice means, from the perspective of those who have problems for which they are seeking some kind of resolution. As a lawyer it is easy to assume that peoples' demands for access to justice are defined wholly by their desire to have *legal* problems addressed by formal *legal* processes. Beginning in the late 1990s, a group of British researchers began to unpack this concept of "legal problems", recognizing that people do not always experience their everyday problems as legal claims that are eligible to bring to law.[16] To fully appreciate the public's (potential) demand for access to justice, these researchers instead defined "justiciable problems" as "happenings and circumstances that raise legal issues but that people may never think of as legal and with respect to which they may never take any legal action".[17] This characterization allows us to ask basic questions about the nature of legal needs, including: What patterns of problems, in terms of both frequency and intensity, do we actually observe across the population and among different groups? Where do people turn for advice about problems and about the

---

[15] Trevor C.W. Farrow, "What is Access to Justice?" (2014) 51.3 Osgoode Hall L.J. 957 at 959.

[16] Hazel Genn, *Paths to Justice: What People Do and Think About Going to Law* (Oxford: Hart Publishing, 1999).

[17] Rebecca L. Sandefur, "Access to Civil Justice and Race, Class, and Gender Inequality" (2008) 34 Annual Review of Sociology 339 at 341.

available mechanisms to have those problems resolved? Do some kinds of problems go unaddressed or unresolved more often than others? Answers to these questions provide a foundation for debates about the obligations of the state and the legal profession to address access to justice, and they help to inform strategies about how best to meet the challenges of improving access, especially for those in the greatest need.

What do we know about the justiciable problems of Canadians? While several national and regional studies have been conducted over the past decade or more, the most recent data come from a national survey of individuals' legal needs conducted by the Canadian Forum on Civil Justice (CFCJ) in 2014.[18] Overall, these data confirm the persistence of a crisis in access to justice, but also yield some surprising predictions, especially with respect to the magnitude and scope of the crisis. The first insight is that justiciable problems are widespread among Canadians as a whole. Within any three-year period, nearly half — 48% — of adult Canadians will experience at least one justiciable problem that they consider serious and difficult to resolve.[19] 42% of those will face three or more such problems over this same period.[20] These data leave little doubt that Canadians frequently confront justiciable problems, despite the relatively-small percentage of those problems that are dealt with by lawyers, and the even smaller percentage that are adjudicated by courts and tribunals.

Second, the CFCJ's research tells us that more than half of the problems that people experience are likely to fall into only a few legal categories. The most frequently reported problems among those respondents who confronted one or more problems within a three-year period are consumer (23%), debt (21%) and employment (16%) issues.[21] While these numbers alone do not tell us anything about the relative seriousness of the problems that people face or about their real impact on peoples' lives, they do suggest that certain types of problems—and therefore certain types of legal claims—may have a disproportionate impact on the Canadian public as a whole.

---

[18] Trevor C.W. Farrow et al., Everyday Legal Problems and the Cost of Justice in Canada: Overview Report (Toronto: Canadian Forum on Civil Justice, 2016). See also Ab Currie, *Nudging the Paradigm Shift, Everyday Legal Problems in Canada* (Toronto: Canadian Forum on Civil Justice, 2016). For earlier studies in Canada, *see* Ab Currie, "A National Survey of the Civil Justice Problems of Low and Moderate Income Canadians: Incidence and Patterns" (2006) 13.3 International Journal of the Legal Professions 217; Ab Currie, "The Legal Problems of Everyday Life" in Rebecca L. Sandefur, ed., *The Sociology of Law Crime and Deviance: Vol. 12* (UK: Emerald, 2009) 1-42.

[19] Trevor C.W. Farrow et al., *Everyday Legal Problems and the Cost of Justice in Canada: Overview Report* (Toronto: Canadian Forum on Civil Justice, 2016) at 2.

[20] Ab Currie, *Nudging the Paradigm Shift, Everyday Legal Problems in Canada* (Toronto: Canadian Forum on Civil Justice, 2016) at 7.

[21] Trevor C.W. Farrow et al., *Everyday Legal Problems and the Cost of Justice in Canada: Overview Report* (Toronto: Canadian Forum on Civil Justice, 2016) at 7-8. "Consumer problems" admittedly covers a broad range of potential issues related to consuming goods and services—for example, problems with defective goods or problems related to contractual obligations for services purchased.

A third lesson from these data is that when people experience more than one justiciable problem at a time, the problems tend to be related to each other in complex ways. For example, the CFCJ study found that the three most prevalent problem types among Canadians tend to "cluster" together, meaning that experiencing one of consumer, debt or employment issues increases the likelihood of that same individual confronting the other two problems.[22] While the study did not identify other specific clusters, national surveys in other jurisdictions have found evidence of clusters linking problems related to homelessness with police action, and family problems with domestic violence.[23] Likewise, certain problems such as the breakdown of a family relationship have been found to "trigger" other problems in a cascading pattern.[24] Although the root causes of problem clustering and triggering are still poorly understood, we might expect that at least some of these linkages are based on systemic poverty, discrimination and other factors of social exclusion. That hypothesis is supported by the available evidence on the demographic characteristics of those who experience justiciable problems, with income, status as an Indigenous person, status as a visible minority, country of birth, age, (dis)ability, employment, and level of education all shown to be significant predictors for one or more problem types.[25]

Finally, the available evidence gives us some picture of how people tend to respond to justiciable problems when they arise. The CFCJ's study found that only five percent of people in the sample with one or more problems "lumped it", *i.e.*, took no action in response. By comparison, 19% of those with problems obtained advice from a lawyer, 28% obtained non-lawyer assistance of some kind (such as from a union or an advocacy group), 33% searched out relevant information online for themselves, and a full 61% obtained at least some advice from friends or relatives.[26] In other words, it appears that people tend to pursue a range of strategies in response to their problems. And while advice from lawyers no doubt occupies an important place among those strategies, these data suggest that it is unhelpful to simply equate access to justice with access to the legal profession, without accounting for the plurality of pathways that people normally take to pursue a just resolution for their problems.

[b] Identifying Barriers to Access

Merely because a majority of justiciable problems are never brought to lawyers for

---

[22] Ab Currie, *Nudging the Paradigm Shift, Everyday Legal Problems in Canada* (Toronto: Canadian Forum on Civil Justice, 2016) at 10.

[23] *See, e.g.*, Pascoe Pleasence *et al.*, *Causes of Action: Civil Law and Social Justice* (UK: Legal Services Commission, 2004).

[24] Ab Currie, *Nudging the Paradigm Shift, Everyday Legal Problems in Canada* (Toronto: Canadian Forum on Civil Justice, 2016) at 10-13.

[25] Ab Currie, "The Legal Problems of Everyday Life: The Nature, Extent and Consequences of Justiciable Problems Experienced by Canadians" (Ottawa: Department of Justice Canada, 2007), *Department of Justice*, online: http://www.justice.gc.ca/eng/rp-pr/csj-sjc/jsp-sjp/rr07_la1-rr07_aj1/rr07_la1.pdf at 19-25.

[26] Trevor C.W. Farrow *et al.*, *Everyday Legal Problems and the Cost of Justice in Canada: Overview Report* (Toronto: Canadian Forum on Civil Justice, 2016) at 9.

their advice does not necessarily imply that lawyers play a minor part in addressing access to justice, nor does it reveal whether or not people are satisfied with the outcomes of the advice strategies they pursue. An important question is therefore: *why* do people pursue different strategies to resolve their everyday legal problems? More specifically, why do so few people (relative to the number who experience problems) seek legal advice from a qualified legal service provider?

One obvious answer is that many people simply cannot afford to hire a lawyer.[27] The monetary costs of legal services have been a central focus of the several reports on access to justice in Canada in recent years.[28] According to one study, "[t]here is a major gap between what legal services cost and what the vast majority of Canadians can afford",[29] citing the lack of legal aid coverage, the high costs of hiring a lawyer and the length of proceedings for a range of services. Certainly, based on what we know about lawyers' hourly rates and the aggregate cost of many legal proceedings, the monetary cost of legal services for individuals is high compared to other goods and services purchased in private markets. Average estimates from an annual survey of lawyers' fees by *Canadian Lawyer* magazine put the hourly rates of Canadian lawyers practicing predominantly in small firms in the range from $204 per hour for new lawyers, to $325 per hour for lawyers with 10 years of experience.[30] Likewise, in 2015 an average five-day civil trial in Canada cost roughly $56,000.[31]

Other studies on accessing justice, however, arrive at more mixed conclusions about the role of monetary costs in deterring legal advice seeking behaviour. In a 2009 survey of low and middle-income people from Ontario, 31% of respondents who experienced problems accessing legal assistance cited the cost of legal services as a reason for not hiring a lawyer, while another 20% said they were refused or did

---

[27] See Noel Semple, "The Cost of Seeking Civil Justice in Canada" (2015) 93 Can. Bar Rev. 639.

[28] Canadian Bar Association, "Reaching Equal Justice Report: An Invitation to Envision and Act" (Ottawa: Canadian Bar Association, November 2013), online: https://www.cba.org/CBAMediaLibrary/cba_na/images/Equal%20Justice%20-%20Microsite/PDFs/EqualJustice-FinalReport-eng.pdf; Action Committee on Access to Justice in Civil and Family Matters, "Access to Civil & Family Justice: A Roadmap for Change" (November 2013), online: *Canadian Forum on Civil Justice* https://www.cfcj-fcjc.org/sites/default/files/docs/2013/AC_Report_English_Final.pdf; Canadian Bar Association Legal Futures Initiative, "Futures: Transforming the Delivery of Legal Services in Canada" (August 2014), online: https://www.cba.org/CBAMediaLibrary/cba_na/PDFs/CBA%20Legal%20Futures%20PDFS/Futures-Final-eng.pdf.

[29] Action Committee on Access to Justice in Civil and Family Matters, "Access to Civil & Family Justice: A Roadmap for Change" (November 2013), online: *Canadian Forum on Civil Justice* https://www.cfcj-fcjc.org/sites/default/files/docs/2013/AC_Report_English_Final.pdf at 3.

[30] Noel Semple, "The Cost of Seeking Civil Justice in Canada" (2015) 93 Can. Bar Rev. 639 at 650.

[31] Michael McKiernan, "The Going Rate" (June 2015) *Canadian Lawyer*, online: *Canadian Lawyer Magazine* https://www.canadianlawyermag.com/staticcontent/images/canadianlawyermag/images/stories/pdfs/Surveys/2015/CL_June_15_GoingRate.pdf at 33.

not qualify for legal aid.[32] As to aggregated costs, the median cost to respondents in the study who sought legal advice was just over $2,000. 34% of respondents reported that they received legal assistance at no cost, while 23% reported payed less than $1,000. While none of these cost estimates are insignificant, they leave considerable room for debate around questions about whether, when and for whom legal services cost "too much".

Without further data, it is fair to assume that the cost of legal services and the lack of adequate public supports to cover or offset these costs will continue to be important pieces of the puzzle in explaining why so few Canadians take their problems to law. But the relationship between cost and access to justice is by no means a straightforward one, for at least two reasons. First, although we might assume that a person's income is directly related to their ability to afford legal advice, some studies have suggested that people at either end of the income spectrum may currently have comparatively better access to legal services for a given problem than those in the middle, at least for some types of problems (although low-income individuals tend to experience a higher *incidence* of problems overall).[33] Why? Higher-income individuals can afford to pay a lawyer out of pocket, and individuals with the very lowest incomes may qualify for provincial legal aid programs—although legal aid is available only for a limited number of civil and criminal justice matters. This can lead to situations in which middle and lower-middle income earners experience acute financial barriers to affording the services of a lawyer.

The second aspect of complexity in explaining why people rarely seek help from lawyers relative to the high incidence of problems has more to do with perceptions and beliefs than with money. As the justiciable problems approach to studying legal need implicitly recognizes, people only define their everyday problems as "legal" in a narrow subset of cases, meaning that they often do not consider formal legal advice or adjudication as viable pathways to resolve those problems. If, as one group of authors famously put it, the process of formulating a legal dispute involves three stages of "naming, blaming and claiming", many justiciable problems appear never to be "named" as legal problems at all.[34] Based on her research in "Middle City" America, legal sociologist Rebecca Sandefur observes that:[35]

> [A]mong the most surprising findings of contemporary research in the U.S. context is that people do not typically highlight the cost of legal services as a main reason for not turning to law for the justice problems that they face. . . In Middle City in

---

[32] Environics Research Group, "Civil Legal Needs of Lower and Middle-Income Ontarians: Quantitative Research" (Toronto: Ontario Civil Legal Needs Project, 2009) at 31-32.

[33] Pascoe Pleasence & Nigel Balmer, "Caught in the Middle: Justiciable Problems and the Use of Lawyers" in Michael Trebilcock, Anthony Duggan & Lorne Sossin, eds., *Middle Income Access to Justice* (Toronto: University of Toronto Press, 2012) at 49-50.

[34] William Felstiner, Richard Abel & Austin Sarat, "The Emergence and Transformation of Disputes: Naming, Blaming, Claiming. . ." (1980) 15 Law & Society 631.

[35] Rebecca L. Sandefur, "What We Know and Need to Know About the Legal Needs of the Public" (2015) 67 S.C.L. Rev. 443 at 449-450.

2013, cost explained the failure to seek assistance for 17% of reported justice problems; the reason for not seeking further help for the other 83% of problems was something else, not cost. In Middle City, the most common reasons people reported for not seeking help are revealed to be variants on, "I don't need any."

Similar findings have been made by Canadian researchers studying legal representation in family law disputes, who observe that an inability to afford a lawyer is a major factor in the lack of representation, but litigants' motivations for not having a lawyer are often complex, including the rise of "do it yourself" social attitudes and a perception of some self-represented litigants that having a lawyer will not result in a significantly better outcome.[36] As Sandefur notes, these findings do not minimize the significant role of cost in making justice inaccessible, but they do "suggest that the role it plays is more subtle than we might expect".[37]

One lesson from recent research on this issue is that advice-seeking behaviour is heavily influenced by the type of justiciable problems people face. Across several countries, individuals have been shown to consult lawyers more frequently about problems such as family breakdown, housing, and drafting a will compared to other types.[38] Another lesson is that once a justiciable problem *is* characterized by the person experiencing it as a "legal" problem, they are much more likely to seek out help from lawyers and other legal professionals.[39] On the other hand, the characterization of problems as "legal" has not been found to affect the frequency with which individuals seek advice from other sources — a finding that may have significant implications for expanding our conception of possible solutions.[40]

Finally, the monetary costs of lawyers' fees are almost certainly not the only set of cost factors that influence peoples' decisions about how to respond to their justiciable problems. Other supply-side barriers have also been identified as significant impediments to access to justice. The complex and often confusing structure of justice systems themselves can act as a deterrent for people to have their disputes formally adjudicated. This is true not only of civil and criminal justice systems that tend to be the focus of much policy reform, but also of modern administrative systems that have traditionally been rationalized as low-cost forums for people to resolve many everyday legal problems. The tendency of these

---

[36] Rachel Birnbaum, Nicholas Bala & Lorne Bertrand, "The Rise of Self-Representation in Canada's Family Courts: The Complex Picture Revealed in Surveys of Judges, Lawyers and Litigants" (2012) 91 Can. Bar Rev. 67 at 71.

[37] Rebecca L. Sandefur, "What We Know and Need to Know About the Legal Needs of the Public" (2015) 67 S.C.L. Rev. 443 at 450.

[38] Pascoe Pleasence, Nigel Balmer & Stian Reimers, "What Really Drives Advice Seeking Behaviour? Looking Beyond the Subject of Legal Disputes" (2011) 1.6 Oñati Socio-Legal Series at 3.

[39] Pascoe Pleasence, Nigel Balmer & Stian Reimers, "What Really Drives Advice Seeking Behaviour? Looking Beyond the Subject of Legal Disputes" (2011) 1.6 Oñati Socio-Legal Series at 14.

[40] Pascoe Pleasence, Nigel Balmer & Stian Reimers, "What Really Drives Advice Seeking Behaviour? Looking Beyond the Subject of Legal Disputes" (2011) 1.6 Oñati Socio-Legal Series at 17.

problems to "cluster" suggests that organization of many boards and tribunals into isolated silos does not accurately reflect the actual experiences of justice systems users, nor does it offer cost-effective means for these users to meet their legal needs.[41] Recent empirical work has also drawn attention to the spatial or geographic barriers to accessing justice — especially for those living in rural and remote regions with small and often dwindling numbers of lawyers and other legal advice providers.[42]

Compounding these challenges is the recognition that, especially for members of marginalized communities, "law is all too often an author of oppression" instead of a viable response to justiciable problems.[43] From this perspective, simply providing "more" access to law and legal systems is clearly insufficient. In other words, what needs to be taken into account is not only the quantity but also the quality of responses to justiciable problems, measured at least in part by the experiences— including the historical and inter-generational experiences—of people and communities with and within systems of justice. For example, in a study of the experiences of Arab and Muslim individuals with Canadian human rights law between 2002 and 2017, Reem Bahdi found that using the legal system to address human rights problems caused a "spiraling and multiplying effect" for some claimants that negatively impacted their lives.[44] These findings raise the troubling prospect that not only do unaddressed justiciable problems cluster together, but efforts to address those problems by going to law may themselves cause or compound clustering effects. The challenges associated with law's oppressive rather than remedial consequences are closely bound up with the important question, discussed next, of how one defines "access to justice".

[c] Defining Access to Justice

Although we still have much to learn about the problems people confront and about why they bring their problems to law so infrequently, the role of legal consciousness in formulating legal claims and the various cost barriers in play suggest that any attempt to define "access to justice" is likely to be highly subjective. A recent study in the Ontario that asked participants to define access to justice in their own words, and to discuss barriers to access identified no less than 10 broad themes related to these questions. Participants in this study offered some of the following reflections:

> "Access to justice means everyone can . . . join into it, enjoy it, and participate. And . . . have the responsibility."

> "Access to justice is ... access to lawyers."

> "I think there are a lot of people who don't ... understand what the justice system

---

[41] Lorne Sossin & Jamie Baxter, "Ontario's Administrative Tribunal Clusters: A Glass Half-Full or Half-empty for Administrative Justice?" (2012) 12 O.U.C.L.J. 157.

[42] Jamie Baxter & Albert Yoon, "No Lawyer for a Hundred Miles? Mapping the New Geography of Access of Justice in Canada" (2014) 52 Osgoode Hall L.J. 9.

[43] Sarah Buhler, "'Don't Want to Get Exposed': Law's Violence and Access to Justice" (2017) 26 J. L. & Soc. Pol'y 68 at 68.

[44] Reem Bahdi, "Arabs, Muslims, Human Rights and Access to Justice and Institutional Trustworthiness: Insights from Thirteen Legal Narratives" (2018) 96 Can. Bar Rev. 72.

is or how to use it — struggling to earn a living, dealing with addictions ... . Unless we address the living conditions that they're dealing with there really is a fundamental issue with access."

"People with money have access to more justice than people without."

"Access to justice looks really different depending on who you are and where you come from . . . because so much of justice and so much of anything related to justice . . . intersects [with] . . . class, gender, race. . . ."

"I know horrendous stories about people seeking justice and they went eighteen, twenty years before it was decided. And when it was finished, when all was said and done, they didn't really get justice. They might have . . . got their day in court."[45]

One way to reflect on these first-person perspectives is to compare them to recent attempts to provide a more formal definition of "access to justice" as the basis for identifying how to respond and who is responsible for doing so. Former Supreme Court Justice Thomas Cromwell, who served as Chair of the Action Committee on Access to Justice in Civil and Family Matters, has offered a definition of access to justice as "the knowledge, resources and services to deal effectively with civil and family legal matters", while at the same time rejecting a "court-centric" view of what such knowledge, resources and services might entail.[46] This approach—while significantly broader than definitions used in the past—focuses attention on meeting the needs of justice system users and satisfying their private interests in achieving access. Others have emphasized the public dimension in defining access to justice. Hazel Genn offers the following perspective, which resonates closely with Chief Justice McLachlin's observations above:

> My starting point is that the civil justice system is a public good that serves more than private interests. The civil courts contribute quietly and significantly to social and economic well-being. They play a part in the sense that we live in an orderly society where there are rights and protections, and that these rights and protections can be made good. In societies governed by the rule of law, the courts provide the community's defence against arbitrary government action. They promote social order and facilitate the peaceful resolution of disputes. In publishing their decisions, the courts communicate and reinforce civic values and norms. Most importantly, the civil courts support economic activity. Law is pivotal to the functioning of markets. Contracts between strangers are possible because rights are fairly allocated within a known legal framework and are enforceable through the courts if they are breached. Thriving economies depend on a strong state that will secure property rights and investments.[47]

A full understanding and definition of access to justice therefore incorporates both the subjective experiences and private demands of system users and a view of access as itself a public good. Keep both of these dimensions in mind as we turn to the next

---

[45] Trevor C.W. Farrow, "What is Access to Justice?" (2014) 51.3 Osgoode Hall L.J. 957 at 969-971.

[46] Hon. Thomas A. Cromwell, "Access to Justice: Towards a Collaborative and Strategic Approach" (2012) 63 U.N.B.L.J. 38 at 39.

[47] Hazel Genn, "What is Civil Justice for? Reform, ADR, and Access to Justice" (2012) 24 Yale J.L. & Human. 397 at 397.

question: who is responsible for addressing and fostering access to justice?

NOTES AND QUESTIONS

1. How should "access to justice" be defined? What are the consequences of your definition for understanding obligations to address access to justice and identifying the possible solutions that might be pursued?

2. The available data on access to justice described above suggest that there is a great deal of work to be done to improve the "supply" of legal advice and other means of problem-solving for those in need. But do these data also suggest opportunities to reduce the "demand" for such services? If so, how?

[3] OBLIGATIONS TO ADDRESS ACCESS TO JUSTICE

[a] The State

To what extent does the Canadian state have a specific obligation to address or foster access to justice? The cases in this section suggest some of the different ways in which constitutional obligations binding on the state and enforced by the courts might (or might not) be engaged.

BRITISH COLUMBIA (ATTORNEY GENERAL) v. CHRISTIE

[2007] S.C.J. No. 21, 2007 SCC 21
(S.C.C., McLachlin C.J.C., Bastarache, Binnie, LeBel, Deschamps,
Fish, Abella, Charron and Rothstein JJ.)

[Dugald Christie was a lawyer in British Columbia who provided legal services at low or no cost to individuals in downtown Vancouver. In the years 1991–1999, his income never exceeded $30,000. Mr. Christie's practice ran into financial difficulties after the imposition of a seven per cent tax on legal services by the British Columbia government. Because his clients did not pay him, Mr. Christie was unable to meet his tax payments as they became due, and the government seized funds from his bank account. Mr. Christie also had difficulties affording the cost of setting up an appropriate accounting system to manage the tax. Mr. Christie brought a constitutional challenge to the tax. He was successful at trial and partially successful at the Court of Appeal. The British Columbia government appealed to the Supreme Court of Canada and Mr. Christie cross-appealed.]

The following is the judgment delivered

BY THE COURT:—

. . . . .

II. Analysis

The respondent's claim is for effective access to the courts which, he states, necessitates legal services. This is asserted not on a case-by-case basis, but as a general right. What is sought is the constitutionalization of *a particular type of access to justice* — access aided by a lawyer where rights and obligations are at stake before a court or tribunal . . . . In order to succeed, the respondent must show that the Canadian constitution mandates this particular form or quality of access. The question is whether he has done so. In our view, he has not.

We take as our starting point the definition of the alleged constitutional principle offered by the majority of the Court of Appeal . . . the right to be represented by a lawyer in court or tribunal proceedings where a person's legal rights and obligations are at stake, in order to have effective access to the courts or tribunal proceedings.

We will first discuss what the proposed right entails. We will then ask whether the right, thus described, is prescribed by the constitution.

This general right to be represented by a lawyer in a court or tribunal proceedings where legal rights or obligations are at stake is a broad right. It would cover almost all — if not all — cases that come before courts or tribunals where individuals are involved. Arguably, corporate rights and obligations would be included since corporations function as vehicles for individual interests. Moreover, it would cover not only actual court proceedings, but also related legal advice, services and disbursements. Although the respondent attempted to argue otherwise, the logical result would be a constitutionally mandated legal aid scheme for virtually all legal proceedings, except where the state could show this is not necessary for effective access to justice.

This Court is not in a position to assess the cost to the public that the right would entail. No evidence was led as to how many people might require state-funded legal services, or what the cost of those services would be. However, we do know that many people presently represent themselves in court proceedings. We also may assume that guaranteed legal services would lead people to bring claims before courts and tribunals who would not otherwise do so. Many would applaud these results. However, the fiscal implications of the right sought cannot be denied. What is being sought is not a small, incremental change in the delivery of legal services. It is a huge change that would alter the legal landscape and impose a not inconsiderable burden on taxpayers.

The next question is whether the constitution supports the right contended for. In support of this contention, two arguments are made.

First, it is argued that access to justice is a fundamental constitutional right that embraces the right to have a lawyer in relation to court and tribunal proceedings. This argument is based on *B.C.G.E.U. v. British Columbia (Attorney General)*, [1988] 2 S.C.R. 214, where this Court affirmed a constitutional right to access the courts, which was breached by pickets impeding access. It is argued that a tax on legal services, like pickets, prevents people from accessing the courts. It follows, the argument concludes, that a tax on legal services also violates the right to access the courts and justice.

The right affirmed in *B.C.G.E.U.* is not absolute. The legislature has the power to pass laws in relation to the administration of justice in the province under s. 92(14) of the *Constitution Act, 1867*. This implies the power of the province to impose at least some conditions on how and when people have a right to access the courts. Therefore *B.C.G.E.U.* cannot stand for the proposition that every limit on access to the courts is automatically unconstitutional.

A second argument is that the right to have a lawyer in cases before courts and tribunals dealing with rights and obligations is constitutionally protected, either as an aspect of the rule of law, or a precondition to it.

. . . . .

The rule of law embraces at least three principles. The first principle is that the "law is supreme over officials of the government as well as private individuals, and thereby preclusive of the influence of arbitrary power" . . . The second principle "requires the creation and maintenance of an actual order of positive laws which preserves and embodies the more general principle of normative order" . . . The third principle requires that "the relationship between the state and the individual . . . be regulated by law".

. . . . .

It is clear from a review of these principles that general access to legal services is not a currently-recognized aspect of the rule of law. However, in *Imperial Tobacco*, this Court left open the possibility that the rule of law may include additional principles. It is therefore necessary to determine whether general access to legal services in relation to court and tribunal proceedings dealing with rights and obligations is a fundamental aspect of the rule of law.

Before examining this question, it is important to note that this Court has repeatedly emphasized the important role that lawyers play in ensuring access to justice and upholding the rule of law . . . This is only fitting. Lawyers are a vital conduit through which citizens access the courts, and the law. They help maintain the rule of law by working to ensure that unlawful private and unlawful state action in particular do not go unaddressed. The role that lawyers play in this regard is so important that the right to counsel in some situations has been given constitutional status.

The issue, however, is whether *general* access to legal services in relation to court and tribunal proceedings dealing with rights and obligations is a fundamental aspect of the rule of law. In our view, it is not. Access to legal services is fundamentally important in any free and democratic society. In some cases, it has been found essential to due process and a fair trial. But a review of the constitutional text, the jurisprudence and the history of the concept does not support the respondent's contention that there is a broad general right to legal counsel as an aspect of, or precondition to, the rule of law.

The text of the Charter negates the postulate of the general constitutional right to legal assistance contended for here. It provides for a right to legal services in one specific situation. Section 10(*b*) of the Charter provides that everyone has the right to retain and instruct counsel, and to be informed of that right "on arrest or detention". If the reference to the rule of law implied the right to counsel in relation to all proceedings where rights and obligations are at stake, s. 10(*b*) would be redundant.

Section 10(*b*) does not exclude a finding of a constitutional right to legal assistance in other situations. Section 7 of the Charter, for example, has been held to imply a right to counsel as an aspect of procedural fairness where life, liberty and security of the person are affected . . . But this does not support a general right to legal assistance whenever a matter of rights and obligations is before a court or tribunal.

674

Thus in *New Brunswick*, the Court was at pains to state that the right to counsel outside of the s. 10(*b*) context is a case-specific multi-factored enquiry.

. . . . .

Nor has the rule of law historically been understood to encompass a general right to have a lawyer in court or tribunal proceedings affecting rights and obligations. The right to counsel was historically understood to be a limited right that extended only, if at all, to representation in the criminal context . . .

We conclude that the text of the constitution, the jurisprudence and the historical understanding of the rule of law do not foreclose the possibility that a right to counsel may be recognized in specific and varied situations. But at the same time, they do not support the conclusion that there is a general constitutional right to counsel in proceedings before courts and tribunals dealing with rights and obligations.

. . . . .

[Appeal allowed and cross-appeal dismissed.]

TRIAL LAWYERS ASSOCIATION OF BRITISH COLUMBIA v. BRITISH COLUMBIA (ATTORNEY GENERAL)

[2014] S.C.J. No. 59, [2014] 3 S.C.R. 31, 2014 SCC 59
(S.C.C., McLachlin C.J.C., LeBel, Abella, Rothstein, Cromwell, Moldaver, Kara-katsanis JJ.)

[This case arose in the context of a family custody dispute in which the claimant asked the judge to waive her court hearing fees amounting to $3,600 for a 10-day hearing. The Trial Lawyers Association of British Columbia and the provincial branch of the Canadian Bar Association intervened in the case to challenge the hearing fee regime as unconstitutional, and the Attorney General of British Columbia intervened in support of the regime. The trial judge ruled that the province's hearing fee regime was unconstitutional, and the Court of Appeal agreed, but found that it could be saved if an exception provision in the legislation was expanded by reading in the words "or in need". The Trial Lawyers Association and the Canadian Bar Association appealed that remedy to the Supreme Court, and the Attorney General cross-appealed on the issue of the hearing fee regime's constitutionality.]

McLACHLIN C.J.C. [for the majority]:—

. . . . .

In *British Columbia (Attorney General) v. Christie*, 2007 SCC 21, [2007] 1 S.C.R. 873 (S.C.C.), this Court said:

> The legislature has the power to pass laws in relation to the administration of justice in the province under s. 92(14) of the *Constitution Act, 1867*. This implies the power of the province to impose at least some conditions on how and when people have a right to access the courts. Therefore, *B.C.G.E.U.* cannot stand for the proposition that every limit on access to the courts is automatically unconstitutional. [Emphasis added; para. 17]

Hearing fees fall squarely within the "administration of justice" and may be used to defray some of the cost of administering the justice system, to encourage the efficient use of court resources, and to discourage frivolous or inappropriate use of the courts.

It was argued that *all* hearing fees are unconstitutional; as courts are a "first charge on government", charging fees for time in court is as offensive to democracy as charging fees for voting. However, this argument is flawed because it focuses on the type of the fee, rather than the real problem — using fees to deny certain people access to the courts. Moreover, the argument raises policy issues relating to how governments should generate revenue and allocate their funds. Hearing fees paid by litigants who *can* afford them may be a justifiable way of making resources available for the justice system and increasing access to justice overall.

I conclude that levying hearing fees is a permissible exercise of the province's jurisdiction under s. 92(14) of the *Constitution Act, 1867*.

B. The Provinces' Power to Impose Hearing Fees Is Not Unlimited

On its face, s. 92(14) does not limit the powers of the provinces to impose hearing fees. However, that does not mean that the province can impose hearing fees in any fashion it chooses. Its power to impose hearing fees must be consistent with s. 96 of the *Constitution Act, 1867* and the requirements that flow by necessary implication from s. 96. . . .

. . . . .

It is not suggested that legislating hearing fees that prevent people from accessing the courts would abolish or destroy the existence of the courts. The question is rather whether legislating hearing fees that prevent people from accessing the courts infringes on the core jurisdiction of the superior courts.

The historic task of the superior courts is to resolve disputes between individuals and decide questions of private and public law. Measures that prevent people from coming to the courts to have those issues resolved are at odds with this basic judicial function. The resolution of these disputes and resulting determination of issues of private and public law, viewed in the institutional context of the Canadian justice system, are central to what the superior courts do. Indeed, it is their very book of business. To prevent this business being done strikes at the core of the jurisdiction of the superior courts protected by s. 96 of the *Constitution Act, 1867*. As a result, hearing fees that deny people access to the courts infringe the core jurisdiction of the superior courts.

. . . . .

While this suffices to resolve the fundamental issue of principle in this appeal, the connection between s. 96 and access to justice is further supported by considerations relating to the rule of law. This Court affirmed that access to the courts is essential to the rule of law in *B.C.G.E.U., Re*, [1988] 2 S.C.R. 214 (S.C.C.). As Dickson C.J. put it, "[t]here cannot be a rule of law without access, otherwise the rule of law is replaced by a rule of men and women who decide who shall and who shall not have access to justice" (p. 230). The Court adopted, at p. 230, the B.C. Court of Appeal's statement of the law ((1985), 20 D.L.R. (4th) 399 (B.C. C.A.), at p. 406):

> ... access to the courts is under the rule of law one of the foundational pillars protecting the rights and freedoms of our citizens. ... Any action that interferes with such access by any person or groups of persons will rally the court's powers to ensure the citizen of his or her day in court. Here, the action causing interference happens to be picketing. As we have already indicated, <u>interference from whatever source</u> falls into the same category. [Emphasis added]

As stated more recently in *Hryniak v. Mauldin*, 2014 SCC 7, [2014] 1 S.C.R. 87 (S.C.C.), *per* Karakatsanis J., "without an accessible public forum for the adjudication of disputes, the rule of law is threatened and the development of the common law undermined" (para. 26).

The s. 96 judicial function and the rule of law are inextricably intertwined. As Lamer C.J. stated in *MacMillan Bloedel Ltd.*, "[i]n the constitutional arrangements passed on to us by the British and recognized by the preamble to the *Constitution Act, 1867*, the provincial superior courts are the foundation of the rule of law itself" (para. 37). The very rationale for the provision is said to be "the maintenance of the rule of law through the protection of the judicial role": *Provincial Judges Reference*, at para. 88. As access to justice is fundamental to the rule of law, and the rule of law is fostered by the continued existence of the s. 96 courts, it is only natural that s. 96 provide some degree of constitutional protection for access to justice.

In the context of legislation which effectively denies people the right to take their cases to court, concerns about the maintenance of the rule of law are not abstract or theoretical. If people cannot challenge government actions in court, individuals cannot hold the state to account — the government will be, or be seen to be, above the law. If people cannot bring legitimate issues to court, the creation and maintenance of positive laws will be hampered, as laws will not be given effect. And the balance between the state's power to make and enforce laws and the courts' responsibility to rule on citizen challenges to them may be skewed: *Christie v. British Columbia (Attorney General)*, 2005 BCCA 631, 262 D.L.R. (4th) 51 (B.C. C.A.), at paras. 68-9, *per* Newbury J.A.

This Court's decision in *Christie* does not undermine the proposition that access to the courts is fundamental to our constitutional arrangements. The Court in *Christie* — a case concerning a 7 per cent surcharge on legal services — proceeded on the premise of a fundamental right to access the courts, but held that not "every limit on access to the courts is automatically unconstitutional" (para. 17). In the present case, the hearing fee requirement has the potential to bar litigants with legitimate claims from the courts. The tax at issue in *Christie*, on the evidence and arguments adduced, was not shown to have a similar impact.

Nor does the argument that legislatures generally have the right to determine the cost of government services undermine the proposition that laws cannot prevent citizens from accessing the superior courts. (Indeed, the Attorney General does not assert such a proposition.) The right of the province to impose hearing fees is limited by constitutional constraints. In defining those constraints, the Court does not impermissibly venture into territory that is the exclusive turf of the legislature. Rather, the Court is ensuring that the Constitution is respected.

I conclude that s. 92(14), read in the context of the Constitution as a whole, does not give the provinces the power to administer justice in a way that denies the right of Canadians to access courts of superior jurisdiction. Any attempt to do so will run afoul of the constitutional protection for the superior courts found in s. 96.

. . . . .

[Appeal allowed and cross-appeal dismissed.]

R. v. MOODIE

[2016] O.J. No. 2727, 2016 ONSC 3469
Nordheimer J.

The applicant is twenty-three years old. He graduated from high school and has a diploma from George Brown College in social work. He has no prior criminal record. For the past few years, the applicant has worked for the St. Alban's Boys and Girls Club on a part-time basis. In 2014, the applicant's gross income was $12,547. In 2015, the applicant's gross income was $16,211. The applicant has little in the way of savings and does not own any assets. He lives at home with his mother. He contributes $300-$400 per month to household expenses. The applicant's chequing account is overdrawn and he also owes money on his credit cards.

The applicant was denied legal aid. He appealed that decision and the appeal was denied. He asked for reconsideration of those decisions and the reconsideration was denied. In refusing legal aid to the applicant, I am advised that Legal Aid Ontario cited its threshold income levels of $9,000 per year for a boarder (as they initially characterized the applicant) and $12,000 per year for a single income person (as they latterly characterized the applicant). Because the applicant's income exceeded these thresholds, legal aid was denied.

It should be obvious to any outside observer that the income thresholds being used by Legal Aid Ontario do not bear any reasonable relationship to what constitutes poverty in this country. As just one comparator, in a report issued last year, Statistics Canada calculated the low income cut-off, before tax, for a single person living in a metropolitan area (more than 500,000 people) for 2014 at $24,328, or more than twice the figure that Legal Aid Ontario uses. The low income cut-off is the level of income below which persons are paying a disproportionate amount of their income for basic necessities (food, shelter and clothing). Some people equate this figure with the "poverty line" although Statistics Canada expressly states that this is not a measure of poverty. The reason for that is simple. There is no accepted definition of "poverty". As Statistics Canada says "Decisions on what defines poverty are subjective and ultimately arbitrary". Nevertheless, the fact that a person, below the low income cut-off, has his or her income largely consumed by those basic necessities obviously means that they do not have sufficient income to allow for extraordinary expenses, such as the fees necessary to retain a criminal defence lawyer to provide representation in a criminal jury trial.

The Crown submitted that the applicant had failed to take adequate steps to try and find other sources of funds to pay defence counsel. Obtaining a bank loan, having a family member co-sign for a loan, getting a second job, borrowing against credit cards and other suggestions were made. None of those suggestions are, in my view, realistic ones. No financial institution is going to loan the applicant money given his income level, his lack of exigible assets, and his outstanding credit card debt. The applicant's father has made it clear that he is not going to assist his son in any way. Unfortunately, the applicant's mother is no better situated financially, than is the applicant, in terms of co-signing for a loan. The applicant has looked for a second job but he has been unable to find one, at least in part because of his bail conditions that include a curfew. There is no realistic prospect that the applicant could borrow any further amounts against his credit cards, certainly not the amounts necessary to fund a retainer. The costs of the trial were estimated by counsel for the applicant, using the lowest hourly rate permitted by Legal Aid Ontario, at more than $11,000. The applicant has asked family members for monies to fund counsel but, save for $500 he received from his godmother, nothing has been forthcoming.

The Crown says that the mere fact that an accused person is denied legal aid, because they are above the income thresholds established by Legal Aid Ontario, should not automatically entitle them to state-funded counsel. To a certain extent, I agree with that submission, although it would be a more persuasive submission if the income thresholds utilized by Legal Aid Ontario were realistic ones. In any event, I accept that a denial by Legal Aid Ontario, based on income levels alone, would not be a sufficient basis for the court to intervene and order a stay of proceedings. The Province is entitled to set income thresholds to qualify for legal aid, even if those thresholds are arbitrary ones. That means that if the charge that an accused person is facing is less serious, or if the factual circumstances are straight forward, it may well be that an accused person, in that situation, will be compelled to proceed to trial unrepresented.

But that is not this case. The Crown has conceded that this is a complex case that requires the applicant to have counsel. There are Charter applications to be argued involving the admissibility of evidence. There is a severance application to be argued. The Crown intends to rely on the co-conspirator's exception to the hearsay rule regarding certain statements made by the person who actually sold the drugs to the undercover officer. Given the Charter issues and the fact that it is a jury case with a challenge for cause, the trial itself will take, at a minimum, five to seven days. Of course, if the severance application is granted, then there will be two trials to contend with. There is no dispute that the applicant would face a term of imprisonment, if convicted, that could range from a high reformatory term to a low penitentiary term.

. . . . .

It is necessary for the applicant to have counsel in order to have a fair trial. The applicant has satisfied me that he does not have access, on any reasonable basis, to other sources of funds in order to retain counsel. It is therefore necessary that he be provided with state-funded counsel.

NEWFOUNDLAND AND LABRADOR (ATTORNEY GENERAL) v. UASHAUNNUAT (INNU OF UASHAT AND OF MANI-UTENAM)

[2020] S.C.J. No. 4, 2020 SCC 4, 443 D.L.R. (4th) 1
(S.C.C., Wagner C.J.C., Abella, Moldaver, Karakatsanis, Gascon, Côté, Brown, Rowe, Martin JJ.)

[In 2013, the Innu of Uashat and of Mani-Utenam and the Innu of Matimekush-Lac John as well as a number of chiefs and councillors representing their respective families, bands and nations filed suit in the Superior Court of Quebec for a permanent injunction, damages and a declaration of Aboriginal title and rights in the context of a large mining project spanning the border between the provinces of Quebec and Newfoundland and Labrador. The defendant mining companies brought motions to strike, arguing that portions of the claim concerned real property rights situated in Newfoundland and Labrador and were therefore beyond the Quebec courts. Had this motion succeeded, the claimants would likely have been forced into duplicate proceedings in Newfoundland and Labrador. In upholding the lower courts' decisions dismissing the motions, the Supreme Court considered the role of access to justice concerns in complex proceedings involving Aboriginal rights and title.]

WAGNER C.J.C., ABELLA AND KARAKATSANIS JJ. [Gascon and Martin JJ. concurring]:—

. . . . .

D. Access to Justice

The motions judge asked the question — [TRANSLATION] "[c]an we say that it is in the interest of justice that essentially the same debate should take place in two jurisdictions that must both apply the same law, when the courts that will hear the cases are both federally appointed?" The answer in this case is no.

As to the suggestion that the approach chosen by the Innu is problematic and may not facilitate access to justice, in our respectful view, this Court should not second-guess a litigant's strategic choice to sue in one jurisdiction rather than in another. The Innu have argued that separating their claim along provincial borders will result in higher — perhaps prohibitive — costs caused by "piecemeal" advocacy, and inconsistent holdings that will require further resolution in the courts. Both the motions judge and the Court of Appeal acknowledged the potential risk of these outcomes derailing the entire proceedings.

These are compelling access to justice considerations, especially when they are coupled with the pre-existing nature of Aboriginal rights.

As Chief Justice McLachlin affirmed in *Trial Lawyers Association of British Columbia*, s. 96 courts, notably, have a special constitutional role to play in terms of access to justice:

> The s. 96 judicial function and the rule of law are inextricably intertwined. As Lamer C.J. stated in *MacMillan Bloedel*, "[i]n the constitutional arrangements

passed on to us by the British and recognized by the preamble to the *Constitution Act, 1867*, the provincial superior courts are the foundation of the rule of law itself" (para. 37). The very rationale for the provision is said to be "the maintenance of the rule of law through the protection of the judicial role": *Provincial Judges Reference*, at para. 88. As access to justice is fundamental to the rule of law, and the rule of law is fostered by the continued existence of the s. 96 courts, it is only natural that s. 96 provide some degree of constitutional protection for access to justice.

In *Hunt v. T & N plc*, [1993] 4 S.C.R. 289 (S.C.C.), this Court stated that, "[a]bove all, it is simply *not just* to place the onus on the party affected to undertake costly constitutional litigation in another jurisdiction": p. 315 (emphasis added). As the Court noted, this concern over fairness was not new, given that the predecessor judgment of *Morguard Investments Ltd. v. De Savoye*, [1990] 3 S.C.R. 1077 (S.C.C.), was concerned with "tempering ... unfairness and inconvenience to litigants in conformity with the changing nature of the world community and, in particular, in light of the Canadian constitutional structure": p. 321.

These holdings apply with greater force to the context of Indigenous claimants generally and the Innu in this case. Where a claim of Aboriginal rights or title straddles multiple provinces, requiring the claimant to litigate the *same issues* in separate courts multiple times erects gratuitous barriers to potentially valid claims. We agree with the intervener the Tsawout First Nation that this is particularly unjust given that the rights claimed pre-date the imposition of provincial borders on Indigenous peoples. We reiterate that the legal source of Aboriginal rights and title is *not* state recognition, but rather the realities of prior occupation, sovereignty and control: see, e.g., *Delgamuukw*, at para. 114. We do not accept that the later establishment of provincial boundaries should be permitted to deprive or impede the right of Aboriginal peoples to effective remedies for alleged violations of these pre-existing rights.

In the specific context of s. 35 claims that straddle multiple provinces, access to justice requires that jurisdictional rules be interpreted flexibly so as not to prevent Aboriginal peoples from asserting their constitutional rights, including their traditional rights to land: see, generally, *Canada (Attorney General) v. TeleZone Inc.*, 2010 SCC 62, [2010] 3 S.C.R. 585 (S.C.C.), at para. 18; *Trial Lawyers Association of British Columbia*, at paras. 39-40; *B.C.G.E.U., Re*, [1988] 2 S.C.R. 214 (S.C.C.), at pp. 229-230; *Hryniak v. Mauldin*, 2014 SCC 7, [2014] 1 S.C.R. 87 (S.C.C.), at paras. 1 and 23 et seq.

Moreover, the honour of the Crown requires increased attention to minimizing costs and complexity when litigating s. 35 matters and courts should approach proceedings involving the Crown practically and pragmatically in order to effectively resolve these disputes.

Requiring the Innu to bifurcate their claim would undermine the twin constitutional imperatives of access to justice and the honour of the Crown.

NOTES AND QUESTIONS

1. To what extent do the courts' approaches to state obligations in these cases turn on their definition of access to justice? How do you think the courts in each case would define that term?

2. Some commentators have suggested that the Supreme Court's decision in *Trial Lawyers Association of British Columbia* softens or even reverses the Court's position governing barriers to access in *Christie*. Do you agree? See Paul Vayda "Chipping Away at Cost Barriers: A Comment on the Supreme Court of Canada's Trial Lawyers Decision" (2015) 36 Windsor Review of Legal & Social Issues 207.

3. The tax at issue in *Christie* applied to the provision of private legal services, whereas the "tax" in *Trial Lawyers Association of British Columbia* applied to court hearings, *i.e.*, access to public institutions. Do you think this distinction influenced the Court's reasoning in these cases?

4. What role do the individual's Charter rights play in the conclusion reached by the court in *Moodie*? Might human rights play a broader role in grounding the state's obligations to foster access to justice? See David Luban, "Is There a Human Right to a Lawyer?" (2014) 17 Leg. Ethics 371.

5. In light of the Supreme Court's insistence in *Uashaunnuat* that the honour of the Crown demands consideration of the costs and complexity of litigating claims to Aboriginal rights and title, we might also ask to what extent the Court's own doctrinal developments in this area have contributed to problems of access to justice for Indigenous peoples. For example, as Professor Borrows points out, the Court's Aboriginal title jurisprudence rests on fundamental assumptions about Crown sovereignty but eschews the assumption of valid title in the hands of claimant Indigenous communities, who bear the burden of proving their claims in common law courts via what are inevitably long, complex and enormously costly proceedings. John Burrows, "Aboriginal title in *Tsilhqot'in v. British Columbia*" (August 2014) Māori Law Review, online: https://maorilawreview.co.nz/2014/08/aboriginal-title-in-tsilhqotin-v-british-columbia-2014-scc-44/.

6   The role of honour of the Crown has received more intensive focus in the context of ethical principles applicable to government lawyers involved in disputes over Aboriginal rights and title, see Chapter 8.

[b] Lawyers and the Legal Profession

The courts have gone some distance toward recognizing that the Canadian state has an obligation to ensure accessible justice systems. But a longstanding debate persists about whether or not such obligations also extend to individual lawyers and/or to the legal professional as a whole. As you saw in Chapter 10, provincial and territorial law societies are typically empowered to regulate the legal profession in pursuit of the public interest. Surely, that public interest must include regulating lawyers to ensure and improve access to justice and consequently, law societies—as well as law schools, lawyers' associations and other organizations—have embraced, at least in part, the idea that the profession plays a crucial role in addressing the current crisis in access. The past few years have seen an outpouring of activity by these organizations to identify reforms and new initiatives that may help to bring lawyers' services within reach of more people. Several of these ideas and initiatives are discussed below. But, as Richard Devlin has pointed out, the reports and studies produced by these actors have not been very precise or explicit about the respective roles and obligations of law societies and lawyers to address access to justice.[48] Without a clearer picture of these obligations and their underlying rationales, it is difficult if not impossible to answer the question of whether or not lawyers and law societies are "doing enough" to respond. Such a lack of clarity may also be producing a checkerboard system of policy responses across the country, resulting in regional disparities and persistent gaps.[49]

Those who argue that lawyers and the legal profession are obligated to foster access to justice have offered several different arguments in support of their position, but each includes some version of the assertion that lawyers' special obligations in this domain are distinct from those of other actors and groups in society. Which, if any, of the arguments below provide a persuasive foundation for grounding the obligations of lawyers and the legal profession in this context? The rationales behind these arguments are crucial for evaluating the various initiatives being undertaken by lawyers and law societies, which are discussed in the next section.

[i] Vocation

Richard Devlin has suggested that Canadian lawyers' obligations to foster access to justice flow from a self-reflective understanding of their own ethical identity — what he refers to as a model of "Public Interest Vocationalism" that embraces lawyering as a professional calling or vocation. For Devlin, the return to a discourse of "vocation" carries with it an aspirational commitment to promoting the public interest and therefore to fostering access to justice, as well as a commitment to developing the technical competencies to achieve this end:

> As a discourse, vocationalism has had a significant influence on a number of professions, particularly nursing and medicine, as well as law. From the multi-disciplinary literature on vocationalism, we can identify two main variations in what is seen to be the essence of a vocation—the aspirational and the technical. When one thinks of vocation in its aspirational sense it is normally used in contradistinction to "a job" or "a career". Thus deployed, vocation is often aligned with the discourses of goals, values, and norms. The technical conception of vocation takes a different tack. Here "vocation" is identified with practical and functional abilities. In this sense "vocation" is used in contradistinction to "academic", which is often characterized as abstract, conceptual and theoretical. Thus deployed, vocation is often aligned with the discourses of skills, competencies, and proficiencies. Professor Downie and I have argued that the distinction between these two conceptions of vocation should not be overblown in the context of the Canadian legal profession. While each of the two conceptions is different, they can be conceived of as complementary rather than contradictory. One can be characterized as the ends (aspirational—the value of the public interest) and the other as the means (technical—the ability to effectively practice law). We should not seek to prefer one over the other but rather we should embrace both and

---

[48] Richard Devlin, "Bend or Break: Enhancing the Responsibilities of Law Societies to Promote Access to Justice" (2016) 38 Man. L.J. 1 at 15-16.

[49] Richard Devlin, "Bend or Break: Enhancing the Responsibilities of Law Societies to Promote Access to Justice" (2016) 38 Man. L.J. 1 at 22.

understand them as being not in opposition but rather in creative tension.[50]

One challenge with this approach is identifying in precise terms the kinds of commitments and practices that lawyering-as-vocation requires in pursuit of access to justice. As Devlin explains:

> The idea of "the public interest" might strike some as being so amorphous and indeterminate as to provide little guidance for discerning substantive content for a revised conception of vocationalism. I resist such skepticism on two grounds. First, the statutory mandate to promote the public interest concretely rules out certain powerful (and perhaps disturbingly pervasive) approaches to the practice of law. For example, it makes it clear, at the level of principle, that membership in the legal profession is not just a private preference, a personal career choice, or exercise of an individual's liberty right. Rather, it is a publically conferred privilege, a "public asset" contingent on a larger social calling, which entails the fulfilment of certain obligations.
>
> Second, in the Canadian context, I would argue that the public interest in the practice of law can be given substantive content by reference to Canada's constitutional principles and values. In the course of the last two decades, in a series of decisions, the Supreme Court of Canada has outlined a number of written and unwritten constitutional values including:
>
> - Federalism
>
> - Democracy
>
> - Constitutionalism and the Rule of Law
>
> - Respect for Minorities
>
> - The Honour of the Crown and a Duty of Reconciliation with Aboriginal Peoples
>
> - Respect for the Inherent Dignity of the Human Person
>
> - Commitment to Social Justice and Equality
>
> - Accommodation of a Wide Variety of Beliefs
>
> - Respect for Cultural and Group Identity
>
> These constitutional values give content to the concept of the public interest. They provide the juris-generative foundation for public interest vocationalism tailored to the unique history and current context of Canada. Several of these principles — especially the rule of law, respect for minorities, respect for the inherent dignity of the human person, commitment to social justice and equality, and faith in institutions which enhance participation of individuals and groups in society — dovetail quite closely with the concerns of access to justice. As such, they help us to conceptualize the ethical identity of the contemporary Canadian lawyer, and comprehend how fostering access to justice is a constitutive component of that identity.[51]

---

[50] Richard Devlin, "Bend or Break: Enhancing the Responsibilities of Law Societies to Promote Access to Justice" (2016) 38 Man. L.J. 1 at 16-18.

[51] Richard Devlin, "Bend or Break: Enhancing the Responsibilities of Law Societies to Promote Access to Justice" (2016) 38 Man. L.J. 1 at 18-20.

[ii] Trusteeship

In arguing that vocationalism should ground lawyers' obligations to foster access to justice, Professor Devlin points to law societies' statutory mandates to regulate in the public interest. An alternative set of arguments about lawyers' obligations in this context might start with the statutory provisions in each province that afford law societies the exclusive power to regulate entry into the practice of law, and thereby establish a monopoly over the provision of legal services. This feature of lawyers' self-regulatory regimes, it has been argued, places lawyers in the position of special responsibility or "trusteeship". David Luban, perhaps the most outspoken advocate of this argument, explains as follows:

> First and foremost, the bar and the legal academy must recognise that as legal professionals they have a special obligation to support initiatives that enhance ordinary people's access to law and law's protection of human rights. This is not as obvious as it might seem. Strictly speaking, it might be objected that the legal system's overall efficacy is not the special responsibility of lawyers more than any other citizens. To say otherwise is like saying that eliminating hunger is the special responsibility of café owners. Just as owning a café does not make me specially responsible for the food distribution system, so practising law should not make me specially responsible for the legal system. Or so the objection goes.
>
> In reply, I suggest that lawyers are not like other private business people. If we are to think of lawyers in market terms, we should say that society has granted lawyers an exclusive license to market the law itself, a good manufactured by the political community for the joint and shared benefit of its citizens. In effect, lawyers are like trustees—agents designated by a principal to administer a good that the principal has created for the benefit of a third party. Here, the principal is the political community taken collectively, the beneficiary is its members—all its members— and the good is law. The community compensates lawyers for their efforts as trustees of the law by granting them an exclusive license to charge money for dispensing legal representation, as well as by moulding the law to the special skills and training of lawyers, in effect giving lawyers an oligopoly on the provision of legal services. Call this the trusteeship model of the legal profession.[52]

In this "trusteeship model", lawyers have a special obligation to foster access to justice because they are collectively and exclusively empowered to provide legal services — at least, those legal services that have traditionally been supplied by lawyers. But this view of lawyers' obligations has not gone uncontested. In the following excerpt, Alice Woolley explains Luban's trusteeship model more fully, and outlines some of the key challenges and problems attached to this perspective.

ALICE WOOLLEY

"Imperfect Duty: Lawyers' Obligation to Foster Access to Justice"
(2008) 45 Alta. L. Rev. 107
[footnotes omitted]

The most common argument advanced for lawyers' special obligation. . . starts from the "monopoly" granted to lawyers to provide legal services. In its simple

---

[52] David Luban, "Is There a Human Right to a Lawyer?" (2014) 17 Leg. Ethics 371 at 379-380.

form, this argument points to the "government-sanctioned monopoly status" of lawyers which grants to them "significant anticompetitive economic advantage". At points, including at the very outset of the American debate with the 1972 publication of the American Bar Foundation's *The Lawyer, the Public, and Professional Responsibility*, the position of lawyers has been analogized to that of the public utility granted a monopoly and, consequentially, placed under a universal service obligation to customers.

The issue with this simple form of the monopoly argument, however, is obvious, and has been pointed out by numerous critics: with thousands of lawyers available for hire — according to the 2001 Census, there were 64,445 lawyers and Quebec notaries in Canada, and in 2006 there were approximately 3000 law school graduates — lawyers are not a monopoly in an economic sense. Simply put, the legal profession has a monopoly, but individual lawyers do not. Since the competition in the market for legal services operates primarily at the individual level, the profession's monopoly does not result in the enjoyment of monopoly rents by individual lawyers. There are more than sufficient numbers of lawyers to ensure that, absent other forms of market failure, the price for legal services will be set by properly operating competitive forces. It should be noted in this respect that after admittance to law school, the barriers to entering the Canadian profession are relatively insignificant. Unlike some American jurisdictions, for example New York and California, no Canadian province has high failure rates on its bar examinations. It is true that obtaining an articling position can be difficult for some students; however, the availability of such positions is set by the market, and not by the law societies.

In essence, lawyers are no different from pharmacists, dentists, speech therapists, physiotherapists, accountants, or any other licensed practitioner who has educational and licensing requirements, after the satisfaction of which they compete for clients. Lawyers have none of the attributes of the natural monopoly associated with increasing returns to scale such as subadditivity (in which having more than one participant in a market decreases the efficiency of delivering the service in question) and capital intensiveness (in which entering the market is costly, because it requires very significant capital investment — for example, construction of a pipeline). Absent some other form of market failure, lawyers will be subject to competitive forces and will earn no more than is warranted by their "human capital: knowledge, skill, education, experience, reputation, discretion and good judgment". The attempt to ensure that consumers are protected from charlatans asserting knowledge of the law "does not warrant a decision to place a special burden on lawyers to meet the legal needs of the poor".

. . . .

Several attempts have been made, however, to refine the monopoly argument and to make it more convincing. The most influential of these is the argument presented by David Luban in his seminal 1988 work, *Lawyers and Justice: An Ethical Study*. Luban argues that the moral duty of lawyers to provide pro bono services arises not just from the fact they have a monopoly, but more importantly from what it is they have a monopoly to. The legal system is a construct of the human mind and a creation of the state. It does not, like our need for health or dental care, inhere in the human condition, such that a lawyer's work could be done absent state support. As a consequence, when lawyers are given the exclusive right to access that system, they are also given a special trusteeship role within it. Additionally, as trustees of the legal system, lawyers have an obligation to ensure that its benefits are distributed equally and fairly, and "that no members of the community be excluded from the law".

. . . . .

Other commentators have refined the monopoly argument by looking at the question of improper benefit, but by defining that benefit differently. Specifically, they have pointed to particular aspects of the rights given to lawyers by the state and argued that those rights — in particular, confidentiality and privilege — are public assets which lawyers sell for profit. Although those rights, or goods, are in general created to benefit consumers, they provide economic rents to lawyers which it is appropriate to require lawyers to redistribute. In particular, it is appropriate to make lawyers redistribute those rents to rectify the impairment of access to justice which their attainment of those rents creates. . . . .

These refinements of the simple monopoly theory defuse many of the criticisms noted above. In these versions, the obligations of lawyers arise not from the fact of their monopoly *per se*, but rather from what it is they have a monopoly to and from the features of that monopoly. It is not simply that lawyers are extracting monopoly rents which they must disgorge; rather, it is the two-fold claim that the role of lawyers within the legal system places them under a special moral or fiduciary-type duty relative to society as a whole, and that lawyers gain economic benefits from certain aspects of their role within that system, which justify holding lawyers especially responsible for ensuring access to justice. As a consequence, these theories are not rebutted simply by pointing out the existence of competitive forces within the market for legal services and the low probability of monopoly rents being extracted in these circumstances.

There are nonetheless significant issues with these theories. Most fundamentally, Luban's primary characterization of the legal system as a product of the state and as therefore distinct from, for example, the licensing of other professionals providing services not created by the state, is problematic. In making his argument, Luban contrasts lawyers to grocers operating with a license on the basis that the lawyer's monopoly is "manufactured by the state", while the grocer's business could exist without the participation of the state. At first glance this seems correct: our need for food is absolute and part of our individual humanity; the system of laws is external to any need we have as individuals. As a consequence, a person could sell food to us without state support but could not supply us with legal services. On further examination, though, this distinction seems less clear-cut. While the individual considered alone may have no inherent need for a system of laws, any individual hoping to co-exist in a social order will require rules of social interaction (laws) and a means of dispute resolution: every human society will have these features in some form and people who participate in delivering them. How these important human needs are met by a society — whether the need for the food or the need for a means of peaceful co-existence — will be determined by the particular society in question. It will determine how food sources are distributed, and it will determine how disputes and other questions of social interaction and formation are resolved. In our society, the licence of the grocer and the licence of the lawyer represent a societal decision as to how to meet an inherent human need. They are inescapably both inherent and socially constructed, and in practice no obvious philosophical distinction can be made between them. Moreover, no obvious philosophical distinction can be made between the individuals acting in furtherance of those social responses to an important human need.

It thus seems more accurate to characterize licensed service providers, whatever their particular form, as meeting both important human needs and as benefiting from a particular socially constructed response to those needs. But when characterized in this way, the obvious difference between lawyers and other licensed service providers disappears, and so does the justification for the special social obligation of lawyers that goes with it. If lawyers are trustees in distributing law, so too are physicians in distributing health care, dentists in distributing dental care, and even teachers in distributing education.

Another issue with the refined monopoly arguments is that it is not obvious that the property attributed to lawyers by some of these theories — in particular, confidentiality and privilege — is properly so attributed. It is clear in law that the rights of confidentiality and privilege are the rights of the client, not the rights of the lawyer. These rights exist to preserve the dignity of individuals intersecting with the legal system and to ensure that those individuals are able to access the system effectively. Costs associated with those rights, such as less efficient litigation and higher prices for lawyers, are not rents extracted by lawyers at the expense of consumers. Rather, they are simply the costs associated with those protections, much as the need for regulatory approvals drives up the cost of certain pharmaceuticals. If those costs are unacceptably high, it might be worthwhile to check or amend the regulatory rules which give rise to them, but imposing a tax on lawyers, whether in the form of money or a service obligation, has only a loose logical connection to those costs.

With respect to the social benefit of low tuition fees, these are benefits received by everyone who attends a public post-secondary institution in Canada. If it is appropriate to require a reimbursement for the increased economic returns associated with that education (and it may well be that it is), that argument, again, is not limited to lawyers. Further, low tuition fees may actually have a positive impact on access to justice. As law school tuition rises, graduates might simply be unwilling to take on less remunerative employment. A law school graduate with low student debt may be more willing to consider working at a legal clinic than one with debt of close to CDN $100,000.

Finally, underlying these theories is an assertion of lawyers as "gatekeepers" to the legal system. While it would be difficult to assert that an unrepresented individual can access the legal system as efficiently and effectively as one with legal counsel, it is not true that the absence of a lawyer absolutely precludes access to the system. This is most obviously true when individuals operate under the shadow of the legal system in forming relationships which are as of yet nonconflictual: getting married, starting a business, or buying a car. But it can also be true in circumstances of legal conflict. Indeed, significant efforts have been made in a variety of forums — for example, at Alberta Small Claims Court and in the Tax Court of Canada's informal dispute resolution proceedings — to allow people to access the justice system effectively without a lawyer. Undoubtedly, having a lawyer helps, even in those circumstances, but it is not absolutely necessary.

. . . . .

Traditional arguments thus fail to justify imposing a special obligation on lawyers to foster access to justice. The most convincing are the refined monopoly arguments, but even these have numerous problems related to their conception of the legal system and of the role of lawyers within that system, and to their doubtful assertion that lawyers are earning economic rents as a consequence of their clients' legal rights.

. . . . .

C) Market Failure

A third approach to the question of whether individual lawyers and the legal profession as a whole have a special obligation to address access to justice, turns on the nature of markets for legal services. We have already seen that lawyers' monopoly on entry into the legal profession plays a central role in Luban's trusteeship model of professional obligation, but of course this feature of self-regulation does not necessarily prevent active competition for clients among individual lawyers and firms. If legal services markets are fully competitive, then the price of those services will accurately reflect lawyers' own costs (education, overhead, *etc.*) and will largely be governed by the level of potential clients' demands for legal advice. But if, on the other hand, these competitive dynamics are absent or impeded by inherent features of legal services markets, then these "market failures" may determine in part why lawyers' fees are too high and thus why access to lawyers is too limited. To the extent that lawyers themselves benefit directly from such market failures, these windfall gains may justifiably ground lawyers' obligations to foster access for those who are priced out of the marketplace as a result.

GILLIAN K. HADFIELD

"The Price of Law: How the Market for Lawyers Distorts the Justice System"
(2000) 98 Mich. L. Rev. 953*
[footnotes omitted]

Why do lawyers cost so much? Surprisingly, we have few insights into this basic question. Conventional popular culture has one suggestion: lawyers are an avaricious lot who will bleed you dry. Conventional economics has another: legal training is expensive. And conventional professional wisdom has another: lawyers enjoy a state-granted monopoly over which they control entry for the purposes of protecting the public. None of these is particularly compelling. While each seems to hold some grain of truth, each also raises more questions than it answers. How is it that the profession has come to be dominated by vice? Why is law so complicated that legal training is so expensive? Is the public better off with inexpensive low quality legal advice or high quality legal advice it cannot afford?

---

* Reproduced with permission.

The profession has long been both uneasy and defensive about its relationship to the market. Concerns about the commercialization of law practice date back almost as far as the profession itself, and certainly characterize the modern bar. The profession is entrusted with guardianship of the justice system, and so imbued with the qualities of public service, but it also primarily distributes its goods via commercial, private markets. This dual role causes internal conflict in the profession. The American Bar Association's ("ABA") 1986 Commission on Professionalism, for example, saw the fundamental question of professionalism to be, "Has our profession abandoned principle for profit, professionalism for commercialism?"

The relative inattention to the basic question of the economic causes of the high cost of legal services may, paradoxically, be precisely attributable to the fact that the relationship between the lawyers and the market is at the heart of modern conceptions of professionalism. As defined by the ABA's Commission on the Profession, for example, the attributes of a "profession" are primarily found in its relation to the market:

> The profession receives special privileges from the state.
>
> Its practice requires substantial intellectual training.
>
> Clients must trust the professional because their lack of training prevents them from evaluating his or her work.
>
> The client's trust presupposes that the practitioner's self-interest is overbalanced by devotion to serving both the client's interest and the public good.
>
> The profession is self-regulating.

By making the relationship between legal practice and the market constitutive of the "profession", definitions such as these cast that relationship as a matter of professional ethics, not economics. Seen in this light, the high cost of legal services is a problem of virtue, not incentives: the very concept of professionalism requires that a disregard of economic incentives be a moral duty for the professional. Lawyers charge high fees only to the extent that they fail at their professional obligation to the public interest. Conversely, fees charged by ethical attorneys are not "high".

The claim of "professionalism" in the relationship between the practice of law and the market is actually a series of linked normative claims derived from the basic fact of legal complexity. Law requires substantial intellectual training. It is therefore in the public interest that law be practised only by those with such training. Only those with training can judge the capacity of others to practise and the quality of practice delivered to clients, and therefore entry into practice and regulation of practice is delegated to those with training. Set apart from the control of both the state and the market, the obligation then falls to the profession not to take advantage of the absence of external controls: to put public and client interest ahead of self-interest. The profession is first conceptualized and then justified as a practice apart from the market economy.

But the practice of law is not apart from the economy. The concept of a profession may set the practice apart as a normative ideal, but the structuring of the profession is still the structuring of a market. As the question, "Has the profession abandoned principle for profit?" suggests, it is not at all evident that practitioners, even highly

690

ethical professionals, resist market incentives in any systematic way. The question then is, if practitioners are behaving as market actors, what kind of market is this? Is it competitive, in the sense that its prices reflect costs and competitive returns to an efficient use of resources such as training and human capital? Or are there systematic features of this market that lead to noncompetitive prices or that otherwise raise the cost of legal services to levels that should trigger concern ?

. . . . . .

Hadfield suggests that any special obligation on the part of lawyers to foster access to justice should rest not on ideals of professionalism or vocationalism, but should instead be understood as a justified response to systematic failures in the market for legal services. Following on Hadfield's reasoning, Alice Woolley has identified several specific features of the market for legal services that may lead to such competitive failures, thereby creating opportunities for lawyers to charge excessive fees and justifying more direct interventions by regulators or the state to make legal services more accessible.[53]

First, while we sometimes speak about "the" market for legal services, the actual services (*i.e.*, the products) that lawyers provide can vary dramatically from one context and individual to another. In other words, as Woolley explains, "[w]hat one lawyer is capable of providing is inherently dissimilar to that which another lawyer can provide, and what one client needs is inherently dissimilar to what another client needs".[54] This insight accurately reflects much of the data generated by recent legal needs surveys as discussed in Part [1]. Moreover, clients generally lack good information about what type and extent of work is needed to address their problems, leaving them at a distinctive disadvantage in evaluating the quality of services being provided.

Second, because the practice of law requires extensive training and because entry into the profession is tightly regulated, the supply of lawyers and thus legal services in the market at any given time is relatively inflexible, or unresponsive to the level of demand from clients. While the legal needs of the population may change rapidly as the result of changing social, political or economic conditions, the number of qualified lawyers available to address the needs of clients will inevitably be much slower to adjust. Finally, as described by Hazel Genn above, the provision of legal services can be understood as a public as well as private good, meaning that the services purchased from lawyers by private clients also cause wide-ranging effects or "externalities" on society as a whole. Although individual clients are likely to price lawyers' services based on the value of those services in resolving the immediate disputes, legal outcomes in any given case can have both positive and negative effects in terms of the use of public resources, establishing legal precedents, *etc.*

Overall, these various imperfections in the market for legal services can create

---

[53] Alice Woolley, "Imperfect Duty: Lawyers' Obligation to Foster Access to Justice" (2008) 45 Alta. L.R. 107.

[54] Alice Woolley, "Imperfect Duty: Lawyers' Obligation to Foster Access to Justice" (2008) 45 Alta. L.R. 1 at 121.

opportunities and incentives for lawyers to charge unjustifiably high fees that ultimately restrict access to justice. But as Woolley is careful to point out, the conceptualization of these various market imperfections does not unambiguously show that lawyers' fees will be higher (instead of lower) than the competitive market price, nor does the available evidence strongly support the empirical conclusion that lawyers actually set their fees too high in practice.

NOTES AND QUESTIONS

1. Recall that the types of problems most frequently experienced by Canadians involve consumer, debt and employment issues. Should these data influence which of the justifications above are most persuasive?

2. If one accepts one or more of the justifications for lawyers' special obligation to address access to justice discussed above, what does this suggest about *how* lawyers or the profession should respond? Debates on this question have conventionally turned on whether or not lawyers should be required to offer *pro bono* services or to reduce the cost of their services in other ways. But given what we know about the problems that people confront and about their advice-seeking behaviour, might other, more systemic, reforms be needed?

Scenario One

In a 2011 interview for the Canadian Bar Association's *National* magazine, Canada's Governor-General David Johnston suggested to Canadian lawyers, "I would be inclined to say that we should see 10% of our time devoted to *pro bono* causes as part of our professional responsibility. The figure is about three per cent now . . ."[55] In 2012, the State of New York became the first jurisdiction in the United States to require the completion of 50 hours of *pro bono* service as a condition for admission to the state bar.[56] Should Canadian law societies impose a mandatory *pro bono* requirement? If so, what should that requirement be? How could this requirement be justified, if at all, using one or more of the theories described above?

[4] RESPONDING TO THE CRISIS

[a] An Overview

In 2013, the Action Committee on Access to Justice in Civil and Family Matters — a group established by the Chief Justice of the Supreme Court of Canada and made up of actors from across the civil and family justice system — published its first comprehensive report in the form of a "roadmap" for reforms to address access to justice. This roadmap provides a broad overview of potential reform initiatives, with the Committee's first three recommendations addressing specific innovation goals related to everyday legal problems, access to essential legal services, and the role of

---

[55] Quoted in, Adam Dodek, "Mandated or Mandatory Pro Bono" (May 3, 2012), slaw.ca. Online: http://www.slaw.ca/2012/05/03/mandated-or-mandatory-pro-bono/.

[56] *See* Justin Hansford, "Lippman's Law: Debating the Fifty-Hour Pro Bono Requirement for Bar Admission" (2014) 41 Fordham Urb. L.J. at 1141.

courts and tribunals. Consider the objectives, feasibility and audience of these proposed responses in light of Patricia Hughes' critique that follows.

ACCESS TO CIVIL & FAMILY JUSTICE: A ROADMAP FOR CHANGE

Action Committee on Access to Justice in Civil and Family Matters
(Ottawa, 2013)*
[footnotes omitted]

A) Refocus the Justice System to Reflect and Address Everyday Legal Problems – By 2018

(i) Widen the Focus from Dispute Resolution to Education and Prevention

As we saw earlier in part 1, people experience and deal with most everyday legal problems outside of the traditional formal justice system; or put differently, only a small portion of legal problems — approximately 6.5 per cent — ever reach the formal justice system.

The justice system must acknowledge this reality by widening its focus from its current (and expensive) court-based "emergency room" orientation to include education and dispute prevention. As one member of the public recently commented, it would be helpful if "a little more money can be spent on education ... to prevent heading to jail or court, to prevent it before it starts...." This shift in focus is designed to help the most people in the most efficient, effective and just way at the earliest point in the process.

To achieve this shift, the justice system must be significantly enhanced so that it provides a flexible continuum of justice services, which includes court services of course, but which is not dominated by those more expensive services. The motto might be: "court if necessary, but not necessarily court."

(ii) Build a Robust "Front End": Early Resolution Services Sector

A key element of this expanded continuum of services is a robust, coherent and coordinated "front end" (prior to more formal court and tribunal related services), which is referred to by the Action Committee as the Early Resolution Services Sector (ERSS). It is the ERSS that will provide accessible justice services at a time and place at which most everyday legal problems occur.

(iii) Improve Accessibility to and Coordination of Public Legal Information

Providing access to legal information is an important aspect of the ERSS. The good news is that there is an enormous amount of publicly available legal information in Canada and that there are active and creative information providers.

But there are significant challenges. It is not always clear to the user what information is authoritative, current or reliable. There is work to be done to improve the accessibility and in some cases the quality of these resources. The biggest challenge, however, is the lack of integration and coordination among information providers. A much greater degree of coordination and integration is required to avoid duplication of effort and to provide clear paths for the public to reliable information.

---

* Reproduced with permission.

This could be achieved through enhanced coordination and cooperation among providers, the development of regional, sector or national information portals, authoritative online information hubs, virtual self-help information services, certification protocols, a complaints process, *etc.*

(iv) Justice Continuum Must Be Reflective of the Population it Serves

Services within the justice continuum must reflect and be responsive to Canada's culturally and geographically diverse population. We need to focus on the needs of marginalized groups and communities and to recognize that there are many barriers to accessing the formal and informal systems — language, financial status, mental health capacity, geographical remoteness, gender, class, religion, sexual orientation, immigration status, culture and aboriginal status. We need to identify these barriers to access to justice and take steps to eliminate them.

B) Make Essential Legal Services Available to Everyone – By 2018

(i) Modernize and Expand the Legal Services Sector

Many everyday problems require legal services from legal professionals. For many, those services are not accessible. Innovations are needed in the way we provide essential legal services in order to make them available to everyone. The profession — including the Canadian Bar Association, the Federation of Law Societies of Canada, law societies, regional and other lawyer associations — will, together with the national and local access to justice organizations discussed below, take a leadership role in this important innovation process.

Specific innovations and improvements that should be considered and potentially developed include:

- limited scope retainers – "unbundling";
- alternative business and delivery models;
- increased opportunities for paralegal services;
- increased legal information services by lawyers and qualified non-lawyers;
- appropriate outsourcing of legal services;
- summary advice and referrals;
- alternative billing models;
- legal expense insurance and broad-based legal care;
- pro bono and low bono services;
- creative partnerships and initiatives designed to encourage expanding access to legal services – particularly to low income clients;
- programs to promote justice services to rural and remote communities as well as marginalized and equity seeking communities; and
- programs that match unmet legal needs with unmet legal markets.

(ii) Increase Legal Aid Services and Funding

Legal services provided by lawyers, paralegals and other trained legal service providers are vital to assuring access to justice in all sectors, particularly for low and moderate income communities and other rural, remote and marginalized groups in society. To assist with the provision of these services for civil and family legal problems, it is essential that the availability of legal aid services for civil and family legal problems be increased.

(iii) Make Access to Justice a Central Aspect of Professionalism

Access to justice must become more than a vague and aspirational principle. Law societies and lawyers must see it as part of a modern — "sustainable"— notion of legal professionalism. Access to justice should feature prominently in law school curricula, bar admission and continuing education programs, codes of conduct, etc. Mentoring will be important to sustained success. Serving the public — in the form of concrete and measurable outcomes — should be an increasingly central feature of professionalism.

B) Make Courts and Tribunals Fully Accessible Multi-Service Centres for Public Dispute *Resolution – By 2019*

(i) Courts and Tribunals Must Be Accessible to and Reflective of the Society they Serve

The Canadian justice system is currently served by excellent lawyers, judges, courts and tribunals. The problem is not their quality, but rather their accessibility. While many of the goals and recommendations considered elsewhere in this report focus on the parts of the justice system that lie outside of formal dispute resolution processes, there is still a central role for robust and accessible public dispute resolution venues. Justice — including a robust court and tribunal system — is very much a central part of any access to justice discussion. However, to make courts and tribunals more accessible to more people and more cases, they must be significantly reformed with the user centrally in mind.

While maintaining their constitutional and administrative importance in the context of a democracy governed by the rule of law, courts and tribunals must become much more accessible to and reflective of the needs of the society they serve. Put simply, just, creative and proportional processes should be available for all legal problems that need dispute resolution assistance. We recognize that much has been done.

We also recognize that much more can be done. Further, the resources and support that are needed for initiatives discussed elsewhere in this report should not come at the expense of service to the public and respect for other important and ongoing initiatives that are working to improve access to justice in courts and tribunals.

(ii) Courts and Tribunals Should Become Multi-Service Dispute Resolution Centres

In the spirit of the "multi-door courthouse", a range of dispute resolution services — negotiation, conciliation and mediation, judicial dispute resolution, mini-trials, *etc.*, as well as motions, applications, full trials, hearings and appeals — should be offered within most courts and tribunals. Some form of court-annexed dispute resolution process — mediation, judicial dispute resolution, etc. — should be more readily available in virtually all cases. While masters, judges and panel members will do some of this work, some of it can also be offered by trained court staff, duty counsel, dispute resolution officers, court-based mediators and others.

Building on the current administrative law model, specialized court services — *e.g.*, mental health courts, municipal courts, commercial lists, expanded and accessible small claims and consumer courts, *etc.* — should be offered within the court or tribunal structure.

Online dispute resolution options, including court and non-court-based online dispute resolution services, should also be expanded where possible and appropriate, particularly for small claims matters, debt and consumer issues, property assessment appeals and others. As Lord Neuberger, President of the U.K. Supreme Court recently stated, "We may well have something to learn from online dispute resolution on eBay and elsewhere...."

(iii) Court and Tribunal Services Must Provide Appropriate Services for Self-Represented

Litigants

Appropriate and accessible processes must be readily available for litigants who represent themselves on their own, or with limited scope retainers. All who work in the formal dispute resolution system must be properly trained to assist litigants in ways that meet their dispute resolution needs to the extent that it is reasonably possible to do so. To achieve this goal, courts and tribunals must be coordinated and integrated with the ERSS information and service providers (some of which may be located within courts and tribunal buildings). Law and family law information centres should be expanded and integrated with all court services. Civil and family duty counsel and pro bono *programs (including lawyers and students) should also be expanded.*

(iv) Case Management Should be Promoted and Available in All Appropriate Cases

Timely — often early — judicial case management should be readily available. In addition, where necessary, case management officers, who may be lawyers, duty counsel, or other appropriately trained people, should be readily available at all courts and tribunals for all cases, with the authority to assist parties to manage their cases and to help resolve their disputes.

Parties should be encouraged to agree on common experts; to use simplified notices; to plead orally where appropriate (to reduce the cost and time of preparing legal materials); and, generally, to talk to one another about solving problems in a timely and cost-effective manner. Judges and tribunal members should not hesitate to use their powers to limit the number of issues to be tried and the number of witnesses to be examined. Scheduling procedures should also be put into place to allow for fast- track trials where possible.

Overall, judges, tribunal members, masters, registrars and all other such court officers should take a strong leadership role in promoting a culture shift toward high efficiency, proportionality and effectiveness through the management of cases. Of course, justice according to law must always be the ultimate guide by which to evaluate the efficiency and effectiveness of judicial and tribunal processes.

(v) Court and Tribunal Processes and Procedures Must Be More Accessible and User-*Friendly*

The guiding principles in part two of the report — specifically including putting the public first, simplification, coherence, proportionality and sustainability, and a focus on outcomes – must animate court and tribunal innovations and reforms. The technology in all courts and tribunals must be modernized to a level that reflects the electronic needs, abilities and expectations of a modern society. Interactive court forms should be widely accessible. Scheduling, e-filing and docket management should all be simplified and made easily accessible and all court and tribunal documents must be accessible electronically (both on site and remotely). Courts and tribunals should be encouraged to develop the ability to generate real time court orders. Courthouse electronic systems should be integrated with other ERSS electronic and self-help services.

Teleconferencing, videoconferencing and internet-based conferencing (*e.g.* Skype) should be widely available for all appearance types, including case management, status hearings, motions, applications, judicial dispute resolution proceedings, mediation, trials and appeals, *etc.*

Better public communication, including through the use of social and other media, should be encouraged to demystify the court and tribunal process. Overall, and in all cases, rules and processes should be simplified to promote and balance the principles of proportionality, simplification, efficiency, fairness and justice.

(vi) Judicial Independence and Ethical Responsibilities

The innovations advanced in this report do not and must not undermine the importance of judicial independence or the ethical standards that judges strive to meet. Rather, they must complement and reinforce these important principles.

PATRICIA HUGHES

"Advancing Access to Justice through Generic Solutions:
The Risk of Perpetuating Exclusion"
(2013) 31 *Windsor Yearbook of Access Justice* 1*
[footnotes omitted]

In many of the recent studies and reports about the problems facing the legal system the predominant focus has been on the lack of affordable legal services and the complexity of the legal process. Several reports have made recommendations for increased availability of unbundled and *pro bono* legal services, more self-help materials, greater reliance on technology, more consensual settlement processes at or in connection with the courthouse and greater opportunity for early resolution of disputes.

There is a rush to implement these recommendations in order to fix what is widely perceived to be a system "in crisis". One report decries "a serious access to justice problem in Canada", serious enough that the system requires "major change". Another warns that "substantive change in the civil justice system has a particular urgency and timeliness". More specifically, one report finds that despite a number of recent reforms, "family law disputants in Ontario continue to face difficulties that include gaps in responding to the province's diverse population, difficulties in understanding and using information, lack of affordable representation and inad-

---

* Reproduced with permission.

equate response to the multidisciplinary nature of family issues". Still another study laments the "dramatic increases in the numbers of people representing (self-represented litigants or SRL's) themselves in family and civil court over the past decade, across North America", referring to numbers reaching up to 80 per cent in some family courts. Yet another emphasizes that it is not only low income but also middle income earners who have difficulty addressing their legal needs, in large measure because of the high cost of legal services, but cautions that the same responses might not be suitable for both.

These recent reports have taken centre stage in efforts to reform the civil legal system, in particular the family law system. Too often, however, the studies pay little attention to a more holistic analysis of the "access to justice" problem, one which explores the meaning of the concept of "access to justice", and which scrutinizes the system from the viewpoint of particular groups (such as members of Aboriginal communities, persons with disabilities, women or racialized women). The reports attracting attention consider "justice" almost in a vacuum; while making brief and, in some cases, mere passing references to particular grounds of marginalization, they place their recommendations in an ostensibly neutral legal system. They do not identify the frameworks within which they promote changes. For example, generally speaking, they do not explain how their reforms would promote a particular form of equality and thus do not consider how these reforms would effect broader change. This is not their purpose: their purpose is to propose practical reforms that can be applied in the legal system, specifically in the courts or in the delivery of legal services and the like and sometimes more broadly to include non-legal actors.

The task of "reimaging" the legal system to include appropriate responses to the challenges faced by all groups is a significant one and it is not surprising that reports seeking to bring about changes do not always address the complex web of factors that create barriers to justice. The list of disadvantaged or excluded groups is long. Mary Anne Noone offers the following concise articulation of these barriers, coupled with institutional barriers:

> Access to justice may be restricted because of geographical factors; institutional limitations; racial, class and gender biases; cultural differences as well as economic factors. The way legal services are delivered by the legal profession, the nature of court proceedings, including procedural requirements and the language used, are also barriers limiting people's opportunity to obtain justice.

Few would dispute that this list accurately – if perhaps incompletely – describes the barriers today. And probably most people would agree that "something needs to be done" to remedy the injustices that result. In itself, it is of concern that these problems exist, but what is even more disheartening about this list is that it was published in 1992, over 20 years ago, and yet it is still valid. Indeed, some of these issues seem to pose even greater challenges than ever.

A number of studies have identified particular forms of disadvantage that constitute barriers to access to justice, recognizing that enhancing access to justice requires responses that take into account these contextual barriers. A recent American Access to Justice Index has focused on low income, disability, limited English proficiency, and gender, race and ethnicity. A New South Wales study identified a much longer list of characteristics: living with a disability, including intellectual, physical, sensory, psychiatric or acquired disabilities; cultural and linguistic diversity; Indigenous Australian status; young and older age; geographic location (remote and rural areas and disadvantaged urban environments); low levels of education and lower levels of literacy; being gay, lesbian or transgendered; women; living in an institution (prisoners, juvenile corrective and psychiatric institutions, immigration detention centres and nursing homes) and having been released from an institution; low income or other financial support; homelessness; not being able to obtain legal representation for family law or violence matters (men); and living with multiple disadvantages. A U.S. study that identified 193 separate tasks that self-represented litigants needed to complete during litigation concluded that whether litigants could carry out certain tasks themselves depended on a variety of characteristics, such as "level of education, familiarity with computers, language skills [whether English is the first language and level of literacy], cognitive abilities and communication skills".

In contrast to these studies, recent Canadian studies, such as Roadmap for Change or the Final Report in the National Self-Represented Litigants Project, have, for the most part, named "generic" solutions, such as an increased reliance on technology, pro bono representation and limited scope retainers (otherwise known as unbundled services), meant to make the system easier to access, and have only occasionally considered the efficacy of these solutions for specific groups who are at a higher risk of exclusion from the legal system. The goal in most of these reports is that people seeking to access their legal rights have sufficient help in order to get a fair result. To that end, their proposals are designed to make it easier to obtain legal help or to do without legal help, to find courts easier to deal with, or to avoid courts altogether. Occasionally, there is also a recognition that individuals' legal problems affect and are affected by other experiences in their lives.

The recommendations in these reports range from very specific recommendations for simpler court forms to calls for more expansive steps, such as being open "to re-thinking and re-working the way that legal and court services are conceived and offered to enhance Access to Justice" or for "Refocus[ing] the Justice System to Reflect and Address Everyday Legal Problems". Clearly, some proposed solutions are more attainable than others and some can be accomplished quite quickly and easily if there is a will, while others are more about the objectives of the legal system, rather than any specific part of it. We might disagree with some of them, some may be too vague, one or two may seem "pie-in-the-sky". Regardless, they all have their place. They all add something to the conversation, they all have had their turn in the media spotlight and they all have as their goal increasing access to justice. Because they offer seemingly "simple" solutions, they are appealing to those anxious to "stop talking" and to "start acting" to reform the system.

Despite referring to various disadvantaged groups, the reports too often present "generic" solutions as an option for everyone who cannot afford representation (and are not eligible for legal aid) or to increase the efficiency and effectiveness of the system. At best, they gloss over the significant differences among excluded groups. Furthermore, although most people who could not afford legal representation were historically those with low income, today many people in the middle class face the same challenge. As one lawyer explained to the Law Commission of Ontario in its project on accessing the family justice system,

> Many of my clients are middle class. They have no significant savings so they live off debt or have to sell their homes, borrow money etc. They are often living pay cheque to pay cheque before the relationship breakdown. Things generally do not improve financially after the breakdown. Their children are left during this difficult time in their lives with having parents who are additionally stressed by the judicial system and the lack of a speedy and effective remedy.

Yet those who cannot afford full legal representation, while similar in this respect, may be otherwise quite different. And those who are portrayed as communities distinct from each other may share characteristics in common. Aboriginal persons and persons with disabilities have different histories, experiences and approaches to the legal system, yet a great many persons in these two "groups" may share similar characteristics ("factors of similarity"), such as living in poverty or low income, having difficulty with obtaining transportation to benefit from legal services or having disproportionate numbers of people with low literacy skills. Of course, the reasons for and appropriate solutions to increase literacy rates or compensate for low rates may differ between the two groups, and it may not be enough simply to identify these other grounds (such as low literacy) without appreciating the unique factors that contribute to low literacy in each group. Thus a full appreciation of these barriers (such as literacy, easy access to transportation and so on) requires reference to the considerable work that has been done in compiling these "portraits" of disadvantaged groups. Appropriate attention to these "factors of similarity" may provide a means to bridge the gap between more complex explorations and the desire to implement specific solutions that are not necessarily dedicated to particular groups.

My purpose here is to argue that some of these common traits (low "traditional" literacy skills (reading and understanding the written word), low computer literacy, lack of trust in the system, residence in remote areas of the province, isolation or lack of family or community support, among others) need to be taken into account in designing or implementing otherwise "generic" solutions to increase access to justice. These traits constitute a very small piece of recognizing "diversity" while at the same time cutting across different grounds of marginalization. Without care, generic solutions can pose unintended barriers to people with characteristics such as low literacy skills. We might call these impediments "operational barriers", since they result from the way initiatives to increase access to justice may operate or be structured. For example, literacy and place of residence (rural or remote) are factors that may significantly affect how some individuals can benefit from the generic solutions of use of technology and unbundled legal services.

It is not that those concerned with reform of the legal system do not know that generic solutions do not work for everyone. Rather, they do not usually differentiate between those who can use them effectively and those who cannot, presumably expecting that this will be addressed after the reforms are implemented. However, it is only through deliberate and systematic analysis of how these characteristics affect the effectiveness or accessibility of the proposed solutions to increase access to justice that their purpose can be achieved by putting in place appropriate measures to counteract their non-availability to vulnerable litigants. The risk is that these solutions will be viewed as providing the answer – or at least a partial answer. For example, unbundled legal services have already gained the imprimatur of several law societies who have primarily identified the concerns as those related to their institutional governance issues rather than their effectiveness for some litigants.

The failure to take more specific but common traits into account when designing and implementing these changes will create an underclass of people still excluded from the legal system. The system risks leaving them behind because it is believed that the solutions are responsive primarily to a single factor, lack of the economic means required to access the legal system, and to some extent, the complexity of the system. Unless a more nuanced approach is taken when designing and implementing solutions to increase access to justice in the current movement for reform, those most in need of help will continue to have the greatest difficulty in obtaining it.

NOTES AND QUESTIONS

1. In what ways is the Action Committee's *Roadmap for Change* vulnerable to Hughes' critique of "generic solutions"?

2. Based on your understanding of the structures and contexts of provincial and territorial law societies discussed in Chapter 10, what types of responses to access to justice are these bodies best positioned to design and implement? For example, to what extent should concerns about access to justice shape bar admissions requirements that address issues of representation, diversity and inclusion in the legal profession?

· · · · ·

[b] Case Study: "Low Bono" Legal Incubators[57]

Law schools, especially in the United States, are playing a growing role in supporting post-graduate initiatives for new lawyers to undertake access to justice work–especially in providing services to lower and middle income clients. According to Luz Herrera:

> Most law students do not see themselves as entrepreneurs or anticipate becoming small business owners. When they become lawyers, they generally lack a roadmap on how to use their professional training to generate their own salaries. In addition to helping law students think about creating viable business plans, law schools can offer post–graduate programs to support new lawyers who launch their law practices and incentivize the offering of low bono rates.[58]

One promising model of post-graduate law school support is the "legal incubator", the first of which was established at CUNY School of Law in New York City in 2007:

> The Community Legal Resource Network (CLRN), an attorney listserv that connects more than 300 attorneys who are otherwise isolated in solo and small

---

[57] Many thanks to Bart Soroka, JD Candidate '17, Schulich School of Law, Dalhousie University for suggesting this case study and for his thoughtful insights on this topic.

[58] Luz Herrera, "Encouraging the Development of 'Low Bono' Law Practices" (2014) 14.1 University of Maryland Law Journal of Race, Religion, Gender and Class 1 at 28-30.

firms, is based at CUNY School of Law. The community allows alumni to support and mentor each other while CUNY staff facilitates continuing legal education, discounts on law office management software and products, and opportunities for low bono work.

The work of CLRN led CUNY to develop its Incubator for Justice—a post-graduate program that houses self-employed graduates as they start their law practices and encourages low bono fees. CUNY's Incubator, established in 2007, trains CLRN members in general law office management issues such as "billing, record-keeping, technology, bookkeeping and taxes while, at the same time, facilitating Incubator participants' involvement in larger justice initiatives and in subject-based training." The CUNY Incubator supports up to twelve attorneys who are starting their law firms. The attorneys operate independently from their law firms but CUNY supports them by providing office space at an affordable rate for up to eighteen months. CUNY alumni pay $500 in rent for office space in downtown Manhattan, which is shared with an adjunct faculty member and alumna, Laura Gentile, who teaches law office management and is available to answer questions about law office procedures. Participants in CUNY's Incubator receive training to launch solo practices in underserved New York City communities. CLRN and the CUNY Incubator use their network to provide low-cost legal services to individuals in New York that would not otherwise have access to lawyers. CUNY's Incubator has served as a model for other law schools seeking to support their graduates' entrepreneurial development and the provision of affordable legal services.[59]

Scenario Two

Design a legal incubator supported by your law school. As you do so, consider the following questions:

- Should your law school support an incubator? Why or why not?

- What should be the relationship between the law school and the incubator (*e.g.*, formal affiliation, level of funding or other support)?

- How should participants in the incubator be selected and what should be the terms of their participation (*e.g.*, restrictions on fees, length of participation)?

- How should success of the incubator be measured?

- What broader opportunities and challenges do incubators offer in terms of addressing the barriers to access to justice discussed above?[60]

[c] Case Study: Paralegal Service Providers

One of the most challenging issues for regulatory reform in pursuit of access to justice returns to questions surrounding lawyers' monopoly on the provision of legal services in Canada. Should lawyers be the only professionals authorized to provide legal advice, especially if their advice is too expensive or otherwise inaccessible for many members of the public? If not, who else should be included, and which

---

[59] Luz Herrera, "Encouraging the Development of 'Low Bono' Law Practices" (2014) 14.1 University of Maryland Law Journal of Race, Religion, Gender and Class 1 at 27.

[60] *See* Patricia Salkin *et al.*, "Law School Based Incubators and Access to Justice— Perspectives from Deans" (2015) 202 Journal of Experiential Learning 202.

governing authorities will provide the appropriate level of oversight in order to protect the public interest? Law societies in some Canadian jurisdictions have already opened the door to paralegals, notaries and other individuals who are not licenced lawyers by regulating them to supply at least some legal advice services, while other jurisdictions are actively considering their options. Several commentators have supported these movements, though some have noted that changes will also require a shift in "our collective willingness to embrace the role of new legal service providers as "lawgivers" — as persons who, albeit to a more discrete and defined extent — occupy the same social role that lawyers do as intermediaries between the citizen and the state".[61]

REPORT OF THE LEGAL SERVICES REGULATORY FRAMEWORK TASK FORCE

Law Society of British Columbia (2014)*
[footnotes omitted]

Access to legal services and to justice is best accomplished where there is access to qualified, and regulated, providers of legal services. Law is complex. Ensuring that legal advice is given by individuals who have studied the law and are trained in its application is important. There is no point in creating a system that enables people to access uninformed legal advice, because more often than not, that advice will simply lead to further legal problems.

By and large, lawyers are currently the predominant providers of paid legal services. Lawyers are well-educated, credentialed, and regulated both as to competence and conduct. However, it is clear that not everyone can afford to retain a lawyer when faced with the need for legal advice. It is also clear that, as it is expensive to become a lawyer, some areas of practice in which advice is needed are simply uneconomical for lawyers to provide legal services. It can therefore be very difficult to find a lawyer to provide advice in some areas of practice.

If there is an unmet need for legal services, and lawyers are the only group that can provide legal services, then either lawyers have to review the way they offer services or some other group or groups will need to be trained to provide services to meet those areas of unmet need. Otherwise, "access to justice" becomes a meaningless ideal to a large segment of the population. This could have significant consequences on the maintenance of the rule of law.

The Task Force has been very aware of the link between its mandate and the need to develop ways to improve access. Expanding the market of legal service providers is one method of addressing access concerns. Expanding the market will not, however, by itself solve the access to justice problem. There will be individuals who (as discussed below) will still not be able to afford the services of new categories of legal service providers that may be created.

---

[61] Alice Woolley & Trevor C.W. Farrow, "Addressing Access to Justice Through New Legal Service Providers: Opportunities and Challenges" (2016) 3 Texas A&M L. Rev. 549 at 551.

* Reproduced with permission.

Moreover, expanding the market of service providers must not come at a cost of harming the public's ability to obtain helpful advice. An unregulated market, leaving the public to assess the value of the services they have contracted, is not in the overall public interest, as is elaborated on in the section below.

Public Interest

At each stage of its analysis, the Task Force has considered whether establishing new classes of legal service provider is in the public interest. The Task Force recognizes that implementing such a proposal will likely be viewed by some legal service providers as a bad idea for reasons of principle, and will be opposed by others out of a desire to prevent competition in the market place. Other legal service providers will welcome the reforms if they achieve the desired object of improving access to justice. External opinions are important to consider, but the Benchers ultimately must be guided by their determination of what is in the public interest.

When analyzing the public interest in connection with the mandate given to the Task Force, two essential elements must be considered.

First, does the existing model of reserving the right to practise law to lawyers (with few exceptions) contribute to the access to justice problem by creating a market place in which a sizeable portion of the public cannot afford lawyers' services, while simultaneously limiting competition from other service providers? If the answer to that question is *yes*, then s. 3 of the *Legal Profession Act* requires that the Benchers take steps to improve the public's access to legal services. Second, how is the public protected properly in a model that expands permitted practice of law to non-lawyers?

The Task Force has explored information gathered in the course of its research to assess whether creating new classes of legal service provider might improve access to justice.

The reasons why the services are unaffordable are complex. This is not an expression of moral blameworthiness for lawyers charging fees that the market can support.

In its 2008 report, "Towards a New Regulatory Model" the Law Society's Futures Committee reached a consensus that "it is in the public interest to expand the range of permissible choices of paid legal service provider to enable a reasonably informed person to obtain the services of a provider who is adequately regulated with respect to any or all of training, accreditation, conduct, supervision and insurance, and who can provide services of a quality and at a cost commensurate to the individual and societal interests at stake in a given matter".

Importantly, the Task Force noted that the 2009 IPSOS Reid survey found that about 66% of British Columbians experienced at least one serious and difficult to resolve problem in the three year period preceding the survey. Despite this, 70% seek no assistance in trying to resolve the problem, preferring to "go it alone" rather than to seek the services of a professional. The three main reasons for seeking no assistance were: (1) legal assistance was not required or necessary, (2) legal assistance was too costly, and (3) legal assistance was too difficult to access.

In fact, the survey indicated that of the 30% who do seek assistance with their legal problems, only half (15% of the total surveyed) sought assistance from a lawyer. Those who sought help from someone who was not a lawyer did so because of a desire to avoid court, as well as the expectation that non-lawyers are cheaper than lawyers. Most respondents who sought assistance from a lawyer had a monetary gain or loss at stake of, on average, $121,000, while those who sought help from a non-lawyer had at stake, on average, $47,000.

The main reason people seek no assistance is because they did not consider they needed help with their problem. However, cost and not knowing how to obtain assistance were also key indicators. An English study has suggested that while most "inaction" in dealing with a legal problem is "rational inaction", (that is, people make rational choices about whether to seek representation or not depending on a number of variables) "a significant minority of cases of inaction are characterized by helplessness or powerlessness" and that "cost (or at least perceived cost) is evidently an important factor in decisions concerning sources of help."

Further, the IPSOS Reid survey indicates that a lack of knowledge was the most difficult issue for respondents to overcome in resolving legal problems. This was broken down into (1) not knowing what to do, (2) thinking nothing could be done, and (3) being uncertain of their rights.

The Task Force, after considering these findings, believes that it is reasonable to conclude that if access could be provided to non-lawyer legal service providers in areas of law that created high(er) incidence of legal problems for British Columbians, or for which lack of legal assistance was most disruptive to people's lives or leads to a cascading of other problems, people would be more likely to seek some assistance or advice and thereby be better informed of their options about what could be done to address their problem. They may still choose to do nothing, but at least then their choice would be a better informed one.

On the other hand, they may be better guided about the range of options available, what rights are involved, and what it may be worth to them to pursue the matter with proper assistance.

The Task Force therefore concludes that it is in the public interest to permit non-lawyer legal service providers to provide certain legal services. It believes this conclusion will increase the number of people who seek legal advice by targeting the 70% of British Columbians who do not do so now, as well as at least some of the 15% who seek advice from non-lawyers now (recognizing that some of this advice comes from unregulated providers with no training or qualifications).

The Task Force does not, however, suggest it is in the public interest for there to be a completely unregulated market of non-lawyer legal service providers. Public protection arises from ensuring that people who provide legal services are properly trained, regulated, and carry liability insurance in circumstances where the absence of such safeguards create an unacceptable level of risk. The discussions about the types of legal services that new classes of service providers ought to be able to provide are frequently challenged by the absence of having created the education, regulation and liability schemes. A default position for many people is to express concern and suggest limits on what non-lawyer legal service providers ought to be able to do on the basis of the argument that the matters that need to be addressed are too complex for non-lawyers. This was a frequent refrain in previous examinations by the Law Society concerning the credentialing of paralegals.

The Task Force suggests that the better way to approach concerns about new classes of legal service provider is to start by identifying what legal services the public needs but to which it does not currently have adequate access. The identification of this gap creates the moral imperative to act. The next stage will be to identify the training that is required to ensure that non-lawyer providers can competently provide those services and to create courses to train people to the expected standard. This requires consultation with education providers and practitioners. It provides an opportunity to take the best of our current approach to legal education and also push forward to address gaps in the current model of legal education. As that work is being done, the regulatory and insurance framework for new categories of providers can be developed. However, as noted, it is premature to engage in the work of credentials and regulation frameworks unless the Benchers are convinced that the public's access to justice requires opening up the market place for legal services. Concerns about existing levels of (or lack of) competency of non-lawyer service providers ought not to dictate the answer, as those concerns are properly addressed by creating the credentials and regulatory schemes addressing these categories of provider.

If the Benchers are convinced that creating new categories of legal service providers is in the public interest, and have some sense of the areas of practice that are being contemplated for these providers, the next step is to seek a legislative amendment to permit the Law Society to develop the credentialing and regulatory scheme for such a change. If the government agrees to such a scheme, in-depth work will be required to identify the specific types of legal services that the public requires and the type of training that is necessary to provide those services in a competent manner. A regulatory and governance scheme would also have to be developed at that time.

Although the Task Force's mandate contemplates that the Law Society should develop the regulatory scheme rather than create another regulatory body to take on that role, the Task Force spent some time considering whether the Law Society was the right body to act as regulator of all legal service providers. In this discussion, the Task Force was largely guided by the work of the Legal Service Providers Task Force, which came to the conclusion that the Law Society was the proper body to assume control of the regulatory functions of lawyers and notaries, should those functions be merged under the head of a single organization.

Much like the Legal Service Providers Task Force, the Task Force rejected the approach that exists in England, where there are multiple legal service regulatory bodies operating under an omnibus regulator, or the approach in British Columbia of the regulation of the many health care providers, all operating under the aegis of an omnibus regulator. In order to best ensure consistency of standards and provide maximum transparency for the public regarding how legal services are regulated in British Columbia, the Task Force agrees with the Legal Service Providers Task Force that the Law Society is the proper body to regulate new classes of legal service providers who are engaged in the practice of law.

. . . . .

NOTES AND QUESTIONS

1. Is the approach to regulating paralegals taken by the Law Society of British Columbia supported by the data presented in Part [1] on the most pressing areas of legal need?

2. If law societies increasingly pursue an expanded scope of regulation for non-lawyer legal service providers, what are the implications for arguments underpinning lawyers' obligations to foster access to justice in Part [2]?

3. *See also* Jennifer Bond, David Wiseman & Emily Bates, "The Cost of Uncertainty: Navigating the Boundary between Legal Information and Legal Services in the Access to Justice Sector" (2016) 25 Journal of Law and Social Policy 1.

Scenario Three

From 2003 to 2007, a group of volunteers in Ottawa provided legal assistance to street-involved people charged with minor provincial or municipal offences — such as vagrancy offences — as part of an initiative called the Ticket Defence Program (TDP). None of these volunteers were licensed to practise law in Ontario. Suzanne Bouclin describes the TDP as follows:

> The TDP was a small group of committed volunteers, comprised of antipoverty activists, service providers, and street-involved people. Its approach was implicitly and explicitly inter-disciplinary. Members were law students, social workers, union representatives, criminologists, political scientists, small business owners, home-makers, representatives from the non-profit sector, and front-line service providers. Each member relied on the expertise of the others, and each brought unique political, legal, and social capital to the group. Each TDP volunteer participated in mandatory training on process, such as filing documents, obtaining disclosure, and filling out appropriate forms; substantive matters, such as negotiating with the prosecutor, understanding legal terminology, and constructing sound arguments; norms, such as effective presentation skills, courtroom decorum, and demeanour; and ethical questions, such as how to protect vulnerable clients.

> . . .

> Street-involved people are often transient and experience homelessness in a cyclical manner. It would have been unrealistic to expect clients to meet with TDP volunteers in a "legal clinic" setting or in a law office located outside of Ottawa's downtown. Initial meetings with TDP liaisons generally took place at one of three drop-off points. These were located in downtown adult and youth drop-in centres with which the TDP had established relationships. Liaisons were essentially "trusted intermediaries" — people with whom clients have long-term trusting relationship and who serve to connect them with appropriate supports, including legal supports. According to the Law Commission of Ontario, trusted intermediaries "have a knowledge of and sensitivity to the challenges posed by the diverse needs of their constituents". Trusted intermediaries may well have lacked "the appropriate information and training" that would enable them to play a more direct role in addressing their clients' legal needs, but they nevertheless served as important "conduits for the delivery of legal services". Each TDP liaison received training from more experienced TDP volunteers (who worked in collaboration with

lawyers and law students) on the ticketing process and played a vital triaging role. When a street-involved person would present a ticket to the liaison, the two would work together to examine possible outcomes and generate options regarding how to proceed with a ticket. The TDP liaisons endeavoured first to provide information and resources to enable street-involved people to defend tickets themselves.

Should a client not wish to dispute the charge, they could simply pay the fine and all applicable surcharges. Liaisons would ensure that clients understood that such an election amounted to a guilty plea. Liaisons would further impart that should a client want to plead guilty to the offence, they could also appear before a justice themselves to make submissions in an effort to obtain a reduced fine or additional time to pay. Finally, should clients wish to plead not guilty, the liaison would help the client fill out a "notice to appear" in court. The liaisons would highlight that should they opt for the latter, a failure to appear could result in an automatic conviction. They would also explain that should they opt to self-represent, a TDP agent could offer court support by sharing information about the process, assisting clients in preparing for proceedings, helping with travel to and from the courthouse, and accompanying the client to court should that be desired and appropriate.

. . . . .

When a client wanted to defend a ticket but felt ill equipped or too overwhelmed to do so, the liaison would explain that they may have a volunteer (TDP agent) to act on their behalf to avoid being tried in absentia. When informed consent to have a TDP agent appear was established, the liaison would collect the ticket, review and explain the TDP authorization form with the client, and request the client's signature or verbal consent in the presence of a witness. When the TDP was originally organized, the agents did direct outreach at drop-off locations and got their instructions directly from clients. This practice was eventually abandoned as the TDP's reputation was quickly established among street-involved people and the group began to receive a steady flow of tickets. The group deferred to the expertise of trained service providers to meet clients and assist them in generating options for legal representation when appropriate. This is not to suggest that the TDP agents did not have direct and ongoing contact with clients; some certainly did. Others, as one TDP volunteer explains, "have personal relationships with several clients, but ... don't hold formal meetings with them". Instead, agents would informally engage with street-involved people they would run into "around the city and talk with them about their current circumstances and how they wanted to proceed on their legal matters". Finally, when a street-involved person had a legal question beyond the scope of the TDP's mandate or its agents' training, liaisons or other TDP volunteers would share information regarding the eligibility criteria of other programs (especially the mental health court, the drug court, and reports on *R. v. Gladue*) and referred clients to a roster of sympathetic lawyers (the TDP's legal advisory committee).[62]

Like other non-lawyer paralegal service providers in Ontario at the time, the TDP operated beyond the authority of a governing regulatory body. But in passing the *Access to Justice Act* in 2007, the Province granted the Law Society of Upper Canada (LSUC) the power to regulate all paralegals in the province, which included TDP volunteers who appeared on behalf of street-involved people before adjudica-

---

[62] Suzanne Bouclin, "Regulated Out of Existence: A Case Study of Ottawa's Ticket Defence Program" (2014) 11 J.L. & Equality 35 at 35.

tive bodies. After the *Act* was passed, the TDP applied to the LSUC's Paralegal Committee for an exemption under the new regulatory regime that would allow TDP volunteers to continue operating without obtaining a paralegal licence. The TDP argued that the costs associated with paralegal licencing and insurance were prohibitive. This application was denied, and the TDP discontinued its operations in 2007.[63]

Assume that you are a member of the Law Society of British Columbia's Legal Services Regulatory Framework Task Force. How would you recommend that the Law Society address the unique circumstances a program like the TDP in British Columbia as the regulator pursues a new framework for paralegal regulation? What opportunities and concerns related to access to justice are raised by a program like the TDP?

. . . . .

[5] FURTHER READING

Devlin, Richard, "Access to Justice and the Ethics and Politics of Alternative Business Structures" (2012) Can. Bar Rev. 483.

Devlin, Richard, "Breach of Contract?: The New Economy, Access to Justice and the Ethical Responsibilities of the Legal Profession" (2002) 25:2 Dal. L.J. 335.

Eltis, Karen, "Courts in the Digital Age: 'Adaptive Leadership' for Harnessing Technology and Enhancing Access to Justice" (November 30, 2020), C. Hunt & R. Diab (eds.), *Digital Privacy and the Charter* (Thompson Reuters, Forthcoming 2021), Available at SSRN: https://ssrn.com/abstract=3739994.

Farrow, Trevor & Lesley Jacobs, *The Justice Crisis: The Cost and Value of Accessing Law* (Vancouver: UBC Press, 2021).

Leering, Michele M. "Enhancing the Legal Profession's Capacity for Innovation: The Promise of Reflective Practice and Action Research for Increasing Access to Justice" (2017) 34:1 Windsor Y.B. Access Just. 189.

Mackenzie, Brooke, "Developments in Access to Justice: *Trial Lawyers' Association of British Columbia* and the Supreme Court's use of the Constitution to Protect Public Access to the Courts", (2016) 72 S.C.L.R. (2d) 485.

Moore, Lisa & Trevor Farrow, "Investing in Justice: A Literature Review in Support of the Case for Improved Access" (Toronto: Canadian Forum on Civil Justice, August 2019), online: https://cfcj-fcjc.org/wp-content/uploads/Investing-in-Justice-A-Literature-Review-in-Support-of-the-Case-for-Improved-Access-by-Lisa-Moore-and-Trevor-C-W-Farrow.pdf.

Salyzyn, Amy *et al.*, "Literacy Requirements of Court Documents: An Underexplored Barrier to Access to Justice" (2017) 33:2 Western Yearbook of Access to Justice 1.

---

[63] Suzanne Bouclin, "Regulated Out of Existence: A Case Study of Ottawa's Ticket Defence Program" (2014) 11 J.L. & Equality 35 at 64.

CHAPTER 12

CHALLENGES FOR LAWYER REGULATION: CURRENT ISSUES AND DEBATES

[1] INTRODUCTION

As previous chapters in this book demonstrate, there is a strong tradition of Canadian lawyers debating issues confronting the profession and working together to improve the profession. What constitutes improvement, and how to create it, can vex lawyers, their regulators and other stakeholders, but the impetus to make things better is real, and has resulted in positive change. 50 years ago, for example, no meaningful regulation of lawyer conflicts of interest existed; today, a comprehensive body of law and regulation exists in an effort to protect client confidentiality and to ensure lawyers' loyalty to their clients' interests.

This Chapter introduces some of the current issues and debates in legal services regulation. It addresses issues related to technology, articling and licensing reform, ethical infrastructure and entity regulation, self-regulation and alternative business structures. Other key issues and debates in lawyer regulation, including diversity and access to justice, were addressed in Chapters 10 and 11.

In reviewing these sections consider the following questions:

- What does the public interest in the practice of law require in these areas? Do the interests of lawyers, clients, the courts or the general public align or do they differ? In what way?

- For each area, what are the strengths and weaknesses of the current regulatory regime? What are the strengths and weaknesses of the proposed reforms? In particular, how would you assess the efficiency and effectiveness of each?

- What role should regulation play in relation to these issues? What role should market forces play?

[2] TECHNOLOGY AND REGULATION

Like everything else in modern society, legal services and the practice of law are subject to technological change. Within a 50-year span, lawyers have gone from an entirely paper-based model of legal practice to one with computers, a variety of digital tools (including e-mail, computer-based research programs and practice management software) and, increasingly, virtual meetings and hearings. Today, technological innovation continues, with particularly complex innovations seeming possible from artificial intelligence and the use of large data analytics to assist with and shape lawyer advocacy. For example, AI-powered e-discovery software is now used in large litigation matters to allow lawyers to much more quickly review thousands (if not millions) of documents to determine which documents need to be disclosed in civil matters. Advanced contract analysis tools are now available and can quickly highlight pertinent information for lawyers (like deviations from standard language) and assist with due diligence reviews.

Other emerging digital tools aim to assist the public directly with their legal needs, either as a replacement to, or supplement for, lawyer help. For example, an American-based app called "DoNotPay," which bills itself as "the world's first robot lawyer," offers a significant range of functions for users, including appealing parking tickets, initiating small claims court lawsuits, and cancelling services and subscriptions.[1]

These innovations in turn create complex issues for both legal practitioners and legal regulators. The use of technology by lawyers raises questions in relation to lawyers' professional duties to provide efficient and competent services, keep client confidences and exercise appropriate supervision.[2] Technological tools that are meant to be used directly by the public raise different issues, including how such tools should intersect with law societies' jurisdiction over the unauthorized practice of law (UPL) and concerns about the quality of service provided and the privacy and security of sensitive user information.[3]

The next two readings identify some of the recent technological innovations and resulting challenges, related in particular to technological or innovation-based alternatives to traditional legal services. Note that "alternative legal structures" in this context does not refer to lawyers practicing outside of traditional law firms (which we discuss later in this Chapter); rather, it refers to legal services being provided through means other than by – or supplementary to – human lawyers.

JUDITH BENNETT, TIM MILLER, JULIAN WEBB, RACHELLE BOSUA, ADAM LODDERS, & SCOTT CHAMBERLAIN

"Current State of Automated Legal Advice Tools"
(2018) Networked Society Institute Discussion Paper 1
[Citations Omitted]

This paper focuses on the current state of automated legal advice tools (ALATs); that is, technologies whose major purpose is "giving legal advice" as regulated by the legal profession.. . . We include ALATs that use legal analysis, legal reasoning, and prediction functions:

- To give legal advice on their own;

---

[1] DoNotPay, "DoNotPay Community" (2021), online: *DoNotPay* https://donotpay.com.

[2] Amy Salyzyn, "AI and Legal Ethics" in *Artificial Intelligence and the Law in Canada*, *in* Florian Martin-Bariteau & Teresa Scassa, (eds.) (Toronto: LexisNexis Canada, 2021) at 310-314.

[3] Amy Salyzyn, "AI and Legal Ethics" in *Artificial Intelligence and the Law in Canada*, *in* Florian Martin-Bariteau & Teresa Scassa, (eds.) (Toronto: LexisNexis Canada, 2021) at 314-318.

- To give advice supervised or reviewed by a lawyer;
- To assist or augment legal advice given by a lawyer; and
- To offer limited or partial legal advice by unbundling transactions into smaller discrete tasks.

Advice-giving ALATs are currently at the leading edge of new information technologies and are still at a relatively early stage of adoption by lawyers and the legal industry. ALATs rely on advances in big data, interconnectivity and processing power combined with logic techniques variously known as artificial intelligence, intelligent automation, cognitive computing, natural language processing and machine learning.

. . . . .

Artificial Intelligence includes several sets of technologies, applications and consequences. It is used here as an umbrella concept to encompass the AI ecosystem. Artificial refers to machines, and Intelligence is also used in a broad sense as to "learn, reason and act in a rational way."

. . . . .

AI techniques such as text mining, knowledge based self-learning, machine learning and natural language processing are coming into play as a means not just of enhancing accuracy and efficiency of existing services, but in creating new value-added services, such as automated legal prediction. They can analyse huge amounts of data with descriptive, diagnostic, predictive and prescriptive analytics tools.

. . . . .

Recent advances see even more sophisticated AI technologies with even more complex machine learning and artificial intelligence including technologies such as neural networks, natural language generation and social intelligence solutions often layered together. Blockchain technologies add further dimension to automation, as they provide for transactions to be completed in a decentralised, distributed manner with no intermediaries or human involvement.

Earlier innovations, like word processing, email and the internet have significantly transformed legal practice. It would be fundamentally unwise to assume that current technological innovations will have effects that are ultimately any less profound. At the same time, however, the hype (and fear) around automation is loud. Some champions of change argue that "AI and machine learning have reached a critical tipping point" and will increasingly augment and extend virtually every technology enabled service, thing or application". [Yet] while AI and machine learning are at the tip of the hype cycle, they are still at least some two to ten years away from significant adoption.

. . . . .

A critical issue is that the cutting edge of fourth wave applications is fundamentally different from second wave expert systems and third wave automated process technology that used more causal, defined logic. A key difference is that the rules by which machine learning technology recommends decisions are not explicitly programmed by a human, rather the machines "self-learn" from data using statistical reasoning. The machines are provided with gigabytes of data from selected databases and use algorithms to find concepts and patterns in the data, form and test hypotheses, and develop recommendations with analysis of that data.

The more intelligent systems can learn, adapt and potentially act autonomously rather than simply execute pre-defined instructions. The capacity for self-learning in turn enables these systems to build more complex, dynamic and adaptive models, and "improve" their performance over time on specific tasks. However, these machine systems do not "understand" their hypotheses in any sense of human understanding, nor do they reason about the causality in a strong or human-like way. They also do not aim to mimic human intelligence. One vision of AI is to have systems that can learn the causal rules, using for example, inductive learning. However, such technology does not scale nor generalise as well as current statistically-based methods.

. . . . .

There are scales of "smart" in the underlying technologies. Some ALATs are simple, being non-AI tools relying solely on hard-coded decisions. More ALATs integrate some concepts of AI, with most being "smart", using simple pre-programmed causal rules and automated reasoning to make decisions. Smarter ALATs add machine learning where a computer can make decisions with minimal programming, that is, rather than following pre-set rules about how to interpret a set of data, the computer uses learning algorithms for solving particular problems that allow it to determine the rules itself. Deep learning uses more advanced algorithms to perform more abstract tasks. With experience, data, and feedback, computers become better at the relevant tasks. "Smarter" to "more intelligent" sophisticated technologies can parse text, learn causations and correlations from data, and reason about these to make predictions.

. . . . .

A new regulatory issue for legal advice is created by the "black box problem". This refers to the fact that legal decisions, or support for them, may be provided by an algorithm that does not provide any reason or explanation for this decision. The ability to give reasons is critical to sophisticated advice-giving by human lawyers. Decisions made by opaque algorithms are "analogous to evidence offered by an anonymous expert, whom one cannot cross-examine".

The issue is that extracting and presenting reasons for AI-based decisions is a challenging task. Where logic is causal and structural, such as with process automation, this can allow lawyers and clients to see the reasoning and assess how the technology delivered the legal advice. However, an explanation is not as simple as extracting a chain of causal reasoning: it needs to be presented to a person, answer the specific question that the person has, and select the most pertinent causes.

However, the problem becomes even more difficult with many machine learning techniques. First, most of these techniques learn associations using statistical methods, while people present and evaluate explanations using causality. Second, many of these techniques, such as neural networks, learn models that are difficult even for experts to understand. Making these models transparent to non- expert

714

users would be a pointless exercise. Instead that they would require post-hoc explanation that justifies decisions based on input parameters.

With smarter and more intelligent automation where machines are increasingly learning using big legal data, and dynamically so, this is more complex, leaving big questions: How can we trace legal reasoning logic? What legal data has been considered, seen as relevant, and how was it sourced? How did learning occur and were there any biases? And further, deeper questions arise. What values lie within the logic? What conscious or unconscious assumptions have been made that are not explicated? Why has the data chosen been so chosen? This becomes more complex where the ALAT is a commercial service and the owners seek to protect their intellectual property by keeping the logic and data confidential.

LAWPRO

"How Does the Legal Profession Respond to Alternative Legal Services Providers?"
Lawpro Magazine, February 2018

At the most basic level, there are just three options for dealing with alternative legal service providers. They are:

1.   prosecute them for the unauthorized practice of law;

2.   ignore them; or

3.   bring them into the legal services tent.

When it comes to dealing with a human being providing legal services [who is not licensed to do so], the first inclination of most lawyers is that the human being be prosecuted for the unauthorized practice of law (UPL). This is not necessarily a practical option for several reasons. First, there is the challenge of determining whether the startup is engaged in the practice of law. Is a company that owns a website that generates a will engaged in the practice of law? Does the answer change depending on whether it is a simple will with very basic clauses for an individual or a very complicated will that includes family trust provisions? Is a company that owns a web-based service that predicts litigation outcomes or gives strategy advice engaged in the practice of law? What about a company that solely does document review for eDiscovery or due diligence purposes?

UPL prosecutions tend to be very time-consuming and expensive. Most legal regulators do not likely have the resources at present to launch large numbers of UPL prosecutions, and it's probably safe to assume members of the profession are unwilling to pay significantly higher annual dues to give their regulators the resources to do so. It's also important to keep in mind that UPL prosecutions are not intended to protect lawyers' turf; rather they are intended to protect the public from suffering damages due to incompetent legal services. Last but not least, human beings see UPL prosecutions as self-serving and protectionist, and alternative legal services providers helping individuals that were otherwise not getting help from lawyers and paralegals would likely argue that access to justice is being thwarted.

In some ways the second option is the status quo. As a profession we are mostly ignoring alternative legal services providers. This option is easier and far less expensive than the UPL prosecution option, but it isn't in the best interest of the legal consumer. Almost universally, the terms of service on alternative legal services provider websites state that the forms or services offered are not legal advice and are offered without warranty on an "as is" basis. The terms of service also specify that there are limitations to the liability of the provider, at best, a limitation to the cost of the service, and more typically, there is a provision that says there will be no liability whatsoever. Lawyers and paralegals may not like this option as it leaves the door open for the alternative legal services providers to encroach on the work that is currently done by lawyers and paralegals.

To address the public protection shortcomings of the previous option we could consider bringing the alternative legal services providers into the regulatory tent. As the current regulatory regime operates by licensing individuals, this option might involve exploring some form of entity regulation. Another option would be to bring in selected types of services based on an assessment of where client protection or other regulatory needs are important or necessary. Client protection would likely be less of a concern when dealing with a parking ticket but a greater concern where a will was being drafted. Some providers may like pursuing this option as they will feel falling under the regulatory umbrella will give them more credibility with consumers. Others, likely in larger numbers, perceive this will increase their costs and decrease their ability to provide access to justice. So there are various options for less regulation to consider and evaluate.

NOTES AND QUESTIONS

1. How might the technological innovations discussed above impact the legal profession? What do you see as potential benefits and downsides?

2. How is the public interest served or challenged by these technological innovations? Do you think a self-regulated legal profession is well positioned to identify that public interest and ensure that it is protected?

3. Based on your own experiences as a participant and consumer in the digital world, what other technological innovations do you think may affect how legal services are delivered to the public? What advantages or disadvantages do you think may rise from those innovations?

4. An issue that has been identified with artificial intelligence is with respect to the ethics of artificial intelligence, and whether it reflects and accounts for societal diversity (See, for example, Paresh Dave and Jeffrey Dastin, "Google fires second AI ethics leader as dispute over research, diversity grows", Reuters, February 19, 2021, Online: https://www.reuters.com/article/us-alphabet-google-research-idUSKBN2AJ2JA). How might those concerns be relevant to the use of artificial intelligence in legal practice settings?

5. Several jurisdictions in North America have established "sandboxes" where new model of legal service delivery, including models that involve technological innovation, can be test run under the supervision of lawyer regulators. The goal of these test runs is to gather data to see whether regulatory changes might benefit the public interest, and what types of specific regulatory changes may be beneficial. See, for example, the sandboxes set up in Utah (https://utahinnovationoffice.org), in British Columbia (https://www.lawsociety.bc.ca/our-initiatives/innovation-sand-

box/), and in Ontario (https://lso.ca/news-events/news/latest-news-2021/law-society-to-launch-innovative-technological-leg).

Scenario One

Canadian governments collect roughly $740 billion dollars per year in taxes; this is equal to almost $20,000 per Canadian. Many people are strongly motivated to reduce the amount of tax that they, or their businesses, must pay to the various levels of government. Canadian lawyers have long played a central role in helping clients reduce their tax liability.

There are legal opportunities for individuals and corporations to reduce tax liabilities, using opportunities created by the *Income Tax Act* and other legislation. There is also, however, client demand (and some lawyer supply) for tax-reduction opportunities beyond what the law allows. Lawyers who provide such assistance to clients risk legal sanction and adverse consequences (see, e.g., *Guindon v. Canada*, [2015] S.C.J. No. 41, 2015 SCC 41).

Suppose that TaxPro.com is an online service which offers tax advice to Canadians. Users upload their tax returns, and answer a series of questions about their financial situation. TaxPro.com then provides customized advice about how to pay less tax. TaxPro.com is a company incorporated in California. It owns no assets and has no employees within Canada. It offers similar services in multiple countries around the world. The service for Canadian users is based on the *Income Tax Act* and other Canadian tax legislation.

TaxPro.com offers three service packages, priced between $19.99 per year (bronze tier) and $499.99 per year (gold tier). Bronze tier customers are told how much they can save by maximizing contributions to legitimate tax shelters such as RRSPs and TFSAs. However, TaxPro.com also gives users advice about how to engage in illegal tax evasion. For example, they are advised about how to get employers and customers to pay them in cash, so that income can go unreported and undetected.

TaxPro.com's gold tier package is designed for financially sophisticated, high-net-worth clients. It relies on artificial intelligence and machine learning. The program asks users to upload all of their prior tax returns and extensive additional financial information. TaxPro.com has also analyzed information about all of the cases in which the Canada Revenue Agency (CRA) has investigated or prosecuted a taxpayer. It provides a customized plan for gold-tier clients to structure their finances so as to minimize tax. This includes not only structures which are legal under the *Income Tax Act*, but also others which are illegal but unlikely to be caught by the CRA. Depending on the user's situation, this may include using offshore tax havens, the dark web, and cryptocurrency to hide income and assets.

Would a Canadian law society be able to take any action against TaxPro.com? Should it? What regulatory or policy reforms might allow Canadian law societies to better respond to TaxPro.com? Are provincial and territorial law societies the best regulatory vehicle to respond to an alternative legal provider such as TaxPro.com? If not, what regulatory mechanisms would be most effective?

Scenario Two

Sadiq is a Canadian accountant. He reads with interest about TaxPro.com. He is disgusted by the illegal tax evasion that the company promotes. However, Sadiq is inspired by the potential of artificial intelligence to provide customized information to ordinary Canadians about our tax system. In Sadiq's experience, the complexity of this system is a source of inequality. Financially sophisticated taxpayers, who are able to pay for the advice of tax lawyers and accountants, are able to legally reduce the amount they owe. Everyone else is stuck paying higher taxes.

Sadiq wants to start a company called CanTax.ca. Like TaxPro.com, it will ask users to upload their personal financial information, and then offer ideas to reduce tax liability. However, CanTax.ca will only offer lawful advice and ideas. Sadiq wants to hire a small team of Canadian tax lawyers to help "train" CanTax.ca so that it will recognize opportunities to propose certain ideas to users based on their input.

Are there any rules or regulations that you have learned about in this course that would prevent Sadiq from carrying out this plan? In answering this question, review the discussion in Chapter 10, with respect to unauthorized practice of law.

How would you design a regulatory regime that prosecutes TaxPro.com but permits CanTax.ca?

Scenario Three

Ontario's *Law Society Act* states that "a person provides legal services if the person engages in conduct that involves the application of legal principles and legal judgment with regard to the circumstances or objectives of a person."[4] This includes "giv[ing] a person advice with respect to the legal interests, rights or responsibilities of the person or of another person."[5] Similar definitions are found in the law of other provinces. Is Sadiq, or CanTax.ca, engaging in the practice of law as that term is defined in Ontario's *Law Society Act*?

Scenario Four

Now suppose that, instead of hiring Canadian lawyers, Sadiq programs CanTax.ca so that it depends on machine learning. The algorithm examines tens of thousands of tax returns, reported tax law decisions, and CRA documents. It is designed to learn which types of tax-reduction efforts are, and are not, likely to trigger audits and/or enforcement from the CRA. Instead of offering this service to the public, Sadiq offers it to tax lawyers. The idea is that tax lawyers will use the service to inform the advice that they give to their clients. However, the CanTax.ca algorithm simply reports a percentage likelihood that a certain proposed structure will trigger a CRA audit. It does not indicate why or how it reached this result. Would this business plan breach any rules or regulations that you have learned about in this course? Would a tax lawyer using CanTax.ca in order to advise their clients breach any rules or regulations? Do you think that Canadian law societies should regulate entities such as CanTax.ca? Why or why not? Should a different public sector entity regulate them?

[3] LICENSING REFORM: THE ARTICLING PROCESS AND LICENSING INTERNATIONALLY-TRAINED LAWYERS

Law, like some other professions and occupations, is subject to a licensing regime.

---

[4] *Law Society Act*, R.S.O. 1990, c. L.8, 1(5).

[5] *Law Society Act*, R.S.O. 1990, c. L.8, 1(6).

Not only must one abide by established rules while practicing law, one must fulfil certain requirements before beginning to practice. In Canada, this includes, in addition to the completion of an approved law degree or equivalent and meeting the good character requirement, completing a period of experiential training (articling or an alternative such as the Ontario's Law Practice Program). Additionally, individuals who have received their legal education outside of Canada must go through a process established by the National Committee on Accreditation (NCA), a standing committee of the Federation of Law Societies of Canada, which "first assesses an individual's unique academic training and professional experience, and then, using a uniform standard as a guide, assigns exams or law studies to fill the individual's knowledge gaps."[6]

Licensing is meant to ensure that only those who have undergone training and demonstrated their aptitude are allowed to provide legal services.[7] Licenses can also be revoked for those found to be incompetent or unethical. Nevertheless, excessively stringent licensing regimes can also increase prices, suppress access to justice, and deprive disadvantaged groups of career opportunities. Most Canadian provinces have struggled with having a greater number of candidates eligible to complete articles than articling positions available. Internationally-trained candidates have expressed concerns about barriers in Canada's licensing and employment processes. The next two readings develop these critiques. In reading these excerpts consider:

1) What is the public interest in relation to an articling requirement? How does the current approach serve the public interest? What reforms, if any, might better serve the public interest?

2) What might articling provide that law school does not in terms of ensuring competence? Are there other ways for achieving those goals?

3) What are the costs of articling for entrants into the legal profession, for the general public and for lawyers providing articling positions? Who should bear those costs? Does the current system allocate those costs fairly?

4) What barriers do internationally-trained lawyers experience in licensing and employment processes? What role should law societies play in addressing these barriers?

NOEL SEMPLE

"Bridges Over the Chasm: Licensing Design and the Abolition of Articling"
Slaw.ca, July 27 2018
[Citations omitted]

What should people who want to practice law have to do before they are licensed? This perennial debate has bloomed once again. The Law Society of Ontario (LSO) is seeking feedback on its *Options for Lawyer Licensing* consultation paper . . .

---

[6] National Committee on Accreditation, Federation of Law Societies of Canada, "About", online: https://nca.legal/about/.

[7] Noel Semple, *Legal Services Regulation at the Crossroads: Justitia's Legions* (Cheltenham, UK: Edward Elgar, 2015) at 35-36.

Two of the LSO's four options would abolish articling. Candidates would instead have to pass exams covering both legal skills and substantive knowledge. There would also be a law practice program, either required for all candidates (LSO's Option 4) or only for those practicing in smaller firms (Option 3).

Thinking of licensing in terms of footbridges over a chasm may help clarify what is at stake, and why the LSO should in fact abolish the articling requirement.

Bridges over the Chasm

A licensing regime creates a legal chasm. Aspiring legal professionals start out on one side. The people and corporations who would like to receive their services stand on the other side. Disregarding the chasm means falling into the "unauthorized practice of law," a sharp set of rocks maintained by the law societies.

Licensing creates bridges over this chasm. Those who successfully cross the bridges are allowed to serve the clients waiting on the other side. To complete the traditional (and still dominant) domestic path to a full lawyer license in most provinces, one must:

1. forego seven years of income and time to obtain the necessary university degrees;

2. typically pay $90,000 or more in combined undergraduate and law school tuition;

3. achieve strong LSAT and undergraduate GPA scores

4. pass licensing exams, and

5. find an articling position and complete articles.

Canada's licensing footbridges are narrow and arduous, relative to those of most comparable countries. For example, only one university degree (not two) is required in countries like England and Australia. In the United States the LSAT scores and GPAs necessary to get into an accredited law school are much lower than they are here. Finally, mandatory apprenticeships akin to articling are very rare abroad.

What's at Stake in Licensing Design?

Suppose you are asked to design licensing footbridges from scratch. What considerations would guide you? That such decisions should be made in the "public interest" is uncontroversial, but what does that mean in this context?

Client interests generally have pride of place within the public interest. Ensuring the baseline competence of licensees to practice law is job #1, as Malcolm Mercer explains. If the bridges are insufficiently challenging, candidates will be able cross them without demonstrating or learning enough of what is necessary in order to be competent practitioners. They could do serious damage to the clients on the other side of the chasm. Quality beyond baseline competence is obviously also desirable, and licensing requirements can also serve this goal.

Quality isn't Everything

However the public interest involves more than just the client interest in quality. Clients also have interests in service price, and in having a broad range of choice in the market. The interests of licensing candidates — especially those who have already invested many years and dollars in efforts to cross the licensing chasm — must also be protected as much as possible in the design process.

Every time you, as designer, make the licensing footbridges longer or harder to cross, several bad things can happen:

- First, some people who *would* become excellent lawyers are deterred from trying to cross the chasm. Many people of modest means would be willing to spend four years and $40,000 in order to become a lawyer (as in the UK), but would balk at eight years and $90,000 plus a mandatory apprenticeship requirement (as in most Canadian provinces).

- Second, the more onerous the licensing requirements are, the more debt and the more foregone income those who do succeed in crossing the chasm will have when they begin serving clients.

- Access to justice therefore suffers as licensing becomes more onerous. Service prices are higher due to increased practitioner debt and reduced numbers of practitioners. There are many thousands of people on the far side of the licensing chasm, who would like to be clients, but cannot afford the rates charged by the select group of licensees who succeed.

- Equity-seeking candidates may be especially disadvantaged. Less affluent people from less privileged backgrounds are more likely to be deterred from legal careers by expensive and arduous licensing requirements. Thus, longer and more arduous licensing footbridges make it more difficult to achieve professional diversity.

- To the extent that lawyers from disadvantaged or equity-seeking groups are more likely to serve clients from those same groups, the people deprived of affordable assistance may be those who need it most.

Building Better Footbridges

The key question for licensing design is: how can we "buy" large and consistent quality benefits for candidates and their clients, for the lowest possible cost in terms of candidates' money and time? Licensing reform that makes it easier to cross the chasm, without any deleterious effect on quality, is good for both clients and candidates. In two commendable recent reforms, the LSO has (i) decided to give paralegals practice rights in some family law matters, and (ii) created alternative pathways to licensure (the Law Practice Program and the Integrated Practice Curriculum). Both decisions created new footbridges across the chasm. Both decisions make it easier for a group of aspiring legal professionals, who are more likely than articled lawyers to be racialized and equity-seeking, to have satisfying careers helping people. They should also produce access to justice benefits, by giving clients access to a new and more affordable class of licensed practitioners.

Exams and practice programs can be designed to optimize their cost-benefit profile for candidates and the clients they will serve. Surveys of practicing lawyers, analyses of complaints data, and emerging methodologies for measuring legal service value can be used to identify baseline knowledge and skills. The risks arising from legal practice can also be identified and quantified.

Practice programs and exam questions can then be calibrated to inculcate the most important skills and knowledge, and minimize the gravest risks. The passing score on a licensing exam or practice program can be set at the level where further increases would have costs greater than their benefits. They can also be calibrated for the context in which different groups of candidates will practice. LSO's Option 3 reflects this insight, by prescribing a law practice program only for the category of licensees (small and solo practitioners) thought to need it most. On the other hand, Option 4's premise that *all* licensees need these skills may also be defensible. The decision between Option 3 and Option 4 should be based on a thorough empirical understanding of real law practice and the value that the law practice program offers to different candidates.

Whither Articling?

How does articling look from this point of view? The question is *not* whether people will still begin legal careers by doing the sorts of things that articling students do today. Undoubtedly they will. The question is whether regulators should require some or all candidates to find and complete articles before granting them a license to practice where and how they wish.

The effect of the articling requirement in fostering candidate quality is questionable. The nature of articling depends on the lightly-regulated decisions and resources of articling principals, so it is necessarily inconsistent. In a worryingly high proportion of cases, the articling requirement subjects candidates to harassment and unprofessional conduct. This may be due to the power imbalance created by the articling principal's status as gatekeeper on the licensing footbridge. Because offering articles is a voluntary decision made by firms, success in obtaining a position can depend to a large extent on factors beyond the candidate's control, such as racial prejudice and market conditions.

Even articling programs that succeed admirably in preparing one to practice in the particular context of that firm may do very little to prepare the candidate to practice in other practice contexts. It is true that articling is "real world" experience and a law practice program's world is simulated, but the "real world" in which one articles doesn't necessarily bear any resemblance to the real world in which one will practice. A simulated world can be designed to develop the skills that are most essential in *all* of the disparate real worlds of law practice today.

Licensing is here to stay. That means there will always be a chasm between people who want to provide legal services, and the people who are ready and willing to pay for those services. It is very important to design appropriate footbridges across the licensing chasm. They must maximize the quality, price, and choice interests at stake. Articling, as a regulatory requirement, is haphazard and arbitrary and therefore inappropriate. The Law Society should abolish it, in favour of well-designed and evidence-based alternatives such as exams and the law practice program.

LAUREN HEUSER

"6 Degrees-CIGI Final Report: Closed Shops: Opening Canada's
Legal Profession to Foreign-Educated Lawyers"
Cigionline.org, December 7, 2017
[Citations omitted]

Introduction

Miriam El Ofir was born and raised in Casablanca, Morocco. The daughter of a
Moroccan father and French-Canadian mother, she is fluent in Arabic, English and
French. After graduating from Casablanca American School in 2009, she — like
most of her peers — decided to go abroad for university.

In 2012, Miriam began studying law at Queen Mary University of London, a law
program that *The Guardian's* 2018 University Guide ranks as the third best in the
United Kingdom, and first in Greater London. In the course of her studies, the
British government started changing its visa requirements, making it more difficult
for international students — and in particular non- Europeans like Miriam — to
obtain work visas after graduating.

. . . . .

So Miriam set her sights on Canada. A Canadian citizen by birthright, she knew she
would not face any immigration hurdles. And since Canada is a predominantly
common-law country, she was confident her legal education had equipped her to
practise here — in particular since she had taken a number of the Canadian law
courses that Queen Mary offers to the Canadian students who study there.

When asked if she was aware of the challenges she would face becoming a lawyer
in Canada, Miriam's refrain was one the author heard repeatedly in her conversations with internationally educated lawyers. "Not at all," she said emphatically. She
had thought that, if anything, coming from England would lend an element of
prestige to her qualifications. And surely being fluent in both official languages
could not hurt either.

. . . . .

Starting a Dialogue About Canada's Closed Legal Shop

Nearly two years after immigrating to Canada, and tens of thousands of dollars
poorer, Miriam is currently still looking for employment. She is one of the hundreds
of internationally educated lawyers who come to Canada each year with the goal of
practising law. Many of these lawyers are Canadian citizens; many are new
immigrants. In general, these individuals will face far more obstacles to becoming
licensed and employed as lawyers than those who come up through the Canadian
legal education system.

Some of these internationally educated lawyers will get there eventually — often
after years of trying and considerable expense. Others will never make it. As David
Ben, a French lawyer observed: "When you come here, the feeling from the NCA
[National Committee on Accreditation] is that you're not welcome: we'll make your
life so hard, we'll either break you and you leave; or maybe you'll pass the
requirements, but it will be almost impossible to find a job."

. . . . .

This report aims to start a dialogue about the key barriers internationally educated lawyers face in Canada's licensing and employment processes, and makes recommendations for how *unnecessary* barriers can be mitigated or dismantled. Barriers are considered unnecessary if they are not relevant to testing an individual's professional competency, or make it unduly difficult for internationally trained lawyers to achieve licensure or employment relative to their Canadian counterparts. These recommendations are directed at a variety of stakeholders, including the NCA, provincial law societies, law schools, fairness commissioners, legal employers, immigration officials and internationally trained lawyers themselves.

Crucially, these recommendations are not aimed at getting the legal profession to relax its high standards, either directly or indirectly. It is assumed that the public is well served by a profession that holds all lawyers to exacting educational, experiential and ethical requirements. And it is recognized that this commitment to high standards will mean, in some cases, that internationally educated lawyers are not able to practise as lawyers in Canada.

However, as conversations with internationally trained lawyers and members of Canada's legal community made clear, many internationally educated lawyers are struggling to become accredited, not due to a lack of ability, but because they lack many of the supports that Canadian- educated lawyers enjoy.

. . . . .

This report begins by discussing some of the data on disparities between Canadian and internationally educated lawyers, as well as important industry trends. It then reviews the processes for becoming a lawyer in Canada — both as a student in the Canadian legal system and as a foreign entrant — and highlights the ways in which foreign lawyers face unique barriers in these processes. Finally, it makes a series of recommendations for how these barriers could be addressed.

The Challenge: Match Rates

Canada's immigrant population is, in general, highly educated. But skilled immigrants are frequently underemployed and undercompensated. One 2011 study found that foreign education is valued at about 70 percent of a Canadian credential, while international work experience is frequently not rewarded at all.

Within the legal profession, hundreds of internationally trained lawyers immigrate to Canada each year, and hundreds of Canadian citizens return to Canada after obtaining law degrees abroad.

Many of these internationally educated lawyers will never practise in Canada. A 2010 study evaluated 2006 census data to determine how well individuals' fields of study matched their occupations in Canada (what the study calls "match rates"). . . Only 12 percent of internationally educated lawyers were "matched" to legal jobs, compared to an average match rate of 24 percent for all occupations, and a match rate of 84 percent for internationally educated chiropractors.

. . .[T]he disparity between Canadian- educated and internationally trained lawyers is also substantial at 57 percent. In other words, Canadian-educated lawyers are far more likely to practise as lawyers. Of course, it is significant that the match rate for

Canadian-educated lawyers is only 69 percent; this likely reflects the fact that the supply of lawyers exceeds demand in some markets and the fact that many lawyers leave legal practice to work in other fields.

. . . . .

The Licensing Process for Internationally Educated Lawyers

Given the high educational and experiential standards Canadian-educated lawyers must meet, it is appropriate — indeed necessary — for internationally educated lawyers to meet these exacting requirements as well.

It would create an unfair double standard if foreign lawyers could qualify as Canadian lawyers by meeting less rigorous standards elsewhere. The reputation of the legal profession and the interests of the public could also suffer as well. It is therefore appropriate for the provinces' law societies to establish standards for internationally educated lawyers that ensure these candidates have the competence to practise as lawyers in accordance with Canadian standards.

Each year, there are between 4,000 and 5,000 candidates completing the licensing process in Canada. Internationally educated lawyers make up roughly one-quarter to one-third of this cohort, and their number has been increasing over the past five years.

. . . . .

Recommendations

The purpose of the licensing process — for both Canadian and internationally educated candidates — should be to ensure professional competency. The process should not penalize foreign-trained candidates simply because they are coming from a foreign jurisdiction.

Currently, most of the requirements applicable to international candidates are, on their surface, equivalent to the standards imposed on Canadian-educated lawyers. Indeed, an NCA- issued Certificate of Qualification certifies that the holder's education is equivalent to that of a Canadian-educated law graduate.

Nonetheless, foreign lawyers can be uniquely disadvantaged by the formal licensure requirements in various ways. They lack clarity about the licensure process: what will be demanded of them, what it will cost and how long it will take. They lack institutional and social support when preparing for exams, which use examination methods that are often unfamiliar to foreign students. They are often working full-time, low- paying jobs while trying to meet these exacting, expensive requirements.

In addition, once internationally educated lawyers have obtained their Certificate of Qualification, they often face barriers to lining up articling positions to fulfill their experiential requirement, and, after that, to lining up employment within the legal job market. There are a number of reasons for this. Internationally educated lawyers operate outside of the campus hiring processes that facilitate Canadian law students' entry into the legal market. They face skeptical prospective employers, who generally prefer to hire students from Canadian law programs. In some cases, they also lack the learned social behaviours one needs to impress prospective employers.

. . . . .

[The report's recommendations, which are available in full in the online version, include (i) Increasing student awareness of labour market conditions and options, (ii) offering better NCA exam materials for foreign-trained candidates, (iii) making the NCA exams more transparent, (iv) micro-loans for licensing candidates.]

. . . . .

Currently, Canada's legal system is not structured to ensure all competent lawyers — regardless of their jurisdiction of training — are able to make their best contribution to Canadian organizations and society. To far too great an extent, Canadian licensing and employment processes present obstacles to foreign individuals practising as lawyers, whether it is by layering on hefty licensure fees while turning a blind eye to the financial constraints they face, or offering them expensive educational programs without disclosing their slim odds of landing legal jobs through them, or ignoring the difficulties they face passing exams when they are offered little guidance on how to succeed on them.

Of course Canada must ensure its licensing and hiring processes verify that lawyers from Canada and abroad are competent. No one is suggesting otherwise. But a profession that is committed to ideals like justice and equality should not be comfortable with so-called entry processes that really function as walls — walls that make it difficult for talented outsiders to get in.

NOTES AND QUESTIONS

1. Do you think that reform to the Canadian lawyer licensing system is needed? Should the articling requirement be abolished? In answering this question, consider that no state in the United States requires lawyers to complete articles (but also that bar examinations in some American states have much higher failure rates than those of any Canadian province).

2. Do you think that all of the licensing requirements that J.D. students must fulfil (undergraduate degree, three years of law school, mandatory law school courses, etc.) are necessary? Do you think any of them should be eliminated or made less onerous? Alternatively, are there any requirements that should be added?

3. Who do you think should decide the licensing requirements for Canadian lawyers? Law societies? Provincial legislatures? Universities? In practice, who does decide?

4. Do you think that imposing requirements additional to the completion of a law degree discriminates against internationally-trained lawyers, relative to those who attend law school in Canada? What process for accrediting internationally-trained lawyers would be fair to those candidates, and advance the public interest in the provision of legal services?

5. Would it be appropriate to distinguish between Canadians who have gone abroad to pursue their legal education and non-Canadians who have qualified as lawyers in their home country, and then successfully immigrated to Canada?

6. In England & Wales, appearing in court and some other activities are

reserved for licensees, but giving advice about the law does not generally require a license. In Canada, by contrast, giving legal advice is considered part of the practice of law, and therefore reserved for lawyers in most cases. Do you think that Canada should reform its system to allow non-licensees to give advice, and/or do other things currently reserved for licensees?

Scenario Five

You have been approached by your provincial law society for your thoughts, as a prospective lawyer and current student of law, about how the licensing system could be improved. They have asked for you to identify five proposed reforms with an assessment of the costs and benefits of each proposed reform. They are interested in particular in your assessment of the ability of those reforms to reduce the barriers to entry into the profession, while also ensuring the competence of the lawyers who complete the requirements and are admitted to the profession.

[4] COMPLIANCE-BASED REGULATION: ENTITIES AND ETHICAL INFRASTRUCTURE

Lawyer regulation in Canada has traditionally focused on two things: individual lawyers and sanctioning bad conduct. That is, it is a reactive individual-based model of regulatory oversight. Both these aspects of traditional lawyer regulation have, however, come under critical scrutiny. Specifically, critics ask whether law societies need to also regulate the entities where lawyers work, and proactively evaluate how well legal workplaces implement systems that encourage ethical conduct and, where necessary, suggest improvements.

This section considers the opportunities and options for supplementing a reactive, individual based regulatory model with a pro-active, entity based regulatory model which focuses on encouraging compliance rather than disciplining non-compliance. Several Canadian jurisdictions have already made this shift. For example, in Nova Scotia, all law firms are required to self-assess their "Management Systems for Ethical Legal Practice" every three years.[8] The Law Society of Saskatchewan has also adopted a proactive approach to law firm regulation.[9] These approaches include requirements such as, for example, mandating that law firms (including sole practitioners) review and assess their management systems to determine whether they are properly designed to encourage ethical legal practice.

As context for your review of these materials about the desirability of a shift to entity and compliance-based regulation, picture a law student who has the makings of a terrific lawyer, perhaps a law school classmate. Your classmate has all of the virtues and abilities demanded by legal professionalism. They have the inherent skills, and the right attitude, to practice law with competence and integrity. You firmly believe that your classmate will not only do excellent work for their future

---

[8] Nova Scotia Barristers' Society, "Self-Assessing your Law Firm (MSELP)", online: https://nsbs.org/legal-profession/your-practice/practice-support-resources/mselp/.

[9] The Law Society of Saskatchewan, "Innovating Regulation", online: https://www.lawsociety.sk.ca/initiatives/innovating-regulation/.

clients, but also make significant contributions to the Canadian legal profession, perhaps even as a Supreme Court of Canada judge.

Now that classmate has graduated and been called to the bar. They are hired by a law firm called Dewey, Cheatem, & Howe LLP. The partners and associates at this law firm have never been disciplined by the Law Society. However, after practicing there for a few months your classmate discovers:

- Associates are expected to work 2800 hours per year, excluding non-billable time.

- Senior lawyers offer little or no assistance to new associates. Mentoring is unavailable and new lawyers do not receive the guidance necessary to do good work on individual files.

- Associates rarely become partners.

- There is a culture of bullying. Racist and sexist comments are not uncommon.

- Two of the partners have sexually harassed lawyers and staff on repeated occasions. Because these partners bring in lucrative files, nothing is done to stop them.

Dewey, Cheatem & Howe is not a real law firm. However, these are all things that happen in some Canadian law firms.

Your classmate is a cautious person, and somewhat introverted. They have never worked in any other law firms, so they assume that the environment at Dewey, Cheatem, & Howe LLP is typical. In law school, you and most of your colleagues considered your classmate to have almost unlimited potential as a lawyer. It seems significantly less likely that they will live up to this potential, now that they have started their career at this firm.

Your classmate is, in other words, one of the people critics have in mind when they suggest that lawyer regulation needs to expand its attention beyond reaction to misconduct to individual lawyers. In addition, however, these critics also argue that other aspects of the public interest could be fostered by an expanded regulatory focus. They suggest that lawyers, clients, the administration of justice and the general public would all benefit from a shift in the focus of lawyer regulation.

The following readings explore these questions. They ask whether protecting client interests, and advancing legal professionalism, require going beyond individual-focused, reactive regulation. The first reading contains two parts of a 2015 Discussion Paper prepared by the Prairie Law Societies on the issue of entity regulation and compliance-based regulation. The third reading is an academic paper arguing in favour of ethical infrastructure as a model for facilitating lawyers' ethics.

LAW SOCIETIES OF ALBERTA, SASKATCHEWAN AND MANITOBA
"Innovating Regulation Discussion Paper"
November 2015
[Citations omitted]

. . . . .

III. ENTITY REGULATION

. . . . .

c) Why regulate entities?

Regulation of entities would close a gap in the current regulatory framework. Professor Adam Dodek is of the view that: "The absence of law firm regulation creates a problem of legitimacy for Law Societies mandated to regulate the practice of law in the public interest. This regulatory gap also raises Rule of Law concerns and may threaten public confidence if the public believes that the most powerful groups of lawyers escape regulation... Consequently, the failure to regulate law firms may threaten self-regulation of the legal profession in Canada."

It is recognized that firms play a considerable role when examining what drives the behaviour of their members. As Professor Adam Dodek has observed: "...the law firm is an independent actor exerting significant influence on the practice of law...". He points out that, "Law firms are front and center in the lawyer-client relationship."

It has been suggested that the law firm is now the intermediary between client and lawyer.

Professor Dodek notes that:

> This is certainly true in terms of advertising, solicitation, client intake, conflicts of interest, retainer agreements, billings and many other interactions that clients and potential clients have with the delivery of legal services via 'the firm'. With larger law firms, the influence of a collective culture may be even stronger.

The American Bar Association's Model Rules regarding law firms recognize that *"the ethical atmosphere of a firm can influence the conduct of all its members."*

This reality underscores the need to examine the regulation of firms.

i) Advantages of Entity Regulation

There are several advantages that could be gained if entity regulation became a reality:

- the regulator could encourage those who control the entity to develop and monitor training, supervision, and quality control systems;

- there would likely be improved management and cultures of law firms, as a whole;

- overall, there would be greater accountability to the regulator;

- effective entity regulation may enhance individual accountability by creating an "ethical infrastructure" for lawyers within a firm;

- the public would have increased confidence that regulators have the ability to self-regulate in the public interest;

- there would be increased protection of the public;
- since entity regulation may result in the regulation of lawyers and non-lawyers (who work within an entity), barriers could be removed which may increase:
  - ○ access to justice; and
  - ○ regulatory effectiveness.

ii) Disadvantages of Entity Regulation

Possible disadvantages of entity regulation require consideration of the following:

1) An expanded regulatory regime will require firms to focus on ethical behavior and conduct at a firm level. While some firms may do this already, others don't and smaller firms, in particular, may find this to be a difficult adjustment.

2) Buy-in from the profession will be needed as the concept represents a departure from the traditional approach to lawyer regulation.

3) Effective planning for entity regulation will require consultation with the profession which represents a time commitment and utilization of resources.

4) Creating compliance systems within firms will require time and money.

5) Some jurisdictions may require legislative amendments in order to bring about such changes but changes take time and require support of stakeholders.

6) There is a danger associated with creating another layer of regulation for what is an otherwise highly regulated profession.

. . . . .

IV. COMPLIANCE-BASED REGULATION

a) Introduction

As we consider transforming the regulation of the legal profession to include the regulation of entities, a related issue to be examined is how those entities should be regulated. Currently, the regulatory frameworks of a number of law societies across Canada have several rules that regulate law firms with respect to specific issues, such as trust accounts or client identification. However, the traditional regulatory regimes that are in place are designed to regulate the individual lawyer. They are not designed to regulate the law firm itself. Therefore, in the current regulatory approach taken by law societies, if entities are to be regulated, then a gap exists with respect to how those entities should be regulated.

This paper discusses a compliance-based approach to the regulation of entities that is proactive, principled and proportionate. Compliance-based regulation is an outcomes-based approach that articulates expected objectives and outcomes with which a firm must comply and, rather than prescribing how a firm must achieve compliance with those objectives and goals, provides the firm with the flexibility and autonomy to determine how it will do so. By passing responsibility to the firm, the firm engages in an educative process to arrive at the policies, procedures and systems — an ethical infrastructure — that will enable it to achieve compliance with the stated objectives and outcomes of the regulatory model. Compliance-based regulation is a shift from the traditional, reactive, prescriptive rules and complaints-based regulation toward a proactive, flexible and outcomes-based regulation.

. . . . .

There are two significant criticisms of the traditional, rules-based, complaints-driven model of regulation. One criticism is that it is a reactive system. That is, the law society only reacts when a complaint is received that a lawyer's conduct failed to meet the professional standards as prescribed by set rules. The law society implements the complaints process, investigates the complaint and, where appropriate, enforces the standards by disciplining the lawyer. Therefore, the criticism is that rather than taking steps to prevent the conduct from occurring in the first place, the law society intervenes after the fact and then only to sanction the lawyer for the conduct that occurred. . . .

Another significant criticism of complaints-driven, rules-based regulation is that it focuses exclusively on the conduct of individual lawyers, while failing to recognize that many lawyers work in law firms. As discussed previously in the context of entity regulation, the firm sets the standards for the lawyers acting within the firm and those lawyers tend to make decisions that comply with the firm's systems and processes. Despite the law firm being responsible for setting the environment in which the individual lawyer makes such decisions, the individual lawyer, rather than the firm, is regulated by the law society.

Law societies can no longer afford to continue to ignore law firms in the regulation of the legal profession, hence the previous discussion on entity regulation. The issue then is how to regulate the legal entity.

. . . . .

d) Compliance-based regulation

Requiring a law firm to implement an ethical infrastructure could be achieved by prescriptive regulation of firms — that is, telling a firm what and how to do it. However, proactive approaches to regulation have been attracting considerable interest and attention. Proactive models of regulation comprise an educative component whereby the firm develops an ethical infrastructure — the systems and processes — to ensure lawyers comply with their ethical duties.

Compliance-based regulation is such a model and is premised on the regulation of the entity using an outcomes-based approach. In this model, the expected objectives and outcomes with which a firm must comply are articulated. That is, a firm is told what it must do. However, it is not given prescriptive rules that tell the firm how it must achieve compliance. Rather, the firm is given the flexibility and autonomy to take into account its size, practice areas and client base in order to determine the systems and processes that will be appropriate for it to achieve regulatory compliance with the outcomes.

For example, a law society may set as an expected outcome or objective for firms that they develop competent practices but without telling them how to do that.

731

Therefore, to achieve the outcome of developing competent practices, the firm could institute a continuing education program.

The key tenet is that the firm has the responsibility to determine how to achieve compliance with that outcome. By giving an entity the autonomy to determine and implement the systems and processes in order to achieve compliance with the regulatory goals or objectives, compliance-based regulation enables a firm to develop its own unique ethical infrastructure in order to promote ethical behaviour.

Compliance-based regulation is a regulatory approach that represents a fundamental shift from the existing rules-based, one-size fits all model of regulation that focuses on the individual lawyer to an outcomes-based, proportionate model that focuses on the culture and behaviour of a firm. It is described as a shift in "regulatory emphasis from responding to complaints and enforcement through discipline to a proactive approach in which goals, expectations and tools for licensees are established".

. . . . .

f) Benefits of compliance-based regulation

There are a number of advantages to implementing a compliance-based approach to entity regulation.

First, the compliance-based approach to regulation is proactive and preventative rather than reactive as it focuses on results rather than rules. That is, instead of focusing on prescriptive rules and reacting to a complaint when a rule is breached, in a compliance-based regulatory model, the regulator sets out the expected outcomes that the regulator expects firms to achieve by adopting systems and processes. The result is that rather than complying with prescriptive and rigid rules, this model of regulation seeks to prevent problems from arising in the first place.

Second, with compliance-based regulation, firms are provided the "incentive, tools and authority to take steps to improve the delivery of legal services". The management and culture of the firm as a whole is improved by implementing an ethical infrastructure that will allow the firm to comply with the regulatory objectives. The implementation of an ethical infrastructure creates an ethical firm culture that promotes and improves the ethical best practices of both the firm and of the lawyers acting within it.

Third, in a compliance-based approach, the individual lawyer is not singled out. Instead, as discussed previously, the firm organization and culture often sets the tone and environment in which lawyers practise. Compliance-based regulation recognizes that the firm has a role to play in ensuring that the ethical behaviour of lawyers is promoted and that a firm may be accountable for system failures that resulted in the lawyer's conduct.

Fourth, although firms are required to comply with the set objectives and outcomes, not all firms will face the same risks. Therefore, firms are not required to implement the same systems and processes in order to achieve compliance regardless of their size. Instead, compliance-based regulation provides firms the flexibility and autonomy to develop the internal systems and processes that are appropriate to their own practices in order to achieve compliance with the regulatory objectives. Rather than implementing a "one-size fits all" approach, which may not necessarily be appropriate for all entities, firms can tailor their systems and processes by taking their own specific circumstances, such as size, practice type and client base, into account. A potential advantage of doing so is that "if you allow entities to develop their own rules, they are more likely to regard those rules as reasonable and, as a result, compliance may be improved".

Fifth, compliance-based regulation is flexible and responsive by utilizing general principles that can adapt to a changing legal environment. Unlike rules that are rigid and prescriptive, a compliance-based approach allows for "future-proofing", which enables the regulator to respond to new issues as they arise without the necessity of having to create new rules.

Sixth, a compliance-based regime enables the regulator to proactively partner with law firms by working with — not against — them. In moving away from prescriptive regulatory requirements and setting expected outcomes and objectives, the regulator focuses on helping law firms improve their ethical practices by assisting them in developing the systems and processes to achieve compliance with regulatory objectives, resulting in ethical outcomes and the delivery of quality legal services.

Finally, compliance-based regulation will serve to enhance public confidence in the legal profession and protect the public interest. The jurisdictions that have implemented this model of regulation, specifically NSW [New South Wales, Australia], have shown a significant reduction in the number of complaints made against regulated entities likely due to more ethically-managed legal practices arising as a result of the self-assessment regime. Therefore, a compliance-based model of proactive regulation, where the regulated entity must determine the ethical infrastructure that will enable it to comply with the stated objectives and outcomes, will certainly raise consciousness about professional ethical obligations. This should translate into more ethical legal practices of the firm and highly ethical behaviours of the lawyers, which will only benefit the public.

g) Concerns with compliance-based regulation

Although the benefits of compliance-based regulation are numerous, concerns have been raised about implementing this regulatory model for the regulation of the legal profession.

The principal concern is that as compliance-based regulation is focused on outcomes rather than rules, there is more ambiguity and less certainty for firms as to what they must actually do to achieve compliance. Generally, lawyers prefer to know exactly what they are required to do rather than figuring it out by themselves. Professor [Julia] Black states:

> "Detailed rules, it is often claimed, provide certainty, a clear standard of behaviour and are easier to apply consistently and without retrospectivity." However, she explains that rules can "lead to gaps, inconsistencies, rigidity and are prone to "creative compliance", to the need for constant adjustment to new situations and to the ratchet syndrome, as more rules are created to address new problems or close new gaps, creating more gaps and so on."

Although the outcomes-focused approach of compliance-based regulation does not tell firms how to achieve compliance, there are opportunities for law societies to work with and provide educational and assessment opportunities for firms so that they can develop systems and processes to achieve compliance with the stated outcomes and objectives of the law society. By using these resources, firms should have greater clarity as to what is expected of them.

Another challenge is the concern that compliance-based regulation would "dilute" individual lawyers' perceptions of their obligations to abide by professional rules and ethics, or their duties to the court, with lawyers blaming the firm for their conduct. Regulation of the ILPs in Australia, at the time, and outcomes-based regulation of the firms in England and Wales, did not replace the traditional model of regulating individual lawyers. At this time, the prairie law societies have not considered replacing the current, traditional model of individual lawyer regulation. Rather, compliance-based regulation is currently being reviewed as a means of regulating the entity, in addition to the current model of regulating the lawyer.

A concern has also been expressed about compliance-based regulation accompanied by self-assessment of the firm's ethical infrastructure — the systems and processes it has in place. The concern is that the self-assessment process will act as a checklist whereby the criteria for the outcomes are simply implemented or, worse, it will result in "ritualistic and ineffective 'box-ticking'", replacing professional values and ethical judgment.

The study conducted in Australia indicates that while a small percentage agreed that the self-assessment amounted to meaningless "box-ticking", which may imply they reported compliance without actually reviewing their systems and processes, a large number reported the self-assessment was a learning process they used to review and revise existing policies and to adopt new ones. The study concluded that the self-assessment process acted as an educational exercise towards compliance for directors in developing their ethical infrastructure.

Although the concerns with implementing compliance-based regulation are understandable, given that it is an approach that is on the other end of the regulation spectrum, these concerns are allayed by the numerous benefits that compliance-based regulation provides to the regulation of the legal profession.

. . . . .

AMY SALYZYN

"What if We Didn't Wait? Regulating Ethical Infrastructure"
(2015) 92 Can Bar Rev 3
[footnotes omitted]

1. Introduction

Canadian law societies primarily regulate lawyer behaviour by responding to complaints made against individual lawyers. Although this complaints-based regime is necessary, in particular to address cases of lawyer misfeasance or extreme incompetence, it is limited in its ability to target a significant determinant of ethical lawyer conduct: the presence of institutional policies, procedures, structures and workplace culture within a law practice that help lawyers fulfill their ethical duties. Given the importance of these formal and informal measures – referred to collectively as "ethical infrastructure" – this article explores whether and how law societies might become more active in promoting effective ethical infrastructures within Canadian law practices.

Ensuring effective ethical infrastructures within law practices seems self-evidently good; we want lawyers to work in environments that facilitate compliance with their ethical duties. It is less obvious, however, that it would be a good thing for law societies to regulate the ethical infrastructures of Canadian legal practices. Decisions about a practice's ethical infrastructure, like what policies and procedures to put in place, are typically thought to fall to private ordering and the decisions of law firm managers (influenced by insurer and client demands) rather than to the domain of public regulators like law societies. Indeed, many Canadian lawyers are likely to be suspicious of proposals to add an additional layer of regulator involvement in their practices.

What justifies regulatory intervention in this area? The case presented in this article for expanded law society involvement in the ethical infrastructures of Canadian law practices is three-fold: (1) there are reasons to believe that these infrastructures could, as a general matter, be improved; (2) this improvement would, in turn, lead to improved outcomes in relation to lawyers' ethical duties; and (3) current law society regulatory efforts are not optimally situated to assist with this improvement. Stated otherwise, law societies should become more involved in the ethical infrastructures of Canadian law practices because neither the market nor current regulatory efforts are effectively addressing this important aspect of law practice.

. . . . .

2. What is Ethical Infrastucture?

The first use of the term "ethical infrastructure" in the law practice context is widely attributed to Ted Schneyer, a University of Arizona law professor. In a 1991 article about professional discipline for law firms, Schneyer notes that "a law firm's organization, policies, and operating procedures constitute an 'ethical infrastructure' that cuts across particular lawyers and tasks .... [and] which may have at least as much to do with causing and avoiding unjustified harm as do the individual values and practice skills of their lawyers." Twenty years later, in a 2011 article, Schneyer provides a similar, slightly elaborated definition:

> Ethical infrastructures consists of the policies, procedures, systems, and structures—
> in short, the "measures" that ensure lawyers in their firm comply with their ethical
> duties and that nonlawyers associated with the firm behave in a manner consistent
> with the lawyers' duties.

Following Schneyer, other legal ethics scholars, mostly in America and Australia, have used and developed this term in their work.

Those who use the term ethical infrastructure often identify measures like conflicts check systems, template retainer letters, and billing policies as part of a law practice's ethical infrastructure. As Schneyer observes, however, the diversity of law practices and the evolving nature of the legal industry make any sort of fixed master-list of everything that could be considered part of a law practice's ethical infrastructure elusive and, indeed undesirable. For this reason, it is helpful to consider the concept of ethical infrastructure from a functional perspective, as intended to capture "organizational policies and procedures designed to impose some regularity on how lawyers in a firm practice."

. . . . .

Although the duties that lawyers owe to clients are an important target of a law practice's ethical infrastructure, lawyers also owe broader duties to the public and to the administration of justice that should be given attention in the formulation of ethical infrastructure. An understanding of ethical infrastructure that encompasses measures relating to such things as fostering the rule of law and access to justice can work to capture this broader ambit of duties. . ..

Additionally, a law practice's ethical infrastructure is best understood not only in relation to measures that impact outcomes for external subjects (clients, the public or the justice system more generally) but also in terms of measures directed to lawyers and other employees who work within the firm. Research on behaviour within organizations suggests that "what might seem to be solely 'business' or 'human resource' decisions, which do not relate directly to lawyers' professional responsibilities, may nonetheless have a significant impact on attitudes and behaviors that do." More specifically, research suggests that the degree to which individuals within an organization perceive that they are being treated fairly can be an important driver of ethical compliance.

. . . . .

In this article, the term "ethical infrastructure" is used inclusively and is adopted here essentially as short-hand for "everything within a law practice that impacts how members of that law practice relate to, or fulfill, the duties owed to clients, the justice system and the public more generally."

. . . . .

A) Ethical Infrastructure in Canadian Law Practices

. . . . .

[I]t is safe to assume that many law practices now implement formalized conflicts checks systems. Indeed, close to 60 per cent of participants in a 2014 survey of the 30 largest Canada-based firms identified conflicts as their top risk management concern. Additionally, the fact that Canadian law societies engage in substantial trust account regulation suggests widespread use of appropriate accounting systems that allow for the tracking of trust account funds and other monies received.

. . . . .

. . . Presumably, one good way to determine if ethical infrastructures in Canadian law practices are currently effective is to consider regulatory outcomes. Although we may not know with much precision what Canadian law practices are doing when it comes to developing their ethical infrastructures, we do know that there are a number of persistent and pressing problems related to the delivery of legal services in Canada. For the purposes of advancing the argument here, three representative areas of concern are discussed. From a client perspective, we know from complaints statistics that what might be called "client service issues" – things like delay or failures to communicate – have persistently been a top area of dissatisfaction. To look beyond clients, we also know that access to justice and diversity in the legal profession remain deep and chronic problems. The continuing problems in these three areas – client service, access to justice and diversity in the legal profession – suggests that the market is not "taking care of itself" and, importantly for the case being made here, that current regulatory efforts are inadequate.

For the most part, the current efforts to regulate lawyer behaviour in Canada revolve around a complaints-based model. They involve disciplinary apparatuses that tend to focus on investigating and, if deemed necessary, prosecuting "after the fact" complaints against individual lawyers about alleged breaches of codes of professional conduct. As a number of other scholars have already noted, this model has several inherent limitations including its focus on individual behaviour (rather than institutional practices) and on whether individuals are complying with minimum standards as well as its reactive nature. A consideration of how this conventional approach interacts with the three areas highlighted above can help to bring some particularity to these observed limitations.

To look at client service issues first, responsibility within a law firm for things like delay and poor communication may be diffused such that no single lawyer within the law firm has acted so egregiously to warrant being sanctioned within the disciplinary system. There may also be underlying workplace culture issues that contribute to client service problems but which are outside the jurisdiction of the conventional approach. Studies on the impact of "bottom-line mentality" (BLM) or "one-dimensional thinking that revolves around securing bottom-line outcomes to the neglect of competing priorities," for example, demonstrate how decision frames adopted by organizations can impact individual behaviour. In the law firm context, one might think of the potential negative impacts in cases where there is too much focus on financial bottom lines like firm profits and/or billable hour targets. The broader research on this topic notes that adoption of a BLM frame can result in employees becoming "so focussed on meeting bottom-line productivity requirements that they cut corners without considering the quality of their work or the ethical consequences of their behaviours." The research supports what many lawyers likely intuit: making billable hours a major, if not singular, determinant of lawyer compensation and promotion can have negative ethical consequences. Yet internal policies like compensation schemes do not generally attract the attention of regulators under the conventional disciplinary model, nor are they necessarily good subjects for regulation under this model which is built largely around a "pass-fail system [where] either the rules are found to be broken or they are not" rather than promoting best practices.

Improving client service outcomes requires regulatory attention to elements of a law practice's ethical infrastructure that impact client service in addition to using lawyer disciplinary regimes to mete out sanctions in individual cases of abject failures to serve. What measures does the practice take to ensure that clients and lawyers have the same understanding of the scope of the retainer? What is done to ensure that clients are kept regularly updated? Does the law practice have formal billing and evaluation policies? These types of questions can help get to the root of client service issues.

A brief consideration of the issues of access to justice and diversity in the legal profession demonstrates that these issues, too, are not optimally addressed by the conventional approach. To the extent that lawyer codes of professional conduct and accompanying disciplinary regimes address these topics, it is through singling out overt and especially egregious forms of lawyer behaviour such as charging unreasonable fees or engaging in discrimination. Most manifestations of these issues are subtle and complex and, thus, fall outside the conventional approach (and, arguably rightly so, given its punitive nature). In these areas, regulatory efforts to promote effective ethical infrastructures and thereby encourage best practices would again seem to be better suited to achieving meaningful change rather than the "quasi-criminal" disciplinary mechanisms at the heart of the conventional approach. To be sure, concerns surrounding access to justice and diversity involve systemic issues that reach beyond what happens within law practices. Nonetheless, the ethical infrastructures of law practices remain important sites to consider when contemplating solutions. For example, ensuring that there are appropriate parental leave policies in place and making evaluation and promotions systems free of bias (both conscious and unconscious) are important steps in eliminating structural barriers faced by women and racialized lawyers in the legal workplace. For access to justice, firm facilitation of pro bono work (through, for example, billable hour credits) and support for creative delivery of legal services (like, perhaps, unbundling) could be helpful institutional level initiatives. Here, again, there is reason to believe that regulator attention to ethical infrastructure might lead to improved outcomes.

. . . . .

5. Conclusion

Improving ethical outcomes in the delivery of legal services requires attention to what happens, both formally and informally, at an institutional level in law practices. Canadian law societies have already recognized this insofar as they do such things as regulate trust firm accounts, engage in practice reviews and develop practice management materials. If one looks to what is happening in other jurisdictions, however, it is clear that law societies could do more when it comes to promoting effective ethical infrastructures in Canadian law practices. This article has sought to make out the case for enhanced law society involvement in the ethical infrastructures of Canadian law practices and to outline some of the policy considerations that law societies should take into account if they decide to become more robustly engaged.

NOTES AND QUESTIONS

1. Do you agree with the assessment of the advantages and disadvantages of entity regulation in the Discussion Paper? Are there other advantages or disadvantages that you can think of? In answering this question recall the definition of regulation provided at the outset of Chapter 10, "the consistent and sustained effort to create particular behaviour and to achieve particular outcomes", and also the benchmarks of effectiveness and efficiency. Will entity regulation achieve particular outcomes well? If so, which ones? Are there other outcomes it will not achieve effectively? If so, which ones? In general, how efficient and effective in each of those areas do you think entity regulation will be relative to individual-focused regulation?

2. One of the points of the definition of regulation offered in Chapter 10, was

to show that regulation can be done in diverse ways; there does not need to be an exclusively command-control regulatory approach, and the ethics of lawyers are affected by a broad variety of forces and events. This allows the possibility of thinking of regulation as a 'menu' of different ways to achieve different outcomes. Considered in this way, which regulatory approaches do you think are most likely to be effective for these ethical behaviours and goals: 1) ensuring lawyers give advice to clients that provides a good faith assessment of what the law permits and requires; 2) ensuring lawyers respect client confidentiality; 3) avoiding conflicts of interest; 4) ensuring diversity in the legal profession; and 5) reducing barriers to access to justice?

3. Considering those same topics, do you think those ethical behaviours and goals would be more likely to be achieved if lawyers worked within an ethical infrastructure? Are some more likely to be improved by ethical infrastructure than others? If so, which ones and why?

4. In thinking about reactive vs. proactive regulation, an underlying question is: what outcomes should the regulator be trying to achieve? Or, to put it slightly differently, what should the regulator be reacting to, or seeking compliance for? Having studied a range of ethical issues, and knowing that regulation ought in general to be directed towards the public interest in the provision of legal services, what do you think legal regulators should be trying to achieve? What should be their priorities? And which of reactive or proactive regulation is most likely to accomplish those priorities?

5. Do you think ethical infrastructure requires entity regulation? Is the possibility for requiring and regulating ethical infrastructure a reason to adopt entity regulation? In thinking about this question, consider the example of the Statement of Principles, discussed in Chapter 10. Was that an example of non-entity based ethical infrastructure? What other examples can you think of?

6. Some take the view that regulation of entities would close a gap in the regulatory framework. In modern economies, business entities are typically regulated as entities, not as collections of individuals. Food safety regulation of a grocery store, for example, does not focus on the conduct of the individuals who work within a particular store. Instead, the corporate entity that owns the store, and its management, are responsible for ensuring that the store, as an entity, complies with its regulatory obligations. Should regulation of ethical conduct by lawyers be similarly directed?

7. In your past work experiences (not just in legal workplaces), have you found that the "ethical infrastructure" affects the success of the organization and the performance of the individual employees?

8. A criticism sometimes levied at entity-based regulation is that it is unfair or burdensome for small law firms. What could be done to ameliorate those concerns?

9. Among Canadian jurisdictions, Nova Scotia has moved furthest towards

"entity-based" or "law-firm regulation". As mentioned above, firms in that province are required, among other things, to conduct regular self-assessments and implement a "management system for ethical legal practice."[10] By contrast in Ontario, most regulation is targeted at individuals, but firms with more than 10 licensees are required to provide information to the Law Society about their equality, diversity and inclusion practices on an annual basis.[11] Entity regulation is well-established in jurisdictions such as the United Kingdom and Australia.

Scenario Six

The Benchers of a Canadian law society of have reviewed the above Discussion Paper, as well as Salyzyn's paper. They are considering whether to adopt entity regulation. In particular, they are deciding whether to adopt the Nova Scotia Barristers' Society requirement that each law firm have a "Designated Lawyer" responsible for communicating with the regulator and for ensuring that the law firm complies with its regulatory obligations. The Benchers are also considering adopting Nova Scotia's requirement that all law firms complete a "self-assessment", which requires that the firm assess whether it has in place appropriate policies, practices and systems to support the elements for a management system for ethical legal practice.

What are the strengths and weaknesses of each of those requirements? Should the Benchers vote to adopt them? What other innovations would you recommend that the Benchers consider with respect to entity regulation or ethical infrastructure?

For more on the Nova Scotia Barristers' Society's approach see NSBS Regulations, Part 4 – Obligations of Lawyers and Law Firms. Online: https://nsbs.org/legal-profession/nsbs-regulations/part-4/.

[5] ALTERNATIVE BUSINESS STRUCTURES

The prior section assessed the advantages and disadvantages of supplementing a reactive individual-focused model of lawyer regulation with a proactive entity-based model. One question not considered, however, was with respect to the nature of the entities within which lawyers provide legal services. That issue, of the business structures within which lawyers provide legal services, is considered here.

Traditionally, lawyers providing legal services to the public have been required to provide those services exclusively through entities owned by lawyers themselves and structured without the benefits of corporate limits on personal liability. That is, through a partnership in which the partners are lawyers.

Alternative business structures ("ABS") challenge that traditional model for the provision of legal services. An ABS is defined for our purposes (and generally) as any entity through which lawyers provide services to the public, but which lawyers do not entirely own and manage. Examples of ABS law firm models include:

---

[10] Nova Scotia Barristers' Society Regulations (Made pursuant to the *Legal Profession Act,* S.N.S 2004, c. 28), ss. 4.6.1, 8.3.2.

[11] Online: https://lso.ca/about-lso/initiatives/edi/measuring-progress/self-assessment-questions.

i)   a law firm which is a publicly traded corporation,

ii) a law firm which is a privately held corporation, with non-lawyers holding some or all of the shares, and

iii) a law firm which is a partnership of equals between lawyers and non-lawyers.

An ABS could include everything from an accounting firm hiring a lawyer to provide services to the public, to the Real Canadian Superstore selling lawyer services to shoppers, to four friends, a lawyer, an accountant, a social worker and a psychologist, owning a firm that provides a full spectrum of services to separating couples and their children.

ABS firms are permitted in jurisdictions such as Australia and the United Kingdom. In Canada, ABS firms are generally forbidden, apart from a few narrow exceptions. For example, Ontario's *Law Society Act* allows a lawyer to practice through a professional corporation but requires all of the shares in the corporation to be owned by licensed lawyers or paralegals.[12] Also relevant is *Model Code* Rule 3.6-7(a), which forbids lawyers to split or share their fees with non-lawyers. Some of the ABS law firm models which might otherwise be adopted would be inconsistent with this Rule.

The following three readings represent different perspectives on the ABS debate. The first reading, from Gillian Hadfield, suggests that the failure to adopt ABS inhibits regulation in the delivery of legal services. The second, from an Ontario lawyer professional association "for plaintiff lawyers and staff", explains why it opposes the adoption of ABS. The third, co-authored by one of leaders of an Australian ABS firm, Slater and Gordon, makes the case for why ABS offers more benefits than potential risks.

As you read each excerpt, identify the arguments you find most convincing both for and against ABS. In doing so, consider in particular the following questions:

a)   What regulatory restrictions, if any, on the type of entities that can provide legal services are most likely to foster and protect the public interest in the provision of legal services?

b)   Which types of entities are most likely to be susceptible to effective entity regulation, and to the imposition of ethical infrastructures?

c)   Which type of entities are most likely to be consistent with the satisfaction of the ethical obligations addressed earlier in this book – for example, with respect to avoiding conflicts of interest, ensuring effective and resolute advocacy in courts, and protecting client confidentiality?

GILLIAN HADFIELD

Rules for a Flat World: Why Humans invented Law and How to Reinvent it for a Complex Global Economy
(Oxford: Oxford University Press, 2016).

Today's markets for legal goods and services are some of the most closed and

---

[12] R.S.O. 1990, c. L.8, s. 61.0.1(4).

constrained in the entire economy. As a result they fail to do what markets can do: harness the capacity for markets to produce transformative solutions to complex and changing circumstances.

So here's the lesson from the history of search for law. Imagine that in 1996 professional librarians had controlled library science the way the legal profession today controls law: deciding who can practice, how practitioners must be educated, what business and financing models they have to use to sell their services. In that strange universe, [Google founders Larry] Page and [Sergey] Brin would have had to be licensed librarians with master's degrees in library science, following the rules of the librarians' professional bodies, before they could have offered to the world a transformative solution to the librarians' problem of how to organize and find information.

Believing that lawyers alone will innovate the transformative solutions we need to the problems of legal infrastructure is like believing that librarians alone would have eventually invented Google.

. . . . .

Why can't even a small number of risk-happy lawyers break through? The reason is a lack of access to what innovators in every other sector of the economy depend on—risk capital. Among the rules that the ABA[13] put in place as it was seeking to rationalize and control the legal profession in the early twentieth century were rules that said no one other than a lawyer can invest in a legal business. Under these rules only businesses that are 100 percent owned and financed by lawyers can deliver legal products and services. These rules mean that legal innovators have no access to venture capital. They can't take money from friends and family and promise a share in the business when it gets big. Angel investors can't sprinkle any stardust on their endeavor. They can't dream of an IPO. They can't share risk with the tech wizard or business genius who wants to partner up with them. They can't access the billions of dollars in investment money floating through global capital. No other industry or sector in the economy could innovate in those circumstances either.

ONTARIO TRIAL LAWYERS ASSOCIATION

"Submission to Law Society of Upper Canada on Alternative Business Structures,"
December 15, 2014

I. Introduction

In September 2011, following the Bencher election, the Law Society of Upper Canada ("LSUC") held a strategic session in which it set out its priorities for the upcoming term (2011-2015). One of these priorities was to examine alternative business structures ("ABS").

. . . . .

As discussed in depth below, OTLA is of the position that there is not enough empirical evidence available from the jurisdictions in which ABS is currently

---

[13] The ABA is the American Bar Association. State bar regulators in the United States, like Canada's law societies, forbid almost all alternative business structures.

permitted to endorse permitting ABS in our jurisdiction. At this stage, OTLA cannot support ABS.

. . . . .

II. Access Considerations

. . . . .

One of the means put forth to "liberalize" the delivery of legal services is non-lawyer ownership or equity in law practices. OTLA cautions that there is insufficient data and research to support the proposition that non-lawyer ownership will improve access to justice.

. . . . .

Certain litigation is inherently expensive. The costs are driven by protracted timelines and other vagaries of the legal process itself. ABS will not materially contribute to the efficiency of the legal process or reduce the costs inherent in the litigation model, without the nature of litigation changing dramatically.

. . . . .

The Trickle Down Theory: Assuming Savings will be Passed onto the Consumer

Even accepting that greater competition or innovation will streamline legal services, and potentially reduce the overall cost of providing those services, there is no proof, beyond conjecture, that those savings will be passed along to the consumer of legal services.

. . . . .

Even where savings are passed onto consumers, in many cases the savings will be marginal with the result that legal services will continue to be inaccessible to individuals identified as having access issues. For example, for someone who struggles with providing the necessities of daily life, an hourly rate "reduction" to $130 is just as out of reach as an hourly rate of $150.

. . . . .

V. Ethical Considerations

A key part of mandate of the Law Society is to protect the public interest and increase access to justice. Public interest is protected when professionalism standards are maintained and ethical considerations enforced. OTLA is concerned that ABS will erode the ability of the LSUC to ensure that ethical and profession-alism standards are maintained. [ABS] may well change the focus from access to justice to 'access to profits', and relegate lawyers from professionals to 'profiteers'. There is simply too great a potential to compromise the sacred values upon which the legal profession has been built over centuries.

. . . . .

ABS will shift the focus away from individual clients and redirect it toward maximizing profits. Investors rarely direct their minds to long term goals or intangibles when assessing an investment. . . . Investors seek profits. Lawyers seek professionalism, as we are duty-bound to do.

743

Professionalism is an intangible quality that is not easily understood by non-lawyers. Lawyers are often challenged – at times vilified – by the public for representing the interests of unpopular clients, particularly in the criminal law field. How can you represent a murderer? A rapist? A drunk driver? The public does not understand our motivation. How do we justify to non-lawyer investors the importance of intangibles like the rule of law, the presumption of innocence, and other requirements of the due administration of justice, if it does not ensure profits?

. . . . .

Ethical issues in personal injury work

The ethical and professionalism issues that arise particularly in personal injury work are bound to be a quagmire under ABS. There will be subtle, if not overt, pressure to prefer the most profitable cases and the most profitable route to resolution. OTLA is concerned that the cost of referral fees to non-lawyers, if permitted, will ultimately be a cost passed on to the consumer.

The insurance industry is dealing with serious fraud complaints as a result of health practitioners paying entities like towing companies to direct consumers to their rehabilitation services instead of getting medical advice from their own treatment providers. OTLA is concerned that ABS will amplify this ethical issue.

. . . . .

When lawyers' independence is lost to overriding investor interests, control is given up and, inevitably, the ability of lawyers and the Law Society to maintain the highest standards of professional integrity is seriously impaired.

Professionalism in personal injury work

Lawyers are unique in placing ethics and professionalism above profit. The two models of motivation - professionalism and capitalism - are incompatible. Personal injury work, like most areas of law, attracts individuals who are socially-minded. Lawyers regularly engage in *pro bono* work, promote safety for the public, take test cases to trial, contribute time and expertise to charitable organizations or service providers for their clients, and act as an independent check on government and corporate power. As professionals, lawyers put their client's interest first. Lawyers take pride in representing victims against Goliaths like insurance companies. Many of these socially-responsible and community-based activities require substantial outlays of time. It is unlikely that investors will find the time spent with such activities, rather than on files, profit-worthy or inspiring of shareholder confidence.

. . . . .

When the driving interest is financial success, professionalism suffers. While there is nothing inherently wrong with seeking a return on investment, it does not synchronize well with the professional's goal, indeed duty, to fearlessly advocate the client's interests. There is an inescapable tension and conflict in maintaining professionalism and ethics under ABS models that include non-lawyer equity holders, controlling or otherwise.

Confidentiality

. . . Maintaining client confidences is a fundamental part of [client] trust. Yet, it will be much more difficult to contain and safeguard information when that information is important to both the investor and the client. Investors want control. They will want input into the decisions made on cases and will need access to confidential information to make informed decisions. Whether it is implicit or explicit, subtle or overt, the pressure will be there. They will be watching the bottom line. Will non-lawyers, not subject to regulation, protect confidentiality? There is huge potential for breaches. It is a complicated area of law. No amount of regulation can protect confidentiality unless the entity breaching confidentiality is subject to that regulation.

. . . . .

Competence

There is a reason lawyers train and study for years in order to provide competent and ethical legal services. Law, by its nature, is complicated and is not amenable to standardization of services. . . . Diluting professional responsibilities by creating a structure that allows work to be done in an environment controlled or influenced by non-lawyers in order to provide cheaper, standardized services and thus maximize profits, is plainly not in the public interest .

. . . . .

ANDREW GRECH & TAHLIA GORDON

"Should Non-Lawyer Ownership Be Endorsed and Encouraged?"
Slater and Gordon and Creative Consequences Pty Ltd. Working Paper, 2015

Introduction

Over the past few years a succession of academic and discussion papers have been published either forthrightly opposing or forthrightly supporting non-lawyer ownership of law firms. The papers opposing the concept of non-lawyer ownership hold to an outdated article of faith - that non-lawyer ownership erodes core values of the legal profession and leads to a corporatized legal services marketplace that sees business and profit motives taking precedence over professional obligations. This outdated article of faith is not supported by any empirical evidence and amount to little more than a self-serving argument designed to protect the status quo and regulatory structures that tend to be more focussed on entrenching privileges of the legal profession much more for their own sake, than for the sake of the community the legal profession exists to serve

. . . . .

As lawyers we have a duty to seek out ways to provide meaningful, innovative and accessible solutions to a key problem which undermines the proper administration to justice - the lack of access to legal services. . . . Whilst it is not the panacea to ending barriers to the justice system for ordinary citizens, liberalising the ownership structures of legal firms can contribute to improving access to the legal system and can also place the profession in a better position to compete with the current array of unqualified providers and new enterprises providing legal or quasi legal services.

This paper argues that statements alleging that ethics and professionalism will be eroded as a result of non-lawyer ownership are completely misguided. If regulated appropriately as Australia, England and Wales have done, the authors argue that non-lawyer owners of law firms present no risk to the professions core values and indeed reduces the risk to clients of unethical behaviour. The greatest threat to the legal profession and the ethical practice of law is not the innovation and capital base that non-lawyer ownership allows, but the steady increase in the market of legal service providers and enterprises offering cheaper, unregulated legal services.

. . . . .

Part 1: Concerns raised about non-lawyer ownership of law firms: protecting core values or protecting core work?

"The fundamental problem with the opposition to external ownership is that ethics is a state of mind, not a state of ownership."

In Australia, like most other jurisdictions around the world, the cost of accessing the legal system significantly limits the capacity of many to initiate action or respond to legal problems. . . . Regulations prohibiting the involvement of non-lawyers in legal services, such as the rules in the United States preventing lawyers from sharing fees, also perpetuate the access to justice gap.

According to several academics, strict licencing regulations for the legal profession is another barrier to providing affordable legal services. The inability of law firms to obtain external investment as a result of strict regulatory frameworks prohibiting non-lawyer ownership of law firms is considerable. According to Noel Semple, the "insulation" of law firms from non-lawyer investment impedes the accessibility of justice in three ways:

> First, they constrain the supply of capital for law firms, thereby increasing the cost which the firms must pay for it. To the extent that this cost of doing business is passed along to consumers, it will increase the price of legal services. Second, bigger firms might be better for access to justice, due to risk-spreading opportunities and economies of scale and scope. Individual clients must currently rely on small partnerships and solo practitioners, and allowing non-lawyer capital and management into the market might facilitate the emergence of large consumer law firms. Large firms would plausibly find it easier than small ones to expand access through flat rate billing, reputational branding, and investment in technology. Finally, insulating lawyers from non-lawyers precludes potentially innovative inter-professional collaborations, which might bring the benefits of legal services to more people even if firms stay small.

Semple is on the mark. Traditional professional partnerships within law firms do not typically concentrate on capital growth and are therefore capital constrained. They focus on attempting to maximise the income for the partners in each year, thereby reducing the opportunity for longer-term planning and growth in the underlying value of the practice.

. . . . .

Part 2: Protecting core values: robust regulatory frameworks in practice

Australia

On 1 July 2001 legislation was enacted in New South Wales, Australia permitting legal practices, including multidisciplinary practices (MDPs) to incorporate, share receipts and provide legal services either alone or alongside other legal service providers who may, or may not be legal practitioners.

. . . . .

The impact of these regulations on ethical and professional standards

Incorporated legal practices have now been permitted in New South Wales for close to 15 years. During this period a number of remarkable things have occurred. Firstly, the legislation has now been adopted by all States and Territories in Australia permitting the non-lawyer ownership of law firms nationally. Secondly, a considerable number of law firms Australia-wide (approximately 30%) have incorporated. Firms of all sizes have incorporated.

. . . . .

Third, the framework for regulating incorporated legal practices has resulted in an effective coregulatory partnership between the OLSC, the Law Society of NSW [New South Wales, Australia] and the financial services regulator and a reduction in red tape. It has not led to a loss of self-regulation by the professional associations.

. . . . .

Fourth, the regulatory framework has been lauded for its ability to curb unethical behaviour and improve law firm management because it is 'proactive' rather than 'reactive'. The framework is a radical departure from the traditional regulatory approach in which certain behaviours or conduct standards are defined and lawyers are disciplined if the behaviours and standards are not met. Rather than the regulator reacting after a complaint against a lawyer is made, the framework in Australia is designed to help firm leaders detect and avoid problems by focusing on management systems and processes designed to entrench ethical behaviours. This can occur because the framework allows firms to develop their own process and management systems and develop internal planning and management practices designed to achieve regulatory goals. This type of framework is referred to as "proactive, management based regulation."

The success of the framework is outlined in a series of research projects. In 2008, a research study by Dr. Christine Parker of the University of Melbourne Law School in conjunction with the NSW regulator assessed the impact of ethical infrastructure and the self-assessment process in NSW to assess whether the process is effective and whether the process is leading to "better conduct" by firms required to self-assess. The research focused on the number of complaints relating to incorporated legal practices after incorporation and comparing this with prior to incorporation. The research found that complaints rates for incorporated legal practices were two-thirds lower than non-incorporated legal practices after the incorporated legal practice completed their initial self assessment. The research also revealed that the complaints rate for incorporated legal practices that self-assessed was one-third of the number of complaints registered against similar nonincorporated legal practices.

Moreover, in another recent research study conducted on incorporated legal practices in NSW, by Professor Susan Saab Fortney of Hofstra University, New York, in conjunction with the NSW regulator, revealed that a majority (84%) of respondents reported that they had revised policies and procedures related to the delivery of legal services. Seventy-one percent of the respondents indicated that they had actually revised firm systems, policies and procedures. Close to half (47%) of the respondents reported that they had adopted new systems, policies, and procedures. In terms of encouraging training and initiatives, 29% indicated that their firms devoted more attention to ethics initiatives and 27% implemented more training for firm personnel.

Finally, the framework regulating incorporated legal practices is being recognised by jurisdictions around the world as the best way to curb unethical behaviour and increase professionalism. The framework adopted in NSW has been replicated to varying extents in the United Kingdom . . . and Canada and is being considered by a number of jurisdictions in the United States.

. . . . .

NOTES AND QUESTIONS

1. The authors of these readings seem to imply some impurity of motive in those who disagree with them, suggesting the pro-ABS side is motivated by profiteering, and the anti-ABS side is motivated by protectionism. Do you think that is fair? What might a person with no direct financial stake in the issue – say a consumer of legal services, an economist, a sociologist, or a judge – say with respect to the advantages and disadvantages of ABS?

2. The OTLA refers to the "sacred values" of the legal profession. Do you think language of that type is helpful or harmful in understanding the nature and extent of lawyers' professional obligations?

3. Another premise of the OTLA is that lawyer's professionalism depends at least somewhat on their having an ownership stake in the firm, and not being subject to external firm ownership. What are the implications of that view for lawyers who practice as in-house counsel, or as government lawyers?

4. In Chapter 10, you read an excerpt from an article by Woolley suggesting that the OTLA's promotion of a "slate" of candidates for bencher based on their position on ABS was problematic for a self-regulated profession's claims to regulate in the public interest. Having read the OTLA's submissions, are you more or less sympathetic to that critique?

5. Do you think the type of entity in which lawyers provide is likely to make a meaningful difference to access to justice? In answering this question, consider the definition of the scope of the access to justice problem set out in Chapter 11, and the barriers to access identified there.

6. In a 2018 blog on Slaw.ca reviewing the results of 5 years of ABS in England – "What can we learn from the English ABS experience after five years? – Malcolm Mercer noted:

> So the implication of the first five years of ABS liberalization in England is that it has not led to much accessing of external capital nor to much innovation. At the same time, it does not appear that ABS liberalization has led to significant problems either. That said, spending substantial

regulatory time and effort to enable a significant regulatory change of rather limited impact does not seem like a great use of resources.

Does that result surprise you? How, if at all, does it change your opinion on the merits of the position taken by the OTLA on the one hand, and by Grech and Gordon on the other?

7. Consider again the questions posed in Scenario Six re the recommendations to the Law Society of Saskatchewan. Based on these readings, and taking into account the limits on available regulatory resources, would you recommend that the Law Society of Saskatchewan permit ABS?

[6] SELF-REGULATION

When we talk about lawyer self-regulation, we mean something quite specific. Lawyer self-regulation refers to the grant of primary regulatory authority over lawyers to lawyers themselves. Each provincial law society has a statutory mandate that gives it the power to determine who gets admitted to the profession, to write the rules of conduct that govern the profession, to adjudicate cases of professional misconduct, to sanction lawyers who commit professional misconduct, and to prosecute people who practise law without a license from the law society. Further, each provincial law society is governed by benchers, the majority of whom are lawyers elected to the position by other lawyers. Lawyers self-regulate both by acting as benchers, and through having the power to choose who gets to be (and to remain) a bencher. Every Canadian lawyer has a role in, and responsibility for, professional governance.

This section considers the merits of the self-regulatory model. Why do we give lawyers the power to regulate themselves? Why might we think it would be better to have someone other than lawyers control regulation of the profession? And how well does the self-regulatory model work?

In reading each of the next three excerpts, bear in mind that Canada now stands alone amongst common law countries in having such a strong commitment to self-regulation. In the United States, the judiciary has always played a significant role in regulation of the profession, and the United Kingdom, Australia and New Zealand have all moved regulation to a model in which lawyers do not play the primary role in setting or enforcing standards for lawyer conduct.

In addition, in reading these excerpts think about the question of self-regulation in light of the regulatory problems and issues raised in this Chapter, and in the two that preceded it. Is a self-regulation model the most likely to result in progress on the complex challenges related to diversity, access to justice and regulatory innovation?

The first excerpt sets out the case in favour of self-regulation.

LAW SOCIETY OF BRITISH COLUMBIA

"Report of the Independence and Self-Governance Committee" March 20, 2008[*]
[modified, footnotes omitted]

Introduction

This Report of the Independence and Self-Governance Committee is the result of the Committee's consideration of the importance of lawyer independence to the protection and maintenance of the rule of law, and thereby to the maintenance of an underlying cornerstone of Canadian democracy.

The first part of this Report addresses the meaning of and reason for lawyer independence, and examines why, in the Committee's view, lawyer independence is best preserved, for the benefit of the public interest, through self-governance. . . .

Part I - Lawyer Independence and Self-Governance

What is "Lawyer Independence?"

"Lawyer independence" is not a well-defined concept, and the Committee spent some considerable time discussing, for the purposes of this Report, how to define it.

Lawyer independence is often presumed by the general public to confer a right upon lawyers. In reality, however, it is a public right necessary (as will be discussed below) to protect the rule of law. The public has a right to be able to obtain legal advice from a lawyer whose primary duty is to his or her client, not to any other person, and certainly not to the state. The public's right to lawyer independence is therefore closely associated with the obligation on the profession to self-govern, in a responsible and effective manner, in order to ensure that lawyers are free from interference or control by the state.

The Committee recognized, however, that, to be useful, the definition needed to be relatively straightforward and free from obscure legal language. The Committee has settled on the following definition:

> Lawyer independence is the fundamental right guaranteeing that lawyers may provide legal assistance for or on behalf of a client without fear of interference or sanction by the government, subject only to the lawyer's professional responsibilities as prescribed by the Law Society, and the lawyer's general duty as a citizen to obey the law. . ..

The Rule of Law

The Rule of Law is a fundamental principle underlying Canadian democracy. The preamble of the *Charter of Rights and Freedoms* states that the rule of law is one of the principles upon which Canada is founded. The rule of law has always been recognized as a fundamental principle. *In Roncarelli v. Duplessis*, for example, Mr. Justice Rand noted that the rule of law is a "fundamental postulate of our constitutional structure".

Briefly stated, the rule of law means that everyone is subject to the law or, put another way, that no one is above the law. Rich or poor, individuals, corporations,

---

[*] Reproduced with permission.

and governments alike are all subject to and governed by the law. The rule of law means that the law is supreme over officials of the government as well as private individuals, and thereby preclusive of the influence of arbitrary power.

The rule of law is required to provide for impartial control of the use of power by the state. It guards against arbitrary governance. Therefore, to be effective, the rule of law requires not only the submission of all to the law, but also the separation of powers within the state. Because the rule of law is devised, in part, to control the powers of the state, there must be a division amongst those who make the law, those who interpret and apply it, and those who enforce it. This requires "an independent judiciary, which in turn requires an efficient, functioning court system and a strong, independent, properly qualified legal profession to support it. An independent legal profession is also fundamental to the maintenance of citizens' rights and freedoms under the rule of law, so that they are guaranteed access to independent, skilled, confidential and objective legal advice...[if the highest standards of skill, professionalism and integrity amongst the legal profession are not maintained] confidence in the legal process will be undermined, so will the necessary respect for the rule of law, and the executive and legislative branches will be both tempted and enabled to interfere in the processes which protect their independence."

A failure to maintain the separation of powers described above, resulting in the interference by the executive with the independence of the judiciary and lawyers, can have severe ramifications on the rule of law and the protections it affords, as has been demonstrated within the past year in both Venezuela and Pakistan.

In an article entitled *The Independence of the Bar*, Jack Giles Q.C. explained the connection between lawyer independence and the rule of law as follows:

> It is simply inconceivable that a constitution which guarantees fundamental human rights and freedoms should not first protect that which makes it possible to benefit from such guarantees, namely every citizen's constitutional right to effective, meaningful and unimpeded access to a court of law through the aegis of an independent bar...While a court of law worthy of its name is impossible without an independent judiciary, meaningful access and the effective use of such a court is impossible without an independent bar. In the result, both an independent bar and an independent judiciary are necessary to maintain and preserve the supremacy of law.

The Committee has therefore concluded that the independence of lawyers is necessarily linked to the preservation of the rule of law. Independent lawyers are therefore necessary to preserve a fundamental principle of the Canadian Constitution.

The Law Society and Self-Governance of Lawyers

Accepting that lawyer independence is necessary to preserve the rule of law, the next question is how can that independence be assured? The Committee believes that self-governance is a necessary condition of this independence, and that this has generally been recognized in Canada by the courts and the legislatures.

The motto of the Law Society is *lex liberorum rex*, which means "the law is king of free men" (a more contemporary translation is "the law is ruler of free people"). This motto has been in place for well over a century, and reflects the importance of the rule of law and of the Law Society's role in protecting it.

The object and duty of the Law Society, set out in s. 3 of the *Legal Profession Act*, S.B.C. 1998, c. 9, is to uphold and protect the public interest in the administration of justice by, amongst other things,

- preserving and protecting the rights and freedoms of all persons, and
- ensuring the independence of lawyers.

The independence of lawyers as a general concept is not, however, well understood, let alone regarded as a fundamental protection of the rule of law and, thereby, the rights and freedoms of citizens. At best, the independence of lawyers is an abstract principle to most people, including to many lawyers. In a recent article, W. Wesley Pue noted that to the general public, "(t)he idea of independence [of lawyers] from state regulation strikes many as undemocratic, if not a prescription for lawlessness."

The *Legal Profession Act* requires the Law Society to ensure the independence of lawyers. The Law Society must therefore discharge this task assiduously. This is particularly important given the essential role that lawyer independence has in the maintenance of the rule of law, and, through it, the administration of justice in Canada. The Supreme Court of Canada has commented on this principle a number of times, perhaps as a reflection of the importance of lawyer independence to the preservation of the rule of law. . . .

The Committee therefore believes that self-regulation and self-governance is essential to lawyer independence. Self-governance most clearly distances the profession from the state, thereby assuring the public of lawyers' independence and freedom from conflicts with the state. Lawyers, who are often retained to act on behalf of clients who are in conflict with the state, would find themselves in an untenable conflict of interest with their client should the lawyer be regulated by the state. If lawyers were not governed and regulated in a manner independent of the state, clients could not be assured that their lawyer would be providing them with independent representation, particularly (for instance) if the client's case required a direct challenge to the state's authority. In such cases, it is necessary that individuals can obtain legal advice and representation that is independent of state control.

There are other models that have been or are being devised by which to regulate and govern lawyers, and not all of these are as clearly self-governing as those in Canada. While some of these models operate in countries that are best described as liberal democracies,

> . . . the fact that liberal, pluralistic democracy A functions without a safeguard does not mean that liberal, pluralistic democracy B functions *better* without it. Nor... does it necessarily follow that liberal, pluralistic democracy B should try to function without the safeguard. The question for liberal, pluralistic democracy B is whether or not the safeguard is desirable in the public interest of pluralistic democracy B (Emphasis in original).

The Committee agrees with this assessment. Models of lawyer regulation that are not self-governing less clearly demonstrate and preserve the independence of lawyers, which is "an important [some would say necessary] component of the fundamental legal framework of Canadian society".

With self-regulation and self-governance, however, comes a responsibility to demonstrate that the Law Society is discharging its mandate in the public interest, rather than in the interest of those it regulates:

> The necessary external condition is that the public and the government consider self-regulation to be in the public interest....Here it is the **perception** that the system operates, or at least is intended to operate, in the public interest that counts, but such a perception is not likely to continue for long if the system is in fact operated for the private interest of the profession... (Emphasis in original).

. . . . .

The next two excerpts criticize self-regulation, the first challenging the normative justification for self-regulation, the second suggesting that the self-regulatory model has not been successful in practice.

R. DEVLIN & P. HEFFERNAN

"The End(s) of Self Regulation(?)"
(2008) 45 Alta. L. Rev. 169
[modified, footnotes omitted]

Introduction

All around the world jurisdictions are reconsidering and ultimately abandoning self-regulation as a model for the governance of the legal profession. Whether it be Australia, New Zealand, Scotland, England and Wales, South Africa or Ireland a wide range of advanced liberal democratic societies have assessed self-regulation and found it wanting as a defensible regime. By contrast, in Canada self-regulation by the legal profession appears to be a sacred cow. Governments, the general public, the judiciary and the profession itself all appear to believe that self-regulation is *de facto* and *de jure* the only game in town and that substantive consideration of alternatives would be unnecessary, fruitless and pointless.

It is time to consider whether such complacency is warranted in Canada. Have there been any failures by the regulatory bodies in Canada? Have law societies in Canada established all the appropriate standards, adequately monitored lawyers' conduct and enforced suitable penalties? Do we have all the ethical rules and principles that we need in Canada? Are there any rules and principles that are missing? Are there any rules and principles that are superfluous?...

The Well-Tilled Field: Arguments Pro and Con Self-Regulation

The arguments pro and con self-regulation have been developed over many decades, by many authors, in many different fora. It is therefore unnecessary to rehearse them in detail. However, a brief overview is helpful in order to set the context for the remainder of this section and to highlight the complexity of the problem of designing a suitable regulatory regime. Regulation is not just about techniques and institutions, it is also about the underlying values of the society in which it operates: democracy, accountability, equality, transparency, effectiveness and efficiency. Consequently it is incumbent on analysts to both question their taken-for-granted assumptions and avoid overly hasty conclusions.

The essence of the argument in favour of self-regulation can be captured in a formula, A+E=I: autonomy plus expertise = independence from state regulation and market forces. The essence of the critique is the old latin maxim: *quis custodiet*, or more polemically: should we allow the fox to guard the chickens . . . or is it wise to put Dracula in charge of the bloodbank?

. . . . .

Arguments in Favour

[The detailed review of arguments in favour of self-regulation is omitted. The authors describe arguments related to the independence of the bar, independency of the judiciary, democracy, public confidence, tradition, expertise, efficiency, higher standards and commitment to the public good]

Arguments Against

There are, however, a significant number of arguments that cast doubt on the foregoing claims. The essence of the critique is that self-regulation is a privilege (not a right) that was granted to the legal profession as part of a "regulative bargain" and in return the profession would promote and protect the public interest. The legal profession, the critics claim, has failed to live up to the regulative bargain on a number of levels.

Conflict of Interest

The key concern of the conflict of interest claim is that it is not possible for a single organization to fulfil both a representative function and a regulatory function. According to the critics it is just too convenient that the public interest in accessing legal services should be presumed to dovetail with the professional interest in providing such services. The legal profession prohibits individual lawyers from benefitting from conflicts of interest, but is oblivious to its own constitutive conflict of interest. For example, if one analyses the sorts of pitches that are made by candidates seeking election to bar council they overwhelmingly reflect the interests and concerns of lawyers, not the public.

Critics of self-regulation, just like the defenders, also play the public perception card: even if there is no actual conflict of interest and the profession does successfully put the public interest ahead of its own, the public is not likely to see it that way and that perception is just as important as reality. If confidence in the rule of law really is at stake, then it should be beyond doubt that the guardian of the rule of law, the legal profession, must itself be free of the taint of impartiality.

. . . . .

Monopoly/Market Control

Although this argument is informed by the economic analysis of law, it is worth noting that it is embraced by critics on both the left and right of the political spectrum. On this view the legal profession is a "conspiratorial cartel" and self-regulation is anti-competitive because it limits the supply of legal services thereby artificially inflating prices. Many legal services could be supplied by others, for example paralegals, and there is no empirical evidence to suggest that the removal of self-regulation would either diminish the quality or availability of legal services. More specifically, comparative empirical research confirms that in many jurisdictions there is a fundamental "lack of a consumer orientation" on the part of the legal profession and, more importantly, that law societies have done little to try to improve this. Thus it is argued that competition might well increase both the possibility of lower prices and improve the quality of services. In short, it engenders competitiveness in quality control. In the long run this should enhance the level of consumer satisfaction. Other analysts go further and suggest that we are witnessing the phenomenon of "regulation-for-competition" whereby regulatory innovation is seen to be a competitive asset in an increasingly globalized world.

Independence: Really . . . and From Whom?

Critics of self-regulation tend to make three broad claims in response to the independence argument: the first calls for analytical clarity; the second suggests a reality check; and the third pleads for historical accuracy.

. . . . . .

Second, critics call for a reality check. Traditional arguments for independence focus on the threat of the state, but in the modern world the state is not the only, or even major, centre of power and control in society. Corporations also wield great influence. Not only are in-house counsel especially vulnerable to their economic masters, so too are law firms that service corporations, especially corporations who are repeat clients -- he who pays the piper -- as the aphorism goes. The independence of the legal profession, in other words, is more apparent than real.

Third, from a historical perspective, critics point out that the legal profession has been somewhat less than enthusiastic in its pursuit of independence than it is often asserted. Many of the elements of self-regulation cannot be traced back to the mystical origins of the common law but are relatively recent, *i.e.*, twentieth century, developments. Furthermore, at times the profession has been aligned with repressive forces as much as with democracy and the rule of law. During the Winnipeg General Strike some members of the legal profession engaged in outrageous behaviour. In Quebec during the Duplessis regime many lawyers refused to provide legal services to Mr. Roncarelli, a Jehovah's Witness, to fight the padlock laws. Many lawyers did little to protest the invocation of the *War Measures Act* and, currently, there are allegations that a significant number of marquee criminal defence lawyers made themselves scarce when the Toronto 17 were arrested. And then again there is Ms. Finney who [when challenging the conduct of the Barreau du Quebec] only got *pro bono* assistance when the case went to the Supreme Court of Canada. As to the argument that there is threat to the independence of the judiciary it has been noted that a significant number of judges come from government or universities, yet there is nothing to indicate that they are less independent or impartial.

Undemocratic

In response to the claim that self-regulation is essential for democracy, critics point out that the causal connection is missing: there are many liberal democratic societies where there is no self-government by the legal profession, yet they seem to be flourishing as well as Canada. Conversely, there are jurisdictions that have a self-regulating legal profession but are deeply authoritarian, for example, Singapore. Moreover, critics insist that the demand for self-regulation comes from the profession itself, not the general public and as such is, in fact, an exercise in "regulatory imperialism". The concern that the public will lose confidence in the legal profession if self-regulation is abolished is conjecture, devoid of any empirical support. To the contrary, at least one commentator suggests that self-regulation may be only a contingent and transitional moment in the development of a profession as it seeks to establish its legitimacy, but once that legitimacy has been consolidated, self-regulation can be relinquished as the profession becomes more mature. Moreover, it is argued that the governors within the legal profession are rarely representative of a cross section of an increasingly diversified and fragmented profession, let alone society. Given this, it is difficult to imagine how their conception of the public interest could authentically and democratically capture the (increasingly complex) reality of the public interest.

Protection Racket

There are a couple of dimensions to this concern. The first is that despite the fact that Codes of Conduct both allow and demand whistle blowing on fellow lawyers, it is very rare for lawyers to report the misconduct of other lawyers. So, while it is true that lawyers may have the expertise to distinguish between proper and improper conduct, that does nothing to ensure that they will in fact exercise that expertise in the public interest. . . .

Moreover, critics also argue that when discipline proceedings are instituted the penalties are too lenient because lawyers are too sensitive to their colleague's situation . . . "there but for the grace of god go I" ... Mr. Hunter [who had a sexual relationship with his client] is but one example of this. Another concern is that few lawyers are ever disciplined for excessive billing, a common practice that is the most significant complaint from clients.

Still others argue that the complaints processes run by law societies are not especially consumer friendly. Furthermore, even if people do pursue their concerns, the disciplinary system occupies the field, crowding out other remedial avenues (civil or criminal). The consequence is that discipline is a sop, it funnels complaints away and often, miscreant lawyers get off the hook, or receive only minimal discipline.

Reactive and Inefficient Institutional Culture

Because the self-regulatory process is beholden to the lawyers themselves in the form of fees, law societies are significantly underfunded and understaffed. Consequently they operate reactively, primarily on the basis of complaints, rather than actively seeking out problematic behaviour, before it is too late. While law societies are empowered to conduct spot audits and can commence an investigation without a complaint, these actions are the exception rather than the rule.

From a slightly different perspective it might also be suggested that law societies' regulatory structures are inefficient/sub-optimal. While it is true that the costs are internalized to the profession, some [commentators] indicate that the bureaucracies created by law societies may not be particularly efficient. The argument is that they are run by lawyers, not professional regulators, and consequently they do not get the best bang for the regulatory buck. An independent regulatory body can provide greater professionalism, rationality, accessibility and efficiency . . . .

. . . . .

ADAM M. DODEK

"Taking Self-Regulation for Granted?"
July 2016 on slaw.ca

"It is not a right. Self-regulation is very much a privilege." So declared Premier Christy Clark at the end of June when she announced that the BC government would take over regulation of the real estate industry in that province.

As those in BC know, the BC housing market has been on fire over the past year. Potential home buyers face a crisis of affordability. Questionable practices by some real estate agents and a failure to respond by the Real Estate Council of British Columbia (RECBC) fuelled a crisis of confidence in the regulator. And the government stepped in.

We need to be cautious about any lessons to be drawn from the BC real estate experience. It is certainly not fair to attribute the crisis of affordability to alleged lax regulation by the self-regulating RECBC. The RECBC was, perhaps, an easy target in the midst of a political firestorm. 2017 is an election year in BC and it is likely that housing affordability will continue to be a top campaign issue.

But yet self-regulation of the legal profession in Canada faces remarkably similar vulnerabilities. We have a largely unaffordable justice system where costs continue to spiral out of control. It is surprising that no grassroots indignation has yet to boil over into the political realm. Law Societies purport to regulate lawyers' fees (Model Code Rule 3.6) but have completely abdicated responsibility on this front. The public may rightly ask why?

To their credit, Law Societies have belatedly embraced access to justice as a regulatory concern. But as [civility] cases like *Groia* in Ontario and *Laarakker* in BC show, Law Societies continue to be distracted by concerns that are unlikely to be priorities to clients or members of the public. Christy Clark could have been reminding law societies when she lectured: "The point of regulation is to protect people, to protect consumers." All regulators need to heed this lesson, but particularly those who are self-regulating like Canadian law societies.

Law Societies have never had a problem articulating their mission; it has been uniform and consistent for over two hundred years in Canada — to regulate the practice of law in the public interest. What has been more problematic historically is how Law Societies have interpreted this mission and how they have arguably strayed from it. Regulating legal services in the public interest means protecting the public and protecting consumers; it does not mean protecting the profession against competition or protecting it against reputational harm. For everything that Law Societies do, they should be judged against this public interest mandate. Law Societies should be asked — and should be asking themselves — how their actions in a particular area and in any case protect people or protect consumers. This is why I find cases like *Groia* and *Laarakker* so frustrating. In *Groia*, the Law Society of Upper Canada has spent a decade prosecuting a lawyer for conduct in the courtroom that had no impact on the public or on clients. The cost to the Law Society in terms of staff time, bencher time and legal fees must be enormous; the opportunity cost of what could have been done in its stead staggering. On *Laarakker*, the Law Society of British Columbia completely missed the boat, targeting a lawyer who stood up for members of the public against a practice described by Alice Woolley as "extortion with letterhead". Law Societies should be going after the abusive practice of shoplifting demand letters that has been well-documented by my colleague Amy Salyzyn. Instead, they have done nothing and allowed this abusive practice to persist for decades.

Law Societies would be wise to remember Premier Clark's words or they may end up finding themselves listening to a similar lecture from another premier one day.

NOTES AND QUESTIONS

1. Do you think self-regulation better protects democracy, the rule of law and independence of the bar than other models? Do you think there are other principles that support a self-regulatory approach?

2. In their article, Devlin and Heffernan discuss the argument that lawyers have greater expertise than non-lawyers about what ought to be considered professional conduct. Lawyers best understand both what lawyers ought to do, and what should be considered misconduct. Do you think non-lawyers understand the lawyer's role? Why or why not?

3. In addition to giving lawyers regulatory power, a self-regulatory model also looks to lawyers to pay for the cost of regulation. Lawyers pay annual fees to law societies of around $2500-5000 per year, not including the cost of insurance. In addition, lawyers found to have committed professional misconduct have to pay at least a part of the costs incurred by the law society in prosecuting the case which, depending upon the circumstances, can be considerable, reaching into the tens or even hundreds of thousands of dollars. Does that affect your assessment of the merits of self-regulation? Do you think if Canada moved away from a self-regulatory model that funding structure would change? Ought it to change?

4. Dodek discusses the civility cases that you considered in Chapter 5 to critique self-regulation. He wrote his article prior to the Supreme Court's decision in *Groia*. Given the Supreme Court's decision, do you agree that those examples suggest weaknesses in the self-regulatory model? More specifically, do you think that law societies erred in prosecuting Groia or Laarakker? And do you think whether they did so was related to the law societies being self-regulated? Based on the ethical issues discussed in previous chapters of the casebook, which ethical issues do you think ought to be the focus of the law societies' concern?

5. If you were asked to give a 30-second elevator pitch in favour of self-regulation what would you say? If you were asked to give a 30-second elevator pitch against self-regulation what would you say? Which one seems more compelling to you?

6. As noted earlier, law societies determine standards for admission to the profession, they set standards for conduct, they investigate and adjudicate allegations of misconduct, they sanction lawyers for misconduct and they prosecute persons who practice law without being licensed to do so. They

also try to resolve public policy issues in relation to legal practice, through decisions such as whether to approve of TWU's law school, or through initiatives to support diversity and encourage equality in the legal profession. Which areas of the law societies' mandate are enhanced by the self-regulatory model? Which areas are undermined by the self-regulatory model? Why?

Scenario Seven

Most law societies have a leader (known as a President or Treasurer) who is elected by the Benchers. In 2020, the Law Society of Ontario elected a new Treasurer. The two leading candidates were Benchers Teresa Donnelly and Philip H. Horgan. Below are the election statements of each candidate. Review each statement and consider the following questions:

1. What concept of the public interest in the practice of law does each statement reflect?

2. What effect, if any, do these statements have on your view of the merits of self-regulation?

3. If you were voting in the bencher election, which candidate would you vote for? Why?

4. Most other professional regulators (e.g. the bodies that regulate health care professionals and teachers) have leadership which is appointed by the government, not elected. Do you think that elections in which lawyers vote are a good way to choose Benchers?

5. Phillip Horgan was part of the "Stop SOP" slate of candidates discussed in a previous Chapter 10. Do you think that slates of candidates – which are somewhat akin to political parties – are a helpful feature of self-regulatory elections? In answering this question, consider Woolley's critique of the OTLA anti-ABS slate in Chapter 10.

Teresa Donnelly:

I am seeking re-election and ask for your support. I would be honoured to continue to work for you.

Priorities for our profession include:

- Promoting equality, diversity, and inclusion and implementing the Challenges report

- Ensuring fiscal accountability

- Regulating in the public interest and achieving effective oversight through our governance structure

- Facilitating access to justice including through collaboration with stakeholders

- Embracing opportunities and confronting challenges of technology and globalization

- Supporting all lawyers, with a focus on sole and small practices to ensure access to supports and resources

- Implementing enhancements to Articling and Law Practice Program to reduce barriers and to ensure quality placements free from harassment and discrimination

. . .

While I am a government lawyer, I work in Goderich which is a small town and I understand the challenges facing sole and small firms and rural practitioners. As a Prosecutor, I have dedicated my career to providing access to justice for victims of domestic and sexual violence – the majority of whom are women and children. As the West Region Sexual Violence Crown, I am one of seven Prosecutors in the province dedicated to enhancing the quality of sexual violence prosecutions and the victim's experience in the criminal justice system.

. . .

Like the majority of lawyers, they are hardworking, dedicated, committed professionals who enhance the reputation of the profession and the administration of justice. I believe in the dignity and integrity of the profession and that each of us must uphold those standards.

Philip Horgan:

The Law Society has strayed from its governance role, and from protecting the public from unscrupulous actors, toward an activist engagement to demand compelled speech from its members on ideological viewpoints.

In recent years, the Society has forced members to adopt an "accelerated culture shift" by adopting a Statement of Principles, which overreaches into our freedoms, however well intentioned. Its denial of accreditation of the previously approved Trinity Western law school was contrary to positions taken by other provincial law societies and the previous approval of that school's program. The Society continues to engage as a government actor into areas where legitimate differences should be allowed. These are all examples of a Law Society that is advancing critical legal theory by imposing a "politically correct" viewpoint on its members.

We must value our independence as individuals and as a profession, and remain focused on the Society's core roles.

The Law Society should support our deeply cherished constitutional freedoms, including the allowance of lawyers to make their own decisions on matters of public debate. Its civic "totalist" advocacy risks sacrificing our independence and freedom as a profession to the next roll-out of ideological demands. I share the views of www.stopsop.ca.

The Society needs to remain frugal. Why are our fees the highest of any similar jurisdiction? I stand for holding the line or reducing dues, which in turn will allow for greater pro bono options, and enhanced access to justice.

I believe that we need to elect benchers who recognize the importance of our independence as a profession, both as lawyers, and in recognition of the role we play for our clients in defending and advancing their interests.

Scenario Eight

In a 2018 post on slaw.ca, "The Bencher from Amazon", Malcolm Mercer observed the potential for technology to "provide legal services where legal services are not now being provided". Based on the assumption that this was a desirable outcome, the question then is: how do you regulate such service providers? He noted that one method would be to include technology providers as a new class of licensees for each provincial law society. He then said,

> If self-regulation is to be maintained, wouldn't the logical consequence of regulating technological providers be to have their elected representatives on the board. Said more plainly, if Amazon provided technologically based legal services, should there be a bencher from, or elected by, Amazon? This would of course change the nature of the Law Society by adding new types of providers to the Convocation table, benchers who are not professionals in the traditional sense of the word.

> But this is not the only possible approach. Another is to take the English approach (or the Canadian approach for health professions such as doctors and nurses) and to have different regulators for different types of providers. There could be a separate regulator of technological providers.

> A third approach would be to adopt the English approach to reserved and unreserved activities and to reduce the scope of the regulatory sphere so as to allow technology to deliver legal services outside of the reserved space subject only to general consumer regulation.

> To be clear, I do not contend for any conclusion in this column but rather seek to highlight that the decision to move beyond legal service delivery by one established profession has its complexities. Those complexities can be managed in different ways and that complexity exists is not a sufficient reason to avoid change in the public interest. But there are things to think about.

Is a natural consequence of expanding the range of legal service providers, while maintaining self-regulation, that the type of people involved in self-regulation must evolve? If so (or if not) how does that effect your assessment of the merits of self-regulation?

[7] FURTHER READING

Arthurs, Harry, "The Dead Parrot: Does Professional Self Regulation Exhibit Vital Signs?" (1995) 33 Alta. L. Rev. 800.

Devlin, Richard & Albert Cheng, "Re-Calibrating, Re-Visioning and Re-Thinking Self-Regulation" (2011) 17(3) International Journal of the Legal Profession 233.

Fischer, James M., "External Control Over the American Bar" (2006) 19 Geo. J. Leg. Ethics 59.

Furlong, Jordan, "The Coming End of Lawyer Control Over Legal Regulation" (February 8, 2019), online: *slaw.ca,* http://www.slaw.ca/2019/02/08/the-coming-end-of-lawyer-control-over-legal-regulation/.

Hurlburt, William, *The Self Regulation of the Legal Profession in Canada and in England and Wales* (Law Society of Alberta and the Alberta Law Reform Institute, 2000).

Law Society of British Columbia, "Anticipating Changes in the Delivery of Legal Services and the Legal Profession: The Final Report of the Futures Task Force", (September 10, 2020), online: https://www.lawsociety.bc.ca/Website/media/Shared/docs/initiatives/2020FuturesTaskForceReport.pdf.

Law Society of Upper Canada, "Alternative Business Structures and the Legal

Profession in Ontario: A Discussion Paper" (September 2014), online: https://www. advocates.ca/Upload/Files/PDF/Advocacy/Submissions/LawSocietyofUpperCanada/ LSUC_ABS_Working_Group_Discussion_Paper.pdf.

Mercer, Malcolm, "Utopia, Dystopia and Alternative Business Structures" (November 11, 2013), online: *slaw.ca* http://www.slaw.ca/2013/11/11/utopia-dystopia-and-alternative-business-structures/.

Mercer, Malcolm, "Thoughts About Self-Regulation in the Public Interest" (November 5, 2019), online: *slaw.ca* http://www.slaw.ca/2019/11/05/thoughts-about-self-regulation-in-the-public-interest/.

Pearson, John, "Canada's Legal Profession: Self-Regulating in the Public Interest" (2015) 92 Can. Bar Rev. 555.

Salyzyn, Amy "AI and Legal Ethics" in *Artificial Intelligence and the Law in Canada, in* Florian Martin-Bariteau & Teresa Scassa, (eds.) (Toronto: LexisNexis Canada, 2021).

Semple, Noel, *Legal Services Regulation at the Crossroads: Justitia's Legions* (Cheltenham: Edward Elgar Publishing, 2015).

Semple, Noel, "Legal Services Regulation in Canada: Plus ca change?" in Andy Boon, ed., *International Perspectives on the Regulation of Lawyers and Legal Services*, (Oxford: Hart Publishing, 2017).

Semple, Noel, "A Good Day for Self-Regulation: The LSO's Family Law Paralegal Proposal" (July 30, 2020), online: *slaw.ca*, http://www.slaw.ca/2020/07/30/a-good-day-for-self-regulation-the-lsos-family-law-paralegal-proposal/.

Turriff, Gordon, "Self-Governance as a Necessary Condition of Constitutionally-Mandated Lawyer Independence in British Columbia" (September 17, 2009), online: http://www.lawsociety.bc.ca/docs/publications/reports/turriff-speech.pdf.

CHAPTER 13

JUDICIAL ETHICS

[1] INTRODUCTION

Judges are lawyers, but they are not members of law societies. Furthermore, the roles and responsibilities of judges are distinct from those of lawyers. Consequently, judges inhabit a discrete and distinctive ethical domain from that of lawyers. In Chapter 1, it was suggested that three core principles structure the lawyer's world: loyal advocacy, lawyers as moral agents in the pursuit of justice and integrity. For judges, the Canadian Judicial Council stipulates that there are five core principles: (1) judicial independence; (2) integrity and respect; (3); diligence and competence; (4) equality; and (5) impartiality.[1]

The range of potential issues to be discussed under the rubric of judicial ethics is quite large, ranging from pre-appointment behaviour, through conduct while serving as a judge (including matters arising in both one's public and private life), to post-retirement activities. It is not possible to cover all such issues in one chapter; indeed, they could be the subject matter of a book.[2] In what follows we will provide only an introduction to this broad and dynamic domain of ethics.

[2] THE GOVERNING REGIME

Judicial ethics are governed by three key mechanisms: constitutional norms, case law and ethical guidelines. First, foundational ethical ideas such as judicial independence and impartiality are said to be part of the constitutional order, both written and unwritten. Second, the courts have sought (with some difficulty) to develop legal rules to govern judicial behaviour, most significantly in the realm of bias and recusal. Third, the Canadian judiciary itself has articulated a series of principles to guide the ethical conduct of judges. While all three dimensions are important, for the purposes of this chapter we will focus on the third.

Canadian judges fall into one of two categories: those who are appointed by provincial or territorial governments, and those who are appointed by the federal government.[3] Most judges in the first category are not bound by a code of conduct. In fact, only four provinces have a code of conduct for judges: Newfoundland and

---

[1] Canadian Judicial Council, *Ethical Principles for Judges* (Ottawa: 2021). The *Ethical Principles* were first published in 1998 and revised in 2021.

[2] Pierre Noreau & Emmanuelle Bernheim, *Applied Judicial Ethics*, 3rd ed. (Montréal: Wilson & Lafleur, 2014).

[3] Provincial judges are appointed under the authority of s. 92(14) and federal judges are appointed under the authority of s. 96 of the *Constitution Act, 1867* (U.K.), 30 & 31 Vict., c. 3, reprinted in R.S.C. 1985, App. II, No. 5.

Labrador, Ontario, Quebec and British Columbia. Is this surprising to you? Is it justifiable? Consider the Quebec *Judicial Code of Ethics*:

1. The judge should render justice within the framework of the law.

2. The judge should perform the duties of his office with integrity, dignity and honour.

3. The judge has a duty to foster his professional competence.

4. The judge should avoid any conflict of interest and refrain from placing himself in a position where he cannot faithfully carry out his functions.

5. The judge should be, and be seen to be, impartial and objective.

6. The judge should perform the duties of his office diligently and devote himself entirely to the exercise of his judicial functions.

7. The judge should refrain from any activity which is not compatible with his judicial office.

8. In public, the judge should act in a reserved, serene and courteous manner.

9. The judge should submit to the administrative directives of his chief judge, within the performance of his duties.

10. The judge should uphold the integrity and defend the independence of the judiciary, in the best interest of justice and society.[4]

How helpful is such a code of conduct? Is it better than no code at all, or is it so general that it provides little assistance to those in need?

Federally-appointed judges are in a different situation. In 1998, the Canadian Judicial Council created a 52-page handbook called *Ethical Principles for Judges*.[5] The Canadian Judicial Council substantially revised the *Ethical Principles,* releasing a streamlined version in 2021. Compare the *Ethical Principles* with the Quebec Code of Conduct. Which is the better document? Why?

The fourth paragraph of the *Ethical Principles* is especially important. It states:

> The ethical principles articulated in this document are aspirational. They are not intended to be a code of conduct that sets minimum standards. They are advisory in nature and are designed to (i) describe exemplary behaviour which all judges strive to maintain; (ii) assist judges with the difficult ethical and professional issues that confront them; and (iii) help members of the public better understand the judicial role. The guidance provided in *Ethical Principles* does not preclude reasonable disagreements about their application in particular cases or imply that any departure from them necessarily warrants disapproval. The ethical principles are intended to be applied in light of all of the relevant circumstances and consistently with the requirements of judicial independence and the law. They should not be viewed as an exhaustive expression of the ethical considerations that judges may face in their professional or personal lives.

---

[4] CQLR, c. T-16, r. 1, ss. 1-10. *Judicial Code of Ethics* available online: http://legisquebec. gouv.qc.ca/en/ShowDoc/cr/T-16,%20r.%201%20/.

[5] Online: https://cjc-ccm.ca/cmslib/general/news_pub_judicialconduct_Principles_en.pdf.

The following two extracts discuss the merits of providing judges with guidance relative to providing them with rules. Both were written prior to the 2021 revisions to the *Ethical Principles*. The first, by a justice of the Saskatchewan Court of Appeal, provides four justifications in support of the guidelines approach. The second, by two academics, argues that judges ought to be guided by rules.

THE HONOURABLE GEORGINA R. JACKSON

"The Mystery of Judicial Ethics: Deciphering the 'Code' "
(2005) 68 Sask. L. Rev. 1[*]
[footnotes omitted]

There are four policy reasons that support this interpretation [in the *Ethical Principles*]. First and foremost, it is not necessary to interpret the *Ethical Principles* as creating standards of conduct. The *Ethical Principles* booklet is written for an independent judiciary. Canadian judges have earned their status first through rigorous training, and then by the respect and approval of their peers prior to appointment. A disciplinary code may be more important in a judicial system where judges are elected or enjoy less status than Canadian judges, but it is not needed for a judiciary that is free from political and financial pressures.

Second, it is commonly believed that the test for sanctionable conduct is now established at a level that maximizes the exercise of impartial judicial thought. If the *Ethical Principles* are interpreted as creating a standard of conduct for disciplinary purposes, the ambit of what is considered sanctionable conduct may be broadened. This may result in an increase in complaints. As Professor Morissette indicates, "a series of complaints is likely to affect the judge where he or she is most vulnerable, namely in the ability to make impartial decisions with the appropriate degree of detachment on questions of general interest that are both very difficult and very controversial."

Third, one can, in my opinion, accomplish more with ethical principles than with a code of prohibited behaviours. Ethical principles are, by their nature, more stringent than any standard of conduct can ever be. They represent the ceiling to which judges strive. Justice Thomas states:

> Some standards can be prescribed by law, but the spirit of, and quality of the service rendered by, a profession depends far more on its observance of ethical standards. These are far more rigorous than legal standards . . . They are learnt not by precept but by the example and influence of respected peers. Judicial standards are acquired, so to speak, by professional osmosis. They are enforced immediately by conscience.

In *Ruffo v. Conseil de la magistrature*, Gonthier J., speaking for the majority in the Supreme Court of Canada, makes the same point:

> Ethical rules are meant to aim for perfection. They call for better conduct not through the imposition of various sanctions, but through compliance with the personally imposed constraints. A definition, on the other hand, sets out fixed rules and thus tends to become an upper limit, an implicit authorization to do whatever is not prohibited. There is no doubt that these two concepts are difficult to reconcile,

---

[*] Reproduced with permission.

and this explains the general nature of the duty to act in a reserved manner: as an ethical standard, it is more concerned with providing general guidance about conduct than with illustrating specifics and the types of conduct allowed.

Ethical principles leave more to the individual good conscience of the judge than a code that can lead simply to a legalist ritual.

Fourth, any attempt to use the *Ethical Principles* as a standard of behaviour for discipline overlooks the fact that the booklet omits matters that we take for granted as sanctionable conduct and addresses matters which could be considered innocuous. For example, there is no mention of gifts, but there is extensive treatment of the circumstances in which a judge can give a letter of reference.

AMY SALYZYN & RICHARD DEVLIN

"Judges Need Ethics Rules, Not Just Ethical Guidance"
Slaw.ca, 28 January 2020
[citations omitted]

Canada is extremely fortunate to be served by a highly competent and responsible judiciary. But judges, like all of us, experience ethical challenges as they fulfill their vitally important social functions. However, many Canadian judges are not subject to a binding code of conduct that can shepherd their behaviour. Instead, they are only offered advice to assist them in navigating ethical issues. We suggest that this should change . . .

In March 2019, the CJC invited public feedback as part of its review of the *EPJs*. The goal of the review, as described in a Background Paper published by CJC, is to "to ensure [the *EPJs*] continue to provide guidance for judges in a manner that reflects evolving public expectations." This is the first review of the *EPJs* in over two decades.

The Board of the Canadian Association for Legal Ethics/Association canadienne pour l'éthique juridique (CALE/ACEJ), of which we are the President and Chair, respectively, provided both written and in-person feedback to the CJC on the *EPJs*. One of CALE/ACEJ's major submissions is that the *EPJs* should be reconstituted as a binding code of conduct. In its feedback, the Canadian Bar Association's Judicial Issues Committee similarly stated that it "believes that modern guidance on judicial ethics requires more than aspirational guidelines."

In November 2019, the CJC released a draft revised version of the *EPJs*. The draft represents, overall, a thoughtful and thorough revision of the *EPJs*. The draft also meaningfully adopts stakeholder feedback in several major respects. The draft does not, however, shift the *EPJs* from aspirational guidelines to a binding code of conduct. The draft continues to state that the *EPJs* are "advisory in nature" and explicitly cautions that the document is "not intended to be a code of conduct that sets out minimum standards of behaviour."

The CJC has welcomed feedback on the draft revised EPJs and has stated that its goal is to produce a final version in Spring 2020. So, there's still time for the *EPJs* to become a binding ethics code for federally appointed judges in Canada. We believe that such a change is necessary for the reasons that follow, which are drawn from CALE/ACEJ's previous submissions to the CJC.

First, public confidence in the judiciary requires that judges be subject to binding ethical rules. As *Roncarelli v. Duplessis* made clear, all holders of public power must be subject to the principles of the rule of law. This applies to members of the judiciary as much as it applies to others who exercise public power. If the *EPJs* are not the source of standards by which judges can be assessed in their exercise of public power, then what are the relevant standards, and where can they be found? How can the public have confidence in the judiciary if there are no clearly articulated and enforceable standards by which to assess judicial behaviour? In a mature democracy in the twenty-first century, a binding code of conduct is a vital mechanism that provides public accountability and enhances the legitimacy of the judiciary as an independent and self-regulating institution.

Second, judges themselves need clearly articulated standards to guide their behaviour and upon which they can rely to avoid allegations of misconduct. The judiciary would benefit from a document that "sets out minimum standards of behaviour", something which is explicitly disavowed in the draft revised *EPJs*, as noted above.

Third, there is a fundamental contradiction. Although, the EPJs state that they "are not and shall not be used as a code or a list of prohibited behaviours . . . . [and] do not set out standards defining judicial misconduct," the reality is that they have in fact been deployed by the CJC as part of the disciplinary process in at least two cases – those dealing with the behaviour of Justices Theodore Matlow and Patrick Smith. Stating that the *EPJs* are advisory only but then referring to them in disciplinary processes is inconsistent, creating confusion for both judges and the general public and undermining public confidence in the administration of justice.

Fourth, one concern that has been raised in relation to creating binding *EPJs* is that such an approach would be a threat to judicial independence. Indeed, the draft revised *EPJs* take care to note that "[n]othing in *Ethical Principles* can or is intended to limit or restrict . . . judicial independence in any manner." We believe this concern to be unfounded. Many jurisdictions around the world have enforceable judicial codes of conduct and there is no reason to believe that they pose a threat to judicial independence. Most civil law countries have such codes, as do several of our common law cousins including the United States, South Africa and Nigeria.[6] Indeed, as of March 2019, in England and Wales the Judicial Complaints Investigation Office, the Lord Chancellor and the Lord Chief Justice are all explicitly permitted to have recourse to their *Guide to Judicial Conduct* "in exercising their disciplinary powers." Moreover, in our own front yard, Quebec's provincial court judges are bound by a Code of Conduct and there is nothing to suggest that they lack independence.

Fifth, another objection against binding *EPJs* is that an advice-based approach allows for the setting of high aspirational standards, on the understanding that they may not be met in all circumstances, while a code approach would necessitate lower or minimal standards to ensure compliance. This is a false dichotomy. Proper

---

[6] See Richard Devlin & Adam Dodek, *Regulating Judges: Beyond Independence and Accountability* (Northampton, MA: Edward Elgar, 2016).

drafting, such as distinguishing between "shall" and "should", can allow a binding code to both establish minimum standards and including more aspirational goals. This is evident in other binding statements of judicial ethics and also in many lawyer codes of conduct. Moreover, there are many elements of the draft revised *EPJs* that cannot be considered merely aspirational. Take, for example, the statements that "judges must be and must appear to be impartial in their performance of their judicial duties" or "all partisan political activity must cease upon appointment." Shouldn't Canadians be assured that these are "minimum standards of conduct" to which judges must adhere?

Sixth, we have heard it argued that binding *EPJs* are untenable because there may be situations where two principles are perceived as contradictory, and it would be unfair to potentially discipline a judge who chooses one rather than the other. But the success of judicial codes in other jurisdictions, and the experience of binding codes in other professions, including lawyers, shows that this concern is not well founded. A well-drafted code can achieve a realistic balancing of obligations.

Canadian judges should be proud of the high ethical standards under which they operate. Clearly articulating and enforcing such standards as required behaviour enhances not only public confidence in the judiciary but also provides more clarity and certainty to members of the judiciary themselves. The ship has not sailed. The CJC should revise its draft *EPJs* to make clear that it is a binding code of ethical conduct for judges. It might be another two decades before this error can be rectified.

NOTES AND QUESTIONS

1. Which of these two analyses do you find more persuasive? Provide reasons for your decision.

2. Does the current system mean that Canadian judges have even greater self-regulatory authority than Canadian lawyers? Why might this be the case? Is it appropriate?

In the remainder of this chapter, we will use the five core principles from the *Ethical Principles for Judges* — (1) judicial independence; (2) integrity and respect; (3); diligence and competence; (4) equality; and (5) impartiality — to structure our analysis.[7]

[3] IMPARTIALITY

[a] The Standard

Impartiality is the most significant of the *Ethical Principles for Judges*. The Statement is very straightforward:

> Judges are impartial and appear to be impartial in the performance of their judicial duties.

However, the principles and commentaries elaborating upon this statement continue

---

[7] The *Ethical Principles for Judges* puts the chapter on impartiality last. For the purposes of our analysis in this book, we have put it first because we understand impartiality to be the lodestar of judicial ethics.

for another 20 pages and are subdivided into 20 categories: General; Judicial Duties; Restraints; Political Activity; Public Statements; Judicial Promotion and Opportunities; Public Engagement, Civic and Charitable Activity; Social Media; Gifts and Remuneration; Speeches and Conferences; Attendance at Events; Conflicts of Interest; Acting as Executors; Judges' Former Legal Practice; Personal Relationships; Judges in Financial Difficulty; Disclosure and Consent; Extraordinary Circumstances: Interests of Justice; Public Education Activities; and Post-Judicial Careers. The following decision of the Canadian Judicial Council illustrates both how this self-regulatory body interprets the impartiality principle and the operation of the complaints process against judges.

CANADIAN JUDICIAL COUNCIL

Report of the Canadian Judicial Council to the Minister of Justice in the Matter Concerning Justice Cosgrove (March 30, 2009),
online: http://www.cjc-ccm.gc.ca/cmslib/general/ Report_to_Minister_Justice_Cosgrove.pdf

INTRODUCTION

. . . After inquiring into the conduct of the Honourable Paul Cosgrove, we find that he has failed in the due execution of his office to such an extent that public confidence in his ability to properly discharge his judicial duties in the future cannot be restored. In the result, we conclude that a recommendation be made to the Minister of Justice that Justice Cosgrove be removed from office.

BACKGROUND

. . . . .

From 1997 to 1999, Justice Cosgrove presided over the murder trial of Julia Elliott. A stay of proceedings was granted on 7 September 1999 after Justice Cosgrove concluded that there had been over 150 violations of Ms Elliott's rights under the *Canadian Charter of Rights and Freedoms.*[8] On appeal, the stay of proceedings was set aside, and a new trial was ordered. The Court of Appeal remarked . . . :

> . . . The trial judge made numerous legal errors as to the application of the Charter. He made findings of misconduct against Crown counsel and police officers that were unwarranted and unsubstantiated. He misused his powers of contempt and allowed investigations into areas that were extraneous to the real issues in the case.

. . . . .

In its review of the judge's conduct, the Inquiry Committee adopted the reasoning of the Supreme Court of Canada in *Moreau-Bérubé v. New Brunswick (Judicial Council)* 2002 SCC 11:

> In some cases, however, the actions and expressions of an individual judge trigger concerns about the integrity of the judicial function itself. When a disciplinary process is launched to look at the conduct of an individual judge, it is alleged that an abuse of judicial independence by a judge has threatened the integrity of the judiciary as a whole. The harm alleged is not curable by the appeal process.

---

[8] Part I of the *Constitution Act, 1982*, being Schedule B to the *Canada Act 1982* (U.K.), 1982, c. 11.

The Inquiry Committee found that the judge's conduct included: an inappropriate aligning of the judge with defence counsel giving rise to an apprehension of bias; an abuse of judicial powers by a deliberate, repeated and unwarranted interference in the presentation of the Crown's case; the abuse of judicial powers by inappropriate interference with RCMP activities; the misuse of judicial powers by repeated inappropriate threats of citations for contempt or arrest without foundation; the use of rude, abusive or intemperate language; and the arbitrary quashing of a federal immigration warrant.

The members of the Inquiry Committee then agreed unanimously as follows . . . :

> In our opinion, the evidence we have characterized as lack of restraint, abuse of judicial independence, or abuse of judicial powers fully warrants a recommendation for removal from office, subject to whatever effect may be given to the judge's statement [of apology] of 10 September 2008.

After considering the judge's statement and the submissions, four out of the five members of the Inquiry Committee concluded as follows . . . :

> . . . [Justice Cosgrove's words and conduct] give rise to a reasonable and irremediable apprehension of bias. . . .

. . . . .

In his statement to Council, Justice Cosgrove confirmed that his personal statement of 10 September 2008 to the Inquiry Committee was intended to be an unqualified recognition of his judicial misconduct and an unqualified apology. He repeated these sentiments in his statement before us. . . .

*   *   *   *   *

ISSUES

. . . . .

. . . There can be no doubt that Justice Cosgrove engaged in serious judicial misconduct, within the meaning of the *Judges Act.*

Accordingly, it remains for Council to proceed to the second stage and determine if public confidence in the judge's ability to discharge the duties of his office has been undermined to such an extent that a recommendation for removal is warranted. In this regard, we adopt the standard identified by Council in the Marshall matter and widely applied in other cases since then:

> Is the conduct alleged so manifestly and profoundly destructive of the concept of the impartiality, integrity, and independence of the judicial role, that public confidence would be sufficiently undermined to render the judge incapable of executing the judicial office?

. . . . .

The Apologies

. . . . .

As found by the Inquiry Committee, the judge's conduct included: giving rise to an apprehension of bias; repeated and unwarranted interference in the presentation of the Crown's case; inappropriate interference with RCMP activities; inappropriate

770

threats of citations for contempt or arrest without foundation; the use of rude, abusive or intemperate language; and the arbitrary quashing of a federal immigration warrant. These are not mere judicial errors.

. . . . .

. . . [W]e must consider an additional – more important – aspect in deciding whether a recommendation for removal is warranted: the effect upon public confidence of the actions of the judge in light of the nature and seriousness of the misconduct.

For Council, therefore, the key question is whether the apology is sufficient to restore public confidence. . . . :

> . . . In discharging its function, the Council must be acutely sensitive to the requirements of judicial independence, and it must ensure never to kill the expression of unpopular, honestly held views in the context of court proceedings. It must also be equally sensitive to the reasonable expectations of an informed dispassionate public that holders of judicial office will remain at all times worthy of trust, confidence and respect.

. . . . .

In this case, it is our conclusion that the misconduct by Justice Cosgrove was so serious and so destructive of public confidence that no apology, no matter its sincerity, can restore public confidence in the judge's future ability to impartially carry out his judicial duties in accordance with the high standards expected of all judges. This was not a single instance of misconduct but, rather, misconduct that was pervasive in both scope and duration.

. . . . .

While it is not strictly necessary to address this issue, given the decision just made, we make the following points. It was open to Justice Cosgrove to offer, at any time, an apology about his conduct but he did not. It appears that the judge did not, for years after the fact, appreciate that he had engaged in serious misconduct.

. . . . .

The tardiness of the judge's apology reveals both his lack of insight and his lack of appreciation of the impact of his egregious misconduct on public confidence in the judiciary.

. . . . .

DECISION

We agree with the conclusions reached by the majority of the members of the Inquiry Committee, as outlined in paragraph 189 of their report, which we now repeat:

> For the reasons given above, the words used and the conduct engaged in by Justice Cosgrove, over a prolonged period of time, constitute a failure in the due exercise of his office by abusing his powers as a judge. They give rise to a reasonable and irremediable apprehension of bias. Regrettably, his statement is insufficient to offset the serious harm done to public confidence in the concept of the judicial role, as described in the Marshall test. He has rendered himself incapable of executing the judicial office.

We find that Justice Cosgrove has failed in the execution of the duties of his judicial office and that public confidence in his ability to discharge those duties in future has been irrevocably lost. We find that there is no alternative measure to removal that would be sufficient to restore public confidence in the judge in this case. Therefore, we hereby recommend to the Minister of Justice, in accordance with section 65 of the *Judges Act*, that Justice Cosgrove be removed from office.

NOTES AND QUESTIONS

1. Justice Cosgrove resigned from the bench before the Minister of Justice exercised their authority to commence the removal proceedings.

2. What should a lawyer do if they believe that a judge is:

    (a) inappropriately aligning themselves with counsel for the other side;

    (b) deliberately, repeatedly and unwarrantedly interfering in your presentation of the evidence;

    (c) inappropriately threatening you with citations for contempt or arrest without foundation; or

    (d) using rude, abusive or intemperate language?

[b] Recusal

If a lawyer has concerns about the impartiality of a judge, the lawyer can request for the judge to recuse themselves from the case. It is up to the individual judge to decide whether to accede to this request. Identify the challenges that this might create for a lawyer. Should Canadian judges adopt a rule which requires that recusal requests be heard by another judge?

If self-recusal is the most appropriate process when a judge sits alone, is it also the most appropriate process in a multi-person court, for example, a court of appeal or the Supreme Court of Canada? Consider the following two decisions from the Supreme Court of Canada.

In *Arsenault-Cameron v. Prince Edward Island*,[9] parents in a Prince Edward Island town demanded the French Language Board provide a facility that offered French-language instruction at the primary level in the community. The Government of P.E.I. refused, and instead offered transport services to a nearby community that had the desired facility. The case reached the Supreme Court of Canada. Sitting on the case was Bastarache J. Justice Bastarache was a long-time supporter of French-language rights.

The respondent filed a motion directed at Bastarache J. The motion claimed that, because of Bastarache J.'s history of promoting French-language rights, his presence on the bench gave rise to a reasonable apprehension of bias. Justice Bastarache heard the motion and, alone, decided not to recuse himself. In his reasons, he stated "[t]he test for apprehension of bias takes into account the presumption of impartiality. A real likelihood or probability of bias must be demonstrated . . . I find nothing in the material submitted by the applicant that would cause a reasonable

---

[9] [1999] S.C.J. No. 75, [1999] 3 S.C.R. 851 (S.C.C.).

person who understands the complex and contextual issues to believe that I would not entertain the various points of view with an open mind."

In *Wewaykum Indian Band v. Canada*,[10] two Indian bands filed a motion to have a decision of the Supreme Court of Canada set aside. The judgment was written by Binnie J. and received unanimous approval from the other eight justices. The motion was filed after the decision. It was only then that one of the bands learned Binnie J. was previously involved with the same case, as an Associate Deputy Minister in the Department of Justice, during its early stages in the 1980s. The bands claimed his prior involvement produced a reasonable apprehension of bias that warranted disqualifying the Court's decision.

Once the motion was received, Binnie J. recused himself from further proceedings. The remaining eight justices examined whether a reasonable apprehension of bias was raised and, if it was, what impact it could have on the decision of the Court. The court ultimately decided "we are convinced that the reasonable person, viewing the matter realistically, would not come to the conclusion that the limited administrative and supervisory role played by Binnie J. in this file, over 15 years ago, affected his ability, even unconsciously, to remain impartial in these appeals . . . We thus conclude that no reasonable apprehension of bias is established and that Binnie J. was not disqualified in these appeals."

QUESTIONS

1. Which process is more legitimate: for the allegedly tainted judge to make the decision whether to recuse themselves, or for their colleagues to do so?

2. Would it be better for another independent panel composed of judges from the same court to make the recusal decision?[11]

3. If such a panel could not be constituted would it be wise to create an *ad hoc* panel of other judges? How does one balance the demands of judicial impartiality with norms of efficiency and accountability? Do you think that the "fully informed reasonable person" test is analytically strong?

4. A judge assesses whether or not to recuse themselves based on the judge's own assessment of the application of the *Ethical Principles* and case law. A survey of provincially appointed judges across Canada showed wide variation in both how judges approached issues of recusal and the actual decisions that they made on whether or not to recuse themselves. See P. Bryden & J. Hughes, "The Tip of the Iceberg: A Survey of the Philosophy and Practice of Canadian Provincial and Territorial Judges Concerning Judicial Disqualification" (2011) 48 Alta. L. Rev. 569. Does this type of empirical research suggest to you that more needs to be done to provide guidance to judges on when it is appropriate or inappropriate to recuse? If yes, what should be done, and who should do it?

5. After *Wewaykum*, the Supreme Court enacted Rule 23(1)(4) which states, "if a judge's previous involvement or connection with the case may result

---

[10] [2003] S.C.J. No. 50, 2003 SCC 45 (S.C.C.).

[11] *In re Pinochet*, [1999] UKHL 1, [2000] 1 A.C. 119 (H.L.).

in it being inappropriate for that judge to take part in the adjudication on the proceedings in the Court"[12] counsel must file a certificate in Form 23C setting out the issues. Does this Rule go far enough? Or does it give guidance only on how to raise an issue of recusal, not the basis on which a judge or the Court ought to resolve it?

Scenario One

A group of 16 Hispanic employees of We-Rent-A-Car are alleging racial discrimination against We-Rent-A-Car and are being represented by the Hispanic Canadian Civil Liberties Association. The case is assigned to Judge Reyes, who used to be involved with the Hispanic Canadian Civil Liberties Association but ceased their involvement once they were appointed to the bench. However, Judge Reyes' spouse is on the board of the Hispanic Canadian Civil Liberties Association Trust, which is a charitable organization that raises money for the Association. Judge Reyes has a reputation as a judge who is skeptical of discrimination lawsuits. Does the judge's association raise an apprehension of bias as a matter of law?

Scenario Two

The federal government has enacted legislation eliminating the "Long-Gun Registry". An advocacy group, Mums Against Guns, has filed an application seeking a declaration that the legislation is unconstitutional. The trial judge, Justice Jake Fudge, summarily dismissed their application, and upheld the legislation. In *obiter* he said that, even without the new legislation, he would have struck down the Long-Gun Registry as unconstitutional. He unequivocally rejected Mums Against Guns' arguments. Two months later, it comes to light that for the last 10 years, Justice Fudge has been a member of the Canuck Hunters' Association, which objects to the long-gun registry, but was not part of the litigation. Is there an apprehension of bias here? Would your answer be different if the judge was not just a member of the Association, but was himself an avid collector of long-guns?[13]

Scenario Three

Justice Jo has been assigned to a case in which the province is seeking to evict an Indigenous activist from the lawn in front of the legislature. The activist has set up a tepee and inside there is an altar to hold sacred objects and a sacred fire. The activist has also begun a ceremonial fast. The purpose of the protest is to draw public attention to the disproportionately high number of suicides among Indigenous youth. Would any of the following actions generate concerns about Justice Jo's impartiality?

a) Prior to rendering their decision, the judge:

   i) Visits the encampment and simply walks around the outside of the tepee;

   ii) Goes inside the tepee to look at the altar and sacred fire, with the consent of the activist;

---

[12] *Rules of the Supreme Court of Canada*, SOR/2002-156.

[13] See also Beverley Smith, *Professional Conduct for Lawyers and Judges*, 4th ed. (Fredericton: Maritime Law Book, 2011) ch. 14, at para. 52.

b) After rendering a decision denying the eviction request by the province:

    i) Visits the encampment and simply walks around the outside of the tepee;

    ii) Goes inside the tepee to have a conversation with the activist;

    iii) Receives a ceremonial sash from supporters of the activist.[14]

[c] The Ethical Challenges of Judicial Community Engagement

Historically in Canada, judges were seen as a special constituency, separate and distinct from other members of society. As a consequence, judges were considered a cloistered community and therefore disengaged from involvement with the larger society. One Supreme Court judge made the analogy to monks,[15] a perhaps less apt comparison given Canada's increasingly diverse judiciary, but one that does convey an image of judicial isolation from the broader society. While this conception of the judicial role certainly had its defenders, over time it was realized that it also caused some problems: it encouraged judges to be aloof; it insulated judges from the changing dynamics and norms of an increasingly pluralistic society; and it reinforced the public perception that judges were elitist and unconcerned with the lived realities of the ordinary person on the street. Consequently, it has been increasingly accepted that judges can, and perhaps should, be involved with the larger community. But the question is: to what extent?

The Impartiality chapter of the *Ethical Principles for Judges* seeks to provide guidance.[16] It begins with several "General Guiding Principles":

A. Judges ensure that their conduct at all times maintains and enhances confidence in their impartiality and that of the judiciary.

B. Judges avoid conduct which could reasonably cause others to question their impartiality.

C. Judges conduct their affairs so as to avoid real or apparent conflicts of interest between their private interests and their judicial duties.

These are very general and the *EPJs* supplement them with more specific guidelines on "Political Activity" and "Public Engagement, Civic and Charitable Activity". Please review the principles at page 38 and the additional set of guidelines at pages 43-44 for Political Activity and pages 45-47 for Public Engagement, Civic and Charitable Activity. Are these guidelines too general, too specific, or about right? Provide reasons to support your analysis.

Consider the following summary[17] of a decision from the Ontario Judicial Council

---

[14] See Canadian Judicial Council, "Canadian Judicial Council completes its review of the matter involving the Honourable Graeme Mitchell", (April 13, 2021), online: https://cjc-ccm.ca/en/news/cjc-completes-review-matter-involving-honourable-graeme-mitchell.

[15] John Sopinka, "Must a Judge Be a Monk – Revisited" (1996) 45 U.N.B.L.J. 167.

[16] Canadian Judicial Council, *Ethical Principles for Judges* (Ottawa: Canadian Judicial Council, 19982021) ch. 5 at 38.

[17] Ontario Judicial Council, "A complaint respecting The Honourable Justice Donald

regarding the matter of Justice Donald McLeod:

> Following a tragic shooting, Justice Donald McLeod helped found and was a prominent voice for the Federation of Black Canadians ("FBC"). As a leading member of the Black community, Justice McLeod was determined to act to address the issues facing the Black community that were the underlying causes of violence and contact with the criminal justice system. The FBC has the goal of promoting greater equality and inclusion for persons of African descent in Canada. Its activities included the identification of issues confronting Black Canadians and meeting with politicians and government officials with a view to addressing those issues and improving the circumstances of African-Canadians.

> The Ontario Court of Justice *Principles of Judicial Office* encourage judges to engage in community activities provided those activities are not inconsistent with judicial office. Before and after his judicial appointment, Justice McLeod has been an active member of the Black community. He was at all times motivated by the highly laudable goal of helping members of the Black community to overcome the historic barriers of racism and poverty.

> While community activity is encouraged, judges must conduct themselves in a manner consistent with the principles of judicial impartiality, integrity and independence. Justice McLeod participated in a process that aimed to identify policy issues to be addressed. He then initiated meetings with senior government officials and politicians, including MPs, Ministers of the Crown, and elected municipal officials, and advocated specific policy changes and the allocation of government resources to achieve those policy changes. By participating in these activities while he was a judge, Justice McLeod engaged in a form of advocacy and political activity that is inconsistent with judicial office.

> It is well-established in law that the purpose of judicial conduct proceedings is not punitive but remedial. A finding of judicial misconduct can only be made where any breach of the standards of judicial conduct by the judge was so seriously contrary to judicial impartiality, integrity and independence that it has undermined the public's confidence in the judge's ability to perform the duties of office or in the administration of justice generally.

> The panel concludes that although Justice McLeod's conduct was incompatible with judicial office, when all the relevant circumstances are taken into account, his conduct has not undermined public confidence in his capacity to carry out his judicial functions or in the administration of justice generally.

> The advocacy and political activity that Justice McLeod engaged in were not prolonged and they were conducted in a measured and respectful manner. The problems confronting Black Canadians that the FBC identified are well-documented and have been recognized by Canadian courts. Justice McLeod's life experiences make him uniquely aware of the problem of Black over-representation in the criminal justice system. He is highly regarded as a judge and he serves as a role model for young Black males. He was genuinely motivated to promote public confidence in the justice system. He acted in good faith, sought ethical advice, and attempted to respect the limits that his judicial role imposed. There is no question of his ability to judge with integrity in an impartial and independent manner.

McLeod", (December 2018), online: https://www.ontariocourts.ca/ocj/ojc/public-hearings-decisions/#Justice_Donald_McLeod (Summary).

This decision clarifies the issue of advocacy and political activity by judges and defines a boundary that all judges must respect in the future, however laudable their motives. In all the circumstances, a finding of judicial misconduct is not required to restore public confidence in Justice McLeod or in the administration of justice generally. Accordingly, the complaint is dismissed.

The Panel noted the difference between education and advocacy. While education is allowed, advocacy is not:

> We do not accept Justice McLeod's position that these activities can be fairly characterized as being merely educative or intended to inform politicians of the difficulties facing Black Canadians. We acknowledge that many of Justice McLeod's community activities, including some of his work with the FBC, were focused on education. We also accept that in his own mind, Justice McLeod saw his work as being primarily focused on education. However, we are satisfied that the line between education and advocacy was crossed. As we have noted, the PowerPoint presentation the FBC delivered to the Prime Minister and other politicians at the June 28, 2017 meeting included "asks" for policy change and resource allocation in each of the areas of mental health, corrections and education . . .[18]

NOTES AND QUESTIONS

1. Are you convinced by the panel's distinction between "education" and "advocacy"?

2. Are you persuaded by the argument that although Justice McLeod had engaged in conduct "incompatible with judicial office" that such conduct did not undermine public confidence in his impartiality or in the justice system?

3. One commentator has argued that "Justice McLeod [is] the victim of systemic and attitudinal racism. He deserves support, not condemnation"[19]. In another analysis, a lawyer suggests:

    > . . . it will become increasingly more common for judicial applicants to have publicly expressed their views one way or another on a range of issues, some of which may come before them. Is there any reason that we cannot expect them to have the capacity to assess disputes before them impartially, just as we expected party workers to do the same? Or, put another way, haven't we long recognized that no one comes to the bench without predispositions developed throughout their life?[20]

    Do you agree? Others have argued that, in fact, Justice McLeod should be

---

[18] Ontario Judicial Council, "A complaint respecting The Honourable Justice Donald McLeod", (December 2018), online: https://www.ontariocourts.ca/ocj/ojc/public-hearings-decisions/#Justice_Donald_McLeod (Summary).

[19] Frances Henry, "Justice McLeod is a victim of systemic and attitudinal racism", *The Star* (December 18, 2018), online: https://www.thestar.com.

[20] Patricia Hughes, "Do We Need to Think About Judges' Roles Differently?" (December 11, 2018), *Slaw* (blog), online: http://www.slaw.ca/2018/12/11/do-we-need-to-think-about-judges-roles-differently/.

commended.[21] Again, do you agree? Provide reasons.

4. Do the rules limiting judicial engagements with the community have a disparate impact on judges who come from historically disadvantaged/oppressed backgrounds?

5. In August 2019 a further complaint was brought against Justice McLeod alleging that he had mislead the first panel and had not discontinued his involvement with the Federation of Black Canadians. A hearing was held in late 2020 and early 2021. In her closing remarks, Justice McLeod's lawyer, Sheila Block, said:

> He is deeply honest, full of integrity and trying to do the right thing. If he's crossed over the line, if he's made a mistake, it was not . . . deliberately false, it was not intending to mislead . . .
>
> We are asking that all these counts be dismissed and, to the extent there is anything you can do, to repair what is the inevitable damage of being accused of having committed perjury . . .
>
> The issue is the struggle . . . lives of Black people are lived out as advocacy. It's overly restrictive and an unfair lens, frankly our white privilege lens . . . Frankly none of us [White lawyers and judges] can really talk about (this) in any . . . deep way.[22]

In June 2021, in an extensive 236-page decision, the Panel found that these allegations were "not made out" (Ontario Judicial Council, "In the Matter of a Hearing Under Section 51.6 of the *Courts of Justice Act*, R.S.O. 1990, c. C. 43, as amended Concerning a Complaint about the Conduct of the Honourable Justice Donald McLeod", (2 June 2021), online: https://www.ontariocourts.ca/ocj/ojc/public-hearings-decisions/#Justice_Donald_McLeod at para. 19.).

In light of the *McLeod* case, consider the following scenarios. For each situation, consider the following questions:

1. Do the *Ethical Principles* provide any assistance?
2. Assume you are the close friend of the judge and they seek your advice for each of the situations. What advice would you give them?

Scenario Four

Judge A has been sitting for 15 years and has issued a number of decisions interpreting various *Charter* provisions. The Canadian Forum for Constitutional Equality (CFCE) invites Judge A to give a keynote speech at its annual conference addressing the theme of "The Judicial Role in Canada's Democracy." The CFCE describes itself on its website as a "forum for citizens to come together for the promotion of equality, diversity and inclusion in Canadian society."

Scenario Five

Judge C has been a judge for 25 years and is now supernumerary. He graduated from

---

[21] Royson James, "Judge should be commended not disciplined over role in Federation of Black Canadians", *The Star* (December 7, 2018), online: thestar.com.

[22] Betsy Powell, " 'He is Deeply Honest': lawyers asks panel to dismiss complaint against judge Donald McLeod", *The Star* (March 18, 2021), online: thestar.com.

Munhousie University's Department of Economics in the late 1970's. Since that time, he has been a proud alumnus, attending various events and making donations of $1,500 to the annual fund every year. Munhousie University opened the doors of its new law school in 2015. Over the course of four years, the school has had two law deans, both of whom left after disagreements with the central university administration.

Judge C, over the course of a year, has received a number of requests from the Chair of the Board at Munhousie:[23]

a) To serve as the Chancellor of the University;

b) To participate in a one-week educational programme in China;

c) To take on the role of Interim Dean for six months until the school is able to appoint a permanent Dean.

Scenario Six

The Civil Engagement Society (CES) is an organization devoted to "promoting public engagement with the most pressing issues of our times." It is in the process of organizing a public debate that will be live-streamed on the following topic: "Climate Change: Fake News, or the End of Civilization as We Know it?" The structure of the debate will be modelled on the CBC's "Debaters." CES has recruited two of Canada's leading litigators, GG Rob and MM Sheman, to argue each side of the debate.

CES has written a letter of invitation to Justice D asking her to take on the role of moderator for the debate. They explain that they have chosen Justice D because of her well-known capacity to balance firm trial management with an engaging sense of humour.

Scenario Seven

Justice E's family have owned a cottage on the east end of the beautiful Willows Beach for more than 60 years. There are 20 neighbours with similar properties, and participation in the Willows Beach Lot Owners Association (WBLA) is mandatory, including an annual road maintenance fee of $600. Approximately 40% of the beach, at the west end, is Crown land. The only access point to this land is at the end of the WBLA's private road. Recently the province and the municipality have announced that they have been approached by a local Indigenous community with a request to transfer the Crown land to them to enhance the economic development of the community. The tentative plan is to build both a resort hotel and an R.V. site. The province and municipality have asked for feedback on the proposal. The WBLA has called a meeting of all members to discuss the proposed project. Justice E has been invited to the WBLA meeting. Advise Justice E on each of the following developments:

---

[23] *Smith v. Canada*, [2020] F.C.J. No. 628, 2020 FC 629 (F.C.). See also Stephen Pitel, "Justice Patrick Smith's Conduct Should Remain a Cautionary Tale" (August 17, 2020), *Slaw* (blog), online: http://www.slaw.ca/2020/08/17/justice-patrick-smiths-conduct-should-remain-a-cautionary-tale// [perma.cc/W8TN-2ZVT].

a) Assume that Justice E attends the meeting. After the first five minutes it becomes obvious that all the other members of the WBLA are opposed to the transfer of the land to the Indigenous community, and the proposed development.

b) After about an hour, all the members of the WBLA have spoken, except Justice E. One of the neighbours then asks Justice E for their opinion.

c) Towards the end of the meeting, it is proposed that the WBLA send a petition to the province and municipality expressing its profound objections to the proposal.

d) It is also proposed that the WBLA contact the local media to express their concerns. They ask for volunteers to take the lead on this.

e) It is also proposed to start a Facebook page and a Twitter account to mobilize support for their campaign against the proposal.

f) The province and municipality announce that they plan to hold a townhall on the proposal. The WBLA encourages all members to attend and voice their concerns.

g) In spite of the objections of the WBLA, the province and municipality announce that they plan to go ahead with the transfer of the land to the Indigenous community. The WBLA decides that it will seek an injunction against the transfer.

h) A few days later, before any transfer of the land takes place, three members of the Indigenous community set up a camp on the Crown land. They have put out a call to other Indigenous people and their allies to join them. The WBLA is concerned by this initiative. They propose that the WBLA erect a lockable gate on their road thereby blocking access to the Crown land and preventing anyone else from joining the encampment.

Scenario Eight

Justice F has been legally blind since birth. Throughout their adult life—at university, during law school and in legal practice—they were actively engaged in advancing the rights of visually impaired Canadians. In 2013, F was appointed to the bench.

In 2015, a visually impaired woman was raped and killed by a group of four young men. Public outrage ensued.

a) Soon thereafter Justice F received a call from a good friend of 30 years with whom they had worked previously in advancing the rights of visually impaired Canadians. The friend told Justice F that a group was forming under the tentative title Voices of Visually Impaired Women (VOVIW). The group wanted Justice F to help establish the organization.

b) Assume that Justice F agreed to attend the first meeting of VOVIW. The first item on the agenda was to constitute an executive steering committee of nine members. Everyone encouraged Justice F to volunteer.

c) The next agenda item was to develop a mission statement. The following was agreed upon:

"VOVIW is a national non-profit organization that advances the social, economic, political, legal and cultural interests of Visually Impaired Women."

d) The next agenda item was to identify a number of action steps to give the organization focus and direction.

  i) To commence a media campaign to inform Canadians of the social, economic, and legal discrimination experienced by visually impaired women.

  ii) To provide mentorship and support for visually impaired women.

  iii) To educate both private sector and public sector organizations on the multiple forms of discrimination experienced by visually impaired women.

  iv) To inform Canada's police forces on the extent of the violence against visually impaired women and to demand more active responses.

  v) To prepare information packages for all levels of government to advance the rights of visually impaired women.

  vi) To organize a series of three "action days" where members of the VOVIW would press municipal, then provincial and territorial, and finally federal politicians to recognize and take specific steps to remedy the multiple forms of discrimination experienced by visually impaired women.

  vii) To host a series of "Awareness Dinners" across the country with keynote speakers, at $100 per ticket, to help support VOVIW and its activities.

Scenario Nine

Assume Justice I has been a judge for five years. The Dean of the law school calls him up and asks if he would be willing to serve on the Advisory Board for the Indigenous Blacks and Mi'kmaq Initiative?

a) Does this raise any ethical issues?

b) Would it make a difference if Justice I had been a student who had participated in that Initiative?

c) Would it make a difference if Justice I was White?

d) What if the Dean were to ask Judge I to serve on the Advisory Committee for the Marine and Environmental Law Institute or the Law and Technology Institute?

Scenario Ten

Munhousie Law School has just opened a chapter of the National Self-Represented Litigants Project, to be known as NSRLP East. The Dean has asked Justice J to become a member of the seven-person Advisory Board. Does this raise any ethical issues?

Scenario Eleven

Justice K's spouse is a minister in the government, but she is not a lawyer. Some judicial vacancies have arisen on the court. Justice K's spouse says, "We are trying to make some decisions on who to appoint. I don't really know who would make a good judge. You know them all, who would you recommend?" Can Justice K share his opinion with his spouse?

Now assume that Judge K did share his thoughts and his spouse forwarded Judge K's suggestions to the Minister of Justice. A few days later, the spouse comes home and is irritated. She tells Justice K that the minister has disregarded the recommendations. She then asks, "Would you write a letter to the Minister of Justice explaining why these recommendations make so much sense?" What response should Justice K give, and why?[24]

[d] Social Media and Judicial Ethics

One issue that has given rise to concern in recent years is judges' familiarity with, and competence to use, social media. Because the *EPJs* were originally drafted in 1998, they did not address the issue of social media. This changed when the *EPJs* were amended in 2021. They now provide guidance in Commentaries 5.B.15-5.B.18 (pages 47-48).

Consider the following scenarios. What advice would you give the judge in each of the following situations?

Scenario Twelve

For Judge K's birthday, their children gift them a blue "Make America Even Greater Again" T-shirt. After Judge K tries it on, the children ask to take a selfie with them. Judge K's children are very active on social media.

Would your opinion differ if it was a "Black Lives Matter" T-shirt?

A "Respect" T-shirt?

Would your answer to these questions change if the judge was from a BIPOC community?

When you pictured the judge, what assumptions did you make about their race, gender or other personal characteristics?

Scenario Thirteen

Judge L separated from their spouse 18 months ago. They have been finding it difficult to meet other people and are a little disconsolate. A good friend suggests that L post a profile on an online dating website. They say it has worked for them.

Scenario Fourteen

After divorce, as part of Judge L's effort to meet people, they buy an annual membership to the Live Dance Theatre group. Last night Live Dance held a wine and cheese fundraiser. Judge L attended and had a good time chatting with other

---

[24] J. Michael MacDonald, "Letter closing the matter involving Justice Suche", *CJC News* (May 4, 2020), online: cjc-ccm.ca [perma.cc/6CZJ-CN6J].

attendees. However, in the course of the evening, Judge L noticed that one of the organizers had been taking photographs.

Scenario Fifteen

Judge Z is a basketball fan. After the sudden accidental death of Kobe Bryant, a Facebook post went viral with the title "One of the Greatest Men of All Time has Passed." The post asks people to "Like" it. Should Judge Z click "Like" on this post?

[4] JUDICIAL INDEPENDENCE

[a] The Standard

Independence is of course a foundational ethical principle for judges:

Statement:

An independent judiciary is indispensable to impartial justice under law. Judges uphold and exemplify judicial independence in both its individual and institutional aspects.

Principles:

1. Judges exercise their judicial functions independently and free of extraneous influence.

2. Judges firmly reject improper attempts to influence their decisions in any matter before the Court.

3. Judges exhibit and promote high standards of judicial conduct so as to reinforce public confidence in the independence of the judiciary.

4. Judges encourage and uphold arrangements and safeguards to maintain and enhance the institutional and administrative independence of the judiciary.

An important question is whether some judges might take advantage of judicial independence to advance their own view of the world or to advance their own positions. Independence and impartiality are closely linked because judicial independence is said to exist in order to protect judicial impartiality. The extent to which these two concepts are intertwined is demonstrated in the topic below.

[b] Judges Returning to Practice

One issue that has raised concern in recent years is judges returning to legal practice after retirement. Historically this was not a problem in Canada because judges simply did not do so; it was a norm that judicial office was the capstone of a legal career. However, increasingly, judges have been returning to practice after they retire from the bench.[25] This has generated a variety of concerns, including questions about the independence of the judiciary. In 2019, the role of former Supreme Court of Canada judges became a topic of popular discussion when four retired Supreme Court justices became involved in the SNC-Lavalin affair, each providing opinions or advice for parties in the case.[26] This involvement has been

---

[25] Stephen Pitel & Will Bortolin, "Revising Canada's Ethical Rules for Judges Returning to Practice" (2011) 34 Dal. L.J. 483.

[26] Kathleen Harris, "How 4 ex-Supreme Court justices got caught up in SNC-Lavalin

considered inappropriate by some commentators, reflecting a larger discussion on the activities of retired judges. In her blog "Against Supreme Lawyering", Professor Amy Salyzyn discusses the issue of judges returning to practice more generally:

> It is reasonable for John Q. Plaintiff to feel that he's not going to get a fair shake when he sees that his lawyer (or he, himself!) is up against a retired SCC judge on the other side. It is also reasonable for the public to feel uneasy about any court decision that stems from such a case. SCC judges hold an enormous amount of prestige and power by virtue of their judicial position, which doesn't simply evaporate upon retirement. A retired SCC judge acting as an advocate in the courtroom brings legitimate concerns about bias or undue deference from the bench or jury.[27]

However, this opinion is not universal. In her blog "Retirement from SCC should not be a life sentence", Kyla Lee writes:

> [T]here is something to be said for how distasteful the idea of pitting one retired SCC judge against another is. And while the optics of that are bad, the reality is that is all it is: optics. If the SCC retirees were not available as a pool of potential lawyers to politicians and their ilk, nothing would change. Instead of retired SCC judges the politicians will just hire high-profile litigators, senior partners at national firms or retired Court of Appeal judges . . . There is no shortage of lawyers to arm oneself with in a legal battle. Removing SCC retirees from the pool changes nothing about how distasteful the practice of battling legal opinions in political discourse has become.[28]

The revised *Ethical Principles for Judges* of 2021 attempt to address the issue of judges returning to practice in sections 5.E.1-5.E.4 (pages 57-58). Do these Commentaries more closely align with the position of Salyzyn or Lee? What are the strengths of these Commentaries? What are the weaknesses?

Consider the following scenario.

Scenario Sixteen

Assume a lawyer is taking a case to the Court of Appeal in their province. The firm representing the other side has recently hired a former Court of Appeal judge who, three years ago, sat on a panel which issued the leading precedent on the matter in dispute. Does this raise any concerns? Would it make a difference if the prior decision had been unanimous? Was it a majority decision, with the retired judge writing for the majority? Was it the retired judge who wrote the dissenting decision? Would it make a difference if that retired judge argues the case before their former colleagues?

The Federation of Law Societies of Canada is currently considering amendments to the *Model Code* on this issue. Check their website to see the status of this

---

affair", *CBC News* (August 15, 2019), online: cbc.ca/news [perma.cc/3BZD-QQYR].

[27] Amy Salyzyn, "Against Supreme Lawyering" (March 29, 2019), *Slaw* (blog), online: http://www.slaw.ca/2019/03/29/against-supreme-lawyering/ [perma.cc/RHZ4-98DT].

[28] Kyla Lee, "Retirement from SCC should not be a life sentence" (August 20, 2019), *The Lawyer's Daily* (blog), online: https://www.thelawyersdaily.ca/articles/14618/retirement-from-scc-should-not-be-a-life-sentence-kyla-lee [perma.cc/B23G-46PF].

consultation and whether they have made any changes to the *Model Code.* See online: http://flsc.ca/national-initiatives/model-code-of-professional-conduct/. How do the amendments adopted by the Federation differ from those proposed above? Which do you prefer and why?

[5] INTEGRITY AND RESPECT

[a] The Standard

Integrity and Respect are also core in the *Ethical Principles for Judges.*

Statement:

Judges conduct themselves respectfully and with integrity so as to sustain and enhance public confidence in the judiciary.

This is elaborated upon through seven principles on page 18 of the *Ethical Principles for Judges.* Please review these as you consider the following subsections.

[b] Judge-Lawyer Tensions

Practising law, either as a lawyer or as a judge, can lead to moments of stress, frustration, exasperation and even anger. Occasionally, judges and lawyers cross swords and the consequences can be disturbing. In addition to the foregoing, the Impartiality Principle attempts to address this as follows:

A. Judges ensure that their conduct at all times maintains and enhances confidence in their impartiality and that of the judiciary.

These are expanded upon in Commentaries 2.C.1 and 2.C.3 (pages 21-22).

The following case illustrates the failure of a judge to fulfil these obligations, the riposte of the lawyer, the admonition of the Canadian Judicial Council to the judge, and the Barreau du Québec's disciplining of the lawyer.

DORÉ v. BARREAU DU QUÉBEC

[2012] S.C.J. No. 12, 2012 SCC 12
(McLachlin C.J.C. and Binnie, LeBel, Fish, Abella, Rothstein and Cromwell JJ.)

ABELLA J.:— The focus of this appeal is on the decision of a disciplinary body to reprimand a lawyer for the content of a letter he wrote to a judge after a court proceeding.

. . . . .

Background

Gilles Doré was counsel for Daniel Lanthier in criminal proceedings. On June 18 and 19, 2001, Mr. Doré appeared before Boilard J. in the Superior Court of Quebec seeking a stay of proceedings or, in the alternative, the release of his client on bail. In the course of Mr. Doré's argument, Justice Boilard said about him that [TRANSLATION] "an insolent lawyer is rarely of use to his client". In his written reasons rejecting Mr. Doré's application on June 21, Boilard J. levied further criticism (*R. v. Lanthier*, 2001 CanLII 9351). He accused Mr. Doré of [TRANSLATION] "bombastic rhetoric and hyperbole" and said that the court must "put aside" Mr. Doré's "impudence". Justice Boilard characterized Mr. Doré's request for a stay as "totally ridiculous" and one of his arguments as "idle quibbling". Finally, he said that "fixated on or obsessed with his narrow vision of reality, which is not consistent with the facts, Mr. Doré has done nothing to help his client discharge his burden".

On June 21, Mr. Doré wrote a private letter to Justice Boilard, stating:

[TRANSLATION]

WITHOUT PREJUDICE OR ADMISSION

Sir,

I have just left the Court. Just a few minutes ago, as you hid behind your status like a coward, you made comments about me that were both unjust and unjustified, scattering them here and there in a decision the good faith of which will most likely be argued before our Court of Appeal.

Because you ducked out quickly and refused to hear me, I have chosen to write a letter as an entirely personal response to the equally personal remarks you permitted yourself to make about me. This letter, therefore, is from man to man and is outside the ambit of my profession and your functions.

If no one has ever told you the following, then it is high time someone did. Your chronic inability to master any social skills (to use an expression in English, that language you love so much), which has caused you to become pedantic, aggressive and petty in your daily life, makes no difference to me; after all, it seems to suit you well.

Your deliberate expression of these character traits while exercising your judicial functions, however, and your having made them your trademark concern me a great deal, and I feel that it is appropriate to tell you.

Your legal knowledge, which appears to have earned the approval of a certain number of your colleagues, is far from sufficient to make you the person you could or should be professionally. Your determination to obliterate any humanity from your judicial position, your essentially non-existent listening skills, and your propensity to use your court - where you lack the courage to hear opinions contrary to your own - to launch ugly, vulgar, and mean personal attacks not only confirms that you are as loathsome as suspected, but also casts shame on you as a judge, that most extraordinarily important function that was entrusted to you.

I would have very much liked to say this to your face, but I highly doubt that, given your arrogance, you are able to face your detractors without hiding behind your judicial position.

Worst of all, you possess the most appalling of all defects for a man in your position: You are fundamentally unjust. I doubt that that will ever change.

Sincerely,
Gilles Doré

P.S. As this letter is purely personal, I see no need to distribute it.

. . . . .

The next day, June 22, 2001, Mr. Doré wrote to Chief Justice Lyse Lemieux, with a copy to Justice Boilard. He made it clear that he was not filing a complaint with her against Justice Boilard. Instead, Mr. Doré respectfully requested that he not be required to appear before Justice Boilard in the future since he was concerned that he could not properly represent his clients before him.

On July 10, 2001, Mr. Doré complained to the Canadian Judicial Council about Justice Boilard's conduct. On July 13, Chief Justice Lemieux sent a copy of the letter Mr. Doré had sent to Justice Boilard to the Syndic du Barreau, the body that disciplines lawyers in Quebec.

In March 2002, the Assistant Syndic filed a complaint against Mr. Doré based on his letter to Justice Boilard. The complaint alleged that Mr. Doré had violated both art. 2.03 of the *Code of ethics of advocates*, R.R.Q. 1981, c. B-1, r.1, and Mr. Doré's oath of office. Art. 2.03 stated: "[T]he conduct of an advocate must bear the stamp of objectivity, moderation and dignity."

In the interval between the filing of the Assistant Syndic's complaint against Mr. Doré and the actual proceedings against him, a committee of judges appointed by the Judicial Council to look into Mr. Doré's complaint communicated its conclusions to Mr. Doré and Justice Boilard in letters sent on July 15, 2002. The committee found that Justice Boilard had made [TRANSLATION] "unjustified derogatory remarks to Mr. Doré" stating, in part:

[TRANSLATION]

. . . to use the words "bombastic rhetoric and hyperbole" and "impudence" in referring to counsel arguing a case before you, quite clearly in good faith, is unnecessarily insulting. To reply to counsel who submits that you have not allowed him to argue his case "that an insolent lawyer is rarely of use to his client" not only is unjustified in the circumstances, but could tarnish counsel's professional reputation in the eyes of his client, his peers and the public. To say to counsel arguing a case before you that "I have the impression this is going to be tiresome" is to gratuitously degrade him. To describe a procedure before the court as "totally ridiculous" is unnecessarily humiliating. It is the panel's opinion that such comments would seem to show contempt for counsel not only as an individual but also as a professional.

The evidence reveals a flagrant lack of respect for an officer of the court, namely Mr. Doré, who was nevertheless at all times respectful to the court. The evidence also shows signs of impatience on your part that are surprising in light of every judge's duty to listen calmly to the parties and to counsel. It is the panel's opinion that in so abusing your power as a judge, you not only tarnished your image as a dispenser of justice, but also undermined the judiciary, the image of which has unfortunately been diminished. The panel reminds you that your independence and your authority as a judge do not exempt you from respecting the dignity of every individual who argues a case before you. Dispensing justice while gratuitously insulting counsel is befitting neither for the judge nor for the judiciary.

Having also read the judgments of the Quebec Court of Appeal in *R. v. Proulx, R. v. Bisson* and *R. v. Callochia*, the panel observed that you tend to use your platform to unjustly denigrate counsel appearing before you. The transcript of the hearing of April 9, 2002 in *Sa Majesté la Reine v. Sébastien Beauchamp*, which contains evidence of personal attacks on another lawyer, also confirmed that the case raised in Mr. Doré's complaint is neither unique nor isolated, but shows that extreme conduct and comments seem to form part of a more generalized attitude. In the panel's view, the fact that such an attitude could persist despite warnings from the Court of Appeal is troubling.

The panel finds that the impatience you showed and the immoderate comments you made to an officer of the court, Mr. Doré, are unacceptable and merit an expression of the panel's disapproval under subsection 55(2) of the Canadian Judicial Council By-Laws.

The panel notes that you have deferred to its decision and assumes that the fact that Mr. Doré has made a complaint will lead you to reflect on this and will remind you of your duty as a judge to show respect and courtesy to all counsel who appear before you.

On July 22, 2002, after receiving this reprimand, Justice Boilard recused himself from a complex criminal trial involving the Hell's Angels, a trial related to the trial of Daniel Lanthier in which Mr. Doré had acted. As a result of this recusal, the Attorney General of Quebec requested the Canadian Judicial Council to conduct an inquiry. The Judicial Council concluded that Justice Boilard's recusal had not constituted misconduct.

As for Mr. Doré, the proceedings before the Disciplinary Council of the Barreau du Québec took place between April 2003 and January 2006. In its January 18, 2006 decision, the Disciplinary Council found that Mr. Doré's letter was [TRANSLATION] "likely to offend and is rude and insulting" (2006 CanLII 53416, at para. 58). It concluded that his statements had little expressive value, as they were "merely opinions, perceptions and insults" (para. 62). The Disciplinary Council rejected Mr. Doré's submission that his letter was private, since it was written by him as a lawyer. It also concluded that Justice Boilard's conduct could not be relied on as justification for the letter.

. . . . .

Analysis

Mr. Doré's argument rests on his assertion that the finding of a breach of the *Code of ethics* violates the expressive rights protected by s. 2(*b*) of the *Charter*. Because the 21-day suspension had already been served when he was before the Court of Appeal, he did not appeal the penalty. The reasonableness of its length, therefore, is not before us.

[The Court then engaged in a lengthy discussion of the relationship between the *Charter* and administrative bodies such as the Barreau du Québec and concluded the following.]

If, in exercising its statutory discretion, the decision-maker has properly balanced the relevant *Charter* value with the statutory objectives, the decision will be found to be reasonable.

Application

The *Charter* value at issue in this appeal is expression, and, specifically, how it should be applied in the context of a lawyer's professional duties.

At the relevant time, art. 2.03 of the *Code of ethics* . . . stated that "[t]he conduct of an advocate must bear the stamp of objectivity, moderation and dignity". This provision, whose constitutionality is not impugned before us, sets out a series of broad standards that are open to a wide range of interpretations. The determination of whether the actions of a lawyer violate art. 2.03 in a given case is left entirely to the Disciplinary Council's discretion.

No party in this dispute challenges the importance of professional discipline to prevent incivility in the legal profession, namely "potent displays of disrespect for the participants in the justice system, beyond mere rudeness or discourtesy" . . . The duty to encourage civility, "both inside and outside the courtroom", rests with the courts and with lawyers (*R. v. Felderhof* (2003), 68 O.R. (3d) 481 (C.A.), at para. 83).

As a result, rules similar to art. 2.03 are found in codes of ethics that govern the legal profession throughout Canada. . . .

But in dealing with the appropriate boundaries of civility, the severity of the conduct must be interpreted in light of the expressive rights guaranteed by the *Charter*, and, in particular, the public benefit in ensuring the right of lawyers to express themselves about the justice system in general and judges in particular . . .

In *Histed v. Law Society of Manitoba*, 2007 MBCA 150, 225 Man. R. (2d) 74, where Steel J.A. upheld a disciplinary decision resulting from a lawyer's criticism of a judge, the critical role played by lawyers in assuring the accountability of the judiciary was acknowledged:

> Not only should the judiciary be accountable and open to criticism, but lawyers play a very unique role in ensuring that accountability. As professionals with special expertise and officers of the court, lawyers are under a special responsibility to exercise fearlessness in front of the courts. They must advance their cases courageously, and this may result in criticism of proceedings before or decisions by the judiciary. The lawyer, as an intimate part of the legal system, plays a pivotal role in ensuring the accountability and transparency of the judiciary. To play that role effectively, he/she must feel free to act and speak without inhibition and with courage when the circumstances demand it. [Emphasis added; para. 71]

Proper respect for these expressive rights may involve disciplinary bodies tolerating a degree of discordant criticism. As the Ontario Court of Appeal observed in a different context in *R. v. Kopyto* [(1976) 62 O.R. (2d) 449], the fact that a lawyer is criticizing a judge, a tenured and independent participant in the justice system, may raise, not lower, the threshold for limiting a lawyer's expressive rights under the *Charter*. This does not by any means argue for an unlimited right on the part of lawyers to breach the legitimate public expectation that they will behave with civility.

We are, in other words, balancing the fundamental importance of open, and even forceful, criticism of our public institutions with the need to ensure civility in the profession. Disciplinary bodies must therefore demonstrate that they have given due regard to the importance of the expressive rights at issue, both in light of an individual lawyer's right to expression and the public's interest in open discussion. As with all disciplinary decisions, this balancing is a fact-dependent and discretionary exercise.

In this case, the 21-day suspension imposed on Mr. Doré is not before this Court, since Mr. Doré did not appeal it either to the Court of Appeal or to this Court. All we have been asked to determine is whether the Disciplinary Council's conclusion that a reprimand was warranted under art. 2.03 of the *Code of ethics* was a reasonable one. To make that assessment, we must consider whether this result reflects a proportionate application of the statutory mandate with Mr. Doré's expressive rights.

Lawyers potentially face criticisms and pressures on a daily basis. They are expected by the public, on whose behalf they serve, to endure them with civility and dignity. This is not always easy where the lawyer feels he or she has been unfairly provoked, as in this case. But it is precisely when a lawyer's equilibrium is unduly tested that he or she is particularly called upon to behave with transcendent civility. On the other hand, lawyers should not be expected to behave like verbal eunuchs. They not only have a right to speak their minds freely, they arguably have a duty to do so. But they are constrained by their profession to do so with dignified restraint.

A reprimand for a lawyer does not automatically flow from criticizing a judge or the judicial system. As discussed, such criticism, even when it is expressed robustly, can be constructive. However in the context of disciplinary hearings, such criticism will be measured against the public's reasonable expectations of a lawyer's professionalism. As the Disciplinary Council found, Mr. Doré's letter was outside those expectations. His displeasure with Justice Boilard was justifiable, but the extent of the response was not.

The Disciplinary Council recognized that a lawyer must have [TRANSLATION] "total liberty and independence in the defence of a client's rights", and "has the right to respond to criticism or remarks addressed to him by a judge", a right which the Council recognized "can suffer no restrictions when it is a question of defending clients' rights before the courts" (paras. 68-70). It was also "conscious" of the fact that art. 2.03 may constitute a restriction on a lawyer's expressive rights (para. 79). But where, as here, the judge was called [TRANSLATION] "loathsome", arrogant and "fundamentally unjust" and was accused by Mr. Doré of "hid[ing] behind [his] status like a coward"; having a "chronic inability to master any social skills"; being "pedantic, aggressive and petty in [his] daily life"; having "obliterate[d] any humanity from [his] judicial position"; having "non-existent listening skills"; having a "propensity to use [his] court — where [he] lack[s] the courage to hear opinions contrary to [his] own — to launch ugly, vulgar, and mean personal attacks", which "not only confirms that [he is] as loathsome as suspected, but also casts shame on [him] as a judge"; and being "[un]able to face [his] detractors without hiding behind [his] judicial position", the Council concluded that the "generally accepted norms of moderation and dignity" were "overstepped" (para. 86).

In the circumstances, the Disciplinary Council found that Mr. Doré's letter warranted a reprimand. In light of the excessive degree of vituperation in the letter's context and tone, this conclusion cannot be said to represent an unreasonable balance of Mr. Doré's expressive rights with the statutory objectives.

I would dismiss the appeal with costs.

NOTES AND QUESTIONS

1. Do you agree that the letter was not a private letter? Do you see any issues arising from Doré writing a letter to the Court in a contested matter without including opposing counsel?

2. To what extent does this decision encourage or discourage lawyers from

criticizing judges? Are you relieved to discover that you do not have to behave like a "verbal eunuch"? Do you think lawyers typically act with "dignified restraint"?

3. Rule 5.1-5 of the *Model Code* provides that a "lawyer must be courteous and civil and act in good faith to the tribunal and all persons with whom the lawyer has dealings". The Commentary adds: "Legal contempt of court and the professional obligation outlined here are not identical, and a consistent pattern of rude, provocative or disruptive conduct by a lawyer, even though unpunished as contempt, may constitute professional misconduct."

    Does Doré's letter meet the thresholds identified in this Rule and Commentary? Rather than treating this as a disciplinary matter, would it have been better for Boilard J. to cite Doré for contempt of court?

4. In what way was the decision of the Barreau to discipline Doré in the public interest?

5. Do you agree with the sanction imposed by the Barreau?

[c]   Civility and Candour

We have seen in Chapter 5 that there has been significant debate on the civility standards to be required of lawyers. A similar challenge faces judges. It is obvious that in accordance with the Equality chapter of the *Ethical Principles for Judges*, that judges should not make statements that are discriminatory—although of course some judges have done so, and some others continue to do so.

However, judges, in delivering their decisions, need to be clear as to the reasoning they employ. Sometimes this may require them to be candid and direct.

In the following situations, on a scale of one to five with one being "ethically unproblematic" and five being "ethically problematic", rank the following statements by judges.

[i]   Comments Critical of Lawyers

1. In the course of a case involving a dispute over renovations to a home, the judge says to one of the lawyers:

    a. "English is not your forte. It is your first language, right?"

    b. "You did study contract law during law school, didn't you? Now if you need more time to study up on these aspects I will give it to you, but I'm tired"[29]

Would your answer differ if, in fact, the lawyer was an immigrant from a non-English speaking country?

2. In the case of a break and enter case, the judge says:

    a. "Both the defence and the prosecution seem to be playing games, and dragging out the proceedings unnecessarily . . ."

    b. "Our courts, at the moment, are understaffed and shorthanded . . .

---

[29] *R. v. Said,* [2019] O.J. No. 2375 at para. 9, 2019 ONCA 378 (Ont. C.A.).

so it is my job to work all the time . . . yet you counsel continue to mess around . . ."

[ii] Comments on Expert Witnesses

1. In a case involving bigamy charges, the judge says:

    a. "I now turn to the expert evidence of Professor Wright. They have an impressive CV—a gold medalist from law school, a graduate degree from an Ivy League school, and numerous publications in peer-reviewed journals. However, I found their evidence pertaining to the lives of the women in Gilead unhelpful. They were only able to provide the most abstract and generalized accounts which failed to shed any light on the present case."

    b. "Their manner of address and response to questions was full of unintelligible academic jargon."

    c. "When pushed they seemed testy, combative, and even petulant."

    d. "At times, their accounts seemed filtered through some feminist ideology."

    e. "In sum, I find their evidence to be devoid of objectivity and therefore of no assistance to this court."[30]

2. In a case of alleged medical malpractice, the judge says:

    a. "Dr. Pink was unprepared."

    b. "Dr. Pink offered expert opinions that were not appropriate, not within his knowledge and expertise, and incorrect."

    c. "Dr. Pink's evidence is contaminated by confirmation bias."

    d. "Of course, I am not questioning Dr. Pink's integrity or expertise, for their confirmation bias seems to be unconscious . . . but this case is a compelling illustration of how easy it is to fall into these errors."

    e. "But what concerns me is the willingness of Dr. Pink to take on an extreme and rigid position, while knowing that he had not done any research to back it up."

    f. "Dr. Pink has been disingenuous."

[iii] Delivering an Oral Decision

1. "I have seen the impact of crystal meth in my community, in our schools, and on the children of my friends and neighbours."

2. "The problem is that, to a certain extent, there are members of certain communities in Canada who appear before the court in unusual numbers charged with crystal meth production. Hence the importance of deterrence."

3. "Defence Counsel sought to explain the behaviour by emphasizing the accused's troubled background. But I don't need to hear another tale of woe. We do not need to go through their life histories."

---

[30] *R. v. Stephan*, [2021] A.J. No. 318, 2021 ABCA 82 (Alta. C.A.).

4. "I know counsel was looking for a little bit of sympathy, and I'll balance that with the charges. But we don't need to hear their life stories since kindergarten. There are all sorts of people who come from awful social backgrounds . . . Indigenous people, Black people, people who come from war-torn countries who were child soldiers."

5. "So I am sympathetic to people who come before me with a lot of social baggage, but at some point they have to stop blaming others."

[iv]   Court of Appeal Critical of Trial Judge

Sometimes there are tensions between trial level judges and court of appeal judges. Occasionally, trial level judges are expressly critical of appellate court decisions and, by the same token, appellate courts are critical of trial level judges. This is most obvious when they are overruling them. The challenge is for the appellate court to be unvarnished in explaining its reasons for reversing the decision of the trial level judge but maintaining courtesy and respect. Consider the following statements by a court of appeal:

1. "Judge Blue has essentially gutted the leading case on conditional discharges."

2. "Judge Blue expressly refused to follow any court decisions on sentencing which they themselves did not fully approve. This is a unilateral declaration of independence."

3. "Judge Blue is wilful, obdurate, and ungovernable."

4. "This is not the first time Judge Blue has gone off on a frolic of their own."

5. "We hope that the clarity of our decision will put an end to Judge Blue's frequent flyer status."

[d]   Judicial Fundraising

It is often thought that if a person donates their time, energy and creativity into fundraising for a charitable organization, then this is a manifestation of their integrity. However, such conduct might run up against the impartiality principle. Consider the following scenario:

Scenario Seventeen

Every year Judges Joy and Funn host a fundraising event for their city's charitable organization, the Legal Information Society [LIS]. The event is a dinner prepared by the two judges at one of their homes on a Saturday night. Law firms are invited to bid on the dinner. The successful firm will be entitled to send three members plus their guests. Does this situation raise any concerns?

NOTES AND QUESTIONS

1. In response to concerns about judicial fundraising, Stephen Pitel and Michal Malecki proposed the following amendment:

    C. Civic and Charitable Activity

        1. Judges are free to participate in civic, charitable and religious activities, subject to the following considerations:

(a)   Judges should avoid any activity or association that could reflect adversely on their impartiality or interfere with the performance of judicial duties.

(b)   Judges should not solicit funds (except from judicial colleagues <u>or family members</u> or for appropriate judicial purposes) or lend the prestige of judicial office to such solicitations. <u>However, judges may:</u>

(i)   <u>assist a civic, charitable or religious organization or an organization concerned with the law, the legal system or the administration of justice in planning relating to fund raising.</u>

(ii)   <u>appear or speak at or receive an award or other recognition at a fund-raising event for an organization concerned with the law, the legal system or the administration of justice, and in connection with that event be featured in its promotion.</u>

(c)   Judges should avoid involvement in causes or organizations that are likely to be engaged in litigation.

(d)   Judges should not give legal or investment advice.[31]

The revised *Ethical Principles for Judges* in 2021 includes the following Commentary:

> **2.F.2** Judges should not allow the prestige of judicial office to be used in aid of fundraising for particular causes, however worthy. They should not solicit funds (expect from judicial colleagues or from family members) or lend the prestige of their judicial office to such solicitations.

Do you prefer the Commentary in the *Ethical Principles for Judges* or the proposal by Pitel and Malecki? Why or why not?

[e]   Miscellaneous

The following scenarios probe a variety of circumstances that might call upon the principles of Integrity and Respect.

Scenario Eighteen

When a lawyer is appointed to the bench, their membership with the law society is held in abeyance while they are a judge. If they want to return to practice after ceasing to be a judge, they must apply to the law society to have their membership and their licence to practise law restored.

Alex Jones was appointed to the Provincial Court of British Columbia in 1999. Between 2006 and 2008, the Judicial Council launched complaints about Judge Jones' behaviour on the bench. The complaints centred on improper sexual touching

---

[31]   Stephen Pitel & Michal Malecki, "Judicial Fundraising in Canada" (2015) 52:3 Alta. L. Rev. 519 at 542.

and inappropriate remarks made by Judge Jones. In 2008, Judge Jones was also charged with sexual assault. They were later acquitted. The same year, the Judicial Council issued its decision. It concluded that Judge Jones engaged in misconduct. Before the Judicial Council was able to issue a penalty, Judge Jones resigned from the bench.[32]

Less than two months later, Jones applied to the Law Society to have their membership as a lawyer in the Society restored. A restoration hearing has been set up and proceedings commenced. Should the Law Society restore Jones' licence to practise law? The factors for consideration of restoration of one's licence are similar to the "good character" requirements discussed in Chapter 11.

Scenario Nineteen

In 2017, the CJC recommended that Justice Robin Camp be removed from the bench because of inappropriate remarks he made to a complainant in a sexual assault case. Justice Camp resigned before he was removed.

Mr. Camp applied to the Law Society of Alberta to be readmitted to the practice of law.[33]

Should he be admitted? Why or why not?

Scenario Twenty

A highly publicized murder trial has been going on for several months. The trial is by jury and is of considerable financial and emotional cost to taxpayers and the parties involved. Suddenly, the trial judge recuses themself from the case. In explaining their decision, the trial judge simply states that they had considered the matter carefully and are fully aware of the consequences of their decision. They also indicate that they plan to retire. With that, they direct the case to be adjourned in order for an alternative judge to preside over the case.

Were the judge's actions acceptable? Should the judge have done anything more? If so, what? Do you anticipate any disciplinary action against the trial judge? If so, of what nature? What do you think should happen to the trial judge and why? Does it matter that this was a trial by jury? What if it were only a trial by judge? What if, a month later, the trial judge who had recused themself resumes their judicial duties and appears in court in an unrelated case?

Scenario Twenty-one

Consider a spousal murder case. The details of the case are grave, and the trial was emotionally exhausting for the victim's family. The trial ends in a first-degree murder conviction of the husband. When the judge releases their decision, it reads:

A scream from the victim: an emission of agony. A knife with blood and prints: an

---

[32] See *Law Society of Upper Canada v. Evans*, [2007] L.S.D.D. No. 27 (L.S.U.C.).

[33] Law Society of Alberta Practice Review Committee, "In the Matter of the *Legal Profession Act* and In the Matter of a Section 116 Reinstatement Application by Robin Brian Camp, A Former Member of the Law Society of Alberta", *Law Society of Alberta* (May 22, 2018), online: https://dvbat5idxh7ib.cloudfront.net/wp-content/uploads/2018/05/Camp_Robin_HE20170223_HCR_No-Signatures1.pdf [perma.cc/H59R-3BA9].

admission of guilt. September 24, 2010. At dusk, with the light dimming in the sky and on her life, Mrs. Smith came home from work. A 12-hour shift. Exhausted. As she entered the kitchen what she didn't expect was exactly what Mr. Smith had planned. A hand brandishing a blade. An arm set on auto-stab. A heart pierced. Fatally. The end of a marriage. The end of a life.

What are your thoughts on how this decision was written? To whom or to what institutions would the victim's family file a complaint, if they had one?[34]

Legal scholars have stressed the importance of writing judicial decisions carefully to consider all audiences: the parties, the public, and the legal community.[35] Professor Elaine Craig argues that in particular, when it comes to gender-based violence,

> Writing judgments involving gender-based violence for a public audience should trigger consideration of two interrelated factors specific to this type of case. The first involves the current crisis of public faith in the legal system's ability to respond appropriately to incidents of gender-based harm. The second, related, factor involves the importance of recognizing the social context and dynamics that produce gender-based violence.[36]

How might each audience react to this decision? Should the judge have written their decision differently because of the gender dynamics in this case?

Scenario Twenty-two

Judge Bob loves the street he lives on. The municipal transit authority has recently decided to build a station at the end of this street. All the residents are opposed to the project, including Judge Bob. At a community meeting, Judge Bob agrees to take a leadership role in protesting the development project. Judge Bob writes letters to the municipal council, the Attorney General, the local newspaper and makes several media appearances. When writing these letters, he often addressed himself as "Judge Bob".

Several months later, the municipal transit authority has become involved in litigation involving a different development project. Judge Bob has been assigned to this case. Identify the challenges this might create for the parties in this case. Should Judge Bob remain the judge on this case?[37]

---

[34] Kirk Makin, "The judge who writes like a paperback novelist", *The Globe and Mail* (March 10, 2011), online: https://www.theglobeandmail.com/news/national/the-judge-who-writes-like-a-paperback-novelist/article570811/.

[35] Elaine Craig, "Judicial Audiences: A Case Study of Justice David Watt's Literary Judgments" (2018) 64:2 McGill L.J. 309.

[36] Elaine Craig, "Judicial Audiences: A Case Study of Justice David Watt's Literary Judgments" (2018) 64:2 McGill L.J. 309 at para. 13.

[37] See, *e.g.*, Canadian Judicial Council, Inquiry Committee Decision, *Proceedings and reports regarding Mr. Justice Theodore Matlow of the Ontario Superior Court of Justice* (December 2008), online: http://www.cjc-ccm.gc.ca/cmslib/general/CJC_20080528.pdf. See also Canadian Judicial Council, "Report of the Review Panel Constituted by the Judicial Council Regarding the Honourable F.J.C. Newbould", (February 13, 2017), online: https://www.cjc-ccm.gc.ca/english/news_en.asp?selMenu=news_2017_0213_en.asp.

NOTES AND QUESTIONS

1. Until the 2021 revisions, the *Ethical Principles* did not mention any duty of confidentiality by judges. Stephen Pitel and Liam Ledgerwood proposed that the Integrity Principle be amended as follows:

    > Information that is not public and that is acquired by a judge in his or her judicial capacity or office shall be confidential and shall not be used or disclosed by the judge, during or subsequent to his or her term of judicial office, for any purpose that is not related to the performance of his or her legal duties.[38]

    The CJC amended the *Ethical Principles* in 2021 to include Principle 2B on page 18:

    > Judges are discreet and do not use or disclose confidential information acquired in their judicial capacity for any purpose not related to judicial duties.

    This principle is elaborated in the commentaries on "Confidentiality and Discretion" on page 21.

    Which version of the confidentiality principle do you prefer? Why?

[6] DILIGENCE AND COMPETENCE

[a] The Standard

Diligence and Competence is an additional ethical principle for judges:

Statement:

Judges perform their duties with diligence and competence.

Principles:

A.   Judges devote themselves to their judicial duties, broadly defined, which include presiding in court and making decisions, as well as those duties essential to court operations and to the administration of justice. Judges do not engage in activities incompatible with the diligent discharge of judicial duties.

B.   Judges perform all judicial duties, including the delivery of reserved judgments, with punctuality and reasonable promptness, having due regard to the urgency of the matter and other special circumstances.

C.   Judges maintain and enhance their knowledge, skills, sensitivity to social context and the personal qualities necessary to perform their judicial duties.

D.   Judges strive to maintain their wellness to optimize the performance of judicial duties.

[b] The Standard Applied

Scientific research has shown that our energy levels ebb and flow over the course of

---

[38] Stephen Pitel & Liam Ledgerwood, "Judicial Confidentiality in Canada" [forthcoming]. See also Adam Dodek, "Judicial Confidentiality" (June 13, 2016), *Slaw* (blog), online: http://www.slaw.ca/2016/06/13/judicial-confidentiality/.

the day. Not everyone has the same patterns, but many people lose focus before lunch because their blood sugar is low and they need to eat and are tired in the afternoons after lunch and their energy levels (and their attention) pick up later in the afternoon. Anyone who has taken (or taught) an early-morning class has noticed that it takes time for students to "wake-up" and be able to focus and participate. In Canada, court hours tend to begin at 9 or 10 in the morning, take a mid-morning break and then a lunch break and return for afternoon proceedings.

Many lawyers have noticed that the focus of some judges differs over the course of the day, as it does for other people. What are the ethical obligations of an individual judge who finds that their attention or their stamina fluctuates over the course of the day? What are the ethical obligations of court administrators who determine scheduling when faced with such scientific evidence? In extreme circumstances, a judge might fall asleep during the course of a proceeding. What should the judge do if they realize that they are falling asleep or that they have nodded off for a moment? What would you do if you were counsel and you saw a judge close his eyes for a few minutes? See *Leader Media Productions Ltd. v. Sentinel Hill Alliance Atlantis Equicap Limited Partnership.*[39]

. . . . .

NOTES AND QUESTIONS

1. In *Leader Media*, the Ontario Court of Appeal said that a lawyer has a responsibility to "bring the judge's inattention home to him" at the moment it is happening. Describe exactly how you would go about fulfilling this responsibility. What sort of responses might your approach elicit from the inattentive judge? Does your answer change if you are a second-year associate or a senior partner? Does your answer depend upon whether the judge appeared distracted or sleepy or whether the judge was clearly asleep (*e.g.*, snoring)?

2. What is the ethical obligation of the individual judge in question after the Court of Appeal's decision in *Leader Media*? What would you do if you were that judge's Chief Justice?

3. In 2020, during the COVID-19 pandemic, many courts moved to proceedings by videoconference, using platforms such as "Zoom". Many commentators have noted the phenomenon of "zoom fatigue", where it is more tiring participating in such videoconferences than it is in person meetings. There are multiple explanations for this, but one explanation is that it is more work for our brain to concentrate. What ethical obligations arise for judges and for the judiciary in light of this?

Scenario Twenty-three

When the judge issues their written decision after a trial, the plaintiff wins. However, it is soon apparent that the judge substantially reproduced 80% of the

---

[39] [2008] O.J. No. 2284, 90 O.R. (3d) 561 (Ont. C.A.), leave to appeal refused [2008] S.C.C.A. No. 394 (S.C.C.).

plaintiff's lawyer's written arguments as part of their reasons for decision. What are some ethical concerns here?[40]

Scenario Twenty-four

Recently, Justice LeBlanc has become distracted and confused. They frequently forget their clerks' names and sometimes calls them by the wrong names. They never used to do this before. At times when discussing cases or issues, Justice LeBlanc seems to get lost and refer to wrong information. One clerk is supporting Justice LeBlanc in their work on a bench-bar committee. The clerk attends the meeting of the committee. At one point, Justice LeBlanc appears to be distracted and says something that is completely irrelevant. Some of the lawyers on the committee appear quite concerned. The clerk is worried when a journalist friend contacts them mentioning the local newspaper is writing a story about Justice LeBlanc's odd behaviour. The journalist wants the clerk to confirm anonymously if the story is accurate. Should the clerk initiate a conversation with Justice LeBlanc?

[c] Independent Research

In the contemporary world, most people turn to the Internet to fill in information gaps. Some judges, in order to be diligent, efficient and contextual, have turned to the Internet. On the one hand, this seems eminently sensible. On the other hand, it might raise some ethical concerns. The revised *Ethical Principles for Judges*, when addressing social media, includes Commentary 5.B.18, which provides that:

> In a digital world, out-of-court information is much more accessible and the acquisition of such information by a judge is more readily discoverable. Accordingly, judges should be vigilant to avoid inappropriately acquiring or receiving out-of-court information related to the parties, witnesses or issues under consideration in matters before them. Fairness issues may need to be considered by the judge should this happen.

Consider the following scenario.

Scenario Twenty-five

The Sapphire Hill psychiatric hospital is being sued by Robin Lanni, an inpatient at the hospital. Lanni is claiming that the hospital's medication policy prevents them from getting the medical care they need. Lanni has acid reflux, and has been prescribed an antacid pill to be taken before every meal. Sapphire Hill has a policy only to give out medication first thing in the morning and right before lights out, and patients are punished for attempting to "cheek" their pills or not take them at those times. Lanni is claiming that their acid reflux medication does not work properly when taken so far in advance of mealtime. Lanni is self-represented. The judge who is hearing the case interrupts the hospital's expert witness and explains that they read on WebMD that antacid medication works best if taken 30-60 minutes before meals, and dissolves in the blood if taken earlier than that. The judge wants the expert witness to comment on this. No evidence about the medication's dissolution in blood has yet been presented in court. Should the judge have conducted this

---

[40] See also *Cojocaru v. British Columbia Women's Hospital and Health Centre*, [2013] S.C.J. No. 30, [2013] 2 S.C.R. 357 (S.C.C.).

independent research? What if the judge said that they looked online because Lanni could not realistically be expected to mount a case and bring this evidence on their own without representation? Would it make a difference if Lanni had visited the same website and was about to bring this evidence forward?[41]

Consider your answer with reference to Principle 2D and Commentaries 2.D.1, 2.D.2 (pages 23-24), 5.A.8, and 5.A.9 (page 41) regarding self-represented litigants.

[7] EQUALITY

[a] The Standard

Equality is a further ethical principle for judges.

Statement:

Judges conduct themselves and the proceedings before them to ensure equality according to law.

---

[41] Debra Weiss, "Dissenter blasts Posner's internet research in inmate's suit over acid reflux treatment", *ABA Journal* (August 20, 2015), online: http://www.abajournal.com/news/article/posners_internet_research_in_inmates_gerd_suit_leads_to_sparring_in_7th_cir/.

Principles:

    A.   Judges carry out their duties with respect for all persons, including parties, counsel, witnesses, court personnel and judicial colleagues, without discrimination or prejudice.

    B.   Judges refrain from discriminatory behaviour. They disassociate themselves from and disapprove of offensive or discriminatory comments or conduct by court staff, counsel or any other person involved in judicial proceedings.

    C.   Judges are sensitive to and are not influenced by attitudes based on stereotype, myth or prejudice. They make meaningful efforts to recognize and dissociate themselves from such attitudes.

    D.   Judges do not belong to any organization that engages in or countenances any form of discrimination that contravenes the law.

[b] Equality and Impartiality

Equality according to law is, undoubtedly, a social good. But what is the relationship between equality and impartiality? Sometimes equality and impartiality are seen to be mutually supporting, at other times they are seen to be in tension. In the following case, the Supreme Court of Canada has addressed this issue, as well as what conduct by the judge in the courtroom will cross the line and call the judge's impartiality into question.

YUKON FRANCOPHONE SCHOOL BOARD, EDUCATION AREA #23 v. YUKON (ATTORNEY GENERAL)

[2015] S.C.J. No. 25, 2015 SCC 25 (S.C.C.)

The judgment of the Court was delivered by ABELLA J. —

After a trial involving claims by the Yukon Francophone School Board about minority language education rights, the trial judge found that the Yukon government had failed to comply with its obligations under s. 23 of the *Canadian Charter of Rights and Freedoms*. Based largely on the conduct of the trial judge, the Court of Appeal concluded that there was a reasonable apprehension of bias and ordered a new trial. That conduct is at the centre of this appeal . . .

Background

. . .

In 2009, the Board sued the Yukon government for what it claimed were deficiencies in the provision of minority language education. The trial took place in two phases. A number of incidents occurred during the trial which set the stage for the bias argument in the Court of Appeal. It is worth noting that, even during the course of the trial, the Yukon was concerned about bias and brought a recusal motion on the ground that certain comments and decisions by the trial judge, as well as his involvement in the francophone community in Alberta both before and during his time as a judge, gave rise to a reasonable apprehension of bias. The trial judge dismissed the motion, finding that many of the acts complained of by the Yukon were procedural in nature and involved decisions of a discretionary nature. He also concluded that his involvement in the francophone community created no reasonable apprehension of bias, observing that counsel for the Yukon did not raise the issue when the case was assigned nor at an earlier point in the proceedings.

. . . . .

On appeal, the Court of Appeal noted that an apprehension of bias can arise either from what a judge says or does during a hearing, or from extrinsic evidence showing that the judge is likely to have strong predispositions preventing him or her from impartially considering the issues in the case. After reviewing the transcript and the trial judge's written rulings, the Court of Appeal concluded that, based on a number of incidents as well as on the trial judge's involvement in the francophone community, the threshold for a finding that there was a reasonable apprehension of bias had been met. It referred to a number of problematic occurrences during the trial.

. . . . .

Analysis

The test for a reasonable apprehension of bias is undisputed and was first articulated by this Court as follows:

> . . . what would an informed person, viewing the matter realistically and practically — and having thought the matter through — conclude. Would he think that it is more likely than not that [the decision-maker], whether consciously or unconsciously, would not decide fairly. [Citation omitted;

Committee for Justice and Liberty v. National Energy Board, [1978] 1 S.C.R. 369, at p. 394, per de Grandpré J. (dissenting)]

. . . . .

The objective of the test is to ensure not only the reality, but the *appearance* of a fair adjudicative process. The issue of bias is thus inextricably linked to the need for impartiality. In *Valente*, Le Dain J. connected the dots from an absence of bias to impartiality, concluding "[i]mpartiality refers to a state of mind or attitude of the tribunal in relation to the issues and the parties in a particular case" and "connotes absence of bias, actual or perceived": p. 685. Impartiality and the absence of the bias have developed as both legal and ethical requirements. Judges are required — and expected — to approach every case with impartiality and an open mind: see *S. (R.D.)*, at para. 49, per L'Heureux-Dubé and McLachlin JJ.

. . . . .

Because there is a strong presumption of judicial impartiality that is not easily displaced (*Cojocaru v. British Columbia Women's Hospital and Health Centre*, [2013] 2 S.C.R. 357, at para. 22), the test for a reasonable apprehension of bias requires a "real likelihood or probability of bias" and that a judge's individual comments during a trial not be seen in isolation: see *Arsenault-Cameron v. Prince Edward Island*, [1999] 3 S.C.R. 851, at para. 2; *S. (R.D.)*, at para. 134, per Cory J.

The inquiry into whether a decision-maker's conduct creates a reasonable apprehension of bias, as a result, is inherently contextual and fact-specific, and there is a correspondingly high burden of proving the claim on the party alleging bias: see *Wewaykum*, at para. 77; *S. (R.D.)*, at para. 114, per Cory J. As Cory J. observed in *S. (R.D.)* . . .

That said, this Court has recognized that a trial judge's conduct, and particularly his or her interventions, can rebut the presumption of impartiality. In *Brouillard v. The Queen*, [1985] 1 S.C.R. 39, for example, the trial judge had asked a defence witness almost sixty questions and interrupted her more than ten times during her testimony. He also asked the accused more questions than both counsel, interrupted him dozens of times, and subjected him and another witness to repeated sarcasm. Lamer J. noted that a judge's interventions by themselves are not necessarily reflective of bias. On the contrary,

> it is clear that judges are no longer required to be as passive as they once were; to be what I call sphinx judges. We now not only accept that a judge may intervene in the adversarial debate, but also believe that it is sometimes essential for him to do so for justice in fact to be done. Thus a judge may and sometimes must ask witnesses questions, interrupt them in their testimony and if necessary call them to order. [p. 44]

. . . . .

[As for how to assess the impact of a judge's identity, experiences and affiliations on a perception of bias, Cory J.'s comments in *S. (R.D.)* helpfully set the stage:

> Regardless of their background, gender, ethnic origin or race, all judges owe a fundamental duty to the community to render impartial decisions and to appear impartial. It follows that judges must strive to ensure that no word or action during the course of the trial or in delivering judgment might leave the reasonable, informed person with the impression that an issue was predetermined or that a question was decided on the basis of stereotypical assumptions or generalizations. [para. 120]

But it is also important to remember the words of L'Heureux-Dubé and McLachlin JJ. in *S. (R.D.)*, where they compellingly explained the intersecting relationship between a judge's background and the judicial role:

> . . . judges in a bilingual, multiracial and multicultural society will undoubtedly approach the task of judging from their varied perspectives. They will certainly have been shaped by, and have gained insight from, their different experiences, and cannot be expected to divorce themselves from these experiences on the occasion of their appointment to the bench. In fact, such a transformation would deny society the benefit of the valuable knowledge gained by the judiciary while they were members of the Bar. As well, it would preclude the achievement of a diversity of backgrounds in the judiciary. The reasonable person does not expect that judges will function as neutral ciphers; however, the reasonable person does demand that judges achieve impartiality in their judging.

> It is apparent, and a reasonable person would expect, that triers of fact will be properly influenced in their deliberations by their individual perspectives on the world in which the events in dispute in the courtroom took place. Indeed, judges must rely on their background knowledge in fulfilling their adjudicative function. [paras. 38-39]

Judicial impartiality and neutrality do not mean that a judge must have no prior conceptions, opinions or sensibilities. Rather, they require that the judge's identity and experiences not close his or her mind to the evidence and issues. There is, in other words, a crucial difference between an open mind and empty one. Bora Laskin noted that the strength of the common law lies in part in the fact that the judges who administer it represent in themselves and in their work a mix of attitudes and a mix of opinions about the world in which they live and about the society in which they carry on their judicial duties. It is salutary that this is so, and eminently desirable that it should continue to be so.

["The Common Law is Alive and Well — And, Well?" (1975), 9 *L. Soc'y Gaz.* 92, at p. 99]

The reasonable apprehension of bias test recognizes that while judges "must strive for impartiality", they are not required to abandon who they are or what they know: *S. (R.D.)*, at para. 29, per L'Heureux-Dubé and McLachlin JJ.; see also *S. (R.D.)*, at para. 119, per Cory J. A judge's identity and experiences are an important part of who he or she is, and neither neutrality nor impartiality is inherently compromised by them. Justice is the aspirational application of law to life. Judges should be encouraged to experience, learn and understand "life" — their own and those whose lives reflect different realities. As Martha Minow elegantly noted, the ability to be open-minded is enhanced by such knowledge and understanding:

> None of us can know anything except by building upon, challenging, responding to what we already have known, what we see from where we stand. But we can insist on seeing what we are used to seeing, or else we can try to see something new and fresh. The latter is the open mind we hope for from those who judge, but not the mind as a sieve without prior reference points and commitments. We want judges and juries to be objective about the facts and the questions of guilt and innocence but committed to building upon what they already know about the world, human beings, and each person's own implication in the lives of others. Pretending not to know risks leaving unexamined the very assumptions that deserve reconsideration. ["Stripped Down Like a Runner or Enriched by Experience: Bias and Impartiality of Judges and Jurors" (1992), 33 *Wm. & Mary L. Rev.* 1201, at p. 1217]

This recognition was reinforced by Cameron A.J. of the Constitutional Court of South Africa in *South African Commercial Catering and Allied Workers Union v. Irvin & Johnson Ltd. (Seafoods Division Fish Processing)*, 2000 (3) S.A. 705:

> . . . "absolute neutrality" is something of a chimera in the judicial context. This is because Judges are human. They are unavoidably the product of their own life experiences and the perspective thus derived inevitably and distinctively informs each Judge's performance of his or her judicial duties. But colourless neutrality stands in contrast to judicial impartiality . . . . Impartiality is that quality of open-minded readiness to persuasion — without unfitting adherence to either party or to the Judge's own predilections, preconceptions and personal views — that is the keystone of a civilised system of adjudication. Impartiality requires, in short, "a mind open to persuasion by the evidence and the submissions of counsel"; and, in contrast to neutrality, this is an absolute requirement in every judicial proceeding. [Citations omitted; para. 13.]

Impartiality thus demands not that a judge discount or disregard his or her life experiences or identity, but that he or she approach each case with an open mind, free from inappropriate and undue assumptions. It requires judges "to recognize, consciously allow for, and perhaps to question, all the baggage of past attitudes and sympathies": Canadian Judicial Council, *Commentaries on Judicial Conduct* (1991), at p. 12. As Aharon Barak has observed:

> The judge must be capable of looking at himself from the outside and of analyzing, criticizing, and controlling himself . . . .

The judge is a product of his times, living in and shaped by a given society in a given era. The purpose of objectivity is not to sever the judge from his environment . . . [or] to rid a judge of his past, his education, his experience, his belief, or his values. Its purpose is to encourage the judge to make use of all of these personal characteristics to reflect the fundamental values of the society as faithfully as possible. A person who is appointed as a judge is neither required nor able to change his skin. The judge must develop sensitivity to the dignity of his office and to the restraints that it imposes. [Footnote omitted.]

But whether dealing with judicial conduct in the course of a proceeding or with "extra-judicial" issues like a judge's identity, experiences or affiliations, the test remains

whether a reasonable and informed person, with knowledge of all the relevant circumstances, viewing the matter realistically and practically, would conclude that the judge's conduct gives rise to a reasonable apprehension of bias . . . .[T]he assessment is difficult and requires a careful and thorough examination of the proceeding. The record must be considered in its entirety to determine the cumulative effect of any transgressions or improprieties. [Citations omitted; *Miglin*, at para. 26.]

[Applying this test to the trial judge's conduct throughout the proceedings, I agree with the Court of Appeal that the threshold for a finding of a reasonable apprehension of bias has been met.]

[The Court found a reasonable apprehension of bias based on the trial judge's conduct during the trial. The Court also addressed arguments about whether a reasonable apprehension of bias was created as a result of the trial judge's involvement with various community organizations.]

. . . I respectfully part company with the Court of Appeal when it concluded that the trial judge's current service as a governor of the Fondation franco-albertaine substantially contributed to a reasonable apprehension of bias. The trial judge had been appointed to the Alberta Court of Queen's Bench in 2002 and the Supreme Court of Yukon in 2005. Before being appointed to the bench, the trial judge played a key role in the creation of École du Sommet in St. Paul, Alberta and served as a school trustee on the Conseil scolaire Centre-Est de l'Alberta from 1994 until 1998. From 1999 to 2001, he served as a member of the executive of the Association canadienne-française de l'Alberta, an organization that lobbies on behalf of and promotes the francophone community in Alberta. He was a governor of the Fondation franco-albertaine while he was a judge. Its "mission" is to [TRANSLA-TION] "[e]stablish charitable activities to enhance the vitality of Alberta's franco-phone community", and its "vision" is for "[a] francophone community in Alberta that is autonomous, dynamic and valued". It is this latter affiliation that triggered the Court of Appeal's admonition.

While the Court of Appeal acknowledged that the Fondation franco-albertaine was not directly involved with the community whose rights were being determined in the litigation and had no affiliation with any organization implicated in the trial, it concluded that

[t]he parallels between the situations of s. 23 rights-holders in Alberta and those in Yukon are direct and obvious. Further, the expressed visions of the [Fondation franco-albertaine] would clearly align it with some of the positions taken by the

[Board] in this case. We are unable, therefore, to accept that the judge's position as governor of the [Fondation franco-albertaine] was innocuous. [para. 199]

It also acknowledged, however, that the Fondation franco-albertaine "appears to be largely a philanthropic organization rather than a political group", and that its goals are primarily charitable, not partisan. Nevertheless, it was of the view that

the organization's mission statement and philosophy shows that it has a particular vision of the francophone community. In continuing to be a governor of the organization, the judge was, in effect, publicly declaring his support for that vision. [para. 193]

While I fully acknowledge the importance of judges avoiding affiliations with certain organizations, such as advocacy or political groups, judges should not be required to immunize themselves from participation in community service where there is little likelihood of potential conflicts of interest. Judges, as Benjamin Cardozo said, do not stand on "chill and distant heights": *The Nature of the Judicial Process* (1921), at p. 168. They should not and *cannot* be expected to leave their identities at the courtroom door. What they *can* be expected to do, however, is remain, in fact and in appearance, open in spite of them. I find the following observations by Lord Bingham of Cornhill C.J., Lord Woolf M.R. and Sir Richard Scott V.-C. in *Locabail (U.K.) Ltd. v. Bayfield Properties Ltd.*, [2000] Q.B. 451 (C.A.), to provide a persuasive instructional template on how to view the relationship between a judge's identity, organizational affiliation, and impartiality:

We cannot . . . conceive of circumstances in which an objection could be soundly based on the religion, ethnic or national origin, gender, age, class, means or sexual orientation of the judge. Nor, at any rate ordinarily, could an objection be soundly based on the judge's social or educational or service or employment background or history, nor that of any member of the judge's family; or previous political associations; or membership of social or sporting or charitable bodies; or Masonic associations; or previous judicial decisions; or extra-curricular utterances (whether in textbooks, lectures, speeches, articles, interviews, reports or responses to consultation papers); or previous receipt of instructions to act for or against any party, solicitor or advocate engaged in a case before him; or membership of the same Inn, circuit, local Law Society or chambers . . . . By contrast, a real danger of bias might well be thought to arise if there were personal friendship or animosity between the judge and any member of the public involved in the case; or if the judge were closely acquainted with any member of the public involved in the case, particularly if the credibility of that individual could be significant in the decision of the case; or if, in a case where the credibility of any individual were an issue to be decided by the judge, he had in a previous case rejected the evidence of that person in such outspoken terms as to throw doubt on his ability to approach such person's evidence with an open mind on any later occasion; or if on any question at issue in the proceedings before him the judge had expressed views, particularly in the course of the hearing, in such extreme and unbalanced terms as to throw doubt on his ability to try the issue with an objective judicial mind . . . or if, for any other reason, there were real ground for doubting the ability of the judge to ignore extraneous considerations, prejudices and predilections and bring an objective judgment to bear on the issues before him. [Citations omitted; para. 25.]

(See also *S. (R.D.)*, at paras. 38-39, per L'Heureux-Dubé and McLachlin JJ.)

The *Ethical Principles for Judges* provide guidance to federally appointed judges.

They advise that while judges should clearly exercise common sense about joining organizations, they are not prohibited from continuing to serve their communities outside their judicial role:

> A judge is appointed to serve the public. Many persons appointed to the bench have been and wish to continue to be active in other forms of public service. This is good for the community and for the judge, but carries certain risks. For that reason, it is important to address the question of the limits that judicial appointment places upon the judge's community activities.
>
> The judge administers the law on behalf of the community and therefore unnecessary isolation from the community does not promote wise or just judgments. The Right Honourable Gerald Fauteux put the matter succinctly and eloquently in *Le livre du magistrat* (translation):
>
>> [there is no intention] to place the judiciary in an ivory tower and to require it to cut off all relationship with organizations which serve society. Judges are not expected to live on the fringe of society of which they are an important part. To do so would be contrary to the effective exercise of judicial power which requires exactly the opposite approach.
>
> The precise constraints under which judges should conduct themselves as regards civic and charitable activity are controversial inside and outside the judiciary. This is not surprising given that the question involves balancing competing considerations. On one hand, there are the beneficial aspects, both for the community and the judiciary, of the judge being active in other forms of public service. This needs to be assessed in light of the expectations and circumstances of the particular community. On the other hand, the judge's involvement may, in some cases, jeopardize the perception of impartiality or lead to an undue number of recusals. If this is the case, the judge should . . . avoid the activity. [*Ethical Principles for Judges*, at p. 33]

Membership in an association affiliated with the interests of a particular race, nationality, religion, or language is not, without more, a basis for concluding that a perception of bias can reasonably be said to arise. We expect a degree of mature judgment on the part of an informed public which recognizes that not everything a judge does or joins predetermines how he or she will judge a case. Canada has devoted a great deal of effort to creating a more diverse bench. That very diversity should not operate as a presumption that a judge's identity closes the judicial mind.

In this case, the Court of Appeal found that the trial judge's involvement as a governor of the Fondation franco-albertaine was problematic. There is, however, little in the record about the organization. In particular, it is difficult to see how, based on the evidence, one could conclude that its vision "would clearly align" with certain positions taken by the Board in this case or that the trial judge's involvement in the organization foreclosed his ability to approach this case with an open mind. Standing alone, vague statements about the organization's mission and vision do not displace the presumption of impartiality. While I agree that consideration of the trial judge's current role as a governor of the organization was a valid part of the contextual bias inquiry in this case, I am not persuaded that his involvement with an organization whose functions are largely undefined on the evidence, can be said to rise to the level of a contributing factor such that the judge, as the Court of Appeal said, "should not have sat on [this case]" (at para. 200).

. . . . .

The appeal from the Court of Appeal's conclusion that there was a reasonable apprehension of bias requiring a new trial is accordingly dismissed . . .

Scenario Twenty-six

Justice Smart is legally blind. Prior to becoming a judge, Smart served as legal counsel for the National Institute for Blind Persons for several years, primarily advancing human rights claims. Subsequently, Smart became a professor at McOz Law School and wrote numerous articles and one book on the rights of persons who are visually impaired. After being appointed to the bench, they agreed to serve as the Honorary Chair of the National Institute for Blind Persons.

Palhousie University is currently being sued by a group of visually impaired students for providing inadequate accommodation. The National Institute for Blind Persons is seeking intervenor status. It soon comes to light that Judge Smart has been assigned to the case. Palhousie University is very concerned. What are some red flags?

NOTES AND QUESTIONS

1. In light of the decision of the Court in *Yukon Francophone Schoolboard*, do you think the judges crossed the line when they made the following comments?

    A. Justice Moreau-Bérubé made the comments below after hearing a breaking and entering and theft case that featured two repeat offenders and allegations of drug use. Within days of making the comments Moreau-Bérubé J. informed the Judicial Council about her remarks and issued an apology at a hearing. Her apology was in reference to the following comment:

    > These are people who live on welfare and we're the ones who support them; they are on drugs and they are drunk day in and day out. They steal from us left, right and centre and any which way, they find others as crooked as they are to buy the stolen property. It's a pitiful sight. If a survey were taken in the Acadian Peninsula, of the honest people as against the dishonest people, I have the impression that the dishonest people would win. We have now got to the point where we can no longer trust our neighbour next door or across the street. In the area where I live, I wonder whether I'm not myself surrounded by crooks. And, that is how people live in the Peninsula, but we point the finger at outsiders. Ah, we don't like to be singled out in the Peninsula. And it makes me sad to say this because I live in the Peninsula now. It's my home. But look at the honest people in the Peninsula, they are very few and far between, and they are becoming fewer and fewer. And do you think these people care that it cost hundreds and thousands of dollars to repair that? They don't give a damn. Are they going to pay for it? No, not a dime. All the money is spent on coke. These people, they don't give a damn. It doesn't bother them one bit, they just – do you think you are going to

arouse their sorrow and sympathy by saying that it costs hundreds and thousands of dollars. We, it bothers us because we are the ones who pay, because we have to wake up every morning and go to work. When we receive our paycheck, three quarters are taken away to support these people. They, don't care. They have nothing to do. They party all day and party all night and that's all they do. They don't care, not one bit. We on the other hand, we have to care because it is our property. These people, if they don't have enough they go to welfare and they get even more and that is how it works. So, I do not want to interrupt you, but I understand what you mean when you say that it cost thousands of dollars and counsel here understand, but the type of people we are dealing with here today in this courtroom, they couldn't care less. Whether it cost one thousand dollars to repair it or whether it cost only two cents, whether it requires six police officers to investigate, they find it funny. Their mentality is that "The pigs will not be at Tim's while they are chasing after us."[42]

B. Writing for a majority that dismissed the Crown's appeal in a sexual assault case, McClung J.A. of the Alberta Court of Appeal made the following remarks:

(i) [I]t must be pointed out that the complainant did not present herself to Ewanchuk or enter his trailer in a bonnet and crinolines.

(ii) [S]he was the mother of a six-month-old baby and that, along with her boyfriend, she shared an apartment with another couple.

(iii) There is no room to suggest that Ewanchuk knew, yet disregarded, her underlying state of mind as he furthered his romantic intentions. He was not aware of her true state of mind. Indeed, his ignorance about that was what she wanted. The facts, set forth by the trial judge, provide support for the overriding trial finding, couched in terms of consent by implication, that the accused had no proven preparedness to assault the complainant to get what he wanted.

(iv) [Describing the sexual assault]: [Ewanchuk's actions were] clumsy passes . . . [actions that] would hardly raise Ewanchuk's stature in the pantheon of chivalric behaviour.

(v) [E]very advance he made to her stopped when she spoke against it. . . . there was no evidence of an assault or even its threat. . . . [T]he sum of the evidence indicates that Ewanchuk's advances to the complainant were far less criminal than hormonal.

---

[42] *Moreau-Bérubé v. New Brunswick*, [2000] N.B.J. No. 368, 2000 NBCA 12 at para. 5 (N.B.C.A.).

(vi)   In a less litigious age going too far in the boyfriend's car was better dealt with on site — a well-chosen expletive, a slap in the face or, if necessary, a well-directed knee.[43]

C.   An accused was convicted of sexual assault, including forced intercourse. The Crown requested a sentence of three years in jail. The judge issued a conditional sentence. In justifying the lesser sentence the judge indicated that the accused is not as culpable as other rapists because "he was a clumsy Don Juan", "sex was in the air [that night]", and that the "victim was wearing a tube top without a bra, high heels and plenty of make-up".[44]

D.   On May 10, 1983, the Court of Appeal rendered its judgment in an appeal investigating the wrongful conviction of Donald Marshall, Jr. for murder. The court quashed Marshall's conviction and directed an acquittal. At the end of its judgment, the court makes the following comments:

> Donald Marshall, Jr. was convicted of murder and served a lengthy period of incarceration. That conviction is now to be set aside. Any miscarriage of justice is, however, more apparent than real.
>
> In attempting to defend himself against the charge of murder Mr. Marshall admittedly committed perjury for which he still could be charged.
>
> By lying he helped secure his own conviction. He misled his lawyers and presented to the jury a version of the facts he now says is false, a version that was so far-fetched as to be incapable of belief.
>
> By planning a robbery with the aid of Mr. Seale he triggered a series of events which unfortunately ended in the death of Mr. Seale.
>
> By hiding the facts from his lawyers and the police Mr. Marshall effectively prevented development of the only defence available to him, namely, that during a robbery Seale was stabbed by one of the intended victims.
>
> He now says that he knew approximately where the man lived who stabbed Seale and had a pretty good description of him. With this information the truth of the matter might well have been uncovered by the police.
>
> Even at the time of taking the fresh evidence, although he had little more to lose and much to gain if he could obtain his acquittal, Mr. Marshall was far from being straightforward on the stand. He continued to be evasive about the robbery and

---

[43] *R. v. Ewanchuk*, [1998] A.J. No. 150, 1998 ABCA 52 at paras. 4, 5, 8, 11, 15 and 21 (Alta. C.A.).

[44] Mia Rabson, "Board raps judge for comments – Council lets Dewar stay on bench" *Winnipeg Free Press* (November 10, 2011).

811

assault and even refused to answer questions until the court ordered him to do so.

There can be no doubt but that Donald Marshall's untruthfulness through this whole affair contributed in large measure to his conviction.[45]

Scenario Twenty-seven

Justice Redd has been assigned to hear a high-profile human rights lawsuit on the basis of sexual orientation. Justice Redd's daughter recently married her partner Jane Jessop and asked Justice Redd to officiate. Justice Redd declined, indicating that his religious faith did not countenance same-sex marriage. What are some concerns you or the involved parties may have about this judge's involvement in the human rights lawsuit?[46]

Reconsider your answer in light of 4.D.1 and 4.D.2 (page 37) of the *Ethical Principles for Judges*.

Scenario Twenty-eight

A parent is in court for a contested divorce case. They have a young baby who is still nursing and have brought the baby into the courtroom with them. Before proceedings begin, the parent starts breastfeeding the baby. The judge tells them that they are not allowed to breastfeed in court, as it is distracting and inappropriate.[47] Does this raise any concerns?

NOTES AND QUESTIONS

1. Given ongoing concerns about the behaviour of some judges in some sexual assault cases, in 2017 the House of Commons unanimously passed Bill C-337 "to restrict eligibility for judicial appointment to individuals who have completed comprehensive education in respect of matters related to sexual assault laws and social context".[48] The Bill was strenuously opposed by organizations representing the judiciary. It died at the Senate. Do you believe it is justifiable for government to try and pass such a Bill? Does it threaten the separation of powers? In May 2021, Royal Assent was given to *An Act to amend the Judges Act and the Criminal Code*,[49] which

---

[45] *MacKeigan v. Hickman*, [1989] S.C.J. No. 99, [1989] 2 S.C.R. 796 at para. 35 (S.C.C.).

[46] "Analyzing the same-sex marriage advice" (August 2015), *Judicial Ethics and Discipline*, online: https://ncscjudicialethicsblog.org/2015/08/.

[47] Alyssa Rahey, "Nova Scotia Judge Accused of Discrimination in the Courtroom", *Rights Watch Blog*, online: http://rightswatch.ca/2015/11/08/nova-scotia-judge-accused-of-discrimination-in-the-courtroom/.

[48] Catharine Tunney, "Proposed bill on sexual assault awareness training for judges 'above politics,' Ambrose says", *CBC News* (Feb 4, 2020), online: cbc.ca/news [perma.cc/PQL5-HZKH].

[49] S.C. 2021, c. 8. For critical commentary see Elizabeth Sheehy & Elaine Craig, "The new sexual assault training law is a meaningless political gesture", *The Globe and Mail* (May 11, 2021), online: https://www.theglobeandmail.com/opinion/article-the-new-sexual-assault-training-law-is-a-meaningless-political-gesture/.

took a different tack. It "restrict[s] eligibility for judicial appointment to persons who undertake to participate in continuing education on matters related to sexual assault law and social context". It also explains that "social context" includes systemic racism and discrimination. Does this assuage or exacerbate concerns raised by organizations representing the judiciary? Do you think it constitutes a threat to, or an enhancement of, the three ethical principles of independence, impartiality, and equality?

[8] FURTHER READING

American Bar Association, *Model Code of Judicial Conduct.*

Alfini, James, *et al.*, *Judicial Conduct and Ethics*, 4th ed. (Newark: Matthew Bender & Co., 2007).

Bryden, Philip & Jula Hughes, "The Tip of the Iceberg: A Survey of the Philosophy and Practice of Canadian Provincial and Territorial Judges Concerning Judicial Disqualification" (2011) 48 Alta. L. Rev. 569.

Devlin, Richard, Adèle Kent & Susan Lightstone, "The Past, Present and Future of Judicial Ethics in Canada" (2013) 16 Leg. Ethics 1.

Devlin, Richard & Adam Dodek, *Regulating Judges: Beyond Independence and Accountability* (Northampton, MA: Edward Elgar, 2016).

Devlin, Richard & Sheila Wildeman, *Disciplining Judges: Contemporary Challenges and Controversies* (Cheltenham: Edward Elgar, 2021)

Dodek, Adam & Lorne Sossin, *Judicial Independence in Context* (Toronto: Irwin Law, 2010).

Friedland, Martin, *A Place Apart: Judicial Independence and Accountability in Canada* (Ottawa: Canadian Judicial Council, 1995).

Hughes, Jula & Philip Bryden, "From Principles to Rules: The Case for Statutory Rules Governing Aspects of Judicial Disqualification" (2016) 53 Osgoode Hall L.J. 853.

Mahoney, Kathleen & Sheilah Martin, *Equality and Judicial Neutrality* (Toronto: Carswell, 1987).

Marshall, The Honourable Mr. Justice T. David, *Judicial Conduct and Accountability* (Scarborough, ON: Carswell, 1995).

McGill, Jena & Amy Salyzyn, "Judging by Numbers: How will judicial analytics impact the justice system and its stakeholders?" (2021) 44:1 Dal. L.J. [forthcoming]

Pitel, Stephen & Liam Ledgerwood, "Judicial Confidentiality in Canada" (2017) 43:1 Queen's L.J. 123.

Pitel, Stephen & Michal Malecki, "Judicial Fundraising in Canada" (2015) 52:3 Alta. L. Rev. 519.

Pitel, Stephen & Will Bortolin, "Revising Canada's Ethical Rules for Judges Returning to Practice" (2011) 34 Dal. L.J. 483.

Shetreet, Shimon & Sophie Turenne, *Judges on Trial: Judicial Independence and Accountability*, 2d ed. (Cambridge: Cambridge University Press, 2013).

Smith, Abbe. "Nice work if you can get it: 'Ethical' Jury Selection in Criminal Defence" (1998) 67 Fordham L. Rev. 523.

Smith, Beverley, *Professional Conduct for Lawyers and Judges*, 4th ed. (Fredericton: Maritime Law Book, 2011).

Thomas, The Honourable Mr. Justice, *Judicial Ethics in Australia* (Agincourt: Carswell, 1988).

TABLE OF CASES

Table of Cases

INDEX

[References are to chapter and section.]

A

ACCESS TO JUSTICE
Generally . . . 11[1]
Barriers to access, identifying . . . 11[2][b]
Constitutional right, as . . . 11[3][a]
   British Columbia (Attorney General) v.
     Christie . . . 11[3][a]
   Charter right, as . . . 11[3][a]
   Counsel in court, right to . . . 11[3][a]
   R. v. Moodie . . . 11[3][a]
   Rule of law and . . . 11[3][a]
   Trial Lawyers Association of British Co-
     lumbia v. British Columbia (Attorney
     General), . . . 11[3][a]
Cost of lawyer . . . 11[3][b][ii]
Defining . . . 11[2][c]
Governments, role and responsibility of
   . . . 11[3][a]
Judges, role and responsibility of . . . 11[4][a]
Lawyer-client relationship and . . . 2[2][b][i]
Lawyers, role and responsibility of . . . 11[3][b]
   Generally . . . 11[3][b]
   Cost of lawyers, reasons for
     . . . 11[3][b][ii]
   Market failure argument . . . 11[3][b][ii]
   Monopoly argument . . . 11[3][b][ii]
   Pro bono services . . . 11[3][b][ii]
   Trusteeship argument . . . 11[3][b][ii]
   Vocation/ethical identity argument
     . . . 11[3][b][i]
Legal aid system . . . 11[1]; 11[2][b]; 11[3][a];
   11[4][a]; 11[4][c]
"Legal" need, understanding . . . 11[2][a]
Meaning of . . . 11[2][a]
Paralegal service providers . . . 11[4][c]
   L.S.B.C. Legal Services Regulatory Frame-
     work Task Force Report . . . 11[4][c]
   Ottawa Ticket Defence Program
     . . . 11[4][c]
Pro bono law school models . . . 11[4][b]
Pro bono work . . . 11[3][b][ii]; 11[4][a]
Response to problem . . . 11[4][a]
   Generally . . . 11[4][a]721
   Action Committee on Access to Justice
     strategy . . . 11[4][a]
   Generic solutions approach . . . 11[4][a]

ADMINISTRATION OF JUSTICE
Lawyer-client relationship and . . . 2[2][b][i]

ADVERTISING
Lawyer-client relationship and . . . 2[2][a]-
   2[2][a][i]

ADVOCACY (See also OFFICERS OF THE COURT)
Generally . . . 5[1]
Advocate's role . . . 5[1]
Civility . . . 5[5]
   Best practice civility codes . . . 5[5]
   CBA *Principles of Civility for Advocates*
     . . . 5[5]
   Clients' interests principle . . . 5[5]
   "Conduct unbecoming a lawyer" . . . 5[5]
   Courtesy as moral good . . . 5[5]
   Definitions . . . 5[5]
   Ethical principles involved . . . 5[5]
   Fundamental ethical values and . . . 5[5]
   Groia v. Law Society of Upper Canada
     . . . 5[5]
   Internet posting . . . 5[5]
   Law Society of British Columbia v. Laarak-
     ker . . . 5[5]
   Meaning of . . . 5[5]
   Model Code rule . . . 5[5]
   Professional misconduct, as . . . 5[5]
   Rudeness and . . . 5[5]
   Schreiber v. Mulroney . . . 5[5]
   Sources of obligation . . . 5[5]
   Trial fairness and . . . 5[5]
Cross-examination . . . 5[4][b]
   Evidentiary foundation requirement, no
     . . . 5[4][b]
   Fair trial imperative . . . 5[4][b]
   Good faith basis . . . 5[4][b]
   Humiliating and contemptuous questioning
     . . . 5[4][b]
   Improper and prejudicial questioning
     . . . 5[4][b]
   R. v. Lyttle . . . 5[4][b]
   R. v. R. (A.J.) . . . 5[4][b]
Demand letters . . . 5[2]
Discovery . . . 5[3][b]
   Civil procedure rules re . . . 5[3][b]
   Duty of prompt discovery . . . 5[3][b]
   Excessive zeal . . . 5[3][b]
   Grossman v. Toronto General Hospital
     . . . 5[3][b]
   Stonewalling . . . 5[3][b]
Negotiation . . . 5[3][c]
Pleadings . . . 5[3]-5[3][a]
   D.C.B. v. Zellers Inc. . . . 5[3][a]
   Demand letters . . . 5[3][b]
   Drafting, *Model Code* rule . . . 5[2]
   Scenarios . . . 4[3][a]
   Unmeritorious/improper steps . . . 5[2]
   Zealousness . . . 5[2]

CONFIDENTIALITY DUTY—Cont.
Disclosure exceptions—Cont.
Innocence at stake (See subhead: Innocence at stake exception)
Non-payment of fees context . . . 3[7][a]
Public safety (See subhead: Public safety exception)
Duty of confidentiality
Generally . . . 3[2][b]
Solicitor-client privilege and, differences between . . . 3[2][c]
Evidentiary context, custody and control . . . 3[7][b]
Concealment of physical evidence . . . 3[7][b]
Model Code rule . . . 3[7][b]
R. v. Murray . . . 3[7][b]
Federal of Law Societies of Canada v. Canada (Attorney General) . . . 3[6][c]
Goodis v. Ontario (Minister of Correctional Services) . . . 3[6][c]
In-house counsel . . . 9[4][a]
Innocence at stake exception . . . 3[6][b]
Full answer and defence, right to . . . 3[6][b]
R. v. Brown . . . 3[6][b]
R. v. McClure . . . 3[6][b]
Solicitor-client privilege vs. . . . 3[6][b]
Law society investigations . . . 3[6][d]
Law Society of Saskatchew v. E.F.A. Merchant, Q.C. . . . 3[6][c]
Loyal advocacy and (See LEGAL ETHICS)
Model Code . . . 3[2][b]
Model Code rule . . . 3[4]; 3[5]; 3[6][a]; 3[6][c]; 3[7][b]; 3[8]
Money-laundering (proceeds of crime) regime . . . 3[6][c]
Negotiation . . . 6[3][b]
Obstruction of justice (See subhead: Evidentiary context)
Public safety exception . . . 3[6][b]
Generally . . . 3[6]
Children and . . . 3[6][a]
Extent of disclosure . . . 3[6][a]
Imminence issue . . . 3[6][a]
Scenarios . . . 3[6][a]
Seriousness factor . . . 3[6][a]
Smith v. Jones . . . 3[6][a]
Rationale for . . . 3[1]; 3[3]
Scope of . . . 3[6][b]
Solicitor-client privilege
Generally . . . 3[2][a]
Class privilege . . . 3[6][b]
Confidentiality duty vs. . . . 3[2][c]
Evolution of . . . 3[6][b]
Full answer and defence vs. . . . 3[6][b]
Innocence at state test for . . . 3[6][b]
Limitations . . . 3[6][a]

CONFIDENTIALITY DUTY—Cont.
Solicitor-client privilege—Cont.
Rationale for . . . 3[6][b]
Scope of . . . 3[6][b]
Substantive rule, as . . . 3[6][b]
Types of . . . 3[6][b]
Statutory exceptions to . . . 3[6][c]
Money laundering . . . 3[6][c]
National security . . . 3[6][c]
Technology, risks arising from use of . . . 3[8]
Waiver . . . 3[5]
Withdrawal from representation context . . . 3[7][a]

CONFLICTS OF INTEREST
Generally . . . 4[1]; 4[2][a]
"Bright line" rule . . . 4[2][c]; 4[2][d]
Chinese Wall/cone of silence approach . . . 4[2][b]; 4[2][c]
Client-client conflicts . . . 4[2][a]-4[2][e]
Alberta Code of Professional Conduct . . . 4[2][c]
Business vs. legal conflicts . . . 4[2][c]
Canadian National Railway Co. v. McKercher LLP. . . . 4[2][d]
CBA Code commentaries . . . 4[2][b]
Client representation, effects on . . . 4[2][d]
Codes of professional conduct rules . . . 4[2][c]; 4[2][d]
Competing commercial entities, acting for . . . 4[2][d]
Confidential information issue . . . 4[2][d]
Contractual duties, conflicting . . . 4[2][d]
Current clients, duties to . . . 4[2][c]
Fiduciary duties . . . 4[2][b]; 4[2][c]; 4[2][d]
Former client conflicts . . . 4[2][e] (See subhead: Former client conflicts)
Former clients, duties to . . . 4[2][b]
Irrebutable presumption test . . . 4[2][b]
Issues involved . . . 4[1]
Lawyer-client conflicts . . . 4[3][a]
Generally . . . 4[3][a]
Client property, possession and control of . . . 4[3][a]
Confidential information, disclosure of . . . 4[3][a]
Discipline proceedings . . . 4[3][a]
Duties in play, generally . . . 4[3][a]
Examples . . . 4[3][a]
Fiduciary duties . . . 4[3][a]
Law Society of Saskatchewan v. Balon . . . 4[3][a]
Law Society of Upper Canada v. Hunter . . . 4[3][a]
Loyalty, duty of . . . 4[3][a]
Model Code . . . 4[3][a]

I

ILLEGALITY (See CONFIDENTIALITY DUTY; COUNSELLING; DEFENCE COUNSEL)

IMPARTIALITY (See JUDGES' ETHICS)

INCOMPETENCE (See COMPETENCE)

INDEPENDENCE
Judges (See JUDGES' ETHICS)
Lawyers (See COUNSELLING; IN-HOUSE COUNSEL; SELF REGULATION)

IN-HOUSE COUNSEL
Generally . . . 9[1]
Corporate citizenship . . . 9[4][d][ii]
Corporate counsel function, history of . . . 9[2]
Corporate gatekeeper . . . 9[4][c]
Decision-making influences . . . 9[5]
Diversity . . . 9[4][d][ii]
Ethical/professionalism complications encountered
    Generally . . . 9[4]
    Canada (and other Common Law countries) . . . 9[4][a][i]
    Confidentiality/privilege considerations . . . 9[4][a]
    Corporate citizenship . . . 9[4][d][ii]
    Corporate gatekeeper . . . 9[4][c]
    Diversity . . . 9[4][d][ii]
    European Union's approach . . . 9[4][a][ii]
    Loyalty issues from potential gatekeeping and reporting roles . . . 9[4][c]
    Multiple clients . . . 9[4][b]
History of . . . 9[2]
Key role issues . . . 9[5]
Loyalty issues from potential gatekeeping and reporting roles . . . 9[4][c]
Non-legal advice in addition to legal advice, providing
    Generally . . . 9[4][d]
    Conscience and leadership roles, potential . . . 9[4][d][ii]
    Risk/crisis assessment and management issues . . . 9[4][d][i]
Professionalism, maintaining . . . 9[3]
Role of . . . 9[2]
Tunnel vision, avoiding . . . 9[3]

INNOCENCE AT STAKE (See CONFIDENTIALITY DUTY)

INTEGRITY
Judges (See JUDGES' ETHICS)
Lawyers (See IN-HOUSE COUNSEL; LEGAL ETHICS; OFFICERS OF THE COURT)

J

JUDGES (See ACCESS TO JUSTICE; JUDGES' ETHICS)

JUDGES' ETHICS
Generally . . . 13[1]
Advisory function of codes . . . 13[2]
Bias (See subhead: Equality)
Civility and candour
    Generally . . . 13[5][c]
    Court of Appeal critical of trial judge . . . 13[5][c][iv]
    Critical of lawyers, comments . . . 13[5][c][i]
    Delivering oral decision . . . 13[5][c][iii]
    Expert witnesses, comments on . . . 13[5][c][ii]
CJC *Ethical Principles for Judges* . . . 13[2]
Codes of conduct, lack of . . . 13[2]
Comments
    Critical of lawyers . . . 13[5][c][i]
    Expert witnesses . . . 13[5][c][ii]
Constitutional norms . . . 13[1]
Court of Appeal critical of trial judge . . . 13[5][c][iv]
Diligence . . . 13[6][a]-13[6][c]
    Independent research by judge . . . 13[6][c]
    Lawyer's responsibility . . . 13[6][b]
    Leader Media Productions Ltd. v. Sentinel Hill Alliance . . . 13[6][b]
    Principle stated . . . 13[6][a]
    Sleeping judge . . . 13[6][b]
    Standard . . . 13[6][a]
    Standard applied . . . 13[6][b]
Equality . . . 13[7][a]-13[7][b]
    Impartiality, presumption of . . . 13[7][b]
    Impartiality vs. . . . 13[7][b]
    Principle stated . . . 13[7][a]
    Reasonable apprehension of bias . . . 13[7][b]
    Stereotyping/implicit bias, examples of . . . 13[7][b]
    Yukon Francophone School Board, Education Area #23 v. Yukon (Attorney General) . . . 13[7][b]
Federal vs. provincial appointed judges . . . 13[2]
Impartiality . . . 13[3][a]-13[3][d]
    Abuse of power . . . 13[3][a]
    Apprehension of bias, test re . . . 13[3][b]
    Arsenault-Cameron v. Prince Edward Island . . . 13[3][b]
    Cosgrove case . . . 13[3][a]
    Judicial community engagement, ethical challenges of . . . 13[3][c]
    Judicial misconduct, example . . . 13[3][a]